TENTH EDITION

Exceptional Learners

Introduction to Special Education

Daniel P. Hallahan
University of Virginia

James M. Kauffman
University of Virginia

PEARSON

Boston   New York   San Francisco
Mexico City   Montreal   Toronto   London   Madrid   Munich   Paris
Hong Kong   Singapore   Tokyo   Cape Town   Sydney

Executive Editor: *Virginia Lanigan*
Editorial Assistant: *Scott Blaszak*
Developmental Editor: *Alicia R. Reilly*
Executive Marketing Manager: *Amy Cronin Jordan*
Production Administrator: *Judith Fiske*
Cover Coordinator: *Linda Knowles*
Composition Buyer: *Linda Cox*
Manufacturing Buyer: *AndrewTurso*
Copyeditor: *Barbara Willette*
Editorial Production Service: *Barbara Gracia*
Electronic Composition: *Publishers' Design and Production Services, Inc.*
Photo Research: *Sarah Evertson*

Between the time website information is gathered and published, some sites may have closed. Also the transcription of URLs can result in typographical errors. The publisher would appreciate notification where these occur so that they may be corrected in subsequent editions.

Library of Congress Cataloging-in-Publication Data

Hallahan, Daniel P., 1944–
    Exceptional learners: introduction to special education / Daniel P. Hallahan, James M. Kauffman—10th ed.
    p.   cm.
    Includes bibliographical references and indexes.
    ISBN 0-205-44421-0
    1. Special education—United States.   I. Kauffman, James M.   II. Title.
    LC3981.H34 2005
    371.9'0973—dc22

2004065977

Printed in the United States of America

10 9 8 7 6 5 4 3 2 1—WC—09 08 07 06 05

Chapter Quotes

Page 3 from Richard H. Hungerford (1950). "On Locusts," *America Journal of Mental Deficiency,* 54, pp. 415–418. Page 39 from Bob Dylan, "The Times They Are A-Changin'." Copyright © 1963, 1964 by Warner Bros., Inc. Copyright renewed 1991 by Special Rider Music. All rights reserved. International copyright secured. Reprinted by permission. Page 79 from Ronald Takaki (1994). Interview: Reflections from a different mirror. *Teaching Tolerance, 3*(1), 11–15. Page 105 from Emily Perl Kingsley (1987). "Welcome to Holland," *Kids Like These.* CBS TV movie. Copyright © 1987 by Emily Perl Kingsley. All rights reserved. Reprinted by permission of the author. Page 131 from Sandra Z. Kaufman (1999). *Retarded Isn't Stupid, Mom!* (Rev. ed.). Baltimore: Paul H. Brooks. Page 167 from Lynn Pelkey (2001). In the LD bubble. In P. Rodis, A. Garrod, & M. L. Boscardin (Eds.), *Learning Difficulties and Life Stories.* Boston: Allyn and Bacon. Page 207 from Heinrich Hoffman (1940). The Story of Fidgety Philip in (Author) *Slovenly Peter or Cheerful Stories and Funny Pictures for Good Little Folks*

(Chapter Quotes and Photo Credits are continued on page iv and are considered an extension of the copyright page.)

Brief Contents

Chapter Quotes (Continued)

Philadelphia: John C. Winston. Page 245 Anonymous (1994). First person account: Schizophrenia with childhood onset. *Schizophrenia Bulletin, 20,* 287–288. Page 285 from David Shields (1989). *Dead Languages.* New York: Alfred A. Knopf, Inc. Page 319 from Martha Sheridan (2001). *Inner Lives of Deaf Children: Interviews and Analysis.* Washington, DC: Gallaudet University Press. Page 357 Stephen Kuusisto, "Elegy for Ray Charles" from *Ragged Edge* (June 2004). Copyright © 2004 by Stephen Kuusisto. Reprinted with permission of the author. Page 395 from Stephen Shore (2003). My life with Asperger syndrome. In R. W. Du Charme & T. P. Gullotta (Eds.), *Asperger syndrome: A guide for professionals and families.* New York: Kluwer Academic/Plenum Publishing. Page 429 from Cathy Crimmins (2000). *Where Is the Mango Princess?* New York: Alfred A. Knopf, pp. 3–4. Copyright © 2000 by Cathy Crimmins. All rights reserved. Page 465 from Tony Early (2000). *Jim the Boy.* Boston: Little Brown. Page 497 from *The Autobiography of Mark Twain,* edited by Charles Neider. Copyright © 1927, 1940, 1958, 1959 by the Mark Twain Company, copyright 1924, 1952, 1955 by Clara Clemens Somossoud, copyright 1959 by Charles Neider. New York: HarperCollins Publishers.

Photo Credits

Contents

Chapter 3 Multicultural and Bilingual Aspects of Special Education   78

Chapter 6   Learners with Learning Disabilities   166

Chapter 9 — *Learners with Communication Disorders* — 284

Chapter 12

Learners with Autism Spectrum Disorders 394

Chapter 13 Learners with Low-Incidence, Multiple, and Severe Disabilities   428

Chapter 14   Learners with Physical Disabilities and Other Health Impairments   464

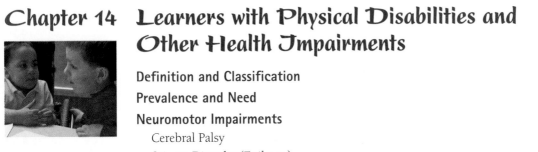

Chapter 15 Learners with Special Gifts and Talents   496

Selected Features

Casebook Reflections

FOCUS ON CONCEPTS

MAKING IT WORK

Personal Perspectives

RESPONSIVE INSTRUCTION

Preface

Exceptional Learners: Introduction to Special Education, Tenth Edition, is a general introduction to the characteristics of exceptional learners and their education. (*Exceptional* is the term that traditionally has been used to refer to people with disabilities as well as to those who are gifted.) This book emphasizes classroom practices as well as the psychological, sociological, and medical aspects of disabilities and giftedness.

We have written this text with two primary audiences in mind: those individuals who are preparing to be special educators and those who are preparing to be general educators. Given the current movement toward including students with disabilities in general education classrooms, general educators must be prepared to understand this special student population and be ready to work with special educators to provide appropriate educational programming for these students. This book also is appropriate for professionals in other fields who work with exceptional learners (e.g., speech-language pathologists, audiologists, physical therapists, occupational therapists, adapted physical educators, counselors, and school psychologists).

In Chapter 1, we begin with an overview of exceptionality and special education, including definitions, basic legal requirements, and the history and development of the field. In Chapter 2, we discuss major current issues and trends, such as inclusion, collaboration and co-teaching, early childhood programming, transition to adulthood programming, inclusion of students with disabilities in general assessments of progress, discipline of students with disabilities, and access of people with disabilities to new technologies. In Chapter 3, we address multicultural and bilingual aspects of special education. In Chapter 4, we consider the significant issues pertaining to parents and families of people with disabilities. In the next eleven chapters, we examine each of the major categories of exceptionality: Chapter 5, mental retardation; Chapter 6, learning disabilities; Chapter 7, attention deficit hyperactivity disorder; Chapter 8, emotional or behavioral disorders; Chapter 9, communication disorders; Chapter 10, deafness or hard of hearing; Chapter 11, blindness or low vision; Chapter 12, autism spectrum disorders; Chapter 13, low-incidence and multiple and severe disabilities; Chapter 14, physical disabilities and other health impairments; and Chapter 15, special gifts and talents.

We believe that we have written a text that reaches the heart as well as the mind. It is our conviction that professionals working with exceptional learners need to develop not only a solid base of knowledge, but also a healthy attitude toward their work and the people whom they serve. Professionals must constantly challenge themselves to learn more theory, research, and practice in special education and to develop an ever more sensitive understanding of exceptional learners and their families.

New Content and Features in the Tenth Edition

In addition to new discussion of IDEA (Individuals with Disabilities Education Act) 2004 and the No Child Left Behind Act, we have made extensive revisions to virtually every aspect of the tenth edition's fifteen chapters (including over 400 new references bearing a copyright date from 2000 and beyond.)

NEW CHAPTER: LEARNERS WITH AUTISM SPECTRUM DISORDERS

In previous editions, we covered autism spectrum disorders (ASD) in the chapters on communication disorders and low-incidence disabilities. Given that the reported prevalence of ASD is increasing dramatically, research activity is vigorous, and there are numerous controversial issues being hotly debated in this field, we thought it time to devote a separate chapter to ASD.

CASEBOOK REFLECTIONS

At several points in each chapter, connections (contributed by Stephen Byrd, doctoral student at the University of Virginia) are made to the outstanding *Cases for Reflection and Analysis*. This is a collection of cases that accompanies this text, pinpointing the specific ways in which special education theories, concepts, and practices play out in the lives and education of real students, their teachers, and their families.

CEC STANDARDS AND INTASC PRINCIPLES.

The Council for Exceptional Children (CEC) Knowledge and Skills Standards and the Interstate New Teacher Assessment and Support Consortium (INTASC) Core Principles provide a framework for all general and special educators. Dr. Elizabeth Martinez of the Council for Exceptional Children has selected the appropriate standards and principles and has noted their application to content in each chapter. The specific relevance of these standards and principles is highlighted in every chapter of this text via the following features, which together serve as a great reference for students to keep as future teachers and use in preparation for licensure exams such as PRAXIS II.

Standards and Principles in This Chapter   Each chapter opens with a primer on CEC Standards (the responsibilities of special educators) and INTASC Principles (the responsibilities of all educators) to be addressed in the upcoming chapter.

Understanding the Standards and Principles   Margin notes throughout each chapter; phrased as questions, highlight key connections between text discussions and standards and principles.

> **UNDERSTANDING THE STANDARDS AND PRINCIPLES**   Why are members of minority groups more apt to be identified as disabled? *(CEC Knowledge and Skills Standard CC1K5)*
>
> Council for Exceptional Children

Applying the Standards and Principles   This feature concludes each chapter and asks readers to apply their understanding of chapter material with questions and activities meant to show the practical relevance of the standards.

Standards Appendix   This appendix at the end of the book is an easy reference to the CEC Core Content Standards and INTASC Principals.

SUCCESS STORIES: SPECIAL EDUCATORS AT WORK (NEW FORMAT AND CONTENT!)

Special educators work in a variety of settings, ranging from general education classrooms to residential institutions. Although their main function involves teaching, these professionals also engage in a variety of activities, such as counseling, collaborating, and consulting. To illustrate this variety, each of the eleven categorical chapters (Chapters 5–15) includes an example of a special educator at work. Written by Dr. Jean B. Crockett of Virginia Tech University, an experienced special education administrator and teacher educator, each story focuses on a special educator's work with an individual student and shows readers the wide range of challenges faced by special educators, the dynamic nature of their positions, and the competent, hopeful practice of special education. In this edition, these features have been revised to reflect a new focus on education for students with special needs that is *intensive, relentless, and specific*. These features have also been updated to include questions for students that relate to CEC Standards.

CHAPTER PREVIEW AND REVIEW FEATURES

Questions to Guide Your Reading of This Chapter   This feature introduces each chapter by highlighting in question form the major topics to be covered.

Chapter Summary   The summary uses the chapter opening questions to structure a streamlined, efficient reference for chapter review.

FOCUS ON CONCEPTS

These features stimulate critical thinking about current research and special topics that are of interest to all educators.

PERSONAL PERSPECTIVES

These features present the human side of having a disability, showing how text topics affect the personal lives of students, teachers, parents, and others.

EXPANDED COVERAGE OF MAJOR ISSUES

As in previous editions, we discuss major features of the Individuals with Disabilities Education Act (IDEA), including the 1997 reauthorization as well as the latest 2004 reauthorization. We inform students about the major requirements of this important federal law. We suggest that you consult the Companion Website, where updates will be made available about future changes in the requirements of federal law.

Since the last edition, another major new federal law—the No Child Left Behind Act (NCLB)—was enacted. We discuss the implications of this new law for special education. We also discuss the President's Commission on Excellence in Special Education (PCESE), which was appointed in 2001 by President George W. Bush. The PCESE submitted its report in 2002. The NCLB and the PCESE are part of an issue that has become prominent in public schools in the early twenty-first century: accountability for results.

Continuing Features of the Tenth Edition

CHAPTER-OPENING QUOTES

Going back to our first edition is the practice of opening each chapter with an excerpt from literature or song. Students continue to tell us that they find these quotes to be effective at grabbing their attention and leading them into some of the issues contained in the text.

MISCONCEPTIONS ABOUT EXCEPTIONAL LEARNERS: MYTHS AND FACTS BOXES

We start each chapter with a feature that juxtaposes several myths and facts about the subject of the chapter. This popular feature, familiar to longtime users of previous editions, serves as an excellent advance organizer for the material to be covered.

RESPONSIVE INSTRUCTION: MEETING THE NEEDS OF STUDENTS

It is our firm belief that most students with disabilities require intensive instruction in order to maximize their potential. Located throughout the eleven categorical chapters (Chapter 5–15) are 36 boxes, authored by Dr. Kristin Sayeski of the University of Virginia, that feature a variety of sound, research-based strategies for teaching students with disabilities. Although these strategies cannot possibly take the place of a full-blown course and text in teaching methods, we think they offer practical suggestions for meeting the needs of exceptional learners through intensive instruction. In keeping with this era of accountability, these boxes stress teaching practices that have a sound research base.

MAKING IT WORK: COLLABORATION AND CO-TEACHING

Each of the categorical chapters (Chapter 5–15) includes a feature, authored by Dr. Margaret Weiss of the University of North Carolina, devoted to co-teaching and collaboration among special and general education teachers, families, and other professionals. Because we believe that it is important for all teachers to understand what expertise special educators can contribute to collaborative, general education classrooms, the first section of each box includes information about knowledge and skills special educators should possess as they enter the field, as identified by the Council for Exceptional Children (CEC) in its Performance-Based Professional Standards (2001). The second section contains examples of research-based instructional practices that teachers can use when collaborating or descriptions of successful collaborations in real classrooms. Each box contains specifics about how to get more information about the strategy or classroom described.

MARGIN NOTES

The marginal glossary of key terms and concepts has been supplemented with information about interesting and relevant websites. All of these websites are also included as hot links on the Companion Website for the tenth edition.

Supplements

Hallahan and Kauffman's Instructor Supplements: A Complete Instructional Package!

Allyn and Bacon is committed to preparing the best quality supplements for its textbooks, and the supplements for Hallahan and Kauffman's *Exceptional Learners* show that commitment. The following supplements provide an outstanding array of resources that facilitate learning about students with disabilities and their families. For more information about the instructor and student supplements that accompany and support the text, ask your local Allyn and Bacon representative, or contact the Allyn and Bacon Sales Support Department (1-800-852-8024).

INSTRUCTOR'S RESOURCE MANUAL AND TEST BANK

The Instructor's Resource Manual section of this supplement was prepared by Dr. Melody Tankersley of Kent State University. Each chapter of the Manual includes an at-a-glance grid that correlates all instructor and student supplementary material to the text outline, a chapter outline, a chapter overview, and an annotated outline wherein the major headings of the chapter are summarized in detail. Included in the annotated outline are suggestions for lecture ideas, discussion points, and activities. The IRM also keys each chapter to appropriate videos, transparencies, and digital images available with this text. Also included are references to related media, films, journals, and websites.

The test bank section, written by Dr. Kerri Martin consists of over 1,300 test questions, including multiple-choice, true/false, and essay formats. Each chapter also includes an interpretive exercise that presents case descriptions or scenarios involving individuals with special needs, followed by questions that require students to apply, analyze, evaluate, or synthesize concepts from the text.

TESTGEN COMPUTERIZED TEST BANK

The printed test bank is also available electronically through our computerized testing system: TestGen. Instructors can use TestGen to create exams in just minutes by selecting from the existing database of questions, editing questions, or writing original questions

POWERPOINT® PRESENTATION

Prepared by Dr. Virginia Dudgeon of the State University of New York at Cortland and ideal for lecture presentations or student handouts, the PowerPoint® presentation created for this text provides dozens of ready-to-use graphic and text images (including many illustrations that appear in the text) to guide and enhance lecture presentation. Go to www.suppscentral. ablongman.com to register for access to this and other online supplements.

ALLYN AND BACON TRANSPARENCIES FOR SPECIAL EDUCATION

The transparencies package include 100 acetates, over half in full-color.

THE "SNAPSHOTS" VIDEO SERIES FOR SPECIAL EDUCATION

- *Snapshots Video: Inclusion* (© 1995, 22 minutes in length; close-captioned) profiles three students of differing ages and with various levels of disability in inclusive class settings. In each case, parents, classroom teachers, special education teachers, and school administrators talk about the steps they have taken to help the students succeed in inclusive settings.

- *Snapshots Categorical Videos.* Each 10- to 12-minute segment profiles an individual with an exceptional condition, his family, teachers, and experiences.
- *Snapshots Video: Behavior Disorders, Learning Disabilities, Mental Retardation* (© 1995, 20–25 minutes in length; close-captioned)
- *Snapshots Video: Traumatic Brain Injury, Hearing Impairments, and Visual Impairments* (© 1995, 20–25 minutes in length; close-captioned)

PROFESSIONALS IN ACTION VIDEOTAPE: TEACHING STUDENTS WITH SPECIAL NEEDS

This *Professionals in Action* video (© 2000, 120 minutes in length; close-captioned) consists of five 15- to 30-minute modules presenting viewpoints and approaches to teaching students with various disabilities in general education classrooms, separate education settings, and various combinations of the two. Each module explores its topic via actual classroom footage and interviews with general and special education teachers, parents, and students themselves.

ONLINE COURSE MANAGEMENT SYSTEM FOR INTRODUCTION TO SPECIAL EDUCATION AND INCLUSION

Powered by Blackboard and hosted nationally, Allyn and Bacon's own course management system, CourseCompass, helps you manage all aspects of teaching your course. The course features preloaded premium content to support Introduction to Special Education and Inclusion courses, and instructor supplements for individual texts. Organized into course topics, the premium content includes practice tests, learning objectives, suggested readings, VideoWorkshop clips, and digital media archive resources. The course seamlessly links to additional special education resources including an interactive timeline and *New York Times* articles as well as to ResearchNavigator. For colleges and universities with WebCT™ and Blackboard™ licenses, special course management packages are available in these formats as well.

Hallahan and Kauffman's Student Supplements: An Integrated Learning System!

Building on the study aids found in the text, Allyn and Bacon offers a number of supplements for students.

CASES FOR REFLECTION AND ANALYSIS—NEW EDITION!

The past several editions of *Exceptional Learners* have included a free casebook with every new copy of the text purchased from Allyn and Bacon. The overwhelming popularity of this supplement motivated us to revise it again for the tenth edition. Four of the thirteen cases are new to this edition. We've also included text references to the cases within each chapter of this text (Casebook Reflections). We hope these will make the booklet an even more helpful learning tool for students. These cases reflect both the joy and the pain teachers experience while working with exceptional children. What professors of education and commentators in the popular press write about teaching is often wondrously abstract, hypothetical, or idealistic and does not always ring true for those who teach in classrooms every day. These cases are neither abstract descriptions nor conjecture, nor do they reflect an idealism that is detached from the realities of the classroom. These are true stories—what really happened as told from the perspectives of real teachers and how they thought and felt about what was happening. We hope that you will enjoy reading and discussing them as much as we have.

STUDENT STUDY GUIDE

Written by Dr. Paula Crowley of Illinois State University the study guide reinforces for students conceptual and factual text material and includes key points, learning objectives, exercises, practice tests, and enrichment activities.

COMPANION WEBSITE

(www.ablongman.com/hallahan10e) Prepared by Dr. Paige Pullen of the University of Virginia, this dynamic, interactive Companion Website includes an online study guide for students that provides, on a chapter-by-chapter basis, learning objectives, study questions with text page references, hot links to relevant websites (including those referenced and highlighted in the text), audio and video clips, and additional enrichment material. Other features of the website include an interactive Special Education Timeline, which highlights the people and events that have shaped special education through history, and a collection of current *New York Times* articles of relevant topics. The Companion Website also features a syllabus builder that allows instructors to create and customize course syllabi online.

Discover where the classroom comes to life! From video clips of teachers and students interacting to sample lessons, portfolio templates, and standards integration, Allyn and Bacon brings students the tools they will need to succeed in the classroom—with content easily integrated into your existing course. Delivered within CourseCompass, Allyn and Bacon's course management system, this program gives your students powerful insights into how real classrooms work and a rich array of tools that will support them on their journey from their first class to their first classroom.

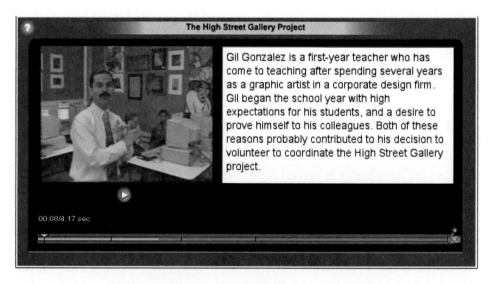

Available free when packaged with the textbook, the CD-ROM contains ten modules of three- to five-minute digitized video clips featuring real classroom settings. The Video-Workshop CD comes with a Student Study Guide, which contains all the materials needed to help students get started. With questions for reflection before, during, and after viewing, this guide extends classroom discussion and allows for more in-class time spent on analysis of material. An Instructor's Teaching Guide is also available to provide ideas and exercises to assist faculty in incorporating this convenient supplement into course assignments and assessments. (Visit www.ablongman.com/videoworkshop for more details.)

"WHAT'S BEST FOR MATTHEW?" INTERACTIVE CD–ROM CASE STUDY FOR LEARNING TO DEVELOP IEPS, VERSION 2.0

This CD-ROM helps preservice and in-service teachers to develop their IEP writing skills through the case study of Matthew, a 9-year-old boy with autism. It is sold separately and is also available at a reduced price as a "value package" with the textbook.

Research Navigator™ (www.researchnavigator.com) is the easiest way for students to start a research assignment or research paper. Complete with extensive help on the research process and three exclusive online databases of credible and reliable source material, including EBSCO's ContentSelect™ Academic Journal Database, New York Times Search by Subject Archive, and "Best of the Web" Link Library, Research Navigator™ helps students quickly and efficiently make the most of their research time. Research Navigator™ is free when packaged with the textbook and requires an access code.

Acknowledgements

We are grateful to those individuals who provided valuable comments on the ninth edition and the drafts of our tenth edition chapters:

Jose Luis Alvarado, San Diego State University
Peggy L. Anderson, Metropolitan State College of Denver
William N. Bender, University of Georgia
David F. Conway, University of Nebraska at Omaha
Rhoda Cummings, University of Nevada
Gary A. Davis, University of Wisconsin at Madison
Stephen D. Dempsey, University of Wisconsin–Eau Claire
Beverly A. Doyle, Creighton University
Mary K. Dykes, University of Florida at Gainesville
Cynthia Ewers, Wilmington College
Scott Fike, D'Youville College
Laura Gaudet, Towson State University
Amy Stevens Griffith, University of Texas at Tyler
Herbert Grossman, University of Wisconsin at Platteville

Dick Heimann, Northland Pioneer College
Jack Hourcade, Boise State University
Karen N. Janssen, Eastern Kentucky University
Craig Kennedy, Vanderbilt University
Frank Kersting, Western Kentucky University
Kathryn A. Lund, Arizona State University
Nancy Mamlin, Appalachian State University
Angela S. McIntosh, San Diego State University
Festus E. Obiakor, University of Wisconsin at Milwaukee
Debra P. Price, Sam Houston State University
Thomas F. Reilly, Chicago State University
Michael A Rettig, Washburn University
Karen E. Santos, James Madison University
Richard L. Simpson, University of Kansas
Albert A. Stramiello, Mercer University
Frances Elliott Ulrich, Notre Dame College
Phillip Waldrop, Middle Tennessee State University
Elizabeth M. Werre, Pensacola Junior College
George J. Yard, University of Missouri at St. Louis

We thank Stephen Byrd, currently a doctoral student at the University of Virginia, who oversaw the tedious task of securing permissions for quoted material. We are once again thankful for the wonderful support and assistance we received from the folks at Allyn and Bacon. Alicia Reilly, our Developmental Editor, continues to amaze us with her ability to balance family responsibilities while attending to all the details of our book. We simply can't thank her enough for all she does for us. She is a gem. Judy Fiske, a new Production Editor for this edition, stepped in seamlessly and brought the project to completion in a timely fashion. Editorial Assistant Scott Blaszak's responsiveness to our e-mails and phone calls was critical to meeting deadlines. Thanks to Amy Cronin Jordan, Executive Marketing Manager, for once again taking such a sincere interest in the success of our text and for understanding the need for translating research into practice. We once again thank Barbara Gracia, Production Coordinator, for gracefully coordinating the many eyes that pored over the page proofs—and for doing this all in the middle of a move across country. Our copy editor, Barbara Willette, of Barbara A. Willette Book Production Services did a terrific job of keeping us stylistically and grammatically correct. We thank Sarah Evertson, Photo Researcher, for such a splendid job of finding just the right photos. We're sure readers will agree that the extra attention you gave to the project has paid off—the photos are terrific. And finally, Virginia Lanigan, Executive Editor, continues to possess that rare combination of competence, professionalism, sensitivity, and a sense of humor. She's "all business" but with a heart. Thank you, Virginia.

SOME FINAL THOUGHTS

Given that this is our tenth edition, several people have alluded to it as some kind of "milestone." We assure you that we didn't approach this edition any differently than we did the first. For those loyal users of previous editions, we assure you that we weighed carefully each change or update. We hope you agree that our revisions reflect the myriad changes in the field of special education over the past few years as well as the information explosion brought about by ever more accessible computer databases and the Internet. We also hope you will agree that we have not failed in our continuing commitment to bring you the best that research has to offer with regard to educating exceptional learners.

DPH
JMK

Exceptional Learners

Chapter 1

Exceptionality and Special Education

Only the brave dare look
upon the gray—
upon the things which
cannot be explained easily,
upon the things which often
engender mistakes,
upon the things whose cause
cannot be understood,
upon the things we must
accept and live with.
And therefore only the brave
dare look upon difference
without flinching.

Richard H. Hungerford
"On Locusts"

QUESTIONS TO GUIDE YOUR READING OF THIS CHAPTER . . .

- HOW can we get oriented to exceptionality and special education?
- WHAT is the educational definition of exceptional learners?
- WHAT is the prevalence of exceptional learners?
- WHAT is the definition of special education?
- HOW is special education provided?
- WHAT are teachers' roles in special education?
- WHAT are the origins of special education?
- WHAT legislation and litigation have affected special education?
- HOW is the intent of special education law implemented in individualized education for students with disabilities?
- WHAT is our perspective on the progress of special education?

STANDARDS AND PRINCIPLES IN THIS CHAPTER

SPECIAL EDUCATORS . . .

- **understand the field as an evolving and changing discipline** based on philosophies, evidence-based principles and theories, relevant laws and policies, diverse and historical points of view, and human issues that have historically influenced and continue to influence the field of special education and the education and treatment of individuals with exceptional needs both in school and society *(from CEC Content Standard #1)*.

- **understand the similarities and differences in human development** and the characteristics between and among individuals with and without exceptional learning needs *(from CEC Content Standard #2)*.

- **realize that individualized decision making and instruction are at the center** of special education practice; develop long-range individualized instructional plans anchored in both general and special education curricula, and, in addition systematically translate these individualized plans into carefully selected shorter-range goals and objectives taking into consideration an individual's abilities and needs, the learning environment, and a myriad of cultural and linguistic factors *(from CEC Content Standard #7)*.

ALL TEACHERS . . .

- **understand the central concepts,** tools of inquiry, structures of the discipline(s) he or she teaches and can create learning experiences that make these aspects of subject matter meaningful for students *(INTASC Principle #1)*.

- **understand how children learn and develop,** and can provide learning opportunities that support the intellectual, social and personal development of each learner *(INTASC Principle #2)*.

The study of exceptional learners is the study of differences. The exceptional learner is different in some way from the average. In very simple terms, such a person might have problems or special talents in thinking, seeing, hearing, speaking, socializing, or moving. More often than not, he or she has a combination of special abilities or disabilities. Today, over five million such different learners have been identified in public schools throughout the United States. About one out of every ten students in U.S. schools is considered exceptional. The fact that even many so-called normal students have school-related problems makes the study of exceptionality very demanding.

The study of exceptional learners is also the study of similarities. Exceptional individuals are not different from the average in every way. In fact, most exceptional learners are average in more ways than they are not. Until recently, professionals—and laypeople as well—tended to focus on the differences between exceptional and nonexceptional learners, almost to the exclusion of the ways in which all individuals are alike. Today, we give more attention to what exceptional and nonexceptional learners have in common—to similarities in their characteristics, needs, and ways of learning. As a result, the study of exceptional learners has become more complex, and many so-called facts about children and youths with disabilities and those who have special gifts or talents have been challenged.

Getting Oriented to Exceptionality and Special Education

Students of one of the hard sciences might boast of the difficulty of the subject matter because of the many facts they must remember and piece together. The plight of students of special education is quite different. To be sure, they study facts, but the facts are relatively few compared to the unanswered questions. Any study of human beings must take into account inherent ambiguities, inconsistencies, and unknowns. In the case of the individual who deviates from the norm, we must multiply all the mysteries of normal human behavior and development by those pertaining to the person's exceptionalities. Because there is no single accepted theory of normal development, it is not at all surprising that relatively few definite statements can be made about exceptional learners.

REASONS FOR OPTIMISM

There are patches of sunshine in the bleak gray painted by Hungerford (1950) in his classic but still highly relevant essay (see the excerpt on p. 3). In the vast majority of cases, we are unable to

Misconceptions about Exceptional Learners

MYTH Public schools may choose not to provide education for some students with disabilities.

FACT Federal legislation specifies that to receive federal funds, every school system must provide a free, appropriate education for every student regardless of any disabling condition.

MYTH By law, the student with a disability must be placed in the least restrictive environment (LRE). The LRE is always the regular classroom.

FACT The law does require the student with a disability to be placed in the LRE. However, the LRE is *not* always the regular classroom. What the LRE does mean is that the student shall be separated as little as possible from home, family, community, and the regular class setting while appropriate education is provided. In many but not all instances, this will mean placement in the regular classroom.

MYTH The causes of most disabilities are known, but little is known about how to help individuals overcome or compensate for their disabilities.

FACT In most cases, the causes of disabilities are not known, although progress is being made in pinpointing why many disabilities occur. More is known about the treatment of most disabilities than about their causes.

MYTH People with disabilities are just like everyone else.

FACT First, no two people are exactly alike. People with disabilities, just like everyone else, are unique individuals. Most of their abilities are much like those of the average person who is not considered to have a disability. Nevertheless, a disability is a characteristic that is not shared by most people. It is important that disabilities be recognized for what they are, but individuals with disabilities must be seen as having many abilities—other characteristics that they share with the majority of people.

MYTH A disability is a handicap.

FACT A *disability* is an inability to do something, the lack of a specific capacity. A *handicap*, on the other hand, is a disadvantage that is imposed on an individual. A disability might or might not be a handicap, depending on the circumstances. For example, the inability to walk is not a handicap in learning to read, but it can be a handicap in getting into the stands at a ball game. Sometimes handicaps are needlessly imposed on people with disabilities. For example, a student who cannot write with a pen but can use a typewriter or word processor would be needlessly handicapped without such equipment.

UNDERSTANDING THE STANDARDS AND PRINCIPLES Why is the study of exceptional learners said to be the study of *differences* and *similarities*? (CEC Knowledge and Skills Standard CC2K5)

Council for
Exceptional
Children

Down Syndrome

A condition resulting from an abnormality with the twenty-first pair of chromosomes; the most common abnormality is a triplet rather than a pair (the condition sometimes referred to as trisomy 21); characterized by mental retardation and such physical signs as slanted-appearing eyes, hypotonia, a single palmar crease, shortness, and a tendency toward obesity.

Retinopathy of prematurity (ROP)

A condition resulting from administration of an excessive concentration of oxygen at birth; causes scar tissue to form behind the lens of the eye.

Phenylketonuria (PKU)

A metabolic genetic disorder caused by the inability of the body to convert phenylalanine to tyrosine; an accumulation of phenylalanine results in abnormal brain development.

Cystic fibrosis

An inherited disease affecting primarily the gastrointestinal (GI) tract and respiratory organs; characterized by thick, sticky mucous that often interferes with breathing or digestion.

Hydrocephalus

A condition characterized by enlargement of the head because of excessive pressure of the cerebrospinal fluid.

identify the exact reason why a person is exceptional, but progress is being made in determining the causes of some disabilities. In a later chapter, for example, we discuss the detection of causal factors in **Down syndrome**, a condition that results in the largest number of children classified as having moderate mental retardation. Likewise, the incidence of **retinopathy of prematurity**, at one time a leading cause of blindness, has been greatly reduced since the discovery of its cause. The cause of mental retardation associated with the metabolic disorder **phenylketonuria (PKU)** has been discovered. Soon after birth, infants are now routinely tested for PKU so that mental retardation can be prevented if they should have the disorder. More recently, the gene responsible for **cystic fibrosis**, an inherited disease characterized by chronic respiratory and digestive problems, has been identified. In the future, the specific genes governing many other diseases and disorders will also likely be located. The location of such genes raises the possibility of gene therapy to prevent or correct many disabling conditions. Surgery to correct some identifiable defects can now sometimes be done on a fetus before birth (in utero), completely avoiding some conditions, such as **hydrocephalus** (an accumulation of fluid around the brain that can cause mental or physical disabilities if not corrected). And before long, research might lead to the ability to grow new organs from tissues taken from a person or from stem cells, perhaps allowing a poorly functioning lung, pancreas, or other internal organ to be replaced and the associated physical disabilities to be avoided.

Besides these and other medical breakthroughs, research is bringing us a more complete understanding of the ways in which the individual's psychological, social, and educational environments are related to learning. For example, special educators, psychologists, and pediatricians are increasingly able to identify environmental conditions that increase the likelihood that a child will have learning or behavior problems (see Bolger & Patterson, 2001; Hallahan, Lloyd, Kauffman, Weiss, & Martinez, 2005; Hart & Risley, 1995; Kauffman, 2005a).

Educational methodology has also made strides. In fact, compared to what we know about causes, we know a lot about how exceptional learners can be taught and managed effectively in the classroom. Although special educators constantly lament that not all the questions have been answered, we do know considerably more today about how to educate exceptional learners than we did ten or fifteen years ago (e.g., Hallahan et al., 2005; Heward, 2003; Lloyd, Forness, & Kavale, 1998; Stein & Davis, 2000).

We know more about educating exceptional learners than we did ten or fifteen years ago. An aid helps this six-year-old boy, who is blind, in a general education writing lesson.

Before moving to the specific subject of exceptional learners, we must point out that we vehemently disagree with Hungerford on an important point: We must certainly learn to live with disabling exceptionalities, but we must never accept them. We prefer to think there is hope for the eventual eradication of many of the disabling forms of exceptionality. In addition, we believe that it is of paramount importance to realize that even individuals whose exceptionalities are extreme can be helped to lead fuller lives than they would without appropriate education.

THE IMPORTANCE OF ABILITIES

We must not let people's disabilities keep us from recognizing their abilities. Many people with disabilities have abilities that go unrecognized because their disabilities become the focus of our concern and we do not give enough attention to what they can do. We must study the disabilities of exceptional children and youths if we are to learn how to help them make maximum use of their abilities in school. Some students with disabilities that are not obvious to the casual observer need special programs of education and related services to help them live full, happy, productive lives. However, we must not lose sight of the fact that the most important characteristics of exceptional learners are their abilities, not their disabilities.

DISABILITY VERSUS HANDICAP

Most exceptional individuals have disabilities, and these individuals have often been referred to as "handicapped" in laws, regulations, and everyday conversations. In this book, we make an important distinction between disability and handicap. A disability is an inability to do something, a diminished capacity to perform in a specific way. A handicap, on the other hand, is a disadvantage imposed on an individual. Thus, a disability might or might not be a handicap, depending on the circumstances. Likewise, a handicap might or might not be caused by a disability. For example, blindness is a disability that can be any-

 YOU CAN VISIT
the site of the virtual world congress and exposition on disability at **www.vwcdexpo.com**
For news about special education, see **www. specialednews.com**

A focus on abilities should be a guiding principle for all educators. This museum exhibit includes a raised version of a Van Gogh painting for people with visual impairments.

thing but a handicap in the dark. In fact, in the dark, the person who has sight is the one who is handicapped. Needing to use a wheelchair might be a handicap in certain circumstances, but the disadvantage may be caused by architectural barriers or other people's reactions, not the inability to walk. Other people can handicap those who are different from themselves (in color, size, appearance, language, and so on) by stereotyping them or not giving them opportunities to do the things they are able to do. When working and living with exceptional individuals who have disabilities, we must constantly strive to separate their disabilities from the handicaps. That is, our goal should be to confine their handicaps to those characteristics and circumstances that cannot be changed and to make sure that we impose no further handicaps by our attitudes or our unwillingness to accommodate their disabilities.

DISABILITY VERSUS INABILITY

Another important distinction is that between inability and disability. All disabilities are an inability to do something. However, not every inability to do something is a disability. Disability is a subset of inability. "A disability is an inability to do something that most people, with typical maturation, opportunity, or instruction, can do" (Kauffman & Hallahan, 2005a, p. 30). Think about age and ability. Most 6-month-olds cannot walk or talk, but they are not thought of as having a disability because their inability is age-appropriate. However, if that inability extends well past the time that most children learn to walk and talk, then we consider their inability a disability. Consider the role of instruction. An adult's inability to read is not a reading disability if she or he has not had reading instruction. Weigh the factor of typical adult human abilities. A typical adult male might not be able to lift 400 pounds, but this is not considered a disability because most men simply cannot lift 400 pounds. Judge inability in the context of old age. The average 70-year-old cannot run ten miles, but most 70-year-olds can walk a considerable distance. Not being able to run ten miles is not considered a disability for a 70-year-old, but being unable to walk at all is. Our point is simply that disability is a significant difference from what we expect most people to be able to do, given their age, opportunities, and instruction.

Educational Definition of Exceptional Learners

For purposes of their education, exceptional learners are those who require special education and related services if they are to realize their full human potential (Kauffman & Hallahan, 2005a). They require special education because they are markedly different from most students in one or more of the following ways: They may have mental retardation, learning or attention disabilities, emotional or behavioral disorders, physical disabilities, disorders of communication, autism, traumatic brain injury, impaired hearing, impaired sight, or special gifts or talents. In the chapters that follow, we define as exactly as possible what it means to have an exceptionality.

Two concepts are important to our educational definition of exceptional learners: (1) diversity of characteristics and (2) need for special education. The concept of diversity is inherent in the definition of exceptionality; the need for special education is inherent in an educational definition. The exceptional learner is very different from most (typical or average) individuals in a particular way that is relevant to their education. Their particular educationally relevant difference demands instruction that is different from what most (typical or average) learners require (Kauffman & Hallahan, 2005a).

Consider the case described in the Personal Perspectives on page 9. The story illustrates a matter we have mentioned and discuss further in Chapter 2: how our focus on persons with disabilities must be on what they can do and how they should be integrated into the larger society as much as possible.

Personal Perspectives

BLAIR SMITH

BLAIR SMITH is different . . . Her legs look like they could snap beneath her at any moment, and she is so short that her perspective barely changes when she rises from her wheelchair.

Still, she always rises.

Smith is among the 20,000 to 50,000 people in the United States with the bone disorder osteogenesis imperfecta (OI). She is also a relentlessly giddy cheerleader at Monticello High School.

There are at least four forms of OI, representing extreme variations in severity from one individual to another. Smith's case falls somewhere in the fairly severe category. OI has rendered her bones soft and brittle, leaving her literally fragile. When she walks, she relies on the support of her crutches and leg braces to keep from breaking a leg or two. Her growth was stunted drastically. . . .

As a ninth-grader at Albemarle High School, Smith cheered from the stands like most of the other Patriot students. But for her sophomore year, she moved to brand-new Monticello . . . and joined the junior varsity team for the Mustangs.

And as a junior this past fall, Smith made the varsity squad, serving as a headliner for Monticello's act from September to February. She takes the floor in her wheelchair—Smith's parents had to solicit the aid of [her physical education teacher] to make her use the chair—and participates in the routines in her own way. Stunts are definitely out, but Smith manages to make her indelible mark on the show without the tools of gymnastic display. . . .

"It's been unbelievable," Debbie Smith [Blair's mother] said. "The kids have just been wonderful. They have been wonderful the whole time she has been in school about accepting her for the way she is."

Blair Smith—just another young girl full of life.

Added Ralph Smith [Blair's father]: "People are always pushing her forward and letting her do things and not putting her in a shell." . . .

She is just another young girl full of life.

That is all. And that makes you want to stand up and cheer. ■

Source: "Something to Cheer About" by Tom Gresham, *The Daily Progress,* May 7, 2000, pp. E1, E6, Charlottesville, VA. Reprinted with permission.

Blair Smith typically, but not always, uses a wheelchair because of a physical disability. However, that does not stop her from being a high school cheerleader or from being included with her peers in many typical teenage activities. For her, appropriate education requires a few reasonable accommodations that allow her access to places and activities. Most of all, she needs—and receives—an attitude of acceptance on the part of teachers and peers.

Sometimes seemingly obvious disabilities are never identified, and the consequences for the person and his or her family, as well as for the larger society, are tragic. Sometimes disabilities are identified but special education is not provided, and opportunities for the child's development are thus squandered. Although early identification and intervention hold the promise of preventing many disabilities from becoming worse, preventive action often is not taken (Kauffman, 1999b, 2005b).

Consider the case of author Martha Randolph Carr (Carr, 2004). She describes her own son's learning disability, related to his attention deficit/hyperactivity disorder and her inability, until he was in high school, to see the disability. Her unwillingness to see his disability was motivated by the typical objections: labels and self-image.

> When Louie was in first grade it became obvious to me that he was having difficulty reading. To avoid labels being placed on my young son, I did what I thought was best: I started reading to Louie. . . . Through elementary and middle school, Louie grew into a thoughtful, intelligent, articulate boy who earned mostly Bs , but who had trouble comprehending the little he could read. No one else knew, and Louie and I rarely talked about it.
>
> His reading difficulty was the only problem I saw, and I accepted that everything else was fine. I told myself that I was doing the right thing because Louie might feel badly about himself if he thought there was something wrong and be-

Personal Perspectives

AN IEP FOR ALICE: WHAT CAN HAPPEN WHEN SPECIAL EDUCATION WORKS

ALICE'S first-grade teacher called about five minutes after the educational planner left my room. Both the first-grade teacher and the educational planner informed me that at the eligibility meeting the day before, it was determined that Alice qualified for services in my class for children with mild mental retardation.

"It would be great if you could write the IEP for Alice soon, so we could have her start right after Christmas," her teacher suggested. "She cries so much. I feel so bad for her. She's no problem, but she just can't do the work." . . .

The father flatly refused to have her placed in my class. "Alice can do the work. I know she can," he said.

So Alice started out the year with new clothes, a smile, and the fine-motor skills of a two-year-old. And although she was from a loving, attentive family that read to her and paid a lot of attention to her, her skills were seriously delayed compared to the other students in the first grade. It wasn't that she didn't learn. She just took so much longer than the other children in her class. Even though Alice participated in the resource program, the speech program, the occupational therapy program (all done in the general education classroom and including other classmates in her lessons), she could not keep up with even the slowest group in her class.

It wasn't long before Alice was asking her mother, "Why can't I do what the other kids do? I want to do it." Motivation did not seem to be a problem initially, but after a few months, Alice decided not to try to try. Can't say that I much blame her. After a while, she made her misery known to all, both at home and at school. She became a helpless blob that cried most of the time. Her teacher said, "As far as I know, no one in my class has ever been mean to Alice. She just purely hates school now," she sighed. Alice's mother agreed with the teacher. "I've asked her over and over again if anyone has been mean to her. She says no, and I believe her." After reading her folder and talking with teachers who worked with Alice, I felt bad for her too.

The parents and I wrote an educational plan for Alice, stating that she would begin attending my class after Christmas. Dad still wasn't so sure that he approved, but knew that something had to be done. "But you have to promise to push her. She can be really manipulative," he warned.

After a few weeks of Alice's placement in my room, the parents and I met again. They seemed much happier. "Alice enjoys coming to school now," they let me know. The dad, much to his credit, wished that he had not denied her services in the fall. "She feels so much better about herself now," he said.

Two years later, Alice's father and I talked about his reaction to the eligibility meeting (the one deciding that Alice qualified for my services). "There were so many people," he said, "and they were all saying that there was something terribly wrong with my daughter. I wondered who in the hell they were talking about! My pretty little girl is so loving and funny. How could they say she was retarded?"

"Does it matter what label they put on her? Isn't she still a pretty, funny, loving little girl?"

"Yeah," he laughed. "Except now she can read!" ■

Source: Kauffman, J. M., & Pullen, P. L. (1996). Eight myths about special education. *Focus on Exceptional Children, 28*(5), 7–8. Reprinted with permission.

cause mainstream colleges wouldn't accept a kid with learning disabilities. Fortunately, time and high school caught up with both of us.

Finally, in high school, Mrs. Carr and Louie could no longer cover up his disability. But his response to recognizing his disability—to its finally being diagnosed—was very different from what she had anticipated.

When I told Louie about the diagnosis, he didn't look hurt or confused. Instead, his face relaxed and he shouted, "You mean I'm not stupid?!" I was so taken aback that I started to cry. Louie said, still very relieved, "Were you worried, too?" I cried harder.
    By denying the truth to myself and thus keeping it from Louie, I had left him with the only other plausible answer that he could come up with as to why he always worked so much harder than his friends and didn't get the same grades.

Special education does not always work as it should, but when it does, a student's disability is identified early, and effective special education is provided in the least restrictive environment. The student's parents are involved in the decision about how to address the student's needs, and the outcome of special education is the student's improved achievement and behavior. Consider the case of Alice, presented in the Personal Perspectives on page 10.

Students with exceptionalities are an extraordinarily diverse group in comparison to the general population, and relatively few generalizations apply to all exceptional individuals. Their exceptionalities can involve sensory, physical, cognitive, emotional, or communication abilities or any combination of these. Furthermore, exceptionalities may vary greatly in cause, degree, and effect on educational progress, and the effects may vary greatly depending on the individual's age, sex, and life circumstances. Any individual we might present as an example of our definition is likely to be representative of exceptional learners in some respects but unrepresentative in others.

The typical student who receives special education has no immediately obvious disability. He (more than half of the students served by special education are males) is in elementary or middle school and has persistent problems in learning and behaving appropriately in school. His problems are primarily academic and social or behavioral. These difficulties are not apparent to many teachers until they have worked with the student for a period of weeks or months. His problems persist despite teachers' efforts to meet his needs in the regular school program in which most students succeed. He is most likely to be described as having a learning disability or to be designated by an even broader label indicating that his academic and social progress in school is unsatisfactory owing to a disability.

By federal law, an exceptional student is not to be identified as eligible for special education until careful assessment indicates that he or she is unable to make satisfactory progress in the regular school program without special services designed to meet his or her extraordinary needs. Federal special education laws and regulations include definitions of several conditions (categories such as learning disability, mental retardation, and hearing impairment) that might create a need for special education. These laws and regulations require that special services be provided to meet whatever special needs are created by a disabling condition and cannot be met in the regular educational program. They do not require that special education be provided simply because a student has a disability.

UNDERSTANDING THE STANDARDS AND PRINCIPLES What special services must be provided when a student is identified with a disability? *(CEC Knowledge and Skills Standard CC1K6)*

Council for Exceptional Children

Prevalence of Exceptional Learners

Prevalence refers to the percentage of a population or number of individuals having a particular exceptionality. The prevalence of mental retardation, for example, might be estimated at 2.3 percent, which means that 2.3 percent of the population, or twenty-three

Casebook Reflections 1.1

Refer to the case *Should I Take Juanita Pope?* in your booklet. Many critics of special education say that too many students are identified for services. What characteristics make you think that she has a disability?

FOR ADDITIONAL INFORMATION about annual reports to Congress on IDEA, see **www.edgov/about/offices/list/osers/osep/index.html?sro-mr**

Autism or autistic spectrum disorder
A pervasive developmental disability characterized by extreme withdrawal, cognitive deficits, language disorders, self-stimulation, and onset before the age of thirty months.

Traumatic brain injury (TBI)
Injury to the brain (not including conditions present at birth, birth trauma, or degenerative diseases or conditions) resulting in total or partial disability or psychosocial maladjustment that affects educational performance; may affect cognition, language, memory, attention, reasoning, abstract thinking, judgment, problem solving, sensory or perceptual and motor disabilities, psychosocial behavior, physical functions, information processing, or speech.

---

people in every thousand, are assumed to have mental retardation. If the prevalence of giftedness is assumed to be between 3 percent and 5 percent, we would expect somewhere between thirty and fifty people in a sample of a thousand to have special gifts of some kind. Obviously, accurate estimates of prevalence depend on our ability to count the number of people in a given population who have a certain exceptionality.

At first thought, the task of determining the number of students who have exceptionalities seems simple enough, yet the prevalence of most exceptionalities is uncertain and a matter of considerable controversy. A number of factors make it hard to say with great accuracy and confidence just how many exceptional individuals there are, including vagueness in definitions, frequent changes in definitions, and the role of schools in determining exceptionality—matters that we discuss in later chapters (see also Kauffman & Hallahan, 2005a).

Government figures show that about ten students out of every hundred were receiving special education in the early twenty-first century (U.S. Department of Education, 2002). Beginning in the mid-1970s, there was steady growth in the number of students served by special education, from about 3.75 million in 1976 to more than 5 million by the early twenty-first century. Most of the children and youths who are served by special education are between the ages of 6 and 17. Although preschoolers and youths ages 18 to 21 are being identified with increasing frequency as having disabilities, school-age children and youths in their early teens make up the bulk of the identified population.

The percentage of the special education population who are identified as having certain disabilities has changed considerably over several decades. For example, the number of students who are identified as having learning disabilities has more than doubled since the mid-1970s; these students now make up about half of the number of students receiving special education. In contrast, the percentage of students whose primary disability is "speech or language impairments" has declined substantially, and the percentage identified as having "mental retardation" is now about half of what it was in 1976. No one has an entirely satisfactory explanation of these changes. However, they might in part reflect alterations in definitions and diagnostic criteria for certain disabilities and the social acceptability of the "learning disabilities" label. In subsequent chapters, we discuss the prevalence of specific categories of exceptionality.

HIGH-INCIDENCE AND LOW-INCIDENCE CATEGORIES

Some disabilities occur with a relatively high frequency. These are called *high-incidence* disabilities because they are among the most common. Learning disabilities, communication (speech and language) disorders, emotional disturbance, and mild mental retardation are among those that are usually considered high-incidence. Other disabilities occur relatively rarely and are considered *low-incidence*. These include disabilities such as low vision and blindness, deafness, deaf-blindness, severe mental retardation, and autism.

Although the rates of occurrence of most of the high-incidence disabilities have remained relatively stable in the early twenty-first century, there have been dramatic increases in some of the low-incidence categories. For example, there has been a dramatic increase in the identification of **autism** or **autistic spectrum disorder** since about 1995, a matter that we discuss further in Chapter 12. Other low-incidence categories that are showing substantial increases in numbers include **traumatic brain injury (TBI)** and orthopedic impairments, much of this due to increases in spinal cord injury and in survival of severe physical trauma, owing to better medical care.

Much of the increase in autism probably represents improved identification procedures and identification of milder cases of autism, not an epidemic (National Research Council,

2001). Although some of the increase in TBI might represent better diagnosis, it might also reflect actual increases in brain injuries, as we will discuss in Chapter 13. The increases in orthopedic impairments might reflect the increasing survival rate of infants born with significant physical anomalies and children who have been involved in accidents. Increases in hearing and vision impairments might represent better diagnosis of these disabilities, too.

Definition of Special Education

Special education means specially designed instruction that meets the unusual needs of an exceptional student. Special materials, teaching techniques, or equipment and/or facilities might be required. For example, students with visual impairments might require reading materials in large print or braille; students with hearing impairments might require hearing aids and/or instruction in sign language; those with physical disabilities might need special equipment; those with emotional or behavioral disorders might need smaller and more highly structured classes; and students with special gifts or talents might require access to working professionals. Related services—special transportation, psychological assessment, physical and occupational therapy, medical treatment, and counseling—might be necessary if special education is to be effective. The single most important goal of special education is finding and capitalizing on exceptional students' abilities. To highlight successes in special education, we have included Success Stories: Special Educators at Work, in each chapter having to do with a particular disability. A sample Success Stories appears below.

SUCCESS STORIES

Introduction

Molly, a student with mental retardation, is a student council representative at her school. Eliot, a student with a learning disability, is finally learning how to read. Josh, a student with attention deficit/hyperactivity disorder, hopes to play football at a Division I school. Through the use of technology, David, a quadriplegic who relies on a ventilator, participates in every aspect of his special school.

These are the stories of success in special education. The critics of special education abound, and we are sure you have heard many of them (e.g., Bolick, 2001; Finn & Rotherham, 2001; Fisher, 2001). Reform movements in the 1980s and 1990s cited a parallel system that was failing students and that needed radical reform (Stainback & Stainback, 1984; Will, 1986). We disagree (e.g., Crockett, 1999–2000; Hockenbury, Kauffman, & Hallahan, 1999–2000; Kauffman, Bantz, & McCullough, 2002; Kauffman & Hallahan, 2005a). Our view of special education is one of challenge and one of the individual, much as Zigmond described:

Special education is, first and foremost, instruction focused on individual need. It is carefully planned. It is intensive, urgent, relentless, and goal-directed. (Zigmond, 1997, pp. 384–385)

We include a Success Stories box in each disability chapter to highlight the intensive, relentless, and specific instruction that is necessary to bring about change in individuals with disabilities. In addition, we include questions at the end of each story that ask you to reflect on your professional development and your beliefs about students with disabilities. Finally, the Success Stories boxes include a section entitled "Using the CEC Standards" to help you integrate the major concepts of the chapters and the Success Stories with the professional requirements of new special educators. Our intent is to provide you with examples of how special education that includes high-quality instruction, hard work, and appropriate collaboration can make for student success. ■

The best general education cannot replace special education. Compared to general education, special education is more precisely controlled in pace or rate, intensity, relentlessness, structure, reinforcement, teacher-pupil ratio, curriculum, and monitoring or assessment (Kauffman & Hallahan, 2005a). We think it is a good idea to improve the education of all children, an objective of the federal No Child Left Behind Act of the early twenty-first century. However, good or reformed general education does not and cannot replace special education for those students who are at the extremes of the range of disabilities (Kauffman & Hallahan, 2005a; Kauffman & Wiley, 2004).

Providing Special Education

Several administrative plans are available for the education of exceptional learners, from a few special provisions made by the student's regular teacher to twenty-four-hour residential care in a special facility. Who educates exceptional students and where they receive their education depend on two factors: (1) how and how much the student differs from average students and (2) what resources are available in the school and community. We describe various administrative plans for education according to the degree of physical integration—the extent to which exceptional and nonexceptional students are taught in the same place by the same teachers.

Beginning with the least specialized environment, the regular classroom teacher who is aware of the individual needs of students and is skilled at meeting them may be able to acquire appropriate materials, equipment, and/or instructional methods. At this level, the direct services of specialists might not be required—the expertise of the regular teacher might meet the student's needs. Some students with disabilities can be accommodated in this way; no truly special educaiton is required to meet their needs.

Alternatively, the regular classroom teacher might need *consultation* with a special educator or other professional (e.g., the school psychologist) in addition to acquiring the special materials, equipment, or methods. The special educator might instruct the regular teacher, refer the teacher to other resources, or demonstrate the use of materials, equipment, or methods. Thus, the special education that is required is minimal.

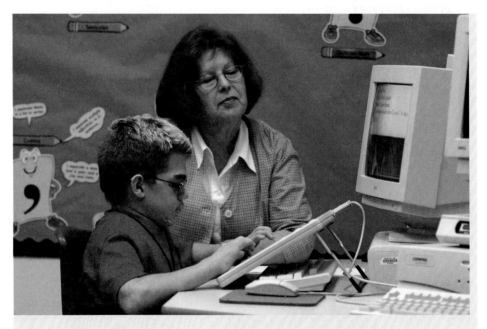

Special education is precisely controlled in pace or rate, intensity, relentlessness, structure, reinforcement, teacher-pupil ratio, curriculum, and monitoring or assessment.

A special educator may provide *itinerant* services to the exceptional student and/or the regular classroom teacher. The itinerant teacher establishes a consistent schedule, moving from school to school and visiting classrooms to instruct students individually or in small groups. This teacher provides materials and teaching suggestions for the regular teacher to carry out and consults with the regular teacher about special problems. The level of specialization is still not high.

A *resource* teacher provides services for the students and teachers in only one school. The students being served are enrolled in the regular classroom and work with the specially trained teacher for a length of time and at a frequency determined by the nature and severity of their particular problems. The resource teacher continually assesses the needs of the students and their teachers and usually works with students individually or in small groups in a special classroom where special materials and equipment are available. Typically, the resource teacher also serves as a consultant to the regular classroom teacher, advising on the instruction and management of the student in the classroom and perhaps demonstrating instructional techniques. The flexibility of the plan and the fact that the student remains with nondisabled peers most of the time make this a particularly attractive and popular alternative.

One of the most visible—and, in recent years, controversial—service alternatives is the special *self-contained class.* Such a class typically enrolls fifteen or fewer exceptional students with particular characteristics or needs. The teacher ordinarily has been trained as a special educator and provides all or most of the instruction. The students who are assigned to such classes usually spend most or all of the school day separated from their nondisabled peers. Often, students with disabilities are included with nondisabled students during part of the day (perhaps for physical education, music, or some other activity in which they can participate well).

Special *day schools* provide an all-day special placement for exceptional learners who need this level of specialization or dedication to their needs. The day school is usually organized for a specific category of exceptional students and may contain special equipment necessary for their care and education. These students return to their homes during nonschool hours.

Hospital or homebound instruction is most often required by students who have physical disabilities, although it is sometimes employed for those with emotional or behavioral disorders or other disabilities when no alternative is readily available. Typically, the youngster is confined to the hospital or the home for a relatively short time, and the hospital or homebound teacher maintains contact with the regular teacher.

In a *residential school,* exceptional students receive twenty-four-hour care away from home, often at a distance from their communities. This is the highest level of specialization or dedication on the continuum of alternative placements required by Individuals with Disabilities Education Act (IDEA). These students might make periodic visits home or return each weekend, but during the week, they are residents of the institution, where they receive academic instruction in addition to management of their daily living environment.

Figure 1.1 illustrates the idea of variation in the separation of children from their regular classrooms and peers. It also

Casebook Reflections

Refer to the case *Least Restrictive for Whom?* in your booklet. Hearing-impaired and a teacher for students with hearing impairments in high school, Andy commented on Brian's situation: "How can you consider this [the general education classroom] the least restrictive environment for Brian when he can only communicate with one person in the whole school?"(p. 31). How should one interpret the notion of "least restrictive environment" in Brian's case? Does his case make understanding the concept more difficult?

A special self-contained class, typically enrolls fifteen or fewer students with particular disability characteristics or exceptional needs.

FIGURE 1.1 Continuum of placement options showing hypothetical relationship between degree of separateness from regular classroom peers and degree of specialness of education

Least specialized   Most specialized

Special
day school

Residential
school

Self-contained
special class

Homebound
or hospital
instruction

Itinerant
teacher

Resource
teacher

Regular
class
only

Regular
class with
consultation

Least separate   Most separate

UNDERSTANDING THE STANDARDS AND PRINCIPLES Briefly describe the continuum of placement and services available for individuals with disabilities. *(CEC Knowledge and Skills Standard GC1K5)*

Council for
Exceptional
Children

Least restrictive environment (LRE)
A legal term referring to the fact that exceptional children must be educated in as normal an environment as possible.

illustrates the increasing specialization of environments. As Kauffman and Hallahan (2005a) point out, the degree to which education is "special" is a continuum. That is, education can be "sort of" special or very, very specialized.

Many school systems, in the process of trying to find more effective and economical ways of serving exceptional students, combine or alter these alternatives and the roles special educators and other professionals play in service delivery. There are wide variations among school systems in the kinds of placements made for particular kinds of students.

As we noted earlier, special education law requires placement of the student in the **least restrictive environment (LRE)**. What is usually meant is that the student should be separated from nondisabled classmates and from home, family, and community as little as possible. That is, the student's life should be as normal as possible, and the intervention should be consistent with individual needs and not interfere with individual freedom any more than is absolutely necessary. For example, students should not be placed in special classes if they can be served adequately by resource teachers, and they should not be placed in a residential school if a special class will serve their needs just as well.

Although placement of exceptional students in the least restrictive environment is laudable, the definition of least restrictive is not as simple as it seems. Long ago, Cruickshank (1977) pointed out that greater restriction of the physical environment does not necessarily mean greater restriction of psychological freedom or human potential (see also Crockett & Kauffman, 1999, 2001). In fact, it is conceivable that some students could be more restricted in the long run in a regular class where they are rejected by others and fail to learn necessary skills than in a special class or day school where they learn happily and well (Gliona, Gonzales, & Jacobson, 2005; Kauffman, Bantz, & McCullough, 2002). Over half a century ago, Stullken stated, "School administrators should realize that an exceptional child may be more harmfully segregated when kept in a regular class which does not meet his needs than when assigned to a special class which meets his needs much better" (1950, p. 299).

It is important to keep the ultimate goals for the students in mind and to avoid letting the term *least restrictive* become a hollow slogan that results in shortchanging them in their education (Crockett & Kauffman, 1999, 2001; Kauffman, 1995; Kauffman, McGee, & Brigham, 2004). As Morse noted many years ago, "The goal should be to find the most productive setting to provide the maximum assistance for the child" (1984, p. 120). Gliona and colleagues (2005) have suggested that the term *segregated* not be used to describe the necessary and helpful placement of students in environments that are *dedicated* to highly specialized education. The term *segregated,* they point out, is neither accurate nor appropriate for describing the placement of students in the specialized environments they need. Gliona and his colleagues also suggest a "Direct Access Model" for concpetualizing LRE. As depicted in Figure 1.2, the student is at the center and can access any of the alternative placement options that meet his or her needs. Figure 1.2 shows LRE choices for two different students. In the first case, the student's LRE has been determined to be a special school. In the second case, the student's LRE has been determined to be a combination of resource room services and regular class placement with consultation.

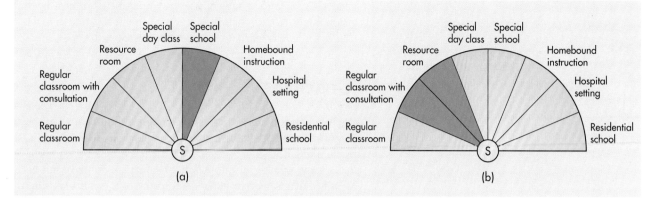

FIGURE 1.2   Direct access model of placement in the least restrictive environment (LRE). (a) a student whose LRE is a special school. (b) a student whose LRE is a combination of programs

Source: Gliona, M. F., Gonzales, A. K., & Jacobson, E. S. (2005). Dedicated, not segregated: Suggested changes in thinking about instructional environments and in the language of special education. In J. M. Kauffman & D. P. Hallahan (Eds.), *The illusion of full inclusion: A comprehensive critique of a current special education bandwagon* (2nd ed., p. 144). Austin, TX: Pro-Ed. Reprinted by permission.

Since the late 1980s, there has been a steady trend toward placing more students with disabilities in regular classes and a corresponding trend toward placing fewer students with disabilities in resource rooms, separate classes, and separate facilities (U.S. Department of Education, 1995, 1997, 2002). Placing more students in regular classes and schools reflects an aim of educational reform, a topic to which we return in Chapter 2.

Considerable variation in the placement of students with disabilities is found from state to state and among school systems within a given state. However, most exceptional students are now educated in regular classes. Nationwide, nearly 50 percent of exceptional children and youths are now served primarily in regular classes. Relatively few students with disabilities are placed outside of regular schools. Figure 1.3 shows the approximate percentage of students served in each type of placement in the early twenty-first century.

Children under the age of six less often receive education in regular classes and more often attend separate schools than do children who have reached the usual school age. Special classes, separate schools, and other environments such as homebound instruction are used more often for older teenagers and young adults than for students of elementary and high school age. We can explain these differences with several facts:

- Preschoolers and young adults who are identified for special education tend to have more severe disabilities than do students in kindergarten through grade 12.
- Some school systems do not have regular classes for preschoolers and young adults; therefore, placements in other than regular classes are typically more available and more appropriate.
- Curriculum and work-related educational programs for older teens and young adults with disabilities are frequently offered off the campuses of regular high schools.

The environment that is least restrictive depends in part on the individual's exceptionality. There is almost never a need to place in a separate class or separate school a student whose primary disability is a speech impairment. Likewise, most students with learning disabilities can be appropriately educated primarily in regular classes. On the other hand, the resources that are

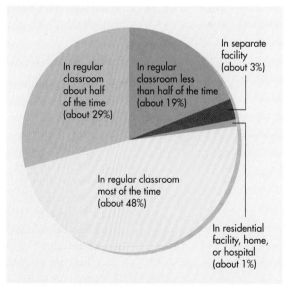

FIGURE 1.3   Approximate percentages of students with disabilities in various placement options in the early twenty-first century

Source: Data from the annual reports of the U.S. Department of Education to Congress on Implementation of the Individuals with Disabilities Education Act.

Casebook Reflections

Refer to the case *Should I Take Juanita Pope?* in your booklet. Consider the factors that might contribute to Juanita's failure in school. In what ways does she fit the description of a child who is at risk?

needed to teach students with severe impairments of hearing and vision might require that these students attend separate schools or classes for at least part of their school careers.

Teachers' Roles

We have noted that most students in public schools who have been identified as exceptional are placed in regular classrooms for at least part of the school day. Furthermore, there is good reason to believe that a large number of public school students who have not been identified as disabled or gifted share many of the characteristics of those who are exceptional. Thus, all teachers must obviously be prepared to deal with exceptional students, although it is unreasonable to expect all teachers to teach all exceptional students (Kauffman & Hallahan, 2005a; Mock & Kauffman, 2002).

The roles of general and special education teachers are not always clear in a given case. Sometimes, uncertainty about the division of responsibility can be extremely stressful; for example, teachers may feel uneasy because it is not clear whose job it is to make special adaptations for a pupil or just what they are expected to do in cooperating with other teachers.

RELATIONSHIP BETWEEN GENERAL AND SPECIAL EDUCATION

During the 1980s, the relationship between general and special education became a matter of increasing concern to policymakers, researchers, and advocates for exceptional children. Radical reformers have recommend that special education be eliminated as a separate, identifiable part of education. They call for a single, unified educational system in which all students are viewed as unique, special, and entitled to the same quality of education. Although many of the suggested reforms have great appeal and some could produce benefits for exceptional students, the basis for the integration of special and general education and the ultimate consequences they might bring have been questioned (Crockett & Kauffman, 1999, 2001; Fuchs & Fuchs, 1994; Hockenbury, Kauffman, & Hallahan, 1999–2000; Kauffman, 1995, 1999–2000; Kauffman & Hallahan, 2005a, 2005b; Martin, 1995; Mock & Kauffman, 2002, 2005).

SPECIAL EDUCATION AND STUDENTS AT RISK

One reason behind reform proposals is concern for pupils who are considered to be at risk. The term *at risk* is often not clearly defined, but it generally refers to students who perform or behave poorly in school and appear likely to fail or fall far short of their potential. Some advocates of reform suggest that at-risk students cannot be or should not be distinguished from those with mild disabilities. Others argue that the problems of at-risk students tend to be ignored because special education siphons resources from general education. Should special education and general education merge for the purpose of making general education better able to respond to students who are at risk? Or should special education maintain its separate identity and be expanded to include these students? Should general education be expected to develop new programs for at-risk students without merging with special education?

There are no ready answers to these and other questions about the education of students who are at risk. Regardless of where one draws the line separating those who are considered to be at risk from those with disabilities, the line is arbitrary and leads to doubts about some students. In other words, there is no entirely clear distinction between *at risk* and *disability* because educational achievement and social competence can vary from a little to a lot, and there is no sudden, dramatic break in people's level of attainment (Kauffman & Hallahan, 2005a).

Uncertainty exists as to how educators should respond to students who are at risk of school failure and/or of developing a disability and the respective roles of general versus special educators in this regard.

THE INCLUSION CONTROVERSY

Inclusion is a term that is often used to describe teaching students with disabilities in the same environment as their age peers who do not have disabilities. We discuss inclusion and its implications further in Chapter 2. Regardless of one's views, the controversy about the relationship between special and general education has made teachers more aware of the problems of deciding just which students should be taught specific curricula, which students should receive special attention or services, and where and by whom these should be provided (Crockett & Kauffman, 1999, 2001; Kauffman & Hallahan, 1997, 2005b; Mock & Kauffman, 2005).

EXPECTATIONS FOR ALL EDUCATORS

There are no pat answers to the questions about how special and general education should work together to see that every student receives an appropriate education. Yet it is clear that the relationship between them must be one of cooperation and collaboration. They must not become independent or mutually exclusive educational tracks, nor can we deny that general and special educators have somewhat different roles to play. To address some specific issues of inclusion for each disability area, we have included a special feature called Making it Work to describe successful partnerships. An introductory sample of this feature appears on page 20.

Regardless of whether a teacher is specifically trained in special education, he or she may be expected to participate in educating exceptional students in any one of the following ways:

1. *Make maximum effort to accommodate individual students' needs.* Teaching in public schools requires dealing with diverse students in every class. All teachers must make an effort to meet the needs of individuals who might differ in some way from the average or typical student. Flexibility, adaptation, accommodation, and special attention are to be

UNDERSTANDING THE STANDARDS AND PRINCIPLES Why is it important for all teachers to have a basic understanding of ways in which disabilities impact learning and development? *(INTASC 2.01)*

Council for Exceptional Children

Collaboration and Co-Teaching of Students with Disabilities

"I have to do what?!"

According to the *17th Annual Report to Congress,* 40.53% of students with disabilities in the United States were served in regular classrooms in the 1992–93 school year (U.S. Department of Education, 1995). In the *24th Annual Report to Congress,* 47% of all students with disabilities spent less than 21% of their school time outside of the general education classroom, the most inclusive category reported (U.S. Department of Education, 2002). With the inclusion of more students with disabilities in the general education classroom, special educators are asking a greater number of general educators to work with them to deliver instruction. This collaboration can take many forms, such as collaborative consultation, working with itinerant teachers or paraprofessionals, and co-teaching. According to the National Center on Educational Restructuring and Inclusion (1995), co-teaching is the collaborative model that is used most often by schools.

To address the issues of collaboration and co-teaching, we have included a feature called "Making It Work" to give readers some how-tos and cautions. The feature boxes in each chapter contain two separate sections: What Does It Mean to Be a Teacher of Students with . . . and Successful Strategies for Co-Teaching or Collaboration. The first section includes information about knowledge and skills special educators should possess as they enter the field, as identified by the Council for Exceptional Children (CEC) in its Performance Based Professional Standards. CEC is the largest professional organization for special educators and is made up of smaller divisions representing professionals and parents from all disability categories. We believe that it is important for all teachers to understand what expertise special educators can contribute to collaborative classrooms. For more information, go to www.cec.sped.org.

The second section contains examples of research-based instructional practices that teachers could use when collaborating or descriptions of successful collaborations in real classrooms. Each box contains specifics about how to get more information about the strategy or classroom described. ■

expected of every teacher. Special education should be considered necessary only when a teacher's best efforts to meet a student's individual needs are not successful.

2. *Evaluate academic abilities and disabilities.* Although a psychologist or other special school personnel might give a student formal standardized tests in academic areas, adequate evaluation requires the teacher's assessment of the student's performance in the classroom. Teachers must be able to report specifically and precisely how students can and cannot perform in all academic areas for which they are responsible.

3. *Refer for evaluation.* By law, all public school systems must make extensive efforts to screen and identify all children and youths of school age who have disabilities. Teachers must observe students' behavior and refer those they suspect of having disabilities for evaluation by a multidisciplinary team. We stress here that a student should not be referred for special education unless extensive and unsuccessful efforts have been made to accommodate the student's needs in regular classes. Before referral, school personnel must document the strategies that have been used to teach and manage the student in general education. Referral is justified only if these strategies have failed. (See the Focus on Concepts on p. 21.)

4. *Participate in eligibility conferences.* Before a student is provided special education, an interdisciplinary team must determine his or her eligibility. Therefore, teachers must be ready to work with other teachers and with professionals from other disciplines (e.g., psychology, medicine, or social work) in determining a student's eligibility for special education.

5. *Participate in writing individualized education programs.* A written individualized education program (IEP) must be on file in the records of every student with a disability. Teachers must be ready to participate in a conference (possibly including the student and/or parents as well as other professionals) in which the program is formulated.

FOCUS ON CONCEPTS

Teachers' Roles: What Should I Do Before I Make a Referral?

IF you are thinking about referring a student, probably the most important thing you should do is contact the student's parents. If you cannot reach them by phone, try a home visit or ask the visiting teacher (or school social worker, psychologist, or other support personnel) to help you set up a conference. It is very important that you discuss the student's problems with the parents before you refer. Parents should never be surprised to find that their child has been referred; they should know well in advance that their child's teachers have noticed problems. One of the most important things you can do to prevent conflict with parents is to establish and maintain communication with them regarding their child's progress.

Before making a referral, check all the student's school records. Look for information that could help you understand the student's behavioral or academic problems. Has the student ever:

- Had a psychological evaluation?
- Qualified for special services?
- Been included in other special programs (e.g., programs for disadvantaged children or speech or language therapy)?
- Scored far below average on standardized tests?
- Been retained?

Do the records indicate:

- Good progress in some areas and poor progress in others?
- Any physical or medical problem?
- That the student is taking medication?

Talk to the student's other teachers and professional support personnel about your concern for him or her. Have other teachers:

- Also had difficulty with the student?
- Found ways of dealing successfully with the student?

The analysis of information obtained in these ways can help you to teach and manage the student successfully or help you justify to the parents why you believe their child might need special education.

Before making a referral, you will be expected to document the strategies that you have used in your class to meet the student's educational needs. Regardless of whether the student is later found to have a disabling condition, your documentation will be useful in the following ways:

- You will have evidence that will be helpful to or required by the committee of professionals who will evaluate the student.
- You will be better able to help the student's parents understand that methods used for other students in the class are not adequate for their child.
- You will have records of successful and/or unsuccessful methods of working with the student that will be useful to you and any other teacher who works with the student in the future.

Your documentation of what you have done might appear to require a lot of paperwork, but careful record keeping will pay off. If the student is causing you serious concern, then you will be wise to demonstrate your concern by keeping written records. Your notes should include items such as the following:

- Exactly what you are concerned about
- Why you are concerned about it
- Dates, places, and times you have observed the problem
- Precisely what you have done to try to resolve the problem
- Who, if anyone, helped you devise the plans or strategies you have used
- Evidence that the strategies have been successful or unsuccessful

In summary, make certain that you have accomplished the following before you make a referral:

- Held at least one conference to discuss your concerns with the parents (or made extensive and documented efforts to communicate with the parents)
- Checked all available school records and interviewed other professionals involved with the child
- Documented the academic and behavioral management strategies that you have tried

Remember that you should refer a student only if you can make a convincing case that the student might have a disability and probably cannot be served appropriately without special education. Referral for special education begins a time-consuming, costly, and stressful process that is potentially damaging to the student and has many legal ramifications. ■

General and special education teachers are expected to share responsibility for educating students with special needs and might need to collaborate with other professionals, depending on students' needs or disabilities.

6. *Communicate with parents or guardians.* Parents (sometimes surrogate parents) or guardians must be consulted during the evaluation of their child's eligibility for special education, formulation of the individualized education program, and reassessment of any special program that may be designed for their child. Teachers must contribute to the school's communication with parents about their child's problems, placement, and progress.

7. *Participate in due process hearings and negotiations.* When parents, guardians, or students with disabilities themselves are dissatisfied with the school's response to educational needs, they may request a due process hearing or negotiations regarding appropriate services. Teachers might be called on to offer observations, opinions, or suggestions in such hearings or negotiations.

8. *Collaborate with other professionals in identifying and making maximum use of exceptional students' abilities.* Finding and implementing solutions to the challenges of educating exceptional students is not the exclusive responsibility of any one professional group. General and special education teachers are expected to share responsibility for educating students with special needs. In addition, teachers might need to collaborate with other professionals, depending on the given student's exceptionality. Psychologists, counselors, physicians, physical therapists, and a variety of other specialists might need teachers' perspectives on students' abilities and disabilities, and they often rely on teachers to implement critical aspects of evaluation or treatment.

A high level of professional competence and ethical judgment is required to conform to these expectations. Teaching demands a thorough knowledge of child development and expertise in instruction. Furthermore, teachers are sometimes faced with serious professional and ethical dilemmas in trying to serve the needs of students and their parents, on the one hand, and in attempting to conform to legal or administrative pressures, on the other (Crockett & Kauffman, 1999; Howe & Miramontes, 1992). For example, when there are indications that a student might have a disability, should the teacher refer that student for evaluation and possible placement in special education, knowing that only inadequate or inappropriate services will be provided? Should a teacher who believes strongly that teenage students with mild retardation need sex education refrain from giving students any information because sex education is not part of the prescribed curriculum and is frowned on by the school board?

EXPECTATIONS FOR SPECIAL EDUCATORS

In addition to being competent enough to meet the expectations for *all* teachers, special education teachers must attain special expertise in the following areas:

1. *Academic instruction of students with learning problems.* The majority of students with disabilities have more difficulty learning academic skills than do those without disabilities. This is true for all categories of disabling conditions because sensory impairments, physical disabilities, and mental or emotional disabilities all tend to make academic learning more difficult. Often, the difficulty is slight; sometimes it is extreme. Special education teachers must have more than patience and hope, though they do need these qualities; they must also have the technical skill to present academic tasks so that students with disabilities will understand and respond appropriately. Exceptional instruction is the key to improving special education (Kauffman & Hallahan, 2005a).

2. *Management of serious behavior problems.* Many students with disabilities have behavior problems in addition to their other exceptionalities. Some, in fact, require special education primarily because of their inappropriate or disruptive behavior. Special education teachers must have the ability to deal effectively with more than the usual troublesome behavior of students. Besides having understanding and empathy, special education teachers must master the techniques that will allow them to draw out particularly withdrawn students, control those who are hyperaggressive and persistently disruptive, and teach critical social skills. Positive, proactive behavior intervention plans are essential for all students who receive special education and exhibit serious behavior problems, regardless of their diagnostic label or classification (Kauffman, Mostert, Trent, & Pullen, 2006).

3. *Use of technological advances.* Technology is increasingly being applied to the problems of teaching exceptional students and improving their daily lives. New devices and methods are rapidly being developed, particularly for students with sensory and physical disabilities. Special education teachers need more than mere awareness of the technology available; they must also be able to evaluate its advantages and disadvantages for teaching the exceptional children and youths with whom they work.

4. *Knowledge of special education law.* For good or ill, special education today involves many details of law. The rights of students with disabilities are spelled out in considerable detail in federal and state legislation. The laws, as well as the rules and regulations that accompany them, are constantly being interpreted by new court decisions, some of which have widespread implications for the practice of special education. Special education teachers do not need to be lawyers, but they do need to be aware of the law's requirements and prohibitions if they are to be adequate advocates for students with disabilities (Yell, in press).

The knowledge and skills that every special education teacher is expected to master have been detailed by the primary professional organization of special educators, the Council for Exceptional Children (1998). We caution here that the specific day-to-day expectations for special education teachers vary from school system to school system and from state to state. What are listed here are the general expectations and areas of competence with which every special educator will necessarily be concerned. Nevertheless, we emphasize that special educators have the responsibility to offer not just good instruction but instruction that is highly individualized, intensive, relentless, urgent, and goal directed (Kauffman & Hallahan, 2005a; Zigmond, 1997, 2003; Zigmond & Baker, 1995). To this end, we include special features entitled Responsive Instruction: Meeting the Needs of Students in each categorical chapter, which provide information about research-based practices to help make instruction intensive, relentless, and goal directed. A sample of this feature is shown on page 24.

Origins of Special Education

There have always been exceptional learners, but there have not always been special educational services to address their needs. During the closing years of the eighteenth century, following the American and French Revolutions, effective procedures were devised for teaching children with sensory impairments—those who were blind or deaf (Winzer, 1986, 1993, 1998). Early in the nineteenth century, the first systematic attempts were made to educate "idiotic" and "insane" children—those who today are said to have mental retardation and **emotional** or behavioral disorders (Kauffman & Landrum, 2006).

In the prerevolutionary era, the most society had offered most children with disabilities was protection—asylum from a cruel world into which they did not fit and in which they could not survive with dignity, if they could survive at all. But as the ideas of democracy, individual freedom, and egalitarianism swept across America and France, there was a change in attitude. Political reformers and leaders in medicine and education began to champion the cause of children and adults with disabilities, urging that these "imperfect" or "incomplete" individuals be taught skills that would allow them to become independent,

Special Education Means Special Instruction

It [special education] is empirically supported practice, drawn from research. To provide special education means to set priorities and select carefully what needs to be taught. It means teaching something special and teaching it in a special way. (Zigmond, 1997, pp. 384–385)

Classwide peer tutoring, community-based instruction, mnemonics, direct instruction, self-monitoring, reducing cursing, instructional adaptations, and adapted physical education—all are research-based practices that are used in today's classrooms. Research in special education has come a long way in the past twenty years (Gersten, Schiller, & Vaughn, 2000). There is now a more substantial research base of effective practices for use with students with disabilities. As in all endeavors, the current research base has limitations, and knowledge is added to it daily. That, combined with many other factors, makes it difficult for teachers to stay current in their knowledge of appropriate instructional practices (Schiller & Malouf, 2000).

Because we believe that effective, empirically supported practice is essential for teachers who work with students with disabilities, we have included a special feature in each disability chapter entitled Responsive Instruction. This feature describes a research-based practice in relative detail, what implications it has for the classroom, and where a teacher can get more information. The practices described within the Responsive Instruction boxes coincide with the CEC Standards for new special educators and provide valuable information for general educators as well. The purpose of the Responsive Instruction boxes is to assist students in connecting the theoretical information provided in the text with current, best-practices in the classroom. For students who are in the early stages of their special education preparation, the feature provides an example of a practical application; for students who are currently teaching or engaged in fieldwork, the feature can direct them to strategies or curricula for classroom use or further exploration. ■

productive citizens. These humanitarian sentiments went beyond a desire to protect and defend people with disabilities. The early leaders sought to normalize exceptional people to the greatest extent possible and confer on them the human dignity they presumably lacked.

The historical roots of special education are found primarily in the early 1800s. Contemporary educational methods for exceptional children can be traced directly to techniques that were pioneered during that era. And many (perhaps most) of today's vital, controversial issues have been issues ever since the dawn of special education. Some contemporary writers believe that the history of special education is critically important to understanding today's issues and should be given more attention because of the lessons we can learn from our past (e.g., Kauffman, 1999a; Kauffman & Landrum, 2006 Smith, 1998a, 1998b). In our discussion of some of the major historical events and trends since 1800, we comment briefly on the history of people and ideas, the growth of the discipline, professional and parent organizations, and legislation.

PEOPLE AND IDEAS

Most of the originators of special education were European physicians. They were primarily young, ambitious people who challenged the wisdom of the established authorities, including their own friends and mentors (Kanner, 1964; see also Winzer, 1998).

Jean-Marc-Gaspard Itard (1775–1838), a French physician who was an authority on diseases of the ear and on the education of students who were deaf, is the person to whom most historians trace the beginning of special education as we know it today. In the early years of the nineteenth century, this young doctor began to educate a boy of about 12 years of age who had been found roaming naked and wild in the forests of France. Itard's mentor, Philippe Pinel (1745–1826), a prominent French physician who was an early advocate of humane treatment of insane people, advised Itard that his efforts would be unsuccessful because the boy, Victor, was a "hopeless idiot." But Itard persevered. He did not eliminate Victor's disabilities, but he did dramatically improve the wild child's behavior through patient, systematic educative procedures (Itard, 1962).

One of Itard's students, Édouard Séguin (1812–1880), immigrated to the United States in 1848. Before that, Séguin had become famous as an educator of so-called idiotic children, even though most thinkers of the day were convinced that such children could not be taught anything of significance.

The ideas of the first special educators were truly revolutionary for their times. These are a few of the revolutionary ideas of Itard, Séguin, and their successors that form the foundation for present-day special education:

- Individualized instruction, in which the child's characteristics, rather than prescribed academic content, provide the basis for teaching techniques
- A carefully sequenced series of educational tasks, beginning with tasks the child can perform and gradually leading to more complex learning
- Emphasis on stimulation and awakening of the child's senses, the aim being to make the child more aware of and responsive to educational stimuli
- Meticulous arrangement of the child's environment, so that the structure of the environment and the child's experience of it lead naturally to learning
- Immediate reward for correct performance, providing reinforcement for desirable behavior
- Tutoring in functional skills, the desire being to make the child as self-sufficient and productive as possible in everyday life
- Belief that every child should be educated to the greatest extent possible, the assumption being that every child can improve to some degree

Special educators have the responsibility to offer not just good instruction, but also instruction that is highly individualized, intensive, relentless, urgent, and goal directed.

So far, we have mentioned only European physicians who figured prominently in the rise of special education. Although much of the initial work did take place in Europe, many U.S. researchers contributed greatly during those early years. They stayed informed of European developments as best they could, some of them traveling to Europe for the specific purpose of obtaining firsthand information about the education of children with disabilities.

Among the young U.S. thinkers who were concerned with the education of students with disabilities was Samuel Gridley Howe (1801–1876), an 1824 graduate of Harvard Medical School. Besides being a physician and an educator, Howe was a political and social reformer, a champion of humanitarian causes and emancipation. He was instrumental in founding the Perkins School for the Blind in Watertown, Massachusetts, and was also a teacher of students who were deaf and blind. His success in teaching Laura Bridgman, who was deaf and blind, greatly influenced the education of Helen Keller. In the 1840s, Howe was also a force behind the organization of an experimental school for children with mental retardation and was personally acquainted with Séguin.

When Thomas Hopkins Gallaudet (1787–1851), a minister, was a student at Andover Theological Seminary, he tried to teach a girl who was deaf. He visited Europe to learn about educating the deaf and in 1817 established the first American residential school, in Hartford, Connecticut, for students who were deaf (now known as the American School of the Deaf). Gallaudet University in Washington, D.C., the only liberal-arts college for students who are deaf, was named in his honor.

The early years of special education were vibrant with the pulse of new ideas. It is not possible to read the words of Itard, Séguin, Howe, and their contemporaries without being captivated by the romance, idealism, and excitement of their exploits. The results they

Jean-Marc-Gaspard Itard (1775–1838) is the person to whom most historians trace the beginning of special education as we know it today.

UNDERSTANDING THE STANDARDS AND PRINCIPLES How did Itard, Séguin, Howe, and Gallaudet shape the field of special education? *(CEC Knowledge and Skills Standard GC1K3)*

Council for Exceptional Children

YOU MIGHT want to explore the website of the Council for Exceptional Children at **www.cec.sped.org**

For more information about the history of special education, see **www.npr.org/programs/disability** and **www.disabilityhistory.org**

achieved were truly remarkable for their era. Today, special education remains a vibrant field in which innovations, excitement, idealism, and controversies are the norm. Teachers of exceptional children—and that includes all teachers, as we noted earlier—must understand how and why special education emerged as a discipline (Kauffman & Hallahan, 2005a).

GROWTH OF THE DISCIPLINE

Special education did not suddenly spring up as a new discipline, nor did it develop in isolation from other disciplines. The emergence of psychology and sociology and especially the beginning of the widespread use of mental tests in the early years of the twentieth century had enormous implications for the growth of special education. Psychologists' study of learning and their prediction of school failure or success by means of tests helped to focus attention on children with special needs. Sociologists, social workers, and anthropologists drew attention to the ways in which exceptional children's families and communities responded to them and affected their learning and adjustment. Anecdotal accounts of mental retardation or other mental disabilities can be found in the nineteenth century literature, but they are not presented within the conceptual frameworks that we recognize today as psychology, sociology, and special education (see, for example, Hallahan & Kauffman, 1977; Kauffman & Landrum, in 2006; Richards & Singer, 1998). Even in the early twentieth century, the concepts of disability seem crude by today's standards (see Trent, 1998).

Development of the Council for Exceptional Children As the education profession itself matured and as compulsory school attendance laws became a reality, there was a growing realization among teachers and school administrators that a large number of students must be given something beyond the ordinary classroom experience. Elizabeth Farrell, a teacher in New York City in the early twentieth century, was highly instrumental in the development of special education as a profession. She and the New York City superintendent of schools attempted to use information about child development, social work, mental testing, and instruction to address the needs of children and youths who were being ill served in or excluded from regular classes and schools. Farrell was a great advocate for services for students with special needs (see Safford & Safford, 1998). Her motives and those of the teachers and administrators who worked with her were to see that every student—including every exceptional child or youth—had an appropriate education and received the related health and social services necessary for optimum learning in school (Hendrick & MacMillan, 1989; MacMillan & Hendrick, 1993). In 1922, Farrell and a group of other special educators from across the United States and Canada founded the Council for Exceptional Children, which is still the primary professional organization of special educators.

Contemporary special education is a professional field with roots in several academic disciplines—especially medicine, psychology, sociology, and social work—in addition to professional education. It is a discipline that is sufficiently different from the mainstream of professional education to require special training programs but sufficiently like the mainstream to maintain a primary concern for schools and teaching.

Development of Other Professional and Parent Organizations Individuals and ideas have played crucial roles in the history of special education, but it is accurate to say that much of the progress that has been made over the years has been achieved primarily by the collective efforts of professionals and parents. Professional groups were organized first, beginning in the nineteenth century. Effective national parent organizations have existed in the United States only since 1950.

Although parent organizations offer membership to individuals who do not have exceptional children of their own, they are made up primarily of parents who do have such children and concentrate on issues that are of special concern to them. Parent organizations have typically served three essential functions: (1) providing an informal group for parents who understand one another's problems and needs and help one another deal with anxi-

In 1817, Thomas Hopkins Gallaudet (1787–1851) established the first American residential school for students who were deaf. Gallaudet University in Washington, D.C., the only liberal arts college for students who are deaf, was named in his honor.

eties and frustrations, (2) providing information regarding services and potential resources, and (3) providing the structure for obtaining needed services for their children. Some of the organizations that came about primarily as the result of parents' efforts include the ARC (formerly the Association for Retarded Citizens), the National Association for Gifted Children, the Learning Disabilities Association, the Autism Society of America, and the Federation of Families for Children's Mental Health.

Legislation and Litigation

Laws have played a major role in the history of special education. In fact, much of the progress in meeting the educational needs of children and youths with disabilities is attributable to laws requiring states and localities to include students with special needs in the public education system. We focus here on recent legislation that represents a culmination of decades of legislative history. However, litigation (lawsuits or court decisions) has also played a major role in special education.

LEGISLATION

A landmark federal law was passed in 1975: the **Education for All Handicapped Children Act**, also commonly known as PL 94-142.* In 1990, this law was amended to become the **Individuals with Disabilities Education Act (IDEA)**. In 1997, the law was amended again, but its name was not changed (see Bateman & Linden, 1998; Huefner, 2000; and Yell, in press, for details). The law was reauthorized again in 2004, as the Individuals with Disabilities Education Improvement Act. IDEA ensures that all children and youths with disabilities have the right to a free, appropriate public education.

Another landmark federal law, enacted in 1990, is the **Americans with Disabilities Act (ADA)**. ADA ensures the right of individuals with disabilities to nondiscriminatory treatment in other aspects of their lives; it provides protections of civil rights in the specific areas of employment, transportation, public accommodations, state and local government, and telecommunications.

IDEA and another federal law focusing on intervention in early childhood (PL 99-457) now mandate a free, appropriate public education for every child or youth between the ages of three and twenty-one years regardless of the nature or severity of the disability he or she may have. PL 99-457 also provides incentives for states to develop early intervention programs for infants with known disabilities and those who are considered to be at risk. Together, these laws require public school systems to identify all children and youths with disabilities and to provide the special education and related services they may need.

The law that we know today as IDEA was revolutionary. It was the first federal law mandating free, appropriate public education for all children with disabilities. Its basic provisions, as amended most recently in 2004, are described in the Focus on Concepts on p. 28.

Historically, legislation has been increasingly specific and mandatory. Beginning in the 1980s, however, the renewed emphasis on states' rights and local autonomy, plus a political strategy of federal deregulation, led to attempts to repeal some of the provisions of IDEA (then still known as PL 94-142) and loosen federal rules and regulations. Federal disinvestment in education and deregulation of special education programs remain popular ideas. It is not surprising that federal mandates for special education have come under fire. Dissatisfaction with federal mandates is due in part to the fact that the federal government contributes relatively little to the funding of special education. Although the demands of

Education for All Handicapped Children Act
Also known as Public Law 94-142, which became law in 1975 and is now known as the Individuals with Disabilities Education Act (IDEA).

Individuals with Disabilities Education Improvement Act (IDEA)
The Individuals with Disabilities Education Act was enacted in 1990 and reauthorized in 1997 and 2004; it replaced PL 94-142, enacted in 1975. This federal law requires that to receive funds under the act, every school system in the nation must provide a free, appropriate public education for every child between the ages of three and twenty-one, regardless of how or how seriously he or she may be disabled.

Americans with Disabilities Act (ADA)
Civil rights legislation for persons with disabilities ensuring nondiscrimination in a broad range of activities.

 You can access current information about IDEA at: **www.ideapractices.org** and at **www.ed.gov/inits/commissionsboards/whspecialeducation/index.html**

*Legislation is often designated PL (for public law), followed by a hyphenated numeral, the first set of digits representing the number of the Congress that passed the bill and the second set representing the number of that bill. Thus, PL 94-142 was the 142nd public law passed by the 94th Congress.

Major Provisions of IDEA

Each state and locality must have a plan to ensure*:

Identification	Extensive efforts to screen and identify all children and youths with disabilities.
Free, Appropriate Public Education (FAPE)	Every student with a disability has an appropriate public education at no cost to the parents or guardian.
Due Process	The student's and parents' rights to information and informed consent before the student is evaluated, labeled, or placed, and the right to an impartial due process hearing if they disagree with the school's decisions.
Parent/Guardian Surrogate Consultation	The student's parents or guardian are consulted about the student's evaluation and placement and the educational plan; if the parents or guardian are unknown or unavailable, a surrogate parent must be found to act for the student.
Least Restrictive Environment (LRE)	The student is educated in the least restrictive environment consistent with his or her educational needs and, insofar as possible, with students without disabilities.
Individualized Education Program (IEP)	A written individualized education program is prepared for each student with a disability, including levels of functioning, long-term goals, extent to which the student will *not* participate in the general education classroom and curriculum, services to be provided, plans for initiating and evaluating the services, and needed transition services (from school to work or continued education).
Nondiscriminatory Evaluation	The student is evaluated in all areas of suspected disability and in a way that is not biased by his or her language or cultural characteristics or disabilities. Evaluation must be by a multidisciplinary team, and no single evaluation procedure may be used as the sole criterion for placement or planning.
Confidentiality	The results of evaluation and placement are kept confidential, though the student's parents or guardian may have access to the records.
Personnel Development, Inservice	Training for teachers and other professional personnel, including inservice training for regular teachers, in meeting the needs of students with disabilities. ■

*Detailed federal rules and regulations govern the implementation of each of these major provisions.

IDEA are detailed, state and local governments must pay most of the cost of special education programs. Some have characterized the legal history of special education as a long, strange trip (Yell, Rogers, & Rogers, 1998).

Special education law is highly controversial, and battles over IDEA are ongoing. The amendment and continuation of IDEA in 1997 and 2004 represented a sustained commitment to require schools, employers, and government agencies to recognize the abilities of people with disabilities. IDEA and ADA require reasonable accommodations that will allow those who have disabilities to participate to the fullest extent possible in all the activities of daily living that individuals without disabilities take for granted. The requirements of ADA are intended to grant equal opportunities to people with disabilities in employment, transportation, public accommodations, state and local government, and telecommunications.

In the early twenty-first century, under the administration of President George W. Bush, the federal No Child Left Behind Act (NCLB) became a major factor in the focus of public schooling. NCLB was an attempt to improve the academic performance of all students, including those with disabilities. In fact, under NCLB and the 2004 reauthorization of IDEA, most students with disabilities are expected to take standard tests of academic achievement and to achieve at a level equal to that of students without disabilities. Whether this expectation is reasonable and achievable is an open question (Kauffman, 2004; in press; Kauffman & Wiley, 2004; Yell & Drasgow, 2005).

LITIGATION

Laws often have little or no effect on the lives of individuals with disabilities until courts interpret exactly what the laws require in practice. Exceptional children, primarily through the actions of parent and professional organizations, have been getting their day in court more frequently since IDEA and related federal and state laws were passed. Therefore, we must examine litigation to complete the picture of how the U.S. legal system may safeguard or undermine appropriate education for exceptional children.

The Individuals with Disabilities Act (IDEA), passed in 1990 and renewed in 1997 and 2004, requires public schools to provide equal education opportunities for all students with disabilities.

Zelder (1953) noted that in the early days of public education, school attendance was seen as a privilege that could be awarded to or withheld from an individual child at the discretion of local school officials. During the late nineteenth and early twentieth centuries, the courts typically found that disruptive children or those with mental retardation could be excluded from school for the sake of preserving order, protecting the teacher's time from excessive demands, and sparing children the discomfort of seeing others who are disabled. In the first half of the twentieth century, the courts tended to defend the majority of schoolchildren from a disabled minority. But now the old excuses for excluding students with disabilities from school are no longer thought to be valid.

Today, the courts must interpret laws that define school attendance as the right of every child, regardless of his or her disability. Litigation is now focused on ensuring that every child receives an education that is appropriate for his or her individual needs. As some legal scholars have pointed out, this does not mean that laws or litigation support full inclusion of all children with disabilities in general education (Dupre, 1997).

Litigation may involve legal suits filed for either of two reasons: because special education services are not being provided for students whose parents want them or because students are being assigned to special education when their parents believe that they should not be. Suits for special education have been brought primarily by parents whose children are unquestionably disabled and are being denied any education at all or are being given very meager special services. The parents who file these suits believe that the advantages of their children's identification for special education services clearly outweigh the disadvantages. Suits against special education have been brought primarily by parents of students who have mild or questionable disabilities and who are already attending school. These parents believe that their children are being stigmatized and discriminated against rather than helped by special education. Thus, the courts today are asked to make decisions in which individual students' characteristics are weighed against specific educational programs.

Parents want their children with disabilities to have a free public education that meets their needs but does not stigmatize them unnecessarily and that permits them to be taught in the regular school and classroom as much as possible. The laws governing education recognize parents' and students' rights to such an education. In the courts today, the burden of proof is ultimately on local and state education specialists, who must show in every instance that the student's abilities and disabilities have been completely and accurately assessed and that appropriate educational procedures are being employed. Much of the special education litigation has involved controversy over the use of intelligence (IQ) and other standardized testing to determine students' eligibility for special education. Although there has been much acrimony in the debate about IQ tests, some scholars have found that IQ scores themselves have not been the primary means of classifying children as eligible for special education (MacMillan & Forness, 1998).

FOR UPDATES on legal issues in special education, see the website maintained by legal expert Dixie Snow Huefner and click on "Chapter Updates" **www.ed.utah.edu/~huefner/ sped-law/spdlawlbk.htm**

One historic court case of the 1980s deserves particular consideration. In 1982, the U.S. Supreme Court made its first interpretation of PL 94-142 (now IDEA) in *Hudson* v. *Rowley,* a case involving Amy Rowley, a child who was deaf. The Court's decision was that appropriate education for a deaf child with a disability does not necessarily mean education that will produce the maximum possible achievement. Amy's parents had contended that she might be able to learn more in school if she were provided with a sign language interpreter. But the Court decided that because the school had designed an individualized program of special services for Amy and she was achieving at or above the level of her nondisabled classmates, the school system had met its obligation under the law to provide an appropriate education. Future cases will undoubtedly help to clarify what the law means by *appropriate education* and *least restrictive environment* (Crockett & Kauffman, 1999; Huefner, 1994; Yell, in press).

The Intent of Special Education Law: Individualized Education for Students with Disabilities

The primary intent of the special education laws passed since 1975 has been to require educators to focus on the needs of individual students with disabilities. The **individualized education program (IEP)** is the most important aspect of this focus; it spells out just what teachers plan to do to meet an exceptional student's needs, and the plan must be approved by the student's parents or guardian. IEPs vary greatly in format and detail from one child to another and from one school district to another. Some school districts use computerized IEP systems to help teachers determine goals and instructional objectives and to save time and effort in writing the documents. Legally, such cut-and-paste IEPs might be questionable because they lack sufficient attention to the particular needs of individuals (see Bateman & Linden, 1998). Many school systems, however, still rely on teachers' knowledge of students and curriculum to complete handwritten IEPs on the district's forms. Federal and state regulations do not specify exactly how much detail must be included in an IEP, only that it must be a written statement that is developed in a meeting of a representative of the local school district, the teacher, the parents or guardian, and, whenever appropriate, the child and that it must include certain elements (see Table 1.1).

The IEPs that are written in most schools contain much information related to the technical requirements of IDEA in addition to the heart of the plans: their instructional components. Figure 1.4 is an IEP provided by Bateman and Linden (1998). Curt "is a ninth-grade low achiever who was considered by the district to be a poorly motivated disciplinary problem student with a 'bad attitude.' His parents recognized him as a very dis-

Individualized education program (IEP)
IDEA requires an IEP to be drawn up by the educational team for each exceptional child; the IEP must include a statement of present educational performance, instructional goals, educational services to be provided, and criteria and procedures for determining that the instructional objectives are being met.

Despues Esto

TABLE 1.1   IEP Components

For All Students	For Some Students
■ Present levels of performance	■ Transition—including transfer of parental rights to students
■ Measurable goals and objectives	■ Behavior plan
■ Assessment status	■ ESL needs
■ Nonparticipation with nondisabled students	■ Braille
■ All needed services fully described (amount, frequency, etc.)	■ Communication needs
■ Progress reporting	■ Assistive technology

Source: Reprinted with permission from Bateman, B. D., & Linden, M. A. (1998). *Better IEPs: How to develop legally correct and educationally useful programs* (3rd ed.). Longmont, CO: Sopris West. All rights reserved.

couraged, frustrated student who had learning disabilities, especially in language arts" (Bateman & Linden, 1998, p. 126).

As we mentioned earlier, there is no standard IEP format that is used by all schools. An entire IEP might be a document of ten pages or more, depending on the format and the extent and complexity of the student's disabilities. The emphasis should be on writing an IEP that is clear, useful, and legally defensible, not on the IEP format (Bateman & Linden, 1998). Clear and explicit relationships among IEP components are required to make sure that the focus of the individualized program—special, individually tailored instruction to meet unique needs—is not lost. In Curt's IEP (Figure 1.4), the relationships among the components are maintained by the alignment of information across columns. Reading across the form, we find first a description of the unique characteristic or need and present level of performance, then the special services and modifications that are needed to address that need, and then the annual goals and objectives or benchmarks related to the need. Under IDEA 2004, not all IEPs must include short-term objectives. That is, if the student is participating in standard (not alternate) assessments of academic achievement required by NCLB, then his or her IEP does not have to include short-term objectives.

The process of writing an IEP and the document itself are perhaps the most important features of compliance with the spirit and letter of IDEA. Bateman and Linden (1998) summarize compliance with both the spirit and the letter of the law. When the IEP is prepared as intended by the law, it means that:

- The student's needs have been carefully assessed.
- A team of professionals and the parents have worked together to design a program of education to best meet the student's needs.
- Goals and objectives are clearly stated so that progress in reaching them can be evaluated.

Writing IEPs that meet all the requirements of the law and that are also educationally useful is no small task. Computerized IEPs and those based only on standardized testing or developmental inventories are likely to violate the requirements of the law, be of little educational value, or both (Bateman & Linden, 1998; Goodman & Bond, 1993). Much of the controversy about IEPs and the disappointment in them appear to result from misunderstanding of the law, lack of instructional expertise, or both. Within the framework of IDEA and other regulations, it is possible to write IEPs that are both legally correct and educationally useful. In Table 1.2 (page 34), Bateman and Linden (1998) summarize do's and don'ts of IEPs.

Government regulation of the IEP process has always been controversial. Some of the people who were influential in formulating the basic law (IDEA) have expressed great disappointment in the results of requiring IEPs (Goodman & Bond, 1993, p. 413). Others question whether the requirement of long-term and short-term objectives is appropriate:

> The IEP assumes that instructors know in advance what a child should and can learn, and the speed at which he or she will learn. . . . This is a difficult projection to make with nondisabled children of school age—for preschool children with cognitive, emotional, and social disabilities, it is near impossible. (Goodman & Bond, 1993, p. 415)

A major problem is that the IEP is too often written at the wrong time and for the wrong reason (Bateman & Linden, 1998). As Figure 1.5 (page 35) illustrates, the legal IEP is written after evaluation and identification of the student's disabilities and before a placement decision is made; what the student needs is determined first, and then a decision is made about placement in the least restrictive environment in which the needed services can be provided. Too often, we see the educationally wrong (and illegal) practice of basing the IEP on an available placement; that is, the student's IEP is written after available placements and services have been considered.

UNDERSTANDING THE STANDARDS AND PRINCIPLES Who should be involved in the development of a student's IEP? *(INTASC 1.11)*

Council for Exceptional Children

Individualized Education Program

Student: __Curt__   Age: __15__   Grade: __9__   Date: __1998__

Unique Educational Needs, Characteristics, and Present Levels of Performance (PLOPs) *(including how the disability affects the student's ability to progress in the general curriculum)*	Special Education, Related Services, Supplemental Aids & Services, Assistive Technology, Program Modifications, Support for Personnel *(including frequency, duration, and location)*	Measurable Annual Goals & Short-Term Objectives or Benchmarks • To enable student to participate in the general curriculum • To meet other needs resulting from the disability *(including how progress toward goals will be measured)*
Present Level of Social Skills: Curt lashes out violently when not able to complete work, uses profanity, and refuses to follow further directions from adults. Social Needs: • To learn anger management skills, especially regarding swearing • To learn to comply with requests	1. Teacher and/or counselor consult with behavior specialist regarding techniques and programs for teaching skills, especially anger management. 2. Provide anger management instruction to Curt. Services 3 times/week, 30 minutes. 3. Establish a peer group which involves role playing, etc., so Curt can see positive role models and practice newly learned anger management skills. Services 2 times/week, 30 minutes. 4. Develop a behavioral plan for Curt which gives him responsibility for charting his own behavior. 5. Provide a teacher or some other adult mentor to spend time with Curt (talking, game playing, physical activity, etc.). Services 2 times/week, 30 minutes. 6. Provide training for the mentor regarding Curt's needs/goals.	*Goal:* During the last quarter of the academic year, Curt will have 2 or fewer detentions for any reason. Obj. 1: At the end of the 1st quarter, Curt will have had 10 or fewer detentions. Obj. 2: At the end of the 2nd quarter, Curt will have had 7 or fewer detentions. Obj. 3: At the end of the 3rd quarter, Curt will have had 4 or fewer detentions. *Goal:* Curt will manage his behavior and language in a reasonably acceptable manner as reported by faculty and peers. Obj. 1: At 2 weeks, asked at the end of class if Curt's behavior and language were acceptable or unacceptable, 3 out of 6 teachers will say "acceptable." Obj. 2: At 6 weeks, asked the same question, 4 out of 6 teachers will say "acceptable." Obj. 3: At 12 weeks, asked the same question, 6 out of 6 teachers will say "acceptable."

FIGURE 1.4 An IEP for Curt

Source: Reprinted with permission from Bateman, B.D., & Linden, M.A. (1998). *Better IEPs: How to develop legally correct and educationally useful programs* (3rd ed.). Longmont, CO: Sopris West. All rights reserved.

Legislation and litigation were initially used in the 1960s and 1970s to include exceptional children in public education with relatively little regard for the quality of the education. Since the 1980s, laws and lawsuits have been used to try to ensure individualized education, cooperation, and collaboration among professionals; parental participation; and accountability of educators for providing high-quality, effective programs.

IDEA, for example, is noteworthy for its expansion of the idea of individualized planning and collaboration among disciplines. PL 99-457 mandated an individualized family service plan (IFSP) for infants and toddlers with disabilities. An IFSP is similar to an IEP for older children in that it requires assessment and statement of goals, needed services, and plans for implementation. As we will discuss in Chapter 2, an IFSP also requires more in-

Individualized Education Program

Unique Educational Needs, Characteristics, and Present Levels of Performance (PLOPs) *(including how the disability affects the student's ability to progress in the general curriculum)*	Special Education, Related Services, Supplemental Aids & Services, Assistive Technology, Program Modifications, Support for Personnel *(including frequency, duration, and location)*	Measurable Annual Goals & Short-Term Objectives or Benchmarks • To enable student to participate in the general curriculum • To meet other needs resulting from the disability *(including how progress toward goals will be measured)*
Study Skills/ Organizational Needs: How to read text Note taking How to study notes Memory work Be prepared for class, with materials Lengthen and improve attention span and on-task behavior Present Level: Curt currently lacks skill in all these areas.	1. Speech/lang. therapist, resource room teacher, and content area teachers will provide Curt with direct and specific teaching of study skills, i.e. Note taking from lectures Note taking while reading text How to study notes for a test Memorization hints Strategies for reading text to retain information 2. Assign a "study buddy" for Curt in each content area class. 3. Prepare a motivation system for Curt to be prepared for class with all necessary materials. 4. Develop a motivational plan to encourage Curt to lengthen his attention span and time on task. 5. Provide aide to monitor on-task behaviors in first month or so of plan and teach Curt self-monitoring techniques. 6. Provide motivational system and self-recording form for completion of academic tasks in each class.	Goal: At the end of academic year, Curt will have better grades and, by his own report, will have learned new study skills. Obj. 1: Given a 20–30 min. lecture/oral lesson, Curt will take appropriate notes as judged by that teacher. Obj. 2: Given 10–15 pgs. of text to read, Curt will employ an appropriate strategy for retaining info.—i.e., mapping, webbing, outlining, notes, etc.—as judged by the teacher. Obj. 3: Given notes to study for a test, Curt will do so successfully as evidenced by his test score. Goal: Curt will improve his on-task behavior from 37% to 80% as measured by a qualified observer at year's end. Obj. 1: By 1 month, Curt's on-task behavior will increase to 45%. Obj. 2: By 3 months, Curt's on-task behavior will increase to 60%. Obj. 3: By 6 months, Curt's on-task behavior will increase to 80% and maintain or improve until end of the year.

volvement of the family, coordination of services, and plans for making the transition into preschool. IDEA mandates the inclusion of plans for transition from school to work for older students as part of their IEPs. Other provisions of IDEA are intended to improve the quality of services received by children and youths with disabilities.

In the early twenty-first century, some people have expressed considerable unhappiness with the results of federal legislation and litigation. Critics have charged that laws that were intended to ensure the appropriate education of students with disabilities have gone awry and that new legislation and federal rules are required (e.g., Finn, Rotherham, & Hokanson, 2001). Others have suggested that the right instruction is actually the key to improving special education (e.g., Kauffman, 2002; Kauffman & Hallahan, 2005a; Zigmond, 2003).

Individualized Education Program *(continued)*

Unique Educational Needs, Characteristics, and Present Levels of Performance (PLOPs) *(including how the disability affects the student's ability to progress in the general curriculum)*	Special Education, Related Services, Supplemental Aids & Services, Assistive Technology, Program Modifications, Support for Personnel *(including frequency, duration, and location)*	Measurable Annual Goals & Short-Term Objectives or Benchmarks • To enable student to participate in the general curriculum • To meet other needs resulting from the disability *(including how progress toward goals will be measured)*
Academic Needs/ Written Language: Curt needs strong remedial help in spelling, punctuation, capitalization, and usage. Present Level: Curt is approximately 2 grade levels behind his peers in these skills.	1. Provide direct instruction in written language skills (punctuation, capitalization, usage, spelling) by using a highly structured, well-sequenced program. Services provided in small group of no more than four students in the resource room, 50 minutes/day. 2. Build in continuous and cumulative review to help with short-term rote memory difficulty. 3. Develop a list of commonly used words in student writing (or use one of many published lists) for Curt's spelling program.	*Goal:* Within one academic year, Curt will improve his written language skills by 1.5 or 2 full grade levels. Obj. 1: Given 10 sentences of dictation at his current level of instruction, Curt will punctuate and capitalize with 90% accuracy (checked at the end of each unit taught). Obj. 2: Given 30 sentences with choices of usage, at his current instructional level, Curt will perform with 90% accuracy. Obj. 3: Given a list of 150 commonly used words in writing. Curt will spell with 90% accuracy.

Adaptations to Regular Program:

- In all classes, Curt should sit near the front of the class.
- Curt should be called on often to keep him involved and on task.
- All teachers should help Curt with study skills as trained by spelling/language specialist and resource room teacher.
- Teachers should monitor Curt's work closely in the beginning weeks/months of his program.

FIGURE 1.4 *(Continued)*

TABLE 1.2 Do's and Don'ts for Individualized Education Programs (IEPs)

Do	Don't
Guarantee full and equal parent participation	Fail to individualize the program to fit the student
Truly individualize instruction to fit the student	Fail to address all the student's needs
Make sure present levels of performance (PLOPs), needs, and characteristics are carefully specified	Fail to describe sufficiently and specify all necessary services
Fully detail all services, modifications, and supports to meet the student's needs	Fail to write clear, objective, meaningful, and reasonable PLOPs, objectives, and goals
Make certain that goals and objectives are measurable, real, and taken seriously	

Source: From information contained in Bateman, B. D., & Linden, M. A. (1998). *Better IEPs: How to develop legally and educationallyl useful programs* (3rd. ed.). Longmont, CO: Sopris West. All rights reserved.

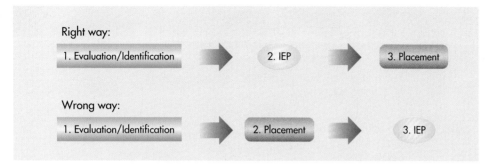

Our Perspective on the Progress of Special Education

Special education has come a long way since it was introduced into U.S. public education over a century ago. It has become an expected part of the public education system, a given rather than an exception or an experiment. Much progress has been made since IDEA was enacted a quarter century ago. Now parents and their children have legal rights to free, appropriate education; they are not powerless in the face of school administrators who do not want to provide appropriate education and related services. The enactment of IDEA was one of very few events in the twentieth century that altered the power relationship between schools and parents (Sarason, 1990). The basic requirements of IDEA are summarized in Table 1.3.

Although IDEA and related laws and court cases have not resulted in flawless programs for exceptional children, they have done much to move U.S. public schools toward providing better educational opportunities for those with disabilities. Laws enacted in the twentieth century have helped to ensure that all infants and toddlers with disabilities will receive early intervention. Laws such as ADA help to ensure that children and adults with disabilities will not be discriminated against in U.S. society. Laws and court cases cannot eliminate all problems in our society, but they can certainly be of enormous help in our efforts to equalize opportunities and minimize handicaps for people with disabilities.

We have made much progress in special education, but making it all that we hope for is—and always will be—a continuing struggle. In Chapter 2, we will discuss current trends and issues that highlight dissatisfaction with the way things are and represent hope for what special education and related services might become.

TABLE 1.3 IDEA Requirements

1. Eligibility decisions based on professional judgment, not quantitative formulas or test scores alone
2. Service and placement for every eligible student
3. Service decisions *not* based on a student's category
4. An IEP based soley on the student's needs, not on availability of services
5. IEPs that are truly individualized, and therefore not ready-made
6. A full continuum of alternative placements, with no type of placement prohibited
7. Inclusion of parents in decision making involving their children
8. Services at no cost to parents
9. Participation in regular assessments of academic progress under NCLB, unless explanation of the need for alternative assessment is provided.

SUMMARY

HOW can we get oriented to exceptionality and special education?

- Exceptionality involves similarities and differences.
- Reasons for optimism include better treatment and education, medical breakthroughs, and prevention.
- Abilities as well as disabilities must be recognized.
- A disability is an inability to do something; a handicap is a limitation that is imposed on someone.
- Not all inabilities are disabilities; a disability is an inability to do something that most people, with typical maturation, opportunity, or instruction, can do.

WHAT is the educational definition of exceptional learners?

- Exceptional learners are those who require special education to reach their full potential.
- Many individuals with disabilities require special education, but some do not.

WHAT is the prevalence of exceptional learners?

- About 10 students in every 100 (about 10 percent of the student population) are identified as exceptional for special education purposes.
- Some categories of disability are considered high-incidence because they are found relatively frequently (e.g., learning disabilities, communication disorders, emotional or behavioral disorders).
- Some categories of disability are considered low-incidence because they occur relatively rarely (e.g., blindness, deafness, deaf-blindness).

WHAT is the definition of special education?

- Special education means specially designed instruction that meets the unusual needs of an exceptional student. It may include special materials, teaching techniques, or equipment and/or facilities.

HOW is special education provided?

- Special education may range from a few special provisions made by the student's regular teacher to twenty-four-hour residential care in a special facility. The plan that is chosen depends on two factors:
  - How and how much the student differs from average students
  - What resources are available in the school and community

- Different placement options include the following, plus combinations:
  - Regular class placement with the regular teacher making accommodations
  - Regular class with consultation
  - Itinerant services from a specialist
  - Resource room services
  - Special self-contained class
  - Special day school
  - Hospital or homebound instruction
  - Residential school
- Federal law (IDEA) calls for placement in the least restrictive environment (LRE) that is compatible with the student's individual needs.
- The trend is toward placement in environments that are closer to the regular classroom in format, especially for younger children.

WHAT are teachers' roles in special education?

- All teachers must be prepared to work with exceptional learners.
- The relationship between general and special education is becoming closer.
- Students who are at risk are becoming an increasingly important issue.
- Inclusion is a controversial and important issue.
- All educators are expected to do the following:
  - Make maximum effort to accommodate individual students' needs
  - Evaluate academic abilities and disabilities
  - Refer students for further evaluation when appropriate
  - Participate in eligibility conferences
  - Participate in writing individualized education programs
  - Communicate with parents or guardians
  - Participate in due process hearings and negotiations
  - Collaborate with other professionals in identifying and making maximum use of exceptional students' abilities
- In addition, special educators are expected to provide or be expert in:
  - Academic instruction of students with learning problems
  - Management of serious behavior problems
  - Technological advances
  - Special education law

WHAT are the origins of special education?

- Special education became common in institutions and in major cities' public education in the nineteenth century.
- Physicians and psychologists played important roles in the early formation of special education.
- The Council for Exceptional Children and many important parent and professional organizations were formed in the twentieth century.

WHAT legislation and litigation have affected special education?

- The primary federal law affecting special education is the Individuals with Disabilities Education Act (IDEA), enacted in the 1970s and reauthorized by the U.S. Congress in 2004.
- Also important is the Americans with Disabilities Act (ADA), which prohibits discrimination against persons with disabilities in employment and communications.
- In the twenty-first century, the No Child Left Behind Act (NCLB) also is important in the education of exceptional learners.
- Lawsuits (litigation) have added to interpretation of the meaning and application of the law.
- Some parents sue to keep their children from being identified for special education or to have them edu-

cated in less atypical situations; others sue because they want their children to be identified for special education or placed in more specialized environments.

HOW is the intent of special education law implemented in individualized education for students with disabilities?

- The primary concern of the law (IDEA) is that every child with a disability be given a free, appropriate public education.
- The primary instrument for achieving this is the individualized education program or IEP.
- The IEP is an attempt to make certain a program has been written for each child with a disability and that:
  - The student's needs have been carefully assessed
  - A team of professionals and the parents have worked together to design a program of education to best meet the student's needs
  - Goals and objectives are clearly stated so that progress in reaching them can be evaluated

WHAT is our perspective on the progress of special education?

- Special education has made great progress, but making it better is a continuing struggle.

APPLYING THE STANDARDS AND PRINCIPLES

- **HOW** has the **history of special education** shaped the field today? Identify and describe at least one current theory, law, point of view, or human issue [refer to Chapter 2] and explain how it might affect the **future of special education.** *(CEC Content Standard #1)*

- **IDENTIFY** and describe **major laws and policies** that support students with disabilities. *(INTASC 1.04 & 1.12)*

- **WHAT** distinguishes **special** educators from **general** educators? *(CEC Content Standard #2 & INTASC Principle #2)*

- **WHAT** are the components of an individualized education program (IEP)? *(CEC Content Standard #7)*

Council for Exceptional Children

INTASC

Chapter **2**

Current Trends and Issues

*C*ome writers and critics
Who prophesy with your pen
And keep your eyes wide,
The chance won't come again.
And don't speak too soon
For the wheel's still in spin
And there's no tellin' who
That it's namin'
For the loser now
Will be later to win
For the times they are a-changin'.

Bob Dylan
"The Times They Are A-Changin'"

*Q*UESTIONS TO GUIDE YOUR READING OF THIS CHAPTER

- WHAT are the trends and issues in integrating people with disabilities into the larger society?

- WHAT are the trends and issues in integrating students with exceptionalities into schools?

- WHAT are the trends and issues in participation in general assessments of progress?

- WHAT are the trends and issues in access to new technologies?

- WHAT are the trends and issues in early intervention?

- WHAT are the trends and issues in transition to adulthood?

- WHAT are the trends and issues in discipline of students with disabilities?

- WHAT are our concluding thoughts about trends and issues?

STANDARDS AND PRINCIPLES IN THIS CHAPTER

SPECIAL EDUCATORS . . .

- **understand the field as an evolving and changing discipline** based on philosophies, evidence-based principles and theories, relevant laws and policies, diverse and historical points of view, and human issues that have historically influenced and continue to influence the field of special education and the education and treatment of individuals with exceptional needs both in school and society *(from CEC Content Standard #1)*.

- **use collaboration** to facilitate the successful transitions of individuals with exceptional learning needs across settings and services *(from CEC Content Standard #10)*.

 Council for Exceptional Children

ALL TEACHERS . . .

- **fosters relationships** with school colleagues, families, and agencies in the larger community to support students' learning and well being *(INTASC Principle #10)*.

 INTASC

ob Dylan could have written "The Times They Are A-Changin" (see the excerpt on p. 39) for special education, which has a rich history of controversy and change. Controversy and change make teaching and studying disabilities challenging and exciting. The history of special education is replete with unexpected twists and turns. Many of today's events and conditions will undoubtedly have consequences that we do not foresee (see Jakubecy, Mock, & Kauffman, 2003; Kauffman, 1999a, 1999–2000, 2005a; Kauffman & Landrum, 2006; Mock, Jakubecy, & Kauffman, 2003; Smith, 1998).

In the 1980s and 1990s and the early twenty-first century, especially dramatic changes occurred in the education of people with disabilities, and current thinking indicates that the field is poised for still more changes in the next decade. One critically important trend and issue for the new century is the movement toward multicultural special education. Because that topic is so important, it is the subject of Chapter 3. In this chapter, we explore seven other major trends:

1. Integration of people with disabilities into society
2. Integration of students with disabilities into schools
3. Participation of students with disabilities in assessments of educational prgress
4. Access of people with disabilities to new technologies
5. Early intervention with children who have disabilities
6. Transition from secondary school to adulthood
7. Discipline of students with disabilities

Integration into the Larger Society

The trend of integrating people with disabilities into the larger society began decades ago and is stronger than ever today. Champions of integration are proud that they have reduced the number of people who live in institutions and the number of students who attend special schools and special classes. Some of the radical proponents of integration, however, will not be satisfied until virtually all institutions, special schools, and special classes are eliminated. They recommend placing all students with disabilities in regular classes. Even today's more conservative advocates of integration recommend much greater interaction between students with and without disabilities than most special educators recommended in the 1960s and 1970s.

NORMALIZATION

A key principle behind the trend toward more integration of people with disabilities into society is normalization. First espoused in Scandinavia (Bank-Mikkelsen, 1969) before being popularized in the United States, **normalization** is the philosophy that we should use "means which are as culturally normative as possible, in order to establish and/or maintain personal behaviors and characteristics which are as culturally normative as possible" (Wolfensberger, 1972, p. 28). In other words, both the means and the ends of education

Normalization
A philosophical belief in special education that every individual, even the most disabled, should have an educational and living environment as close to normal as possible.

Misconceptions about Learners with Disabilities

MYTH Normalization, the principle that the means and ends of education for students with disabilities should be as culturally normative as possible, is straightforward, needing little interpretation.

FACT There are many disagreements pertaining to the interpretation of the normalization principle. As just one example, some educators have interpreted it to mean that all people with disabilities must be educated in regular classes, whereas others maintain that a continuum of placements (residential schools, special schools, special classes, resource rooms, regular classes) should remain available as options.

MYTH All professionals agree that technology should be used to its fullest to aid people with disabilities.

FACT Some believe that technology should be used cautiously because it can lead people with disabilities to become too dependent on it. Some professionals believe that people with disabilities can be tempted to rely on technology instead of developing their own abilities.

MYTH All students with disabilities must now be included in standardized testing, just like students without disabilities.

FACT Most students with disabilities will be included in standardized testing procedures, but for some, a given test will be judged inappropriate. Some students will require adaptations of the testing procedure to accommodate their specific disabilities. However, students with disabilities can no longer be automatically excluded from participation in standardized assessment procedures.

MYTH Research has established beyond a doubt that special classes are ineffective and that mainstreaming is effective.

FACT Research comparing special versus mainstream placement has been inconclusive because most of these studies have been methodologically flawed. Researchers are now focusing on finding ways of making mainstreaming work more effectively.

MYTH Professionals agree that labeling people with disabilities, (e.g., "retarded," "blind," "behavior disordered") is more harmful than helpful.

FACT Some professionals maintain that labels help them to communicate, explain the atypical behavior of some people with disabilities to the public, and spotlight the special needs of people with disabilities for the general public.

MYTH People with disabilities are pleased with the media's portrayal, especially about their extraordinary achievements.

FACT Some disability rights advocates are disturbed by what they believe are too frequent overly negative and overly positive portrayals in the media.

MYTH Everyone agrees that teachers in early intervention programs need to assess parents as well as their children.

FACT Some authorities now believe that although families are an important part of intervention programming and should be involved in some way, special educators should center their assessment efforts primarily on the child, not the parents.

MYTH Everyone agrees that good early childhood programming for students with or without disabilities should be the same.

FACT There is considerable disagreement about whether early intervention programming for children with disabilities should be child directed, as is typical of regular preschool programs, or more teacher directed.

MYTH Professionals agree that all students with disabilities in secondary school should be given a curriculum focused on vocational preparation.

FACT Professionals are in conflict over how much vocational versus academic instruction students with mild disabilities should receive.

MYTH There are completely different rules of discipline for students with disabilities.

FACT In most cases, the same discipline rules apply to students with and without disabilities. However, the law does not allow discontinuation of education for a student with a disability. Even if the student is not allowed to return to the school, education must be provided in an alternative setting.

YOU CAN SEARCH major newspaper websites for articles about issues in special education. The *New York Times* site is **www.nytimes.com** and the *Washington Post* site is **www.washingtonpost.com**

Deinstitutionalization A social movement of the 1960s and 1970s whereby large numbers of persons with mental retardation and/or mental illness were moved from large mental institutions into smaller community homes or into the homes of their families; recognized as a major catalyst for integrating persons with disabilities into society.

for students with disabilities should be as much like those for nondisabled students as possible. Regarding the means, for example, we should place students with disabilities in educational settings that are as similar to those of nondisabled students as possible. We should also use treatment approaches that are as close as possible to the ones we use with the rest of the student population. Regarding the ends, we should strive to weave people with disabilities into the larger fabric of society.

Although normalization seems simple enough in principle, it has sparked numerous controversies. Many of these controversies have involved deinstitutionalization, self-determination, and—particularly important for teachers—full inclusion. Here, we mention only a few of the more hotly contested issues.

The phrase *as culturally normative as possible* is open to interpretation. Even though the originators of the normalization principle saw the need for a variety of service delivery options—including residential institutions, special schools, and special classes—more recently, some have interpreted normalization to mean abolishing all such separate settings.

Some groups of people with disabilities are leery about being too closely integrated into nondisabled society. For example, some people who are deaf, because of their difficulty in communicating with the hearing world, prefer associating with other people who are deaf. For them, normalization does not translate into integration into the larger society. (We will discuss this further in Chapter 10.) Others have pointed out that a diversity of settings and groupings of people is itself normal in most societies (Kauffman & Hallahan, 1997).

Some disability rights advocates suggest that the assessment of normalization is wrong-headed, as it begins with the idea that nondisabled people should be seen as the norm to which those with disabilities are compared. For example, a representative of the organization Disabled People's International has called for "the elimination of the value concept of normalization as a measurement and the use of non-disabled people as the norm" (Mathiason, 1997, p. 2). Christopher Reeve (the late actor who fell from a horse and was paralyzed from the neck down) was criticized for refusing to give up the goal of being able to walk again like a "normal" person (Groopman, 2003).

Some have questioned whether the rapidly expanding use of technology to assist people with disabilities actually works against the goal of normalization. Certainly, there is little doubt that technology has made it possible for more and more people with disabilities to take part in activities that previously were inaccessible to them. Thus, in many instances, technology serves as a means for achieving normalization. Some people with disabilities, however, have expressed concern that individuals might be too quick to rely on technology instead of working to improve their own abilities. Reliance on artificial means of interacting with the environment when more natural means are possible could jeopardize a person's quest for normalization.

It is now commonplace to find individuals with disabilities participating in a wide variety of activities. Craig Timm, an arm amputee, makes a cut to the ramp during the jump portion of the 2004 U.S. National Disabled Water Ski Championships.

DEINSTITUTIONALIZATION

At one time, it was common to place nearly all children and adults with mental retardation and/or mental illness in residential institutions. In the 1960s and 1970s, systematic efforts were made to move people out of institutions and back into closer contact with the community. Referred to as **deinstitutionalization**, this movement caused more children with disabilities to be raised by their families. Today, smaller facilities, located within local neighborhoods, are common. Halfway houses exist for individuals with emotional difficulties who no longer are thought to need the more isolated environment of a large institution. For people with mental retardation, group homes house small numbers of individuals whose mental retardation may range from mild to severe. More people with disabilities are now working, with assistance from "job coaches," in competitive employment situations (Stroman, 2003).

Some have asserted that in certain cases, deinstitutionalization has been implemented without much forethought (Crissey & Rosen, 1986; Lamb & Weinberger, 2001; Landesman & Butterfield, 1987; Zigler, Hodapp, & Edison, 1990). They maintain that although deinstitutionalization has the potential to improve the quality of life for most people who, in previous generations, would have lived in institutions, it has failed because of poor planning. They argue that institutions can be humane, effective alternative placements for some individuals.

Some people with disabilities have been turned out of institutions onto the streets or into assisted living facilities that are every bit as abusive as larger institutions. A four-part exposé of community-based assisted living homes was published in the *The Washington Post* in May 2004 (Fallis, 2004a, 2004b, 2004c, 2004d).

> For nearly three decades, Viginia has been emptying its large institutions for the mentally ill and mentally retarded, moving those patients into much smaller settings in communities across the state—often to assisted living facilities. Since the early 1980s, the number of beds in public institutions has been cut by more than half, triggering a search for housing for former patients, some of whom have violent histories. (Fallis, 2004b, p. A6)

Virginia, like other states, implemented deinstitutionalization on a broad scale, beginning in the 1970s. However, the more local community facilities or group homes into which people with disabilities were moved have often been understaffed, poorly managed, delapidated, dangerous, and abusive.

A review of research on deinstitutionalization between 1980 and 1999 suggested that many people with intellectual disabilities have improved their adaptive behavior by moving into small community homes (University of Minnesota, 1999). However, research also indicates that much still needs to be done to improve the quality of life for some people with disabilities who have been released from institutions. In fact, many people who were or formerly would have been in institutions are now homeless or in jail (see Lamb & Weinberger, 2001).

There is no inexpensive or easy way to provide humane care for people with disabilities. However, it seems clear now from exposés and research that simply changing the location of people from institutions to communities does little or nothing to improve the quality of their lives.

SELF-DETERMINATION

Deinstitutionalization has fostered increasing recognition that people with and without disabilities have a right to exercise **self-determination**—the right to make one's own decisions about important aspects of one's life. Examples are where to work and live, with whom to become friends, and what education to pursue. **Person-centered planning** has become an important aspect of self-determination (Stroman, 2003).

Schwartz, Jacobson, and Holburn (2000) suggest that the primary hallmark of person-centered planning is that "the person's activities, services and supports are based upon his or her dreams, interests, preferences, strengths, and capacities" (p. 238). The main idea is that people with disabilities should exercise personal control of their lives (Stancliffe, Abery, & Smith, 2000).

Self-determination
The ability to make personal choices, regulate one's own life, and be a self-advocate; a prevailing philosophy in education programming for persons with mental retardation.

Person-centered planning
Planning for a person's self-determination; planning activities and services based on a person's dreams, aspirations, interests, preferences, strengths, and capacities.

A key goal for individuals with disabilities is learning skills that allow them self-determination.

COMMUNITY integration and educational inclusion are topics with many associated websites, including **www.normemma.com/index. htm** and **www.dssc.org**

For the latest information about AAMR's definition and policies on mental retardation, visit the website at

www.aamr.org

Other people, such as psychologists, counselors, physicians, parents, teachers, and administrators, should not make decisions for people with disabilities.

There is growing recognition that self-determination is learned and should be taught in schools, even in the elementary grades (Agran, Blanchard, & Wehmeyer, 2000; Browder, Wood, Test, Karvonen, & Algozzine, 2001; Palmer & Wehmeyer, 2003; Wehmeyer, Palmer, Agran, Mithaug, & Martin, 2000). Making schools places where all children have a significant voice or say in important decisions is seen as critical.

In general, self-determination means taking charge of one's life. Teachers can play an important role in promoting the abilities and attitudes individuals will need to take charge of their lives through providing instruction in self-determination skills and creating school environments where these skills can be practiced (Browder et al., 2001, p. 233). Some professional organizations have policy statements regarding self-determination. For example, you might want to visit the home page of the American Association on Mental Retardation for statements on self-determination and other issues of interest.

The idea of self-determination, like so many other concepts related to ability and disability, is culturally embedded. In working toward self-determination, as well as any other goal, we must be aware of cultural differences in the meaning of self, independence, and success, as we will discuss further in Chapter 3 (see also Cronin, 2000).

Integration into Schools

The most controversial issue about integration of students with disabilities in schools is that of inclusion. Especially controversial is what is known as **full inclusion**. Actually, integration or inclusion has been an issue with all exceptional students, including those with special gifts or talents. Here, we discuss inclusion related to disabilities; we will discuss inclusion of gifted and talented students further in Chapter 15.

FULL INCLUSION

Full inclusion
All students with disabilities are placed in their neighborhood schools in general education classrooms for the entire day; general education teachers have the primary responsibility for students with disabilities.

Writers have different ideas about exactly what full inclusion means (Kauffman & Hallahan, 2005b; Stainback & Stainback, 1992). However, most definitions contain the following key elements:

- All students with disabilities—regardless of the types or severities of disabilities—attend only classes in general education. In other words, there are no separate special education classes.
- All students with disabilities attend their neighborhood schools (i.e., the ones they would go to if they had no disabilities).
- General education, not special education, assumes primary responsibility for students with disabilities.

Individuals with Disabilities Education Improvement Act (IDEA)
The Individuals with Disabilities Education Act was enacted in 1990 and reauthorized in 1997 and 2004; it replaced PL 94-142, enacted in 1975. This federal law requires that to receive funds under the act, every school system in the nation must provide a free, appropriate public education for every child between the ages of three and twenty-one, regardless of how or how seriously he or she may be disabled.

Some advocates of full inclusion propose the total elimination of special education. Others hold that professionals such as special teachers are still needed but that their main duties should be carried out in general education classrooms.

CURRENT TRENDS

Least restrictive environment (LRE)
A legal term referring to the fact that exceptional children must be educated in as normal an environment as possible.

Full Inclusion Versus a Continuum of Alternative Placements   Educational programming for students with disabilities has historically been built on the assumption that a variety of service delivery options need to be available (Crockett & Kauffman, 1999, 2001). As was mentioned in Chapter 1, federal special education law, the **Individuals with Disabilities Education Improvement Act (IDEA)**, stipulates that schools place students with disabilities in the **least restrictive environment (LRE)**, which is to be chosen from a **continuum of alternative placements (CAP)**.

Most people have conceptualized LRE as involving only a physical location of the child, with alternatives along a continuum of restrictiveness ranging from residential institutions on one end to regular classes on the other (you might want to review Figure 1.1). They have viewed the LRE concept as subordinate to the concept of a **free appropriate public education (FAPE)**. Before LRE was enacted into law, school personnel were free to claim that they did not have services for children with disabilities and to deny these children access to regular classes. Now, however, some of the advocates of full inclusion would like to make FAPE subordinate to LRE—to do away with the concept of LRE and deny access to special classes or schools to children with disabilities (Laski, 1991). The argument of Laski and some of the others who advocate full inclusion is that the general education classroom is the LRE for all students, whether they have disabilities or not. In fact, it is our observation that in some school districts, special classes have been closed down in favor of full inclusion, leaving no continuum of placement options.

Some have suggested that the restrictiveness of an environment is not simply a matter of location. Restrictiveness also is determined by what is taught and how it is presented—the instructional and social contexts of a place (e.g., Crockett & Kauffman, 2001; Cruickshank, 1977; Rueda, Gallego, & Moll, 2000). The argument can then be made that some special classes or schools are, for some students, less restrictive of their academic, emotional, and social development than is a general education classroom (e.g., Carpenter & Bovair, 1996; Gliona, Gonzales, & Jacobson, 2005; Kauffman, Bantz, & McCullough, 2002; Mock & Kauffman, 2002, 2005).

Arguments Favoring Full Inclusion   Those who advocate full inclusion base their position on at least the following four premises:

1. Labeling people is harmful.
2. Separate special education has been ineffective.
3. People with disabilities should be viewed as a minority group.
4. Ethics are more important than empirical evidence.

We consider each of these premises in the sections that follow.

Labeling as Harmful   Some people fear that a "special education" label can cause a child to feel unworthy or to be viewed by the rest of society as a deviant and hence grow to feel

Continuum of alternative placements (CAP)
The full range of alternative placements, from those assumed to be least restrictive to those considered most restrictive; the continuum ranges from regular classrooms in neighborhood schools to resource rooms, self-contained classes, special day schools, residential schools, hospital schools, and home instruction.

Free appropriate public education (FAPE)
The primary intent of federal special education law, that the education of all children with disabilities will in all cases be free of cost to parents (i.e., at public expense) and appropriate for the particular student.

When labels take precedence over recognizing individual characteristics, labels themselves become disabling.

unworthy. This fear is not entirely unfounded. Any label that designates a student as needing special education carries negative connotations, simply because any disability is something we want to prevent or remediate if possible. Disabilities are conditions that most people would rather avoid; they are not seen by most people as good things to have (Kauffman, 2003). Consequently, being described as having a disability can lower a person's self-esteem or cause others to behave differently toward him or her. Understandably, advocates for people with disabilities have suggested using different labels or, to the extent possible, avoiding labels altogether.

Antilabeling sentiment is based in part on the theory that disabilities are a matter of social perceptions and values, not inherent characteristics. Bogdan (1986) suggested that disability is a socially created construct. Its existence depends on social interaction. Only in a very narrow sense, according to Bogdan, does a person have a disability. For example, the fact that a person cannot see only sets the stage for his or her being labeled "blind."

Bogdan's theory suggests that once we call a person "blind," a variety of undesirable consequences occur. Our interactions are different because of the label. That is, we view the person primarily in terms of the blindness. We tend to interpret everything he or she can or cannot do in terms of the blindness, and the label takes precedence over other things we might know about the individual. This labeling opens the door for viewing the person in a stereotypical and prejudicial manner because, once a label has been applied, we tend to think of all people with blindness as being similar to one another but different from the rest of society.

Research on the effects of labeling has been inconclusive. On the one hand, studies indicate that people tend to view labeled individuals differently from nonlabeled ones. People are more likely both to expect deviant behavior from labeled individuals and to see abnormality in nondisabled individuals if told (incorrectly) that nondisabled people are deviant. On the other hand, labels can also make nondisabled people more tolerant of those with disabilities. That is, labels can provide explanations or justifications for differences in appearance or behavior for which the person with a disability otherwise might be blamed or stigmatized even more (Fiedler & Simpson, 1987). For example, it is probably fairly common for the nondisabled adult to tolerate a certain degree of socially immature behavior in a child with mental retardation while finding the same behavior unacceptable in a nondisabled child.

In addition to serving as an explanation for unusual behavior, the use of labels is defended on other grounds by some special educators. First, they argue that the elimination of one set of labels would only prompt development of another set. In other words, they believe that individuals with special problems will always be perceived as different. Second, these special educators contend that labels help professionals communicate with one another. In talking about a research study, for example, it helps to know with what type of population the study was conducted. Third, they assert that labels help to spotlight the spe-

FOR BETTER OR FOR WORSE©   by Lynn Johnston

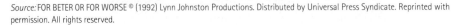

Source: FOR BETER OR FOR WORSE © (1992) Lynn Johnston Productions. Distributed by Universal Press Syndicate. Reprinted with permission. All rights reserved.

cial needs of people with disabilities for the general public: "Like it or not, it is a fine mixture of compassion, guilt, and social consequence that has been established over these many years as a conditioned response to the label 'mental retardation' that brings forth . . . resources [monies for specialized services]" (Gallagher, 1972, p. 531). The taxpayer is more likely to react sympathetically to something that can be labeled.

Finally, some people have pointed out that any time we use an intervention that is not universal—used with all students regardless of their characteristics—we automatically apply a label. That is, labels are an inescapable part of preventive practices unless those practices are universal—applied to all children without regard to their individual characteristics (Kauffman, 2001, 1999b). The decision, then, is whether we will recognize and talk about the differences we call disabilities or will ignore them (Kauffman, 2003, 2005a, 2005b; Kauffman & Hallahan, 2005a). You might recall from Chapter 1 the excerpts from an article by Martha Randolph Carr (2004) about her son. Labeling and addressing his problem brought her and her son relief, not more stigma.

Ineffectiveness of Separate Special Education   Some special educators assert that research shows separate **pull-out programs** to be ineffective. These educators maintain that students with disabilities have better, or at least no worse, scores on cognitive and social measures if they stay in regular classes than if they are put in special education for all (self-contained classes) or part (resource rooms) of the school day. Adding fuel to this argument are studies showing that the instruction that is received in separate placements is not what one would expect if special education were being implemented appropriately (e.g., Vaughn, Moody, & Schumm, 1998).

Many research studies have compared students with disabilities in more and less separate settings; over the past thirty years, there have been more than fifty such studies. Results, when taken at face value, have not been very supportive of separate settings. Critics of this research, however, argue that taking these investigations at face value is highly questionable. The biggest problem with this line of research is that most of the studies are methodologically flawed. Furthermore, some studies do show that some students with disabilities make better progress in more specialized settings and that full inclusion does not serve all children best (see Mock & Kauffman, 2005).

Research findings and logical analysis challenge the idea that full inclusion is best for all children (Kauffman & Hallahan, 2005a, 2005b). The place where the child is taught should not be seen as more important than meeting the child's needs (Zigmond, 2003).

People with Disabilities as a Minority   Advocates of full inclusion tend to see people with disabilities as members of a minority group rather than as individuals who have difficulties as an inherent result of their disabilities. In other words, the problems that people with disabilities face are seen as the result of society's discrimination and prejudice (Stainback & Stainback, 1992).

Thinking of people with disabilities as a minority is consistent with the views of disability rights activists. These activists are a part of the **disability rights movement**, which is patterned after the civil rights movement of the 1960s. Disability activists claim that they, like African Americans and other ethnic minority groups, are an oppressed minority. They have coined the term **handicapism**, a parallel of racism.

Although more and more people with disabilities—and nondisabled professionals too—are supporting the disability rights movement, some believe that the political climate in the United States has not been conducive to fostering yet another rights movement. Whereas the civil rights movement of the 1960s was spawned in an era of liberal ideology, the disability rights movement has coincided with a more conservative political climate.

The disability rights movement is international and is addressing a wide range of issues. It includes a spectrum of views on controversial topics, and not every statement of every person with a disability is representative of the majority of people with disabilities (Michalko, 2002; Switzer, 2003; Tregaskis, 2004). For example, some express negative sentiments about finding a cure for spinal cord injuries that would allow people with paralysis

Pull-out programs
Special education programs in which students with disabilities leave the general education classroom for part or all of the school day (e.g., to go to special classes or resource room).

Disability rights movement
Patterned after the civil rights movement of the 1960s, this is a loosely organized effort to advocate for the rights of people with disabilities through lobbying legislators and other activities. Members view people with disabilities as an oppressed minority.

Handicapism
A term used by activists who fault the unequal treatment of individuals with disabilities. This term is parallel to the term *racism*, coined by those who fault unequal treatment based on race.

to walk; others find optimism about reversing the effects of spinal cord injuries laudable and heartening (Groopman, 2003; Kastor, 1997).

Activists themselves have been unable to agree on the best ways to meet the movement's general goals. Some believe that individuals with disabilities should receive special treatment in such things as tax exemptions or reduced public transportation fares; others maintain that such preferential treatment fosters an image of people with disabilities as dependent (Gartner & Joe, 1986; Martin, 2001).

People with disabilities are an incredibly heterogeneous population. General goals can be the same for all people with disabilities, but specific needs vary greatly. Clearly, the particular problems that an adolescent with severe mental retardation and blindness faces are considerably different from those of a combat veteran who has lost the use of his or her legs. Although activists admit that it would not be good for the public to believe that all people with disabilities are alike—any more than they already do—this heterogeneity makes it difficult for people with disabilities to join forces on specific issues.

Consider the case of Kathy Buckley, described in the Personal Perspectives on page 49. Her deafness is obviously not as important as her positive self-perception, can-do attitude, personal charm, and keen wit.

People in the disability rights movement have been active on a variety of fronts, ranging from lobbying legislators and employers to criticizing the media for being guilty of representing people with disabilities in stereotypical and inaccurate ways. Disability activists have been particularly critical of television and movies (see Kuppers, 2001; Longmore & Umansky, 2001; Safran, 1998, 2001). Some argue that the depictions of people with disabilities are typically overly negative or overly positive. On the negative side, electronic media often treat people with disabilities as criminals, monsters, potential suicides, maladjusted people, or sexual deviants. These portrayals offer the viewer absolution for any difficulties faced by people with disabilities and allow blaming the victims for their own problems. Rarely do movie themes acknowledge society's role in creating attitudinal barriers for people with disabilities.

When television attempts to portray people with disabilities in a positive light, it often highlights phenomenal accomplishments—a one-legged skier, a wheelchair marathoner, and so forth. The superhero image is a mixed blessing. It promotes the notion that being disabled does not automatically limit achievement. However, such human interest stories make ordinary people with disabilities feel inferior because they have not achieved such superhuman goals. These stories also imply that people with disabilities can prove their worth only by achieving superhuman goals. Hence, among some disability rights advocates, portraying anyone with a disability doing something that most people without disabilities cannot do reinforces the stereotype of people with disabilities as "heroic" (see Ravitch, 2003).

Most disability advocates have been displeased with TV dramas' portrayal of disabilities, but they have been more complimentary of advertising that uses characters with disabilities, especially when the characters blend into the fabric of society rather than being singled out. More actors with disabilities are now seen in TV advertising, either out of corporate desire to be socially responsive or out of recognition of the large market of buyers with disabilities.

Ethics   Full-inclusion proponents emphasize discrimination against people with disabilities. They tend to approach integration from an ethical perspective without considering evidence. For them, empirical data on the comparative effectiveness of full inclusion versus spearate programs are irrelevant. Apparently, even if well-controlled research shows that separate programs lead to better academic and social outcomes than do full-inclusion programs, these advocates would still favor full inclusion on ethical grounds (see Kavale & Forness, 2000; Sasso, 2001 for comment on this tactic).

The rationale for full inclusion is based on presumptive moral values, not research data. However, the presumed moral values are not based on realities, making the assumed values meaningless (see Kauffman & Landrum, 2005; Mock & Kauffman, 2005). The ideology of full inclusion suggests that this equal access can be achieved only when each and

Personal Perspectives

LAUGHING OUT LOUD: TURNING A DEAF EAR TO COMEDY

WHEN it comes to comedy, Kathy Buckley takes center stage. Billed as "America's First Hearing Impaired Comedienne," she was nominated "Best Female Stand-Up Comedienne" for the 1997 American Comedy Awards, the third year in a row Buckley has made the award list.

Buckley never aspired to be a comedienne. "I didn't know what I wanted to do," she says. "I wanted to be a nurse when I was a kid, but because of my hearing impairment they said I couldn't." Actually, her performing career started almost by accident. "I did it on a dare," Buckley admits, speaking of the first time she performed on stage. It was in 1988 at a charity benefit called "Stand-up Comics Take a Stand" in Encino, California. "I was a nervous wreck," she admits. Even though she could not hear the audience's laughter except by feeling the stage floor vibrations, Buckley says what really made her nervous was competing against other comedians with years of experience. Despite that, she won fourth place.

Since then Kathy Buckley has turned the comedy world "on its ear." She is popular at "Catch a Rising Star" in Las Vegas and

"I truly believe that the only disability out there today is attitude."

"The Improv" and "The Comedy Store" in Hollywood and has appeared several times on HBO comedy specials and such television shows as *The Tonight Show Starring Jay Leno, The Howard Stern Show*, and *Phil Donahue*. Much of her comic material is based on her hearing loss.

"My comedy disarms people. I truly believe that the only disability out there today is attitude," she says. "I love to make people laugh, but I love even more if I can teach them something at the same time."

And that is just what she does. In her nightly performance she jokes about what it is like to be hearing impaired and about how others treat her. She performs for many charity events and benefits.

Buckley says that although she tries to entertain and enlighten all kinds of people, her heart belongs to children. "Kids mean everything to me," she says. "Every single child deserves to have a real childhood, and they should have healthy role models to show them that people do care about them deeply." ■

Source: D'Agostino, D. (1997). Laughing out loud: Turning a deaf ear to comedy. *Exceptional Parent, 27*(3), 44–45. Reprinted by permission.

every student is included in neighborhood schools and regular classes, taking his or her rightful places alongside age peers who have not been identified as having disabilities.

Arguments Against Full Inclusion   The notion of full inclusion has met with considerable resistance. At least six arguments against full inclusion have been offered:

1. General educators, special educators, and parents are largely satisfied with and see the continuing need for the continuum of alternative placements.
2. General educators are unwilling and/or unable to cope with all students with disabilities.
3. Justifying full inclusion by asserting that people with disabilities are a minority is flawed.
4. Full-inclusion proponents' unwillingness to consider empirical evidence is professionally irresponsible.
5. The available empirical evidence does not support full inclusion.
6. In the absence of data to support one service delivery model, special educators must preserve the continuum of placements.

Satisfaction with Continuum of Placements   Defenders of the full continuum of alternative placements point out that most teachers, parents, and students are satisfied with the current degree of integration into general education. Repeated polls, surveys, and interviews have indicated that the vast majority of students with disabilities and their parents are satisfied with the special education system and placement options (e.g., Guterman, 1995; Semmel, Abernathy, Butera, & Lesar, 1991). Many students say that they prefer separate classes (Klinger, Vaughn, Schumm, Cohen, & Forgan, 1998). Parents have banded together to keep special schools open for their children (Gliona, Gonzalez, & Jacobson, 2005). Although many students are no doubt unhappy with the stigma of the label "learning disabilities," the majority seem not to regret that they are not educated in general education classes. As one student summed up:

> [Full inclusion] would make it worse. Basically it would be embarrassing for that person (a student with learning disabilities). It (an inclusive classroom) would be egging it more. People would be getting into a lot more fights because somebody is always going to joke around and say something like, "He's a retard." (Guterman, 1995, p. 120)

Critics of full inclusion claim that it is being championed by only a few radical special educators, primarily those who teach children with the most severe disabilities (Fuchs & Fuchs, 1994). Some point out that most students with severe disabilities are taught primarily in special classes; students with the most mild disabilities are the most likely to be fully included (Palmer, Fuller, Arora, & Nelson, 2001). Palmer and colleagues studied the comments of parents of children with severe disabilities about inclusion, finding that although some were supportive of inclusion, others were skeptical. Given parents' thoughts on the matter, it is not surprising to encounter the argument that parents' thinking has been ignored by those who push hardest for full inclusion. Consider the responses of parents in the Personal Perspectives on page 51.

Although a majority of parents of children with disabilities—if one includes the entire range of disabilities from none to severe—might have positive attitudes toward inclusion, there are parents with serious reservations and concerns (Duhaney & Salend, 2000). Those who question full inclusion do not oppose inclusion in all cases. They see it as inappropriate for *some* students (Kauffman & Hallahan, 2005a, 2005b).

Attitudes of General Educators   The attitudes of many general educators toward including students with disabilities in regular classes have been less than enthusiastic. In a synthesis of over two dozen surveys of general educators' views on integrating students with disabilities into their classes, only about half thought that integration could provide some benefits (Scruggs & Mastropieri, 1996). Furthermore, only about one fourth to one third thought that they had sufficient time, skills, training, and resources for working with students with disabilities. Most critics of full inclusion sympathize with the classroom teacher's already arduous job. Although some critics blame teachers for their unwillingness to accommodate more students with disabilities, many agree that their hesitation to do so is justified and that training all teachers to be able to meet the needs of all students with disabilities is simply impossible from a practical standpoint (see Lieberman, 1992; Mock & Kauffman, 2002, 2005; Palmer et al., 2001).

A logical analysis of the problem of full inclusion indicates its infeasability because of the demands on general education teachers. As Zigmond (2003) summarized:

> General educators cannot imagine focusing intensively on individual students to the extent that different instructional activities for different students are being implemented at the same time. This is simply impractical in a classroom of 25 to 35 students. Moreover, special education's most basic article of faith, that instruction must be individualized to be truly effective, is rarely contemplated, let alone observed in most general education classrooms. Mainstream teachers must consider

Personal Perspectives

PARENTS' THOUGHTS ON INCLUSION OF THEIR CHILDREN WITH SEVERE DISABILITIES

PARENTS of children with severe disabilities have suggested the following reasons for supporting inclusion:

1. The child acquires more academic or functional skills because of higher expectations and greater stimulation in the regular classroom.
2. Nondisabled students benefit by learning to know children with disabilities; they become more sensitive to people with disabilities.
3. Being around "normal" kids helps students with disabilities acquire social skills.
4. Siblings with and without disabilities go to the same school.
5. Segregation of any kind is morally wrong; inclusion is morally right.

Parents of children with severe disabilities have suggested the following reasons for *not* supporting inclusion:

1. The type or severity of the child's disability precludes benefits from inclusion.
2. Inclusion would overburden or negatively affect regular classroom teachers and students.

3. The curriculum of the general education classroom doesn't match the needs of the child.
4. The child does not get the needed teacher attention or services in general education.
5. The child is unlikely to be treated well by nondisabled children in the regular classroom.
6. The child is not likely to benefit but [is likely] to be overwhelmed by the surroundings in the regular classroom.
7. The child is too young (and needs more supervision or structure) or too old (having become used to a special class) to benefit from inclusion.
8. The child needs to be around other children with similar disabilities; he or she fits in better, feels less stigmatized or different, and has more real friends in a special setting.
9. The child is too disruptive or aggressive or has too many behavior problems for a regular class.
10. Teachers and others in general education don't have the appropriate training for dealing with the child's needs. ■

Source: From Taking sides: Parent views on inclusion for their children with severe disabilities by D. S. Palmer, K. Fuller, T. Arora, & M. Nelson, *Exceptional Children, 67,* 2001, 467–484. Copyright © 2001 by the Council for Exceptional Children. Reprinted with permission.

---

the good of the group and the extent to which the learning activities they present maintain classroom flow, orderliness, and cooperation. In addition, they generally formulate teaching plans that result in a productive learning environment for 90% or more of their students. General education settings are best for learning what most students need to learn.

For many of the remaining 10% of students, however, a different orientation will probably be needed. These students need to learn something different because they are clearly not learning what everyone else is learning. Interventions that might be effective for this group of students require a considerable investment of time and effort, as well as extensive support. (p. 197)

People with Disabilities as a Minority   Many critics of full inclusion do not deny that in many ways, people with disabilities have been treated similarly to oppressed minority groups such as African Americans, Hispanics, and women. They have experienced discrimination on the basis of their disability and therefore can be considered an oppressed minority group.

These critics, however, do not see that this minority group status translates into the same educational placement decisions as it does for African Americans, Hispanics, and

Critics of full inclusion assert that it is unrealistic to expect the general education system, with its fast, competitive pace and whole-group focus, to provide the individualized instruction that is often needed by students with disabilities.

women (Dupre, 1997; Gliona et al., 2005; Hallahan & Kauffman, 1994; Kauffman & Hallahan, 1993; Kauffman & Lloyd, 1995). They argue that separation of students with disabilities from the mainstream can be defended on educational grounds. Students with disabilities are sometimes placed in special classes or resource rooms to better accommodate their educational needs. Placement in separate educational environments is inherently unequal, these critics maintain, when it is done for factors that are irrelevant to learning (e.g., skin color), but such placements may result in equality when done for instructionally relevant reasons (e.g., the student's ability to learn, difficulty of material being presented, preparation of the teacher).

Finally, critics of full inclusion argue that the most important civil right of students with disabilities and their parents is the right to choose where to be taught. That is, IDEA gives parents—and students themselves, when appropriate—the right to choose the environment they, not advocates of full inclusion, consider most appropriate and least restrictive (Crockett & Kauffman, 1998, 1999, 2001; Gliona et al., 2005).

Unwillingness to Consider Empirical Evidence Unfortunately, full inclusion ignores the considerable evidence that children and adults need affiliation, for at least some of the time, with others like themselves (Hall, 2002). Some professionals see as folly the disregard of empirical evidence espoused by some proponents of full inclusion (Fuchs & Fuchs, 1991; Kauffman, 1989, 1999a, 2002; Kauffman & Hallahan, 1997, 2005b; Kauffman, Lloyd, Hallahan, & Astuto, 1995; Kavale & Forness, 2000; Mock & Kauffman, 2005). They believe that ethical actions are always of the utmost importance. They assert, however, that decisions about what is ethical should be informed by research. Some critics maintain that proponents of full inclusion have resorted to rhetoric rather than reason. These critics assert that backers of full inclusion have traded in their credentials as scientific researchers in favor of becoming advocates and lobbyists (Mostert, Kauffman, & Kavale, 2003; Sasso, 2001).

Lack of Empirical Support for Full Inclusion There are few rigorous studies of full inclusion, but those that are available suggest that full inclusion has not led to social or academic benefits for all students (Mock & Kauffman, 2005; Zigmond, 2003). For example, one study found that students with disabilities in full-inclusion classrooms were not very well liked by their general education peers (Sale & Carey, 1995); another found that attempts to implement full inclusion did not produce the expected results (Fox & Ysseldyke, 1997); and others found that full inclusion did not serve all children appropriately (Baxter, Woodward, & Olson, 2001; Cook, Gerber, & Semmel, 1997; Mills et al., 1998; Vaughn, Elbaum, & Boardman, 2001). The authors concluded that their results were similar to those of previous studies of students with disabilities who were served in resource rooms. With respect to academics, the combined results of three longitudinal studies indicate that even after tremendous amounts of financial and professional resources were invested, 40 percent of fully included students with learning disabilities "were slipping behind at what many would consider a disturbing rate" (Zigmond et al., 1995, p. 539). More recent research has found that teachers tend to have unmanageable case loads in resource rooms and that the instruction that teachers are able to give in such circumstances leaves children with learning disabilities without important reading skills (Moody, Vaughn, Hughes, & Fischer, 2000).

In perhaps the most extensive study of full inclusion, researchers interviewed school personnel and students and observed in classrooms in five full-inclusion sites around the United States (Baker & Zigmond, 1995; Zigmond, 1995; Zigmond & Baker, 1995). On the basis of their data, the researchers claimed that teachers did not individualize instruction or plan ahead for how to accommodate the needs of students with disabilities. In fact, the individualization that did occur was most often carried out by peers (using peer tutoring—see page 00) or paraprofessionals (teacher aides). Besides, special education focuses on individuals, whereas general education focuses on the group (Johns, 2003).

"Students with severe reading-related LD [learning disabilities] require *specific, intensive, and explicit reading instruction individually or in small groups* if they are to make significant progress" (McCray, Vaughn, & Neal, 2001, p. 17, emphasis added). McCray and colleagues studied middle school students with reading disabilities, finding that most did not receive such instruction but instead received instructional supports in the form of tutoring or strategy training designed to help them survive in the general middle school curriculum. Yet McCray and colleagues (2001) note that "intensive and highly structured reading programs can make a qualitative difference in students' reading performance, even for students with a history of reading failure" (p. 29). Regarding socialization, Vaughn et al. (2001) found that inclusion might be appropriate for some students with learning disabilities, but for others it is ill advised. There appears to be no substitute for case-by-case determination of the best placement of students with disabilities.

On the basis of research to date, we conclude that intensive instruction is required for many students with disabilities if they are to make substantial progress. Such intensive instruction will sometimes need to be delivered in separate special education settings, such as special classes or resource rooms. Unfortunately, teachers in general education classrooms often find it difficult to provide enough intensive instruction, even with supports that are intended to help students survive the general education curriculum. The current structure of resource room programs, in which teachers have heavy case loads and cannot provide the instruction students need, is a setup for failure (Moody et al., 2000). Besides, as Zigmond (2003) suggests, asking *where* students should be taught is the wrong question; asking *how well* they are taught should be the focus of special education (Kauffman & Hallahan, 2005a; Kauffman & Landrum, 2005).

Preserving the Continuum of Placements   Critics of full inclusion argue that, given the empirical evidence, it is wise to be cautious about changing the current options too quickly or drastically. They admit that there are problems with current special education and that there might even be a need for more integration of students with disabilities, including inclusion of some. They are leery, however, about eliminating the range of service delivery options that are currently available to school personnel and parents (Crockett & Kauffman, 1999, 2001; Gliona et al., 2005; Martin, 1994; Kauffman, McGee, & Brigham, 2004; Vaughn et al., 2001).

One group of advocates has suggested a change in thinking and talking about special education placements (Gliona et al., 2005). Whereas it has been common to refer to any placement outside the regular classroom as *segregated,* Gliona and colleagues suggest using the word *dedicated* in referring to such placements. And there is no heirarchy of placements. Any one or a combination of alternative placements should be seen as equally appropriate, depending on the student's needs. Gliona and colleagues (2005) also point out that "*every option on the continuum of alternative placements is some child's least restrictive environment*" (p. 138).

Casebook Reflections

Refer to the case *The Red Belt* in your booklet. Because Tyler is extremely explosive and verbally abusive, what are the arguments for and against including him in the general education class for mathematics? How can the present debate on inclusion and the reality of Tyler's needs be resolved?

UNDERSTANDING THE STANDARDS AND PRINCIPLES   What is your opinion about full inclusion? *(CEC Knowledge and Skills Standard CC1S1)*

Council for Exceptional Children

Collaboration and Participation in General Education Classrooms

Whether or not one supports the concept of full inclusion, the fact is that most educators are in favor of some degree of integration of students with disabilities with nondisabled students. For participation in general education classrooms to be successful, special educators, general educators, and other professionals must provide some form of support for the student. There are generally five ways in which teachers help students with disabilities to participate in the general education classroom:

1. Prereferral teams and response to intervention models
2. Collaborative consultation
3. Cooperative teaching and other team arrangements
4. Curricula and instructional strategies
5. Accommodations and adaptations

PREREFERRAL TEAMS AND RESPONSE TO INTERVENTION

Prereferral teams (PRTs)

Teams made up of a variety of professionals, especially regular and special educators, who work with regular class teachers to come up with strategies for teaching difficult-to-teach children. Designed to influence regular educators to take ownership of difficult-to-teach students and to minimize inappropriate referrals to special education.

Prereferral teams (PRTs) are groups of professionals (e.g., special education teachers, counselors, administrators, psychologists) who work with general education teachers to help identify alternative educational strategies for students who are struggling in the classroom before a referral for special education evaluation is made. As the name implies, when a prereferral team is consulted, the student has not yet been identified as a student with a disability. A teacher usually asks for help when he or she has exhausted her own bag of tricks for helping a difficult-to-teach student. The team reviews the information about a student that the teacher brings to the group and then offers suggestions about what the teacher might try to do to help the student. These suggestions might include (but are not limited to) such things as behavioral contracts, instructional changes, or additional assessment of the child. The team might also provide assistance through model lessons, one-on-one tutoring, or referral to other school programs. One of the primary goals is to establish ownership of these children by general educators. In other words, PRTs try to keep down the number of referrals to special education by encouraging general educators to try as many alternative strategies as possible before deciding that difficult-to-teach students need to become the primary responsibility of special educators. In addition, prereferral teams are an attempt by school officials to meet the IDEA requirement that a student not be found eligible for special education services because of poor or missing instruction. Although PRTs have become popular, there has been little research on their effectiveness (see Hallahan, Lloyd, Kauffman, Weiss, & Martinez, 2005).

In the most recent reauthorization of IDEA, Congress has included an additional option for determining eligibility for special education in the case of suspected learning disabilities that forces varying levels of support in general education before referral to special education. Specifically, IDEA 2004 says that, "in determining whether a child has a specific learning disability, states may rely on a process that determines whether the child responds to scientific, research-based intervention as a part of the evaluation. In practice, this concept has been termed **response to intervention (RTI)**. Similar to the concept of prereferral teams in some ways, RTI usually provides for about three standard levels of intervention for students who are experiencing difficulties. There are varying forms, but generally, the first level includes verification of quality, research-based instruction with some standard changes and various other supports for a student in the general education classroom. The teacher monitors the student's progress in the curriculum and in relation to peers. If student achievement improves, no other action is taken. If the student's performance does not improve, the student moves to level 2. Level 2 usually includes individual or peer instruction in the areas of difficulty (e.g., reading or writing) or some other form of remediation. If the student's performance does not improve at this level, the student moves to level 3,

Response to intervention (RTI)

or response-to-treatment approach. A way of determining whether a student has a learning disability; increasingly intensive levels of instructional intervention are delivered, and if the student does not achieve, at some point, he or she is determined to have a learning disability or is referred for special education evaluation.

which is often a referral to special education services. Throughout the process, professionals monitor the student's progress in the curriculum, and these results are used (with other information) to determine special education eligibility (Vaughn & Fuchs, 2003). The difference between RTI and PRTs is that in RTI, students move through steps that are predetermined and progress is monitored closely, whereas in PRTs, interventions are determined on an individual basis and a student's progress might or might not be as closely monitored.

Advocates of RTI claim that it will reduce the number of referrals for special education and provide more options for students with disabilities to participate in general education classrooms. The argument is that because high-quality instruction is provided at every level, RTI helps to determine whether a student is truly a student with a disability and not a student who has been subjected to poor or missing instruction. Unfortunately, little research evidence is available to determine whether RTI is effective. In fact, it has been used on a wide scale in only a few school districts in the country (Fuchs, Mock, Morgan, & Young, 2003). Nevertheless, IDEA 2004 gives school the option of using RTI.

COLLABORATIVE CONSULTATION

Once it has been determined that a student is in fact a student with a disability, he or she may receive special education services within the general education classroom through collaborative consultation, cooperative teaching, curricula and other instructional strategies, and accommodations and adaptations. In **collaborative consultation**, the special education teacher or psychologist acts as an expert who provides advice to the general education teacher. The special educator might suggest changes to instruction or additional supports, such as behavior plans or school-home notes. This special educator might see the student with a disability in a resource room or other special education setting also, or the student might receive all of his instruction in the general education class. In essence, the special educator might have little direct contact with the student but rather provides support to the teachers of the student. Research suggests that collaborative consultation is a promising approach to meeting the needs of many students with disabilities in general education settings if the consultant provides frequent follow-up and feedback on intervention (Noell et al., 2000). Nevertheless, much remains unknown about what makes it work.

Collaborative consultation
An approach in which a special educator and a general educator collaborate to come up with teaching strategies for a student with disabilities. The relationship between the two professionals is based on the premises of shared responsibility and equal authority.

CO-TEACHING

Sometimes referred to as collaborative teaching or **cooperative teaching**, co-teaching takes mutuality and reciprocity in collaborative consultation one step further (see Fennick, 2001; Vaughn, Schumm, & Arguelles, 1997; Walsh & Jones, 2004). **Co-teaching** between general and special educators means "two or more professionals delivering substantive instruction to a diverse, or blended, group of students in a single physical space" (Cook & Friend, 1998, p. 454).

Proponents argue that co-teaching is a viable model for the effective inclusion of students with disabilities into regular classes for at least two reasons. First, co-teaching allows a special educator to be directly involved in the instructional support of the general educator, planning and teaching lessons together, instead of following a consultation model in which the special educator offers suggestions or helps in modifications without direct support (Cook & Friend, 1998). Second, it is thought that co-teaching provides a direct means of special education service delivery that neither stigmatizes nor isolates special education students. It also helps special educators to know exactly what is taking place in the general education classroom.

Many forms of co-teaching occur in schools (Weiss & Lloyd, 2002). Sometimes, teachers find it very effective and workable. Other times, co-teaching can present incredible challenges to teachers and to students. Unfortunately, research on cooperative teaching is lacking (Murawski & Swanson, 2001; Weiss & Brigham, 2000). Of the research that is available, results indicate that its success depends on at least two factors. First, enough time needs to be built into the general and special educators' schedules for cooperative planning.

Cooperative teaching
An approach in which general educators and special educators teach together in the general classroom; it helps the special educator know the context of the regular classroom better.

Co-teaching
A special educator working side-by-side with a general educator in a classroom, both teachers providing instruction to the group.

Second, the two teachers' personalities and working styles need to be compatible (Kauffman, Mostert, Trent, & Pullen, 2006). Because of the importance of interpersonal skills in making cooperative teaching and collaborative consultation successful, some researchers have cautioned teachers about neglecting teaching (Vaughn, Bos, & Schumm, 1997). Teachers who are engaged in cooperative teaching or collaborative consultation need to get along but not neglect teaching or the needs of their students.

CURRICULA AND INSTRUCTIONAL STRATEGIES

In addition to teacher cooperation, there are curricula and instructional strategies that help in making some students with disabilities successful in the general education classroom. **Cooperative learning** is an instructional strategy that many proponents of inclusion believe is an effective way of integrating students with disabilities into groups of nondisabled peers. In cooperative learning, students work together in heterogeneous small groups to solve problems or practice responses. The emphasis is on assisting each other in learning rather than on competition. Some educators have suggested that cooperative learning leads to better attitudes on the part of nondisabled students toward their peers with disabilities as well as to better attitudes of students with disabilities toward themselves. However, studies of cooperative groups also indicate that some students with disabilities, particularly those with emotional or behavioral disorders and those with mental impairments, do not work very well with others in groups that demand cooperation (Pomplun, 1997).

Another instructional strategy to enhance the integration of students with disabilities that is recommended by research is peer-mediated instruction (Fuchs et al., 2001; Gardner et al., 2001; Maheady, Harper, & Mallette, 2001; see also Fulk & King, 2001 and the websites they list). **Peer-mediated instruction** may refer to **peer tutoring**, the use of peer confederates in managing behavior problems, or any other arrangement in which peers are deliberately recruited and trained to help teach an academic or social skill to a classmate (Falk & Wehby, 2001). This is quite different from cooperative learning, in which students simply work together to accomplish a task. In most examples of peer-mediated instruction, professionals have advocated having students with disabilities act as tutors as well as tutees. When the student with a disability assumes the role of tutor, the tutee is usually a younger peer.

When the whole class is involved, the strategy is referred to as **classwide peer tutoring (CWPT)**. In this procedure, peer tutoring is routinely done by all students in the general education classroom for particular subject matter, such as reading or math (Greenwood et al., 2001). CWPT does not mean that the teacher provides no instruction. On the contrary, teachers must provide instruction in how to do peer tutoring and in the content of the tutoring sessions. Peers tutor each other to provide drill and practice of skills they already have.

Research on the effectiveness of various peer tutoring and cooperative learning strategies suggests that these methods can be very helpful for some students with disabilities and virtually useless for others (see Greenwood et al., 2001; Utley, Mortweet, & Greenwood, 1997). This leads us to emphasize the importance of carefully monitoring the progress of each individual student to assess the effectiveness of any instructional approach.

Partial participation, another instructional strategy, means having students with disabilities participate, on a reduced basis, in virtually all activities experienced by all students in the general education classroom. It questions the assumption that including students with severe mental and physical limitations is a waste of time because they cannot benefit from the activities in the same way that nondisabled students can. Instead of excluding anyone from these activities, advocates of partial participation recommend that the teacher accommodate the student with disabilities by such strategies as "providing assistance for more difficult parts of a task, changing the 'rules' of the game or activity to make it less difficult, or changing the way in which a task or activity is organized or presented" (Raynes, Snell, & Sailor, 1991, p. 329). The objectives of partial participation are twofold. First, pro-

Cooperative learning
A teaching approach in which the teacher places students with heterogeneous abilities (for example, some might have disabilities) together to work on assignments.

Peer-mediated instruction
The deliberate use of a student's classroom peer(s) to assist in teaching an academic or social skill.

Peer tutoring
A method that can be used to integrate students with disabilities in general education classrooms, based on the notion that students can effectively tutor one another. The role of learner or teacher may be assigned to either the student with a disability or the nondisabled student.

Classwide peer tutoring (CWPT)
An instructional procedure in which all students in the class are involved in tutoring and being tutored by classmates on specific skills as directed by their teacher.

Partial participation
An approach in which students with disabilities, while in the general education classroom engage in the same activities as nondisabled students but on a reduced basis; the teacher adapts the activity to allow each student to participate as much as possible.

ponents maintain that it provides exposure to academic content that the student with disabilities might otherwise miss. Second, it helps students with disabilities to achieve a greater degree of social interaction with nondisabled peers.

ACCOMMODATIONS AND ADAPTATIONS

Modifications can occur in either instruction or assessment of students with disabilities or in both. Modifications usually take the form of accommodation or adaptation and are different from changes in curricula or instructional strategies. **Accommodations** might be changes in instruction, student response, or assessment that do not change the content or conceptual difficulty level of the curriculum significantly. Alternatively, **adaptation** might involve more significant modifications of instruction than accommodations (Miller, 2002).

Instructional accommodations most often include changes in time, input, output, participation, and level of support. For example, during a history lecture, the teacher might use a graphic organizer to indicate important points and to graphically display how information is related. For a math problem-solving project, the teacher might give a student a few extra days to complete the requirements. The critical feature of accommodations is that the content of instruction is not changed, and the objective stays the same. The route to get to the objective might have to be changed or shifted for students with disabilities.

Instructional adaptations, by contrast, make the objectives for students with disabilities different from those for their peers. Therefore, changes may be made by creating alternative goals or using a substitute curriculum. For example, a teacher might allow a student with learning disabilities to use notes or an open book for an activity in which other students are not permitted to do so. In this case, the objective is for the student to use the information and to be able to find the information when needed, not to have the information committed to memory.

Tiered assignments (Tomlinson, 2001) are yet another example of adaptations. In tiered assignments, teachers provide choices for assignments on a single topic that vary in difficulty. For example, when studying *Huckleberry Finn,* some students might write paragraphs that identify and describe the characters; others might write paragraphs or papers that analyze the traits of each character, using examples from the book. In this case, both the assignment and the subsequent grading are different.

Research on the individual impact of program and testing modifications is hindered by the fact that students with disabilities are such a heterogeneous group and that some accommodations are built into instructional programs. Because of this, curricular or instructional modifications might show little impact for a large sample of students with disabilities but show quite an impact for a smaller subgroup. Unfortunately, much of the research on modifications has been done on the use of accommodations for classroom and high-stakes assessment (e.g., Fuchs, Fuchs, Eaton, Hamlett, & Karns, 2000; Helwig & Tindal, 2003; Johnson, Kimball, Brown & Anderson, 2001). This research seems to indicate that teachers are not terribly efficient at determining which student is the best candidate for accommodations and that some accommodations might actually hinder student performance. Obviously, with the increased focus on standard curricula and high-stakes testing in general education, more research is necessary in this area.

CONTINUING ISSUES

As the twenty-first century unfolds, the full-inclusion controversy is sharpened by emphasis on school reform, especially reforms that set higher standards that all students are expected to meet. The direction the controversy will take is anyone's guess (see Kauffman, 1999a, 1999–2000, 2004; Kauffman & Hallahan, 2005b; Kauffman & Wiley, 2004; Hoover & Patton, 2004). However, three dimensions of the controversy appear likely to dominate.

Modifications
Changes made in instruction or assessment to make it possible for a student with a disability to respond more normally.

Accommodations
Changes in the delivery of instruction, type of student performance, or method of assessment which do not significantly change the content or conceptual difficulty of the curriculum.

Adaptations
Changes in curricular content or conceptual difficulty or changes in instructional objectives and methods.

Tiered assignment
Assignments varying in difficulty but on a single topic.

First, there is the question of the legitimacy of atypical placements: Do special classes and special schools have a legitimate, defensible place in the alternatives that are provided to students with disabilities at public expense? If the answer to this question is "yes," then we are likely to see renewed emphasis on the advantages that such special placements offer.

Second, if a student is not able to function adequately in the general education curriculum, achieving what is judged to be "success" in general education, then should that student remain in the general education environment or be taught in an alternative place with other students who have similar learning needs? If the answer to this question is "remain in the general education environment," then ways must be found to remove the stigma of failure in that environment from both the student and the teacher, who might be judged to have failed to measure up to expectations.

Third, for students who are placed in alternative environments, increasing attention must be given to the quality of instruction that is provided there. Vaughn and colleagues (1998) and Moody and colleagues (2000) found that the instruction that was offered in the resource rooms they studied was not the intensive, individualized, relentless, and effective instruction that should characterize special education. The critical problem of today's special education might not be that students with disabilities are sometimes taught in separate settings but that special education teachers too seldom use the opportunity of such settings to offer the instruction that students need (Kauffman & Hallahan, 2005a; Zigmond, 2003). We cannot overemphasize the importance of intensive instruction in meeting the needs of children with disabilities. In our opinion, children with disabilities should be placed where such instruction is most likely to be provided.

Participation in General Assessments of Progress: IDEA and NCLB

In the 1990s, state and federal policymakers became concerned about what they perceived as a general decline in students' educational achievement. As a result, they emphasized "standards-based" reforms. These reforms involve setting standards of learning that are measured by standardized tests. The reformers believed that teachers' expectations have been too low and that all students should be held to higher standards (see Finn, Rotherham, & Hokanson, 2001; Hoover & Patton, 2004; Pugach & Warger, 2001; Thurlow, 2000; Thurlow, Nelson, Teelucksingh, & Draper, 2001).

Concerns of special educators were expressed primarily in the 1997 amendments to IDEA. Concerns of general educators were expressed primarily in the 2002 No Child Left Behind Act (NCLB), which was actually a reauthorization of the Elementary and Secondary Education Act (Yell & Drasgow, 2005). Both laws had the intention of improving the instruction of students with disabilities by making sure that these students are included in the assessments of educational progress that are demanded of all students. The NCLB requires that the average scores of various subgroups of students be reported and that all groups, including students with disabilities, show progress. The NCLB also requires that gaps in the performance of various groups be closed so that the averages for the various subgroups are not significantly different. Although this objective appears to be impossible to achieve in the case of students with disabilities, it is nonetheless an assumption of NCLB, IDEA 2004, and the President's Commission on Excellence in Special Education, that was appointed in 2001 by President George W. Bush and that submitted its report in 2002 (see Kauffman, 2004; Kauffman & Wiley, 2004).

CURRENT TRENDS

Because special education is an integral part of public education in the United States, students with disabilities were included in the concern for higher standards. That is, the feeling was that expectations have been too low for all students, including those receiving special education, and that students with disabilities should not only be expected to learn the general curriculum, but also be expected to perform at a level comparable to that of students without disabilities. Moreover, reformers argued, no school or state should be allowed to avoid responsibility for demonstrating that its students with disabilities are making acceptable progress in the general education curriculum.

The standards-based reform movement of the late twentieth and early twenty-first centuries brought with it a heavy emphasis on access to the general education curriculum for students with disabilities (Hoover & Patton, 2004; Pugach & Warger, 2001; Thurlow, 2000). The curriculum for students with disabilities often has been different from the curriculum in general education. Failure to teach students with disabilities the same things that are taught in general education has been interpreted to mean that the expectations for these students are lower, resulting in their low achievement and failure to make a successful transition to adult life.

IDEA 2004 and the 2002 No Child Left Behind act say that progress in the general education curriculum must be addressed in every IEP. Do you think that the same assessment standards should apply to all students, regardless of their disability?

Furthermore, students with disabilities often have not been included in statewide or national assessments of educational progress. Consequently, we have little information about how they have been progressing in comparison to the normative group or how education reforms might affect them. IDEA 2004 and the 2002 NCLB both required the inclusion of students with disabilities in assessments of educational progress with the exception of students with the most severe disabilities.

Understandably, the standards-based reform movement has generated much controversy: What constitutes curriculum? What should be the curriculum? What should the standards be (just how high should they be, and in what areas of the curriculum should they be set)? Who should set the standards? How should achievement of or progress toward the standards be measured? What should be the consequences for students—and for schools or states—if standards are not met? What should be given up in music, art, poetry, physical education, and other areas to ensure progress on standardized tests in core curriculum areas of reading and math?

These are not trivial questions for general or special educators. Dobbs (2004) reports that some schools are indeed dropping classes in art, foreign language, and other electives to give more time and attention to the standards required by NCLB. He described public schools in Indiana specifically, but noted:

> Budget cuts in many states have compounded the problem [of insufficient funds to maintain programs not tested by NCLB], forcing principals and superintendents to make tough decisions on how to focus their resources. Faced with a financial shortfall, other Indiana districts have cut extracurricular activities, from school newspapers to the swim team to cheerleading coaches.
>
> "It's the lopsidedness that I worry about," said Anne Young, principal of Clark Elementary School in Franklin, a rural community near Indianapolis. "The pressure on teachers [to improve test results] is enormous. Some young teachers only know the world of data. I want teachers to see faces, not numbers." (Dobbs, 2004, p. A12)

Another writer complained that his poetry-writing class in a Washington, D.C., middle school was eliminated because of NCLB standards (Grim, 2004). He noted also:

> The library is locked because the school can't afford a librarian. Probably nothing in those books would teach the kids how to pass the standardized tests anyway.
>
> Many educators and policymakers supported the No Child Left Behind Act because it was supposed to increase school funding. But that promise turned out to be empty. The act was not funded as promised, and now educators are stuck with an unfunded mandate to constantly improve their test scores. (Grim, 2004, p. B8)

For students with disabilities, additional questions arise: Should all standards apply to all students, regardless of their disability? What should be the consequences of failing to meet a given standard if the student has a disability? Under what circumstances are alternative standards appropriate? Under what circumstances should special accommodations be made in assessing progress toward a standard? Answering questions like these requires professional judgment in the individual case, and such judgment is required by law (see Bateman & Linden, 1998; Huefner, 2000; Johns, 2003; Kauffman & Hallahan, 2005a; Thurlow, 2000; Yell, 1998). Moreover, assuming that IDEA and NCLB require the same things of students with disabilities is erroneous (Johns, 2003), and expecting students with disabilities to score the same, on average, as students without disabilities is expecting the impossible (Kauffman, 2004; Kauffman & Wiley, 2004). As special education teacher Melissa Gogel, a sixth-grade special education teacher is reported to have said, "We [special educators and their students] will always fail. . . . The governmnent is trying to put eveybody in one melting pot and say that everybody has to pass the same test" (Dobbs, 2004, p. A12).

We might ask what NCLB is actually interpreted to mean. Is the same level of performance expected of all students? Following is one educational consultant's view:

> Teachers say they have to teach the students where they are, which means at sixth-grade level in high school if they can't read well. Their attitude may be compassionate, but it is misguided. There's ample evidence that accelerating instruction works better than retarding it in the name of remediation. Observations made in the Dallas Unified School District show that students who score well have teachers who cover the curriculum appropriate to the grade level. These teachers spend little time on drill and practice, and don't remediate in the classroom but rather get help for students outside of class. (Mitchell, 2004, p. A21)

If this view is taken as defensible, then what happens to remedial programs and to special education during the school day? Is it a good idea to provide instruction that is advanced beyond the student's level of ability to understand and perform successfully? One noted special educator said that in her opinion, Mitchell's educational philosophy could be stated in a nutshell: "Teach the best and shoot the rest" (Janet Lerner, personal communication, April 27, 2004; see also Kauffman & Landrum, 2006). The issue is of obvious importance to general education, but it is of particular concern to special education for two reasons: First federal regulations allow only a small minority of students with disabilities to be excluded from the same testing as students without disabilities (1 percent of the school population, about one tenth of those with disabilities). Second, some of the programs that are being eliminated (e.g., art, music, physical education, and other "noncore" or extracurricular activities) are those in which students with disabilities are most likely to experience success and be successfully included.

By current federal law, the inclusion of students with disabilities in assessments of progress in the general education curriculum must be addressed in every individualized education program (IEP). Although the law recognizes that some students with disabilities have educational needs that are not addressed in the general education curriculum, each

 FOR UPDATES on legal issues in special education, see the website maintained by legal expert Dixie Snow Huefner and click on "Chapter Updates": **www.ed.utah.edu/~huefner/ sped-law/spdlawbk.htm** or **www.wrightslaw.com**

student's IEP must include a statement of how and when the student's educational progress will be measured.

Accommodations for evaluation procedures might involve altering the time given for responding, changing the setting in which the assessment is done, or using an alternative format for either the presentation of tasks or the type of response required. Examples of the kinds of accommodations that might be made for students with disabilities who are taking tests are shown in Table 2.1. Such accommodations can make a significant difference in how students with some disabilities are able to perform on standardized tests (Tindal, Heath, Hollenbeck, Almond, & Harniss, 1998). Therefore, making sure that students are assessed with appropriate accommodations for their disabilities will be extremely important when they are included in evaluations of progress. However, inappropriate accommodations merely undercut reasonable expectations for students with disability and misrepresent students' true capabilities (Kauffman et al., 2004).

CONTINUING ISSUES

No doubt the current standards-based reform movement, including NCLB and IDEA 2004, will entail enormous difficulties in regard to all students but particularly those with disabilities. Moreover, although some people argue that uniform standards or expectations will result in greater equity for students, others worry that new inequalities for ethnic minority students and those with disabilities will be created by standards-based reforms (e.g., Johns, 2003; Kauffman, 2004; Kauffman & Wiley, 2004; McNeil, 2000; Thurlow, 2000; Thurlow et al., 2001). Some of the controversy generated by NCLB and IDEA 2004 is highlighted in the Focus on Concepts on page 62.

In any area of performance, setting a standard that very few individuals fail will eventually be perceived as "low." Setting a standard that many individuals cannot reach will be perceived, at least after a time, as "high." Who will be blamed for a given person's failure to meet a standard and who will be congratulated when someone meets or exceeds a standard depend on our assessment of the effort expended by teacher and student. However, one thing seems certain: Standards will not homogenize achievement or expectations. The consequences of standards-based reform such as NCLB for students with and without disabilities will become clearer as reforms are implemented and standards are set. Some commentators have noted that the basc premises and language of NCLB are seductive. As Raspberry (2004) put it, it is "an idea that seems so right you wonder how any decent-

FOR INFORMATION about universal design, see **www.cec.sped.org/spotlight/udl/**

ISSUES RELATED to accessibility of the World Wide Web to people with disabilities are found at **www.seriweb.com**
For websites and radio related to disability, see **www.ican.com/channels/on_a_roll/index.cfm**

TABLE 2.1   **Examples of Accommodations for Assessments**

Flexible Time	Flexible Setting	Alternative Presentation Format	Alternative Response Format
Extended time	Test alone in test carrel or separate room	Braille or large-print edition	Pointing to response
Alternating lengths of test sections (e.g., shorter and longer)	Test in small-group setting	Signing of directions	Using template for responding
More frequent breaks	Test at home (with accountability)	Interpretation of directions	Giving response in sign language
Extended testing sessions over several days	Test in special education classroom	Taped directions	Using a computer
	Test in room with special lighting	Highlighted keywords	Allow answers in test book

Source: Reprinted with permission from Yell, M. L, & Shriner, J. G. (1997). The IDEA amendments of 1997: Implications for special and general education teachers, administrators, and teacher trainers. *Focus on Exceptional Children, 30*(1), p. 8. All rights reserved.

FOCUS ON CONCEPTS

Testing Matthew

THE following is excerpted from a transcript of PBS's *The NewsHour with Jim Lehrer* of April 20, 2004:

Jim Lehrer: Now testing students with disabilities under No Child Left Behind. John Merrow, the NewsHour special correspondent for education, reports. . . .

John Merrow: What's happening in West Hartford is happening all over the country. Thousands of schools have been singled out because of the poor performance of students with disabilities. Some say that's exactly the wakeup call the system needed.

Eugene Hickok [Deputy Secretary of Education, U.S. Department of Education]: Fact is, a group of students were being left behind. And now they know that and they will be fine. They're going to turn that around. But they needed to know. . . . Isn't a public school supposed to serve the entire public? I mean, to me the answer is yes.

[Ohio] Rep. Ted Strickland: Give me a break. Let me tell you what they're doing over at the Department of Education. They're engaging in a lot of fanciful rhetoric. Fanciful rhetoric.

John Merrow: Representative Ted Strickland of Ohio voted for No Child Left Behind. But with 70 percent of students with disabilities failing in his own state, he's now come out hard against the law.

Rep. Ted Strickland: Every child can learn, but not every child can learn at the same pace or reach the same level of achievement. That is the truth. . . .

John Merrow: Testing students like Matt Petrone [a student with Down syndrome] is generating the most heat. No Child Left Behind does provide exemptions but only for students with the most severe disabilities. Thousands of students like Matt do not qualify for exemptions and therefore will be tested.

Rep. Ted Strickland: It is unreasonable to take a child with significantly diminished cognitive abilities and expect them to achieve at an average level. It is not defensible.

John Merrow: At first, Cathy Petrone [Matt's mother] also thought the idea of testing her son was indefensible.

Then she changed her mind. To her, No Child Left Behind represents a turning point in education for students with disabilities. Only ten years ago, Connecticut routinely sent students like Matthew to separate schools.

Cathy Petrone: I don't think in general, the educational system really did have that high expectations for Matthew. I mean, there was definitely issues of special education teachers saying, to me, you know, that your son is not going to read. He is only going to read sight words so we are not going to teach him this. And I was like, well how can you know that? How do you know that?

John Merrow: Today, Matthew can read, not as well as his peers but better than most people expected.

Cathy Petrone: He's kind of like a mirror in terms of the way you react towards him is kind of the way he'll act towards you. If you have low expectations or dismiss him, he'll basically act that way. I've seen this from when he was a child or if you meet him where he is and bring him up to a higher level, generally he will try to do that within his ability. The hope is that, you know, the law will help change expectations and change people's minds.

Eugene Hickok: Certainly this has never been tried before. We think this is the next logical step in making sure that special education is part of American public education.

John Merrow: Secretary Hickok said No Child Left Behind is forcing schools to take seriously the business of educating kids with special needs.

Rep. Ted Strickland: Well, there is some truth to that, but the way you correct that problem is not to create a system where students are set up to fail.

Cathy Petrone: I do not really have expectation that he will pass, but the idea that everyone should have standards, that's a good idea. This is not just about us. This is about everybody who is coming up behind us, and I hope, you know, that they'll get more opportunities. ■

Source: Excerpted from the PBS News Hour transcript of April 20, 2004. Reprinted by permission.

minded legislator could oppose it" (p. A21). Yet, Raspberry also notes, the law has a fatal flaw, which is its focus on punishing those who do not meet its standards: "its underlying assumption that school failure is willful, and that if you put the fear of God in the people who run the schools, they'll do their jobs a lot better" (p. A21).

Requiring all students with disabilities and those for whom the tests are inappropriate for other reasons to take state exams can be considered by some to be cruel to both students and teachers (Kauffman, 2002, 2004; Kauffman & Wiley, 2004). Special education teacher Pixie Holbrook describes the agony of a state-mandated test for herself and one of her pupils, Sarah, a fourth-grader with a learning disability. She describes Sarah as a good and diligent student, but because of her learning disability, Sarah does not have the skills required for the test.

> She knows she doesn't know. And she knows that I know she doesn't know. This is so very humiliating.
>
> Her eyes are wet now, but she's silent and stoic. I check in, and she reassures me she's fine. She appears to be on the verge of weeping, but she will not be deterred. I cannot help her in any way; I can only sit nearby and return a false smile. I can offer a break, nothing more. Later, I calculated the reading level of this selection. Sarah reads like a second-grader, and the poem is at the high end of the fifth-grade scale. Her eyes are not just scanning the paragraphs. I know she has stopped reading and is just glancing and gazing. It's meaningless, and it hurts. Yet she attempts to answer every question. It is now $2\frac{1}{2}$ hours, and my anger is growing. This is immoral and has become intolerable. And it's only the first day. (Holbrook, 2001, p. 783)

The potential for bias in testing must be taken seriously. However, objecting to all testing and standards is likely to be counterproductive. As Thurlow and colleagues remark:

> Despite the potential hazards of results-based education systems, there are some potential benefits for all students, including those students with disabilities from multicultural backgrounds. Only with information on how these students are doing, information like that obtained on other students, will we know that our education system is or is not working. This information appears necessary as we begin to adjust and improve the educational opportunities provided to these students, so that they achieve all of the important educational outcomes. (2001, p. 169)

As Kauffman (2002) explains, "The only way to know whether a program is working is by testing" (p. 238). If we want to know whether programs for students with disabilities are "working," then testing to determine outcomes is necessary. Standardized tests have a legitimate place in assessing outcomes, and demonizing the tests themselves is not helpful. However, it is also important to understand that "Testing is useful only if you make the right comparisons for the right reasons" (Kauffman, 2002, p. 240). When it comes to special education, it is wrong to compare outcomes for students with disabilities to outcomes for students without disabilities. The right comparison is comparing students with disabilities who receive special education or any given treatment to those who do not receive it (Kauffman, 2004; Kauffman & Hallahan, 2005a).

Access to New Technologies

As technology becomes ever more sophisticated, the issue of independence will become ever more important. One general guideline might be that if the technology allows people with disabilities to do something they could not do without it, then the technology is in their best interest. However, if it allows them to do something new or better but at the same time imposes new limitations, then one might need to rethink the technology's benefits.

Technological advances of all types can have implications for people with disabilities. Two types stand out as particularly important: advances in medical and communications

Raymond J. Witte III, who is a college student learning to teach special education students, practices with a head-mounted pointer. Advances in electronics and computers are making it easier for special education students to be taught in regular classes.

Cochlear implantation
A surgical procedure that allows people who are deaf to hear some environmental sounds; an external coil fitted on the skin by the ear picks up sound from a microphone worn by the person and transmits it to an internal coil implanted in the bone behind the ear, which carries it to an electrode implanted in the cochlea of the inner ear.

technologies. Some of these advances, particularly those in the medical field, are very controversial. The controversy is typically about whether something that can be done should be done. For example, should **cochlear implantations**—artificial inner ears, which we will discuss further in Chapter 10—be used to allow deaf children to hear whenever possible? Should disabilities be corrected surgically before birth (in utero) if that is possible? Should the findings of fetal stem cell research be applied to cure or correct physical disabilities if possible? These are some of the controversial ethical issues that we will discuss in later chapters.

Communication technologies sometimes overlap with medical technologies (e.g., cochlear implants), but ordinarily, they do not. Usually, they involve hardware or software applications that allow someone to use equipment or media. Perhaps the most obvious issue today is making the World Wide Web accessible to people with disabilities. For some, this means adaptations that allow a person to use a keyboard or mouse or read a visual display. We discuss some of these adaptations in Chapters 13 and 14.

CURRENT TRENDS

As the pace of technology quickens, so do applications of these technologies to the daily lives of people with disabilities. In many ways, technologies expand the abilities of people with or without disabilities to access information, communicate, travel, and accomplish many other everyday tasks. Technological applications can also allow some people with disabilities to function like those without disabilities. For example, Michalko (2002) notes the importance of students with visual impairments getting together in a resource room to share ideas about assistive computer technology:

What brings these disabled students together is their need for technology. What keeps them together, both informally and formally, is their need to share ideas and information about technology. Without technology, these visually impaired stu-

dents would not be able to do the ordinary things of university life; they would not
be able to read books, write papers, take notes in class, and so on. (p. 157)

The current trend is toward considering the needs of all potential users in developing
a technology. This is often called **universal design** (Pisha & Coyne, 2001). In architecture,
the design of new tools and the design of instructional programs, the trend is toward making technologies or products usable by the widest possible population of potential users.

Access to the World Wide Web by people with disabilities is a current trend that has
significant implications for design. You might want to visit the website of the Web Accessibility Initiative sponsored by the U.S. Department of Education's National Institute on
Disability and Rehabilitation Research and other agencies. You might also want to visit the
website of the Center for Applied Special Technology and its Universal Design for Learning. Section 508 of the Rehabilitation Act requires access to electronic and information
technology procured by federal agencies, which further enhances the abilities of people
with disabilities to participate.

CONTINUING ISSUES

One of the major issues concerning technologies is cost. Technologically advanced equipment or surgical procedures typically are very costly at first. Their immediate application to
people of any description is beyond the financial reach of most consumers. However, as
technological advances become incorporated into everyday life and mass produced, their
cost typically falls dramatically.

An issue that is likely to become more controversial is whether we should do things
that we can with new technologies. The moral and ethical dilemmas that are created by the
availability of the means to eliminate limitations, whether they are considered disabilities or
not—for example, being unable to hear, see, walk, or communicate—will increase in years
to come.

Another issue that is bound to arise as new technologies are created is when to assume
that the limits of universal design have been reached and go ahead with production. In-
ventors and designers may do their best to be "smart from the start" (Pisha & Coyne,
2001), but perhaps no one can be certain that no potential user's needs have been overlooked. At some point, someone decides to put a gadget or technology into production
under the assumption that the design is as universal as it can be made at that time. Perhaps
the term *universal,* like the term *all,* must not be taken too literally, or it becomes self-
defeating.

Early Intervention

Many educators and social scientists believe that the earlier in life a disability is recognized
and a program of education or treatment is started, the better the outcome will be for the
child (e.g., Kaiser, 2000; Walker, Ramsey, & Gresham, 2004). They also see an important
federal role in ensuring early intervention. Three basic arguments underlie early
intervention:

1. A child's early learning provides the foundation for later learning, so the sooner a
   special program of intervention is begun, the further the child is likely to go in
   learning more complex skills.
2. Early intervention is likely to provide support for the child and family that will
   help prevent the child from developing additional problems or disabilities.
3. Early intervention can help families adjust to having a child with disabilities; give
   parents the skills they need to handle the child effectively at home; and help families find the additional support services they may need, such as counseling, medical assistance, or financial aid.

Universal design
The design of new buildings,
tools, and instructional programs to make them usable by
the widest possible population
of potential users.

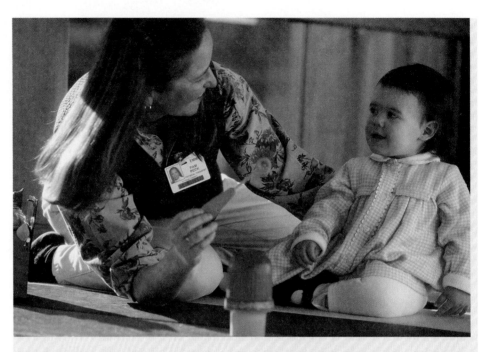

Federal laws now require that a variety of early intervention services be available to all infants and toddlers who are identified as having disabilities. Such services include special education instruction, physical therapy, speech and language therapy, and medical diagnostic services.

Developmental delay

A term often used to encompass a variety of disabilities of infants or young children indicating that they are significantly behind the norm for development in one or more areas such as motor development, cognitive development, or language.

Children whose disabilities are diagnosed at a very young age tend to be those with specific syndromes (e.g., Down syndrome) or obvious physical disabilities. Many have severe and multiple disabilities. Up through the primary grades, children with disabilities may be categorized under the broad label **developmental delay** rather than identified as having a more specific disability (e.g., mental retardation, learning disability, or emotional disturbance). Typically, such a child's needs cannot be met by a single agency or intervention, so many professionals must work together closely and with parents if the child is to be served effectively (Gallagher, Rhodes, & Darling, 2004). If the child's disabilities are recognized at an early age and intervention by all necessary professionals is well coordinated, the child's learning and development can often be greatly enhanced.

In the area of emotional and behavioral disorders, particularly those involving children who are highly oppositional or disobedient and aggressive from a young age, early intervention shows enormous promise (Walker et al., 2004). Long-term follow-up data suggest that the life course of children who are at high risk for becoming aggressive and disruptive can be changed dramatically through early behavioral intervention (Strain & Timm, 2001).

Federal laws now require that a variety of early intervention services be available to all infants and toddlers who are identified as having disabilities. Such services include special education instruction, physical therapy, speech and language therapy, and medical diagnostic services. In addition, laws require the development of an **individualized family service plan (IFSP)** (see Bateman & Linden, 1998). As we discussed in Chapter 1, an IFSP is similar to an IEP for older children, but it broadens the focus to include the family as well as the child. In fact, federal regulations stipulate that the family be involved in the development of the IFSP. Other important requirements are that the IFSP must contain statements of the following:

Individualized family service plan (IFSP)

A plan mandated by PL 99-457 to provide services for young children with disabilities (under three years of age) and their families; drawn up by professionals and parents; similar to an IEP for older children.

- The child's present levels of functioning in cognitive, physical, language and speech, psychosocial, and self-help development
- The family's resources, priorities, and concerns relating to the child's development

- The major expected outcomes for the child and family, including criteria, procedures, and time lines for assessing progress
- The specific early intervention services necessary to meet the child's and the family's needs, including frequency, intensity, location, and method of delivery
- The projected dates for initiating and ending the services
- The name of the case manager
- The steps needed to ensure a smooth transition from the early intervention program into a preschool program

Figure 2.1 shows the relationship between age of children in months and the writing of IFSPs. The figure shows that although children first had IFSPs at every age from one month through thirty-six months, most first had IFSPs very soon after birth or soon after their second birthday. This is likely because the disabilities of young children tend, on the one hand, to be obvious at birth or very soon thereafter or, on the other hand, to become obvious when the child is not learning to talk or walk. If a child is not talking and walking by age 2, then a developmental delay is suspected.

TYPES OF PROGRAMS

One common way of categorizing the variety of early intervention programs is to consider whether the primary location of the services is in a center, a home, or a combination of the two. The earliest early intervention programs for children with disabilities were center-based. In **center-based programs**, the child and the family come to the center for training and/or counseling. One advantage of center-based programs is that center staff can see more children. Furthermore, some professionals believe that this program allows center staff to have more influence over what goes on in the interaction between parent and child.

Center-based program
A program implemented primarily in a school or center, not in the student's home.

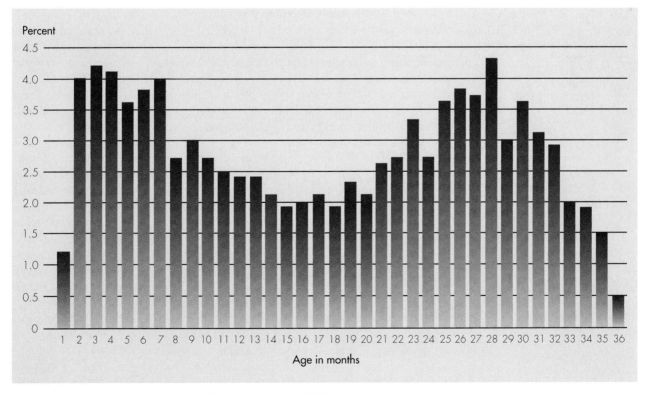

FIGURE 2.1 Age at time of Individualized Family Service Plan (IFSP)

Source: National Early Intervention Longitudinal Study. (2000).

Home-based program
A program delivered primarily in a student's home rather than in a school or center.

RESOURCES for Early Childhood Special Education has a useful site at **www.mcps. k12.md.us/curriculum/pep/ pz.html**

The National Information Center for Children and Youth with Disabilities has a useful website at **www.nichcy.org**

In more recent years, authorities have advocated **home-based programs** or a combination of center- and home-based approaches. There are several advantages to approaches that take place in the home. A couple of the most important are that (1) with the increase in mothers working outside the home and single-parent families, home-based programs are more convenient for more family members, and (2) skills and techniques learned by children and adults at the center need to be transferred to the home, but when these skills are learned in the natural environment—that is, the home—this transfer is not necessary.

As preschool programs and daycare become more pervasive, more and more young children with disabilities are being included in "natural" environments with their nondisabled or typically developing peers. The integrated or inclusionary daycare or preschool program is thus another type of program.

CURRENT TRENDS

Compared to most of special education, that for infants, toddlers, and preschoolers has had few controversial issues. This is probably because so many professionals have fought for so long to get the needs of very young children recognized that they have not had time to engage in many debates about specific details involved in early intervention. In a sense, early childhood special educators have been bound together by the common goal of securing legislation and programming for young children with disabilities. Nevertheless, there have been and continue to be some areas of disagreement among early childhood special education professionals. Three of the most compelling issues are the following:

1. The appropriate role of the family in early intervention
2. Whether it is better to have a child- or a adult-directed curriculum
3. Whether full inclusion is best for all young children.

We devote all of Chapter 4 to family issues, so we discuss only the second and third issues here.

Child–Directed Versus Adult-Directed Programs   Tension exists between early childhood educators who are concerned with nondisabled populations and those who are focused on children with disabilities over the degree of adult direction that is most appropriate, whether the adult is a parent or teacher. Heavily influenced by the theories of the noted Swiss psychologist Jean Piaget, most early childhood teachers are oriented toward a curriculum that allows children to explore their environment relatively freely. These teachers advocate a developmental approach, assuming that children's development will unfold naturally with encouragement, guidance, and support from the teacher.

Many early interventionists, on the other hand, come from a tradition that assumes that children with disabilities need a heavy dose of direction from adults if they are to learn the skills they lack. Furthermore, early childhood special educators have generally had a greater focus on individualizing instruction for preschoolers through task analysis, adaptation of materials and activities, and systematic assessment (Carta, 1995; Carta & Greenwood, 1997). As more and more children with disabilities have been integrated with nondisabled preschoolers, the issues of adult direction and individualization have come to the fore.

A major task facing early childhood special educators is to reach agreement with mainstream early childhood educators on programming for preschoolers with disabilities. Both sides can undoubtedly learn from each other. On the one hand, researchers have known for a long time that preschoolers with disabilities do better in highly structured, teacher-directed, individualized programs (Abt Associates, 1976–1977). On the other hand, authorities have noted that moving from a highly structured preschool intervention program to a traditional kindergarten can present problems.

Inclusive Education   Virtually all early childhood educators suggest that children with identifiable disabilities and those who are considered at risk for school failure should be included in programs that are designed to serve diverse groups of learners, including young children without disabilities. In fact, most preschoolers with disabilities now receive their education totally or primarily in regular classrooms. However, the extent to which the practices in programs for typically developing young children are appropriate for children with disabilities has been a matter of considerable controversy (Odom, 2000).

A radical philosophy of inclusive education will not necessarily serve all young children well (Garrett, Thorp, Behrmann, & Denham, 1998; Mills et al., 1998). However, some research has suggested that with proper adjustment for the individual needs of children, inclusion of young children with disabilities is always or nearly always beneficial (Odom, 2000; Strain, 2001). Certainly, there is more evidence supporting the inclusion of very young children in groups with typically developing students than there is supporting the inclusion of older students.

CONTINUING ISSUES

We hope that early childhood education will continue to play an important role in eliminating and lessening the impact of disability on children and their families. We caution, however, not to assume that early intervention alone will mean fewer children with disabilities (see Kauffman, 2005b). Although educators are devising more effective programs of early intervention, the number of children with disabilities is increasing. The reasons for this increase are many and complex and are related to changes in economic and social conditions in the United States. Today, we know of these factors in the twenty-first century:

- A high percentage of young children and their mothers live in poverty, have poor nutrition, and are exposed to environmental conditions that are likely to cause disease and disability.
- Many babies are born to teenage mothers.
- Many babies are born to mothers who receive inadequate prenatal care, have poor nutrition during pregnancy, and abuse substances that can harm the fetus.
- Many babies are born with a low birth weight.
- Environmental hazards, both chemical and social, are increasing.
- Millions of children are subjected to abuse and to environments in which violence and substance abuse are pervasive.
- Substantial cuts in, and revisions of, social programs have widened the gap between needs and the availability of social services.

Early intervention seems to hold great promise for prevention of disabilities, but there are strong forces working against prevention, including the revulsion many people feel for labels and propositions of education reformers that work against identifying problems early and intervening to stop them from getting worse (Kauffman, 1999b, 2005a, 2005b). Besides prevention, other issues for the new millennium include the use of computer technology with young children, the changing roles of special educators, emerging philosophies of early childhood education, cultural and linguistic diversity, and access to community resources (Lerner et al., 1998).

𝒯ransition to 𝒜dulthood

Preparing students for continued education, adult responsibilities, independence, and employment has always been a goal of public secondary education. Most students complete high school and find jobs, enter a vocational training program, or go to college without experiencing major adjustment difficulties. We know that dropout and unemployment rates are far too high for all youths, especially in economically depressed communities, but the outlook for students with disabilities is perhaps even worse.

Published figures on dropout rates must be viewed with caution because there are many different ways of defining the term *dropout* and computing the statistics (MacMillan

UNDERSTANDING THE STANDARDS AND PRINCIPLES What are some trends and issues in early childhood education and early childhood special education? *(CEC Knowledge and Skills Standard EC1K2)*

Council for Exceptional Children

FIGURE 2.2   Percentage of students ages 17 through 21+ with disabilities graduating with a standard diploma: 1994–95 to 1997–98

Source: U.S. Department of Education, Office of Special Education Programs, Data Analysis System (DANS). Washington, DC: Author.

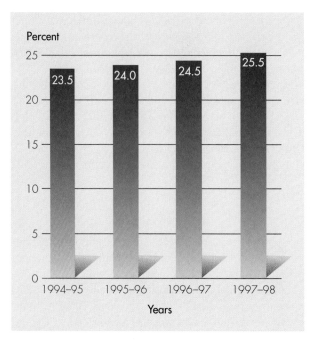

et al., 1992). Studies of what happens to students with disabilities during and after their high school years strongly suggest, however, that a higher percentage of them, compared to students without disabilities, have difficulty in making the transition from adolescence to adulthood and from school to work. Many students with disabilities drop out of school, experience great difficulty in finding and holding jobs, do not find work that is suited to their capabilities, do not receive further training or education, or become dependent on their families or public assistance programs.

Figure 2.2 shows the gradual increase in students with disabilities who graduated from high school with a standard diploma. These overall rates of graduation with a diploma mask the outcomes for particular categories of disability. Overall outcomes for students with disabilities are disappointing, but those in some categories of disability fare much better than others. Students with severe and multiple disabilities and those with emotional or behavioral disorders typically have the poorest outcomes. Those with specific learning disabilities or speech and language impairments tend to have comparatively better outcomes.

FEDERAL INITIATIVES

Federal laws, including IDEA, require attention to transition plans for older students, and these must be incorporated in students' IEPs. Transition services include a coordinated set of outcome-oriented activities, that promotes movement from school to post-secondary education, vocational training, integrated employment (including supported employment), continuing adult education, adult services, independent living, or community participation.

IDEA 2004 requires that each student's IEP contain a statement of needed transition services for him or her, beginning no later than 16 years of age and annually thereafter. (For students for whom it is appropriate, the statement is to be included in the IEP at a younger age.) In addition, the IEP must include a statement of the linkages and/or responsibilities of each participating agency before the student leaves the school setting.

An important aspect of this legislation is that it recognizes that transition involves more than just employment. Many authorities have applauded this broad emphasis on independent living, community adjustment, and so forth. For example, some have championed the idea that transition programming should be aimed at improving the quality of life for people with disabilities (e.g., Chadsey-Rusch & Heal, 1995). Although quality of life is difficult to define, Halpern (1993) points to personal choice as its underlying principle. He

UNDERSTANDING THE STANDARDS AND PRINCIPLES   What should professionals and parents consider when planning students' transition to adulthood? *(CEC Knowledge and Skills Standard GC10S4)*

Council for Exceptional Children

Students with disabilities must have preparation for life after high school, including further education, work, and independent living. Working with a job coach and with the cooperation of a local business, a student is integrated into this work staff.

also identifies three important quality-of-life domains: (1) physical and material well-being; (2) performance of adult roles (e.g., employment, leisure, personal relationships, social responsibility); and (3) personal fulfillment (e.g., happiness).

An increase in supported employment has come with the federal mandate for transition services. **Supported employment** is designed to assist people with disabilities who cannot function independently in competitive employment. It is a method of ensuring that they are able to work in integrated work settings alongside people without disabilities. In a typical supported employment situation, an employment specialist, or **job coach**, places the individual in a job with a business. The job coach then provides on-site training that is gradually reduced as the worker is able to function more independently on the job. Competitive employment is usually defined as working at least twenty hours per week at a type of job usually filled by a person without disabilities. (We discuss supported employment further in Chapter 5.)

Although employment is a goal, some adults with disabilities attend activity centers or day care. Table 2.2 describes the range of adult service and community employment alternatives that might be considered for an individual with severe disabilities.

CURRENT TRENDS

As with early intervention programming, little controversy surrounds the basic premise of transition programming for students as they move from secondary school to work or post-secondary education. All special educators agree that transition programming is critical for the successful adjustment of adults with disabilities (see Kohler, 1998; Moon & Inge, 2000; Sitlington et al., 2000). However, there is some controversy about the specifics of transition. Much of this has to do with trying to meet the diverse requirements of the federal mandate. A few states have achieved a high degree of compliance with federal law and have implemented excellent transition policies, but many others have not (Furney, Hasazi, & DeStefano, 1997). Many IEPs are in technical compliance with the IDEA mandate for transition but lack key elements, reflecting a lack of thoughtful planning (Grigal, Test, Beattie, & Wood, 1997).

Supported employment
A method of integrating people with disabilities who cannot work independently into competitive employment; includes use of an employment specialist, or job coach, who helps the person with a disability function on the job.

Job coach
A person who assists adult workers with disabilities (especially those with mental retardation), providing vocational assessment, instruction, overall planning, and interaction assistance with employers, family, and related government and service agencies.

TABLE 2.2 Typical Adult Service and Community Employment Alternatives

1. *Competitive (unsupported) employment*—on company payroll with benefits and without trainer or support from a human services agency.

2. *Job placement, or transitional support into regular employment*—short-term help from an agency, such as the state vocational rehabilitation agency, in finding and getting adjusted to a job.

3. *Supported employment*—job placement, training, and continuing support for as long as necessary in an integrated community business. Supported employment can be in the form of an individual placement or a group model of several workers, such as an enclave or mobile work crew. Workers earn minimum wage or better.

4. *Volunteer work*—unpaid work that is preferred or chosen by an individual for reasons other than "daily support." This is usually done for community service organizations, such as the SPCA, a hospital, or the National Cancer Society. Labor laws define what types of work are considered volunteer. Workers with disabilities cannot volunteer to do work that would pay a wage to employees without disabilities.

5. *Sheltered work*—work done in a sheltered workshop where the majority of workers are disabled and earn subminimum wages. Sheltered workshops can offer a variety of employment and evaluation services, such as work activity, work adjustment training, vocational evaluation, long-term sheltered employment, and work activity programs.

6. *Work activity center–based or nonintegrated day programs*—focus on "prevocational" skills, such as motor tasks or self-care skills.

7. *Day activity or adult day care center–based, nonintegrated programs*—usually have a therapeutic or nonvocational emphasis, depending on the funding source.

Source: Moon, M. S., & Inge, K. (2000). Vocational preparation and transition. In M. E. Snell & F. Brown (Eds.), *Instruction of students with severe disabilities* (5th ed., p. 595). Upper Saddle River, NJ: Merrill. Reprinted with permission.

Some professionals are debating how best to build a curriculum that covers education, employment, independent living, and community participation. This concern for meeting the diverse needs of students is manifested somewhat differently for students with more severe disabilities than for those with milder disabilities.

Students with Severe Disabilities For students with severe disabilities, much of the concern focuses on the coordination and linkage of the many agencies outside the school setting (Moon & Inge, 2000). Many special education personnel are unaccustomed to working with nonschool agencies. For example, the relationship between vocational and special education has traditionally been ambiguous. Federal regulations, however, now require that special education work with vocational education as well as with other agencies in the community.

For a number of years, special educators at the secondary level have been moving toward more involvement in the community, but the federal transition mandate has hastened the need for these outreach efforts. Approaches such as supported employment, for example, require that special educators work with local employers in setting up and instituting training and working environments for students with disabilities. Not all special educators have been trained for this expanded role, however. We are still in the infancy stage of knowing how best to accomplish this interface between the school and community environments. There is a need for experimentation with approaches to educating special educators for this broader role.

Students with Mild Disabilities For students with mild disabilities, much of the concern centers on attempting to meet their academic as well as their vocational needs. Teachers of secondary students are constantly faced with the decision of how much to stress academics versus vocational preparation. Because their disabilities are milder, many children with learning disabilities, for example, may be able to go on to postsecondary educational institutions, such as community colleges or universities. It is often difficult to tell as early as tenth grade (when such decisions need to be made) whether to steer students with learning disabilities toward college preparatory or more vocationally oriented curricula. Co-teaching is one approach to helping students with disabilities in general education settings learn skills related to employment (Fennick, 2001). That is, general and special education teachers can work together to help students learn about career possibilities, prepare their résumés, search for jobs, write letters of application, interview for jobs, and so on.

It might seem intuitive that successful transition for young people with severe disabilities is harder to achieve than for young people with relatively mild disabilities. However, this is not necessarily the case. Finding employment at which people with relatively mild mental retardation can be successful is not as easy as it might seem (see Leahy, 2004). People with relatively mild disabilities may have multiple problems that make their successful employment more challenging than one might assume.

Some authorities believe that too many students with learning disabilities have been sold short on how much they can achieve academically. These authorities believe that such students are written off as academic failures who can never achieve at the college level. This diminished expectation for academic success translates into a curriculum that makes few academic demands on students. For example, one study of students in learning disabilities classrooms at the secondary level found an "environmental press against academic content" (Zigmond & Miller, 1992, p. 25)—hence the recent emphasis we have already discussed on access to and progress in the general education academic curriculum.

Other authorities maintain that an overemphasis on academics leaves many students with learning disabilities unprepared to enter the world of work on leaving school. They believe that the learning problems of students with learning disabilities tend to be minimized. They assert that just because students with learning disabilities are characterized as having mild disabilities, they do not necessarily have insignificant learning impairments.

Along these same lines, some professionals think that far too few support services are available to students with mild disabilities. Whereas transition services such as supported employment are available to people with severe disabilities, individuals with milder disabilities are often left to fend for themselves once they graduate from secondary school.

CONTINUING ISSUES

It is still too early to tell how much impact the emphasis on standards-based reform and the inclusion of students with disabilities in general education curriculum and assessment procedures (as mandated by NCLB and IDEA 2004) will have on students with disabilities. However, despite some of the unresolved issues, we can be encouraged by all the attention that special educators have given to the area of transition. A variety of transition opportunities are available now that were unavailable just a few years ago. However, it is increasingly clear that successful transition takes early and sustained effort, and it is not clear just how such support can best be provided (see Moon & Inge, 2000; Peck, 2004; Sitlington et al., 2000).

In considering transition issues, it is helpful to keep in mind that a smooth and successful transition to adult life is difficult for any adolescent. Individuals find many different routes to adulthood, and we would be foolish to prescribe a single pattern of transition. Our goal must be to provide the special assistance needed by adolescents and young adults with disabilities that will help them to achieve the most rewarding, productive, independent, and integrated adult lives possible. This goal cannot be achieved by assuming that all adolescents and young adults with disabilities, or even all individuals who fall into a given special education category, will need the same special transition services or that all will achieve the same level of independence and productivity. One of education's great challenges is to devise an effective array of programs that will meet the individual needs of students on their paths to adulthood.

Discipline of Students with Disabilities

In the late twentieth and early twenty-first centuries, safe schools and orderly learning environments became paramount concerns of many school administrators and legislators (e.g., Dupre, 2000; Dwyer, Osher, & Hoffman, 2000; Skiba & Peterson, 2000; Smith, 2000; Sprague & Walker, 2000; Yell, Rozalski, & Drasgow, 2001). Dramatic shootings in schools and statistics on the presence of weapons, violence, and drugs in schools led to severe measures that are intended to improve discipline, decrease violence, and eliminate drugs in schools.

One of the most dramatic and controversial measures involving discipline for serious offenses is known as **zero tolerance**. Zero tolerance was introduced by the federal Gun-Free Schools Act of 1994, which led to corresponding state legislation. Under most of these state laws, school boards and other school administrators could use discretion in applying the zero-tolerance policy. In the case of discipline, zero tolerance means that the circumstances surrounding a particular incident are not weighed in deciding what the consequences should be; only the act itself is to be questioned. For example, if a student brings a weapon to school, the circumstances leading up to the incident are not considered relevant in determining the punishment (see Kauffman, 2002; Kauffman & Brigham, 2000; Skiba & Peterson, 2000).

School administrators and teachers have been assumed to abuse their discretion in determining the punishment for certain serious offenses, such as bringing a weapon to school. Therefore, higher authorities (e.g., boards of education) in many cases removed discretion from the hands of teachers and lower administrators, prescribing a given punishment (e.g., long-term suspension or expulsion) for a particular offense (e.g., bringing a knife or a drug to school) regardless of the circumstances surrounding the act. For example, if an elementary school child accidentally brings a paring knife to school in her lunch box, she will be expelled. If a high school student forgets to remove a roofing knife from his pocket and turns it in at the office because he knows he should not have it in school, he will be expelled. If a toy gun is brought to school by a student with mental retardation who does not understand that a gun is a weapon and even toy weapons are forbidden in school or if a child is found to possess a single dose of aspirin, he or she will be expelled. Decisions like these have actually been made by school authorities under the zero-tolerance rationale.

Violence, disorder, and drugs in schools are serious problems that must be addressed. However, zero tolerance and standardization of penalties present particular problems for special education. Special educators recognize the need for schoolwide discipline that brings a high degree of uniformity to consequences for particular acts (e.g., Martella, Nelson, & Marchand-Martella, 2003). Nevertheless, special educators also argue for exceptions based on the relevance of the student's disability to the event in question (see Skiba & Peterson, 2000; Zurkowski, Kelly, & Griswold, 1998; Yell et al., 2001).

Zero tolerance
A school policy, supported by federal and state laws, that having possession of any weapon or drug on school property will automatically result in a given penalty (usually suspension or expulsion) regardless of the nature of the weapon or drug or any extenuating circumstances.

Casebook Reflections

Refer to the case *What Do We Do with Jim?* in your booklet. Jim was leaving school in handcuffs for shoving the psychologist into the door. How should the school handle Jim's instruction with the present zero-tolerance policy for school discipline?

CURRENT TRENDS

The discipline of students with disabilities is highly controversial, and many teachers and school administrators are confused about what is legal. Special rules apply to managing some of the serious misbehavior of students who are identified as having disabilities. In some cases, the typical school rules apply, but in others, they do not (see Bateman & Linden, 1998; Huefner, 2000; Yell, in press; Yell & Shriner, 1997; Yell et al., 2001). In any case, much of the special education advocacy regarding discipline is based on finding alternatives to suspension and expulsion for bringing weapons or drugs to school or for endangering others, as keeping students out of school is not an effective way of helping them learn to behave acceptably.

Three concepts and related procedures provide the basis for much of the controversy surrounding the discipline of students with disabilities: (1) determining whether the behavior is or is not a manifestation of the student's disability, (2) providing an alternative placement for the student's education for an interim period if temporary removal from the student's present placement is necessary, and (3) developing positive, proactive behavior intervention plans. We discuss these issues further in Chapter 8, as they most frequently arise in the case of students with emotional or behavioral disorders.

Deciding whether a student's misbehavior is or is not a manifestation of disability is called a **manifestation determination**. The idea behind this part of IDEA 2004 is that it would be unfair to punish a student for engaging in a misbehavior that is part of his or her disability. However, if the misbehavior is not a manifestation of disability, then the usual punishment for students without disabilities should apply. For example, if a misbehavior is the result of a seizure or other neurological disorder or a manifestation of mental incapacity or emotional disturbance, then the student should not be punished for doing it. The manifestation determination is a highly controversial issue, and some writers believe that it is more political than educational in purpose (Dupre, 2000; Katsiyannis & Maag, 2001). Some people argue that the process actually undermines fairness because the rules or procedures for the manifestation determination are not entirely objective, requiring subjective judgment about the causes of misbehavior.

Perhaps the most critical part of the discipline provisions of IDEA 2004 is the requirement that teachers must devise **positive behavioral intervention** plans for students with disabilities who have behavior problems. The emphasis of this requirement is on creating proactive and positive interventions (Artesani & Millar, 1998; Buck, Polloway, Kirkpatrick, Patton, & Fad, 2000; Ruef, Higgins, Glaeser, & Patnode, 1998; Sugai & Horner, 1999–2000; Sugai et al., 2000). When special discipline is involved, the school must reevaluate the student's IEP and make efforts to address the misconduct that led to the problem. Also required is a **functional behavioral assessment (FBA)**, in which educators attempt to determine and alter the factors that account for the student's misconduct (Condon & Tobin, 2001; McConnell, Hilvitz, & Cox, 1998). Although the notion of functional assessment is itself a controversial issue, it is clear that the intent of the legal requirement is to encourage proactive problem solving rather than reactive punishment of misconduct (Nelson, Roberts, Mather, & Rutherford, 1999; Sasso, Conroy, Stichter, & Fox, 2001).

Positive behavioral supports (PBS), also known as positive behavioral intervention and supports, are procedures required under IDEA to help students behave as desired (Bradley, 2001). The emphasis is on positive (rewarding) consequences for appropriate behavior rather than punishment for misbehavior.

PBS uses systemic and individualized strategies to prevent problem behavior and achieve positive social and learning outcomes. It integrates valued outcomes, the science of human behavior, validated procedures, and systems change to enhance quality of life and reduce problem behavior. Its primary goal is to improve the link between research-validated practices and the environments in which teaching and learning occur. This behaviorally based systems approach enhances the capacity of schools, families, and communities to design effective teaching and learning environments that improve lifestyle results (personal, health, social, family, work, recreation, etc.) for all children and youth. These environments apply contextually and culturally appropriate interventions to make problem behavior less effective, efficient, and relevant and to make desired behavior more functional (Sugai et al., 2000).

CONTINUING ISSUES

The struggle to resolve discipline issues involving students with disabilities is ongoing. On the one hand, school administrators want the highest possible degree of uniformity of expectations (i.e., the same high expectations for all students). On the other hand, special educators and other advocates for students with disabilities see the uniformity of disciplinary rules as failure to accommodate students' individual abilities and needs. The legal

UNDERSTANDING THE STANDARDS AND PRINCIPLES   What does the law say with respect to discipline of students with disabilities? *(CEC Knowledge and Skills Standard CC1K2)*

Manifestation determination
Determination that a student's misbehavior is or is not a manifestation of a disability.

Functional behavioral assessment (FBA)
Evaluation that consists of finding out the consequences (purposes), antecedents (what triggers the behavior), and setting events (contextual factors) that maintain inappropriate behaviors; this information can help teachers plan educationally for students.

Positive behavioral intervention and supports (PBIS)
Positive reinforcement (rewarding) procedures intended to support a student's appropriate or desirable behavior.

requirements regarding discipline, including suspension and expulsion, will continue to evolve as educators find more productive ways of dealing with serious misconduct.

Some Concluding Thoughts Regarding Trends and Issues

If you are feeling overwhelmed by the controversial nature of special education, that is understandable. We, too, are constantly amazed by the number of unanswered questions our field faces. It seems that just as we find what we think are the right answers to a certain set of questions about how to educate students with disabilities, more challenging questions emerge.

It would be easy to view this inability to reach definitive conclusions as indicative of a field in chaos. We disagree. We see this constant state of questioning as a sign of health and vigor. The controversial nature of special education makes it exciting and challenging. We would be worried (and we believe people with disabilities and their families would be worried, too) if the field suddenly decided that it had reached complete agreement on all important issues. We should constantly be striving to find better ways to provide education and related services for people with disabilities. In doing this, it is inevitable that there will be differences of opinion.

SUMMARY

WHAT are the trends and issues in integrating people with disabilities into the larger society?

- The major trends and issues involve normalization, deinstitutionalization, and self-determination.
  - Normalization dictates that both the means and the ends of education for people with disabilities should be as normal as possible.
  - Some researchers question the wisdom of complete deinstitutionalization, as some people who return to community placements do not fare well, and the death rate might be higher for these people in community placements than in institutions.
  - Self-determination is based on the philosophy that people with disabilities should make decisions about their own lives.

WHAT are the trends and issues in integrating students with exceptionalities into schools?

- Full inclusion is a major controversy based on four assumptions:
  - Labeling of people is harmful.

- Special education pull-out programs have been ineffective.
- People with disabilities should be viewed as a minority group.
- Ethics should take precedence over empiricism.
- Opponents of full inclusion put forth the following arguments:
  - Professionals and parents are largely satisfied with the current level of integration.
  - General educators are unwilling and/or unable to cope with all students with disabilities.
  - Although equating disabilities with minority group status is in many ways legitimate, it has limitations when it comes to translation into educational programming recommendations.
  - An unwillingness to consider empirical evidence is professionally irresponsible.
  - Available empirical evidence does not support full inclusion.
  - In the absence of data to support one service delivery model, special educators must preserve the continuum of placements.

WHAT are the trends and issues in participation in general assessments of progress?

- Both IDEA and NCLB require the participation of most students with disabilities in general assessments of educational progress.
  - Proponents of participation suggest that special education has not been held accountable for students' progress.
  - Some educators point out that the average achievement of students with disabilities will always be—even with good instruction—lower than the average for students without disabilities.

WHAT are the trends and issues in access to new technologies?

- The major technologies that are controversial for people with disabilities involve medical advances and communications.
  - There is controversy about whether we should do something just because we can.
  - New technologies are often created with concern for universal design—the principle that the technological device or program should be workable for as many potential users as possible.

WHAT are the trends and issues in early intervention?

- Early intervention is now mandated by law, and a cornerstone of early intervention is the individualized family service plan (IFSP).
- Three issues pertaining to early childhood intervention are the following:
  - The appropriate role of the family
  - Whether the curriculum should be teacher centered or child centered
  - Whether full inclusion is best for all young children

WHAT are the trends and issues in transition to adulthood?

- Issues focus largely on coordinating and linking the many agencies outside the school setting.
- *Transition* is defined as including a variety of postschool activities, including postsecondary education, vocational training, integrated employment, continuing and adult education, adult services, independent living, or community participation.
- Transition plans must, by law, be incorporated into the IEPs of students with disabilities.
- Interventions often involve supported employment or job coaches.

WHAT are the trends and issues in discipline of students with disabilities?

- Concern for safe and orderly schools resulted in controversial policies related to the discipline of students with disabilities.
- Much of the controversy regarding discipline has to do with zero tolerance for certain behaviors, such as bringing a weapon or drugs to school.
  - Disciplinary action the school may take might depend on determining whether the student's misbehavior was or was not a manifestation of his or her disability.
  - In most cases, the same rules of discipline apply to students with disabilities as apply to all other students.

What are our concluding thoughts about trends and issues?

- We belive controversy indicates that the field of special education is alive and well.
- We should be constantly striving to make special education better.

APPLYING THE STANDARDS AND PRINCIPLES

- **DO** you agree that the **continuum of placement and services available** for individuals with disabilities should be preserved? Why or why not? *(CEC Content Standard #1)*

 Council for Exceptional Children

- **DESCRIBE** ways in which **teachers can collaborate** with each other, with other professionals, and with families to ensure that students with disabilities are valued members of society. *(CEC Content Standard #10 & INTASC Principle #10)*

INTASC

Chapter 3

Multicultural and Bilingual Aspects of Special Education

I think schools are a crucial—probably the most crucial—site for inviting us to view ourselves in a different mirror. I think schools have the responsibility to teach Americans about who we are and who we have been. This is where it's important for schools to offer a more accurate, a more inclusive multicultural curriculum. The classroom is the place where students who come from different ethnic or cultural communities can learn not only about themselves but about one another in an informed, systematic and non-intimidating way. I think the schools offer us our best hope for working it out. I would be very reluctant to depend upon the news media or the entertainment media, which do not have a responsibility to educate.

RONALD TAKAKI
"Reflections from a Different Mirror"

QUESTIONS TO GUIDE YOUR READING OF THIS CHAPTER . . .

- IN what ways do we see universality of cultural pride and shame?

- WHAT is American about multiculturalism?

- WHAT are the important concepts about cultural diversity for education?

- WHAT are the most important aspects of multicultural and bilingual special education?

SPECIAL EDUCATORS . . .

- are active and resourceful in seeking to **understand how primary language, culture, and familial backgrounds** interact with the individual's exceptional condition to impact the individual's academic and social abilities, attitudes, values, interests, and career options *(from CEC Content Standard #3).*

- **foster environments in which diversity is valued** and individuals are taught to live harmoniously and productively in a culturally diverse world *(from CEC Content Standard #5).*

- **match their communication methods to an individual's language proficiency and cultural and linguistic differences**; provide effective language models; and use communication strategies and resources to facilitate understanding of subject matter for individuals with exceptional learning needs whose primary language is not English *(from CEC Content Standard #6).*

Council for Exceptional Children

ALL TEACHERS . . .

- **understand how students differ** in their approaches to learning and create instructional opportunities that are adapted to diverse learners *(INTASC Principle #3).*

INTASC

Many nations and regions are splintered into factions, clans, tribes, and gangs. In some cases, this splintering has been accompanied by extreme cruelty of individuals or groups toward others. Differences—especially those of national origin, religion, ethnic origin, color, custom, sexual orientation, social class, and disability—are too often the basis for viciousness.

No personal characteristic of skin color, ethnic identity, sexual identity, nationality, religion, disability—or any other cultural marker—immunizes anyone against the mistreatment of others. This remains a central problem of humankind. In the early twenty-first century, slavery is still practiced in some nations of the world, and "civilized" people mistreat prisoners who might or might not differ from their guards in nationality, ethnicity, religion, or other cultural features. Suicide bombers kill and maim others. Terrorists kill, maim, and threaten, and acts of war do the same. Not so long ago, systematic efforts were made in a highly "civilized" society to exterminate people with disabilities, and we would be wise to learn the lessons our history can teach us about our personal and collective capacity for brutality (Mostert, 2002).

Universality of Cultural Pride and Shame

All cultures and ethnic groups of the world can take pride in much of their heritage, but all also bear a burden of shame because at some time, they have engaged in the ruthless treatment or literal enslavement of others. For example, see Hirsch (2004) for a report of twenty-first century mistreatment of Iraqi prisoners by U.S. armed forces or Jones (2003) for a novel based on the fact that some African Americans were slaveholders in the nineteenth century. Sometimes this treatment has extended to minority members of their own larger group whose differences have been viewed as undesirable or intolerable. Not only is religion the basis for conflict in places such as Northern Ireland and Iraq, but just the appearance of being different or assumptions about appearances have been sufficient to trigger discrimination. For example, in his memoir *Angela's Ashes*, Frank McCourt (1996) describes how in the mid-twentieth century, some Catholics in Ireland looked askance at what they called "Protestant hair":

> Come here till I comb your hair, said Grandma. Look at that mop, it won't lie down. You didn't get that hair from my side of the family. That's that North of Ireland hair you got from your father. That's the kind of hair you see on Presbyterians. If your mother had married a proper decent Limerickman you wouldn't have this standing up, North of Ireland, Presbyterian hair. (p. 128)

In virtually every nation, society, religion, ethnic group, tribe, or clan, discrimination exists against those who are different. It is therefore critically important that we learn to

Misconceptions about
Multicultural and Bilingual Aspects of Special Education

MYTH Multicultural education addresses the concerns of ethnic minorities who want their children to learn more about their history and the intellectual, social, and artistic contributions of their ancestors.

FACT This is a partial truth. In FACT, multicultural education seeks to help the children of all ethnic groups appreciate their own and others' cultural heritages—plus our common American culture that sustains multiculturalism.

MYTH Everyone agrees that multicultural education is critical to our nation's future.

FACT Some people, including some who are members of ethnic minorities, believe that multicultural education is misguided and diverts attention from our integration into a distinctive, cohesive American culture.

MYTH Implementing multicultural education is a relatively simple matter of including information about all cultures in the curriculum and teaching respect for them.

FACT Educators and others are struggling with how to construct a satisfactory multicultural curriculum and multicultural instructional methods. Nearly every aspect of the task is controversial: which cultures to include, how much attention to give to each, and what and how to teach about them.

MYTH Multiculturalism includes only the special features and contributions of clearly defined ethnic groups.

FACT Ethnicity is typically the focal point of discussions of multiculturalism, but ethnicity is sometimes a point of controversy if it is defined too broadly (for example, by lumping all Asians, all Africans, or all Europeans together). Besides ethnic groups, other groups and individuals—such as people identified by gender, sexual orientation, religion, and disability—need consideration in a multicultural curriculum.

MYTH Disproportionate representation of ethnic minorities in special education is no longer a problem.

FACT Some ethnic minorities are still underrepresented or overrepresented in certain special education categories. For example, African American students, especially males, are overrepresented in programs for students with emotional disturbance and underrepresented in programs for gifted and talented students.

MYTH Disability is never related to ethnicity.

FACT Some disabilities are genetically linked and therefore more prevalent in some ethnic groups. For example, sickle-cell disease (a severe, chronic, hereditary blood disease) occurs disproportionately in children with ancestry from Africa, Mediterranean and Caribbean regions, Saudi Arabia, and India.

MYTH If students speak English, there is no need to be concerned about bilingual education.

FACT Conversational English is not the same as the more formal and sometimes technical language used in academic curriculum and classroom instruction. Educators must make sure that students understand the language that is used in teaching, not just informal conversation.

Multicultural education
Aims to change educational institutions and curricula so they will provide equal educational opportunities to students regardless of their gender, social class, ethnicity, race, disability, or other cultural identity.

accept the principle that those who differ from us are equals as human beings. Furthermore, it is necessary for all educators to understand the purpose of **multicultural education**, which aims for educational institutions and curricula that provide equal educational opportunities to students regardless of their gender, social class, ethnicity, race, disability, or other cultural identity. It also seeks to socialize students to a multicultural norm: acceptance of and respect for those whose culture is different from one's own and knowledge of our shared history. Schools play a central role in multicultural education, as Takaki notes in his comments on page 79.

Nevertheless, the problem of multiculturalism also involves the spectre of *collective* versus individual pride and guilt in behavior. Is the entire group of people that make up a culture justified in taking pride in the fact that one of their group has accomplished something notable? Is an entire group of people—perhaps a nation—guilty for the acts of some of its members? To what extent does an entire group deserve commendation or condemnation because of what some of its members have done? For example, are all Islamic people guilty of acts of terror because some Islamists commit terrorist acts? Are all Americans guilty of the abuse of human rights because some members of its armed forces committed barbaric acts against Iraqui prisoners (see Kennicott, 2004)? Clearly, the assignment of *collective* guilt is a convenient, time-honored way of perpetuating discrimination, ethnic clensing, genocide, and other acts of violence. *Collective* pride can blind people to the faults of members of a group and create a false sense of worthiness.

America and Multiculturalism

Our desire as Americans should be to build a diverse but just society in which the personal freedom and pride of all cultural groups and respect for others' cultural heritage are the norm, a society in which fear, hate, and abuse are eliminated and in which guilt or accomplishment is not determined by association. Working toward this ideal demands a multicultural perspective, one from which we can simultaneously accomplish two tasks. First, as a nation of increasing cultural diversity, we must renew our efforts to achieve social justice and take specific steps to understand and appreciate one another's cultures. Second, in doing so, we must pledge our first loyalty to common cultural values that make diversity a strength rather than a fatal flaw. We seek a commitment to our common humanity and to democratic ideals that bind people together for the common good and give all of them freedom for the rightful honoring of their heritage. Nobel laureat and Holocaust survivor Elie Wiesel explained why he loves the United States, a nation of imigrants, in spite of its mistakes: "America has always seemed concerned with other people's welfare" but "Self-criticism remains its second nature" (2004, p. 5).

Multicultural education has its critics, some of whom see it as eroding the moral foundations of society and undermining the central purpose of schooling: ensuring the academic competence of students. A newspaper columnist wrote, "For 40 years, American public education has pressed children into a humanistic, secular, multicultural mold" (Thomas, 1998, p. A8). Although multiculturalism is sometimes distorted into indefensible ideology (Ravitch, 2003), we do not understand how the multicultural education that we advocate can be anything but helpful in students' academic learning and socialization to American ideals.

Since the civil rights movement of the 1960s, educators have become increasingly aware of the extent to which differences among cultural and ethnic groups affect children's schooling. Gradually, educators and others are coming to understand that the cultural diversity of the United States and the world demands multicultural education. Progress in constructing multicultural

Casebook Reflections

Refer to the case *What Do We Do with Jim?* in your booklet. Jim's mother claims that the reason he doesn't do well "is because he is African-American and the teachers are prejudiced" (p. 49). In what way(s) do you think the issues about Jim's behavior are culturally based or are related to cultural diversity? What else might be the case?

The cultural diversity of the United States and the world is reflected in our schools and is something that educators can, with good planning, put to very good use.

education has been slow, however, in part because of the way in which all cultural groups tend to view themselves as the standard against which others should be judged.

Education that takes full advantage of the cultural diversity in our schools and the larger world requires much critical analysis and planning. It can be very difficult for all cultural or ethnic groups to find common satisfaction in any specific curriculum, even if they are all seeking what they consider the multicultural ideal. Moreover, some argue that the more important goal is finding the common American culture and ensuring that our children have a common cultural literacy (Hirsch, 1996; Ravitch, 2003). Even the metaphors that we use for dealing with cultural diversity and cultural unity are points of controversy. The United States has often been called a "cultural melting pot," but some now reject the notion of total melding or amalgamation—they reject the metaphor of an alloy in which metals are dissolved in each other and fused into a new substance. Those who reject the alloy or melting pot metaphor want each identifiable group to be recognized as separate, distinct, and legitimate in its own right.

That racism and discrimination remain serious problems in the United States and most other nations and societies of the world is obvious. These problems have no simple resolution, and they are found among virtually all ethnic groups (Wiesel, 2004). People of every cultural description struggle with the meaning of differences that might seem trivial or superficial to some but elicit powerful emotional responses and discrimination from others. Many have commented on the discrimination that is practiced not only between people with very light skin and people with very dark skin but also among people who vary in hue in every ethnic group (e.g., King, 2004).

As Anne Lewis points out on page 84, the problems of desegregating schools have remained in the face of the May, 1954 *Brown versus Board of Education* Supreme Court decision that ended legal racial segregation. The No Child Left Behind Act can be seen as another law making "white flight" possible.

Misunderstanding and suffering are still often associated with differences in color as well as in gender, religion, sexual orientation, family affiliation, abilities and disabilities, and political beliefs. Anti-Semitism and other racist attitudes still exist in all regions of America as well as in all nations of the world, and no cultural group is entirely free of prejudice and other racist sentiments. Consider the experience of Susie Kay, a Jewish teacher in a Washington, D.C., high school where all the students are African American:

> Kay's students say they know about white culture mainly from television shows; hardly any interact regularly with whites—"Caucasians," as they call them. Most have never met a Jewish person, except for Miss Kay, who wears her Star of David necklace every day. Prompting students to ask, "Isn't that the star of the Devil?"
>
> "And what's the difference between a white person and a Jew anyway?" asks another. Both are rich, right? (Horwitz, 1998, p. F1)

The solution is not as simple as becoming sensitized to differences. Too often, Eurocentrism is met with Europhobia, Afrocentrism with Afrophobia, homocentrism with homophobia, sensitivity to difference with hypersensitivity about being different. Nor is the solution to become "blind" to difference (see Schofield, 1997; Williams, 1998a, 1998b). In discussing people of color, Spencer (1997) concludes that "we need the current racial classifications in order to fight racism, because as soon as we discard the racial classifications black people are still going to be discriminated against" (p. 148). Glazer (1997, 1998) also observes that loss of racial identity in the service of equal opportunity for minorities cannot work. Likewise, eliminating labels for individuals with disabilities inevitably results in the loss of their equal educational opportunity (Hallahan & Kauffman, 1994; Kauffman, 1999, 2001, 2003). A simple reality is that we cannot accept or accommodate what we do not see and label. Perhaps the solution must include both engendering sensitivity to differences and building confidence that one's own differences will not be threatened by others'. The solution might also require transforming the curriculum in ways that help students understand how knowledge is constructed and how to view themselves and others from different perspectives.

We are optimistic about multicultural education because it is an opportunity to face our shared problems squarely and to extract the best human qualities from each cultural heritage. We have the opportunity to develop an appreciation of our individual and shared cultural treasures and to engender acceptance, if not love, of all differences that are not destructive of the human spirit. The best antidote for cultural insularity is inclusiveness. Insularity will be overcome by adherence to truly American values of multiculturalism.

Personal Perspectives

DESEGREGATION AND DEGENERATION

WITH a shortage of smart teachers (and any teachers in some areas), it is not surprising that the least experienced and lowest-scoring teachers are teaching the neediest students. Districts want to keep middle-class parents and good teachers happy, so they rarely challenge union seniority policies that allow the best teachers to clump together in less needy schools. When resources are scarce, the least powerful get the least.

Choice is the new euphemism for white flight. Now that those who desire schools that enroll "our kind" have pushed suburban sprawl to its limit, they have turned to parental choice, including vouchers, as a way to use public funds for private purposes. The parental choice provisions of the No Child Left Behind (NCLB) act were almost an afterthought in many urban school districts, which already catered to primarily middle-class parents through extensive choice programs. Charters are another form of separation, as a recent study found in Boston: no English-language learner was enrolled in a charter school, only half of the charter school students were low-income compared to three-fourths in the traditional Boston schools, and only one in 10 had a disability. Charter schools now seem to offer a new haven for the advantaged. ■

Source: Lewis, A. C. (2004). Desegregation and Degeneration. *Phi Delta Kappan, 85* 643–644. Reprinted by permission.

Personal Perspectives

IN LIVING BLACK AND WHITE

My son used to attend a small nursery school. Over the course of a year, three different teachers in his school assured me that he was colorblind. Resigned to this diagnosis, I took my son to an ophthalmologist who tested him and pronounced his vision perfect. I could not figure out what was going on until I began to listen carefully to what he was saying about color.

As it turned out, my son did not misidentify color. He resisted identifying color at all. "I don't know," he would say when asked what color the grass was; or, most peculiarly, "It makes no difference." This latter remark, this assertion of the greenness of grass making no difference, was such a precociously cynical retort that I began to suspect some social complication in which he somehow was invested.

The long and short of it is that the well-meaning teachers at his predominantly white school had valiantly and repeatedly assured their charges that color makes no difference. "It doesn't matter," they told the children, "whether you're black or white or red or green or blue." Yet upon further investigation, the very reason that the teachers had felt it necessary to impart this les-

son in the first place was that it did matter, and in predictably cruel ways: Some of the children had been fighting about whether black people could play "good guys."

My son's anxious response was redefined by his teachers as physical deficiency—illustrative, perhaps, of the way in which the liberal ideal of colorblindness is too often confounded. That is to say, the very notion of blindness about color constitutes an ideological confusion at best, and denial at its very worst. I recognize, certainly, that the teachers were inspired by a desire to make whole a division in the ranks. But there is much overlooked in the move to undo that which clearly and unfortunately matters just by labeling it that which "makes no difference." The dismissiveness, however unintentional, leaves those in my son's position pulled between the clarity of their own experience and the often alienating terms in which they must seek social acceptance. ■

Source: Excerpt from "The Emperor's New Clothes" from *Seeing a Color-Blind Future: The Paradox of Race* by Patricia J. Williams. Copyright © 1997 by Patricia J. Williams. Reprinted with permission of Farrar, Strauss & Giroux, Inc.

Multiculturalism is now a specialized field of study and research in education, and its full exploration is far beyond the scope of this chapter. Of particular concern to special educators is how exceptionalities are related to cultural diversity and the way in which special education fits within the broader general education context in a multicultural society. Cultural diversity presents particular challenges for special educators in three areas: assessment of abilities and disabilities, instruction, and socialization. Before discussing each of these challenges, we summarize some of the major concepts about education and cultural diversity that set the context for multicultural and bilingual special education.

UNDERSTANDING THE STANDARDS AND PRINCIPLES   What challenges might educators face in striving to accomplish the general purposes of multicultural education? *(CEC Knowledge and Skills Standard CC6K2)*

Council for Exceptional Children

Education and Cultural Diversity

Culture has many definitions. However, most definitions include the following elements:

1. Values and typical behavior
2. Languages or dialects
3. Nonverbal communication
4. Awareness of one's cultural identity
5. World views or general perspectives

These elements can together make up a national or shared culture. Within the larger culture are many **subcultures** that share the common characteristics of the larger culture. The term *subculture* should not be interpreted to mean anything other than a part (not the

Subculture
A culture that is associated with or part of a larger culture; a culture that is not the entire culture of a nation or other entity. Sometimes called "microculture," but a subculture is not necessarily small or a minority of a larger culture.

FIGURE 3.1 Individuals belong to many different subcultural groups.

Source: From J. A. Banks, *Cultural Diversity and Education: Foundations, Curriculum, and Teaching,* p. 76. Copyright © 1994 by Allyn & Bacon. Reprinted/adapted with permission.

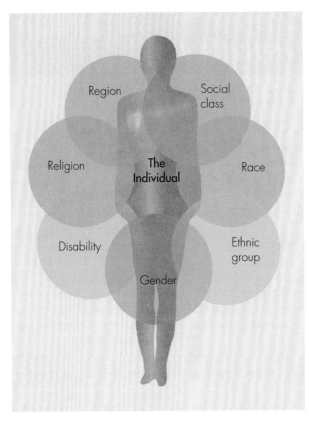

total) of the larger or general culture. *Subculture* does not mean lesser in importance, nor does it indicate that one group is dominated by another. We prefer the term *subculture* to *microculture*, a term that Banks (1997) uses, simply because "sub" can mean *associated with or part of* whereas "micro" means *small.* Some subcultures are not small and may, in fact, be the majority group in a given region, state, organization, or other group. European Americans are a subculture in the United States of America, although they have to date been the majority of Americans. But, of course, European Americans can be considered as subcultures described by their region or nation of origin, as well as by other categories.

Subcultures include all of the various subcategories of citizens that one might name, including various political parties, ethnic identities, gender, sexual orientation, age, and disability (and subcultures include the largest subgroup in any given area, which, although perhaps the largest in its region, is not all of the larger culture). Subcultures may have unique values, behavior, languages or dialect, nonverbal communication, awareness, identity, and views. Some subcultures are voluntary (e.g., religion, political party), and some are involuntary (e.g., skin color, gender). An individual might identify with the larger, general culture and also belong to many different subcultures, as shown in Figure 3.1. The variety of subcultures to which a person belongs affects his or her behavior. The larger, general culture in the United States consists of certain overarching values, symbols, and ideas, such as justice, equality, and human dignity. Within the United States, subcultures might share these common values but differ in many other ways.

The number of subcultures represented in U.S. schools has increased in recent decades because of the variety of immigrants from other countries, particularly Southeast Asia. However, it has also increased because of increased recognition of and sensitivity to subcultures, such as those represented by disability, age, sexual orientation, religion, and so on.

Many American children live in poverty. The United States gained more immigrants in the 1990s than in any previous decade. Poverty clearly places children at higher risk of disability compared to children who are reared in conditions of economic advantage (Fujiura & Yamaki, 2000). The United States is increasingly home to refugees from other nations

(Harrison, 2000), and many urban children spend a great deal of time on the streets or are homeless (Walker, 2000). Thus, the United States in the twenty-first century is more diverse than ever in the subcultures it includes—diverse in ethnic groups, economic status, lifestyles, and disabilities.

Students from some subcultures in U.S. society do extremely well in school, but others do not. The factors accounting for the school performance of subcultures are complex, and social scientists are still searching for the attitudes, beliefs, traditions, and opportunities that foster the success of specific cultural groups. The 2002 No Child Left Behind Act (NCLB) was intended, in part, to eliminate differences in achievement among various ethnic groups and other subgroups.

Although there is considerable evidence that various ethnic minority communities have a strong influence on students' achievement and school behavior, we offer three cautions. First, we need to guard against stereotypes—assumptions that one's cultural identity is sufficient to explain academic achievement or economic success. The "Doonesbury" cartoon on page 88 makes the point rather well. Second, the fact that minority communities may have a strong influence on school success does not relieve schools of the obligation to provide a multicultural education. All students need to feel that they and their cultural heritage are included in the mainstream of American culture and schooling. Third, unless teachers and other school personnel value minority students—see value and promise in them and act accordingly by setting challenging but not unreachable expectations—the support of families and the minority community may be insufficient to improve the academic success of minority students. Too often, minority students are devalued in school, regardless of their achievements and behaviors.

The general purposes of multicultural education are to promote pride in the positive aspects of one's own cultural heritage and understanding of cultures that are different from one's own, foster positive attitudes toward cultural diversity, and ensure equal educational opportunities for all students. These purposes cannot be accomplished unless students develop an understanding and appreciation of their own cultural heritage, as well as an awareness and acceptance of cultures different from their own. Understanding and appreciation are not likely to develop automatically through unplanned contact with members of other cultures. Rather, teachers must plan experiences that teach about culture and provide models of cultural awareness and acceptance and the appreciation of cultural diversity.

On the surface, teaching about cultures and engendering an acceptance and appreciation of cultural diversity appear to be simple. However, two questions immediately complicate things: Which cultures shall we include? What and how shall we teach about them? The first question demands that we consider all the cultures that might be represented in the school and the difficulties inherent in including them all. For example, a letter to the editor of *The Washington Post* on April 14, 2004, included the following in response to an article about Blair High School in Maryland (Mui, 2004):

> Students are divided by the categories of "white," "black," "Hispanic" and "Asian." But for Arab Americans, Indian Americans, Persian Americans and numerous Middle Eastern students at Blair, no race distinction is available.
> Middle Easterners are not racially white or black, and while we are technically Asian, we are not allowed to mark this as our race because we are not ethnically Chinese, Japanese, Korean, Vietnamese or other classically "Asian" nationalities. (Hadadi, 2004, p. A24)

But the diversity of Blair High School's student body was seen as inadequate for multicultural education. Another letter writer concluded that there is still segregation at Blair and commented:

> Some classes were primarily made up of black and Latino students; others had almost all white and Asian American students. Because of this, Blair is not truly multicultural. As a former board member of the National Association for Multicultural

Doonesbury   BY GARRY TRUDEAU

Education and an associate professor of multicultural education at Gallaudet University, I would describe Blair as racially diverse. (DeGarcia, 2004, p. A24)

In some urban school districts with large numbers of immigrant children, more than twenty different languages may be spoken in students' homes. If any subgroup is not represented in any given class or school activity or if the proportion of students in any given class or school activity is not the same as the proportion of that group in the student body, then some people will consider it to be segregated.

Ethnic or national origin is only one dimension of cultural diversity, one branch of many in the multicultural program. Ethnicity is not the only representation of culture, and there is much variation of culture within any ethnic group (Keogh, 2003; Keogh, Gallimore, & Weisner, 1997). In fact, assuming that all individuals of a particular racial, ethnic, disability, or other cultural group have the same values and perspectives is a form of stereotyping.

Many advocates of multiculturalism consider gender, sexual orientation, religion, disability, and so on to be additional dimensions of cultural diversity that require explicit attention. Moreover, some cultural groups find the traditions, ceremonies, values, holidays, and other characteristics of other cultures unacceptable or even offensive. That is, when it comes to what and how to teach about other cultures, the stage may be set for conflict. Treating all cultures with equal attention and respect can present substantial or seemingly insurmountable logistical and interpersonal problems.

One of the most controversial aspects of multicultural education is the use of language. For instance, is it appropriate to refer to a *minority* or *minorities* when the group to which we refer constitute half or more of the population in a given school, district, region, or state? What labels and terms are acceptable for designating various groups? What languages or dialects should be used for instruction? With the arrival of many immigrants to the United States, the issue of bilingual education and its relationship to multiculturalism has become increasingly important. As we discuss later, bilingual education is of even greater concern when children with disabilities are considered (Gersten & Baker, 2000; Gersten, Brengelman, & Jimenez, 1994).

Given the multiplicity of subcultures, each wanting—if not demanding—its precise and fair inclusion in the curriculum, it is not surprising that educators sometimes feel caught in a spiral of factionalism and feuding. Furthermore, additional questions about cultural values inevitably must be addressed: Which cultural values and characteristics should we embrace? Which, if any, should we shun? Would we, if we could, fully sustain some cultures, alter some significantly, and eliminate others? Consider, for example, cultures in which women are treated as chattel, as well as the drug culture, the culture of street gangs, and the culture of poverty. To what extent does every culture have a right to perpetuate itself? How should we respond to some members of the Deaf culture, for example, who reject the prevention of deafness or procedures and devices that enable deaf children to hear, preferring deafness to hearing and wishing to sustain the Deaf culture deliberately (see Mundy, 2002)? How should educators view and react to subcultures that reject studying and school achievement (see Welsh, 2004)?

Depending on how we define culture, the values of our own cultural heritage, and our role in multicultural education, we might find ourselves embroiled in serious cultural conflicts. No wonder that some describe the late twentieth and early twenty-first centuries as an era of "culture wars." To deal effectively with the multicultural challenge, we must focus on the challenges that are most pertinent to special education.

Multicultural and Bilingual Special Education

The subcultures that are of particular importance for special education are ethnic groups and exceptionality groups. Banks (1997) notes that an ethnic group "has a historic origin and a shared heritage and tradition" (p. 66). It has value orientations, behavioral patterns, and often political and economic interests that differ from those of other groups in the larger society. An ethnic group may be a majority or a minority of people in a given country or region. We define an exceptionality group as a group sharing a set of specific abilities or disabilities that are especially valued or that require special accommodation within a given subculture. Thus, a person may be identified as exceptional in one ethnic group (or other subculture defined by gender, social class, religion, etc.) but not in another. The inability to read or speak standard English, for example, may identify a student as having a disability in an English-speaking culture, but the same student would not be considered disabled in a culture in which English-language skills are unimportant.

We still do not know much about how best to train teachers to be aware of their own cultural histories and biases. However, because of the relatively poor performance of many students of color in schools, many parents and policymakers, as well as teacher educators, see better teacher education as critically important. Making certain that every classroom is

One of the most controversial aspects of multicultural education is the use of language. With the arrival of many immigrants to the United States, the issue of bilingual education has become increasingly important.

FOR MORE INFORMATION about bilingual education and linguistic diversity in education, see **www.ed. gov/about/offices/list/oela/ index.html?src=mr**

staffed by a "highly qualified" teacher is one of the objectives of the NCLB, but "highly qualified" is a concept that is open to question (Gelman, Pullen, & Kauffman, in press).

Part of the better training of teachers is helping them to be more knowledgeable about and responsive to both their own and their students' cultures. Some teacher educators suggest that this can be accomplished only if teachers are helped to understand their own culture's history of community, rules, ways of handling tasks, language, and values related to people and outcomes (Artiles, Trent, Hoffman-Kipp, & Lopez-Torres, 2000; Osher et al., 2004).

Ethnicity and exceptionality are distinctly different concepts. In fact, multicultural special education must focus on two primary objectives that go beyond the general purposes of multicultural education:

1. Ensuring that ethnicity is not mistaken for educational exceptionality
2. Increasing understanding of the subculture of exceptionality and its relationship to other cultures

UNDERSTANDING THE STANDARDS AND PRINCIPLES Why are members of minority groups more apt to be identified as disabled? *(CEC Knowledge and Skills Standard CC1K5)*

Council for Exceptional Children

Ethnicity can be mistaken for exceptionality when one's own ethnic group is viewed as setting the standard for all others. For example, patterns of eye contact, physical contact, use of language, and ways of responding to people in positions of authority may vary greatly from one ethnic group to another. Members of each ethnic group must realize that what they see as deviant or unacceptable in their own group might be normal and adaptive in another ethnic group. That is, we must not mistakenly conclude that a student has a disability or is gifted just because he or she is different.

Students may be particularly likely to be identified or not identified as having certain disabilities depending on their gender and ethnicity. The disproportional representation of males and ethnic minority students in special education is a problem of long standing. Boys make up considerably more than half of the students with certain disabilities (e.g., about 75 percent of those with emotional disturbance), and the percentage of students with certain disabilities who are ethnic minorities is disproportionately high—or, in some cases, disproportionately low. Table 3.1 shows the discrepancies between the percentages of all public school students who are white, black, Asian/Pacific Islander, Hispanic, and American Indian and the percentages of these minorities who are identified as having certain disabilities.

Notice that white, Asian/Pacific Islander, and Hispanic students receive special education at percentages somewhat below their representation in the general population, while black and American Indian students are overrepresented in special education. One has to be careful not to misinterpret these figures. For example, a common misinterpretation is that 20 percent of black students are receiving special education (MacMillan & Reschly, 1998; Reschly, 2001). Such grotesque misinterpretations demean the image of minority students and undermine the seriousness of the problem of overrepresentation. The actual meaning of the figures shown in Table 3.1 is that about 20 percent of the students receiving special education are black, a far different matter than the common misinterpretation.

TABLE 3.1 Percentage of Students of Various Ethnic Groups in the Total School Population and Their Percentage of Those Receiving Special Education

	White	Black	Asian/Pacific Islander	Hispanic	American Indian
Percent of total school population	66.2	14.8	3.8	14.2	1.0
Percent of those receiving special education	63.6	20.2	1.7	13.2	1.3

Source: U.S. Department of Education (2000). *Twenty-second annual report to Congress on the implementation of the Individuals with Disabilities Education Act.* Washington, DC: Author.

It is also important to recognize that disproportionality is not an equal problem in all special education categories, schools, localities, or states for any given ethnic group. The problem of overrepresentation varies with ethnic group and the proportion of the school population that is minority (see Artiles & Zamora-Duran, 1997; Coutinho & Oswald, 2000; Osher et al., 2004; Oswald & Coutinho, 2001).

Important civil rights are involved in the issue of disproportional representation in special education. On the one hand, children with disabilities have a right to appropriate education regardless of their ethnicity, even if their ethnic group is statistically overrepresented in special education. On the other hand, however, children also have a right to freedom from discrimination and segregation. The disproportional placement of ethnic minority students in special education strongly suggests that in some cases, students are misidentified and wrongly placed (and stigmatized and segregated) in special education, while in other cases, ethnic minority students' disabilities are ignored (and the students are therefore denied appropriate education).

The reasons for the disproportional representation of certain groups in special education might involve assessment of students' abilities, but other factors such as community standards and resources might be implicated as well. There is little argument that children of color disproportionately experience poverty or that poverty is a risk factor for disability. Moreover, data suggest that low academic achievement is a significant predictor of identification for special education, and it is well recognized that disproportionate numbers of children of color receive substandard schooling and score relatively low on tests of academic achievement (Hosp & Reschly, 2004). However, the problem of disproportionality is very complex and there are no simple solutions (Oswald & Coutinho, 2001). IDEA 2004 directs schools to address the problem but does not say precisely how.

The complexity of this issue requires an integrated and multifaceted effort to promote greater educational access and excellence for racial/ethnic minority students that involves policymakers, educators, researchers, parents, advocates, students, and community representatives. The disproportionate representation of racial/ethnic minority students in special education programs and classes points to the need to do the following:

- Have available strong academic programs that foster success for all students in regular and special education
- Implement effective, appropriate special education policies and procedures for early intervention, referral, assessment, eligibility, classification, placement, and reevaluation
- Increase the level of home, school, and community involvement in education
- Use diverse community resources to enhance and implement educational programs for all students

Disproportionality is not the only multicultural issue in special education. People with certain exceptionalities can develop their own subcultures (Gollnick & Chinn, 1994). Those with severe hearing impairments, for example, are described by some as belonging to a Deaf culture that is not well understood by most normally hearing people and that results in feelings of isolation or separation from people with normal hearing. An important aspect of multicultural special education is developing an increased awareness, understanding, and appreciation of cultural differences involving disabilities. Multicultural special education is not merely a matter of overcoming students' prejudice and stereotyping. We must also educate ourselves as teachers to improve methods of assessment, provide effective instruction, and foster appropriate socialization.

ASSESSMENT

Assessment is a process of collecting information about individuals or groups for the purpose of making decisions. In education, assessment ordinarily refers to testing, interviewing, and observing students. The results should help us to decide whether problems exist

Traditional assessment practices have frequently been viewed to be in violation of the American ideals of fairness and equal opportunity regardless of culture, ethnicity, gender, or disability.

in a student's education and, if problems are identified, what to do about them. Clearly, assessment often results in important decision about people's lives. Therefore, in the U.S. culture, there is great concern for accuracy, justice, and fairness.

Unfortunately, the accuracy, justice, and fairness of many educational assessments, especially those involving special education, are open to question (McDonnell, McLaughlin, & Morison, 1997; Utley & Obiakor, 2001b). Particularly when ethnic subcultures are involved, traditional assessment practices have frequently violated the U.S. ideals of fairness and equal opportunity regardless of ethnic origin, gender, or disability. That is, the assessment practices of educators and psychologists have frequently come under attack as being biased, resulting in misrepresentation of the abilities and disabilities of ethnic minorities and exceptional students, and useless, resulting only in labeling or classification rather than improved educational programming (Council for Exceptional Children, 1997; Ford, 1998). Even prereferral practices, in which the objective is to find solutions to educational problems before referral for evaluation, are subject to bias.

The problems in assessing students are numerous and complex, and there are no simple solutions (MacMillan, & Reschly, 1998; MacMillan, Gresham, Lopez, & Bocian, 1996; Thurlow, Nelson, Teelucksingh, & Draper, 2001; Utley & Obiakor, 2001b). Many of the problems are centered on traditional standardized testing approaches to assessment that have serious limitations: (1) They do not take cultural diversity into account, (2) they focus on deficits in the individual alone, and (3) they do not provide information useful in teaching. Although these problems have not been entirely overcome, awareness of them and the use of more appropriate assessment procedures for diverse learners are increasing. Assessment must not result in the misidentification of children whose language or other characteristics are merely different, but it must also identify those whose differences represent disabilities.

Standardized tests may be biased because most of the test items draw on specific experiences that students from different subcultures may not have had. Tests may, for example, be biased in favor of the likely experiences of white, middle-class students or be couched in language that is unfamiliar to members of a certain subculture (Singh, Baker, Winton, & Lewis, 2000). Tests may be administered in ways that penalize students with impaired vision, hearing, or ability to answer in a standard way. Because test scores are often the basis for deciding that a student qualifies for special education, many scholars suspect that test bias accounts for the disproportionate representation of certain groups in special education, especially males and children of color, and the neglect of many children of color who are gifted.

At best, test scores represent a sample of an individual's ability to respond to a standard set of questions or tasks; they do not tell us all the important things an individual has learned or how much he or she can learn. Controversy over the biases that are inherent in standardized tests and the search for so-called culture-free and culture-fair tests is long standing (Taylor, 1997). Three cautions are in order:

1. Tests give only clues about what a student has learned.
2. Test scores must be interpreted with recognition of the possible biases the test contains.
3. Testing alone is an insufficient basis for classifying a student or planning an instructional program.

Traditional assessment procedures focus on the student, not on the environment in which he or she is being taught. Critics of traditional assessment have decried the assumption that any deficit that is identified will be a deficit of the student. So in addition to assessing the student's behavior or performance, many educators now suggest assessing the instructional environment. This might involve classroom observation and interviews with the student and teacher. It focuses on such items as whether instruction is presented clearly and effectively, the classroom is effectively controlled, the teacher's expectations are appropriate, appropriate curriculum modifications are made, thinking skills are being taught, effective motivational strategies are used, the student is actively engaged in academic responding and given adequate practice and feedback on performance, and progress is directly and frequently evaluated. The purpose of assessing the instructional environment is to make sure that the student is not mistakenly identified as the source of the learning problem (see Hallahan, Lloyd, Kauffman, Weiss, & Martinez, 2005; Utley & Obiakor, 2001b). An underlying assumption is that this approach will decrease the likelihood that cultural differences will be mistaken for disabilities.

Traditional assessment procedures result in test scores that may be useful in helping to determine a student's eligibility for special education or other special services. These testing procedures do not, however, typically provide information that is useful in planning for instruction. A variety of alternative assessment procedures were devised in the late 1980s and early 1990s that focus on students' performance in the curriculum or on tasks in everyday contexts, rather than on to how well they did on standardized tests (see Rueda & Kim, 2001). The intent of these procedures is to avoid the artificiality and biased nature of traditional testing and obtain a more fair and instructionally useful assessment of students' abilities. These procedures can be useful in some respects, but they are not a solution to all problems of assessment (Terwilliger, 1997; Utley & Obiakor, 2001b).

One particularly useful alternative approach that emerged in the 1980s is **curriculum-based assessment (CBA)** (Fuchs & Fuchs, 1997; Jones, 2001a, 2001b). This method of assessment contrasts sharply with traditional testing, in which students are tested infrequently and may never before have seen the specific items on the test. CBA involves students' responses to their usual instructional materials; it entails direct and frequent samples of performance from the curriculum in which students are being instructed. (We discuss curriculum-based assessment in more detail in Chapter 6.) This form of assessment is thought to be more useful for teachers than traditional testing and to decrease the likelihood of cultural bias.

Finally, we note that fair and accurate assessment is an issue in identifying special gifts and talents as well as disabilities. Too often, the extraordinary abilities of students of color or other ethnic difference and students with disabilities are overlooked because of bias or ignorance on the part of those who are responsible for assessment. In Chapter 1, we emphasized the importance of identifying the abilities as well as the disabilities of students. To that, we add the importance of being aware of culturally relevant gifts and talents and recognizing and valuing the abilities of minority students.

INSTRUCTION

A major objective of multicultural education is ensuring that all students are instructed in ways that do not penalize them because of their cultural differences and that, in fact, capitalize on their cultural heritage (see Council for Exceptional Children, 2000). The methods that are used to achieve this objective are among the most controversial topics in education today. All advocates of multicultural education are concerned with the problem of finding instructional methods that help to equalize educational opportunity and achievement for all cultural groups—that is, methods that break down the inequities and discrimination that have been part of the U.S. public education system, which NCLB and IDEA 2004 seek to eliminate. Yet there is considerable debate over the question of what instructional methods are most effective in achieving this goal.

Curriculum-based assessment (CBA)
A formative evaluation method designed to evaluate performance in the particular curriculum to which students are exposed; usually involves giving students a small sample of items from the curriculum in use in their schools; proponents argue that CBA is preferable to comparing students with national norms or using tests that do not reflect the curriculum content learned by students.

If students' differences are ignored, then the students will probably be given instruction that is not suited to their needs. They will likely fail to learn many skills, which will in turn deny them power and opportunity in the larger culture. For example, if we ignore non-English-speaking students' language and cultural heritage and force them to speak English, they may have great difficulty in school.

However, the answer to this problem is not necessarily recognition of students' differences, for instruction that is geared to individual students' subculture might teach only skills that are valued by their own subculture. Because the larger or more general culture does not value these skills, the students' difference will be perpetuated. For example, if non-English-speaking students are taught in their native language and are not required to learn English, then their progress in the English-speaking society will be slowed.

Should a student who speaks no English be forced to give up his or her native language in school and learn to use only English (ignoring the cultural-linguistic difference)? Or should the student's native language be used as the primary vehicle of instruction while English is taught as a second language (acknowledging the cultural-linguistic difference)? We could pose similar questions for students with severe hearing impairments: Should we teach them by using primarily sign language or spoken language? The same dilemma appears in providing instruction for students with other disabilities: To what extent should they be treated as different and provided with special accommodations, and to what extent should they be treated just like everyone else (Kauffman, McGee, & Brigham, 2004)?

Clearly, the problem of instruction in multicultural education is not easily resolved, especially for bilingual students in special education (Gersten & Baker, 2000). Most authorities now agree, however, that accepting and fostering cultural diversity must not be used as an excuse for not teaching students the skills they need to survive and prosper in the larger context of American culture.

Among the multicultural controversies of our time are Afrocentric instruction and special African American programs and schools. Afrocentric instruction is an alternative to the Eurocentrism of the prevailing curriculum and methods of instruction; it highlights African culture and seeks distinctively African modes of teaching and learning. Some critics suggest that Afrocentrism is a regressive practice that detaches students from the realities of their

To what extent should students with diverse backgrounds and abilities be provided with special accommodations, and to what extent should they be treated just like everyone else?

American social environment (Wortham, 1992). Others call for instructional practices that are culturally sensitive—attuned to the particular cultural characteristics of African American learners (Ford, Obiakor, & Patton, 1995; Franklin, 1992; Van Keulen, Weddington, & DeBose, 1998). The assumption underlying culturally sensitive instruction is that students with different cultural backgrounds need to be taught differently, that certain aspects of a student's cultural heritage determine to a significant extent how he or she learns best. For example, Franklin (1992) suggests that African American students differ from others in the cultural values of their homes and families, their language and patterns of movement, their responses to variety and multiplicity of stimulation, and their preference for divergent thinking.

Perhaps it is understandable that when emphasis is placed on differences in the ways in which students learn, there is also emphasis on devising special programs and schools that cater to these differences. Furthermore, the greater is the diversity of cultural backgrounds of students in one class, the greater is the difficulty in teaching all students effectively—if we assume that cultural background determines how students are best taught. Of course, we might hypothesize that certain methods of instruction are equally effective for all students in a culturally diverse group (see Council for Exceptional Children, 2000; Singh, Ellis, Oswald, Wechsler, & Curtis, 1997). That is, some instructional approaches (e.g., direct instruction, cooperative learning, peer tutoring, and cross-age grouping) allow teachers to provide culturally sensitive instruction to all members of a diverse group at once. **Classwide peer tutoring** may, in fact, be particularly useful in helping children at the elementary school level who are not proficient in English to learn English more efficiently (Fulk & King, 2001; Greenwood, Arrega-Mayer, Utley, & Gavin, Terry, 2001).

Nevertheless, the notion that certain curricula and instructional practices are more appropriate for students of one ethnic origin than for those of another may be used to justify distinctive programs, including African American immersion schools, in which all instruction is geared to the presumed particular learning characteristics of a single ethnic group (see Ascher, 1992). Such schools are often said to be segregationist in practice and intent, but Leake and Leake (1992) suggest that their philosophy opposes the concept of segregation:

> True integration occurs naturally when the differences between peers are minimal. Therefore, the bane of segregation is a culturally and ethnically diverse population of academically competent and self-confident individuals. The African-American immersion schools were designed to provide academically challenging and culturally appropriate experiences for their students. It was hoped that the anticipated increase in student achievement would work to vitiate the African-American students' feelings of inadequacy and impotence. (p. 784)

Do special programs that are designed with specific learning characteristics in mind help students learn more than they otherwise would and increase their self-esteem? This is a central controversy for both special education and multicultural general education, and research has not provided a clear answer for special programs of either type. Given that ethnicity and disability are two separate dimensions of human difference, however, special programming might be much more appropriate and effective for one dimension of difference than the other.

Many questions about instruction and the teachers who offer it are not easily answered in a multicultural society. Are the instructional methods that evidence suggests are effective with one cultural group effective for all? "Specific teacher behaviors (e.g., positive reinforcement, questioning techniques) have been shown to lead to better student outcomes, and we assume that the absence of these behaviors has a deleterious effect on student learning" (Tyler, Yzquierdo, Lopez-Reyna, & Flippin, 2004, pp. 27–28). Do children of one cultural affliation learn better when taught by a particular method but others learn better when taught in a different way? If so, which is the lesser evil: grouping students for instruction based on their cultural affiliation or shortchanging some by using a particular

UNDERSTANDING THE STANDARDS AND PRINCIPLES What are some challenges associated with addressing the differing ways in which students from culturally diverse backgrounds learn? *(CEC Knowledge and Skills Standard CC3K5)*

Council for Exceptional Children

Classwide peer tutoring
An instructional procedure in which all students in the class are involved in tutoring and being tutored by classmates on specific skills as directed by their teacher.

instructional method? Can either evil be avoided entirely? Do students learn best when they are taught by someone who shares their cultural heritage? If so, what does that mean for recruiting and assigning teachers, and what does it mean for grouping students for instruction? How do we best address the problem of increasing the cultural and linguistic diversity of special education teachers (see Tyler et al., 2004)? Which is more important in a teacher: instructional competence or cultural affiliation? If neither is more important than the other, how should teachers be recruited and trained?

What is not an open question, however, is this: Must both special and general education adopt instructional programs that value all students and help all to be as successful as possible in American society, regardless of their specific cultural heritage? This question has been answered resoundingly in the affirmative, not by research but by our common commitment to the American values of equality of opportunity and fairness for all (see Singh, 1996). The pursuit of equality and fairness has led educational reformers toward four instructional goals:

1. Teaching tolerance and appreciation of difference
2. Working cooperatively with families
3. Improving instruction for language-minority students
4. Adopting effective teaching practices

TEACHING TOLERANCE
magazine and teaching ideas can be found at **www.tolerance.org/teach** and the Gay, Lesbian and Straight Network (GLSEN) can be found at **www.glsen.org**

UNDERSTANDING THE STANDARDS AND PRINCIPLES How can special educators teach students to appreciate those who are different from themselves? *(CEC Knowledge and Skills Standard CC5K7)*

Teaching Tolerance and Appreciation   By *tolerance*, we do not mean merely toleration of others who are seen as undesirable, nor does the publication *Teaching Tolerance* mean such toleration. Tolerance in our sense, and in the sense of *Teaching Tolerance*, means an appreciation and valuing, the opposite of rejection, denigration, or toleration of a necessary evil. It means working for equity and fair treatment, seeing those who are different in culture from ourselves as equal. Still, mere toleration would be a step away from the hostile rejection, ridicule, and subjugation that intolerance breeds.

Noted historian Ronald Takaki (1994), writing in *Teaching Tolerance*, recalls that his grandparents were Japanese immigrant plantation laborers in Hawaii. Nobel laureate and author Elie Wiesel (2004), writing in the Sunday magazine *Parade*, recalls his rescue from a concentration camp. Both suggest that the American promise of equality and fairness can become a reality only if we free ourselves from a legacy of racism and prejudice. We can do so by acknowledging the reality of our past and learning more about ourselves and our heritage.

Overcoming prejudice and teaching students to appreciate those who are different from themselves is by no means easy. Moreover, this is not an area in which research can provide definitive guidelines. Yet proposed methods for how teachers can help students learn both self-esteem and tolerance of difference seem promising (Artiles & Zamora-Duran, 1997; Banks, 1997; Utley & Obiakor, 2001a). Some schools focus on how to incorporate diversity by design or organizing antibias clubs that encourage understanding and tolerance of others (e.g., Bennett, 2000; Collins, 2000; McAfee, 2000).

Teaching tolerance and appreciation of difference is not, of course, limited to ethnic, regional, sexual orientation, or language differences but includes differences of all types, including disabilities.

Working with Families   Schools have always depended, in part, on family involvement and support for their success. Because working with families is so important, we have devoted Chapter 4 to the topic.

Different cultural traditions mean that parents have different views of exceptionality and disability and different ways of accommodating these differences in their children (Cho, Singer, & Brenner, 2000; Pullen, 2004). An understanding of the cultural basis for parents' attitudes and wishes is therefore critical, particularly for families that have recently come to the United States. When combined with other differences, difficulties for students with disabilities are increased, as pointed out in the description of GLESN on page 97.

FOCUS ON CONCEPTS

GLSEN in Tough Times

Training Educators about LGBT Issues in a Challenging Political, Economic, and Educational Climate

TEACHERS of today's youth must be especially aware of the individual needs that each child brings to the classroom, and develop strategies to make the classroom a safe environment in which to address these needs. Among the youth in each class, an unknown population are lesbian, gay, bisexual or transgender (LGBT), and they bring special concerns to school similar to other students who experience harassment and acts of violence because they are different. According to the 2003 National School Climate Survey by The Gay, Lesbian and Straight Education Network, or GLSEN, harassment continues at unacceptable levels and is too often ignored: 84% of LGBT students report being verbally harassed because of their sexual orientation and 82.9% of students report that faculty never or rarely intervene when present. The survey also found that unchecked harassment correlates with poor performance and diminished aspirations: LGBT youth who report significant verbal harassment are twice as likely to report they do not intend to go to college and their GPAs are significantly lower. When youths with behavior disorders are also LGBT, their personal and school-related problems are likely to be compounded while their ability to deal effectively with these problems is diminished. ■

Source: Bell, K. (2004). GLSEN in tough times: Training educators about LGBT issues in a challenging political, economic, and educational climate. *Beyond Behavior, 13*(2), 29–30.

Improving Instruction for Language-Minority Students   Students for whom English is a second language face the simultaneous demands of learning a new language and mastering traditional subject matter. Those who have disabilities encounter the third demand of coping with the additional hurdles imposed by their exceptionalities. Bilingual special education is therefore particularly controversial, presenting difficult dilemmas and paradoxes. Moreover, the demand of the NCLB of 2002 that students who are not fluent in English score on average the same as those who are fluent in English created extraordinary controversy about langugé learning.

Language-minority students with disabilities face the paradox of simultaneous overrepresentation and underrepresentation. Ethnic- and language-minority students may be overrepresented in special education if they are referred and misidentified for problems that are not disabilities. At the same time, students from language-minority groups may be underreferred. They may "truly need specialized assistance, but . . . languish in general education classrooms, benefiting little from conventional instruction" (Gersten & Woodward, 1994, p. 312).

One approach to teaching language-minority students is to emphasize use of their native languages. In this approach, all academic instruction is initially provided in each student's native language, and English is taught as a separate subject. Later, when the student has demonstrated adequate fluency in English, he or she makes the transition to instruction in English in all academic subjects.

Another approach is to offer content-area instruction in English from the beginning of the student's schooling but at a level that is "sheltered," or constantly modified to make sure the student understands it. The goal of this approach is to help the student learn English while learning academic subjects as well.

In the first approach—**native-language emphasis**—students are taught for most of the day in their native languages and

Casebook Reflections

Refer to the case *Who Will Help Patrick?* in your booklet. Margaret's approach to parenting is shouting, fear, and intimidation. Is socioeconomic status also a cultural issue in this case? To what extent might Margaret's attitudes and discipline of Patrick be explained by cultural factors? Could Margaret's approach to dealing with Patrick be justified as culturally acceptable and appropriate?

Different cultural traditions mean that parents have different views of exceptionality and disability and different ways of accommodating these differences in their children.

Native-language emphasis

An approach to teaching language-minority pupils in which the students' native language is used for most of the day and English is taught as a separate subject.

Sheltered-English approach

A method in which language-minority students are taught all their subjects in English at a level that is modified constantly according to individuals' needs.

Scaffolded instruction

A cognitive approach to instruction in which the teacher provides temporary structure or support while students are learning a task; the support is gradually removed as the students are able to perform the task independently.

later make a transition to English. In the second approach, the **sheltered-English approach**, students receive instruction in English for most of the school day from the beginning of their schooling. The question as to which approach is better for students with disabilities has not been answered, although it is clear that changing from one approach to the other when students change schools creates particular difficulties (Gersten & Baker, 2000; Gersten & Woodward, 1994).

Another issue for language-minority instruction is whether an emphasis on the natural uses of language or, alternatively, on skills such as vocabulary and pronunciation is most effective. However, this controversy might be based on a false dichotomy. What students need is an effective balance between skill building and language that is meaningful and relevant to their lives and interests (Gersten & Baker, 2000; Ovando, 1997; Van Keulen et al., 1998). Moreover, instruction of language-minority students needs to be consistent with effective teaching.

Adopting Effective Teaching Practices   In a sense, effective multicultural education requires only that we implement what we know about effective instruction. Effective teaching practices are sensitive to each student's cultural heritage, sense of self, view of the world, and acquired knowledge and skills. Teaching about various cultures, individual differences, and the construction of knowledge should permeate and transform the curriculum (Banks, 1997). Nonetheless, for language-minority students—indeed, for all students—we can articulate more specific components of effective teaching. We offer the following description of six components of effective teaching outlined by Gersten et al. (1994, p. 9):

1. *Scaffolding and strategies.* Students learn more efficiently when they are provided a scaffold, or structure, for ideas and strategies for problem solving. In **scaffolded instruction**, the teacher assists the student in learning a task and then phases out the help as the student learns to use the strategy independently. (See Chapter 6 for further discussion.) Means of helping students learn more easily include stories, visual organizers (e.g., pictures, diagrams, outlines), **mnemonics** (tactics that aid memory, such as rhymes or images), and **reciprocal teaching** (in which the student sees the teacher use a learning strategy and then tries it out).

2. *Challenge.* Too much of education, even special education, is not appropriately challenging for students. All students—including those who are from cultural minorities, who are at high risk for failure, and who have disabilities—need to be given challenging tasks. Appropriately challenging tasks are those that a given student finds just manageable. Although these tasks are not impossible, they do require serious effort and stretch the student's capabilities. Too often, teachers underestimate the capabilities of minority and exceptional students and underteach them (Delpit, 1995; Ford, 1998; Patton, 1997).

3. *Involvement.* Students must be engaged in extended conversations, in which they use complex linguistic structures. Verbal exchanges between teachers and pupils must not always be short, simple, and direct (although such exchanges have their place). Rather, teachers must probe with questions, share experiences, and elicit from pupils the kind of language that demonstrates their active involvement in learning (Kline, Simpson, Blesz, Myles, & Carter, 2001).

4. *Success.* Students who are at the highest risk of failure and dropping out are those who have low rates of success in daily school activities. All students need to experience frequent success, and teachers must present challenging tasks at which the student can be successful (Kauffman, Mostert, Trent, & Pullen, 2006). Failure should not be perpetuated.

5. *Mediation and feedback.* Too often, students work for long periods without receiving feedback, or are given feedback that is not comprehensible, or are asked for rote responses to which they attach little or no meaning. Providing frequent, comprehensible feedback on performance is vital to effective teaching, as is focusing on the meanings of responses—how evidence and logic are used to construct questions and their answers.

6. *Responsiveness to cultural and individual diversity.* The content of instruction must be related to students' experiences, including those as individuals and as members of various cultural groups. The issues of cultural and individual diversity cannot be adequately considered in a few special lessons; rather, they must be included routinely in all curriculum areas.

Of all the academic skills, reading is most important. Research increasingly points to the importance of an environment in which children have the opportunity to listen to reading, examine books, engage in activities such as saying nursery rhymes, writing, and seeing and talking about printed materials (Hammill, 2004; Peck & Scarpati, 2004). This means encouraging such literacy-related activities in the home, which cannot occur unless the teacher is competent in addressing cultural differences among families.

Of all the academic skills, reading is most important. Teachers should encourage literacy-related activities in the home, so they must be aware of and competent in addressing cultural differences among families.

It also means teaching with a sense of urgency, as described on page 100, and understanding that effective instruction is special education's bottom line (Kauffman & Hallahan, 2005).

A viable multicultural curriculum cannot be created and handed out to teachers (Banks, 1997). Teachers must be invested in the endeavor, as their values, perspectives, and teaching styles will affect what is taught and how. The effective implementation of a multicultural curriculum requires teaching strategies that are involvement oriented, interactive, personalized, and cooperative.

This perspective applies to our own teaching and writing as well. In any textbook, the adequate treatment of multicultural issues cannot be confined to a single chapter. A chapter like this one—devoted specifically to multicultural education—may be necessary to ensure that the topic is given sufficient focused attention. Our intention in this book, however, is to prompt consideration of multicultural issues in every chapter.

Mnemonics
Techniques that aid memory, such as using rhymes, songs, or visual images to remember information.

Reciprocal teaching
A method in which students and teachers are involved in a dialogue to facilitate learning.

SOCIALIZATION

Academic instruction is one of two primary purposes of education. The other, socialization, involves helping students develop appropriate social perceptions and interactions with others and learn how to work for desirable social change. Socializing the student does not mean that any kind of behavior or attitude is acceptable in school; nor does it mean ignoring the student's cultural heritage. Cartledge and Loe (2001) conclude that the commonalities among children are greater than their differences but that cultural and linguistic differences nonetheless pose significant challenges for teachers, who must make the classroom an affirming place for students. Osher and colleagues (2004) express similar views.

In some cases, helping children learn appropriate social skills might require helping parents learn how to teach their children (Elksnin & Elksnin, 2000). This requires understanding the cultural and linguistic diversity of families.

FOCUS ON CONCEPTS

A Common Sense of Urgency

WE need to exercise caution with well-intended but general concepts, for much very poor instruction has occurred as a result of misguided interpretations. To illustrate, we often stress that good teachers should care about and demonstrate concern for their students. One teacher who was brought to my attention would display very caring behaviors by taking time on her weekends to expose some of her poor urban students to community cultural events such as art shows, museums, and libraries. On the other hand, extensive observations in her general education elementary classroom revealed constant chaos and little meaningful instruction. Although she wanted to be effective, she was incapacitated by her lack of skill, and her students suffered accordingly. To be specific, I would propose that a school with a sense of community is one that is united in the urgency of helping each child master the grade-level curriculum. Classroom time is not wasted, teachers are well trained in teaching strategies that work, children's progress is monitored constantly, remedial actions are taken when needed, and there is the clear expectation that all children can and will meet mastery.

Schools with underachieving culturally diverse students clearly need this common sense of urgency. Most educators will say that they care about their students and have no racial or cultural animus, but relatively few teachers are aware that one of the best examples of the absence of bias is to teach with this sense of urgency, fully expecting children to learn. Schools that fail to be alarmed when two thirds to three quarters of their students are two to three grades behind academically are consciously or unconsciously subscribing to this bias

Source: Cartledge, G. (2004). Another look at the impact of changing demographics on public education for culturally diverse learners with behavior problems: Implications for teacher preparation. In L. M. Bullock & R. A. Gable (Eds.), *Quality personnel preparation in emotional/behavioral disorders: Current perspectives and future directions* (pp. 64–69). Denton, TX: Institute for Behavioral and Learning Differences at the University of North Texas. Reprinted with permission. ■

Destructive and stereotypic social perceptions and interactions among differing subcultural groups are long-standing problems in schools and communities in the United States, particularly when there are cultural differences among students in language and social behavior (Ishii-Jordan, 1997; Osher et al., 2004). The cartoon on page 101 illustrates how stereotypes have affected the way we think about people and the ideas that are embedded in our language. Part of the process of multicultural socialization is giving students experiences that make them question the way we think about other cultures.

The most obvious examples involve racial discrimination, although sex discrimination and discrimination against people of differing religions and disabilities are also common in our society. Consider the case of Adelaide Ruffner, a woman with cerebral palsy, who was thought not to be acceptable as a teacher in the 1960s but went on to earn a master's degree and to be recognized for her extraordinary work with children with disabilities and their families. In a report of Ruffner's award-winning work, Dadurka (2004) included the following:

> Though her family was supportive, others were not always so accepting. When Ruffner began her student-teaching term at Johnson Elementary in the 1960s, she was let go after six weeks.
> "The parents complained. Back then you were judged by your exterior. . . . People were scared," she said. "It was like segregation." (p. A2)

There is no guarantee that discrimination such as that experienced by Adelaide Ruffner will not be encountered today. Teachers and teacher educators must become keenly aware of their own cultural heritages, identities, and biases before they can help their students deal with cultural diversity in ways that enhance democratic ideals, such as human dignity,

justice, and equality (Banks, 1997). Becoming comfortable with one's own identity as a member of subcultural groups is an important objective for both teachers and students. Depending on the cultural context, accepting and valuing one's identity can be quite difficult.

Teaching about different cultures and their value may be important in reducing racial and ethnic conflict and promoting respect for human differences. Equally important, however, is structuring classroom interactions to promote the understanding and appreciation of others. One of the most effective ways of breaking down prejudice and encouraging appropriate interaction among students with different characteristics is **cooperative learning**. In cooperative learning, students of different abilities and cultural characteristics work together as a team, fostering interdependence.

Teachers of exceptional children and youths must be aware of the variety of subcultural identities their students may be developing and struggling with. Review the multiple aspects of cultural identity suggested by Figure 3.1 (page 86) and reflect on the combinations of these and other subcultures that a given student might adopt. One of the cultural identities that is not included in Figure 3.1 is sexual orientation, yet many children and adolescents, including many with educational exceptionalities, experience serious difficulties with what some have called the invisible culture of gay and lesbian youth. Students who are "straight" might struggle with their own prejudices against homosexuals, prejudices that are all too often fostered by both their peers and adults and sometimes given justification by identification with a religious or political subculture. Gay and lesbian students are often harassed and abused verbally and physically in school and may suffer from serious depression or other psychological disorders as a result; even the appearance or assumption of being gay can lead to abuse (see Associated Press, 2004; Bell, 2004). Gay students need to be able to be themselves without fear of harassment or discrimination (Elliot, 2000). Consider also that a student might be both gay or lesbian and gifted, physically disabled, or mentally retarded or have any other educational exceptionality.

Our point is that the task of socialization in a multicultural society demands attention to the multitude of identities that students may assume. It also demands an awareness that any of these identities may carry the consequence of social rejection, isolation, and alienation. Many children with disabilities are lonely and need to develop friendships (Pavri, 2001). Our task as educators is to promote understanding of cultural differences and acceptance of individuals whose identities are different from one's own. Building pride in one's cultural identity is a particular concern in teaching exceptional students. As we have noted elsewhere, many people in the Deaf community prefer to be called *the Deaf*, which runs contrary to the current use of terms such as *hearing impaired*. Deaf people and blind people have begun to express pride in their identities and cultures and, at the same time, foster multicultural experiences involving other languages and customs (Gallucci, 2000). In fact, for increasing numbers of people with disabilities, labels are to be embraced, not hidden.

People from many segments of society—such as parents of children with disabilities, senior citizens, religious groups, and recovering alcoholics—find that congregating for mutual support and understanding enhances their feelings of self-worth. Educators need to

Cooperative learning
A teaching approach in which the teacher places students with heterogeneous abilities (for example, some might have disabilities) together to work on assignments.

Schools should be places where students from different cultural and ethnic groups can learn about themselves and one another in natural, nonintimidating ways.

consider the possible value of having students with disabilities congregate for specific purposes.

By trying to avoid labels and insisting that students with disabilities always be placed with those who do not have disabilities, perhaps we risk giving the message that those who have disabilities are less desirable or even not fit to associate with as peers. Bateman (1994) suggests that "something is terribly and not very subtly insulting about saying a bright learning disabled student ought not attend a special school with other students who have learning disabilities because he needs to be with non-disabled students" (p. 516). In striving for true multicultural awareness, we might learn that it is more productive in the long run to embrace identities associated with exceptionalities, while working to increase tolerance and understanding of differences, than it is to avoid labels or refrain from congregating students with specific characteristics.

One of the most difficult tasks of teaching is socializing students through classroom discipline—that is, through the management of classroom behavior. Managing classroom behavior presents a serious challenge for nearly all teachers and a particularly difficult challenge for most special education teachers (see Evertson & Weinstein, in press; Kauffman et al., 2006). Two considerations are critical: the relationship between the teacher's approach to classroom discipline and the parents' child-rearing practices and the teacher's sensitivity to cultural differences in responses to discipline.

Teachers might have an approach to classroom discipline that they consider effective and humane but that differs radically from some cultures' accepted child-rearing practices. Educators, like everyone else, are often ethnocentric, believing that their views are correct and those of others are not. In a given case, they might be right, in that their view is more humane or effective, but they might also be biased and wrong. In the case of discipline involving students of culturally diverse backgrounds, the teacher might face difficult ethical decisions about child abuse or neglect. When do one's own beliefs about the treatment of children demand that a culturally condoned disciplinary practice be confronted as abuse or neglect? Answering this question is not easy.

Finally, we note that education should not merely socialize students to fit into the existing social order. The goals of multicultural education include teaching students to work for social change, which entails helping students who are members of oppressed minorities become advocates for themselves and other members of their subcultures (Banks, 1997; Banks & Banks, 1997; Utley & Obiakor, 2001c).

SUMMARY

IN what ways do we see universality of cultural pride and shame?

■ People of every identity take justifiable pride in aspects of their heritage.

■ People of every identity have conducted themselves in ways that bring shame to their group.

■ Collective guilt and collective pride are problems for every group.

WHAT is American about multiculturalism?

■ The United States is a very diverse society that seeks justice for all.

■ Ideally, American culture is one that celebrates diversity within a framework of clearly defined common values.

WHAT are the important concepts about cultural diversity for education?

■ American society is made of many subcultures (cultures that are a part, not all, of the larger society), each of which is characterized by:

  ■ Values and typical behavior

  ■ Languages or dialects

  ■ Nonverbal communication

  ■ Awareness of one's cultural identity

  ■ World views or general perspectives

■ Special education must foster achievement in the context of cultural diversity.

WHAT are the most important aspects of multicultural and bilingual special education?

■ Three aspects of cultural diversity that are particularly important for special education are the following:

  ■ Assessment that honors the student's cultural heritage and does not penalize the student

  ■ Instruction that that uses the student's cultural strengths and that involves teaching tolerance and appreciation of culture, working with families, improving language instruction for language-minority students, and adopting effective teaching practices

  ■ Socialization to multicultural norms

APPLYING THE STANDARDS AND PRINCIPLES

■ **DESCRIBE** ways in which students from **culturally diverse backgrounds** might differ in the ways they learn. What strategies might a special educator use to address those differences? *(CEC Content Standard #3)*

■ **HOW** might a lack of attention to cultural, ethnic, gender, and linguistic differences affect the **identification of students** for special services? *(INTASC 3.04 & 3.09)*

■ **HOW** might having a child with disabilities influence a **family's view** of themselves as caregivers and as members of their communities? *(INTASC 3.06)*

■ **HOW** can special educators **foster environments in which diversity is valued** and individuals are taught to live harmoniously and productively in a culturally diverse world? *(CEC Content Standard #5)*

Council for Exceptional Children

INTASC

Chapter 4

Parents and Families

I am often asked to describe the experience of raising a child with a disability—to try to help people who have not shared that unique experience to understand it, to imagine how it would feel. It's like this. . . .

When you're going to have a baby, it's like planning a fabulous vacation trip—to Italy. You buy a bunch of guide books and make your wonderful plans. The Coliseum. The Michelangelo David. The gondolas in Venice. You may learn some handy phrases in Italian. It's all very exciting.

After months of eager anticipation, the day finally arrives. You pack your bags and off you go. Several hours later, the plane lands. The stewardess comes in and says, "Welcome to Holland."

"*Holland*?!?" you say. "What do you mean Holland?? I signed up for Italy! I'm supposed to be in Italy. All my life I've dreamed of going to Italy."

But there's been a change in the flight plan. They've landed in Holland and there you must stay.

The important thing is that they haven't taken you to a horrible, disgusting, filthy place, full of pestilence, famine and disease. It's just a different place.

So you must go out and buy new guide books. And you must learn a whole new language. And you will meet a whole new group of people you would never have met.

It's just a *different* place. It's slower-paced than Italy, less flashy than Italy. But after you've been there for a while and you catch your breath, you look around. . . . and you begin to notice that Holland has windmills. . . . and Holland has tulips. Holland even has Rembrandts.

But everyone you know is busy coming and going from Italy . . . and they're all bragging about what a wonderful time they had there. And for the rest of your life, you will say "Yes, that's where I was supposed to go. That's what I had planned."

And the pain of that will never, ever, ever, *ever* go away . . . because the loss of that dream is a very very significant loss.

But . . . if you spend your life mourning the fact that you didn't get to Italy, you may never be free to enjoy the very special, the very lovely things . . . about Holland.

EMILY PERL KINGSLEY
"Welcome to Holland"

QUESTIONS TO GUIDE YOUR READING OF THIS CHAPTER . . .

- HOW have professionals' views of parents changed?
- WHAT are the effects of a child with a disability on the family?
- WHAT are the best ways for families to be involved in treatment and education?

STANDARDS AND PRINCIPLES IN THIS CHAPTER

SPECIAL EDUCATORS

- **facilitate instructional planning in a collaborative context** including the individuals with exceptionalities, families, professional colleagues, and personnel from other agencies as appropriate *(from CEC Content Standard #7).*

- Special educators **routinely and effectively collaborate** with families, other educators, related service providers, and personnel from community agencies in culturally responsive ways *(from CEC Content Standard #10).*

ALL TEACHERS

- **plans instruction** based on knowledge of subject matter, students, the community and curriculum goals *(INTASC Principle #7).*

Council for Exceptional Children

- **fosters relationships** with school colleagues, families, and agencies in the larger community to support students' learning and well being *(INTASC Principle #10).*

INTASC

As Emily Perl Kingsley—the mother of a child with Down syndrome—points out (see p. 105), the birth of a child with a disability can have a profound effect on the family. But the exact nature of the effect is not always certain. Reactions of family members to the individual with a disability can run the gamut from absolute rejection to absolute acceptance, from intense hate to intense love, from total neglect to overprotection. And most important, a child with disabilities does not always threaten the family's well-being. In fact, some parents and siblings assert that having a family member with a disability has strengthened the family bonds.

In this chapter, we explore the dynamics of families with children who are disabled and discuss parental involvement in their treatment and education. Before proceeding further, however, it is instructive to consider the role of parents of children who are disabled from a historical perspective.

Professionals' Changing Views of Parents

Today, knowledgeable professionals who work with exceptional learners are aware of the importance of the family. They recognize that the family of the person with a disability can help in their educational efforts. To ignore the family is shortsighted because it can lessen the effectiveness of teaching.

Even though we now recognize how crucial it is to consider the concerns of parents and families in treatment and educational programs for individuals who are disabled, this was not always the case. Professionals' views of the role of parents have changed dramatically. In the not too distant past, some professionals pointed to the parents as the primary cause of the child's problems or as a place to lay blame when practitioners' interventions were ineffective. For at least two reasons, we now know that automatically holding parents responsible for their children's problems is inappropriate.

First, research has shown that the direction of causation between child and adult behavior is a two-way street (Bell & Harper, 1977). Sometimes the parent changes the behavior of the child or infant; sometimes the reverse is true. With specific regard to children who are disabled, some researchers point out that these children, even as infants, sometimes have difficult temperaments, which influence how parents respond to them (Brooks-Gunn & Lewis, 1984; Mahoney & Robenalt, 1986). Some infants who are disabled, for example, are relatively unresponsive to stimulation from their parents, making it more difficult to interact with these children. With an understanding of the reciprocal nature of parent–child interaction, we are thus more likely, for example, to sympathize with a mother's frustration in trying to cuddle an infant with severe mental retardation or a father's anger in attempting to deal with his teenager who has an emotional or behavior disorder.

Second, researchers have found that the family can have a positive influence on the educational process. Although at first many authorities tended to think that parents needed training to achieve a positive effect on their children, more and more educators now have recognized that parents often have as much or more to offer than professionals regarding

Misconceptions about
Parents and Families of Persons with Disabilities

MYTH Parents are to blame for many of the problems of their children with disabilities.

FACT Parents can influence their children's behavior, but so, too, can children affect how their parents behave. Research shows that some children with disabilities are born with difficult temperaments, which can affect parental behavior.

MYTH Parents must experience a series of reactions—shock and disruption, denial, sadness, anxiety and fear, and anger—before adapting to the birth of a child with a disability.

FACT Parents do not go through emotional reactions in lockstep fashion. They may experience some, or all, of these emotions but not necessarily in any particular order.

MYTH Many parents of infants with disabilities go from physician to physician, "shopping" for an optimistic diagnosis.

FACT Just the opposite is often true. Parents frequently suspect that something is wrong with their baby but are told by professionals not to worry—that the child will outgrow the problem. Then they seek another opinion.

MYTH The father is unimportant in the development of the child with a disability.

FACT Although they are frequently ignored by researchers and generally do experience less stress than mothers, fathers can play a critical role in the dynamics of the family.

MYTH Parents of children with disabilities are destined for a life of stress and misery.

FACT Some parents experience high degrees of disruption and stress, but over time many come to learn to cope. And some actually gain unanticipated positive benefits from having a child with a disability.

MYTH Siblings are usually unaffected by the addition of a child with a disability to the family.

FACT Siblings often experience the same emotional reactions as parents do, and their lack of maturity can make coping with these emotions more difficult.

MYTH The primary role of the early intervention professional should be to provide expertise for the family.

FACT Many authorities now agree that professionals should help parents become more involved in making decisions for the family.

MYTH The typical family in the United States has two parents, is middle class, and has only the father working outside the home.

FACT Demographics are changing rapidly. There are now many more families with both parents working outside the home as well as more single-parent families and families living in poverty.

MYTH Parents who elect not to be actively involved in their child's education and treatment are neglectful.

FACT Although it is desirable for parents to be involved, it is sometimes very difficult for them to do so because of their commitments to other family functions (e.g., work and child care).

MYTH Professionals are always in the best position to help families of people with disabilities.

FACT Informal sources of support, such as extended family and friends, are often more effective than formal sources of support, such as professionals and agencies, in helping families adapt to a family member with a disability.

MYTH Teachers should respect the privacy of parents and communicate with them only when absolutely necessary—for example, when their child has exhibited serious behavior problems.

FACT Teachers should initiate some kind of contact with parents as soon as possible, so that if something like a serious behavior infraction does occur, some rapport with the parents will already have been established.

Federal law stipulates that schools must make a concerted effort to involve parents and families in the education of their children with disabilities.

suggestions for the treatment of their children. The prevailing philosophy now dictates that whenever possible, professionals should seek the special insights that parents can offer by virtue of living with their children. Furthermore, authorities today are less likely to view the purpose of early intervention to be training parents to assume the role of quasi-therapist or quasi-teacher (Berry & Hardman, 1998). Instead, many believe that the goal should be to develop and preserve the natural parent–child relationship as much as possible. In sum, a healthy parent–child relationship is inherently beneficial.

The fact is that parents and teachers have a symbiotic relationship. Each group can benefit enormously from the other. (See Table 4.1).

Recognizing the importance of the family, Congress has passed several federal laws stipulating that schools make a concerted effort to involve parents and families in the education of their children with disabilities. Current law mandates that schools attempt to include parents in crafting their children's individualized education programs (IEPs) (see Chapter 1). In the case of children under 3 years of age, schools must involve parents in developing **individualized family service plans (IFSPs)**. The focus of the IFSP is to be family-centered. In other words, the IFSP not only addresses the needs of the individual child who has a disability, but also focuses on the child's family by specifying what services the family needs to enhance the child's development.

Individualized family service plan (IFSP)
A plan for services for young children with disabilities (under three years of age) and their families; drawn up by professionals and parents; similar to an IEP for older children; mandated by PL 99-457.

The Effects of a Child with a Disability on the Family

The birth of any child can have a significant effect on the dynamics of the family. The parents and other children must undergo a variety of changes to adapt to the presence of a new member. The effects on the family of the birth of a child who has a disability can be even more profound.

The everyday routines that most families take for granted are frequently disrupted in families with children who are disabled (Keogh, Garnier, Bernheimer, & Gallimore, 2000).

TABLE 4.1   Importance of Families to Teachers and Teachers to Families

Families . . .

- Provide teachers with personal information that can explain why certain students' behaviors are occurring in the classroom.

- Provide background information and medical histories to teachers and to the school that can help teachers understand why a student behaves or learns in certain ways.

- Reinforce directives that teachers give their students, especially on homework assignments.

- Support teachers by serving as chaperones or volunteers in the classroom.

- Help teachers determine students' interests so that long-term education or vocation goals can be established.

- Tell teachers about which types of discipline and learning strategies work best with their children.

- Help teachers determine each student's strengths and needs so that appropriate instructional goals are created.

Teachers . . .

- Provide families with documented evidence of their children's progress and successes.

- Help families become more actively involved in their children's education.

- Help families determine where a student's interests lie so that appropriate long-term goals can be established.

- Teach and reinforce social skills that are needed for students to be successful, contributing members of the communities in which families live.

- Tell families when their children exhibit inappropriate behaviors or academic needs in the classroom.

- Provide important educational and community data to help families stay current and knowledgeable about opportunities available for children.

- Lend a helping hand, a supportive ear, and a friendly face to all families served.

Source: Adapted from O'Shea, D. J., & O'Shea, L. J. (2001). Why learn about students' families? In D. J. O'Shea, L. J. O'Shea, R. Algozzine, D. J. Hammitte (Eds.), *Families and teachers of individuals with disabilities: Collaborative orientations and responsive practices* (pp. 5–24). Austin: Pro-Ed, Inc. Copyright © 2001. Adapted by permission of Pro Ed, Inc.

For example, the child with a disability might require alterations in housing (e.g., the family might decide to move closer to therapists), household maintenance schedules (e.g., chores might not be done as quickly because of lack of time), and even parents' career goals (e.g., a parent might pass up a promotion to spend more time with the child).

In addition to affecting family dynamics, a child with a disability can influence family members' employment. One survey, for example, found that over half the families reported that one or more family members altered their work hours, worked fewer hours, changed jobs, or quit working altogether because of having a child with a disability (Anderson, Larson, Lakin, & Kwak, 2002).

It is important to note that the child with a disability can have an impact on both parents and siblings and in different ways. We discuss parental reactions first and then sibling reactions.

PARENTAL REACTIONS

A Stage Theory Approach   Traditionally, researchers and clinicians have suggested that parents go through a series of stages after learning they have a child with a disability. Some of these stages parallel the proposed sequence of responses that accompany a person's reactions to the death of a loved one. Based on interviews of parents of infants with serious

UNDERSTANDING THE STANDARDS AND PRINCIPLES How might parents react to having a child with a disability? *(CEC Knowledge and Skills Standard CC10K3)*

Council for Exceptional Children

The birth of any child has a profound effect on his or her family, and when the child is born with a disability, the effect is even more so.

physical disabilities, a representative set of stages includes shock and disruption, denial, sadness, anxiety and fear, anger, and finally adaptation (Drotar, Baskiewicz, Irvin, Kennell, & Klaus, 1975).

Several authorities have questioned the wisdom of this stage approach in understanding parental reactions. It is clear that parents should not be thought of as marching through a series of stages in an identical and predictable way. It would be counterproductive, for example, to think, "This mother is now in the anxiety and fear stage. We need to encourage her to go through the anger stage so that she can finally adapt."

One argument against a strict stage model comes from the fact that many parents report that they do not engage in denial. In fact, they are often the first to suspect a problem. It is largely a myth that parents of children who are disabled go from physician to physician, "shopping" for a more favorable diagnosis. In fact, all too frequently, they have to convince the doctor that there is something wrong with their child.

Although parents might not go through these reactions in a rigid fashion, some do experience some or all these emotions at one time or another. A commonly reported reaction is guilt.

The Role of Guilt   The parents of a child with a disability frequently wrestle with the terrifying feeling that they are in some way responsible for their child's condition. Even though there is absolutely no basis for such thoughts in the vast majority of cases, guilt is one of the most commonly reported feelings of parents of exceptional children.

The high prevalence of guilt is probably due to the fact that the primary cause of so many disabilities is unknown. Uncertainty about the cause of the child's disability creates an atmosphere that is conducive to speculation by the parents that they themselves are to blame. Mothers are particularly vulnerable. As Featherstone (1980), the mother of a boy who was blind and had hydrocephaly, mental retardation, cerebral palsy, and seizures, stated:

> Our children are wondrous achievements. Their bodies grow inside ours. If their defects originated in utero, we blame our inadequate bodies or inadequate caution. If . . . we accept credit for our children's physical beauty (and most of us do, in our hearts), then inevitably we assume responsibility for their physical defects.
>
> The world makes much of the pregnant woman. People open doors for her, carry her heavy parcels, offer footstools and unsolicited advice. All this attention seems somehow posited on the idea that she is creating something miraculously fine. When the baby arrives imperfect, the mother feels she has failed not only herself and her husband, but the rest of the world as well.
>
> Soon this diffuse sense of inadequacy sharpens. Nearly every mother fastens on some aspect of her own behavior and blames the tragedy on that. (pp. 73–74)

Dealing with the Public   In addition to ambivalence about the cause of the child's disability, parents can feel vulnerable to criticism from others about how they deal with their child's problems. Parents of children with disabilities sometimes sense, whether correctly or not, that others are scrutinizing their decisions about their child's treatment, educational placement, and so forth.

The public can sometimes be cruel in their reactions to people with disabilities. People with disabilities—especially those who have disabilities that are readily observable—are inevitably faced with inappropriate reactions from those around them. And understandably, parents often assume the burden of responding to inappropriate or even cruel reactions from the public. The following experience of the mother of a child with autism is illustrative:

Worn out, I toss my purse under the seat and look absently out the window onto the dark tarmac. Last to board, a woman and a girl of about ten struggle to get into the small, crowded plane. The girl flaps her hand frantically near her face. The pair move in a sort of lunging, shuffling duet. The mother's eyes are firmly fixed toward the rear of the plane and her hand is vise-gripped to the girl's wrist. I know this scenario: mother and child with autism traveling. Small world.

Loud guttural sounds, almost a moan, almost a scream, come from the girl. Her first utterance causes the people near me to shift around in their seats and nervously clear their throats.

I glance back. The mother is working overtime to get her daughter to settle down and stay calm as we take off and gain altitude. It is hard for anyone to stay calm on a little airplane. I look down as the brightly lit buildings of Portland give way to the faint lights of small towns and farms.

The girl's sounds begin to escalate as the plane hits some turbulence. Fellow passengers murmur. To me, of course, this feels like home. . . .

More NOISE. The child is obviously upset and uncomfortable. At least that's obvious to me. The pressure in her ears is probably giving her excruciating pain. I am jarred from my internal reflection by a man's cold remark.

"Why can't she make her be quiet?" the passenger behind me complains loudly.

"Why the hell did she bring her on a plane," hisses the other. Passengers in the seats next to them chuckle.

It's all I can do not to turn around and shout, "Be glad that you aren't that uncomfortable. Be glad that you aren't that child's caretaker, having to dread taking a short, forty minute flight because of cutting remarks from jerks like you. Aren't you glad she isn't your child because if she was you couldn't just get off a plane and walk away from her!" But I stew in silence.

The plane is descending. We will touch ground soon. The people behind me will get off the plane and glide down to their baggage and their cars. Perhaps they will stop for a martini before they go home, with only themselves to worry about.

The mother in the rear of the plane will wait until everyone else is off, struggle down the rickety steps, carrying too many bags and trying to keep her grip on the tired, crotchety girl. A week from now the others will not even remember this flight or the girl who was making so much noise. I will not be able to forget her. (Gerlach, 1999, pp. 108–110)

Dealing with the Child's Feelings   In addition to dealing with the public's reactions to their child's disability, parents are faced with the delicate task of talking with their child about his or her disability. This can be a difficult responsibility because parents need to address the topic without making the disability seem more important than it actually is. In other words, parents do not want to alarm the child or make the child more concerned about the disability than is necessary.

Nevertheless, the child with a disability usually has questions about it: How did I get it? Will it go away? Will it get worse?

People with disabilities are inevitably faced with inappropriate reactions from those around them, and parents often must help their children respond to such behavior.

Will I be able to live independently as an adult? If possible, parents should wait for the child to ask specific questions to which they can respond, rather than lecturing about generalities. However, it is a good idea for parents to talk with the child at as early an age as possible, especially before the teenage years, when so many parents and children have problems communicating. Finally, most authorities recommend that parents be honest in their responses. Here is advice from an adult with cerebral palsy:

> Some parents have a tendency to hold back information, wanting to spare their son's or daughter's feelings. What they fail to realize is that, in the long term, being given correct information at an early age is very good for healthy development. And, if kids are informed, they can answer questions themselves, rather than depending on Mom or Dad to speak up for them. (Pierro, 1995, p. 92)

 THE FATHERS NETWORK is a website devoted to information for fathers of children with disabilities and special health needs: **www.fathersnetwork.org**

Parental Adjustment Evidence is abundant that parents of children with disabilities undergo more than the average amount of stress (Lessenberry & Rehfeldt, 2004). The stress is usually not the result of major catastrophic events but rather the consequence of daily responsibilities related to child care. A single event, such as a family member coming down with a serious illness, can precipitate a family crisis, but its effects will be even more devastating if the family was already under stress because of a multitude of daily hassles.

There is not a clear consensus on whether mothers and fathers of children with disabilities experience the same degree of stress. Earlier studies suggested that fathers are not under as much stress as mothers, but as fathers have assumed more child-care responsibilities than was once the case, there appears to be a trend toward fathers and mothers experiencing relatively equal amounts of stress (Dyson, 1997).

Parental Reaction to Stress There is no universal parental reaction to the added stress of raising a child with a disability. Although one would think that stress would be strongly related to the severity of the disability, there is little evidence to support this assumption. For example, parents of children with more severe disabilities might have greater child-care burdens, but parents of children with milder disabilities might be more likely to experience additional stress related to that felt by parents of children without disabilities (e.g., stress pertaining to school achievement, dating, driving a car).

Two factors that appear to be most predictive of how parents will cope with the stress are their prior psychological makeup and marital happiness and the quality and degree of informal support they receive from others. Although there are exceptions, it is fair to say that parents who were well adjusted and happily married before the birth of the child have a better chance of coping with the situation than do those who were having psychological or marital problems.

Social support that parents receive from each other, extended family members, friends, and others can be critical in helping them cope with the stress of raising a child with a disability (Duis, Summers, & Summers, 1997; Gavidia-Payne & Stoneman, 1997; Singer, 2002). The support can be physical, such as offering child care, or it can be psychological. Just having someone to talk to about problems can be helpful.

Changing Views of Parental Adjustment At one time, most professionals assumed that parents of children with disabilities were destined for a life of stress and misery. Whereas at one time it was popular to blame parents for their children's disabilities, it then became commonplace to go overboard in assuming that children with disabilities almost invariably caused parents to become dysfunctional or neurotic (Ferguson, 2002). In recent years, however, authorities have begun to find that many parents of children with disabilities end up adjusting quite well. In the early years of raising a child with a disability, some may experience high degrees of disruption and stress, but over time, many learn to cope (Seltzer, Greenberg, Floyd, Pettee, & Hong, 2001).

Some parents, in fact, report that adding a child with a disability to the family actually has some unanticipated positive results (Ferguson, 2002; Scorgie & Sobsey, 2000; Skinner,

Bailey, Correa, & Rodriguez, 1999). They report undergoing life-changing experiences, which include becoming:

- More tolerant of differences in other people
- More concerned about social issues
- Better parents
- A closer-knit family
- More philosophical or spiritual about life

Elizabeth King Gerlach's philosophical outlook on society's obsession with normalcy was undoubtedly shaped by her having a child with a disability:

Society views disability as a "tragedy." In fact, the greater tragedy is society's larger and erroneous view that there is such a state as "normal." . . .

"Normal" does exist, but you have to look for it. It is a place that is somewhere between the middle of two extremes. For instance, [a] good example of normal can be found on my clothes dryer, between "fluff," and "shrink it." This area is marked "normal." I use this setting because it is the closest to normal that my life usually gets.

The truth is, "normal" is not a word that should apply to the human condition. People are different, and they constantly change. A close approximation to "normal" might be "balanced." . . . And some of us endeavor to maintain a balanced state within ourselves, our families, and our communities. We have to discover what this means for ourselves, and this too changes over time.

I used to think there was such a thing as a "normal, happy family" and that it was something attainable. I hadn't experienced that as a child, so I set out to create it as an adult. Autism bombed that notion. Just as well. I'm not pretending that autism, in its varying degrees of severity, isn't painful in many ways for everyone

Some parents report that having a child with a disability in the family has unanticipated positive results, including greater tolerance of differences in other people, being better parents, and having a closer knit family.

involved. It is. I'm simply saying that some of that pain is relieved with understanding and acceptance. Having a child with a disability has shown me how precious life really is and that being human means learning to love. The simplicity and complexity of this understanding never cease to amaze me. (Gerlach, 1999, pp. 4–6)

This is not to minimize the fact that the added stress a child with a disability often brings can have a devastating impact on the stability of the family. It is dangerous to assume, though, that the birth of a child with a disability automatically spells doom for the psychological well-being of the parents or for the stability of their marriage.

SIBLING REACTIONS

Although a relatively large body of literature pertains to parental reactions, there is much less information about siblings of people with disabilities. What is available, however, indicates that siblings can and frequently do experience the same emotions—fear, anger, guilt, and so forth—that parents do. In fact, in some ways, siblings might have an even more difficult time than their parents in coping with some of these feelings, especially when they are younger. Being less mature, they might have trouble putting some of their negative thoughts into proper perspective. And they might be uncomfortable asking their parents the questions that bother them. Table 4.2 provides examples of sibling concerns.

Although some feelings about their siblings' disabilities might not appear for many years, a substantial number of accounts indicate that nondisabled siblings are aware at an early age that their brothers or sisters are different in some way. For example, in Personal Perspectives on page 115, Abigail Seaver recalls feeling the sting of prejudice toward her brother when she was only about 5 or 6 years old. Even though young children might have a vague sense that their siblings with disabilities are different, they might still have misconceptions about the nature of their siblings' conditions, especially regarding what caused them.

TABLE 4.2 Sibling Concerns About . . .

Their sibling with a disability	■ What caused the disability? ■ Why does my brother behave so strangely? ■ Will my sister ever live on her own?
Their parents	■ Why do they let my brother get away with so much? ■ Why must all their time be given to my sister? ■ Why do they always ask me to babysit?
Themselves	■ Why do I have such mixed feelings about my sister? ■ Will I catch the disability? ■ Will we have a normal brother–sister relationship?
Their friends	■ How can I tell my best friend about my brother? ■ Will my friends tell everyone at school? ■ What should I do when other kids make fun of people with disabilities?
Their school and community	■ What happens in special education classes? ■ Will I be compared with my sister? ■ What should I tell strangers?
Adulthood	■ Will I be responsible for my brother when my parents die? ■ Do I need genetic counseling? ■ Should I join a parents' and/or siblings' group?

Source: Adapted from *Brothers & sisters—A special part of exceptional families* (2nd ed.), by T. H. Powell & P. A. Gallagher, 1993, Baltimore, MD: Paul H. Brookes (P.O. Box 10624, Baltimore, MD 21285–0624). Reprinted by permission.

Personal Perspectives

FIGHTING PREJUDICE

My older brother, Justin, 19, was born with Down syndrome. When he was young, he learned a little more slowly than others, but he could do a lot of things. When he was 2, he had a blood clot in his brain and had a stroke. After that he needed to use a walker, and he couldn't talk. The clot killed the left side of his brain. Now he can only make noises because he uses a trache to breathe. When he got older, his legs got worse, and he needed a wheelchair to get around. I remember something else that happened to Justin a few years ago. He experienced prejudice.

One day, when I was about 5 or 6, my mom and dad took Justin, my friend, Tony, and me to McDonald's. After we ate we went to the restaurant playroom. As we played, there was a group of boys that began to laugh at Justin. They were calling him a pig, a loser, an idiot, retarded, and stupid. Justin didn't know they were being mean to him so he laughed right along.

I was dumbstruck. I didn't know what to do. I wanted to yell at them and tell them they didn't know him—that they should be quiet. When we left the restaurant, I told my mom and she told me about prejudice. That day I learned that people should

Abigail, 10, and Justin live with their parents, Cynthia and David, in Wallingford, CT. Abigail attends Rock Hill School and Justin works at a local Wal-Mart.

try to get to know other people before they make fun of them. After that, I was always protective of my brother.

To this day, Justin still doesn't know if people are making fun of him. If I saw anyone doing that to him again, I would go up to them and tell them that if they knew him and knew what a great friend he is, they wouldn't make fun of him. Then I'd ask if they would like to meet him.

What happened to my brother was very mean, and it still makes me feel like crying when I think about it. Prejudice is so cruel. Nobody makes fun of him anymore: my friends have gotten to know him and they like him, and some of them are even learning to sign so they can talk with him. Next time you think of making fun of someone different, think about my brother Justin. ∎

Source: Abigail Seaver. (2001). Fighting prejudice. *Exceptional Parent, 31(4),* 116. Reprinted with the expressed consent and approval of *Exceptional Parent*, a monthly magazine for parents and families of children with disabilities and special health care needs. Subscription cost is $39.95 per year for 12 issues; call (877) 372-7368. Offices at 65 E. Rte. 4, River Edge, N.J. 07661.

As nondisabled siblings grow older, their concerns often become more focused on how society views them and their siblings who are disabled. Adolescence can be a particularly difficult period. Teens, fearing rejection by peers, often do not want to appear different, and having a sibling with a disability can single a person out.

Siblings' Adjustment   Children, like parents, can adapt well or poorly to having family members with disabilities. Research indicates that some siblings have trouble adjusting, some have no trouble adjusting, and some actually appear to benefit from the experience. Like parents, however, siblings of children with disabilities are at a greater risk than siblings of nondisabled children to have difficulties in adjustment.

Why some individuals respond negatively whereas others do not is not completely understood. Although not definitive, there is some evidence that birth order, gender, and age differences between siblings have some bearing on adjustment (Berry & Hardman, 1998). A nondisabled sister who is older than her sibling who has a disability, for example, might have a negative attitude when she reaches adolescence because she often has to shoulder child-care responsibilities (Burke, 2004).

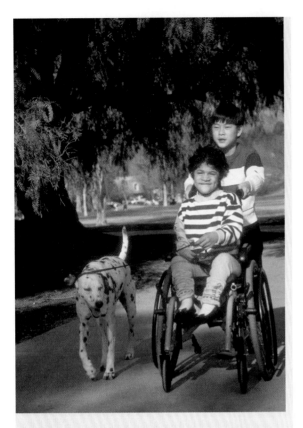

Siblings of children with disabilities often recount being aware at a very early age that something was different about their brothers or sisters. Siblings' attitudes change at different stages of their own lives; for example, adolescents become more concerned about public peception of themselves and their siblings with disabilities.

Sibshops
Workshops for siblings of children with disabilities; designed to help siblings answer questions about the disability and learn to adjust to having a sister or brother with a disability.

Family-centered model
A consumer-driven model that encourages the family to make its own decisions with respect to services while mobilizing resources and supports for the family's goals.

Siblings of the same gender and siblings who are close in age are more likely to experience conflicts. At older ages, however, when siblings are adults, there is evidence that women show more favorable attachments than men do to their sibling with a disability, and adults who are of the same gender as their sibling with a disability experience more favorable emotional responses (Orsmond & Seltzer, 2000).

Access to information is one key to adjustment for siblings of children with disabilities. As is noted in Table 4.2, siblings have myriad questions pertaining to their sibling's disability. Straight-forward answers to these questions can help them to cope with their fears.

Teachers, as well as parents, can provide answers to some of these questions. Teachers, for example, can talk with students about the materials and contents of programs for their siblings with disabilities (Powell & Gallagher, 1993). Another excellent resource for providing information and support to siblings is sib-shops (Meyer & Vadasy, 1994). **Sibshops** are workshops that are specifically designed to help siblings of children with disabilities.

Family Involvement in Treatment and Education

As was noted earlier, today's professionals are more likely to recognize the positive influence parents can have on their exceptional children's development. This more positive attitude toward parents is reflected in how parents are now involved in the treatment and education of their children.

At one time, most early intervention programs for families who had children with disabilities operated according to the philosophy that the professionals had the expertise and that the families needed that expertise to function. Most authorities today, however, advocate a **family-centered model** (Blue-Banning, Summers, Frankland, Nelson, & Beegle, 2004; Dunst, 2002; Kraus, Maxwell, & McWilliam, 2001). According to these authorities, a family-centered model is a consumer-driven model that encourages the family to make its own decisions with respect to services while mobilizing resources and supports for the family's goals. Another way of describing the family-centered approach is to say that it is a model in which the professionals work for the family.

The use of family-centered models reflects a change from viewing parents as passive recipients of professional advice to viewing them as equal partners in the development of treatment and educational programs for their children. The notion is that when professionals do not just provide direct services but also encourage the family to help themselves and their children, the family takes more control over their own lives and avoids the dependency that is sometimes associated with typical professional–family relationships.

Achieving the right balance between offering assistance and allowing families to make independent decisions can be challenging. For example, interviews with parents have resulted in the following recommendations:

- Be direct—but don't tell us what to do.
- Tell the truth and be honest—but also be hopeful and encouraging.
- Be knowledgeable—but admit when you don't know the answer.
- Don't overwhelm—but don't hold back information. (Meadow-Orlans, Mertens, & Sass-Lehrer, 2003)

Table 4.3 lists several tips for teachers that are consistent with a family-centered approach.

The effort to build professional–parent partnerships is consistent with the thinking of child development theorists who stress the importance of the social context within which child development occurs. Urie Bronfenbrenner (1979, 1995), a renowned child development and family theorist, has been most influential in stressing that an individual's behavior cannot be understood without understanding the influence of the family on that behavior. Furthermore, the behavior of the family cannot be understood without considering the influence of other social systems (e.g., the extended family, friends, and professionals) on the behavior of the family. The interaction between the family and the surrounding social system is critical to how the family functions. A supportive network of professionals (and especially friends) can be beneficial to the family with a child who has a disability.

Casebook Reflections

Refer to the case *The Reluctant Collaborator* in your booklet. There is no mention of Peter's parents in this case. How might this information be relevant in deciding what to do on his behalf?

FAMILY SYSTEMS THEORY

The emphasis on the individual's behavior being understood in the context of the family and the family's behavior being understood in the context of other social systems is the basic principle underlying **family systems theory** (Lambie, 2000). There are several family system theories, all of which assume that the more treatment and educational programs

Family systems theory
Stresses that the individual's behavior is best understood in the context of the family and the family's behavior is best understood in the context of other social systems.

TABLE 4.3 Suggestions for Teachers to Involve Families in Class and School Activities

- Empathize with students and family members to understand what they may be experiencing and act according to their needs instead of personal needs.

- Value individual families, cultures, and their uniqueness instead of trying to categorize and stereotype families.

- Take time each morning to speak with students. Communicate regularly with family members.

- Allow options when communicating with families. Use a variety of contacts, including phone, face to face, notebook, or home visits. Determine the school professional with whom the family members may feel most comfortable.

- Communicate with both households when there is a joint custody arrangement. Don't assume that the information from school is reaching both parents.

- Be considerate of home arrangement facts when assigning homework. There might be no one at home to help with projects or difficult assignments that would need adult supervision.

- Plan alternative conference times in addition to school hour conferences. Think convenience for the families instead of teachers only. Hold conferences frequently. Avoid talking over or under the parents' heads: Avoid educational jargon.

- Make every conference meaningful and productive. Include the student in some of the conferences. Begin and end every conference, conversation, meeting, with a positive fact or work sample.

- Invite families into the classroom as much as possible. Value any and all contributions or suggestions family members make. Use lessons to incorporate family customs, rituals, and traditions.

- Value the diversity of all students and their family compositions. Even though a family composition might seem unstructured or confusing, there are lessons and a contribution they can make to the class. Set up programs that benefit all students and all types of households.

Source: Adapted from O'Shea, D. J., & Riley, J. E. (2001). Typical families: Fact or fiction? In D. J. O'Shea, L. J. O'Shea, R. Algozzine, D. J. Hammitte (Eds.), *Families and teachers of individuals with disabilities: Collaborative orientations and responsive practices* (pp. 25–50). Austin: Pro-Ed, Inc. Copyright © 2001. Adapted by permission of Pro-Ed, Inc.

UNDERSTANDING THE STANDARDS AND PRINCIPLES Why is it important to involve families? *(CEC Knowledge and Skills Standards CC10K2, CC10K3, CC10S2, CC10S3, & CC10S4)*

Council for Exceptional Children

take into account the relationships and interactions among family members, the more likely it is they will be successful. One model that has been developed specifically with people with disabilities in mind is that of the Turnbulls. Their model includes four interrelated components: family characteristics, family interaction, family functions, and family life cycle (Turnbull & Turnbull, 2001).

Family Characteristics   **Family characteristics** provide a description of basic information related to the family. They include characteristics of the exceptionality (e.g., the type and severity), characteristics of the family (e.g., size, cultural background, and socioeconomic status), personal characteristics (e.g., coping styles), and special conditions (e.g., spousal abuse, maternal depression). Family characteristics help to determine how family members interact with themselves and with others outside the family. For example, it could make a difference whether the child is mentally retarded or hearing impaired, is an only child or has five siblings, is of the upper middle class or lives in poverty, and so forth.

Recent trends in U.S. society make it even more important to take into account family characteristics. In particular, teachers should be attentive to the expanding ethnic diversity in the United States. (See the Focus on Concepts on p. 119 for suggestions on facilitating involvement of culturally and linguistically diverse families in the education of their children.) In addition to wider diversity with regard to ethnicity, there are also increases in the numbers of families in which both parents work outside the home, single-parent families, same-sex unions, and families who are living in poverty.

Coupled with these demographic changes—and to a certain extent influenced by them—families today live under a great deal more stress than they did in previous decades. Adding to this stress is the threat of terrorism subsequent to the attacks on the World Trade Center and the Pentagon on September 11, 2001. On the one hand, children need attention and reassurance more than ever; but on the other hand, because of pressures to earn a living, parents have fewer resources to draw on to provide comfort to their children.

These dramatic societal changes present formidable challenges in working with families of children with disabilities. As the family configurations change, professionals need to alter their approaches. For example, the same approaches that are successful with two-parent families might not be suitable for single mothers. Also, professionals need to understand that today's parent is living under more and more stress and might find it increasingly difficult to devote time and energy to working on behalf of his or her child.

Family Interaction   Family members can have a variety of functional and dysfunctional ways of relating to one another. Some authorities point to the degree of responsiveness of the parent to the child as key to healthy child development (Mahoney, Boyce, Fewell, Spiker, & Wheeden, 1998). The more the parent responds appropriately to the young child's body language, gestures, facial expressions, and so forth, the more the child's development will flourish.

In the Turnbulls' model, **family interactions** point to family cohesion and adaptability as important determinants of how family members interact with each other. In general, families are healthier if they have moderate degrees of cohesion and adaptability.

Cohesion   *Cohesion* refers to the degree to which an individual family member is free to act independently of other family members. An appropriate amount of family cohesion permits the individual to be his or her own person while at the same time drawing on other family members for support as needed. Families with low cohesion might not offer the child with a disability the necessary support, whereas the overly cohesive family might be overprotective.

It is often difficult for otherwise healthy families to find the right balance of cohesion. They sometimes go overboard in wanting to help their children and, in so doing, limit their children's independence. A particularly stressful time can be adolescence, when it is normal for teenagers to loosen their familial bonds. What makes the situation difficult for many families of children with disabilities is that because of her or his disability, the child has

---

Family characteristics
A component of the Turnbulls' family systems model; includes type and severity of the disability as well as such things as size, cultural background, and socioeconomic background of the family.

FIESTA EDUCATIVA is a project focused on providing information for Spanish speaking families that have a child with a disability: **www.fiestaeducativa.org**

Family interaction
A component of the Turnbulls' family systems model; refers to how cohesive and adaptable the family is.

FOCUS ON CONCEPTS

Facilitating Involvement of Culturally and/or Linguistically Diverse Families

THE increasing ethnic diversity of schools has resulted in a wider mismatch between the ethnicity of teachers and students, especially students in special education. (See Chapter 3.) One of the things that many special education teachers, who are often white, have difficulty with is knowing how to involve families from a different culture. Here are several suggestions based on the work of Howard Parette and Beverly Petch-Hogan (2000), two professors at Southeast Missouri State University.

CONTACTS WITH FAMILIES

- *Problem:* Families from culturally and/or linguistically diverse backgrounds often defer to professionals as the "experts." *Possible solution:* Do not assume that school personnel should always take the lead in providing information or contacting families.
- *Problem:* Some families mistrust school personnel. *Possible solutions:* Identify trusted people in the community (e.g., a minister, physician, retired teacher) to contact the family; establish a Family Advisory Council where parents can present issues; make use of interpreters in the case of parents who are English language learners.

LOCATION OF MEETINGS

- *Problem:* Meetings typically take place in a school building, which can present problems for parents without transportation and may be perceived as aversive or intimidating. *Possible solutions:* Provide transportation, or hold the meeting at a neutral site, e.g., neighborhood church or community center.

SUPPORTS DURING THE MEETING

- *Problem:* Child care for families can make it difficult to attend a meeting. *Possible solution:* Provide child care.

PROVISION OF INFORMATION/TRAINING

- *Problem:* Professionals often deliver information to families via lectures and printed materials. *Potential solution:* Consider that culturally and linguistically diverse families are often more comfortable obtaining information in less formal settings, such as parent support groups.
- *Problem:* Typically, parents alone are the targets of information and training. *Potential solution:* Consider involving siblings or extended family members because they often assume significant responsibility for childcare.

KNOWLEDGE OF FAMILY PRIORITIES, NEEDS, RESOURCES

- *Problem:* Some families may find the implementation of intervention programs results in too much stress for the family. *Potential solution:* Be sensitive to families' desire not to get involved too deeply in intervention efforts.
- *Problem:* Some families do not view time in the same way as many professionals do. *Potential solution:* Be flexible in scheduling meeting times and consider video-or audio-taping parts of meetings missed by families. ■

Source: Parette, H. P., & Petch-Hogan, B. (2000). Approaching families: Facilitating culturally/linguistically diverse family involvement. *Teaching Exceptional Children*, 33(2), 4–10. Reprinted by permission.

---

often by necessity been more protected. In fact, there is research to suggest that in the early years, the more supportive the parent is with the child, the better. For example, in one study mothers of toddlers with Down syndrome who during play engaged in more helpful behaviors, such as steadying objects and otherwise making it more likely that the children would experience success, had children who were more likely to play and vocalize (Roach, Barratt, Miller, & Leavitt, 1998).

Cohesion can also be an issue for adults with disabilities. Current thinking dictates that people with disabilities should live in the community, but many will also need support from their families to do this successfully. They will need a number of daily living skills, such as managing personal finances, keeping to a work schedule, and planning and

Adults with mental retardation, especially those who live at home, often have special problems finding the right degree of independence from their families. When they do live away from home, parents are often concerned about providing enough support so their children don't become socially isolated.

preparing meals, that do not always come easily even to nondisabled young adults. Finding the right degree of independence from the family for young adults with disabilities can be a significant challenge. As one mother who was interviewed about future living arrangements for her daughter, who is severely mentally retarded, explained:

> I would like to see her live fairly close. . . . She's going to have to have some support, I know that. . . . And I would like to see her close enough so that we always have the constant, not constant, [sic] but we will always be there if she needs us. And both Tim and I agree that that's something we will always do. We will be here. But, on the other hand, if we want to go away for a month, we'll know there are other people that can be called upon to give her the support she needs. (Lehmann & Baker, 1995, p. 30)

Adaptability *Adaptability* refers to the degree to which families are able to change their modes of interaction when they encounter unusual or stressful situations. Some families are so chaotic that it is difficult to predict what any one member will do in a given situation. In such an unstable environment, the needs of the family member who is disabled might be overlooked or neglected. At the other end of the continuum are families that are characterized by extreme rigidity. Each family member has his or her prescribed family role. Such rigidity makes it difficult to adjust to the addition of a new family member, especially one with a disability. For example, the mother's involvement in transporting the child with a disability to therapy sessions might necessitate that the father be more involved taking care of the other children.

Family Functions   **Family functions** are the numerous routines in which families engage to meet their many and diverse needs. Economic, daily care, social, medical, and educational needs are just a few examples.

An important point for teachers to consider is that education is only one of several functions in which families are immersed. For some students, especially those with multiple disabilities, several professionals might be vying for the parents' time. It is only natural, of course, that teachers should want to involve parents as much as possible. Positive benefits can occur when parents are part of the treatment program. At the same time, however, they need to respect the fact that education is just one of the many functions to which families must attend.

Several authorities have reported that many families of students with disabilities prefer a passive, rather than an active, degree of involvement in their children's education (Turnbull & Turnbull, 2000). There are often legitimate reasons for playing a more passive role. For example, in their culture, it might be customary for parents to refrain from interfering with the roles of school personnel in educational matters. Furthermore, some parents might simply be so busy attending to other family functions that they are forced to delegate most of the educational decisions to teachers. Teachers should respect the parents' desire to play a relatively passive role in their child's education.

Family Life Cycle   Several family theorists have noted that the impact of a child with a disability on the family changes over time (Berry & Hardman, 1998; O'Shea, O'Shea, Algozzine, & Hammitte, 2001). For this reason, some have pointed to the value of looking at families with children with a disability from a **family life cycle** perspective. Most family

Family functions
A component of the Turnbulls' family systems model; includes such things as economic, daily care, social, medical, and educational needs.

Family life cycle
A component of the Turnbulls' family systems model; consists of birth and early childhood, childhood, adolescence, and adulthood

theorists consider four stages in the lives of families: early childhood, childhood, adolescence, and adulthood.

Transitions between stages in the life cycle are often stressful for families, especially families with children who are disabled. We have already mentioned the difficulties facing families at the transition point when their child, as an adult, moves into more independent work and living settings. A particularly difficult issue for some parents of children with disabilities who are entering adulthood is that of mental competence and guardianship. Parents who decide that their children are not competent to make rational choices without endangering themselves can go through legal channels to obtain guardianship of their children. **Guardianship** means that one person has the authority, granted by the courts, to make decisions for another person. Guardianship can range in degree from total to more limited or temporary authority to make decisions.

Another particularly troublesome transition can be from the relatively intimate confines of an infant or preschool program to the larger context of a kindergarten setting, which requires more independence on the part of the child. As one parent relates:

> As my daughter's third birthday approached, I lived in dread. . . . The infant program had become home away from home for me. It was supportive and intimate. I had made some lifelong friendships, as well as having established a comfortable routine in our lives. I saw making the transition to a preschool program in the school district as an extremely traumatic experience, second only to learning of Amy's diagnosis. . . .
>
> First, I was concerned that my husband and I, along with professionals, would be deciding the future of our child. How could we play God? Would our decisions be the right ones? Second, I feared loss of control, as I would be surrendering my child to strangers—first to the school district's intake assessment team and then to the preschool teacher. The feeling of being at the mercy of professionals was overwhelming. In addition, I had more information to absorb and a new system with which to become familiar. . . . (Hanline & Knowlton, 1988, p. 116)

Transitions between stages are difficult because of the uncertainty that each new phase presents to the family. One of the reasons for the uncertainty pertains to replacements of the professionals who work with the child who is disabled. In particular, parents of a child with multiple disabilities, who requires services from multiple professionals, can be anxious about the switches in therapists and teachers that occur many times throughout the child's life, especially at transition points.

Guardianship
A legal term that gives a person the authority to make decisions for another person; can be full, limited, or temporary; applies in cases of parents who have children who have severe cognitive disabilities.

Social support
Emotional, informational, or material aid provided to a person or a family; this informal means of aid can be very valuable in helping families of children with disabilities.

SOCIAL SUPPORT FOR FAMILIES

Authorities now recognize that families can derive tremendous benefit from social support provided by others (Singer, 2002). **Social support** refers to emotional, informational, or material aid that is provided to persons in need. In contrast to assistance that comes from professionals and agencies, social support is informal, coming from such sources as extended family, friends, church groups, neighbors, and social clubs.

Ethnicity and Social Support   Interestingly, there is evidence in ethnic minority families of familial and religious support (Harry, 2002). The values of some minority groups place heavy emphasis on caring for one's own family members, disabled or not. And the family's church plays a major social support role for many minorities, again regardless of whether they are disabled or not. In addition, research suggests that ethnic minority parents

A particularly difficult issue for some parents of children with disabilities who are entering adulthood is that of mental competence and guardianship.

tend to be more accepting of their children with disabilities than European American parents are—and less stressed.

Parental Support Groups   One common type of social support, especially for parents of recently diagnosed children, is parental support groups that consist of parents of children with the same or similar disabilities. Such groups can be relatively unstructured, meeting infrequently with unspecified agendas, or they can be more structured. They serve as a means for parents to share their experiences, thus providing educational and emotional support. Parental support groups, however, are not of benefit to everyone. Some parents actually experience more stress from sharing problems and listening to the problems of others (Berry & Hardman, 1998).

Internet Resources for Parents   The Internet is an excellent resource for parents of children with disabilities. Dozens of electronic mailing lists, newsgroups, and World Wide Web sites are now devoted to disability-related topics. Through mailing lists, newsgroups, and web boards, parents of children with disabilities can communicate with each other, with people who have disabilities, and with professionals concerning practical as well as theoretical issues. There are lists and newsgroups for specific disabilities (e.g., Down syndrome, attention deficit/hyperactivity disorder, cerebral palsy, cystic fibrosis) as well as more general ones.

POSITIVE BEHAVIORAL SUPPORT FOR CHALLENGING BEHAVIORS

Some children with disabilities engage in behaviors that are particularly challenging for professionals and family members alike. Children with emotional or behavioral disorders and those with autism, for example, sometimes exhibit outbursts of aggressive or self-injurious behavior. As one team of researchers documented, such behaviors can have a profound impact on the family:

> The families we interviewed described a family life that was deeply and pervasively affected. . . . The entire family system was engaged in multiple accommodations

Positive behavior support (PBS) for families might include mealtimes, seasonal celebrations, visits to relatives, etc. as opportunities for reinforcing positive or appropriate behavior.

in response to the child's problem behavior. . . . These families were changed as a result of the persistent and overwhelming demands of physically intervening with their child or worrying about their child's problem behavior. As researchers, we found it difficult to construct the prose that would adequately convey the emotional, physical, and structural impact of problem behavior on family life. Problem behavior relentlessly affected family relationships, physical circumstances, social networks, and daily activities. (Fox, Vaughn, Wyatte, & Dunlap, 2002, p. 448)

Such extreme behaviors often require more than just social support from friends and the community. In such cases, authorities recommend that social support be integrated with positive behavioral supports (Singer, Goldberg-Hamblin, Peckham-Hardin, Barry, & Santarelli, 2002). In Chapter 2, we introduced the practice of **positive behavioral supports (PBS)**, the use of positive reinforcement procedures for appropriate behavior.

To apply PBS with families, authorities recommend focusing on **family activity settings**, routines that families engage in, such as mealtimes, seasonal celebrations, visits to relatives, shopping, going on vacations, and eating in restaurants (Lucyshyn, Horner, Dunlap, Albin, & Ben, 2002; Singer et al., 2002). The frequency and importance of such activities for families make them a logical place to use PBS. Under the guidance of professionals, families typically begin by concentrating on just one or two settings before expanding to more.

COMMUNICATION BETWEEN PARENTS AND PROFESSIONALS

Virtually all family theorists agree that no matter what particular approach one uses to work with parents, the key to the success of a program is how well parents and professionals are able to work together. Even the most creative, well-conceived model is doomed to fail if professionals and parents are unable to communicate effectively.

Unfortunately, such communication does not come easily. This is not too surprising, considering the ingredients of the situation. On the one hand, there are the parents, who are trying to cope with the stresses of raising a child with a disability in a complex and changing society. On the other hand, there are the professionals—teachers, speech therapists, physicians, psychologists, physical therapists, and so forth—who might be frustrated because they do not have all the answers to the child's problems.

One of the keys to avoiding professional–parent misunderstandings is communication. It is critical that teachers receive information from parents as well as providing information to them. Given that the parents have spent considerably more time with the child and have more invested in the child emotionally, they can be an invaluable source of information about the child's characteristics and interests. And by keeping parents informed of what is going on in class, teachers can foster a relationship in which they can call on parents for support should the need arise.

One area in particular that requires the cooperation of parents is homework. For mainstreamed students who are disabled, homework is often a source of misunderstanding and conflict. The Focus on Concepts on p. 124 offers some strategies for enhancing the homework experience for students with disabilities.

Most authorities agree that the communication between the teacher and parents should start taking place as soon as possible and that it should not be initiated only by negative behavior on the part of the student. Parents, especially those of students with behavior disorders, often complain that the only time they hear from school personnel is when their child has misbehaved (Hallahan & Martinez, 2002). To establish a degree of rapport with parents, some teachers make a practice of sending home a brief form letter at the beginning of the school year, outlining the goals

Positive behavior supports (PBS) Positive reinforcement (rewarding) procedures that are intended to support a student's appropriate or desirable behavior.

Family activity settings Activities that families routinely engage in, such as mealtimes and seasonal celebrations; can be focal points for the implementation of PBSs.

UNDERSTANDING THE STANDARDS AND PRINCIPLES How can teachers better communicate with families? *(CEC Knowledge and Skills Standards CC7S2 & CC7S3)*

Council for Exceptional Children

Casebook Reflections

Refer to the case *Least Restrictive for Whom?* in your booklet. At the first meeting with Brian's parents, they were angry when Mary suggested that they consider placement in a residential institution for the deaf. How might Mary have communicated with Brian's parents so that this meeting would have been more cordial and constructive? What do you think the parents thought Mary was communicating about them as parents?

FOCUS ON CONCEPTS

Homework: Tips for Teachers and Administrators

GIVE CLEAR AND APPROPRIATE ASSIGNMENTS

If the homework is too hard, is perceived as busy work, or takes too long to complete, students might tune out and resist doing it. Never send home any assignment that students cannot do. Homework should be an extension of what students have learned in class.

- Make sure students and parents have information regarding the policy on missed and late assignments, extra credit, and available adaptations. . . .
- Remind the students of due dates periodically.
- Coordinate with other teachers to prevent homework overload.
- Establish a routine at the beginning of the year for how homework will be assigned.
- Assign homework at the beginning of class. . . .
- Explain how to do the homework, provide examples, and write directions on the chalkboard.
- Have students begin the homework in class, check that they understand, and provide assistance as necessary.

MAKE HOMEWORK ACCOMMODATIONS

- Provide additional one-on-one assistance to students. . . .
- Allow alternative response formats (e.g., allow the student to audiotape an assignment).
- Adjust the length of the assignment.
- Provide a peer tutor or assign the student to a study group.
- Provide learning tools (e.g., calculators).
- Adjust evaluation standards.
- Give fewer assignments. . . .

ENSURE CLEAR HOME–SCHOOL COMMUNICATION

Recommended ways in which teachers can improve communications with parents include

- Providing a list of suggestions on how parents might assist with homework. For example, ask parents to check with their children about homework daily.
- Providing parents with frequent written communication about homework.

Ways in which administrators can support teachers in improving communication include

- Supplying teachers with the technology needed to aid communication (e.g., telephone answering systems, email, homework hotlines).
- Providing incentives for teachers to participate in face-to-face meetings with parents (e.g., release time, compensation).
- Suggesting that the school district offer after school and/or peer tutoring sessions to give students extra help with homework.

RESOURCES

Bryan, Nelson, & Mathur (1995); Bryan & Sullivan-Burstein (1997); Epstein, Munk, Bursuck, Polloway, & Jayanthi (1999); Jayanthi, Bursuck, Epstein, & Polloway (1997); Jayanthi, Sawyer, Nelson, Bursuck, & Epstein (1995); Klinger & Vaughn (1999); Polloway, Bursuck, Jayanthi, Epstein, & Nelson (1996)

Source: Adapted from Warger, C. (2001, March). Five homework strategies for teaching students with disabilities. ERIC Clearinghouse on Disabilities and Gifted Education. Retrieved October 20, 2001 from the World Wide Web: www.ericec.org/digests/e608.html. Reprinted by permission.

---

for the year. Others send home periodic newsletters or make occasional phone calls to parents. By establishing a line of communication with parents early in the year, the teacher is in a better position to initiate more intensive and focused discussions should the need arise. Three such methods of communication are parent–teacher conferences, home-note programs, and traveling notebooks.

Parent–Teacher Conferences Parent–teacher conferences can be an effective way for teachers to share information with parents. Likewise, they are an opportunity for teachers to learn more about the students from the parents' perspective. In addition to regularly scheduled meetings open to all parents, teachers might want to hold individual conferences with the parents of particular students. A key to conducting successful parent–teacher conferences is planning. How the teacher initiates the meeting, for example, can be crucial.

Some recommend that the first contact be a telephone call that proposes the need for the meeting, without going into great detail, followed by a letter reminding the parents of the time and place of the meeting (Hallahan & Martinez, 2002). Table 4.4 presents some suggestions for effective parent–teacher conferences.

If the focus of the meeting is the student's poor work or misbehavior, the teacher will need to be as diplomatic as possible. Most authorities recommend that the teacher find something positive to say about the student while still providing an objective account of what the student is doing that is troubling. The teacher needs to achieve a delicate balance of providing an objective account of the student's transgressions or poor work while demonstrating advocacy for the student. If parents detect that the teacher is angry, this can make them apprehensive about the treatment the child might be receiving. Conveying only good news can also lose the parents' sense of trust. If the parents only hear good news, then they will be taken by surprise if a serious incident does occur.

Home-Note Programs   Sometimes referred to as *home-contingency programs*, **home-note programs** are a way of communicating with parents and having them reinforce behavior that occurs at school (Cottone, 1998; Kelley, 1990; Kelley & McCain, 1995; McCain & Kelley, 1993). By having parents dispense the reinforcement, the teacher takes advantage of the

UNDERSTANDING THE STANDARDS AND PRINCIPLES   How can teachers learn more about parents' perspectives? *(CEC Knowledge and Skills Standard CC10S5)*

Council for Exceptional Children

Home-note program. A system of communication between the teacher and parents; the teacher evaluates the behavior of the student using a simple form, the student takes the form home, gets the parents' signatures, and returns the form the next day.

TABLE 4.4   Guidelines for Parent–Teacher Meetings and Conferences

Lay the Foundation

- Review the student's cumulative records.
- Familiarize yourself with the student and family's culture.
- Consult with other professionals about the student.
- Establish rapport with the parents and keep them informed.
- Collect information to document the student's academic progress and behavior.
- Share positive comments about the student with parents.
- Invite the parents to observe or volunteer in your classroom.

Before the Meeting

- Discuss the goals of the meeting with the parents and solicit their input.
- Involve the student, as appropriate.
- Schedule a mutually convenient day and time for the meeting.
- Provide written notice prior to the meeting.

During the Meeting

- Welcome the parents and speak informally with them before beginning.
- Reiterate the goals of the meeting.
- Begin with a discussion of the student's strengths.
- Support your points with specific examples and documentation.
- Encourage the parents to ask questions.
- Encourage parents to share insights.
- Ask open-ended questions.
- Avoid jargon.
- Practice active listening (e.g., show interest, paraphrase comments, avoid making judgments, etc.).
- Review the main points of the meeting and determine a course of action.
- Provide additional resources (e.g., support groups, family resource centers, websites).

After the Meeting

- Document the results of the meeting.
- Share results with colleagues who work with the student.
- Follow up with the parents as needed to discuss changes.

Source: Hallahan, D. P., & Martinez, E. A. (2002). Working with families. From James M. Kauffman, Mark P. Mostert, Stanley C. Trent, & Daniel P. Hallahan (Eds.), *Managing classroom behavior: A reflective case-based approach* (3rd ed., pp. 124–140). Published by Allyn and Bacon, Boston, MA. Copyright © 2002 by Pearson Education. Reprinted by permission of the publisher.

Sara,   9/15

We witnessed an apparently significant moment in her oral communication: She'll try to say "all done" after a meal. The execution is imperfect, to say the least, but she gets an "A" for effort. Could you please reinforce this after snack? Just ask her, "What do you say after you finish your snack?"

Thanks,
Lynn

9/28

Lauren had an esp. good day! She was jabbering a lot! Being very expressive with her vocalness & jabbering. I know she said "yes," or an approximate thereof, several times when asked if she wanted something. She was so cute with the animal sounds esp. pig & horse – she was really trying to make the sounds. It was the first time we had seen such a response. Still cruising a lot! She walked with me around the room & in the gym. She used those consonant and vowel sounds: dadada, mamama – her jabbering was just so different & definitely progressive.

Sara

9/29

I want to bring in some different spoons next week to see if she can become more independent in scooping with a large handle spoon or a spoon that is covered.

Joan

Joan —   10/1

Although Lauren would very much approve of your idea for making her more independent during feeding, we'd rather not initiate self-feeding with an adaptive spoon at this time. Here's why:

1. When I feed Lauren or get her to grip a spoon and then guide her hand, I can slip the entire bowl of the spoon into her mouth and get her to close her lips on it. When Lauren uses a spoon without help, she turns it upside-down to lick it or inserts just the tip of it into her mouth and then sucks off the food…

2. Lauren has always been encouraged to do things "normally." She never had a special cup or a "Tommy Tippee," for instance. Of course it took a year of practice before she could drink well from a cup, and she still dribbles a little occasionally; but she's doing well now. We really prefer to give Lauren practice in using a regular spoon so that she doesn't get dependent on an adaptive utensil.

Lynn

2/26

Good news! Lauren walked all the way from the room to the gym & back – She also walked up & down the full length of the gym!

Several other teachers saw her and were thrilled. She fell maybe twice! But picked herself right up —

Sara

3/2

Lauren had a great speech session! We were playing with some toys and she said "I want help" as plain as day. Later she said "I want crackers" and at the end of the session, she imitated "Cindy, let's go." Super!

Marti

FIGURE 4.1   A traveling notebook. These short excerpts are taken at random from a notebook that accompanies 2-year-old Lauren, who has cerebral palsy, back and forth to her special class for preschoolers. The notebook provides a convenient mode for an ongoing dialogue among her mother, Lynn; her teacher, Sara; her occupational therapist, Joan; and her speech therapist, Marti. As you can see from this representative sample, the communication is informal but very informative in a variety of items relating to Lauren.

fact that parents usually have a greater number of reinforcers at their disposal than do teachers.

There are a number of different types of home notes. A typical one consists of a simple form on which the teacher records "yes," "no," or "not applicable" to certain categories of behavior (e.g., social behavior, homework completed, homework accurate, in-class academic work completed, in-class academic work accurate). The form also may contain space for the teacher and the parents to write a few brief comments. The student takes the form home, has his or her parents sign it, and returns it the next day. The parents deliver reinforcement for the student's performance. The teacher often starts out sending a note home each day and gradually decreases the frequency until the notes are being sent once a week.

Although home-note programs have a great deal of potential, researchers have pointed out that they require close communication between the teacher and parents (Cottone, 1998). Additionally, both teachers and parents need to agree philosophically with a behavioral approach to managing student behavior. If either is opposed to using reinforcement as a means of shaping behavior, the home-note program is unlikely to succeed.

Traveling Notebooks   Less formal than home notes and particularly appropriate for students who see multiple professionals are traveling notebooks. A **traveling notebook** goes back and forth between school and home. The teacher and other professionals, such as speech and physical therapists, can write brief messages to the parents and vice versa. In addition, a traveling notebook allows the different professionals to keep up with what each is doing with the student. See Figure 4.1 for excerpts from a traveling notebook of a 2-year-old with cerebral palsy.

PARENT ADVOCACY

Another important way that parents and other family members can become involved in treatment and education is through advocacy. **Advocacy** is action that results in benefit to one or more persons (Alper, Schloss, & Schloss, 1996). Advocacy can be a way of getting needed or improved services for children while helping parents gain a sense of control over outcomes for their children. Although sometimes associated with the notion of confrontations between parents and professionals, advocacy need not be adversarial. In fact, ideally, parents and professionals work together in their advocacy efforts.

Parents can focus their advocacy on helping their own children as well as other people with disabilities. The latter might involve volunteering for advisory posts with schools and agencies as well as political activism—for example, campaigning for school board members who are sympathetic to educational issues pertinent to students with disabilities.

One of the most common ways of advocating for one's own child is by means of the IEP meeting. Table 4.5 lists several ways in which parents can help to make IEP meetings more effective. And the Personal Perspectives on p. 128 offers suggestions on how parents can prepare themselves to advocate for their child.

As important as advocacy is, not all parents have the personalities or the time to engage in such activities. Also, engaging in advocacy may be more or less suitable to some parents at various stages in their child's development. For example, some parents might be heavily involved in such efforts when their children are young but become exhausted over the years and reduce their involvement. Likewise, some parents might not see the need for intervening on behalf of their children until they encounter problems later on—for example, in transition programming in the teenage years. The best advice for teachers is to encourage parents to be advocates for their children but respect their hesitancy to take on such responsibilities.

Traveling notebook
A system of communication in which parents and professionals write messages to each other by way of a notebook or log that accompanies the child to and from school.

Advocacy
Action that is taken on behalf of oneself or others; a method parents of students with disabilities can use to obtain needed or improved services.

 THE NATIONAL Information Center for Children and Youth with Disabilities, funded by the U.S. Department of Education's Office of Special Education Programs, has information on the IEP process that parents should find valuable: **www.nichcy.org/basic-par.htm**

There are now several websites focused on helping parents and advocates understand special education and the law. Following are some examples:
www.reedmartin.com
www.wrightslaw.com
www.edlaw.net
www.specialedlaw.net/index.mv
www.cleweb.org

TABLE 4.5   Hints for Parents for a More Effective IEP Meeting

■ Take the initiative to set the date, time, and place of the meeting. Consider holding the meeting in your own home or in a community setting that feels comfortable to you.

■ Before the meeting, ask the organizer to clarify the purpose and provide you with information you may need ahead of time. Also, find out who will be attending the meeting so that you may suggest other potential team members.

■ Call the organizers to let them know what items you would like to have included on the agenda.

■ Write down ideas about your child's present and future goals, interests, and needs, and bring these with you to share at the meeting.

■ During the meeting, ask to have discussion items and lists of actions written down on large pieces of flip-chart paper so that all team members can see them.

■ Be a "jargon buster"—ask to have unfamiliar terms clarified for you and other team members during the meeting.

■ Ask team members to set a regular meeting schedule (e.g., monthly, bimonthly, semiannually, etc.) for the purpose of reviewing and evaluating your child's progress.

■ After the meeting, ask to have the minutes sent to you and other team members.

■ Help promote ongoing communication by asking other team members to call or write you on a regular basis.

Source: Salembier, G. B., & Furney, F. S. (1998). Speaking up for your child's future. *Exceptional Parent, 28(7),* 62–64. Reprinted with permission.

Personal Perspectives

ADVOCACY IN ACTION: YOU CAN ADVOCATE FOR YOUR CHILD

GET ALL THE INFORMATION YOU CAN

The first step to successful advocacy is to gather information. Learn what is happening in the school, . . . and talk with your child's teacher to learn his or her view of areas of concern.

You should also learn about special education law and its protections. You can obtain this information from the school's special education or guidance director, state departments of education, or parent information and training centers, as well as organizations such as CEC (Council for Exceptional Children). . . .

Talk with your child to learn his or her view of the situation and what he or she thinks will help. Even young children have a keen sense of their stress points and what could be done to make it easier for them to succeed.

WHAT DO YOU WANT THE SCHOOL TO DO?

As your child's advocate, you need to be clear about what you want the school to do. Be able to explain what you are happy with, unhappy with, what you want changed, and how you want it changed.

BE A GOOD COMMUNICATOR

Communicating well with your child's teacher and other school personnel is essential to your advocacy efforts. . . . Be honest and develop a positive relationship with the teacher and other staff. Start where the concern is, usually the classroom teacher. Only move up the chain of command if you must.

Being diplomatic can be hard when you are concerned about your child's welfare—you want to get feisty. But get feisty only if that is what it takes.

BRING A COMPANION TO MEETINGS

. . . This person can help you listen, take notes so you are free to concentrate on what is happening, and help you understand what happened afterwards. In addition, your companion can help slow you down if things get too emotional.

DON'T BE AFRAID TO SAY NO

Don't be pressured into making a bad decision. You can always say no, ask for more information, or for more time to consider a proposed solution. Take the time to consult with experts and people you trust. . . .

MAKING YOUR VOICE STRONGER

One of the best ways to make your voice stronger is to band together with other parents facing similar situations. . . .

When you meet with other parents, share your experiences. As a group, develop some proposals to solve the problem. The parents should then meet with the individual(s) who will be affected. For example, a group of parents who wanted to get computers in the resource room would meet first with the resource room teacher. . . . Then teachers and parents can build an alliance, which can be particularly effective in creating change. ■

Source: Osher, T. (1997). Advocacy in action: You can advocate for your child! *CEC Today,* 4(4) 4. Reprinted by permission.

In Conclusion

Today's knowledgeable educators recognize the tremendous impact a child with a disability can have on the dynamics of a family. They appreciate the negative as well as the positive influence such a child can exert. Today's knowledgeable educators also realize that the family of a child with a disability can be a bountiful reservoir of support for the child as well as an invaluable source of information for the teacher. Although tremendous advances have been made, we are just beginning to tap the potential that families have for contributing to the development of their children with disabilities. We are just beginning to enable families to provide supportive and enriching environments for their children. And we are just beginning to harness the expertise of families so we can provide the best possible programs for their children.

SUMMARY

HOW have professionals' views of parents changed?

- Professionals' views of parents are more positive than they once were for at least two reasons:
  - Not only can parent behavior influence child behavior, but the reverse can also occur.
  - The family can have a positive effect on the educational process.
- Congress has recognized the potentially positive influence by passing legislation mandating that families be involved in developing IEPs and IFSPs.

WHAT are the effects of a child with a disability on the family?

- The addition of a child with a disability to a family can have significant effects on family dynamics and work patterns.
- Parental reactions to the birth of a child with a disability can involve a variety of reactions; guilt (even though unfounded) tends to be one that is frequent.
- Parents must also deal with public reactions to their child as well as the child's feelings about having a disability.
- There is substantial research to show that parents of children with disabilities undergo a great deal of stress.
  - How parents deal with the stress is dependent on their prior psychological makeup and marital happiness as well as the quality and quantity of social support they receive.
  - Current research indicates that many parents adjust well to having a child with a disability; some even benefit from the experience.
- Siblings of children with disabilities often experience some of the same emotions as the parents.
  - Siblings of the same gender and those who are close in age tend to have more conflicts, and at older ages, there is some evidence that women have a closer attachment to their sibling with a disability.
  - Having access to accurate information helps siblings to achieve a more positive adjustment.

WHAT are the best ways for families to be involved in treatment and education?

- Most authorities advocate a family-centered model, whereby the families assume more decision making and professionals provide supports for families to achieve their goals.
- Most authorities also stress family systems theory. One such model (the Turnbulls') is composed of family characteristics, family interaction, family functions, and family life cycle.
- Social support, which involves emotional, informational, or material aid provided by nonprofessionals, is important for families.
  - There is evidence suggesting that some ethnic minority groups provide especially good social support.
  - Two common types of social support are parental support groups and Internet sites devoted to parents of children with disabilities.
- Positive behavior supports, the use of positive reinforcement, is an important tool for parents who have children with challenging behavior problems.
- Communication between professionals and families is critical to involving families.
  - Parent–teacher conferences are an important means of communication, and preparation is a key to making them successful.
  - Home-note programs are a means for communication and a way for teachers to encourage parents to reinforce behavior that occurs at school.
  - Traveling notebooks are a way for one or more professionals to communicate with parents.
- Parent advocacy is an important way for families to become involved in the treatment and education of their children.
  - Advocacy need not be confrontational.
  - A common way to advocate is through active involvement in IEP meetings.
  - Teachers should encourage parent advocacy but respect parents who do not wish to be involved in this way.

APPLYING THE STANDARDS AND PRINCIPLES

- **HOW** might teachers **encourage parents** to maintain an active role in their child's education? *(CEC Content Standard #7 & INTASC Principle #7)* | **INTASC**

- **WHAT** do you think are the keys to **effective collaboration** with parents? *(CEC Content Standard #10 & INTASC Principle #10)*

Council for Exceptional Children

Chapter 5

Learners with Mental Retardation

W henever I step back and consider how "normal" . . . Nicole's life is, I am struck by how different her adulthood is from what Matt and I had thought it would be. [Recently] I paid a visit to the Regional Center. . . .

What a different world it is out there these days, I mused. Parents of a baby or child who is identified as having—or even at risk of having—developmental delays can turn to the Regional Center system for assessments, counseling, intervention therapies, respite care, and a host of other programs for both family and child. . . .

A mother with a crying baby entered the library. As I watched her trying to talk with the volunteer over the din, I thought of the things that haven't changed at all: the gut-wrenching adjustment to the actuality of giving birth to an "imperfect" infant, the exhaustion of caring for the vulnerable son or daughter. . . .

I followed [Colleen Mock] upstairs. . . . She segued into an explanation of the current perspective among professionals. . . . Professionals try to regard children or adults they see as whole people, capable of making decisions for themselves about things that affect their lives. Consumers . . . are encouraged—are empowered—to set goals and make choices. . . . When the appropriate supports are in place as a child grows older, his or her role as the determiner of what is wanted supplants the parents' function as advocate. Support services continue, but consumers are encouraged to use community resources to solve problems that arise, the rationale being that the process of engaging "natural supports"—family members, friends, neighbors, or fellow employees—is controlled by the consumer and integrates him or her in the community far more than dependence on service personnel.

SANDRA Z. KAUFMAN
Retarded Isn't Stupid, Mom!

QUESTIONS TO GUIDE YOUR READING OF THIS CHAPTER . . .

- HOW do professionals define mental retardation?

- WHAT is the prevalence of mental retardation?

- WHAT causes mental retardation?

- WHAT methods of assessment are used to identify individuals with mental retardation?

- WHAT are some of the psychological and behavioral characteristics of learners with mental retardation?

- WHAT are some educational considerations for learners with mental retardation?

- WHAT are some things to consider with respect to early intervention for learners with mental retardation?

- WHAT are some things to consider with respect to transition to adulthood for learners with mental retardation?

Standards and Principles in This Chapter

SPECIAL EDUCATORS . . .

- **understand the field** as an evolving and changing discipline *(from CEC Content Standard #1)*.

- **understand the similarities and differences in human development** and the characteristics [of] individuals with and without exceptional learning needs *(from CEC Content Standard #2)*.

- **possess a repertoire** of evidence-based instructional strategies *(from CEC Content Standard #4)*.

- develop a variety of **individualized transition plans** *(from CEC Content Standard #7)*.

- **use the results of assessments** to help identify exceptional learning needs *(from CEC Content Standard #8)*.

- **use collaboration** to facilitate the successful transitions of individuals with exceptional learning needs *(from CEC Content Standard #10)*.

ALL TEACHERS

- **understand the central concepts, tools of inquiry, structures of the discipline(s) they teach** and can create learning experiences that make these aspects of subject matter meaningful *(INTASC Principle #1)*.

- **understand how children learn and develop,** and can provide learning opportunities that support the . . . development of each learner *(INTASC Principle #2)*.

- **understand and use a variety of instructional strategies** to encourage students' development of critical thinking, problem solving, and performance skills *(INTASC Principle #4)*.

- **understand and use formal and informal assessment strategies** to evaluate and ensure the continuous intellectual, social and physical development of the learner *(INTASC Principle #8)*.

- foster relationships with school colleagues, families, and agencies in the larger community *(from INTASC Principle #10)*.

Council for Exceptional Children

INTASC

---

s Sandra Kaufman (1999) points out (see p. 131), in many ways, there is a world of difference in the quantity and quality of services for people with mental retardation now, compared to just a few years ago. At the same time, though, she poignantly reminds us that some things related to mental retardation are likely never to change. For parents, having a child with mental retardation means facing a set of lifelong challenges. The main difference, however, is that today, although parents of a child with mental retardation are very likely to feel overwhelmed initially, they can look around them and see signs of hope. They can see examples of adults with mental retardation who are leading relatively independent lives, holding jobs in competitive or semicompetitive work environments and living independently or semi-independently in the community.

As Mock explained to Kaufman, much of the success being achieved by people with mental retardation is attributed to a change in philosophy that includes respecting their rights to be a part of decisions affecting their lives and that involves the use of **natural supports**. Later in the chapter, we discuss the important philosophical changes that have brought about the emphasis on self-determination and natural supports.

It takes more than well-intentioned philosophies to ensure that people with mental retardation reach their full potential with respect to independent employment and community living. We hasten to point out that it often takes years of intensive instruction from special educators, working in tandem with other professionals, including general educators, to put the philosophies of self-determination and natural supports into effect.

There have been other changes, too, that have had a profound effect on the field of mental retardation in the past several years; perhaps the most significant one is the fact that designating someone as mentally retarded has become much more difficult. Today, professionals are more reluctant to apply the label of mental retardation than they once were. At least three reasons account for this more cautious attitude toward identification of students as being mentally retarded:

1. Professionals became concerned about the misdiagnosis of children from ethnic minority groups as mentally retarded. Twenty to thirty years ago, it was much more common for children from ethnic minorities, especially African American and Hispanic students, to be labeled mentally retarded because they did not achieve well in school and they scored poorly on intelligence tests.

2. Some people believe that the diagnosis of mental retardation results in a stigma that causes children to have poor self-concepts and to be viewed negatively by others.

3. Some professionals now believe that to a certain extent, mental retardation is a socially constructed condition. For example,

Misconceptions about Learners with Mental Retardation

MYTH Mental retardation is defined by how a person scores on an IQ test.

FACT The most commonly used definition specifies that in order for a person to be considered mentally retarded, he or she must meet two criteria: (1) low intellectual functioning *and* (2) low adaptive skills.

MYTH Once diagnosed as mentally retarded, a person remains within this classification for life.

FACT A person's level of mental functioning does not necessarily remain stable; this is particularly true for those individuals who are mildly mentally retarded. With intensive educational programming, some persons can improve to the point that they are no longer mentally retarded.

MYTH Professionals are in agreement about the definition of mental retardation.

FACT There is considerable disagreement about definition, classification, and terminology; in fact, some people have proposed doing away with the term *mental retardation*.

MYTH It is easy to identify the cause of mental retardation in most cases.

FACT Although the mapping of the human genome has increased our knowledge about causes of mental retardation, it is still difficult to pinpoint the cause of mental retardation in many people, especially those with mild mental retardation.

MYTH Psychosocial factors are the cause of the vast majority of cases of mild mental retardation.

FACT Exact percentages are not available, but researchers are finding more and more genetic syndromes that result in mild mental retardation; hereditary factors are also involved in some cases.

MYTH The teaching of vocational skills to students with mental retardation is best reserved for secondary school and beyond.

FACT Many authorities now believe it appropriate to introduce vocational content in elementary school to students with mental retardation.

MYTH When workers with mental retardation fail on the job, it is usually because they do not have adequate job skills.

FACT When they fail on the job, it is more often because of poor job responsibility (poor attendance and lack of initiative) and social incompetence (interacting inappropriately with co-workers) than because of incompetence in task production.

MYTH People with mental retardation should not be expected to work in the competitive job market.

FACT More and more people who are mentally retarded hold jobs in competitive employment. Many are helped through supportive employment situations, in which a job coach helps them and their employer adapt to the workplace.

Natural supports
Resources in person's environment that can be used for support, such as friends, family, co-workers.

 AN EXAMPLE of an organization that has changed its name to avoid using the term *mental retardation* is the Arc. Formerly known as the Association for Retarded Citizens, it also uses the acronym, the Arc, as its name. The Arc is primarily a parent organization and a strong advocate for rights for those with mental retardation: www.thearc.org

the American Association on Mental Retardation (AAMR) conceives of mental retardation not as a trait residing in the individual but as the product of the interaction between a person and his or her environment.

The last point has not gone uncontested. Some authorities think that the AAMR has gone too far in denying the existence of mental retardation as an essential feature within a person. In fact, there has been recent discussion within the AAMR, the major professional organization concerned with mental retardation, about doing away with the label *mental retardation* altogether and renaming the organization (See the Focus on Concepts below.) There are those who vehemently oppose such a change. However, even if the name change does not occur, the fact that it is being debated indicates the level of concern about terminology and definition, topics to which we now turn.

Definition

A more conservative approach to identifying students as mentally retarded is reflected in changes in definition that have occurred over the years. Since 1950, the AAMR has endorsed seven official definitions of mental retardation.

FOCUS ON CONCEPTS

What's in a Name?

THE February 2002 issue of *Mental Retardation*, a journal published by the AAMR, featured several articles under the collective title "Symposium on 'What's in a Name?'" Authors shared their views on whether to eliminate *mental retardation* from the name of the organization. Following are very different perspectives taken by two of the authors.

IN FAVOR OF A NAME CHANGE

The term *mental retardation* . . . long ago escaped from the clinical realm of classification into universal English usage as a potent, utterly dismissive invective in the mouths of adults and school children. The injurious nominal form *retard* became a term of opprobrium alongside *moron, imbecile,* and *idiot.* As a descriptive, *retarded* is a commonly heard teen epithet to label someone or something as deserving ridicule, as in, "Those shoes are so *retarded.*" (Gelb, 2002, p. 55)

OPPOSED TO A NAME CHANGE

The relentless and fanatical emphasis on language and terminology in recent years has obscured the fact that

much of people's attitudes toward any human condition—such as the condition we call mental retardation, and the people who "have" it or "are retarded"—derives either *not* from language at all, or only in part so. Instead, it derives heavily from such things as the settings in which such people are commonly found; their personal appearance, hygiene, social graces, and demeanor; the people with whom they are grouped and associated; their activities; the imagery associated with fund-raising appeals on their behalf; how people personally experience contact with them, and with those who represent such persons; how such persons are portrayed in the arts; and so on. In *all* of these areas, actions could be taken that would improve attitudes toward mentally retarded people. (Wolfensberger, 2002a, p. 77)

Although a few years have passed, AAMR's membership is still divided on the issue, and there is still talk of changing the name. A few that have been suggested are American Association on Cognitive Disabilities, American Association on Intellectual Disabilities, and American Association for Community Living. But as yet there is no consensus. ■

Professionals are cautious about identifying and labeling mental retardation due to concerns about misidentification and what are seen as the limitations of traditional definitions.

THE AAMR DEFINITION

The current AAMR definition reads as follows:

> Mental retardation is a disability characterized by significant limitations both in intellectual functioning and in adaptive behavior as expressed in conceptual, social, and practical adaptive skills. This disability originates before age 18. (AAMR Ad Hoc Committee on Terminology and Classification, 2002, p. 1)

The AAMR also states that the following five assumptions are essential to the application of the definition:

1. Limitations in present functioning must be considered within the context of community environments typical of the individual's age peers and culture.
2. Valid assessment considers cultural and linguistic diversity as well as differences in communication, sensory, motor, and behavioral factors.
3. Within an individual, limitations often coexist with strengths.
4. An important purpose of describing limitations is to develop a profile of needed supports.
5. With appropriate personalized supports over a sustained period, the life functioning of the person with mental retardation generally will improve. (AAMR Ad Hoc Committee on Terminology and Classification, 2002, p. 1)

The AAMR definition underscores two important points: Mental retardation involves problems in adaptive behavior not just intellectual functioning, and the intellectual functioning and adaptive behavior of a person with mental retardation can be improved.

Adaptive Behavior At one time, it was common practice to diagnose individuals as mentally retarded solely on the basis of an IQ score. Today, we recognize that IQ tests are

UNDERSTANDING THE STANDARDS AND PRINCIPLES Why are professionals generally more cautious about identifying students as mentally retarded? *(CEC Knowledge and Skills Standard MR1K1)*

Council for Exceptional Children

TABLE 5.1 Examples of Conceptual, Social, and Practical Adaptive Behavior Skills

Conceptual Skills	
■ Receptive and expressive language	■ Money concepts
■ Reading and writing	■ Self-directions

Social Skills	
■ Interpersonal	■ Naivete
■ Responsibility	■ Follows rules
■ Self-esteem	■ Obeys laws
■ Gullibility (likelihood of being tricked or manipulated)	■ Avoids victimization

Practical Skills	
■ Personal activities of daily living, such as eating, dressing, mobility, and toileting	■ Occupational skills
■ Instrumental activities of daily living such as preparing meals, taking medication, using the telephone, managing money, using transportation and doing housekeeping activities	■ Maintaining a safe environment

Source: Adapted from AAMR. (1999–2004). Fact Sheet: Frequently Asked Questions About Mental Retardation. Retrieved June 4, 2004 from the World Wide Web: **www.aamr.org/Policies/faq_mental_retardation.shtml**. Reprinted by permission.

Founded in 1876, the American Association on Mental Retardation is one of the oldest professional organizations focused on mental retardation in the world. Its mission is to "promote progressive policies, sound research, effective practices, and universal human rights for people with intellectual disabilities." Visit its Web site at **www.aamr.org/index.shtml** for information related to mental retardation. For example, you can access past issues of AAMR's newsletter, *News & Notes.*

Adaptive behavior
Conceptual, social, and practical skills that people have learned so that they can function in their everyday lives; along with intellectual functioning are considered in making a determination of mental retardation.

Supports
Resources and strategies that promote a person's development, education, interests, and personal well-being; critical to the AAMR's conceptualization of mental retardation

far from perfect and that they are but one indication of a person's ability to function. Professionals came to consider adaptive behavior in addition to IQ in defining retardation because they began to recognize that some students might score poorly on IQ tests but still be "streetwise"—able to cope, for example, with the subway system, with an after-school job, with peers.

The AAMR defines **adaptive behavior** as

> the collection of conceptual, social, and practical skills that people have learned so that they can function in their everyday lives. Significant limitations in adaptive behavior impact a person's daily life and affect the ability to respond to a particular situation or to the environment. (AAMR, 1999–2004)

Table 5.1 contains examples of conceptual, social, and practical adaptive behavior skills.

People with Mental Retardation Can Improve In the past, many authorities held little hope for significantly enhancing the functioning of people with mental retardation; they essentially believed mental retardation to be incurable. Today, however, the prevailing opinion is that the functioning of virtually all people with mental retardation can be improved and that some, especially those with mild mental retardation, can eventually improve to the point at which they are no longer classified as mentally retarded.

In agreement with the notion that mental retardation is improvable and not necessarily permanent, the developers of the current AAMR definition hold that how well a person with mental retardation functions is directly related to the amount of support he or she receives from the environment. With enough support, the person can improve and possibly overcome the mental retardation.

The concept of supports is integral to the AAMR's conceptualization of mental retardation. They define **supports** as

> resources and strategies that aim to promote the development, education, interests, and personal well-being of a person and that enhance individual functioning (AAMR Ad Hoc Committee on Terminology and Classification, 2002, p. 151).

TABLE 5.2 Levels of Support for People with Mental Retardation

Intermittent Supports on an as-needed basis, characterized by their episodic (the person does not always need the supports) or short-term nature (supports are needed during life-span transitions, e.g., job loss or acute medical crisis). Intermittent supports may be high or low intensity when provided.
Limited An intensity of supports characterized by consistency over time, time-limited but not of an intermittent nature, may require fewer staff members and less cost than more intense levels of support (e.g., time-limited employment training or transitional supports during the school-to-adult period).
Extensive Supports characterized by regular involvement (e.g., daily) in at least some environments (e.g., school, work, or home) and not time-limited nature (e.g., long-term support and long-term home living support).
Pervasive Supports characterized by their constancy, high intensity, provision across environments, potentially life-sustaining nature. Pervasive supports typically involve more staff members and intrusiveness than do extensive or time-limited supports.

Source: Adapted from AAMR Ad Hoc Committee on Terminology and Classification. (2002). *Mental retardation: Definition, classification, and systems of supports* (10th ed, p. 152). Washington, DC: American Association on Mental Retardation. Reprinted by permission.

According to the AAMR, sources of supports can be either natural or service based. *Natural supports* are those that typically occur in one's environment, such as oneself, family members, or friends. *Service-based supports* are those provided by professionals, such as teachers, counselors, psychologists. Table 5.2 lists the various **levels of supports** that people with mental retardation might need.

CLASSIFICATION OF MENTAL RETARDATION

Most school systems classify students with mental retardation according to the severity of their condition. And although the AAMR does not advocate such a classification scheme, two other prominent professional organizations do (the American Psychological Association and the American Psychiatric Association). Most school systems use the American Psychological Association's classifications of mild, moderate, severe, and profound mental retardation or a close approximation: **mild mental retardation** (IQ of about 50 to 70, **moderate mental retardation** (IQ of about 35 to 50), **severe mental retardation** (IQ of about 20 to 35), and **profound mental retardation** (IQ below about 20).

Prevalence

The average (mean) score on an IQ test is 100. Theoretically, we expect 2.27 percent of the population to fall two standard deviations (IQ = 70 on the Wechsler Intelligence Scale for Children Fourth Edition [WISC-IV]) or more below this average. This expectation is based on the assumption that intelligence, like so many other human traits, is distributed along a normal curve. Figure 5.1 shows the hypothetical normal curve of intelligence. This curve is split into eight areas by means of standard deviations. One standard deviation equals 15 IQ points; 2.14 percent of the population scores between 55 and 70, and 0.13 percent scores below 55. Thus, it would seem that 2.27 percent should fall between 0 and 70. (See p. 145 for more on intelligence tests.)

However, the actual prevalence figures for students who are identified as mentally retarded are much lower. In recent years, they have been somewhere around 1 percent.

Levels of support
The basis of the AAMR classification scheme; characterizes the amount of support needed for someone with mental retardation to function as competently as possible as (1) intermittent, (2) limited, (3) extensive, or (4) pervasive.

Mild mental retardation
A classification used to specify an individual whose IQ is approximately 55–70.

Moderate mental retardation
A classification used to specify an individual whose IQ is approximately 40–55.

Severe mental retardation
A classification used to specify an individual whose IQ is approximately 25–40.

Profound mental retardation
A classification used to specify an individual whose IQ is below approximately 25.

UNDERSTANDING THE STANDARDS AND PRINCIPLES What do we know about the causes of mental retardation? *(CEC Knowledge and Skills Standards MR2K1 & MR2K2)*

To see the complete address of Sharon Davis, a representative from the Arc, visit **www.ornl.gov/hgmis/resource/arc.html**

For further information on the Human Genome Project visit **www.ornl.gov/sci/techresources/Human_Genome/home.shtml**

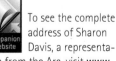

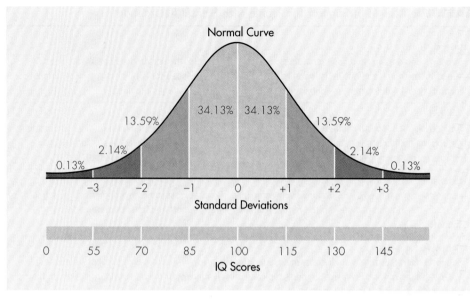

FIGURE 5.1   Theoretical distribution of IQ scores based on normal curve

Prenatal causes of mental retardation
Causes occurring during fetal development; some examples include chromosomal disorders, inborn errors of metabolism, developmental disorders affecting brain formation, and environmental influences.

Perinatal causes of mental retardation
Causes at birth; some examples are anoxia, low birthweight, and infections such as syphilis and herpes simplex.

Postnatal causes of mental retardation
Causes occurring after birth; can be biological (e.g., traumatic brain injury, infections) or psychosocial (an unstimulating environment).

Chromosomal disorder
Any of several syndromes resulting from abnormal or damaged chromosome(s); can result in mental retardation.

Down syndrome
A condition resulting from an abnormality with the twenty-first pair of chromosomes; the most common abnormality is a triplet rather than a pair (the condition sometimes referred to as trisomy 21); characterized by mental retardation and such physical signs as slanted-appearing eyes, hypotonia, a single palmar crease, shortness, and a tendency toward obesity.

Authorities surmise that this lower prevalence figure is due to school personnel considering adaptive behavior or a broader definition of intelligence in addition to an IQ score to diagnose mental retardation. There is also evidence that in cases in which the student's IQ score is in the 70s, thus making identification as mentally retarded a close call, parents and school officials might be more likely to identify children as learning disabled than as mentally retarded because *learning disabled* is perceived as a less stigmatizing label (MacMillan, Gresham, Bocian, & Lambros, 1998).

Causes

As recently as the mid-1990s, most experts estimated that only in about 10 to 15 percent of cases was the cause of mental retardation known. However, the mapping of the human genetic code by the Human Genome Project has brought a wealth of information related to causes of mental retardation. (These advances have also engendered a number of thorny issues; see the Focus on Concepts on p. 139.) However, not all causes of mental retardation are genetically related, so there still remains a large percentage of cases (probably over 50 percent) in which we cannot pinpoint the cause of a child's mental retardation.

A common way of categorizing causes of mental retardation is according to the time at which the cause occurs: **prenatal** (before birth), **perinatal** (at the time of birth), and **postnatal** (after birth).

PRENATAL CAUSES

We can group prenatal causes into (1) **chromosomal disorders**, (2) inborn errors of metabolism, (3) developmental disorders affecting brain formation, and (4) environmental influences.

Chromosomal Disorders   As was noted above, scientists are making great strides in identifying genetic causes of mental retardation. At least 750 genetic syndromes have been

FOCUS ON CONCEPTS

The Human Genome Project: Ethical Issues Pertaining to Mental Retardation

STARTED in 1990, the U.S. Human Genome Project's goals have been to

- *Identify* all the approximately 30,000 genes in human DNA
- *Determine* the sequences of the 3 billion chemical base pairs that make up human DNA
- *Store* this information in databases
- *Improve* tools for data analysis
- *Transfer* related technologies to the private sector
- *Address* the ethical, legal, and social issues (ELSI) that may arise from the project (Human Genome Project, 2004a)

The mapping of the human genome was completed in the summer of 2000.

One of the practical benefits noted by the project's administrators is the development of revolutionary ways to diagnose, treat, and eventually prevent genetic conditions. However, such potential breakthroughs have made some people uneasy. For example, some have asserted that to use genetic information to prevent mental retardation devalues the lives of those who are mentally retarded:

Then, in a world where disability is not valued, people with disabilities are also not valued, rendering our efforts towards "normalization" impossible. How do we cope with a culture that teaches us, with an emphasis on "success," to devalue individuals whose disabilities render their chances of achievement, in its usual meaning, as less than likely? What of the ethical issues surrounding potential genetic therapies that may eventually "cure" mental retardation? Do people with disabilities lead fulfilling lives with their disability or in spite of it? How do professionals . . . assist and support individuals when the

shifting climate indicates more than ever their worth, or lack thereof, in society? (Kuna, 2001, pp. 159–160)

On the other hand,

the major argument in favor of gene therapy is based on its potential for treating individuals severely affected by their condition. A perfect example is Lesch-Nyhan disease, which is characterized by communication deficits, writhing movements, and involuntary self-injurious behavior. Males who have this disorder have to be restrained constantly to prevent them from inflicting severe damage on themselves. Most have their teeth removed to keep from biting their lips off. If we have a new medical technology that will cure this condition, don't we have an obligation to use it? (Davis, 1997)

The Human Genome Project's website contains papers on several ethical issues of relevance to mental retardation, as well as other areas of disability (Human Genome Project, 2004b). Following are some of the concerns they address:

- Who should have access to personal genetic information, and how will it be used?
- How does personal genetic information affect an individual and society's perceptions of that individual?
- How does genomic information affect members of minority communities?
- Should testing be performed when no treatment is available?
- Should parents have the right to have their minor children tested for adult-onset diseases? ■

For more information on these papers, you can visit the following website: www.ornl.gov/sci/techresources/Human_Genome/elsi/elsi.shtml.

identified as causes of mental retardation (Dykens, Hodapp, & Finucane, 2000). Just a few of the most common of these genetic syndromes are Down syndrome, Williams syndrome, fragile X syndrome, and Prader-Willi syndrome.

Down Syndrome   Many, but not all, genetic syndromes are transmitted hereditarily. In fact, by far the most common of these syndromes, **Down syndrome**, is usually not an inherited condition. Down syndrome involves an anomaly at the twenty-first pair of

FOCUS ON CONCEPTS

Down Syndrome and Alzheimer's Disease

IT has been well over a century since researchers first noted a high prevalence of senility in persons with Down syndrome (Fraser & Mitchell, 1876, cited in Evenhuis, 1990). And it was in the early twentieth century that postmortem studies of the brains of people with Down syndrome revealed neuropathological signs similar to those of people with Alzheimer's disease (Carr, 1994). It was not until the 1980s and 1990s, however, that scientists started to address this correlation seriously.

Postmortem studies of the brains of people with Down syndrome indicate that virtually all who reach the age of 35 have brain abnormalities very similar to those of persons with Alzheimer's disease (Wisniewski, Silverman, & Wegiel, 1994; Hof et al., 1995). And behavioral signs of dementia, or mental deterioration, occur in more than half of people with Down syndrome over 50 years of age.

Findings that link Down syndrome to Alzheimer's disease have made researchers optimistic about uncovering the genetic underpinnings of both conditions. For example, researchers have found that some types of Alzheimer's disease are related to mutations of the twenty-first pair of chromosomes (Bush & Beail, 2004). ■

Chromosome
A rod-shaped entity in the nucleus of the cell; contains genes, which convey hereditary characteristics; each cell in the human body contains 23 pairs of chromosomes.

Trisomy 21
A type of Down syndrome in which the twenty-first chromosome is a triplet, making forty-seven, rather than the normal forty-six, chromosomes in all.

Amniocentesis
A medical procedure that allows examination of the amniotic fluid around the fetus; sometimes recommended to determine the presence of abnormality.

Spina bifida
A congenital midline defect resulting from failure of the bony spinal column to close completely during fetal development.

chromosomes. In the vast majority of cases of Down syndrome, the twenty-first set of chromosomes (the normal human cell contains twenty-three pairs of chromosomes) is a triplet rather than a pair; hence, Down syndrome is also referred to as **trisomy 21**. Estimated to account for about 5 to 6 percent of all cases of mental retardation (Beirne-Smith, Ittenbach, & Patton, 2002), Down syndrome is the most common form of mental retardation that is present at birth.

Down syndrome is associated with a range of distinctive physical characteristics that vary considerably in number from one individual to another. People with Down syndrome may have thick epicanthal folds in the corners of the eyes, making the eyes appear to slant upward slightly. Other common characteristics include small stature, decreased muscle tone (hypotonia), hyperflexibility of the joints, a small oral cavity that can result in a protruding tongue, short and broad hands with a single palmar crease, heart defects, and susceptibility to upper respiratory infections (Taylor, Richards, & Brady, 2005). There is also evidence of a link between Down syndrome and Alzheimer's disease (see the Focus on Concepts above.)

The degree of mental retardation varies widely among peo-

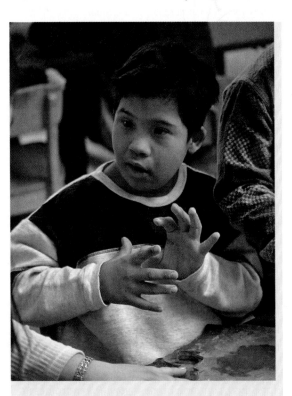

Down syndrome is associated with certain physical characteristics. Children with Down Syndrome have shown an increase in IQ scores into the mildly mentally retarded range since special education programming.

ple with Down syndrome; most individuals fall in the moderate range. In recent years, more children with Down syndrome have achieved IQ scores in the mildly mentally retarded range than previously, presumably because of intensive special education programming.

The likelihood of having a child with Down syndrome increases with the age of the mother. For example, for mothers who are 45 years of age, there is about a 1 in 30 chance of giving birth to a child with Down syndrome (Beirne-Smith et al., 2002). In addition to the age of the mother, researchers are pointing to other variables as possible causes, such as the age of the father, exposure to radiation, and exposure to some viruses. Research on these factors is still preliminary, however.

Methods are available for screening for Down syndrome and some other birth defects during pregnancy. Four such methods are amniocentesis, chorionic villus sampling, a nuchal translucency sonogram, and maternal serum screening:

- In **amniocentesis**, the physician takes a sample of amniotic fluid from the sac around the fetus and analyzes the fetal cells for chromosomal abnormalities. In addition, the amniotic fluid can be tested for the presence of proteins that may have leaked out of the fetus's spinal column, indicating the presence of **spina bifida** (a condition in which the spinal column fails to close properly).
- In **chorionic villus sampling (CVS)**, the physician takes a sample of villi (structures that later become the placenta) and tests them for chromosomal abnormalities. One advantage of CVS is that it can be done earlier than amniocentesis.
- Another procedure that can be done earlier than amniocentesis is a **nuchal translucency sonogram**–a measure of fluid behind the fetus's neck as well as proteins in the mother's blood.
- In **maternal serum screening (MSS)**, a blood sample is taken from the mother and screened for the presence of certain elements that indicate the possibility of spina bifida or Down syndrome. If the results are positive, the physician can recommend a more accurate test, such as amniocentesis or CVS.

Williams Syndrome   Williams syndrome is caused by the absence of material on the seventh pair of chromosomes. The range of IQs for people with Williams syndrome is approximately 40 to 70 (Semel & Rosner, 2003). In addition, they often have heart defects, an unusual sensitivity to sounds, and "elfin" facial features.

Fragile X Syndrome   Fragile X syndrome is the most common known hereditary cause of mental retardation (Taylor et al., 2005). In association with mental retardation, it occurs in 1 in 4,000 males and at least half as many females (Turner, Webb, Wake, & Robinson, 1996). In association with milder cognitive deficits, such as learning disabilities, the prevalence may be as high as 1 in 2,000 (Hagerman, 2001). It is associated with the X chromosome in the twenty-third pair of chromosomes. In males, the twenty-third pair consists of an X and a Y chromosome; in females, it consists of two X chromosomes. This disorder is called fragile X syndrome because in affected individuals, the bottom of the X chromosome is pinched off in some of the blood cells. Fragile X occurs less often in females because they have an extra X chromosome, giving them better protection if one of their X chromosomes is damaged. People with fragile X syndrome may have a number of physical features, such as a large head; large, flat ears; a long, narrow face; a prominent forehead; a broad nose; a prominent, square chin; large testicles; and large hands with nontapering fingers. Although this condition usually results in moderate rather than severe mental retardation, the effects are highly variable, some people having less severe cognitive deficiencies and some, especially females, scoring in the normal range of intelligence (Dykens et al., 2000).

Chorionic villus sampling (CVS)
A method of testing the unborn fetus for a variety of chromosomal abnormalities, such as Down syndrome; a small amount of tissue from the chorion (a membrane that eventually helps form the placenta) is extracted and tested; can be done earlier than amniocentesis but the risk of miscarriage is slightly higher.

Nuchal translucency sonogram
A method of screening for Down syndrome; fluid from behind the fetus's neck and protein from the mother's blood are analyzed.

Maternal serum screening (MSS)
A method of screening the fetus for developmental disabilities such as Down syndrome or spina bifida; a blood sample is taken from the mother and analyzed; if it is positive, a more accurate test such as amniocentesis or CVS is usually recommended.

Williams syndrome
A condition resulting from deletion of material in the seventh pair of chromosomes; often results in mild to moderate mental retardation, heart defects, and elfin facial features; people affected often display surprising strengths in spoken language and sociability while having severe deficits in spatial organization, reading, writing, and math.

Fragile X syndrome
A condition in which the bottom of the X chromosome in the twenty-third pair of chromosomes is pinched off; can result in a number of physical anomalies as well as mental retardation; occurs more often in males than females; thought to be the most common hereditary cause of mental retardation.

Prader-Willi syndrome
Caused by inheriting from one's father a lack of genetic material on the fifteenth pair of chromosomes; leading genetic cause of obesity; degree of mental retardation varies, but the majority fall within the mildly mentally retarded range.

Sleep apnea
Cessation of breathing while sleeping.

Scoliosis
Curvature of the spine.

Inborn errors of metabolism
Deficiencies in enzymes used to metabolize basic substances in the body, such as amino acids, carbohydrates, vitamins, or trace elements; can sometimes result in mental retardation; PKU is an example.

Phenylketonuria (PKU)
A metabolic genetic disorder caused by the inability of the body to convert phenylalanine to tyrosine; an accumulation of phenylalanine results in abnormal brain development.

Microcephalus
A condition causing development of a small, conical-shaped head; proper development of the brain is prevented, resulting in mental retardation.

Hydrocephalus
A condition characterized by enlargement of the head because of excessive pressure of the cerebrospinal fluid.

Fetal alcohol syndrome (FAS)
Abnormalities associated with the mother's drinking alcohol during pregnancy; defects range from mild to severe.

Prader-Willi Syndrome   People with **Prader-Willi syndrome** have inherited from their father a lack of genetic material on the fifteenth pair of chromosomes (Dykens et al., 2000). There are two distinct phases to Prader-Willi. Infants are lethargic and have difficulty eating. Starting at about one year of age, however, they become obsessed with food. In fact, Prader-Willi is the leading genetic cause of obesity. Although a vulnerability to obesity is usually their most serious medical problem, people with Prader-Willi are also at risk for a variety of other health problems, including short stature due to growth hormone deficiencies; heart defects; sleep disturbances, such as excessive daytime drowsiness and **sleep apnea** (cessation of breathing while sleeping); and **scoliosis** (curvature of the spine). The degree of mental retardation varies, but the majority fall within the mildly mentally retarded range, and some have IQs in the normal range (Taylor et al., 2005).

Inborn Errors of Metabolism   **Inborn errors of metabolism** result from inherited deficiencies in enzymes used to metabolize basic substances in the body, such as amino acids, carbohydrates, vitamins, or trace elements (Thomas, 1985). One of the most common of these is **phenylketonuria (PKU)**. PKU involves the inability of the body to convert a common dietary substance—phenylalanine—to tyrosine; the consequent accumulation of phenylalanine results in abnormal brain development. All states routinely screen babies for PKU before they leave the hospital. Babies with PKU are immediately put on a special diet, which prevents the occurrence of mental retardation. At one time, it was thought that the diet could be discontinued in middle childhood. However, authorities now recommend that it be continued indefinitely, for two important reasons: Those who stop the diet are at risk for developing learning disabilities or other behavioral problems, and over 90 percent of babies born to women with PKU who are no longer on the diet will have mental retardation and may also have heart defects (The Arc, 2001).

Developmental Disorders of Brain Formation   There are a number of conditions, some of which are hereditary and accompany genetic syndromes and some of which are caused by other conditions such as infections, that can affect the structural development of the brain and cause mental retardation. Two examples are microcephalus and hydrocephalus. In **microcephalus**, the head is abnormally small and conical in shape. The mental retardation that results usually ranges from severe to profound. There is no specific treatment for microcephaly, and life expectancy is short (National Institute of Neurological Disorders and Stroke, 2001).

   Hydrocephalus results from an accumulation of cerebrospinal fluid inside or outside the brain. The blockage of the circulation of the fluid results in a buildup of excessive pressure on the brain and enlargement of the skull. The degree of mental retardation depends on how early the condition is diagnosed and treated. Two types of treatment are available: surgical placement of a shunt (tube) that drains the excess fluid away from the brain to abdomen or insertion of a device that causes the fluid to bypass the obstructed area of the brain.

Environmental Influences   There are a variety of environmental factors that can affect a woman who is pregnant and thereby affect the development of the fetus she is carrying. One example is maternal malnutrition. If the mother-to-be does not maintain a healthy diet, fetal brain development might be compromised.

   We are also now much more aware of the harmful effects of a variety of substances, from obvious toxic agents, such as cocaine and heroin, to more subtle potential poisons, such as tobacco and alcohol. In particular, researchers have exposed **fetal alcohol syndrome (FAS)** as a significant health problem for the unborn children of expectant mothers who consume large quantities of alcohol. Children with FAS are characterized by a variety of physical deformities as well as mental retardation. There is evidence that women who drink moderately during pregnancy are at risk of having babies who, although not exhibiting full-blown FAS, nevertheless show more subtle behavioral abnormalities. These children are now being referred to as having **fetal alcohol effect (FAE)** (Drew & Hardman, 2004).

We have recognized the hazards of radiation to the unborn fetus for some time. For example, physicians are cautious not to expose pregnant women to X-rays unless absolutely necessary, and the public has become concerned over the potential dangers of radiation from improperly designed or supervised nuclear power plants.

Infections in the mother-to-be can also affect the developing fetus and result in mental retardation. **Rubella (German measles)**, in addition to being a potential cause of blindness, can also result in mental retardation. Rubella is most dangerous during the first trimester (three months) of pregnancy.

PERINATAL CAUSES

A variety of problems that can happen during the process of giving birth can result in brain injury and mental retardation. For example, if the child is not positioned properly in the uterus, brain injury can result during delivery. One problem that sometimes occurs because of difficulty during delivery is **anoxia** (complete deprivation of oxygen).

Another potential cause is low birthweight. **Low birth weight (LBW)** can result in a variety of behavioral and medical problems, including mental retardation (Taylor, Klein, Minich, & Hack, 2000). Because most babies with LBW are premature, the two terms— LBW and *premature*—are often used synonymously. LBW is usually defined as 5.5 pounds or lower, and it is associated with a number of factors: poor nutrition, teenage pregnancy, drug abuse, and excessive cigarette smoking. In addition, LBW is more common in mothers living in poverty.

Infections such as **syphilis** and **herpes simplex** can be passed from mother to child during childbirth. These venereal diseases can potentially result in mental retardation.

Casebook Reflections

Refer to the case *Who Will Help Patrick?* in your booklet. Patrick's mother abused alcohol and drugs during her pregnancy, and Patrick was moved to a foster home when he was 6 months old. For the past three years of preschool, he has demonstrated a variety of troubling academic and social problems. Patrick is currently identified as developmentally delayed and impaired in speech language. Do you think he will later be identified as a student with mental retardation? Why or why not?

Fetal alcohol effect (FAE)
Abnormalities that are more subtle than those of FAS; caused by the mother drinking alcohol during pregnancy.

Rubella (German measles)
A serious viral disease, which, if it occurs during the first trimester of pregnancy, is likely to cause deformity in the fetus.

Anoxia
Deprivation of oxygen; can cause brain injury.

Low birth weight (LBW)
Babies who are born weighing less than 5.5 pounds; usually premature; at risk for behavioral and medical conditions, such as mental retardation.

Syphilis
A venereal disease that can cause mental subnormality in a child, especially if it is contracted by the mother-to-be during the latter stages of fetal development.

Herpes simplex
A viral disease that can cause cold sores or fever blisters; if it affects the genitals and is contracted by the mother-to-be in the later stages of fetal development, it can cause mental subnormality in the child.

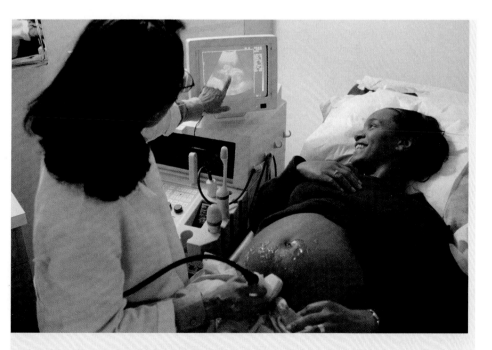

A variety of environmental factors can affect a woman who is pregnant and, thereby, affect the development of the fetus she is carrying.

Traumatic brain injury (TBI)
Injury to the brain (not including conditions present at birth, with trauma, or degenerative diseases or conditions) resulting in total or partial disability or psychosocial maladjustment that affects educational performance; may affect cognition, language, memory, reasoning, abstract thinking, judgment, problem solving, sensory or perceptual and motor abilities, psychosocial behavior, physical functions, information processing, or speech.

Meningitis
A bacterial or viral infection of the linings of the brain or spinal cord.

(Herpes simplex, which shows as cold sores or fever blisters, is not usually classified as a venereal disease unless it affects the genitals.)

POSTNATAL CAUSES

We can group causes of mental retardation occurring after birth into two very broad categories: those that are biological in nature and those that are psychosocial in nature.

Biological Postnatal Causes   Examples of biological postnatal causes are **traumatic brain injury (TBI)**, infections, malnutrition, and toxins. TBI refers to head injuries that result from such things as blows to the head, vehicular accidents, or violent shaking. (We discuss TBI in more detail in Chapter 12.) **Meningitis** and **encephalitis** are two examples of infections that can cause mental retardation. Meningitis is an infection of the covering of the brain that may be caused by a variety of bacterial or viral agents. Encephalitis, an inflammation of the brain, results more often in mental retardation and usually affects intelligence more severely. One of the toxins, or poisons, that has been linked to mental retardation is lead. Although lead in paint is now prohibited, infants still become poisoned by eating lead-based paint chips, particularly in impoverished areas. The effect of lead poisoning on children varies; high lead levels can result in death. To lower the risk of inhaling lead particles from auto exhaust, the federal government now requires that automobile manufacturers produce cars that use only lead-free gasoline.

FOCUS ON CONCEPTS

The Nature–Nurture Controversy

FOR many years, theoreticians tended to view the nature–nurture issue from an either/or perspective: Either you believed that heredity held the key to determining intellectual development or you believed that the environment was the all-important factor. Today, however, most authorities believe that both heredity and the environment are critical determinants of intelligence. Some scientists have tried to discover how much of intelligence is determined by heredity and how much by the environment, but many view this quest as futile. They assert that heredity and environment do not combine in an additive fashion to produce intelligence. Instead, the interaction between genes and environment results in intelligence.

The following exchange between a professor of biopsychology and his student points out the importance of viewing intelligence in this way—that is, as the result of an interaction between genetics and experience and not a simple addition of the two:

One of my students told me that she had read that intelligence was one-third genetic and two-thirds experience, and she wondered whether this was true. She must have been puzzled when I began my response by describing an alpine experience. "I was lazily wandering up a summit ridge when I heard an unexpected sound. Ahead, with his back to me, was a young man sitting on the edge of a precipice, blowing into a peculiar musical instrument. I sat down behind him on a large sun-soaked rock, and shared his experience with him. Then, I got up and wandered back down the ridge, leaving him undisturbed.

I put the following question to my student: "If I wanted to get a better understanding of the music, would it be reasonable for me to begin by asking how much of it came from the musician and how much of it came from the instrument?"

"That would be dumb," she said, "The music comes from both; it makes no sense to ask how much comes from the musician and how much comes from the instrument. Somehow the music results from the interaction of the two, and you would have to ask about the interaction."

"That's exactly right," I said. "Now, do you see why . . ."

"Don't say any more," she interrupted. "I see what you're getting at. Intelligence is the product of the interaction of genes and experience, and it is dumb to try to find how much comes from genes and how much comes from experience." (Pinel, 2003, p. 23) ■

Psychosocial Postnatal Causes Children who are raised in poor environmental circumstances are at risk for mental retardation. It should be obvious that extreme cases of abuse, neglect, or understimulation can result in mental retardation. However, most authorities believe that less severe environmental factors, such as inadequate exposure to stimulating adult-child interactions, poor teaching, and lack of reading materials, can also result in mental retardation, especially mild mental retardation. For example, in one large-scale study of 267,277 children, those who were born to teenage mothers who had fewer than twelve years of education were at increased risk for mild and moderate mental retardation (Chapman, Scott, & Mason, 2002).

Although environmental causes of mild mental retardation are undeniable, heredity can also play a role. For example, in a major study of heredity and mild mental retardation, researchers looked at the degree of similarity in intellectual performance of monozygotic twins versus similarity in performance of dizygotic twins (Spinath, Harlaar, Ronald, & Plomin, 2004). Monozygotic, or identical, twins come from the same egg and have the same genetic makeup. Dizygotic, or fraternal, twins come from separate eggs. In those who scored in the mildly mentally retarded range, the degree of similarity was much higher in monozygotic twins than in dizygotic twins, thus indicating high heritability.

It is important to point out that even though it is tempting to ask how much a person's intelligence is due to the environment versus heredity, it is virtually impossible to disentangle the influence of one from that of the other. (See the Focus on Concepts on p. 144.)

For many years, it has been assumed that psychosocial factors are the cause of the vast majority of cases of mild mental retardation whereas organic, or biological, factors are the cause of more severe mental retardation. In recent years, however, authorities are beginning to suspect that many cases of mild mental retardation might be caused by specific genetic syndromes (Dykens et al., 2000). They point to the many cases of people with Prader-Willi syndrome and Williams syndrome, as well as females with fragile X syndrome, who have mild mental retardation, and they speculate that in the near future, new genetic syndromes will be discovered as causes of mild mental retardation.

Assessment

Two major areas are assessed to determine whether a person is mentally retarded: intelligence and adaptive skills.

INTELLIGENCE TESTS

There are many types of IQ tests. Because of their accuracy and predictive capabilities, practitioners prefer individually administered tests to group tests. One of the most commonly used IQ tests for children is the Wechsler Intelligence Scale for Children—Fourth Edition (WISC-IV) (Wechsler, 2003). The WISC-IV consists of a Full-Scale IQ, as well as four composite scores: Verbal Comprehension, Perceptual Reasoning, Working Memory, and Processing Speed.

Although not all IQ tests call for this method of calculation, we can get a rough approximation of a person's IQ by dividing **mental age** (the age level at which a person is functioning) by **chronological age** and multiplying by 100. For example, a 10-year-old student who performs on an IQ test as well as the average 8-year-old (and thus has a mental age of eight years) would have an IQ of 80.

Compared to many psychological tests, IQ tests such as the WISC-IV are among the most valid. By *validity*, we mean whether

Encephalitis
An inflammation of the brain; can affect the child's mental development adversely.

UNDERSTANDING THE STANDARDS AND PRINCIPLES How do professionals determine whether a person is mentally retarded? *(CEC Knowledge and Skills Standards MR8K1 & MR8K3)*

Mental age
Age level at which a person performs on an IQ test; used in comparison to chronological age to determine IQ. IQ = (mental age ÷ chronological age) × 100.

Chronological age
Refers to how old a person is; used in comparison to mental age to determine IQ. IQ = (mental age ÷ chronological age) × 100.

Casebook Reflections

Refer to the case *Should I Take Juanita Pope?* in your booklet. Juanita has been shifted from program to program. Her IQ score on her last evaluation was above 70, and she was found ineligible for services. Nevertheless, she is experiencing serious difficulties in school in all academic areas as well as behavioral problems. Do you think the committee made a mistake?

the instrument measures what it is supposed to measure. A good indicator of the validity of an IQ test is the fact that it is generally considered the best single index of how well a student will do in school. It is wise to be wary, however, of placing too much faith in a single score from any IQ test. There are at least four reasons for caution:

1. Although this is not common, an individual's IQ can change from one testing to another, and sometimes the change can be dramatic.
2. All IQ tests are culturally biased to a certain extent. Largely because of differences in language and experience, people from minority groups are sometimes at a disadvantage in taking such tests.
3. The younger the child, the less validity the test has. Infant intelligence tests are particularly questionable.
4. IQ tests are not the absolute determinant when it comes to assessing a person's ability to function in society. A superior IQ does not guarantee a successful and happy life, nor does a low IQ doom a person to a miserable existence. Other variables are also important determinants of a person's coping skills in society. That is why, for example, professionals also assess adaptive skills.

ADAPTIVE BEHAVIOR SKILLS

There are a number of commonly used adaptive behavior measures. The basic format of these instruments requires that a parent, teacher, or other professional answer questions related to the person's ability to perform adaptive skills. An example is the AAMR Adaptive Behavior Scale—School Edition: 2 (Lambert, Nihira, & Leland, 1993). It consists of two parts: independence and daily living skills and maladaptive behavior in such things as social interaction, trustworthiness, and self-abusive behavior.

Psychological and Behavioral Characteristics

Some of the major areas in which people with mental retardation are likely to experience deficits are attention, memory, language development, self-regulation, social development, and motivation. In considering the psychological and behavioral characteristics of persons with mental retardation, we hasten to point out that a given individual with mental retardation may not display all of these characteristics.

The importance of attention for learning is critical. A person must be able to attend to the task at hand before she or he can learn it. For years, researchers have posited that we can attribute many of the learning problems of persons with mental retardation to attention problems (Tomporowski & Tinsley, 1997). Often attending to the wrong things, they have difficulty allocating their attention properly.

One of the most consistent research findings is that people with mental retardation have difficulty remembering information. Their deficits are widespread, but they often have particular problems with working memory (Bray, Fletcher, & Turner, 1997). **Working memory** involves the ability to keep information in mind while simultaneously doing another cognitive task. Trying to remember an address while listening to instructions on how to get there is an example of working memory.

In general, the language of people who are mentally retarded follows the same developmental course as that of nonretarded people, but their language development starts later, progresses at a slower rate, and ends up at a lower level of development (Warren & Yoder, 1997). They often experience problems with the ability both to understand and to produce language.

Self-regulation is a broad term referring to an individual's ability to regulate his or her own behavior. People who are mentally retarded also have difficulties with metacognition, which is closely connected to the ability to self-regulate (Bebko & Luhaorg, 1998). **Metacognition** refers to a person's awareness of what strategies are needed to perform a

UNDERSTANDING THE STANDARDS AND PRINCIPLES What should teachers know about the psychological and behavioral characteristics of individuals with mental retardation? *(CEC Knowledge and Skills Standard MR2K3)*

Council for
Exceptional
Children

Working memory
The ability to remember information while also performing other cognitive operations.

Self-regulation
Refers generally to a person's ability to regulate his or her own behavior (e.g., to employ strategies to help in a problem-solving situation); an area of difficulty for persons who are mentally retarded.

Metacognition
A person's (1) awareness of what strategies are necessary to perform a task and (2) ability to use self-regulation strategies.

task, the ability to plan how to use the strategies, and the evaluation of how well the strategies are working. Self-regulation is thus a component of metacognition. (We discuss metacognition again in Chapter 6.)

People with mental retardation are candidates for a variety of social problems. They often have problems making and keeping friends for at least two reasons: First, many do not seem to know how to strike up social interactions with others, and this difference is evident as early as preschool (Kasari & Bauminger, 1998). Second, even when they are not attempting to interact with others, they may exhibit behaviors that put their peers off. For example, people with mental retardation display higher rates of inattention and disruptive behavior than their nonretarded classmates do.

Friendships and peer relationships are no less important to individuals with mental retardation than they are to anyone else.

Many of the problems pertaining to attention, memory, language development, self-regulation, and social development place people who are mentally retarded at risk to develop problems of motivation. If these individuals have experienced a long history of failure, they can be at risk of developing **learned helplessness**—the feeling that no matter how hard they try, they will still fail. Believing that they have little control over what happens to them and that they are primarily controlled by other people and events, some people with mental retardation tend to give up easily when faced with challenging tasks.

LINKING GENETIC SYNDROMES TO PARTICULAR BEHAVIORAL PHENOTYPES

Until recently, most authorities paid little attention to the type of mental retardation a person had in considering behavioral characteristics. However, researchers have begun to find general patterns of behavioral characteristics associated with some of the genetic syndromes. These patterns of behavior are referred to as **behavioral phenotypes**.

Researchers have identified the four genetic syndromes that we discussed under prenatal causes of mental retardation—Down syndrome, Williams syndrome, fragile X syndrome, and Prader-Willi syndrome—as being ones that have relatively distinctive behavioral phenotypes (Abbeduto et al., 2003; Dykens, 2001; Dykens et al., 2000; Fidler, Hodapp, & Dykens, 2002; Hatton et al., 2003; Hodapp & Fidler, 1999; Moldavsky, Lev, & Lerman-Sagie, 2001). For example, people with Down syndrome often have significant impairments in language and grammar compared to visual-spatial skills, whereas for individuals with Williams syndrome, the reverse is often true. In fact, the storytelling ability of the latter, including their ability to modulate the pitch and volume of their voices to interject emotional tone in their stories, together with their sociability and elflike faces, have led to some speculation that the pixies, elves, or fairies depicted in folktales were people with Williams syndrome. (See the Personal Perspectives on p. 148.)

Table 5.3 lists some of the major behavioral characteristics associated with Down syndrome, Williams syndrome, fragile X syndrome, and Prader-Willi syndrome. Although much research has been done to link these behavioral phenotypes with each of the syndromes, there is far from a one-to-one correspondence between the diagnosis and the char-

THE NATIONAL Association for Down Syndrome (NADS), was founded in 1961 by a group of parents. Its website at **www.nads.org** provides information on resources as well as links to other sites devoted to Down syndrome.

The Williams Syndrome Association is devoted to providing information to affected families: **www. williams–syndrome.org**

The National Fragile X Foundation is devoted to providing information to affected families: **www.fragilex.org/html/home. shtml**

The Prader-Willi Association (USA) is devoted to providing information to affected families: **www.pwsausa.org/** The propensity for those with Prader-Willi to crave food has raised ethical issues pertaining to allowing then to eat and the concept of least restrictive environment. The Prader-Willi Association (USA) has issued a policy statement on the subject. See: **www.pwsausa.org/ postion/ps002.htm**

Learned helplessness
A motivational term referring to a condition wherein a person believes that no matter how hard he or she tries, failure will result.

Behavioral phenotype
A collection of behaviors, including cognitive, language, and social behaviors as well as psychopathological symptoms, that tend to occur together in people with a specific genetic syndrome.

Personal Perspectives

WILLIAMS SYNDROME: AN INSPIRATION FOR SOME PIXIE LEGENDS?

FOLKTALES from many cultures feature magical "little people"—pixies, elves, trolls, and fairies. A number of physical and behavioral similarities suggest that at least some of the fairies in the early tales might have been modeled on people who had Williams syndrome. Such a view is in keeping with the contention of historians that a good deal of folklore and mythology is based on real life.

The facial traits of Williams people are often described as pixielike. In common with pixies in folklore and art, many people with Williams syndrome have small, upturned noses, a depressed nasal bridge, "puffy" eyes, oval ears, and broad mouths with full lips accented by a small chin. Indeed, those features are so common that Williams children tend to look more like one another than their relatives, especially as children. The syndrome also is accompanied by slow growth and development, which leads most Williams individuals to be relatively short.

The "wee, magical people" of assorted folktales often are musicians and storytellers. Fairies are said to "repeat the songs they have heard" and can "enchant" humans with their melodies. Much the same can be said of people with Williams syndrome, who in spite of typically having subnormal IQs, usually display vivid narrative skills and often show talent for

The children in the photograph, who are unrelated, display elfin facial features that clinicians associate with Williams syndrome.

music. (The large pointed ears that are so often associated with fairies might symbolically represent the sensitivity of those mythical individuals—and of Williams people—to music and to sound in general.)

As a group, Williams people are loving, trusting, caring, and extremely sensitive to the feelings of others. Similarly, elves are frequently referred to as the "good people" or as kind and gentle-hearted souls. Finally, Williams individuals, much like the fairies of legend, require order and predictability. In Williams people, this need shows up as rigid adherence to daily routines and a constant need to keep abreast of future plans.

In the past, storytellers created folktales about imaginary beings to help explain phenomena that they did not understand—perhaps including the distinguishing physical and behavioral traits of Williams syndrome. Today researchers turn to Williams people in a quest to understand the unknown, hoping to decipher some of the secrets of how the brain functions. ■

acteristics. Not all individuals with each of these conditions will have all of the symptoms. In other words, not all people who have a syndrome are exactly alike.

Educational Considerations

In recent years, there has been a dramatic philosophical change toward educational programming for students with mental retardation. This change has involved two related movements: a greater emphasis on inclusion and the teaching of useful skills and a greater emphasis on self-determination (Westling & Fox, 2000).

TABLE 5.3   Links between Genetic Syndromes and Behavioral Phenotypes

Genetic Syndrome	Behavioral Phenotype	
	Relative Weaknesses	Relative Strengths
Down syndrome	Receptive and expressive language, especially grammar Problems interpreting facial emotions Cognitive skills tend to worsen over time Early onset of Alzheimer's disease	Visual-spatial skills Visual short-term memory
Williams syndrome	Visual-spatial skills Fine-motor control Anxieties, fears, phobias Overly friendly	Expressive language, vocabulary Facial recognition and memory Musical interests and skills
Fragile X syndrome	Short-term memory Sequential processing Repetitive speech patterns Social anxiety and withdrawal	Verbal skills, including vocabulary Long-term memory for information already acquired Adaptive behavior
Prader-Willi syndrome	Auditory processing Feeding problems in infancy Overeating, obesity in childhood and adulthood Sleep disturbances Obsessive-compulsive behaviors	Relatively high IQ (average about 70) Visual processing Facility with jigsaw puzzles

Source: Based on the following studies and reviews: Abbeduto et al., 2003; Belser & Sudhalter, 2001; Dimitropoulos, Feurer, Butler, & Thompson, 2001; Dykens, Hodapp, & Finucane, 2000; Fidler, Hodapp, & Dykens, 2002; Hatton et al., 2003; Kasari, Freeman, & Hughes, 2001; Mervis, Klein-Tasman, & Mastin, 2001; Moldavsky, Lev, & Lerman-Sagie, 2001.

INCLUSION AND USEFUL SKILLS

As we noted previously, more and more students with mental retardation are being edu-cated in regular schools alongside students without disabilities. The Success Stories on p. 150 describes Molly, a student with mental retardation, who has been included in gen-eral education classrooms since first grade. Her curriculum is modified, but she is able to participate in most activities with the help of high-quality instruction, a special educator, and a classroom aide.

To help facilitate integration into the mainstream environment, inclusion advocates note the importance of teaching students with mental retardation using a curriculum that promotes practical, age-appropriate skills. In the past, the tendency was to provide such students with a curriculum that was more suited to their mental age than to their chrono-logical age. Most authorities agree that this is demeaning. In addition, it does not prepare the students for functioning alongside their nondisabled peers.

SELF-DETERMINATION

Because people with mental retardation have reduced cognitive capacity, professionals and parents alike have traditionally considered them incapable of making decisions on their own. In a sense, this paternalistic attitude often resulted in a self-fulfilling prophecy by not providing persons with mental retardation an opportunity to take more control over their lives. However, as we noted in Chapter 2, many professionals and parents now champion the notion of promoting self-determination in persons who are mentally retarded. In fact, the major parent organization in the field, The Arc, and the major professional organization, the AAMR, have adopted position statements supporting the idea of self-determination. (See the Focus on Concepts on p. 152 for an excerpt from AAMR's policy.)

UNDERSTANDING THE STANDARDS AND PRINCIPLES   What educational approaches are most appropriate for students with mental retardation? *(CEC Knowledge and Skills Standards MR4K1 & MR7S1)*

Council for Exceptional Children

THE ARC has also issued a policy state-ment on self-deter-mination: **www.thearc.org/ posits/2002positions.doc**

Special Educators at Work

Dave Berry, Molly's father: "We don't expect the classroom teachers to do it all."
Thirteen-year-old Molly Berry has been included in general education classes since preschool.
These are the keys to her success:
- *Intensive collaboration and classroom support*
- *Relentless focus on communication and teamwork*
- *Specific interventions for math and reading, initiating tasks, and improving attention and behaviors*

Special educator Lisa Douville and general educator Mike Morcom are collaborating to maximize learning for Molly Berry before she leaves elementary school. Lisa Douville sees improvement in Molly's ability to focus, and Karen and Dave Berry agree that Molly has made gains socially in the mainstream. All agree that Molly has gained from intensive, relentless, and specific special education.

Intensive Collaboration and Classroom Support   Molly is one of four special needs students among the twenty-two members of Mike Morcom's fifth-grade class. It would be hard to manage instruction without support from a special educator and a classroom aide, says Morcum, who sees collaboration as key to Molly's success. Janet Metcalf, a certified teacher, has worked as the educational technician with Molly's class for two years. So has special educator Douville who supervises Metcalf, works directly with Molly on reading and math skills in the resource room, and manages her educational plan. Douville and Morcom jointly track Molly's progress.

"We started to work as a team when the second grade teacher identified the supports Molly needed in the classroom," Dave Berry recalls. "Her fourth and fifth grade teachers have

been terrific at working closely *with* special educators. We don't expect the classroom teachers to do it all, but we do expect them to have help."

Relentless Focus on Communication and Teamwork
According to Dave Berry, "When parents and professionals are both well informed, then they're on even ground." Karen Berry makes sure that IEPs are available to all Molly's teachers. "Then," she says, "I check to see if they are being used."

For the Berrys, the key issue in Molly's education is effective communication and team work from year to year. That means that teachers exchange information and that parents and educators listen carefully to each other. "Everyone needs to know it's okay to speak up for the real needs of the child, despite the costs or inconveniences," says Mr. Berry. "We've all worked hard to help Molly make progress."

Karen and Dave Berry are strong advocates for Molly. Together with the team, they crafted an IEP that carefully describes her unique learning needs:

Molly exhibits delays in the development of perceptual-motor skills, a mild to moderate phonological disorder, a

Self-determination
The ability to make personal choices, regulate one's own life, and be a self-advocate; a prevailing philosophy in education programming for people with mental retardation. Having control over one's life, not having to rely on others for making choices about one's quality of life; develops over one's life span.

Self-determination involves the ability to make personal choices, to regulate one's life, and to be a self-advocate (Westling & Fox, 2000). A person who is self-determined exhibits four characteristics:

- *Autonomy*, acting according to one's own preferences, interests, and abilities, independently and free from undue external influences
- *Self-regulation*, deciding what strategies and tactics to use in particular situations, in setting goals, in problem solving, and in monitoring one's own performance in these tasks
- *Psychological empowerment*, a belief that one has control over important circumstances, and a belief that one has the skills to achieve desired outcomes, and that by applying those skills, the desired outcome will occur

moderate to severe expressive language delay, and difficulties comprehending complex verbal material. When compared to her peers, Molly has difficulties in the following areas: working independently, and initiating and completing tasks. Off-task behaviors consist of unpredictable episodes of physical and visual wandering, and ignoring teacher requests. This behavior is compounded in situations when tasks are perceived by Molly as being difficult. Her levels of performance are consistent with test results and classroom observations.

Specific Interventions: Math and Reading, Initiating Tasks, and Improving Attention and Behaviors Molly's math program is carried out by the classroom aide with guidance and resource support from Douville. If the class is working as a group or taking a test, Metcalf adapts the activity. She might pull the next item from Molly's individualized math packet or develop a criterion reference test based on Molly's third-grade level goals. For social studies and science, Metcalf adapts Morcom's materials and activities for the special needs students in the class. She also keeps a daily school–home journal with the Berrys.

Molly's reading and spelling programs are also directed by Douville and carried out by Metcalf in the classroom. Molly has difficulty decoding words, and her comprehension is better when she gets information orally. Says Douville, "Molly is embarrassed to be seen with the second/third-grade level books she is able to read. She is aware of her social environment and needs help with handling sensitive issues appropriately."

As they plan for the future, this team of parents and professionals hope that Molly will be able to remain included in classes with nondisabled peers as much as is appropriate for her.

Says Dave Berry, "I think it must be said that while this approach works for my child, inclusion in a regular class might not be appropriate for someone else's child." Karen Berry agrees. "I don't want her just to be included. It's what is done for her in the classroom that counts."

CEC'S STANDARDS: PAVING THE WAY TO SUCCESS

Council for Exceptional Children

ASSESS YOUR STEPS TO SUCCESS in meeting the CEC knowledge and skill base for all beginning special education teachers of students with mental retardation or developmental disabilities. Use the following questions to reflect on the growth of your own professional knowledge, skills, and dispositions.

REFLECTING ON YOUR OWN PROFESSIONAL DEVELOPMENT

If you were Molly's teacher . . .

- WHAT are some areas about educating students with mental retardation or developmental disabilities that you would need to know more about?
- WHAT are some specific skills that would help you address her academic and behavioral challenges?
- WHAT personal dispositions do you think are most important for you to develop in teaching students with limited cognitive abilities?

Using the CEC Standards . . .

- WHAT are some behavioral problems associated with individuals with mental retardation or developmental delays? (MR1K6)
- WHAT approaches could you utilize to create positive learning environments for individuals with mental retardation and developmental disabilities? (MR5K1)
- WHAT are some ways to foster respectful and beneficial relationships between families and professionals? (CC10S3) ■

By Jean Crockett

- *Self-realization*, one has a reasonably accurate knowledge of himself[/herself] and his[/her] strengths and his[/her] limitations and acts in a way that capitalizes on this knowledge (Westling & Fox, 2000, p. 34)

We should not assume that self-determination will develop on its own in people who are mentally retarded. On the basis of our previous discussion of their history of learning deficits and vulnerability for developing learned helplessness, it should be obvious that people with mental retardation will find it difficult to become self-determined. Investigators have just begun to look into ways of fostering self-determination (e.g., Wehmeyer, Palmer, Agran, Mithaug, & Martin, 2000), but much more research is needed to determine the best ways to cultivate self-determination in students with mental retardation.

FOCUS ON CONCEPTS

AAMR Policy Statement on Self-Determination

THE following are excerpts from the American Association on Mental Retardation's Self-Determination Policy Statement:

POSITION

- AAMR will uphold the right to self-determination as the right to act as the primary causal agent in one's life, to pursue self-defined goals and to participate fully in society. Self-determining individuals control their lives, make choices and decisions based on their interests, abilities and preferences, and take responsibility for their lives.
- People with mental retardation must have the opportunity to advocate for themselves, without fear of punish-

ment, and with the knowledge that their demands and suggestions will be heard and given fair consideration.

- AAMR recognizes and supports the right of individuals with mental retardation to self-determination in every aspect of decision making that affects them as individuals, including living arrangements, work, religious participation, personal relationships and control of their private funds and public funds designated for the purchase of services for them as individuals. . . . ■

Source: American Association on Mental Retardation, 1998 (revised 2000), posted on the World Wide Web: http://aamr.org/Policies/Pol_self_determination.shtml. Reprinted with permission.

Perhaps the most important issue pertaining to self-determination involves deciding just how far to go in allowing people with disabilities to make decisions solely on their own. Some believe that the notion of self-determination can be carried too far. (See the Personal Perspectives on p. 153.) Also, as we discussed in Chapter 3, we need to keep in mind that self-determination will be defined differently depending on the particular culture of the individual. Some cultures are more oriented toward valuing individuality and autonomy; others are less so (Cronin, 2000).

Educational programs for students with mental retardation vary according to the degree of mental retardation and how much support is required. The overall goal is to achieve the proper blend of academic and functional skills instruction.

INSTRUCTIONAL METHODS

In general, the focus of educational programs varies according to the degree of the student's mental retardation or how much the student requires support services. For example, the lesser the degree of mental retardation, the more the teacher emphasizes academic skills; and the greater the degree of mental retardation, the more stress there is on self-help, community living, and vocational skills. Keep in mind, however, that, in practice, all students who are mentally retarded, no matter the severity level, need some instruction in academic, self-help, community living, and vocational skills. We focus on the elementary school level here; we discuss preschool and secondary programming in later sections.

A major issue facing special educators is how to ensure that students with mental retardation have access to the general education curriculum, as dictated by the Individuals With Disabilities Education Act (see Chapter 1), while still being taught functional skills. The more severe the level of mental retardation, the more this is an issue. Authorities recommend that there be a merger of functional and academic curricular standards. This notion of blending academics and functional skills is embodied in functional academics. **Functional academics** involve teaching academics in the context of daily living skills (Drew & Hardman, 2004). Whereas the nonretarded child is taught academics, such as reading, to learn other academic content, such as history, the child with mental retardation is often taught reading to learn to function independently. In functional reading, the child learns academics to do such things as read a newspaper, read the telephone book, read labels on goods at the store, make change, and fill out job applications. Examples of functional math, taken from Colorado's performance indicators, are as follows:

> "make and read simple graphs representing meaningful information and relationships," demonstrate a beginning sense of measurement (e.g., big, little, heavy, light, etc.)," "match number symbols with appropriate amount," and "find months and dates on the calendar." (Browder et al., 2004, p. 216.)

Educational programming for students with mental retardation, especially those with more severe mental retardation, often includes the following three features: systematic instruction, instruction in real-life settings with real materials, and functional behavioral assessment and positive behavioral support.

Systematic Instruction   Effective teaching of students with mental retardation involves systematic instruction. **Systematic instruction** is the use of instructional prompts,

Functional academics
Practical skills (e.g., reading a newspaper or telephone book) rather than academic learning skills.

Systematic instruction
Teaching that involves instructional prompts, consequences for performance, and transfer of stimulus control; often used with students with mental retardation.

Personal Perspectives

SELF-DETERMINATION:
TOO MUCH OF A GOOD THING?

SOME people are beginning to question seriously whether self-determination can be carried too far. For example, some see it as a way to save resources:

> Call it "self-determination," call it "choice," but call it "less." That creative service coordinators can do more with less given enough flexibility is an attractive but fanciful notion when presented as a system-wide solution. The idea has been oversold through the use of success stories involving exceptionally supportive families, friends, and/or communities. How many people or their families really want to, or are really capable of, managing all their supports? A large segment of the population in public service are adults with families whose time is already taxed to the hilt. They live in disinterested communities. . . .
>
> It is time to wake up to the fact that self-determination is increasingly being used to cover for cutbacks in funding where it can be least afforded—among the front-line agencies upon which consumers depend. (Ashbaugh, 2002, pp. 416–417.

Others see it as an impractical panacea that promises too much:

> Human decency and so-called natural law . . . inform us that impaired people need to have competent advocates at their side who, if the occasion requires it, are willing and able to make wise decisions on their behalf, even if these do not always please a person of limited, disturbed, or diminished mentality. (Wolfensberger, 2002b, p. 257)

In response to those who would question the utility of self-determination practices, some have evoked ethical principles:

> Ashbaugh . . . pointed to the lack of empirical evidence supporting many of the basic assumptions offered in arguments for self-determined systems of support. . . . Certainly, we do not need research to tell us what is moral and ethical: People with disabilities should be in charge of their own life. How to best position service delivery systems to make this a reality is, however, in our opinion, still in need of empirical demonstration. (Romer, Richardson, Aigbe, & Porter, 2003, p. 293) ■

Community-based instruction focuses on everyday living skills learned in actual settings.

Constant time delay
An instructional procedure whereby the teacher makes a request while simultaneously prompting the student and then over several occasions makes the same request and waits a constant period of time before prompting; often used with students with mental retardation.

Progressive time delay
An instructional procedure whereby the teacher makes a request while simultaneously prompting the student and then over several occasions gradually increases the latency between the request and the prompt; often used with students with mental retardation.

Functional behavioral assessment
The practice of determining the consequences (what purpose the behavior serves), antecedents (what triggers the behavior), and setting events (in what contexts the behavior occurs) of inappropriate behavior.

Positive behavioral support (PBS)
Systematic use of the science of behavior to find ways of supporting the desirable behavior of an individual rather than punishing the undesirable behavior.

consequences for performance, and strategies for the transfer of stimulus control (Davis & Cuvo, 1997). Students who are mentally retarded often need to be prompted or cued to respond in the appropriate manner. These prompts can be verbal, gestural, or physical, or modeling may be used (Davis & Cuvo, 1997). A verbal prompt can be a question such as "What do you need to do next?" or a command such as "Put your socks in the top dresser drawer." A gestural prompt might involve pointing to the socks and/or the dresser drawer while stating the question or the command. Taking the student's hand and placing it on the socks and/or drawer would be an example of a physical prompt. The adult might also model putting the socks in the drawer before then asking the student to do it.

With respect to consequences, research has consistently shown that students who are positively reinforced for correct responses learn faster. Positive reinforcers can range from verbal praise to tokens that can be traded for prizes or other rewards. For students with severe mental retardation, the more immediate the reinforcement, the more effective it is. Once the student demonstrates the desired behavior consistently, the goal is to wean the student from reliance on external reinforcers as soon as possible.

The goal of transfer of stimulus control is to reach a point at which the student does not have to rely on prompts and can be more independent. To transfer the control away from the prompts to more naturally occurring stimuli, several techniques are used, including delaying the time between a request and the prompt (Browder & Snell, 2000; Wolery & Schuster, 1997). For example, with **constant time delay**, the adult starts by making a request ("Please put your clothes away") and giving a prompt simultaneously ("Put your clothes in the top dresser drawer"). On subsequent occasions, the adult might wait a set period of time (e.g., five seconds) between the request and the prompt. With **progressive time delay**, the adult also starts with a simultaneous prompt and request, but the latency period between the two is then increased gradually.

Instruction in Real-Life Settings with Real Materials   Instruction can take place in the classroom, under simulated conditions, or in real-life settings. It is generally better to teach daily living skills to students with mental retardation in the actual settings where they will be using these skills. Because it is easier to hold instruction in classrooms than in real-life settings, the teacher might start out with instruction in the classroom and then supplement it with instruction in real-life situations (Browder & Snell, 2000). For example, the teacher might use worksheets and photos of various shopping activities in class or set up a simulated store with shelves of products and a cash register (Morse & Schuster, 2000). These classroom activities could then be supplemented with periodic visits to real grocery stores. Likewise, it is preferable to use real cans of food and real money in teaching students to read product labels and to make change.

Functional Behavioral Assessment and Positive Behavioral Support   One of the major reasons some students with mental retardation have difficulty being included in general education classrooms is that they sometimes exhibit inappropriate behavior, such as hitting, biting, or screaming. Authorities recommend that teachers use a combination of **functional behavioral assessment (FBA)** and **positive behavioral support (PBS)** to reduce or eliminate these behaviors. FBA involves determining the consequences, antecedents, and setting events that maintain such behaviors (Horner, Albin, Sprague, & Todd, 2000). *Consequences* refer to the purpose the behavior serves for the person. For example, some students behave inappropriately to gain attention. *Antecedents* refer to things that trigger the behavior. For example, the student might become aggressive only toward certain peers. Setting events take into account broader contextual factors. For example, the student might be more likely to exhibit inappropriate behavior when sick or in hot, humid weather. On the basis of a functional assessment, the teacher can make changes in consequences, antecedents, and/or contextual factors and monitor the effectiveness of these changes.

On the basis of results from FBA, teachers can develop a PBS plan for students. As we discussed in Chapter 4, PBS involves finding ways to support positive behaviors of students instead of punishing negative behaviors. PBS focuses on the total environment of the student, including instruction. Some proponents of PBS place an emphasis on implementing schoolwide plans to promote positive behavior in all students, not just those with disabilities (Sugai et al., 2000). Under such a plan, all school personnel are prepared to deliver positive reinforcement for appropriate behavior in virtually all settings: classrooms, cafeteria, hallways, playground, school buses, and so on.

SERVICE DELIVERY MODELS

Placements for school-age students with mental retardation range from general education classes to residential facilities. Although special classes for these students tend to be the norm, more and more students with mental retardation are being placed in more integrated settings. The degree of integration tends to be determined by the level of severity, students who are less severely mentally retarded being the most integrated. An example of instructional practice that includes students with mild mental retardation in reading instruction is Classwide Peer Tutoring. See the Responsive Instruction on p. 156 for details.

However, as we discussed in Chapter 2, some professionals believe that all students with mental retardation should be educated in the general education classroom and that schools should provide the necessary support services (e.g., a special aide or special education teacher) in the class. Recent research in the area of mathematics indicates that using certain instructional procedures, with support in the general education classroom, can help students with mental retardation improve their computation and problem solving skills. See the Responsive Instruction box on p. 157.

Although not all authorities agree on how much inclusion should be practiced, virtually all agree that placement in a self-contained class with no opportunity for interaction with nondisabled students is inappropriate. At the same time, even parents who favor integrated settings often believe that it is good for their children to interact with other children with disabilities too and that being the only student in the class with a disability has its drawbacks (Guralnick, Connor, & Hammond, 1995).

Early Intervention

We can categorize preschool programs for children with mental retardation as those whose purpose is to prevent mental retardation or those that are designed to further the development of children who have already been identified as mentally retarded. In general, the former address children who are at risk for mild mental retardation, and the latter are for children with more severe mental retardation.

EARLY CHILDHOOD PROGRAMS DESIGNED FOR PREVENTION

The 1960s witnessed the birth of infant and preschool programs for at-risk children and their families. Three such projects are the Perry Preschool Project, the Chicago Child-Parent Center (CPC) Program, and the Abecedarian Project. The first two focused on preschool children from low-income environments who were at risk for a variety of negative outcomes, including mental retardation. Both have demonstrated that early intervention can have positive long-term effects on participants, including reduction in rates of mental retardation. In the case of the Perry Preschool Project (Schweinhart & Weikart, 1993), when

TASH, an organization that has been perhaps the most vocal in advocating for full inclusion of students with disabilities, identifies itself as a "civil rights organization for, and of, people with mental retardation, autism, cerebral palsy, physical disabilities and other conditions that make full integration a challenge": **www.tash.org**

Meeting the Needs of Students with Mental Retardation

Classwide Peer-Tutoring

WHAT THE RESEARCH SAYS

In an effort to meet the instructional needs of students with mild mental retardation within inclusive settings, researchers have explored instructional methods that provide the necessary structure, individualization, and level of corrective feedback critical for success for this population. One such method is classwide peer tutoring (CWPT) (Delquadri, Greenwood, Stretton, & Hall, 1983). CWPT involves the use of peers to provide instruction and feedback in a reciprocal format. That is, paired students have the opportunity to serve as a tutor and as a tutee during each session. CWPT procedures were designed to address the need for higher levels of active, academic engagement for all students, but particularly for students with the greatest academic deficits (Greenwood, 1991).

RESEARCH STUDY

A team of researchers conducted a study to examine the effectiveness of CWPT on the spelling performance of eight students (four students with mild mental retardation and four nondisabled students) participating in a general education class (Mortweet et al., 1999). The students with mild mental retardation were included in general education classrooms for spelling, a social activity period, and lunch. The CWPT model was compared to traditional teacher-led instruction during the spelling period.

The investigators used the following structure for the CWPT sessions:

1. Each student with mild mental retardation was paired with a nondisabled peer.
2. Tutoring sessions occurred four times a week for twenty minutes per day.
3. Tutoring materials included the list of spelling words, point sheets, and practice sheets.
4. The teacher assigned each pair to one of two competing classroom teams. (Points earned by the pairs contributed to daily team point totals.) Partners and teams were reassigned on a weekly basis.
5. During each session, students served as the tutor for ten minutes and as the tutee for the other ten minutes.
6. Instruction consisted of the tutor reading the spelling word to the tutee. The tutee wrote the spelling word while saying each letter aloud. If the word was spelled

correctly, the tutor awarded the tutee two points; if the word was spelled incorrectly, the tutor spelled the word correctly and the tutee wrote the word three times while naming each letter. The tutee could receive one point for correctly spelling the practice word. After ten minutes, the roles were reversed.

7. The teacher assigned bonus points for pairs that were working cooperatively and following the instructional protocol.
8. When the twenty-minute session was over, the teacher calculated team points on the basis of partner points. The winning team received such privileges as lining up for recess first.
9. Modifications made for the students with mild mental retardation included: shortened word lists, enlarged practice sheets, and tutee reading of words when the student with mild mental retardation was the tutor and was unable to read the word.

RESEARCH FINDINGS

When compared to the teacher-led condition, the CWPT resulted in improved academic performance for all students, increased amount of engaged academic time (approximately five to ten minutes more per student per session), and positive acceptance from the teachers and students. Thus, CWPT provides teachers with a flexible instructional strategy to meet the varying needs of an inclusive classroom.

APPLYING THE RESEARCH TO TEACHING

Given the effectiveness of CWPT, teachers can establish similar procedures in their classes. Tasks such as math facts, spelling, letter sounds, and word identification make great CWPT topics. Following the model established in the study, teachers can create their own tutoring materials. Key features of CWPT include partnering of a higher and lower skilled student, explicit instruction in the tutoring activities (i.e., ample training prior to independent partner work), structured tasks for the tutor to guide the tutee in completing, reciprocal roles so the tutee has the opportunity to be a tutor, and use of points to reward desired behavior. ■

By Kristin L. Sayeski

Meeting the Needs of Students with Mental Retardation

Strategies for Effective Instruction in Mathematics

WHAT THE RESEARCH SAYS

Although many professionals use the catchall term *mildly disabled* when referring to both students with learning disabilities and students with mild-to-moderate mental retardation, research on instruction for these two groups reveals differences in learning that have implications for classroom practices (Butler, Miller, Lee, & Pierce, 2001; Parmar, Cawley, & Miller, 1994). Current research demonstrates quantitative and qualitative differences between the performances of students with mental retardation and students with learning disabilities (Parmar et al., 1994; Scott, Greenfield, & Partridge, 1991). Questions about what topics should be taught, when topics should be introduced, how much time should be spent on certain topics, and whether students with different IQ levels can be equally served by the same methods drive this current research.

RESEARCH STUDY

A study conducted with large groups of students with mental retardation and learning disabilities (206 and 295, respectively) revealed differences between the groups in the areas of basic concepts, listening vocabulary, problem solving/reasoning, and fractions (Parmar et al., 1994). The students with mental retardation scored lower on all subtest areas (concepts, vocabulary, problem solving, and fractions) when compared to the students with learning disabilities. Overall, both groups performed poorly on the problem-solving and application-of-concepts problems. Researchers attributed problem-solving difficulties to lack of instruction in real-world problem solving. The generally depressed scores of the students with mental retardation, however, reflect the need for more intense and differentiated instructional practices for this group of students.

RESEARCH FINDINGS

In answer to the questions of when, how, and with what intensity certain mathematics topics should be taught, the students with mental retardation scored significantly lower than the students with learning disabilities (e.g., 14-year-old students with mental retardation performed at levels similar to or lower than those of 10-year-olds with learning disabilities). They also failed to attain the same steady growth rates exhibited by students with learning disabilities (e.g., gains in problem solving/reasoning by students with learning disabilities were more than twice those of students with mental retardation (Parmar et al., 1994). Thus, it is reasonable to conclude that instruction for these groups of students should differ in terms of pace, type of instruction, and level of practice.

APPLYING THE RESEARCH TO TEACHING

Historically, mathematics instruction for students with mental retardation emphasized memorization of algorithms and abstract routines—a practice that is clearly reflected in the above study. Yet a recent review of studies on mathematics instruction for students with mental retardation identified specific instructional practices that resulted in increased competence in both basic-skills computation and problem solving/application (Butler et al., 2001).

On the basis of recommended practices, a team of researchers designed the following instructional sequence that could be implemented in a general education classroom that includes students with mental retardation (Butler et al., 2001):

1. A one-minute math time trial to promote fluency and retention of previously learned facts. These trials would be specific to the particular skills a student is working on.
2. Step-by-step strategy instruction provided to the whole class using direct instruction.
3. Small-group work that involves applying the strategy. Problems for each group would be commensurate with the computational skill level of students within the group. Work at the concrete, representational, and abstract levels would be introduced during this time at the appropriate pace and sequence.
4. Final individual instruction in basic skills or computation could be provided via the computer, peers, or teacher-directed methods such as constant time delay or multisensory methods. ■

By Kristin L. Sayeski

Early intervention programs can have positive long-term effects on participants, including reduction in rates of mental retardation.

students who had received preschool intervention were studied again at age 27, a number of differences favored them over those who had not received the intervention:

- More had completed the twelfth grade.
- Fewer had been arrested.
- More owned their own homes.
- Fewer had ever been on welfare.
- They had a lower teenage pregnancy rate.
- They earned a better-than-average income.
- Classification as disabled or mentally retarded was less likely.

Furthermore, a cost-benefit analysis that took into account such things as costs of welfare and the criminal justice system and benefits of taxes on earnings showed a return of $7.16 for every dollar invested in the Perry Preschool Project.

The most recent follow-up of participants in the CPC Program at age 20 indicates similar results: higher school completion rates, lower juvenile arrest rates, and lower rates of grade retention and identification for special education. In fact, the rate of identification for special education was almost half that of the comparison group, which had not received early intervention (Reynolds, Temple, Robertson, & Mann, 2001).

One of the best-known infant stimulation programs is the Abecedarian Project (Ramey & Campbell, 1984, 1987). Participants were identified before birth by selection of children from a pool of pregnant women living in poverty. After birth, the infants were randomly assigned to one of two groups: half to a day-care group that received special services and half to a control group that received no such services. The day-care group participated in a program that provided experiences to promote perceptual-motor, intellectual, language, and social development. The families of these children also received a number of social and medical services. Results of the Abecedarian Project, reported through the age of 21, indicate that the infants from the day-care group have attained better scores on intellectual and academic measures and are more likely to have attended a four-year college (Campbell, Ramey, Pungello, Sparling, & Miller-Johnson, 2002).

EARLY CHILDHOOD PROGRAMS DESIGNED TO FURTHER DEVELOPMENT

Early childhood programs designed to enhance the development of children already identified as mentally retarded place a great deal of emphasis on language and conceptual development. Because these children often have multiple disabilities, other professionals—for example, speech therapists and physical therapists—are frequently involved in their education. Also, many of the better programs include opportunities for parent involvement. Through practice with their children, parents can reinforce some of the skills that teachers work on. For example, parents of infants with physical disabilities, such as cerebral palsy, can learn from physical therapists the appropriate ways of handling their children to further their physical development. Similarly, parents can learn appropriate feeding techniques from speech therapists.

UNDERSTANDING THE STANDARDS AND PRINCIPLES Transition programming for individuals with mental retardation involves what two related areas? *(CEC Knowledge and Skills Standards MR7K1 & MR10S1)*

Council for Exceptional Children

Transition to Adulthood

Most authorities agree that, although the degree of emphasis on transition programming should be greater for older than for younger students, such programming should begin in the elementary years. Table 5.4 depicts some examples of curriculum activities pertaining to domestic, community living, leisure, and vocational skills.

Authorities are now recommending that transition planning be person centered. **Person-centered planning** is similar to family-centered planning that we discussed in Chapter 4 except that it is focused more on the individual than on the family. In other words, person-centered planning is a consumer-driven model that encourages the individual to make his or her own decisions with respect to services while mobilizing resources and supports to meet the person's goals.

Transition programming for individuals with mental retardation involves two related areas: community adjustment and employment.

COMMUNITY ADJUSTMENT

For people with mental retardation to adjust to living in the community, they need to acquire a number of skills, many of which are in the area of self-help. For example, they need to be able to manage money, use public transportation, and keep themselves well groomed and their living quarters well maintained. They also need to have good social skills so that they can get along with other people in the community. In general, research has shown that attempts to train for community survival skills can be successful, especially when the training occurs within the actual setting in which the individuals live. For a specific example about shopping for groceries, see the Responsive Instruction on p. 160.

Person-centered planning
A type of transition model; consumer-driven in that professionals are viewed as working for individuals.

TABLE 5.4 Examples of Curriculum Activities Across the School Years for Domestic, Community Living, Leisure, and Vocational Skills

Skill Area			
Domestic	**Community Living**	**Leisure**	**Vocational**
Elementary school student: Tim			
Washing dishes	Eating meals in a restaurant	Climbing on swing set	Picking up plate, silverware, and
Dressing	Using restroom in a local	Playing board games	glass after a meal
Grooming	restaurant	Playing tag with neighbors	Returning toys to appropriate
Toileting skills	Giving the clerk money for	Tumbling activities	storage space
Sorting clothes	item he wants to purchase	Running	
Junior high school student: Mary			
Washing clothes	Crossing streets safely	Taking aerobics classes	Waxing floors
Cooking a simple hot meal	Purchasing an item from a	Playing checkers with a friend	Hanging and bagging clothes
(soup, salad, and sandwich)	department store	Playing miniature golf	Bussing tables
Raking leaves	Using local transportation	Cycling	Operating machinery (such as
Purchasing items from a list	system to get to and from	Attending high school or	dishwasher, buffer, etc.)
Vacuuming and dusting living	recreational facilities	local college basketball	Following a job sequence
room		games	
High school student: Sandy			
Cleaning all rooms in place	Utilizing bus system to move	Jogging	Performing required janitorial
of residence	about the community	Archery	duties at J.C. Penney
Developing a weekly budget	Depositing checks into bank	Watching college basketball	Performing laundry duties at
Cooking meals	account	Video games	Moon's Laundromat
Maintaining personal needs	Using community health	Card games (Uno)	Performing photography at
Caring for and maintaining	facilities (physician,	Athletic club swimming class	Virginia National Bank
clothing	pharmacist)	Gardening	Headquarters

Source: Adapted from P. Wehman, M. S. Moon, J. M. Everson, W. Wood, & J. M. Barcus, (1988) *Transition from school to work: New challenges for youth with severe disabilities* (Baltimore: Paul H. Brookes), pp. 140–142. Reprinted with permission.

Meeting the Needs of Students with Mental Retardation

Computer-Based Video to Teach Grocery Shopping

For many individuals with moderate mental retardation, the focus of their transition plan is on increased independence. For some, this goal might come in the form of independent or semi-independent living. Grocery shopping can be a key skill that leads to greater self-sufficiency and autonomy. The freedom to make choices about which foods are purchased and the ability to locate and retrieve those items from the store can dramatically influence a person's self-determination.

OVERVIEW OF THE STUDY

Many studies have been conducted to determine efficient and effective strategies for teaching individuals with mental retardation to shop for groceries. One recent and promising study explored the use of computer-based video to assist students in locating items in a grocery store (Mechling, Gast, & Langone, 2002). In this study, Mechling and colleagues used a computer-based video to teach students how to read words found on grocery store aisle markers and to locate particular items within the corresponding aisle.

Four students (ages 9–17) with moderate mental retardation learned to touch aisle sign words on the computer screen and then to select target items from the aisle (again by touching the screen). A system of least prompts was employed to teach the students the steps and reinforce correct responses. Least prompts procedures involve moving from less intrusive to more intrusive guiding. In this study, the least prompt was a command to touch the aisle sign word that corresponded to the student's list (e.g., "Touch potato chip"). If the student did not respond after five seconds, the next level prompt was employed (e.g., a repeat of the command with a gesture toward the screen). The final and most intrusive prompt was to physically guide the student's hand to the screen paired with the command. This least prompts instructional procedure has been demonstrated through research to be very effective in teaching new skills to students who are mentally retarded. Correct selection of the words on aisle signs were followed by praise and a ten-second video clip of scanning the aisle and viewing the item on the shelf. The computer-based instruction occurred in three phases. During each phase, four additional items were added to the list (i.e., four words for phase 1, eight words for phase 2, and twelve words for phase 3). After the computer-based training in each phase, the teacher took the students to a grocery store, where they were asked to locate all twelve items.

RESEARCH FINDINGS

Mechling and colleagues found that all four students in the study were able to generalize the reading of aisle sign markers and locating items from the computer session to the grocery store probes. In addition, parents noted that their children tended to locate those items independently when shopping after the study had concluded. The researchers believe that teaching students to make use of the aisle markers enhances grocery-shopping efficiency when compared to traveling up and down all aisles to locate items.

APPLYING THE RESEARCH TO TEACHING

Teachers whose students have transition IEP goals that are community focused can use the tools employed in the study: computer-based video training linked with community-based practice. The researchers created the computer-based video by using Hyperstudio and importing still photos of aisle marker signs and short video clips of scanning and walking down the aisles. The researchers were able to create training videos of three different grocery stores. Frequently, restraints such as scheduling difficulties, time limitations, and access limit a teacher's ability to provide community-based instruction in more than one setting (Mechling et. al, 2002). The computer-based training allowed the researchers to include greater variation into the instruction. In addition, the use of the computer allowed for more teaching opportunities without having to go out into the community to provide that support. In summary, the use of computer-based simulations can be a powerful way for teachers to enhance their community-based instruction. ■

By Kristin L. Sayeski

Although large residential facilities for people with mental retardation still exist, they are fast disappearing. There is a trend toward smaller **community residential facilities (CRFs)**. CRFs, or group homes, accommodate small groups (three to ten people) in houses under the direction of "house parents." Placement can be permanent, or it can serve as a temporary arrangement to prepare the individuals for independent living. In either case, the purpose of the CRF is to teach independent living skills in a more normal setting than a large institution offers.

Some professionals are questioning whether CRFs go far enough in offering opportunities for integration into the community. They are recommending **supported living**, in which persons with mental retardation receive supports to live in more natural, noninstitutional settings, such as their own home or apartment. There is some evidence that supported living arrangements lead to a higher level of self-determination in people with mental retardation than do CRFs (Stancliffe, Abery, & Smith, 2000).

More and more authorities point to the family as a critical factor in determining whether persons with mental retardation will be successful in community adjustment and employment. Even though many hold up supported living as an ideal, the fact is that the vast majority of adults with mental retardation live with their families (MR/DD Data Brief, 2001). Even for those who live away from home, the family can still be a significant source of support for living in the community and finding and holding jobs.

EMPLOYMENT

Surveys show that adults with mental retardation have high rates of unemployment (National Organization on Disability & Harris, 2000). Even though employment statistics for workers who are mentally retarded have been discouraging, most professionals working in this area are optimistic about the potential for providing training programs that will lead to meaningful employment for these adults. Research indicates that with appropriate training, individuals with mental retardation can hold down jobs with a good deal of success, measured by such things as attendance, employer satisfaction, and length of employment (McDonnell, Hardman, & McDonnell, 2003).

When people with mental retardation are not successful on the job, the cause more often involves behaviors related to job responsibility and social skills than job performance per se (Butterworth & Strauch, 1994; Heal, Gonzalez, Rusch, Copher, & DeStefano, 1990; Salzberg, Lignugaris/Kraft, & McCuller, 1988). In other words, the problem is not so much that people with mental retardation cannot perform the job as it is that they have difficulty with such issues as attendance, initiative, responding to criticism, and interacting socially with coworkers and supervisors. This latter problem—social interaction—most consistently distinguishes workers who are mentally retarded from those who are not.

A variety of vocational training and employment approaches for individuals with mental retardation are available. Most of these are subsumed under two very different kinds of arrangements: the sheltered workshop and supported competitive employment.

Sheltered Workshops   The traditional job-training environment for adults with mental retardation, especially those who are classified as more severely mentally retarded, has been the sheltered workshop. A **sheltered workshop** is a structured environment where a person receives training and works with other workers with disabilities on jobs requiring relatively low skills. This can be either a permanent placement or a transitional placement before a person obtains a job in the competitive job market.

More and more authorities are voicing dissatisfaction with sheltered workshops. Among the criticisms are the following:

1. Workers make very low wages because sheltered workshops rarely turn a profit. Usually managed by personnel with limited business management expertise, they rely heavily on charitable contributions.
2. There is no integration of workers who are disabled with those who are nondisabled. This restricted setting makes it difficult to prepare workers who are

Community residential facility (CRF)
A place, usually a group home, in an urban or residential neighborhood where about three to ten adults with mental retardation live under supervision.

Supported living
An approach to living arrangements for those with mental retardation that stresses living in natural settings rather than institutions, big or small.

Sheltered workshop
A facility that provides a structured environment for persons with disabilities in which they can learn skills; can be either a transitional placement or a permanent arrangement.

Collaboration and Co-teaching of Students with Mental Retardation

"Why Should This Student Be in My Classroom?"

WHAT DOES IT MEAN TO BE A TEACHER OF STUDENTS WITH MENTAL RETARDATION?

Collaboration for students with mental retardation can include general and special educators and often other related service personnel and parents. Coordinating all of these participants is the responsibility of the special educator, and this requires both management and interpersonal skills. Teachers of students with mental retardation are expected to do the following:

1. Plan instruction in a variety of placement settings.
2. Use and maintain assistive technologies.
3. Select and use specialized instructional strategies appropriate for students with mental retardation.
4. Plan and implement age- and ability-appropriate instruction.
5. Design, implement, and evaluate instructional programs that enhance social participation across environments (Council for Exceptional Children, 2001).

SUCCESSFUL STRATEGIES FOR COLLABORATION

Collaboration between professionals and parents was very important to Pat Daniels, the mother of Will, a high school student with Down syndrome. She worked with Will's teachers and coaches to make his experience in general and special education successful. Will received his special education diploma and was awarded one of the school's ten faculty awards. Pat describes their experiences:

> Open lines of communication between the teachers and the parent were extremely important. I made a point to meet each teacher before the school year began. French was one of the more successful classes. The teacher was unaware of what she was getting with Will, but she was willing and eager to learn. She began by getting to know him, not his weaknesses. She let him try activities, putting him in situations in which he was successful and

---

Competitive employment
A workplace that provides employment that pays at least minimum wage and in which most workers are nondisabled.

Supported competitive employment
A workplace where adults who are disabled earn at least minimum wage and receive ongoing assistance from a specialist or job coach; the majority of workers in the workplace are nondisabled.

Job coach
A person who assists adult workers with disabilities (especially those with mental retardation), providing vocational assessment, instruction, overall planning, and interaction assistance with employers, family, and related government and service agencies.

mentally retarded for working side by side with nondisabled workers in the competitive workforce.

3. Sheltered workshops offer only limited job-training experiences. A good workshop should provide opportunities for trainees to learn a variety of new skills. All too often, however, the work is repetitive and does not make use of current industrial technology.

Supported Competitive Employment In contrast to sheltered employment, **competitive employment** is an approach that provides jobs for at least the minimum wage in integrated work settings in which most of the workers are not disabled. In **supported competitive employment**, the person with mental retardation has a competitive employment position but receives ongoing assistance, often from a **job coach**. In addition to on-the-job training, the job coach might provide assistance in related areas, such as finding an appropriate job, interactions with employers and other employees, use of transportation, and involvement with other agencies.

Although more research is needed, thus far research indicates that supported competitive employment leads to better employment outcomes (McDonnell et al., 2003). Although the ultimate goal for some adults with mental retardation might be competitive employment, many will need supported employment for some period of time or even permanently.

In comparison to sheltered workshops, supported competitive employment is more in keeping with the philosophy of self-determination, which we discussed in Chapter 2 and earlier in this chapter. However, to achieve the goal of self-determination, it is important that clients not become too dependent on their job coach. For this reason, the role of the job coach has been changing in recent years. Many now advocate that the job coach involve coworkers of persons with mental retardation as trainers and/or mentors (Mank, Cioffi, &

challenged. He had a textbook and did homework with the class, taking tests aimed at what he had learned. She helped find a volunteer study-buddy. This teacher understood that he was working at his own level, but she, like others, was often surprised and delighted by his contributions to the class.

The general education teachers and I communicated most frequently about tests and special projects. For example, one history teacher would call me before a test, and we would generate specific review questions. Another teacher would send the class's study sheets home with specific items highlighted. Phone calls by teachers describing class projects helped establish exactly what Will was expected to accomplish. (Will was not always accurate about the specific instructions given orally in class.) When the special education teachers knew of a project, they incorporated time to work on that project into Will's special classes.

Will's drama class was also successful. The teacher let him participate as he was able, even performing at a teachers' meeting. Students' positive attitudes were important to both the French and drama classes. These teachers set the example. Will sat among other students, teachers called on him, and they assigned him to teams to participate in activities. Will's participation was valued, as was every other student's.

Will was also the manager for two girls' varsity teams and was a member of the track team. The special education teacher was the assistant coach of the volleyball team, so she was able to work with the coach to teach Will the duties of a manager. The basketball coach saw Will in action and asked for his help. The coaches expected Will to do what any manager would do, including filling in at practice for missing players and riding the bus to away games. The coaches would communicate with me, and I would discuss any of Will's frustrations with them. The coaches made decisions based on Will's abilities, resulting in two "good finishes" each meet. At many track meets, the encouragement to "RUN" came from teammates and from participants and spectators from the opposing team. Our collaboration with coaches encouraged a student with a hearing impairment and his interpreter to join the team! ■

By Margaret P. Weiss

Yovanoff, 2003). After a period of time, the worker can be weaned from relying on the job coach and can learn to use more natural supports. Recall the quotation at the beginning of the chapter (p. 131), in which Sandra Kaufman talks about the change in philosophy toward the use of natural supports in the form of relatives, neighbors, friends, and coworkers rather than social agency personnel.

The use of supported competitive employment has grown dramatically. However, the number of workers in sheltered workshops still far outnumbers those in competitive employment. According to a recent study of national data on people with mental retardation receiving vocational services, only 16 percent were in competitive employment, whereas 50 percent were in noncompetitive employment (Olney & Kennedy, 2001).

PROSPECTS FOR THE FUTURE

Current employment figures and living arrangements for adults with mental retardation might look bleak, but there is reason to be optimistic about the future. Evidence shows that employers are taking a more favorable attitude toward hiring workers who are mentally retarded (Nietupski, Hamry-Nietupski, VanderHart, & Fishback, 1996). And outcomes for adults with mental retardation are improving, albeit slowly, with respect to employment and living arrangements (Frank & Sitlington, 2000). As Kaufman noted at the beginning of the chapter, with the development of innovative transition programs, many people with mental retardation are achieving levels of independence in community living and employment that were never thought possible. Most of this success requires the collaboration of parents, students, and many professionals. For a description of a successful program from a parent's perspective, read about Will in Making It Work.

Summary

HOW do professionals define mental retardation?

- The American Association on Mental Retardation defines mental retardation as "a disability characterized by significant limitations both in intellectual functioning and in adaptive behavior as expressed in conceptual, social, and practical adaptive skills. This disability originates before age 18."
- The definition reflects two principles: (1) Mental retardation involves problems in adaptive behavior, not just intellectual functioning, and (2) persons with mental retardation can improve.
- Most schools and several professional organizations use the following classifications: mild (IQ of about 50 to 70), moderate (IQ of about 35 to 50), severe (IQ of about 20 to 35), and profound (IQ below about 20).

WHAT is the prevalence of mental retardation?

- From a purely statistical-theoretical perspective and relying only on scores on IQ tests, 2.27 percent of the population would be mentally retarded; however, only about 1 percent of the school-age population is identified as mentally retarded.
- The reason for the lower prevalence in the schools is probably due to (1) schools using low adaptive behavior as well as low IQ as criteria and (2) a preference by some to identify students as *learning disabled* rather than *mentally retarded* because they perceive a learning disability to be less stigmatizing.

WHAT causes mental retardation?

- Prenatal causes include (1) chromosomal disorders, (2) inborn errors of metabolism, (3) developmental disorders affecting brain formation, and (4) environmental influences. Chromosomal disorders include Down syndrome, Williams syndrome, fragile X syndrome, and Prader-Willi syndrome.
  - Down syndrome results from chromosomal abnormalities; fragile X syndrome and Prader-Willi syndrome are inherited.
  - Phenylketonuria (PKU) is an example of a cause of mental retardation due to an inborn error of metabolism.
  - Microcephalus and hydrocephalus are examples of disorders of brain formation.
  - Prenatal environmental influences include maternal malnutrition, fetal alcohol syndrome, and rubella (German measles).
  - Prenatal screening for Down syndrome and other conditions is available.
- Perinatal causes include anoxia (lack of oxygen), low birth weight, and infections such as syphilis and herpes simplex.
- Postnatal causes include those that are biologically or psychologically based.
  - Biological causes include traumatic brain injury and infections such as meningitis and encephalitis.
  - Psychosocial causes (e.g., unstimulating adult–child interactions) are thought to be the most common reasons for mild mental retardation.
  - Although environmental causes of mild mental retardation are undeniable, heredity can also play a role. Most authorities now believe that heredity and environment interact to determine intelligence.
  - Recent research suggests that many cases of mild mental retardation are caused by specific genetic syndromes.

WHAT methods of assessment are used to identify individuals with mental retardation?

- Individual IQ tests are used to assess intelligence. The following cautions are important: (1) An individual's IQ score can change; (2) all IQ tests are culturally biased to some extent; (3) the younger the child, the less valid are the results; and (4) a person's ability to live a successful and fulfilling life does not depend solely on his or her IQ.
- Adaptive behavior measures usually involve a parent, teacher, or other professional answering questions related to the person's independence and daily living skills and maladaptive behavior.

WHAT are some of the psychological and behavioral characteristics of learners with mental retardation?

- Major areas of problems for people with mental retardation are attention, memory (especially working memory), language, self-regulation, social development, and motivation.
- Researchers are beginning to link genetic syndromes to particular behavioral patterns, or phenotypes.
  - Down syndrome is linked to relatively low expressive language, relatively high visual-spatial skills.
  - Williams syndrome is linked to relatively low visual spatial skills, relatively high expressive language.

- Fragile X syndrome is linked to relatively low short-term memory, relatively high adaptive behavior.
- Prader-Willi syndrome is linked to relatively low auditory processing and compulsive eating, relatively high visual processing.

WHAT are some educational considerations for learners with mental retardation?

- Promoting self-determination has become a major guiding principle in educating people with mental retardation.
- The lesser the degree of mental retardation, the more the teacher emphasizes academic skills; and the greater the degree of mental retardation, the more stress there is on self-help, community living, and vocational skills.
- Authorities recommend a merger of functional and academic curricular standards, which can be accomplished by teaching functional academics.
- Effective teaching of students with mental retardation involves systematic instruction, that is, instructional prompts, consequences for performance, and strategies for the transfer of stimulus control.
- With respect to behavioral problems, authorities recommend using functional behavioral assessment (FBA) and positive behavioral support (PBS).
- Although special classes for these students tend to be the norm, more and more students with mental retardation are being placed in more integrated settings.

WHAT are some things to consider with respect to early intervention for learners with mental retardation?

- Preschool programs differ in their goals according to whether they are aimed at preventing mental retardation or furthering the development of children who have already been identified as mentally retarded.
- In general, prevention programs are aimed at children who are at risk of developing mild mental retardation, whereas programs for children who have been identified as mentally retarded focus on children with more severe mental retardation.
- Research supports the clear link between such interventions and success later in life.

WHAT are some things to consider with respect to transition to adulthood for learners with mental retardation?

- A guiding principle for transition programs is the promotion of person-centered planning.
- Transition programming involves two related areas: community adjustment and employment.
  - Community skills include such things as managing money, using public transportation, and maintaining living environments. Large residential institutions are fast disappearing in favor of smaller community residential facilities (CRFs). Some people favor supported living, whereby people with mental retardation live in their own apartment or home, over CRFs.
  - Two common types of employment models are the sheltered workshop and supported competitive employment. Sheltered workshops offer structured training with other workers with disabilities on jobs requiring relatively low skills. Supported competitive employment involves receiving at least minimum wage in settings in which most of the workers are not disabled, accompanied by ongoing assistance from a job coach.

APPLYING THE STANDARDS AND PRINCIPLES

- **ONE** of your colleagues, whose background is in general education, asks, **"What does it really mean to have mental retardation?"** How would you respond? *(CEC Content Standard #1 & #2; INTASC Principle #1 & #2)*

- **HOW** should teachers determine what **instructional methods** to use with students with mental retardation? *(CEC Content Standard #4 & INTASC Principle #4)*

- **IS** it prudent to rely heavily on **IQ test results** to gauge how well a student with mental retardation will do in school? Why or why not? *(CEC Content Standard #8 & INTASC Principle #8)*

- **HOW** would you **respond to parents** who approached you expressing concern about the future of their high school student with mental retardation? *(CEC Content Standard #7 & #10; INTASC Principle #7 & #10)*

Council for Exceptional Children

INTASC

Chapter 6

Learners with Learning Disabilities

As much as I want to find the perfect words to express what it is like to be dyslexic, I cannot. I can no more make you understand what it is like to be dyslexic than you can make me understand what it is like not to be. I can only guess and imagine. For years, I have looked out, wanting to be normal, to shed the skin that limits me, that holds me back. All the while, others have looked upon me, as well. There were those who have pitied me and those who have just given up on me, those who stood by, supporting me and believing in me, and those who looked at me as if I were an exhibit in a zoo. But, in general, people have shown a desire to understand what dyslexia is and how to teach those afflicted with it. Each side, it seems, longs to understand the other.

LYNN PELKEY
"In the LD Bubble"

QUESTIONS TO GUIDE YOUR READING OF THIS CHAPTER . . .

- HOW do professionals define learning disabilities?
- HOW do professionals identify students with learning disabilities?
- WHAT is the prevalence of learning disabilities?
- WHAT causes learning disabilities?
- WHAT assessment practices do professionals use with students with learning disabilities?
- WHAT are some of the psychological and behavioral characteristics of learners with learning disabilities?
- WHAT are some educational considerations for learners with learning disabilities?
- WHAT are some things to consider with respect to early intervention for learners with learning disabilities?
- WHAT are some things to consider with respect to transition to adulthood for learners with learning disabilities?

SPECIAL EDUCATORS . . .

- **understand how changes in the field of special education influence professional practice,** including assessment, instructional planning, implementation, and program evaluation *(from CEC Content Standard #1).*

- **understand the similarities and differences in human development** and the characteristics between and among individuals with and without exceptional learning needs *(from CEC Content Standard #2).*

- **possess a repertoire of evidence-based instructional strategies** to individualize instruction for individuals with exceptional learning needs *(from CEC Content Standard #4).*

- **use the results of assessments to** help identify exceptional learning needs and to develop and implement individualized instructional programs, as well as to adjust instruction in response to ongoing learning progress *(from CEC Content Standard #8).*

ALL TEACHERS . . .

- **understand the central concepts, tools of inquiry, structures of the discipline(s) they teach** and can create learning experiences that make these aspects of subject matter meaningful for students *(INTASC Principle #1).*

- **understand how children learn and develop,** and can provide learning opportunities that support the intellectual, social and personal development of each learner *(INTASC Principle #2).*

- **understand and use a variety of instructional strategies** to encourage students' development of critical thinking, problem solving, and performance skills *(INTASC Principle #4).*

 Council for Exceptional Children

- **understand and use formal and informal assessment strategies** to evaluate and ensure the continuous intellectual, social and physical development of the learner *(INTASC Principle #8).*

 INTASC

Lynn Pelkey's (2001) comment about having dyslexia, or reading disability (see p. 167), should provide some degree of solace to researchers, teachers, parents, and policymakers, who have struggled to define learning disabilities since its formal recognition by the federal government in the 1960s. Pelkey has one specific (albeit the most common) form of learning disabilities: a reading disability. Yet even after living with the condition for thirty-five years, she is still unable to articulate its essence.

That she and the best of theoreticians and practitioners are unable to define learning disabilities in precise language, however, does not mean that her disability is not real. If you were to go on to read the rest of her story, you would find that like the millions of others who have learning disabilities, she faced tremendous challenges not only academically but also socially. You would also find that Pelkey was able eventually to overcome her feelings of rejection, successfully hold a job, and receive an associate's degree with honors from a community college. Her success, however, came not only from hard work and the support of others (as she notes in the quote on p. 167), but also from coming to terms with her learning disability: "Not long ago, it became very clear to me that I would have to come face-to-face with my feelings about being stupid if I was going to find peace within myself" (Pelkey, 2001, p. 27). As we discuss later in this chapter, being able to take control of one's life is what often separates people with learning disabilities who function successfully as adults from those who do not.

The struggle to elucidate the nature of learning disabilities has traditionally led to professional turmoil over the best ways to educate such students. Although the field of learning disabilities has had to struggle to overcome its penchant for questionable practices and to survive the intense scrutiny of professionals and the lay public, most who work within this field are happy to be part of it. For them, controversy and ambiguity only add excitement to the already challenging task of educating students with learning disabilities. As the field has matured, much more consensus has developed about key issues. For example, research evidence has converged to help us understand the causes of learning disabilities as well as the best educational treatment approaches.

Two related controversies that have continued to nag the field are those of definition and identification procedures.

Definition

At a parents' meeting in New York City in the early 1960s, Samuel Kirk proposed the term *learning disabilities* as a compromise because of the confusing variety of labels that were then being used to describe the child with relatively normal intelligence who was

Misconceptions About
Learners with Learning Disabilities

MYTH IQ–achievement discrepancy is a straightforward, error-free way of determining whether a student has a learning disability.

FACT There are numerous conceptual problems in using an IQ–achievement discrepancy.

MYTH Response-to-Intervention (RTI) is a straightforward, error-free way of determining whether a student has a learning disability.

FACT Little research exists on RTI, especially when implemented on a large-scale; therefore, many questions remain regarding how best to implement it.

MYTH All students with learning disabilities are brain damaged.

FACT Many authorities now refer to students with learning disabilities as having central nervous system (CNS) *dysfunction*, which suggests a malfunctioning of the brain rather than actual tissue damage.

MYTH The fact that so many definitions of *learning disabilities* have been proposed is an indicator that the field is in chaos.

FACT Although at least eleven definitions have been proposed at one time or another, professionals have settled on two: the federal definition and the National Joint Committee on Learning Disabilities definition. And although they differ in some ways, these two definitions have a lot in common.

MYTH The rapid increase in the prevalence of learning disabilities is due solely to sloppy diagnostic practices.

FACT Although poor diagnostic practices may account for some of the increase, there are plausible social/cultural reasons for the increase. In addition, there is evidence that school personnel may "bend" the rules to identify students as learning disabled instead of the more stigmatizing identification of "mentally retarded."

MYTH We know very little about what causes learning disabilities.

FACT Although there is no simple clinical test for determining the cause of learning disabilities in individual cases, recent research strongly suggests causes related to neurological dysfunction resulting from genetic, teratogenic, or medical factors.

MYTH Standardized achievement tests are the most useful kind of assessment for teachers of students with learning disabilities.

FACT Standardized achievement tests do not provide much information about *why* a student has achievement difficulties. Formative, informal, and authentic assessments give teachers a better idea of the particular strengths and weaknesses of a student.

MYTH Math disabilities are relatively rare.

FACT Math disabilities are second only to reading as an area of academic difficulty for students with learning disabilities.

MYTH We need not be concerned about the social-emotional well-being of students with learning disabilities because their problems are in academics.

FACT Many students with learning disabilities also develop problems in the social-emotional area.

MYTH Most children with learning disabilities outgrow their disabilities as adults.

FACT Learning disabilities tend to endure into adulthood. Most individuals with learning disabilities who are successful must learn to cope with their problems and make extraordinary efforts to gain control of their lives.

MYTH For persons with learning disabilities, IQ and achievement are the best predictors of success in adulthood.

FACT The best predictors of success for adults with learning disabilities are perseverance, goal-setting, realistic acceptance of weaknesses and ability to build on strengths, exposure to intensive and long-term educational intervention, and especially the ability to take control of their lives.

For first-person accounts of having a learning disability, visit **www.ldonline.org/ first_person/first_person_ archives.html**

This is a page contained on the LD-Online website. LD-Online is a service of the Learning Project of WETA in Washington, DC. Visit the LD-Online home page for more information on learning disabilities: **www.ldonline.org**

Educators have struggled to formulate a clear and comprehensive definition of the term *learning disability*, which generally describes children of seemingly normal intelligence who, nevertheless, have learning problems.

Minimal brain injury

A term used to describe a child who shows behavioral but not neurological signs of brain injury; the term is not as popular as it once was, primarily because of its lack of diagnostic utility (i.e., some children who learn normally show signs indicative of minimal brain injury).

The Learning Disabilities Association of America remains the major parent organization for learning disabilities. Its website at **www.ldanatl.org** contains a variety of information on learning disabilities for parents and professionals.

having learning problems. Such a child was likely to be referred to as *minimally brain injured*, a *slow learner*, *dyslexic*, or *perceptually disabled*.

Many parents as well as teachers believed the label "minimal brain injury" to be problematic. **Minimal brain injury** refers to individuals who show behavioral but not neurological signs of brain injury. They exhibit behaviors (e.g., distractibility, hyperactivity, and perceptual disturbances) similar to those of people with real brain injury, but their neurological examinations are indistinguishable from those of nondisabled individuals.

Historically, the diagnosis of minimal brain injury was sometimes dubious because it was based on questionable behavioral evidence rather than on more solid neurological data. Moreover, minimal brain injury was not an educationally meaningful term because such a diagnosis offered little real help in planning and implementing treatment. The term *slow learner* described the child's performance in some areas but not in others—and besides, intelligence testing indicated that the ability to learn existed. *Dyslexic*, too, fell short as a definitive term because it described only reading disabilities, and many of these children also had problems in other academic areas, such as math. To describe a child as *perceptually disabled* just confused the issue further, for perceptual problems might be only part of a puzzling inability to learn. So the New York parents' group finally agreed on the educationally oriented term *learning disabilities*. Accordingly, they founded the Association for Children with Learning Disabilities, now known as the Learning Disabilities Association of America. A few years later, following the lead of the parents, professionals and the federal government officially recognized the term.

The interest in learning disabilities evolved as a result of a growing awareness that a large number of children were not receiving needed educational services. Because they tested within the normal range of intelligence, these children did not qualify for placement in classes for children with mental retardation. And although many of them did show inappropriate behavior disturbances, some of them did not. Therefore, placement in classes for students with emotional disturbance was thought to be inappropriate. Parents of children who were not achieving at their expected potential—children who are learning disabled—wanted their children's academic achievement problems corrected.

Eleven different definitions of learning disabilities have enjoyed some degree of acceptance since the field's inception in the early 1960s (Hammill, 1990). Created by individual professionals and committees of professionals and lawmakers, each definition provides a slightly different slant. The two most influential definitions have been the federal definition and the definition of the National Joint Committee on Learning Disabilities (NJCLD).

THE FEDERAL DEFINITION

The majority of states use a definition that is based on the federal government's definition. This definition, first signed into law in 1977, was—with a few minor wording changes—adopted again in 1997 by the federal government and reauthorized in 2004. As we discuss in the next section, changes have occurred in identification procedures. However, the IDEA 2004 did not change the definition contained in the 1997 reauthorization.

> GENERAL—The term "specific learning disability" means a disorder in one or more of the basic psychological processes involved in understanding or in using language, spoken or written, which disorder may manifest itself in an imperfect ability to listen, think, speak, read, write, spell, or do mathematical calculations.
>
> DISORDERS INCLUDED—Such term includes such conditions as perceptual disabilities, brain injury, minimal brain dysfunction, dyslexia, and developmental aphasia.
>
> DISORDERS NOT INCLUDED—Such term does not include a learning problem that is primarily the result of visual, hearing, or motor disabilities, of mental retardation, of emotional disturbance, or of environmental, cultural, or economic disadvantage. (Individuals with Disabilities Education Act Amendments of 1997, Sec. 602(26), p. 13.)

THE NATIONAL JOINT COMMITTEE FOR LEARNING DISABILITIES DEFINITION

The NJCLD, made up of representatives of the major professional organizations involved with students with learning disabilities, came up with an alternative definition. They deemed it necessary to present their own definition because of their dissatisfaction with the following factors in the federal definition:

1. *Reference to psychological processes.* Many of the early pioneers in the learning disabilities field believed that the processing of visual and auditory information, or the making sense of this information (as distinct from visual and auditory acuity problems of those identified as blind or deaf), was the underlying cause of academic problems, such as reading disabilities. Furthermore, they believed that training students in visual- and auditory-processing skills in isolation from academic material would help them conquer their reading problems (Frostig & Horne, 1964; Kephart, 1971; Kirk & Kirk, 1971). Researchers ultimately determined that these perceptual and perceptual-motor exercises did not result in benefits for students' reading achievement (see Hallahan, 1975, and Hallahan & Cruickshank, 1973, for reviews). It was in reaction to the widespread adoption of unproven perceptual training programs that the NJCLD objected to the "basic psychological processes" phrase.

2. *Omission of the intrinsic nature of learning disabilities.* The federal definition makes no mention of causal factors, but the NJCLD considered learning disabilities to be due to central nervous system dysfunction within the individual.

3. *Omission of adults.* The NJCLD responded to the growing awareness that learning disabilities was not just a disability of childhood. It is a lifelong condition.

UNDERSTANDING THE STANDARDS AND PRINCIPLES Why has defining the term *learning disabilities* been so controversial? *(CEC Knowledge and Skills Standards CC1K5 & LD1K5)*

Council for Exceptional Children

TO SEE an executive summary of each of the papers from the Learning Disabilities Summit, as well as videos of the presenters, visit **www.air.org/ LDsummit/default.htm**

The full papers, as well as those of respondents, are included in: Danielson, L., Bradley, R., & Hallahan, D. P. (Eds.), (2002). *Identification of learning disabilities: Research to practice.* Mahwah, NJ: Lawrence Erlbaum.

The fact that students with learning disabilities have apparently normal intelligence but still experience learning problems can be frustrating for teachers and parents.

4. *Omission of self-regulation and social interaction problems.* The NJCLD responded to the growing awareness that students with learning disabilities often experience difficulties in self-regulation and social interaction.

5. *Inclusion of terms that are difficult to define.* The NJCLD believed that the federal definition was confusing because of its inclusion of terms such as *perceptual handicaps, dyslexia,* and *minimal brain dysfunction,* which have been so difficult to define (Hammill, Leigh, McNutt, & Larsen, 1981).

6. *Confusion about the exclusion clause.* The federal definition excludes a learning *problem* that is primarily due to other disabling conditions, such as mental retardation, but it is vague with respect to whether one could have both a learning disability and another disability. The NJCLD preferred to be explicit about the possibility that someone with another disabling condition, such as mental retardation, could also have a learning disability.

7. *Inclusion of spelling.* The NJCLD believed that there was no need to mention spelling because it thought it to be included in writing.

On the basis of these seven purported weaknesses of the federal definition, the NJCLD proposed the following definition:

> *Learning disabilities* is a general term that refers to a heterogeneous group of disorders manifested by significant difficulties in the acquisition and use of listening, speaking, reading, writing, reasoning, or mathematical abilities. These disorders are intrinsic to the individual, presumed to be due to central nervous system dysfunction, and may occur across the life span. Problems in self-regulatory behaviors, social perception and social interaction may exist with learning disabilities but do not by themselves constitute a learning disability.
>
> Although learning disabilities may occur concomitantly with other handicapping conditions (for example, sensory impairment, mental retardation, serious emotional disturbance) or with extrinsic influences (such as cultural differences, insufficient or inappropriate instruction), they are not the result of those conditions or influences. (National Joint Committee on Learning Disabilities, 1989, p. 1)

Identification Procedures

Identification procedures for learning disabilities are currently in a state of transition. As we noted in Chapter 2, the federal government reauthorized the Individuals with Disabilities Education Act (IDEA) in 2004. With this reauthorization the way in which students may be found eligible for special education services as learning disabled has changed dramatically. First, we discuss achievement–ability discrepancy—the traditional approach to identifying learning disabilities. Then we discuss response to intervention—an alternative *option* to identifying learning disabilities contained in the reauthorization. In other words, the 2004 reauthorization of IDEA allows states to choose between using achievement-ability discrepancy or RTI as a means of identifying students as learning disabled.

Casebook Reflection

Refer to the case *Should I Take Juanita Pope?* in your casebook. Juanita was in a second grade when she was found eligible for services as a student with a learning disability. However, when she was in fifth grade, she was found ineligible because of her significant gains academically. Are Juanita's gains the result of inappropriate diagnosis or because the special education services she was receiving had been helpful? Did the eligibility committee make a mistake?

ACHIEVEMENT–ABILITY DISCREPANCY

Shortly after presenting its definition in 1977, the federal government published regulations on how to identify students with learning disabilities. The key element in these regulations was that to be identified as learning disabled, the student needed to exhibit a "severe discrepancy between achievement and intellectual ability." In other words, a child who was achieving well below his or her potential would be identified as learning disabled.

The federal government left it up to individual states to decide precisely how they determined whether a student had a severe discrepancy. Most states relied on an **IQ–achievement discrepancy**—a comparison between scores on standardized intelligence and achievement tests. Many states adopted different statistical formulas for identifying IQ–achievement discrepancies. Over the years, however, considerable objection to the use of such formulas has developed. Some of the formulas are statistically flawed and lead to inaccurate judgments, and those that are statistically adequate are difficult and expensive to implement. Furthermore, they give a false sense of precision. That is, they tempt school personnel to reduce to a single score the complex and important decision of identifying a learning disability.

> **IQ–achievement discrepancy**
> Academic performance markedly lower than would be expected on the basis of a student's intellectual ability.

In addition to the problem of using formulas, some authorities have objected to using an IQ–achievement discrepancy to identify learning disabilities on other conceptual grounds (Fletcher et al., 2002). For example, some authorities have pointed out that IQ is not a very strong predictor of reading ability. Furthermore, IQ scores of students with learning disabilities are subject to underestimation because performance on IQ tests is dependent on reading ability, to some extent. In other words, students with poor reading skills have difficulty expanding their vocabularies and learning about the world. As a result, they get lower-than-average scores on IQ tests, which lessen the discrepancy between IQ and achievement. Finally, some educators have pointed out that the idea of discrepancy is practically useless in the earliest elementary grades. In the first or second grade, a child is not expected to have achieved very much in reading or math, so it is difficult to find a discrepancy. Because of this delay in identification, the IQ–achievement discrepancy approach has been called a "wait-to-fail" model.

RESPONSE TO INTERVENTION OR RESPONSE TO TREATMENT

On the basis of the above-mentioned criticisms of IQ–achievement discrepancy, researchers have proposed an alternative means of identifying students as learning disabled. Referred to as a **response-to-intervention (RTI)** or **response-to-treatment approach**, this way of determining a learning disability involves the following components:

> **Response-to-intervention (RTI)** or **response-to-treatment approach**
> A way of determining whether a student has a learning disability; increasingly intensive levels of instructional intervention are delivered, and if the student does not achieve, at some point, he or she is determined to have a learning disability or is referred for special education evaluation.

1. Students are provided with "generally effective" instruction by their classroom teacher;
2. Their progress is monitored;
3. Those who do not respond get something else, or something more, from their teacher or someone else;
4. Again, their progress is monitored; and
5. Those who still do not respond either qualify for special education or for special education evaluation. (Fuchs, Mock, Morgan, & Young, 2003, p. 159)

FOCUS ON CONCEPTS

Response to Intervention: Many Unanswered Questions Remain

ALTHOUGH many researchers support a Response to Intervention (RTI) approach in theory, they are concerned that not enough research has been done on how best to implement it. Even Lynn and Doug Fuchs of Vanderbilt University, who are credited with providing much of the conceptual work behind RTI (Fuchs & Fuchs, 1998a), have raised questions that they believe need to be addressed before we can be sure that RTI will be successful (Fuchs, Fuchs, McMaster, Yen, & Svenson, 2004; Fuchs, Mock, Morgan, & Young, 2003; Fuchs, 2003; Vaughn & Fuchs, 2003).

Here are just a few of the questions that have been raised:

- What should the nature of the intervention be? Should it be individualized or should all students receive the same intervention; that is, should it be a standard protocol?
- How will RTI be implemented with students with math disabilities? So far, RTI has been used only with students who are experiencing reading problems.
- Should the intervention be the ordinary instruction that is delivered in the general education classroom, or should it be a more specialized type of instruction, such as one-on-one tutoring above and beyond the ordinary instruction?
- Who should deliver the intervention: a general education or special education teacher?
- What criterion or criteria will be used to determine responsiveness? For example, should it be level of achievement, rate of progress, or a combination of the two?
- How intense should the intervention be (e.g., 30 minutes per day, every day, 50 minutes per day, three times a week)?
- How long should the intervention last (e.g., 10 weeks, one semester)?

- How many levels of intensity of instruction should a student fail to respond before he or she is identified as learning disabled? For example, in some models, the student is identified after only one level of intervention, whereas in others, several levels are provided before the student is referred or found eligible for special education.
- If a student receives supplemental intensive instruction and responds to it, does this guarantee that he or she will continue to progress with the less intensive instruction that is typically delivered in the general education classroom?

With respect to the last three points, some people are concerned that RTI might end up being subject to the same "wait-to-fail" criticism that is leveled at the IQ–achievement discrepancy approach. Unfortunately, one study has indicated that this is indeed a potential problem (Vaughn, Linan-Thompson, & Hickman, 2003). Students who had received and responded well to ten weeks of supplemental reading instruction were returned to the general education classroom. Those who did not respond received an additional ten weeks of supplemental instruction. Of those who responded well after either ten or twenty weeks, 33 percent failed to progress well once they returned to the general education classroom.

Given the above sample of unanswered questions, it will be interesting to see how school systems respond to the challenges they will undoubtedly face if they choose to implement RTI rather than ability-achievement discrepancy as a method of determining eligibility for learning disabilities services. ■

Advocates of the RTI approach state that in addition to avoiding the previously mentioned pitfalls with the achievement–ability discrepancy approach, one of its major advantages is that it ensures that the student's low achievement is not simply due to having received ineffective instruction.

A variety of RTI models have been proposed and implemented. (See Fuchs et al., 2003, for a discussion of some of these models.) However, so far very little research has been done on any of these models, and many questions remain about how best to implement RTI. This lack of research has led some to worry about what will happen in those states that choose the RTI option. (See Focus on Concepts on p. 174.)

Prevalence

According to figures kept by the U.S. government, the public schools have identified as learning disabled between 5 and 6 percent of students 6 to 17 years of age. Learning disabilities is by far the largest category of special education. More than half of all students that the public schools have identified as needing special education are learning disabled.

INCREASE IN PREVALENCE

Since 1976–1977, when the federal government first started keeping prevalence figures, the size of the learning disabilities category has more than doubled. Many authorities maintain that the rapid expansion of the learning disabilities category reflects poor diagnostic practices. They believe that children are being overidentified, that teachers are too quick to label students with the slightest learning problem as "learning disabled" rather than entertain the possibility that their own teaching practices are at fault. Others, however, argue that some of the increase might be due to social and cultural changes that have raised children's vulnerability to develop learning disabilities (Hallahan, 1992). For example, the number of children living in poverty doubled between 1975 and 1993. Although these numbers have been on the decline since 1993, there are still over two million children living in poverty (National Center for Children in Poverty, 2002), and poverty is associated with higher rates of social and learning problems. Furthermore, even families who are not in poverty are under more stress than ever before, which takes its toll on the time children have for concentrating on their schoolwork and on their parents' ability to offer social support.

Still others maintain that there is a causal relationship between the decrease in the numbers of students who are being identified as mentally retarded and the increase in the numbers of students who are being identified as learning disabled. There is suggestive evidence that when faced with a student who could qualify as mentally retarded, school personnel often bend the rules to apply the label of "learning disabilities" rather than the more stigmatizing label of "mental retardation" (MacMillan, Gresham, & Bocian, 1998; MacMillan & Siperstein, 2002).

GENDER DIFFERENCES

Boys outnumber girls by about three to one in the learning disabilities category. Some researchers have suggested that the prevalence of learning disabilities among males is due to their greater biological vulnerability. The infant mortality rate for males is higher than that for females, and males are at greater risk than females for a variety of biological abnormalities. Other researchers have contended, however, that the higher prevalence of learning disabilities among males might be due to referral bias. They suggest that academic difficulties are no more prevalent among boys than among girls but that boys are more likely to be referred for special education when they do have academic problems because of other behaviors that bother teachers, such as hyperactivity. Research on this issue is mixed (Clarizio & Phillips, 1986; Leinhardt, Seewald, & Zigmond, 1982; Shaywitz, Shaywitz, Fletcher, & Escobar, 1990). So at this point, it is probably safest to conclude that

UNDERSTANDING THE STANDARDS AND PRINCIPLES What do we know about the causes of learning disabilities? *(CEC Knowledge and Skills Standards LD2K1 & LD2K2)*

Council for Exceptional Children

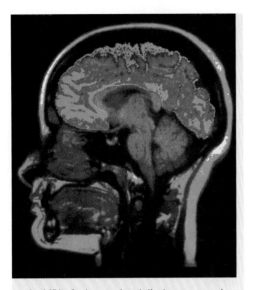

An MRI of a human head displays a normal brain with color coded regions. In recent years researchers have focused on technological assessments of brain activity in search of CNS dysfunction as a basis for learning disabilities, rather than just behavioral symptoms.

Magnetic resonance imaging (MRI)

A neuroimaging technique whereby radio waves are used to produce cross-sectional images of the brain; used to pinpoint areas of the brain that are dysfunctional.

Functional magnetic resonance imaging (fMRI)

An adaptation of the MRI used to detect changes in the brain while it is in an active state; unlike a PET scan, it does not involve using radioactive materials.

Functional magnetic resonance spectroscopy (fMRS)

An adaptation of the MRI used to detect changes in the brain while it is in an active state; unlike a PET scan, it does not involve using radioactive materials.

some bias does exist but that the biological vulnerability of males also plays a role. For example, the federal government's figures indicate that all disabilities are more prevalent in males, including conditions that are difficult to imagine resulting from referral or assessment bias, such as hearing impairment (53% are males), orthopedic impairment (54% are males), and visual impairment (56% are males). (Hallahan, Lloyd, Kauffman, Weiss, & Martinez, 2005, p. 35)

Causes

For years, many professionals suspected that neurological factors were a major cause of learning disabilities. Many of the theoretical concepts and teaching methods associated with the field of learning disabilities grew out of work done in the 1930s and 1940s with children who were mentally retarded and brain injured (Werner & Strauss, 1941; see Hallahan & Mercer, 2002, for a review). When the field of learning disabilities was emerging, professionals noted that many of these children displayed behavioral characteristics (e.g., distractibility, hyperactivity, language problems, perceptual disturbances) similar to those exhibited by people who were known to have brain damage, such as those who had suffered a stroke or a head wound.

In the case of most children with learning disabilities, however, there is little neurological evidence of actual *damage* to brain tissues. Therefore, today, the term *dysfunction* has come to replace *injury* or *damage*. Thus, a child with learning disabilities is now often referred to as having central nervous system (CNS) dysfunction rather than brain injury. Dysfunction does not necessarily mean tissue damage; instead, it signifies a malfunctioning of the brain or central nervous system.

At one time, there was little evidence, other than behavioral symptoms, that children with learning disabilities actually had CNS dysfunction. However, in recent years, researchers have begun to harness advanced technology to assess brain activity more accurately. The most recent technology being used by researchers to document neurological dysfunction in some people with learning disabilities includes **magnetic resonance imaging (MRI)**, **functional magnetic resonance imaging (fMRI)**, **functional magnetic resonance spectroscopy (fMRS)**, and **positron emission tomography (PET) scans**.

- An MRI sends magnetic radio waves through the head and creates cross-sectional images of the brain.
- fMRI and fMRS are adaptations of the MRI. Unlike an MRI, they are used to detect changes in brain activity while a person is engaged in a task, such as reading.
- A PET scan, like an fMRI or fMRS, is used while the person is performing a task. The subject is injected with a substance containing a low amount of radiation, which collects in active neurons. Using a scanner to detect the radioactive substance, researchers can tell which parts of the brain are actively engaged during various tasks.

Using these neuroimaging techniques, researchers are accumulating evidence for structural and functional differences between the brains of those with and without learning disabilities, especially reading disabilities (Kibby & Hynd, 2001; Richards, 2001). Structural differences refer to such things as the size of the various areas of the brain. Function refers to activity in the brain. With respect to the functional differences, for example, researchers have found that different areas of the brain are activated during reading tasks for individuals with dyslexia versus nondyslexics. See Focus on Concepts on page 177 for a summary of the major findings.

Taken as a whole, these studies are not definitive evidence of a neurological basis for all students who are identified as learning disabled. Some researchers have noted that for the most part, the studies have been conducted on individuals with severe learning disabilities. However, the results have turned many people who were formerly skeptical into believers that CNS dysfunction could be the cause of many cases of learning disabilities.

Even in cases in which one can be fairly certain that the person with learning disabilities has neurological dysfunction, the question still remains: How did the person come to have the neurological dysfunction? Possible reasons fall into three general categories: genetic, teratogenic, and medical factors.

GENETIC FACTORS

Over the years, evidence has accumulated that learning disabilities can be inherited. The two most common types of studies that are used to look at the genetic basis of learning disabilities are familiality studies and heritability studies.

Positron emission tomography (PET) scans
A computerized method for measuring bloodflow in the brain; during a cognitive task, a low amount of radioactive dye is injected in the brain; the dye collects in active neurons, indicating which areas of the brain are active.

FOCUS ON CONCEPTS

Neuroimaging and Reading Disabilities: Major Findings

SEVERAL teams of researchers have been studying the structural and functional differences between the brains of those with and without reading disabilities. These scientists have used different neuroimaging methods, used different measures of reading, and studied different populations, adults as well as children.

Even with these many methodological differences among research teams, their conclusions have been remarkably consistent. It appears that the left side of the brain is the site of abnormal structure and function in most individuals with severe reading disabilities. Scientists have also begun to pinpoint specific areas within the left side. Figure A depicts some of the areas that have generally received the most support as being abnormal in individuals with severe reading disabilities. (See Richards, 2001, for a review of some of this research.) We should be cautious, however, about concluding that any of these is (are) *the* site(s) of dysfunction in individual cases. Not

all of those studied have had abnormalities in the same areas. Furthermore, some have shown an abnormality in only one area, whereas others have had disturbances in several of the areas. As neuroimaging techniques are perfected further, researchers will undoubtedly refine their conclusions with respect to the areas of the brain responsible for reading disabilities. ∎

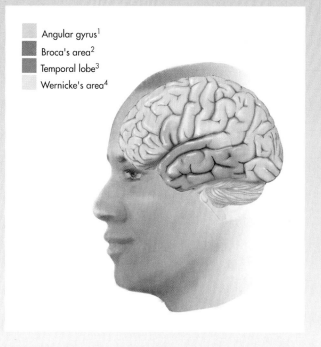

Angular gyrus[1]
Broca's area[2]
Temporal lobe[3]
Wernicke's area[4]

FIGURE A   Areas of the brain associated with reading difficulties

Studies supporting these sites as involved in individuals with reading disabilities:
[1]*Angular gyrus:* Flowers, Wood, & Naylor, 1991; Pugh et al., 2000; Rumsey et al., 1999; Shaywitz et al., 1998
[2]*Broca's area:* Georgiewa et al., 1999; Shaywitz et al., 1998
[3]*Temporal lobe:* Hagman et al., 1992; McCrory et al., 2000; Paulesu et al., 2001
[4]*Wernicke's area:* Brunswick, McCrory, Price, Frith, & Frith, 1999; Flowers, 1993; Flowers, Wood, & Naylor, 1991; Kushch et al., 1993; Shaywitz et al., 1998

Familiality studies
A method of determining the
degree to which a given condition is inherited; looks at the
prevalence of the condition in
relatives of the person with the
condition.

Familiality studies examine the degree to which a certain condition, such as a learning disability, occurs in a single family (i.e., the tendency for it to "run in a family"). Researchers have found that about 35 to 45 percent of first-degree relatives of individuals with
reading disabilities—that is, the immediate birth family (parents and siblings)—have reading disabilities (Hallgren, 1950; Olson, Wise, Conners, Rack, & Fulker, 1989; Pennington,
1990), and the risk for having reading disabilities goes up for children who have both parents with reading disabilities (Raskind, 2001). The same degree of familiality has also been
found in families of people with speech and language disorders (Beichtman, Hood, & Inglis, 1992; Lewis, 1992) and spelling disabilities (Schulte-Korne, Deimel, Muller, Gutenbrunner, & Remschmidt, 1996).

The tendency for learning disabilities to run in families may also be due to environmental factors. For example, it is possible that parents with learning disabilities will pass on
their disabilities to their children through their child-rearing practices. Given this, a more
convincing method of determining whether learning disabilities are inherited is **heritability
studies**—comparing the prevalence of learning disabilities in identical (monozygotic, from
the same egg) versus fraternal (dizygotic, from two eggs) twins. Researchers have found that
identical twins are more concordant than are fraternal twins for reading disabilities and
speech and language disorders (DeFries, Gillis, & Wadsworth, 1993; Lewis & Thompson,
1992; Reynolds et al., 1996). In other words, if an identical twin and a fraternal twin each
has a learning disability, the second identical twin is more likely to have a learning disability than the second fraternal twin.

There have also been studies attempting to pinpoint the precise gene or genes that are
involved in learning disabilities. There is suggestive evidence implicating genes located on
chromosomes 6 and 15 in reading disabilities (Grigorenko, Wood, Meyer, & Pauls, 2000;
Kaplan et al., 2002; Petryshen et al., 2001; Schulte-Korne, 2001).

TERATOGENIC FACTORS

Teratogens are agents that can cause malformations or defects in the developing fetus. In
Chapter 5, we discussed **fetal alcohol syndrome (FAS)** and lead as two potential causes
of mental retardation. Authorities have also speculated that some people may be exposed
to levels of these substances that are not high enough to result in mental retardation but are
high enough to cause learning disabilities.

MEDICAL FACTORS

There are several medical conditions that can have such a negative impact on children that
they develop learning disabilities. Again, many of these can also result in mental retardation, depending on the severity of the condition. For example, premature birth places children at risk for neurological dysfunction, and pediatric AIDS can result in neurological
damage such that learning disabilities result.

Assessment

Four types of assessment are popular in the field of learning disabilities:

1. Standardized achievement assessment
2. Formative assessment
3. Informal assessment
4. Authentic assessment

STANDARDIZED ACHIEVEMENT ASSESSMENT

Teachers and psychologists commonly use **standardized achievement assessment** with
students who are learning disabled because achievement deficits are the primary charac-

Heritability studies
A method of determining the
degree to which a condition is
inherited; a comparison of the
prevalence of a condition in
identical (i.e., monozygotic,
from the same egg) twins
versus fraternal (i.e., dizygotic,
from two eggs) twins.

Teratogens
Agents, such as chemicals, that
can disrupt the normal development of the fetus; a possible
cause of learning disabilities
and other learning and behavioral problems.

**Fetal alcohol syndrome
(FAS)**
Abnormalities associated with
the mother's drinking alcohol
during pregnancy; defects
range from mild to severe.

**Standardized
achievement
assessment**
A method of evaluating a
person that has been applied
to a large group so that an
individual's score can be compared to the norm, or average.

teristic of these students. Several standardized achievement tests are currently in use. For example, the Wechsler Individual Achievement Test, Second Edition (WIAT®-II), assesses achievement in all the areas pertaining to the federal definition of learning disabilities: basic reading, reading comprehension, spelling, written expression, mathematics reasoning, numerical operations, listening comprehension, and oral expression. The developers of the WIAT designed the test so it could be used in conjunction with the Wechsler Intelligence Scale for Children (WISC) to look for discrepancies between achievement and ability. There are also examples of achievement tests focused on specific areas, among them the KeyMath-Revised-Normative Update (KeyMath-R/NU) and the Test of Written Language, Third Edition (TOWL-III).

One limitation of most standardized instruments is that they cannot be used to gain much insight into why students have difficulty. Teachers and clinicians use these tests primarily to identify students with learning problems and to provide gross indicators of academic strengths and weaknesses.

The notion of using assessment information to help plan educational strategies has gained much of its popularity from professionals working in the area of learning disabilities. Three methods of assessment—formative assessment, informal assessment, and authentic assessment—are better suited to the philosophy that evaluation is more useful to teachers if it can be translated into educational recommendations. We discuss each in following sections.

FORMATIVE ASSESSMENT

Formative assessment directly measures a student's behavior to keep track of his or her progress (Choate, Enright, Miller, Poteet, & Rakes, 1995; Deno, 1985; Fuchs & Fuchs, 1997). Formative evaluation is less concerned with how the student's performance compares with that of other students and more concerned with how the student performs in light of his or her abilities. Although there are a variety of formative evaluation models, they have at least five features in common:

1. The assessment is usually done by the child's teacher, rather than a school psychologist or diagnostician.

Formative assessments focus on how students perform in light of their own abilities, rather than as compared with other students.

> **UNDERSTANDING THE STANDARDS AND PRINCIPLES** Describe the features of the four general types of assessments that practitioners use with students with learning disabilities. *(CEC Knowledge and Skills Standards CC8K1)*

Council for Exceptional Children

Formative assessment Measurement procedures used to monitor an individual student's progress; they are used to compare how an individual performs in light of his or her abilities, in contrast to standardized tests, which are primarily used to compare an individual's performance to that of other students.

2. The teacher assesses classroom behaviors directly. For instance, a teacher who is interested in measuring the student's pronunciation of the letter *l* looks at that particular behavior and records whether the child can pronounce that letter.
3. The teacher observes and records the student's behavior frequently and over a period of time. Most other kinds of tests are given once or twice a year at the most. In formative evaluation, performance is measured at least two or three times a week.
4. The teacher uses formative evaluation to assess the pupil's progress toward educational goals. After an initial testing, the teacher establishes goals for the student to reach in a given period of time. For example, if the student can orally read twenty-five words correctly in one minute out of a certain book, the teacher may set a goal, or criterion, of being able to read 100 words correctly per minute after one month. This aspect of formative evaluation is sometimes referred to as **criterion-referenced testing**.
5. The teacher uses formative evaluation to monitor the effectiveness of educational programming. For instance, in the preceding example, if after a few days the teacher realizes that it is unlikely that the child will reach the goal of 100 words, the teacher can try a different educational intervention.

One particular model of formative evaluation is **curriculum-based assessment (CBA)**. Although it draws heavily on earlier research, CBA was developed largely by Deno and his colleagues (Deno, 1985; Fuchs, Deno, & Mirkin, 1984).

Because it is a type of formative evaluation, CBA has the five features just listed. In addition, it has two other distinguishing characteristics:

1. It is designed to measure students' performances on the particular curriculum to which they are exposed. Proponents of CBA state that this reliance on the curriculum is an advantage over commercially available standardized achievement tests, which are usually not keyed to the curriculum in any particular school. In math, for example, the teacher might give students two minutes to compute samples of problems from the basal text and record the number of digits computed correctly. In reading, the teacher might ask the student to read for one minute from the basal reader and record the number of words read correctly. (See Figure 6.1.)
2. CBA compares the performance of students with disabilities to that of their peers in their own school or school division. Deno and his colleagues suggest that the teacher take CBA measures on a random sample of nondisabled students so that this comparison can be made. Comparison with a local reference group is seen as more relevant than comparison with the national norming groups used in commercially developed standardized tests.

INFORMAL ASSESSMENT

A common method of assessment used by teachers is to ask students to work on their academic assignments as the teacher takes note of what the students do well and where they have difficulty. In the area of reading, for example, teachers can use an **informal reading inventory (IRI)**, a series of reading passages or word lists graded in order of difficulty. The teacher has the student read from the series, beginning with a list or passage that is likely to be easy for the student. The student continues to read increasingly more difficult lists or passages while the teacher monitors the student's performance. After the results of the IRI have been compiled, the teacher can use them to estimate the appropriate difficulty level of reading material for the student.

In using an IRI or other means of informal assessment, the teacher can also do an error analysis of the student's work (Lopez-Reyna & Bay, 1997). Sometimes referred to as miscue analysis, an **error analysis** is a way of pinpointing particular areas in which the student

---

Criterion-referenced testing

Assessment wherein an individual's performance is compared to a goal or standard of mastery; differs from norm-referenced testing wherein an individual's performance is compared to the performance of others.

Curriculum-based assessment (CBA)

A formative evaluation method designed to evaluate performance in the particular curriculum to which students are exposed; usually involves giving students a small sample of items from the curriculum in use in their schools; proponents argue that CBA is preferable to comparing students with national norms or using tests that do not reflect the curriculum content learned by students.

Informal reading inventory (IRI)

A method of assessing reading in which the teacher has the student read progressively more difficult series of passages or word lists; the teacher notes the difficulty level of the material read and the types of errors the student makes.

Error analysis

An informal method of teacher assessment that involves the teacher noting the particular kinds of errors a student makes when doing academic work.

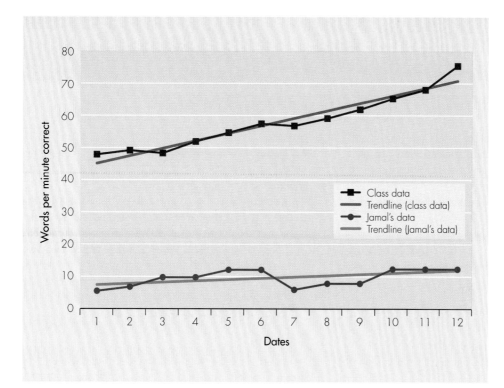

FIGURE 6.1 Example of curriculum-based assessment of reading rate
Jamal, a first grader with learning disabilities, was asked to read from his basal reader for one minute 12 times over three weeks. His rate of reading, as well as his growth rate (trend line) over this period were well below that of his class as whole.

Source: Adapted from Hallahan, D. P., Lloyd, J. W., Kauffman, J. M., Weiss, M. P., & Martinez, E. A. (2005). *Learning disabilities: Foundations, characteristics, and effective teaching.* Boston: Allyn & Bacon.

has difficulty. In reading, for example, it might show that the student typically substitutes one vowel for another or omits certain sounds when reading aloud. See the Personal Perspectives on page 182 for an example of an error analysis.

AUTHENTIC ASSESSMENT

Some educators question the authenticity of typical test scores—especially those from standardized tests—asserting that the scores do not reflect what students do in situations in which they work with, or receive help from, teachers, peers, parents, or supervisors. The purpose behind **authentic assessment** is to assess students' critical thinking and problem-solving abilities in real-life situations.

An example of authentic assessment is portfolios. **Portfolios** are a collection of samples of a student's work done over time. Students of music or art have used portfolios, but their use in academic areas is relatively recent (Meese, 2001). Portfolios allow for a broader-based evidence of students' work, evidence that is more closely related to real-life skills. For example, the following might be included:

- Essays or other writing samples, such as letters, instructions, or stories
- Videotapes or audiotapes of speeches, or oral responses to questions
- Audiotapes or videotapes of recitals or other performances
- Experiments and their results or reports

Portfolio assessment, however, is more difficult and time consuming than many educators realize (Hallahan et al., 2005). Teachers need to help students decide what to put in their portfolios and need to give careful attention to criteria for evaluating the portfolios. However, done properly, they can be a rich source of information about a student's strengths and interests. Furthermore, portfolios can be of particular value for culturally diverse students, for whom traditional standardized tests may not reflect their true abilities (Rueda & Garcia, 1997).

Authentic assessment
A method that evaluates a student's critical-thinking and problem-solving ability in real-life situations in which he or she may work with or receive help from peers, teachers, parents, or supervisors.

Portfolios
A collection of samples of a student's work done over time; a type of authentic assessment.

Personal Perspectives

MS. LOPEZ CONDUCTS AN ERROR ANALYSIS

TEACHERS often use curriculum-based assessment and student work samples to analyze student errors and plan for instruction. Let's listen to a conversation in Ms. Lopez's room during a spelling lesson with Travis:

Ms. Lopez: Travis, let's look at the work you completed yesterday in spelling.

Travis: Okay.

Ms. Lopez: It looks like you had some trouble with the new vowel pattern we've been working on this week. What is your new vowel pattern?

Travis: Uh . . . the "ay?"

Ms. Lopez: That's right. Tell me the rule for the "ay" pattern.

Travis: Um . . . a long /a/ sound is spelled A-Y.

Ms. Lopez: Travis, a long /a/ sound at the end of a one-syllable word is spelled A-Y.

Travis: Oh yeah!

Ms. Lopez: Tell me some words on the list that have the "ay" pattern.

Travis: Um . . . "hay" and "play."

Ms. Lopez: Good. Those are some of the words with the "ay" pattern. Let's look through your spelling list again. The "ay" words are the only words that gave you trouble. I think you've figured out the "ee" words pretty well. We'll do a practice activity tomorrow on just the "ay" words, and I'll test you on just those words before we do the whole spelling list again. Okay, now let's take another look at those tricky "ay" words. . . . ■

Source: Meese, R. L. (2001). *Teaching learners with mild disabilities: Integrating research and practice* (2nd ed., p. 137). Stamford, CT: Wadsworth.

Psychological and Behavioral Characteristics

Before discussing some of the most common characteristics of people with learning disabilities, we point out two important features of this population: People with learning disabilities exhibit a great deal of both interindividual and intraindividual variation.

INTERINDIVIDUAL VARIATION

In any classroom of students with learning disabilities, some will have problems in reading, some will have problems in math, some will have problems in spelling, some will be inattentive, and so on. One term for such interindividual variation is *heterogeneity*. Although heterogeneity is a trademark of children from all the categories of special education, the old adage "No two are exactly alike" is particularly appropriate for students with learning disabilities. This heterogeneity makes it a challenge for teachers to plan educational programs for the diverse group of children they find in their classrooms.

INTRAINDIVIDUAL VARIATION

UNDERSTANDING THE STANDARDS AND PRINCIPLES What should teachers know about the psychological, social, and emotional characteristics of individuals with learning disabilities? *(CEC Knowledge and Skills Standard LD2K3)*

Council for
Exceptional
Children

In addition to differences among one another, children with learning disabilities also tend to exhibit variability within their own profiles of abilities. For example, a child might be two or three years above grade level in reading but two or three years behind grade level in math. Such uneven profiles account for references to *specific* learning disabilities in the literature on learning disabilities.

Some of the pioneers in the field of learning disabilities alerted colleagues to what is termed *intraindividual* variation. Samuel Kirk was one of the most influential in advocating the notion of individual variation in students with learning disabilities. He developed the

Illinois Test of Psycholinguistic Abilities, which purportedly measured variation in processes important for reading. Researchers ultimately found that Kirk's test did not measure processes germane to reading (Hallahan & Cruickshank, 1973; Hammill & Larsen, 1974), and the test is rarely used today. Nonetheless, most authorities still recognize intraindividual differences as a feature of many students with learning disabilities.

We now turn to a discussion of some of the most common characteristics of persons with learning disabilities.

Casebook Reflections

Refer to the case *More than LD: Shannon* in your casebook. As you read this section, compare it with the areas in which Shannon is struggling.

ACADEMIC ACHIEVEMENT PROBLEMS

Academic deficits are the hallmark of learning disabilities. By definition, if there is no academic problem, a learning disability does not exist.

Reading   Reading poses the most difficulty for most students with learning disabilities. Students with reading disabilities are likely to experience problems with three aspects of reading: decoding, fluency, and comprehension (Hallahan et al., 2005). **Decoding** is the ability to convert print to spoken language. It is largely dependent on phonological awareness and phonemic awareness. **Phonological awareness** is the understanding that speech consists of small units of sound, such as words, syllables, and phonemes (Pullen, 2002; Troia, 2004). Phonemic awareness, is particularly important (Blachman, 2001). Children with **phonemic awareness** understand that words are made up of sounds, or phonemes. For example, the word *bat* consists of three phonemes: *b, a, t.*

Eliot, the student in the Success Stories on page 184, is someone with difficulties in this area. He became extremely frustrated with his inability to learn to read because he was so successful in other areas.

Interestingly, there is suggestive evidence that readers of English are more susceptible than readers of some other languages to problems with phonological awareness. Some have speculated that this is why reading disabilities are more prevalent in English-speaking countries than in some other countries (See the Focus on Concepts on p. 186).

Students who have difficulty decoding invariably have problems with fluency. **Reading fluency** refers to the ability to read effortlessly and smoothly. Recall that Figure 6.1 showed the reading rate for one student compared to the reading rates of his classmates. Reading rate and the ability to read with appropriate expression are components of reading fluency.

Problems with reading fluency are a major reason why students have difficulties with reading comprehension (Good, Simmons, & Kame'enui, 2001). **Reading comprehension** refers to the ability to gain meaning from what one has read. In other words, reading too slowly or in a halting rather manner interferes with a person's ability to comprehend text.

Written Language   People with learning disabilities often have problems in one or more of the following areas: handwriting, spelling, and composition (Hallahan et al., 2005). Although even the best students can have less-than-perfect handwriting, the kinds of problems that are manifested by some students with learning disabilities are much more severe. These children are sometimes very slow writers, and their written products are sometimes illegible. Spelling can be a significant problem because of the difficulty (noted in the previous section) in understanding the correspondence between sounds and letters.

In addition to the more mechanical areas of handwriting and spelling, students with learning disabilities frequently have difficulties in the more creative aspects of composition (Montague & Graves, 1992). For example, compared to nondisabled peers, students with learning disabilities use less complex sentence structures; include fewer types of words; write paragraphs that are less well organized; include fewer ideas in their written products; and write stories that have fewer important components, such as introducing main characters, setting scenes, describing a conflict to be resolved (Hallahan et al., 2005).

Decoding
The ability to convert print to spoken language; dependent on phonological awareness and phonemic awareness; a significant problem for many people with reading disabilities.

Phonological awareness
The ability to understand that speech flow can be broken into smaller sound units such as words, syllables, and phonemes; generally thought to be the reason for the reading problems of many students with learning disabilities.

Phonemic awareness
One's ability to understand that words are made up of sounds, or phonemes.

Reading fluency
The ability to read effortlessly and smoothly; consists of the ability to read at a normal rate and with appropriate expression; influences one's reading comprehension.

Reading comprehension
The ability to understand what one has read.

Special Educators at Work

Eliot: "Learning that stuff is not fun, but it works!"
Like many students across the country, fifth grader Eliot Danner attends a private school without any special education services. His parents had to look elsewhere for specialized training to help him learn to read.
These are the keys to his success:
- *Intensive focus on reading*
- *Relentless engagement and practice with language*
- *Specific instruction to meet his reading problems*

"Teaching kids with learning disabilities is not a casual engagement," says Nancy Pietrefesa. She believes that her son Eliot's success began when he met Dr. Nancy Cushen White and Mia Callahan Russell, special educators who were trained to address language disabilities. These specialists accurately described his problems, articulated his strengths and weaknesses, and prescribed intense remedial instruction. As a result, Eliot assumed greater control and self-acceptance. He began to understand himself as a reader through intensive, relentless, and specific special education.

Intensive Focus on Reading Eliot met Nancy Cushen White in the summer before second grade when he attended an intensive special education program to address language disabilities. Everyone knew he had trouble reading, but no one was sure what to do about it. Since kindergarten, Eliot has attended independent schools designed for high academic achievers, not for students with learning disabilities. Eliot always had passionate interests and easily memorized stories that were read to him. But for all his curiosity, Eliot could not read by himself. A psychological evaluation identified problems with spatial orientation, word attack, spelling, and composition skills. After one year of tutoring in phonological awareness to complement his school's whole language approach, Eliot was still anxious and unsure whether he would ever learn to read. "We needed to respond to that, or we feared we would lose him as a reader," says his mother. Eliot's parents considered enrolling him in another school, but Dr. White pointed out that changing schools was not the answer. "This wasn't a question of settings but of strategies. Eliot is a child with dyslexia who needed to learn how to read."

Relentless Engagement and Practice with Language Eight-year-old Eliot soon began a three-week, half-day, summer program of daily direct instruction in language skills that has paid off. Getting students to think through the process of language is the program's goal. Teachers keep sessions lively, and students are expected to be active, self-checking, and always thinking. "Nobody should just sit!" says White. "Success hinges on developing the association of hearing, saying, seeing, and writing. Students are taught there is a system and they can use

Syntax
The way words are joined together to structure meaningful sentences (i.e., grammar).

Semantics
The study of the meanings attached to words.

Phonology
The study of how individual sounds make up words.

Spoken Language Many students with learning disabilities have problems with the mechanical and social uses of language. Mechanically, they have trouble with **syntax** (grammar), **semantics** (word meanings), and, as we have already noted, **phonology** (the ability to break words into their component sounds and blend individual sounds together to make words).

With regard to social uses of language—commonly referred to as **pragmatics**—students with learning disabilities are often inept in the production and reception of discourse. In short, they are not very good conversationalists. They are unable to engage in the mutual give-and-take that conversations between individuals require.

For instance, conversations of individuals with learning disabilities are frequently marked by long silences because they do not use the relatively subtle strategies that their nondisabled peers do to keep conversations going. They are not skilled at responding to others' statements or questions and tend to answer their own questions before their companions have a chance to respond. They tend to make task-irrelevant comments and make

it!" Skills are taught in specific sequence and students are taught to see how the rules of the English language fit together. "There is emphasis on repetition and practice, much like in sports or in music," says Eliot's mother. "Have you ever seen how football coaches make kids practice plays over and over?"

Specific Instruction to Meet His Reading Problems
Nancy White trained teacher Mia Russell to tailor her intensive tutorial work specifically to Eliot's individual patterns and errors. "Eliot does not have a weakness in any one modality. He has great difficulty with auditory, visual, and kinesthetic integration, particularly in association with his long-term visual memory," says White. "His phonological awareness is poor, and he has difficulties with visual discrimination. Because he can't rely on his memory, it all becomes a jumble when he has to write things down."

According to Eliot, this training was just "fiddle faddle!" until the end of the summer, when he saw himself improve. To keep up the pace for second and third grades, a creative schedule was developed with Eliot's private school. Monday through Thursday he attended classes from 9:00 to 12:00, and each afternoon, he was tutored at home for two and one-half hours. He attended school all day on Friday. With the benefit of more summer training, in fourth grade, Eliot worked with Mia Russell eight hours a week in a room provided for them at his school. The sessions were reduced to three hours a week in fifth grade. "The staff at the school is very cooperative," says Russell. "They see him as a bright, articulate student who needs specific interventions they are not equipped to offer."

Eliot has worked hard to become an expert on how he learns, and he is eager to start sixth grade. "He has really knocked himself out," says his mom. He is an independent learner, conscious of which strategies he needs to use to get at what he wants to know. Says Eliot, "Learning that stuff is not fun, but it works!"

CEC'S STANDARDS: PAVING THE WAY TO SUCCESS

Council for Exceptional Children

ASSESS YOUR STEPS TO SUCCESS in meeting the CEC Knowledge and Skill Base for All Beginning Special Education Teachers of Students with Learning Disabilities. Use the following questions to reflect on the growth of your own professional knowledge, skills, and dispositions.

REFLECTING ON YOUR OWN PROFESSIONAL DEVELOPMENT

If you were Eliot's teacher . . .

- WHAT are some areas about educating students with learning disabilities that you would need to know more about?
- WHAT are some specific skills that would help you to address his learning challenges?
- WHAT personal dispositions do you think are most important for you to develop in teaching students with learning disabilities to be successful in mastering new skills?

Using the CEC Standards:

- WHAT are some procedures you might use to identify young children who may be at risk for learning disabilities? (LD8K3)
- WHAT are some instructional methods you would use with students with learning disabilities to strengthen and compensate for deficits in perception, comprehension, memory, and retrieval? (LD4S5)
- WHAT are some sources of specialized curricula, materials, and resources for individuals with learning disabilities? (LD7K2) ■

By Jean Crockett

those with whom they talk uncomfortable. In one often-cited study, for example, children with and without learning disabilities took turns playing the role of host in a simulated television talk show (Bryan, Donahue, Pearl, & Sturm, 1981). Analysis of the verbal interactions revealed that in contrast to nondisabled children, children with learning disabilities playing the host role allowed their nondisabled guests to dominate the conversation. Also, their guests exhibited more signs of discomfort during the interview than did the guests of nondisabled hosts.

Math Although disorders of reading, writing, and language have traditionally received more emphasis than problems with mathematics, the latter are now gaining a great deal of attention. Authorities now recognize that math difficulties are second only to reading disabilities as an academic problem area for students with learning disabilities. The types of problems these students have include difficulties with computation of math facts (Cawley, Parmar, Yan, & Miller, 1998) as well as word problems (Woodward & Baxter,

Pragmatics
The study within psycholinguistics of how people use language in social situations; emphasizes the functional use of language, rather than mechanics.

FOCUS ON CONCEPTS

Dyslexia: Same Brains, Different Languages

PITY the poor speakers of English. New research suggests that they may be especially prone to manifest dyslexia, the language disorder that makes reading and writing a struggle, simply because their language is so tricky.

The distinctive pattern of spelling and memory problems that characterizes dyslexia has a strong genetic basis, suggesting that some neurological oddity underlies the disorder. But there appears to be a cultural component to the [condition] as well, because dyslexia is more prevalent in some countries than others; for instance, about twice as many people fit the definition of dyslexic in the United States as in Italy. Researchers have suspected that certain languages expose the disorder while others allow dyslexics to compensate. Now a brain imaging study backs this theory up.

A multinational team of researchers used positron emission tomography (PET) scans to observe brain activity in British, French, and Italian adults while they read [Paulesu et al., 2001]. Regardless of language, . . . people with symptoms of dyslexia showed less neural activity in a part of the brain that's vital for reading.

"Neurologically, the disease looks very much the same" in people who speak different languages, says neurologist Eraldo Paulesu of the University of Milan Biocca in Italy. "Therefore, the difference in prevalence of clinical manifestations [among different countries] must be attributed to something else." The

researchers blame language. English consists of just 40 sounds, but these phonemes can be spelled, by one count, in 1120 different ways. French spelling is almost as maddening. Italian speakers, in contrast, must map 25 different speech sounds to just 33 combinations of letters. Not surprisingly, Italian schoolchildren read faster and more accurately than do those in Britain. And it's no surprise that people have a harder time overcoming reading disorders if their language, like English or French, has a very complex, arbitrary system for spelling. . . .

Compared to normal readers, dyslexics from all three countries showed less activation in parts of the [left] temporal lobe while reading. [See the figure in the Focus on Concepts box on p. 177.] The underutilized areas are familiar to neurologists: Patients with strokes in this area often lose the ability to read and spell, even though they still speak fluently. . . .

This research doesn't supply ready solutions for how to help dyslexic students overcome their reading disability, Paulesu says, short of moving to Italy, Turkey, or Spain, where spelling is simple and straightforward. So sympathize when English- or French-speaking students complain about having to memorize arbitrarily spelled words; they're right to feel wronged. ■

Source: Reprinted with permission from Helmuth, L. (2001). Dyslexia: Same brains, different languages. *Science, 291,* 2064–2065. Copyright © 2001 by American Association for the Advancement of Science.

TO SEE the full text for the Helmuth article from *Science,* see **www.sciencemag.org/ content/vol291/issue5511/ index.shtml**

1997); trouble with the latter is often due to the inefficient application of problem-solving strategies.

PERCEPTUAL, PERCEPTUAL–MOTOR, AND GENERAL COORDINATION PROBLEMS

Studies indicate that some children with learning disabilities exhibit visual and/or auditory perceptual disabilities (see Hallahan, 1975, and Willows, 1998, for reviews). A child with visual perceptual problems might have trouble solving puzzles or seeing and remembering visual shapes, for example, or he or she might have a tendency to reverse letters (e.g., mistake a *b* for a *d*). A child with auditory perceptual problems might have difficulty discriminating between two words that sound nearly alike (e.g., *fit* and *fib*) or following orally presented directions.

Teachers and parents have also noted that some students with learning disabilities have difficulty with physical activities involving motor skills. They describe some of these children as having "two left feet" or "ten thumbs." The problems may involve both fine motor (small motor muscles) and gross motor (large motor muscles) skills. Fine motor skills often involve coordination of the visual and motor systems.

DISORDERS OF ATTENTION AND HYPERACTIVITY

Students with attention problems display such characteristics as distractibility, impulsivity, and hyperactivity. Teachers and parents of these children often characterize them as being unable to stick with one task for very long, failing to listen to others, talking nonstop, blurting out the first things on their minds, and being generally disorganized in planning their activities in and out of school.

Individuals with learning disabilities often have attention problems (Kotkin, Forness, & Kavale, 2001), and they are often severe enough to be diagnosed as having **attention deficit hyperactivity disorder (ADHD)**. ADHD, characterized by severe problems of inattention, hyperactivity, and/or impulsivity, is a diagnosis made by a psychiatrist or psychologist, using criteria established by the American Psychiatric Association (2001). (See Chapter 7 for a full discussion of ADHD.) Although estimates vary, researchers have consistently found an overlap of 10–25 percent between ADHD and learning disabilities (Forness & Kavale, 2002).

MEMORY, COGNITIVE, AND METACOGNITIVE PROBLEMS

We discuss memory, cognitive, and metacognitive problems together because they are closely related. A person who has problems in one of these areas is likely to have problems in the other two as well.

Memory   Parents and teachers are well aware that students with learning disabilities have problems remembering such things as assignments and appointments. In fact, these adults often exclaim in exasperation that they can't understand how a child who is so smart can forget things so easily. Furthermore, early researchers in learning disabilities documented that many students with learning disabilities have a real deficit in memory (Hallahan, 1975; Hallahan, Kauffman, & Ball, 1973; Torgesen, 1988; Torgesen & Kail, 1980).

Students with learning disabilities have problems that affect at least two types of memory: **short-term memory (STM)** and **working memory (WM)** (Swanson & Sachse-Lee, 2001). Problems with STM involve difficulty recalling information shortly after having seen or heard it. A typical STM task requires a person to repeat a list of words that are presented visually or aurally. Problems with WM affect a person's ability to keep information in mind while simultaneously doing another cognitive task. Trying to remember an address while listening to instructions on how to get there is an example of WM.

Researchers have found that one of the major reasons that children with learning disabilities perform poorly on memory tasks is that, unlike their nondisabled peers, they do not use strategies. For example, when presented with a list of words to memorize, most children will rehearse the names to themselves. They will also make use of categories by rehearsing words in groups that go together. Students with learning disabilities are not likely to use these strategies spontaneously. However, they can be taught memory strategies, which research indicates can enhance their academic performance. One such strategy is **mnemonics**, the use of memory-enhancing cues to help persons remember. For a description of mnemonics and how it can be used in the classroom, see the Responsive Instruction feature on page 188.

Cognition   The deficiency in the use of strategies on memory tasks also indicates that children with learning disabilities have problems in cognition. **Cognition** is a broad term that covers many different aspects of thinking and problem solving. Students with learning disabilities often exhibit disorganized thinking that results in problems with planning and organizing their lives at school and at home.

Metacognition   Closely related to these cognitive problems are problems in metacognition. **Metacognition** has at least three components: the ability to (1) recognize task requirements, (2) select and implement appropriate strategies, and (3) monitor and adjust performance (Butler, 1998).

Attention deficit hyperactivity disorder (ADHD)
A condition characterized by severe problems of inattention, hyperactivity, and/or impulsivity; often found in people with learning disabilities.

Short-term memory (STM)
The ability to recall information after a short period of time.

Working memory (WM)
The ability to remember information while also performing other cognitive operations.

Mnemonics
The use of memory-enhancing cues to help one remember something.

Cognition
The ability to solve problems and use strategies; an area of difficulty for many persons with learning disabilities.

Metacognition
One's understanding of the strategies available for learning a task and the regulatory mechanisms needed to complete the task.

Meeting the Needs of Students with Learning Disabilities

Mnemonics

WHAT ARE MNEMONICS?

The term *mnemonic* comes from the name of the Greek goddess of memory, Mnemosyne. Mnemosyne's name was derived from *mnemon*, meaning mindful. Today, a mnemonic refers to any memory-enhancing strategy. Almost everyone has used a mnemonic at one time or another. To remember the order of the planets, many students learn the phrase "My Very Educated Mother Just Served Us Nine Pizzas." Music students trying to remember scales learn "Every Good Boy Deserves Fudge." Rhymes are another form of mnemonic—"I before E, except after C, or when pronounced as A as in *neighbor* and *weigh*." Mnemonics come in a variety of forms, but what defines a mnemonic is its ability to aid in the retention of certain information.

WHAT THE RESEARCH SAYS

It is well documented that many students with learning disabilities have difficulty remembering information and do not spontaneously engage in memory-enhancing strategies, such as rehearsal (Mastropieri & Scruggs, 1998). By the early 1980s, researchers had begun to conduct studies to identify strategies that would address these deficit areas. Although rehearsal was found to be an effective tool for increasing the retention of information, researchers found that memory strategies involving pictures and elaboration had greater potential (Mastropieri & Scruggs, 1998). Using mnemonic strategies to help children with memory problems remember curriculum content, the teacher transforms abstract information into a concrete picture that depicts the material in a more meaningful way.

Researchers have studied mnemonics and students with learning disabilities in both laboratory settings (i.e., one-to-one with trained experimenters rather than classroom teachers) and classroom settings. Findings from these studies reveal the following gains made by students who were taught using mnemonics:

- Mnemonic keyword method resulted in increased recall of information.
- Small groups of students with learning disabilities could be taught using a variety of mnemonic strategies over a period of days without diminishing the effectiveness of the specific mnemonics.
- Mnemonic pictures aided in the comprehension and recall of information presented in science and history texts.
- Students with learning disabilities could be taught to create their own mnemonics and apply them successfully.
- Students with learning and behavior disorders benefited from teacher-created mnemonics and were able to retain the information longer than students who were not provided mnemonics.
- Mnemonics appeared to result in increased motivation, efficacy, and willingness to learn. (Mastropieri & Scruggs, 1998)

Regarding the first component—ability to recognize task requirements—students with learning disabilities frequently have problems judging how difficult tasks can be. For example, they might approach the reading of highly technical information with the same level of intensity as they experience when reading for pleasure.

An example of problems with the second component—ability to select and implement appropriate strategies—occurs when students with learning disabilities are asked questions such as "How can you remember to take your homework to school in the morning?" they do not come up with as many strategies (e.g., writing a note to oneself, placing the homework by the front door) as students without disabilities do.

An example of the third component of metacognition—ability to monitor or adjust performance—is comprehension monitoring. **Comprehension monitoring** refers to the abilities employed while one reads and attempts to comprehend textual material. Many students with reading disabilities have problems, for example, in being able to sense when they are not understanding what they are reading (Butler, 1998). Good readers are able to sense this and make necessary adjustments, such as slowing down and/or rereading difficult passages. Students with reading problems are also likely to have problems in picking out the main ideas of paragraphs.

Comprehension monitoring
The ability to keep track of one's own comprehension of reading material and to make adjustments to comprehend better while reading; often deficient in students with learning disabilities.

IMPLEMENTING MNEMONICS IN THE CLASSROOM

Two effective mnemonic techniques are the keyword and pegword methods (Lasley, Matczynski, & Rowley, 2002). When using a keyword approach, students are taught how to transform an unfamiliar word to a familiar word. For example, the word *accolade* could be associated with the keyword *Kool-Aid*. To associate Kool-Aid with the definition of accolade, students can think of someone making a toast to a guest of honor with a cup of Kool-Aid. Thus, the definition "giving praise" will be closely associated with *accolade* (Levin, 1993).

To use the pegword strategy, students learn to correlate numbers with familiar rhyming words. The teacher creates a picture that incorporates the pegword along with the content associations. Teachers use this strategy when students need to remember the order of information or when there is a number association with the fact. For example, a student who is trying to remember that Monroe was the fifth president could combine the keyword *money* for Monroe and the pegword *hive* for five. The image of bees carrying money to a hive would be the mnemonic (Mastropieri & Scruggs, 1998).

Teachers working in inclusive settings find that mnemonics can be a useful strategy for both their special needs and general education students (see Mastropieri, Sweda, & Scruggs, 2000 for examples of inclusive classroom implementations).

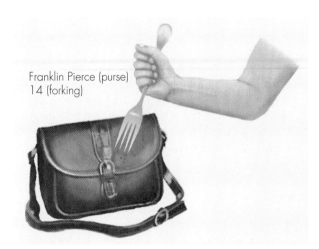

Franklin Pierce (purse)
14 (forking)

FIGURE A Mnemonic representation of Franklin Pierce, fourteenth president of the United States.

Source: Adapted from Mastropieri, M. A., Scruggs, T. E., & Whedon, C. (1997). Using mnemonic strategies to teach information about U.S. Presidents: A classroom-based investigation. *Learning Disability Quarterly, 20,* 13–21. Copyright 1994 by Thomas E. Scruggs and Margo A. Mastropieri.

EXAMPLE MNEMONIC

Figure A is an example of a mnemonic based on the keyword *purse* for Franklin Pierce and the pegword *forking* for *fourteen*. The "action" of the fork piercing the purse reinforces the connection between the two items and enhances the association students will need to recall. ■

By Kristin L. Sayeski

SOCIAL-EMOTIONAL PROBLEMS

Although not all, perhaps not even a majority, of children with learning disabilities have significant social-emotional problems, they do run a greater risk than do their nondisabled peers of having these types of problems. For those who experience behavioral problems, the effects can be long-lasting and devastating. In their early years, these children are often rejected by their peers and have poor self-concepts (Bryan, Burstein, & Ergul, 2004). In adulthood, the scars from years of rejection can be painful and not easily healed (McGrady, Lerner, & Boscardin, 2001). See the Personal Perspectives on page 190 for testimony to the depth of the emotional scars experienced by some people with learning disabilities.

One plausible reason for the social problems of some students with learning disabilities is that these students have deficits in social cognition. That is, they misread social cues and may misinterpret the feelings and emotions of others. Most children, for example, can tell when their behavior is bothering others. Students with learning disabilities sometimes act as if they are oblivious to the effect their behavior is having on their peers. They also have difficulty taking the perspective of others, of putting themselves in someone else's shoes.

Personal Perspectives

LEARNING DISABILITIES AND THE PAIN OF REJECTION

THE following excerpt from the autobiography of a 34-year-old man with learning disabilities poignantly illustrates how difficult it can be for some people with learning disabilities to make and keep friends:

Making new friends was a most difficult process, one I rarely attempted. I had been so shy in the first grade that the other kids saw me as a freak and avoided contact with me. I was socially blackballed from the get-go. When my father, a man without many friends, heard of my social problems he passed along some less than sage advice. He said, "If they don't like you, dazzle them with bullshit." Once I was clear on what bullshit was, I embarked on a destructive path that ruined my prospects of making true friends. In order to keep people interested in maintaining a friendship, I jazzed myself up. When given the opportunity to advance my image in someone else's eyes, I leapt on it, no matter how outrageous the lie. . . .

All too soon, the practice began to backfire as my peers, not nearly as stupid as I believed, began to challenge my lies. For a while, I stood by my stories, unable to address why I told them or the effect they might have on others. But time and the constant doubt of my classmates eventually wore me down. By the third grade, I was beaten, defenseless, and had nowhere to retreat, so I publicly recanted. After that, word of my confession spread like pink eye through the school yard, and I was left alone. No one at school would befriend the known liar, the boy who could not tell the truth. As my peers rolled down the path of socialization, I was left standing in their dust. Early on, I had tried being myself and it had gotten me alienated. I tried being everything to everyone, and it cost me any hope of social acceptance. I was left with nothing, both socially and emotionally. (Queen, 2001, p. 5) ■

Nonverbal learning disabilities
A term used to refer to individuals who have a cluster of disabilities in social interaction, math, visual-spatial tasks, and tactual tasks.

Locus of control
A motivational term referring to how people explain their successes or failures; people with an internal locus of control believe that they are the reason for success or failure, whereas people with an external locus of control believe that outside forces influence how they perform.

Researchers have noted that problems with social interaction tend to be more evident in children who also have problems in math, visual-spatial tasks, tactual tasks, and self-regulation and organization (Rourke, 1995; Worling, Humphries, & Tannock, 1999). In laypersons' terms, such children are sometimes described as "spacey" or "in a fog." Individuals who exhibit this constellation of behaviors are referred to as having **nonverbal learning disabilities**. However, the term is somewhat of a misnomer because these people often exhibit subtle problems in using language, especially in social situations. Researchers have speculated that nonverbal learning disabilities are caused by malfunctioning of the right half of the brain because of known linkages of math, visual-spatial, and tactual skills to the right cerebral hemisphere.

There is also evidence that individuals with nonverbal learning disabilities are at risk for depression, presumably because of the social rejection and isolation they may experience. In extreme cases, they have an increased risk of suicide (Bender, Rosenkrans, & Crane, 1999).

MOTIVATIONAL PROBLEMS

Another source of problems for many people with learning disabilities is their motivation, or feelings about their abilities to deal with many of life's challenges and problems. People with learning disabilities may appear content to let events happen without attempting to control or influence them. These individuals have what is referred to as an *external*, rather than an *internal*, **locus of control**. In other words, they believe that their lives are controlled by external factors such as luck or fate rather than by internal factors such as determination or ability (Hallahan, Gajar, Cohen, & Tarver, 1978; Short & Weissberg-Benchell, 1989). People with this outlook sometimes display **learned helplessness**: a tendency to give up and expect the worst because they think that no matter how hard they try, they will fail (Seligman, 1992).

What makes these motivational problems so difficult for teachers, parents, and individuals with learning disabilities to deal with is the interrelationship between cognitive and motivational problems (Montague, 1997). A vicious cycle develops: The student learns to expect failure in any new situation on the basis of past experience. This expectancy of failure, or learned helplessness, might then cause the student to give up too easily when faced with a difficult or complicated task. As a result, not only does the student fail to learn new skills; she or he also has another bad experience, reinforcing feelings of helplessness and even worthlessness—and so the cycle goes.

THE CHILD WITH LEARNING DISABILITIES AS AN INACTIVE LEARNER WITH STRATEGY DEFICITS

Many of the psychological and behavioral characteristics we have described can be summed up by saying that the student with learning disabilities is an inactive learner, lacking in strategies for attacking academic problems (Hallahan & Bryan, 1981; Hallahan & Reeve, 1980; Torgesen, 1977). Specifically, research describes the student with learning disabilities as someone who does not believe in his or her own abilities (learned helplessness), has an inadequate grasp of what strategies are available for problem solving (poor metacognitive skills), and has problems producing appropriate learning strategies spontaneously.

The practical implications of this constellation of characteristics is that students with learning disabilities can have difficulties working independently. They are not likely to be "self-starters." Assignments or activities requiring them to work on their own may cause problems unless the teacher carefully provides an appropriate amount of support. As we discussed in Chapter 4, homework is a major problem for many students with disabilities; this is especially true for those with learning disabilities (Bryan & Sullivan-Burstein, 1998; Epstein, Munk, Bursuck, Polloway, & Jayanthi, 1998). Students' difficulties range from failing to bring home their homework to being distracted while doing homework to forgetting to turn in their homework.

Educational Considerations

In this section, we consider two major approaches to alleviating the academic problems of students with learning disabilities: cognitive training and direct instruction. Although we look at these approaches individually, in practice they are often combined. In addition, we discuss service delivery models.

COGNITIVE TRAINING

The approach termed **cognitive training** involves three components: (1) changing thought processes, (2) providing strategies for learning, and (3) teaching self-initiative. Whereas behavior modification focuses on modifying observable behaviors, cognitive training is concerned with modifying unobservable thought processes, prompting observable changes in behavior. Cognitive training has proven successful in helping a variety of academic problems for many students with learning disabilities (Hallahan et al., 2005).

Authorities give at least two reasons as to why cognitive training is particularly appropriate for students with learning disabilities—namely, it aims at helping them overcome

1. Cognitive and metacognitive problems, by providing them with specific strategies for solving problems

IN 1999, two mothers of daughters with nonverbal learning disabilities started a website devoted to information on nonverbal learning disabilities: **www.nldontheweb.org**

Learned helplessness
A motivational term referring to a condition in which a person believes that no matter how hard he or she tries, failure will result.

THE DIVISION for Learning Disabilities of the Council for Exceptional Children maintains a website devoted to research-based, teaching practices: **www.TeachingLD.org**
    Another professional organization providing information on learning disabilities is the Council for Learning Disabilities: **www.cldinternational. org**

Cognitive training
A group of training procedures designed to change thoughts or thought patterns.

UNDERSTANDING THE STANDARDS AND PRINCIPLES What educational approaches are most appropriate for students with learning disabilities? *(CEC Knowledge and Skills Standards LD4S1, LD4S2, & LD4S13)*

Council for Exceptional Children

Self-instruction
A type of cognitive training technique that requires individuals to talk aloud and then to themselves as they solve problems.

Self-monitoring
A type of cognitive training technique that requires individuals to keep track of their own behavior.

Scaffolded instruction
A cognitive approach to instruction in which the teacher provides temporary structure or support while students are learning a task; the support is gradually removed as the students are able to perform the task independently.

2. Motivational problems of passivity and learned helplessness, by stressing self-initiative and involving them as much as possible in their own treatment

A variety of specific techniques and approaches fall under the heading of cognitive training. We briefly discuss four: self-instruction, self-monitoring, scaffolded instruction, and reciprocal teaching.

Self-Instruction The purpose of **self-instruction** is to make students aware of the various stages of problem-solving tasks while they are performing them and to bring behavior under verbal control. Typically, the teacher first models the use of the verbal routine while solving the problem. Then the teacher closely supervises the students using the verbal routine while doing the task. Then the students do it on their own.

One study using self-instruction as an integral feature of instruction involved fifth- and sixth-grade students with learning disabilities solving math word problems (Case, Harris, & Graham, 1992). The five-step strategy that the students learned to use involved saying the problem out loud, looking for important words and circling them, drawing pictures to help explain what was happening, writing the math sentence, and writing the answer. Furthermore, students were prompted to use the following self-instructions:

1. *Problem definition*: "What do I have to do?"
2. *Planning*: "How can I solve this problem?"
3. *Strategy use*: "The five-step strategy will help me look for important words."
4. *Self-evaluation*: "How am I doing?"
5. *Self-reinforcement*: "Good job. I got it right."

Self-Monitoring **Self-monitoring** involves students keeping track of their own behavior. Self-monitoring often consists of two components: *self evaluation* and *self-recording*. The student evaluates his or her behavior and then records whether the behavior occurred. For example, after working on several math problems, the student can check his or her answers and then record on a graph how many of the answers were correct. After several days, the student and teacher have an observable record of the student's progress. Teachers and students can use self-monitoring for various academic tasks in addition to math. For example, self-monitoring has been used to increase the number of words spelled correctly and to increase the length and the quality of written stories (Harris, Graham, Reid, McElroy, & Hamby, 1994).

In addition to monitoring academic performance, teachers have also had students monitor their on- and off-task behavior. The students are instructed to ask themselves "Was I paying attention?" every time they hear a tone on a tape recorder. (The teacher has prepared a tape with tones that occur randomly every thirty to ninety seconds.) Not only has the students' on-task behavior increased, but their academic productivity has also increased (Lloyd, Hallahan, Kauffman, & Keller, 1998; Mathes & Bender, 1997).

Scaffolded Instruction In **scaffolded instruction**, assistance is provided to students when they are first learning tasks and then is gradually reduced so that eventually students do the tasks independently. For example, in one study, the teacher modeled a three-step strategy for writing, saying the steps aloud:

1. *Think*, who will read this, and why am I writing it?
2. *Plan* what to say using *TREE* (note *Topic* sentence, note *Reasons, Examine* reasons, note *Ending*).
3. *Write* and *Say More*. (Sexton, Harris, & Graham, 1998, p. 300)

While modeling the strategy, the students and teacher discussed various aspects of it, and the students gradually memorized the strategy and implemented it on their own.

In scaffolded instruction, assistance is provided to students when they are first learning tasks and then is gradually reduced, so that eventually students perform tasks independently.

Reciprocal Teaching   Like scaffolded instruction, **reciprocal teaching** involves an interactive dialogue between the teacher and students in which the teacher–student relationship is similar to that of an expert (teacher) and an apprentice (student). The teacher gradually relinquishes her or his role as the sole instructor and allows the student to assume the role of co-instructor for brief periods. The teacher models and then encourages and prompts the students to use four strategies: predicting, questioning, summarizing, and clarifying:

> During reciprocal teaching, teachers begin reading selections by having students make predictions based on story titles, headings, or other appropriate passage features. In this way, students are encouraged to activate background knowledge and information and to set a purpose for reading. Teachers then foster practice of good questioning strategies by requiring students to ask "teacher-like" questions rather than fill-in-the-blank questions. In addition, if students are unable to ask a question, the teacher might provide an appropriate question word as a prompt. Summarizing strategies for students include finding the main idea and supporting details and stating this information in their own words without looking at the text. Students are told to look for a topic sentence or to give a name to a list of items as ways to identify main ideas. Finally, students point out information that is unclear or unknown as they clarify new vocabulary, unfamiliar expressions, or ambiguous information. (Meese, 2001, p. 318)

DIRECT INSTRUCTION

The **Direct Instruction (DI)** method focuses on the details of the instructional process. Advocates of DI stress a systematic analysis of the concept to be taught, rather than analysis of the characteristics of the student. A critical component of DI is task analysis. **Task analysis** involves breaking down academic problems into their component parts so that teachers can teach the parts separately and then teach the students to put the parts together in order to demonstrate the larger skill.

Reciprocal teaching
A cognitive teaching strategy whereby the student gradually assumes the role of co-instructor for brief periods; the teacher models four strategies for the students to use: (1) predicting, (2) questioning, (3) summarizing, and (4) clarifying.

Direct Instruction (DI)
A method of teaching academics, especially reading and math; emphasizes drill and practice and immediate feedback; lessons are precisely sequenced, fast-paced, and well-rehearsed by the teacher.

Task analysis
The procedure of breaking down an academic task into its component parts for the purpose of instruction; a major feature of Direct Instruction.

Direct Instruction programs, which consist of precisely sequenced, fast-paced lessons taught to small groups of four to ten students, may bring both immediate and long-term academic gains in students with learning disabilities.

A variety of DI programs are available for reading, math, and language (Engelmann, Carnine, Engelmann, & Kelly, 1991; Engelmann, Carnine, Johnson, & Meyers, 1988, 1989). These programs consist of precisely sequenced, fast-paced lessons that are taught to small groups of four to ten students. There is a heavy emphasis on drill and practice. The teacher teaches from a well-rehearsed script, and pupils follow the lead of the teacher, who often uses hand signals to prompt participation. The teacher offers immediate corrective feedback for errors and praise for correct responses. See Responsive Instruction on page 195 for more information about DI in the classroom.

Direct Instruction programs are among the best-researched commercial programs available for students with learning disabilities. Use of these programs not only results in immediate academic gains, but also may bring long-term academic gains (see Lloyd, 1988, for a review of this research).

BEST PRACTICES IN TEACHING STUDENTS WITH LEARNING DISABILITIES

FOR MORE INFORMATION on DI, visit the Association for Direct Instruction website: **www.adihome.org**

Authorities have concluded that neither cognitive training nor DI, by itself, is the answer to instructing all students with learning disabilities. Instead, teachers should be prepared to use both. Students need teachers to teach them strategies and skills directly through DI, but they also need the chance to practice these strategies on their own, using cognitive training techniques such as self-instruction, self-monitoring, scaffolded instruction, and reciprocal teaching (Rosenshine & Meister, 1994; Swanson, 2001; Swanson & Hoskyn, 1998; Vaughn, Gersten, & Chard, 2000). The Responsive Instruction box on page 196 gives an example of how peers can work together to practice both self-instruction and content skills using Peer-Assisted Learning Strategies (PALS). See Making it Work on page 198 for a description of how general and special educators can work together to make PALS happen successfully.

Meeting the Needs of Students with Learning Disabilities

Direct Instruction

WHAT IS DIRECT INSTRUCTION?

Direct instruction (DI) is a highly structured, teacher-directed method of instruction. The main features of DI programs are as follows:

- Field-tested, scripted lesson plans
- Curriculum based upon the theory of mastery learning (i.e., students do not move on until they have mastered the concept)
- Rapid pace of instruction highly dependent upon frequent teacher questioning and student response
- Achievement grouping
- Frequent assessments

Siegfried Englemann developed DI in the 1960s on the basis of studies of beginning reading. Since the development of his early DI programs such as DISTAR (Direct Instructional System for Teaching and Remediation), published in 1968, DI programs have been developed in the areas of reading, language arts, mathematics, science, and social studies. One of the defining features of DI programs is that virtually every aspect of instruction undergoes careful evaluation before it is approved for inclusion in the program. Researchers evaluate everything from group size to teacher directions to method of student response to achieve optimal effectiveness. As a result, DI programs have received the highest ranking for program effectiveness in an independent analysis of instructional programs (Ellis, 2001).

WHAT THE RESEARCH SAYS

To obtain in an idea of the overall effectiveness of a program, researchers conduct what is called a meta-analysis. To conduct a meta-analysis, researchers identify all studies that have been conducted on a specific technique or program and statistically determine how effective the technique is as a whole. Since the inception of DI, several of these comprehensive evaluations have been conducted in regard to DI curriculum. A recent meta-analysis made over 173 comparisons between DI and other programs. Results showed that *(1)* 64 percent of the comparisons resulted in statistically significant differences in favor of the groups using DI, *(2)* 35 percent of the comparisons showed no differences among programs, and *(3)* 1 percent showed differences in favor of programs other than DI (Adams & Englemann, 1996). In short, the overall effectiveness of DI programs is among the highest in the field of education.

IMPLEMENTING THE CURRICULUM

To implement DI, teachers need to receive training in the program. Because of the highly structured nature of DI materials, many educators and administrators incorrectly assume that DI is "teacher-proof"; that is, anyone could be effective using the materials. Nothing could be farther from the truth. Using the materials with ease, understanding the rationale for each component and therefore being able to communicate that to students, and pacing the instruction to meet the unique needs of a group of students requires teaching skills that cannot come from a script. After initial training, coaches or facilitators provide ongoing support for teachers who use DI programs to ensure that teachers are maximizing the effectiveness of the curriculum.

WHAT DOES DI LOOK LIKE?

The sample script in Figure A is an excerpt from Corrective Reading, an accelerated reading program for students in grades 3.5 through 12 who have not mastered the basics of decoding and comprehension. In this decoding lesson, students work on phonemic awareness, letter–symbol identification, and sounding out words. The use of choral response increases opportunities for student engagement, and individual questioning ensures individual mastery. ■

By Kristin L. Sayeski

EXERCISE 3

Say the Sounds

Note: **Do not write the words on the board. This is an oral exercise.**

1. Listen: **fffēēē**. (Hold up a finger for each sound.)
2. Say the sounds in (pause) **fffēēē**. Get ready. (Hold up a finger for each sound.) *fffēēē*. (Repeat until the students say the sounds without stopping.)
3. Say it fast. (Signal.) *Fee.*
4. What word? (Signal.) *Fee.* Yes, **fee.**
5. (Repeat steps 2–4 for **if, fish, sam, at, me, rim, she, we, ship, fat, miff.**)

FIGURE A

Meeting the Needs of Students with Learning Disabilities

PALS—Peer-Assisted Learning Strategies

WHAT THE RESEARCH SAYS

In response to increasing student academic diversity within general education settings, researchers at Vanderbilt University have developed a framework for instruction that results in increased individualization, higher levels of student engagement, and greater teacher accountability for student learning (Fuchs & Fuchs, 1998b). The program, Peer-Assisted Learning Strategies (PALS), is based on research-proven, best practices in reading, such as phonological awareness, decoding, and comprehension activities. PALS curriculum is effective for students with and without learning disabilities at all grade levels (Fuchs, Fuchs, & Burish, 2000).

OVERVIEW OF FIRST-GRADE PALS

All PALS programs involve the pairing of a higher-performing student with a lower-performing student. The pairs participate in three highly structured tutoring sessions lasting thirty-five minutes each per week. During each session, students take turns being the Coach (the tutor) and the Reader (the tutee).

The first-grade PALS curriculum includes two main activities: working with sounds and words and reading connected text. During the sounds-and-words part of the lesson, there is both a teacher-directed component and the partnering component. Teacher-directed instruction involves instruction in sounds, segmenting, and blending (i.e., breaking words apart into their individual sounds and blending individual sounds

into words). Partnering activities include saying sounds, sounding out, identifying sight words, and reading PALS stories. For the final activity, students take turns reading out of big books or other trade books.

IMPLEMENTING THE CURRICULUM

To implement PALS in the classroom, teachers first rank order all of their students from lowest to highest, then divide the class into high performers and low performers. The highest performer is matched to the highest student in the low-performer group. This matching continues until all students are matched. In addition to rank, teachers should consider student personality when making these matches. After the pairs are assigned, the teacher then assigns the pairs to one of two teams. The pairs earn points during each session and these points are added to overall team points. Students stay with their partner for about four weeks.

During the first couple of weeks of implementation, the students are taught how to work with their partner using the PALS materials. Teachers use scripts to assist them in teaching students the rules for PALS, correcting mistakes, and assigning points for the various activities.

SAMPLE SCRIPT

The following is part of the script a teacher would use when teaching students the PALS procedures. The sample comes

---

FOR MORE INFORMATION on PALS, visit their website: **http://kc.vanderbilt.edu/kennedy/pals**

SERVICE DELIVERY MODELS

For many years, the most common form of educational placement for students with learning disabilities was the resource room. In the mid-1990s, however, in keeping with the trend toward inclusion, the regular classroom surpassed the resource room as the most popular placement. In addition, the number of placements in separate classrooms has gradually diminished. Forty-five percent of students with learning disabilities between the ages of 6 and 21 are educated primarily in the regular classroom, with 38 percent being educated in resource rooms and 16 percent in separate classrooms (U.S. Department of Education, 2002).

As we discussed in Chapter 2, more and more schools are moving toward some kind of cooperative teaching arrangement, in which regular and special education teachers work together in the regular classroom. Some advocates believe that this model is particularly appropriate for students with learning disabilities, since it allows them to stay in the regular classroom for all or almost all of their instruction. However, the research base for cooperative teaching is still in its infancy (Murawski & Swanson, 2001).

Because students with learning disabilities make up the largest category of special education students and because their academic and behavioral problems are not as severe as

from Training Lesson 3, the "Saying Sounds" part of the lesson (Mathes, Torgeson, Allen, & Allor, 2001).

Saying Sounds

Teacher: You did a nice job of saying sounds in words and reading them. Now you're going to practice "Saying Sounds" with your partner. Readers, open your folders and take out Lesson 3. [*Place the PALS Lesson 3 transparency on the overhead.*] We have a new sound today. The new sound today is /sss/. What sound?

Students: sss

Teacher: Coaches, when there is a new sound in a box, remember to tell your partner the new sound for the day. You should say, "The new sound for today is /sss/. What sound?" Then Readers will say the sounds. Coaches, use a soft voice to tell your partners the new sound for the day. Readers, say the sound in a soft voice. [*Award points to pairs following directions.*] Great job saying the new sound. If I'm the Coach, what do I say as I touch each letter?

Students: What sound?

Teacher: Great! And what do I say when I point to a star?

Students: Good job! Great! Super!

Teacher: Great! You're ready to practice with your partner. You'll do "Saying Sounds." Remember to make some mistakes so your partner can practice helping you. Don't forget to mark your happy faces and 5 points, then switch jobs. Stop when the timer rings.

Begin. [*Set the timer for 4 minutes. Monitor and give points. Stop when the timer rings.* (See Figure A.)]

After about two weeks, students should be able to follow the PALS procedures with less teacher support. Teachers, however, should continue to move around the classroom and support pairs as well as assign points to reinforce appropriate behaviors.

In summary, the PALS components—partnering of high and low performers, structured sessions, effective reading practices, and frequent positive reinforcement—result in a comprehensive approach to address critical reading skills for all students. ■

By Kristin L. Sayeski

		LESSON 3				Coach says:
[s]	t	s	a	★	m	"What sound?"
s	m	t	a	s	★	
t	m	a	t	s	★	
				☺	☺	
				5	5	
				points	points	

FIGURE A

those of students with mental retardation or behavior disorders, they are often candidates for full inclusion. However, all the major professional and parent organizations have developed position papers against placing all students with learning disabilities in full-inclusion settings. There is also evidence that students with learning disabilities themselves prefer resource placements over full inclusion, although many such students also think that inclusion meets their needs (Klingner, Vaughn, Schumm, Cohen, & Forgan, 1998). Research on the effectiveness of inclusion for students with learning disabilities also argues against using full inclusion for all students with learning disabilities (Klingner, Vaughn, Hughes, Schumm, & Elbaum, 1998; Vaughn, Elbaum, & Boardman, 2001). In conclusion, evidence indicates that the legal mandate of IDEA requiring the availability of a full continuum of placements is sound policy for students with learning disabilities.

Early Intervention

Very little preschool programming is available for children with learning disabilities because of the difficulties in identifying them at such a young age. When we talk about testing

THE COORDINATED CAMPAIGN for Learning Disabilities, consisting of the major professional and parent organizations in learning disabilities, has focused on public awareness of learning disabilities. In particular, it has emphasized making parents of young children aware of the benefits of early identification of learning disabilities: **www.focusonlearning.org**

MAKING IT WORK

Collaboration and Co-Teaching of Students with Learning Disabilities

"How can she help me if she doesn't know science like I do?"

Co-teaching with a special educator to meet the needs of students with learning disabilities (LD) can and should take many forms in the classroom. Experts on co-teaching have identified at least five different models for use in the classroom, many of them incorporating the special educator as an equal partner in instruction (see Vaughn, Schumm, & Arguelles, 1997). But how can this work if the special educator is not as much of a content area specialist as the general educator, a frequent occurrence at the secondary level? Though you might think that would mean an end to equal collaboration in, say, a biology or advanced literature course, teachers of students with learning disabilities have knowledge and skills about learning that can be used across content areas to make them an active part of any co-teaching team.

WHAT DOES IT MEAN TO BE A TEACHER OF STUDENTS WITH LEARNING DISABILITIES?

Most training programs for teachers of students with learning disabilities do not focus on content area information. Rather, they focus on understanding learning and effective strategies to promote learning across the content areas. Specifically, the Council for Exceptional Children (2001) has identified the following skills as those necessary for beginning teachers of students with learning disabilities:

1. Modify the pace of instruction, and provide organizational cues.
2. Identify and teach basic structures and relationships within and across curricula.
3. Use instructional methods to strengthen and compensate for deficits in perception, comprehension, memory, and retrieval.
4. Identify and teach essential concepts, vocabulary, and content across the general curriculum.
5. Implement systematic instruction in teaching reading comprehension and monitoring strategies.
6. Teach learning strategies and study skills to acquire academic content.

preschool children for learning disabilities, we are really talking about prediction rather than identification (Keogh & Glover, 1980). In other words, because preschool children do not ordinarily engage in academics, it is not possible, strictly speaking, to say that they are "behind" academically. Unfortunately, all other things being equal, prediction is always less precise than identification.

At least two factors make predicting later learning disabilities particularly difficult at the preschool age:

1. In many cases of learning disabilities, the problems are relatively mild. Many of these children seem bright and competent until they are faced with a particular academic task, such as reading or spelling. Children with learning disabilities are not as immediately identifiable as many other children with disabilities.
2. It is often difficult to determine what is a true developmental delay and what is merely maturational slowness. Many nondisabled children show slow developmental progress at this young age but soon catch up with their peers.

There has been growing sentiment among some professionals not to use the "learning disability" label with preschoolers. Noting that this label implies deficits in academics, which are not ordinarily introduced until kindergarten or first grade, these professionals favor using more generic labels for preschool children, such as "developmentally delayed" or "at risk." Those who favor using the "learning disability" label argue that the sooner a child's specific problems can be identified, the sooner teachers and parents can make plans for the long-term nature of the condition.

To aid parents and professionals, research is needed for developing better predictive tests at the preschool level. At present, we know that the most accurate predictors are pre-

Most of these skills can help all students in the classroom. These skills are supported by instructional strategies that have been researched and used in the general education classroom for students with learning disabilities and others—strategies that each co-teacher can use to improve learning in his or her classroom.

SUCCESSFUL STRATEGIES FOR CO-TEACHING

As you read in the Responsive Instruction box on page 196, the Peer Assisted Learning Strategies (PALS) program is a form of peer tutoring that has been shown to improve reading skills for students with LD, as well as low and average-achieving students. In addition to the first-grade PALS described in the Responsive Instruction box, PALS in reading has been used successfully in general education classrooms from grades 2 to 6, and in high school (Fuchs et al., 2001).

In the older elementary grades, students are organized in pairs and given specific tasks (partner reading, paragraph shrinking, and prediction relay) to complete as both tutor and tutee, all of which are upper-level skills that are necessary in content area reading. There are three main activities in PALS:

partner reading, paragraph shrinking, and prediction relay. In partner reading, pairs take turns reading text and correcting errors. In paragraph shrinking, students take turns reading text and summarizing it. During prediction relay, pairs take turns reading text, summarizing it, and then predicting what the next block of text will be about.

For all tasks, tutors provide feedback for tutees. Teachers provide direct instruction in how to complete the PALS tasks, how to give corrective and appropriate feedback, and how to interact appropriately. The dyads are also on teams, and points are awarded for correct or corrected responses that help the team.

In the general education classroom, the teacher of students with LD could be responsible for teaching and implementing the component pieces of PALS on an ongoing basis while the general educator could be responsible for providing the content area reading material and the extension of the information read to projects and so on. There would also be double the sets of hands to put peer tutoring in motion! More information about PALS is available at www.vanderbilt.edu/kennedy/pals. ■

By Margaret P. Weiss

---

academic skills (Foorman, Francis, Shaywitz, Shaywitz, & Fletcher, 1997). **Preacademic skills** are behaviors that are needed before formal instruction can begin, such as identification of numbers, shapes, and colors. A particularly important preacademic skill for reading is phonological awareness (Torgesen, 2002), a skill that we discussed earlier (see p. 183). Phonological awareness is the ability to understand that speech flow can be broken into smaller sound units such as words, syllables, and phonemes. Nondisabled children generally develop phonological awareness in the preschool years. Preschoolers who exhibit problems in phonological awareness are at risk of having reading disabilities when they enter elementary school.

Preacademic skills
Behaviors that are needed before formal academic instruction can begin (e.g., ability to identify letters, numbers, shapes, and colors).

Transition to Adulthood

At one time, professionals thought that children outgrew their learning disabilities by adulthood. We now know that this is far from the truth. Although the long-term prognosis for individuals with learning disabilities is generally more positive than that for children with some other disabilities (e.g., behavior disorders), there is still the potential for difficulty. There is a danger, for example, that students with learning disabilities will drop out of school in their teenage years. The majority of students with learning disabilities do not drop out of school. Nonetheless, their futures can be uncertain. Many adults with learning disabilities have persistent problems in learning, socializing, holding jobs, and living independently (Blackorby & Wagner, 1997; Gerber, 1997;

Casebook Reflections

Refer to the case *More than LD: Shannon* in your casebook. Her academic problems in school began immediately. Could more have been done to prevent her failure earlier? Why or why not?

The most accurate predictors of learning problems in preschool that may show up later are preacademic skills, such as counting and identifying letters, numbers, shapes, and colors.

Goldstein, Murray, & Edgar, 1998; Witte, Philips, & Kakela, 1998). Even those individuals who are relatively successful in their transition to adulthood often must devote considerable energy to coping with daily living situations.

For example, in an intensive study of adults with learning disabilities, one of the subjects (S3), an assistant dean of students at a large urban university, found it

essential that organization and routines remain constant. For example, she recounted that her kitchen is arranged in a specific fashion. Most implements are visible rather than put away because she would not be able to remember where to find them. Once, when her roommate changed the kitchen setup, S3 had great difficulty finding anything, and when she did, she couldn't remember where to return it. She had to reorganize the kitchen to her original plan. When she moved from her home state to the New Orleans area, she kept her kitchen set up in exactly the same way as previously. "I don't know if that's just because I'm stubborn or because it's comfortable."

The need for organization and structure seems to pervade her daily living. She mentioned that she imposes structure on everything from the arrangement of her medicine cabinet to her professional life. She has her work day carefully organized and keeps close track of all her appointments. She has trouble coping with unannounced appointments, meetings or activities. She said that if her work routine is interrupted in such a fashion, "I can't get it together." (Gerber & Reiff, 1991, p. 113)

FACTORS RELATED TO SUCCESSFUL TRANSITION

How any particular adult with learning disabilities will fare depends on a variety of factors and is difficult to predict. Several researchers have addressed the topic of what contributes to successful adjustment of adults with learning disabilities (Gerber, Ginsberg, & Reiff, 1992; Kavale, 1988; Lindstrom & Benz, 2002; Raskind, Goldberg, Higgins, & Herman, 1999; Reiff, Gerber, & Ginsberg, 1997; Spekman, Goldberg, & Herman, 1992). Although it would seem that IQ and achievement would be the best predictors of success, according to successful adults with learning disabilities, the things that set them apart from those who are not as successful are the following:

- An extraordinary degree of perseverance
- The ability to set goals for oneself
- A realistic acceptance of weaknesses coupled with an attitude of building on strengths
- Access to a strong network of social support from friends and family
- Exposure to intensive and long-term educational intervention
- High quality on-the-job or postsecondary vocational training
- A supportive work environment
- Being able to take control of their lives

The last attribute, in particular, is a consistent theme among the successful. They have not let their disability rule them; rather, they have taken the initiative to control their own destiny. As one adult remarked, on looking back at his days in secondary school:

Having an LD is much akin to being blind or losing the use of an appendage; it affects all aspects of your life. In dealing with this, you have two choices. One, you can acknowledge the parasitic relationship the LD has with you and consciously strive to excel despite its presence. . . . The other path let[s] the LD slowly dominate you and become[s] the scapegoat for all your failings. Can't find a good job? Must be the LD. Relationships always fail? It's the LD. If you follow this destructive path, you spend the remainder of your life being controlled by your LD. (Queen, 2001, p. 15)

SECONDARY PROGRAMMING

Approaches to educating students with learning disabilities at the secondary level differ, depending on whether the goal is to prepare students for college or work. In general, there are seven different program options for students with learning disabilities at the secondary level: functional skills, work-study, basic skills remediation, tutorial in subject areas, learning strategies, inclusion or co-teaching, and consultation (Bender, 2004). The first two are oriented more toward preparing students for the world of work than the others. However, schools often offer a blend of these models.

Functional Skills   The functional skills model concentrates on adaptive skills, such as on-the-job behavior, filling out job applications, and balancing a checkbook. It is often combined with a work-study and/or a basic skills model.

Work-Study   The work-study option provides supervised work experiences during the school day. Ideally, the student is able to explore a variety of jobs that might be of interest to her or him.

Basic Skills   With this approach, the special education teacher provides instruction in basic academic skills in math, language arts, and reading. The amount of instruction, delivered by a special educator in a separate classroom, varies according to need.

A major difficulty faced by students with learning disabilities in the transition from high school to college is the decrease in the amount of guidance provided by adults, and the greater demand on self-discipline.

Casebook Reflections

Refer to the case *More than LD: Shannon* in your casebook. Shannon wants to be a teacher or work for a TV station. What supports might be available to her in college to help her be more successful?

FOR MORE INFORMATION on the University of Kansas Center for Research on Learning, visit **www.ku-crl.org/iei/index.html**

For specific information on the Strategic Instruction Model developed for adolescents with learning disabilities, visit **www.kucrl.org/iei/sim/index.html**

Tutorial   The special education teacher tutors the student in the content areas—history, math, English, and so forth. One disadvantage is that the special educator is stretched to teach in areas in which he or she might not have a great deal of expertise.

Learning Strategies   The learning strategies model was developed at the University of Kansas Center for Research on Learning and focuses on teaching students to overcome their metacognitive deficits by using learning strategies (Deshler et al., 2001). The Kansas group has developed a variety of strategies that students can use to help them organize information and learn it more efficiently.

Inclusion and Co-Teaching   In this model, the special educator and general educator teach together in the general education classroom. As we noted in Chapter 2, there are various co-teaching models, ranging from the general educator delivering the main content and the special educator supplementing the instruction with tutorial help to both teachers taking turns delivering the content.

Consultation   In the consultation model, the special education teacher consults with the general education teacher on ways to modify the general education curriculum to meet the needs of students with learning disabilities. The general educator delivers the instruction rather than the special educator.

POSTSECONDARY PROGRAMMING

Postsecondary programs include vocational and technical programs as well as community colleges and four-year colleges and universities. More and more individuals with learning disabilities are enrolling in colleges and universities, and more and more universities are establishing special programs and services for these students. In the 1990s, for example, the percentage of entering first-year college students with learning disabilities nearly tripled—from 1.2 percent to 3.5 percent (Henderson, 1999, as cited in Hitchings et al., 2001).

Secondary-school teachers should prepare their students to make the right choices of colleges and help them to delineate what accommodations they will need in their programs. Students and their families may take advantage of published guides to college programs for students with learning disabilities (Cobb, 2003; Peterson, 2003; Wax & Kravets, 2003). Also, students can avail themselves of the special accommodations available for students who are learning disabled when they take the Scholastic Aptitude Test (SAT) and the American College Test (ACT).

In selecting a college, students and their families should explore what kinds of student support services are offered. Section 504 of the Vocational Rehabilitation Act of 1973 (Public Law 93-112) requires that colleges make reasonable accommodations for students with disabilities so that they will not be discriminated against because of their disabilities. Some typical accommodations are extended time on exams, allowing students to take exams in a distraction-free room, providing tape recordings of lectures and books, and assigning volunteer note-takers for lectures. In addition, two key ingredients are *comprehensiveness* and *individualization*.

With these support services in mind, there are two overall considerations in selecting a college program: comprehensiveness and individualization. The prospective student should consider the comprehensiveness of services offered. A service plan that includes some type of summer orientation and training program, tutoring in various classes, assessment as needed, emotional support, and accommodations in program planning should meet the needs of most students. However, even when comprehensive services are provided, an individually tailored program is critical. Students should not settle for a program that attempts to fit all students with learning disabilities into one standard program. Rather, case managers should meet with the student with learning disabilities to individually plan appropriate services. (Bender, 2004, p. 384)

A potentially useful skill for college students with learning disabilities can be self-advocacy: the ability to understand one's disability, be aware of one's legal rights, and communicate one's rights and needs to professors and administrators (Hitchings et al., 2001). Although ideally, self-advocacy skills should be taught to students with learning disabilities in secondary school, many students come to college in need of guidance in how to go about advocating for themselves in a confident but nonconfrontational manner.

There is little doubt that much remains to be learned about programming effectively for students with learning disabilities at the postsecondary level. However, the field has made great strides in opening windows of opportunity for these young adults. Authorities have noted that many college applicants with learning disabilities try to hide their disabilities for fear that they will not be admitted (Skinner, 1998). If the burgeoning interest in postsecondary programming for individuals who are learning disabled continues, we may in the near future see the day when students and colleges routinely collaborate to use information about students' learning disabilities in planning their programs.

SUMMARY

HOW do professionals define learning disabilities?

- The most common definition is that of the federal government, which has been in effect since 1977 (with a few minor wording changes in 1997).
- The National Joint Committee on Learning Disabilities presented a definition that differs from the federal government's with respect to (1) no reference to psychological processes, (2) inclusion of intrinsic nature of learning disabilities, (3) inclusion of adults, (4) inclusion of self-regulation and social interaction problems, (5) omission of terms difficult to define, (6) purportedly less confusion regarding the exclusion clause, and (7) omission of spelling.

HOW do professionals identify students with learning disabilities?

- Since the late 1970s, the major method of identifying learning disabilities has been by looking for an IQ–achievement discrepancy.
- More recently, professionals have proposed that a Response to Intervention (RTI) approach be used.
  - A variety of RTI models have been proposed and implemented.
  - Very little research has been conducted on any of these models.

- Many questions remain regarding large-scale implementation of RTI.

WHAT is the prevalence of learning disabilities?

- Between 5 and 6 percent of school-age students are identified as learning disabled, making learning disabilities the largest category of special education by far.
- The prevalence of learning disabilities has more than doubled since the late 1970s.
  - Some believe this increase reflects poor diagnostic practices.
  - Some believe that some of the increase may be due to social and cultural changes.
- Boys with learning disabilities outnumber girls about 3 to 1.
  - Some believe that this is due to gender bias in referrals.
  - Some believe that this is partly due to boys being more vulnerable biologically.

WHAT causes learning disabilities?

- With the advance of neuroimaging techniques, most authorities now believe that central nervous system dysfunction underlies learning disabilities.

- There is strong evidence that many cases of learning disabilities are inherited.
- Teratogens (e.g., fetal alcohol syndrome) and medical factors (premature birth) can also result in learning disabilities.

WHAT assessment practices do professionals use with students with learning disabilities?

- Standardized achievement tests provide an indication of where a student stands relative to others, but they do not help much in planning educational strategies.
- Formative assessment measures student performance directly and frequently, and teachers can use it to assess pupil progress toward educational goals as well as to evaluate the effectiveness of educational programming.
  - Curriculum-based assessment (CBA), a type of formative assessment, measures the child's progress in the curriculum.
  - CBA can be used to compare the student with disabilities to his or her peers in the classroom or the school.
- Informal assessment includes having students do academic work in order to analyze where they have problems.
- Authentic assessment, an example being portfolios, is designed to assess students' critical thinking and problem-solving ability in real-life situations.

WHAT are some of the psychological and behavioral characteristics of learners with learning disabilities?

- Persons with learning disabilities exhibit interindividual and intraindividual variability.
- Academic deficits are the hallmark of learning disabilities.
  - Reading disabilities are the most common form of academic disability and can be manifested in decoding, fluency and comprehension problems.
    - Phonological awareness, the understanding that speech consists of units of sound (words, syllables, phonemes), underlies the ability to decode.
    - Phonemic awareness—understanding that words are made up of sounds or phonemes—is particularly important for learning to decode.
  - Writing disabilities, including handwriting, spelling and composition, are common in students with learning disabilities.
  - Spoken language disabilities include problems with syntax (grammar), semantics (word meanings), phonology, and pragmatics (social uses of language).
  - Math disabilities include problems with computation and word problems.
- Some students with learning disabilities experience problems with perceptual, perceptual-motor, and general coordination.

- Many students with learning disabilities have problems with attention, and there is an overlap of 10 to 25 percent between learning disabilities and attention deficit hyperactivity disorder.
- Memory problems include problems with short-term memory and working memory.
- Cognitive problems include thinking and problem-solving deficits.
- Metacognitive problems include deficits in recognizing task requirements, selecting and using appropriate strategies, and monitoring and adjusting performance.
- Social-emotional problems include peer rejection, poor self-concepts, and poor social cognition.
  - Problems with social interaction are more prevalent in students with problems with math, visual-spatial and tactual tasks, and self-regulation; such students are sometimes referred to as having nonverbal learning disabilities.
- Motivational problems can include having an external locus of control and learned helplessness.
- Some authorities believe that a composite of many of the preceding characteristics indicates that many students with learning disabilities are passive rather than active learners.

WHAT are some educational considerations for learners with learning disabilities?

- Cognitive training focuses on (1) changing thought processes, (2) providing strategies for learning, and (3) teaching self-initiative.
  - Self-instruction involves having students say out loud what it is they are to do.
  - Self-monitoring involves having students self-evaluate and self-record while they are doing academic work.
  - Scaffolded instruction involves providing students with teacher support while they perform academic work.
  - Reciprocal teaching involves teacher modeling correct performance and then having the student assume the role of co-teacher while using four strategies: predicting, questioning, summarizing, and clarifying.
- Direct instruction (DI) focuses even more directly on academics than does cognitive training; a critical component of DI is task analysis, as well as the following:
  - Field-tested scripted lessons
  - Curricula based on mastery learning
  - Rapid instructional pace
  - Achievement grouping
  - Frequent assessments
- Best practices in teaching students with learning disabilities include a combination of cognitive training and DI.

- With respect to service delivery models, available research evidence indicates that a full continuum of placements is sound policy for students with learning disabilities.

WHAT are some things to consider with respect to early intervention for learners with learning disabilities?

- Little preschool programming exists for children with learning disabilities because it is so hard to predict at that age which children will later develop academic problems.
- Certain preacademic skills, such as letter, shape, and color recognition and especially phonological awareness, are the best predictors of later academic learning.

WHAT are some things to consider with respect to transition to adulthood for learners with learning disabilities?

- Factors related to successful transition include the following:
  - Extraordinary perseverance

- Setting goals
- Acceptance of weaknesses, combined with building on strengths
- Strong network of social support
- Intensive and long-term educational intervention
- High-quality on-the-job or postsecondary vocational training
- Supportive work environment
- Taking control of one's life
- Seven programming options at the secondary level include those oriented toward functional skills, work-study, basic skills, tutoring, learning strategies, inclusion and co-teaching, or consultation.
- Postsecondary programs include vocational and technical programs as well as community colleges and four-year colleges and universities.
- More and more students with learning disabilities are attending college; two key components to look for in college programs are comprehensiveness and individualization.

APPLYING THE STANDARDS AND PRINCIPLES

- **ONE** of your colleagues, whose background is in general education, asks, "**What does it really mean to have a learning disability?**" How would you respond? *(CEC Content Standard #1 & #2; INTASC Principle #1 & #2)*

- **DISCUSS** the benefits and limitations of **standardized achievement assessments.** *(CEC Content Standard #8 & INTASC Principle #8)*

- **THE parent of a second grader** with a learning disability approaches you to discuss her son's difficulties in reading. "My son doesn't seem to understand that words are made up of sounds. What approaches would work with him?" How would you respond? *(CEC Content Standard #4 & INTASC Principle #4)*

Council for Exceptional Children

INTASC

Chapter 7

Learners with Attention Deficit Hyperactivity Disorder

L et me see if Philip can
      Be a little gentleman.
Let me see, if he is able
To sit still for once at table;
Thus Papa bade Phil behave;
And Mamma look'd very grave.
But fidgety Phil,
He won't sit still;
He wriggles
And giggles,
And then, I declare
Swings backwards and forwards
And tilts up his chair,
Just like any rocking horse;
"Philip! I am getting cross!"

HEINRICH HOFFMANN
"The Story of Fidgety Philip"

Questions to Guide Your Reading of This Chapter

- WHAT are the historical origins of ADHD?

- WHAT is the current definition of ADHD?

- WHAT is the prevalence of ADHD?

- WHAT methods of assessment are used to identify individuals with ADHD?

- WHAT causes ADHD?

- WHAT are some of the psychological and behavioral characteristics of learners with ADHD?

- WHAT are some educational considerations for learners with ADHD?

- WHAT are some medication considerations for learners with ADHD?

- WHAT are some things to consider with respect to early intervention for learners with ADHD?

- WHAT are some things to consider with respect to transition to adulthood for learners with ADHD?

SPECIAL EDUCATORS . . .

- **understand the similarities and differences in human development** and the characteristics between and among individuals with and without exceptional learning needs *(from CEC Content Standard #2).*

- **understand the effects that an exceptional condition can have** on an individual's learning in school and throughout life *(from CEC Content Standard #3).*

- **possess a repertoire** of evidence-based instructional strategies *(from CEC Content Standard #4).*

- **use the results of assessments** to help identify exceptional learning needs *(from CEC Content Standard #8).*

- **use collaboration** to facilitate the successful transitions of individuals with exceptional learning needs across settings and services *(from CEC Content Standard #10).*

ALL TEACHERS . . .

- **understand the central concepts, tools of inquiry, structures of the discipline(s) they teach** and can create learning experiences that make these aspects of subject matter meaningful *(INTASC Principle #1).*

- **understand how children learn and develop** and can provide learning opportunities that support the intellectual, social and personal development of each learner *(INTASC Principle #2).*

- **Understand and use a variety of instructional strategies** to encourage students' development of critical thinking, problem solving, and performance skills *(INTASC Principle #4).*

- **Understand and use formal and informal assessment strategies** to evaluate and ensure the continuous intellectual, social and physical development of the learner *(INTASC Principle #8).*

- **Foster relationships** with school colleagues, families, and agencies in the larger community to support students' learning and well being *(INTASC Principle #10).*

Council for Exceptional Children

INTASC

idgety Phil, the character in the poem by the German physician Heinrich Hoffmann (1865) (see p. 207) is generally considered one of the first allusions in Western literature to what today is referred to as attention deficit hyperactivity disorder (ADHD) (Barkley, 1998). Phil's lack of impulse control bears an uncanny similarity to today's conceptualization of ADHD as less a matter of inattention than a matter of regulating one's behavior. We discuss this conceptualization more fully later, but it is also important to point out here that Phil's excessive motor activity, or hyperactivity, may be characteristic of many children with ADHD but not all. Interestingly, Hoffman also wrote another poem, "The Story of Johnny Head-in-Air," about a child who fits to a T children with ADHD who do not have problems with hyperactivity.

The fact that the condition was recognized as early as the mid-nineteenth century, albeit only in the form of a "poetic case study," is important. Today, ADHD is often the subject of criticism, being referred to as a phantom or bogus condition—sort of a fashionable, trendy diagnosis for people who are basically lazy and unmotivated. Such thinking is probably behind some of the reasons why ADHD is not recognized as its own separate category (as are mental retardation, learning disabilities, and so forth) by the U.S. Department of Education; students with ADHD are served by special education under the category of "other health impaired."

Although there are undoubtedly a few people who hide behind an inappropriate diagnosis of ADHD, evidence indicates that the condition is extremely real for those who have it. And as we point out in the next section, ADHD is not a recently "discovered," trendy diagnosis.

Brief History

In addition to Hoffmann's account of Fidgety Phil, published in the mid-nineteenth century, we have evidence of a more scientific nature of the existence of ADHD, dating back to the beginning of the twentieth century.

STILL'S CHILDREN WITH "DEFECTIVE MORAL CONTROL"

Dr. George F. Still, a physician, is credited with being one of the first authorities to bring the condition we now call ADHD to the attention of the medical profession. Still delivered three lectures to the Royal College of Physicians of London in 1902 in which he described cases of children who displayed spitefulness, cruelty, disobedience, impulsivity, and problems of attention and hyperactivity. He referred to them as having "defective moral control."

Misconceptions about Learners with Attention Deficit Hyperactivity Disorder

MYTH All children with ADHD are hyperactive.

FACT Psychiatric classification of ADHD includes (1) ADHD, Predominantly Inattentive Type, (2) ADHD, Predominantly Hyperactive-Impulsive Type, or (3) ADHD, Combined Type. Some children with ADHD exhibit no hyperactivity and are classified as ADHD, Predominantly Inattentive.

MYTH The primary symptom of ADHD is inattention.

FACT Although the psychiatric classification includes an Inattentive Type, recent conceptualizations of ADHD place problems with behavioral inhibition, executive function, time awareness and management, and goal-directed behavior as the primary behavioral problems of ADHD.

MYTH ADHD is a fad, a trendy diagnosis of recent times in the United States with little research to support its existence.

FACT Reports of cases of ADHD go back to the mid-nineteenth century and the beginning of the twentieth century. Serious scientific study of it began in the early and mid-twentieth century. There is now a firmly established research base supporting its existence. And the prevalence of ADHD in several other countries is at least as high as it is in the United States.

MYTH ADHD is primarily the result of minimal brain injury.

FACT In most cases of ADHD there is no evidence of actual damage to the brain. Most authorities believe that ADHD is the result of neurological dysfunction, which is often linked to hereditary factors.

MYTH The social problems of students with ADHD are due to their not knowing how to interact socially.

FACT Most people with ADHD know how to interact, but their problems with behavioral inhibition make it difficult for them to implement socially appropriate behaviors.

MYTH Using psychostimulants, such as Ritalin, can easily turn children into abusers of other substances, such as cocaine and marijuana.

FACT There is no evidence that using psychostimulants for ADHD leads directly to drug abuse. In fact, there is evidence that those who are prescribed Ritalin as children are less likely to turn to illicit drugs as teenagers. However, care should be taken to make sure that children or others do not misuse the psychostimulants prescribed for them.

MYTH Psychostimulants have a "paradoxical effect" in that they subdue children rather than activate them. Plus, they have this effect only on those with ADHD.

FACT Psychostimulants, instead of sedating children, actually *activate* parts of the brain responsible for behavioral inhibition and executive functions. In addition, this effect occurs in persons without ADHD, too.

MYTH Because students with ADHD react strongly to stimulation, their learning environments should be highly unstructured in order to take advantage of their natural learning styles.

FACT Most authorities recommend a highly structured classroom for students with ADHD, especially in the early stages of instruction.

YOU CAN SEE the "Fidgety Philip" and "Johnny-Head-in-Air" nursery rhymes complete with illustrations at **www.fln.vcu.edu/struwwel/guck_e.html**

In 1998, The National Institutes of Health brought together a panel of experts from a variety of disciplines, including medicine, psychology, and special education, to arrive at consensus regarding identification and treatment of ADHD. Although they concluded that more research was needed on various issues, they affirmed the validity of ADHD: "Although an independent diagnostic test for ADHD does not exist, there is evidence supporting the validity of the disorder." To see the complete NIH consensus statement, go to **http://odp.od.nih.gov/consensus/cons/110/110_statement.htm**

Moral control involves inhibitory volition—the ability to refrain from engaging impulsively in inappropriate behavior:

> Volition, in so far as it is concerned in moral control, may be regarded as inhibitory; it is the overpowering of one stimulus to activity—which in this connection is activity contrary to the good of all—by another stimulus which we might call the moral idea, the idea of the good of all. There is, in fact, a conflict between stimuli, and in so far as the moral idea prevails the determining or volitional process may be regarded as inhibiting the impulse which is opposed to it. (Still, 1902, p. 1088)

Although Still's words are more than a century old, they still hold currency. For example, one of the most influential current psychological theories is based on the notion that an essential impairment in ADHD is a deficit involving behavioral inhibition (Barkley, 1997, 1998; 2000a, 2000b).

Still's cases were also similar to today's population of persons with ADHD in at least five ways:

1. Still speculated that many of these children had mild brain pathology.
2. Many of the children had normal intelligence.

The Goulstonian Lectures

ON

SOME ABNORMAL PSYCHICAL CONDITIONS IN CHILDREN.

Delivered before the Royal College of Physicians of London on March 4th, 6th, and 11th, 1902.

BY GEORGE F. STILL, M.A., M.D. CANTAB., F.R.C.P. LOND.,

ASSISTANT PHYSICIAN FOR DISEASES OF CHILDREN, KING'S COLLEGE HOSPITAL;
ASSISTANT PHYSICIAN TO THE HOSPITAL FOR SICK CHILDREN, GREAT ORMOND-STREET.

LECTURE I.

Delivered on March 4th.

MR. PRESIDENT AND GENTLEMEN,—The particular psychical conditions with which I propose to deal in these lectures are those which are concerned with an abnormal defect of moral control in children. Interesting as these disorders may be as an abstruse problem for the professed psychologist to puzzle over, they have a very real practical—shall I say social?—importance which I venture to think has been hardly sufficiently recognised. For some years past I have been collecting observations with a view to investigating the occurrence of defective moral control as a morbid condition in children, a subject which I cannot but think calls urgently for scientific investigation.

Source: Still, G. F. (1902). Some abnormal psychical conditions in children. *The Lancet, 1,* 1008–1012.

A reproduction of Dr. George Still's opening remarks for his classic lectures on children with defective moral control.

3. The condition was more prevalent in males than females.
4. There was evidence that the condition had a hereditary basis.
5. Many of the children and their relatives also had other physical problems, such as depression and tics.

We return later to Barkley's theory and to these five points. Suffice it to say here that Still's children with "defective moral control" today would very likely be diagnosed as having ADHD by itself or ADHD with **conduct disorder**. (Conduct disorder, which we discuss more fully in Chapter 8, is characterized by a pattern of aggressive, disruptive behavior.)

GOLDSTEIN'S BRAIN-INJURED SOLDIERS OF WORLD WAR I

Kurt Goldstein reported on the psychological effects of brain injury in soldiers who had suffered head wounds in combat in World War I. Among other things, he observed in his patients the psychological characteristics of disorganized behavior, hyperactivity, **perseveration**, and a "forced responsiveness to stimuli" (Goldstein, 1936, 1939). Perseveration, the tendency to repeat the same behaviors over and over again, is often cited today by clinicians as a characteristic of persons with ADHD. Goldstein found that the soldiers' forced responsiveness to stimuli was evident in their inability to concentrate perceptually on the "figure" without being distracted by the "ground." For example, instead of focusing on a task in front of them (the figure), they were easily distracted by objects on the periphery (the background).

THE STRAUSS SYNDROME

Goldstein's work laid the foundation for the investigations of Heinz Werner and Alfred Strauss in the 1930s and 1940s. Having emigrated from Germany to the United States after Hitler's rise to power, they teamed up to try to replicate Goldstein's findings. Werner and Strauss noted the same behaviors of distractibility and hyperactivity in some children with mental retardation.

In addition to clinical observations, Werner and Strauss used an experimental task consisting of figure/background slides that were presented at very brief exposure times. The slides depicted figures (e.g., a hat) embedded in a background (e.g., wavy lines). Werner and Strauss found that the children with supposed brain damage, when asked what they saw, were more likely than those without brain damage to say that they had seen the background (e.g., "wavy lines") rather than the figure (e.g., "a hat") (Strauss & Werner, 1942; Werner & Strauss, 1939, 1941). After these studies, professionals came to refer to children who were apparently hyperactive and distractible as exhibiting the **Strauss syndrome**.

CRUICKSHANK'S WORK

William Cruickshank, using Werner and Strauss's figure/background task, found that children with cerebral palsy were also more likely to respond to the background than to the figure (Cruickshank, Bice, & Wallen, 1957). There were two important ways in which this research extended the work of Werner and Strauss. First, whereas Werner and Strauss had largely assumed that their children were brain damaged, Cruickshank's children all had **cerebral palsy**, a condition that is relatively easy to diagnose. Cerebral palsy is characterized by brain damage that results in impairments in movement (see Chapter 13). Second, the children who were studied were largely of normal intelligence, thus demonstrating that children without mental retardation could display distractibility and hyperactivity.

Cruickshank is also important historically because he was one of the first to establish an educational program for children who today would meet the criteria for ADHD. (We discuss his educational program later in the chapter.) At the time (the late 1950s), however, many of these children were referred to as "minimally brain injured."

Conduct disorder
A disorder characterized by overt, aggressive, disruptive behavior or covert antisocial acts such as stealing, lying, and fire setting; may include both overt and covert acts.

Perseveration
A tendency to repeat behaviors over and over again; often found in people with brain injury, as well as those with ADHD.

Strauss syndrome
Behaviors of distractibility, forced responsiveness to stimuli, and hyperactivity; based on the work of Alfred Strauss and Heinz Werner with children with mental retardation.

Cerebral palsy
A condition characterized by paralysis, weakness, incoordination, and/or other motor dysfunction because of damage to the brain before it has matured.

MINIMAL BRAIN INJURY AND HYPERACTIVE CHILD SYNDROME

At about the same time as Cruickshank's extension of Werner and Strauss's work to children of normal intelligence, the results of a now classic study were published (Pasamanick, Lilienfeld, & Rogers, 1956). This study of the aftereffects of birth complications revived Still's notion that subtle brain pathology could result in behavior problems, such as hyperactivity and distractibility. Professionals began to apply the label of **minimal brain injury** to children who were of normal intelligence but who were inattentive, impulsive, and/or hyperactive. Although popular in the 1950s and 1960s, the "minimal brain injury" label fell out of favor as professionals pointed out that it was difficult to document actual tissue damage to the brain (Birch, 1964).

Minimal brain injury was replaced in the 1960s by the label "hyperactive child syndrome" (Barkley, 1998). **Hyperactive child syndrome** was preferred because it was descriptive of behavior and did not rely on vague and unreliable diagnoses of subtle brain damage. This label's popularity extended into the 1970s. By the 1980s, however, it too had fallen out of favor as research began to point out that inattention, not hyperactivity, was the major behavioral problem experienced by these children. In fact, some exhibited attention problems without excessive movement.

This recognition of inattention as more important than hyperactivity is reflected in the current definition of ADHD and its immediate predecessors. However, as we discuss later, some authorities are now recommending that deficits in behavioral inhibition replace inattention as the primary deficit in ADHD. In any case, most authorities do not view hyperactivity as the primary deficit in ADHD.

Minimal brain injury
A term used to refer to children who exhibit inattention, impulsivity, and/or hyperactivity; popular in the 1950s and 1960s.

Hyperactive child syndrome
A term used to refer to children who exhibit inattention, impulsivity, and/or hyperactivity; popular in the 1960s and 1970s.

Definition

Most professionals rely on the American Psychiatric Association's (APA's) *Diagnostic and Statistical Manual of Mental Disorders (DSM)* for the criteria that are used to determine whether an individual has ADHD. Over the years, researchers and practitioners have debated whether ADHD is a single syndrome or whether there are subtypes. Partly as a result of this debate, the name for the condition has changed from time to time. For example, for several years, the APA used the general term *attention deficit disorder* (ADD) to refer to all people with the condition. It then allowed for the subtypes of ADD with Hyperactivity and ADD without Hyperactivity.

The current DSM uses ADHD as the general term and subdivides individuals into *(1)* ADHD, Predominantly Inattentive Type; *(2)* ADHD, Predominantly Hyperactive-Impulsive Type; and *(3)* ADHD, Combined Type (American Psychiatric Association, 2000). See Table 7.1.

Prevalence

UNDERSTANDING THE STANDARDS AND PRINCIPLES Briefly describe the diagnostic criteria for attention deficit hyperactivity disorder as outlined in the *Diagnostic and Statistical Manual of Mental Disorders. (CEC Knowledge and Skills Standard GC1K1)*

ADHD is widely recognized as one of the most frequent reasons, if not the most frequent reason, why children are referred for behavioral problems to guidance clinics. From one-third to one-half of cases referred to guidance clinics are for ADHD (Richters et al., 1995). Most authorities estimate that from 3 to 5 percent of the school-age population have ADHD (National Institute of Mental Health, 2003). However, because the U.S. Department of Education does not recognize ADHD as a separate category of special education, it is difficult to estimate how many students with ADHD are served in special education. (See Focus on Concepts on p. 214.)

ADHD occurs much more frequently in boys than girls, with estimates as high as 5 to 1 in community-based samples (Barkley, 1998). This has led some to suggest that boys

TABLE 7.1   Diagnostic Criteria for Attention Deficit Hyperactivity Disorder

A. Either (1) or (2):

   (1) six (or more) of the following symptoms of *inattention* have persisted for at least 6 months to a degree that is maladaptive and inconsistent with developmental level:

     Inattention

     (a) often fails to give close attention to details or makes careless mistakes in schoolwork, work, or other activities

     (b) often has difficulty sustaining attention in tasks or play activities

     (c) often does not seem to listen when spoken to directly

     (d) often does not follow through on instructions and fails to finish schoolwork, chores, or duties in the workplace (not due to oppositional behavior or failure to understand instructions)

     (e) often has difficulty organizing tasks and activities

     (f) often avoids, dislikes, or is reluctant to engage in tasks that require sustained mental effort (such as schoolwork or homework)

     (g) often loses things necessary for tasks or activities (e.g., toys, school assignments, pencils, books, or tools)

     (h) is often easily distracted by extraneous stimuli

     (i) is often forgetful in daily activities

   (2) six (or more) of the following symptoms of hyperactivity-impulsivity have persisted for at least 6 months to a degree that is maladaptive and inconsistent with developmental level:

     Hyperactivity

     (a) often fidgets with hands or feet or squirms in seat

     (b) often leaves seat in classroom or in other situations in which remaining seated is expected

     (c) often runs about or climbs excessively in situations in which it is inappropriate (in adolescents or adults, may be limited to subjective feelings of restlessness)

     (d) often has difficulty playing or engaging in leisure activities quietly

     (e) is often "on the go" or often acts as if "driven by a motor"

     (f) often talks excessively

     Impulsivity

     (g) often blurts out answers before questions have been completed

     (h) often has difficulty awaiting turn

     (i) often interrupts or intrudes on others (e.g., butts into conversations or games)

B. Some hyperactive-impulsive or inattentive symptoms that caused impairment were present before age 7 years.

C. Some impairment from the symptoms is present in two or more settings (e.g., at school [or work] and at home).

D. There must be clear evidence of clinically significant impairment in social, academic, or occupational functioning.

E. The symptoms do not occur exclusively during the course of a Pervasive Developmental Disorder, Schizophrenia, or other Psychotic Disorder and are not better accounted for by another mental disorder (e.g., Mood Disorder, Anxiety Disorder, Dissociative Disorder, or a Personality Disorder).

Code based on type

■ Attention-Deficit/Hyperactivity Disorder, Combined Type: if both Criteria A1 and A2 are met for the past 6 months

■ Attention-Deficit/Hyperactivity Disorder, Predominantly Inattentive Type: if Criterion A1 is met but Criterion A2 is not met for the past 6 months

■ Attention-Deficit/Hyperactivity Disorder, Predominantly Hyperactive-Impulsive Type: if Criterion A2 is met but Criterion A1 is not met for the past 6 months

Coding note: For individuals (especially adolescents and adults) who currently have symptoms that no longer meet full criteria, "In Partial Remission" should be specified.

Source: Reprinted with permission from the *Diagnostic and Statistical Manual of Mental Disorders, Fourth Edition, text revision,* pp. 92–93. Copyright 2000 American Psychiatric Association.

FOCUS ON CONCEPTS

How Many Students with ADHD Are Served in Special Education?

BECAUSE ADHD is such a prevalent condition, one would think that it would be relatively easy to find out how many students with ADHD receive special education services. Federal law, after all, requires that schools report how many students with a given disability have been identified for special education services. However, when Public Law 94-142 (the Education for All Handicapped Children Act) was passed in 1975, ADHD was not included as one of the separate categories of special education. This was due in part to two interrelated factors: (1) The research on this condition was still in its infancy, and (2) the advocacy base for children with ADHD was not yet well developed. For example, the *Diagnostic and Statistical Manual of Mental Disorders* that was in use at the time, the *DSM-II*, published in 1968, was vague in its criteria for identifying children with these problems. And the major advocacy organization for people with ADHD, CHADD (Children and Adults with Attention Deficit Disorder), was not founded until 1987.

By the time of the reauthorization of the law as the Individuals with Disabilities Education Act (IDEA) in 1990, however, there was substantial research on ADHD, and CHADD's membership was well on its way to its present level of 18,000 members. CHADD lobbied hard for ADHD to be considered a separate category, arguing that children with ADHD were being denied services because they could qualify for special education only if they also had another disability, such as learning disabilities or emotional disturbance. Their lobbying was unsuccessful. However, in 1991, the U.S. Department of Education determined that students with ADHD would be eligible for special education under the category other health impaired (OHI) "in instances where the ADD is a chronic or acute health problem that results in limited alertness, which adversely affects educational performance." Students with ADHD can also qualify for accommodations under another law (Section 504).

Many professionals are still disappointed with the decision not to include ADHD as a separate category because they say that using the OHI category is too roundabout a means of identification, and Section 504 is not completely satisfactory because it does not require an individualized education program (IEP). (See pp. 28–33 in Chapter 1 for a discussion of IEPs.)

However, the growth of the OHI category since 1991 suggests that more and more students with ADHD are being iden-

tified as OHI (see Figure A). Although numbers in the OHI category have more than quadrupled in ten years, the 0.44 percent reported for 2000–2001 is still well below the prevalence estimates of 3 to 5 percent. Many authorities think that fewer than half of students with ADHD are receiving special education services. As long as ADHD is not recognized as a separate category of special education, however, it will be virtually impossible to know exactly how many school-age children with ADHD are receiving special education services. ■

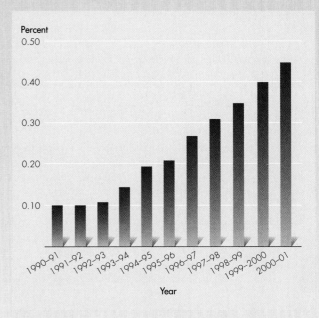

FIGURE A Percentage of students aged 6 to 21 receiving special education services in the category of "other health impaired."

Source: U.S. Department of Education. (1992, 1993, 1994, 1995, 1996, 1997, 1998, 1999, 2000, 2001, 2002). *Fourteenth, Fifteenth, Sixteenth, Seventeenth, Eighteenth, Nineteenth, Twentieth, Twenty-first, Twenty-second, Twenty-third, and Twenty-fourth annual reports to Congress on the implementation of the individuals with Disabilities Education Act.* Washington, DC: Author.

FOCUS ON CONCEPTS

Ethnicity and ADHD

MANY practitioners and researchers suspect that African-American children, especially boys, are more likely to be identified as ADHD than are white children. Unfortunately, there are no definitive, large-scale epidemiological studies on this topic. What scanty evidence does exist suggests that they are no more likely to be formally identified as ADHD than their white peers (Rowland et al., 2001).

Even though we do not have evidence that African-American students are formally identified as ADHD more often than their white peers, we do know that there are differences in how teachers rate African-American versus white children with respect to inattentive and hyperactivity behaviors (Arnold et al., 2003; Reid et al., 2000; Reid, Casat, Norton, Anastopoulos, & Temple, 2001). For example, in one study, African-American boys had the most severe symptoms of ADHD, white girls had the least severe symptoms, and African-American girls and white boys were in between and were indistinguishable from one another (Reid et al., 2000). And in another study, African-American boys were 2.5 times more likely to have behaviors indicative of ADHD than were white boys, and African-American girls were 3.5 times more likely to have ADHD symptoms than were white girls (Reid et al., 2001).

An important question is whether these differences are due to actual differences in behavior or rater bias. That rater bias might be operating is suggested by the finding that white teachers were more likely than African-American teachers to rate African-American students as highly inattentive and hyperactive (Reid et al., 2001). ■

---

might be overidentified as ADHD and/or that girls might be underidentified as ADHD. That the latter may be the case is suggested by the fact that the gap between the prevalence rates of ADHD for girls and boys is narrowing (Robison, Skaer, Sclar, & Galin, 2002).

Some have speculated that boys are identified more often than girls because boys tend to exhibit the highly noticeable hyperactive or impulsive type of ADHD, whereas girls are more likely to exhibit the inattentive type. Some gender bias in referral may exist, but our best research evidence suggests that it is not enough to account for the wide disparity in prevalence rates between boys and girls. Gender differences are likely due to constitutional, or biological, differences (Barkley, 1998).

Some critics have asserted that ADHD is primarily a U.S. phenomenon, a result of our society's emphasis on achievement and conformity. However, statistics do not bear this out. Although it is difficult to compare prevalence rates cross-culturally because of differing diagnostic criteria, sampling techniques, and cultural expectations, the evidence strongly suggests that prevalence rates at least as high as those in the United States are found in several other countries, including Canada, Australia, New Zealand, Germany, Japan, China, and Brazil (Baumgaertel, Wolraich, & Dietrich, 1995; Esser, Schmidt, & Woerner, 1990; Fergusson, Horwood, & Lynskey, 1993; Kanbayashi, Nakata, Fujii, Kita, & Wada, 1994; Leung et al., 1996; Rohde et al., 1999; Schaughency, McGee, Raja, Freehan, & Silva, 1994; Szatmari, 1992; Wilens, Biederman, & Spencer, 2002).

Some critics have also suggested that African-American children, especially boys, are diagnosed disproportionately as ADHD. (See Focus on Concepts above)

Assessment

Most authorities agree that there are four important components to assessing whether a student has ADHD: a medical

Casebook Reflections

Refer to the case *More Than LD: Shannon* in your booklet. Shannon's diagnosis of ADHD did not come until she was in the sixth grade. We know from research that girls can be overlooked for having ADHD. Why do you think that is?

In addition to medical exams and clinical interviews, rating scales filled out by teachers, parents, and in some case children, can help quantify the process of identifying children who might have ADHD.

UNDERSTANDING THE STANDARDS AND PRINCIPLES What are the three important components to assessing whether a student has ADHD? *(CEC Knowledge and Skills Standards CC8K3, CC8K4, & GC8S3)*

 Council for Exceptional Children

Continuous performance test (CPT) A test measuring a person's ability to sustain attention to rapidly presented stimuli; can help in the diagnosis of ADHD.

 THE MAGAZINE *Scientific American* has an excellent article on causes by the noted ADHD authority, Russell Barkley. You can find it by looking up the September, 1998 issue in the archives on the *Scientific American* website: **www.sciamarchive.org/ www.sciam.com/1998/0998 issue/0998barkley.html**

examination, a clinical interview, teacher and parent rating scales, and behavioral observations. The medical examination is necessary to rule out medical conditions, such as brain tumors, thyroid problems, or seizure disorders, as the cause of the inattention and/or hyperactivity (Barkley, 1998).

The clinical interview of the parent(s) and the child provides information about the child's physical and psychological characteristics, as well as family dynamics and interaction with peers. Although the interview is essential to the diagnosis of ADHD, clinicians need to recognize the subjective nature of the interview situation. Some children with ADHD can look surprisingly "normal" in their behavior when in the structured and novel setting of a doctor's office.

In an attempt to bring some quantification to the identification process, researchers have developed rating scales to be filled out by teachers, parents, and, in some cases, the child. Some of the most reliable and popular are the Conners scales and the ADHD-Rating Scale—IV. There are now several versions of the Conners scale for parents or teachers in use (Conners, 1989a, 1989b, 1997). The ADHD-Rating Scale—IV (DuPaul, Power, Anastopoulos, & Reid, 1998) is based on the DSM-IV criteria. Raters, who can be either parents or teachers, rate the child on items pertaining to each of the eighteen criteria listed in the DSM-IV (see Table 7.1). For example, for the first item, "Fails to give close attention to details or makes careless mistakes in his/her work," they rate 0 (never or rarely), 1 (sometimes), 2 (often), or 3 (very often), and so forth. Assessment scales for adults are more recent. An example is the Conners Adult ADHD Rating Scales (Conners, 1999).

Whenever possible, the clinician should behaviorally observe the student. This can be done in the classroom, or clinicians who specialize in diagnosing and treating children with ADHD sometimes have specially designed observation rooms in which they can observe the child while he or she performs tasks requiring sustained attention. In addition, professionals can use a **continuous performance test (CPT)** in the clinic. A typical CPT consists of stimuli (e.g., Xs and Os) presented one at time on a screen rapidly (about 1 per second), with the individual pressing a button every time a particular stimulus (e.g., X) appears or a particular sequence (e.g., O followed by an X) appears. The computer

FOCUS ON CONCEPTS

Controversial Causal Theories of ADHD

OVER the years, a number of myths have sprung up about what causes hyperactive behavior or ADHD. Most of these have little if any substantial scientific support. A good example is sugar. Parents and teachers have often complained that young children become more hyperactive when they ingest sugar in the form of soft drinks, cakes, and candies. However, careful research has demonstrated that this is not the case (Wolraich, Wilson, & White, 1995). The mistaken notion that sugar causes hyperactivity probably originated from the observation that children are hyperactive in situations in which sweets are served. Being relatively stimulating and unstructured, these situations, such as parties, are likely to elicit hyperactive behavior.

Another example is that of television and video games. Many people in the general public believe that by watching too much television or playing too many video games, children will become ADHD. One study did find that children who watch more television as preschoolers are rated as more inattentive at 7 years of age (Christakis, Zimmerman, DiGiuseppe, & McCarty, 2004). However, this is not proof that watching television *causes* ADHD or even higher rates of inattention. It could be that parents who let their children watch more television contribute in some other ways to their children's inattentive behavior. Perhaps they provide less supervision generally.

Other environmental agents that some believe cause ADHD are artificial food colorings and additives. The original proponent of this theory was Benjamin Feingold, a pediatric allergist (Feingold, 1975) who proposed a strict diet devoid of these additives. However, substantial research has shown that putting all children with ADHD on the diet is not beneficial (Kavale & Forness, 1983). However, a recent research study presents some provocative data suggesting that when young children are on a diet containing food colorings and additives, their parents rate them higher in inattention and hyperactivity than when they are on a diet free of colorings and additives (Bateman et al., 2004). A particular strength of this study is that the parents were "blind" to when the children's diet did or did not contain colorings and additives. However, a major caveat is that the children's behavior did not differ with or without the diet on arguably more objective measures of inattention and hyperactivity that were administered by researchers in the clinic.

Another caveat is that this study still falls short of demonstrating a *causal* link between diet and formal *diagnosis of ADHD*. However, further research is definitely warranted to determine whether there might be a subgroup of children with ADHD, however small, who might benefit from a diet restricting certain food additives and colorings. In the meantime, there is no support for automatically placing all children with ADHD on such restricted diets. ■

keeps track of the number of correct responses, failures to respond to a correct stimulus (omission errors), and incorrect responses or responses to the wrong stimulus (commission errors).

Causes

Probably because there is no simple diagnostic test, such as a blood test, for ADHD, there has been much controversy over what actually causes ADHD and a history of questionable causal theories. (See Focus on Concepts above) We now know, however, that there is strong evidence linking neurological abnormalities to ADHD.

As we noted earlier, authorities in the early and middle parts of the twentieth century attributed problems of inattention and hyperactivity to neurological problems resulting from brain damage. When researchers were unable to verify actual tissue damage in cases of ADHD, many professionals soured on the idea that ADHD was neurologically based. However, as we noted in our discussion of learning disabilities (see Chapter 6), the development of neuroimaging techniques such as MRIs, PET scans, and fMRIs in the 1980s and

UNDERSTANDING THE STANDARDS AND PRINCIPLES What do we know about the causes of ADHD? *(CEC Knowledge and Skills Standard GC2K3)*

Council for Exceptional Children

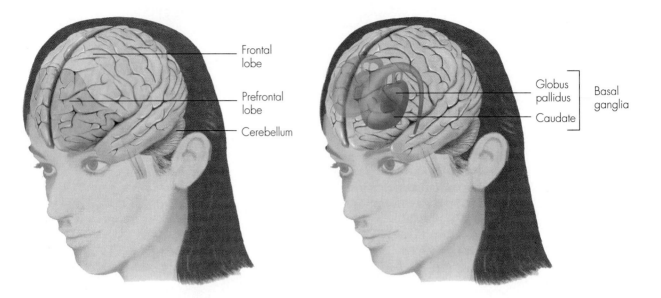

FIGURE 7.1   Areas of the brain (frontal lobes, prefrontal lobes, cerebellum, globus pallidus and caudate of the basal ganglia) that some researchers have identified as abnormal in people with ADHD.

Frontal lobes
Two lobes located in the front of the brain; responsible for executive functions; site of abnormal development in people with ADHD.

Prefrontal lobes
Two lobes located in the very front of the frontal lobes; responsible for executive functions; site of abnormal development in people with ADHD.

Basal ganglia
A set of structures within the brain that include the caudate, globus pallidus, and putamen, the first two being abnormal in people with ADHD; generally responsible for the coordination and control of movement.

Caudate
A structure in the basal ganglia of the brain; site of abnormal development in persons with ADHD.

Globus pallidus
A structure in the basal ganglia of the brain; site of abnormal development in people with ADHD.

1990s allowed scientists for the first time to obtain more detailed and reliable measures of brain functioning. Using these techniques, researchers have made great strides in documenting the neurological basis of ADHD. As is the case with learning disabilities, the research indicates that ADHD most likely results from neurological dysfunction rather than actual brain damage. Again like learning disabilities, evidence points to heredity as playing a very strong role in causing the neurological dysfunction, with teratogenic and other medical factors also implicated to a lesser degree.

AREAS OF THE BRAIN AFFECTED: FRONTAL LOBES, BASAL GANGLIA, AND CEREBELLUM

Using neuroimaging techniques, several teams of researchers have found consistent abnormalities in three areas of the brain in people with ADHD: the frontal lobes, basal ganglia (specifically, the caudate and the globus pallidus), and cerebellum (Castellanos, 2001; Castellanos et al., 2002; Filipek et al., 1997; Hynd et al., 1993; Teicher et al., 2000). (See Figure 7.1.) Specifically, researchers have found that the size of each of these areas is smaller in children and adults with ADHD than in those who are nondisabled. Although not always consistent, several of the studies point to the abnormality occurring on the right side of the brain, especially the right basal ganglia (Castellanos, 1997). In addition, PET scans suggest reduced metabolic activity in the frontal lobes and basal ganglia in people with ADHD (Lou, Henriksen, & Bruhn, 1984; Lou, Henriksen, Bruhn, Borner, & Nielsen, 1989).

Frontal Lobes   Located in the front of the brain, the **frontal lobes**, and especially the very front portion of the frontal lobes—the **prefrontal lobes**—are responsible for what are referred to as executive functions. Among other things, executive functions involve the ability to regulate one's own behavior. (We discuss executive functions more fully later.)

Basal Ganglia   Buried deep within the brain, the **basal ganglia** consist of several parts, the **caudate** and the **globus pallidus** being the structures that are abnormal in persons with ADHD. The basal ganglia are responsible for the coordination and control of motor behavior (Pinel, 2003).

Cerebellum   The **cerebellum** is also responsible for the coordination and control of motor behavior. Although it is relatively small, constituting only about 10 percent of the mass of the brain, the fact that it contains more than half of all the brain's neurons attests to its complexity (Pinel, 2003).

NEUROTRANSMITTERS INVOLVED: DOPAMINE AND NOREPINEPHRINE

Much exciting research is being conducted on what neurotransmitter abnormalities might cause ADHD. **Neurotransmitters** are chemicals that help in the sending of messages between neurons in the brain. Researchers have found that abnormal levels of two neurotransmitters—**dopamine** and **norepinephrine**—appear to be involved in ADHD (Barkley, 2000b; Solanto, 2002).

HEREDITARY FACTORS

Most authorities agree that there is a hereditary basis to ADHD. Evidence for the genetic transmission of ADHD comes from at least three sources: family studies, twin studies, and molecular genetic studies.

Family Studies   Generally, studies indicate that if a child has ADHD, the chance of his or her sibling having ADHD is about 32 percent (Barkley, 1998). Children of adults with ADHD run a 57 percent risk of having ADHD (Biederman et al., 1995). In addition, several studies demonstrate that parents of children with ADHD are two to eight times more likely to also be ADHD than are parents of non-ADHD children (Faraone & Doyle, 2001).

Twin Studies   There are several studies comparing the prevalence of ADHD in identical (monozygotic, from the same egg) versus fraternal (dizygotic, from two eggs) twins, when one of the members of the pair has ADHD. These studies consistently show that if an identical twin and a fraternal twin each have ADHD, the second identical twin is much more likely to have ADHD than is the second fraternal twin (Gillis, Gilger, Pennington, & De-Fries, 1992; Sherman, Iacono, & McGue, 1997; Stevenson, 1992).

Molecular Genetic Studies   With the mapping of the human genome have come advances in **molecular genetics**, the study of the molecules (DNA, RNA, and protein) that regulate genetic information. Molecular genetic research on ADHD is in its early stages, but several studies have already implicated several genes as possibly being involved in causing ADHD (Faraone & Doyle, 2001).

TOXINS AND MEDICAL FACTORS

In Chapters 5 and 6, we discussed **toxins**—agents that can cause malformations in the developing fetus of a pregnant woman—as the cause of some cases of mental retardation or learning disabilities. Although the evidence for toxins is not as strong as that for heredity, some of these same substances have been shown to be related to ADHD. For example, exposure to lead and the abuse of alcohol or tobacco (Faraone & Doyle, 2001) by pregnant women does place the unborn child at increased risk of developing ADHD.

Other medical conditions may also place children at risk for having ADHD. Again, the evidence is not as strong as it is for heredity, but complications at birth and low birth weight are associated with ADHD (Levy, Barr, & Sunohara, 1998; Milberger, Biederman, Faraone, Guite, & Tsuang, 1997).

Cerebellum
An organ at the base of the brain responsible for coordination and movement; site of abnormal development in persons with ADHD.

Neurotransmitters
Chemicals involved in sending messages between neurons in the brain.

Dopamine
A neurotransmitter, the levels of which may be abnormal in people with ADHD.

Norepinephrine
A neurotransmitter, the levels of which may be abnormal in people with ADHD.

Molecular genetics
The study of the organization of DNA, RNA, and protein molecules containing genetic information.

Toxins
Poisons in the environment that can cause fetal malformations; can result in cognitive impairments.

Casebook Reflections

Refer to the case *More Than LD: Shannon* in your booklet. After the consultation with their doctor, Shannon's father felt that he had had the same problems in school: lack of attention, disorganization, problems keeping up with schoolwork. Do you think he had ADHD but was never diagnosed? What do these remarks reveal?

THE AMERICAN Academy of Pediatrics has an excellent website containing information on several kinds of medical and health-related conditions. For example, the Academy issues policy statements and press releases on diagnosis and treatment of various disabilities, e.g., blindness, deafness, ADHD, and so forth. It also provides synopses of selected articles appearing in its journal, *Pediatrics* at **www.aap.org**

Psychological and Behavioral Characteristics

One can use the DSM-IV criteria discussed earlier (see Table 7.1) to get a sense of some of the typical behaviors of students with ADHD. Although most people think that inattention is the key characteristic of ADHD, there is a growing consensus that inattention, hyperactivity, and impulsivity are actually the result of problems in behavioral inhibition.

BARKLEY'S MODEL OF ADHD

There is an abundance of research pointing to problems with behavioral inhibition in people with ADHD (Barkley, 1997, 1998, 2000a, 2000b; Semrud-Clikeman et al., 2000; Schachar, Mota, Logan, Tannock, & Klim, 2000; Willcutt et al., 2001). As we noted earlier, Russell Barkley, in particular, has proposed a model of ADHD in which behavioral inhibition is key. In its simplest form, this model proposes that problems in behavioral inhibition set the stage for problems in executive functions and time awareness and management, which then disrupt the person's ability to engage in persistent goal-directed behavior.

Behavioral Inhibition   **Behavioral inhibition** involves the ability to do the following:

1. delay a response,
2. interrupt an ongoing response, if one detects that the response is inappropriate because of sudden changes in the demands of the task, or
3. protect a response from distracting or competing stimuli (Lawrence et al., 2002).

Behavioral inhibition
The ability to stop an intended response, to stop an ongoing response, to guard an ongoing response from interruption, and to refrain from responding immediately; allows executive functions to occur; delayed or impaired in those with ADHD.

Problems in behavioral inhibition can be reflected in the ability to wait one's turn, to refrain from interrupting conversations, to resist potential distractions while working, or to delay immediate gratification to work for larger, long-term rewards (Tripp & Alsop, 2001). In addition, there is evidence that problems with behavioral inhibition in children with ADHD is related to abnormalities of the caudate in the brain that we discussed earlier (Semrud-Clikeman et al., 2000). In the classroom, difficulties with behavioral inhibition

Students with ADHD may experience difficulties with behavioral inhibition, including the ability to wait one's turn, recognize inappropriate responses, or resist distractions.

Meeting the Needs of Students with Attention Deficit Hyperactivity Disorder

Task Switching: Preparing Students with ADHD for Change

WHAT THE RESEARCH SAYS

Many researchers contend that the primary deficit of students with ADHD is deficient behavioral inhibition (see p. 220). In other words, once a student with ADHD begins a task, it is difficult for him or her to mentally switch to a new activity. Researchers hypothesize that the executive controls needed to "inhibit" the current activity and "start up" the next are different for students with ADHD compared to students who do not have ADHD.

RESEARCH STUDY

A group of researchers examined task-switching ability of students with and without ADHD (Cepeda, Cepeda, & Kramer, 2000). Results from the study indicated that clear performance deficits existed for unmedicated students with ADHD in the first trial after a task switch, even when the tasks were considered compatible, such as both tasks involving numbers. All students with ADHD, unmedicated or medicated, had higher "switch costs"—increased response time—when the new task was incompatible with the old task (e.g., switching from a number-identification task to a word-identification task). This type of task required the inhibition of thinking about numbers and the preparation for thinking about letters

and sounds. The findings suggest that differences do exist between students with and without ADHD in the ability to efficiently and effectively task switch.

APPLYING THE RESEARCH TO TEACHING

Studies such as the one presented here indicate the need to support students with ADHD as they transition from one activity to another. Cognitive support for such transitions can include the following:

- Allowing for time between asking a student to do or say something and expecting the response (i.e., increasing wait time)
- Avoiding overloading a students' working memory (Barkley, Murphy, & Kwasnik, 1996) by limiting the number of steps or sequence of procedures a student must keep in working memory or by providing a visual for students to refer to
- Creating routinized procedures for daily transitions
- Preparing students for the type of response that will be required when asking a question
- Dividing instruction into consistent, predictable sequences throughout the day ■

By Kristin L. Sayeski

---

can present themselves during task-switching or transitions. See the Responsive Instruction above for a description of research on this topic and how to apply this research to the classroom.

Executive Functions   The delay allowed by behavioral inhibition permits the individual to self-regulate his or her behavior. This ability to engage in a variety of self-directed behaviors involves what are referred to as **executive functions**. The fact that there is a wealth of evidence that executive functions are controlled by the prefrontal and frontal lobes of the brain fits nicely with the neuroimaging studies pointing to these areas of the brain being abnormal in persons with ADHD.

In Barkley's model, persons with ADHD can exhibit problems with executive function in four general ways. First, they often have problems with working memory (WM). As we noted in Chapter 5, WM refers to a person's ability to keep information in mind that "can be used to guide one's actions either now or in the near future" (Barkley & Murphy, 1998, p. 2). In the case of students with ADHD, deficiencies in WM can result in forgetfulness, a lack of hindsight and forethought, and problems with time management.

Second, people with ADHD frequently have delayed inner speech. **Inner speech** is the inner "voice" that allows people to "talk" to themselves about various solutions when in the midst of solving a problem. Students with ADHD who have deficient inner speech have

Executive functions
The ability to regulate one's behavior through working memory, inner speech, control of emotions and arousal levels, and analysis of problems and communication of problem solutions to others; delayed or impaired in people with ADHD.

Inner speech
An executive function; internal language used to regulate one's behavior; delayed or impaired in people with ADHD.

221

Special Educators at Work

Josh: "It's not like the work is hard; it's just getting it done!"

High school sophomore Josh Bishop hopes to play football on a team in the National Collegiate Athletic Association's Division I, despite his struggles with organization and time management.

These could be the keys to his success:
- *Intensive classroom structure and consistent expectations*
- *Relentless positive reinforcement and behavioral support*
- *Specific accommodations and self-advocacy*

Special educator Jane Warner coordinates services for college students with disabilities at the university where Josh Bishop hopes to play football. She guides many students like Josh and encourages incoming freshman with ADHD to begin their self-advocacy early. Josh doesn't find school work hard to do, but he finds it hard to get done. Although her son does not receive special education services, Josh's mother, Joni Poff, encourages him to seek out structures and supports so that he can meet his future goals.

Intensive Classroom Structure and Consistent Expectations. Josh is a successful athlete, but in the classroom, he faces challenges. "I never have been very organized. I got by in elementary school, but middle school was a real wake-up call. In sixth grade, I'd get all my homework done *in* class. In seventh grade, I had homework due for *every* class."

Josh keeps an assignment book but admits that he doesn't use it faithfully. "When I've missed a deadline, sometimes I don't turn the work in at all. I know I need to do homework and I keep saying I'm going to do it, and then I don't turn it in and I get a zero. I can get work done at school, but I just can't get it done at home." According to his mother, "Josh does better with shorter time segments in a more structured setting. At home, he has trouble following through with sustained work. His pediatrician told me to back off. Josh takes medication during the day, and it's harder for him to concentrate in the evening."

Josh mentioned his medication but did not refer to his difficulties with completing written work, organizational skills, or attentiveness as being out of the ordinary. He would rather not be treated differently from other students, but he says that only a few teachers have provided the classroom structure that he needs. His mother thinks that the most successful teachers for Josh have been those who were very organized and made their expectations very clear. "They weren't wishy-washy. They were sympathetic that some things were difficult for Josh. They understood that he wasn't being purposefully lazy or disrespectful, but they still held high expectations for him."

problems in guiding their behavior in situations that demand the ability to follow rules or instructions.

Third, children and adults have problems controlling their emotions and their arousal levels. They often overreact to negative or positive experiences. On hearing good news, for example, they might scream loudly, unable to keep their emotions to themselves. Likewise, they are often quick to show their temper when confronted with frustrating experiences.

Fourth, children and adults with ADHD have difficulty analyzing problems and communicating solutions to others. They are less flexible when faced with problem situations, often responding impulsively with the first thing that comes to mind.

Josh, the student described in the Success Stories above, has many of the executive function difficulties we have just discussed. He has problems with completing homework, solving problems, and organizing himself to keep up with his work. Josh hopes to play sports in college, so he must figure out how to organize and study to get better grades.

Relentless Positive Reinforcement and Behavioral Support Josh was diagnosed by his pediatrician with ADHD when he was 7 years old. "Josh always had a high activity level," recalls his mother. "In kindergarten, he was put on a behavior contract with stickers as positive reinforcement, but his first grade teacher didn't follow through with his behavior management." By second grade, medication was recommended. Josh's family moved to a small school district where the local high school he attends has only 650 students. Contact between home and school has been close. But as he has matured and the academic demands have increased, says his mother, "high school has been difficult for Josh. Recently, I asked him to take advantage of a tutor or some structured support to help reinforce his behavior, but he seems determined to do it alone."

Specific Accommodations and Self-Advocacy Doing it alone is not always the answer, says Jane Warner. Students with ADHD frequently need support when they move from high school to college. "Study skills and time management are troublesome for students with ADHD. Things can start to fall apart. Students might miss several classes and think they can never go back, so they just sit out and their grades go down, their self-esteem starts to slip, and they hit the wall." Warner encourages students to disclose their learning needs confidently and make the primary contact with the office for disability services on campus. Students with ADHD who have not received special services in high school are advised to get the documentation they need for colleges to provide them with appropriate accommodations. "We prefer comprehensive evaluations that have been done by a qualified professional within the previous three years," says Warner. "IEPs are part of the puzzle but IEPs can't be used as the only documentation for post-secondary accommodations."

Warner points out that current evaluations provide a clear picture of strengths and weaknesses, especially if the evaluator explains what the results mean in lay terms and makes specific educational recommendations. "Sometime between now and high school graduation," she says, "getting a current clinical evaluation will be a very important strategy for developing his self-advocacy and for moving Josh closer to reaching his goals."

CEC'S STANDARDS: PAVING THE WAY TO SUCCESS

ASSESS YOUR STEPS TO SUCCESS in meeting the CEC Knowledge and Skill Base for All Beginning Special Education Teachers. Use the following questions to reflect on the growth of your own professional knowledge, skills, and dispositions.

REFLECTING ON YOUR OWN PROFESSIONAL DEVELOPMENT

If you were Josh's teacher . . .

- WHAT are some areas about educating students with ADHD about which you would need to know more?
- WHAT are some specific skills that would help you to address his academic and behavioral challenges?
- WHAT personal dispositions do you think are most important for you to develop in teaching students with challenging behaviors posed by ADHD?

Using the CEC Standards

- HOW would you describe the psychological and social-emotional characteristics of individuals with ADHD? (GC2K4)
- WHAT are the effects of various medications on individuals with ADHD? (CC2K7)
- WHAT type of procedures would you use to increase self-awareness, self-management, self-control, self-reliance, and self-esteem in a student with ADHD? (CC4S5) ■

By Jean Crockett

Time Awareness and Management Barkley (2000a) sees the deficit in time awareness and management shown by people with ADHD as crucial:

> Understanding time and how we organize our own behavior within and toward it is a major key to the mystery of understanding ADHD. . . . I now believe that the *awareness of themselves across time is the ultimate yet nearly invisible disability afflicting those with ADHD.* (p. 30)

Persistent Goal-Directed Behavior The many problems with executive functions experienced by people with ADHD lead to deficits in engaging in sustained goal-directed activities:

> The poor sustained attention that apparently characterizes those with ADHD probably represents an impairment in goal- or task-directed persistence arising

THE NATIONAL Institutes of Health has funded several studies on the genetics of ADHD. One team of researchers at UCLA has created a website that summarizes its findings in layperson's language. This website is useful for both professionals and families. For families, it provides opportunities to participate in the research effort. **www.adhd.ucla.edu**

from poor inhibition and the toll it takes on self-regulation. And the distractibility ascribed to those with ADHD most likely arises from poor interference control that allows other external and internal events to disrupt the executive functions that provide for self-control and task persistence. The net effect is an individual who cannot persist in effort toward tasks that provide little immediate reward and who flits from one uncompleted activity to another as disrupting events occur. The inattention in ADHD can now be seen as not so much a primary symptom as a secondary one; it is the consequence of the impairment that behavioral inhibition and interference control create in the self-regulation or executive control of behavior. (Barkley, 1997, p. 84)

With diminished self-regulation or executive control abilities, students with ADHD find it exceedingly difficult to stay focused on tasks that require effort or concentration but which are not inherently exciting (e.g., many school-related activities).

ADAPTIVE SKILLS

Adaptive skills
Skills needed to adapt to one's living environment (e.g., communication, self-care, home living, social skills, community use, self-direction, health and safety, functional academics, leisure, and work); usually estimated by an adaptive behavior survey; one of two major components (the other is intellectual functioning) of the AAMR definition.

The concept of **adaptive skills** (e.g., self-help, community use, home use, and so forth) has traditionally been associated with the area of mental retardation. The American Association on Mental Retardation's definition, for example, stipulates that mental retardation be defined as impairments in intelligence and adaptive behavior (see Chapter 5). In recent years, authorities in the ADHD field have discovered that many children and adults with ADHD also have difficulties in adaptive behavior (Barkley, 1998). A good example is that they have more problems related to driving as adolescents and young adults: more accidents and traffic violations (Cox, Merkel, Kovatchev, & Seward, 2000; Woodward, Fergusson, & Horwood, 2000). Furthermore, those who do have problems with adaptive skills run a much greater risk of having a variety of learning and behavioral problems at school and home (Shelton et al., 2000).

PROBLEMS SOCIALIZING WITH PEERS

UNDERSTANDING THE STANDARDS AND PRINCIPLES Describe the social status experienced by many students with ADHD. *(CEC Knowledge and Skills Standard CC3K1)*

Some authorities have argued that the social problems that students with ADHD experience are so common that they should be considered the defining characteristic of the condition (Landau, Milich, & Diener, 1998). Although the evidence might not warrant asserting that all persons with ADHD experience problems getting along with others, it is probably safe to say that the majority experience significant problems in peer relations. In fact, it usually does not take long for others to find students with ADHD uncomfortable to be around. For example, one team of researchers found that after just one day in a summer camp, many children with ADHD were rejected by other campers (Erhardt & Hinshaw, 1994).

Unfortunately, the negative social status experienced by students with ADHD is difficult to overcome and is usually long lasting. The enduring nature of social rejection leads easily to social isolation. The result is that many children and adults with ADHD have few friends, even though they may desperately want to be liked. This can set up a vicious circle in which they attempt to win friends by latching onto the least chance for interaction with others. But their frantic need for friendship, coupled with their deficient impulse control, ends up leading them to bother or pester the very people they are trying to befriend.

Given the problems in behavioral inhibition, it is not surprising that so many children and adults with ADHD end up socially ostracized. Unable to regulate their behavior and emotions, they are viewed as rude by others. It may not be that they do not know how to behave appropriately so much as that they are unable to do so (Landau et al., 1998). In other words, if asked what the appro-

Casebook Reflections

Refer to the case *More Than LD: Shannon* in your booklet. Her parents thought that they saw signs of something more than a learning disability. How does this comment reflect the difficulty of separating learning disabilities and ADHD?

priate behavior in a given situation should be, they can often give the socially acceptable answer. But when faced with choices in the actual situation, their deficits in behavioral inhibition lead them to make choices impulsively and to overreact emotionally.

COEXISTING CONDITIONS

ADHD often occurs simultaneously with other behavioral and/or learning problems, such as learning disabilities or emotional or behavioral disorders. In addition, persons with ADHD run a higher risk than the general population for substance abuse.

Learning Disabilities   Studies using careful diagnostic criteria have found an overlap of 10 to 25 percent between ADHD and learning disabilities (Forness & Kavale, 2002). Some authorities maintain that the relationship is strongest for students who have ADHD, Predominantly Inattentive Type (Marshall, Hynd, Handwerk, & Hall, 1997; Willcutt, Chhabildas, & Pennington, 2001).

Emotional or Behavioral Disorders   Estimates of the overlap with ADHD vary widely, but it is safe to say that 25 to 50 percent of people with ADHD also exhibit some form of emotional or behavioral disorder (Hallahan & Cottone, 1997; Forness & Kavale, 2002). Some people with ADHD can exhibit aggressive, acting-out behaviors; whereas others can have the types of withdrawn behaviors that accompany anxiety or depression.

Substance Abuse   Adults with ADHD are about twice as likely as the general population to abuse alcohol or to become dependent on drugs, such as cocaine (Biederman, Wilens, Mick, Faraone, & Spencer, 1998; Lambert & Hartsough, 1998). Children with ADHD who also have externalizing types of behavior disorders are especially vulnerable for early drug use (Chilcoat & Breslau, 1999). In addition, adults with ADHD are about twice as

Children with ADHD who also have externalizing types of behavior disorders are especially vulnerable for early drug use.

likely to be cigarette smokers (Lambert & Hartsough, 1998). Some reports in the popular media have claimed that the treatment of ADHD with psychostimulants such as Ritalin leads children to take up the use of illegal substances. However, there is no research to back up this claim (DuPaul, Barkley, & Connor, 1998).

Exactly why ADHD co-occurs with so many other learning and behavioral disabilities remains largely a mystery. Researchers are just beginning to attempt to tease out which of several possibilities are the most likely reasons for so much overlap between ADHD and other disabilities. For example, does having ADHD put one at risk for developing another disability, such as learning disabilities or depression? Or do ADHD and the other disability occur independent of each other? Is there a genetic basis to the coexistence of so many of these conditions? Research over the next few years should begin to provide more definitive answers to these questions.

Educational Considerations

In this section, we consider two aspects of effective educational programming for students with ADHD:

- Classroom structure and teacher direction
- Functional behavioral assessment and contingency-based self-management

Casebook Reflections

Refer to the case *Never Give Up* in your booklet. Does Ryan's behavior reflect a student with ADHD, or does his behavior reflect a student with emotional and behavioral disorders? Could he have both? Why or why not?

CLASSROOM STRUCTURE AND TEACHER DIRECTION

William Cruickshank, whom we discussed earlier, was one of the first to establish a systematic educational program for children who today would meet the criteria for ADHD. Two hallmarks of Cruickshank's program were reduction of stimuli that are irrelevant to learning and enhancement of materials that are important for learning, and a structured program with a strong emphasis on teacher direction.

Because Cruickshank assumed that children with attention problems were susceptible to distraction, irrelevant stimuli were reduced as much as possible. For example, students' workspaces consisted of three-sided cubicles to reduce distractions. On the other hand, teachers were encouraged to use attractive, brightly colored teaching materials.

The emphasis on classroom structure and teacher direction can be summed up by the following:

Specifically, what is meant by a structured program? For example, upon coming into the classroom the child will hang his hat and coat on a given hook—not on any hook of his choice, but on the same hook every day. He will place his lunch box, if he brings one, on a specific shelf each day. He will then go to his cubicle, take his seat, and from that point on follow the teacher's instructions concerning learning tasks, use of toilet, luncheon activities, and all other experiences until the close of the school day. The day's program will be so completely simplified and so devoid of choice (or conflict) situations that the possibility of failure experience will be almost completely minimized. The learning tasks will be within the learning capacity and within the limits of frustration and attention span of the child. . . . If it is determined that he has an attention span of four minutes, then all teaching tasks

Teacher-directed general education classes, with colorful visual aids, enclosed teaching areas, and proximity to the teacher have been successful learning environments for students with ADHD.

should be restricted to four minutes. (Cruickshank, Bentzen, Ratzeburg, & Tannhauser, 1961).

It is rare today to see teachers using all the components of Cruickshank's program, especially the cubicles. Many authorities now believe that not all children with ADHD are distracted by things in their environment. For those who are distractible, however, some authorities recommend the use of such things as cubicles to reduce extraneous stimulation.

The degree of classroom structure and teacher direction advocated by Cruickshank is also rarely seen today. First, this intensity of structure could be achieved only in a self-contained classroom. As we discuss later, most students with ADHD are in general education settings. Second, most authorities today believe that a structured program is important in the early stages of working with many students with ADHD but that these students gradually need to learn to be more independent in their learning.

Nevertheless, many of Cruickshank's ideas are still alive in the educational recommendations of today's professionals. For example:

> *All* children, and particularly, those with ADHD, benefit from clear, predictable, uncomplicated routine and structure. It helps if the day is divided into broad units of time and if this pattern is repeated daily. Within each block of lesson time there should be a similar breaking down of tasks and activities into subtasks/activities. Presenting the student with an enormously detailed list of tasks and subtasks should be avoided. An important goal should be to create a simple overarching daily routine that the student will eventually learn by heart. The number of tasks should be kept small and tight timelines should be avoided. Complexities of timetabling and working structures merely confuse students with ADHD, because a major difficulty that goes with this condition is a poorly developed ability to differentiate between and organize different bits of information. This clearly makes the formal curriculum difficult to manage, without having to struggle with the organizational arrangements that surround the curriculum. Once a workable daily timetable has been established this should be publicly displayed and/or taped to the student's desk or inside his or her homework diary. (Cooper, 1999, p. 146)

For more specifics about planning for students with ADHD in the classroom, see Responsive Instruction on page 230. For recommendations on how to introduce, conduct, and conclude lessons see Table 7.2.

FUNCTIONAL BEHAVIORAL ASSESSMENT AND CONTINGENCY-BASED SELF-MANAGEMENT

As we noted in Chapter 5, **functional behavioral assessment (FBA)** is an important aspect of dealing with behavioral problems of students with mental retardation. It is also extremely useful in educational programming for students with ADHD. FBA involves determining the consequences, antecedents, and setting events that maintain inappropriate behaviors (Horner & Carr, 1997). Examples of typical functions of inappropriate behavior of students with ADHD are to avoid work and to gain attention from peers or adults (DuPaul & Ervin, 1996).

Contingency-based self-management approaches usually involve having people keep track of their own behavior and then receive consequences, usually in the form of rewards, based on their behavior (Davies & Witte, 2000; Shapiro, DuPaul, & Bradley-Klug, 1998). For example, the teacher might have students use self-monitoring to record how many times they left their seats during a class period. For directions about how to use self-monitoring in the classroom, see Responsive Instruction on page 232 and Chapter 6.

A combination of FBA and contingency-based self-management techniques has proven successful in increasing appropriate behavior of elementary and secondary students with ADHD (DuPaul, Eckert, & McGoey, 1997; Ervin, DuPaul, Kern, & Friman, 1998; Shapiro

Functional behavioral assessment (FBA)
The practice of determining the consequences (what purpose the behavior serves), antecedents (what triggers the behavior), and setting events (in what contexts the behavior occurs) of inappropriate behavior.

Contingency-based self-management
Educational techniques that involve having students keep track of their own behavior, for which they then receive consequences (e.g., reinforcement).

TABLE 7.2 Introducing, Conducting, and Concluding Lessons

Introducing Lessons

- **Provide an advance organizer.** Prepare students for the day's lesson by quickly summarizing the order of various activities that are planned.
- **Review previous lessons.** Review information about previous lessons on this topic.
- **Set learning expectations.** State what students are expected to learn during the lesson. For example, explain to students that a language arts lesson will involve reading a story about Paul Bunyan and identifying new words in the story.
- **State needed materials.** Identify all materials that the children will need during the lesson rather than leaving them to figure out on their own the materials required. For example, specify that children will need their journals and pencils for journal writing or their crayons, scissors, and colored paper for an art project.
- **Explain additional resources.** Tell students how to obtain help in mastering the lesson. For example, refer children to a particular page in the textbook for guidance on completing a worksheet.
- **Simplify instructions, choices, and scheduling.** The simpler the expectations communicated to an ADHD student, the more likely it is that he or she will comprehend and complete them in a timely and productive manner.

Conducting Lessons

- **Be predictable.** Structure and consistency are very important for children with ADHD; many do not do well with change. Minimal rules and minimal choices are best for these children. They need to understand clearly what is expected of them, as well as the consequences for not adhering to expectations.
- **Support the student's participation in the classroom.** Provide students with ADHD with private, discreet cues to stay on task and advance warning that they will be called on shortly. Avoid bringing attention to differences between ADHD students and their classmates. At all times, avoid the use of sarcasm and criticism.
- **Check student performance.** Question individual students to assess their mastery of the lesson. For example, you can ask students who are doing seatwork to demonstrate how they arrived at the answer to a problem, or you can ask individuals

to state, in their own words, how the main character felt at the end of the story.

- **Perform ongoing student evaluation.** Identify students who need additional assistance. Watch for signs of lack of comprehension, such as daydreaming or visual or verbal indications of frustration. Provide these students with extra explanations, or ask another student to serve as a peer tutor for the lesson.
- **Follow-up directions.**
  - *Oral directions.* After giving directions to the class as a whole, provide additional oral directions for a child with ADHD. For example, ask the child if he or she understood the directions and repeat the directions together.
  - *Written directions.* Provide follow-up directions in writing. For example, write the page number for an assignment on the chalkboard and remind the child to look at the chalkboard if he or she forgets the assignment.
- **Divide work into smaller units.** Break down assignments into smaller, less complex tasks. For example, allow students to complete five math problems before presenting them with the remaining five problems.
- **Eliminate or reduce frequency of timed tests.** Tests that are timed might not allow children with ADHD to demonstrate what they truly know owing to their potential preoccupation with elapsed time.

Concluding Lessons

- **Provide advance warnings.** Provide advance warning that a lesson is about to end. Announce five or ten minutes before the end of the lesson (particularly for seatwork and group projects) how much time remains. You might also want to tell students at the beginning of the lesson how much time they will have to complete it.
- **Check assignments.** Check completed assignments for at least some of the students. Review what they have learned during the lesson to get a sense of how ready the class was for the lesson and how to plan the next lesson.
- **Preview the next lesson.** Instruct students on how to begin preparing for the next lesson. For example, inform the students that they need to put away their textbooks and come to the front of the room for a large-group spelling lesson.

Source: Adapted from U.S. Department of Education, Office of Special Education and Rehabilitative Services, Office of Special Education Programs. (2004). *Teaching Children with Attention Deficit Hyperactivity Disorder: Instructional Strategies and Practices.*

et al., 1998). In one study, for instance, a combination of FBA and contingency-based self-management increased the on-task behavior of two adolescents with ADHD. For example, for one of the students, the FBA phase consisted of interviews with the teacher and observations in the classroom, which led the researchers and teachers to conclude that an adolescent boy's disruptive behavior was a function of gaining peer attention (Ervin et al., 1998). They based this assumption on evidence that the antecedents to his inattentive behavior consisted of such things as peers looking his way, calling out his name, and making gestures toward him and that the consequences of his inattention were such things as the peers laughing or returning comments to him.

The contingency-based self-management phase involved the student evaluating his on-task behavior on a five-point scale (0 = unacceptable to 5 = excellent) at the end of each math class. The teacher also rated the student's behavior, and the student was awarded points based on how closely the ratings matched. During writing class, the teacher awarded negative or positive points to members of the class depending on whether or not they responded to attention-seeking behaviors from any member of the class. In both classes, the points could be used for privileges.

The Role of Reinforcement   Authorities have pointed to the crucial role that contingency plays in contingency-based self-management. In other words, they point out that reinforcement of some kind, such as social praise or points that can be traded for privileges, is especially important for self-management techniques to be effective. For example, an extensive review of research found that contingency-based self-management strategies were more effective than self-management strategies without contingencies in leading to positive behavioral changes in students with ADHD (DuPaul & Eckert, 1997).

Although the use of behavioral procedures such as reinforcement and punishment is somewhat controversial—that is, there are those who are opposed to their use (Kohn, 1993)—many authorities consider them almost indispensable in working with students with ADHD. For example, they are an integral part of a set of intervention principles advocated by one team of authorities (see Table 7.3).

SERVICE DELIVERY MODELS

Because the U.S. Department of Education does not recognize ADHD as a separate special education category, we do not have statistics on how many students are served in different classroom environments. It is safe to assume, however, that one can find students with ADHD across the entire continuum, from residential schools to full inclusion in general education classrooms. But because, as we noted earlier, there is reason to believe that fewer than half receive any special education services (Forness & Kavale, 2002), it is logical to assume that most students with ADHD spend most of their time in general education classrooms. Making It Work on page 234 describes different ways to use co-teaching to help meet the needs of these students, whether they receive special education services or not.

As with all students with disabilities, the best placement for students with ADHD should be determined on an individual basis. Although full inclusion in a general education

UNDERSTANDING THE STANDARDS AND PRINCIPLES   Describe effective educational programming for students with ADHD. *(CEC Knowledge and Skills Standards CC4S3 & CC4S5)*

Council for Exceptional Children

TABLE 7.3   Pfiffner and Barkley's Intervention Principles for ADHD

1. Rules and instructions must be clear, brief, and often delivered through more visible and external modes of presentation.

2. Consequences must be delivered swiftly and immediately.

3. Consequences must be delivered more frequently [than for students without ADHD].

4. The types of consequences must often be of a higher magnitude, or more powerful [than for students without ADHD].

5. An appropriate and often richer degree of incentives must be provided.

6. Reinforcers, or particularly, rewards must be changed or rotated more frequently.

7. Anticipation is the key. Teachers must be mindful of planning ahead, particularly during phases of transition across activities or classes, to ensure that the children are cognizant of the shift in rules (and consequences) that is about to occur.

Source: Condensed from L. J. Pfiffner & R. A. Barkley, Treatment of ADHD in school settings. In R. A. Barkley, *Attention-deficit hyperactivity disorder: A handbook for diagnosis and treatment,* 2nd ed. (New York: Guilford Press, 1998), pp. 462–464. Reprinted with permission.

Meeting the Needs of Students with Attention Deficit Hyperactivity Disorder

Planning for Students with ADHD in the General Education Classroom

WHAT THE RESEARCH SAYS

The majority of students with ADHD are served in general education classrooms. Through adding key modifications or supports to their traditional instructional routines, teachers can address the needs of students with ADHD without taking away from the instruction of students without disabilities in their class.

The following lesson sequence includes a description of research-supported supports that can be provided at each stage of instruction and a rationale for how those supports meet the needs of students with ADHD.

APPLYING THE RESEARCH TO TEACHING

Stage 1: Pre-planning—Divide Instruction into Meaningful "Chunks"

Description Before instruction, break your instructional sequence into meaningful chunks or steps (Rosenshine, 1995). By dividing your instructional sequence into small, meaningful sections, you ensure that all students do not move on until they understand and that ample practice and teacher feedback has been provided at each step (Hudson, 1997).

Rationale Long tasks can be overwhelming for students with ADHD. Chunking allows for shorter periods of focused attention, activity changes as you move through the instructional sequence, focused practice, and reduced reliance on working memory (Kemp, Fister, & McLaughlin, 1995).

Stage II: Introduction

Description During this stage, the teacher introduces the day's instructional objectives. Information or activities that should be included in the introduction are (1) a rationale for the lesson, (2) an explanation or presentation of a model of what the end result of the lesson will be, and (3) an advance organizer that informs students of the sequence of instructional activity (Allsopp, 1999).

Rationale These activities provide a "road map" for students to follow. For students with ADHD who have difficulty focusing on the main task or goal (Barkley, 1997), explicit identification of lesson goals or outcomes and clearly delineated steps create an external goal-setting guide.

Stage III: Instruction and Modeling

Description After the teacher has set the stage for learning, the instructional part of the lesson begins. During this stage, a teacher might demonstrate a procedure or phenomenon, present students with a problem scenario to be solved, or have students engage in an activity that will then be linked to key instructional concepts. Regardless of the particular method the teacher is using to teach, students should have a clear understanding of what the teacher is doing and what they should be doing in response. Strategies for effective teaching include the teacher (1) thinking aloud as he or she presents the initial part of the lesson, (2) modeling the exact steps the students will complete, and (3) soliciting feedback from students during the instructional phase (Mercer & Mercer, 1998).

Psychostimulants
Medications that activate dopamine levels in the frontal and prefrontal areas of the brain that control behavioral inhibition and executive functions; used to treat persons with ADHD.

classroom might be appropriate for some students with ADHD, the estimate that over half do not receive any special education services can be viewed with some concern. This is especially true in light of the fact that studies have shown that positive behavioral changes in students with ADHD are much more likely to occur in special education than in general education settings (DuPaul & Eckert, 1997).

Medication Considerations

One of the most controversial topics in all of special education is the treatment of ADHD with medication. **Psychostimulants**, which stimulate or activate neurological functioning,

Rationale A student with ADHD might have difficulty making connections between the instructional phase of a lesson and the activity, assignment, or worksheet that follows. By providing a clear model of what needs to be done, demonstrating the type of inner speech that should be guiding their thinking (via the think-aloud), and checking students for understanding, the teacher increases the likelihood of students making connections between the instruction and the practice or application of the concept (Kucan & Beck, 1997).

Stage IV: Guided Practice

Description The guided practice (GP) stage is the critical transition stage between instruction and independent practice. During GP, students have the opportunity to practice or work with the concept being taught while the teacher is actively providing feedback (Allsopp, 1999; Kemp et al., 1995). GP can consist of students working several problems at the board or on whiteboards at their desks, students explaining (in their own words) to the class what was previously presented, or groups of students doing the first part of a task and reporting their work to the class. The key element of GP is that the teacher has the opportunity to correct or reteach before students are engaged in IP.

Rationale The GP stage provides an important bridge for students with ADHD who may need to be actively engaged in the task to be receptive to instructional guidelines or recommendations provided during instruction (Kemp et al., 1995). GP also provides an opportunity for positive reinforcement as the student makes initial attempts at understanding. Given the chunking of the lesson, teachers could go through the Instruction/Modeling and GP stages two to three times during a given lesson. Providing frequent shifts in activity creates additional support for such ADHD characteristics as short atten-

tion span, task-completion difficulty, and short-term memory problems (Rooney, 1995).

Stage V: Independent Practice

Description Independent practice (IP) comes in many forms, ranging from individual to pair or small-group work to homework. The purpose of IP is for students to apply what was taught. At this point in the instructional sequence, students should understand the task requirements and be able to perform the task with competence (Rosenshine, 1995).

Rationale Work presented at students frustration level can be a trigger for common ADHD behaviors—out of seat or verbal or physical disruptions. By establishing clear expectations for IP, ensuring students are capable of the work, and providing support, teachers increase the likelihood of meaningful student engagement.

Stage VI: Closure and Review

Description At the end of every lesson, time should be permitted to "recap" the main ideas of the lesson. For closure, teachers can review key vocabulary, have students state something they learned, or have students complete a brief journal activity. During closure, the lesson's "big idea" should be reinforced as well as connections made to past and future learning (Kameenui & Carnine, 1998).

Rationale Students with ADHD may have difficulty with synthesizing information (Barkley, 1994). Providing closure at the end of a lesson creates the support necessary for students to make connections among the day's concepts (Rosenshine, 1995).

In summary, teachers can serve many students with ADHD effectively within the general education setting, providing the instruction is responsive to their unique needs. ■

By Kristin L. Sayeski

are by far the most frequent type of medication prescribed for ADHD. The most common stimulant prescribed for ADHD is methylphenidate, or **Ritalin**. The fact that physicians would prescribe a psychostimulant for someone who exhibits hyperactivity is, at first blush, counterintuitive. In fact, for years professionals referred to the **paradoxical effect of Ritalin** because its effects appeared to be the opposite of those one would expect in the case of someone who does not have ADHD. Researchers have concluded, however, that Ritalin influences the release of the neurotransmitter dopamine, thus enabling the brain's executive functions to operate more normally (Swanson, Castellanos, Murias, LaHoste, & Kennedy, 1998; Swanson et al., 1998). Furthermore, it is now believed that Ritalin has the same chemical and behavioral effect on people who do not have ADHD as it does on those with ADHD (Solanto, 1998).

Ritalin
The most commonly prescribed psychostimulant for ADHD; its generic name is methylphenidate.

Paradoxical effect of Ritalin
The now discredited belief that Ritalin, even though a stimulant, acts to subdue a person's behavior and that this effect of Ritalin is evident in people with ADHD but not in those without ADHD.

Meeting the Needs of Students with Attention Deficit Hyperactivity Disorder

The Benefits of Self-Monitoring and Group Contingency

WHAT THE RESEARCH SAYS

Many students with ADHD lack the ability to self-monitor. Self-monitoring requires the ability to appraise a situation and consider alternative ways of responding as well as possible outcomes associated with the various forms of responding (Shapiro, DuPaul, & Bradley-Klug, 1998). This inability to "think" before acting creates problems for students with ADHD in the areas of paying attention in class, responding to social situations appropriately, and finishing assigned tasks. To address these issues, teachers can teach students to use self-management procedures wherein the student monitors, records, analyzes, and reinforces her or his own behavior (Davies & Witte, 2000). Many studies have been conducted in the area of self-management, and these studies have repeatedly demonstrated the effectiveness of teaching students such strategies (Cole & Bambara, 1992; Lloyd, Hallahan, Kauffman, & Keller, 1998; Mathes & Bender, 1997; Reid & Harris, 1992; Shimabukuro, Prater, Jenkins, & Edelen-Smith, 1999; Smith, Nelson, Young, & West, 1992).

Although teaching self-management to students with ADHD has been proven to be effective, many teachers prefer whole-class or group-contingency plans. Within a group-contingency model, the behavior of one student is tied to the outcome of the whole group. Group-contingency models promote interdependence, as group members must work together to meet their goal (Tankersley, 1995). Under a group contingency, teachers can use the same behavior management approach for all students and do not have to differentiate their treatment of the few students who need help with self-management. Thus, group contingencies can be very effective for general education teachers who have students with ADHD in their classrooms.

RESEARCH STUDY

One study examined the effects of a management program with third-graders that included both self-management and group contingency on the behaviors of students with ADHD in a general education classroom (Davies & Witte, 2000). All students—those with ADHD as well as nondisabled students—were responsible for monitoring their own behavior, and contingencies were established for group performance. Sample procedures for the group intervention were:

1. If any student displayed the target behavior [inappropriate verbalizations], she or he moved one dot from his/her group's chart from the green section into the blue section. If the child did not move the dot after about ten seconds, then the teacher moved a dot into the red section of the chart.
2. The rewards a group received were related to how many dots the group had in the green section of their chart at the end of the intervention period. Each group needed to have at least one dot left in the green section at the end of the intervention period to receive the reinforcer. [Each group started with five dots.] (Davies & Witte, 2000, p. 141)

RESEARCH FINDINGS

Results from the study demonstrated a decrease in the talking out behaviors of the four students with ADHD. In addition, there was no evidence of possible negative side effects of peer pressure, such as threats or negative verbal comments (Davies & Witte, 2000).

APPLYING THE RESEARCH TO TEACHING

Findings from this study demonstrate the effectiveness of using self-management within the context of a group contingency. Teachers can implement similar management strategies through (1) targeting specific undesirable behaviors to be eliminated or specific desirable behaviors to be reinforced, (2) creating a chart for students to use for self-management, (3) communicating the procedures for recording behaviors on the chart (e.g., "If you do X, mark your chart" or "When the beeper beeps, check to see if you are doing X, then mark your chart accordingly"), or (4) connecting the self-management procedures to a group contingency (e.g., "If all students get over X points during the lesson, all students will get a homework pass"). ∎

By Kristin L. Sayeski

Programs that allow students to monitor their own behavior and performance may encourage them to maintain appropriate behavior at school.

Ordinarily, Ritalin takes about one hour to take effect, the optimal effect occurring at about two hours. The effects of Ritalin usually wear off after about four hours. Responsiveness to Ritalin is highly individual, so the dosage level and number of doses per day vary from person to person.

Adderall is another stimulant that is sometimes prescribed. Some research suggests that it is at least as effective as Ritalin and that its effects are longer lasting, meaning that it does not have to be administered as often (Faraone, Pliszka, Olvera, Skolnik, & Biederman, 2001; Manos, Short, & Findling, 1999; Pliszka, Browne, Olvera, & Wynne, 2000).

More recently, the U.S. Food and Drug Administration has approved **Strattera**, a nonstimulant, for use with ADHD. Strattera affects the neurotransmitter norepinephrine, whereas the stimulants primarily affect dopamine. There are not yet any studies comparing Strattera to Ritalin or Adderall.

Adderall
A psychostimulant for ADHD; its effects are longer acting than those of Ritalin.

Strattera
A nonstimulant medication for ADHD; affects the neurotransmitter norepinephrine.

OPPOSITION TO RITALIN

Not all professionals, parents, and laypeople are in favor of using pyschostimulants for ADHD. In fact, Ritalin has been the subject of numerous assaults by the media. Starting in the late 1980s and continuing into the 1990s, several critics appeared on nationally broadcast television shows, such as *Oprah, Donahue, Geraldo,* and *20/20,* as well as evening and morning news shows. Although some criticisms have been relatively mild, others have ranged from assertions that ADHD is a bogus diagnosis to claims that professionals are trying to control children with medication and make them overly docile.

THE RESEARCH EVIDENCE

Dozens of research teams around the world have been studying the effects of several medications on ADHD. Most of this research has focused on the psychostimulant, Ritalin.

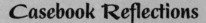

Casebook Reflections

Refer to the case *More Than LD: Shannon* in your booklet. After Shannon's teachers had made several modifications for instruction, Mrs. Morgan recommended talking to Dr. Rodriguez about putting Shannon on medicine. Do you think that was an appropriate suggestion? Why or why not?

Collaboration and Co-Teaching of Students with ADHD

"How can I get this student focused?!"

WHAT DOES IT MEAN TO BE A TEACHER OF STUDENTS WITH ATTENTION DEFICIT HYPERACTIVITY DISORDER?

Currently, the Council for Exceptional Children does not have specific competencies for teachers of students with ADHD because it is not a separate category of disability under IDEA. Often, these students have additional disabling conditions, such as a learning disability or an emotional/behavioral disorder and are served by teachers with expertise in those areas.

SUCCESSFUL STRATEGIES FOR CO-TEACHING

Co-teaching can take many forms in a classroom with students with ADHD. Vaughn, Schumm, and Arguelles (1997) describe five basic models of co-teaching that provide co-teachers with opportunities to use the instructional strategies described in this chapter and in Table 7.3. The decision to use a certain strategy should be based on instructional goals and student needs.

One Teach, One Drift   In this model, one teacher is responsible for instruction, and the other teacher drifts, monitoring students. This model allows the drifting teacher to redirect students who are off task, to observe and mark student monitoring forms, to provide feedback on individual students' attention and participation, and to deliver reinforcers or consequences on a frequent basis.

Station Teaching   In station teaching, co-teachers split content into two parts and students into three groups. Each teacher teaches one of the two content pieces at a station to a small group of students, and the other group works independently. The student groups move to each station. In this model, teachers can break content down to smaller tasks that maintain the attention of all students. Each teacher can work with a small group of students, making it easier to ensure that the students are focused and learning. It is also easier to help students work together and to provide reinforcers and consequences more frequently. The difficulty lies in making sure that students with ADHD can work appropriately at the independent station.

Parallel Teaching   In parallel teaching, the two teachers split the class into two groups and teach the same content to a smaller group of students. This model provides the same opportunities as station teaching, along with the chance to modify the instructional delivery of the same content material to meet the needs of the students.

Alternative Teaching   The alternative teaching model includes content instruction by one teacher to a large group of students and remedial or supplementary instruction by the other teacher to a small group of students. In this model, the teacher of the small group can modify delivery of content, control the delivery of consequences and rewards, and closely monitor and observe students. In addition, the teacher of the small group can incorporate instruction in strategies such as self-monitoring.

Team Teaching   In team teaching, co-teachers alternate or "tag team" in delivering instruction to the entire class. In this model, co-teachers can both be on the lookout for misconceptions, confusion, inattention, and disruption. These can then be addressed in the flow of instruction rather than afterward or on an individual basis. In addition, co-teachers can work together to present both content and learning strategies in unison to better meet the needs of all students.

In All Models   Teachers working together can discuss and better evaluate whether rules and instructions are clear, brief, and delivered in appropriate formats for students with ADHD. Co-teachers can also work together to better anticipate rough spots for students with ADHD, particularly during transition times, changes in routines, or complex tasks (see Table 7.3). The varying models of co-teaching provide the flexibility for teachers to adjust instructional delivery to meet the objectives of the teachers and the needs of the students with ADHD. ■

By Margaret P. Weiss

Effectiveness   Despite all the negative publicity in the media, most authorities in the area of ADHD are in favor of Ritalin's use. After hundreds of studies, the research is overwhelmingly positive on its effectiveness in helping students to have more normalized behavioral inhibition and executive functioning (Barkley, 1998; Crenshaw, Kavale, Forness, & Reeve, 1999; Evans et al., 2001; Forness, Kavale, & Crenshaw, 1999). Moreover, Ritalin not only leads to better results on parent and teacher rating scales, but also leads to improved performance in academic achievement as well as classroom behavior, such as better note-taking, on-task behavior, quiz scores, homework completion, and written-language work (Evans et al., 2001).

     In fact, even though there was a wealth of evidence showing the effectiveness of Ritalin and other medications, the National Institute of Mental Health decided to play it safe because of the controversy surrounding medication for ADHD. It embarked on a large-scale, well-controlled, extensive study on the effects of medication and behavioral management treatments (see Focus on Concepts on p. 236). Again, the results demonstrated the effectiveness of medication.

Nonresponders and Side Effects   Ritalin is not effective for everyone. Somewhere around 30 percent of those who take Ritalin do not have a favorable response (Spencer et al., 1996). In addition, some side effects are possible, including insomnia, reduction in appetite, abdominal pain, headaches, and irritability. There has also been speculation on the possibility that in a very small number of cases, Ritalin causes tics or increases their intensity in those who already have tics (DuPaul, Barkley, & Connor, 1998). There have also been many anecdotal reports of a "rebound effect," in which a child exhibits irritability as the Ritalin wears off. In most cases, these side effects are mild and can be controlled. For example, in the case of the two most common side effects—insomnia and reduction in appetite—care should be taken not to take the Ritalin too close to mealtime or bedtime. In the case of the rebound effect, some physicians recommend using a time-release form of Ritalin.

Drug Abuse   A popular misconception is that by taking Ritalin, children with ADHD are more likely to become abusers of drugs such as marijuana or cocaine as adolescents or young adults. There is little, if any, documented evidence that this occurs (Barkley, 1998). In fact, there is suggestive evidence that those with ADHD who are prescribed Ritalin as children are less likely to turn to illicit drugs as teenagers (Biederman, Wilens, Mick, Spencer, & Faraone, 1999). Some have speculated that perhaps those who are not medicated with Ritalin turn to other drugs to try to find "peace of mind" or to "chill out."

CAUTIONS REGARDING MEDICATION

Although the research is overwhelmingly positive on the effectiveness of medication for increasing appropriate behavior, there are still a number of cautions:

- Medication should not be prescribed at the first sign of a behavioral problem. Only after careful analysis of the student's behavior and environment should medication be considered. The use of psychostimulants for ADHD in the United States has doubled every four to seven years since 1971 (Wilens & Biederman, 1992). Furthermore, rates of Ritalin usage vary substantially from one country to another. For example, Ritalin is administered in the United States at more than twice the rate of its use in Great Britain and Australia (Kewley, 1998). Although the lower rates of Ritalin usage in other countries might indicate that many people with ADHD are not being treated properly, it is also very likely that at least some children in the United States are being medicated inappropriately.
- Although research has demonstrated the effectiveness of medication on behavioral inhibition and executive functions, the results for academic

RESEARCHERS and other professionals have begun to fight back against what they consider inappropriate media coverage of ADHD. On February 7, 2002, the National Attention Deficit Disorder Association issued a statement on the media and ADHD: **www.add. org/content/research/media. htm**

TWO ARTICLES in the *Archives of General Psychiatry*, summarizing the results of the NIMH MTA study, are available on-line at **http://archpsyc.ama-assn.org /content/vol56/issue12/ index.dt**

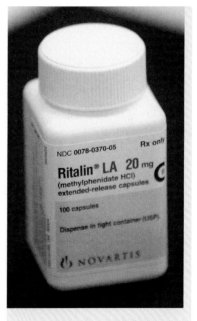

Psychostimulants, especially Ritalin, have sparked a national controversy over the treatment of ADHD. Although Ritalin is not effective for everyone and can have side effects, the bulk of research evidence supports its effectiveness.

FOCUS ON CONCEPTS

Is Medication Effective for Children with ADHD?
The National Institute of Mental Health's MTA Study

THE National Institute of Mental Health (NIMH) Collaborative Multisite Multimodal Treatment Study of Children with Attention-Deficit/Hyperactivity Disorder (MTA), cosponsored by the U.S. Department of Education, has been the most ambitious study yet conducted on the efficacy of medication for children with ADHD. (MTA Cooperative Group, 1999). It involved a total sample of 579 children between the ages of 7 and 9.9 years from seven sites around North America: Berkeley, California; Durham, North Carolina; Irvine, California; Montreal, Quebec; New York City; Pittsburgh, Pennsylvania; and Queens, New York,

Researchers randomly assigned students to one of four groups:

- *Medication Management (MedMgt)*: This group received carefully monitored medication. Most received Ritalin, but those who reacted unfavorably to Ritalin were given an alternative medication.
- *Behavioral Treatment (Beh)*: This intensive behaviorally oriented program involved a school-based intervention, including teacher training in behavior management, a classroom aide, and a daily report card linked to home consequences; twenty-seven sessions of parent training in child behavior management; individual parent training sessions; child-focused therapy; and an eight-week all-day behaviorally oriented summer program.
- *Combined Medication Management and Behavioral Treatment (Comb)*:
- *Community Care (CC)*: Families in this group were provided a list of mental health resources in their community. (Sixty-seven percent ended up on medication at some point; however, the medication was not managed as closely.)

The study lasted for fourteen months, during which an extensive battery of measures and ratings were taken.

RESULTS

Using a composite score of teacher and parent ratings of core ADHD symptoms, the researchers rated whether each of the treatments could be considered a success (Swanson et al., 2001). The ranking of the groups with respect to success rates at the end of the fourteen months was as follows:

- Comb: 68%
- MedMgt: 56%
- Beh: 34%
- CC: 25%

CONCLUSIONS

The findings clearly point to the impressive effects of medication. They also suggest that using medication in combination with behavioral method is the most powerful treatment.

The findings are a bit less clear with respect to the value of the behavioral treatment alone. Although a 34 percent success rate is not as high as one would like, some observers have noted that this is an average of the seven sites studied (Swanson et al., 2001). Some students improved much more than others. Furthermore, there was considerable variability in how intensively the behavioral treatment was delivered from school to school within each site (Pelham, 2000). In other words, it still makes sense for teachers to use behavior management, especially because we know that the behavior problems of many children with ADHD are likely to deteriorate without intensive behavioral interventions.

FURTHER RESEARCH

Currently, NIMH is conducting a similar study focusing on preschool children. The Preschool ADHD Treatment Study is looking at the effects of psychostimulant medications on young children with ADHD in addition to attempting to provide criteria for physicians to use in diagnosing ADHD in preschool children. ■

Source: A 14-Month Randomized Clinical Trial of Treatment Strategies for Attention-Deficit/Hyperactivity Disorder, *Archives of General Psychiatry*, vol. 56, Dec. 1999, pp. 1073-1086. Reprinted with permission.

outcomes have not been as dramatic. Although important academic measures, such as work completed or accuracy on assignments, have shown substantial improvement, the impact on achievement tests has been much (Forness et al., 1999). Thus, teachers should not assume that medication will take care of all the academic problems these students face.

- Parents, teachers, and physicians should monitor dosage levels closely so that the dose that is used is effective but not too strong. Proper dosage levels vary considerably (Hale et al., 1998).
- Teachers and parents should not lead children to believe that the medication serves as a substitute for self-responsibility and self-initiative.
- Teachers and parents should not view the medication as a panacea; they, too, must take responsibility and initiative in working with the child.
- Parents and teachers should keep in mind that psychostimulants are a controlled substance. There is the potential for siblings, peers, or the child himself or herself, to attempt to experiment with them.
- The final key to the effective use of medication is communication among parents, physicians, teachers, and the child himself or herself.

UNDERSTANDING THE STANDARDS AND PRINCIPLES What are the pros and cons of treating ADHD with medication? *(CEC Knowledge and Skills Standard CC2K7)*

Council for
Exceptional
Children

Early Intervention

Diagnosis of young children with ADHD is particularly difficult because many children who do not have ADHD tend to exhibit a great deal of motor activity and a lack of impulse control. For the very reason that excessive activity and impulsivity are relatively normal for young children, preschoolers with ADHD can be particularly difficult to manage. Thus, those preschoolers who really do have ADHD are a great challenge to parents and teachers.

Because of the severity of the symptoms of preschoolers who have been diagnosed with ADHD, the importance of the educational principles of classroom structure, teacher direction, functional behavioral assessment, and contingency-based self-management that we discussed above are all the more important. Given that even young children who do not have ADHD lack fully developed self-management skills, most recommend an even stronger emphasis on the use of contingencies in the form of praise, points, and tangible rewards.

In the case of preschoolers with ADHD and high rates of aggression, even implementing very intensive early intervention procedures, including highly structured classrooms with strong contingencies, leads only to limited behavioral and academic improvements that do not endure (Shelton et al., 2000). In other words, even high-quality early intervention is not likely to remediate completely the symptoms of children with ADHD and severe aggression. Such children need long-term programming.

Transition to Adulthood

Not too long ago, most professionals assumed that ADHD diminished in adolescence and usually disappeared by adulthood. Authorities now recognize about two thirds of individuals who are diagnosed with ADHD in childhood will continue to have significant symptoms in adulthood (Faraone & Doyle, 2001). And with the greater recognition of ADHD by the scientific community as well as by the popular media, many people are being diagnosed with ADHD in adulthood. The few studies of prevalence that have been conducted report a prevalence rate of about 4 to 5 percent (Barkley, 1998), which mirrors that for children.

DIAGNOSIS IN ADULTHOOD

The diagnosis of ADHD in adults is controversial. Because of the long-held assumption that ADHD did not persist into adulthood, there is not a very long history of research on ADHD

For learners with ADHD, coaching beyond high school, through either a job coach, therapist, or teacher counselor is highly recommended.

in adults. In recent years, however, professionals have begun to make progress in identifying and treating ADHD in adults. Because there is no test for ADHD, most authorities hold that the person's history is of utmost importance. As one authoritative team has put it:

> This is old-fashioned medicine, not high-tech. This is a doctor talking to a patient, asking questions, listening to answers, drawing conclusions based on getting to know the patient well. These days we often don't respect or trust anything medical that doesn't depend upon fancy technology. Yet the diagnosis of [ADHD] depends absolutely upon the simplest of all medical procedures: the taking of a history. (Hallowell & Ratey, 1994, pp. 195–196)

> The best test for [ADHD] is the oldest test in the history of medicine: the patient's own story. . . . If possible, the history should always be taken from at least two people—the identified patient plus a parent or spouse or friend. (Hallowell & Ratey, 1996, p. 188)

An abbreviated history of an adult with ADHD is presented in the Personal Perspectives on page 239.

As crucial as the history is, however, its subjective nature does make it vulnerable to misinterpretation. Therefore, clinicians have come up with guidelines for diagnosis. Table 7.4 contains a set of suggested diagnostic criteria for adults.

ADULT OUTCOMES

Many adults with ADHD have antisocial, anxiety, and depression disorders and experience more school failure, employment problems, and automobile accidents than do adults who do not have ADHD (Faraone et al., 2000). Those who have a coexisting condition, such as depression or aggression, tend to have less positive outcomes than do those who do not. Although people with ADHD are at risk for poorer outcomes, it is important to point out that there are many adults with ADHD who have highly successful careers and jobs, and many have happy marriages and families.

Personal Perspectives

AN ADULT WITH ADHD: ANN'S STORY

I **GREW** up not feeling very good about myself. In school, it was hard for me to stay on the subject or to finish anything. . . . Teachers would be on my back. They said I was such a good child—they couldn't understand it. And I tried so hard. I just couldn't finish anything. . . . I was distracted very easily by practically everything. If someone sneezed, I'd look at him and my mind would go off in a million directions. I'd look out the window, wondering why he had sneezed. . . .

The situation has persisted into adulthood. I'm very disorganized. Take housekeeping, for example. After dinner, when I start the dishes, I'll wash a little, then run and wipe off the table, wipe the cabinet, talk on the phone, and never get anything completed. I have to really concentrate and tell myself "You are going to get the dishes done." Then they get done, but I still get the urge to stop and go wash off the dining room table. Just like someone is pulling me. My closet and drawers are still a mess, just like when I was a kid.

What's really hard is to stay with any kind of paper work—bills, for example. It's my husband's job to do the bills. If it were mine, we'd probably be in jail. . . . Only recently at age forty-five have I been able to sit down and write a letter. I usually write small postcards.

I'm the most impulsive person in the world. It gets me in trouble. If I see something I know I shouldn't buy, I'll buy it any-

way. Or, I'll say something that I know the minute it comes out of my mouth I'm going to regret. . . .

I wish I could just slow down and relax. I have problems sitting still. . . . People say I make them nervous, but I don't even realize I'm doing anything. That hurts my feelings. I don't want to be different.

My dream has always been to be some kind of counselor, but I felt like I wasn't college material, so I got married and had two children. I have a real estate license now. I don't know how I passed the test. I must have guessed right. What I like about selling is that I'm always on the move and I love people. I'm tuned into them. But I'm too sensitive to have a sense of humor. I think I have a thin skin. I get my feelings hurt easily. When that happens, I cry and go into my shell.

My mood swings from high to low. I either feel very good or very down. I feel up if the house looks good. If I get everything done that I think I should, it makes me feel good about myself. I feel responsible for a lot of people. If my husband is in a bad mood, or if things aren't going right for my kids, my mother, or my sister, I feel bad. I don't know what's wrong with me. ■

Ann Ridgley

Source: Weiss, L. (1992). *Attention deficit disorder in adults* (pp. 11–14). Lanham, MD: Taylor Publishing Co. Reprinted by permission.

Employment   One of the keys to successful employment for all people, but especially for persons with ADHD, is to select a job or career that maximizes the individual's strengths and minimizes her or his weaknesses. Success is often dependent on pursuing a job that fits a person's needs for structure versus independence. It is recommended that those who work best with structure look for jobs with organizations that have a clear mission and lines of authority, with an emphasis on oversight from supervisors who have an understanding of ADHD. Those who find formal structures too confining should look for work environments that are flexible, have variety, and allow one to be independent (Hallowell & Ratey, 1996).

Marriage and Family   Given some of the behavioral characteristics of ADHD, it is not surprising that husbands and wives of people with ADHD frequently complain that their spouse is a poor listener, preoccupied, forgetful, unreliable, messy, and so forth (Murphy, 1998). A person's ADHD can have a negative impact on the entire family. Parents who have ADHD may find it difficult to manage the daily lives of their children. As one parent put it, "I couldn't remember to brush my teeth when I was a kid, and now I can't remember to tell my kid to brush his teeth." (Weiss, Hechtman, & Weiss, 2000, p. 1060)

Many authorities recommend that the first step to treatment is to have all family members become educated about the facts associated with ADHD. Because ADHD is a family

TABLE 7.4   Suggested Diagnostic Criteria for Attention Deficit Disorder in Adults

Note: Consider a criterion met only if the behavior is considerably more frequent than that of most people of the same mental age.

A. A chronic disturbance in which at least twelve of the following are present:
- A sense of underachievement, of not meeting one's goals (regardless of how much one has actually accomplished).
- Difficulty getting organized.
- Chronic procrastination or trouble getting started.
- Many projects going simultaneously; trouble with followthrough.
- A tendency to say what comes to mind without necessarily considering the timing or appropriateness of the remark.
- A frequent search for high stimulation.
- An intolerance of boredom.
- Easy distractibility, trouble focusing attention, tendency to tune out or drift away in the middle of a page or a conversation, often coupled with an ability to hyperfocus at times.
- Often creative, intuitive, highly intelligent.
- Trouble in going through established channels, following "proper" procedure.
- Impatient; low tolerance of frustration.
- Impulsive, either verbally or in action, as in impulsive spending of money, changing plans, enacting new schemes or career plans, and the like; hot-tempered.
- A tendency to worry needlessly, endlessly; a tendency to scan the horizon looking for something to worry about, alternating with inattention to or disregard for actual dangers.
- A sense of insecurity.
- Mood swings, mood lability, especially when disengaged from a person or a project.
- Physical or cognitive restlessness.
- A tendency toward addictive behavior.
- Chronic problems with self-esteem.
- Inaccurate self-observation.
- Family history of ADD or manic-depressive illness or depression or substance abuse or other disorders of impulse control or mood.

B. Childhood history of ADD. (It may not have been formally diagnosed, but in reviewing the history, one sees that the signs and symptoms were there.)

C. Situation not explained by other medical or psychiatric condition.

Source: From *Driven to distraction: Recognizing and coping with attention deficit disorder from childhood through adulthood.* by Edward M. Hallowell, M.D. and John J. Ratey, M.D., copyright © 1994 by Edward H. Hallowell, M.D. and John J. Ratey, M.D. Used by permission of Pantheon Books, a division of Random House, Inc.

 ADULTS and children with ADHD, as well as parents of children with ADHD, can find a wealth of useful information from organizations devoted to ADHD. The oldest organization devoted to ADHD is the Children and Adults with Attention-Deficit/Hyperactivity Disorder (CHADD). A more recent organization is the National Attention Deficit Disorder Association (National ADDA). Their respective websites are **www.chadd.org** and **www.add.org**

For more personal stories about ADHD visit the following link on the National ADDA website: **www.add.org/content/stories1.htm**

UNDERSTANDING THE STANDARDS AND PRINCIPLES   What do we know about transition to adulthood for students with ADHD? *(CEC Knowledge and Skills Standards CC10K2 & CC10K3)*

Coaching
A technique whereby a friend or therapist offers encouragement and support for a person with ADHD.

issue, they also recommend that all members of the family should be partners in its treatment:

> Unlike some medical problems, [ADHD] touches everybody in the family in a daily, significant way. It affects early-morning behavior, it affects dinner-table behavior, it affects vacations, and it affects quiet time. Let each member of the family become a part of the solution, just as each member of the family has been a part of the problem. (Hallowell & Ratey, 1996, p. 303)

IMPORTANCE OF COACHING

One highly recommended therapeutic technique is that of coaching (Hallowell & Ratey, 1994). **Coaching** involves identifying someone whom the person with ADHD can rely on for support. The term *coach* is used because this person can be visualized as someone "standing on the sidelines with a whistle around his or her neck barking out encouragement, directions, and reminders to the player in the game" (Hallowell & Ratey, 1994,

p. 226). The coach, who can be a therapist or a friend, is someone who spends ten to fifteen minutes each day helping to keep the person with ADHD focused on his or her goals. The coach provides the structure needed to plan for upcoming events and activities and heaps on praise when tasks are accomplished.

Although ADHD is a lifelong struggle for most people with the condition, with the appropriate combination of medical, educational, and psychological counseling, satisfactory employment and family adjustment are within the reach of most people with ADHD. Now that most authorities recognize that ADHD often continues into adulthood, more and more research will be focused on treatment of ADHD in adults. With this research should come an even more positive outlook for adults with ADHD.

SUMMARY

WHAT are the historical origins of ADHD?

- In the mid-nineteenth century, Dr. Heinrich Hoffman wrote nursery rhymes about "Fidgety Phillip" and "The Story of Johnny Head-in-Air."
- In 1902, Dr. George F. Still reported on children whom he referred to as having "defective moral control."
- In the 1930s, Kurt Goldstein reported on soldiers who had head wounds in World War I.
- In the 1930s and 1940s, Heinz Werner and Alfred Strauss reported on children with mental retardation who were assumed to be brain-injured, referred to as having the "Strauss syndrome."
- In the 1950s, William Cruickshank extended Werner and Strauss's work to children with normal intelligence.
- In the 1950s and 1960s, the term *minimal brain injury* was used to refer to children who were of normal intelligence but who were inattentive, impulsive, and/or hyperactive.
- In the 1960s and 1970s, the term *hyperactive child syndrome* was popular.

WHAT is the current definition of ADHD?

- Most professionals rely on the American Psychiatric Association's *Diagnostic and Statistical Manual of Mental Disorders*, which uses ADHD as the general term and subdivides individuals into (1) ADHD, Predominantly Inattentive Type; (2) ADHD, Predominantly Hyperactive-Impulsive Type; and (3) ADHD, Combined Type.

WHAT is the prevalence of ADHD?

- The best estimates are that 3 to 5 percent of the school-age population has ADHD.
- Boys with ADHD outnumber girls, most likely owing to biological differences and perhaps some referral bias.

WHAT methods of assessment are used to identify individuals with ADHD?

- Professionals usually use four methods of assessment: (1) a medical examination, (2) a clinical interview, (3) teacher and parent rating scales, and (4) behavioral observations. The behavioral observations can be done in the classroom and/or in the clinician's office using a computerized continuous performance test.

WHAT causes ADHD?

- Neuroimaging studies have identified three areas of the brain that might be affected in people with ADHD: the frontal lobes, the basal ganglia, and the cerebellum.
  - The frontal lobes are responsible for executive functions, or the ability to regulate one's behavior.
  - The basal ganglia and cerebellum are involved in coordination and control of motor behavior.
- Research has identified an imbalance in two neurotransmitters: dopamine and norepinephrine.
- Family studies, twin studies, and molecular genetic studies indicate that heredity may also be a significant cause of ADHD.

■ Exposure to toxins such as lead and abuse of alcohol and tobacco, as well as medical factors such as complications at birth and low birth weight, can also be a cause of ADHD.

WHAT are some of the psychological and behavioral characteristics of learners with ADHD?

■ Barkley's theory of ADHD points to problems with (1) behavioral inhibition, (2) executive functioning, (3) time awareness and management, and (4) persistent goal-directed behavior.

■ People with ADHD also often experience problems in adaptive behavior and in their relationships with peers.

WHAT are some educational considerations for learners with ADHD?

■ Good educational programming for students with ADHD involves a high degree of classroom structure and teacher-directed activities.

■ Good educational programming for students with ADHD involves functional assessment and contingency-based self-management.
  ■ Functional behavioral assessment involves determining the consequences, antecedents, and setting events that maintain inappropriate behaviors.
  ■ Such approaches might also include self-monitoring or self-management programs, wherein students record their own behaviors.

WHAT are some medication considerations for learners with ADHD?

■ Psychostimulants, such as Ritalin, are prescribed most often; Strattera, a nonstimulant, has recently been introduced.

■ Psychostimulants work on the neurotransmitter dopamine; Strattera works on the neurotransmitter norepinephrine.

■ Scientific studies (including a large-scale study sponsored by the National Institute for Mental Health) support the effectiveness of medication, and most authorities on ADHD favor its use.

■ Some cautions about medication are that some people are non-responders, dosage levels should be monitored closely, some people experience side effects (although these usually are not serious), children should not be encouraged to see the medication as a replacement for self-initiated behavioral control, and medication should not be the first response to problem behavior.

WHAT are some things to consider with respect to early intervention for learners with ADHD?

■ Diagnosing ADHD in early childhood is difficult, partly because very young children typically have short attention spans and are motorically active.

■ Principles of classroom structure, teacher direction, functional behavioral assessment, and contingency-based self-management are important for preschoolers with ADHD.

■ Because young children typically do not have strong self-management skills, contingencies in the form of praise, points, and tangible rewards are important.

WHAT are some things to consider with respect to transition to adulthood for learners with ADHD?

■ The taking of a thorough clinical history is critical in diagnosing ADHD in adults.

■ Although exceptions exist, adults with ADHD tend to have less positive outcomes than the general population in terms of employment, marriage and family, and general social well-being.

■ Coaching is a therapeutic technique often recommended for adults with ADHD.

APPLYING THE STANDARDS AND PRINCIPLES

- **ONE** of your colleagues, whose background is in general education, asks, **"What does it really mean to have ADHD?"** How would you respond? *(CEC Content Standard #1 & #2; INTASC Principle #1 & #2)*

- **WHAT** should teachers know about the **psychological and behavioral characteristics** of students with ADHD? *(CEC Content Standard #3)*

- **HOW** should teachers determine what **instructional methods** to use with students with ADHD? *(CEC Content Standard #4 & INTASC Principle #4)*

- **HOW** easy or difficult is it to **identify ADHD**? *(CEC Content Standard #8 & INTASC Principle #8)*

- **HOW** would you **respond to parents** who approached you expressing concern about the future of their **high school student with ADHD**? *(CEC Content Standard #10 & INTASC Principle #10)*

Council for
Exceptional
Children

INTASC

Chapter 8

Learners with Emotional or Behavioral Disorders

*I*t has always been hard for me to have friends. I want friends, but I don't know how to make them. I always think people are being serious when they are just joking around, but I don't figure that out until a lot later. I just don't know how to adapt.

I get into fights with people all the time. I take their teasing seriously and get into trouble. I don't remember having as much trouble getting along with kids when I was little. They seemed to feel sorry for me or thought I was weird. I used to run away from kids and hide in the bathroom at school or under my desk.

After I got back from the hospital, I really couldn't get along with anyone. That was when kids first began calling me "retard." I am not retarded, but I get confused and can't figure out what is going on. At first I couldn't figure out what they were saying to me. Finally one girl in my special education class became my friend. She kind of took care of me. I had another friend in junior high who was also nice and kind to me. But my best friend is my dog Cindie. Even though I give her a hard time, she is always ready to love me.

I like to play by myself best. I make up stories and fantasies. My mother says it is too bad I have such a hard time writing, because with my imagination and all the stories I have created in my mind I could write a book.

ANONYMOUS

QUESTIONS TO GUIDE YOUR READING OF THIS CHAPTER . . .

- WHAT terminology is used to describe emotional and behavioral disorders?

- WHAT is the definition of emotional and behavioral disorder?

- HOW are emotional and behavioral disorders classified?

- WHAT is the prevalence of emotional and behavioral disorders?

- WHAT are the causes of emotional and behavioral disorders?

- HOW are emotional and behavioral disorders identified?

- WHAT are the major educational considerations regarding emotional and behavioral disorders?

SPECIAL EDUCATORS . . .

- **understand the field** as an evolving and changing discipline *(from CEC Content Standard #1).*

- understand the **similarities and differences** in human development *(from CEC Content Standard #2).*

- **possess a repertoire** of evidence-based instructional strategies *(from CEC Content Standard #4).*

- **actively create learning environments** for individuals with exceptional learning needs that foster cultural understanding, safety and emotional well-being, positive social interactions, and active engagement *(from CEC Content Standard #5).*

- **use the results of assessments** to help identify exceptional learning needs *(from CEC Content Standard #8).*

- **use collaboration** to facilitate the successful transitions of individuals with exceptional learning needs across settings and services *(from CEC Content Standard #10).*

ALL TEACHERS . . .

- understand **how children learn and develop** *(from INTASC Principle #2).*

- understand and use a variety of **instructional strategies** *(from INTASC Principle #4).*

- **use an understanding of individual and group motivation and behavior** to create a learning environment that encourages positive social interaction, active engagement in learning, and self-motivation *(INTASC Principle #5).*

- **Understand and use formal and informal assessment strategies** to evaluate and ensure the continuous intellectual, social and physical development of the learner *(INTASC Principle #8).*

- **foster relationships** with school colleagues, families, and agencies in the larger community to support students' learning and well being *(INTASC Principle #10).*

Council for Exceptional Children

INTASC

Children and youths who have emotional or behavioral disorders are not typically good at making friends. Their most obvious problem is failure to establish close and satisfying emotional ties with other people who can help them. As the youth in the excerpt on page 245 describes, it can be easier for these individuals to hide, both physically and emotionally. If they do develop friendships, it is often with deviant peers (Farmer, 2000; Farmer, Farmer, & Gut, 1999; Farmer, Quinn, Hussey, & Holahan, 2001; Walker, Ramsey, & Gresham, 2004).

Some of these children are withdrawn. Other children or adults might try to reach them, but these efforts are usually met with fear or disinterest. In many cases, quiet rejection continues until those who are trying to make friends give up. Because close emotional ties are built around reciprocal social responses, people lose interest in others who do not respond to social overtures.

Many other children with emotional or behavioral disorders are isolated from others not because they withdraw from friendly advances but because they strike out with hostility and aggression. They are abusive, destructive, unpredictable, irresponsible, bossy, quarrelsome, irritable, jealous, defiant—anything but pleasant. Naturally, other children and adults choose not to spend time with children like this unless they have to. Some strike back at youngsters who show these characteristics. It is no wonder that these children and youths seem to be embroiled in a continuous battle with everyone. The reaction of most other children and adults is to withdraw to avoid battles, but rejected children then do not learn to behave acceptably. "In the case of [the] rejected child, parents, teachers, and peers simply withdraw from the child, and 'teaching opportunities' are greatly reduced, along with the opportunity for the rejected child to redeem himself in the eyes of parents, teachers, and mainstream peers" (Ialongo, Vaden-Kiernan, & Kellam, 1998, p. 210).

Where does the problem start? Does it begin with behavior that frustrates, angers, or irritates other people? Or does it begin with a social environment so uncomfortable or inappropriate that the child can only withdraw or attack? These questions cannot be answered fully on the basis of current research. The best thinking today is that the problem is not always just in the child's behavior or just in the environment. The problem arises because the social interactions and transactions between the child and the social environment are inappropriate. This is an ecological perspective—an interpretation of the problem as a negative aspect of the child and the environment in which the child lives.

Special education for these students is in many ways both confused and confusing. The terminology of the field is inconsistent, and there is much misunderstanding of definitions (Cullinan, 2004; Kauffman, 2005a). Reliable classifications of children's behavior problems have only recently emerged from research. The large number of theories about the causes and the best treatments of emotional and behavioral disorders makes it difficult to sort out

Misconceptions about
Learners with Emotional or Behavioral Disorders

MYTH   Most children and youths with emotional or behavioral disorders are not noticed by people around them.

FACT   Although it is difficult to identify the types and causes of problems, most children and youths with emotional or behavioral disorders, whether aggressive or withdrawn, are quite easy to spot.

MYTH   Students with emotional or behavioral disorders are usually very bright.

FACT   Relatively few students with emotional or behavioral disorders have high intelligence; in fact, most have below-average IQs.

MYTH   Youngsters who exhibit shy, anxious behavior are more seriously impaired than those whose behavior is hyperaggressive.

FACT   Youngsters with aggressive, acting-out behavior patterns have less chance for social adjustment and mental health in adulthood. Neurotic, shy, anxious children and youths have a better chance of getting and holding jobs, overcoming their problems, and staying out of jails and mental hospitals, unless their withdrawal is extreme. This is especially true for boys.

MYTH   Most students with emotional or behavioral disorders need a permissive environment, in which they feel accepted and can accept themselves for who they are.

FACT   Research shows that a firmly structured and highly predictable environment is of greatest benefit for most students.

MYTH   Only psychiatrists, psychologists, and social workers are able to help children and youths with emotional or behavioral disorders overcome their problems.

FACT   Most teachers and parents can learn to be highly effective in helping youngsters with emotional or behavioral disorders, sometimes without extensive training or professional certification. Many of these children and youths do require services of highly trained professionals as well.

MYTH   Undesirable behaviors are only symptoms; the real problems are hidden deep in the individual's psyche.

FACT   There is no sound scientific basis for belief in hidden causes; the behavior and its social context are the problems. Causes may involve thoughts, feelings, and perceptions.

MYTH   Juvenile delinquency and the aggressive behavior known as conduct disorder can be effectively deterred by harsh punishment if children and youths know that their misbehavior will be punished.

FACT   Harsh punishment, including imprisonment, not only does not deter misbehavior, but also creates conditions under which many individuals become even more likely to exhibit unacceptable conduct.

the most useful concepts. Therefore, study of this area of special education demands more than the usual perseverance and critical thinking. In fact, children and youths with emotional or behavioral disorders present some of the most difficult social problems that our society has to solve (Kauffman, 2005a; Walker, Forness, Kauffman, Epstein, Gresham, Nelson, & Strain, 1998).

Terminology

UNDERSTANDING THE STANDARDS AND PRINCIPLES Why has defining emotional and behavioral disorders always been problematic? *(CEC Knowledge and Skills Standards CC1K5 & BD1K1)*

Council for
Exceptional
Children

Many different terms have been used to designate children who have extreme social-interpersonal and/or intrapersonal problems, including *emotionally handicapped, emotionally impaired, behaviorally impaired, socially/emotionally handicapped, emotionally conflicted,* and *seriously behaviorally disabled.* These terms do not designate distinctly different types of disorders; that is, they do not refer to clearly different types of children and youths. Rather, the different labels appear to represent personal preferences for terms and slightly different theoretical orientations. The terminology of the field is so variable and confusing that it is possible to pick a label of choice simply by choosing one or more of the overlapping terms from set A and combining it with one of those from set B in Figure 8.1 (and, if it seems appropriate, adding other qualifiers, such as *serious* or *severe*). Thus, one could have *emotional disturbance, behavioral disorder, emotional or behavioral disorder, social disability,* and so on.

Until 1997, *seriously emotionally disturbed* was the term used in federal special education laws and regulations. *Seriously* was dropped from the terminology in 1997. *Emotionally disturbed* is the term used in the Individuals with Disabilities Education Act (IDEA), but it has been criticized as inappropriate. *Behaviorally disordered* is consistent with the name of

FIGURE 8.1 Possible combinations of terms. Choose one or more in set A combined with one in set B.

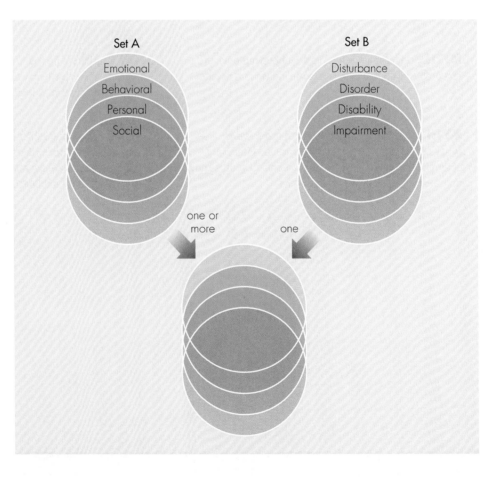

the Council for Children with Behavioral Disorders (CCBD, a division of the Council for Exceptional Children) and has the advantage of focusing attention on the clearly observable aspect of these children's problems: disordered behavior. Many authorities favor terminology indicating that these children may have emotional or behavioral problems or both (Cullinan, 2002, 2004; Kauffman, 2005a; Kavale, Forness, & Mostert, 2005).

In 1990, the National Mental Health and Special Education Coalition, representing over thirty professional and advocacy groups, proposed the new term *emotional or behavioral disorder* to replace *emotional disturbance* in federal laws and regulations (Forness & Knitzer, 1992). *Emotional or behavioral disorder* could become the generally accepted terminology of the field, although changes in federal and state laws and regulations may be slow in coming.

THE COUNCIL for Children with Behavioral Disorders (CCBD) maintains a website at **www.ccbd.net**

Definition

Defining emotional and behavioral disorders has always been problematic. Professional groups and experts have felt free to construct individual working definitions to fit their own professional purposes (Cullinan, 2004; Forness & Kavale, 1997; Kauffman, Brigham, & Mock, 2004; Kauffman & Landrum, 2006; Landrum & Kauffman, 2003). For practical reasons, we might say that someone has had an emotional or behavioral disorder whenever an adult authority has said so. Until recently, no one has come up with a definition that a majority of professionals understand and accept.

DEFINITIONAL PROBLEMS

There are valid reasons for the lack of consensus about definition. Defining emotional and behavioral disorders is somewhat like defining a familiar experience—anger, loneliness, or happiness, for example. We all have an intuitive grasp of what these experiences are, but forming objective definitions of emotional or behavioral disorders is difficult for the following reasons:

- We lack precise definitions of mental health and normal behavior.
- There are substantial differences among conceptual models.
- Measurement of emotions and behavior is imprecise.
- Emotional or behavioral disorders often overlap with other disabilities.
- Professionals who diagnose and serve children and youths often disagree.

Consider each of these problems in turn. Mental health and normal behavior have been hard to define precisely. It is no wonder, then, that the definition of emotional or behavioral disorder presents a special challenge. Conceptual models—assumptions or theories about why people behave as they do and what we should do about it—may offer conflicting ideas about just what the problem is (Kauffman, 2005a, 2005b). Measurement is basic to any definition, and emotions and behavior—the disorders, in this case—are notoriously difficult to measure precisely. Emotional or behavioral disorders tend to overlap a great deal with other disabilities, especially learning disabilities and mental retardation. Finally, each professional group has its own reasons for serving individuals with emotional or behavioral disorders. For example, clinical psychologists, school psychologists, social workers, teachers, and juvenile justice authorities all have their particular concerns and language. Differences in the focuses of different professions tend to produce differences in definition as well (Cullinan, 2002, 2004; Forness & Kavale, 1997; Kauffman, 2005a; Kavale et al., 2005).

CURRENT DEFINITIONS

Although the terminology that is used and the relative emphasis that is given to certain points vary considerably from one definition to another, it is possible to extract several common features of current definitions. There is general agreement that emotional or behavioral disorder refers to the following:

- Behavior that goes to an extreme—that is not just slightly different from the usual
- A problem that is chronic—one that does not quickly disappear
- Behavior that is unacceptable because of social or cultural expectations

The Federal Definition   In the federal rules and regulations governing the implementation of IDEA, the term *emotionally disturbed* is defined as follows:

i. The term means a condition exhibiting one or more of the following characteristics over a long period of time and to a marked extent, which adversely affects educational performance:
  A. An inability to learn that cannot be explained by intellectual, sensory, or health factors;
  B. An inability to build or maintain satisfactory relationships with peers and teachers;
  C. Inappropriate types of behavior or feelings under normal circumstances;
  D. A general pervasive mood of unhappiness or depression; or
  E. A tendency to develop physical symptoms or fears associated with personal or school problems.
ii. The term includes children who are schizophrenic. The term does not include children who are socially maladjusted unless it is determined that they are emotionally disturbed.

The federal definition is modeled after one proposed by Bower (1981), but his definition does not include the statements found in part (ii) of the federal definition. These inclusions and exclusions are, as Bower (1982) and Kauffman (2005a) point out, unnecessary. Bower's five criteria for emotional disturbance indicate that schizophrenic children must be included and that socially maladjusted children cannot be excluded. Furthermore, the clause *which adversely affects educational performance* makes interpretation of the definition impossible, unless the meaning of educational performance is clarified. Does educational performance refer only to academic achievement? If so, then children with other listed characteristics who achieve on grade level are excluded.

UNDERSTANDING THE STANDARDS AND PRINCIPLES Why has the federal definition of the term *emotionally disturbed* been widely criticized? *(CEC Knowledge and Skills Standards CC1K5 & BD1K1)*

Council for
Exceptional
Children

Developing objective criteria for defining emotional and behavioral disorders can be problematic, partly because feelings of unhappiness or anger are familiar—or "normal"—to all people.

The federal definition has been widely criticized, and the federal government has more than once mandated study of it. One of the most widely criticized and controversial aspects of the definition is its exclusion of children who are socially maladjusted but not emotionally disturbed. Strong moves have been made in some states and localities to interpret social maladjustment as **conduct disorder**—aggressive, disruptive, antisocial behavior. This is the most common type of problem exhibited by students who have been identified as having emotional or behavioral disorders. Cline (1990) notes that excluding students with conduct disorder is inconsistent with the history of IDEA. Moreover, the American Psychological Association and the CCBD have condemned this practice, which has no empirical basis (Costenbader & Buntaine, 1999; Kauffman, 2005a).

An Alternative to the Federal Definition The National Mental Health and Special Education Coalition proposed an alternative definition in 1990. The coalition's proposed definition is as follows:

i. The term emotional or behavioral disorder means a disability characterized by behavioral or emotional responses in school so different from appropriate age, cultural, or ethnic norms that they adversely affect educational performance. Educational performance includes academic, social, vocational, and personal skills. Such a disability:
  A. is more than a temporary, expected response to stressful events in the environment;
  B. is consistently exhibited in two different settings, at least one of which is school-related; and
  C. is unresponsive to direct intervention in general education, or the child's condition is such that general education interventions would be insufficient.
ii. Emotional and behavioral disorders can co-exist with other disabilities.
iii. This category may include children or youths with schizophrenic disorders, **affective disorder**, **anxiety disorder**, or other sustained disorders of conduct or adjustment when they adversely affect educational performance in accordance with section (i). (Forness & Knitzer, 1992, p. 13)

Advantages of the proposed definition over the federal definition include the following:

- It uses terminology that reflects current professional preferences and concern for minimizing stigma.
- It includes both disorders of emotions and disorders of behavior and recognizes that they may occur either separately or in combination.
- It is school-centered but acknowledges that disorders exhibited outside the school setting are also important.
- It is sensitive to ethnic and cultural differences.
- It does not include minor or transient problems or ordinary responses to stress.
- It acknowledges the importance of prereferral interventions but does not require slavish implementation of them in extreme cases.
- It acknowledges that children and youths can have multiple disabilities.
- It includes the full range of emotional or behavioral disorders of concern to mental health and special education professionals without arbitrary exclusions.

Classification

Because emotional or behavioral disorders are evidenced in many ways, it seems reasonable to expect that individuals could be grouped into subcategories according to the types of problems they have. Still, there is no universally accepted system for classifying emotional or behavioral disorders for special education.

Conduct disorder
A disorder characterized by overt, aggressive, disruptive behavior or covert antisocial acts such as stealing, lying, and fire setting; may include both overt and covert acts.

Affective disorder
A disorder of mood or emotional tone characterized by depression or elation.

Anxiety disorder
A disorder characterized by anxiety, fearfulness, and avoidance of ordinary activities because of anxiety or fear.

Psychiatric classification systems have been widely criticized for several decades. Those found in publications of the American Psychiatric Association have little meaning for teachers. Many psychologists and educators have recommended relying more on individual assessment of the child's behavior and situational factors than on the diagnostic classifications used by psychiatrists.

An alternative to psychiatric classifications is the use of statistical analyses of behavioral characteristics to establish dimensions of disordered behavior. Using sophisticated statistical procedures, researchers look for patterns of behavior that characterize children who have emotional or behavioral disorders. By using these methods, researchers have been able to derive descriptive categories that are less susceptible to bias and unreliability than the traditional psychiatric classifications are (Achenbach, 1985; Cullinan, 2004; Richardson, McGauhey, & Day, 1995).

Researchers have identified two broad, pervasive dimensions of disordered behavior: externalizing and internalizing. **Externalizing** behavior involves striking out against others (see Furlong, Morrison, & Jimerson, 2004). **Internalizing** behavior involves mental or emotional conflicts, such as depression and anxiety (see Gresham & Kern, 2004). Some researchers have found more specific disorders, but all of the more specific disorders can be located on these two primary dimensions.

Individuals may show behaviors characteristic of both dimensions; that is, the dimensions are not mutually exclusive. A child or youth might exhibit several behaviors associated with internalizing problems (e.g., short attention span, poor concentration) and several of those associated with externalizing problems as well (e.g., fighting, disruptive behavior, annoying others). Actually, **comorbidity**—the co-occurrence of two or more conditions in the same individual—is not unusual (Cullinan, 2004; Tankersley & Landrum, 1997). Few individuals with an emotional or behavioral disorder exhibit only one type of maladaptive behavior. The federal government estimates that about one third of children with emotional

Externalizing
Acting-out behavior; aggressive or disruptive behavior that is observable as behavior directed toward others.

Internalizing
Acting-in behavior; anxiety, fearfulness, withdrawal, and other indications of an individual's mood or internal state.

Comorbidity
Co-occurrence of two or more conditions in the same individual.

Researchers differentiate between the externalizing and internalizing dimensions of behavioral disorders, externalizing behavior referring to striking out against others, damaging property, and other disruptive actions.

or behavioral disorders have another disability as well (U.S. Department of Education, 2000).

Furthermore, children may exhibit characteristic types of behavior with varying degrees of intensity or severity. That is, either dimension of behavior may be exhibited to a greater or lesser extent; the range may be from normal to severely disordered. For example, an individual might have a severe conduct disorder, an externalizing problem defined by overt, aggressive, disruptive behavior or covert antisocial acts such as stealing, lying, and fire setting. Severe emotional or behavioral disorders include the extremes of any externalizing or internalizing problem. Individuals with **schizophrenia** have a severe disorder of thinking. They might believe that they are controlled by alien forces or might have other delusions or hallucinations. Typically, their emotions are inappropriate for the actual circumstances, and they tend to withdraw into their own private worlds. Childhood schizophrenia is a disorder that typically begins after a normal period of development during early childhood. It is distinguished from **autism** or **autistic spectrum** disorders, which we discuss in Chapter 12, in several ways:

1. Children with schizophrenia usually have delusions (bizarre ideas) and hallucinations (seeing or hearing imaginary things), whereas children with autism usually do not.
2. Children with schizophrenia tend to have psychotic episodes interspersed with periods of near-normal behavior, whereas children with autism tend to have more constant symptoms.
3. About 25 percent of children with autism have epileptic seizures, whereas children with schizophrenia seldom have seizures (Rutter & Schopler, 1987).

In summary, the most useful classifications of emotional or behavioral disorders describe behavioral dimensions. Dimensions described in the literature involve a wide range of externalizing and internalizing problems. The typical student with emotional or behavioral disorders has multiple problems (Cullinan, 2004; Gresham et al., 2001).

Schizophrenia
A disorder characterized by psychotic behavior manifested by loss of contact with reality, distorted thought processes, and abnormal perceptions.

Autism
A pervasive developmental disability characterized by extreme withdrawal, cognitive deficits, language disorders, self-stimulation, and onset before the age of 30 months.

Autistic spectrum disorder
A range of disorders characterized by symptoms of autism that can range from mild to severe.

Prevalence

Estimates of the prevalence of emotional or behavioral disorders in children and youths have varied tremendously because there has been no standard and reliable definition or screening instrument. For decades, the federal government estimated that 2 percent of the school-age population was emotionally disturbed. However, the government's estimate was extremely conservative. Credible studies in the United States and many other countries have consistently indicated that at least 6 to 10 percent of children and youths of school age exhibit serious and persistent emotional/behavioral problems (Kauffman, 2005a). However, only about 1 percent of schoolchildren in the United States are identified as emotionally disturbed for special education purposes. A report on children's mental health from the U.S. Surgeon General has also indicated that a very small percentage of children with serious emotional or behavioral disorders receive mental health services (U.S. Department of Health and Human Services, 2001).

The most common types of problems exhibited by students who are placed in special education for emotional or behavioral disorders are externalizing—that is, aggressive, acting-out, disruptive behavior. Boys outnumber girls in displaying these behaviors by a ratio of 5 to 1 or more. Overall, boys tend to exhibit more aggression and conduct disorder than girls do, although antisocial behavior in girls is an increasing concern (Furlong et al., 2004; Kazdin, 1997; Talbott & Callahan, 1997).

THE U.S. Surgeon General's 2001 report on children's mental health is found at **www. surgeongeneral.gov/topics/ cmh**

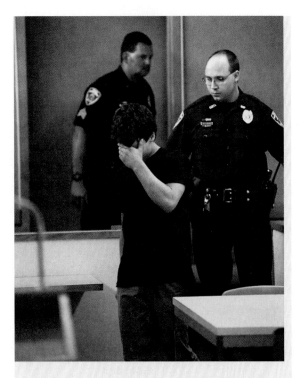

Viewpoints differ as to whether juvenile delinquent youths should automatically be considered to have emotional or behavioral disorders.

Juvenile delinquency and the antisocial behavior known as conduct disorder present particular problems in estimating prevalence. Delinquent youths constitute a considerable percentage of the population. About 3 percent of U.S. youths are referred to a juvenile court in any given year, a disproportionate number of whom are African American males (Miller, 1997). Many others engage in serious antisocial behavior but are not referred to the courts. One point of view is that all delinquent and antisocial youths should be thought of as having emotional or behavioral disorders. Some people argue that most youths who commit frequent antisocial acts are socially maladjusted, not emotionally disturbed. However, we cannot clearly distinguish social maladjustment from emotional disturbance.

Disabling conditions of various kinds are much more common among juvenile delinquents than among the general population (Nelson, Leone, & Rutherford, 2004; O'Mahony, 2005). Moreover, the social and economic costs of delinquency and antisocial behavior are enormous. Adolescent males account for a disproportionately high percentage of serious and violent crime in U.S. society. Those who exhibit serious antisocial behavior are at high risk for school failure as well as other negative outcomes (Walker et al., 2004; Walker, Forness, et al., 1998; Walker, Kavanaugh, Stiller, Golly, Severson, & Feil, 1998). If schools are to address the educational problems of delinquent and antisocial children and youths, then the number served by special education must increase dramatically.

Causes

UNDERSTANDING THE STANDARDS AND PRINCIPLES Briefly describe four major factors to which the causes of emotional or behavioral disorders have been attributed. *(CEC Knowledge and Skills Standards BD2K1)*

Council for Exceptional Children

The causes of emotional or behavioral disorders have been attributed to four major factors:

1. Biological disorders and diseases
2. Pathological family relationships
3. Undesirable experiences at school
4. Negative cultural influences

Although in the majority of cases, there is no conclusive empirical evidence that any of these factors is directly responsible for the disorder, some factors might give a child a predisposition to exhibit problem behavior, and others might precipitate or trigger it. That is, some factors, such as genetics, influence behavior over a long time and increase the likelihood that a given set of circumstances will trigger maladaptive responses. Other factors (such as observing one parent beating the other) might have a more immediate effect and might trigger maladaptive responses in an individual who is already predisposed to problem behavior.

Another concept that is important in all theories is the idea of contributing factors that heighten the risk of a disorder. It is extremely unusual to find a single cause that has led directly to a disorder. Usually, several factors together contribute to the development of a problem. In almost all cases, the question of what specifically has caused the disorder cannot be answered because no one really knows. However, we often do know the factors that place children at risk—the circumstances or conditions that increase the chances that a child will develop the disorder. Figure 8.2 illustrates how risk factors accumulate to place children and youths at risk for antisocial and violent behavior—often called conduct disorder—which is one of the most common and troubling emotional-behavioral problems of young people (see also Kazdin, 1997).

FOR A SITE with links to articles about children's health, including emotional and behavioral problems, see **www.mcleanhospital.org**

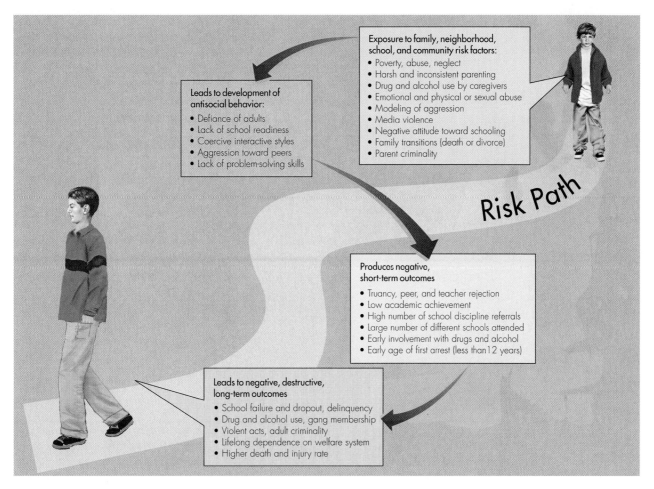

FIGURE 8.2 Risk pathway to antisocial and violent behavior. It reflects the effects of exposure to known risk factors and developmental outcomes.

Source: From Early identification and intervention for youth with antisocial and violent behavior by Jeffrey Sprague and Hill Walker. *Exceptional Children, 66,* 371. Copyright © by the Council of Exceptional Children. Reprinted with permission.

BIOLOGICAL FACTORS

Behaviors and emotions may be influenced by genetic, neurological, or biochemical factors or by combinations of these. Certainly, there is a relationship between body and behavior, and it would therefore seem reasonable to look for a biological causal factor of some kind for certain emotional or behavioral disorders (Cooper, 2005; Forness & Kavale, 2001). We do know, for example, that prenatal exposure to alcohol can contribute to many types of disability, including emotional or behavioral disorders. But only rarely is it possible to demonstrate a relationship between a specific biological factor and an emotional or behavioral disorder.

For most children with emotional or behavioral disorders, there simply is no real evidence that biological factors alone are at the root of their problems. For those with severe and profound disorders, however, there is evidence to suggest that biological factors may contribute to their conditions. Moreover, there is increasing evidence that medications are helpful in addressing the problems of many or most students with emotional or behavioral disorders if they receive state-of-the-art psychopharmacology (Konopasek & Forness, 2004).

All children are born with a biologically determined behavioral style, or temperament. Although children's inborn temperaments may be changed by the way they are reared,

Substance abuse may contribute to emotional and behavioral problems, but it is difficult to determine when or whether it is the direct cause.

Tourette's syndrome (TS)

A neurological disorder beginning in childhood (about three times more prevalent in boys than in girls) in which stereotyped, repetitive motor movements (tics) are accompanied by multiple vocal outbursts that may include grunting noises or socially inappropriate words or statements (e.g., swearing).

some people have long believed that children with so-called difficult temperaments are predisposed to develop emotional or behavioral disorders. There is no one-to-one relationship between temperament and disorders, however. A difficult child might be handled so well or a child with an easy temperament so poorly that the outcome will be quite different from what one would predict on the basis of initial behavioral style (Keogh, 2003). Other biological factors besides temperament—disease, malnutrition, and brain trauma, for example—can predispose children to develop emotional or behavioral problems. Substance abuse also can contribute to emotional and behavioral problems. Except in rare instances, it is not possible to determine that these factors are direct causes of problem behavior (see Kauffman, 2005a).

As biological and psychological research has become more sophisticated, it has become apparent that biological factors cause or set the stage for many disorders that formerly were widely assumed to be caused mostly or entirely by social interactions. Schizophrenia is the foremost example. Another is **Tourette's syndrome (TS)**, which is characterized by multiple motor tics (repetitive, stereotyped movements) and verbal tics (the individual makes strange noises or says inappropriate words or phrases). Although we now understand that schizophrenia, Tourette's syndrome, attention deficit/hyperactivity disorder (ADHD), some forms of depression, and many other disorders are caused wholly or partly by brain or biochemical dysfunctions, these biological causal factors remain poorly understood. That is, we do not know exactly how genetic, neurological, and other biochemical factors contribute to these disorders, nor do we know how to correct the biological problems that are involved in these disorders.

Four points are important to remember about biological causes:

1. The fact that disorders have biological causes does not mean that they are not emotional or behavioral disorders. An emotional or behavioral disorder can have a physical cause; the biological malfunction is a problem because of the disorder it creates in the individual's emotions or behavior.

2. Causes are seldom exclusively biological or psychological. Once a biological disorder occurs, it nearly always creates psychosocial problems that then also contribute to the emotional or behavioral disorder.

3. Biological or medical treatment of the disorder is seldom sufficient to resolve the problem. Medication may be of great benefit, but it is seldom the only intervention that is needed (Forness & Kavale, 2001; Forness, Kavale, Sweeney, & Crenshaw, 1999; Konopasek & Forness, 2004). The psychological and social aspects of the disorder must also be addressed.

4. Medical or biological approaches are sometimes of little or no benefit and the primary interventions are psychological or behavioral, even though the disorder is known to have primarily a biological cause. Medications do not work equally well for all cases, and for some disorders, no generally effective medications are known.

FAMILY FACTORS

Even in cases of severe emotional or behavioral disorders, it is not possible to find consistent and valid research findings that allow the blame for the children's problem behavior to be placed primarily on their parents (Kauffman, 2005a). Very good parents sometimes have children with very serious emotional or behavioral disorders, and incompetent, neglectful, or abusive parents sometimes have children with no significant emotional or behavioral disorders. The relationship between parenting and emotional or behavioral disorders is not simple, but some parenting practices are definitely better than others.

Sensitivity to children's needs, love-oriented methods of dealing with misbehavior, and positive reinforcement (attention and praise) for appropriate behavior unquestionably tend to promote desirable behavior in children. Parents who are generally lax in disciplining their children but are hostile, rejecting, cruel, and inconsistent in dealing with misbehavior are likely to have aggressive, delinquent children. Broken, disorganized homes in which the parents themselves have arrest records or are violent are particularly likely to foster delinquency and lack of social competence.

In the mid-1990s, Harris (1995) proposed a theory of group socialization, suggesting that the role of parents is minimal in the development of their children's personality or social behavior. Popularization of her theory led many laypeople to the conclusion that family environment has little influence on social development and that the child's peer group is the primary factor in socialization. Although socialization by peers is undeniably an important factor in the development of emotional or behavioral disorders, other research already cited indicates that parents and families can have a significant causal influence on some disorders.

Educators must be aware that most parents of youngsters with emotional or behavioral disorders want their children to behave more appropriately and will do anything they can to help them. These parents need support resources—not blame or criticism—for dealing with very difficult family circumstances. The Federation of Families for Children's Mental Health was organized in 1989 to help provide such support and resources, and parents are organizing in many localities to assist each other in finding additional resources (Jordan, Goldberg, & Goldberg, 1991). In the Personal Perspectives on page 258, one of the founding members shares her perspective on why parents are so often blamed for their children's emotional or behavioral disorders.

SCHOOL FACTORS

Some children already have emotional or behavioral disorders when they begin school; others develop such disorders during their school years, perhaps in part because of damaging experiences in the classroom itself. Children who exhibit disorders when they enter school may become better or worse according to how they are managed in the classroom (Furlong, Morrison, & Fisher, 2005; Walker, 1995; Walker et al., 2004). School experiences are no doubt of great importance to children, but as with biological and family factors, we cannot justify many statements about how such experiences contribute to the child's behavioral difficulties. A child's temperament and social competence can interact with the behaviors of classmates and teachers in contributing to emotional or behavioral problems.

There is a very real danger that a child who exhibits problem behavior will become trapped in a spiral of negative interactions, in which he or she becomes increasingly irritating to and irritated by teachers and peers. The school can contribute to the development of emotional problems in several rather specific ways. For instance, teachers might be insensitive to children's individuality, perhaps requiring a mindless conformity to rules and routines. Educators and parents alike might hold too high or too low expectations for the child's achievement or conduct, and they might communicate to the child who disappoints them that the child is inadequate or undesirable.

Discipline in the school might be too lax, too rigid, or inconsistent. Instruction might be offered in skills for which the child has no real or imagined use. The school environment might be such that the misbehaving child is rewarded with recognition and special attention (even if that attention is criticism or punishment), whereas the child who behaves properly is ignored. Finally, teachers and peers might be models of misconduct—the child might misbehave by imitating them (Farmer et al., 2001; Kauffman, 2005a; Kauffman, Mostert, Trent, & Pullen, 2006).

 THE HOME PAGE of the PACER (Parent Advocacy Coalition for Educational Rights) Center is **www.pacer.org**
For the Federation of Families for Children's Mental Health, see **www.ffcmh.org**

Personal Perspectives

FAMILY FACTORS

DIXIE JORDAN is the parent of a 19-year-old son with an emotional and behavioral disorder. She is director of the Families and Advocates Partnership for Education at the PACER Center in Minneapolis (a resource center for parents of children with disabilities) and a founding member of the Federation of Families for Children's Mental Health. She is also a Systems of Care coach for Four Directions Consulting.

Why do you think there is such a strong tendency to hold parents responsible for their children's emotional or behavioral disorders?

I am the parent of two children, the younger of which has emotional and behavioral problems. When my firstborn and I were out in public, strangers often commented on what a "good" mother I was, to have such an obedient, well-behaved, and compliant child. Frankly, I enjoyed the comments and really believed that those parents whose children were throwing tantrums and generally demolishing their environments were simply not very skilled in child-rearing. I recall casting my share of reproachful glances in those days and thinking with some arrogance that raising children should be left to those of us who knew how to do it well. Several years later, my second child and I were on the business end of such disdain, and it was a lesson in humility that I shall never forget. Very little that I had learned in the previous 3 three years as a parent worked with this child; he was neurologically different, hyperactive, inattentive, and noncompliant even when discipline was consistently applied. His doctors, his neurologist, and finally his teachers referred me to parenting classes, as though the experiences I had had with my older child were nonexistent; his elementary principal even said that there was nothing wrong that a good spanking wouldn't cure. I expected understanding that this was a very difficult child to raise, but the unspoken message was that I lacked competence in basic parenting skills, the same message that I sent to similarly situated parents just a few years earlier.

Most of us in the world today are parents. The majority of us have children who do not have emotional or behavioral problems. Everything in our experience suggests that when our children are successful and obedient, it is because of our parenting. We are reinforced socially for having a well-behaved child from friends, grandparents, even strangers. It makes sense, then, to attribute less desirable behaviors in children to the failure of their parents to provide appropriate guidance or to set firm limits. Many parents have internalized that sense of responsibility or blame for causing their child's emotional problems, even when they are not able to identify what they might have done wrong. It is a very difficult attitude to shake, especially when experts themselves cannot seem to agree on causation. With most children, the "cause" of an emotional or behavioral disorder is more likely a complex interplay of multiple factors than "parenting styles," "biology," or "environmental influences" as discrete entities, but it is human nature to latch onto a simple explanation—and inadequate parenting is, indeed, a simple explanation. When systems blame parents for causing their child's emotional or behavioral disorders, the focus is no longer on services to help the child learn better adaptive skills or appropriate behaviors, but on rationalizing why such services may not work. When parents feel blamed, their energies shift from focusing on the needs of their child to defending themselves. In either instance, the child is less well served.

Another reason that people hold parents responsible for their children's emotional or behavioral disorders is that parents may be under such unrelenting stress from trying to manage their child's behavior that they may resort to inappropriate techniques because of the failure of more conventional methods. A parent whose 8-year-old hyperactive child smashes out his bedroom window while being timed out for another problem may know that tying the child to a chair is not a good way to handle the crisis, but may be out of alternatives. It may not have been the "right" thing for the parent to do, but [he or she] is hardly responsible for causing the child's problems in the first place. It would be a mistake to attribute the incidence of abuse or neglect as "causing" most emotional or behavioral disorders without consideration that difficult children are perhaps more likely to be abused due to their noncompliant or otherwise difficult behaviors. ■

Source: Reprinted with the permission of Merrill Prentice Hall from *Characteristics of emotional and behavioral disorders of children and youth* (8th ed.), by James M. Kauffman. Copyright © 2005 by Pearson Education, Inc.

In considering how they might be contributing to disordered behavior, teachers must ask themselves questions about their academic instruction, expectations, and approaches to behavior management. Teachers must not assume blame for disordered behavior to which they are not contributing, yet it is equally important that teachers eliminate whatever contributions they might be making to their students' misconduct.

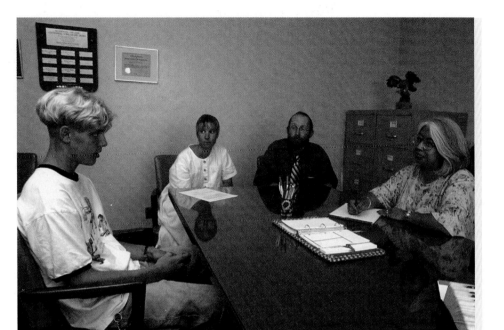

There is a danger that a child who exhibits problem behavior may become trapped in a spiral of negative interactions, resulting in worsening problems with teachers and peers.

CULTURAL FACTORS

Children, their families, and schools are embedded in cultures that influence them (Walker et al., 2004). Aside from family and school, many environmental conditions affect adults' expectations of children and children's expectations of themselves and their peers. Values and behavioral standards are communicated to children through a variety of cultural conditions, demands, prohibitions, and models. Several specific cultural influences come to mind: the level of violence in the media (especially television and motion pictures), the use of terror as a means of coercion, the availability of recreational drugs and the level of drug abuse, changing standards for sexual conduct, religious demands and restrictions on behavior, and the threat of nuclear accidents or war. Peers are another important source of cultural influence, particularly after the child enters the upper elementary grades (Farmer, 2000; Farmer et al., 2001).

Undoubtedly, the culture in which a child is reared influences his or her emotional, social, and behavioral development. Case studies of rapidly changing cultures bear this out. Other studies suggest cultural influences on anxiety, depression, and aggression. The level of violence depicted on television and in movies is almost certainly a contributing factor in the increasing level of violence in U.S. society (see Walker et al., 2004).

The changing cultural conditions in the United States might predispose children to develop emotional or behavioral disorders and a variety of other disabling conditions or to be mistakenly identified as having such disorders. Among these changes are increases in the number of children living in poverty and those being born to teenage mothers and to mothers who engage in substance abuse. At the same time, medical and social services available to poor children and their families have been cut substantially. In short, we are living in an era of enormous affluence for some Americans but also a period in which poverty and related problems continue to grow rapidly. Moreover, dramatic increases in the ethnic diversity of most communities might contribute to the mistaken identification of behavioral differences as behavioral disorders (see Osher, Cartledge, Oswald, Sutherland, Artiles, & Coutinho, 2004).

Abuse and other forms of extreme trauma are known to contribute significantly to the emotional or behavioral disorders of many children in our society today. Racial bias and discrimination are also known to be deeply embedded in our culture and to play a part in the disproportionate rate of imprisonment of African American males. Emphasis on imprisonment and punishment, especially for relatively minor offenses, combined with lack of economic and educational opportunities, appear to perpetuate if not exacerbate the harsh conditions of life that contribute to emotional or behavioral disorders and delinquency. Americans seem much more willing to pay for prisons than for schools (see Block & Weisz, 2004).

Clearly, cultural influences affect how children behave in school and whether they are identified as having emotional or behavioral disorders. But even when culture is considered as a cause, we must be aware of interactive effects. Schools and families influence culture; they are not simply products of it. Finally, refer back to Chapter 3 for a discussion of the importance of a multicultural perspective.

Identification

UNDERSTANDING THE STANDARDS AND PRINCIPLES What should teachers consider when screening students for emotional or behavioral problems? *(CEC Knowledge and Skills Standard CC8K3 & BD8K2)*

Council for Exceptional Children

It is much easier to identify disordered behaviors than it is to define and classify their types and causes. Most students with emotional or behavioral disorders do not escape the notice of their teachers. Occasionally, such students will not bother anyone and thus will be invisible, but it is usually easy for experienced teachers to tell when students need help. Teachers often fail to assess the strengths of students with emotional or behavioral disorders. However, it is important to include assessment of students' emotional and behavioral competencies, not just their weaknesses or deficits (Epstein & Sharma, 1997; Jones, Dohrn, & Dunn, 2004).

The most common type of emotional or behavioral disorder—conduct disorder, an externalizing problem—attracts immediate attention, so there is seldom any real problem in identification. Students with internalizing problems might be less obvious, but they are not difficult to recognize. Students with emotional or behavioral disorders are so readily identified by school personnel, in fact, that few schools bother to use systematic screening procedures. Also, the availability of special services for those with emotional or behavioral disorders lags far behind the need—and there is not much point in screening for problems when there are no services available to treat them. Children with schizophrenia are seldom mistaken for those who are developing normally. Their unusual language, mannerisms, and ways of relating to others soon become matters of concern to parents, teachers, and even many casual observers. Children with schizophrenia are a very small percentage of those with emotional or behavioral disorders, and problems in their identification are not usually encountered. However, they might first be identified as having another disorder, such as ADHD or depression, and later be diagnosed with schizophrenia.

Even so, do not conclude that there is never any question about whether a student has an emotional or behavioral disorder. The younger the child, the more difficult it is to judge whether his or her behavior signifies a serious problem. And some children's emotional or behavioral disorders are undetected because teachers are not sensitive to the children's problems or because they do not stand out sharply from other children in the environment who might have even more serious problems. Furthermore, even sensitive teachers sometimes make errors of judgment. Also keep in mind that some students with emotional or behavioral disorders do not exhibit problems at school.

Formal screening and accurate early identification for the purpose of planning educational intervention are complicated by

the problems of definition we have already discussed. In general, however, teachers' informal judgments have served as a reasonably valid and reliable means of screening students for emotional or behavioral problems (as compared with judgments of psychologists and psychiatrists). When more formal procedures are used, teachers' ratings of behavior have turned out to be quite accurate.

Walker and his colleagues have devised a screening system for use in elementary schools, based on the assumption that a teacher's judgment is a valid and cost-effective (though greatly underused) method of identifying children with emotional or behavioral disorders (Walker & Severson, 1990; Walker, Severson, & Feil, 1994; see also Walker, Ramsey, & Gresham, 2003–2004a; Walker et al., 2004). Although teachers tend to over-refer students who exhibit externalizing behavior problems (i.e., those with conduct disorders), they tend to underrefer students with internalizing problems (i.e., those characterized by anxiety and withdrawal). To make certain that children are not overlooked in screening but that time and effort are not wasted, a three-step process is used:

1. The teacher lists and ranks students with externalizing and internalizing problems. Those who best fit descriptions of students with externalizing problems and those who best fit descriptions of those with internalizing problems are listed in order from most like to least like the descriptions.

2. The teacher completes two checklists for the three highest-ranked pupils on each list. One checklist asks the teacher to indicate whether each pupil exhibited specific behaviors during the past month (such as "steals," "has tantrums," "uses obscene language or swears"). The other checklist requires the teacher to judge how often (never, sometimes, frequently) each pupil shows certain characteristics (e.g., "follows established classroom rules" or "cooperates with peers in group activities or situations").

3. Pupils whose scores on these checklists exceed established norms are observed in the classroom and on the playground by a school professional other than the classroom teacher (a school psychologist, counselor, or resource teacher). Classroom observations indicate the extent to which the pupil meets academic expectations; playground observations assess the quality and nature of social behavior. These direct observations of behavior, in

A teacher's judgment is a valid and cost-effective method of identifying children with emotional or behavioral disorders.

addition to teachers' ratings, are then used to decide whether the child has problems that warrant classification for special education. Such carefully researched screening systems can lead to improved services for children with emotional or behavioral disorders. Systematic efforts to base identification on teachers' judgments and careful observation should result in services being directed to those students who are most clearly in need.

PSYCHOLOGICAL AND BEHAVIORAL CHARACTERISTICS

Describing the characteristics of children and youths with emotional or behavioral disorders is an extraordinary challenge because disorders of emotions and behaviors are extremely varied. Remember that individuals may vary markedly in intelligence, achievement, life circumstances, and emotional and behavioral characteristics.

Intelligence and Achievement   The idea that children and youths with emotional or behavioral disorders tend to be particularly bright is a myth. Research clearly shows that the average student with an emotional or behavioral disorder has an IQ in the dull-normal range (around 90) and that relatively few score above the bright-normal range. Compared to the normal distribution of intelligence, more children with emotional or behavioral disorders fall into the ranges of slow learner and mild mental retardation. On the basis of a review of the research on the intelligence of students with emotional or behavioral disorders, Kauffman (2005a) hypothesized distributions of intelligence as shown in Figure 8.3.

Of course, we have been referring to children with emotional or behavioral disorders as a group. Some children who have emotional or behavioral disorders are extremely bright and score very high on intelligence tests. We caution, too, that intensive early behavioral intervention may reveal cognitive abilities that have not been apparent.

There are pitfalls in assessing the intellectual characteristics of a group of children by examining the distribution of their IQs. Intelligence tests are not perfect instruments for measuring what we mean by intelligence, and it can be argued that emotional or behavioral difficulties might prevent children from scoring as high as they are capable of scoring. Still, the lower-than-normal IQs for these students do indicate lower ability to perform tasks that other students perform successfully, and the lower scores are consistent with impairment in other areas of functioning (e.g., academic achievement and social skills). IQ is a relatively good predictor of how far a student will progress academically and socially, even in cases of severe disorders.

Most students with emotional or behavioral disorders are also underachievers at school, as measured by standardized tests (Kauffman, 2005a). A student with an emotional or behavioral disorder does not usually achieve at the level expected for his or her mental age; seldom are such students academically advanced. In fact, many students with severe disorders lack basic reading and arithmetic skills, and the few who seem to be competent in reading or math are often unable to apply their skills to everyday problems.

FIGURE 8.3 Hypothetical frequency distribution of IQ for students with emotional or behavioral disorders as compared to a normal frequency distribution.

Source: Reprinted with the permission of Prentice-Hall Publishing Company from *Characteristics of emotional and behavioral disorders of children and youth* (8th ed.) by James M. Kauffman. Copyright © 2005 by Prentice-Hall Publishing Company.

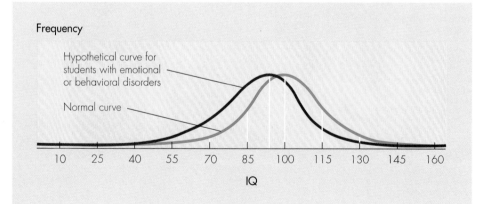

Social and Emotional Characteristics   Previously, we described two major dimensions of disordered behavior based on analyses of behavior ratings: externalizing and internalizing. The externalizing dimension is characterized by aggressive, acting-out behavior; the internalizing dimension is characterized by anxious, withdrawn behavior and depression. Our discussion here focuses on these two types.

A given student might, at different times, show both aggressive and withdrawn or depressed behaviors. Remember that most students with emotional or behavioral disorders have multiple problems (Tankersley & Landrum, 1997; Walker et al., 2004). At the beginning of this chapter, we said that most students with emotional or behavioral disorders are not well liked or identify with deviant peers. Studies of the social status of students in regular elementary and secondary classrooms indicate that those who are identified as having emotional or behavioral disorders may be socially rejected. Early peer rejection and aggressive behavior place a child at high risk for later social and emotional problems (Ialongo et al., 1998). Many aggressive students who are not rejected affiliate primarily with others who are aggressive (Farmer, 2000; Farmer et al., 1999, 2001). The relationship between emotional or behavioral disorders and communication disorders is increasingly clear (Rogers-Adkinson & Griffith, 1999). Many children and youths with emotional or behavioral disorders have great difficulty in understanding and using language in social circumstances. Read about Chrissy, the middle school student with emotional or behavioral disorders described in the Success Stories on page 264. She has great difficulty understanding language. Her teachers focused on positive behavioral supports and increasing her vocabulary to help improve her social skills.

Aggressive, Acting-Out Behavior (Externalizing)   As we noted earlier, conduct disorder is the most common problem exhibited by students with emotional or behavioral disorders. Hitting, fighting, teasing, yelling, refusing to comply with requests, crying, destructiveness, vandalism, extortion—these behaviors, if exhibited often, are very likely to earn a child or youth the label "disturbed." Normal children cry, scream, hit, fight, become negative, and do almost everything else children with emotional or behavioral disorders do, but not as impulsively and not as often. Youngsters of the type we are discussing here drive adults to distraction. These youths are not popular with their peers either, unless they are socialized delinquents who do not offend their delinquent friends. They typically do not respond quickly and positively to well-meaning adults who care about them and try to be helpful. The Responsive Instruction on page 266 provides strategies for classroom teachers who deal with students with oppositional and defiant behavior.

Some of these students are considered to have attention deficit/hyperactivity disorder or brain injury. Their behavior not only is extremely troublesome, but also appears to be resistant to change through typical discipline. Often, these children are so frequently scolded and disciplined that punishment means little or nothing to them. Because of adult exasperation and their own deviousness, these youths get away with misbehavior a lot of the time. These are children who behave horribly not once in a while, but so often that the people they must live with or be with cannot stand them. Of course, aggressive, acting-out children typically cannot stand the people they have to live and be with either, and often for good reason. Such children are screamed at, criticized, and punished a lot. The problem, then, is not just the individual children's behavior. What must be examined if the child or anyone else is to be helped is the interaction between the child's behavior and the behavior of other people in her or his environment (Walker, Kavanagh, et al., 1998).

Aggression has been analyzed from many viewpoints. The analyses that have the strongest support in empirical research are those of social learning theorists, such as Bandura (1973, 1986), and behavioral psychologists, such as Colvin, Patterson, and others, (Colvin, 2004; Patterson et al., 1992; Walker et al., 2004). Their studies take into account the child's experience and his or her motivation, based on the anticipated consequences of aggression. In brief, they view aggression as learned behavior and assume that it is possible to identify the conditions under which it will be learned.

UNDERSTANDING THE STANDARDS AND PRINCIPLES   What do we know about the social characteristics of individuals with emotional or behavioral disorders? *(CEC Knowledge and Skills Standard BD2K3)*

 Council for Exceptional Children

 **FOR MORE INFORMATION** about antisocial children and youth and their management, see **www.oslc.org**

Aggression
Behavior that intentionally causes others harm or that elicits escape or avoidance responses from others.

Special Educators at Work

Chrissy: "I've called you to my office because you are a star!"
Fourteen-year-old Christina Isaacs attends a special public middle school program for students with emotional and behavioral disorders. These are the keys to her success:
- *Intensive instruction in social skills and academics*
- *Relentless positive behavioral support*
- *Specific interventions for academic achievement, reducing reliance on adults, building friendships, and increasing her self-confidence*

Special educator and school principal Teresa Zutter praised eighth grader Chrissy Isaacs for making progress toward her annual goals. Chrissy is included daily in general classes for physical education and teen life, and she sings every afternoon with the middle school chorus. "I want to do well in regular classes because I want to be a cheerleader and get a regular high school diploma," she says with pride. Chrissy started seventh grade as a girl in distress—physically frail and frightened—but she prospered from intensive, relentless, and specific special education.

Intensive Instruction: Social Skills and Academics The Herndon Center serves sixty students in grades seven and eight with emotional and behavioral disorders. These students need close attention, and the program offers a small student–teacher ratio. In addition to Zutter, there are thirteen teachers and a psychologist, a social worker, a guidance counselor, a health awareness monitor, and a conflict resolution teacher. Weekly clinical staff meetings address students' needs and provide a forum for educators and support staff to discuss problems. "This

is such a spirited staff," says Zutter. "We laugh a lot and take care of each other."

Each classroom is equipped with a hot-line telephone connected to the main office. A carpeted quiet room serves as a time-out area for angry students. Zutter works closely with parents, alerting them to misbehaviors and sometimes calling them to take their sons or daughters home. Rules and policies are clear for students, teachers, and families. Gaining trust is critical. For these students, "there is an absolute need for structure and for individualization," says Zutter. "We have so many people here to help and to talk to students that no one has to hit to communicate."

Relentless Positive Behavioral Support: Coping with Stress The center's treatment model assumes that students thrive on positive reinforcement. Nonphysical punishment is used on occasion, but only to the degree necessary, and students are taught mechanisms to cope with their anxieties. "Girls and boys who are stressed can be made to feel better," says Zutter. "They are not just ED for a while but have entrenched be-

Children learn many aggressive behaviors by observing parents, siblings, playmates, and people portrayed on television and in movies. Individuals who model aggression are more likely to be imitated if they are high in social status and are observed to receive rewards and escape punishment for their aggression, especially if they experience no unpleasant consequences or obtain rewards by overcoming their victims. If children are placed in unpleasant situations and they cannot escape from the unpleasantness or obtain rewards except by aggression, they are more likely to be aggressive, especially if this behavior is tolerated or encouraged by others. Aggression is encouraged by external rewards (social status, power, suffering of the victim, obtaining desired items), vicarious rewards (seeing others obtain desirable consequences for their aggression), and self-reinforcement (self-congratulation or enhancement of self-image). If children can justify aggression in their own minds (by comparison to the behaviors of others or by dehumanizing their victims),

haviors; it's a life struggle. They won't be okay without interventions and without being taught how to cope with stress."

Chrissy is a good example. When she started seventh grade, she was out of touch with reality, staring at her own reflection whenever she could and slipping into the protection of fantasy. She was socially awkward and needed to learn how to act in various situations. When she was lost in her own thoughts, she would throw tantrums or provoke fights without seeing the impact her behaviors had on her relationships. She was also becoming oppositional.

As long as she is confronted gently and is not embarrassed in front of other students, Chrissy is responsive to correction. She takes pride in her appearance and musical talents. Socially, she tries to be everybody's friend, but peers are still afraid of her erratic and aggressive behaviors. "Chrissy tends to be overly sensitive to what others are saying, whether it relates to her or not," says her mother. When she is angry, Chrissy resorts to profanity and physical threats. This year she managed to develop some stable and cherished friendships with a few girls.

Specific Interventions: Vocabulary Development, Increased Adult Attention, and Homework Accommodations

Chrissy started seventh grade below grade level in most areas. She could decode words, but she couldn't comprehend what she read. She couldn't organize her thoughts. With frequent reassurance and lots of help to stay on task, Chrissy made gains and performed at grade level in all classes by the end of the year. Speech therapy helped Chrissy to develop vocabulary and use words with multiple meanings, like those in the jokes and riddles she couldn't understand. Accommodations included extra adult attention, additional time to complete class work and tests, shortened assignments, peer/work helpers, and directions stated several times. Although she daydreamed, Chrissy was willing to work hard and to focus when she was provided with support. She is now described as a conscientious student who worries about the quality of her work. According to Zutter,

"Chrissy will always have some difficulties, but with help, she can be eased from her world of fantasy. Hopefully, she'll value herself and stay in reality."

CEC'S STANDARDS: PAVING THE WAY TO SUCCESS

ASSESS YOUR STEPS TO SUCCESS in meeting the CEC Knowledge and Skill Base for All Beginning Special Education Teachers of Students with Emotional and Behavioral Disorders. Use the following questions to reflect on the growth of your own professional knowledge, skills, and dispositions.

REFLECTING ON YOUR OWN PROFESSIONAL DEVELOPMENT:

If you were Chrissy's teacher . . .

- WHAT are some areas about educating students with emotional and behavior disorders that you would need to know more about?
- WHAT are some specific skills that would help you address her academic and behavioral challenges?
- WHAT personal dispositions do you think are most important for you to develop in teaching students with challenging behaviors?

Using the CEC Standards

- WHAT are some functional classroom designs for students with emotional/behavioral disorders? (BD5K2)
- HOW would you identify realistic expectations for Chrissy's personal and social behavior in various settings? (CC5S2)
- WHAT are some professional organizations relevant to the field of emotional/behavioral disorders and how could you participate in their activities? (BD91, BD9S1) ■

By Jean Crockett

---

they are more likely to be aggressive. Punishment can actually increase aggression under some circumstances: when it is inconsistent or delayed, when there is no positive alternative to the punished behavior, when it provides an example of aggression, or when counterattack against the punisher seems likely to be successful.

Teaching aggressive children to be less so is no simple matter, but social learning theory and behavioral research do provide some general guidelines. In general, research does not support the notion that it is wise to let children act out their aggression freely. The most helpful techniques include providing examples (models) of nonaggressive responses to aggression-provoking circumstances, helping the child rehearse or role-play nonaggressive behavior, providing reinforcement for nonaggressive behavior, preventing the child from obtaining positive consequences for aggression, and punishing aggression in ways that involve as little counteraggression as possible (e.g., using time-out or brief social isolation

Meeting the Needs of Students with Emotional or Behavioral Disorders

Strategies for Students with Oppositional Defiant Disorder

UNDERSTANDING ODD

Some children continually act out in specifically defiant ways, such as willfully disobeying an adult's request or blaming others for their poor decision making. Often these children are angry and have a difficult time making friends or receiving positive regard from adults. Such behaviors are associated with the psychological category of oppositional defiant disorder (ODD) (American Psychiatric Association, 1994). Obviously, the acting out (externalizing) behaviors associated with ODD place children in a position to have difficulty in school, and many of these children would be considered to have a behavioral disorder.

To be diagnosed with ODD, children must exhibit at least four of the following behaviors for at least six months: "often loses temper, often argues with adults, often actively defies or refuses to comply with adults' request or rules, often deliberately annoys people, often blames others for his or her mistakes or misbehavior, is often touchy or easily annoyed by others, is often angry and resentful, and is often spiteful or vindictive" (Knowlton, 1995, p. 6). It is important for teachers to recognize that all children will go through periods of defiance in the natural course of development. What differentiates children with ODD from their typically developing peers is the persistent nature of the opposition. Many children will experiment with being defiant—having a temper tantrum in response to an undesirable situation or choosing not to comply with an adult request. These children eventually abandon the disobedience with more adaptive strategies for getting their needs met (Knowlton, 1995). Children with ODD, on the other hand, continue to use maladaptive responses with adults and their peers even though it leads to alienation and rejection.

BEHAVIOR MANAGEMENT AND ODD

Ironically, many of the behavior management strategies that a teacher would employ with most students do not meet the unique needs of students with ODD. One of the most effective behavior management techniques, positive reinforcement, is one such strategy that can have the opposite effect on students with ODD. The following story illustrates this:

> Billy has always had problems walking down the hall. . . . he continually pulls down papers or pictures that other classes have displayed on the walls. Even though he has received several verbal reminders from me and the principal and has as a consequence spent some recess time inside, he continues to exhibit this behavior. On this particular day . . . [w]e walked all the way to the gym without Billy pulling down a single picture. . . . I turned to the group and said to Billy that I was very proud of him. . . . Billy immediately ran to the closest wall and pulled down several pictures. (Knowlton, 1995, pp. 7–8)

CLASSROOM SUGGESTIONS

As you can see from this example, Billy's desire not to be controlled and to do the opposite of what was expected resulted in positive reinforcement failing. Thus, interventions with students who are oppositional must take into consideration the primary response system for ODD students: public opposition. Knowlton (1995) suggests these indirect reinforcement techniques when working with oppositional students:

1. The "walk-by" reinforcement: A brief positive comment or tap as the teacher walks by. This minimizes the need for the student to publicly respond and reduces the chance of the student negatively engaging the teacher.
2. Whispering: Providing the student with a private, positive message gives the student the opportunity not to respond.
3. Leaving notes: Similar to the other strategies, leaving a note in the student's desk reduces the likelihood of getting a negative response from the student.
4. Providing rewards: Like all indirect methods, rewards can be delivered but should be done without any amplification or excessive praise. Responses that are delivered in a matter-of-fact manner can remove the emotion that an oppositional student desires.

Other suggestions include avoiding arguing; reducing perceived teacher control through establishing standardized procedures; offering students choices; anticipating problems; allowing appropriate outlets for anger such as physical, noncompetitive activities; clearly identifying consequences; and providing counseling support from a therapist or trained counselor. The goal of all of these strategies is to retrain the student's negative pattern of interacting so that someday traditional positive reinforcement is just that—positive. ∎

By Kristin Sayeski

Children who act out aggressively or impulsively with frequent negative confrontations often are not well liked by their peers.

rather than spanking or yelling) (Colvin, 2004; Walker et al., 2003–2004b, 2004). The Responsive Instruction box on page 269 provides a description of a schoolwide strategy to reduce aggression.

The seriousness of children's aggressive, acting-out behavior should not be underestimated. It was believed for decades that although these children cause a lot of trouble, they are not as seriously disabled as are children who are shy and anxious. Research has exploded this myth. When combined with school failure, aggressive, antisocial behavior in childhood generally means a gloomy future in terms of social adjustment and mental health, especially for boys (Ialongo et al., 1998). Shy, anxious children are much more likely to be able to get and hold jobs, overcome their emotional problems, and stay out of jails and mental hospitals than are adults who had conduct problems and were delinquent as children (see Kazdin, 1995). Of course, there are exceptions to the rule. Nonetheless, there is a high probability that the aggressive child who is a failure in school will become more of a social misfit as an adult than will the withdrawn child. When we consider that conduct disorders and delinquency are highly correlated with school failure, the importance of meeting the needs of acting-out and underachieving children is obvious (Kauffman, 2005a; Walker et al., 2004).

Immature, Withdrawn Behavior and Depression (Internalizing)
In noting the seriousness of aggressive, acting-out behavior, we do not intend to downplay the disabling nature of immaturity and withdrawal or depression. Such disorders not only have serious consequences for individuals in their childhood years, but also carry a very poor prognosis for adult mental health. The child whose behavior fits a pattern of extreme immaturity and withdrawal or depression cannot develop the close and satisfying human relationships that characterize normal development. Such a child will find it difficult to meet the pressures and demands of everyday life. The school environment is the one in which

Casebook Reflection

Refer to the case *How Did We Miss Jack All These Years?* in your booklet. Jack's situation is very sad because of the problems in his family and with his brother. Jack seems to be internalizing all of his problems. Should Jack have been identified as having a disability? If you think so, at what point in his school career do you think the disability could have been identified?

A particularly important aspect of immature, withdrawn behavior is depression, which has recently been recognized as a serious and widespread problem among children and adolescents.

anxious and withdrawn adolescents in particular experience the most distress (Masia, Klein, Storch, & Corda, 2001). All children exhibit immature behavior and act withdrawn or feel sad once in a while. Children who fit the withdrawn or depressed description, however, might be reluctant to interact with other people. They are often social isolates who have few friends, seldom play with children their own age, and lack the social skills necessary to have fun. Some retreat into fantasy or daydreaming; some develop fears that are completely out of proportion to the circumstances; some complain constantly of little aches and pains and let their supposed illnesses keep them from participating in normal activities; some regress to earlier stages of development and demand constant help and attention; and some become depressed for no apparent reason.

As in the case of aggressive, acting-out behavior, withdrawal and depression can be interpreted in many different ways. Proponents of the psychoanalytic approach are likely to see internal conflicts and unconscious motivations as the underlying causes. Behavioral psychologists tend to interpret such problems in terms of failures in social learning; this view is supported by more empirical research data than other views (Kauffman, 2005a). A social learning analysis attributes withdrawal and immaturity to an inadequate environment. Causal factors may include overrestrictive parental discipline, punishment for appropriate social responses, reward for isolated behavior, lack of opportunity to learn and practice social skills, and models (examples) of inappropriate behavior. Immature or withdrawn children can be taught the skills they lack by arranging opportunities for them to learn and practice appropriate responses, showing models engaging in appropriate behavior, and providing rewards for improved behavior.

A particularly important aspect of immature, withdrawn behavior is depression. Only recently have mental health workers and special educators begun to realize that depression is a widespread and serious problem among children and adolescents (Kaslow, Morris, & Rehm, 1997; Sheras, 2001). Today, the consensus of psychologists is that the nature of depression in children and youths is quite similar in many respects to that of depression in adults. The indications of depression include disturbances of mood or feelings, inability to think or concentrate, lack of motivation, and decreased physical well-being. A depressed child or youth might act sad, lonely, and apathetic; exhibit low self-esteem, excessive guilt, and pervasive pessimism; avoid tasks and social experiences; and/or have physical complaints or problems in sleeping, eating, or eliminating. Sometimes depression is accompanied by such problems as bed-wetting (nocturnal **enuresis**), fecal soiling (**encopresis**), extreme fear of or refusal to go to school, failure in school, or talk of suicide or suicide attempts. Depression also frequently occurs in combination with conduct disorder (Kazdin, 1997).

Suicide increased dramatically during the 1970s and 1980s among young people between the ages of 15 and 24 and is now among the leading causes of death in this age group (Sheras, 2001). Depression, especially when severe and accompanied by a sense of hopelessness, is linked to suicide and suicide attempts. Therefore, it is important for all those who work with young people to be able to recognize the signs. Substance abuse is also a major problem among children and teenagers and may be related to depression.

Depression sometimes has a biological cause, and antidepressant medications have at times been successful in helping depressed children and youths to overcome their problems

Enuresis
Urinary incontinence; wetting oneself.

Encopresis
Bowel incontinence; soiling oneself.

Meeting the Needs of Students with Emotional or Behavioral Disorders

Approaches to Reducing Bullying in Schools

UNDERSTANDING BULLYING

Recent school tragedies directly or indirectly tied to bullying have resulted in increased attention on the part of administrators, teachers, and students to the issue of bullying in schools. One program recommended by researchers addresses bullying through involving key people who can help the aggressor learn more appropriate behaviors and help the victim learn options for responding. In addition to bringing all stakeholders together, the program addresses the issue from several vantage points (Garrity, Jens, Porter, Sager, & Short-Camilli, 1996, 2000).

A COMPREHENSIVE APPROACH TO REDUCING BULLYING

Garrity and colleagues' program involves the entire school (students, teachers, administrators, staff) as well as students' families. Staff members receive training in response procedures, and then teachers implement the program within their classes. A summary of this model follows.

Who Should Be Involved?

1. *Teachers and other staff members.* All school personnel need to be informed of standard procedures and be willing to act. Students, including both the bully and the victim, must know that teachers and staff will respond.
2. *The caring majority.* The caring majority are those students who neither bully nor are bullied. These students know the bullying is occurring but often do not know whether or how to respond.
3. *The bullies.* The bullies need to be addressed in ways that stop their aggression toward other students and direct their need for power into more prosocial directions.
4. *The victims.* Victims need protection and support, but they also need the social and interpersonal skills critical for seeking outside and internal support.
5. *Parents.* Parents should be made aware of school policies and procedures. Informed parents will feel more secure about sending their child to school and know the type of response that will occur when their child is either the bully or the victim.

What Is Involved?

1. *Staff training.* All school personnel are involved in staff training, including bus drivers, after-school workers, media specialists, and others. During staff training, faculty members learn about the different manifestations of bullying (e.g., physical aggression, name calling, gossiping, intimidating phone calls, verbal threats, and locking in confined spaces); explore ways to address both the victim and bully; role-play conflict resolution, particularly how to address the bully in a firm, no-nonsense manner; generate an antibullying curriculum, such as selecting literature on bullies and victims or creating skits or artwork with similar themes; and develop a comprehensive school plan for addressing instances of bullying.
2. *Classroom intervention.* Within the classroom, students are taught rules to eliminate bullying, strategies for reacting to bullying, and steps to follow if they see bullying occurring.

The following rules, strategies, and steps are recommended by Garrity and colleagues (1996, 2000):

a. Rules for Bully-Proofing Our Classroom:
   i. We will not bully other students.
   ii. We will help others who are being bullied by speaking out and by getting adult help.
   iii. We will use extra effort to include all students in activities at our school.
b. What I Can Do if I Am Being Bullied:
   i. HA = Help and assert
   ii. HA = Humor and avoid
   iii. SO = Self-talk and own it
c. What I Can Do if I See Someone Being Bullied:
   i. Creative problem solving
   ii. Adult help
   iii. Relate and join
   iv. Empathy

Finally, Garrity and colleagues suggest the following strategies for empowering victims: (1) Teach a repertoire of friendship-making skills, (2) develop an understanding that self-esteem affects friendships and how one handles bullying, and (3) teach skills that help victims to feel empowered and better able to handle bullies. ∎

By Kristin Sayeski

(Konopasek & Forness, 2004). In many cases, however, no biological cause can be found. Depression can also be caused by environmental or psychological factors, such as the death of a loved one, separation of one's parents, school failure, rejection by one's peers, or a chaotic and punitive home environment. Consider the boy's experience in the following account:

> One terrible morning at my house, my mother woke up next to my father, who had died in his sleep. It was Dec. 5, 1989, the day before my fourth birthday. . . .
>
> My dad's death hit us hard. My mother was left alone with two energetic little boys. She tried to be cheerful, but I knew she was crying every night, and I ached to be the man of the house. Within a few years, I had plunged into a massive depression. I didn't want to live. I couldn't get out of bed, and I stopped eating and playing. A couple of hospitalizations and a long recovery awaited me. (Godwin, 2004, p. C10).

Often, just having someone with whom to build a close relationship—in the case just described, a "big brother" volunteer—can be an important key in recovery from depression. Also, interventions based on social learning theory—instructing children and youths in social interaction skills and self-control techniques and teaching them to view themselves more positively, for example—have often been successful in such cases (Gresham & Kern, 2004).

Educational Considerations

Students with emotional or behavioral disorders typically have low grades and other unsatisfactory academic outcomes, have higher dropout rates and lower graduation rates than other student groups, and are often placed in highly restrictive settings. Moreover, these students are disproportionately from poor and ethnic-minority families and frequently encounter the juvenile justice system (Coutinho, Oswald, Best, & Forness, 2002; Oswald, Coutinho, Best, & Singh, 1999). Consequently, their successful education is among the most important and challenging tasks facing special education today (Landrum, Tankersley, & Kauffman, 2003). Finding a remedy for the disproportionate representation of ethnic minorities in programs for students with emotional or behavioral disorders is a critical issue. However, finding effective intervention strategies for diverse students is equally important (Ishii-Jordan, 2000; Landrum & Kauffman, 2003).

Unfortunately, there has never been a consensus among special educators about how to meet the challenge of educating students with emotional or behavioral disorders. Although a national agenda has been written for improving services to students with emotional or behavioral disorders, it is so vaguely worded that it is of little value in guiding the design of interventions (Kauffman & Landrum, 2006).

Several different conceptual models of education have been described over the decades (Kauffman & Landrum, 2006). A combination of models guides most educational programs today, so we do not describe them here (see Kauffman, 2005a, 2005b, for a description and case illustrations of models.) All credible conceptual models have two objectives: (1) controlling misbehavior and (2) teaching students the academic and social skills they need. They do not focus on one objective to the exclusion of the other. They also see the need for integrating all the educational, psychological, and social services these students require.

BALANCING BEHAVIORAL CONTROL WITH ACADEMIC AND SOCIAL LEARNING

Some writers have suggested that the quality of educational programs for students with emotional or behavioral disorders is often dismal. The focus is often said to be on external control of students' behavior, and academic instruction and social learning are too often secondary or almost entirely neglected (Kauffman, 2005a). Teachers might not have knowledge and skills in teaching basic skills such as reading (Coleman & Vaughn, 2000). Although the quality of instruction is undoubtedly low in too many programs, examples can be found of effective academic and social instruction for students at all levels (Kauffman, Bantz, & McCullough, 2002; Peacock Hill Working Group, 1991; Walker, Forness, et al., 1998).

Behavioral control strategies are an essential part of educational programs for students with externalizing problems (Colvin, 2004). Without effective means of controlling disruptive behavior, it's extremely unlikely that academic and social learning will occur. Excellent academic instruction will certainly reduce many behavior problems as well as teach important academic skills (Falk & Wehby, 2001; Kauffman et al., 2006; Stein & Davis, 2000; Sutherland & Wehby, 2001). Nevertheless, even the best instructional programs will not eliminate the disruptive behaviors of all students. Teachers of students with emotional or behavioral disorders must have effective control strategies, preferably involving students as much as possible in self-control. In addition, teachers must offer effective instruction in academic and social skills that will allow their students to live, learn, and work with others (Farmer et al., 2001; Walker et al., 2004). Teachers must also allow students to make all the choices they can—manageable choices that are appropriate for the individual student (Jolivette, Stichter, & McCormick, 2002; Kauffman et al., 2006). The Responsive Instruction on page 272 gives suggestions about ways to do this to reduce cursing.

IMPORTANCE OF INTEGRATED SERVICES

Children and youths with emotional or behavioral disorders tend to have multiple and complex needs. For most, life is coming apart in more ways than one. In addition to their problems in school, they typically have family problems and a variety of difficulties in the community (e.g., engaging in illegal activities, an absence of desirable relationships with peers and adults, substance abuse, difficulty finding and maintaining employment). Thus, children or youths with emotional or behavioral disorders might need, in addition to special education, a variety of family-oriented services, psychotherapy or counseling, community supervision, training related to employment, and so on. No single service agency can meet the needs of most of these children and youths, but it is clear that school plays an important role (Farmer & Farmer, 1999). Integrating these needed services into a more coordinated and effective effort is now seen as essential (Edgar & Siegel, 1995; Stein & Davis, 2000; Zanglis, Furlong, & Casas, 2000).

STRATEGIES THAT WORK

Regardless of the conceptual model that guides education, we can point to several effective strategies. Successful strategies at all levels, from early intervention through transition, balance concern for academic and social skills and provide integrated services. These strategies include the following elements (Peacock Hill Working Group, 1991; see also Walker, Forness, et al., 1998; Kauffman, 2005a):

- Systematic, data-based interventions—interventions that are applied systematically and consistently and that are based on reliable research data, not unsubstantiated theory
- Continuous assessment and monitoring of progress—direct, daily assessment of performance with planning based on this monitoring
- Provision for practice of new skills—skills are not taught in isolation but are applied directly in everyday situations through modeling, rehearsal, and guided practice
- Treatment matched to the problem—interventions that are designed to meet the needs of individual students and their particular life circumstances, not general formulas that ignore the nature, complexity, and severity of the problem
- Multicomponent treatment—as many different interventions as are necessary to meet the multiple needs of students (e.g., social skills training, academic

Meeting the Needs of Students with Emotional or Behavioral Disorders

Strategies for Reducing Cursing

Many students with emotional or behavioral disorders exhibit acting-out behaviors that may include cursing. Student cursing can range from the occasional outburst in reaction to a situation ("D———, I forgot my homework") to deliberate insults with a racial or cultural bias. For many teachers, any cursing is undesirable, but assaultive, insulting cursing is simply unacceptable. White and Koorland (1996) recommend twelve strategies for reducing cursing:

1. Avoid personalizing, accentuating, and reinforcing cursing when the misbehavior occurs. Respond to cursing in a matter-of-fact manner. This reduces the thrill associated with offending or shocking a teacher.

2. Teach students the differences among assaultive cursing, racial insults and slurs, lewd and sexually assaultive insults and slurs, and profanity and epithets. Explain to students that curses and insults are verbally assaultive and can be as harmful as physical assaults. Such verbal assaults should be dealt with more severely than the non-assaultive epithet (Ouch! D———!) or profanity (S———!).

3. Employ developmentally and culturally appropriate verbal or nonverbal reprimands for cursing to undermine shock value. Respond to students in an age-appropriate manner that does not invite comment or reaction from peers.

4. When teaching students about cursing and cursing control, use verbal or written approximations. Never use the actual curse.

5. Differentially reinforce less offensive profanity. Response positively to students when they depersonalize their cursing.

6. Differentially reinforce cursing by setting or place. Teach students that time and place do matter when cursing, and reinforce them when they choose not to curse in the classroom. This can be taught by telling students to go outside the building if they feel the need to curse.

7. Differentially reinforce lower rates of cursing. Making students aware of their rate of cursing, charting the cursing occurrences, and reinforcing them when the occurrences are reduced can lead to a reduction in, or elimination of, cursing.

8. Use response cost to decelerate cursing and token economies to reinforce appropriate verbalizations. Use a point or token system to provide rewards (earning points for not cursing) and punishments (loss of points for cursing).

9. Use more intensive aversives only if necessary and always in conjunction with a reinforcement program. If a student persists in cursing, an aversive such as time-out may be necessary.

10. Try self-mediated interventions. Students can self-record their occurrences of cursing and be rewarded for accurately monitoring and reducing or eliminating their cursing.

11. Implement group-contingent interventions. Students who are motivated by peer support would benefit from class rewards tied to individual or group reduction in cursing.

12. Use audiovisual recordings for reinforcement and reduction. Student cursing may decrease when a videocamera or audiotape is recording the class session. ◼

By Kristin Sayeski

remediation, medication, counseling or psychotherapy, and family treatment or parent training)

- Programming for transfer and maintenance—interventions designed to promote transfer of learning to new situations, recognizing that quick fixes nearly always fail to produce generalized change
- Commitment to sustained intervention—interventions designed with the realization that many emotional or behavioral disorders are developmental disabilities and will not be eliminated entirely or cured.

SERVICE DELIVERY

Only a relatively small percentage of children and youths with emotional or behavioral disorders are officially identified and receive any special education or mental health services.

Consequently, the individuals who do receive special education tend to have very serious problems, although most (along with those who have mild mental retardation or learning disabilities) have typically been assumed to have only mild disabilities. That is, the problems of the typical student with an emotional or behavioral disorder who is identified for special education are often more serious than many people have assumed. The term *severe* does not apply only to the disorders of autism and schizophrenia; a child can have a severe conduct disorder, for example, and its disabling effects can be extremely serious and persistent (Farmer et al., 2001; Kauffman, 2005a; Kazdin, 1997; Patterson et al., 1992).

Compared to students with most other disabilities, a higher percentage of students with emotional or behavioral disorders are educated outside regular classrooms and schools, probably in part because students with these disorders tend to have more serious problems before they are identified. Emotional or behavioral disorders include many different types of behavioral and emotional problems, which makes it hard to make generalizations about how programs are administered.

Trends Toward Inclusion Even so, the trend in programs for students with emotional or behavioral disorders is toward integration into regular schools and classrooms. Even when students are placed in separate schools and classes, educators hope for reintegration into the mainstream. Integration of these students is typically difficult and requires intensive work on a case-by-case basis (Fuchs, Fuchs, Fernstrom, & Hohn, 1991; Kauffman, Lloyd, Baker, & Riedel, 1995; Walker & Bullis, 1991). Furthermore, some educators, researchers, and parents have made the case that students with emotional and behavioral disorders who are at high risk for continued problems need the structure and support of a special class—that being in a separate class can be better than being included in a regular classroom (Farmer et al., 2001; Kauffman et al., 2006). The Making it Work on page 274 provides suggestions as to how teachers can collaborate to implement positive behavioral supports for students with emotional or behavioral disorders in the general education classroom.

Different Needs Require Different Placements Placement decisions for students with emotional or behavioral disorders are particularly problematic (Kauffman, Lloyd,

UNDERSTANDING THE STANDARDS AND PRINCIPLES Where are most students with emotional or behavioral disorders educated? How should placement decisions be made? *(CEC Knowledge and Skills Standards BD1K6 & BD5K1)*

Council for Exceptional Children

Including students with emotional and behavioral disorders in general education classrooms may sometimes be problematic since social interactions are a primary area of concern.

Collaboration and Co-Teaching of Students with Emotional and Behavioral Disorders:
"I Don't Want Him in My Classroom if He Can't Follow the Rules!"

Statewide standards to improve educational outcomes and policies of zero tolerance to increase the safety of public schools have placed increased pressure on all teachers. These two issues, combined with the fact that many general educators do not receive training in more than routine classroom management, often make a teacher hesitant to collaborate with special educators to include students with emotional/behavioral disorders, even though many students who create discipline problems are not identified as having a disability. The increase in disciplinary concerns in schools is actually a great reason for general educators to collaborate with teachers skilled in assessing and managing behavior.

WHAT DOES IT MEAN TO BE A TEACHER OF STUDENTS WITH EMOTIONAL AND BEHAVIORAL DISORDERS?

The expertise of a teacher of students with emotional and behavioral includes understanding, assessing, and managing behavior to promote learning across the content areas. Specifically, the Council for Exceptional Children (2001) has identified the following as those skills necessary for beginning teachers of students with emotional/behavioral disorders:

1. Know prevention and intervention strategies for individuals who are at risk of emotional and behavioral disorders.
2. Use a variety of nonaversive techniques to control targeted behavior and maintain attention of individuals with emotional and behavioral disorders.
3. Establish a consistent classroom routine, and use skills in problem solving and conflict resolution.
4. Plan and implement individualized reinforcement systems and environmental modifications at levels equal to the intensity of the behavior.
5. Integrate academic instruction, affective education, and behavior management for individuals and groups.
6. Assess appropriate and problematic social behaviors of individuals.

SUCCESSFUL STRATEGIES FOR CO-TEACHING

Recent research has validated the use of positive behavioral supports (PBS) for students with chronically challenging behaviors. Lewis (2000) identifies six steps in developing PBS plans for individual students in any classroom. These steps provide a unique opportunity for collaboration among general and special education faculty. Special and general educators can work together on each step to lighten the workload, provide different perspectives, and improve consistency.

The first step is to define the behavior operationally. Each teacher can provide feedback to the other to pinpoint exactly what the student is doing in the classroom, not just stating, "He's disruptive." Step 2 includes conducting a functional behavioral assessment (FBA). FBAs are time-consuming and include observing, analyzing, and hypothesizing about the behavior. Two (or more) teachers working together can observe the student at different times and in different situations, using both formalized and informal observation systems, without losing time with the rest of the class. They can also analyze data together to move to step 3: developing a hypothesis about why the student engages in the behavior. Step 4 is targeting a replacement behavior—What do the teachers want the student to do instead of the unwanted behavior? Teachers who know the student well then work together to identify this behavior, analyze it, and describe what skills the student has and does not have in order to set up a teaching scheme for this new behavior (step 5). Next, the teachers work together to teach the student the new behavior, reinforce it in the classroom, and verify that it is achieving the goals for both student and teachers. The last step is to modify the environment enough that the previous inappropriate behavior does not result in the same outcome. This can be the most difficult part and require the greatest amount of teamwork. The student will probably still try the old behavior. Teachers will hope to not see it again and can get discouraged if they do. It is at this point that teachers working together will need to support one another and to enlist other collaborators, such as administrators, parents, and other teachers, to keep the plan going. More information about positive behavioral supports is available at Office of Special Education Program's Technical Assistance Center on Positive Behavioral Interventions and Supports at www.pbis.org/english/index.html

■

By Margaret P. Weiss

Hallahan, & Astuto, 1995). Educators who serve students with the most severe emotional or behavioral disorders provide ample justification for specialized environments for these children and youths. That is, it is impossible to replicate in the context of a regular classroom in a neighborhood school the intensive, individualized, highly structured environments with very high adult–student ratios offered in special classes and facilities (see Brigham & Kauffman, 1998; Farmer et al., 2001; Kauffman et al., 2006; Kauffman & Hallenbeck, 1996).

Hence, it is extremely important that the full continuum of placement options be maintained for students with emotional or behavioral disorders and that placement decisions be made on an individual basis after an appropriate program of education and related services has been designed. Students must not be placed outside regular classrooms and schools unless their needs require it. The IDEA mandate of placement in the least restrictive environment applies to students with behavioral disorders as well as those in all other categories. In other words, they are to be taught in regular schools and classes and with their nondisabled peers to the extent that doing so is consistent with their appropriate education. However, students' needs for appropriate education and safety take priority over placement in a less restrictive environment (Bateman & Chard, 1995; Crockett & Kauffman, 1999).

INSTRUCTIONAL CONSIDERATIONS

Before being identified for special education, many students with emotional or behavioral disorders have been in regular classrooms where they could observe and learn from appropriate peer models. In reality, though, these students usually fail to imitate these models. They are unlikely to benefit merely from being with other students who have not been identified as disabled, as incidental social learning is insufficient to address their difficulties (Colvin, 2004; Hallenbeck & Kauffman, 1995; Kauffman & Pullen, 1996; Rhode, Jensen, & Reavis, 1992). For students with emotional or behavioral disorders to learn from peer models of appropriate behavior, most will require explicit, focused instruction about whom and what to imitate. In addition, they might need explicit and intensive instruction in social skills, including when, where, and how to exhibit specific types of behavior (Walker et al., 2004).

The academic curriculum for most students with emotional or behavioral disorders parallels that for most students. The basic academic skills have a great deal of survival value for any individual in society who is capable of learning them; failure to teach a student to read, write, and perform basic arithmetic deprives that student of any reasonable chance for successful adjustment to the everyday demands of life. Students who do not acquire academic skills that allow them to compete with their peers are likely to be socially rejected (Kauffman, 2005a; Walker, 1995).

Need for Social Skills   Students with emotional or behavioral disorders might need specific instruction in social skills as well. We emphasize two points: (1) Effective methods are needed to teach basic academic skills, and (2) social skills and affective experiences are as crucial as academic skills. How to manage one's feelings and behavior and how to get along with other people are essential features of the curriculum for many students with emotional or behavioral disorders. These children cannot be expected to learn such skills without instruction, for the ordinary processes of socialization obviously have failed (Walker et al., 2004). Enlisting the help of peers—including peers with emotional or behavioral disorders who have learned important social skills themselves—can be an effective strategy in some cases (Blake, Wang, Cartledge, & Gardner, 2000; Farmer et al., 2001; Presley & Hughes, 2000).

Students with schizophrenia and other major psychiatric disorders vary widely in the behaviors they exhibit and the learning problems they have. Some might need hospitalization and intensive treatment; others might remain at home and attend regular public schools. Again, the trend today is away from placement in institutions or special schools and toward inclusion in regular public schools. In some cases, students with major psychiatric disorders who attend regular schools are enrolled in special classes.

Needs of Juvenile Delinquents   Educational arrangements for juvenile delinquents are hard to describe in general terms because delinquency is a legal term, not an educational distinction, and because programs for extremely troubled youths vary so much among states and localities. Special classes or schools are sometimes provided for youths who have histories of threatening, violent, or disruptive behavior. Some of these classes and schools are administered under special education law, but others are not because the pupils assigned to them are not considered emotionally disturbed. In jails, reform schools, and other detention facilities that house children and adolescents, wide variation is found in educational practices. Education of incarcerated children and youths with learning disabilities is governed by the same laws that apply to those who are not incarcerated, but the laws are not always carefully implemented. Many incarcerated children do not receive assessment and education appropriate for their needs because of lack of resources, poor cooperation among agencies, and the attitude that delinquents and criminals are not entitled to the same educational opportunities as law-abiding citizens (Katsiyannis & Archwamety, 1999; Kauffman, 2005a; Nelson et al., 2004).

Special Challenges for Teachers   Given all this, it is clear that teachers of students with emotional or behavioral disorders must be able to tolerate a great deal of unpleasantness and rejection without becoming counteraggressive or withdrawn. Most of the students they teach are rejected by others. If kindness and concern were the only things required to help these students, they probably would not be considered to have disabilities. Teachers cannot expect caring and decency always to be returned. They must be sure of their own values and confident of their teaching and living skills. They must be able and willing to make wise choices for students who choose to behave unwisely (Kauffman, 2005a; Kauffman et al., 2006).

SPECIAL DISCIPLINARY CONSIDERATIONS

Disciplining is a controversial topic, especially for students with disabilities, as we discussed in Chapter 2. Many teachers and school administrators are confused about what is legal. Special rules do apply in some cases to students who have been identified as having dis-

Because delinquency is a legal term, not an educational distinction, educational arrangements for juvenile delinquents are not always well delineated.

abilities. In some instances, the typical school rules apply; in others, they do not under the 2004 reauthorization of IDEA. The issues are particularly controversial for students with emotional or behavioral disorders because, although their behavior might be severely problematic, the causes of their misbehavior are often difficult to determine.

Uncertainty or controversy usually involves a change in the student's placement or suspension or expulsion due to very serious misbehavior such as bringing a weapon or illegal drugs to school. The IDEA 2004 discipline provisions for students with disabilities are intended to maintain a safe school environment without violating the rights of students with disabilities to fair discipline, taking the effects of their disability into consideration.

In 2001, the reauthorization of the Elementary and Secondary Education Act (ESEA) allowed local school officials to discipline a student with disabilities just as they discipline students without disabilities when it comes to suspension and expulsion. ESEA does not require that schools suspend or expel children with disabilities as they would those without disabilities, but it does allow it. States and localities were given the option of following the IDEA rules and continuing the education of a student whose placement is changed to an alternative setting. IDEA 2004 also allows suspension and expulsion under some conditions.

Casebook Reflection

Refer to the case *What Do We Do With Jim?* in your booklet. Jim came off nine days of suspension from school. The administration believed that he would not do well in the self-contained class for SED with the "streetwise guy". The principal suggested placing him in the resource room with Frieda, who has her teaching credential in SED. In what ways was this action appropriate, and in what ways was it problematic?

Functional Behavioral Assessment and Positive Behavioral Supports   IDEA 2004, as well as 1997, calls for **functional behavioral assessment (FBA)** if the student's behavior is persistently a problem, but the meaning of *functional asessment* is not entirely clear in the context of the law. You might recall from Chapter 1 that FBA means that *educators attempt to determine and alter the factors that account for the student's misconduct.* Nevertheless, precisely what the law now requires of special educators and other school personnel is uncertain (Landrum, 2000; Mueller, Edwards, & Trahant, 2003; Sasso, Conroy, Stichter, & Fox, 2001; Sugai & Horner, 1999–2000). Apparently, the intent of the law is to require teachers to assess the student's behavior in ways that lead to the selection of effective intervention strategies.

There is now great emphasis on positive behavioral supports and behavior intervention plans for students with emotional and behavioral disorders. Increasingly, researchers recognize that problem behavior occurs less frequently in the classroom when the teacher is offering effective instruction (Kauffman et al., 2006).

Resources for positive behavior management are increasingly available on the World Wide Web. Many sites are being developed, and most provide links to other sites. Following are some that you might want to access:

- The National Center on Education, Disability and Juvenile Justice at www.edjj.org
- The Oregon Social Learning Center at www.oslc.org
- The Technical Assistance Center on Positive Behavioral Interventions and Supports at www.pbis.org

Functional behavioral assessment (FBA) The practice of determining the consequences (what purpose the behavior serves), antecedents (what triggers the behavior), and setting events (in what contexts the behavior occurs) of inappropriate behavior.

UNDERSTANDING THE STANDARDS AND PRINCIPLES   What should teachers know about assessment of behavior? *(CEC Knowledge and Skills Standards BD8S1 & BD8S2)*

Council for Exceptional Children

€arly Jntervention

Early identification and prevention are basic goals of intervention programs for any category of disability (Sprague & Walker, 2000). For students with emotional or behavioral disorders, these goals present particular difficulties—yet they also hold particular promise. The difficulties are related to the definition and measurement of emotional or behavioral disorders, especially in young children; the particular promise is that young children's social-emotional behavior is quite flexible, so preventive efforts seem to have a good chance of success (Kaiser, 2000; Kamps, Tankersley, & Ellis, 2000; Kauffman, 1999, 2005c).

INFORMATION about positive behavioral support and its role in schoolwide discipline and teaching may be obtained from **www.pbis.org**

The principal of Positive Behavioral Supports includes a recognition of the fact that problem behavior occurs less frequently in classrooms where teachers offer consistent, effective instruction.

As was mentioned previously, defining emotional or behavioral disorders in such a way that children can be reliably identified is a difficult task. Definition and identification involving preschool children are complicated by several additional factors:

1. The developmental tasks that young children are expected to achieve are much simpler than those that are expected of older children, so the range of normal behaviors to be used for comparison is quite restricted for young children. Infants and toddlers are expected to eat, sleep, perform relatively simple motor skills, and respond socially to their parents. School-age children, however, must learn much more varied and complex motor and cognitive skills and develop social relations with a variety of peers and adults.

2. There is wide variation in the child-rearing practices of good parents and in family expectations for preschool children's behavior in different cultures, so we must guard against inappropriate norms used for comparison. What is described as immature, withdrawn, or aggressive behavior in one family might not be perceived as such in another.

3. In the preschool years children's development is rapid and often uneven, making it difficult to judge what spontaneous improvements might occur.

4. The most severe types of emotional or behavioral disorders often are first observed in the preschool years. But it is frequently difficult to tell the difference between emotional or behavioral disorders and other conditions, such as mental retardation or deafness. Often, the first signs are difficulty with basic biological functions (e.g., eating, sleeping, or eliminating), inadequate social responses (e.g., problems responding positively to a parent's attempts to offer comfort or "molding" to the parent's body when being held), or delay in learning language. Difficulty with these basic areas or in achieving developmental milestones such as walking and talking indicate that the child might have an emotional or behavioral disability. But these difficulties might also be indicators of other conditions, such as mental retardation, sensory impairment, or physical disability. As Thomas and

Guskin remarked, "Diagnosis of disruptive behaviors in very young children is challenging because they appear to respond to a variety of risk factors with similar hyperactive, aggressive, and defiant behaviors (2001, p. 50).

The patterns of behavior that signal problems for the preschool child are those that bring them into frequent conflict with, or keep them aloof from, their parents or caretakers and their siblings or peers. Many children who are referred to clinics for disruptive behavior when they are seven to twelve years of age showed clear signs of behavior problems by the time they were three or four—or even younger (Loeber, Green, Lahey, Christ, & Frick, 1992; Shaw, Owens, Giovannelli, & Winslow, 2001; Walker et al., 2004). Infants or toddlers who exhibit a very "difficult temperament"—who are irritable; have irregular patterns of sleeping, eating, and eliminating; have highly intense responses to many stimuli and negative reactions toward new situations—are at risk for developing serious behavior problems unless their parents are particularly skillful at handling them. Children of preschool age are likely to elicit negative responses from adults and playmates if they are much more aggressive or much more withdrawn than most children their age. (Remember the critical importance of same-age comparisons. Toddlers frequently grab what they want, push other children down, and throw things and kick and scream when they don't get their way; toddlers normally do not have much finesse at social interaction and often hide from strangers.)

Because children's behavior is quite responsive to conditions in the social environment and can be shaped by adults, the potential for primary prevention—preventing serious behavior problems from occurring in the first place—would seem to be great. If parents and teachers could be taught effective child management skills, perhaps many or most cases could be prevented (Ialongo et al., 1998; Walker et al., 2004; Walker, Kavanagh, et al., 1998). Furthermore, one could imagine that if parents and teachers had such skills, children who already have emotional or behavioral disorders could be prevented from getting worse (secondary prevention). But as Bower (1981) notes, the task of primary prevention is not that simple. For one thing, the tremendous amount of money and personnel that

UNDERSTANDING THE STANDARDS AND PRINCIPLES What interventions might be effective for a preschooler who is exhibiting overly aggressive or withdrawn behavior? *(CEC Knowledge and Skills Standard BD4K4)*

Council for Exceptional Children

Preschool intervention for children with emotional or behavioral disorders has been quite effective in preventing or reducing subsequent problems. However, identifying these disorders between 3 and 5 years can be difficult.

are needed for training in child management are not available. For another, even if the money and personnel could be found, professionals would not always agree on what patterns of behavior should be prevented or on how undesirable behavior could be prevented from developing (Kauffman, 1999, 2005c; Kazdin, 1995).

If overly aggressive or withdrawn behavior has been identified in a preschooler, what kind of intervention program is most desirable? Behavioral interventions are highly effective (see Peacock Hill Working Group, 1991; Strain & Timm, 2001; Strain et al., 1992; Walker, Forness, et al., 1998; Walker et al., 2004). A behavioral approach implies defining and measuring the child's behaviors and rearranging the environment (especially adults' and other children's responses to the problem child) to teach and support more appropriate conduct. In the case of aggressive children, social rewards for aggression should be prevented. For example, hitting another child or throwing a temper tantrum might result in brief social isolation or time-out instead of adult attention or getting one's own way.

In summary, it is possible to identify at an early age those children who are at high risk for emotional or behavioral disorders (Farmer et al., 2001; Walker, Kavanagh, et al., 1998; Walker et al., 2004; Wehby, Dodge, & Valente, 1993). These children exhibit extreme aggression or social withdrawal and may be socially rejected or identify with deviant peers. They should be identified as early as possible, and their parents and teachers should learn how to teach them essential social skills and how to manage their problem behavior using positive, nonviolent procedures (see Kamps et al., 2000; Serna, Lambros, Nielsen, & Forness, 2000; Strain & Timm, 2001; Timm, 1993; Walker et al., 2004). If children with emotional or behavioral disorders are identified very early and intervention is sufficiently comprehensive, intense, and sustained, then there is a good chance that they can recover and exhibit developmentally normal patterns of behavior (Strain & Timm, 2001; Timm, 1993; Walker et al., 2004).

Nevertheless, research suggests that in practice, early intervention typically does not occur. In fact, intervention does usually not begin until the child has exhibited an extremely disabling pattern of behavior for several years (Duncan, Forness, & Hartsough, 1995). The primary reasons given as to why early, comprehensive, intense, and sustained intervention is so rare include worry about labeling and stigma, optimism regarding the child's development (i.e., the assumption that he or she will "grow out of it"), lack of resources required to address the needs of any but the most severely problematic children, and ignorance about the early signs of emotional or behavioral problems (Kauffman, 1999, 2004, 2005c).

Transition to Adulthood

The programs designed for adolescents with emotional or behavioral disorders have varied widely in aims and structure (Cheney & Bullis, 2004; Maag & Katsiyannis, 1998; Nelson et al., 2004). Nelson and Kauffman (1977) describe the following types, which remain the basic options today:

- Regular public high school classes
- Consultant teachers who work with regular teachers to provide individualized academic work and behavior management
- Resource rooms and special self-contained classes to which students may be assigned for part or all of the school day
- Work-study programs in which vocational education and job experience are combined with academic study
- Special private or public schools that offer the regular high school curriculum in a different setting
- Alternative schools that offer highly individualized programs that are nontraditional in both setting and content
- Private or public residential schools

UNDERSTANDING THE STANDARDS AND PRINCIPLES What do we know about transition to adulthood for students with emotional or behavioral disorders? *(CEC Knowledge and Skills Standards BD4K3 & BD10K1)*

 Council for Exceptional Children

Incarcerated youths with emotional or behavioral disorders are an especially neglected group in special education (Nelson et al., 2004). One suspects that the special educational needs of many (or most) of these teenagers who are in prison are neglected because incarcerated youths are defined as socially maladjusted rather than emotionally disturbed. The current federal definition appears to allow denial of special education services to a large number of young people who exhibit extremely serious misbehaviors and have long histories of school failure.

One of the reasons it is difficult to design special education programs at the secondary level for students with emotional or behavioral disorders is that this category of youths is so varied. Adolescents categorized for special education purposes as emotionally disturbed may have behavioral characteristics ranging from autisticlike withdrawal to aggressive delinquency, intelligence ranging from severely retarded to highly gifted, and academic skills ranging from preschool to college level. Therefore, it is hardly realistic to suggest that any single type of program or model will be appropriate for all such youths. In fact, youths with emotional or behavioral disorders, perhaps more than any other category of exceptionality, need a highly individualized, creative, and flexible education. Programs may range from teaching daily living skills in a sheltered environment to advanced placement in college, from regular class placement to hospitalization, and from the traditional curriculum to unusual and specialized vocational training.

FOR INFORMATION about juvenile justice and education, see **www.edjj.org**

Transition from school to work and adult life is particularly difficult for adolescents with emotional or behavioral disorders. Many of them lack the basic academic skills necessary for successful employment. In addition, they often behave in ways that prevent them from being accepted, liked, and helped by employers, coworkers, and neighbors. It is not surprising that students with emotional or behavioral disorders are among the most likely to drop out of school and among the most difficult to train in transition programs (Cheney & Bullis, 2004; Edgar & Siegel, 1995; Malmgren, Edgar, & Neel, 1998).

Many children and youths with emotional or behavioral disorders grow up to be adults who have real difficulties leading independent, productive lives. The outlook is especially grim for children and adolescents who have conduct disorders. Contrary to popular opinion, the child or youth who is shy, anxious, or neurotic is not the most likely to have psychiatric problems as an adult. Rather, it is the conduct-disordered (hyperaggressive) child or youth whose adulthood is most likely to be characterized by socially intolerable behavior and lack of social competence (Kazdin, 1995, 1997; Walker & Stieber, 1998; Walker et al., 2004). About half the children who are hyperaggressive will have problems that require legal intervention or psychiatric care when they are adults.

Successful transition to adult life is often complicated by neglectful, abusive, or inadequate family relationships. A high percentage of adolescents with conduct disorder have family relationships of this nature. However, the emphasis on punishment and imprisonment, particularly of African American males, appears to be counterproductive. The emphasis on punishment contributes to family deterioration and harsh conditions of life that perpetuate undesirable conduct (Miller, 1997).

Examples of relatively successful high school and transition programs are available, most of which employ a behavioral approach (Cheney & Bullis, 2004; Edgar & Siegel, 1995; Peacock Hill Working Group, 1991). However, it is important to stress the term *relatively* because many adolescents and young adults with severe conduct disorder appear to have a true developmental disability that requires intervention throughout their life span (Wolf, Braukmann, & Ramp, 1987). By the time these antisocial youths reach high school, the aim of even the most effective program is to help them accommodate their disabilities. Rather than focusing on remediation of academic and social skills, these programs attempt to teach youths the skills they will need to survive and cope in school and community, to make a transition to work, and to develop vocations (Walker et al., 2004). Well-planned alternative schools appear to offer important options to students at high risk, including those with emotional or behavioral problems (Duke, Griesdorn, & Kraft, 1998; Tobin & Sprague, 1999).

Summary

WHAT terminology is used to describe emotional and behavioral disorders?

- The current term in federal laws is *emotionally disturbed*.
- The terminology of various states and localities is varied and sometimes confusing; it includes a variety of combinations of terms such as *emotional disturbance, behavioral disorder,* and *social maladjustment.*

WHAT is the definition of emotional and behavioral disorder?

- Any definition generally refers to behavior that goes to an extreme, a problem that is chronic, and behavior that is unacceptable because of social or cultural expectations.
- The current federal definition lists five characteristics, any one of which must be exhibited to a marked extent and over a period of time and adversely affect educational performance:
  - Inability to learn
  - Inability to establish satisfactory relationships
  - Inappropriate behavior
  - Pervasive unhappiness or depression
  - Physical symptoms, pains, or fears
- The major points of the definition of the National Mental Health and Special Education Coalition are that the behavior:
  - Is more than a temporary, expected response to stressful events in the environment
  - Is consistently exhibited in two different settings, at least one of which is school
  - Is unresponsive to direct intervention in general education, or the child's condition is such that general education interventions would be insufficient.

HOW are emotional and behavioral disorders classified?

- Psychiatric classifications are not very useful to teachers.
- The most useful and reliable classifications are based on the primary dimensions of externalizing (acting against others) and internalizing (acting against self).

WHAT is the prevalence of emotional and behavioral disorders?

- Most studies suggest that 5–10 percent of the child population have such disorders.

- Special education and mental health serve only a fraction of those needing help for serious disorders (i.e., about 1 percent of the child population).

WHAT are the causes of emotional and behavioral disorders?

- Causes are multiple and complex, and seldom can a single cause be identified.
- Major causal factors include biology, family, school, and culture.

HOW are emotional and behavioral disorders identified?

- Teacher judgment plays the most significant role.
- Most students are below average in tested intelligence and academic achievement.
- Students exhibit externalizing (aggressive toward others) or internalizing (immature, withdrawn, depressed) behavior or a combination of the two.

WHAT are the major educational considerations regarding emotional and behavioral disorders?

- A balance between behavioral control and academic instruction is required.
- Integrated services are important.
- Strategies that work best include the following:
  - Systematic, data-based interventions
  - Continuous assessment and monitoring of progress
  - Provision for practice of new skills
  - Treatment matched to the problem
  - Multicomponent treatment
  - Programming for transfer and maintenance
  - Commitment to sustained intervention
- Service delivery emphasizes inclusion when appropriate and the importance of a full continuum of alternative placements.
- Instruction should be highly structured and relevant to the student's life.
- Special disciplinary considerations include functional behavioral assessment and positive behavioral support.
- Early intervention is often suggested but seldom practiced.
- Transition is difficult but particularly important because the long-term and employment outcomes for most students are not good.

APPLYING THE STANDARDS AND PRINCIPLES

- **ONE** of your colleagues, whose background is in general education, asks, **"What does it really mean to have an emotional or behavioral disorder?"** How would you respond? *(CEC Content Standard #1 & #2; INTASC Principle #1 & #2)*

- **HOW** should teachers determine what **instructional methods** to use with students with emotional or behavioral disorders? *(CEC Content Standard #4 & INTASC Principle #4)*

- **WHAT** is your opinion with respect to **where students with emotional or behavioral disorders**

should be taught? *(CEC Content Standard #5 & IN-TASC Principle #5)*

- **HOW** easy or difficult is it to **identify an emotional or behavioral disorder?** *(CEC Content Standard #8 & INTASC Principle #8)*

- **HOW** would you **respond to parents** who approached you expressing concern about the future of **their high school student** with an emotional or behavioral disorder? *(CEC Content Standard #4 & #10; INTASC Principle #4 & #10)*

Council for Exceptional Children

INTASC

Chapter 9

Learners with
Communication Disorders

*S*tutterers have a tendency to generalize their fear of one word that begins with a particular sound to a fear of all words that begin with the same sound. In the space of the summer I'd effectively eliminated every *F* from my vocabulary, with the exception of the preposition, "for," which for the time being was too small to incite terror. A few weeks later, my fear of *F* ended when another letter—I think it was *L*—suddenly loomed large.

David Shields
Dead Languages

QUESTIONS TO GUIDE YOUR READING OF THIS CHAPTER . . .

- HOW are communication disorders defined?

- WHAT is the prevalence of communication disorders?

- WHAT is the difference between communicative differences and disorders?

- WHAT are the major disorders of language?

- WHAT are the major disorders of speech?

- WHAT are the major features of assessment of communication disorders?

- WHAT are the main educational considerations for communication disorders?

- WHAT are the major aspects of early intervention for communication disorders?

- WHAT is emphasized in transition for students with communication disorders?

SPECIAL EDUCATORS . . .

- understand the similarities and differences in human development and the characteristics between and among individuals with and without exceptional learning needs *(from CEC Content Standard #2).*

- possess a repertoire of evidence-based instructional strategies to individualize instruction for individuals with exceptional learning needs *(from CEC Content Standard #4).*

- understand typical and atypical language development and the ways in which exceptional conditions can interact with an individual's experience with and use of language *(from CEC Content Standard #6).*

- develop a variety of individualized transition plans, such as transitions from preschool to elementary school and from secondary settings to a variety of postsecondary work and learning contexts *from CEC Content Standard #7).*

ALL TEACHERS . . .

- understand how children learn and develop and can provide learning opportunities that support the intellectual, social and personal development of each learner *(INTASC Principle #2).*

- understand and use a variety of instructional strategies to encourage students' development of critical thinking, problem solving, and performance skills students *(INTASC Principle #4).*

- plan instruction based on knowledge of subject matter, students, the community and curriculum goals *(INTASC Principle #7).*

Council for Exceptional Children

INTASC

Communication is such a natural part of our everyday lives that we seldom stop to think about it. Social conversation with families, friends, and casual acquaintances is normally so effortless and pleasant that it is hard to imagine having difficulty with it. Most of us have feelings of uncertainty about the adequacy of our speech or language only in stressful or unusual social situations, such as talking to a large audience or being interviewed for a job. If we always had to worry about communicating, we would worry about every social interaction we had.*

For some people, however, communication is not effortless and pleasant. Their communication may take great effort. For instance, some individuals have serious problems producing a sufficiently clear voice quality, described as a *voice disorder*, and other individuals are unable to comprehend the language that others produce, described as a receptive *language disorder*. The young man described on page 285 was unable to produce fluent speech, or speech of an appropriate rhythm and rate; this is a *fluency disorder*, or stuttering.

Not all communication disorders involve disorders of speech. Not all speech disorders are as handicapping in social interactions as stuttering, nor is stuttering the most common disorder of speech. Stuttering affects only about one person in twenty at any time in their lives, and only about one in a hundred people stutter throughout their lives. Most cases of childhood stuttering are resolved by adulthood (Owens, Metz, & Haas, 2000; Yairi & Ambrose, 1999).

Today, difficulty such as that described by Shields is viewed within the broad context of communication disorders because of the obstacle it presents to social interaction, which is the major purpose of language. The young man's stuttering was an inability to convey his thoughts and feelings, not just a problem of being fearful and unable to say certain words. In thinking about communication disorders, three elements of communication must be considered: the *contexts* in which communication occurs (e.g., in a group, in the classroom), the *functions* expressed by communication or the reasons one communicates (e.g., to request, to comment, to reason), and the actual *execution* of communication comprehension and expression.

Definitions

Speech and language are tools used for communication. Communication is the process of sharing information between

---

*We are indebted to Laura M. Justice, Ph.D., of the University of Virginia for her invaluable assistance in preparing this chapter.

Misconceptions about
Learners with Communication Disorders

MYTH Children with language disorders always have speech difficulties as well.

FACT It is possible for a child to have good speech yet not make any sense when he or she talks; however, most children with language disorders have speech disorders as well.

MYTH Individuals with communication disorders always have emotional or behavioral disorders or mental retardation.

FACT Some children with communication disorders are normal in cognitive, social, and emotional development.

MYTH How children learn language is now well understood.

FACT Although recent research has revealed quite a lot about the sequence of language acquisition and has led to theories of language development, exactly how children learn language is still unknown.

MYTH Stuttering is primarily a disorder of people with extremely high IQs. Children who stutter become stuttering adults.

FACT Stuttering can affect individuals at all levels of intellectual ability. Some children who stutter continue stuttering as adults; most, however, stop stuttering before or during adolescence with help from a speech-language pathologist. Stuttering is primarily a childhood disorder, found much more often in boys than in girls.

MYTH Disorders of phonology (or articulation) are never very serious and are always easy to correct.

FACT Disorders of phonology can make speech unintelligible; it is sometimes very difficult to correct phonological or articulation problems, especially if the individual has cerebral palsy, mental retardation, or emotional or behavioral disorders.

MYTH There is no relationship between intelligence and communication disorders.

FACT Communication disorders tend to occur more frequently among individuals of lower intellectual ability, although they may occur in individuals who are extremely intelligent.

MYTH There is not much overlap between language disorders and learning disabilities.

FACT Problems with verbal skills—listening, reading, writing, speaking—are often central features of learning disabilities. The definitions of language disorders and several other disabilities are overlapping.

MYTH Children who learn few language skills before entering kindergarten can easily pick up all the skills they need, if they have good peer models in typical classrooms.

FACT Early language learning is critical for later language development; a child whose language is delayed in kindergarten is unlikely to learn to use language effectively merely by observing peer models. More explicit intervention is typically required.

Communicative function
Acts of communication, such as requesting, rejecting, commenting, arguing, and reasoning.

Communication disorders
Impairments in the ability to use speech or language to communicate.

Communication
The process of sharing information.

Language
An arbitrary code or system of symbols to communicate meaning.

Expressive language
Encoding or sending messages in communication.

Receptive language
Decoding or understanding messages in communication.

Speech
The formation and sequencing of oral language sounds during communication.

Augmentative or alternative communication (AAC)
Alternative forms of communication that do not use the oral sounds of speech or that augment the use of speech.

Speech disorders
Oral communication that involves abnormal use of the vocal apparatus, is unintelligible, or is so inferior that it draws attention to itself and causes anxiety, feelings of inadequacy, or inappropriate behavior in the speaker.

Language disorders
Oral communication that involves a lag in the ability to understand and express ideas, putting linguistic skill behind an individual's development in other areas, such as motor, cognitive, or social development.

two or among more individuals. It involves many **communicative functions**, such as requesting, rejecting, commenting, arguing, and reasoning. A **communication disorder** may involve language or speech or both, and it impairs a communicative function.

Communication requires *encoding* (sending messages in understandable form) and *decoding* (receiving and understanding messages). It always involves a sender and a receiver of messages, but it does not always involve language. Animals communicate through movements and noises, for example, but their communication does not qualify as true language (see Justice, 2006). Language and speech are important tools for *human* communication.

Language is the communication of ideas—sending and receiving them—through an arbitrary system of symbols used according to certain rules that determine meaning. Encoding or sending messages is referred to as **expressive language**. Decoding or understanding messages is referred to as **receptive language**. When people think of language, they typically think of oral language. **Speech**—the neuromuscular activity of forming and sequencing the sounds of oral language—is the most common symbol system used in communication between humans. Without the rule-governed symbol system that we call language, we would have only grunts and groans, not speech.

Some languages, however, are not based on speech. For example, American Sign Language (ASL) does not involve speech sounds; it is a manual language used by many people who cannot hear speech. **Augmentative or alternative communication (AAC)** for people with disabilities involving the physical movements of speech may consist of alternatives to the speech sounds of oral language (see the discussion of AAC in Chapter 13).

The American Speech-Language-Hearing Association (ASHA) provides definitions of disorders of communication, including speech disorders, language disorders, and variations in communication (differences or dialects and augmentative systems) that are not disorders (see the Focus on Concepts on page 290). **Speech disorders** are impairments in the production and use of oral language. They include disabilities in making speech sounds, producing speech with a normal flow, and producing voice.

Language disorders include problems in comprehension and expression. Remember that language is governed by rules. The problems—rule violations—may involve the form, content, or use of language. **Phonology** refers to the rules governing speech sounds—the particular sounds and how they are sequenced. **Morphology** refers to the rules that govern alterations of the internal organization of words, such as adding suffixes and other grammatical inflections to make proper plurals, verb tenses, and so on. **Syntax** refers to the rules of organizing sentences that are meaningful, including subject and predicate and getting modifiers at the right place, for example. **Semantics** refers to the rules about attaching meanings and concepts to words. **Pragmatics** refers to the rules about using language for social purposes. Language disorders may involve any one or a combination of these five subsystems of language. Differences in speech or language that are shared by people in a given region, social group, or cultural/ethnic group should not be considered disorders. For example, African American English (Ebonics or Black English Vernacular), Appalachian English, and the Cajun dialect are varieties of English, not disorders of speech or language. These differences are governed by their own rules and reflect the cultural and linguistic diversity of North America. As long as speech and language are guided by consistent rules of a language community, they are not disordered even if they are different from what we are accustomed to hearing and saying.

Similarly, the use of AAC systems does not imply that a person has a language disorder. Rather, such systems are used by those who have temporary or permanent inabilities to use speech satisfactorily for communication. Those who use AAC systems might or might not have language disorders in addition to their inability to use speech.

Prevalence

Establishing the prevalence of communication disorders is difficult because they are extremely varied, sometimes difficult to identify, and often occur as part of other disabilities (e.g., mental retardation, brain injury, learning disability, or autism). About a million children—one-fifth of all children who are identified for special education—receive services primarily for language or speech disorders. Speech-language therapy is one of the most frequently provided related services for children with other primary disabilities (e.g., mental retardation or learning disability).

It is probably reasonable to estimate that about 10 to 15 percent of preschool children and about 6 percent of students in elementary and secondary grades have speech disorders; about 2 to 3 percent of preschoolers and about 1 percent of the school-age population have language disorders. Communication disorders of all kinds are predicted to increase during the coming decades, as medical advances preserve the lives of more children and youths with severe disabilities that affect communication. Therefore, there is a need for more speech-language pathologists in the schools as well as for greater knowledge of communication disorders by special and general education teachers and greater involvement of teachers in helping students learn to communicate effectively.

Communication Variations

The fact that a student does not use the speech or language that is expected in school does not necessarily mean that she or he has a language disorder. The most important question for a child whose speech or language is different from what is standard or expected is whether the student is an effective communicator in his or her speech and language community (see Goldstein & Iglesias, 2004; Justice, 2006; Owens, 2004). Someone with a language difference that is also a disorder has difficulty communicating in every language environment, including his or her home language community.

The speech or language of African American children, for example, might mistakenly be judged to indicate disorder when it is merely different from the standard American English. Oetting and McDonald (2001) noted that differences in Southern White English and Southern African American English may lead to the misdiagnosis of a language disorder in either Caucasian or African American children. Of course, an individual may both have a language disorder and exhibit a variation that is not a disorder. Such an individual will be unable to communicate effectively even with others who use the same language variation.

Encouraging the communication of children whose cultural heritage or language patterns are not those of the professionals' subculture is of increasing concern to classroom teachers and speech-language clinicians (see Chapter 3). On the one hand, care must be taken not to mistake a cultural or ethnic difference for a disorder; on the other hand, disorders that exist in the context of a language difference must not be overlooked. When assessing children's language, the professional must be aware of the limitations of normative tests and sources of potential bias.

A child might not have a language disorder yet have a communicative difference that demands special teaching to promote academic achievement and social communication. Children of nondominant cultures must be taught the rules for effective communication in the dominant culture. However, professionals must also understand and accept the effectiveness of the children's home languages in their cultural contexts. Failure to teach children the skills they need to communicate effectively according to the rules of the dominant culture will deny them many opportunities. In effect, children of minority language groups might need to learn to live in two worlds: one in which their home language is used and one in which school language is used.

Phonology
The study of how individual sounds make up words.

Morphology
The study within psycholinguistics of word formation; how adding or deleting parts of words changes their meaning.

Syntax
The way words are joined together to structure meaningful sentences; grammar.

Semantics
The study of the meanings attached to words and sentences.

Pragmatics
The study within psycholinguistics of how people use language in social situations; emphasizes the functional use of language, rather than mechanics.

AN IMPORTANT Website to visit for more information about communication disorders is the home page of the American Speech-Language-Hearing Association at **www.asha.org**

FOCUS ON CONCEPTS

Definitions of the American Speech–Language–Hearing Association

I.   A communication disorder is an impairment in the ability to receive, send, process, and comprehend concepts or verbal, nonverbal and graphic symbol systems. A communication disorder may be evident in the processes of hearing, language, and/or speech. A communication disorder may range in severity from mild to profound. It may be developmental or acquired. Individuals may demonstrate one or any combination of communication disorders. A communication disorder may result in a primary disability or it may be secondary to other disabilities.

A. A speech disorder is an impairment of the articulation of speech sounds, fluency, and/or voice.

1. An articulation disorder is the atypical production of speech sounds characterized by substitutions, omissions, additions, or distortions that may interfere with intelligibility.

2. A fluency disorder is an interruption in the flow of speaking characterized by atypical rate, rhythm, and repetitions in sounds, syllables, words, and phrases. This may be accompanied by excessive tension, struggle behavior, and secondary mannerisms.

3. A voice disorder is characterized by the abnormal production and/or absences of vocal quality, pitch, loudness, resonance, and/or duration, which is inappropriate for an individual's age and/or sex.

B. A language disorder is impaired comprehension and/or use of spoken, written, and/or other symbol systems. The disorder may involve (1) the form of language (phonology, morphology, syntax), (2) the content of language (semantics), and/or (3) the function of language in communication (pragmatics) in any combination.

1. Form of Language

a. Phonology is the sound system of a language and the rules that govern the sound combinations.

b. Morphology is the system that governs the structure of words and the construction of word forms.

c. Syntax is the system governing the order and combination of words to form sentences, and the relationships among the elements within a sentence.

2. Content of Language

a. Semantics is the system that governs the meanings of words and sentences.

3. Function of Language

a. Pragmatics is the system that combines the above language components in functional and socially appropriate communication.

II. Communication Variations

A. Communication difference/dialect is a variation of a symbol system used by a group of individuals that reflects and is determined by shared regional, social, or cultural/ethnic factors. A regional, social, or cultural/ethnic variation of a symbol system should not be considered a disorder of speech or language.

B. Augmentative/alternative communication systems attempt to compensate and facilitate, temporarily or permanently, for the impairment and disability patterns of individuals with severe expressive and/or language comprehension disorders. Augmentative/alternative communication may be required for individuals demonstrating impairments in gestural, spoken, and/or written modalities. ■

Source: American Speech-Language-Hearing Association. (1993). "Definitions of communication disorders and variations." *ASHA, 35*(Suppl. 10), pp. 40–41. Reprinted with permission.

Many students for whom language difference is an issue do not speak entirely different languages, but variations peculiar to certain groups of speakers—that is, dialects. For example, one dialect that is different from standard English (and is not a language disorder) is Appalachian English. People in Appalachia speak a variation of English with features that are not shared by other English dialects. Teachers must understand—and help their students understand—that other dialects are not inferior or limited language systems.

Furthermore, cultural differences must be recognized regardless of the communication device being used. Multicultural issues arise in all communication interactions, including those in which AAC is used (Goldstein & Iglesias, 2004; Soto, Huer, & Taylor, 1997).

Families differ greatly in the ways they talk to children and in the language they expect children to use. Although students might not have language disorders, their language variations could put them at a disadvantage in using language in an academic context. Consequently, some people have suggested that children who come to school without mastery of the English of their textbooks should be taught it directly and consistently (e.g., Raspberry, 2001). Among the recommendations of Goldstein and Iglesias (2004, pp. 368–369) are the following:

- Taking the student's cultural values and learning style into account
- Asking for help from colleagues, parents, and others, if necessary
- Viewing the student in the naturalistic context of the classroom
- Knowing the features of the community's dialects
- Taking the student's dialect into account
- Using the least biased tools for assessment

A major concern today in both special and general education is teaching children who are learning English as a second language, who are non-English proficient, or who have limited English proficiency. Bilingual education is a field of concern and controversy because of the rapidly changing demographics in many American communities (see Butler, 1999b; Justice, 2006; Nelson, 1998; Owens, 2004). Spanish-speaking children make up a rapidly growing percentage of the students in many school districts. Moreover, a large number of children from various nations that do not speak English have immigrated to the United States during the past decade. Many of these children have no proficiency or limited proficiency in English, and some have disabilities as well. Bilingual special education is still a developing field. As we discussed in Chapter 3, finding the best way to teach children to become proficient in English, particularly when they have disabilities as well as language differences, is a special challenge for the twenty-first century.

Language Disorders

Communication disorders cannot be understood without knowledge of normal language development. So before discussing the disorders of language and speech, we provide a brief description of normal language development. Language disorders are discussed first and more extensively than speech disorders, because the primary focus of speech-language pathologists and other specialists in communicative disorders has shifted from speech to language during the evolution of special education and related services (Owens et al., 2000).

The newborn makes few sounds other than cries. The fact that within a few years the human child can form the many complex sounds of speech, understand spoken and written language, and express meaning verbally is one of nature's great miracles. The major milestones in this miraculous ability to use language are fairly well known by child development specialists. The underlying mechanisms that control the development of language

UNDERSTANDING THE STANDARDS AND PRINCIPLES Are cultural and linguistic differences necessarily related to language disorders? Why or why not? *(CEC Knowledge and Skills Standard CC6K1)*

Council for Exceptional Children

FOR INFORMATION about normal speech and language development and the difference between speech disorder and language disorder, visit the Speech-Language Pathology site at **home.ica.net/~fred**

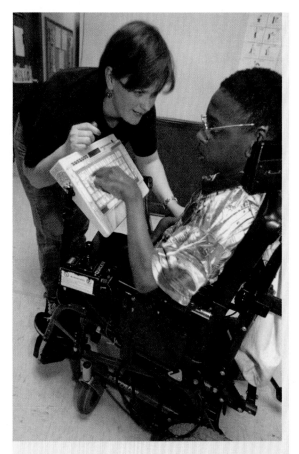

A child may not have a language disorder yet have a communication difference that demands special teaching. Such differences might be related to culture and/or disability.

Casebook Reflection

Refer to the case *Albert* in your booklet. We know nothing from the case about his early developmental history except that his mother took certain pieces out of his school file. What do you think might have been some of the early signs or symptoms of Albert's communication disorder?

are still not well understood, however. What parts of the process of learning language are innate, and what parts are controlled by the environment? What is the relationship between cognitive development and language development? These and many other questions about the origins and uses of language cannot yet be answered definitively.

The typical development of speech, language, and communication is described in Table 9.1. The child with a language disorder may eventually reach many or most of the milestones shown for normal development in Table 9.1 but at a later age than typically developing children. It is important to note that children sometimes seem to "catch up" in language development, only to fall behind typical development again at a later age.

No one knows exactly how or why children learn language, but we do know that language development is related in a general way to physical maturation, cognitive development, and socialization. The details of the process—the particulars of what happens physiologically, cognitively, and socially in the learning of language—are still being debated. Nelson (1998) discusses six theories of language that have dominated the study of human communication

TABLE 9.1 Development of speech, language, and communication

Age	Accomplishments
Newborn	Prefers human face and voice Able to discriminate loudness, intonation, and phonemes
3 months	Begins babbling Responds vocally to partner
6 months	Begins reduplicated babbling "Ba-ba-ba"
8 months	Begins gesturing Begins variegated babbling Imitates tonal quality of adult speech, called jargon
10 months	Adds phonetically consistent forms
12 months	First word spoken. Words fill intentions previously signaled by gestures.
18 months	Begins combining words on the basis of word-order rules
2 years	Begins adding bound morphemes. Average length or mean length of utterance (MLU) is 1.6–2.2 morphemes.
3 years	More adultlike sentence structure. Mean length of utterance (MLU) is 3.0–3.3 morphemes.
4 years	Begins to change style of talking to fit conversational partner. Mean length of utterance (MLU) is 3.6–4.7 morphemes.
5 years	Ninety percent of language form learned
6 years	Begins to learn visual mode of communication with writing and reading
8 years	All American English speech sounds acquired
Adolescence	Able to competently participate in conversations and telling of narratives Knows multiple meanings of words and figurative language Uses a gender style, or genderlect, when talking
Adult	Vocabulary has expanded to 30,000–60,000 words Specialized styles of communicating with different audiences and for diverse purposes

Source: R. E. Owens, Jr., D. E. Evans, & A. Haas. (2000). Introduction to communication disorders: A life span perspective. Boston: Allyn & Bacon.

at various times. The six theories and research based on them have established the following:

1. Language learning depends on brain development and proper brain functioning. Language disorders are sometimes a result of brain dysfunction, and ways to compensate for the dysfunction can sometimes be taught. The emphasis is on *biological maturation*.

2. Language learning is affected by the consequences of language behavior. Language disorders can be a result of inappropriate learning, and consequences can sometimes be arranged to correct disordered language. The emphasis is on *behavioral psychology*.

3. Language can be analyzed as inputs and outputs related to the way information is processed. Faulty processing may account for some language disorders, and more effective processing skills can sometimes be taught. The emphasis is on *information processing*.

4. Language is acquired by a biological process that dictates rules governing the form, content, and use of language. Language disorders are the result of a failure to acquire or employ rule-governed aspects of language, and these disorders may be overcome by helping an individual induce or learn these rules. The emphasis is on a *linguistic or nativist perspective*.

5. Language is one of many cognitive skills. Language disorders reflect basic problems in thinking and learning, and sometimes these disorders can be addressed effectively by teaching specific cognitive skills. The emphasis is on *cognitive development*.

6. Language arises from the need to communicate in social interactions. Language disorders are a breakdown in ability to relate effectively to one's environment, and the natural environment can sometimes be arranged to teach and support more effective interaction. The emphasis is on *social interaction*.

All these theories contain elements of scientific truth, but none is able to explain the development and disorders of language completely. All six theories have advantages and disadvantages for assessing language disorders and devising effective interventions.

UNDERSTANDING THE STANDARDS AND PRINCIPLES How is language development related to physical maturation, cognitive development, and socialization? *(CEC Knowledge and Skills Standard GC2K1 & GC6K3; INTASC 2.06)*

No one knows exactly how or why children learn language, but we do know that language development is related in a general way to physical maturation, cognitive development, and socialization.

Casebook Reflection

Refer to the case *Who Will Help Patrick?* in your booklet. Patrick is labeled as developmentally delayed. Do you foresee him also being labeled with a speech language disorder? Why or why not? What makes this decision difficult?

Advances in neurological imaging technology may lead to better understanding of the biological bases of language (Foundas, 2001). However, pragmatic or social interaction theory is widely viewed as having the most direct implications for speech-language pathologists and teachers because it focuses most directly on how communication skills can be fostered through adult–child interaction (Owens, 2004).

Language involves listening and speaking, reading and writing, technical discourse, and social interaction. Language problems are therefore basic to many of the disabilities discussed in this text, especially hearing impairment, mental retardation, traumatic brain injury, autistic spectrum disorder, and learning disability.

CLASSIFICATION OF LANGUAGE DISORDERS

Primary language disorder
A language disorder that has no known cause.

Secondary language disorder
A language disorder that is caused by another disorder or disability, such as mental retardation, hearing impairment, or brain injury.

Language disorders can be classified according to two primary dimensions: *domain* (subsystem or type) and *etiology* (cause). The ASHA definitions shown in the Focus on Concepts on page 295 suggest a classification scheme involving five subsystems or types of language: phonological (sounds), morphological (word forms), syntactical (word order and sentence structure), semantic (word and sentence meanings), and pragmatic (social use of language). Difficulty with one of these dimensions of language is virtually certain to be accompanied by difficulty with one or more of the others. However, children with language disorders often have particular difficulty with one dimension. Language disorders involving these subsystems are illustrated in the Focus on Concepts on page 295.

Another way of classifying language disorders is based on the presumed cause (etiology) or related conditions. Classification by etiology provides two subtypes: *primary* and *secondary*. A **primary language disorder** has no known cause. A **secondary language disorder** is caused by another condition, such as mental retardation, hearing impairment, autistic spectrum disorder, cerebral palsy, or traumatic brain injury.

Children with language disorders often have particular difficulty with one dimension of language, be it phonology, morphology, syntax, semantics, or pragmatics.

FOCUS ON CONCEPTS

Types of Language Disorders

DISORDERS CAN AFFECT any one or a combination of the *form* (phonology, mophology, or syntax), *content* (semantics), or *use* (pragmatics) of language. Following are illustrations of each of five types of disorders. Remember that in judging what is a disorder, one must keep in mind the individual's age, culture, and linguistic community so that normal development and differences are not mistakenly considered disorders.

PHONOLOGICAL DISORDER

An elementary student might pronounce words with certain sounds omitted or distorted. For example, the student might say *boo* for the color *blue*, *dat* for *that*, *tee* for *teeth*, and *wabba* for *rubber* and in other ways fail to communicate effectively because the sounds of many words are omitted, distorted, or substituted. This same student might also have little awareness of the phonological structure of language, so the student is unable to identify the sounds that make up a word (e.g., the word *bag* contains three sounds). This difficulty has posed problems for the student's reading development, specifically learning the relationship between letters and sounds.

MORPHOLOGICAL AND SYNTACTICAL (OR MORPHOSYNTACTIC) DISORDER

Problems with morphology and syntax tend to occur together. A school-age child or older person with morphological difficulties may have problems inflecting words using suffixes (e.g., making a plural by adding *s*, constructing the present progressive by adding *ing*). The person might not understand how to make the past tense of the word hide (say *hided* instead of *hid*) or how to contract auxillary verbs (e.g., *is, am, are*) to make contracted verbs (e.g., *she's going, I'm waiting, we're going*). The school-age child with syntactic difficulties might leave out important grammatical markers, such as articles (*a, an, the*) and might have problems using pronouns correctly (e.g., say *her did it* instead of *she did it*).

SEMANTIC DISORDER

A school-age child or older person might have a difficult time learning new words or using new words when appropriate. For instance, after hearing the word *rumpus* five times in the story *Where the Wild Things Are*, the child might still react to this word in the future as if he or she has never heard it before. Or when faced with a situation that has rumpuslike characteristics, the child would not be able to use the word to describe the situation. The individual might not be able to make sense of stories, retell them in ways that make sense to listeners, or say things to which others can attach meaning. For example, instead of "On Christmas, we sing songs and open presents and have special things to eat," the person might say, "Sing Merry Christmas, presents, eating lots of stuff."

PRAGMATIC DISORDER

A school-age child or older person might not understand how to use language in social situations. For example, the person might start a conversation with a complete stranger by saying something like "I like planes a lot, and I like to watch them" or say something offensive, such as "You sure are fat!" or, in response to an invitation to take a turn in conversation (e.g., "Burt, what do you think?") give an inappropriate response (e.g., "No! You say."). Individuals with pragmtatic language disorders may not know how to make their needs clear to others or know how to use language for practical purposes (e.g., asking someone to call 911 in an emergency). ■

A scientific approach to problems demands classification, but human beings and their language are very difficult to categorize. Therefore, all classification systems contain ambiguities, and none can account for all cases. In a textbook devoted to language disorders, Owens (2004) notes:

> Many children with [language impairments] cannot be described easily by any of the categories discussed in this chapter. Such children may have either more than one primary diagnostic category or characteristics that do not fit into any category. Each child represents a unique set of circumstances, so language assessment and intervention should be individualized. (p. 20)

Special Educators at Work

Ryan: "When I look back, I realize how slow I was as a result of the head injury." College student Ryan McGarr was severely injured in a Thanksgiving Day car wreck during his junior year in high school. An innovative traumatic brain injury project provided a bridge between his rehabilitation services and school reentry.

These are the keys to his success:

- *Intensive coordination of services and supports*
- *Relentless instruction in academics and vocabulary development*
- *Specific goals for compensatory strategies and teacher training*

Special Educator Nancy Maher-Maxwell directed a specialized traumatic brain injury (TBI) Project for the Nassau County Board of Cooperative Educational Services in New York. When Ryan was injured, she coordinated his medical and educational services. She also trained his teachers to meet his individual needs as he reentered school after the accident. Ryan remained in a coma for three days and his residual difficulties in language and cognitive processing presented academic challenges. He credits his success to intensive, relentless, and specific special education along with spontaneous neurological recovery and a strong desire to achieve.

Intensive Coordination of Services and Supports
Kathy McGarr was grateful that someone at the hospital told her about the TBI project: "Just the trauma, and trying to take care of your other children—the whole family tends to fall apart. I didn't have the concentration or anything to deal with this." According to Maher-Maxwell, "research suggests that kids who have this connection between rehabilitation and school reentry, along with ongoing staff support once they've returned, have greater success rates than those who don't."

Ryan returned to school part-time in April of his junior year. He went to an outpatient rehabilitation center for therapies in the morning and then to his local public high school in the afternoon for English, social studies, art, and resource room. He returned full-time for his senior year, carrying a full program of academic courses with resource room support for 45 minutes daily.

Relentless Instruction in Academics and Vocabulary Development Nancy Maher-Maxwell remembers that when she met Ryan six weeks after the accident, he was determined to graduate with his class and wanted tutoring. "The psychologist at the hospital, who evaluated him nine weeks after the accident, told me Ryan would probably never finish school and that I was overwhelming him with academics," says Mrs. McGarr, "but it was what he wanted, and I had to let him try to do it."

To start the process, Maher-Maxwell contacted Ryan's school district. His former English teacher agreed to be his home tutor. With Maher-Maxwell's help, her lessons were individualized, concentrating on vocabulary and word meanings. She used flashcards and together with Ryan made up funny sentences using mnemonics to help him remember information. Instead of

Specific language impairment (SLI)
A language disorder with no identifiable cause; language disorder not attributable to hearing impairment, mental retardation, brain dysfunction, or other plausible cause; also called specific language disability.

Early expressive language delay (EELD)
A significant lag in the development of expressive language that is apparent by age 2.

Ryan, the student described in the Success Stories above, is a perfect example of this concept. He suffered a brain injury and, with the help of his family and involved professionals, he learned to communicate again. Ryan was fortunate enough to experience a full recovery but his struggles with communication are fresh in his mind.

Primary Language Disorders **Specific language impairment (SLI)** refers to language disorders that have no identifiable cause. These disorders are not due to mental retardation, the perceptual problems that characterize language learning disability, hearing problems, and so on. Often, SLI involves multiple aspects of language. Many children with SLI will have difficulties in their development of vocabulary and grammar (Leonard, 2000).

Early expressive language delay (EELD) refers to a significant lag in expressive language that the child will not outgrow (i.e., the child does not have a fifty-word vocabulary or use two-word utterances by age 2). About half the children whose language development is delayed at age two will gradually catch up developmentally with their age peers; however the other half will not catch up and will continue to have language problems throughout their school years.

giving him a chapter to read in history, she chunked material to be learned by breaking it up into smaller units.

Specific Goals for Compensatory Strategies and Teacher Training   The TBI Project coordinated Ryan's reentry into the regular educational environment by providing workshops as well as ongoing support for his teachers. Training emphasized Ryan's need to take in new information in a variety of ways. Teachers were shown techniques to reinforce study skills, such as taking notes, outlining chapters, and organizing projects. "Often the typical high school teacher will lecture on the subject, expect the kids to take good notes, and evaluate them on a test. Because of the disruptions in the learning systems of students with TBI, there may be a slower rate in processing, so extended time is often necessary both in teaching and in testing," Nancy Maher-Maxwell says.

His mother recalls that it was hard to tell whether Ryan would regain his language abilities. "In speech therapy, he had a terrible time with categorization skills. His therapist asked him to name five green vegetables, and he couldn't do it! What was even more surprising was that he couldn't imagine that anyone could!"

TBI is an acquired injury that demands new adjustments. "If I hadn't spoken with Nancy," says Mrs. McGarr, "I wouldn't have known to put Ryan in a resource room, since he never needed special education before." Head injuries can also make the future harder to predict. "That early neuropsychological evaluation that said he could forget about his academic aspirations never took into account Ryan's determination and the compensatory strategies that special education could provide," says Ms. Maher-Maxwell.

Ryan still finds that he is more easily distracted than he used to be, and he continues to need extended time on some college exams. He remains confident about the future saying, "I'll succeed in the world doing whatever I want to do. I have no doubts about that."

CEC'S STANDARDS: PAVING THE WAY TO SUCCESS

Council for Exceptional Children

ASSESS YOUR STEPS TO SUCCESS in meeting the CEC Knowledge and Skill Base for All Beginning Special Education Teachers of Students in Individualized General Curriculums. Use the following questions to reflect on the growth of your own professional knowledge, skills, and dispositions.

REFLECTING ON YOUR OWN PROFESSIONAL DEVELOPMENT

If you were Ryan's teacher . . .

- WHAT are some areas in educating students with communication and information processing skills that you would need to know more about?
- WHAT are some specific skills that would help you to address Ryan's academic and social challenges?
- WHAT personal dispositions do you think are most important for you to develop in teaching students to regain their functional use of language?

Using the CEC Standards

- WHAT is the impact of language development and listening comprehension on the academic and nonacademic learning of individuals with disabilities? (IC6K1)
- WHAT are the collaborative and/or consultative roles of the special education teacher in the reintegration of individuals with disabilities into the general education environment? (IC10K2)
- HOW can the continuum of placements and services be used in supporting a student's school reentry following a TBI? (IC1K4) ■

By Jean Crockett

Language-based reading impairment involves a reading problem based on a language disorder. This disorder cannot be identified until the child begins learning to read and has problems. Research of such abilities as phonological awareness, alphabet knowledge, and grammatical speech have helped in identifying children who are vulnerable to this kind of disorder (Justice & Schuele, 2004). More than 50 percent of children who show language impairments in kindergarten will have obvious reading problems by second grade (Catts, Fey, Zhang, & Tomblin, 2001).

Language-based reading impairment
A reading problem that is based on a language problem.

Secondary Language Disorders   The literature on language disorders often includes discussion of the particular communication impairments of individuals with other specific disabling conditions, such as mental retardation or autistic spectrum disorder (e.g., Owens, 2004). Difficulty in using language in social interactions and relationships is now seen as a basic problem in many disorders.

Emotional and behavioral disorders, for instance, may range from social reticence or withdrawal to severe acting out and aggression (Butler, 1999a; Rogers-Adkinson & Griffith, 1999). Young children who have language disorders might have special difficulty in developing skills in social interaction because they do not interpret social circumstances correctly and have difficulty expressing themselves. Donahue, Hartas, and Cole (1999) provide an example.

> In a kindergarten classroom, there are two adjacent (unisex) bathroom doors, each sporting almost identical pumpkin face posters. Almost invisible to the adult eye, one pumpkin has the faintest suggestion of eyelashes (instead of triangle eyes, this pumpkin has rectangles with a jagged top). A boy identified as having a language disorder comes out of this bathroom and goes to his table. Another boy approaches him, saying:
>
> Why did you go to the girls' bathroom? (pointing to the pumpkin face)
> Huh?
> You went to the girls' bathroom.
> No—no—. That not girls'.
> Yes it is.
> No way—boys can too. (voice rising)
> Yeah, there's a girl pumpkin on it.
> But—but . . . that not a girl! (getting angry)
> Yeah, look at those eyelashes.
> But—but . . . NOT! (Splutters, jumps up and shoves the other boy. The teacher intervenes, and gives the child with the language disorder a time-out for fighting. He sits angrily, muttering to himself, "not a girl!") (p. 72)

Speech Disorders

Speech disorders are very heterogeneous. That is, there are many different types, degrees, and combinations of them. Speech disorders pose a wide variety of challenges to the communication abilities of school children.

Most speech disorders will be treated primarily by speech-language pathologists, not classroom teachers. Teachers should be aware of possible speech disorders in order to be able to refer students properly.

We provide only brief descriptions of the major disorders affecting the speech of school-age children. Most speech disorders are treated primarily by a speech-language pathologist, not by a classroom teacher. However, both general and special education teachers are expected to work collaboratively with speech-language pathologists in assessment and intervention.

PHONOLOGICAL DISORDERS

Phonological disorders occur in children younger than 9 years. They do not include the normally developing young child's inability to say words correctly. The cause of the disorder is often unknown, but for some reason, the child does not understand the rules for producing the sounds of his or her language. The child's speech sound production is different from age-appropriate, culturally based expectations. The child does not seem to understand how to differentiate and produce the phonemes or sounds of language to construct intelligible words. This disorder occurs in about four or five in one hundred children, somewhat more often in boys than in girls.

Phonological disorders are often confused with articulation disorders (Justice, 2006). Whereas the child with an articulation disorder simply has trouble producing sounds correctly, the child with a phonological disorder seems to have a poor inner representation of the sounds of language. He or she might not understand the contrasts between or the distinctiveness of sound, which results in problems with how speech sounds are produced. For instance, the child who does not have an internal representation of consonants at the end of words produces *hat* as *ha* and *dog* as *do*.

Phonology is critical to literacy. Learning to read requires an understanding of the principle of the alphabet—that letters and combinations of letters represent certain sounds. **Phonological awareness** (the ability to blend sounds into words, to segment words into sounds, and to otherwise manipulate the sounds of spoken words in other ways) and *sound–symbol correspondence* are both critical abilities for reading. Some, but not all, children with phonological disorders lack phonological awareness. Some have serious problems with verbal working memory (remembering what was said or what they want to say) or word learning and word retrieval.

Phonological disorders may occur with a variety of other disorders (Justice, 2006). There are many different theories of phonology and alternative classification systems that are beyond our scope here (see Justice, 2006; Kent, 2004; Vihman, 2004). Suffice to say here that phonological disorders represent a failure of the child to understand the sound system of language at an age-appropriate level and in a culturally appropriate way. This disorder of the phonological *system* of language affects speech sound production and may affect literacy as well.

ARTICULATION DISORDERS

Articulation disorders involve errors in producing words. The problem is not an underlying phonological problem but a disorder in which the individual omits, substitutes, distorts, or adds speech sounds. Lisping, for example, involves a substitution or distortion of the [s] sound (e.g., *thunthine* or *shunshine* for *sunshine*). Missing, substituted, added, or poorly produced word sounds can make a speaker difficult to understand or even unintelligible. Such errors in speech production may also carry heavy social penalties, subjecting the speaker to teasing or ridicule.

When are articulation errors considered a disorder? That depends on a clinician's subjective judgment, which will be influenced by her or his experience, the number and types of errors, the consistency of these errors, the age and developmental characteristics of the speaker, and the intelligibility of the person's speech (see Bernthal & Bankson, 2004).

Young children make frequent errors in speech sounds when they are learning to talk. Many children do not learn to produce all the speech sounds correctly until they are 8 or 9 years old. Furthermore, most children make frequent errors until after they enter school.

Phonological awareness
The ability to understand that speech flow can be broken into smaller sound units such as words, syllables, and phonemes; lack of such awareness is generally thought to be the reason for the reading problems of many students with learning disabilities.

The age of the child is thus a major consideration in judging the adequacy of articulation. Another major consideration is the characteristics of the child's language community, because children learn speech largely through imitation. For instance, a child who is reared in the deep South might have speech that sounds peculiar to residents of Long Island, but this does not mean that the child has a speech disorder. Remember that there are differences that are not disorders.

The number of children who have difficulty producing word sounds decreases markedly during the first three or four years of elementary school. Among children with other disabilities, especially mental retardation and neurological disorders such as cerebral palsy, the prevalence of articulation disorders is higher than that in the general population.

Lack of ability to articulate speech sounds correctly can be caused by biological factors. For example, brain damage or damage to the nerves controlling the muscles that are used in speech may make it difficult or impossible to articulate sounds (Bernthal & Bankson, 1998; Cannito, Yorkston, & Beukelman, 1998). Furthermore, abnormalities of the oral structures, such as a cleft palate, can make normal speech difficult or impossible. Relatively minor structural changes, such as loss of teeth, can produce temporary errors. Poor articulation may also result from a hearing loss.

The parents of a preschool child might refer the child for assessment if he or she has speech that is really difficult to understand. Most schools screen all new pupils for speech and language problems, and in most cases, a child who still makes many articulation errors in the third or fourth grade will be referred for evaluation. Older children and adults sometimes seek help on their own when their speech draws negative attention. A speech-language pathologist will assess not only articulation but also social and developmental history, hearing, general language ability, and speech mechanism.

Although speech-language pathologists' interest in articulation disorders has appeared to decrease in recent years, with more attention being given to language and phonology, persistent articulation disorders may have serious long-term consequences. The decision about whether to include a child in an intervention program will depend on the child's age, other developmental characteristics, and the type and consistency of the articulation errors (Williams, 2001).

Articulation disorders are often accompanied by other disorders of speech or language; therefore, the child might need intervention in multiple aspects of communication (Bauman-Waengler, 2000; Hodson & Edwards, 1997; Nelson, 1998). The decision to include or not include a child in speech-language therapy will also depend on the pathologist's assessment of the likelihood that the child will self-correct the errors and of the social penalties, such as teasing and shyness, the child is experiencing. If the child misarticulates only a few sounds but does so consistently and suffers social embarrassment or rejection as a consequence, an intervention program is usually called for.

VOICE DISORDERS

People's voices are perceived as having pitch, loudness, and quality. Changes in pitch and loudness are part of the stress patterns of speech. Vocal quality is related not only to production of speech sounds, but also to the nonlinguistic aspects of speech.

Larynx
The structure in the throat containing the vocal apparatus (vocal cords); laryngitis is a temporary loss of voice caused by inflammation of the larynx.

Voice disorders, though difficult to define precisely, are characteristics of pitch, loudness, and/or quality that are abusive of the **larynx**; hamper communication; or are perceived as markedly different from what is customary for someone of a given age, sex, and cultural background (Robinson & Crowe, 2001).

Voice disorders can result from a variety of biological and nonbiological causes, including growths in the larynx (e.g., nodules, polyps, or cancerous tissue), infections of the larynx (laryngitis), damage to the nerves supplying the larynx, or accidental bruises or scratches on the larynx (Haynes & Pindzola, 1998). Misuse or abuse of the voice also can lead to a quality that is temporarily abnormal. High school cheerleaders, for example, frequently develop temporary voice disorders due to the formation of nodules (calluses) on their vocal cords (Campbell, Reich, Klockars, & McHenry, 1988). The same kind of problem can be caused by a child's screaming. Teachers and others who constantly use a very loud voice, whether expressing passionate beliefs, talking over noisy conditions, or speaking in a room with poor acoustics, may also develop voice problems.

Disorders resulting from misuse or abuse of the voice can damage the tissues of the larynx. So can smoking or inhaling substances that irritate the vocal folds. Sometimes a person has psychological problems that lead to a complete loss of voice (**aphonia**) or to severe voice abnormalities.

Voice disorders having to do with **resonance**—vocal quality—may be caused by physical abnormalities of the oral cavity (such as **cleft palate**) or damage to the brain or nerves controlling the oral cavity. Infections of the tonsils, adenoids, or sinuses can also influence how the voice is resonated. Most people who have severe hearing loss typically have problems in achieving a normal or pleasingly resonant voice. Finally, sometimes a person simply has not learned to speak with an appropriately resonant voice. There are no biological or deep-seated psychological reasons for the problem; rather, it appears that she or he has learned faulty habits of positioning the organs of speech.

Teachers need to observe children for common symptoms of voice disorders, such as hoarseness, aphonia, breathiness, odd pitch (voice too high or too low pitched), or an inappropriately loud or soft voice. A teacher who notes possible problems should ask a speech-language pathologist to do an evaluation. Teachers should also monitor their own voices for indications of vocal stress.

FLUENCY DISORDERS

Normal speech is characterized by some interruptions in speech flow. Especially when a child is learning to talk, we can expect normal **dysfluencies.** These are the hesitations, repetitions, and other interruptions of normal speech flow that are entirely normal parts of learning to use language. All of us occasionally get speech sounds in the wrong order (e.g., saying *revalent* for *relevant*), speak too quickly to be understood, pause at the wrong place in a sentence, use an inappropriate pattern of stress, or become dysfluent—that is, stumble and backtrack, repeating words or phrases, and fill in pauses with *uh* while trying to think of how to finish what we have to say. It is only when the speaker's efforts are so intense or the interruptions in the flow of speech are so frequent or pervasive that they keep him or her from being understood or draw extraordinary attention that they are considered disorders. Besides, listeners have a greater tolerance for some types of dysfluencies than others. Most of us will more readily accept speech-flow disruptions that we perceive as necessary corrections of what the speaker has said or is planning to say than disruptions that appear to reflect the speaker's inability to proceed with the articulation of what she or he has decided to say (Robinson & Crowe, 2001).

The most frequent type of fluency disorder is **stuttering.** Stuttering is different from normal dysfluency in both the rate and the type of dysfluency. Children who stutter produce dysfluencies at a greater rate than children who do not stutter, with dysfluences making up more than 10 percent of speech (Guitar, 1998). Also, children who stutter produce part-word repetitions (I wa-wa-want . . .), sound prolongations (It is at my hhhhhouse . . .), and sound blocks (My name is L#aura . . .), all of which are types of dysfluencies not normally seen in young children. About 1 percent of children and adults are considered stutterers. More boys than girls stutter. Many children quickly outgrow their childhood dysfluencies. These children generally use regular and effortless dysfluencies, appear to be unaware of their hesitancies, and have parents and teachers who are unconcerned about their speech patterns. Those who stutter for more than a year and a half or two appear to be at risk for becoming chronic stutterers (Conture, 2001).

Stuttering is actually not just dysfluency. It does consist of repetitions prolongations of sounds, and blocks in which the person seems unable to make the intended sound, which are the *core behaviors* of stuttering. But it also consists of related *secondary behaviors* that are intended to avoid or escape the dysfluency, such as gestures, head nods, eye blinks, and so on. It also includes negative feelings about communication on the part of those who stutter.

FOR INFORMATION about cleft lip, cleft palate, and other cranio-facial deformities and effects on speech, see SMILES at **www.cleft.org**

Aphonia
Loss of voice.

Resonance
The quality of the sound imparted by the size, shape, and texture of the organs in the vocal tract.

Cleft palate
A condition in which there is a rift or split in the upper part of the oral cavity; may include the upper lip (cleft lip).

Dysfluencies
Hesitations, repetitions, and other disruptions of normal speech flow.

Stuttering
Speech characterized by abnormal hesitations, prolongations, and repetitions; may be accompanied by grimaces, gestures, or other bodily movements indicative of a struggle to speak, anxiety, blocking of speech, or avoidance of speech.

MORE INFORMATION about stuttering is available at the following sites: National Center for Stuttering at **www.stuttering.com** and the Stuttering Foundation of America at **www.stuttersfa. org**

A child who is thought to stutter should be evaluated by a speech-language pathologist. Early diagnosis is important if the development of chronic stuttering is to be avoided. Unfortunately, many educators and physicians do not refer potential stutterers for in-depth assessment because they are aware that dysfluencies are a normal part of speech-language development. Some experts also advocate a "wait and see" approach (Curlee & Yairi, 1997). But nonreferral is extremely detrimental to children who are at risk for stuttering. If their persistent stuttering goes untreated, it might result in a lifelong disorder that affects their ability to communicate, develop positive feelings about themselves, and pursue certain educational and employment opportunities (Conture, 2001; Curlee & Siegel, 1997).

MOTOR-SPEECH DISORDERS

The muscles that make speech possible are under voluntary control. When there is damage to the areas of the brain that control these muscles or to the nerves leading to the muscles, there is a disturbance in the ability to speak normally. These disorders may involve controlling speech sounds (**dysarthria**) or planning and coordinating speech (**apraxia**). Both disorders (dysarthria and apraxia) affect the production of speech, slow its rate, and reduce intelligibility (Owens et al., 2000). Keep in mind, too, that dysarthria and apraxia are not mutually exclusive. That is, an individual can have both problems. Because these disorders are caused by a neurological problem, they are often called *neurogenic disorders of speech*.

By listening to the person's speech and inspecting his or her speech mechanism, the speech-language pathologist will assess the ability of the person with a motor-speech disorder or neurogenic speech disorder to control breathing, phonation, resonation, and articulatory movements. Medical, surgical, and rehabilitative specialists in the treatment of neurological disorders also must evaluate the person's problem and plan a management strategy. In cases in which the neurological impairment makes the person's speech unintelligible, an AAC system might be required.

Dysarthria   Difficulties in speaking may occur because the muscles controlling breathing, the larynx, the throat, the tongue, the jaw, and/or the lips cannot be controlled precisely.

Dysarthria
A condition in which brain damage causes impaired control of the muscles used in articulation.

Apraxia
The inability to plan and coordinate speech.

There are several ways in which damage to the areas of the brain controlling the muscles used for speech create a disturbance in the ability to speak normally.

Depending on the nature of the injury to the brain, perceptual and cognitive functions may also be affected; the individual may have a language disorder in addition to a speech disorder.

Dysarthria is characterized by slow, labored, slurred, and imprecise speech. As a result of brain injury, the person's respiratory support for making speech sounds is affected, and his or her speech may be characterized by shallow breathing, hoarseness, and reduced loudness. The person might not be able to produce speech sounds precisely because of muscle weakness.

Probably the condition that most frequently accounts for dysarthria in children is **cerebral palsy**—brain injury before, during, or after birth that results in muscular weakness or paralysis. Among the many causes of brain injury are physical trauma, oxygen deprivation, poisoning, diseases, and strokes. Vehicular accidents are a frequent cause of traumatic brain injury in adolescence and young adulthood. Anything that causes brain injury can cause dysarthria.

Apraxia   Apraxia is characterized by a disruption of motor planning and programming so that speech is slow, effortful, and inconsistent. A person with this disorder may recognize that he or she is making errors and try to correct them, but the attempts at correction make it even harder to understand what the person intends to say. Owens et al. (2000) provide the following example of the speech of someone with apraxia:

> O-o-on . . . on . . . on cavation, cavation, cacation . . . oh darn . . . vavation, of, you know, to Ca-ca-caciporenia . . . no, Lacifacnia, vafacnia to Lacifacnion . . . On vacation to Va-cafornia, no darn it . . . to Ca-caliborneo . . . not bornia . . . fornia, Bornfifornia . . . no, Ballifornio, Ballifornee, Balifornee, Californee, California. Phew, it was hard to say Cacaforneo. Oh darn. (p. 416)

Developmental apraxia is a disorder of motor planning that emerges as the child develops speech and language skills. Children with this disorder show significant delays in the ability to produce speech sounds and to organize sounds into words for effective communication. **Acquired apraxia** has similar symptoms but it occurs because of a stroke or other type of brain damage after learning speech. Usually, the person with apraxia knows that he or she is making errors, wants to correct them, knows what he or she wants to communicate, but simply cannot do so. Consequently, apraxia is an unusually frustrating disorder for the speaker.

Cerebral palsy
A condition characterized by paralysis, weakness, lack of coordination, and/or other motor dysfunction; caused by damage to the brain before it has matured.

Developmental apraxia
A disorder of speech or language involving problems in motor planning such that the child has difficulty in producing speech sounds and organizing words and word sounds for effective communication. The cause may be unknown.

Acquired apraxia
As in Developmental apraxia, there are problems in motor planning such that the child has difficulty in producing speech sounds and organizing words and word sounds for effective communication. However, the problem is known to the cause by neurological damage.

Assessment

Two general purposes of language assessment are (1) to determine, in as much detail as possible, what the child's current language abilities are and (2) to observe the ease and speed with which the child learns new language skills (see Owens, 2004; Ruscello, 2001). The first strategy typically involves the use of standardized testing, nonstandardized testing, developmental scales, and behavioral observations. Standardized testing has many dangers and is not always useful in planning an intervention program, but it can sometimes be helpful in making crude comparisons of the child's abilities in certain areas. Development scales are ratings or observations that can be completed by direct observation or based on memory or records of developmental milestones. Nonstandardized tests and behavioral observations are nonnormative in nature, but they can yield the most important assessment information. The subjective judgment of an experienced clinician based on observation of the child's

Casebook Reflection

Refer to the case *Albert* in your booklet. Albert understands what his teachers and mother are saying but is unable to communicate verbally or intelligibly. What assessments might be used to understand his disability?

language in a variety of environments and circumstances can provide the most useful basis for intervention. Because language disorders vary widely in nature and are seen in individuals ranging from early childhood through old age, assessment and intervention are never simple and are always idiosyncratic (Gillam & Hoffman, 2001; Owens, 2004; Ruscello, 2001).

An intervention plan based on assessment must consider the content, form, social context, and use of language. That is, it must consider the following:

- What the child talks about and should be taught to talk about
- How the child talks about things and how he or she could be taught to speak of those things more intelligibly
- How the child functions in the context of his or her linguistic community
- How the child uses language and how the child's language use could be made to serve the purposes of communication and socialization more effectively

In arranging a training sequence based on assessment, one might base instruction on the normal sequence of language development. Other sequences of instruction might be more effective, however, because children with language disorders obviously have not learned in the normal way and research suggests that different sequences of learning may be more effective. It is more and more apparent that effective language intervention must occur in the child's natural environment and involve parents and classroom teachers, not just speech-language pathologists (Justice, 2006; Owens, 2004).

Educational Considerations

Children with all types of disabilities are increasingly placed in general education classrooms. This means that all teachers must become aware of how they can address language problems in the classroom (Owens, 2004; Throneburg, Calvert, Sturm, Paramboukas, & Paul, 2000). Helping children overcome speech and language disorders is not the responsibility of any single professional. Rather, identification is the joint responsibility of the classroom teacher, the speech-language pathologist, and the parents. The teacher can carry out specific suggestions for individual cases. By listening attentively and empathetically when children speak, providing appropriate models of speech and language for children to imitate, and encouraging children to use their communication skills appropriately, the classroom teacher can help not only to improve speech and language, but also to prevent some disorders from developing in the first place.

Casebook Reflection

Refer to the case *Albert* in your booklet. Although Albert does not have expressive language, he demonstrates normal receptive language. He is also able to write his name, to understand his assignments, and to make good grades in school. In light of these factors, what type of placement do you foresee as the least restrictive environment for him? What about in the future?

FACILITATING THE SOCIAL USE OF LANGUAGE

The primary role of the classroom teacher is to facilitate the social use of language. The fact that a student has a language or speech disorder does not necessarily mean that the teacher or clinician must intensify efforts to teach the student about the form, structure, or content of language. Rather, language must be taught as a way of solving problems by making oneself understood and making sense of what other people say.

The classroom offers many possibilities for language learning. It should be a place in which there are almost continuous opportunities for students and teachers to employ language and obtain feedback in constructive relationships. Language is the basic medium through which most academic and social learning takes place in school. Nevertheless, the language of school, in both classrooms and textbooks, is often a problem for students and teachers.

School language is more formal than the language many children use at home and with playmates. It is structured conversation, in which listeners and speakers or readers and writers must learn to be clear and expressive, to convey and interpret essential information quickly and easily. Without skill in using the language of school, a child is certain to fail academically and virtually certain to be socially unsuccessful as well.

Teachers need the assistance of speech-language specialists in assessing their students' language disabilities and in devising interventions. Specifics about how speech-language pathologists work to meet the needs of students with communication disorders is the topic of both the Responsive Instruction box on page 307 and the Making it Work on page 306. Part of the assessment and intervention strategy must also examine the language of the teacher. Problems in classroom discourse involve how teachers talk to students as well as how students use language. Learning how to be clear, relevant, and informative and how to hold listeners' attention are not only problems for students with language disorders but also problems for their teachers. The Personal Perspectives on page 308 offers some general guidelines for how teachers should talk with students.

Casebook Reflection

Refer to the case *Albert* in your booklet. In the case of Albert, the speech-language pathologist works with Albert using sign language, but to no avail. What other approaches might be used?

UNDERSTANDING THE STANDARDS AND PRINCIPLES How can teachers help students improve their speech and language? *(CEC Knowledge and Skills Standard CC4S3)*

Council for Exceptional Children

QUESTION-ASKING STRAGEGIES

One example of the role of the teacher's language in classroom discourse is asking questions. Teachers often ask students too many questions in areas of their identified weaknesses, thereby inadvertently curtailing the students' use of expressive language. For example, a teacher might ask a preschooler who does not know colors to identify colors repeatedly. Or a teacher may overuse yes/no questions (e.g., Is this blue? Are you finished?), which curtail the child's engagement in extended dialogues or provocative conversations. Unfortunately, teachers might not know how to modify their questions to teach concepts effectively, so their questions merely add to children's confusion.

The classroom offers many possibilities for language learning and should provide almost continuous opportunities for students and teachers to employ language and obtain feedback in constructive relationships.

MAKING IT WORK

Collaboration and Co-teaching of Students with Communication Disorders

"Answer me, Amanda. What? Has the cat got your tongue?"

Although throwaway lines like the one in the title might seem harmless, to some students with communication disorders, such statements bring on feelings of fear, shame, and anxiety. Simple misunderstandings during discussion, reluctance to respond to questions for which they have the answers, and an inability to interpret directions are all problems students might have if they have communication disorders. These characteristics might be incorrectly interpreted by the general classroom teacher. The teacher might think that the student is disrespectful, is "not getting it," or "hears when he wants to." Language delays are a thread that run through many disabilities, not just communication disorders (B. Lubker, personal communication). For these reasons, collaboration with a speech-language pathologist or language interventionist is very important for students with communication disorders and their teachers.

WHAT DOES IT MEAN TO BE A TEACHER OF STUDENTS WITH COMMUNICATION DISORDERS?

What is a speech-language pathologist? According to the American Speech-Language-Hearing Association (ASHA), speech-language pathologists help people to develop their communication abilities and treat speech, language, and voice disorders. As you read in the Responsive Instruction on page 307, their services include prevention, identification, evaluation, treatment, and rehabilitation of communication disorders.

ASHA is the professional organization that oversees the certification of speech-language pathologists. This organization has established a set of standards for the newly trained pathologist. The Certificate of Clinical Competence (CCC) is given only to those with a master's or doctoral degree. The CCC includes requirements in basic science courses, professional coursework, 375 clock hours of supervised clinical observation/practice, a clinical fellowship, and a national examination. This is a tremendous amount of coursework in the basics of physiology and audiology, evaluation, and remediation of speech problems.

SUCCESSFUL STRATEGIES FOR COLLABORATION

Speech-language pathologists are encouraged to participate in a variety of collaborative structures, such as co-teaching and collaborative consultation. The general education classroom is one of the environments in which students with language problems must generalize the individual skills they are taught by speech language pathologists, whether they receive instruction in these skills in that classroom or in separate settings. Therefore, the speech-language pathologist can work with the general education teacher, quite often through the special education teacher, to let that teacher know the specific implications of the speech or language disorder for a student's performance in the classroom. The pathologist can also provide guidance in identifying components of a general educator's instruction that may be causing problems and can help modify those components. Finally, the speech language pathologist can work with the general educator to monitor a student's progress, celebrate victories, and work toward a student's independence. For more information, see the American Speech-Language-Hearing Association website at www.asha.org. ∎

By Margaret P. Weiss

Alternative question-asking strategies can be used to help students think through problems successfully. When a student fails to answer a higher-order question because it is beyond his or her level of information or skill, the teacher should reformulate the problem at a simpler level. After the intermediate steps are solved, the teacher can return to the question that was too difficult at first.

Teachers sometimes do not clearly express their intent in questioning students or fail to explicitly delimit the topic of their questions. For example, a teacher might ask "What are you going to tell me?" (not being clear about intention) or "How have you been feeling recently?" (asking a question that is too general or not sufficiently focused). Consequently, students become confused. Teachers must learn to clarify the problems under such circumstances. Teachers must also give unambiguous feedback to students' responses to their questions. Too often, teachers do not tell students explicitly that their answers are wrong, for fear of showing nonacceptance. Lack of accurate, explicit feedback, however, prevents students from learning the concepts involved in instruction.

Meeting the Needs of Students with Communication Disorders

Working with the Speech-Language Pathologist

WHAT IS A SPEECH LANGUAGE PATHOLOGIST?

A speech-language pathologist (SLP) is a specialist in the assessment, treatment, and prevention of communication disorders. Many SLPs work with specific populations or disorders, such as early childhood language development, learning disabilities, developmental delays, autism, articulation/phonology, fluency, voice, swallowing and acquired brain injury.

Tasks of the SLP can include the following:

- Administering screening instruments and making recommendations for treatment:
- Adapting interviewing and testing procedures to meet the needs of a student;
- Assisting teachers and other school professionals as to how to identify children who are at risk for developing problems;
- Working with professionals to help prevent problems before they occur by promoting opportunities for success with spoken and written language at home and school;
- Collaborating with other professionals (e.g. classroom teacher, special educator, administration) on issues relevant to case management and service delivery; and
- Providing direct and indirect services (American Speech-Language-Hearing Association, 2001)

SUPPORTING SPEECH AND LANGUAGE GOALS IN THE CLASSROOM

Traditionally, SLPs have provided services in a clinical, pull-out model. Students on their caseload would come to them to receive intense, directed therapy. Shifts in ideological perspectives toward inclusion, however, are changing that service delivery model. This trend translates into more therapy being conducted within the classroom (Erhen, 2000). Similar to the tensions that exist in the delivery of special education services within general education settings, SLPs must learn to balance the advantages of creating therapy that is responsive to educational demands with the disadvantages of potentially "watering down" the therapy (Erhen, 2000).

To maximize therapy opportunities within classroom settings, SLPs should clearly define their role within the classroom. Role definition should include specific ways in which the SLP will deliver educationally relevant therapy. A guideline for SLPs to follow is as follows:

> In providing in-classroom services the speech-language pathologist's primary responsibility should consist of providing therapeutic services for students on the caseload who need direct service and assisting classroom teachers to meet the needs of these students and others on the caseload who need indirect services. (Erhen, 2000, p. 223)

Examples of therapeutic activities that can be provided in the classroom directly by the SLP include using the classroom text (science, social studies, language arts, etc.) to identify vocabulary, metaphors, idioms, or other language-related concepts; teaching language strategies to all students, while providing cues or guides for students on the caseload to use; and working on therapy goals with a small group of students who may or may not all be on the caseload (Erhen, 2000).

In addition to having the SLP work directly with the classroom, general and special education teachers can support speech and language goals on their own. Through observation, consultation and collaboration with the SLP, classroom teachers can develop a repertoire of strategies that will maintain the work of the SLP. Possible strategies may include the following:

- Developing vocabulary through encouraging naming and describing;
- Promoting comprehension through teaching plot structure, predicting, summarizing strategies, and retelling;
- Creating spelling or reading word lists related to specific articulation goals of a student;
- Connecting speech and written language through having students state responses as well as write them;
- Providing drill and practice in naming objects, following directions, answering questions about stories, etc.;
- Fostering compensatory language skills such as using gestures or writing support or supplant oral communication; or
- Integrating strategies taught by the SLP to encourage language skills such as initiating of conversation, turn-taking, or clarifying communication needs. (American Speech-Language-Hearing Association, 2001)

In summary, many speech and language goals can be addressed within the classroom setting. By understanding the necessary therapeutic role of the SLP, classroom teachers can collaborate with SLPs to identify opportunities for optimal service delivery. ∎

By Kristin L. Sayeski

Personal Perspectives

SUGGESTIONS FOR TALKING WITH STUDENTS

- Choose a topic of interest to the student. Comment on the student's thinking, feelings, and experiences, as he or she describes them by providing models of other words or phrases.
- After initiating the conversation, let the student take the lead. Show interest in and, if appropriate, excitement about what the student says.
- Try not to ask lots of questions, and when you do ask questions, ask open-ended ones for which explanations are appropriate.
- Use appropriate wait-time with your questions; don't demand an immediate response, but give the student enough time to formulate an answer. Be comfortable with some open or empty spaces in the conversation; don't rush.
- Encourage question-asking in return, and give honest and open answers (except, of course, decline politely to, answer inappropriate or highly personal questions).

- Keep your voice at an appropriate level, keep your pace moderate, and keep the conversation light and humorous unless the topic of conversation is serious and humor is inappropriate.
- Avoid being judgmental or making snide remarks about the student's language, simply because if the student thinks you are judgmental or you correct every error he or she will stop talking to you. Demonstrate acceptance of the student's language.
- Do not interrupt the student when he or she is talking, and listen attentively to the student's ideas; show respect.
- Provide as many opportunities as you can for the student to use language in social situations, and respond appropriately to the student's attempts to use language to accomplish his or her goals. ■

Our points here are these:

- The teacher's role is not merely to instruct students about language but also to teach them how to use it. More specifically, the teacher must help students learn how to use language in the context of the classroom.
- The teacher's own use of language is a key factor in helping students learn effectively, especially if students have language disorders.

Teachers need to keep in mind, too, that language disorders can change with the child's development. Just because a child has receptive or expressive language within the normal range at one age does not mean that it will be within the same range at a later age. Figure 9.1 depicts changes with age for Troy, a child whose language problems are shown at various ages (Plante & Beeson, 1999). Language intervention can change the nature and course of a child's language abilities, but even with therapy, a child might have language problems that are persistent. Notice that Troy, who received speech-language services, did not achieve expressive language abilities close to the normal range until age 14 and that only then did his expressive language ability exceed his receptive ability.

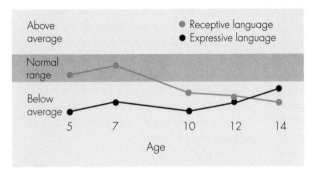

FIGURE 9.1 For children with developmental language disorders, the components of language can change over time. Here we can see receptive and expressive language skills shift over time in a single child relative to typically developing peers.

Source: From Plante, E., & Beeson, P. M. (1999). *Communication and communication disorders: A clinical introduction.* Boston: Allyn & Bacon, p. 155. Copyright © 1999. Reprinted/adapted by permission by Allyn & Bacon.

TEACHING WRITTEN LANGUAGE

Written language or developing literacy is a special problem for many students with speech and language disorders. In fact, as students progress through the grades, written language takes on increasing importance. Students are expected to read increasingly complex and difficult material and understand its meaning. In addition, they are expected to express themselves more clearly in writing. The interactions teachers have with students about their writing—the questions they ask to help students understand how to write for their readers—are critical to overcoming disabilities in written language (Graham, Harris, MacArthur, & Schwartz, 1998). Likewise, the strategies teachers use to help students master the alphabetic system are also critical.

Finally, we note that intervention in language disorders employs many of the same strategies used in intervention in learning disabilities. Metacognitive training, strategy training, and other approaches that we discuss in Chapter 6 are typically appropriate for use with students who have language disorders (see also Hallahan, Lloyd, Kauffman, Weiss, & Martinez, 2005).

Early Intervention

Early intervention is critically important for two primary reasons:

1. The older the child is when intervention is begun, the smaller the chance that he or she will acquire effective language skills (other things being equal).
2. Without having functional language, the child cannot become a truly social being (Warren & Abbaduto, 1992). Of all the skills in which a child may be lagging, language—communication—is the most important, as it is the foundation of academic and social learning.

EARLY DEVELOPMENT AND EARLY INTERVENTION

The study of children's early development has shown that the first several years of life are a truly critical period for language learning. We have known for a long time that much of children's language, literacy, and social development depends on the nature and quantity of the language interactions they have with parents or other caregivers. In the homes of children who come to school ready to learn, the language interactions between parents and children have typically been frequent, focused on encouragement and affirmation of the children's behavior, emphasized the symbolic nature of language, provided gentle guidance in exploring things and relationships, and demonstrated the responsiveness of adults to children. By contrast, children who enter school at a disadvantage tend to have experienced much lower rates of language interaction; to have heard primarily negative, discouraging feedback on their behavior; and to have heard language that is harsh, literal, and emotionally detached.

In a now classic study, Hart and Risley (1995) compared the language experiences of children of professional parents, working-class parents, and parents on welfare. The contrasts in language experiences and the effects observed in children's academic achievement and behavior are stark, but the differences are unrelated to income or ethnicity. Rather, the differences are related to how and how much the parents talked to their children. As summed up by the authors:

> Our data showed that the magnitude of children's accomplishments depends less on the material and educational advantages available in the home and more on the amount of experience children accumulate with parenting that provides language diversity, affirmative feedback, symbolic emphasis, gentle guidance, and responsiveness. By the time children are 3 years old, even intensive intervention cannot make up for the differences in the amount of such experience children have received from their parents. If children could be given better parenting, intervention might be unnecessary. (Hart & Risley, 1995, p. 210)

Thus, it appears that the key to preventing many disabilities related to language development is to help parents improve how they relate to their children when they are infants and toddlers. Nevertheless, for many young children, intervention in the preschool and primary grades will be necessary. But such intervention must be guided by understanding of children's families, particularly mothers' views of language development (Hammer & Weiss, 2000). Preschoolers who require intervention for a speech or language disorder occasionally have multiple disabilities that are sometimes severe or profound.

Language is closely tied to cognitive development, so impairment of general intellectual ability is likely to have a retarding influence on language development. Conversely, lack of language can hamper cognitive development. Because speech is dependent on neurological and motor development, any neurological or motor problem might impair ability to speak. Normal social development in the preschool years also depends on the emergence of language, so a child with language impairment is at a disadvantage in social learning. Therefore, the preschool child's language is seldom the only target of intervention.

EARLY INTERVENTION IN DELAYED LANGUAGE DEVELOPMENT

Children with language disorders may follow the same sequence of development as most children but achieve each skill or milestone at a later-than-average age. Some children with language disorders reach final levels of development that are significantly below those of their peers who do not have disabilities. Still other children may be generally delayed in language development but show great discrepancies in the rate at which they acquire certain features of language.

Some children are late bloomers who in time will catch up with their age peers (Sowell, 1997). Yet many children whose language development is delayed show a developmental lag that they will not outgrow (Owens, 2004). They are frequently diagnosed as having mental retardation or another developmental disability. Sometimes these children come from environments where they have been deprived of many experiences, including the language stimulation from adults that is required for normal language development, or they have been severely abused or neglected. Regardless of the reasons for a child's delayed language, however, it is important to understand the nature of the delay and to intervene to give him or her the optimal chance of learning to use language effectively.

Milieu teaching is an approach that uses naturalistic language to teach functional language skills. In this approach, teaching is built around the child's interests.

Some children 3 years of age or older show no signs that they understand language and do not use language spontaneously. They might make noises, but they use them to communicate in ways that may characterize the communication of infants and toddlers before they have learned speech. In other words, they may use **prelinguistic communication**. For example, they may use gestures or vocal noises to request objects or actions from others, to protest, to request a social routine (e.g., reading), or to greet someone.

When assessing and planning intervention for children with delayed language, it is important to consider what language and nonlanguage behaviors they imitate, what they comprehend, what communication skills they use spontaneously, and what part communication plays in their lives. It is also important, particularly with young children, to provide intervention in contexts in which language is used for normal social interaction. For example, parents or teachers may use a **milieu teaching** approach, "a naturalistic language intervention designed to teach functional language skills" (Kaiser, Hammeter, Ostrosky, Alpert, & Hancock, 1995, p. 40). In this approach, teaching is built around the child's interests. When the child requests some action, object, or activity from the adult, the adult prompts the child's language and makes access to what is requested contingent on an attempt to communicate. Milieu teaching is a naturalistic approach, in that it encourages designing interventions that are similar to the conversational interactions that parents and children ordinarily have. Prelinguistic communication may be a good indication of a child's later ability to use language (Calandrella & Wilcox, 2000). The effectiveness of a milieu teaching approach may depend, at least to some extent, on mothers' responsiveness to their children's prelinguistic communication (Yoder & Warren, 2001).

INVOLVEMENT OF FAMILIES

Researchers have become increasingly aware that language development has its beginning in the earliest mother–child interactions. Concern for the child's development of the ability to communicate cannot be separated from concern for development in other areas. Therefore, speech-language pathologists are a vital part of the multidisciplinary team that evaluates an infant or young child with disabilities and develops an individualized family service plan (IFSP) (see Chapters 2 and 4). Early intervention programs involve extending the role of the parent. This means a lot of simple play with accompanying verbalizations. It means talking to the child about objects and activities in the way most mothers talk to their babies. But it also means choosing objects, activities, words, and consequences for the child's vocalizations with great care so the chances that the child will learn functional language are enhanced (Fey, Catts, & Larrivee, 1995).

Early childhood specialists now realize that prelinguistic intervention is critical for language development—that is, intervention should begin before the child's language emerges. The foundations for language are laid in the first few months of life through the nonverbal dialogues infants have with their mothers and other caretakers (Nelson, 1998). In the early years of implementing IFSPs, emphasis was placed on assessing families' strengths and needs and training parents how to teach and manage their children. More recently, professionals have come to understand that assessing families in the belief that professionals know best is often misguided. Parents can indeed be helped by professionals to play an important role in their children's language development. But the emphasis today is on working with parents as knowledgeable and competent partners whose preferences and decisions are respected (Hammer & Weiss, 2000; see also discussion in Chapter 14).

Intervention in early childhood is likely to be based on assessment of the child's behavior related to the content, form, and especially the use of language in social interaction. For the child who has not yet learned language, assessment and intervention will focus on imitation, ritualized and make-believe play, play with objects, and functional use of objects. At the earliest stages in which the content and form of language are interactive, it is important to evaluate the extent to which the child looks at or picks up an object when it is referred to, does something with an object when directed by an adult, and uses sounds to request or refuse things and call attention to objects. When the child's use of language is

Prelinguistic communication
Communication through gestures and noises before the child has learned oral language.

Milieu teaching
A naturalistic approach to language intervention in which the goal is to teach functional language skills in a natural environment.

The first several years of life are truly critical for language learning.

considered, the earliest objectives involve the child looking at the adult during interactions; taking turns in and trying to prolong pleasurable activities and games; following the gaze of an adult and directing the behavior of adults; and persisting in or modifying gestures, sounds, or words when an adult does not respond. In the preschool, teaching discourse (conversation skills) is a critical focus of language intervention. In particular, emphasis is placed on teaching children to use the discourse that is essential for success in school. Children must learn, for example, to report their experiences in detail and to explain why things happen, not just add to their vocabularies. They must learn not only word forms and meanings, but also how to take turns in conversations and maintain the topic of a conversation or change it in an appropriate way. Preschool programs in which such language teaching is the focus may include teachers' daily individualized conversations with children, daily reading to individual children or small groups, and frequent classroom discussions.

Current trends are directed toward providing speech and language interventions in the typical environments of young children. This means that classroom teachers and speech-language pathologists must develop a close working relationship. The speech-language pathologist might work directly with children in the classroom and advise the teacher about the intervention that he or she can carry out as part of the regular classroom activities. Alternatively, the speech-language pathologist might work with the teacher directly to help her incorporate effective instructional practices for these students. The Responsive Instruction on page 313 provides an example of one successful collaboration. The child's peers may also be involved in intervention strategies. Because language is essentially a social activity, its facilitation requires involvement of others in the child's social environment—peers as well as adults (Audet & Tankersley, 1999; Fey et al., 1995; Prizant, 1999).

Normally developing peers have been taught to assist in the language development of children with disabilities by doing the following during playtimes: establishing eye contact; describing their own or others' play; and repeating, expanding, or requesting clarification of what the child with disabilities says. Peer tutors can help in developing the speech and language of their classmates who may use different dialects (McGregor, 2000). Another intervention strategy involving peers is sociodramatic play. Children are taught in groups of three, including a child with disabilities, to act out social roles such as those people might take in various settings (e.g., a restaurant or shoe store). The training includes scripts that specify what each child is to do and say, which the children can modify in creative ways.

RESPONSIVE INSTRUCTION

Meeting the Needs of Students with Communication Disorders

Collaboration in an Inner-City Classroom

WHAT THE RESEARCH SAYS

Research on early language ability has demonstrated a correlation between early language development and later reading ability (Snow, Burns, & Griffin, 1998). Children from low income homes, with identified language impairments, or who have difficulty speaking English face considerable challenges in learning to read (Snow et al., 1998; Stothard, Snowling, Bishop, Chipchese, & Kaplon, 1998; Walker, Greenwood, Hart, & Carta, 1994).

Given the fact that many inner-city school districts have disproportionately high numbers of students who fall into one of the above "risk factors," school personnel are constantly seeking ways to mediate these risks. Recommendations from professional organizations encourage collaboration among professionals in order to capitalize on specific areas of strength and provide connected interventions across settings. In the area of language, the America Speech-Language-Hearing Association, the professional organization of speech-language pathologists, recommends that speech-language pathologists and the classroom teachers collaborate to intensify language instruction within general education classrooms (American Speech-Language-Hearing Association, 1991).

RESEARCH STUDY

One team of researchers explored the effectiveness of a collaborative, classroom-based intervention to improve the vocabulary and phonological awareness of inner-city kindergartners and first graders (Hadley, Simmerman, Long, & Luna, 2000). Eighty-three percent of the students in this school district were eligible for free or reduced-cost lunch—a marker for low socioeconomic status. In addition, 28 percent of the students were considered limited English proficient.

For the study, four general education classrooms were selected. Two classrooms served as the control groups (i.e., received no intervention) and two served at the experimental groups (i.e., received the intervention). The intervention consisted of the speech-language pathologist teaching language-related lessons two and a half days per week and regularly collaborating with the general education teacher to develop other language-based activities to integrate throughout the day. The control classes followed standard instructional practices with no collaboration or teaching from the speech-language pathologist.

RESEARCH FINDINGS

Following the six-month intervention, students in the experimental groups demonstrated greater gains in the areas of receptive vocabulary, expressive vocabulary, beginning sound awareness, and letter-sound associations when compared to students in the control group. Additionally, the findings demonstrated that both native English speakers and students with nonnative backgrounds benefited from the intensive vocabulary and phonemic awareness instruction.

The study demonstrated the ability of speech-language pathologists to collaborate successfully with general education teachers. This collaboration facilitated the teaching of explicit skills within educationally relevant communication and curricular activities.

APPLYING THE RESEARCH TO TEACHING

The results of this study demonstrate potential benefits of collaboration between speech-language pathologists and general educators. Critical are:

- Creating time for joint planning so that intervention activities are planned and roles are clearly established;
- Identifying specific goals to be addressed and allocating intervention activities by expertise;
- Modeling on the part of the speech-language pathologist so that the classroom teacher can use the strategies throughout the day, not just when the speech-language pathologist is present. (Hadley et al., 2000) ■

By Kristin L. Sayeski

Casebook Reflection

Refer to the case *Albert* in your booklet. The story of Albert ends with his mother stating that her brother has the same condition but is able to conduct a normal life. What does this piece of information say about Albert's transition to adulthood?

UNDERSTANDING THE STANDARDS AND PRINCIPLES What speech-language services should teachers keep in mind when planning students' transition programming? *(CEC Knowledge and Skills Standard GC7K2)*

Council for Exceptional Children

Transition to Adulthood

In the past, adolescents and adults in speech and language intervention programs generally fell into three categories: (1) the self-referred, (2) those with other health problems, and (3) those with severe disabilities. Adolescents or adults might refer themselves to speech-language pathologists because their phonology, voice, or stuttering is causing them social embarrassment and/or interfering with occupational pursuits. These are generally people with long-standing problems who are highly motivated to change their speech and obtain relief from the social penalties their differences impose.

Adolescents and adults with other health problems might have experienced damage to speech or language capacities as a result of disease or injury, or they might have lost part of their speech mechanism through injury or surgical removal. Treatment of these individuals always demands an interdisciplinary effort. In some cases of progressive disease, severe neurological damage, or loss of tissues of the speech mechanism, the outlook for functional speech is not good. However, surgical procedures, medication, and prosthetic devices are making it possible for more people to speak normally. Loss of ability to use language is typically more disabling than loss of the ability to speak. Traumatic brain injury may leave the individual with a seriously diminished capacity for self-awareness, goal setting, planning, self-directing or initiating actions, inhibiting impulses, monitoring or evaluating one's own performance, or problem solving. Recovering these vital language-based skills is a critical aspect of transition of the adolescent or young adult from hospital to school and from school to independent living (Klein & Moses, 1999).

Individuals with severe disabilities might need the services of speech-language pathologists to help them achieve more intelligible speech. They might also need to be taught an alternative to oral language or given a system of augmented communication. One of the major problems in working with adolescents and adults who have severe disabilities is setting realistic goals for speech and language learning. Teaching simple, functional language—such as social greetings, naming objects, and making simple requests—may be realistic goals for some adolescents and adults.

A major concern of transition programming is ensuring that the training and support provided during the school years are carried over into adult life. To be successful, the transition must include speech-language services that are part of the natural environment. That is, the services must be community based and integrated into vocational, domestic, recreational, consumer, and mobility training activities. Speech-language interventions for adolescents and young adults with severe disabilities must emphasize functional communication—understanding and making oneself understood in the social circumstances that are most likely to be encountered in everyday life (Justice, 2006). Developing appropriate conversation skills (e.g., establishing eye contact, using greetings, taking turns, and identifying and staying on the topic), reading, writing, following instructions related to recreational activities, using public transportation, and performing a job are examples of the kinds of functional speech-language activities that may be emphasized.

Today, much more emphasis is being placed on the language disorders of adolescents and young adults who do not fit into other typical categories of disabilities. Many of these individuals were formerly seen as having primarily academic and social problems that were not language related. But now it is understood that underlying many or most of the school and social difficulties of adolescents and adults are basic disorders of language. These language disorders are a continuation of difficulties experienced earlier in the person's development.

Classroom teachers are in a particularly good position to identify possible language-related problems and request help from a communication specialist. The Focus on Concepts

FOCUS ON CONCEPTS

Identifying Possible Language Problems Related to Transition

OLDER CHILDREN and adolescents may need help from a communication specialist if they:

- Fail to understand instructions in typical situations
- Cannot use language effectively to meet their daily living needs

- Frequently violate social rules involving politeness and interpersonal interactions
- Do not have the ability to read important signs and symbols, complete forms, and write simple reports
- Have problems speaking so that others understand ■

above describes for teachers several characteristics exhibited by older children and adolescents that may indicate a need for consultation and intervention. Addressing problems like these as early and effectively as possible is important in helping youngsters make successful transitions to more complex and socially demanding environments.

Some adolescents and adults with language disorders are excellent candidates for strategy training, which teaches them how to select, store, retrieve, and process information (see Hallahan et al., 2005, and Chapter 6). Others, however, do not have the required reading skills, symbolic abilities, or intelligence to benefit from the usual training in cognitive strategies. Whatever techniques are chosen for adolescents and older students, the teacher should be aware of the principles that apply to intervention with these individuals.

SUMMARY

HOW are communication disorders defined?

- Communication involves sharing information between two individuals or among more than two individuals.
- Communicative functions include requesting, rejecting, commenting, arguing, reasoning, and so on.
- Communication disorders may involve language or speech or both, and they impair communicative functions.
  - Language is sending and receiving ideas—expression and reception—through an arbitrary system of symbols used according to rules.
  - Speech is the neuromuscular activity of forming and sequencing the sounds of oral language.

WHAT is the prevalence of communication disorders?

- Reasonable estimates are that about 10 to 15 percent of preschool children and about 6 percent of students in elementary and secondary grades have speech disorders.
- Probably about 2 to 3 percent of preschoolers and about 1 percent of the school-age population have language disorders.

WHAT is the difference between communicative differences and disorders?

- Differences include dialects, regional differences, language of ethnic minority groups, and nondominant languages.

- An individual with a difference that is not a disorder is an effective communicator in his or her language community, whereas someone with a disorder has impaired communication in all language environments.

WHAT are the major disorders of language?

- There are many different theories of language development and the disorders of language.
- Language disorders may be primary (no known cause) or secondary (attributable to another condition or disability).
  - Primary language disorders include specific language impairment (SLI), early expressive language delay (EELD), and language-based reading impairment.
  - Secondary language disorders include those related to emotional or behavioral disorders or any other disability, such as mental retardation or autistic spectrum disorder.

WHAT are the major disorders of speech?

- Speech disorders are a very heterogeneous group of problems related to the production of oral language, including the following:
  - Phonological disorders—problems in understanding the sound system of language
  - Articulation disorders—problems in producing correct speech sounds
  - Voice disorders—problems in producing voice with appropriate pitch, loudness, or quality
  - Fluency disorders—problems in maintaining speech flow
  - Motor-speech—problems in speaking due to neuro-motor damage, including the following:
    - Dysarthria—problems in controlling the production of speech sounds
    - Apraxia—problems in planning and coordinating speech

WHAT are the major features of assessment of communication disorders?

- The two main requirements of assessment are determining the child's current language abilities and observing the ease and speed with which the child learns new language skills.
- Assessment for intervention requires attention to the following:
  - What the child talks about and should be taught to talk about
  - How the child talks about things and how he or she could be taught to speak of those things more intelligibly
  - How the child functions in the context of his or her linguistic community
  - How the child uses language and how his or her use of it could be made to serve the purposes of communication and socialization more effectively

WHAT are the main educational considerations for communication disorders?

- The classroom teacher needs to work with others in three main areas:
  - Facilitating the social uses of language
  - Question-asking
  - Teaching written language

WHAT are the major aspects of early intervention for communication disorders?

- Early intervention is based on early language development.
- Early intervention usually involves working with delayed language.
- Early intervention requires working with families.

WHAT is emphasized in transition for students with communication disorders?

- Transition involves helping students use the language demanded for successful employment.

APPLYING THE STANDARDS AND PRINCIPLES

- **ONE** of your colleagues, whose background is in general education, asks, "**What does it really mean to have a language disorder?**" How would you respond? *(CEC Content Standard #2 & INTASC Principle #2)*

- **WHAT** can teachers do to **help students** overcome speech and language disorders? *(CEC Content Standard #4)*

- **WHY** are **language differences sometimes mistaken for language disorders**? *(CEC Content Standard #6)*

- **WHAT** language-related problems might **older children and adolescents** exhibit that may indicate a need for consultation and intervention? *(CEC Content Standard #7 & INTASC Principle #7)*

Council for Exceptional Children

INTASC

Chapter 10

Learners Who Are Deaf or Hard of Hearing

U pon transitioning to high school, friends dispersed into separate crowds. The new school was much bigger. . . . I found myself becoming increasingly isolated. One afternoon . . ., I sat on the sofa . . . having a mutually desired but laborious conversation with my mother. . . . I asked her why I didn't have as many friends as the other kids. . . . She looked at me with a surprised expression on her face.

"You don't know why?" she asked.

"No."

"It's because you can't hear, and they don't understand that."

That was a revelation and turning point in my life. Until that moment, I had only understood my deafness in a blur. I had never understood this difference between myself and others to be such a determining factor in my life. . . . But still I did not realize all the implications regarding relationships, my future, language, and education. I did not know this wasn't just a hearing problem. The difficulties I faced were not because I had a hearing problem, but because the often-cruel world around me was full of barriers. That understanding was a long way off.

MARTHA SHERIDAN
Inner Lives of Deaf Children: Interviews and Analysis

QUESTIONS TO GUIDE YOUR READING OF THIS CHAPTER. . . .

- HOW do professionals define and classify individuals who are deaf or hard of hearing?

- WHAT is the prevalence of hearing impairment?

- WHAT are some basic anatomical and physiological characteristics of the ear?

- HOW is hearing ability measured?

- WHAT causes hearing impairments?

- WHAT are some psychological and behavioral characteristics of learners with hearing impairments?

- WHAT are some educational considerations for learners with hearing impairments?

- WHAT are some things to consider with respect to early intervention for learners with hearing impairments?

- WHAT are some things to consider with respect to transition to adulthood for learners with hearing impairments?

SPECIAL EDUCATORS . . .

- **understand the field** as an evolving and changing discipline *(from CEC Content Standard #1).*

- understand the similarities and differences in **human development** *(from CEC Content Standard #2).*

- **understand the effects** that an exceptional condition can have on an individual's learning. *(from CEC Content Standard #3).*

- **actively create learning environments** . . . that foster cultural understanding, safety and emotional well-being, positive social interactions, and active engagement *(from CEC Content Standard #5).*

- **use individualized strategies** to enhance language development and teach communication skills *(from CEC Content Standard #6).*

- develop a variety of **individualized transition plans** *(from CEC Content Standard #7).*

- **use the results of assessments** to help identify exceptional learning needs *(from CEC Content Standard #8).*

- **use collaboration** to facilitate the successful transitions of individuals with exceptional learning needs *(from CEC Content Standard #10).*

ALL TEACHERS . . .

- understand the **central concepts, tools of inquiry, structures of the discipline(s)** they teach *(from INTASC Principle #1).*

- understand how **children learn and develop** *(from INTASC Principle #2).*

- **use an understanding of individual and group motivation and behavior** to create a learning environment that encourages positive social interaction, active engagement in learning, and self-motivation *(INTASC Principle #5).*

- **plan instruction** based on knowledge of subject matter, students, the community, and curriculum goals *(INTASC Principle #7).*

- understand and use formal and informal **assessment strategies** *(from INTASC Principle #8).*

- **foster relationships** with school colleagues, families, and agencies *(from INTASC Principle #10).*

INTASC

To be deaf, or even hard of hearing, often places a person in a difficult place somewhere between the world of the hearing and the world of the Deaf. Martha Sheridan's (2001) words (see p. 319) reflect the isolation that can accompany a hearing impairment. And as we see from her experience, this isolation is caused primarily by communication problems. As we will see in this chapter, even if the hearing impairment is not severe enough for the child to be classified as "deaf," but rather as "hard of hearing," the child with a hearing impairment is at a distinct disadvantage in virtually all aspects of English language development. The importance of the English language in U.S. society, particularly in school-related activities, is obvious. Many of the problems that people with hearing impairment have in school are due primarily to their deficiencies in English. We explore this issue in some depth in this chapter.

A related controversy that is inherent in Martha Sheridan's words is the debate concerning whether the child who is deaf should be educated to communicate orally or through manual sign language. Sheridan is typical of the 95 percent of those who are deaf in that her parents are hearing (Mitchell & Karchmer, 2004). Her parents are hearing and had chosen not to learn sign language. Again, this is common. Also common, however, is the fact that Sheridan had difficulty learning to speechread, or to use visual information, including lip movements, from a number of sources to understand what is being said.

Again, like others in the same situation, Sheridan eventually went on to immerse herself in the Deaf community. She found her identity as a Deaf person through her experiences at Gallaudet University, the primary postsecondary institution for students with hearing impairment;

> Gallaudet was a major gateway for me. It was the pot of gold at the end of my search for self, and it represented the beginning of the rest of my life. It was at Gallaudet that I discovered what it means to be deaf. . . . Here, and with sign language, my love for learning blossomed. (Sheridan, 2001, pp. 7–8)

But not all people who are deaf elect to join the Deaf community. Some do become fluent enough in spoken English to function in mainstream society. Others are able to straddle both the world of the hearing and the Deaf. But no matter what the outcome, virtually all people who are deaf, as well as their parents, struggle with critical choices about oral versus manual modes of communication and cultural identity. With respect to the latter, in fact, many members of

Misconceptions About
Learners Who Are Deaf or Hard of Hearing

MYTH People who are deaf are unable to hear anything.

FACT Most people who are deaf have some residual hearing.

MYTH Deafness is not as severe a disability as blindness.

FACT Although it is impossible to predict the exact consequences of a disability on a person's functioning, in general, deafness poses more difficulties in adjustment than does blindness. This is largely due to the effects hearing loss can have on the ability to understand and speak oral language.

MYTH It is unhealthy for people who are deaf to socialize almost exclusively with others who are deaf.

FACT Many authorities now recognize that the phenomenon of a Deaf culture is natural and should be encouraged. In fact, some are worried that too much mainstreaming will diminish the influence of the Deaf culture.

MYTH In learning to understand what is being said to them, people with a hearing impairment concentrate on reading lips.

FACT *Lipreading* refers only to visual cues arising from movement of the lips. Some people who have a hearing impairment not only read lips but also take advantage of a number of other visual cues, such as facial expressions and movements of the jaw and tongue. They are engaging in what is referred to as *speechreading*.

MYTH Speechreading is relatively easy to learn and is used by the majority of people with a hearing impairment.

FACT Speechreading is extremely difficult to learn, and very few people who have a hearing impairment actually become proficient speechreaders.

MYTH American Sign Language (ASL) is a loosely structured group of gestures.

FACT ASL is a true language in its own right, with its own set of grammatical rules.

MYTH People within the Deaf community are in favor of mainstreaming students who are deaf into regular classes.

FACT Some within the Deaf community have voiced the opinion that regular classes are not appropriate for many students who are deaf. They point to the need for a critical mass of students who are deaf in order to have effective educational programs for these individuals. They see separate placements as a way of fostering the Deaf culture.

MYTH Families in which both the child and the parents are deaf are at a distinct disadvantage compared to families in which the parents are hearing.

FACT Research has demonstrated that children who are deaf who have parents who are also deaf fare better in a number of academic and social areas. Authorities point to the parents' ability to communicate with their children in ASL as a major reason for this advantage.

Casebook Reflection

Refer to the case *Least Restrictive for Whom?* in your booklet. Mary Scanlon had learned in a Characteristics of Persons with Disabilities course that "deafness was probably the most difficult disability with which to live." Do you agree with this assessment? Why or why not?

UNDERSTANDING THE STANDARDS AND PRINCIPLES What is the distinction between *deaf* and *hard of hearing?* (CEC Knowledge and Skills Standard DH1K1)

Council for Exceptional Children

Decibels
Units of relative loudness of sounds; zero decibels (0 dB) designates the point at which people with normal hearing can just detect sound.

Congenitally deaf
Deafness that is present at birth; can be caused by genetic factors, by injuries during fetal development, or by injuries occurring at birth.

Adventitiously deaf
Deafness that occurs through illness or accident in an individual who was born with normal hearing.

Prelingual deafness
Deafness that occurs before the development of spoken language, usually at birth.

Postlingual deafness
Deafness occurring after the development of speech and language.

the Deaf community consider themselves part of a cultural minority rather than disabled.

All of these thorny issues make deafness one of the most challenging fields of study in all of special education. As you would surmise from our discussion of other special education areas, this challenge is evident in attempts to arrive at a definition of hearing impairment.

Definition and Classification

There are many definitions and classification systems of hearing impairment. By far the most common division is between *deaf* and *hard of hearing*. Although it is common to think that being deaf means not to be able to hear anything and that being hard of hearing means being able to hear a little bit, this is generally not true. Most people who are deaf have some residual hearing. Complicating things is the fact that different professionals define the two categories differently. The extreme points of view are represented by those with a physiological orientation versus those with an educational orientation.

Those who maintain a strictly physiological viewpoint are interested primarily in the *measurable degree* of hearing impairment. Children who cannot hear sounds at or above a certain intensity (loudness) level are classified as "deaf"; others with a hearing impairment are considered "hard of hearing." Hearing sensitivity is measured in **decibels** (units of relative loudness of sounds). Zero decibels (0 dB) designates the point at which the average person with normal hearing can detect the faintest sound. Each succeeding number of decibels that a person cannot detect indicates a certain degree of hearing impairment. Those who maintain a physiological viewpoint generally consider people with hearing impairments of about 90 dB or greater to be deaf and people with impairments at lower decibel levels to be hard of hearing.

People with an educational viewpoint are concerned with how much the hearing impairment is likely to affect the child's ability to speak and develop language. Because of the close causal link between hearing impairment and delay in language development, these professionals categorize primarily on the basis of spoken language abilities. *Hearing impairment* is a broad term that covers individuals with impairments ranging from mild to profound; it includes those who are deaf or hard of hearing. Following are commonly accepted, educationally oriented definitions for *deaf* and *hard of hearing*:

- A deaf person is one whose hearing disability precludes successful processing of linguistic information through audition, with or without a hearing aid.
- A person who is hard of hearing generally, with the use of a hearing aid, has residual hearing sufficient to enable successful processing of linguistic information through audition (Brill, MacNeil, & Newman, 1986, p. 67).

Educators are extremely concerned about the age of onset of hearing impairment. Again, the close relationship between hearing impairment and language delay is the key. The earlier the hearing impairment occurs in a child's life, the more difficulty the child will have developing the language of the hearing society (e.g., English). For this reason, professionals frequently use the terms **congenitally deaf** (those who are born deaf) and **adventitiously deaf** (those who acquire deafness at some time after birth).

Two other frequently used terms are even more specific in pinpointing language acquisition as critical: **Prelingual deafness** refers to deafness that occurs at birth or early in life before speech and language develop. **Postlingual deafness** is deafness that occurs after the development of speech and language. Experts differ about the dividing point between prelingual and postlingual deafness. Some believe that it should be at about eighteen months; others think it should be lower, at about twelve months or even six months (Meadow-Orlans, 1987).

Some professionals find it useful to classify according to hearing threshold levels, such as the following: mild (26–40 dB), moderate (41–55 dB), moderate-severe (56–70 dB), severe (71–90 dB), and profound (91 dB and above) (Andrews, Leigh, & Weiner, 2004). These levels of severity according to loss of hearing sensitivity cut across the broad classifications of deaf and hard of hearing. The broader classifications are not directly dependent on hearing sensitivity. Instead, they stress the degree to which speech and language are affected.

Some authorities object to adhering too strictly to any of the various classification systems. Because these definitions deal with events that are difficult to measure, they are not precise. Therefore, it is best not to form any hard-and-fast opinions about an individual's ability to hear and speak solely on the basis of a classification of his or her hearing disability.

In considering issues of definition, it is important to point out that there is growing sentiment among people who are deaf that deafness should not even be considered a disability. (See Focus on Concepts on p. 324.) Note that Lane at times uses the term *Deaf* with a capital *D* and at other times does not. Although there is some variance, following is the distinction that is often used by those who view deafness as a cultural difference rather than as a disability:

A current issue in defining deafness is that many people in the Deaf community do not want to be considered as having a disability. Instead, they want to be thought of as members of a cultural group with its own language—American Sign Language (ASL).

The lowercase "deaf" refers to those for whom deafness is primarily an audiological experience. It is mainly used to describe those who lost some or all of their hearing in early or late life, and who do not usually wish to have contact with signing Deaf communities, preferring to try to maintain their membership in the majority society in which they were socialized.

"Deaf" refers to those born Deaf or deafened in early (sometimes late) childhood, for whom the sign languages, communities and cultures of the Deaf collective represents their primary experience and allegiance, many of whom perceive their experience akin to other language minorities. (Ladd, 2003, p. xvii)

Later in the chapter, we discuss more thoroughly the nature and purpose of the Deaf culture. For now, it is enough to be aware of the challenges that have been raised to the very notion of considering deafness a disability.

Prevalence

Estimates of the number of children with hearing impairment vary considerably. Such factors as differences in definition, populations studied, and accuracy of testing contribute to the varying figures. The U.S. Department of Education's statistics indicate that the public schools identify about 0.13 percent of the population from 6 to 17 years of age as deaf or hard of hearing. Although the Department of Education does not report separate figures for the categories of deaf and hard of hearing, there is strong evidence that students who are hard of hearing are far more prevalent than those who are deaf (Meadow-Orlans, Mertens, & Sass-Lehrer, 2003). Furthermore, some authorities believe that many children who are hard of hearing who could benefit from special education are not being served.

An important statistic is that close to 23 percent of students who are deaf in the United States come from Hispanic-speaking homes (Gallaudet Research Institute, 2003). In

MORE INFORMATION on the anatomy of the ear, including drawings, can be found at a website called, Virtual Tour of the Ear: **www.augie.edu/perry/ear/hearmech.htm**

The Virtual Tour of the Ear home page at **http://ctl.augie.edu/perry/ar/ar.htm** contains dozens of links to websites devoted to many topics concerning hearing impairment.

Another excellent website is maintained by the National Institute on Deafness and Other Communication Disorders of the National Institutes of Health: **www.nidcd.nih.gov.** On this site you can access a number of interesting demonstrations, including a video that explains how the ear works.

FOCUS ON CONCEPTS

Deafness: Disability or Cultural Difference?

FOR the vast majority of society, it seems fairly obvious that deafness is a disability. However, it is far from obvious to many people who are deaf, who argue that instead of being considered disabled, people who are deaf should be considered a cultural minority with a language of their own: sign language (Ladd, 2003; Lane, 2002; Padden & Humphries, 1988). As Harlan Lane puts it:

> What is the source of the belief that being a Deaf person entails an inherent biological limitation? Why is *deaf* associated with loss rather than difference or gain (different language, different culture, etc.)? I submit that it is because the society that has elaborated the concept of *deaf* is largely hearing and conceptualizes *deaf* as a loss of hearing. Indeed, the difference in hearing of a person born Deaf and one born hearing is called "hearing loss," although the Deaf person didn't lose anything. (Lane, 2002, p. 366)

Knowing that some within the Deaf community do not believe that deafness is a disability presents an interesting and challenging problem for educators and other professionals. Should their wishes be honored? Special educators, in particular, are trained to help *remediate* differences and to try to make people with such differences as "normal" as possible. Would it

be professionally irresponsible not to find students who are deaf eligible for special education services?

One team of authorities has acknowledged that there has been a history of viewing some behaviors, such as very expressive facial expressions and overt methods of getting someone's attention, of people who are deaf as pathological when, in fact, they are merely cultural differences (Andrews, Leigh, & Weiner, 2004). However, they also note that many within the Deaf community were advocates for equal rights protections under the Americans with Disabilities Act. They further state:

> The point to be made is that the hearing population, including professionals, need to focus on and recognize the . . . positive aspects of deaf people. . . . The pendulum has swung from the time when deafness was viewed as a pathology so severe that Alexander Graham Bell, in a paper published by the prestigious National Academy of Science, proposed that stringent eugenics should be applied to eradicate deafness through genetic and reproductive restrictions (Bell, 1883). This bears testimony to the conditions and attitudes deaf people have faced in the past. It makes understandable their desire to have their culture respected and the focus placed on their abilities, not limitations. (Andrews et al., 2004, p. 12) ■

Tympanic membrane (eardrum)
The anatomical boundary between the outer and middle ears; the sound gathered in the outer ear vibrates here.

Auricle
The visible part of the ear, composed of cartilage; collects the sounds and funnels them via the external auditory canal to the eardrum.

Ossicles
Three tiny bones (malleus, incus, and stapes) that together make possible an efficient transfer of sound waves from the eardrum to the oval window, which connects the middle ear to the inner ear.

addition, there are relatively large numbers of other non-English-speaking immigrants who are deaf. The relatively high numbers of students who are deaf who come from non-English-speaking families creates significant challenges for the schools. Deafness by itself makes spoken language acquisition in the native language very difficult, let alone deafness plus attempting to learn a second language.

Anatomy and Physiology of the Ear

The ear is one of the most complex organs of the body. The many elements that make up the hearing mechanism are divided into three major sections: the outer, middle, and inner ear. The outer ear is the least complex and least important for hearing; the inner ear is the most complex and most important for hearing. Figure 10.1 shows these major parts of the ear.

THE OUTER EAR

The outer ear consists of the auricle and the external auditory canal. The canal ends with the **tympanic membrane (eardrum)**, which is the boundary between the outer and mid-

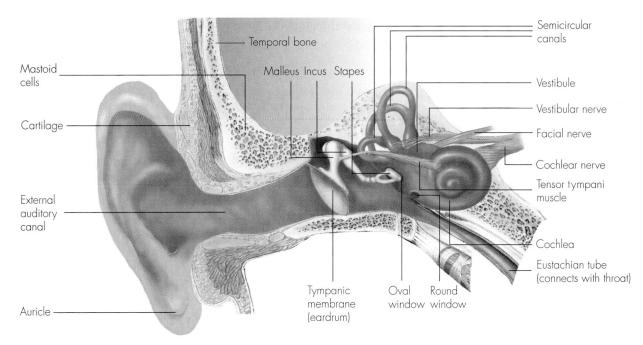

FIGURE 10.1   Illustration of the outer, middle, and inner ear

dle ears. The **auricle** is the part of the ear that protrudes from the side of the head. The part that the outer ear plays in the transmission of sound is relatively minor. Sound is collected by the auricle and is funneled through the external auditory canal to the eardrum, which vibrates, sending the sound waves to the middle ear.

THE MIDDLE EAR

The middle ear comprises the eardrum and three very tiny bones (**ossicles**) called the **malleus** (hammer), **incus** (anvil), and **stapes** (stirrup), which are contained within an air-filled space. The chain of the malleus, incus, and stapes conducts the vibrations of the eardrum along to the **oval window**, which is the link between the middle and inner ears. The ossicles function to create an efficient transfer of energy from the air-filled cavity of the middle ear to the fluid-filled inner ear.

THE INNER EAR

About the size of a pea, the inner ear is an intricate mechanism of thousands of moving parts. Because it looks like a maze of passageways and is highly complex, this part of the ear is often called a *labyrinth*. The inner ear is divided into two sections according to function: the vestibular mechanism and the cochlea. These sections, however, do not function totally independently of each other.

The **vestibular mechanism**, located in the upper portion of the inner ear, is responsible for the sense of balance. It is extremely sensitive to such things as acceleration, head movement, and head position. Information about movement is fed to the brain through the vestibular nerve.

By far the most important organ for hearing is the **cochlea**. Lying below the vestibular mechanism, this snail-shaped organ contains the parts necessary to convert the mechanical action of the middle ear into an electrical signal in the inner ear that is transmitted to the brain. In the normally functioning ear, sound causes the malleus, incus, and stapes of the middle ear to move. When the stapes moves, it pushes the oval window in and out, causing the fluid in the cochlea of the inner ear to flow. The movement of the fluid in turn

Malleus
The hammer-shaped bone in the ossicular chain of the middle ear.

Incus
The anvil-shaped bone in the ossicular chain of the middle ear.

Stapes
The stirrup-shaped bone in the ossicular chain of the middle ear.

Oval window
The link between the middle and inner ears.

Vestibular mechanism
Located in the upper portion of the inner ear; consists of three soft, semicircular canals filled with a fluid; sensitive to head movement, acceleration, and other movements related to balance.

Cochlea
A snail-shaped organ that lies below the vestibular mechanism in the inner ear; its parts convert the sounds coming from the middle ear into electrical signals that are transmitted to the brain.

THE NATIONAL Institute on Deafness and Other Communication Disorders of the National Institutes of Health has been concerned about the fact that many infants with hearing impairment go undetected even though technology exists to identify such impairments. Information on early screening can be found on their website: **www.nidcd.nih.gov**

Audiologist
An individual trained in audiology, the science dealing with hearing impairments, their detection, and remediation.

Otoacoustic emissions
Low-intensity sounds produced by the cochlea in response to auditory stimulation; used to screen hearing problems in infants and very young children.

Pure-tone audiometry
A test whereby tones of various intensities and frequencies are presented to determine a person's hearing loss.

Hertz (Hz)
A unit of measurement of the frequency of sound; refers to the highness or lowness of a sound.

Audiometric zero
The lowest level at which people with normal hearing can hear.

causes a complex chain of events in the cochlea, ultimately resulting in excitation of the cochlear nerve. With stimulation of the cochlear nerve, an electrical impulse is sent to the brain, and sound is heard.

Measurement of Hearing Ability

There are four general types of hearing assessment: screening tests, pure-tone audiometry, speech audiometry, and specialized tests for very young children. Depending on the characteristics of the examinee and the use to which the results will be put, the **audiologist** may choose to give any number of tests from any one or a combination of these four categories.

SCREENING TESTS

There are screening tests for infants and screening tests for school-age children. Over half the states now mandate newborn hearing screening programs. These tests, involving the use of computer technology, measure **otoacoustic emissions**. The cochlea not only receives sounds, but also emits low-intensity sound when stimulated by auditory stimuli. These sounds emitted by the cochlea are known as otoacoustic emissions, and they provide a measure of the how well the cochlea is functioning (Campbell & Derrick, 2001).

Many schools have routine screening programs in the early elementary grades. Hearing screening tests are administered either individually or in groups. These tests, especially those that are group administered, are less accurate than tests administered in an audiologist's office. Children who are detected through screening as having possible problems are referred for more extensive evaluation.

PURE-TONE AUDIOMETRY

Pure-tone audiometry is designed to establish the individual's threshold for hearing at a variety of different frequencies. Frequency, measured in **hertz (Hz)** units, has to do with the number of vibrations per unit of time of a sound wave; the pitch is higher with more vibrations, lower with fewer. A person's threshold for hearing is simply the level at which he or she can first detect a sound; it refers to how intense a sound must be before the person can detect it. As was mentioned earlier, hearing sensitivity, or intensity, is measured in decibels (dB).

Pure-tone audiometers present tones of varying intensities, or loudness (decibel levels), at varying frequencies, or pitch (hertz). Audiologists are usually concerned with measuring sensitivity to sounds ranging from 0 to about 110 dB. A person with average-normal hearing is barely able to hear sounds at a sound-pressure level of 0 dB. The zero decibel level is frequently called the zero hearing-threshold level, or **audiometric zero**. Because the decibel scale is based on ratios, each increment of 10 dB is a tenfold increase in sound level. This means that 20 dB is one hundred times more intense than a 10 dB sound, and 30 dB is one thousand times more intense than a 10 dB sound. Whereas a leaf fluttering in the wind registers about 0 dB, most speech sounds range between 20 and 55 dB, and a power lawnmower would have an intensity of about 100 dB (Schirmer, 2001).

Hertz are usually measured from 125 Hz (low pitch) to 8,000 Hz (high pitch). Frequencies in speech range from 80 to 8,000 Hz, but most speech sounds have energy in the 500- to 2,000-Hz range.

Testing each ear separately, the audiologist presents a variety of tones within the range of 0 to about 110 dB and 125–8,000 Hz until she or he establishes at what level of intensity (dB) the individual can detect the tone at a number of frequencies—125 Hz, 250 Hz, 500 Hz, 1,000 Hz, 2,000 Hz, 4,000 Hz, and 8,000 Hz. For each frequency, there is a measure of degree of hearing impairment. A 50-dB hearing impairment at 500 Hz, for example, means the individual is able to detect the 500-Hz sound when it is given at an intensity level of 50 dB, whereas the average person would have heard it at 0 dB.

SPEECH AUDIOMETRY

Because the ability to understand speech is of prime importance, a technique called **speech audiometry** has been developed to test a person's detection and understanding of speech. The **speech reception threshold (SRT)** is the decibel level at which one is able to understand speech. One way to measure the SRT is to present the person with a list of two-syllable words, testing each ear separately. The dB level at which he or she can understand half the words is often used as an estimate of SRT level.

TESTS FOR YOUNG AND HARD-TO-TEST CHILDREN

A basic assumption for pure-tone and speech audiometry is that the individuals who are being tested understand what is expected of them. They must be able to comprehend the instructions and show with a head nod or raised hand that they have heard the tone or word. None of this might be possible for very young children (under about 4 years of age) or for children with certain disabilities.

Audiologists use a number of different techniques to test the hearing of young and hard-to-test children. For example, some use the otoacoustic emission testing that we mentioned earlier. Others use **play audiometry**. In a gamelike format, using pure tones or speech, the examiner teaches the child to do various activities whenever he or she hears a signal. The activities are designed to be attractive to the young child. For example, the child might be required to pick up a block, squeeze a toy, or open a book. In **tympanometry**, a rubber-tipped probe is inserted in the ear, sealing the ear canal, and the effects of pressure and sound are then measured to assess the functioning of the middle ear. Still another method is **evoked-response audiometry**. Evoked-response audiometry involves measuring changes in brain wave activity by using an electroencephalograph (EEG). All sounds heard by an individual result in electrical signals within the brain, so this method has become more popular with the development of sophisticated computers. Evoked-response audiometry can be used during sleep, and the child can be sedated and thus not be aware that he or she is being tested.

Speech audiometry
A technique that tests a person's detection and understanding of speech, rather than using pure tones to detect hearing loss.

Speech reception threshold (SRT)
The decibel level at which a person can understand speech.

Play audiometry
Use of a gamelike format to test hearing of young and hard-to-test children; the examiner teaches the child to respond to sounds.

Tympanometry
A method of measuring the middle ear's response to pressure and sound.

Evoked-response audiometry
A technique involving electroencephalograph measurement of changes in brain wave activity in response to sounds.

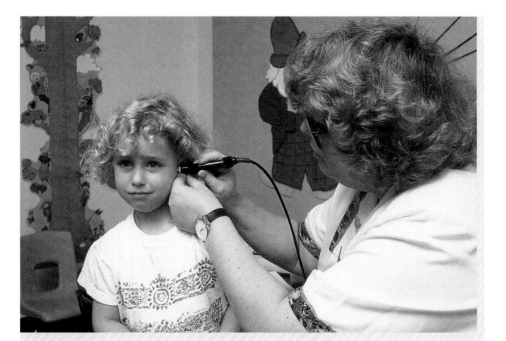

Routine hearing examinations, conducted in schools, often provide the first identification of mild hearing problems.

Causes

We discuss causes with respect to the type (conductive, sensorineural, and mixed) of hearing impairment as well as the location (outer, middle, or inner ear) of the hearing impairment.

CONDUCTIVE, SENSORINEURAL, AND MIXED HEARING IMPAIRMENT

Conductive hearing impairment
A hearing impairment, usually mild, resulting from malfunctioning along the conductive pathway of the ear (i.e., the outer or middle ear).

Sensorineural hearing impairment
A hearing impairment, usually severe, resulting from malfunctioning of the inner ear.

Mixed hearing impairment
A hearing impairment resulting from a combination of conductive and sensorineural hearing impairments.

External otitis
An infection of the skin of the external auditory canal; also called *swimmer's ear*.

Otitis media
Inflammation of the middle ear.

Professionals classify causes of hearing impairment on the basis of the location of the problem within the hearing mechanism. There are three major classifications: conductive, sensorineural, and mixed hearing impairments. A **conductive hearing impairment** refers to an interference with the transfer of sound along the conductive pathway of the middle or outer ear. A **sensorineural hearing impairment** involves problems in the inner ear. A **mixed hearing impairment** is a combination of the two. Audiologists attempt to determine the location of the dysfunction. The first clue may be the severity of the loss. A general rule is that hearing impairments greater than 60 or 70 dB involve some inner-ear problem. Audiologists use the results of pure-tone testing to help determine the location of a hearing impairment, converting the results to an audiogram—a graphic representation of the weakest (lowest-decibel) sound the individual can hear at each of several frequency levels. The profile of the audiogram helps to determine whether the loss is conductive, sensorineural, or mixed.

HEARING IMPAIRMENT AND THE OUTER EAR

Although problems of the outer ear are not as serious as those of the middle or inner ear, several conditions of the outer ear can cause a person to be hard of hearing. In some children, for example, the external auditory canal does not form, resulting in a condition known as atresia. Children may also develop **external otitis**, or "swimmer's ear," an infection of the skin of the external auditory canal. Tumors of the external auditory canal are another source of hearing impairment.

HEARING IMPAIRMENT AND THE MIDDLE EAR

Although abnormalities of the middle ear are generally more serious than problems of the outer ear, they, too, usually result in a person's being classified as hard of hearing rather than deaf. Most middle-ear hearing impairments occur because the mechanical action of the ossicles is interfered with in some way. Unlike inner-ear problems, most middle-ear hearing impairments are correctable with medical or surgical treatment.

The most common problem of the middle ear is **otitis media**—an infection of the middle-ear space caused by viral or bacterial factors, among others. For children under 6 years of age, it is the most common reason for visits to the physician (Schirmer, 2001). Otitis media is linked to abnormal functioning of the eustachian tubes. If the eustachian tube malfunctions because of a respiratory viral infection, for example, it cannot do its job of ventilating, draining, and protecting the middle ear from infection. Otitis media can result in temporary conductive hearing impairment, and even these temporary losses can make the child vulnerable for having language delays (Feldman et al., 2003). If untreated, otitis media can lead to rupture of the tympanic membrane.

HEARING IMPAIRMENT AND THE INNER EAR

The most severe hearing impairments are associated with the inner ear. In addition to problems with hearing sensitivity, a person with inner-ear hearing impairment can have additional problems, such as sound distortion, balance problems, and roaring or ringing in the ears.

Causes of inner-ear disorders can be hereditary or acquired. Genetic or hereditary factors are a leading cause of deafness in children. In fact, over 400 different varieties of hereditary deafness have been identified (Arnos, 2002). Scientists have recently identified mutation in the **connexin-26 gene** as the most common cause of congenital deafness, accounting for about 20 percent of childhood deafness (National Center for Biotechnology Information, 2000).

Acquired hearing impairments of the inner ear include those due to bacterial infections (e.g., meningitis, the second most frequent cause of childhood deafness), prematurity, viral infections (e.g., mumps and measles), anoxia (deprivation of oxygen) at birth, prenatal infections of the mother (e.g., maternal rubella, congenital syphilis, and cytomegalovirus), Rh incompatibility (which can now usually be prevented with proper prenatal care of the mother), blows to the head, side effects of some antibiotics, and excessive noise levels.

Two of the above conditions deserve special emphasis because of their relatively high prevalence. **Congenital cytomegalovirus (CMV)**, a herpes virus, deserves special mention because it is the most frequent viral cause of deafness in newborns. CMV can result in a variety of conditions, such as mental retardation, visual impairment, and especially hearing impairment. In addition, repeated exposure to such things as loud music, gunshots, or machinery can result in gradual or sudden hearing impairment.

Connexin-26 gene
A gene, the mutation of which causes deafness; the leading cause of congenital deafness in children.

Congenital cytomegalovirus (CMV)
The most frequently occurring viral infection in newborns; can result in a variety of disabilities, especially hearing impairment.

Psychological and Behavioral Characteristics

Hearing impairment can have profound consequences for some aspects of a person's behavior and little or no effect on other characteristics. Consider this question: If you were forced to choose, which would you rather be—blind or deaf? On first impulse, most of us would choose deafness, probably because we rely on sight for mobility and because many of the beauties of nature are visual. But in terms of functioning in an English language–oriented society, the person who is deaf is at a much greater disadvantage than is someone who is blind.

SPOKEN LANGUAGE AND SPEECH DEVELOPMENT

By far the most severely affected areas of development in the person with a hearing impairment are the comprehension and production of the English language. We stress English because it is the predominant language in the United States of those who can hear. In other words, people who are hearing impaired are generally deficient in the language used by most people of the hearing society in which they live. (This is not to deny the situation facing other people who are deaf, such as Najia in Success Stories on page 330, whose parents speak Spanish and Arabic in the home.) The distinction is important, because people who are hearing impaired can be expert in their own form of language: sign language.

Nevertheless, it is an undeniable fact that individuals with hearing impairment are at a distinct disadvantage. This is true in terms of language comprehension, language production, and speech. Speech intelligibility is linked to (1) degree of hearing impairment and (2) the age of onset of the hearing impairment. Even after intensive speech therapy, it is rare for children with prelingual profound deafness to develop intelligible speech (Marschark, 2002). Infants who are able to hear their own sounds and those of adults before becoming deaf have an advantage over those who are born deaf. Children who are deaf are handicapped in learning to associate the sensations they feel when they move their jaws, mouths, and tongues with the auditory sounds these movements produce. In addition, these children have a difficult time hearing the sounds of adult speech, which nonimpaired children hear and imitate.

UNDERSTANDING THE STANDARDS AND PRINCIPLES What should teachers know about the psychological and behavioral characteristics of individuals who are deaf or hard of hearing? *(CEC Knowledge and Skills Standards DH2K1, DH3K3, & DH3K4)*

Council for Exceptional Children

Special Educators at Work

Najia's father: "We are so lucky to have found this school."
Six-year-old Najia Elyoumni-Pinedo attends a special school for students who are deaf.
These are the keys to her success:
- *intensive instruction in small, specialized classes*
- *relentless focus on communication*
- *specific interventions to enhance skills in sign language and problem solving*

Special educator Wanda Frankel, and her assistant, Maria Diaz-Schwartz, signed to the six children in their kindergarten class to clean up their snacks. "Najia, what is your job this week?" asked Frankel. A dark-haired girl went to get paper towels as she signed, "To wash the table." Najia was diagnosed as profoundly deaf when she was 2 years old. Since then, she has benefited from intensive, relentless, and specific special education.

Intensive Instruction: Small, Specialized Classes   New York City's Lexington School for the Deaf serves over 350 students from preschool through grade 12. The school's mission is to educate students to become literate, reflective, independent thinking people with the confidence and tools necessary to contribute to society. Classes are small in the elementary grades, with an average of eight students, one teacher, and one assistant. The curriculum follows state standards, and students also have classes in swimming, dance, art, library, keyboarding, and conflict resolution. All classrooms have FM amplification systems available.

Wanda Frankel is certified as a Teacher of the Deaf. She has taught at the Lexington School for twelve years. Effortlessly, she signs and speaks with her students. "Usually I wear a microphone, or an FM system. I can set the mic to amplify my voice louder than other sounds coming through the children's hearing aids. Today, it's broken!" Fortunately, there is an audiology repair shop on campus.

Relentless Focus on Communication   The school serves a large immigrant community, and many parents, like the Elyoumni-Pinedos, must learn both English and sign language. For Najia and her parents, sign is their common language. Says Frankel, "Counselors at the school help parents learn to communicate with their deaf child as well as help deaf children express their feelings and express anger in nonphysical ways."

Najia's mother is from Peru, and her father is from Morocco. They met in an English language class one year before Najia was born. She was 18 months old before her father was convinced that Najia was deaf. "He clapped his hands, he slammed a door, he made a lot of noise, but she didn't hear it," recalls Ms.

Table 10.1 gives general examples of the effects that various degrees of hearing impairment can have on English language development. This is only a general statement of these relationships, since many factors interact to influence language development in the child with hearing impairment.

SIGN LANGUAGE

Sign language
A manual language used by people who are deaf to communicate; a true language with its own grammar.

Although children who are deaf face extraordinary challenges in learning a *spoken* language, with exposure they can easily learn **sign language**. However, historically, sign language has suffered from several misconceptions, including the belief that it is not a true language. The notion that sign language is simply a primitive, visual representation of oral language similar to mime was first challenged by the pioneering work of William Stokoe at Gallaudet University. A linguist, Stokoe submitted that, analogous to the phonemes of spoken English, each sign in ASL consists of three parts: handshape, location, and movement (Stokoe, 1960; Stokoe, Casterline, & Croneberg, 1976). For many years, Stokoe's col-

Pinedo. Before that, there were always other reasons to explain why she didn't talk or respond like other children. Najia and her parents lived with three other Moroccan families and their seven children, so they thought that she was too busy playing to answer. They also thought that she didn't know which language to use. "When Najia was with me and my friends, we spoke Spanish," says her mother. "At home, her father and the other families spoke Arabic." When audiology evaluations confirmed that Najia had a profound hearing loss, the Elyoumni-Pinedos were advised to take Najia to the Lexington School for early intervention services.

Specific Interventions: Sign Language and Problem Solving Skills Sign language is central to instruction in Najia's kindergarten classroom. She has already developed a strong language base and is acquiring beginning reading skills. She knows the alphabet and can sight-read the days of the week and names of favorite people. Najia participates in hands-on math readiness activities in basic addition and subtraction. In addition to academics, a schoolwide curriculum emphasizes independent learning, and children in all grades practice skills in problem solving. "Najia comes up with some great solutions," says Ms. Frankel.

At circle time, Najia and her classmates watched Frankel closely as she talked with her lively hands. "Listen," she signed, encouraging the children to watch each other closely. When it was her turn, Najia signed that she was proud of her artwork hanging on the classroom wall. "She is so artistic," says Frankel. "Last year, she started to draw pictures using perspective! She's very bright." Says Ms. Pinedo, "My husband and I like to think she will be a professional."

The resources of this special school have built a solid foundation for both Najia and her parents. When the Elyoumni-Pinedos' second child was born with a hearing loss, Lexington was able to provide his evaluation and referral to another program for children with less intensive needs. Ms. Pinedo spoke with emotion as she said, "We are so lucky to have found this school. We are so lucky to be in America."

CEC'S STANDARDS: PAVING THE WAY TO SUCCESS

ASSESS YOUR STEPS TO SUCCESS in meeting the CEC Knowledge and Skill Base for All Beginning Special Education Teachers of Students Who Are Deaf and Hard of Hearing. Use the following questions to reflect on the growth of your own professional knowledge, skills, and dispositions.

REFLECTING ON YOUR OWN PROFESSIONAL DEVELOPMENT

If you were Najia's teacher . . .

- WHAT are some areas about educating students who are deaf and hard of hearing that you would need to know more about?
- WHAT are some specific skills that would help you address her academic and behavioral challenges?
- WHAT personal dispositions do you think are most important for you to develop in teaching students with hearing loss?

Using the CEC Standards

- WHAT are some ways that families influence the overall development of the individual who is deaf or hard of hearing? (DH3K3)
- HOW would you design a classroom environment that maximizes opportunities for visual and/or auditory learning for individuals who are deaf or hard of hearing? (DH5S5)
- WHAT are some sources of specialized materials for individuals who are deaf or hard of hearing? (DH4K1)

By Jean Crockett

---

leagues scoffed at him, but research in several areas has proved that he was correct in asserting that sign language is a true language.

Grammatical Complexity of Sign Language Researchers have continued to refine Stokoe's work on sign language grammar, confirming its complexity. For example, like spoken language, sign language has grammatical structure at the sentence level (syntax) as well as the word or sign level (Goldin-Meadow, 2003). Handshapes, location, and movement are combined to create a grammar every bit as complex as that of spoken language.

Nonuniversality of Sign Language Contrary to popular opinion, there is not a single, universal sign language. For example, people who are deaf in France communicate in French Sign Language, and those in the United States use ASL. A person who is deaf visiting a foreign country has difficulties communicating with others who are deaf, much as a hearing person does. This is because sign languages, like spoken languages, evolve over

TABLE 10.1 Degrees of Hearing Impairment and Impact on Communication

Hearing Level	Descriptor	Impact on Communication
−10 to 15 dB	Normal	No impact on communication
16 to 25 dB	Slight	In quiet environments, the individual has no difficulty recognizing speech, but in noisy environments, faint speech is difficult to understand.
26 to 40 dB	Mild	In quiet conversational environments in which the topic is known and vocabulary is limited, the individual has no difficulty in communicating. Faint or distant speech is difficult to hear even if the environment is quiet. Classroom discussions are challenging to follow.
41 to 55 dB	Moderate	The individual can hear conversational speech only at a close distance. Group activities, such as classroom discussions, present a communicative challenge.
56 to 70 dB	Moderate-Severe	The individual can hear only loud, clear conversational speech and has much difficulty in group situations. Often, the individual's speech is noticeably impaired though intelligible.
71 to 90 dB	Severe	The individual cannot hear conversational speech unless it is loud and even then, cannot recognize many of the words. Environmental sounds can be detected, though not always identified. The individual's speech is not altogether intelligible.
91 dB +	Profound	The individual may hear loud sounds but cannot hear conversational speech at all. Vision is the primary modality for communication. The individual's own speech, if developed at all, is not easy to understand.

Source: From Schirmer, B. R. (2001). *Psychological, social, and educational dimensions of deafness.* Boston: Allyn & Bacon. Reprinted/adapted with permission.

time through common usage. In other words, sign language was not invented by any one person or a committee of people. The eighteenth century French clergyman Charles-Michel de l'Eppe is often referred to as the "father of sign language." On hearing this, some people assume that de l'Eppe invented sign language. However, what he did was to take French Sign Language, which already existed within the Deaf community, and promote its usage. This is not to diminish the profound impact he did have on advocating for using sign language in educating students with hearing impairments.

There have been several studies verifying the evolutionary aspect of sign languages. For example, twins who are deaf born to hearing parents soon begin to develop a signing system to communicate with each other. However, even after several years of such communication, their means of communication is still extremely rudimentary and nowhere near as sophisticated as ASL. The Nicaraguan Sign Language Study has also documented how sign languages change over time. (See Focus on Concepts on p. 333.)

Developmental Milestones of Sign Language Considerable evidence indicates that children who are deaf reach the same language development milestones in sign as nondisabled children do in spoken language and do so at about the same time (Emmorey, 2002; Goldin-Meadow, 2003). For example, they manually "babble" at about the same time as hearing infants verbally babble. And infants who are deaf sign their first words and two-word phrases at about the same time that hearing infants verbalize their first words and two-word phrases.

Some professionals have suggested that infants who are deaf and those who are hearing can learn to use some simple signs and gestures earlier than they can learn to use spoken words (Acredolo & Goodwyn, 2002). They have advocated that these signs and gestures, called **baby signs**, be used with hearing infants. (See Focus on Concepts on p. 334.)

Baby signs
A system developed to help hearing parents and their infants communicate with each other before spoken language develops; consists of signs from ASL as well as other gestures.

FOCUS ON CONCEPTS

The Nicaraguan Sign Language Study

As a part of governmental reform, Nicaragua established a school system for the deaf in the 1980s. For the first time, children who were deaf who had previously lived in relative isolation were able to interact with large numbers of other children who were deaf. This provided a rare opportunity for researchers to observe and record the development of sign language among the children, that is, the birth of Nicaraguan Sign Language (Idioma de Señas de Nicaragua—ISN). The well-regarded cognitive scientist Steven Pinker has noted that this has led researchers to have the "ability to witness, in real time, how the structure of a language emerges as the language is being created." (Quoted in Helmuth, 2001, p. 1758.)

One surprising finding has been that over time, the youngest signers have been the ones who have been most influential in changing the grammar of ISN (Kegle, Senghas, & Coppola, 1999). However, the complete development and perpetuation of ISN is dependent on a complex interplay between the generations (Senghas, 2003). The bottom line is that sign

Two Nicaraguan girls communicate using Idioma de Señas de Nicaragua (ISN).

language, like spoken language, changes over time based on intergenerational interactions among users of the language. ■

Neurological Foundations of Sign Language　Further evidence that sign language is a true language comes from studies showing that sign language has the same neurological underpinnings as does spoken language. As you recall, in Chapter 6, we noted that areas within the left cerebral hemisphere of the brain are primarily responsible for language. However, we were referring to *spoken* language. Interestingly, there is substantial evidence that the left hemisphere of the brain is also the primary site responsible for sign language acquisition and use (Emmorey, 2002). For example, patients who are deaf who suffer a stroke are more likely to have deficits in signing if the stroke is to the left hemisphere than if the right hemisphere is damaged. In addition, using neuroimaging techniques, such as **positron emission tomography (PET)** and **functional magnetic resonance imaging (fMRI)**, researchers have found that when people who are deaf sign, the left side of the brain is more active than the right.

INTELLECTUAL ABILITY

For many years, professionals believed that the conceptual ability of individuals who are deaf was deficient because of their deficient spoken language. As was noted earlier, however, we now know that they might not have a spoken language, such as English, but if they use American Sign Language, they are using a true language with its own rules of grammar.

Any intelligence testing that is done with people who are hearing impaired must take their English language deficiency into account. Performance tests, rather than verbal tests, especially if they are administered in sign, offer a much fairer assessment of the IQ of a person with a hearing impairment. When these tests are used, there is no difference in IQ between those who are deaf and those who are hearing (Prinz et al., 1996).

Positron emission tomography (PET) scans
A computerized method for measuring bloodflow in the brain; during a cognitive task, a low amount of radioactive dye is injected in the brain; the dye collects in active neurons, indicating which areas of the brain are active.

Functional magnetic resonance imaging (fMRI)
An adaptation of the MRI used to detect changes in the brain while it is in an active state; unlike a PET scan, it does not involve using radioactive materials.

FOCUS ON CONCEPTS

Baby Signs

ASK most hearing parents, and they will tell you that their hearing infants learned to gesture to make some of their wants known before learning to ask for what they wanted; for instance, they brought their hands up to their mouths to ask for food before verbalizing their desire to be fed. Professors Linda Acredolo and Susan Goodwyn have taken advantage of the power of gesturing in infants to come up with a system of "baby signs," a combination of formal ASL signs and informal gestures that are often used by parents and babies (Acredolo & Goodwyn, 2002).

These researchers have found suggestive evidence that using their system of baby signs with hearing infants might result in better spoken language development (Goodwyn, Acredolo, & Brown, 2000). However, further research is needed before we can conclude that baby signs definitely results in better language development. In the meantime, baby signs do appear to offer a good way for parents and infants to communicate earlier than they do when they rely strictly on spoken language. It might help to alleviate the frustration par-

PIG Press finger to nose.

PLAY With thumb and little finger up, twist hands.

ents and babies often feel in communicating with each other in those early months, when spoken language has not yet begun to emerge.

Above are two examples of baby signs. The sign for "play" is an ASL sign; the one for "pig" is not. ▪

Source: Adapted from Acredolo, L, & Goodwyn, S. (2002). *Baby signs: How to talk with your baby before your baby can talk.* Chicago, IL: Contemporary Books.

ACADEMIC ACHIEVEMENT

Unfortunately, most children who are deaf have extreme deficits in academic achievement. Reading ability, which relies heavily on English language skills and is probably the most important area of academic achievement, is most affected. For example, the average 18-year-old student who is hearing impaired has a fourth-grade reading comprehension level (Traxler, 2000). Even in math, their best academic subject, students with hearing impairment trail their hearing peers by substantial margins.

Several studies have demonstrated that children who are deaf who have parents who are deaf have higher reading achievement and better language skills than do those who have hearing parents. There is not universal agreement on why this is the case (Powers, 2003). However, many authorities speculate that it is because of the positive influence of sign language. Parents who are deaf might be able to communicate better with their children through the use of ASL, providing the children with needed support. In addition, children who have parents who are deaf are more likely to be proficient in ASL, and ASL can aid these children in learning written English and reading.

A supportive home environment is associated with higher achievement in students who are deaf. Families that are more involved in their child's education, seek knowledge about their child's condition to provide guidance, have high expectations for achievement, do not try to overprotect their child, and participate along with their child in the Deaf community are likely to have higher-achieving children (Schirmer, 2001).

SOCIAL ADJUSTMENT

Social development and personality development in the hearing population depend heavily on communication, and the situation is no different for those who are deaf. The hearing person has little difficulty finding people with whom to communicate. The person who is deaf, however, can face problems in finding others with whom he or she can converse. Studies have demonstrated that many students who are deaf are at risk for loneliness (Cambra, 1996; Charlson, Strong, & Gold, 1992). Two factors are important in considering the possible isolation of students who are deaf: inclusion and hearing status of the parents.

Researchers have shown that in inclusionary settings, very little interaction typically occurs between students who are deaf and those who are not (Kluwin, Stinson, & Colarossi, 2002). Furthermore, in inclusionary settings, students who are deaf feel more emotionally secure if they have other students who are deaf with whom they can communicate (Stinson & Whitmire, 1992). This is not always possible, however, because of the low prevalence of hearing impairment. Some interventions using cooperative learning have been successful in increasing the interactions between students who are deaf and their hearing peers (Kluwin et al., 2002).

Some authorities believe that the child who is deaf who has hearing parents runs a greater risk of being unhappy than the child who has parents who are deaf. This is because many hearing parents do not become proficient in ASL and are unable to communicate with their children easily. Given that about 95 percent of children who are deaf have hearing parents (Mitchell & Karchmer, 2004), this problem in communication might be critical.

The need for social interaction is probably most influential in leading many people with hearing impairment to associate primarily with others with hearing impairment. If their parents are deaf, children who are deaf are usually exposed to other deaf families from an early age. Nonetheless, many people who are deaf end up, as adults, socializing predominantly with others who are deaf, even if they have hearing parents and even if they do not come into contact as children with many other children who were deaf. This phenomenon of socializing with others who are deaf is attributable to the influence of the Deaf culture.

Casebook Reflection

Refer to the case *Least Restrictive for Whom?* in your booklet. Brian's parents had used simple signs with him since he was a little boy. However, he could not communicate or socialize with other students in his school or his parents. How might teachers or support personnel have helped to improve this situation?

The Deaf Culture   In the past, most professionals viewed isolation from the hearing community on the part of many people who are deaf as a sign of social pathology. Now more and more professionals agree with the many people who are deaf who believe in the value of having their own Deaf culture. They view this culture as a natural condition emanating from the common bond of sign language.

The unifying influence of sign language is the first of six factors noted by Reagan (1990) as demarcating the Deaf community as a true culture:

1. *Linguistic differentiation* is at the heart of Deaf culture; many within the Deaf community view themselves as bilingual, with individuals possessing varying degrees of fluency in ASL and English (Ladd, 2003). People who are deaf are continually shifting between ASL and English as well as between the Deaf culture and that of the hearing (Padden, 1996).

2. *Attitudinal deafness* refers to whether a person thinks of himself or herself as deaf. It might not have anything to do with a person's hearing acuity. For example, a person with a relatively mild hearing impairment might think of herself or himself as deaf more readily than does someone with a profound hearing impairment.

3. *Behavioral norms* within the Deaf community differ from those in hearing society. A few examples of these norms, according to Lane, Hoffmeister, and Bahan (1996), are that people who are deaf value informality and physical contact in their interactions with one another, often giving each other hugs when greeting and departing, and their leave-takings

Whereas professionals once viewed isolation from the hearing community as a sign of social pathology, many now recognize the value of having a Deaf culture.

often take much longer than those of hearing society. Also, they are likely to be frank in their discussions, not hesitating to get directly to the point of what they want to communicate.

4. *Endogamous marriage patterns* are evident from surveys showing rates of ingroup marriage as high as 90 percent. The Deaf community tends to frown on "mixed marriages" between people who are deaf and those who are hearing.

5. *Historical awareness* of significant people and events pertaining to people who are deaf permeates the Deaf community. They are often deferential to elders and value their wisdom and knowledge pertaining to Deaf traditions.

6. *Voluntary organizational networks* are abundant in the Deaf community. Some examples are the National Association of the Deaf, the World Games for the Deaf (Deaf Olympics), and the National Theatre of the Deaf (See the Personal Perspectives on p. 337).

Concern for the Erosion of Deaf Culture   Many within the Deaf community and some professionals are concerned that the cultural status of children who are deaf is in peril (Gaustad & Kluwin, 1992; Janesick & Moores, 1992; Lane et al., 1996). They believe that the increase in inclusion is eroding the cultural values of the Deaf culture. In the past, much of Deaf culture was passed down from generation to generation through contacts made at residential schools, but if they attend local schools, today's children who are deaf, may have little contact with other children who are deaf. Many authorities now recommend that schools involve members of the Deaf community in developing classes in Deaf history and culture for students who are deaf who attend local schools.

Further evidence of the erosion of the Deaf culture is the fact that **Deaf clubs** are on the decline (Ladd, 2003). Deaf clubs are gathering places where people who are deaf can socialize and participate in leisure activities and entertainment. With the increase in inclusion and the growing popularity of the Internet as a means of gathering information, it will be interesting to see what the future holds for Deaf clubs.

Deaf Activism: The Gallaudet Experience   Even though some might think that the Deaf community is in peril of losing its identity, it is still very active in advocating a variety

Deaf clubs
Gathering spots where people who are deaf can socialize; on the decline in the United States.

VISIT the National Theatre of the Deaf's website to look for upcoming performances in your area: **www.NTD.org**

Personal Perspectives

THE NATIONAL THEATRE OF THE DEAF

The Oldest Continuously Producing Touring Theater Company in the United States

THROUGH its thirty-six year history, the National Theatre of the Deaf stands as testimony to the artistry and capability of its Actors. There have been 64 national tours, performances in all 50 states, all the continents, 31 international tours and over 8,000 performances earning NTD its place in theatrical history as the oldest continually-producing touring theater company in the United States. Through NTD's signature style of visual language, American Sign Language, the audience enjoys a greater appreciation that no other theater company can approach. Through its art, the NTD has created profound social change. The magic of it all has been the National Theatre of the Deaf's remarkable ability to entertain and inform at the same time. As one critic has praised, "sculpture in the air." ■

Source: The National Theatre of the Deaf. (2001, March 19 "About NTD." Retrieved May 24, 2004 from the World Wide Web: www.ntd.org/about.htm. Reprinted with permission.

Actors Tyrone Giordano, left, and Michael McElroy sign a scene during a rehearsal of "Big River", a version of the Tony award-winning musical, which includes deaf, hard-of-hearing, and hearing actors, and weaves together spoken English and American Sign Language (ASL).

of social, educational, and medical policies. A prominent and historic example of Deaf activism occurred in 1988 at Gallaudet University, a liberal arts college for the deaf and hard of hearing, when students and faculty protested the board of trustees' selection of a hearing president. Since its founding in 1864, Gallaudet had never had a deaf president. After students shut down the university for several days, the school's administration acquiesced to their demands for a deaf president and a reconfiguration of the board to include a majority of members who are deaf.

Deaf Activism: The Cochlear Implant Debate   Deaf activists have also been aggressive in attacking what they consider an oppressive medical and educational establishment. An example of just how much this segment of the Deaf community is at odds with many professionals is its opposition to the medical procedure of **cochlear implantation**. This procedure involves surgically implanting electronic elements under the skin behind the ear and in the inner ear. A small microphone worn behind the ear picks up sounds and sends them to a small computerized speech processor worn by the person. The speech processor sends coded signals to an external coil worn behind the ear, which sends them through the skin to the implanted internal coil. The internal coil then sends the signals to electrodes implanted in the inner ear, and these signals are sent on to the auditory nerve. (See Figure 10.2.)

Ever since the U.S. Food and Drug Administration approved the use of cochlear implants for young children in 1990, there have been thousands of operations both in the United States and the rest of the world, especially Australia. The technology is advancing rapidly, but not everyone with hearing impairment is a candidate for implantation. Generally, it is recommended for those who have a severe to profound sensorineural loss in both ears. In the case of children, medical opinions vary, but it is usually not recommended before the age of 12 months (Listening Center at Johns Hopkins, 2004). (Currently, the U.S.

Cochlear implantation A surgical procedure that allows people who are deaf to hear some environmental sounds; an external coil fitted on the skin by the ear picks up sound from a microphone worn by the person and transmits it to an internal coil implanted in the bone behind the ear, which carries it to an electrode implanted in the cochlea of the inner ear.

FIGURE 10.2 A cochlear implant

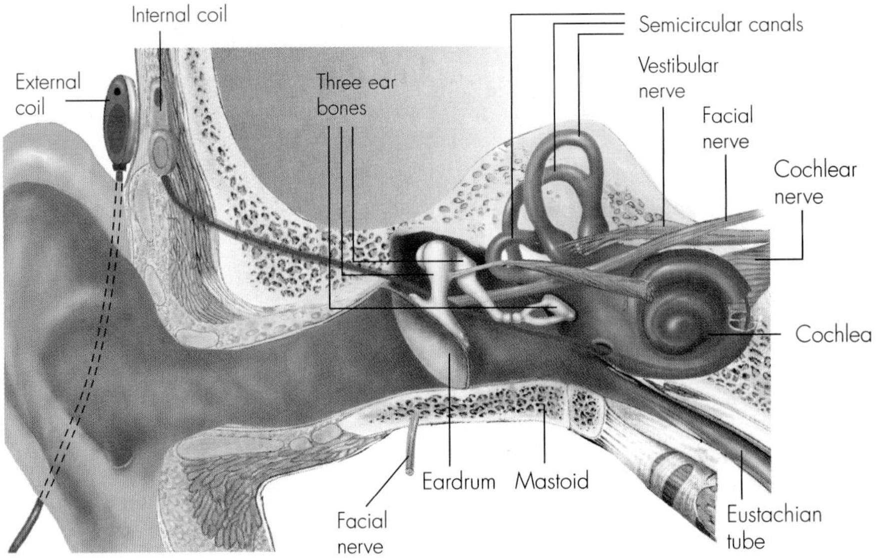

AS NOTED in the feature, "Making Peace with a Threat to 'Deaf Culture' " on page 339, the National Association of the Deaf had for years been opposed to cochlear implants. However, in the fall of 2000, it issued a policy statement that was much more neutral in tone. You can see the policy by using the "search" function on the NAD website: **www.nad.org**.

The Public Broadcasting Service (PBS) has established an excellent website focused on the documentary "Sound and Fury": **www.pbs.org/wnet/soundandfury**. Although the site focuses on the issue of cochlear implants, it also contains useful information pertaining to the Deaf culture and links to other interesting websites.

Food and Drug Administration has not approved cochlear implants for children under the age of 12 months.)

Although the manufacturers of these devices, as well as many within the medical community, have viewed cochlear implants as miraculous, they have engendered vociferous objections from many within the Deaf community, where they are viewed as physically and culturally invasive:

> I expect that most Americans would agree that our society should not seek the scientific tools or use them, if available, to change a child biologically so he or she will belong to the majority rather than the minority—even if we believe that this biological engineering might reduce the burdens the child will bear as a member of a minority. Even if we could take children destined to be members of the African American, or Hispanic American, or Native American, or Deaf American communities and convert them with bio-power into white, Caucasian, hearing males—even if we could, we should not. We should likewise refuse cochlear implants for young deaf children even if the devices were perfect. (Lane, 1992, p. 237)

Until recently, the Deaf community has not had to even come close to confronting the issue, raised by Lane: whether to have the surgery even if it were to result in perfect hearing. Although perfect hearing through cochlear implants might not be just around the corner, enormous strides in technology have resulted in many more cases than ever before of greatly improved hearing for people with implants. These more positive results are making it more difficult for those who are deaf, or their parents, to decide whether to choose cochlear implantation (see the Personal Perspectives on p. 339). Results still vary enormously from individual to individual. For someone who is profoundly deaf, the most common outcome is improvement to the level of severe hearing impairment (i.e., a hearing impairment of about 71 to 90 dB) (Blamey et al., 2001; Spencer, 2002). And to reap the benefits of the improved hearing, the individual needs to engage in intensive oral instruction of the kind that we discuss in the next section (Schery & Peters, 2003). Again, this is a far cry from a cure, but for some, it is enough of an improvement to elect to undergo the surgery.

Deaf Activism: The Genetic Engineering Debate Ironically, deaf activists can also put scientific discoveries to use to help sustain the Deaf culture but not without facing

Personal Perspectives

MAKING PEACE WITH A THREAT TO "DEAF CULTURE"

JAMIE WEINSTEIN-DELAHUNT, a deaf toddler from Jamaica Plain, is a born communicator and a symbol of the profound changes now sweeping the world of the deaf.

Hands flying, the 2-year-old can communicate in American Sign Language, or ASL. But she is also learning to hear and speak standard English, thanks to a controversial device called a cochlear implant that surgeons put in her ear nearly a year ago.

Before long, Jamie and other deaf children who can both speak and sign may accomplish what many of their elders could or would not: Straddle the fiercely separate worlds of people who talk with their voices and those who talk with their hands.

Until a year or so ago, the idea of "fixing" deafness in a child like Jamie was anathema to many proud members of Deaf (they spell it with a capital "D") culture, who feel that deafness is not a disability and that any attempt to remedy it is tantamount to "ethnocide"—the elimination of deaf people and their minority culture and language. Harlan Lane, a psychologist and linguist at Northeastern University, puts this view bluntly:

"If you believe, as I do, that a healthy, deaf child is a healthy child like a healthy, short child, it's just plain wrong to operate on that child."

To hearing people like Jamie's parents the deaf culture's attitude toward implants has been difficult to understand. Even the prospect that Jamie would need years of speech and hearing therapy after getting an implant seemed worth the gamble.

"We had been in the midst of so much loss," says her mother, "that the idea that Jamie could talk, despite being deaf, was the most hopeful news we had heard."

But probably the biggest driving force behind the growing acceptance of implants is that they have improved so much. A generation ago, the devices had only one electrode and the results were decidedly mixed.

Today, implants, which cost about $23,000 and are often covered by insurance, have up to 22 electrodes, which allows different sounds to sound truly different.

Implants "dramatically improve hearing in almost all children and lead to good speech recognition and production in most children who get them before age 4," says Marilyn Neault, director of Boston Children's Hospital.

"More and more individuals are getting implants for their children at younger ages," agrees Barbara Herrmann, an audiologist at the Massachusetts Eye and Ear Infirmary. A series of large studies in Missouri and Indiana shows "very impressive growth of language for children who receive implants."

The decision to get an implant or not to get one is never easy, says Christine Mitchell, director of the office of ethics at Children's Hospital. Hearing parents who opt for ASL instead of

"I can call her name from down the street and she turns to me."—mother of Jamie Weinstein-Delahunt

an implant face not only the burden of learning ASL themselves and teaching it to their child, but the possibility that their child may someday become part of the "deaf community in a way they can't follow or share," Mitchell says.

Since it is "often easier to change the child than the parent," she adds, an implant may give assurance to hearing parents that their child may hear and speak and, therefore, be more like them. It also means that their child may be more likely to become part of mainstream culture.

But is that a good thing? In some ways it is, says Mitchell, but a deaf child with an implant is still deaf, and becoming mainstreamed may not fulfill the deepest yearnings, for "feeling like you genuinely belong."

For Jamie and her parents, it's been a long, but hopeful road. Learning sign language, when Jamie was about a year old, was the first step. "The minute we did that, she completely responded," says Weinstein. "My first story for her was 'Goodnight, Gorilla.' I signed all the animal names. It was so satisfying."

The implant has brought even more joy. Although the family still signs when Jamie gets confused, her hearing, and her speech, grow daily. Now, say Weinstein, "I can call her name from down the street and she turns to me." ■

Source: Excerpted from Foreman, J. (2001, August 28). Making peace with a threat to "deaf culture." *The Boston Globe*, pp. C1–C2. Reprinted with permission.

In vitro fertilization
The procedure of removing eggs from the mother, fertilizing them with the father's sperm in a laboratory, then returning them to the mother's uterus; used to help infertile couples conceive.

Oralism–manualism debate
The controversy over whether the goal of instruction for students who are deaf should be to teach them to speak or to teach them to use sign language.

Total communication approach
An approach for teaching students with hearing impairment that blends oral and manual techniques.

Bicultural-bilingual approach
An approach for teaching students with hearing impairment that stresses teaching American Sign Language as a first language and English as a second language and promotes the teaching of Deaf culture.

Auditory-verbal approach
Part of the oral approach to teaching students who are hearing impaired; stresses teaching the person to use his or her remaining hearing as much as possible; heavy emphasis on use of amplification; heavy emphasis on teaching speech.

Speechreading
A method that involves teaching children to use visual information from a number of sources to understand what is being said to them; more than just lipreading, which uses only visual clues arising from the movement of the mouth in speaking.

thorny ethical concerns (Moores, 2002). Earlier, we noted the discovery of the mutation of the connexin-26 gene as the leading cause of deafness in children. Parents could use such information to increase their chances of having a baby who is deaf. (Contrary to what many in hearing society assume, when both parents are deaf, they usually would prefer to have a baby who is deaf.) For example, they could use **in vitro fertilization**, a procedure that is usually used to help infertile couples, whereby egg cells from the mother are fertilized in the laboratory and then placed in the mother's uterus. Parents who are deaf could choose to retain only fertilized eggs that have the connexin-26 mutation. Another option that has been used is artificial insemination by a donor who has a high probability of carrying genes leading to deafness (Mundy, 2002).

Educational Considerations

Formidable problems face the educator who works with students who are deaf or hard of hearing. As we would expect, one major problem is communication. Dating back to the sixteenth century, there has been a raging debate about how individuals who are deaf should converse (Lane, 1984). This controversy is sometimes referred to as the **oralism–manualism debate** to represent two very different points of view: oralism favors teaching people who are deaf to speak; manualism advocates the use of some kind of manual communication. Manualism was the preferred method until the middle of the nineteenth century, when oralism began to gain predominance. Currently, most educational programs involve both oral and manual methods in what is referred to as a **total communication approach** (Andrews et al., 2004). However, many within the Deaf community believe that the total communication approach is inadequate, and they advocate for a **bicultural-bilingual approach**, which promotes ASL as a first language and instruction in the Deaf culture.

We first discuss the major techniques that make up the oral approach and the oral portion of the total communication approach; then we take up total communication, followed by a discussion of the bicultural-bilingual approach. For information on some of the major best instructional practices, see the Responsive Instruction on p. 341.

ORAL APPROACHES: THE AUDITORY–VERBAL APPROACH AND THE AUDITORY–ORAL APPROACH

The Auditory–Verbal Approach   The **auditory-verbal approach** focuses exclusively on using audition to improve speech and language development (Andrews et al., 2004). It assumes that most children with hearing impairment have some residual hearing that can be used to their benefit. It relies heavily on amplification technology, such as hearing aids and cochlear implants, and it stresses that this amplification technology should be instituted at as young an age as possible. There is also a heavy emphasis on speech training. Because children with hearing impairments have problems hearing their own speech or that of others and often hear speech in a distorted fashion, they must be explicitly instructed in how to produce speech sounds.

The Auditory–Oral Approach   The **auditory-oral approach** is similar to the auditory-verbal approach, but it also stresses the use of visual cues, such as speechreading and cued speech. Sometimes inappropriately called *lipreading*, **speechreading** involves teaching children who are hearing impaired to use visual information to understand what is being said to them. *Speechreading* is a more accurate term than *lipreading* because the goal is to teach students to attend to a variety of stimuli in addition to specific movements of the lips. For example, proficient speechreaders read contextual stimuli so that they can anticipate certain types of messages in certain types of situations. They use facial expressions to help them interpret what is being said to them. Even the ability to discriminate the various speech sounds that flow from a person's mouth involves attending to visual cues from the

Meeting the Needs of Students Who Are Deaf or Hard of Hearing

Advances in Instructional Practices

RESEARCH-BASED RECOMMENDATIONS

Advances in research on effective instructional practices can provide guidance for general education teachers and special education teachers who have little or no training in methods for students with hearing impairment. Among the most promising practices are universal teaching materials; media, materials, and technology; collaborative models; and classroom interactions and instruction (Easterbrooks, 1999).

Universal Design for Learning Universal design, an architectural term referring to the construction of buildings accessible to people with disabilities, denotes instructional materials that meet the needs of diverse learners. Universal design for learning includes multiple ways of representing the content (e.g., electronic text that can be transformed into an outline or linked to graphic supports), strategy prompts built into the instruction to promote active engagement, and options for presentation formats (Pisha & Coyne, 2001).

Media, Materials, and Technology Because of the heavy reliance on visual rather than auditory cues for learning, students who are deaf or hard of hearing can make use of media, materials, and technology that provide explicit visual support for learning (Kaplan, Mahshie, Mosely, Singer, & Winston, 1993).

Collaborative Models Collaborative models encourage multiple perspectives, solutions, and approaches vital for the diverse population of students with hearing impairment. A one-size-fits-all approach can lead to ineffective instruction (i.e., instruction that lacks in necessary support) or inappropriate instruction (i.e., when too many supports place unnecessary restrictions or communication limitations and/or burdens on a student).

Classroom Interactions and Instruction A student's ability to effectively communicate in a classroom has a direct effect on the amount of learning that will occur. Teachers who can sign fluently or are responsive to student communication needs will increase instructional outcomes.

CLASSROOM APPLICATIONS

Specific recommendations for the classroom teacher include the following:

- Modifying the classroom environment:

  - Place students who use amplification devices away from distracting background noise such as doors or windows.
  - Provide ample lighting, particularly on instructional visual aids.
  - Allow the student access to see the teacher's and classmates' faces and the ability to move around the classroom for optimal placement.

- Creating "visual" instruction (Lucker, Bowen, & Carter, 2001):

  - Use sign or fingerspelling or promote speech reading when instructing.
  - Use as many visual supports as possible (bulletin boards, computers, televisions, pictures, graphs, graphic organizers, films with captions, artifacts, etc.).
  - Face students when addressing them. Avoid writing on the chalkboard while talking; use an overhead projector that allows you to face students.
  - Use nonverbal cues to emphasize verbal directions (e.g., gesturing, facial expressions).
  - Avoid note taking. Students who are looking at their desk writing notes will not be able to see an interpreter or read lips.
  - Repeat questions and answers provided by other students.

- Supporting communication:

  - Provide access to student's dominant mode of communication (e.g., manual, cued, or oral).
  - Set up effective communication practices among students. When working in pairs or small groups, students should face each other and have rules for communication, which might include signaling before speaking.
  - Pair figurative language with concrete or familiar examples.
  - Moderate the volume, rate, and complexity of speech.

Finally, the classroom teacher should seek guidance and information from outside experts. Speech/language pathologists, teachers of the deaf and hard of hearing, administrators, and professional organizations can provide a range of instructional recommendations to meet the unique needs of a particular student. ∎

By Kristin L. Sayeski

tongue and jaw as well as the lips. For example, to learn to discriminate among vowels, the speechreader concentrates on cues related to the degree of jaw opening and lip shaping.

Cued speech is a method of augmenting speechreading. In cued speech, the individual uses hand shapes to represent specific sounds while speaking. Eight hand shapes are cues for certain consonants, and four serve as cues for vowels. Some sounds look alike on the lips, and these cues are designed to help the speechreader differentiate these sounds. Although it has some devoted advocates, cued speech is not used widely in the United States.

Criticisms of the Oral Approach

Criticisms of the Oral Approach   Several authorities have been critical of using an exclusively oral approach with students who have hearing impairment (Lane et al., 1996; Padden & Humphries, 1988). In particular, they object to the deemphasis of sign language in this approach, especially for children who are deaf. These critics assert that it is unreasonable to assume that many children with severe or profound degrees of hearing impairment have enough hearing to be of use. Therefore, denying these children access to ASL is denying them access to a language to communicate.

Critics of the oral approach also point out that speechreading is extremely difficult and that good speechreaders are rare (Andrews et al., 2004). It is easy to overlook some of the factors that make speechreading difficult. For instance, speakers produce many sounds with little obvious movement of the mouth. Another issue is that the English language has many **homophenes**—different sounds that are visually identical when spoken. For example, a speechreader cannot distinguish among the pronunciations of [p], [b], and [m]. There is also variability among speakers in how they produce sounds. Finally, such factors as poor lighting, rapid speaking, and talking with one's head turned are further reasons why good speechreading is a rare skill (Menchel, 1988).

TOTAL COMMUNICATION

As we noted previously, most schools have adopted the total communication approach, a combination of oral and manual methods. Total communication involves the simultaneous use of speech with one of what are known as Signing English systems. **Signing English systems** refer to approaches that professionals have devised for teaching people who are deaf

Cued speech
A method to aid speechreading in people with hearing impairment; the speaker uses hand shapes to represent sounds.

Homophenes
Sounds that are different but that look the same with regard to movements of the face and lips (i.e., visible articulatory patterns).

Signing English systems
Used simultaneously with oral methods in the total communication approach to teaching students who are deaf; different from American Sign Language because they maintain the same word order as spoken English.

A total communication approach blends oral and manual methods.

to communicate. **Fingerspelling**, the representation of letters of the English alphabet by finger positions, is also used occasionally to spell out certain words (see Figure 10.3).

There has been growing dissatisfaction with total communication among some professionals and by many within the Deaf community. The focus of the criticism has been on the use of signing English systems rather than ASL. Unlike ASL, signing English systems maintain the same word order as spoken English, thereby making it possible to speak and sign at the same time. Defenders of signing English systems state that the correspondence in word order between signing English systems and English helps students to learn English better. Advocates of ASL assert that the use of signing English systems is too slow and awkward to be of much benefit in learning English. They argue that word order is not the critical element in teaching a person to use and comprehend English.

Fingerspelling
Spelling the English alphabet by using various finger positions on one hand.

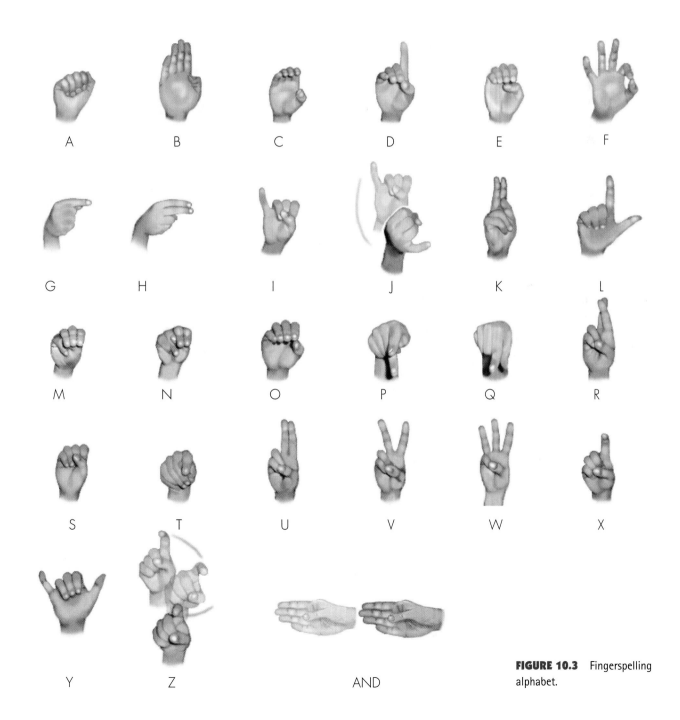

FIGURE 10.3 Fingerspelling alphabet.

THE INTERNET has several sites with animated finger spelling or American Sign Language dictionaries. An example for finger spelling is: **www.pbs.org/wnet/ soundandfury/culture/sign_ basic.html**.

An example for ASL, developed at Michigan State University, is: **http://commtechlab. msu.edu/sites/aslweb**

UNDERSTANDING THE STANDARDS AND PRINCIPLES What are the pros and cons of the total communication approach? *(CEC Knowledge and Skills Standards DH6K4, DH6K5, & DH6K7)*

UNDERSTANDING THE STANDARDS AND PRINCIPLES What are the features of a bicultural-bilingual approach? Does research support its effectiveness? *(CEC Knowledge and Skills Standards DH6K4, DH6K5, & DH6K7)*

Advocates of ASL believe that fluency in ASL provides students with a rich background of information that readies them for the learning of English. Furthermore, they assert that ASL is the natural language of people who are deaf and that it should be fostered because it is the most natural and efficient way for students who are deaf to learn about the world. Unlike ASL, signing English systems are not true languages. They have been invented by one or a few people in a short period of time, whereas true sign languages such as ASL have evolved over several generations of users. Many of the critics of the total communication approach advocate the bicultural-bilingual approach.

THE BICULTURAL-BILINGUAL APPROACH

Although there are several variations of the bicultural-bilingual approach, most of them contain these three features (Schirmer, 2001):

1. ASL is considered the primary language, and English is considered the secondary language.
2. People who are deaf play an important role in the development of the program and its curriculum.
3. The curriculum includes instruction in Deaf culture.

Bilingual education for students who are deaf can be structured so that ASL is learned first, followed by English, or the two can be taught simultaneously. In addition, children who are deaf born to hearing parents usually learn English first before they are exposed to ASL in a bilingual program.

Lending credence to those advocating ASL instruction are studies showing a relationship between ASL usage and academic performance in English (Wilbur, 2000). However, research directly bearing on the efficacy of bicultural-bilingual programs is in its infancy. Even though at least one study has found evidence for the effectiveness of bicultural-bilingual programming (Andrews, Ferguson, Roberts, & Hodges, 1997), it is probably safest to conclude that

> No fail-safe, success-guaranteed method exists for educating deaf children, though periodically through the history of deaf education various methods have been proposed as the pedagogical solution. In the 1960s and 1970s, total communication was considered to be the answer. In the 1980s and 1990s, bilingual education was touted as the solution. With the increase in cochlear implants, greater numbers of children are being educated orally/aurally . . ., and oral/aural approaches have seen renewed interest. Ultimately, the profession may recognize that only a range of approaches can meet the needs of a range of deaf children. (Schirmer, 2001, p. 203)

SERVICE DELIVERY MODELS

Students who are deaf or hard of hearing can be found in settings ranging from general education classes to residential institutions. Starting in the mid-1970s, more and more of these students have been attending local schools in self-contained classes, resource rooms, and regular classes. Currently, about 85 percent of students between the ages of 6 and 21 attend classes in local schools, and 40 percent spend the vast majority of their time in the general education classroom (U.S. Department of Education, 2003). Even though students with hearing impairment are now included to a very high degree in general education classrooms, they are still served in special schools or residential settings more than most other disability categories, with about 7 percent in the former and 9 percent in the latter type of placement.

Many people within the Deaf community have been critical of the degree of mainstreaming or inclusion that is occurring (Aldersley, 2002; Lane et al., 1996; Padden &

Although students who are deaf or hard of hearing are included to a very high degree in general education classrooms, they are still served in separate settings more than any other disability category.

Humphries, 1988; Siegel, 2000). They argue that residential schools (and, to a lesser extent, day schools) have been a major influence in fostering the concept of a Deaf culture and the use of ASL. Inclusion, they believe, forces students who are deaf to lose their Deaf identity and places them in a hearing and speaking environment in which it is almost impossible for them to succeed. In particular, critics of inclusion argue that when a student who is deaf is placed in a setting with nondisabled children, he or she is usually the only student with a hearing impairment in the class. This lack of a "critical mass" of students who are deaf can lead to two interrelated problems: a lack of peers with whom the student who is deaf can communicate and a high degree of social isolation.

Students who are deaf tend to be less socially mature than their hearing peers and find it difficult to interact with their hearing classmates in inclusionary settings (Kluwin et al., 2002). Even though inclusion can present problems for many students who are deaf, by no means is it a negative experience for all students. Research on the effects of integrating students who are deaf with hearing peers has consistently found that social and academic outcomes vary depending on the individual. For some, full integration is beneficial; for others, a separate setting is best. Researchers have found that effective inclusive programming for students who are deaf is related to support from the school administration and parents and opportunities for instruction in the general education classroom by special educators trained in deaf education (Schirmer, 2001). For an example of how this can work, read the Making it Work on page 346.

TECHNOLOGICAL ADVANCES

A number of technological advances have made it easier for persons with hearing impairment to communicate with and/or have access to information from the hearing world. This technological explosion has primarily involved five areas: hearing aids, captioning, telephones, computer-assisted instruction, and the Internet. For information on how to select and integrate assistive technology, read the Responsive Instruction on page 347.

Collaboration and Co-Teaching of Students Who Are Deaf or Hard of Hearing

"If he can't hear me, how can I teach him?"

Working with a teacher of students who are deaf or hard of hearing might mean learning a new language or how to work with interpreters. This can cause anxiety and initial reluctance on the part of the general education teacher to try to collaborate, particularly if there is a concern about planning time. In all cases, the general educator who is being asked to collaborate has the right to a thorough understanding of the abilities of the student (not just the disabilities) and of the goals the special educator has set for the collaboration. This initial step is vital in setting up a successful partnership.

WHAT DOES IT MEAN TO BE A TEACHER OF STUDENTS WHO ARE DEAF OR HARD OF HEARING?

The focus of training for teachers of the deaf or hard of hearing is not in a content area but is on the assessment, characteristics, and management of hearing impairments. Again, these teachers have special skills that they can offer the general educator, such as the following:

1. Providing activities to promote literacy in English or American Sign Language.
2. Modifying incidental language experiences to fit visual and other sensory needs.
3. Selecting, adapting, and implementing classroom management strategies.
4. Designing a classroom environment that maximizes opportunities for visual and/or auditory learning.
5. Facilitating independent communication. (Council for Exceptional Children, 2001)

Tapping into these areas of expertise will certainly help in a collaborative situation, but it takes more than expertise in a teaching area to make a collaboration work, as is evidenced by the following example.

SUCCESSFUL STRATEGIES FOR CO-TEACHING

Cindy Sadonis (a teacher of students who are deaf or hard of hearing) and Connie Underwood (a third-grade teacher) worked collaboratively to include Joe and Brittany. Joe used hearing aids but had language deficits, and Brittany had a profound hearing loss and used both sign and oral language.

Cindy: I teach nine students with hearing impairments in grades K through 5. The students receive a range of special education services. All students, however, are mainstreamed for library, music, PE, guidance, and special events.

Connie: I teach a general education third-grade class. There are seventeen students. I had worked with students with hearing impairments in my general education classroom in the past, and although the experiences were positive in many ways, I felt that I was connecting with the students "at a distance."

Cindy: We were both apprehensive despite being friends, coworkers, and experienced teachers. I went into Connie's room, and she and her third-grade students came into my room.

Connie: I had three main fears. First, was I going to be able to communicate with Joe and Brittany without an interpreter? Yikes! My signing skills were labored, elementary, and painfully wrong at times. Second, how much more planning and time would this take? When I was lead teacher, Cindy interpreted and observed and was ready the following week with lessons on the same theme. I became a support in her room when she became the lead teacher. Third, I was concerned about student relationships. Without prompting, our students began signing as they tried to communicate, and by the latter part of the year, it was amazing how much communication was going on at the lunch table, in PE, and even secretively (or so the kids thought) in the classroom. But there were times when Brittany and Joe still felt different and when my students found it much easier to engage in conversations with their friends without hearing losses.

Cindy: It is important to note that collaborative teaching to this degree is often difficult, largely because of schedule. Positive teacher attitudes are required if inclusion is to succeed. Challenges presented themselves along the way for us, too. Social interaction was always an area of need despite our best efforts. As teachers, we have highs and lows too. Working through them has helped us continue to move in the right direction. ■

By Margaret P. Weiss

Meeting the Needs of Students Who Are Deaf or Hard of Hearing

Assistive Technology

WHAT IS ASSISTIVE TECHNOLOGY?

Assistive technology is defined under IDEA as "any item, piece of equipment or product system, whether acquired commercially off the shelf, modified, or customized, that is used to increase, maintain, or improve the functional capabilities of children with disabilities" (*Federal Register*, August 19, 1991, p. 41272). For students with hearing impairments, assistive technology can offer support for receptive and expressive communication, access to visual instruction, and individualization of instruction critical for their success. To make the most of assistive technology in the classroom, teachers need to be aware of how the technology can be integrated into the context of instruction.

TYPES OF ASSISTIVE TECHNOLOGY

Students who are deaf or hard of hearing may benefit from the following types of assistive technology:

- Amplification devices such as hearing aids or frequency modulated (FM) systems
- Computer-assisted instruction
- Captioned programming
- Telecommunication devices for the deaf (TDD)
- Speech digitizers and synthesizers

CLASSROOM APPLICATIONS

Before introducing assistive technology in the classroom, the teacher should identify instructional goals for the student.

Guiding questions such as "What is it the student cannot do as a result of his or her disability?" and "Would assistive technology enable the student to meet the goal?" facilitate the identification of instructionally relevant technologies (Chambers, 1997).

When selecting technology, teachers should consider whether there is a low-tech alternative that would meet the same instructional goals, the level of support necessary to maintain the technology, the skills required to appropriately use the device, and the potential availability of the technology in other environments outside of the classroom (Garrick-Duhaney & Duhaney, 2000).

Finally, teachers should plan for meaningful integration of the technology into the teaching–learning process. Consideration of environmental demands and task expectations help teachers to determine where and when to use the technologies. Questions can include the following:

- What is the physical arrangement?
- What is the instructional context?
- What supports already exist in the environment?
- What activities support the student's curriculum?
- What are the critical elements of the instructional activities?
- How might the activities be modified to accommodate the student's needs?
- How might the technology support the student's participation in those activities? (Chambers, 1997) ■

By Kristin L. Sayeski

Hearing Aids   There are three main types of hearing aids: those worn behind the ear, those worn in the ear, and those worn farther down in the canal of the ear. The behind-the-ear hearing aid is the most powerful and is therefore used by those with the most severe hearing impairment. It is also the one that children most often use because it can be used with FM systems that are available in some classrooms. With an FM system, the teacher wears a wireless lapel microphone, and the student wears an FM receiver (about the size of a cell phone). The student hears the amplified sound either through a hearing aid that comes attached to the FM receiver or by attaching a behind-the-ear hearing aid to the FM receiver. Whether a student will be able to benefit from a hearing aid by itself depends a great deal on the acoustic qualities of the classroom.

Although hearing aids are an integral part of educational programming for students with hearing impairment, some children who are deaf cannot benefit from them because of the severity and/or nature of the hearing impairment. Generally, hearing aids make sounds louder, not clearer, so if a person's hearing is distorted, a hearing aid will merely amplify the distorted sound.

For those who can benefit from hearing aids, it is critical for the student, parents, and teachers to work together to ensure the maximum effectiveness of the device. This means that the teacher should be familiar with its proper operation and maintenance.

Television, Video, and Movie Captioning At one time, viewers needed a special decoder to access captioned programs. Federal law now requires that TVs over 13 inches must contain a chip to allow one to view captions without a decoder. Federal law stipulates that by January of 2004, 75 percent of television programming had to be captioned. By January 2006, 100 percent of new programming must be captioned (National Association of the Deaf, 2001).

Many videotapes and DVDs available from rental stores are captioned as well. The most recent innovation in captioning is the Rear Window Captioning System, which displays captions on transparent acrylic panels that movie patrons can attach to their seats (National Center for Accessible Media, 2004). The captions are actually displayed in reverse at the rear of the theater, and the viewer sees them reflected on his or her acrylic screen.

Telephone Adaptations At one time, people with hearing impairments had problems using telephones, either because their hearing impairment was too great or because of acoustic feedback (noise caused by closeness of the telephone receiver to their hearing aids). However, this has changed since the invention of **text telephones (TT)**, sometimes referred to as TTYs (teletypes) or TTDs (telecommunication devices for the deaf). A person can use a TT connected to a telephone to type a message to anyone else who has a TT, and a special phone adaptation allows someone without a TT to use the pushbuttons on his or her phone to "type" messages to someone with a TT.

The federal government now requires each state to have a relay service for use by people with TTs. A relay service allows a person with a TT to communicate with anyone through an operator, who conveys the message to a person who does not have a TT. The TT user can carry on a conversation with the non-TT user, or the TT user can leave a message. The latter is useful for carrying out everyday activities, such as scheduling appointments. More and more people with hearing impairments are also making use of other telephone devices: the fax and text messaging on cell phones.

Computer-Assisted Instruction The explosion of microcomputer and related technology (e.g., videodiscs, CD-ROMs) is expanding learning capabilities for people who are deaf and their families. For example, visual displays of speech patterns on a computer screen can help someone with hearing impairment to learn speech. Videodisc programs showing people sign are also available for use in learning ASL.

Another example of computer-based technology is C-Print. With C-Print, a hearing person transcribes on a computer what is being said by, for example, someone lecturing. The student who is deaf can read a real-time text display on her or his computer as well as receive a printout of the text at a later time (Elliot, Stinson, McKee, Everhart, & Francis, 2001).

The Internet The information superhighway has opened up a variety of communication possibilities for people who are deaf. For example, electronic mail allows people who are deaf to communicate with one another as well as with hearing individuals. People who are

Text telephone (TT)
A device connected to a telephone by a special adapter; allows communication over the telephone between people who are hearing impaired and those with hearing; sometimes referred to as a TTY (teletype) or TTD (telecommunication device for the deaf).

UNDERSTANDING THE STANDARDS AND PRINCIPLES How have technological advances helped individuals with hearing impairment communicate? *(CEC Knowledge and Skills Standard DH5S3)*

Council for Exceptional Children

 TWO EXAMPLES of publications devoted to issues of concern to the Deaf community are the magazines, *Silent News* and *Deaf Life*. The former also has a Web version: **www.silentnews.com/index.html**. On the site, it presents itself as "a good glimpse into the Deaf community." *Deaf Life's* website at **www.deaflife.com** has chat rooms for adults and just for children.

Brian Blaisdell, a 15-year-old student at the Rhode Island School for the Deaf, holds up a T-Mobile Sidekick. Cell phone-size messaging devices have caught on quickly with people who are deaf, giving them the freedom to move around and communicate like never before.

deaf may also subscribe to email lists, connect to newsgroups or Web-based boards, and participate in chat rooms devoted to deafness, along with a multitude of other subjects. The ever-expanding World Wide Web provides access to a multitude of information sources.

In addition to providing people who are deaf with a way to access information, educators can use the Internet to help students who are deaf practice reading and writing skills. For instance, teachers can set up newsgroups, mailing lists, Web boards, or Weblogs through which students can communicate with others in the class, the school, or even worldwide.

Early Intervention

Education for infants and preschoolers with hearing impairments is of critical importance. Such programs not only can help facilitate the development of the children, but also may be beneficial in reducing parents' stress levels (Lederberg & Golbach, 2002).

Because language development is such an issue for children who are hearing impaired and because early childhood is such an important time for the development of language, it is not surprising that many of the most controversial issues surrounding early intervention in the area of deafness focus on language. As we indicated in the earlier discussion of oralism versus manualism, some people maintain that English language should be the focus of intervention efforts, and others hold that ASL should be used starting in infancy.

Children who are deaf who have parents who are deaf are likely to do better than children who are deaf who have hearing parents. For example, in infancy, they develop ASL at a rate similar to the rate at which hearing infants of hearing parents develop English. But infants who are deaf who have hearing parents do not develop either English or ASL at as fast a rate. This may be because day-to-day interactions between mothers and infants are more facilitative and natural when both the infant and parents are deaf than when the infant is deaf and the parents are hearing.

In addition to facility with ASL, parents who are deaf also have the advantage of being better prepared to cope with their infant's deafness (Meadow-Orlans, 1990). Most parents who are hearing are unprepared for the birth of a child with hearing impairment, whereas parents who are deaf can draw on their own experiences in order to offer helpful support to their child who is deaf.

Hearing parents, especially if they want to teach their infants sign language, may need help in understanding the importance of the visual modality in communicating with their infants (Bornstein et al., 1999). Hearing parents need to understand, for example, that the eye gaze of the infant who is deaf is extremely important because it is the infant's way of expressing interest and motivation.

Hearing parents of children who are deaf face a quandary over how to provide their children with appropriate sign language models. Both signed English and ASL, especially the latter, are difficult to learn to a high degree of fluency in a relatively short time. And like any language, ASL is harder to acquire as an adult and can rarely be learned to the same degree of fluency as that possessed by a native ASL signer.

The fact that over 95 percent of children who are deaf have parents who are hearing underscores the importance of intervention for many infants who are deaf. In fact, many authorities believe that there is a far greater need for early intervention for families with hearing parents of a child who is deaf than for families in which both the parents and the child are deaf (Andrews & Zmijewski, 1997).

Educators have established preschool intervention projects to teach the basics of sign language to the parents of children who are deaf as well as to the children themselves. Such projects are generally successful at teaching the rudiments of sign to parents and infants. Once the child is ready to progress beyond one- and two-word signed utterances, however, it is important that native signers be available as models. Authorities recommend a practice that is popular in Sweden: that adults who are deaf be part of early intervention efforts because they can serve as sign language models and can help hearing parents form positive expectations about their children's potential (Lane et al., 1996). Even though hearing parents might never be able to communicate fluently in sign language, it is important that they continue to sign with their child. Not only does signing allow parents a means of communicating with the child; it also demonstrates that they value the child's language and the Deaf culture.

Transition to Adulthood

UNDERSTANDING THE STANDARDS AND PRINCIPLES What can individuals with hearing impairment expect as they transition to adulthood? *(CEC Knowledge and Skills Standards DH7K1, DH10K2, & DH10S2)*

Council for Exceptional Children

Unemployment and underemployment (being overqualified for a job) have been persistent problems for persons with a hearing impairment, especially women (Schirmer, 2001). There is some evidence, however, that this bleak picture is slowly beginning to change. The primary reason for this change has been the expansion of postsecondary programming for students with hearing impairment. A fifteen-year follow-up of graduates with hearing impairment from two-year or four-year colleges found that a college education made a substantial difference in having a satisfying career and life (Schroedel & Geyer, 2000).

POSTSECONDARY EDUCATION

Before the mid-1960s, the only institution established specifically for the postsecondary education of students with hearing impairment was Gallaudet College (now Gallaudet University). Except for this one institution, these students were left with no choice but to attend traditional colleges and universities. However, traditional postsecondary schools were generally not equipped to handle the special needs of students with hearing impairment. It is little wonder, then, that a study by Quigley, Jenne, and Phillips (1968) was able to identify only 224 people with hearing impairment who were graduates of regular colleges and universities in the United States between 1910 and 1965.

Findings such as these led to the expansion of postsecondary programs. The federal government has funded a wide variety of postsecondary programs for students with hearing impairment. The two best-known ones are Gallaudet University and the National Technical Institute for the Deaf (NTID) at the Rochester Institute of Technology. The NTID program, emphasizing training in technical fields, complements the liberal arts orientation of Gallaudet University. At NTID, some students with hearing impairment also attend classes with hearing students at the Rochester Institute of Technology.

In addition to Gallaudet and NTID, there are now well over 100 postsecondary programs in the United States and Canada for students with hearing impairment. By law, Gallaudet and NTID are responsible for serving students from all fifty states and territories. Others serve students from several states, from one state only, or from specific districts only.

Although many people who are deaf who enroll in higher education choose to attend Gallaudet, NTID, or colleges with special programs, some go to traditional colleges and universities. These students usually take advantage of the expanding roles of university programs that have been established to facilitate the academic experiences of students with disabilities. One of the accommodations often recommended is to provide sign language interpreters in the classes of students with hearing impairment.

The role of interpreters generates a debate over using ASL versus transliteration. **Transliteration**, which is similar to signed English, maintains the same word order as spoken English. ASL, by contrast, requires the interpreter to digest the meaning of what is said before conveying it through signs. The little research that has been done comparing the two has not provided clear-cut evidence of one being more beneficial than the other.

Most college instructors have limited, if any, experience in working with sign language interpreters. Even so, it is critical that instructors and interpreters work closely together to provide the optimum learning experience for students who are deaf while not disrupting other students in the class. (Seal, 2004). The Focus on Concepts on page 352 provides some tips for working with sign language interpreters.

Transliteration
A method used by most sign language interpreters in which the signs maintain the same word order as that of spoken English; American Sign Language (ASL) is also used by some interpreters.

CHILDREN of Deaf Adults (CODA) is an organization devoted to children of adults who are deaf. You can visit its website at **www.coda-international.org**

As stated on the website, "CODA is an organization established for the purpose of promoting family awareness and individual growth in hearing children of deaf parents. This purpose is accomplished through providing educational opportunities, promoting self-help, organizing advocacy efforts, and acting as a resource for the membership and various communities."

There are now over 100 postsecondary programs in the United States and Canada for students who are deaf or hard of hearing. Many of these students choose to attend traditional colleges and universities as well.

FOCUS ON CONCEPTS

Tips for Working with Sign Language Interpreters

GENERAL PRINCIPLES

- The interpreter must be certified. (The Americans With Disabilities Act specifies different types of acceptable certification.)
- The interpreter must maintain confidentiality.
- The interpreter should match the needs of the student with respect to preference for such things as ASL versus signed English, transliteration versus interpretation, and use of voice while interpreting.
- The interpreter should be available for all school-related activities.
- If at times the student can interact with peers successfully without the interpreter, then he or she should be allowed to do so.
- The interpreter is there to interpret, not to act as a classroom aide or to teach. *(Seal, 2004)*

SPECIFICS

- The interpreter should have copies of all handouts and, if possible, copies of the textbooks.
- The instructor and fellow students should talk directly to the student and not to the interpreter.
- In a lecture class, the instructor should be aware of the pace of his or her delivery, perhaps pausing more frequently than usual.
- In a discussion class, participants should try to talk one at a time and account for the time lag between what is spoken and its signed interpretation.
- The instructor might want to request that the interpreter stop the class if something becomes too complicated to interpret. In fact, the interpreter's need to clarify might very well signal that the rest of the students do not understand the information either. *(Siple, 1993)* ■

Sign language interpreters are also used in elementary and secondary schools, where the issues concerning their use are no less important. There is a tremendous shortage of qualified interpreters for the public schools.

FAMILY ISSUES

With regard to raising a family, people who are deaf often face unique challenges. National statistics indicate that 95 percent of adults who are deaf choose deaf spouses, and 90 percent of the offspring of these marriages have normal hearing (Buchino, 1993). These hearing children often serve as interpreters for their parents. Being called on to interpret for one's parents can help to develop self-confidence around adult authority figures (e.g., doctors, lawyers, insurance agents), but it can also force one to face some unpleasant biases, as the following story from a hearing child of deaf parents demonstrates:

> Curled up in the seat, chin dug into my chest, I noticed there was a lull in the conversation. Dad was a confident driver, but Mom was smoking more than usual.
> "Something happened? That gas station?" Mom signed to me.
> "No, nothing," I lied.
> "Are you sure?"
> "Everything is fine." Dad and I had gone to pay and get directions. The man behind the counter had looked up, seen me signing and grunted, "Huh, I didn't think mutes were allowed to have driver's licenses." Long ago I'd gotten used to hearing those kind of comments. But I never could get used to the way it made me churn inside. (Walker, 1986, p. 9)

These children also sometimes admit to resenting that being called on to interpret for their parents has interfered with their social lives (Buchino, 1993).

There has been a long tradition of preparing students who are deaf for manual trades (Lane, 1992). But unskilled and semiskilled trades are fast disappearing from the workforce in favor of jobs requiring higher-level skills. As a result, adults who are deaf face even greater obstacles when they enter the job market. Although the educational, work, and social opportunities for adults who are deaf are often limited, there are reasons to be optimistic about the future. With the continued expansion of transition programming, postsecondary education, and greater public awareness of the potential of people who are deaf should come a brighter outlook for more adults who are deaf.

Summary

HOW do professionals define and classify individuals who are deaf or hard of hearing?

- Those with a physiological perspective use a decibel loss of 90 dB or greater as the cutoff for deafness.
- Those with an educational perspective classify individuals as deaf if they are unable to process linguistic information, with or without a hearing aid; they classify individuals as hard of hearing if they are able to process this information with the help of a hearing aid.
- Congenital versus adventitious deafness refers to being born deaf versus acquiring deafness after birth; prelingual deafness versus postlingual deafness refers to deafness occurring before versus after speech and language development.
- There is growing sentiment in the Deaf community that those who are deaf should be considered as a cultural/linguistic minority rather than disabled.

WHAT is the prevalence of hearing impairment?

- About 0.13 percent of students from 6 to 17 years of age are identified as hearing impaired, with those classified as hard of hearing being more prevalent than those identified as deaf.
- Close to 23 percent of students who are deaf come from Hispanic-speaking homes.

WHAT are some basic anatomical and physiological characteristics of the ear?

- The outer ear consists of the auricle and external auditory canal.
- The middle ear consists of the eardrum and three tiny bones (ossicles): the malleus, incus, and stapes.

- The inner ear consists of the vestibular mechanism and the cochlea; the former monitors balance, and the latter is the most important for hearing because it is responsible for sending electrical impulses to the brain via the cochlear nerve.

HOW is hearing ability measured?

- Screening tests for infants often measure otoacoustic emissions, low-intensity sound emitted from the cochlea when stimulated.
- Pure-tone audiometry assesses decibel (intensity) and hertz (frequency) levels.
- Speech audiometry assesses the ability to detect and understand speech.
- Specialized tests for young children and those who are hard to test include play audiometry, tympanometry, and evoked-response audiometry.

WHAT causes hearing impairments?

- Conductive hearing impairments involve the middle or outer ear, sensorineural hearing impairments involve the inner ear, mixed hearing impairments involve both.
- Impairments of the outer ear are caused by such things as infections of the external canal or tumors.
- Impairments of the middle ear are often due to malfunctioning of the ossicles; otitis media is a common cause of temporary middle-ear hearing problems.
- Impairments of the inner ear usually result in greater hearing impairment than do those of the middle or outer ear; impairments of the inner ear can be hereditary or acquired, but the former are much more common. Genetic or hereditary factors are the leading cause of

deafness in children, with mutation of the connexin-26 gene now considered the most common cause of congenital deafness.

WHAT are some psychological and behavioral characteristics of learners with hearing impairments?

- The most severely affected area is comprehension and production of English.
- Sign language is the primary language of most people in the Deaf community.
  - Each sign consists of three parts: handshape, location, and movement.
  - Sign language is a true language, as evidenced by the facts that sign language is as grammatically complex as spoken language, there is no universal sign language, children who are deaf reach the same language milestones and at the same times as do those who are hearing, the neurological underpinnings of sign are the same as those for spoken language.
- Deafness does not affect intelligence.
- Most students who are deaf have extreme deficits in academics, especially reading.
  - Students who are deaf who have parents who are deaf do better academically.
  - A supportive home environment is associated with higher achievement.
- Students who are deaf might face limited opportunities for social interaction.
  - The inclusion movement can result in students who are deaf not having peers who are deaf with whom to communicate.
  - About 95 percent of children who are deaf have hearing parents, most of whom are not proficient in sign language.
  - Many authorities recognize the Deaf culture as a means of healthy social communication. There is concern that the Deaf culture might be eroding owing to inclusionary programming. Deaf activists have raised issues with respect to cochlear implants and genetic engineering.

WHAT are some educational considerations for learners with hearing impairments?

- The oral approach consists of the following:
  - The auditory-verbal approach, which focuses on using audition to improve speech and language development.
  - The auditory-oral approach, which is like the auditory-verbal approaches with the addition of using visual cues such as speech reading and cued speech.
- The manual approach stresses sign lanaguge.
- Most educational programs use a total communication approach, a blend of oral and manual techniques, the latter being a type of signing English system in which the English word order is preserved.
- Some advocate for a bicultural-bilingual approach, which consists of three features: ASL is considered the primary language, people who are deaf are involved in the development of the program and curriculum, and the curriculum involves instruction in Deaf culture.
- Educational placement of students who are deaf includes the full continuum, but more inclusive settings are becoming more and more popular, with about 85 percent of students who are deaf attending classes in regular schools and 40 percent spending the vast majority of their time in general education classrooms. Many within the Deaf community are concerned that the inclusion movement results in the absence of a "critical mass" of students who are deaf, which can result in social isolation.
- Numerous technological advances are occurring in hearing aids; television, video, and movie captioning; text telephone technology; computer-assisted instruction; and the Internet.

WHAT are some things to consider with respect to early intervention for learners with hearing impairments?

- Families of children who are deaf who have hearing parents might be in greater need of early intervention programming than families in which the parents are deaf.
- Because it is difficult for hearing parents to become fluent in sign language, native signers are a part of some intervention programs.

WHAT are some things to consider with respect to transition to adulthood for learners with hearing impairments?

- In addition to Gallaudet University and the National Technical Institute for the Deaf, there are now several postsecondary programs for students with hearing impairment.
- A common accommodation in college is the use of sign language interpreters. Transliteration involves maintaining the same word order as English whereas ASL does not.
- Ninety percent of the children of two parents who are deaf are deaf. These children often face challenges of negotiating between the Deaf community and hearing society.
- There has been a long tradition of preparing many students who are deaf for manual trades; however, these trades are disappearing.
- Expanded transition programming, postsecondary education, and public awareness promises a brighter outlook for adults who are deaf.

APPLYING THE STANDARDS AND PRINCIPLES

- **WHAT** should teachers know about how hearing impairment is **defined**? *(CEC Content Standard #1 & INTASC Principle #1)*

- **WHY** is it important for teachers to know about the **causes of hearing impairment**? *(CEC Content Standards #1, #2, & #3; INTASC Principles #1 & #2)*

- **THE parents** of a young child who is hard of hearing ask you to advise them on how their child should be taught to converse. How would you respond? *(CEC Content Standards #5 & #6; INTASC Principle #5)*

- **HOW** is **hearing ability measured**? *(CEC Content Standard #8 & INTASC Principle #8)*

- **HOW** would you **respond to parents** who approached you expressing concern about the future of their deaf high school student? *(CEC Content Standards #7 & #10; INTASC Principles #7 & #10)*

Council for Exceptional Children

INTASC

Chapter 11

Learners with Blindness or Low Vision

R ay, no one knows what it's like to carry water
The way your mother made you carry it—

Even the boy Pharaoh
Wore a yoke on his shoulders

Just to show he was a man.
History doesn't matter much,

At least until your child
"Done gone blind"—your Mama saw it—

"You always got to carry water," she said.
"This ain't no kidding around."

Long time
You carried water

In both hands,
Feeling for the path

With your feet.
Ray, your Mama knew—

A song comes that way—
Or else it never will.

Laugh or cry it's the same.
A Mockingbird listens from a telephone wire.

Long time, water, both hands.

STEPHEN KUUSISTO
"Elegy for Ray Charles And His Mother"

QUESTIONS TO GUIDE YOUR READING OF THIS CHAPTER . . .

- HOW do professionals define and classify learners with blindness and low vision?

- WHAT is the prevalence of visual impairment?

- WHAT are some basic anatomical and physiological characteristics of the eye?

- WHAT are some of the psychological and behavioral characteristics of learners with visual impairments?

- HOW is visual ability measured?

- WHAT causes visual impairments?

- WHAT are some educational considerations for learners with visual impairments?

- WHAT are some things to consider with respect to early intervention for learners with visual impairments?

- WHAT are some things to consider with respect to transition to adulthood for learners with visual impairments?

SPECIAL EDUCATORS . . .

- **understand the field** as an evolving and changing discipline *(from CEC Content Standard #1)*.

- **understand the similarities and differences in human development** and the characteristics between and among individuals with and without exceptional learning needs *(from CEC Content Standard #2)*.

- **understand the effects** that an exceptional condition can have on an individual's learning in school and throughout life *(from CEC Content Standard #3)*.

- develop a variety of **individualized transition plans** *(from CEC Content Standard #7)*.

- use the results of **assessments** *(from CEC Content Standard #8)*.

- **use collaboration** to facilitate the successful transitions of individuals with exceptional learning needs across settings and services *(from CEC Content Standard #10)*.

ALL TEACHERS . . .

- **understand the central concepts, tools of inquiry, structures of the discipline(s) they teach** and can create learning experiences that make these aspects of subject matter meaningful for students *(INTASC Principle #1)*.

- **understand how children learn and develop** and can provide learning opportunities that support the intellectual, social, and personal development of each learner *(INTASC Principle #2)*.

- **plan instruction based on knowledge** of subject matter, students, the community, and curriculum goals *(INTASC Principle #7)*.

- Understand and use formal and informal **assessment strategies** to evaluate and ensure the continuous intellectual, social, and physical development of the learner *(INTASC Principle #8)*.

- **foster relationships** with school colleagues, families, and agencies in the larger community to support students' learning and well being *(INTASC Principle #10)*.

Council for Exceptional Children

INTASC

Stephen Kuusisto, the author of the poem reprinted on page 357, was blind from birth but was well into his adult years before he stopped the charade of trying to "pass" as a sighted person. Once at peace with his blindness, he was able to turn his energies to more productive endeavors, such as being a successful author. As Kuusisto acknowledges in his elegy to Ray Charles, people vary in their response to being blind. Some actually gain an inner strength from adversity, for example, "She'd make me cut wood, wash clothes and build a fire under the pot. . . . People thought that was abusive. My mother had the attitude 'He's got to learn, and just because he's blind doesn't mean he's stupid'" (Charles, 2004). However, a major impediment to being able to accept one's blindness is society's reactions to people who are blind. Visual impairments seem to evoke more awkwardness than most other disabilities. Why are we so uncomfortably aware of blindness? For one thing, blindness is visible. We often do not realize that a person has impaired hearing, for example, until we actually talk to him or her. The person with visual impairment, however, usually has a variety of symbols, such as a cane, thick or darkened glasses, a guide dog.

Another possible reason for being self-conscious around people who are blind is the role that eyes play in social interaction. Poets, playwrights, and songwriters have long recognized how emotionally expressive the eyes can be for people who are sighted. Those of us who are sighted know how uncomfortable it can be to talk with someone who does not make eye contact with us. Think how often we have heard someone say or have ourselves said that we prefer to talk face to face on an important matter, rather than over the telephone.

Another reason we fear loss of vision is that the sense of sight is linked so closely with the traditional concept of beauty. We derive great pleasure from our sight. Our feelings about others are often based largely on physical appearances that are visually perceived.

Finally, our use of language reinforces a negative view of blindness:

> The word blind has always meant more than merely the inability to see. . . . Throughout history of the language and in common usage today, the word [blind] connotes a lack of understanding . . ., a willful disregard or obliviousness, a thing meant to conceal or deceive. In fact, when you stop to listen, the word is far more commonly used in its figurative than its literal sense. And it comes up so often: blind faith, blind devotion, blind luck, . . . blind alley, . . . blind taste test, double-blind study, flying blind, . . . blind submission, blind side, blind spot. . . . Pick up any book or magazine and you will find dozens of similes and

Misconceptions about
Learners with Blindness or Low Vision

MYTH People who are legally blind have no sight at all.

FACT Only a small percentage of people who are legally blind have absolutely no vision. Many have a useful amount of functional vision.

MYTH People who are blind have an extra sense that enables them to detect obstacles.

FACT People who are blind do not have an extra sense. Some can learn to develop an "obstacle sense" by noting the change in pitch of echoes as they move toward objects.

MYTH People who are blind automatically develop better acuity in their other senses.

FACT Through concentration and attention, individuals who are blind can learn to make very fine discriminations in the sensations they obtain. This is not automatic but rather represents learning to use received sensations better.

MYTH People who are blind have superior musical ability.

FACT The musical ability of people who are blind is not necessarily better than that of sighted people; however, many people who are blind pursue musical careers as one way in which they can achieve success.

MYTH Stereotypic behaviors (e.g., body rocking, head swaying) are always maladaptive and should be totally eliminated.

FACT Although more research is needed, there are some authorities who maintain that these behaviors, except when they are extreme, can help persons who are blind regulate their levels of arousal.

MYTH Braille is not very useful for the vast majority of people who are blind; it should only be tried as a last resort.

FACT Very few people who are blind have learned braille, primarily due to fear that using it is a sign of failure and to a historical professional bias against it. Authorities acknowledge the utility of braille for people who are blind.

MYTH Braille is of no value for those who have low vision.

FACT Some individuals with low vision have conditions that will eventually result in blindness. More and more, authorities think that these individuals should learn braille to be prepared for when they cannot read print effectively.

MYTH If people with low vision use their eyes too much, their sight will deteriorate.

FACT Only rarely is this true. Visual efficiency can actually be improved through training and use. Wearing strong lenses, holding books close to the eyes, and using the eyes often cannot harm vision.

MYTH Mobility instruction should be delayed until elementary or secondary school.

FACT Many authorities now recognize that even preschoolers can take advantage of mobility instruction, including the use of a cane.

MYTH The long cane is a simply constructed, easy-to-use device.

FACT The National Academy of Sciences has drawn up specifications for the manufacture of the long cane and its proper use.

MYTH Guide dogs take people where they want to go.

FACT The guide dog does not "take" the person anywhere; the person must first know where he or she is going. The dog is primarily a protection against unsafe areas or obstacles.

MYTH Technology will soon replace the need for braille and for mobility aids such as the long cane and guide dogs. In addition, a breakthrough for restoring complete sight through technology is just around the corner.

FACT As amazing as some of the technology is in the field of vision impairment, it is doubtful that it will be as effective as braille, the long cane, or guide dogs anytime soon. Research on artifical vision is exciting, but it too does not promise to have huge practical benefits for some time.

metaphors connecting blindness and blind people with ignorance, confusion, indifference, ineptitude. (Kleege, 1999, p. 21)

So although blindness is the least prevalent of all disabilities, at least in children, people dread it. It is reportedly the third most feared condition; only cancer and AIDS outrank it (Jernigan, 1992). With a bit of reflection, however, it becomes obvious that our anxieties about blindness are irrational. Most of our apprehension can be attributed to our lack of experience in interacting with individuals with visual impairment. It is not until we talk to people who are blind or read about their appreciation of sounds, smells, and touch that we begin to realize that sight is not the only sense that enables us to enjoy beauty or interact socially with other people.

Like anyone with a disability, the person who is blind wants to be treated like everyone else. Most people who are blind do not seek pity or unnecessary help. In fact, they can be fiercely protective of their independence. See the Personal Perspectives below for tips of etiquette on interacting with someone who is blind.

In this chapter, we hope to dispel several myths about blindness. We start by presenting a fact that most sighted people do not know: The majority of people who are blind can actually see.

Personal Perspectives

SOCIAL INTERACTION WITH PEOPLE WHO ARE BLIND: POINTS OF ETIQUETTE

THE following letter to "Dear Abby" from the president of the American Foundation for the Blind lists some appropriate ways that the sighted can interact with those who are blind. Suggestions such as these help to avoid awkward social situations.

Dear Abby:

You recently ran a letter from a woman who gave a few tips on what sighted people should do when they meet a blind person. As president of the American Foundation for the Blind, and a blind person myself, I believe I can add a few more points of etiquette your readers may find helpful.

1. Speak to people who are blind or visually impaired using a natural conversational tone and speed. Do not speak loudly and slowly unless the person also has a hearing impairment.
2. Address blind people by name when possible. This is especially important in crowded places.
3. Immediately greet blind people when they enter a room or service area. This lets them know you are present and ready to assist.
4. Indicate the end of a conversation with a blind person in order to avoid the embarrassment of

leaving a person speaking when no one is actually there.
5. Feel free to use words that refer to vision when conversing with blind people. Words such as "look," "see," "watching TV," are part of everyday communication. The words "blind" and "visually impaired" are also acceptable in conversation.
6. Do not leave a blind person standing in "free space" when you serve as a guide. Also, be sure that the person you guide has a firm grasp on your arm or is leaning against a chair or a wall if you have to be separated momentarily.
7. Be calm and clear about what to do if you see a blind person about to encounter a dangerous situation. For example, if the person is about to bump into something, calmly and firmly call out, "Wait there for a moment; there is an obstruction in your path.". . .

Carl R. Augusto, President
American Foundation for the Blind, New York. ■

Source: Letter reprinted with permission of the American Foundation for the Blind.

Definition and Classification

The two most common ways of describing someone with visual impairment are the legal and educational definitions. The former is the one laypeople and medical professionals use; the latter is the one educators favor. The two major classifications are blindness and low vision.

LEGAL DEFINITION

The legal definition involves assessment of visual acuity and field of vision. A person who is **legally blind** has visual acuity of 20/200 or less in the better eye even with correction (e.g., eyeglasses) or has a field of vision so narrow that its widest diameter subtends an angular distance no greater than 20 degrees. The fraction 20/200 means that the person sees at 20 feet what a person with normal vision sees at 200 feet. (Normal visual acuity is thus 20/20.) The inclusion of a narrowed field of vision in the legal definition means that a person may have 20/20 vision in the central field but severely restricted peripheral vision. Legal blindness qualifies a person for certain legal benefits, such as tax advantages and money for special materials.

In addition to this medical classification of blindness, there is a category referred to as low vision (sometimes referred to as partially sighted). According to the legal classification system, persons who have **low vision** have visual acuity falling between 20/70 and 20/200 in the better eye with correction.

EDUCATIONAL DEFINITION

Many professionals, particularly educators, have found the legal classification scheme inadequate. They have observed that visual acuity is not a very accurate predictor of how people will function or use whatever remaining sight they have. Although a small percentage of individuals who are legally blind have absolutely no vision, the majority can see to some degree.

Many who recognize the limitations of the legal definition of blindness and low vision favor the educational definition, which stresses the method of reading instruction. For educational purposes, individuals who are blind are so severely impaired they must learn to read braille or use aural methods (audiotapes and records). (**Braille**, a system of raised dots by which blind people read with their fingertips, consists of quadrangular cells containing from one to six dots whose arrangement denotes different letters and symbols.) Educators often refer to those individuals who can read print, even if they need magnifying devices or large-print books, as having low vision. For example, the following educators' definition states that a person with low vision is someone:

> who has difficulty accomplishing visual tasks, even with prescribed corrective lenses, but who can enhance his or her ability to accomplish these tasks with the use of compensatory visual strategies, low vision or other devices, and environmental modifications. (Corn & Koenig, 1996, p. 4)

It is important to note that even though people with low vision can read print, many authorities believe that some of them can benefit from using braille. (We discuss this later in the chapter.) This is why we emphasized above that those who are considered blind *must* use braille to read.

Prevalence

Blindness is primarily an adult disability. Most estimates indicate that blindness is approximately one-tenth as prevalent in school-age children as in adults. The federal government

Legally blind
A person who has visual acuity of 20/200 or less in the better eye even with correction (e.g., eyeglasses) or has a field of vision so narrow that its widest diameter subtends an angular distance no greater than 20 degrees.

Low vision
A term used by educators to refer to individuals whose visual impairment is not so severe that they are unable to read print of any kind; they may read large or regular print, and they may need some kind of magnification.

Braille
A system in which raised dots allow people who are blind to read with their fingertips; each quadrangular cell contains from one to six dots, the arrangement of which denotes different letters and symbols.

 SEVERAL WEBSITES contain sample Snellen charts. Some examples are: **www.gimbel.com/check-yv.htm** **www.saoa.co.za/chart.htm** **www.vision3k.com/snellen.asp**

The website of Prevent Blindness America contains an example of a Web-based measure of near vision: **www.preventblindness.org/eye_tests/near_vision_test.html**

Prevent Blindness America, founded in 1908, is a voluntary organization devoted to eye health and safety. Its website at **www.preventblindness.org** contains a variety of information on blindness prevention.

Cornea
A transparent cover in front of the iris and pupil in the eye; responsible for most of the refraction of light rays in focusing on an object.

Aqueous humor
A watery substance between the cornea and lens of the eye.

Pupil
The contractile opening in the middle of the iris of the eye.

Iris
The colored portion of the eye; contracts or expands, depending on the amount of light striking it.

Lens
A structure that refines and changes the focus of the light rays passing through the eye.

Vitreous humor
A transparent, gelatinous substance that fills the eyeball between the retina and the lens of the eye.

Retina
The back portion of the eye, containing nerve fibers connected to the optic nerve.

classifies only about 0.05 percent of the population ranging from 6 to 17 years of age as "visually impaired," which includes those who are blind or who have low vision. This makes visual impairment one of the least prevalent disabilities in children.

Anatomy and Physiology of the Eye

The anatomy of the visual system is extremely complex, so our discussion here will focus only on basic characteristics. Figure 11.1 shows the functioning of the eye. The physical object being seen becomes an electrical impulse that is sent through the optic nerve to the visual center of the brain, the occipital lobes. Before reaching the optic nerve, light rays reflecting off the object being seen pass through several structures within the eye. The light rays do the following:

1. Pass through the **cornea** (a transparent cover in front of the iris and pupil), which performs the major part of the bending (refraction) of the light rays so that the image will be focused
2. Pass through the **aqueous humor** (a watery substance between the cornea and lens of the eye)
3. Pass through the **pupil** (the contractile opening in the middle of the **iris**, the colored portion of the eye that contracts or expands, depending on the amount of light striking it)
4. Pass through the **lens**, which refines and changes the focus of the light rays before they pass through the **vitreous humor** (a transparent gelatinous substance that fills the eyeball between the retina and lens)
5. come to a focus on the **retina** (the back portion of the eye, containing nerve fibers connected to the **optic nerve**, which carries the information back to the brain)

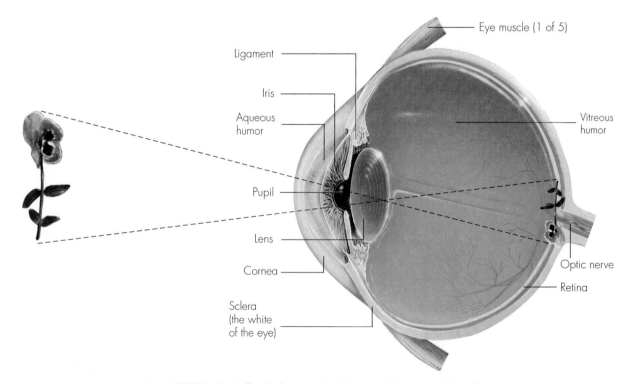

FIGURE 11.1   The basic anatomical features of the eye and the visual process.

Measurement of Visual Ability

Visual acuity is most often measured with the **Snellen chart**, which consists of rows of letters (for individuals who know the alphabet) or Es (for the very young and or those who cannot read). In the latter case, the Es are arranged in various positions, and the person's task is to indicate in what direction the "legs" of the Es face. Each row corresponds to the distance at which a person with normal vision can discriminate the letters or the directions of the Es. (There are eight rows, one corresponding to each of the following distances: 15, 20, 30, 40, 50, 70, 100, and 200 feet.) People are normally tested at the 20-foot distance. If they can distinguish the letters in the 20-foot row, they are said to have 20/20 central visual acuity for far distances. If they can distinguish only the much larger letters in the 70-foot row, they are said to have 20/70 central visual acuity for far distances.

Although the Snellen chart is widely used and can be very useful, it has at least three limitations:

1. It measures visual acuity for distant but not near objects, which is why it is necessary to report the results in terms of central visual acuity for *far* distances. Many educational activities, particularly reading, require visual acuity at close distances. A variety of near-vision tests, consisting of cards with different size print or symbols, are available. For example, a person might be asked to name letters that range in size from smaller to larger than the letters on this page on a card that is at a typical reading distance from the person's eyes.

2. Visual acuity, as measured by the Snellen chart, does not always correspond with visual efficiency. **Visual efficiency** refers to the ability, for example, to control eye movements and to use visual information quickly and accurately (Barraga & Erin, 2001). Teachers often assess visual efficiency by observing the student performing in a variety of settings or by using an instrument designed for this purpose.

3. Visual acuity does not always correspond with how a student actually uses her or his vision in natural settings, which have variable environmental conditions (e.g., fluorescent lighting, windows that emit sunshine, highly reflective tile floors).

To determine how students use their vision in everyday situations, the vision teacher performs a **functional vision assessment**. The vision teacher observes the student in his or her daily activities, taking note of how the student functions under a variety of conditions (e.g. in sunny or cloudy weather) and on a variety of tasks (e.g., reading books, navigating within the classroom or from class to class) (Miller, 1999).

As part of this assessment, teachers should be alert to signs that children might have visual disabilities. Prevent Blindness America (1998–2003) has listed a number of signs of possible eye problems on their website (see the Focus on Concepts p. 364).

Causes

The most common visual problems are the results of errors of refraction. **Refraction** refers to the bending of the light rays as they pass through the various structures of the eye. **Myopia** (nearsightedness), **hyperopia** (farsightedness), and **astigmatism** (blurred vision) are examples of refraction errors that affect central visual acuity. Although each can be serious enough to cause significant impairment (myopia and hyperopia are the most common impairments of low vision), wearing glasses or contact lenses usually can bring vision within normal limits.

Myopia results when the eyeball is too long. In this case, the light rays from the object in Figure 11.2a would be in focus in front of, rather than on, the retina. Myopia affects vision for distant objects, but close vision may be unaffected. When the eyeball is too short, hyperopia (farsightedness) results (see Figure 11.2b). In this case, the light rays from the object in the diagram would be in focus behind, rather than on, the retina. Hyperopia affects vision for close objects, but far vision may be unaffected. If the cornea or lens of the eye is irregular, the person is said to have astigmatism. In this case, the light rays from the object in the figure would be blurred or distorted.

Optic nerve
The nerve at the back of the eye, which sends visual information back to the brain.

Visual acuity
The ability to see fine details; usually measured with the Snellen chart.

Snellen chart
Used in determining visual acuity; consists of rows of letters or Es arranged in different positions; each row corresponds to the distance at which a normally sighted person can discriminate the letters; does not predict how accurately a child will be able to read print.

Visual efficiency
A term used to refer to how well one uses his or her vision, including such things as control of eye movements, attention to visual detail, and discrimination of figure from background; believed by some to be more important than visual acuity alone in predicting a person's ability to function visually.

Functional vision assessment
An appraisal of an individual's use of vision in everyday situations.

Refraction
The bending of light rays as they pass through the structures (cornea, aqueous humor, pupil, lens, vitreous humor) of the eye.

Myopia
Nearsightedness; vision for distant objects is affected; usually results when eyeball is too long.

Hyperopia
Farsightedness; vision for near objects is affected; usually results when the eyeball is too short.

Astigmatism
Blurred vision caused by an irregular cornea or lens.

FOCUS ON CONCEPTS

Signs of Possible Eye Trouble in Children

If one or more of these signs appear, take your child to an eye doctor right away.

What do your child's eyes look like?

- eyes don't line up, one eye appears crossed or looks out
- eyelids are red-rimmed, crusted or swollen
- eyes are watery or red (inflamed)

How does your child act?

- rubs eyes a lot
- closes or covers one eye
- tilts head or thrusts head forward
- has trouble reading or doing other close-up work, or holds objects close to eyes to see
- blinks more than usual or seems cranky when doing close-up work

- things are blurry or hard to see
- squints eyes or frowns

What does your child say?

- "my eyes are itchy," "my eyes are burning" or "my eyes feel scratchy."
- "I can't see very well."
- After doing close-up work, your child says "I feel dizzy," "I have a headache" or "I feel sick/nauseous."
- "Everything looks blurry," or "I see double."

Remember, your child may still have an eye problem even if he or she does not complain or has not shown any unusual signs. ■

Source: Retrieved February 22, 2004 from the World Wide Web: www.preventblindness.org/children/trouble_signs.html. Reprinted with permission from Prevent Blindness America ®. Copyright © 1998–2003.

Among the most serious impairments are those caused by glaucoma, cataracts, and diabetes. These conditions occur primarily in adults, but each, particularly the latter two, can occur in children.

Glaucoma is actually a group of eye diseases that causes damage to the optic nerve. At one time, it was thought to be due exclusively to excessive pressure inside the eyeball; we now know that some cases of glaucoma occur with normal pressure (Glaucoma Research Foundation, 2003). It is referred to as the "sneak thief of sight" because it often occurs with no symptoms. However, glaucoma can be detected through an eye exam; and because it occurs more frequently in older people (and in African Americans), professionals recommend increasingly frequent checkups, starting at age 35 (and even more frequently for African Americans).

Cataracts are caused by a clouding of the lens of the eye, which results in blurred vision. In children, the condition is called *congenital cataracts*, and distance and color vision are seriously affected. Surgery can usually correct the problems caused by cataracts. Dia-

Glaucoma
A condition often, but not always, due to excessive pressure in the eyeball; the cause is unknown; if untreated, blindness results.

Cataracts
A condition caused by clouding of the lens of the eye; affects color vision and distance vision.

FIGURE 11.2 Visual problems: (a) myopia, (b) hyperopia

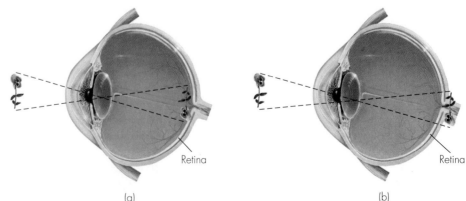

Retina   Retina

(a)   (b)

betes can cause **diabetic retinopathy**, a condition that results from interference with the blood supply to the retina.

Several other visual impairments primarily affect children. Visual impairments of school-age children are often due to prenatal causes, many of which are hereditary. We have already discussed congenital (meaning *present at birth*) cataracts and glaucoma. Another congenital condition is retinitis pigmentosa, a hereditary disease resulting in degeneration of the retina. It can start in infancy, early childhood, or the teenage years. **Retinitis pigmentosa** usually causes the field of vision to narrow (**tunnel vision**) and also affects

Diabetic retinopathy
A condition resulting from interference with the blood supply to the retina; the fastest-growing cause of blindness.

Retinitis pigmentosa
A hereditary condition resulting in degeneration of the retina; causes a narrowing of the field of vision and affects night vision.

Tunnel vision
A condition characterized by problems in peripheral vision, or a narrowing of the field of vision.

(a)   (b)

(c)   (d)

(e)

Consider how people with certain visual impairments see the world: (a) normal vision; (b) glaucoma; (c) cataracts; (d) diabetic retinopathy; (e) retinitis pigmentosa.

Night blindness

A condition characterized by problems in seeing at low levels of illumination; often caused by retinitis pigmentosa.

Cortical visual impairment (CVI)

A poorly understood childhood condition that apparently involves dysfunction in the visual cortex; characterized by large day-to-day variations in visual ability.

Retinopathy of prematurity (ROP)

A condition resulting in abnormal growth of blood vessels in the eye; caused by factors related to premature birth, including the administration of an excessive concentration of oxygen at birth.

Strabismus

A condition in which the eyes are directed inward (crossed eyes) or outward.

Nystagmus

A condition in which there are rapid involuntary movements of the eyes; sometimes indicates a brain malfunction and/or inner-ear problems.

UNDERSTANDING THE STANDARDS AND PRINCIPLES What should teachers know about the psychological and behavioral characteristics of individuals who are visually impaired? *(CEC Knowledge and Skills Standards VI2K4 & VI2K5)*

Council for Exceptional Children

one's ability to see in low light (**night blindness**). Included in the "prenatal" category are infectious diseases that affect the unborn child, such as syphilis and rubella.

A condition that can occur in childhood or adulthood is **cortical visual impairment (CVI)**. CVI results from damage or dysfunction in the parts of the brain that are responsible for vision. The damage or dysfunction can be the result of a variety of causes, such as infection or stroke. Children who have it are characterized by wide fluctuations from day to day in their visual abilities. They often start out blind, with their vision tending to improve over time (Blind Babies Foundation, 2002a).

One of the most dramatic medical discoveries of a cause of blindness involved a condition now referred to as **retinopathy of prematurity (ROP)**. ROP, which results in abnormal growth of blood vessels in the eye, began to appear in the 1940s in premature infants. In the 1950s, researchers determined that excessive concentrations of oxygen often administered to premature infants were causing blindness. The oxygen was necessary to prevent brain damage, but it was often given at too high a level. Since then, hospitals have been careful to monitor the amount of oxygen administered to premature infants. Today, with medical advances, many more premature babies are surviving, but they need very high levels of oxygen and are thus at risk for ROP. Furthermore, many authorities now believe that ROP can result from factors other than excessive oxygen that are related to being born very prematurely (Blind Babies Foundation, 2002b).

Two other conditions, strabismus and nystagmus, resulting in visual problems can be grouped because both are caused by improper muscle functioning. **Strabismus** is a condition in which one or both eyes are directed inward (crossed eyes) or outward. Left untreated, strabismus can result in permanent blindness because the brain will eventually reject signals from a deviating eye. Fortunately, most cases of strabismus can be corrected with eye exercises or surgery. Eye exercises sometimes involve the person's wearing a patch over the good eye for periods of time to force use of the eye that deviates. Surgery involves tightening or loosening the muscles that control eye movement. **Nystagmus** is a condition in which there are rapid involuntary movements of the eyes, usually resulting in dizziness and nausea. Nystagmus is sometimes a sign of brain malfunctioning and/or inner-ear problems.

Psychological and Behavioral Characteristics

LANGUAGE DEVELOPMENT

Most authorities believe that lack of vision does not have a very significant effect on the ability to understand and use language. They point to the many studies showing that students who are visually impaired do not differ from sighted students on verbal intelligence tests. Because auditory more than visual perception is the sensory modality through which we learn language, it is not surprising that studies have found that people who are blind are not impaired in language functioning. The child who is blind is still able to hear language and might even be more motivated than the sighted child to use language because it is the main channel through which he or she communicates with others.

There are, however, a few subtle differences in the way in which language usually develops in children, especially infants, who are visually impaired (Perez-Pereira & Conti-Ramsden, 1999). There appears to be a delay in the very earliest stages of language for some infants with visual impairment; their first words tend to come later. Once they start producing words, however, their vocabulary expands rapidly.

INTELLECTUAL ABILITY

Performance on Standardized Intelligence Tests At one time, it was popular for researchers to compare the intelligence of sighted people with that of persons with blindness. Most authorities now believe that such comparisons are virtually impossible because finding comparable tests is so difficult. From what is known, there is no reason to believe that blindness results in lower intelligence.

Conceptual Abilities   It is also very difficult to assess the performance of children with visual impairment on laboratory-type tasks of conceptual ability. Many researchers, using conceptual tasks originally developed by noted psychologist Jean Piaget, have concluded that infants and very young children who are blind lag behind their sighted peers. This is usually attributed to the fact that they rely more on touch to arrive at conceptualizations of many objects, and touch is less efficient than sight. However, these early delays do not last for long, especially once the children begin to use language to gather information about their environment (Perez-Pereira & Conti-Ramsden, 1999). Touch, however, remains a very critical sense throughout life for those who are blind. As one person who is blind described it, he "sees with his fingers" (Hull, 1997).

Casebook Reflection

Refer to the case *The Reluctant Collaborator* in your booklet. Peter's classroom teacher rarely approached Peter. She preferred to talk about any problems to the itinerant teacher for students with impairment. Do you think this attitude would have changed if she had more information about the language development and intellectual ability of students who are blind or visually impaired?

An important difference between individuals with and without sight is that the latter need to take much more initiative to learn what they can from their environment. Sighted infants and children can pick up a lot of visual information incidentally. In a sense, the world comes to them, whereas children who are visually impaired need to extend themselves out to the world to pick up some of the same information. Exploring the environment motorically, however, does not come easily for infants and young children with visual impairment, especially those who are blind. Many have serious delays in motor skills, such as sitting up, crawling, and walking (Celeste, 2002). Therefore, adults should do as much as possible to encourage infants and young children who are blind to explore their environment.

Cathy Yerian, from San Diego, reads a braille display on a sign at the San Diego Zoo. The increasing availability of such displays enables people with blindness or low vision to experience and explore their environment.

In addition to fostering a sense of exploration in children who are visually impaired, it is critical that teachers and parents provide intensive and extensive instruction, including repetition, in order to help them develop their conceptual abilities:

> When a student cannot see, it takes time to comprehend and identify the front and back of a car, inside *and* out, including the front and back doors. It can be mystifying to comprehend what the front and back of a store are when the student is inside of it. It is especially difficult if the student is thinking of the front and back of his or her own body that, as the student moves, are continually changing relationship to objects and *their* fronts and backs. . . . A gradual approach to teaching concepts, presenting many repetitions over time and in a variety of situations, with repeated opportunities for tactile exploration, will yield the most detailed mental image and the most thorough understanding. (Knott, 2002, p. 69)

ORIENTATION AND MOBILITY

Orientation and mobility (O & M) skills
The ability to have a sense of where one is in relation to other people, objects, and landmarks and to move through the environment.

Orientation and mobility skills are very important for the successful adjustment of people with visual impairment. **Orientation and mobility (O & M)** skills refer to the ability to have a sense of where one is in relation to other people, objects, and landmarks (orientation) and to move through the environment (mobility). O & M skills depend to a great extent on spatial ability. The spatial abilities of people who are blind continue to develop throughout childhood and adolescence; full development does not occur until well into the teenage years (Ochaita & Huertas, 1993).

Authorities have identified two ways in which persons with visual impairment process spatial information: as a sequential route or as a map depicting the general relation of various points in the environment (Webster & Roe, 1998). The latter method, referred to as **cognitive mapping**, is preferable because it offers more flexibility in navigating. Consider three sequential points—A, B, and C. A sequential mode of processing spatial information restricts a person's movement so that the person can move from A to C only by way of B. But a person with a cognitive map of points A, B, and C can go from A to C directly without going through B. Although not impossible, it is more difficult for people who are blind to build these cognitive maps. Vision allows us to

Cognitive mapping
A nonsequential way of conceptualizing the spatial environment that allows a person who is visually impaired to know where several points in the environment are simultaneously; allows for better mobility than does a strictly sequential conceptualization of the environment.

> construct a coherent sense of the physical environment and our place in it, without struggling to remember. On entering an unfamiliar classroom, a sighted child is able to take in something of the whole at a glance, and perhaps work out the overall position of the room in relation to more familiar places, such as the library, computer room. . . . For the child with a visual impairment, constructing an inner map of this new classroom presents a problem of synthesizing information from the integration of small, local details to achieve a functional sense of the whole, which must then be largely memorised. (Webster & Roe, 1998, p. 69)

Mobility skills vary greatly among people with visual impairment. It is surprisingly difficult to predict which individuals will be the best travelers. For example, common sense seems to tell us that mobility would be better among those who have more residual vision and those who lose their vision later in life, but this is not always the case. How much motivation and how much proper instruction one receives are critical to becoming a proficient traveler.

Obstacle sense
A skill possessed by some people who are blind, whereby they can detect the presence of obstacles in their environments; research has shown that it is not an indication of an extra sense, as popularly thought; it is the result of learning to detect subtle changes in the pitches of high-frequency echoes.

Obstacle Sense Some persons who are blind have the ability to detect physical obstructions in the environment. Walking along the street, they often seem able to sense an object in their path. This ability has come to be known as the **obstacle sense**—an unfortunate term in some ways, because many laypeople have taken it to mean that people who are blind somehow develop an extra sense. It is easy to see why this misconception exists. Even people who are blind have a very difficult time explaining the phenomenon (Hull,

1997). A number of experiments have shown that with experience, people who are blind come to learn to detect subtle changes in the pitches of high-frequency echoes as they move toward objects. Actually, they are taking advantage of the **Doppler effect**, a physical principle that says the pitch of a sound rises as a person moves toward its source.

Although obstacle sense can be important for the mobility of someone without sight, by itself it will not make its user a highly proficient traveler. It is merely an aid. Extraneous noises (e.g., traffic, speech, rain, wind) can render obstacle sense unusable. Also, it requires walking at a fairly slow speed to be able to react in time.

The Myth of Sensory Acuteness   Along with the myth that people with blindness have an extra sense comes the general misconception that they automatically develop better acuity in their other senses. However, people who are blind do not have lowered thresholds of sensation in touch or hearing. What they are able to do is make better use of the sensations they obtain. Through concentration and attention, they learn to make very fine discriminations.

Another common belief is that people who are blind automatically have superior musical talent. Some do embark on musical careers, but this is because music is an area in which they can achieve success.

ACADEMIC ACHIEVEMENT

Most professionals agree that direct comparisons of the academic achievement of students who are blind with that of sighted students must be interpreted cautiously because the two groups must be tested under different conditions. There are, however, braille and large-print forms of some achievement tests. The few studies that have been done suggest that both children with low vision and those who are blind are sometimes behind their sighted peers (Rapp & Rapp, 1992). Most authorities believe that when low achievement does occur, it is due not to the blindness itself, but to such things as low expectations or lack of exposure to braille. Patrick, the student described in Success Stories on page 370, has begun to learn braille as an older student. He enjoys reading braille instead of holding his book two inches from his right eye and struggling to use his remaining sight.

With respect to reading, we do know that learning to read braille is similar in some important ways to learning to read print. For example, **phonological awareness** (see Chapter 6, "Learners with Learning Disabilities") is an important component of learning to read print or braille (Barlow-Brown & Connelly, 2002; Gillon & Young, 2002).

SOCIAL ADJUSTMENT

At one time the prevailing opinion of professionals was that people with visual impairment were at risk to exhibit personality disturbances. Authorities now agree that personality problems are not an inherent condition of blindness. The social difficulties that arise are usually due to society's inappropriate reaction to blindness.

Much of this inappropriateness might be because most of us do not have many acquaintances who are blind. Social interactions are often based on subtle cues, such as facial expressions. Research suggests that some who are blind have facial expressions that differ in subtle ways from those who are sighted. For example, they are less able to hide their true feelings, especially when negative ones (Galati, Sini, Schmidt, & Tinti, 2003). Another good example is smiling. Smiling is a strong visual cue that sighted people use to provide feedback to one another. For some people with visual impairment, however, smiling is not as spontaneous a social response as it is for those who are sighted. John M. Hull, whose eyesight deteriorated gradually over several years, kept a diary of his experiences. The following entry pertains to smiling:

> Nearly every time I smile, I am conscious of it. . . . Why is this? It must be because there is no reinforcement. There is no returning smile. . . . Most smiling is

Doppler effect
A term used to describe the phenomenon of the pitch of a sound rising as the listener moves toward its source.

Phonological awareness
The ability to understand that speech flow can be broken into smaller sound units such as words, syllables, and phonemes; generally thought to be the reason for the reading problems of many students with learning disabilities.

Special Educators at Work

Patrick's mother, Audrey Pugh: "All I want anyone to do is give him a fair chance."
Nineteen-year-old Patrick Pugh is a high school junior with impaired vision and multiple disabilities. He is working toward his future with consistent and specialized support.
These are the keys to Patrick's success:
- *Intensive instruction from specialized personnel*
- *Relentless persistence over time*
- *Specific goals for transition and vocational education*

Special educator Ricki Curry, an itinerant teacher of students with visual impairments, has worked closely with Patrick for fourteen years. She credits much of his progress to a key ingredient—time. Since he was 5 years old, she has set high expectations for Patrick, who has no vision in his left eye and only partial sight in his right eye. His speech is slurred, and he does not have functional use of his left arm or leg. "Patrick is eager to learn new things," says Curry, who credits his success to intensive, relentless, and specific special education.

Intensive Instruction from Specialized Personnel   Patrick started vision and physical therapy when he was 2 years old. Ricki Curry remembers the little boy whose eyes would lift aimlessly to the ceiling, not using what vision he had. "Our basic goal was for Patrick to learn to use his sight by tracking objects and looking at pictures, but as a 5-year-old, he was stubborn, difficult, and noncompliant," she recalls. Despite his reluctance, Patrick successfully learned literal information and concrete routines. He was highly distractible, and progress was very slow.

His parents hoped that all he needed was extra time, so he stayed in a preschool for children with special needs until he was 7 years old.

Patrick spent first grade in a self-contained class for children with learning disabilities in the nearest physically accessible elementary school. Curry continued to provide weekly sessions and to supervise his vision services. He was also given a personal aide to assist with mobility and visual modifications. "In some ways, kids with personal aides never encounter problems, so they don't learn any problem solving skills!" says Curry. "On the other hand, there are some effective strategies that can be used by paraeducators." Patrick's hand use was limited, so his aide assisted him with writing. Math was broken down into small steps, reading was individualized, and he was taught to use a large-print word processor.

Relentless Persistence over Time   Patrick finished elementary school two years older than most of his classmates yet only able to do rote math. His reading skills were also concrete;

responsive. You smile spontaneously when you receive a smile. For me it is like sending dead letters. Have they been received, acknowledged? Was I even smiling in the right direction? (Hull, 1997, p. 30)

Unfortunately, some people who are blind feel that they need to go to great lengths to appear "normal." The following account, written by the National Federation of the Blind's president, himself blind, of one man's attempt not to appear different is humorous but poignant:

Dr. Schroeder became a teacher and an administrator of public programs of education, but he was still affected by his beliefs about blindness. With the acquisition of the new job, Dr. Schroeder had the money to buy a house. He faced the problem of how to get the lawn mowed. He thought he might hire somebody to do it, but (he reasoned) if he asked a sighted person to mow his lawn, the neighbors would believe he was not able to do it himself because he was blind. This would reinforce their assessment of him as inferior. However, he was also afraid to mow

he could decode text but had limited comprehension. "He could answer factual questions, but he couldn't make that leap to the abstract," recalls Curry. "Patrick was in a middle school science class learning about mitochondria. That's when it really hit me. Sure, he could learn the definition of mitochondria, but was this functional for him? He'd never use this word again!"

Patrick was 13 years old when his mother and the IEP team decided that he needed a class that emphasized functional academics, such as money skills. "At that point, we all knew this was what he needed," says Curry. "Patrick has multiple learning needs, and it takes him a long time to learn; it takes intensive care and a lot of specific teaching. This class gave him the right information at the right pace. We forgot about the mitochondria and were now reading for comprehension."

Specific Goals for Transition and Vocational Education

Patrick started high school at the age of 17, and a creative program was crafted for him blending functional academics, work experience, and independent living skills. He spends his mornings in two periods of functional English and math. He then boards a van for the vocational center three afternoons a week, where he eats lunch with coworkers. Two afternoons are spent at an independent living center learning to clean, shop, and travel around the community.

Patrick Pugh and Ricki Curry work sixty minutes daily on braille skills geared toward his vocational goals. "I think there's a job out there for Patrick," says Curry. "We've got two years to get those skills really sharp." Patrick enjoys reading braille and translating printed sentences with a unimanual brailler. According to Curry, he's exceeding everybody's expectations. "Every time we've taught him something, he's had some success in learning it." This description of Patrick does not surprise Audrey Pugh. "Opportunity is the main thing," she says. "All I want anyone to do is give him a fair chance."

CEC'S STANDARDS: PAVING THE WAY TO SUCCESS

Council for Exceptional Children

ASSESS YOUR STEPS TO SUCCESS in meeting the CEC Knowledge and Skill Base for All Beginning Special Education Teachers of Students with Visual Impairments. Use the following questions to reflect on the growth of your own professional knowledge, skills, and dispositions.

REFLECTING ON YOUR OWN PROFESSIONAL DEVELOPMENT

If you were Patrick's teacher...

- WHAT are some areas about educating students with blindness or low vision that you would need to know more about?
- WHAT are some specific skills that would help you address Patrick's academic and social challenges?
- WHAT personal dispositions do you think are most important for you to develop in teaching students with blindness or low vision?

Using the CEC Standards

- HOW could the attitudes and actions of teachers affect the behaviors of individuals with visual impairments? (VI3K3)
- HOW would you structure and supervise the activities of paraeducators and tutors who work with individuals with visual impairments? (VI10S2)
- HOW would you help families and other team members understand the impact of a visual impairment on learning and experience? (VI10S1) ■

By Jean Crockett

---

the lawn himself because the neighbors might watch him do it, and if he missed a patch of grass, they would conclude that he was incompetent. He could, of course, cover the lawn in such a way that he would not miss any grass—going over it repeatedly in narrow strips—but this would look unusual and peculiar to the neighbors.

Dr. Schroeder did not want to look peculiar. He decided that the best solution was for him to mow his lawn when the neighbors were not likely to observe. He decided to cut the grass at night. I cannot say how the neighbors reacted to this plan. However, if the objective is to seem normal, I doubt that mowing the lawn at night is the best way to accomplish this purpose.

The efforts of Dr. Fred Schroeder to avoid looking conspicuous and to appear normal remind me of my own embarrassing experiences. How great a premium there is on seeming normal! (Maurer, 2000, p. 294)

An important point is that it should not be only up to people who are visually impaired to change their ways of interacting socially. Sighted people should also be responsible for

THE NATIONAL Federation of the Blind is probably the leading organization devoted to advocacy for people who are blind: **www.nfb.org**

Another important organization is the American Foundation for the Blind: **www.afb.org**

A misconception about people who are blind is that they do not adjust well socially.

Stereotypic behaviors
Any of a variety of repetitive behaviors (e.g., eye rubbing) that are sometimes found in individuals who are blind, severely retarded, or psychotic; sometimes referred to as *stereotypies* or *blindisms*.

instances of faulty communication with people who are blind. Not only might some people with visual impairment profit from instruction in using appropriate visually based cues (e.g., facial expressions, head nods, and gestures), but sighted people also can learn to use their natural telephone skills when communicating with people who are blind. Two sighted people talking on the telephone use a variety of auditory cues to help them communicate, even though they cannot see each other (e.g., responding with "uh-hum" or "yeah," asking for more information, adjusting tone of voice) (Fichten, Judd, Tagalakis, Amsel, & Robillard, 1991). If sighted individuals consciously try to use these strategies when interacting with people who are blind, communication may be smoother.

STEREOTYPIC BEHAVIORS

An impediment to good social adjustment for some students with visual impairment is **stereotypic behaviors**: repetitive, stereotyped movements such as body rocking, poking or rubbing the eyes, repetitive hand or finger movements, and grimacing. These can begin as early as a few months of age. For many years, the term *blindisms* was used to refer to these behaviors because it was thought that they were manifested only in people who are blind; however, they are also sometimes characteristic of children with normal sight who are severely mentally retarded or disturbed.

Several competing theories concern the causes of stereotypic behaviors (McHugh & Lieberman, 2003). For example, some researchers believe that they are an attempt to provide oneself with more stimulation to make up for a relative lack of sensory or social stimulation. Others believe them to be an attempt to self-regulate one's stimulation in the face of overstimulation. In either case, most authorities believe that these behaviors serve to stabilize the person's arousal level (Warren, 1994).

There is even some disagreement about how much one should intervene to reduce or eliminate stereotypic behaviors. On the one hand, when done to the extreme, these behaviors can interfere with learning and socialization, and can even be physically injurious. On the other hand, if not done to the extreme, such behaviors might help maintain an appropriate level of arousal (Warren, 1994). In addition, some have argued for society's need to be more tolerant of stereotypic behaviors: "As researchers and advocates . . ., let us consider the idea that rocking is simply an idiosyncrasy or individual difference that should be ignored or for which we should demand greater awareness, tolerance, and understanding" (McHugh & Lieberman, 2003, p. 472).

Educational Considerations

THE WEBSITE at www.nbp.org/alph. html shows the braille alphabet. This website, maintained by the National Braille Press, allows the user to type in a word or name and have it translated into braille.

Lack of sight can severely limit a person's experiences because a primary means of obtaining information from the environment is not available. What makes the situation even more difficult is that educational experiences in the typical classroom are frequently visual. Nevertheless, most experts agree that students who are visually impaired should be educated in the same general way as sighted children. Teachers need to make some modifications, but they can apply the same general educational principles. The important difference is that students with visual impairment will have to rely on other sensory modalities to acquire information.

Meeting the Needs of Students with Blindness or Low Vision

Instructional Adaptations

RESEARCH-BASED RECOMMENDATIONS

Classroom teachers can accommodate and address the needs of students with visual impairment in a variety of ways. The following guidelines provide information about how general education teachers can promote successful inclusion of students with blindness or low vision through effective adaptations (Cox & Dykes, 2001):

- Understand where and when incidental learning is not taking place and create supports to address students' lack of access to visual cues. For example, students with visual impairment might be unable to pick up cues from schedules written on the board, the classroom clock, or activities that are taking place around them. For these students, teachers need to explicitly teach classroom routines, cues for changes in daily events, and even how to identify classmates.

- Promote independent movement around the classroom and school. Students need to be free to move around the classroom as well as the school to have access to a variety of school experiences. Teaching students school landmarks; the layout of the classroom and building; popular areas such as the cafeteria, library, main office, and gym; and emergency procedures helps students successfully navigate their environment. Different types of mobility systems can support this instruction further (e.g., sighted guides, canes, guide dogs, electronic devices).

- Collaborate with the vision specialist to identify resources and design instructional and curricular adaptations. Strategies for instruction can include designating priority seating, providing copies of notes in large print or braille, reading notes aloud while writing them, providing audio-

tapes of written materials, enlarging books or worksheets, and creating hands-on activities.

- Provide tactile support for learning whenever possible. Students with visual impairment will learn more from charts, maps, graphs, and models that can be "read" through the sense of touch. In addition, teachers should allow students to work with any manipulatives or equipment before an activity so that the student can focus on the concept being taught, rather than the material.

- Check for comprehension of auditory information. Although students with visual impairment can hear, they might not interpret the information in the same way as their sighted peers do. Comprehending auditory language involves creating corresponding mental pictures associated with past verbal input. Frequent checks for understanding, opportunities to develop background knowledge, and provision of auditory cues to emphasize important information can aid in student comprehension of the material.

- Make use of any vision capacity. Most students with visual impairment are not totally blind. They can benefit from braille materials or large-print books, an easel to bring the text closer, felt-tip pens and soft lead pencils for greater contrast, or extra light at their work area.

- Teach social skills such as shaking hands, conversational skills (e.g., smiling, nodding, and making eye contact), and using hand movements in conversation.

Through understanding the various domains in which students with visual impairment might need support, general education teachers can appropriately plan for making key adaptations and identifying instructional supports. ■

By Kristin L. Sayeski

The student with little or no sight will possibly require special modifications in four major areas: (1) braille, (2) use of remaining sight, (3) listening skills, and (4) orientation and mobility training. The first three pertain directly to academic education, particularly reading; the last refers to skills needed for everyday living. The Responsive Instruction above provides a summary of general instructional adaptations for the classroom.

BRAILLE

In nineteenth century France, Louis Braille introduced a system of reading and writing for people who, like him, were blind. Although not the first method that was developed,

Personal Perspectives

CAPTAIN CHARLES BARBIER DE LA SERRE AND LOUIS BRAILLE

THE first person to develop a system of reading and writing for persons who are blind was Captain Charles Barbier de la Serre. However, his original reason for inventing the system was for military purposes. Only after his system was rejected by the military establishment did he suggest it as a system for people who are blind. But they, too, turned down his offer. And, ironically, one of his biggest critics was Louis Braille:

> In 1822, Captain Charles Barbier de la Serre came to present his night-writing code to the [National Institute for the Young Blind]. He was a career military officer of aristocratic background, presumably full of indignation that his code had been rejected by the army, forcing him to offer it instead to this nearly destitute and decidedly distasteful institution. Children at the institute read texts with embossed Roman characters. Since they had to trace each letter with their fingers, reading was slow and inefficient. Barbier's code used patterns of raised dots to represent phonic units, which would reduce the number of characters required for each word and make reading quicker and more accurate. Among the collection of children selected to test the Barbier system was one skinny, pale, thirteen-year-old boy. . . . This boy, when prodded to speak, not only criticized Barbier's code as inferior to the embossed texts already in use but actually enumerated its flaws.
>
> And Barbier must have been an imposing figure, with a voice accustomed to giving orders. To him, this boy Braille, this son of a saddler, this runty bag of bones was the sort of boy one routinely ignored except to have him stoop to give one a leg up onto a horse.
>
> But Braille spoke up anyway. As he analyzed the flaws in Barbier's code, it set into motion the thought process that would lead to his own code. Two years later Braille perfected his own system. He used six dots instead of Barbier's twelve. He made each character represent a letter in the alphabet so that a child who learned to read would also learn to spell. And he made provisions for punctuation, numbers, and musical notation. When he proposed his code to the institute's director, they rejected it too. They cited the same common objections they had to Barbier's system. . . . What seemed particularly threatening about Braille's code was that he produced it himself. When the blind learned to write at all, they used a sort of stencil to make Roman letters. But they could not read what they wrote. Braille's code was easy to write, requiring only a couple of simple tools. It would allow blind children to send messages to each other and to read them without sighted intervention. To give blind children a method of communication that their sighted custodians would not be able to oversee meant trouble. Who knew what messages those blind children might write . . .? It was not until 1847 that Braille's code was authorized for use in the institute. During the twenty-three-year interim, students secretly used and trained each other in the forbidden code even though discovery meant punishment, even expulsion. ■

Source: Kleege, G. (1999). *Sight unseen*. New Haven, CT: Yale University Press, pp. 223–225. Reprinted with permission.

Literary braille
Braille symbols used for most writing situations.

Nemeth Code
Braille symbols used for mathematics and science.

Unified Braille Code
A combination of literary braille and braille codes for technical fields, such as the Nemeth Code for science and mathematics; not yet widely adopted.

Braille's was the one that became widely used. Even his system, however, was not adopted for several years after he invented it. (See the Personal Perspectives above.)

One braille code, called **literary braille**, is used for most everyday situations; other codes are available for more technical reading and writing. The **Nemeth Code**, for example, is used for mathematical and scientific symbols. Some people support adoption of a Unified Braille Code that would combine these several codes into one (International Council on English Braille, 2004). These proponents argue that in our ever more technological society most people, sighted or blind, often need to read and write using technical as well as everyday language (Chong, 2000; Mangold, 2000). At this point, the **Unified Braille Code** has not been adopted widely.

The basic unit of braille is a quadrangular cell, containing from one to six dots (see Figure 11.3). Different patterns of dots represent letters, numbers, and even punctuation marks. Generally, the best method of reading braille involves using both hands:

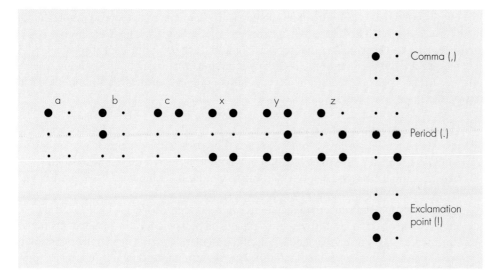

FIGURE 11.3 Examples of symbols from braille

Both hands start at the top left side of the page. Together they move across the letters until they reach the middle. While the right hand continues across, the left hand moves down a line and orients itself at the beginning of that line. When the right hand is finished with the top line, the left hand immediately begins to read the second line. The right hand joins the left until they reach the middle of the second line of text. (Bailey, 2003, p. 324).

Two basic means of writing in braille are the Perkins Brailler and the slate and stylus. The **Perkins Brailler** has six keys, one for each of the six dots of the cell (see Figure 11.4). When depressed simultaneously, the keys leave an embossed print on the paper. More portable than the Perkins Brailler is the **slate and stylus** (see Figure 11.5). The stylus—a pen-shaped instrument—is pressed through the opening of the slate, which holds the paper between its two halves.

Perhaps the most hotly debated topic in the field of visual impairment concerns whether students who are blind should be taught to use braille or one of the other methods of communication, such as a tape recorder or voice-activated computer. At one time, it was fairly common for students with blindness to use braille, but the percentage of students who are blind who use braille has steadily declined since the mid-1960s, when nearly half used braille. Recent estimates indicate that fewer than 10 percent now use braille (P. Mauer, personal communication, June 29, 2001).

Perkins Brailler
A system that makes it possible to write in braille; has six keys, one for each of the six dots of the cell, which leave an embossed print on the paper.

Slate and stylus
A method of writing in braille in which the paper is held in a slate while a stylus is pressed through openings to make indentations in the paper.

FIGURE 11.4 A Perkins Brailler

FIGURE 11.5 A slate and stylus in use

THE AMERICAN FOUNDATION for the Blind has a website, Braille Bug Site, devoted to encouraging young children to learn braille: **www.afb.org/ braillebug**

Braille bills
Legislation passed in several states to make braille more available to students with visual impairment; specific provisions vary from state to state, but major advocates have lobbied for (1) making braille available if parents want it, and (2) ensuring that teachers of students with visual impairment are proficient in braille.

Many within the community of blind people are alarmed at the reduced availability of braille and assert that it has led to a distressing rate of illiteracy (Koenig & Holbrook, 2000; Schroeder, 2002). They charge that too few sighted teachers are proficient in braille and that they do little to discourage the notion held by some that using braille indicates inferiority. Whether a person is comfortable in identifying himself or herself as blind is critical to whether that person will be motivated to learn braille:

> Legally blind children who regard themselves as blind may find that braille facilitates and intensifies group identification and thus leads to the development of self-confidence and self-esteem. . . . Children who do not regard themselves as blind may reject braille because of its relationship to blindness. (Schroeder, 1996, p. 217)

Many authorities are concerned that, even when students do receive braille instruction, it is often not intense enough. In a survey of experts on braille usage, the respondents stated that in the early stages of braille acquisition, in particular, students need daily instruction for several years (Koenig & Holbrook, 2000). The need for intensive braille instruction presents a dilemma for school systems because of the lack of qualified braille instructors.

Advocates of braille also point out that it is essential for most students who are legally blind to learn braille to lead independent lives. Bolstering their argument is research indicating that adults who had learned braille in childhood as their primary medium for reading were employed at twice the rate of those who had used print as their primary medium (Ryles, 1996). A way of ensuring that braille becomes more readily available is through **braille bills**. As of July 2003, thirty-two states had braille bills on the books (National Federation of the Blind, 2003). Although the specific provisions of these bills vary from state to state, the National Federation of the Blind, a major proponent of braille bills, has drafted a model bill that specifies two important components:

1. Braille must be available for students if any members of the individualized education program (IEP) team, including parents, indicate that it is needed.
2. Teachers of students with visual impairment need to be proficient in braille.

Federal law now reinforces the first component above. The Individuals With Disabilities Education Act (IDEA) specifies that braille services and instruction are to be a part of the IEP unless all members of the team, including parents, agree that braille should not be used. To provide a way of determining the braille proficiency of licensed teachers of students who are blind, the Library of Congress has developed the National Literary Braille Competency Test.

Authorities now recommend that some students with low vision who are able to read large print or print with magnification should also be taught braille. There are many students with low vision whose condition dictates that their vision will worsen over the years. Learning braille at an early age prepares them for the time when their eyesight no longer allows them to read print.

USE OF REMAINING SIGHT

For many years, there was a great deal of resistance to having children with visual impairment use their sight in reading and some other activities. Many myths contributed to this reluctance, including beliefs that holding books close to the eyes is harmful, strong lenses hurt the eyes, and using the eyes too much injures them.

It is now recognized that this is true only in very rare conditions. In fact, some professionals believe that teachers can actually train students to use what visual abilities they do have to better advantage (Barraga & Collins, 1979; Collins & Barraga, 1980). Even though some question the efficacy of such vision training (Ferrell & Muir, 1996), most agree on the importance of encouraging people with visual impairment to use what sight they do have but not to the exclusion of braille for those who need it.

Two visual methods of aiding children with visual impairment to read print are large-print books and magnifying devices. **Large-print books** are simply books printed in larger-size type. The text in this book, printed primarily for sighted readers, is printed in 10-point type. Figure 11.6 shows print in 18-point type, one of the most popular sizes for large-print materials. Type sizes for readers with visual impairment may range up to 30-point type.

The major difficulty with large-print books is that they are bigger than usual and therefore require a great deal of storage space. In addition, they are of limited availability, although, along with the American Printing House for the Blind, a number of commercial publishers are now publishing and marketing large-print books.

Although not advocating for the elimination of large-print books, some authorities have stated that they should not be seen as quick fixes. In fact, with respect to reading speed and comprehension, they point out that using **magnifying devices** is at least as effective as using large-print books for many students (Lussenhop & Corn, 2003). Furthermore, students who become dependent on large-print books are at a disadvantage when they encounter situations, such as many jobs, in which large-print materials are unavailable.

Most professionals agree on the importance of encouraging people with visual impairment to use what sight they do have, but not to the exclusion of braille for those who need it.

Magnifying devices can be for close vision or distance vision. Those for close vision range from glasses and handheld magnifiers to closed-circuit television scanners that present enlarged images on a TV screen. For distance vision, people with low vision can use a small hand-held monocular telescope or a binocular telescope that sits on eyeglass-type frames. Authorities highly recommend that students with low vision receive intensive instruction in the use of magnifying devices rather than being left on their own to use them (Corn & Koenig, 2002). They have also determined that in the case of close vision magnifyers, such intensive instruction pays off in faster reading speeds and better reading comprehension (Corn et al., 2002).

LISTENING SKILLS

The importance of listening skills for children who are blind cannot be overemphasized. There is a tendency to assume that listening skills will develop automatically in children who are blind. However, authorities agree that in most cases, these children must be taught how to listen. In addition, teachers should provide a classroom environment as free from auditory distractions as possible.

Large-print books
Books having a font-size that is larger than the usual 10-point type; a popular size for large print books is 18-point type.

Magnifying devices
Often recommended for people with low vision; can be for close vision (e.g., handheld magnifier) or distance vision (e.g., monocular telescope or binocular telescope mounted on eyeglass frames).

This is an example of 10-pt. type.

This is an example of 18-pt. type.

This is an example of 24-pt. type.

FIGURE 11.6 Typefaces come in various sizes. Large-print books often use 18-point type and 24-point type.

UNDERSTANDING THE STANDARDS AND PRINCIPLES How can teachers help with the orientation and mobility of students with visual impairment? *(CEC Knowledge and Skills Standards VI4K11 & VI7S1)*

Council for Exceptional Children

Listening skills are becoming more important than ever because of the increasing accessibility of recorded material. The American Printing House for the Blind and the Library of Congress are major sources for these materials. Listeners can play the material at normal speed, or they can use a compressed-speech device that allows them to listen at about 250 to 275 words per minute. This method works by discarding very small segments of the speech. Some of the more sophisticated compressed-speech devices use a computer to eliminate those speech sounds that are least necessary for comprehension.

ORIENTATION AND MOBILITY (O & M) TRAINING

How well the person with a visual disability can navigate her or his environment will greatly determine how independent and socially integrated she or he will be. There are four general methods to aid the orientation and mobility of people with visual impairment: the long cane, guide dogs, tactile maps, and human guides.

Long cane
A mobility aid used by individuals with visual impairment, who sweep it in a wide arc in front of them; proper use requires considerable training; the mobility aid of choice for most travelers who are blind.

The Long Cane Professionals most often recommend the long cane for those individuals with visual impairments who need a mobility aid. It is called a **long cane** because it is longer than the canes that are typically used for support or balance. Long canes can be straight, folded, or telescopic; the last two types are more compact but not as sturdy as the straight cane (Knott, 2002). By moving the cane along the ground, the user is provided with auditory and tactual information about the environment. It can alert the user to drop-offs, such as potholes or stairs, and can help to protect the lower part of the body from collision with objects.

Although the long cane looks like a simple device, scientists and O & M specialists working under the auspices of the National Academy of Sciences have drawn up specifications for its construction. And although watching a skilled user of the long cane can give the impression that it is easy to manipulate, intensive training in its proper use is often re-

Today, more and more preschoolers are learning cane techniques, though there is considerable debate about whether people who are themselves blind should be used as mobility instructors.

quired. The traveler holds the butt or crook of the long cane at about the height of the navel and sweeps it in an arc wide enough to protect the body, lightly touching the ground in front with the cane tip (Bongers, Schellingerhout, van Grinsven, & Smitsman, 2002). Considerable coordination between the sweeping of the cane and the movement of the feet is required for proper touch technique.

At one time, O & M teachers thought that young children were not old enough to be taught mobility skills. Some parents, especially sighted parents, saw the use of a cane as too stigmatizing. As one person who is blind said:

> The cane was the thing that my parents put off for as long as they could, and they did it with the support of educators. For them the cane was the symbol. It transformed me from being their blind son—which was okay—to being somebody who might grow up to be a blind man. That wasn't okay. So I didn't see a cane until I was about eleven years old. (Wunder, 1993, p. 568)

Today, however, more and more preschoolers are learning cane techniques.

Currently, there is considerable debate about whether people who are themselves blind should be allowed to be mobility instructors. Those who oppose this practice mainly focus on safety concerns, asking, for example, whether instructors who are blind would be able to warn their students of potential dangers in the environment such as hanging tree limbs, icy sidewalks, or construction sites (Millar, 1996). Those who favor having instructors who are blind view such concerns as overprotection. They state that such potential dangers are part of the frequently faced realities of cane travel, and that instructors who are blind are more likely to allow their pupils to encounter such obstacles in training and thereby learn to cope with them (Hill, 1997).

Guide Dogs   **Guide dogs** are not as popular an option as most people tend to think. Extensive training is required to learn how to use guide dogs properly. The extended training—as well as the facts that guide dogs are large, walk relatively fast, and need to be cared for—make them particularly questionable for children. Also, contrary to what most people think, the guide dog does not "take" the person who is blind anywhere. The person must first know where he or she is going; the dog is primarily a safeguard against walking into dangerous areas.

For some adults, however, guide dogs have proven to be valuable aides and companions. Some users of guide dogs point out that the dogs can alert their owners to potential hazards in the environment—such as stairways, entrances, exits, and elevators—sooner than can be detected by a cane (Gabias, 1992). One person who has found a guide dog especially rewarding is author Stephen Kuusisto (see the Personal Perspectives on p. 380).

People who are sighted should keep in mind a few guidelines pertaining to guide dogs and their owners (Ulrey, 1994):

1. Although it might be tempting to pet a guide dog, you should do so only after asking the owner's permission. Guide dogs are not just pets—they are working for their owner.
2. If someone with a guide dog appears to need help, approach on his or her right side (guide dogs are almost always on the left side) and ask whether he or she needs assistance.
3. Do not take hold of the dog's harness, as this may confuse the dog and the owner.

Tactile Maps   **Tactile maps** are embossed representations of the environment. People who are blind can orient themselves to their surroundings by touching raised symbols representing streets, sidewalks, buildings, and so forth. Such maps can also provide specific routes to desired destinations (Harder & Michel, 2002).

THE WEBSITE HowStuffWorks.com has a section devoted to guide dogs: **www. howstuffworks.com/guide-dog.htm**

A NUMBER of organizations and companies focus on raising and training guide dogs and helping people who are blind learn to use guide dogs. Following are some examples:

The Seeing Eye, Inc.: **www.seeingeye.org**

Guide Dogs of America: **www.guidedogsofamerica.org**

Guiding Eyes for the Blind, Inc.: **www.guiding-eyes.org**

Guide Dog Foundation for the Blind, Inc.: **www.guidedog.org**

Guide Dogs for the Blind, Inc.: **www.guidedogs.com**

Guide dogs
Dogs trained for the purpose of helping people who are blind navigate the environment; generally not recommended for children; they require extensive training for the user.

Tactile map
An embossed representation of the environment that people who are blind can use to orient themselves to their surroundings.

Personal Perspectives:

STEPHEN KUUSISTO AND HIS GUIDE DOG, CORKY

STEPHEN KUUSISTO has been almost totally blind since birth as the result of retinopathy of prematurity (ROP). In his memoir, *Planet of the Blind*, Kuusisto chronicles how he spent all of childhood and much of adult life in denial of his blindness. Instrumental in his eventual acceptance of a blind identity has been the freedom of mobility provided by Corky, his guide dog. Kuusisto has also discovered that "guide dogs are still wondrous creatures in the public's imagination, and more than fifty years after their introduction to the United States, they remain a novelty." This novelty serves to attract numerous interactions with the public. Although these interactions are usually positive, at times they highlight the misunderstandings that the sighted have about people who are blind:

Stephen Kuusisto and his guide dog Corky.

How strange it is, sometimes, to be Corky's human appendage. Often people stop our forward progress and speak only to her, as if I do not exist, then, after much baby talk, they vanish. Others are drawn to us because we are totemic. Early one morning I meet two boys with developmental disabilities.

"Hi!" one says. "I knew a blind guy, but he died!"

"He was bigger than you," the other adds. "He had a heart attack!" Then they sweep away down the sidewalk on their Rollerblades, and through it all Corky advances without distraction, my familiar, my Pavlova.

In the supermarket we're spotted by a small child.

"Look, Mommy, there's a dog in the store!"

"Shhhh! Be quiet, dear!"

"But Mommy, that man has a *dog!*"

"That's a blind man! The dog helps him."

"Is the dog blind too?"

"No, the dog sees for the man!"

"What happens if the dog is blind?"

"The dog isn't blind, honey, the dog can see. It's the man who can't see!"

"The man can't see?"

"That's right, blind people can't see."

"If he can't see, how does he know when it's morning?"

"Shhhh! Be quiet! The man gets up because he has to have breakfast!"

The woman hurries her little boy down the cleaning products aisle. I hear his thin voice from some distance.

"How does he eat?"

I'm standing beside an enormous pyramid of cans. Corky has decided to sit down. I have an evangelical desire, a need to reassure these two. I want to recite something from Psalms to them: The Lord is gracious, and full of compassion; slow to anger, and of great mercy."

I want to follow this mother and child through the tall laundry soap displays and tell them that the world doesn't end. I imagine telling them that the blind are not hungry for objects. I want to take strangers by the hand and tell them there is no abyss. ■

Source: From *Planet of the Blind: A Memoir* by Stephen Kuusisto, 1998, New York: The Dial Press, pp. 176–177, 179–180. Copyright © 1998 by Stephen Kuusisto. Used by permission of The Dial Press/Dell Publishing, a division of Random House, Inc.

Embossment, or raised symbols, has also been used to help people who are blind to appreciate environments that are considerably more vast than what are found locally. (See the Focus on Concepts on p. 381.)

Human Guides   Human guides undoubtedly enable people with visual impairment to have the greatest freedom in moving about safely. However, most O & M specialists do not recommend that this be the primary means of navigation because it fosters too much dependence on other people. There are times, however, when the use of a human guide is warranted. Most people who are blind who travel unaccompanied do not need help from

FOCUS ON CONCEPTS

Touch the Universe

WHEN Noreen Grice was an undergraduate working as an intern at the Boston Museum of Science in the 1980s, she happened to ask some students visiting from the Perkins School for the Blind what they thought of the planetarium show (Chandler, 2003). One youngster straight away spoke up, "That stunk!"

Although no doubt taken aback by the student's honesty, Grice immediately asked:

Why does it have to stink?

She decided to write a brochure that could be produced in braille. "Then, I said, 'Wait a minute. That's not what's missing. The thing that's missing is the pictures.' " (Chandler, 2003, p. 104)

The experience with the Perkins' students served as a catalyst for Grice's search for a method of presenting tactile representations of astronomical objects. Now an astronomer and in charge of the Boston Museum of Science's Planetarium, Grice over the years has experimented with various methods of producing tactile images of heavenly bodies. In 2002, her quest culminated in the publication of *Touch the Universe*. Consisting of photographs, embossed shapes, and a combination of braille and large-print captions, the book presents 14 photos taken with the Hubble Space Telescope. Planets, stars, and galaxies come to life for readers who are visually impaired as well as those with sight. As a fellow astronomer who consulted with Grice on the project puts it:

As a radio astronomer (and the world's only blind one at that), I feel a powerful intuitive connection with the astonishing exotic objects in the distant universe. When I touch the tactile image of the Hubble Northern Deep Field of galaxies in *Touch the Universe*, I am overwhelmed by the same astonishment, a sensory connection with the distant cosmos. It has oft been said that a picture is worth a thousand words. Well, for the first time in my career, I get the picture. (From the back cover of *Touch the Universe*, by Noreen Grice (2002), published by Joseph Henry Press, National Academies Press) ■

Noreen Grice has helped many blind students "get the picture."

those around them. However, if a person with visual impairment looks as though he or she needs assistance, you should first ask if help is wanted. If physical guidance is required, allow the person to hold onto your arm above the elbow and to walk a half-step behind you. Sighted people tend to grasp the arms of people with visual impairments and to sort of push them in the direction they are heading. (See Figure 11.7).

(a)   (b)   (c)

FIGURE 11.7   Human guide technique. (a) The child maintains a constant grip on the guide's arm while following the guide around obstacles as they travel through the environment. To maintain a grip that allows active participation in travel, the child must grasp the guide's arm so the thumb is placed on the outside, with the remaining fingers gripping the inside of the arm (b). The child is a half-step behind and to the side of the guide.

A common adaptation for smaller students is to have the student grasp the guide's extended fingers, wrist, or forearm rather than maintaining a grip above the elbow (c). Effective guided travel involves a partnership between guide and child with both participants actively involved.

Source: Gense, D. J., & Gense, M. (2000, July, Revised). The importance of orientation and mobility skills for students who are deaf-blind. *DB-LINK Fact Sheet*, Retrieved March 22, 2004 from the World Wide Web: http://www.tr.wou.edu/dblink/o&m2.htm. Copyright © 2000 DB-LINK. Reprinted with permission. Figure adapted from illustration by Rebecca Marsh-McCannell

TECHNOLOGICAL AIDS

Kurzweil 1000
A computerized device that converts print into speech for persons with visual impairment; the user places the printed material over a scanner that then reads the material aloud by means of an electronic voice.

Braille notetakers
Portable devices that can be used to take notes in braille, which are then converted to speech, braille, or text.

Visual impairment is perhaps the disability area in which the most technological advances have been made. The infusion of technology has occurred primarily in two general areas: (1) communication and information access and (2) orientation and mobility. In addition, there has been some highly experimental research on artificial vision.

Technological Aids for Communication and Information Access   There are now computers and software available that convert printed material into synthesized speech or braille. One such device is the **Kurzweil 1000**. The user places the material on a scanner that reads the material with an electronic voice or renders it in braille. The machines are compatible with the basic editing features of Microsoft Word and WordPerfect, so the user can edit text for customized use. A nice feature is that they can also be used by students with reading disabilities.

Portable **braille notetakers**, such as Braille Lite, BrailleNote, and Braille 'n Speak, can serve the same function as the Perkins Brailler or slate and stylus but offer additional speech-synthesizer and word-processing capabilities. The user enters information with a braille keyboard and can transfer the information into a larger computer, review it using a speech synthesizer or braille display, or print it in braille or text. However, even those who are major proponents of using braille notetakers caution against using them to the exclusion of laptop or desktop computers (Chong, 2004). Computers allow much greater flexibility in producing printed material, and much of what people who are blind produce is for consumption by the sighted community.

Technology has also been used to develop a device for teaching braille skills. The product, called Speech Assisted Learning, comes with a curriculum on diskettes that teaches the sounds of braille letters and words. In addition, it comes with software that teachers can use to create their own lessons.

Millions of people now own hand-held personal data assistants and cell phones. Some manufacturers have responded to the need to make these accessible for people with disabilities, such as blindness. The Voice Mate is a product similar to Palm personal organizers for people who are blind. The Voice Mate has a talking phone book, a voice-activated appointment book that beeps to notify the user of an appointment, a talking alarm clock, and a talking calculator. In addition, several companies now offer cell phones with features such as voice-recognition menu selection, audio cues for main functions, and/or main function keys that are easily distinguishable tactually. The Cellular Telecommunications & Internet Association has a website that provides information on cell phone products and features for people with disabilities: www.accesswireless.org.

Two services available for those who are visually impaired are Newsline and Descriptive Video Service. **Newsline®**, a free service, allows individuals to access several national newspapers (including *USA Today*, the *Chicago Tribune, the New York Times*, the *Wall Street Journal*, the *Washington Post*, the *Los Angeles Times*, and the *Toronto Globe and Mail*) as well as dozens of local newspapers. The user can access the information twenty-four hours a day from any touch-tone telephone. **Descriptive Video Service®** inserts a narrated description of key visual features of programs on television. It is also available in some movie theaters as well as some movies on videotape or DVD.

Great strides have been made in recent years to make computers and the World Wide Web more accessible for people with disabilities, including those who have visual impairments. With respect to computer software, there are **screen readers** that magnify information on the screen, convert on-screen text to speech, or do both. JAWS for Windows is one of the most popular of these screen readers.

With the development of the World Wide Web have come issues pertaining to access for people with disabilities, including those with visual impairments. Unfortunately, what is most attractive to the sighted with respect to web design—that is, images—is often unappealing to those who are blind. In an article with the clever title "[Image] [Image] [Image] [Link] [Link] [Link]: Inaccessible Web design from the perspective of a blind librarian," come the following observations:

During the past few years, advances in Internet technology have greatly enhanced librarian's access to information. Unfortunately, these same advances have made my job more complicated. Just a few years ago,

Casebook Reflection

Refer to the case *The Reluctant Collaborator* in your booklet. There is little mention of using technology with Peter. How might he benefit from technological aids?

Newsline®
A service allowing access via touch-tone phone to several national newspapers; available free of charge to those who are visually impaired.

Descriptive Video Service®
A service for use of people with visual impairment that provides audio narrative of key visual elements; available for several public television programs and some videos of movies.

Screen reader
Software for computers that magnifies images on the screen, converts text on the screen to speech, or both.

Visual impairment is an area of disability in which technological advances continue to be made. Michael May, blind since the age of three, uses braille GPS equipment to get around.

I could surf the Web . . . without thinking twice. Those were the days when everything was text. . . .

With the increased use of graphics, keyboard commands became beveled buttons or cute icons that could be activated with a click. Boring backgrounds became whimsical wallpapers. Important messages could blink or scroll across the screen. The Web became user-friendly. Unfortunately, this user-friendly Web was not very friendly to me. (Lewis & Klauber, 2002, p. 138.)

However, strides are being made to make the Web more accessible for people with visual impairments. The American Foundation for the Blind has published several suggestions for Web developers (American Foundation for the Blind, 2002). And the National Federation of the Blind has established procedures for certifying websites as being accessible to people who are blind.

Technological Aids for Orientation and Mobility Researchers are working on a number of sophisticated electronic devices for sensing objects in the environment. Representative examples are the laser cane and the Miniguide. These devices operate on the principle that human beings can learn to locate objects by means of echoes, much as bats do. The laser cane can be used in the same way as the long cane or as a sensing device that emits beams of infrared light which are converted into sound after they strike objects in the path of the traveler. The Miniguide is a small (1.8-ounce), hand-held device. Research has shown that the Miniguide is useful for such things as avoiding obstacles, locating doorways, avoiding park benches and poles, and detecting overhanging obstacles (Hill & Black, 2003).

Software is available that allows people who are blind to take advantage of information obtained from the Global Positioning System (GPS). Twenty-four GPS satellites are constantly circling the earth and sending back signals, which can be picked up by hand-held receivers. Combining this information with an expanding database now consisting of over 15 million geographic points in the United States, the GPS allows users to determine their whereabouts with considerable accuracy. The makers of the BrailleNote GPS have entered hundreds of thousands of points into the device. In addition, users can enter their own information into the BrailleNote GPS:

You can use this technology for route planning. . . . Maybe you go some place like a barber shop that you don't remember the directions to because you only go every couple of months. In that case you would drop what we call electronic bread crumbs along the way. These are simply GPS locations at every significant turn. For example, Jones Street, Seventh Street, bush is on my right. What will happen is, the next time you walk that route, you will hear within 45 feet of that location, Jones Street, Seventh Street, bush is on my right, 45 feet, 30 feet, 20 feet, and then you make your turn and go on to the next waypoint. (The Sendero Group, 2000–2003)

A variety of other technological developments can be helpful for individuals who are visually impaired. For example, some communities now have acoustic signaling systems, which emit infrared beams. The user points a receiver toward a transmitter and receives a message identifying the location.

Cautions About Technology Words of caution are in order in considering the use of computerized and electronic devices. Supporters of braille argue that although tape recorders, computers, and other technological devices can contribute much to reading and acquiring information, these devices cannot replace braille. For example, finding a specific section of a text and "skimming" are difficult with a tape recording, but these kinds of activities are possible when using braille. Taking notes for class, reading a speech, or looking up words in a dictionary is easier when using braille than when using a tape recorder. Braille proponents are especially concerned that the slate and stylus be preserved as a viable method of taking notes. They point out that just as computers have not replaced paper and pen or pencil for people who are sighted, neither can they take the place of the slate and stylus for people who are blind.

Technological devices designed for orientation and mobility also have limitations. They are best viewed as potential secondary O & M aids. They are not appropriate as substitutes for the long cane, for example.

There has also been remarkable progress in developing an artificial vision system for people who are blind. This involves surgically attaching a digital camera and computer hardware to the visual cortex of the brain (Dobelle, 2000; Groopman, 2003). However, contrary to reports in the popular media, the degree of vision such surgery affords is very far from what sighted people can see. The following is a description of what one patient, who had been totally blind from 3 to 46 years of age, was able to see three years after his surgery:

> His uncorrected vision is roughly 20/1000 and he is near sighted. . . . This means that he can count fingers at 2 to 5 feet depending on the lighting. Mike can read one-inch high letters half a foot away if the contrast is good. He can see colors quite well and get most visual information from colors. People's shapes are recognizable up to 10 to 20 feet but Mike could not tell you if they were short or tall, blonde or dark hair over 15 feet away. (The Sendero Group, 2000–2004)

Although technology might not be the answer to all the difficulties faced by people who are blind, there is no doubt that technology can make their lives easier and more productive. And as technologies develop for society in general, it is important that those who are visually impaired be able to take advantage of them.

SERVICE DELIVERY MODELS

The four major educational placements for students with visual impairment, from most to least segregated, are residential school, special class, resource room, and regular class with itinerant teacher help. In the early 1900s virtually all children who were blind were educated in residential institutions. Today, **itinerant teacher services**, wherein a vision teacher visits several different schools to work with students in their general education classrooms, is the most popular placement for students with visual impairment. The fact is, there are so few students with visual impairment that most schools find it difficult to provide services through special classes or resource rooms. Read Making it Work on page 386 for an example of how an itinerant teacher supports a general education teacher.

Residential placement, however, is still a relatively popular placement model compared to other areas of disability. For example, a little over 7 percent of students with visual impairment between the ages of 6 and 21 years are placed in a residential institution, whereas only about 0.6 percent of students with mental retardation are so placed. The advantage of residential placement is that services can be concentrated to this relatively low-incidence population. In the past, most children who were blind attended such institutions for several years; today some may attend on a short-term basis (e.g., one to four years). The prevailing philosophy of integrating children with visual impairments into classes with sighted children is also reflected in the fact that many residential facilities have established cooperative arrangements with local public schools wherein the staff of the residential facility usually concentrates on training for independent living skills such as mobility, personal grooming, and home management, while local school personnel emphasize academics.

Itinerant teacher services
Services for students who are visually impaired in which the special education teacher visits several different schools to work with students and their general education teachers; the students attend their local schools and remain in general education classrooms.

Early Intervention

Researchers have documented that immediately after birth infants begin processing a wealth of visual information in their environment (Berk, 2005). This fact makes it easy to

Collaboration and Co-Teaching of Students with Blindness or Low Vision

"I don't have time to learn braille!"

WHAT DOES IT MEAN TO BE A TEACHER OF STUDENTS WITH VISUAL IMPAIRMENTS?

Collaboration for students with visual impairments often takes the form of working with itinerant special education teachers. This can be frustrating for general educators in that they are left on their own when the special educator is at another building. Therefore, in planning for collaboration, it is important that the general educator and itinerant teacher have time to plan for student needs that may arise at any time. Working with the general educator to plan for instruction, the teacher of students with visual impairments can offer expertise in the following areas:

1. Designing multisensory learning environments that encourage active participation in group and individual activities
2. Creating learning environments that encourage self-advocacy and independence
3. Teaching individuals with visual impairments to use thinking, problem-solving, and other cognitive strategies
4. Preparing individuals with visual impairments to respond constructively to societal attitudes and actions
5. Obtaining and organizing special materials (including technologies) to implement instructional goals (Council for Exceptional Children, 2001)

SUCCESSFUL STRATEGIES FOR CO-TEACHING

Ricki Curry (an itinerant teacher) and Jenny Garrett (a fourth-grade teacher) talk about how they collaborated to fully include Dennis, a student with a severe visual impairment.

Jenny: My fourth-grade class consisted of twenty-three 9- and 10-year-old students, including two children with learning disabilities, one with severe behavior disorders, and Dennis. They began the year reading anywhere from a first- to a sixth-grade level.

Ricki: Although he has some usable vision, Dennis can see no details from a distance of more than about two feet and uses large-print texts for reading.

Jenny: Dennis has some difficulty making friends because of his immaturity, his compulsive talking, and his inabil-

ity to listen. On the other hand, Dennis has a good sense of humor and is quick with language. Dennis was in my class all day long for every academic subject. Ricki worked with him during language arts block, teaching braille. She would come to school during the last half of my planning period, which gave us a daily opportunity to discuss assignments, homework, curricular adaptations, equipment, and the like. Homework was an enormous issue. Ricki helped Dennis to set up a notebook with a homework contract enclosed and a special highlighter, which he used to mark off completed assignments. He had to write down the assignments himself, remember to take the notebook home, complete the assignments, get a parent's signature, and get it back to school. The hardest part of working with Dennis was the start-up period. I had to get to know him, his visual capabilities, his strengths and weaknesses, and his coping strategies. I began adapting my teaching style, using an easel rather than the blackboard so that he could scoot up to it. I had to decide how hard to push, what to expect from his parents, and what to demand from Dennis.

Ricki: I often found myself overwhelmed by the number of things that Jenny and/or Dennis needed help with in the short time that I was in the building. And so many things seemed to go wrong in the time between when I left one day and when I arrived again the next day! Although I was frustrated by the limitations imposed by time constraints, the beauty of the inclusion model was that I was very aware of the true gestalt of Dennis's program and knew exactly what he was involved in all the time. Had I not had an almost daily view of Dennis's classroom performance, I might not have believed how hard it was to integrate this very bright, verbal, personable child into Jenny's class.

Jenny: Collaboration works best when there is a match of personalities as well as energy, enthusiasm for teaching, and professionalism. ■

By Margaret P. Weiss

understand why intensive intervention should begin as early as possible to help the infant with visual impairment begin to explore the environment. As we noted earlier, many infants who are blind lag behind their peers in motor development. Consequently, O & M training should be a critical component of preschool programming.

Although many people believe that preschoolers with visual impairments should be educated in inclusive settings with sighted children, it is critical that teachers facilitate

RESPONSIVE INSTRUCTION

Meeting the Needs of Students with Blindness or Low Vision

Strategies for Working with Young Children

WHAT RESEARCH SAYS

Children with blindness or low vision learn best through active engagement with their environment. Because these children do not receive visual stimuli to support what they hear, they depend on tactile interactions to promote learning. Research on infants with visual impairment, however, indicates they spend less time exploring and interacting with the environment than do infants without visual disabilities (Chen, 2001). As a result, natural understanding of people, objects, activities, and the environment is limited.

RESEARCH-BASED RECOMMENDATIONS IN EARLY CHILDHOOD SETTINGS

To promote cognitive skills, children with visual impairment require direct instruction (Chen, 2001). Structured experiences that allow children to have repeated interactions with objects, people, or situations promote understanding of cause and effect. For example, an infant with a visual impairment drops a spoon. If someone were to hand the spoon back to the child, the infant would not understand (1) where the spoon went, (2) how the spoon returned to him or her, and (3) that similar phenomena occur every time something is dropped. Repeated exposure to the act of dropping items and showing the child where the item fell will teach the concept of gravity and reinforce the difficulty involved in locating dropped items!

In addition to systematic, repeated learning opportunities, children with visual impairment should interact with real objects rather than models (Chen & Dote-Kwan, 1999). A child who has not previously developed the concept of a banana will be unable to make the connection between a plastic banana and a real one. Instruction therefore should include op-

portunities for conceptual development through repeated interactions with real objects.

Concepts involving spatial relationship can be difficult to learn because they are dependent upon a visual reference to a physical object. For example, concepts of "in front of" and "behind" are frequently taught in relationship to one's body. Similarly, understanding of physical characteristics such as color, size, shape, and texture can be challenging without a visual reference. Children with visual impairment will need many opportunities to manipulate objects to reinforce these abstract concepts. Even the concepts of outside and inside can be misunderstood if children are not explicitly exposed to the differentiating characteristics of each (e.g., walls, ceilings, doors, streets, sidewalks, grass) (Chen, 2001).

Although children with visual impairment develop language in a manner similar to that of children without visual impairment, children with visual impairment have greater difficulty mastering nuances of language that are visually dependent, such as pronouns (Chen, 2001). Imagine how difficult it would be to interpret pronouns if you could not see the person talking, what is being talked about, or other people who are being referenced. Again, direct instruction in language skills is recommended.

Finally, much of what young children learn about the world comes from watching and imitation. The development of play, adaptive behaviors, and social interactions is largely dependent on modeling. Hand-over-hand modeling, hand-under-hand modeling, play or social interaction modeling, and participatory modeling all foster social and emotional development. ■

By Kristin L. Sayeski

interactions between the children. We know from research that merely placing preschoolers who are visually impaired with sighted preschoolers does not lead to their interacting with one another (D'Allura, 2002). Teachers must provide instruction in appropriate interactions, using active engagement and repeated opportunities for learning. Read Responsive Instruction above for a description of these concepts.

Most authorities agree that it is extremely important to involve parents of infants with visual impairment in early intervention efforts. Parents can become actively involved in working at home with their young children, helping them with fundamental skills such as mobility and feeding, as well as being responsive to their infants' vocalizations (Chen, 1996). Parents, too, sometimes need support in coping with their reactions to having a baby with visual impairment.

Casebook Reflection

Refer to the case *The Reluctant Collaborator* in your booklet. Compare Jenny and Ricki's collaboration (see Making It Work on page 386) with the example of Mary Scanlon and Ms. Cunningham. How might Peter's general education and itinerant teachers work more effectively together? How do you think he will fare in the future?

UNDERSTANDING THE STANDARDS AND PRINCIPLES What can individuals with visual impairment expect as they transition to adulthood? *(CEC Knowledge and Skills Standards VI7K2 & VI10K1)*

Council for
Exceptional
Children

Accessible pedestrian signal (APSs)
Devices for people who are blind to let them know when the "walk" signal is on at intersections; can be auditory, tactile, or both.

Raised dome detectable warnings
Bumps in the pavement that are designed to alert people who are blind to unsafe areas.

Transition to Adulthood

Two closely related areas are difficult for some adolescents and adults with visual impairment: independence and employment.

INDEPENDENT LIVING

With proper training, preferably starting no later than middle school, most people who are blind can lead very independent lives. However, there is evidence that many students who are blind are not receiving the necessary training in daily living skills (Lewis & Iselin, 2002; Wolffe et al., 2002). Ironically, some have asserted that the movement toward including students with visual impairment in general education and providing them access to the general education curriculum has led to a diminished emphasis on teaching skills necessary for independence (Spungin, 2003). They say that itinerant teachers often do not have enough time to do much direct teaching of daily living skills.

Many authorities also point out that a major reason why adolescents and adults with visual impairment might have problems becoming independent is because of the way society treats people without sight. A common mistake is to assume that such individuals are helpless. Many people think of blindness as a condition to be pitied. People with visual impairment have a long history of arguing against paternalistic treatment by sighted society. They have often resisted governmental actions that were presumably designed to help them. For example, the National Federation of the Blind recently passed resolutions opposing the universal installation of accessible pedestrian signals and underfoot raised dome detectable warnings. **Accessible pedestrian signals (APSs)** alert people who are blind to when it is safe to walk across an intersection. The most common types provide auditory or tactile cues or a combination of the two. Some operate all the time—for example, whenever the "walk" signal for sighted pedestrians is lit, an auditory cue such as a chirping noise is activated. Some operate only when a button is pushed. **Raised dome detectable warnings** alert people who are blind to unsafe areas, such as ledges next to tracks in subway stations.

The National Federation of the Blind (NFB) has stated that APSs might be needed at some complex intersections, but that they are not needed universally (Maurer, 2003). They claim that APSs can be distracting and that continuously operating APSs add to noise pollution, which can interfere with the person's hearing traffic flow. The NFB asserts that the raised dome detectable warnings are also not needed in many instances and that they can lead to unstable walking conditions.

Underlying the NFB's objection to both of these travel aids is its concern that sighted society will view people who are blind as needing more accommodations than necessary, thus reinforcing the notion that they are helpless. Whether one agress with the NFB or believes that it is being overly sensitive, there is no doubt that sighted society is inclined to view people who are blind in a paternalistic manner. The following account of a trip taken by students from the O & M Program of Louisiana Tech University to the World Trade Center in New York City points out—with considerable irony, given the tragedy of September 11, 2001—how misguided special treatment toward those who are blind can be. Presumably because of their blindness, the group experienced lax security in their trip up to the top of the building. Afterwards, in the words of one of the students,

we made jokes about lax security. If you want to bomb the trade center, just walk in with a white cane, and they will welcome you with open arms. There was a bit of irony in this. In 1993 the World Trade Center had been bombed, but at the moment I had forgotten one important detail about that event. . . .

The thing which I had forgotten about that event was brought back to my attention. I don't remember if it was a graduate student, a center student, or a staff member who said it, but as soon as the words were out, a little piece of irony clicked into place. In a federal penitentiary outside my home town of Springfield, Missouri, sits a blind man. His crime? He masterminded the [1993] bombing of the World Trade Center. When will they ever learn?

Society too loses something when it offers undeserved privileges to people it believes inferior. The general public loses the chance to experience the distinctiveness that we can add to society. Each minority has something to add—to contribute to the mosaic of life. With the mixture we all become stronger. By refusing to acknowledge that we are only a cross-section of themselves, those members of society who believe we need special treatment are missing out as much as we are when we accept their charity. Because of this charity these people expect us all to be the same. They cannot tell the good guys from the bad guys in the blind minority. (Lansaw, 2000, pp. 964–965)

Compounding the problem of paternalism, the public also has a tendency to make superheroes out of people who are blind when they accomplish relatively mundane tasks. Although climbing mountains such as Mount McKinley or Mount Everest are no mundane feats, the sentiments of Erik Weihenmayer point out that the accolades can sometimes be way over the top:

Not all of my time leading up to the climb [of Mount McKinley] was spent on the mountain; as part of their public-education campaign, the [American Foundation for the Blind] asked me to do some TV interviews. One was a cheesy daytime talk show, on which I was showcased among a group of blind people deemed "amazing and inspirational." All the blind people were led onto the stage, canes tapping and dogs' tails wagging, and seated in a row in front of the crowd. I was featured first, and the host opened with, "A blind mountain climber. Isn't that incredible? Even I, who can see just fine, wouldn't think of climbing a mountain." This wasn't the first time I had heard the "even I" statement. It was always meant as a compliment, but it never failed to annoy me. There might be a dozen other factors that prevented the host from excelling in the sport of mountain climbing. She might be fifty pounds overweight, wheezing with every breath, and might never have even set foot on a mountain, but in her mind, success or failure was automatically attributed to one factor: sight or no sight. . . .

Throughout the rest of the segment, I squirmed in my seat. . . . I was simply a blind person who planned to climb a mountain and nothing more. But people sensationalize the lives of blind people when, often, all they did was exhibit a semblance of normalcy. I had been receiving these accolades my whole life: give someone directions to my house—incredible. Make eye contact in a conversation—amazing. Pour a glass of milk without spilling it all over the table—inspiring. Each of us on the panel was being honored for our heroic tales, but the recognition spoke more loudly of low expectations than of accomplishment. My heart burned with the memory of my heroes, people like Helen Keller, who took the world's perceptions about the disabled and shattered them into a million pieces, people whose stories made me hunger for the courage to live in their image. (Weihenmayer, 2001, pp. 166–168)

Erik Weihenmayer receives accolades for his mountain climbing, but bristles when praise for the accomplishments of blind persons appears to mask low expectations.

Even though people who are blind can achieve virtually the same degree of independence as people who are sighted, it would be a mistake to assume that this comes naturally or easily. Many independent living skills that sighted people learn incidentally need to be taught explicitly to those who are visually impaired. The NFB publishes a book that can be useful in this regard (Jernigan, 1994). It has chapters, for example, on cooking, sewing, marking dials, tactile labeling, and shopping ideas.

EMPLOYMENT

Many working-age adults with visual impairment are unemployed, and those who do work are often overqualified for the jobs they hold. For example, surveys indicate that adults who are blind are employed at about half the rate of those who are sighted (Houtenville, 2003; Leonard, 2002). This unfortunate situation is due to a history of inadequate transition programming at the secondary school level rather than to the visual impairment itself. Said another way, with proper transition programming, students with visual impairment, even those who are totally blind, can go on to hold jobs at every level of preparation—teachers, laborers, physicians, engineers. Proper transition programming, however, must be intensive and extensive, including numerous well-supervised work experiences, or internships, while still in secondary school.

High on the list of ways to improve employment possibilities for those who are blind are job accommodations. Employees who are blind report that relatively minor adjustments can go a long way toward making it easier for them to function in the workplace. A sample of suggested adaptations are improved transportation (such as car pools), better lighting, tinted office windows to filter light, prompt snow removal, regularly scheduled fire drills to ensure spatial orientation, hallways that are free of obstacles, and computer software (such as screen magnification programs) and PC-based reading machines that convert print into braille (Rumrill, Roessler, Battersby-Longden, & Schuyler, 1998; Rumrill, Schuyler, & Longden, 1997).

The American Foundation for the Blind has a website (www.afb.org/careerconnect/) devoted to helping people who are blind find jobs. The site, which also has information for employers, has information on such things as career exploration, finding a job, getting

Obtaining gainful, fulfilling employment should not be an unrealistic goal for someone with visual impairment

hired, and keeping a job. It also offers a way to link to other workers who are blind and who can serve as mentors.

Visual impairment no doubt poses a real challenge for adjustment to everyday living. However, people with visual impairment have many similarities with people in the rest of society. Special and general educators need to achieve the delicate balance between providing special programming for students with visual impairment and treating them in the same manner as they do the rest of their students.

SUMMARY

HOW do professionals define and classify learners with blindness and low vision?

- Those using a legal definition use visual acuity and field of vision:
  - Blindness is visual acuity of 20/200 or less in the better eye with correction; low vision is 20/70 to 20/200.
  - Blindness is a field of vision no greater than 20 degrees.
- Those using an educational definition use method of reading:
  - Blindness is needing to use braille or aural methods.
  - Low vision is being able to read print (enlarged or magnified).

WHAT is the prevalence of visual impairment?

- Blindness is primarily an adult disability.
- Fewer than 0.05 percent of students from age 6 to 17 are identified as visually impaired.

WHAT are some basic anatomical and physiological characteristics of the eye?

- Objects are seen when an electrical impulse travels from the optic nerve at the back of the eye to the occipital lobes of the brain.
- Light rays pass through the cornea, aqueous humor, pupil, lens, vitreous humor, and retina before reaching the optic nerve at the back of the brain.

HOW is visual ability measured?

- Visual acuity for far distances is most often measured by using the Snellen chart.
- There are also measures available for measuring visual acuity for near distances.
- Visual efficiency, controlling eye movements, and using visual information, is often assessed by teacher observation.

- Vision teachers can perform functional assessments to determine how students use their vision in everyday situations.

WHAT causes visual impairments?

- The most common visual problems result from errors of refraction:
  - Myopia (nearsightedness)
  - Hyperopia (farsightedness)
  - Astigmatism (blurred vision)
- Some conditions affect both adults and children:
  - Glaucoma is a group of diseases causing damage to the optic nerve.
  - Cataracts cause clouding of the lens of the eye.
  - Diabetic retinopathy results from interference of the blood supply to the retina.
- Some conditions affect primarily children:
  - Retinitis pigmentosa usually causes tunnel vision and night blindness.
  - Cortical visual impairment results from brain damage or dysfunction.
  - Retinopathy of prematurity can be caused by excessive concentrations of oxygen or other factors.
- Improper muscle functioning can cause visual problems:
  - Strabismus refers to the eyes being turned inward (crossed eyes) or outward.
  - Nystagmus refers to rapid involuntary movements of the eyes.

WHAT are some of the psychological and behavioral characteristics of learners with visual impairments?

- Language development is largely unaffected, although there can be subtle developmental delays, especially in infancy.
- There may be early delays in conceptual development, which do not last long.

- Motor delays in infancy are common; it is important that adults encourage them to explore their environment to help overcome these delays.
- Orientation and mobility (O & M) skills depend on spatial abilities:
  - People with visual impairment can process spatial information either sequentially or as a cognitive map; the latter is more efficient.
  - Some people with visual impairment have the obstacle sense, the ability to detect objects by noting subtle changes in high frequency echoes (the Doppler effect).
  - Two myths are that people who are blind have an extra sense and that they automatically develop better acuity in their other senses.
- Studies suggest that some students who are blind experience low academic achievement, which is most likely due to low expectations or lack of exposure to braille.
- Phonological awareness is important for learning to read print or braille.
- The social adjustment problems that people with visual impairment have are largely due to sighted society's reactions to blindness.
- Some people with visual impairment engage in stereotypic (repetitive) behaviors.
  - Most authorities attribute stereotypic behaviors to an attempt to stabilize arousal levels.
  - There is disagreement about whether to intervene with these behaviors.

WHAT are some educational considerations for learners with visual impairments?

- The ability to read braille is a crucial skill.
  - Many authorities believe that the use of braille has slipped to dangerously low levels.
  - Braille bills have helped to ensure that students receive instruction in braille.
  - Federal law requires that braille be available if any member of the IEP team, including parents, think it necessary.
  - Authorities point out that many people with low vision can benefit from braille instruction.
- The use of remaining sight is an important skill.
  - Large-print books are useful, although the need for storage space is a drawback.
  - Magnifying devices can be used for close or distance vision.
- Listening skills are important.
- O & M skills are of critical importance.
  - Learning to use a long cane is very important.
  - Unfortunately, some resist using a long cane because they think it stigmatizing.
  - Preschoolers and young children can learn cane techniques.

- There is debate about whether those who are blind can be good mobility instructors.
- Some find using a guide dog very helpful.
  - Guide dogs are much more practical for adults than for children.
  - Guide dogs do not take the person anywhere; instead, they primarily alert the owner to dangerous areas.
- Tactile maps can be very helpful.
- Human guides, although not recommended as a primary means of mobility, can be helpful at times.
- Technological aids are becoming increasingly important.
  - There are technological aids for communication and information access, such as Braille notetakers, personal data assistants, Newsline®, Descriptive Video Service®, and screen readers for computers.
  - There are technological aids for O & M, such as obstacle detection devices and the Global Positioning System (GPS).
  - Learners with visual impairments should not become so dependent on technology that they neglect basic techniques, such as braille, the slate and stylus, and the long cane.
- Itinerant teacher services is the most common service delivery model, and compared to other areas of disability residential placement is relatively popular.

WHAT are some things to consider with respect to early intervention for learners with visual impairments?

- Intensive intervention should begin as early as possible.
- Inclusive settings can be beneficial, but it is important that the teacher facilitate interactions between students with visual impairments and sighted students.
- It is important to try to involve parents.

WHAT are some things to consider with respect to transition to adulthood for learners with visual impairments?

- Most people who are blind can lead very independent lives.
- The current emphasis on inclusion needs to be viewed with caution to make it does not come at the expense of learning independent living skills.
- Sighted society needs to be careful not to treat those with visual impairments as helpless.
- Explicit teaching of independent living skills is essential.
- Many working-age adults with visual impairments are unemployed or are overqualified for the jobs they hold.
  - Transition programming should be intensive and extensive.
  - Job accommodations are essential.

APPLYING THE STANDARDS AND PRINCIPLES

- **WHAT** should teachers know about how visual impairment is **defined**? *(CEC Content Standard #1 & INTASC Principle #1)*

- **WHY** is it important for teachers to know about the **causes of visual problems**? *(CEC Content Standards #1, #2, & #3; INTASC Principles #1 & #2)*

- **HOW** is visual acuity **measured**? *(CEC Content Standard #8 & INTASC Principle #8)*

- **HOW** would you **respond to parents** who approached you expressing concern about the future of their blind high school student? *(CEC Content Standards #7 & #10; INTASC Principles #7 & #10)*

Council for Exceptional Children

INTASC

Chapter 12

Learners with Autism Spectrum Disorders

For me, hearing birds in the morning feels like their beaks scraping across my eardrum. It's sensory overload or violation. Fortunately, I have the verbal ability to express myself properly and explain these violations. Or I can modify the environment by closing the window. But what about the child in school who is sitting in a classroom and his eyes are actually so sensitive that he can see the fluorescent lights above him flicker?

. . .How can we expect the student to pay attention to his teacher, or do his class work?

As a result, the student gets out of the chair to shut off the lights. . . . This happens a few more times, and he gets sent to the principal's office and is going to have to stay after school for the rest of his life because he's been acting up.

STEPHEN SHORE
Asperger Syndrome: A Guide for Professionals and Families

QUESTIONS TO GUIDE YOUR READING OF THIS CHAPTER . . .

- WHAT is the history behind autism spectrum disorders?
- HOW do professionals define autism spectrum disorders?
- WHAT is the prevalence of autism spectrum disorders?
- WHAT causes autism spectrum disorders?
- WHAT methods of assessment are used to identify individuals with autism spectrum disorders?
- WHAT are some of the psychological and behavioral characteristics of learners with autism spectrum disorders?
- WHAT are some educational considerations for learners with autism spectrum disorders?
- WHAT are some things to consider with respect to early intervention for learners with autism spectrum disorders?
- WHAT are some things to consider with respect to transition to adulthood for learners with autism spectrum disorders?

STANDARDS AND PRINCIPLES IN THIS CHAPTER

SPECIAL EDUCATORS . . .

- **understand the field** as an evolving and changing discipline (*from CEC Content Standard #1*).

- understand the similarities and differences in **human development** (*from CEC Content Standard #2*).

- **possess a repertoire** of evidence-based instructional strategies (*from CEC Content Standard #4*).

- **actively create learning environments** for individuals with exceptional learning needs that foster cultural understanding, safety and emotional well-being, positive social interactions, and active engagement of individuals with exceptional learning needs (*from CEC Content Standard #5*).

- **use the results of assessments** to help identify exceptional learning needs (*from CEC Content Standard #8*).

- **use collaboration** to facilitate the successful transitions of individuals with exceptional learning needs (*from CEC Content Standard #10*).

ALL TEACHERS . . .

- **understand the central concepts, tools of inquiry, structures of the discipline(s) they teach** and can create learning experiences that make these aspects of subject matter meaningful (*INTASC Principle #1*).

- understand how **children learn and develop** (*from INTASC Principle #2*).

- **understand and use a variety of instructional strategies** to encourage students' development of critical thinking, problem solving, and performance skills (*INTASC Principle #4*).

- **use an understanding of individual and group motivation and behavior** to create a learning environment that encourages positive social interaction, active engagement in learning, and self-motivation (*INTASC Principle #5*).

- understand and use formal and informal **assessment strategies** (*from INTASC Principle #8*).

- **foster relationships** with school colleagues, families, and agencies in the larger community to support students' learning and well being (*INTASC Principle #10*).

Council for Exceptional Children

INTASC

As the poignant words of Stephen Shore attest (see p. 395), people with autism are often misunderstood. Their array of bizarre behaviors is a puzzle to peers and to many professionals, and the puzzlement often leads others to misinterpret their actions as willful acts of defiance.

It is important to point out that the peculiar behavior highlighted by Shore—hypersensitivity to light—is but one of myriad aberrant perceptual, cognitive, linguistic, and social behaviors that individuals with autism might display. And although there are some consistent patterns to the deficits that accompany autism, there is also a great deal of variation in symptoms exhibited by those who are autistic. For example, not all have hypersensitive perceptions. And some function in the mentally retarded range, whereas others are quite intelligent. As Shore notes elsewhere in his writing, he has strong verbal ability unlike some with autism. In fact, he has what is referred to as Asperger syndrome. Before turning to the definition of autism and its variants, such as Asperger syndrome, it is helpful to provide some historical context to our discussion.

Historical Context: Kanner's and Asperger's Papers

The seminal work in the field of autism began with the publication of two scientific papers published only one year apart (1943 and 1944) by physicians working independently: Leo Kanner and Hans Asperger. Interestingly, both were born and raised in Vienna; however, Kanner came to the United States and wrote his historic paper in English. Asperger's work went largely ignored for many years, probably because it was published in German at the time of World War II.

Also interestingly, both Kanner and Asperger used the term *autistic* to refer to the children they were observing. Autism was a label that had been coined earlier in the twentieth century (Bleuler, 1916) and was used to refer to individuals who had an extreme narrowing of relationships to people and the outside world: "a withdrawal from the fabric of social life into the self. Hence the words 'autistic' and 'autism' from the Greek word *autos* meaning 'self'" (Frith, 2003, p. 5).

Misconceptions About
Learners With Autism Spectrum Disorders

MYTH Autism is a single, well-defined category of disability.

FACT Autism is a wide spectrum of disorders and ranges from very severe to very mild. Autism spectrum disorder includes conditions that can be difficult to identify with great accuracy.

MYTH People with autism spectrum disorders are mentally retarded and cannot to be involved in higher education or professions.

FACT People with autism spectrum disorders have the full range of intellectual capacity. Although a high percentage of them do have mental retardation as an additional disability, many with milder forms, such as Asperger syndrome, are highly intelligent, earn graduate degrees, and are successful professionals.

MYTH All people with autism are impaired in some cognitive areas but are highly intelligent or geniuses in other areas.

FACT Only a very few people with autism have extraordinary skills. Called autistic savants, these individuals are not geniuses in the traditional sense, but they possess very highly developed splinter skills—skills that are in isolation from functional skills.

MYTH There is an autism epidemic that must be due to something dangerous in our environment, such as a toxin or virus.

FACT There has undoubtedly been an increase in the number of diagnosed cases of autism. Most authorities assert that this can be accounted for by two things: a widening of the criteria that are used to diagnose autism, including the recognition of milder forms such as Asperger syndrome, and a greater awareness of autism in the general public as well as in the medical, psychological, and educational professions.

MYTH The measles, mumps, and rubella vaccine causes autism.

FACT The Institute of Medicine of the National Academies commissioned a review of the available evidence and concluded that the evidence favors rejection of a causal relationship between MMR vaccine and autism.

MYTH Bad parenting, especially cold, nonresponsive mothering ("refrigerator moms") can cause autism.

FACT There is no evidence that bad parenting can cause autism. Furthermore, even if a parent is relatively unresponsive, this might be in reaction to the infant's low level of arousal or because of parental stress regarding the child's abnormal behavior.

Schizophrenia
A disorder characterized by psychotic behavior manifested by loss of contact with reality, distorted thought processes, and abnormal perceptions.

Echolalia
The parroting repetition of words or phrases either immediately after they are heard or later; often observed in individuals with autistic spectrum disorders.

Autism spectrum disorders
Five similar conditions: autism, Asperger syndrome, Rett syndrome, childhood disintegrative disorder, and pervasive developmental disorder not otherwise specified; all involve varying degrees of problems with communication skills, social interactions, and repetitive and stereotyped patterns of behavior.

LEO KANNER'S PAPER

Kanner (1943) reported on the cases of eleven children from the Child Psychiatric Unit at Johns Hopkins University. Some of the major characteristics that distinguished these children were these:

- An inability to relate to others in an ordinary manner
- An extreme autistic aloneness that seemingly isolated the child from the outside world
- An apparent resistance to being picked up or held by the parents
- Deficits in language including . . . echolalia. . . .
- Extreme fear reactions to loud noises
- Obsessive desire for repetition and maintenance of sameness
- Few spontaneous activities such as typical play behavior
- Bizarre and repetitive physical movement such as spinning or perpetual rocking (Scheuermann & Weber, 2002, p. 2)

A major conclusion that Kanner reached was that these children could be set apart from children who had **schizophrenia** in at least three ways:

1. The children with schizophrenia tended to withdraw from the world, whereas the children with autism never seemed to have made any social connections to begin with.
2. The children with autism exhibited some unique language patterns, such as pronoun reversals (e.g., *I* for *it, he* for *she*) and **echolalia**, the repetition of words or phrases.
3. The children with autism did not appear to deteriorate in their functioning over time, as did some children with schizophrenia.

HANS ASPERGER'S PAPER

Asperger (1944) reported on four cases of children he observed in summer camp who preferred to play alone and not interact with the other children. Asperger's children were similar to Kanner's with two notable exceptions. First, they had average intelligence. However, they seemed to channel their intellectual pursuits into obsessive preoccupation in narrow areas, such as machinery or mathematical calculations. Second, their language was perceived as normal. (As we will discuss later in the chapter, later investigators have revealed some subtle language abnormalities.)

Asperger referred to his cases as having "autistic psychopathy." It was nearly forty years later that his work gained scientific notoriety when Lorna Wing (1981) published a paper that referred to Asperger's original paper and sparked interest in the topic. She was the one who suggested calling the condition *Asperger's syndrome*. And it was her paper that drew attention to the condition and was the catalyst for Asperger syndrome's becoming recognized as a condition meriting attention.

Definition of Autism Spectrum Disorders

 AN IMPORTANT and comprehensive report on autism and autistic spectrum disorders is available from the National Academy of Sciences at **www.nap.edu/books/ 0309072697/html**

Although *autism* has been a separate category under the Individuals With Disabilities Education Act (IDEA) since 1990, other disorders that are similar to it in many ways are now typically collected under a broader term: **autism spectrum disorders**. A similar term is *pervasive developmental disorders*, although most professionals are now using the term *autism spectrum disorders*. All of the disorders that are classified as autism spectrum disorders are "characterized by varying degrees of impairment in three areas: (1) communication skills, (2) social interactions, and (3) repetitive and stereotyped patterns of behavior" (Strock, 2004). Table 12.1 lists the five disorders that are included in autism spectrum disorders.

TABLE 12.1   Autism Spectrum Disorders

- **Autism:** extreme social withdrawal and impairment in communication; often includes stereotyped movements, resistance to change, and unusual responses to sensory experiences; usually manifests before three years of age

- **Asperger syndrome (AS) or Asperger disorder:** much like mild autism, but without significant impairments in cognition and language

- **Rett syndrome:** normal development for five months to four years, followed by regression and mental retardation; much more prevalent in females

- **Childhood disintegrative disorder:** normal development for at least two and up to 10 years, followed by significant loss of skills; much more prevalent in males

- **Pervasive developmental disorder not otherwise specified (PDD-NOS):** persons who display behaviors typical of autism but to a lesser degree and/or with an onset later than three years of age

Although most of what we discuss in this chapter applies to all the conditions of the spectrum, we focus primarily on individuals with autism or those with Asperger syndrome. As we note later in our discussion of prevalence, autism and Asperger syndrome are the most prevalent of the disorders covered by the spectrum.

AUTISM DEFINED

Autism, as defined by the Individuals with Disabilities Education Act (IDEA) is

> a developmental disability affecting verbal and nonverbal communication and social interaction, generally evident before age 3, that affects a child's performance. Other characteristics often associated with autism are engagement in repetitive activities and stereotyped movements, resistance to environmental change or change

Children with autism spectrum disorders may be distinguished by many characteristics, often including an aversion to interaction with peers.

Autism
One of five autistic spectrum disorders; characterized by extreme social withdrawal and impairment in communication; other common characteristics are stereotyped movements, resistance to environmental change or change in daily routines, and unusual responses to sensory experiences; usually evident before age of 3 years.

Asperger syndrome
One of five autistic spectrum disorders; a milder form of autism without significant impairments in language and cognition; characterized by primary problems in social interaction.

Rett syndrome
One of five autistic spectrum disorders; normal development for five months to four years, followed by regression and mental retardation; much more prevalent in females.

Childhood disintegrative disorder
One of five autistic spectrum disorders; normal development for at least two and up to ten years, followed by significant loss of skills; much more prevalent in males.

Pervasive developmental disorder not otherwise specified (PDD-NOS)
One of five autistic spectrum disorders; pervasive delay in development that does not fit into any of the other diagnostic categories.

UNDERSTANDING THE STANDARDS AND PRINCIPLES How is autism defined in the Individuals with Disabilities Education Act? *(CEC Knowledge and Skills Standard CC1K5)*

 Council for Exceptional Children

FOR A comprehensive overview of autism spectrum disorders, including definition, causes, and treatments see this National Institute of Mental Health website: **www.nimh.nih.gov/Publicat/autism.cfm**

 FOR A comprehensive overview of Asperger syndrome, including definition, causes, and treatments see this National Institute of Neurological Disorders and Stroke website: **www.ninds.nih.gov/disorders/asperger/asperger.htm**

in daily routines, and unusual responses to sensory experiences. The term does not apply if a child's educational performance is adversely affected primarily because the child has serious emotional disturbance. (34 C.F.R., Part 300, 300.7[b][1])

Although this is not specifically noted in the IDEA definition, autism is also characterized by severe cognitive deficits.

ASPERGER SYNDROME DEFINED

As we have already discussed, persons with Asperger syndrome have higher intelligence and communication skills than those with autism, but they display most, if not all of the other characteristics of autism spectrum disorders, with their primary difficulties being in social interactions. In general, we can think of Asperger syndrome as a milder form of autism.

Prevalence

Prevalence estimates for each of the autism spectrum disorders vary considerably. Recent statistics indicate that 0.15 percent (15 out of 10,000) of the school-age population are receiving special education services under the category of autism. In a review of several studies, it was found that the most reliable data indicate prevalence rates of 60 per 10,000 for autism spectrum disorders and from 8 to 30 per 10,000 for autism (Wing & Potter, 2002, as reported in Frith, 2003). Accurate prevalence figures for Asperger syndrome are harder to come by, but some have estimated an occurrence of about 36 to 48 per 10,000 (Frith, 2003). Rett syndrome (1 per 10,000–15,000) and childhood disintegrative disorder (1 per 50,000) are very rare (Strock, 2004).

Studies are consistent in pointing to a higher prevalence in males than females (about 3:1 or 4:1) in autism spectrum disorders with the exception of Rett syndrome, in which the

Prevalence estimates for each of the autism spectrum disorders vary considerably, though studies are consistent in pointing to a higher prevalence in males than females, except for Rett syndrome, in which the majority affected are females.

FOCUS ON CONCEPTS

Is There an Autism Epidemic?

AT ONE TIME, autism was considered a rare disorder. Today, however, almost everyone knows someone, or the family member of someone, who has been diagnosed with autism or Asperger syndrome. To put it into perspective, there are now five times more people with autism spectrum disorders than with Down syndrome and three times more than those with juvenile diabetes (Nash, 2002).

Research studies have documented that there has been an increase in autism. For example, the first large-scale epidemiological survey of autism, conducted in 1966, found a prevalence rate of 4.5 per 10,000. Because this study was done before the recognition of the entire spectrum of autism, including Asperger syndrome, it is probably fair that it be compared to today's prevalence of classic autism. But with recent rates for autism of between 8 and 30 per 10,000, even this more conservative comparison results in at least a twofold increase in autism.

Such growth in prevalence statistics for autism has led some to speculate that some mysterious toxin in our environment may be the culprit. Others are pointing their fingers at the now widespread use of vaccinations for babies and toddlers (see Focus on Concepts on p. 402). Most scientists, however, conclude that there is no epidemic and, in fact, that there is no increase in the number of actual cases (Fombonne, 1999; Frith, 2003; National Research Council, 2001; Wing & Potter, 2002). Instead, they argue, the increase is due to two things: (1) a widening of the criteria used to diagnose autism, including the recognition of milder forms such as Asperger syndrome, and (2) a greater awareness of autism in the general public as well as the medical, psychological, and educational professions. ■

---

vast majority affected are females. When girls do have autism, however, they are more likely to have cognitive deficits (National Research Council, 2001).

A controversial finding is that prevalence figures for autism have increased dramatically over the past 30 to 40 years, leading some to claim that there is an "autism epidemic." However, most authorities think that such claims are exaggerated. (See Focus on Concepts above and the Focus on Concepts on p. 402.)

Causes

With the rapid increase in autism has come an increase in research into its causes. This research has dramatically altered our understanding of the causes of the condition. Early speculative causal theories have been replaced by a more scientifically based set of theories.

EARLY CAUSAL THEORIES

Asperger conjectured that there was a biological basis for autism, and he believed that heredity played a role (Hewetson, 2002). Kanner too speculated that the cause of autism was biological, but he also noted that the parents of these children were not "warmhearted":

> In the whole group, there are very few really warmhearted fathers and mothers. . . . Even some of the happiest marriages are rather cold and formal affairs. Three of the marriages were dismal failures. The question arises whether or to what extent this fact has contributed to the condition of the children. The children's aloneness from the beginning of life makes it difficult to attribute the whole picture exclusively to the type of the early parental relations with our patients.
>
> We must then assume that these children have come into the world with innate inability to form the usual, biologically provided affective contact with people. (Kanner, 1943; reprinted in Kanner, 1973, pp. 42–43.)

UNDERSTANDING THE STANDARDS AND PRINCIPLES What do we know about the causes of autism? *(CEC Knowledge and Skills Standard IC2K3)*

FOCUS ON CONCEPTS

Is There a Link Between Measles, Mumps, Rubella (MMR) Vaccinations and Autism?

THERE has been a firestorm of controversy about whether the measles, mumps, rubella (MMR) vaccine can cause autism. In particular, there are assertions that the preservative **thimerosal**, which contains small traces of mercury, is the culprit.* In higher doses, mercury is known to cause neurological deficits. Thus far, evidence strongly indicates that there is no connection between this vaccine and autism. Following is a brief synopsis of how this apparently specious theory came to be and the influence it has had on the public at large. It is an interesting lesson in how science, the media, public policy, and the legal system sometimes interact.

THE ORIGINAL WAKEFIELD PAPER

In 1998, Andrew Wakefield, along with twelve coauthors, published a paper in *The Lancet* on twelve cases of children with autism who had been referred for **gastrointestinal** problems to a clinic in England (Wakefield et al., 1998). Wakefield and colleagues reported two major findings. First, several of the children had a particular form of intestinal lesions. Second, parents or physicians of eight of the children attributed the onset of autistic symptoms to MMR vaccination, that is, the symptoms

*In 1999, the American Academy of Pediatrics and the U.S. Public Health Service issued a joint statement recommending the removal of thimerosal from vaccines. Since that time, U.S. drug companies have stopped using thimerosal in vaccines, and it is estimated that no MMR vaccinations containing thimerosal since 2001 have been given in the United States.

suddenly appeared a short time (48 hours to two weeks) after vaccination.

With respect to the latter finding, they concluded: "We did not prove an association between [MMR] vaccine and the syndrome [autism] described. . . . Studies are underway that may help resolve this issue" (Wakefield et al., 1998, p. 641).

In the same issue, the editors of *The Lancet* commissioned a commentary to the Wakefield paper pointing out its limitations. One of the major limitations was that the onset of symptoms shortly after the immunization could very likely have been coincidental:

A first dose of MMR vaccine is given to about 600,000 children every year in the UK, most during the second year of life, the time when autism first becomes manifest. Not surprisingly, therefore, some cases will follow MMR vaccination. (Chen & DeStefano, 1998, p. 612)

PUBLIC REACTION TO THE WAKEFIELD PAPER

Although Wakefield and colleagues admitted that they did not *prove* that the MMR vaccine caused autism and although the commentary cautioned readers against drawing that conclusion, these caveats were lost on much of the public. Once the possible connection between vaccines and autism was reported by the media, public fear spread quickly in Europe as well as North America.

The public reaction immediately prompted many to voice concerns that the public would lose faith in the MMR vaccine,

Thimerosal
A preservative, that up until 1999, was used in vaccines as a preservative; contains small traces of mercury, which in higher doses is known to cause neurological defects.

Gastrointestinal
Pertaining to the stomach, intestines, and/or other related organs.

Even though Asperger and Kanner came down on the side of a biological basis for autism, the prevailing **psychoanalytic** ideas of the 1960s held sway for several years for professionals who were groping to find an answer to the puzzling condition of autism. One psychiatrist in particular was extremely influential in promoting the idea that parents, especially mothers, were the cause of their children's autism. Perhaps influenced by Kanner's anecdotal reference to a handful of parents as not being warmhearted plus his later statement that "emotional refrigeration has been the common lot of autistic children" (Eisenberg & Kanner, 1956), Bruno Bettelheim conceived a theory that cold and unresponsive mothers caused autism (Bettelheim, 1967). And most authorities attribute the term *refrigerator moms* (once used to refer to mothers of children with autism) to Bettelheim.

As we noted in Chapter 4, it was not too long ago that it was common to blame parents for the problems of their children, so Bettelheim's ideas were not viewed as radical. We now recognize that the direction of causation between child and adult behavior is a two-

thus leading to an outbreak of measles. Many researchers and physicians wrote letters to the editors of *The Lancet* about this. Following is a sampling of their concerns:

- *The Lancet* is a prestigious, peer reviewed journal with high public profile. The profession, journalists, the public, and especially distressed parents of ill children suppose that a publication in this journal will be true. In this example you print a commentary, which if it had been a peer reviewer's report, should have led to the rejection of the paper. (Beale, 1998, p. 906)
- We are now at a point when the elimination of measles is a real possibility. If, as a result of this paper, parents reject MMR vaccine, this could lead to a re-emergence of measles infection with the associated deaths and permanent neurological damage among young children, and a resurgence of rubella infection leading to a rise in congenital rubella births and terminations of pregnancies. (Bedford et al., 1998, p. 907)

SEVERAL AUTHORS SUBMIT RETRACTION

Ten of the thirteen authors of the Wakefield paper also voiced concerns about the public reaction and offered a retraction. They pointed out that the major focus of the paper was on the intestinal abnormalities of the children and that their data were "insufficient" to find a causal link between MMR vaccinations and autism. Furthermore, in light of all the press coverage's potentially negative impact on public health, they considered that

"now is the appropriate time that we should together formally retract the interpretation placed upon these findings in the paper" (Murch et al., 2004).

INSTITUTE OF MEDICINE'S COMMISSIONED REPORT

Since publication of the Wakefield paper, there have been several epidemiological studies of the possible autism–MMR vaccine link. In the United States, several federal agencies, including the prestigious Institute of Medicine of the National Academies, commissioned a review of the available evidence. In their third and final report, the committee concluded "**that the evidence favors rejection of a causal relationship between MMR vaccine and autism**" [bold in the original] (Institute of Medicine, 2004, p. 6).

LAWSUITS MULTIPLY

Despite overwhelming scientific epidemiological evidence to the contrary, many parents remain unconvinced that MMR vaccinations did not cause their *particular* child's autism. For example, as of August 2004, over 4,200 lawsuits had been filed in the United States alleging that thimerosal had caused autism. Time will tell whether any of these suits are successful. In the meantime, the vast majority of the research community maintains that the MMR vaccine, with or without thimerosal, does not cause autism. ∎

way street (Bell & Harper, 1977). It is reasonable to conclude that parents of a relatively unresponsive baby would themselves display behaviors that seemed cold and distant. Furthermore, we know that the families and parents of children with autism typically experience considerable stress because they are suddenly and unexpectedly confronted by the child's disability. Usually, their child does not look different from the typical child, and often the child has gone through a short period of months or years of apparently normal development before the parents recognize that something is wrong. It is therefore understandable that parents would behave in ways that reflect stress and concern.

TODAY'S CAUSAL THEORIES

Scientists do not yet know precisely what is wrong with the brain in autism spectrum disorders, but they have established unequivocally that the cause is neurological, not

Psychoanalytic
Related to psychoanalysis, including the assumptions that emotional or behavior disorders result primarily from unconscious conflicts and that the most effective preventive actions and therapeutic intervention involve uncovering and understanding unconscious motivations.

For much of the twentieth century it was widely speculated that parents, especially mothers, were the cause of their children's autism.

interpersonal (National Research Council, 2001; Strock, 2004). Furthermore, they have strong evidence that heredity plays a role in many cases. However, given the range of symptoms and levels of severity of autism spectrum disorders, it is a reasonable guess that there is no single neurological or genetic cause.

Neurological Basis of Autism Spectrum Disorders   That autism spectrum disorders have a neurological basis is suggested by the fact that people with autism have a high incidence of brain seizures and cognitive deficits (Volkmar & Pauls, 2003). Furthermore, postmortem studies and neurological imaging studies, using the same techniques that we discussed in earlier chapters on learning disabilities and attention deficit hyperactivity disorder (ADHD) (e.g., positron emission tomography scans, computerized axial tomographic scans, and magnetic resonance imaging), have implicated a number of areas of the brain (Strock, 2004; Volkmar & Pauls, 2003). Figure 12.1 depicts some of the major brain structures that are affected.

One particularly interesting line of neurological research involves the brain and head size of people with autism (Courchesne, Carper, & Akshoomoff, 2003; Courchesne et al., 2001; Fombonne, Roge, Claverie, Courty, & Fremoile, 1999; Piven, Arndt, Bailey, & Andreason, 1996; Piven et al., 1995). Studies indicate that the brains and heads of young children with autism are actually larger than normal. In his 1943 paper, Kanner noted that many of the children he studied had overly large heads. Since then, large head size has come to be "one of the most replicated neurobiological findings in the disorder (Lainhart, 2003). Recent evidence (Courchesne et al., 2003) strongly suggests the following for many people with autism:

- At birth, their brains are of average size or perhaps even smaller than average.
- Their brains grow suddenly and excessively in the first two years of life.
- After age two, their brain growth slows, and it reaches its maximum size around 4 or 5 years of age.
- After about age five years, their brains decrease in size and become the same size as those of the nondisabled by adolescence or adulthood.

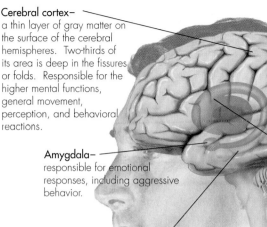

Cerebral cortex–
a thin layer of gray matter on
the surface of the cerebral
hemispheres. Two-thirds of
its area is deep in the fissures
or folds. Responsible for the
higher mental functions,
general movement,
perception, and behavioral
reactions.

Amygdala–
responsible for emotional
responses, including aggressive
behavior.

Hippocampus–
makes it possible to remember
new information and recent events.

Basal ganglia–
gray masses deep in the
cerebral hemisphere that
serve as a connection
between the cerebrum and
cerebellum. Helps to
regulate automatic movement

Corpus callosum–
consists primarily of closely
packed bundles of fibers that
connect the right and left
hemispheres. Allows for
communication between the
hemispheres.

Brain stem–
located in front of the
cerebellum. Serves as a
relay station, passing messages
between various parts of the
body and the cerebral cortex.
Primitive functions essential to
survival (breathing and heart
control) are located here.

Cerebellum–
located at the back of the
brain. Fine tunes motor
activity. Regulates balance,
body movements,
coordination, and the
muscles used in speaking.

FIGURE 12.1   Major brain
structures implicated in
autism

Source: Strock, M. (2004). Autism
Spectrum Disorders (Pervasive Develop-
mental Disorders). NIH Publication No.
NIH-04-5511, National Institute of
Mental Health, National Institutes of
Health, U.S. Department of Health and
Human Services, Bethesda, MD, 40 pp.
Retrieved August 9, 2004, from the
World Wide Web:
www.nimh.nih.gov/publicat/autism.cfm.

The significance of abnormally high rates of brain growth in the first two years is un-
derscored by the fact that this is a time of critical importance to brain organization:

> The organizational events in the brain during the first two years set the neuro-
> developmental stage for the acquisition of language and the capacity for inference,
> a sense of self-awareness (Herschkowitz, 2000), and, eventually, complex infor-
> mation processing (Minshew, Sweeney, & Luna, 2002). (Lainhart, 2003, p. 394)

Hereditary Basis of Autism Spectrum Disorders   The scientific evidence for autism
having a hereditary component is very strong (Strock, 2004; Volkmar & Pauls, 2003). For
example, studies have shown that when one family member is diagnosed with autism, the
chances are 50 to 200 times higher that another family member also has autism than in
the population as a whole. And when a monozygotic (identical, one egg) twin has autism,
the chances are much greater that the other twin will also have autism than is the case with
dizygotic (fraternal, two eggs) twins. Furthermore, even if they are not diagnosed as autistic, family members of those with autism are more likely to exhibit autisticlike characteristics at a subclinical level, such as a lack of close friends, a preoccupation with narrow
interests, and a preference for routines (Volkmar & Pauls, 2003).

Research has not yet identified the exact genes that are involved. However, it is likely that multiple genes are involved and that not the same ones are implicated in all people with autism.

Assessment

UNDERSTANDING THE STANDARDS AND PRINCIPLES How is autism diagnosed? *(CEC Knowledge and Skills Standards CC8K3, CC8K4, & IC8S3)*

 Council for Exceptional Children

There is no universally used diagnostic test for autism or any of the other disorders in the spectrum. The diagnosis of autism is often made by a psychiatrist using criteria established by the American Psychiatric Association (2000) that focus on communication skills, social interactions, and repetitive and stereotyped patterns of behavior (see Table 12.2). In addition to observing the child in the examining room and taking a detailed history from parents, clinicians can use behavioral observation instruments and ask parents and/or teachers to fill out behavior checklists.

Although the diagnosis of autism might sound somewhat vague, the behavioral symptoms are so severe and striking that it is actually relatively easy to diagnose. Asperger syndrome, by contrast, is somewhat more subjective because the symptoms are milder. With Asperger syndrome, the clinician is looking for normal or close to normal communication abilities but problems in social interactions and repetitive and stereotyped patterns of behavior, but to a lesser extent than is seen in classic autism.

TABLE 12.2   Diagnostic Criteria for Autism

A. A total of six (or more) items from (1), (2), and (3), with at least two from (1), and one each from (2) and (3):
1. Qualitative impairment in social interaction, as manifested by at least two of the following:
    a. Marked impairment in the use of multiple nonverbal behaviors such as eye-to-eye gaze, facial expression, body postures, and gestures to regulate social interaction.
    b. Failure to develop peer relationships appropriate to developmental level
    c. A lack of spontaneous seeking to share enjoyment, interests, or achievements with other people (e.g., by a lack of showing, bringing, or pointing out objects of interest).
    d. Lack of social or emotional reciprocity.
2. Qualitative impairments in communication as manifested by at least one of the following:
    a. Delay in, or total lack of, the development of spoken language (not accompanied by an attempt to compensate through alternative modes of communication such as gestures or mime).
    b. In individuals with adequate speech, marked impairments in the ability to initiate or sustain a conversation with others.
    c. Stereotyped and repetitive use of language or idiosyncratic language.
    d. Lack of varied, spontaneous make-believe play or social imitative play appropriate to developmental level.
3. Restricted repetitive and stereotyped patterns of behavior, interests, and activities, as manifested by at least one of the following:
    a. Encouraging preoccupation with one or more stereotypic and restricted patterns of interest that is abnormal either in intensity or focus.
    b. Apparently inflexible adherence to specific, nonfunctional routines or rituals.
    c. Stereotypic and repetitive motor mannerisms (e.g., hand or finger flapping or twisting, or complex whole-body movements).
    d. Persistent preoccupation with parts of objects.

B. Delays or abnormal functioning in at least one of the following areas, with onset prior to age 3 years: (1) social interaction, (2) language as used in social communication, or (3) symbolic or imaginative play.

C. The disturbance is not better accounted for by Rett's Disorder or Childhood Disintegrative Disorder.

Source: American Psychiatric Association. (2000). *Diagnostic and statistical manual of mental disorders* (4th ed., text rev., p. 92). Washington, DC: Author.

Psychological and Behavioral Characteristics

As we noted earlier, there is some variation in the behavioral characteristics that are associated with the different autism spectrum disorders. Our discussion focuses on autism and Asperger syndrome because (1) they are the most prevalent of the autism spectrum disorders; (2) many of the characteristics of autism apply to Rett-syndrome, childhood disintegrative disorder, and pervasive developmental disorder not otherwise specified; and (3) there are some important differences between Asperger syndrome and the other autism spectrum disorders.

AUTISM

We noted that people with autism have deficits in social interaction, communication, and repetitive and stereotyped patterns of behavior. In addition, they display cognitive deficits, and some have abnormal sensory perceptions.

Impaired Social Interaction   Most of the social interaction problems that individuals with autism exhibit pertain to deficits in social responsiveness. Parents of children with autism often notice that their babies or toddlers do not respond normally to being picked up or cuddled. And the young child with autism might not show a differential response to parents, siblings, or their teachers compared to other strangers. They might not smile in social situations, or they might smile or laugh when nothing appears funny. Their eye gaze often differs significantly from that of others; they sometimes avoid eye contact with others or look out of the corners of their eyes. They might show little or no interest in other people but be preoccupied with objects. They might not learn to play normally. These characteristics persist and prevent the child from developing typical attachments to their parents or friendships with their peers. In fact, they often give the impression that they are not interested in making friends.

Impaired Communication   Most children with autism lack **communicative intent**, or the desire to communicate for social purposes; and as many as 50 percent are thought to be **mute**, that is, they use no, or almost no, language (Scheuermann & Webber, 2002). Those who do develop speech typically show abnormalities in intonation, rate, volume, and content of their oral language. Their speech might sound "robotic," or they might exhibit echolalia, a parroting of what they hear. They might reverse pronouns (e.g., confuse *you* and *I* or refer to themselves as *he* or *she* rather than *I* or *me*). Using language as a tool for social interaction is particularly difficult for most people with autism. If they do acquire language, they may have considerable difficulty using it in social interactions because they are unaware of the reactions of their listeners.

Communicative intent The need to communicate for social reasons; thought to be lacking in most children with autism.

Mute Possessing no, or almost no, language; characteristic of many with autism.

Stereotypic behaviors Any of a variety of repetitive behaviors (e.g., eye rubbing) that are sometimes found in individuals who are autistic, blind, severely mentally retarded, or psychotic; sometimes referred to as stereotypies or blindisms.

Repetitive and Stereotyped Patterns of Behavior   Many people with autism display **stereotypic behaviors**: repetitive, ritualistic motor behaviors such as twirling, spinning objects, flapping the hands, and rocking, similar to those that are evident in some people who are blind (see Chapter 11). Another characteristic that is frequently seen in autism and related disorders is extreme fascination or preoccupation with objects and a very restricted range of interests. Children with autism might play ritualistically with an object for hours at a time or show excessive interest in objects of a particular type. They might be upset by any change in the environment (e.g., something out of place or something new in the home or classroom) or any change in routine. That is, some individuals with autism seem intent on the preservation of sameness and have extreme difficulty with change or transition (Adreon & Stella, 2001; Myles & Simpson, 2001).

Casebook Reflections

Refer to the case *Chase* in your booklet. Although Chase is able to perform at grade level academically, he engages in person-specific, ritualistic behaviors and rigid associations, as well as exhibiting a fascination with glass. Do his characteristics resemble those of a student with one of the autism spectrum disorders? Why or why not?

Impaired Cognition Most individuals with autism display cognitive deficits similar to those of people with mental retardation. However, there are some cognitive processing problems that seem to be peculiar to autism:

> Children with autism are thought to display difficulty in coding and categorization of information, . . . relying on literal translations, and they seem to remember things by their location in space rather than concept comprehension (Schuler, 1995). For example, "shopping" means going to a particular store on a particular street, rather than the concept of visiting any type of store, browsing around, perhaps buying something . . ., or various other aspects of the concept of "shopping." In fact, it has been speculated that individuals with autism employ an "echo box-like memory store" (Grandin, 1995; Hermelin, 1976). This would explain why autistic children may excel at putting puzzles together and building things out of blocks, matching tasks, or drawing replicas. However, they tend to perform poorly on tasks requiring verbal comprehension and expressive language. (Scheuermann & Webber, 2002, p. 9)

The striking difference in favor of visual and spatial abilities relative to language and conceptual abilities has been termed *thinking in pictures* by Temple Grandin (see Personal Perspectives on p. 409). Although Grandin is more typical of someone with Asperger syndrome, her description of heightened visual-spatial abilities is applicable to some with autism as well as to some with Asperger syndrome.

There are some individuals with autism who have such extraordinary skills that at first blush, one thinks they are geniuses. These individuals are referred to as autistic savants. An **autistic savant** may have relatively severe autism, in that he or she shows serious developmental delays in overall social and intellectual functioning. However, the person with this condition also shows remarkable ability or apparent talent in particular splinter skills—skills that exist in apparent isolation from the rest of the person's abilities to function. An autistic savant might have extraordinary capabilities in playing music, drawing, or calculating. For example, when given a date that is far into the future, such as September 9, 2016, some autistic savants are immediately able to say that this will be a Friday. The same person, however, might not have the functional mathematical skills to be able to purchase items in a grocery store. The character Raymond, played by Dustin Hoffman, in the movie *Rain Man* was an autistic savant. (See Sacks, 1995, for other examples.)

Because the skills of individuals who are autistic savants are so extraordinary, they are often covered in the media. This fact, along with publicity that accompanies such films as *Rain Man, Shine* (a film loosely based on the life of pianist David Helfgott), and *Mozart and the Whale*, has led to the misconception in the general public that most, if not all, people with autism have such amazing talents. Although we do not have precise figures, we do know that autistic savants represent a very small proportion of people with autism.

Abnormal Sensory Perceptions Some people with autism are either hyperresponsive or hyporesponsive to particular stimuli in their environment. With respect to being hyperresponsive, recall Stephen Shore's hypersensitivity to certain sounds in the quote at the beginning of the chapter (see p. 395). Some experience hypersensitivity to visual stimuli, such as Shore's reference to a child being sensitive to fluorescent lights; and still others can be overly sensitive to touch. Interestingly, some people with autism are totally the opposite of hyperresponsive. They are very *unresponsive* to auditory, visual, or tactile stimuli. In fact, to the casual observer, some appear to be deaf or blind. And some have a combination of hypersensitivity and hyposensitivity, for instance, being oblivious to loud noises such as a fire alarm but overreacting to someone whistling at a great distance.

ASPERGER SYNDROME

People with Asperger syndrome are likely to display impairment or abnormalities in the same areas (i.e., social interaction, communication, repetitive and stereotyped patterns of

Autistic savant
A person with severe autism whose social and language skills are markedly delayed but who also has advanced skills in a particular area, such as calculation or drawing.

Personal Perspectives

FIRST PERSON, MYSELF—TEMPLE GRANDIN

I WAS 2½ years old when I began to show symptoms of autism: not talking, repetitious behavior, and tantrums. Not being able to communicate in words was a great frustration, so I screamed. Loud, high-pitched noises hurt my ears like a dentist's drill hitting a nerve. I would shut out the hurtful stimuli by rocking or staring at sand dribbling through my fingers.

As a child, I was like an animal with no instincts to guide me, I was always observing, trying to work out the best ways to behave, yet I never fit in. When other students swooned over the Beatles, I called their reaction an ISP—interesting sociological phenomenon. I wanted to participate but did not know how. I had a few friends who were interested in the same things I was, such as skiing and riding horses. But friendship always revolved around what I did rather than who I was.

Even today personal relationships are something I don't really understand. I still consider sex to be the biggest, most important "sin of the system," to use my old high school term. From reading books and talking to people at conventions, I have learned that autistic people who adapt most successfully in personal relationships either choose celibacy or marry someone with similar disabilities.

Early education and speech therapy pulled me out of the autistic world. Like many autistics, I think in pictures. My artistic abilities became evident when I was in first and second grade, and they were encouraged. I had a good eye for color and painted watercolors of the beach.

But words are like a foreign language to me. I translate them into full-color movies, complete with sound, which run like a videotape in my head. When I was a child, I believed that everybody thought in pictures. Not until I went to college did I realize that some people are completely verbal and think only in words. On one of my earliest jobs, I thought the other engineer was stupid because he could not "see" his mistakes on his drawings. Now I understand his problem was a lack of visual thinking and not stupidity.

Autistics have trouble learning things that cannot be thought about in pictures. The easiest words for an autistic child to learn are nouns because they relate directly to pictures. Spatial words such as *over* and *under* had no meaning for me until I had a visual image to fix them in my memory. Even now, when I hear the word *under* by itself, I automatically picture myself getting under the cafeteria tables at school during an air-raid

Temple Grandin credits her visualization abilities for her success in designing feed pens.

drill, a common occurrence on the East Coast in the early 1950s.

Teachers who work with autistic children need to understand associative thought patterns. But visual thinking is more than just associations. Concepts can also be formed visually. When I was little, I had to figure out that small dogs were not cats. After looking at both large and small dogs, I realized that they all had the same nose. This was a common visual feature of all the dogs but none of the cats.

I credit my visualization abilities with helping me understand the animals I work with. One of my early livestock design projects was to create a dip-vat and cattle-handling facility for a feed yard in Arizona. A dip vat is a long, narrow, 7-ft. deep swimming pool through which cattle move in single file. It is filled with pesticide to rid the animals of ticks, lice and other external parasites. In 1978 dip-vat designs were very poor. The animals often panicked because they were forced into the vat down a steep, slick decline. They would refuse to jump into the vat and would sometimes flip over backward and drown.

The first thing I did when I arrived at the feedlot was put myself inside a cow's head and see with its eyes. Because their eyes are on the sides of their head, cattle have wide-angle vision. Those cattle must have felt as if they were being forced to jump down an airplane escape slide into the ocean.

One of my first steps was to convert the ramp from steel to concrete. If I had a calf's body and hooves, I would be very scared to step on a slippery metal ramp. The final design had a concrete ramp at a 25° downward angle. Deep grooves in the concrete provided secure footing. The ramp appeared to enter the water gradually, but in reality it abruptly dropped away below the water's surface. The animals could not see the drop-off because the dip chemicals colored the water. When they stepped out over the water, they quietly fell in because their center of gravity had passed the point of no return.

Owners and managers of feedlots sometimes have a hard time comprehending that if devices such as dip vats and restraint chutes are properly designed, cattle will voluntarily enter them. Because I think in pictures, I assume cattle do too. I can imagine the sensations the animals feel. Today half the cattle in the U.S. are handled in equipment I have designed.

Grandin is an assistant professor of animal sciences at Colorado State University ■

Source: Grandin, T. (2002, May 6). First person: Myself. *Time* p.56.

UNDERSTANDING THE STANDARDS AND PRINCIPLES Describe the social characteristics likely to be exhibited by persons with Asperger syndrome. *(CEC Knowledge and Skills Standard IC2K4)*

Hidden curriculum
The dos and don'ts of social interactions that most people learn incidentally or with little instruction but that remain hidden for those with Asperger syndrome.

behavior, cognitive processing, sensory perception) as do those who have autism but to a milder degree. We focus our discussion on impairments in social skills and communication skills because most authorities consider social interaction to be their biggest challenge and because problems in communicating contribute to their social ineptitude.

Impaired Social Interaction   A major reason that people with Asperger syndrome have so much difficulty in social interactions is that they are not adept at reading social cues. In fact, at times, they can appear clueless about what constitutes appropriate social behavior. And because they can be highly verbal and intelligent, others can easily get the impression that they are willfully disregarding social etiquette. By "turning off" those around them, they become further ostracized from their peer group, making it difficult to make and keep friends and to interact with others in the workplace.

The essence of the social problems for individuals with Asperger syndrome is captured by the notion of the hidden curriculum (Myles & Simpson, 2001, 2003). The **hidden curriculum** refers to those dos and don'ts of everyday living that most people learn incidentally or with very little instruction from others. They are behaviors or ways of acting that most of us take for granted. See Table 12.3 for some examples of hidden curriculum items.

For people with Asperger syndrome, these "rules" of how to interact remain hidden. And what makes it all the more difficult for the person with Asperger syndrome is that the hidden curriculum can be different for different settings:

> Everyone knows that Mrs. Robbins allows students to whisper in class as long as they get their work done, whereas Mrs. Cook does not tolerate any level of noise in her class. Similarly, everyone knows that Mr. Johnson, the assistant principal, is a stickler for following the rules, so no one curses or even slouches in his presence. Everyone also knows that the really tough guys (the ones who beat up unsuspecting kids) hang out behind the slide, just out of teachers' view—everyone knows these things—everyone, that is, except the student with Asperger syndrome.
>
> Outside of school, the hidden curriculum is an even bigger issue. What is the hidden curriculum for talking to or taking rides from strangers? The bus driver is a stranger, but it is permissible to accept a ride from her. . . . It is okay to accept candy from the distributor who is giving free samples at Toys "R" Us, yet it is not prudent to take candy from a stranger standing on the street corner. (Myles & Simpson, 2003, p. 132)

TABLE 12.3   Examples of Hidden Curriculum Items

- Do not tell the principal that if she listened better, more kids would like her.
- You should not have to pay students to be your friends.
- Do not talk to other kids in the classroom when the teacher is giving a lesson.
- When the teacher is scolding another student, it is not an appropriate time to ask the teacher a question.
- Do not tell classmates about the "skeletons in your parents' closets."
- Do not draw violent scenes in school.
- During a conversation, face the speaker and position your body in that direction.
- Speak to teachers in a pleasant tone of voice, because they will respond to you in a more positive manner.

Source: Adapted from Myles, B. S., & Simpson, R. L. (2001). Understanding the hidden curriculum: An essential social skill for children and youth with Asperger syndrome. *Intervention in School and Clinic, 36,* 282.

Contributing to their social awkwardness, people with Asperger syndrome also have a tendency to interpret what others say very literally. Stephen Shore, a person with Asperger syndrome whose quote introduced this chapter, provides examples of his struggles with being overly literal:

> A friend of mine . . . said he felt "like a pizza." "What do you mean—'feel like a pizza'?" And it wasn't until college that I realized, "Oh, he meant he felt like EATING a pizza." At this time, idioms usually go zipping past me but I am often able to "pull them back" for further examination before I say something ridiculous. But it takes some additional thinking on my part, to figure out "Well, what's the meaning? How do I interpret this?" . . .
>
> I remember when I was about nineteen, sitting in a restaurant with my parents, and they said to me, "You know, that girl over there, she's got her eye on you; she's giving you the eye." "WHAT DO YOU MEAN SHE'S GIVING ME THE EYE? I DON'T WANT HER EYE! You need two eyes; you see in stereo. She needs HER two eyes, that's gross and sickening anyway and I won't take it." Idioms like that one got away. (Shore, 2003, p. 198)

Impaired Communication Skills   According to the American Psychiatric Association's diagnostic criteria, Asperger syndrome does not involve "clinically significant general delay in language." However, numerous practitioners and researchers have asserted that this statement is misleading (Mesibov, Shea & Adams, 2001). People with Asperger syndrome may be able to express themselves using age-appropriate vocabulary and grammar, but they often exhibit numerous idiosyncratic language and language-related behaviors. They often have problems with **pragmatics**, the social uses of language. For example, they might speak using an abnormal voice inflection, such as a monotone, talk too loudly or too quickly or slowly, not be adept at taking turns talking in a conversation, engage in monologues, or repeat the same thing over and over. In Chapter 6, we noted that people with learning disabilities can also experience problems with pragmatics; however, the pragmatic skills of those with Asperger syndrome are much more severe and pervasive.

Pragmatics
The study within psycholinguistics of how people use language in social situations; emphasizes the functional use of language rather than the mechanics.

The problems with pragmatics of those with Asperger syndrome also extend to non-verbal communication skills:

> such as standing closer to another person than is customarily accepted; intensely staring at another person for long periods; maintaining abnormal body posture; failing to make eye contact or displaying an inexpressive face, thereby failing to signal interest, approval, or disapproval; and failing to use or understand gestures and facial expressions. (Myles & Simpson, 2003, p. 9)

ATTEMPTS TO CONSTRUCT A UNIFYING THEORY OF AUTISM SPECTRUM DISORDERS

Although a wide variety of psychological and behavioral characteristics have been attributed to individuals with autism spectrum disorders, some researchers have attempted to build theories that can account for many of the behaviors they display. The three most prominent theories identify the major impairments as being accounted for by problems in (1) executive functions, (2) weak central coherence, or (3) theory of mind (Frith, 2003; National Research Council, 2001; Volkmar & Pauls, 2003). Even though none of these three theories, by itself, can explain all the myriad problems that are displayed, together they help us begin to build a composite picture of autism spectrum disorders.

Executive functions
The ability to regulate one's behavior through working memory, inner speech, control of emotions and arousal levels, and analysis of problems and communication of problem solutions to others; delayed or impaired in those with ADHD and ASD.

Executive Functions   In Chapter 7, we noted that many people with attention deficit hyperactivity disorder (ADHD) exhibit difficulties in self-directed behaviors. These self-directed behaviors are referred to as **executive functions**, which include such things as working memory, self-regulation of emotions, and the ability to plan ahead. Research indicates that many people with autism have difficulties with executive functions (Ozonoff, 1997). These problems are often more severe than those experienced by people with ADHD.

Central coherence
The inclination to bring meaning to stimuli by conceptualizing it as a whole; thought to be weak in people with ASD.

Central Coherence   Some authorities have identified people with autism as having weak central coherence (Frith, 2003). According to this theory, **central coherence** is the natural inclination for most human beings to bring order and meaning to information in their environment by perceiving it as a meaningful whole rather than as disparate parts. Individuals with autism, on the other hand, are just the opposite. They get caught up in details in classic "not being able to see the forest for the trees" fashion:

> In the normal cognitive system there is a built-in propensity to form coherence over as wide a range of stimuli as possible, and to generalize over as wide a range of contexts as possible. It is this drive that results in grand systems of thought, and it is this capacity for coherence that is diminished in children with autism. (Frith, 2003, pp. 159–160)

Interestingly, some people with autism do not seem to recognize that their way of processing information is disjointed, nor do they appear to have any desire or need to bring coherence to their fragmented perceptions:

> A patient exhibiting autistic symptoms from early childhood obsessively collected information about the addresses of juvenile courts. It is unknown how this extremely odd interest arose. However it came about, it would be less odd if it emerged from a general interest in courts, buildings, or town plans. In this case it would not be just a fragment, however well studied, but part of a bigger picture. But this was definitely not the case for this patient. When asked why he did not want to know about the addresses of nonjuvenile courts, he replied, "They bore me to tears." This was not a joke on his part. The remark showed a total lack of understanding that interests are expected to be justified as part of a coherent pattern of likes and dislikes, and not arbitrary. (Frith, 2003, pp. 157–158)

Theory of mind
The ability to take another's perspective in a social exchange; the ability to infer another person's feelings, intentions, desires, etc.; impaired in those with ASD.

Theory of Mind   **Theory of mind** refers to a person's ability to take the perspective of other people. It is the ability to "read" the mind of other people with respect to such things as their intentions, feelings, beliefs, and desires. Earlier, we discussed how difficult it is for many people with Asperger syndrome to read social cues. The reading of social cues is another way of saying that a person can anticipate and understand what another is probably thinking. Most of us are able to infer the emotional state of those with whom we are conversing by interpreting cues, such as tone of voice and facial expressions. We are able to gauge how others are reacting to what we are saying using similar cues.

People with autism spectrum disorders have varying degrees of difficulty inferring the thoughts of others. Some, in fact, do not seem to understand that their thoughts are different from those of others. See Focus on Concepts on page 413 for a study demonstrating the theory of mind problems that are exhibited by children with autism.

UNDERSTANDING THE STANDARDS AND PRINCIPLES   What type of education is likely to be most appropriate for students with autism spectrum disorders? *(CEC Knowledge and Skills Standards CC4S3, IC4S1, & CC5K5)*

Council for
Exceptional
Children

Educational Considerations

As we have mentioned, the characteristics of autism spectrum disorders are quite varied. When these characteristics are severe, they typically carry a very guarded prognosis, even with early, intensive intervention. A significant percentage of children with severe symptoms are unlikely to recover completely, although they might make substantial progress (Charlop-Christy, Schreibman, Pierce, & Kurtz, 1998; National Research Council, 2001).

Because autism's symptoms are so unusual and so resistant to remediation, autism has been fertile ground for faddish and unproven treatment methods. As one authority has put it:

FOCUS ON CONCEPTS

Theory of Mind: The Sally and Anne Experiment

In what has become regarded as a classic study of theory-of-mind problems, researchers investigated whether children with autism age 6 to 16 years were able to recognize that others can have false beliefs that affect their judgment (Baron-Cohen, Leslie, & Frith, 1985). Using two dolls (Sally and Anne), an investigator acted out the following scenario to three groups of children (autistic, Down syndrome, nondisabled):

Sally has a basket and Anne has a box. Sally has a marble and she puts it into her basket. She then goes out. Anne takes out Sally's marble and puts it into her box while Sally is away. Now Sally comes back and wants to play with her marble. At this point we ask the critical question: "Where will Sally look for her marble?" The answer is, of course, "In the basket." (Frith, 2003, pp. 82, 84)

The vast majority of the nondisabled children and even the children with Down syndrome answered correctly. However, only a few of the children with autism gave the correct response. They were unable to understand that Sally had no way of knowing that the marble had been switched—that to her way of thinking, the marble was where she had left it. ▪

The ASD [autism spectrum disorders] field is particularly well known for its willingness to embrace and/or maintain a liberal tolerance toward unproven and controversial interventions and treatments. A number of these purportedly effective methods appear to have neither empirical nor logical foundation. (Simpson, 2004, p. 139)

A prime example of an unproven technique that continues to claim proponents despite overwhelming evidence of its ineffectiveness is facilitated communication. (We discuss facilitated communication in Chapter 13.)

Largely because of the numerous controversies surrounding interventions for students with autism, the National Research Council of the National Academy of Sciences commissioned and published a report on autism (National Research Council, 2001). In this report, they recommend that six areas of skill should be given priority in education:

1. Functional, spontaneous communication
2. Social skills that are age-appropriate (e.g., with very young children, responding to mother)
3. Play skills, especially play with peers
4. Cognitive (thinking) skills that are useful and applied in everyday life
5. Appropriate behavior to replace problem behavior
6. Functional academic skills, when appropriate to the needs of the child

EDUCATIONAL PROGRAMMING PRINCIPLES FOR STUDENTS WITH AUTISM SPECTRUM DISORDERS

Although educational programming for students with autism spectrum disorders must cover a wide variety of areas, there are some guidelines on which most authorities have agreed. First, generally speaking, many believe that the greatest areas of needed instruction are communication skills for those with autism and social skills for those with Asperger syndrome. Also, most agree that educational programming for students with autism spectrum disorders should include (1) direct instruction of skills, (2) behavior management using functional behavioral assessment and positive behavioral support, and (3) instruction in natural settings. See the Responsive Instruction on page 414 for further strategies for teaching students with autism spectrum disorders.

THE FACILITATED Communication Institute at Syracuse University is the main promoter of facilitated communication (FC) in the United States: **http://soeweb.syr.edu/thefci/**
Most authorities have viewed FC as an unproven technique for several years. For example, in 1994 the American Psychological Association adopted a position statement (see: **http://soeweb.syr.edu/thefci/apafc.htm**) with the conclusion that FC is an "unproved communicative procedure with no scientifically demonstrated support for its efficacy." See also a review of FC in the *Skeptic*: **www.skeptic.com/02.3.green-fc.html**.

Meeting the Needs of Students with Autism Spectrum Disorders

Instructional Strategies

WHAT THE RESEARCH SAYS

Students identified as having autistic spectrum disorders will exhibit great variability in their specific strengths, interests, characteristics, behavioral challenges, and academic needs. In general, however, researchers have found that students with autistic spectrum disorders will require instructional programming to address many of the following areas: desire for routine; limited social awareness; restricted range of interests; problems focusing on toys, people's faces, or information providing prompts; poor motor coordination; academic difficulties; and emotional vulnerability (Barnhill, 2001; Williams, 2001).

APPLYING THE RESEARCH TO TEACHING

To address these characteristics, teachers will need to consider how the learning environment they create and the instructional strategies they choose will affect student growth. Specific suggestions for promoting student success include:

- Create a predictable environment built upon consistent routines.
- Teach students how to read and respond to social cues. Often, students with autism will need to be taught how to "read" emotions, tone of voice, nonverbal gestures, and idioms or abstract expressions. Teachers can use role-play, cue cards, and peers to help teach students these valuable social cues.
- Encourage other students in the class to engage the student with autism. Students with autism can be introverted and prefer their own company. By teaching other students in the class ways to engage and participate with the student with autism, the number of opportunities for learning will be increased.
- Create rules for engaging in discussions or activities that fall within the student's limited interests. Children with Asperger syndrome can have extreme interests and desire to seek only information on that topic. Similarly, a student with autism may want only to play with a certain object.

Teachers should establish "time and place" rules for allowing engagement of those topics or activities so that other interests and learning can be developed.

- Use structured, positive reinforcement to shape desired social interactions and behaviors. For example, giving specific praise (or providing another desired response) to a student who joins a group activity or makes a request will lead the student to more frequently engage in those activities. When a student's behavior is shaped in this way, the student will begin to act in ways determined by the teacher to result in increased learning or positive long-term outcomes.
- Divide instructional tasks into meaningful components and create overt, external stimuli to guide the student. Students with autistic spectrum disorders can be distracted by nonrelevant stimuli (e.g., the pattern on the teacher's dress, the lawn mower outside, the colors in the book) or internal stimuli (e.g., day-dreaming). To support focusing on the task at hand, teachers can create physical cues, such as a chart that is divided into the components of the lesson or a cue card the student selects as he or she finishes each step, to direct the student.
- Create academic experiences that build upon success. Students with autistic spectrum disorders can have intellectual capacities that range from severe and profound mental retardation to giftedness, yet all students will need support in the areas of understanding the nuances of language, multiple levels of meaning, and abstract connections. Explicit and structured instruction create cognitive support for student learning, retention, and concept integration.
- Teach students coping mechanisms to use when confronted with stressor anxiety. Routines and scripts can be helpful in allowing the student to feel as though she or he has regained control (Matson, Benavidez, Compton, Paclwaskyj, & Baglio, 1996; McClannahan & Krantz, 1999; Williams, 2001). ■

By Kristin L. Sayeski

Direct Instruction of Skills Effective instruction for students with autism spectrum disorders usually requires a highly structured, directive approach that uses basic principles of behavioral psychology for analyzing tasks and how best to teach them. Direct instruction means using structured, teacher-led lessons; instruction in small groups or one on one; lessons presented in small steps; frequent use of teacher questions; extensive opportunities for practice; and frequent feedback, reinforcement and correction (Hallahan, Lloyd, Kauffman, Weiss, & Martinez, 2005).

Effective instruction for students with autism spectrum disorders often requires the use of direct instruction in small group or one-on-one settings to teach skills in communication, social interaction, cognition, and functional academics.

Teachers can use direct instruction to teach skills in communication, social interaction, and daily living. The following is an example of direct instruction of communication skills for a student who is autistic:

> First, the teacher gains the student's attention, sometimes indicating what is to be learned (e.g., "Dana, look at me. It's time to work on your words"). Second, the teacher presents a stimulus, usually in the form of a command although it could also be a visual stimulus such as written directions. For example, the teacher may say "Dana, point to the word 'stop'." Third, the teacher may prompt the correct response by guiding the student's hand or by offering visual or verbal cues. Fourth, the teacher waits for the clearly defined student response (e.g., the student will point to the correct word card with the index finger within 10 seconds). Depending on the student's response, the teacher will now give a consequence or feedback as step 5. If the response was correct, the teacher may say "Good." If the response was incorrect, the teacher may not say anything, repeat the stimulus command, and provide more effective prompting. (Scheuermann & Webber, 2002, p. 15)

Teachers or speech clinicians can also use **augmentative or alternative communication (AAC)** systems (see Chapters 9 and 13) for students with autism who are nonverbal or who have very little functional language. One such system that uses pictures to help students initiate and maintain functional communication is the Picture Exchange Communication System (PECS) (see Responsive Instruction on p. 416).

Behavior Management   Students with autism spectrum disorders, especially those with severe levels of autism, sometimes display highly inappropriate behaviors, such as biting, hitting, or screaming. As we mentioned in our discussion of mental retardation, emotional

Augmentative or alternative communication (AAC) Alternative forms of communication that do not use the oral sounds of speech or that augment the use of speech.

Meeting the Needs of Students with Autism Spectrum Disorders

Using the Picture Exchange Communication System to Enhance Social Interactions of Students with Autism

The National Research Council (2001) estimates that one third to one half of children with autism do not use speech functionally. To assist and support these individuals' communication, augmentative and alternative communication systems are employed (Mirenda, 2003). Augmentative systems serve as a supplement to existing communication (e.g., the use of manual signs in addition to limited speech). Alternative systems, by contrast, serve as the primary means of communication (e.g., the use of pictures or line drawings to express communication in the absence of any other speech or communication).

One AAC system is the Picture Exchange Communication System (PECS), which was originally designed by Bondy and Frost to support the communication of students with autism (Bondy & Frost, 2001; Frost & Bondy, 2002). PECS allows individuals to make requests or demands, choose preferred items, and express feelings by using picture cards. The PECS teaches students to exchange the symbols physically for preferred items and build simple communication sentences through the use of picture cards.

WHAT THE RESEARCH SAYS

Several studies examining the acquisition and impact of PECS found that students were able not only to learn the symbols and use them functionally, but also to replace the use of symbols with spontaneous and imitative speech after an extended period of using the cards (Bondy & Frost, 1994; Charlop-Christy, Carpenter, LeBlanc, & Kellit, 2002; Schwartz, Garfinkle, & Bauer, 1998). The advantages of PECS for supporting communication of individuals with autism are as follows:

- Greater flexibility owing to the nonelectrical nature of the system
- Ability of students with poor manual fine motor skills to make use of the system, compared to nonaided communication such as manual signs
- Ease of implementation and acquisition
- Communication that is meaningful and naturally reinforcing
- The potential for increased speech development and production concurrent with the use of the aided symbols (Mirenda, 2003)

APPLYING THE RESEARCH TO TEACHING

Implementing the PECS begins with teaching the student to exchange a picture for a desired item. Students are taught how to discriminate among the symbols and to build communication "sentences." As students progress with the materials, they are also taught to respond to questions and to comment on situations. With PECS, students do not rely on external prompts; rather, they are taught to initiate communication by using the cards. Typically, the PECS is taught in four to six phases:

- Phase I: Teach students to spontaneously request desired items or activities by exchanging a picture card for the item. Students practice with one card at a time. Immediate reinforcement comes from receiving the item or participating in the activity.
- Phase II: Expand the vocabulary of the student by increasing the number of cards used yet still only using one card at a time.
- Phase III: Teach the student to discriminate among many cards to identify the desired card by placing a number of cards on a board.
- Phase IV: Teach basic sentence structure using sentence strips on a board (e.g., "I want" paired with the picture of the desired item).
- Phases V and VI: Add adjectives and other words to expand communication. This includes adding words such as *four, red, I see, I hear,* and *I feel* (Wallin, 2004).

Although PECS was originally designed for preschoolers, research has shown that it can be effective with adolescents and adults. Teachers can learn to use the system by following the PECS Training Manual (Frost & Bondy, 2002; see PECS Product Ordering Information).

Products related to PECS can be purchased from Pyramid Education Products found on-line at www.pyramidproducts.com/index.html. ■

By Kristin L. Sayeski

or behavioral disorders, and ADHD (see Chapters 5, 7, and 8), authorities recommend that such behaviors be dealt with by using a combination of **functional behavioral assessment (FBA)** and **positive behavioral support (PBS)** to reduce or eliminate these behaviors. FBA involves determining the consequences, antecedents, and setting events that maintain such behaviors (Horner, Albin, Sprague, & Todd, 2000). *Consequences* refer to the purpose the behavior serves for the person. *Antecedents* refer to things that trigger the behavior. *Setting events* take into account the contextual factors in which the behavior occurs. For example, the student might be more likely to exhibit inappropriate behavior toward the end of the day when he or she is more tired.

PBS involves finding ways to support positive behaviors of students rather than punishing negative behaviors. It focuses on the total environment of the student, including instruction.

> ## Casebook Reflection
>
>
>
> Refer to the case *Chase* in your booklet. Chase is receiving his schooling in a center for students with emotional/behavior disorders, not his local public school. Do you think this is the best placement for him (the least restrictive environment)? Do you think he would be more successful in the general education classroom?

Instruction in Natural Settings   Educators of students with autism spectrum disorders are putting increasing emphasis on applying behavioral psychology in natural settings and in natural interactions—the kinds of settings and interactions that nondisabled children enjoy. Researchers are constantly trying to make better instructional use of the natural interactions by which children normally learn language and other social skills. In Success Stories on page 418, read about how a combination of these strategies (direct instruction, behavior management, and instruction in natural settings) has helped Wesley, a six-year-old with autism, to reach his preschool and kindergarten goals.

EDUCATIONAL STRATEGIES FOR TEACHING SOCIAL SKILLS TO STUDENTS WITH ASPERGER SYNDROME

Because the needs of students with autism spectrum disorders are primarily focused on social skills and because these students are likely to be the most integrated into general education classrooms, we discuss strategies that focus on social skill development separately.

Students with Asperger syndrome need explicit instruction in social skills that most students pick up through indirect or incidental learning:

> Students with AS are at a disadvantage because they do not understand the hidden curriculum. As a result, they inadvertently break the rules associated with the hidden curriculum and either get in trouble with adults or are further ostracized or hurt by peers. Instruction and interpretation of hidden curriculum items should be an integral part of the education of children and youth with AS. It is through these types of activities that individuals with this exceptionality can learn to understand and function in the world around them. (Myles & Simpson, 2001, p. 285)

Researchers have shown that at least two types of strategies for teaching social skills have been relatively successful: (1) social interpreting and (2) coaching (Myles, 2003).

Social Interpreting   Because students with Asperger syndrome have so much difficulty in reading social cues, some authorities have recommended the use of social interpreters—"someone who can turn a confusing event into a meaningful interaction through explanation and clarification" (Myles, 2003, p. 28). Researchers and practitioners have devised several techniques to train social interpreting skills. For example, one such technique is SODA (Stop, Observe, Deliberate, and Act) (Bock, 2002). The student is taught to ask himself or herself questions such as the following:

> *Stop:* What is the room arrangement?, What is the activity or routine? . . .
> *Observe:* What are the people doing?, What are people saying?, What is the length
>   of a typical conversation . . .?

Functional behavioral assessment (FBA)
Evaluation that consists of finding out the consequences (what purpose the behavior serves), antecedents (what triggers the behavior), and setting events (contextual factors) that maintain inappropriate behaviors; this information can help teachers plan educationally for students.

Positive behavioral support (PBS)
Systematic use of the science of behavior to find ways of supporting desirable behavior of an individual rather than punishing the undesirable behavior.

Special Educators at Work

Mrs Gilmer, Wesley's mother: "His success has helped us feel more encouraged about his future."

Six-year-old Wesley Gilmer has attended a special elementary school program for students with autism. This year, Wesley will participate in the general education kindergarten with specialized supports.

These are the keys to his success:

- *intensive, explicit instruction in social skills and academics*
- *relentless and structured positive behavioral support*
- *specific interventions for skill acquisition and communication*

Special education coordinator Toni Elitharp glows with pride as Wesley Gilmer takes his place as a student in the general education kindergarten program. Wesley has mastered his preschool goals, and he will continue to receive specially designed instruction as he learns the kindergarten curriculum. Wesley doesn't say much about his experiences, but the smile on his face tells the story. Wesley started preschool at 3 years of age with significant difficulties associated with autism, but he prospered from intensive, relentless, and specific special education.

Intensive, Explicit Instruction in Social Skills and Academics   Mountain View Elementary School serves neighborhood students in preschool through fifth grade. The school also provides specialized programming for children with autism who need intensive attention in classes with a small student–teacher ratio. The faculty and staff at Mountain View are active participants in creating a warm, caring, and cooperative climate for learning. "This school is child-centered," says Elitharp, who finds the key to working with students with autism is understanding their unique characteristics.

Toni Elitharp helps teachers learn to use applied behavior analysis (ABA), an educational model that targets individualized skill acquisition and behavior reduction. The ABA approach for teaching children with autism emphasizes the use of task analysis, discrete teaching, positive reinforcement, behavior intervention, and self-monitoring. "Visual strategies are also necessary to guide the students through the daily plan," says Elitharp. "It's a struggle for children with autism to know the sequence of their day without seeing the sequence in a visually explicit way." Mr. Gilmer says, "Wesley is a visual sponge."

Relentless and Structured Positive Behavioral Support
According to Elitharp, "children with autism live by rules, routine, and the predictability of their environment." She sees Wesley as an example of a child with autism who has thrived on relentless and structured support in coping with unpredictable events.

When he started preschool, Wesley had no parallel play skills or appropriate social skills for his age. "I knew there were some peculiarities," says Mrs. Gilmer, "but he also had some unique talents." Now, as long as Wesley is shown a picture schedule of

Deliberate: What would I like to do? What would I like to say? How will I know when others would like to visit longer . . .?

Act: Approach person(s) with whom I'd like to visit. Say, "Hello, how are you?" Listen to person(s) *and* ask related questions. Look for cues that this person would like to visit longer *or* would like to end this conversation. (Myles, 2003, p. 32)

Another technique with considerable research to back it up is cartooning (see Responsive Instruction on p. 420).

Coaching   Whereas social interpreting focuses on events after they have taken place, coaching involves helping persons with Asperger syndrome to prepare ahead of or during a social interaction. For example, the teacher might do the following:

his day and is made aware of any changes before they occur, he is able to participate in all activities. He now takes pride in his work, interacts with peers and adults, and shows a variety of appropriate emotions.

Wesley started preschool as a developmentally delayed child with autism. His communication skills, social skills, and readiness skills were very limited. Through the use of task analysis for each new skill, a predictable manner of presenting each skill, visual strategies, and consistent positive reinforcement, Wesley was able to make gains and perform above grade level by the end of his preschool career.

Specific Interventions: Skill Acquisition and Communication "ABA helps children learn how to learn," says Elitharp. She shows teachers how to break skills down into smaller units for easier understanding, how to practice the small units with each child, and then how to help the child connect the smaller units to something more meaningful. "The use of physical prompts reinforces correct learning, and then the prompts are gradually reduced until skills are self maintained," she explains.

Elitharp also encourages teachers to use assistive technologies and a variety of communication systems to help children with autism gain the ability to generalize skills. Speech therapy has helped Wesley to develop his expressive vocabulary. "As he developed language, he became a happier little boy," says Mrs. Gilmer. "He is now prompting us to help him learn what he wants to learn."

"When you first learn your child has autism, you want to find out what it means, and it's often discouraging," says Mr. Gilmer. "We tried to find encouraging stories. We had so many questions." Mrs. Gilmer remembers, "We'd set little goals for Wesley, hoping they could be accomplished. They have been accomplished because of the willingness and patience of those who have worked with him." According to Toni Elitharp, Wesley has come far from where he began. "He has worked hard, and he will still have to work hard to progress in a world that is some-times foreign to him." With continued effort and help from educators trained to provide specialized instruction, he should continue to succeed.

CEC'S STANDARDS: PAVING THE WAY TO SUCCESS

Council for Exceptional Children ASSESS YOUR STEPS TO SUCCESS in meeting the CEC Knowledge and Skill Base for All Beginning Special Education Teachers of Students in Individualized General Curriculums and of Students in Individualized Independence Curriculums. Use the following questions to reflect on the growth of your own professional knowledge, skills, and dispositions.

REFLECTING ON YOUR OWN PROFESSIONAL DEVELOPMENT

If you were Wesley's teacher ...

- WHAT are some areas about educating students with autism that you would need to know more about?
- WHAT are some specific skills that would help you to address his academic and behavioral challenges?
- WHAT personal dispositions do you think are most important for you to develop in teaching students with autism?

Using the CEC Standards

- WHAT are some research-supported methods for teaching individuals with autism? (GC4S1)
- DESCRIBE how you might use task analysis in planning instruction for a student with autism. (CC7S5)
- WHAT steps would you take in planning and implementing individualized reinforcement systems and environmental modifications for a student with autism? (IC7S1) ■

By Jean Crockett

- Point out another child who is alone and might want to interact socially. *"Johnny is standing over there by himself. I think he might want someone to play with. Why don't you go over and talk to him."*
- Provide the child with a sentence or topic he can use in a social exchange. *"Ask Susan if she has seen* [a current popular movie]. *If she has, you can say 'What did you like about the movie.' If she says that she hasn't seen the movie, say, "What movies have you seen lately?"* (Myles, 2003, p. 37)

People with Asperger syndrome often have a great deal of difficulty initiating conversations. One recommended strategy is to provide them with "conversation starters"—cards that contain topics that might be of interest to same-age and same-sex peers (Myles, 2003).

Meeting the Needs of Students with Autism Spectrum Disorders

Cartooning to Enhance Social Interactions for Students with Asperger Syndrome

WHAT THE RESEARCH SAYS

Students with Asperger syndrome (AS) have difficulty interpreting and responding to social situations. Frequently, the nuances of language and pace of social interactions leave students with AS frustrated and confused. In 1994, Carol Gray developed cartooning as a way to make abstract communication concrete for students with AS (Glaeser, Pierson, & Fritschmann, 2003). Through the use of symbols and stick figure drawings, the cartoons provide a static display of communication. Teachers, parents, and therapists make use of this freezing of the moment in time to help students gain a sense of control in the conversation. Teachers work with the student to understand the interaction, and the student becomes better prepared to enter a similar situation.

Cartooning has been paired with social stories to further enhance the student's understanding of a particular social situation. Social stories are brief, statement-by-statement overviews of a social situation. For example, in one study, the social situation was lunchtime conversation for a male adolescent student with AS. The resource room teacher working with the student created an eight-sentence social story to highlight the important features of the situation:

> I eat lunch with my friends. Sometimes we talk about the Chiefs. . . . Sometime we talk about things that confuse me and make me feel bad. I will remember to tell my teacher during my visit. After lunch, I need to put my ID cards away in my locker and get my notebook. (Rogers & Myles, 2001, p. 311)

The teacher created two comic strips that connected to the social story and elaborated on it further by highlighting particular incidences that occurred during recent lunches. The comic strips included stick drawings of the students involved with language and thought bubbles related to the interaction. Using the comic strips, the teacher could discuss each person's perspective and how statements could have been interpreted differently. In one situation, a female peer had commented that she thought the student with AS had "a cute butt." The student with AS interpreted this as sexual harassment. The teacher used the thought bubble to provide an alternative explanation: "X is cute. I like him." When given this alternative

explanation, the student suggested other, more appropriate ways in which he could have reacted.

The student enjoyed using the comic strip conversations and asked to use them in other situations. In addition, the intervention appeared to reduce his frustrations at lunch. Data collected by the resource teacher demonstrated significantly fewer redirections at lunch and better on-time arrival to his next class, both of which had been problems before the intervention.

APPLYING THE RESEARCH TO TEACHING

Teachers can employ cartooning with a student once a problematic social situation has been identified. Glaeser and colleagues (2003) created a three-step process for using comic strips to enhance positive student interactions:

- **Step I: Introduce and Model**—Once a situation has presented itself, the teacher and student create a picture of what happened. Glaeser and colleagues use a four-panel template for the cartoon. The teacher guides the student through the process by prompting the student to think of words and thoughts for each person's bubbles.
- **Step II: Symbol Dictionary**—The teacher can create a symbol dictionary to assist the student in remembering and using key symbols such as thought bubbles, speech bubbles, emotion faces (e.g., happy, sad, angry), and settings (e.g., playground, classroom).
- **Step III: Reinforcement of Use**—The final step is to encourage the student to create a cartoon strip each day to highlight an interaction. The interactions can be positive or negative. Teachers can work with the student to interpret the pictures and help the student to identify other's perspectives and motives. The strips can be created in a journal that the student takes home to share with parents and caregivers.

Cartooning can be a positive way to assist students in understanding complex social interactions and support them in identifying age-appropriate solutions or actions to take. By creating a permanent record of an incident, students can evaluate the situation on multiple occasions and with different mentors, such as teachers, parents, and even peers. ■

By Kristin L. Sayeski

SERVICE DELIVERY MODELS

The U.S. Department of Education reports that currently, the most popular placement for students with autism is in a self-contained classroom. About 50 percent of school-age students with autism are in separate classes, about 20 to 25 percent are in general education classrooms, about 15 percent are in resource rooms, about 10 to 15 percent are in separate schools, and about 2 percent are in residential facilities.

Partly because of the emphasis on more natural ways of teaching children with autism spectrum disorders, an increasing percentage of such students are being taught in neighborhood schools and general education classrooms, especially at younger ages. In this model, general educators and special educators work together to meet the individual needs of students with autism. However, there is little research describing how this collaboration should look in the classroom. One promising format might be the Autism Spectrum Disorder Inclusion Collaboration model (Simpson, deBoer-Ott, & Smith-Myles, 2003). See Making It Work on page 422 for more information. Nevertheless, some of the effective instruction of children with autism spectrum disorders requires one-on-one teaching or teaching in very small groups, and this often cannot be done effectively in the regular classroom.

Even when such intensive instruction is offered in specialized settings, state-of-the-art teaching emphasizes the most natural possible human interactions. At the preschool level, teachers are putting emphasis on natural interactions with normal peers in regular classrooms. At the elementary level, educators are including more children with autism spectrum disorders in cooperative learning groups with their nondisabled peers in regular classrooms.

Early Intervention

Most early intervention programming is focused on those with relatively severe degrees of autism spectrum disorders, such as autism, rather than milder degrees, such as Asperger syndrome. This is because Asperger syndrome is usually not diagnosed until the child is beyond the preschool years.

To be most effective, education and related interventions for students with autism must be early, intensive, and highly structured and must involve families. Early, intensive intervention may produce remarkable gains in many young children with autism spectrum disorders, although no intervention yet can claim universal success in enabling these children to overcome their disabilities completely. Education increasingly focuses on using natural interactions to teach students in natural environments, including regular classrooms to the extent possible. The National Research Council (2001) reviewed research and practice and found strong consensus that the following are essential features of effective preschool programs for children with autism spectrum disorders:

- Entry into intervention programs as soon as an autism spectrum diagnosis is seriously considered;
- Active engagement in intensive instructional programming for a minimum of the equivalent of a full school day, 5 days (at least 25 hours) a week, with full year programming varied according to the child's chronological age and developmental level;
- Repeated, planned teaching opportunities generally organized around relatively brief periods of time for the youngest children (e.g., 15–20 minute intervals), including sufficient amounts of adult attention in one-to-one and very small group instruction to meet individualized goals;
- Inclusion of a family component, including parent training;
- Low student/teacher ratios (no more than two young children with autistic spectrum disorders per adult in the classroom); and

UNDERSTANDING THE STANDARDS AND PRINCIPLES Where are most students with autism educated? How should placement decisions be made? *(CEC Knowledge and Skills Standard CC1K6)*

Council for Exceptional Children

MAKING IT WORK

Collaboration and Co-Teaching of Students with Autism Spectrum Disorders

WHAT DOES IT MEAN TO BE A TEACHER OF STUDENTS WITH AUTISM SPECTRUM DISORDERS?

The Council for Exceptional Children does not identify separate knowledge and skills requirements for teachers of students with autism spectrum disorders (ASD). In most cases, a teacher who would work with these students would be certified to teach in the area of emotional/behavioral disorders or in either curriculum area under multicategorical licensure. Though there are no specific guidelines for the preparation of teachers of students with ASD, this is a new and growing area of study, and many universities (and other groups) offer specific training programs. TEACCH is but one example of this type of program. More information about TEACCH can be found at www.teacch.com.

SUCCESSFUL STRATEGIES FOR COLLABORATION

Collaboration strategies for students with ASD are rather new, and few have been tested for effectiveness in the general education classroom. Nevertheless, researchers are working to create models that are effective and support both the general and special educators who are working "by the seat of their pants" at this point. One such model is the Autism Spectrum Disorder Inclusion Collaboration model (Simpson, deBoer-Ott, & Smith-Myles, 2003). According to the authors, this model "emphasizes shared responsibility and shared decision making among general educators, special educators, and support personnel. The model also permits consideration of both learner behaviors and instructional factors" (p. 117). The model includes five main components: (1) environmental and curricular modifications, general education classroom support, and instructional methods; (2) attitudinal and social support; (3) coordinated team commitment; (4) recurrent evaluation of inclusion procedures; and (5) home–school collaboration. The model is not prescriptive in its recommendations for how collaboration should look in the classroom. Rather, it includes specific items related to each component that must be in place for a collaborative model to work. These items include:

Environmental and Curricular Modifications

- Availability of appropriately trained support personnel
- Inservice training
- Implementation of appropriate instructional methods
- Availability of paraeducators
- Adequate teacher planning time
- Reduced class size

Attitudinal and Social Support

- Building principal's positive attitude toward inclusion
- Administrative support for those working to include students with ASD
- Dissemination of information about ASD
- Use of curricula and experiences to facilitate understanding and sensitivity toward students with ASD
- Social interaction training for students with ASD

Coordinated Team Commitment

- Clear definition of roles for service delivery personnel
- Effective communication
- Shared decision making

Recurrent Evaluation of Inclusion Practices

- Evaluating appropriate supplemental aides and services, evidence of benefit from participation and education, evidence of appropriate facilitation of membership, the child's demonstration of appropriate participation

Home-school Collaboration

- Meaningful participation
- Suitable administrative supports
- School willingness to listen

For more on the Autism Spectrum Disorder Inclusion Collaboration Model, see Simpson, de Boer-Ott, and Smith-Myles (2003). ■

By Margaret P. Weiss

- Mechanisms for ongoing program evaluation and assessments of individual children's progress, with results translated into adjustments in programming. (p. 175)

Better understanding of the parental role has led to having parents work together with others as co-therapists in many treatment programs. If early intervention is to be as intensive and pervasive as required, family involvement is essential. Without parental participation in training, children are unlikely to acquire and maintain the communication and daily living skills they need for social development and eventual independence.

Transition to Adulthood

We discuss transition to adulthood for those with more severe forms of autism spectrum disorders, such as autism, separately from the less severe form of Asperger syndrome.

TRANSITION PROGRAMMING FOR PEOPLE WITH AUTISM

Transition programming for people with autism follows virtually the same principles as those for people with mental retardation (see Chapter 5). Transition planning should begin as early as the elementary years and become gradually more intensive in the middle school and secondary years. The current prevailing philosophy is **person-centered planning**, whereby the person with the disability is encouraged to make his or her own decisions. More and more people with autism are being integrated into the community in small **community residential facilities** and in **supported living** settings, such as their own homes or apartments. The goal for work settings is for people with autism to be in **competitive employment** or **supported competitive employment** situations.

TRANSITION PROGRAMMING FOR PEOPLE WITH ASPERGER SYNDROME

As with programming at earlier ages, planning for transition to adulthood for people with Asperger syndrome is largely concerned with issues of social interaction. Research suggests that the social interactions issues for people with Asperger syndrome tend to increase as they reach adolescence and adulthood (Myles & Simpson, 2003). Unfortunately, this increase in difficulties in social interactions works against their achieving success in employment. Research also indicates that when people with Asperger syndrome do experience job difficulties, it usually has something to do with inappropriate social interactions rather than job performance (Gerhardt, 2003).

Many persons with autism are being integrated into the community in small community residential facilities and supported living settings, such as their own homes or apartments.

Person-centered planning
Planning for a person's self-determination; planning activities and services on the basis of a person's dreams, aspirations, interests, preferences, strengths, and capacities.

Community residential facility (CRF)
A place, usually a group home, in an urban or residential neighborhood where about three to ten adults with disabilities live under supervision.

Supported living
An approach to living arrangements for those with disabilities that stresses living in natural settings rather than institutions, big or small.

Competitive employment
A workplace that provides employment that pays at least minimum wage and in which most workers are nondisabled.

Supported competitive employment
A workplace where adults who are disabled earn at least minimum wage and receive ongoing assistance from a specialist or job coach; the majority of workers in the workplace are nondisabled.

UNDERSTANDING THE STANDARDS AND PRINCIPLES What do we know about transition to adulthood for students with autism and Asperger syndrome? *(CEC Knowledge and Skills Standards CC10K2 & CC10S9)*

Council for Exceptional Children

Casebook Reflection

Refer to the case *Chase* in your booklet. According to the case, Chase's behavior began to improve over the year through the behavior program worked out by his teachers. How do you foresee Chase's future involvement in school, community, and work?

One way of approaching deficits in social interaction is to consider a continuum from social survival skills to social competence:

For . . . example, we can examine the job interview process both from the point of view of social competence and social survival. Under ideal circumstances, a degree of social competence would be considered highly desirable during a job interview process (e.g., establish rapport, talk about last night's game, discuss alma maters, etc.). But in the absence of these skills, there is some social survival skills (i.e., establishing eye contact, smiling when greeting the interviewer, avoiding controversial discussion topics) that may be sufficient to highlight one's employability and allow one to gain access to employment. (Gerhardt, 2003, p. 160)

The notion here is that therapists or teachers of people with Asperger syndrome should focus first on social survival skills because they are the minimum necessary for independence. Table 12.4 provides other examples of social skills on the continuum from survival to competence.

In transition programming for people with any kind of disability, it is always important that employers, college instructors, and those in similar positions have a solid understanding of the nature of the disability the individual has. In the case of Asperger syndrome, it is critical that they have this understanding. In many cases, the person with Asperger syndrome may be misunderstood because he or she is intelligent but engages in eccentric behaviors.

It is fair to ask just how much the social eccentricities of people with Asperger syndrome should be tolerated or how much these behaviors actually interfere with the culture of the workplace. Most people would agree that there is room for improvement in society's attitudes toward those who behave differently from the norm but do not bother or harm others. In many cases, it is probably reasonable to ask how much it matters that an individual employee does not fit in socially with the rest of the workforce if he or she gets the job done. The following quote expresses well the tension between changing the

TABLE 12.4 Toward Promoting Skills from Social Survival to Social Competence

Emphasis Less Competence More Survival Necessary: Skills upon which independence may depend	Preferred: Skills that support independence but may not be critical	Emphasis Greater Competence Less Survival Marginal: Skills that, while valuable, may be negotiable
Riding mass transit Wait until others get off before you get on	Whenever possible, choose a seat where you are not sitting next to someone	Whenever possible, put a row between you and other passengers
Lunch with coworkers Eat neatly	Respond to interactions from coworkers	Initiate conversations with coworkers
Job interview Eye contact	Ask informed questions about the employer	Comment on items in the office that may be relevant (e.g., is the person someone who likes to fish?)

Source: Gerhardt, P. F. (2003). Transition support for learners with Asperger syndrome: Toward a successful adulthood. In R. W. Du Charme & T. P. Gullotta (Eds.), *Asperger syndrome: A guide for professionals and families* (pp. 157–171). New York: Kluwer Academic/Plenum Publishing (p. 161).

individual with Asperger syndrome and changing society's reaction to people with the condition:

> A sentiment often expressed at the Douglass Group, a support group for adults with AS [Asperger syndrome] that I founded a number of years ago was "If you NTs [neurotypicals—a term coined by those with Asperger syndrome to describe those who do not have neurological disabilities] have all the skills, why don't you adapt for a while?" The perceived professional proclivity to focus solely on somehow "changing" the person with AS was often discussed as similar to expecting a person who is blind to see if only he or she would try harder. Given that, group members instead argued that while the primary focus of intervention should remain on the provision of skills to the learner with AS, the focus should be expanded to include comprehensive community education. (Gerhardt, 2003, p. 158)

Many people with Asperger syndrome, in fact, are becoming advocates for themselves and others who have their condition. For example, numerous websites, created by individuals with Asperger syndrome, offer information and support (see Personal Perspectives below).

THE FOLLOWING website has resources specifically for college students with Asperger syndrome: **www.users.dircon. co.uk/~cns/**.

Personal Perspectives

YOUTH USES WEB TO HELP OTHERS ON "WRONG PLANET"

PEOPLE who suffer from Asperger syndrome often feel like they're on the "wrong planet" and don't fit in. One area teen, however, is trying to ensure they don't feel quite so out of this world. Alex Planck, an 18-year-old rising senior at Charlottesville High School, is the cofounder of a new website for people with Asperger syndrome. . . .

The site, www.wrongplanet.net, was launched last month but already has close to 300 members. It features a chat room, member profiles, articles about Asperger's, personal Web logs, or "blogs," and an online store selling everything from shirts to mouse pads. . . .

"There were other Web sites . . . but they were kind of elitist," he said. His site fosters a sense of community and helps people fit in with society.

"They also didn't have as many features as our site," Planck added.

Creating and maintaining the site has been exciting for Planck. The site has received visits from such far off places as New Zealand, Australia, Denmark, and the Seychelles, a group of islands in the Indian Ocean. . . .

Alex Planck

Although Planck says his greatest passion is learning new things, he confesses that computers are among his most enduring interests.

"It's easy to become obsessed with them because there's so much about them," he explained. Planck's partner in founding the site, Dan Grover, is a 15-year-old from Vermont who has already launched Wonderwarp, his own software group. Planck recently joined the group as a programmer.

Planck's mother, Mary, is a teacher . . . and his father, Doug, . . . is a lawyer.

"I think [the site] is such a neat resource. It's so hard to imagine what these kids deal with," his mother said.

Aside from computers and learning, the teen is also an enthusiastic mountain biker. He's hoping to attend the University of Virginia next year.

"When he wants to do something and he's focused on it, he's amazing," Mary Planck said, "We're proud of him." ■

Source: Cannon, J. (2004, July 22). Youth uses Web to help others on 'wrong planet.' *The Daily Progress*, Charlottesville, VA, p. 00.

SUMMARY

WHAT is the history behind autism spectrum disorders?

- In 1943, Leo Kanner reported on cases of children, whom he labeled as "autistic," who had major problems in communication and social interactions, as well as bizarre repetitive movements and an obsessive dislike of change.
- In 1944, Hans Asperger reported on cases of children, whom he referred to as having autistic psychopathy, who he thought had normal intelligence and language but who were socially isolated and had obsessive interests in extraordinarily narrow areas.

HOW do professionals define autism spectrum disorders?

- Five similar disorders, all of which involve problems with communication skills, social interactions, and repetitive and stereotyped patterns of behavior, are autism, Asperger syndrome, Rett syndrome, childhood disintegrative disorder, and pervasive developmental disorder not otherwise specified.
  - Autism is characterized by severe deficits in communication, social interaction, and cognitive functioning and often involves repetitive, stereotyped movements, resistance to change, and unusual sensory perceptions.
  - People who have Asperger syndrome have higher cognitive and language skills than those with classic autism, but they have problems in the other areas of ASD, especially social interaction.

WHAT is the prevalence of autism spectrum disorders?

- Prevalence estimates vary for each of the disorders in autism spectrum disorders (ASD); the best estimates we have are as follows: ASD (60 per 10,000), autism (8 to 30 per 10,000), Asperger syndrome (36 to 48 per 10,000), Rett's disorder (1 per 10,000 to 15,000), childhood disintegrative disorder (1 per 50,000).
- With the exception of Rett syndrome, which occurs primarily in females, males outnumber females 3:1 or 4:1 in ASD.
- Prevalence figures have risen dramatically for autism in the past 30 to 40 years, leading some to declare an autism "epidemic" and to claim that there must be some mysterious toxin in our environment or that the measles, mumps, rubella (MMR) vaccination may be a cause; the best scientific evidence indicates that:

- The MMR vaccination does not cause autism.
- The increase in autism is due to a widening of the criteria for identification as autistic and a greater awareness of ASD.

WHAT causes autism spectrum disorders?

- Early causal theories were influenced by psychoanalytic thinking and blamed parents, often mothers, for causing autism by being too cold and unresponsive.
- Today's causal theories point to a neurological and hereditary basis of autism.
  - Several areas of the brain are implicated, such as the cerebral cortex, basal ganglia, amygdala, hippocampus, corpus callosum, brain stem, and cerebellum.
  - Recent research suggests that excessive brain growth in the first two years of life might be a factor.
  - Evidence indicates that there is probably no single neurological or hereditary cause for all cases of autism.

WHAT methods of assessment are used to identify individuals with autism spectrum disorders?

- There is no universally used diagnostic test for ASD.
- For autism, the clinician uses criteria that focus on communication skills, social interactions, and repetitive and stereotyped patterns of behavior.
- For Asperger syndrome, the clinician looks for normal or close to normal communication abilities but problems in social interactions and repetitive and stereotyped patterns of behavior, but to a lesser extent than in classic autism.

WHAT are some of the psychological and behavioral characteristics of learners with autism spectrum disorders?

- People with autism have deficits in communication, social interaction, and cognition, as well as repetitive and stereotyped patterns of behavior, and some have abnormal sensory perceptions.
  - Most lack communicative intent, the desire to communicate socially.
  - They have cognitive deficits similar to those of people with mental retardation; some have additional peculiarities, such as processing things visually and spatially rather than conceptually or linguistically.
  - Some, who are called autistic savants, have extraordinary splinter skills.

- Examples of abnormal sensory perceptions are being hyperresponsive and/or hyporesponsive to stimuli.
- Compared to people with autism, those with Asperger syndrome often display a milder degree of impairments or abnormalities in social interaction, communication, repetitive and stereotyped patterns of behavior, cognitive processing, and sensory perceptions.
  - Their main problems are in social interactions, with difficulties in understanding the hidden curriculum (the dos and don'ts of everyday living) and taking things too literally.
  - Their main problems in communication are in pragmatics, the social uses of verbal and nonverbal communication skills.
- Three theories have been proposed to account for many deficits in ASD. No one of them explains all the deficits of all the disorders, but together they begin to build a composite picture of ASD.
  - Problems with executive functions include such things as working memory, self-regulation of emotions, and the ability to plan ahead.
  - Problems with central coherence involve paying too much attention to details or parts in cognitive processing, thereby leading to impairments in conceptualizing coherent wholes.
  - Problems with a theory of mind lead to impairments in taking another person's perspective, or being able to "read" what they might be thinking.

WHAT are some educational considerations for learners with autism spectrum disorders?

- The greatest area of needed instruction is in communication skills for those with autism and in social skills for those with Asperger syndrome.

- Educational programming for students with ASD should include (1) direct instruction of skills, (2) behavior management using functional behavioral assessment and positive behavioral support, and (3) instruction in natural settings.
- Students with Asperger syndrome need explicit instruction in social skills; two general strategies for teaching such skills are social interpreting and coaching.

WHAT are some things to consider with respect to early intervention for learners with autism spectrum disorders?

- The most effective early intervention programs are intensive, are highly structured, and involve families.
- Early intervention programs often use natural interactions to teach students in natural environments, including regular classrooms to the extent possible.

WHAT are some things to consider with respect to transition to adulthood for learners with autism spectrum disorders?

- For those with autism, the emphasis is on person-centered planning, with living arrangements in community residential facilities or supported living settings and placement in competitive employment or supported competitive employment situations.
- For those with Asperger syndrome, the focus is often on improving social interactions both in employment and in postsecondary school settings.

APPLYING THE STANDARDS AND PRINCIPLES

- **HOW** easy or difficult is it to **identify autism?** *(CEC Content Standards #1, #2, & #8; INTASC Principles #1, #2, & #8)*
- **WHAT** should teachers know about the **psychological and behavioral characteristics** of students with autism and Asperger syndrome? *(CEC Content Standard #3)*
- **HOW** should teachers determine what **instructional methods** to use with students with autism spectrum

disorders? *(CEC Content Standards #4 & #5; INTASC Principles #4 & #5)*

- **HOW** would you **respond to parents** who approached you expressing concern about the future of their high school student with autism? *(CEC Content Standard #10 & INTASC Principle #10)*

Council for Exceptional Children

INTASC

Chapter 13

Learners with Low-Incidence, Multiple, and Severe Disabilities

ccidents divide things into the great Before and After.

"Even before his brain injury, Alan had a hard time remembering names," I'll say. "Since Daddy's accident, I have to work more," I tell our daughter, Kelly. The brain injury community marks time by asking how long someone has been "out of" injury, the same way bereavement counselors ask how long your loved one has been dead.

Out of what, exactly?

Out of the giant crevice that has been exploded into the bedrock of your life.

Here's how I see it: One day, you and your family are hiking across a long, solid plain, when out of the sky comes a blazing meteor that just happens to hit one family member on the head. The meteor creates a huge rift in the landscape, dragging the unlucky one down to the bottom of the crevice it has made. You spend the next year on a rescue mission, helping him climb to the top, but when he gets up there, you realize that he has been greatly changed by the hardship. He doesn't know a meteor has hit him. He will never know, really. He only knows that he has spent a lot of time in a dark, confusing place. He left a lot of stuff behind, the stuff he was carrying with him, down in the big hole, and it's impossible to get it all back.

CATHY CRIMMINS
Where Is the Mango Princess?

QUESTIONS TO GUIDE YOUR READING OF THIS CHAPTER . . .

- WHAT is the definition of low-incidence, multiple, and severe disabilities, and what is their prevalence?

- WHAT is traumatic brain injury, and how might it affect education?

- HOW is deaf-blindness defined, and what are the special educational problems it entails?

- WHAT considerations apply to many students with low-incidence, multiple, and severe disabilities?

Standards and Principles in this Chapter

SPECIAL EDUCATORS . . .

- **understand the field** as an evolving and changing discipline (*from CEC Content Standard #1*).

- **understand the similarities and differences in human development** and the characteristics between and among individuals with and without exceptional learning needs (*from CEC Content Standard #2*).

- **possess a repertoire** of evidence-based instructional strategies (*from CEC Content Standard #4*).

- **create learning environments** for individuals with exceptional learning needs that **foster cultural understanding,** safety and emotional well-being, positive social interactions, and active engagement of individuals with exceptional learning needs (*from CEC Content Standard #5*).

- **are familiar with technologies** to support and enhance communication of individuals with exceptional needs (*from CEC Content Standard #6*).

- develop a variety of **individualized transition plans** (*from CEC Content Standard #7*).

ALL TEACHERS . . .

- **understand the central concepts, tools of inquiry, structures of the discipline(s) they teach** and can create learning experiences that make these aspects of subject matter meaningful (*INTASC Principle #1*).

- **understand how children learn and develop** and can provide learning opportunities that support the intellectual, social and personal development of each learner (*INTASC Principle #2*).

- **understand and use a variety of instructional strategies** to encourage students' development of critical thinking, problem solving, and performance skills (*INTASC Principle #4*).

- **create a learning environment** that encourages positive social interaction, active engagement in learning, and self-motivation (*INTASC Principle #10*).

Council for Exceptional Children

INTASC

he definition of any category of exceptionality is controversial. Severe and multiple disabilities are no exception. Disabilities of every type are difficult to understand. The causes, meanings, and life course associated with disabilities are often unknown. People may be even more mystified by disabilities that are severe or profound. The definition of every category of exceptionality is controversial. Low-incidence, severe, and multiple disabilities are no exception.

Definition and Prevalence

The Association for Persons with Severe Handicaps (TASH) uses the following definition of severe disabilities:

> individuals of all ages who require extensive ongoing support in more than one major life activity in order to participate in integrated community settings and to enjoy a quality of life that is available to citizens with fewer or no disabilities. Support may be required for life activities such as mobility, communication, self-care, and learning as necessary for independent living, employment, and self-sufficiency (as quoted in Brown & Snell, 2000, p. 71).

People with a severe disability in any area typically have more than one disability. Furthermore, a combination of mild disabilities may present severe educational problems, as noted in the Individuals with Disabilities Education Act (IDEA): "Multiple disabilities means concomitant impairments . . . the combination of which causes such severe educational problems that they cannot be accommodated in special education programs solely for one of the impairments" [34 CFR, Sec. 300 (b)(6)]. IDEA also includes language stating that

> The term "children with severe disabilities" refers to children with disabilities who, because of the intensity of their physical, mental, or emotional problems, need highly specialized education, social, psychological, and medical services in order to maximize their full potential for useful and meaningful participation in society and for self-fulfillment. The term includes those children with severe emotional disturbance (including schizophrenia), autism, severe and profound mental retardation, and those who have two or more serious disabilities, such as deaf-blindness, mental retardation and blindness, and cerebral palsy and deafness. Children with severe disabilities may experience severe speech, language, and/or perceptual-cognitive deprivations, and evidence abnormal behaviors, such as failure to respond to pronounced social

MISCONCEPTIONS ABOUT
Learners with Low-Incidence, Multiple, and Severe Disabilities

MYTH People with severe and multiple disabilities have problems so severe that the best they can hope for is employment in a sheltered workshop.

FACT With intensive and extensive instruction, many people with severe and multiple disabilities are now able to be employed in more integrated work settings.

MYTH People with severe and multiple disabilities have problems so severe that the best they can hope for is to live under close supervision in a large residential facility.

FACT With intensive and extensive instruction, many people with severe and multiple disabilities are now able to live independently or semi-independently by themselves or in a small community residential facility (CRF).

MYTH A person with traumatic brain injury (TBI) can be expected, with time, to recover completely and function without disabilities.

FACT Some people with TBI do recover completely, but many do not. Usually, a person with TBI has long-term disabilities that may be compensated for in many ways, but these disabilities do not ordinarily disappear completely, even with the best treatment and rehabilitation.

MYTH For students with Usher syndrome whose vision will deteriorate over time, it is best not to introduce braille and training with the long cane while their vision is still relatively good because to do so stigmatizes them.

FACT Braille and orientation and mobility training should not wait until the later stages of vision loss. Getting a head start on learning these complex skills almost always outweighs any stigmatization that might occur.

MYTH Someone who cannot speak will have extreme difficulty making himself or herself understood to others.

FACT With an appropriate augmentative or alternative communication (AAC) system, a person who cannot speak will be able to carry on a normal conversation, sometimes very near the rate at which nondisabled speakers talk. The flexibility, speed, and usefulness in communication of AAC are increasing rapidly with new technologies, and they now often allow a user to approximate the typical verbal exchanges between speakers.

MYTH The only really effective way of controlling the undersirable behavior of people with severe and multiple disabilities is to use punishment.

FACT Functional behavioral assessment and positive behavioral supports are finding more and more ways of replacing undesirable with desirable behavior without the use of punishment. Often, the key is finding out what the person with severe and multiple disabilities is trying to communicate and helping them find a more effective, efficient way of communicating that to others.

MYTH Braille is only for people who are blind.

FACT It is helpful to teach braille to two groups of individuals who are not blind: (1) those who have visual impairments so severe that they cannot read print reliably and (2) those whose condition will worsen with time to the point at which braille will be their only option.

Case book Reflection

Refer to the case, *Who Will Help Patrick?* in your booklet. We are not told much about Patrick's early development except that his mother was a substance abuser. Nevertheless, in what ways does he demonstrate that he has multiple and severe disabilities?

MORE INFORMATION about TBI may be found at the Brain Injury Association of America: **www.biausa.org**

Traumatic brain injury (TBI)

Injury to the brain (not including conditions present at birth, birth trauma, or degenerative diseases or conditions) resulting in total or partial disability or psychosocial maladjustment that affects educational performance; may affect cognition, language, memory, attention, reasoning, abstract thinking, judgment, problem solving, sensory or perceptual and motor disabilities, psychosocial behavior, physical functions, information processing, or speech.

Open head injury

A brain injury in which there is an open wound in the head, such as a gunshot wound or penetration of the head by an object, resulting in damage to brain tissue.

Closed head injury

Damage to the brain that occurs without penetration of the skull; might be caused by a blow to the head or violent shaking by an adult.

stimuli, self-mutilation, self-stimulation, manifestation of intense and prolonged temper tantrums, and the absence of rudimentary forms of verbal control, and may also have intensely fragile physiological conditions. [34 CFR, Sec. 315.4(d)]

Low-incidence, severe, and multiple disabilities are often linked conceptually. They occur in only a relatively small percentage of cases of disability. Furthermore, nearly any low-incidence, severe disability will involve extensive and ongoing support in more than one major life activity. That is, low-incidence, severe, and multiple disabilities tend to go together. True, one can find a severe disability that involves a single life activity (e.g., profound deafness that involves only manual-visual rather than vocal-aural communication) or multiple disabilities, none of which is severe (e.g., relatively mild orthopedic impairment, mild visual impairment, and mild mental retardation). All of the low-incidence, severe, and multiple disabilities that we discuss in the chapter probably affect fewer than 1 percent of the population.

With these considerations in mind, in this chapter, we discuss the categories and problems of traumatic brain injury and deaf-blindness. Then we discuss issues that apply to all categories of low-incidence, multiple, and severe disabilities: augmentative and alternative communication, behavior problems, early intervention, and transition to adulthood.

We discussed severe and profound mental retardation in Chapter 5 and autistic spectrum disorders in Chapter 12. However, much of what we present in this chapter applies to some individuals with autism and to those with severe or profound mental retardation as well. Remember, though, that autistic spectrum disorders can range from mild to severe, as is the case in all other categories of disability.

Traumatic Brain Injury

In Chapter 1, we noted that in 1990 the IDEA created the category of **traumatic brain injury (TBI)**, under which students may be found eligible for special education and related services. Today, there is much greater understanding of the nature of TBI and the educational needs of students who acquire it (Ashley, 2004). Unlike cerebral palsy, TBI is brain damage that is acquired by trauma after a period of normal neurological development. As the passage quoted on page 429 suggests, TBI is a life altering experience. It presents unique educational problems that often have been poorly understood and mismanaged. Recent medical advances have greatly improved diagnosis and treatment.

Definition and Characteristics

Commonly accepted definitions of TBI specify the following:

1. There is injury to the brain caused by an external force.
2. The injury is not caused by a degenerative or congenital condition.
3. There is a diminished or altered state of consciousness.
4. Neurological or neurobehavioral dysfunction results from the injury.

Most definitions also specify that the injury is followed by impairments in abilities required for school learning and everyday functioning.

TBI can result from two categories of injury: open or closed. **Open head injuries** involve a penetrating head wound, from such causes as a fall, gunshot, assault, vehicular accident, or surgery. In **closed head injuries**, there is no open head wound but brain damage is caused by internal compression, stretching, or other shearing motion of neural tissues within the head (Adelson & Kochanek, 1998).

The educational definition of TBI focuses on impairments in one or more areas important for learning. The federal (IDEA) definition of TBI states that it is

> an acquired injury to the brain caused by an external physical force, resulting in total or partial functional disability or psychosocial impairment, or both, that adversely affects a child's educational performance. The term applies to open or closed head injuries resulting in impairments in one or more areas, such as cognition; language; memory; attention; reasoning; abstract thinking; judgment; problem-solving; sensory, perceptual, and motor abilities; psychosocial behavior; physical functions; information processing; and speech. The term does not apply to injuries that are congenital or degenerative, or brain injuries induced by birth trauma. [34 CFR, Sec. 300.7(6)(12)]

The various consequences of TBI create a need for special education; the injury itself is a medical problem. The effects of TBI may range from very mild to profound and may be temporary or permanent. Often, the effects are immediate, and these immediate effects set TBI apart from most other disabilities—the child or youth is literally changed overnight (Council for Exceptional Children, 2001). The sudden change presents particular difficulties to families and teachers, not to mention the individual sustaining the injury (Ashley, 2004; Dell Orto & Power, 2000). However, sometimes the effects of TBI are not seen immediately after the injury but appear months or even years afterward.

The possible effects of TBI include a long list of learning and psychosocial problems, such as the following:

Justin Greenwood, who suffered a brain injury during a football game, works on his short-term memory during a therapy session.

- Problems remembering things
- Problems learning new information
- Speech and/or language problems
- Difficulty sequencing things
- Difficulty in processing information (making sense of things)
- Extremely uneven abilities or performance (able to do some things but not others)
- Extremely uneven progress (quick gains sometimes, no gains other times)
- Inappropriate manners or mannerisms
- Failure to understand humor or social situations
- Becoming easily tired, frustrated, or angered
- Unreasonable fear or anxiety
- Irritability
- Sudden, exaggerated swings of mood
- Depression
- Aggression
- Perseveration (persistent repetition of one thought or behavior)

One of the great difficulties with TBI is that it is often "invisible." Like a learning disability, it is not something that one necessarily notices about a person at first. True, in some

UNDERSTANDING THE STANDARDS AND PRINCIPLES   Explain the federal (IDEA) definition of TBI in your own words. *(CEC Knowledge and Skills Standard IC1K1)*

Council for Exceptional Children

cases, a person with TBI has paralysis, slurred speech, or some other indicator of brain damage that is quickly apparent. But in many cases, the person with TBI looks just like everyone else. In Personal Perspectives on page 435, Cathy Crimmins describes one aspective of life following the TBI of her husband, Alan, who acquired his brain injury in a speedboat accident in 1996. (Bill is Alan's counselor from the Office of Vocational Rehabilitation.) Crimmins's book vividly illustrates not only the sudden change in abilities and behavior with which individuals and families must cope, but also the hidden nature of TBI.

Prevalence

The exact prevalence of TBI is difficult to determine, but we do know that TBI occurs at an alarming rate among children and youths. Estimates are that each year about 0.5 percent of school-age children acquire a brain injury. By the time they graduate from high school, nearly 4 percent of students may have TBI. Of about a million children and adolescents who receive head injuries each year, roughly 15,000 to 20,000 will experience lasting effects (Council for Exceptional Children, 2001).

Males are more prone to TBI than females are, and the age range in which TBI is most likely to occur for both males and females is late adolescence and early adulthood (Christensen, 1996). The Council for Exceptional Children (2001) refers to TBI as a "silent epidemic." It is considered an epidemic because of its increasing prevalence; it is "silent" because many serious head injuries are unreported and many cases of TBI go undetected or are mistaken for other disabilities. The prevalence of TBI is disconcerting because so many of the causes of TBI are entirely preventable or avoidable by following ordinary safety precautions (see Christensen, 1996).

The prevalence of TBI is disconcerting because so many of the causes of TBI are entirely preventable or avoidable by following ordinary safety precautions, such as properly securing infants and children in car safety seats.

Personal Perspectives

TBI: OFTEN A HIDDEN DISABILITY

YESTERDAY Bill and Alan met with Al's employers at the First Union Bank. All systems seem go for a return to work part-time some time in January, and at this point the folks at the bank say they understand Alan's limitations. Part of Bill's job is to act as an advocate and explain brain injury to Al's bosses and coworkers. He will also go to work with Al every day, functioning as a job coach. The biggest accommodation the bank will have to make is to allow Alan to work part-time, at the beginning only twelve hours a week. Alan looks just fine—that's why TBI is often dubbed "the hidden disability"—but everyone must understand why he has to take it slow. The hardest concept to get across is that brain injury is a *physical* condition. "If Al were in a wheelchair or had a cast on his leg, people would understand that something happened," says Crystal Mangir. "But no one can see a broken brain." ■

Source: Crimmins, C. (2000). *Where is the mango princess?* (p. 199). New York: Knopf.

Causes

Under age five, accidental falls are the dominant cause of TBI, with vehicular accidents and child abuse causing substantial injuries as well. After age five, and increasingly through adolescence, vehicular accidents (including accidents involving pedestrians, bicycles, motorcycles, and cars) account for the majority of TBI; assaults and gunshot wounds are increasingly prevalent among youths at older ages. Closed head injuries may be caused by a variety of events besides vehicular accidents, including a fall or abuse such as violent shaking of a child by an adult.

Educational Considerations

The educational implications of TBI can be extremely varied, depending on the nature and severity of the injury and the age and abilities of the individual at the time of injury. A significant issue in educating someone who has experienced TBI is helping family members, teachers, and peers to respond appropriately to the sudden and sometimes dramatic changes that may occur in the student's academic abilities, appearance, behavior, and emotional states (Dell Orto & Power, 2000). Both general and special education teachers need training about TBI and its ramifications if students are to be reintegrated successfully into the schools and classrooms they attended before the injury (DePompei & Tyler, 2004; Tyler & Mira, 1999).

The following characteristics are essential features of appropriate education for students with TBI:

1. Transition from a hospital or rehabilitation center to the school
2. A team approach involving regular and special educators, other special teachers, guidance counselor, administrators, and the student's family
3. An individualized education program (IEP) concerned with cognitive, social/behavioral, and sensorimotor domains
4. Educational procedures to help students solve problems in focusing and sustaining attention for long periods, remembering previously learned facts and skills, learning new things, dealing with fatigue, and engaging in appropriate social behavior

MAKING IT WORK

Collaboration and Co-Teaching of Students with Low-Incidence, Multiple, and Severe Disabilities

"We may have different goals for students. How can we solve that problem?"

SUCCESSFUL STRATEGIES FOR COLLABORATION

Students with severe disabilities often require a wide range of services at school. Many professionals, including teachers, nurses, and aides, must collaborate to provide those services. With so many people involved in a student's education, problems are likely to arise and everyone should be ready to engage in collaborative problem solving.

Partners in collaborative settings should develop a plan to attack problems before they arise. Problems can be related to the student's response to settings and personnel, the student's environment, differences in professional goals, and discrepancies in professional philosophies. Though the causes might be different, a similar step-by-step process can be used to address each one. Mostert (1998) describes the following steps for successful problem solving:

1. *Is there a problem to solve?* This step involves reflection on these questions: Is there really a problem here? Who owns it? Is the problem solvable?

2. *What is the problem?* Once a problem has been identified, participants define it in specific, objective terms. Statements such as "I don't like her attitude" must be refined to describe the situation specifically; "Sofia makes inappropriate comments about other students when I ask her a question in class." After the problem is defined, partners gather data on the frequency, duration, and degree of the problem in a variety of environments.

3. *How can the problem be solved?* All participants generate solutions to the problem. This is the brainstorming step, so all suggestions should be welcomed.

4. *Which solution or combination is best?* Personnel working together must be able to discuss the solutions presented

5. Emphasis on the cognitive processes through which academic skills are learned, not just curriculum content
6. Plans for addressing long-term needs in addition to immediate and annual IEP goals (see DePompei & Tyler, 2004; Savage, 1988; Tyler & Mira, 1999)

TBI is a special case of neurological impairment (which we discuss further in the next chapter), in which there is a sudden alteration in abilities; this can often cause frustration for the student and teachers who must cope with this loss. The student must undergo medical treatment to address the biophysical aspects of the injury, and it is critical that educators understand the implications of the injury for structuring the student's psychological and social environments in school (Bigge, Best, & Heller, 2001; Dell Orto & Power, 2000; Tyler & Mira, 1999).

The teacher must focus on helping the student with TBI to recover cognitive abilities, because these are most critical to academic and social progress. The abilities to remember and to make sense of academic information and social circumstances are key to the student's long-term success. The teacher must help the student learn to use coping mechanisms and alternative strategies, such as using a tape recorder, a planner, or other organizational devices and memory aids for whatever abilities cannot be recovered. TBI also presents particular challenges to teachers in areas of assessment and educational planning. As the Council for Exceptional Children has noted,

the educational needs of the child with TBI will change quickly after the injury. Therefore, the child's IEP goals and objectives must be developed initially for achievement over short periods of time, 4–6 weeks, rather than six months to a year as is traditionally done. Likewise, the child may need more frequent assessments than other children with disabilities. (2001, p. 15)

and evaluate them without emotional attachment. Interventions for students should be judged as to whether there is evidence of previous success (research-based, not anecdotal), whether there are appropriate supports and resources, whether the participants can and will fully implement it, and whether the intervention is truly appropriate for the student. Solutions that do not fit these criteria should be abandoned.

5. *Which solution should we select?* After evaluating all solutions, the partners choose the one to implement.

6. *How will we implement the solution?* This step requires delegating responsibilities for the solution to members of the team. It means specifically stating what the team hopes will happen, setting up how the partners will know if the solution worked, and scheduling a time to reconvene to share data.

7. *Did it work?* This step requires data collection again. Partners must be able to present information as to whether the solution achieved its goals. If not, it is time to start the process again. If the solution worked, the team can move on to another problem!

Problem solving with other professionals requires that participants develop an environment with open communication, overcoming barriers by using effective communication skills. According to Walther-Thomas, Korinek, McLaughlin, and Williams (2000), these skills include the following:

1. *Listening.* Attending to the speaker, paraphrasing content, reflecting feelings, and summarizing.
2. *Repetition.* Sending the same message to partners repeatedly and through different channels.
3. *Empathy.* Making predictions about how a partner will respond to a message you send.
4. *Understanding.* Making sure that the language you use is clear and concise.

When collaborating with other professionals and even with students, there is no way to avoid problems. But to avoid conflict, partners should discuss and set up problem-solving strategies *before* these situations occur. Problem-solving strategies, along with effective communication skills, will help collaborators to provide continuous, appropriate services to students. ∎

By Margaret P. Weiss

A major problem in reentry to school after TBI—at least if the consequences are serious—is that the student tends to see himself or herself as not having changed, whereas peers and teachers are likely to notice that the student with TBI is not the same. Dell Orto and Power (2000) note that our societal emphasis on productiveness, organization, independence, and achievement can contribute to negative attitudes toward a student with TBI. "Academic deficits displayed by survivors of TBI conflict with achievement values, not only causing discomfort in teachers, but frustration and perhaps a sense of rejection in the young person" (p. 22). Many teachers apparently do not want students with TBI in their classrooms, probably because these students exhibit characteristics that teachers find troublesome (just consider the bulleted list on p. 433). Thus, a student's returning to school after TBI is a major issue that typically requires a team approach involving a variety of professionals, as we mentioned in our list of essential features of appropriate educational programs. Collaboration and problem solving by this team are essential to the success of the student's reentry. See Making It Work above for more on team problem solving.

The assessment of a student's academic and social skills following TBI is tricky because it is often difficult or impossible to separate physiological causes or reasons for difficulty with a task from other causes. More important than knowing precisely what difficulties have a physiological cause is pinpointing just what the student's academic and social learning difficulties are. Here again, a team approach is essential. Neurologists can often provide information about the consequences of TBI that helps teachers to set reasonable expectations and teach coping skills that help the student to compensate for abilities that will not return.

LANGUAGE DISORDERS

A student with TBI might acquire a language disorder after a period of normal development, or the student might acquire a more severe language disorder than existed before the injury (see Chapter 9). Individuals with TBI are a very diverse population, although a disproportionate number of students with TBI have a pretrauma history of learning problems or delayed speech and language (Beukelman & Mirenda, 1998; McDonald, Togher, & Code, 1999a, 1999b).

Motor-speech disorder
Loss or impairment of the ability to understand or formulate language because of accident or illness.

Language or speech disorders are the greatest complicating factor in most students' return to school following TBI. A loss of ability to understand and formulate language due to brain injury is sometimes referred to as a **motor-speech disorder**, which we discussed in Chapter 9. The student may have trouble finding or saying words or constructing sentences that are appropriate for the topic of conversation or social context. Problems like these are a source of frustration, anger, and confusion for some students with TBI.

The language problems that are acquired with TBI are primarily related to the cognitive and social demands of communication. The student might have problems with tasks that demand responding quickly, organizing, dealing with abstractions, sustaining attention (especially if there are distractions), learning new skills, responding appropriately in social situations, and showing appropriate affect. In fact, TBI can potentially disrupt all aspects of the give-and-take of social interaction that are required for effective communication.

The effects of TBI on language are extremely variable, and careful assessment of the given individual's abilities and disabilities is critically important. Interventions may range from making special accommodations, such as allowing more response time or keeping distractions to a minimum, to focusing on instruction in the social uses of language.

Depending on the site and degree of brain damage, a person with TBI may have motor control problems that interfere with communication, including the cognitive and social aspects of communication. Some students with TBI cannot communicate orally using the muscles of speech and must rely on alternative or augmentative communication systems, which we describe later in the chapter.

SOCIAL AND EMOTIONAL PROBLEMS

Brain injury may be accompanied by a variety of serious social and emotional effects. We know that TBI can cause violent aggression, hyperactivity, impulsivity, inattention, and a wide range of other emotional or behavioral problems, depending on just what parts of the brain are damaged. The possible effects of TBI include a long list of other psychosocial problems, some of which we listed previously as general characteristics (see Dell Orto & Power, 2000; Light et al., 1998; Tyler & Mira, 1999):

Behavior modification
Systematic control of environmental events, especially of consequences, to produce specific changes in observable responses. May include reinforcement, punishment, modeling, self-instruction, desensitization, guided practice, or any other technique for strengthening or eliminating a particular response.

The emotional and behavioral effects of TBI are determined by more than the physical damage. These effects also depend on the student's age at the time of injury and the social environment before and after the injury occurs. Home, community, or school environments that foster misbehavior of any child or youth are known to be associated with increased risk for acquiring TBI. Such environments are extremely likely to worsen any emotional or behavioral problem resulting from TBI. Creating an environment that is conducive to and supportive of appropriate behavior is one of the great challenges of dealing effectively with the results of brain injury.

Behavior management
Strategies and techniques used to increase desirable behavior and decrease undesirable behavior. May be applied in the classroom, home, or other environment.

Many of the typical **behavior modification** or **behavior management** strategies that are used with other students who have emotional or behavioral difficulties are appropriate for use with students who have TBI. Consistency, predictability, and reinforcement (praise, encouragement, and other rewards) are particularly important (Persel & Persel, 2004), as is developing rapport with the student. Developing a good personal relationship with a student with TBI can be particularly challenging, as such students can be unpredictable, irritable, and angry at those who are trying to help (see Kauffman, Mostert, Trent, & Pullen, 2006; Tyler & Mira, 1999).

TBI often shatters an individual's sense of self. Recovering one's identity can require a long period of rehabilitation and can be a painstaking process requiring multidisciplinary efforts (Dell Orto & Power, 2000; Fraser & Clemmons, 2000). Effective education and treatment often require not only classroom behavior management, but also family therapy,

The emotional issue involved in TBI can be especially complex. Eileen Vosper, 12, enjoys holding "Kelli," a six-year-old collie who serves in a pet therapy program for children and adults with brain-injury related disabilities. The visits with the dogs are short, but meaningful.

medication, cognitive training, and communication training (Light et al., 1998; Tyler & Mira, 1999).

A great deal of information about TBI is now available on the World Wide Web. For further information, you might want to visit the website of the Brain Injury Association of America (www.biusa.org).

Deaf-Blindness

A VARIETY of information about deaf-blindness is found at **www.deafblind.com** and at **www.tr.wou.edu/ dblink**

In Chapters 10 and 11, we noted that, depending on the level of severity, blindness or deafness can have a substantial impact on a person's ability to function independently. For those who are both deaf and blind, the impact can be even more profound than simply adding the effects of each disability. Because the primary avenues for receiving information—sight and sound—are limited, those who are deaf-blind are at risk for having extensive problems in communicating and in navigating their environments.

Although being cut off from the sights and sounds of daily life makes deaf-blindness one of the most challenging of all multiple disabilities (Scheetz, 2001), this does not mean that a person with deaf-blindness is doomed to a poor-quality life. In general, outcomes for individuals with deaf-blindness depend on at least three things:

1. The quality and intensity of instruction the person receives is critical. Teachers of students with deaf-blindness "must make the most of every opportunity for learning. All interactions with adults and all aspects of the environment will be harnessed to help the child overcome the restrictions imposed by sensory impairments" (Hodges, 2000, p. 167).

2. The degree and type of visual impairment and auditory impairment can vary dramatically in individuals with deaf-blindness. The term *deaf-blindness* covers those with visual impairments ranging from low vision (20/70 to 20/200 in the better eye with correction) to those who are totally blind. Likewise, the term covers those with hearing impairments ranging from mild to profound. Although there are some very notable exceptions, in general, the more severe the impairments, the greater is the impact on a person's ability to adapt.

3. The vast majority of students who are deaf-blind have other disabilities and medical conditions. For example, approximately 11 percent of children between birth and age twenty-two who are deaf-blind also have mental retardation (Hembree, 2000). In general, the more numerous and severe these other disabilities, the greater is the impact on a person's ability to adapt.

Definition

CHARGE syndrome
A genetic syndrome resulting in deaf-blindness; characterized by physical anomalies, often including coloboma (abnormalities of the pupil, retina and/or optic nerve), cranial nerves, heart defects, atresia (absence or closure) of the chonae (air passages from nose to throat), retardation in growth and mental development, genital abnormalities, ear malformation and/or hearing loss.

Usher syndrome
An inherited syndrome resulting in hearing loss and retinitis pigmentosa, a progressive condition characterized by problems in seeing in low light and tunnel vision; there are three different types of Usher syndrome, differing with respect to when it occurs developmentally and the range of the major symptoms of hearing impairment, vision impairment, and balance problems.

As we discussed in Chapters 10 and 11, there is considerable controversy over the definitions of deafness and blindness. As one might expect, this means that defining deaf-blindness is even more controversial than defining deafness or blindness by itself. Following is the federal government's definition of deaf-blindness contained in IDEA:

> Deaf-blindness means concomitant hearing and visual impairments, the combination of which causes such severe communication and other developmental and educational needs that they cannot be accommodated in special education programs solely for children with deafness or children with blindness. (U.S. Department of Education, 1999, p. 12422)

Many states have found this definition too vague and have either developed their own definitions or added other criteria to the federal definition. For example, Alaska has added the following criteria:

> *Vision*: Visual acuity of 20/70 or less in the better eye with correction; visual field restriction of 20 degrees or less; functional vision which is virtually absent or unmeasurable for purposes of learning; need for special services requiring the use of non-standard instructional materials or aids designed to facilitate the child's learning; temporary impairment or loss of vision due to illness, accidents, temporary treatments; a diagnosis of a syndrome or disorder associated with progressive vision loss.
>
> *Hearing*: Hearing impairment of 30dB or greater unaided in the better ear; recurrent otitis media or documented history of recurrent otitis media affecting language or learning abilities; functional hearing which is absent or unmeasurable for purposes of learning; diagnosis of a syndrome or disorder associated with a progressive hearing loss. (National Information Clearinghouse on Children Who Are Deaf-Blind, 2001)

Prevalence

The fact that definitions and criteria vary from state to state, coupled with the fact that so many students with deaf-blindness also have other disabling conditions, has made it very difficult to get an accurate picture of prevalence rates. However, a recent census indicates that there are about 10,000 individuals from birth to twenty-two years of age who are deaf-blind (Hembree, 2000). The number of adults with deaf-blindness is estimated to be about 35,000–40,000 (Baldwin, 1994, as cited in Miles, 1998).

Causes

Causes of deaf-blindness can be grouped into three broad categories: (1) genetic/chromosomal syndromes, (2) prenatal conditions, and (3) postnatal conditions.

GENETIC/CHROMOSOMAL SYNDROMES

As we discussed in Chapter 5, researchers are making enormous strides in discovering genetic/chromosomal mental retardation syndromes. Some of these syndromes are inherited, and some result from damaged genetic and/or chromosomal material. This is also the case with respect to deaf-blindness. There are now over fifty genetic/chromosomal syndromes associated with deaf-blindness. The most common are **CHARGE syndrome**, **Usher syndrome**, and **Down syndrome**.

CHARGE Syndrome   CHARGE syndrome is characterized by a number of physical anomalies that are present at birth. The exact cause of CHARGE is still being debated, but there is growing evidence that it results from a genetic abnormality (Aitken, 2000; Oley, 2001). The reason for the uncertainty is probably that the condition was not identified in the medical literature until 1979 (Hall, 1979). The letters in CHARGE refer to some of the most common characteristics of this condition: C = coloboma, cranial nerves; H = heart defects; A = atresia of the choanae; R = retardation in growth and mental development; G = genital abnormalities; E = ear malformation and/or hearing loss.

    Coloboma refers to a condition in which the child is born with an abnormally shaped pupil and/or abnormalities of the retina or optic nerve (CHARGE Syndrome Foundation, 2001). Coloboma can result in a variety of visual problems, including deficits in visual acuity and extreme sensitivity to light.

    The **cranial nerves** supply information between the brain and various muscles and glands in the body. Individuals with CHARGE syndrome often have paralysis or weakness of facial muscles as well as swallowing problems because of abnormal development of some of the cranial nerves.

    The vast majority of children with CHARGE syndrome are born with heart defects. Some of these problems are relatively minor, but some are life threatening and require surgery (CHARGE Syndrome Foundation, 2001).

    An **atresia** is the absence or closure of a body opening present at birth. The **choanae** are air passages from the nose to throat. When the choanae are blocked or narrowed, the ability to breathe is affected. Surgery can help to correct these breathing problems.

    Most children with CHARGE syndrome are of normal size at birth but may experience growth problems because of nutrition, heart problems, and/or growth hormone abnormalities (CHARGE Syndrome Foundation, 2001). In addition, some are mentally retarded.

    Genital anomalies include incomplete or underdeveloped genitals. This is more common in males than in females (Brown, 1996).

    CHARGE syndrome can result in a variety of structural abnormalities of the outer, middle, and/or inner ear. The consequent hearing impairment may be conductive, sensorineural, or mixed (both conductive and sensorineural).

Usher Syndrome   Usher syndrome, an inherited condition, is characterized by hearing impairment and **retinitis pigmentosa**. As you recall from Chapter 10, retinitis pigmentosa can result in vision problems starting in infancy, early childhood, or the teenage years, with the condition becoming progressively worse. It results in problems in seeing in low light, referred to as **night blindness**, and as it progresses, it results in a narrowing of the field of vision, referred to as **tunnel vision**.

    There are three types of Usher syndrome, varying with respect to the type and time of occurrence of the major symptoms of hearing loss, vision loss, and balance problems. For example, depending on the type of Usher syndrome, the person can be born profoundly deaf, hard of hearing, or with normal hearing that deteriorates over time. Some experience

---

Down syndrome
A condition resulting from a chromosomal abnormality; characterized by mental retardation and such physical signs as slanted-appearing eyes, hypotonia, a single palmar crease, shortness, and a tendency toward obesity; the most common type of Down syndrome is trisomy 21.

Coloboma
A condition of the eye in which the pupil is abnormally shaped and/or there are abnormalities of the retina or optic nerve; can result in loss of visual acuity and extreme sensitivity to light.

Cranial nerves
Twelve pairs of nerves that connect the brain with various muscles and glands in the body.

Atresia
Absence or closure of a part of the body that is normally open.

Choanae
Air passages from the nose to the throat.

Retinitis pigmentosa
A hereditary condition resulting in degeneration of the retina; causes a narrowing of the field of vision and affects night vision.

Night blindness
A condition characterized by problems in seeing at low levels of illumination; often caused by retinitis pigmentosa.

Tunnel vision
A condition characterized by problems in peripheral vision, or a narrowing of the field of vision.

night blindness starting in infancy; others have night blindness starting in the teenage years. Some have severe balance problems, due to inner-ear problems, starting in infancy; some have no balance problems; and some are born with normal balance that deteriorates over time.

People researching genetics have been finding more and more genes that cause the three types of Usher syndrome. As of February 2001, researchers had localized six genes causing six subtypes of Usher I, three genes causing three subtypes of Usher II, and one gene causing Usher III (Boys Town National Research Hospital Genetics Department, 2001).

Although Usher syndrome is one of the most common hereditary conditions causing deaf-blindness, its overall prevalence is very low. There are only about 300 people from birth to age twenty-two who have been identified as having Usher syndromes I–III (Hembree, 2000). However, the genetics of Usher syndrome show an interesting demographic pattern (see Focus on Concepts on p. 443).

Down Syndrome Most often noted as a cause of mental retardation (see Chapter 5), Down syndrome is also sometimes associated with deaf-blindness. Unlike Usher syndrome, which is inherited, Down syndrome results from damaged chromosomal material.

PRENATAL CONDITIONS

Like Down syndrome, two of the most common types of **prenatal** conditions—**rubella**, sometimes referred to as **German measles**, and congenital **cytomegalovirus (CMV)**—can cause mental retardation and/or deaf-blindness. When rubella occurs in a pregnant woman, especially in the first trimester, it can lead to a variety of disabilities, including deaf-blindness. Children born with CMV, a herpes virus, are also at risk for a variety of disabilities, including deaf-blindness.

POSTNATAL CONDITIONS

Among the most common **postnatal** conditions that can cause deaf-blindness are **meningitis** and traumatic brain injury (TBI). As we learned in Chapter 5, meningitis, which is an infection of the covering of the brain, can also cause mental retardation. And TBI, as we discussed earlier in this chapter, can result in a variety of other disabilities, as well as deaf-blindness.

Psychological and Behavioral Characteristics

People who are deaf-blind can have significant problems in at least three areas: (1) accessing information, (2) communicating, and (3) navigating the environment (Aitken, 2000).

PROBLEMS ACCESSING INFORMATION

People who are sighted and have hearing are able to access a variety of information about their world, whether it be from the media (e.g., newspapers, television, the Internet) or other people. For people who are deaf-blind, however, access to this information is much harder to obtain. And because communication is largely dependent on the availability of information, restricted access to information can have a negative impact on the ability to communicate:

> The consequence of not being able to access information is that life experiences are reduced. Lack of everyday ordinary experiences—how to make a sandwich, knowing that water comes from a tap—makes it more difficult for the person who

Prenatal
Occurring or developing in the fetus before birth.

Rubella (German measles)
A serious viral disease, which, if it occurs during the first trimester of pregnancy, is likely to cause a deformity in the fetus.

Cytomegalovirus (CMV)
A herpes virus; can cause a number of disabilities.

Postnatal
Occurring in an infant after birth.

Meningitis
A bacterial or viral infection of the linings of the brain or spinal cord; can cause a number of disabilities.

UNDERSTANDING THE STANDARDS AND PRINCIPLES What should teachers know about the psychological and behavioral characteristics of individuals who are deaf-blind? *(CEC Knowledge and Skills Standard IC2K4)*

Council for Exceptional Children

FOCUS ON CONCEPTS

The Genetics of Usher Syndrome and Its Geographic Distribution

ABOUT one in seventy-five people carries an Usher gene, but most do not realize that they have it. Usher syndrome is an *autosomal-recessive disorder*, meaning that for a child to have the condition, both parents must be carriers of the gene. And with each such pregnancy, there is a one-in-four chance of the child having Usher syndrome. Thus, the chance of having a child with Usher syndrome is relatively rare even among those who carry the gene, and that is why the prevalence of Usher syndrome is so low. However, the odds of producing an offspring with Usher syndrome rise dramatically among people who are related:

> Each of us, regardless of family history, is thought to silently carry five or more recessive genes that have the potential to cause genetic disorders in the next generation. But the chance of conceiving a child with a recessive disorder is low because most unrelated couples do not carry the exact same recessive genes. Conversely, because members of one's immediate or extended family share a similar genetic makeup, it becomes easier for two autosomal recessive genes to match up to cause a particular disorder. Thus, children conceived by parents who are related to each other are at higher than average risk for being affected by autosomal recessive disorders. And in certain cultures in which marriages between relatives are the norm or in which many people preferentially choose partners with the same inherited trait (e.g., marriage between two people with deafness), recessive conditions occur more commonly than expected. (Dykens, Hodapp, & Finucane, 2000, p. 46)

Unfortunately, social forces have operated historically to make the likelihood of intermarriage higher among a certain cultural group: the Acadian French of south Louisiana. This has resulted in a relatively higher number of people with Usher syndrome in this area of the country. Following is an excerpt from a retired teacher who had worked at the Louisiana School for the Deaf for twenty-seven years:

> To begin with, Usher syndrome among the Acadian French people in south Louisiana was something people knew the "about" of, but not the "what" or "why" of. They knew that generation after generation of children were struck mysteriously with deafness and eventually with

partial-to-full blindness. It was something that was dreaded, but had to be endured. Again and again, cousins, aunts, uncles, and sometimes two or three children in a family were found to have the condition, but no one knew what to do, or what to call it.

The "what" and "why" of it was that the Acadian parishes of south Louisiana have a far higher percentage of Usher syndrome than anywhere else in the United States. This extraordinarily high percentage has been documented in several studies. . . . For example, [Kloepfer, Laguaite, and McLaurin, 1966] estimated that 30 percent of the deaf population in the parishes of Lafayette, Vermillion, and Acadia had Usher syndrome. The high incidence is a result of several hundred years of intermarriage among this close-knit ethnic group. Inevitably, two individuals, both carrying a recessive gene for Usher syndrome transmitted to them by a common ancestor, marry and have children with this condition.

The Acadians, or Cajuns, as they are called, were originally from Acadia (Nova Scotia) in Canada. In the 1700s they were expelled from that area by the English. They moved down along the east-coast of America, finally settling along the bayous of several south Louisiana parishes. At first they were not readily accepted by people in the area and were somewhat isolated both by language and by culture. With time, however, the Cajuns came into their own and have won admirers around the world for their music, love of fun, and never-to-be-forgotten cuisine.

Many students at the Louisiana School for the Deaf (LSD) come from the Acadian parishes resulting in a high incidence of Usher syndrome at the school. . . . Fifteen to twenty percent of children on the Louisiana deaf-blind census for children birth through age 21 are known to have Usher syndrome [Type 1] as compared to an average of 3 percent for all other states in the nation. (Melancon, 2000, p. 1)

The high prevalence of Usher syndrome in south Louisiana is also the subject of a video narrated by the well-known neurologist Oliver Sacks, *The Ragin' Cajun Usher Syndrome*, produced by the British Broadcasting Company. ■

is deaf-blind to build up a store of world knowledge. Without that store of world knowledge what is there to communicate about? (Aitken, 2000, p. 3)

PROBLEMS COMMUNICATING

Most authorities agree that the biggest obstacle faced by people with deaf-blindness is communication (Aitken, 2000; Ford & Fredericks, 1995; Miles, 1998). Without a strong commitment by teachers and other professionals and parents to providing a variety of opportunities for communication, the child who is deaf-blind can easily become socially isolated. The pattern for this isolation can begin at birth. The baby

> may not be able to make and sustain eye contact or to respond to a soothing voice. His mother's face may be invisible or only a blur and her speech only a low sound which he cannot pick out from the background of other noises. The deafblind baby may register little of the world around him, or may find it a frightening place full of half-registered shapes and sounds. He will not hold his mother's attention with a ready gaze and will not be able to play the games of sight, sound and movement which other babies enjoy. If his vision and hearing are so seriously damaged that he cannot use visual or auditory cues to warn him that someone is coming to pick him up, or that a particular activity is about to happen, contact with other people may even become threatening. (Pease, 2000, p. 38)

Once this pattern of isolation has been established, it is difficult to reverse. Therefore, it is critical that professionals and parents work together to provide an environment that is as supportive and rich in communication opportunities as possible.

No better example of the importance of providing a language-rich environment exists than the classic case of Helen Keller (1880–1968) and her teacher Annie Sullivan (1866–1936). Popularized by the classic movie *The Miracle Worker*, Helen Keller's accomplishments are now familiar to most of us. Having lost her sight and hearing at the age of nineteen months, Keller went on to extraordinary achievements, including graduating cum laude from Radcliffe College in 1904, publishing essays and books (including the much acclaimed *The Story of My Life*, written while she was in college and available in over fifty languages), touring the country lecturing on blindness, being a spokesperson for women's right to vote, and receiving the Presidential Medal of Freedom, the nation's highest civilian award.

Helen Keller is testimony to the power of the human spirit to overcome overwhelming odds. However, just as important, she is testimony to the power of intensive and extensive special education instruction. As remarkable as she was, it is doubtful that Keller would have conquered her condition without the prolonged instruction from Annie Sullivan, who devoted nearly fifty years to being Keller's teacher and constant companion. Sullivan, herself born blind, had had some of her sight restored through several operations. She arrived at the home of the Kellers in 1887 to meet a not yet seven-year-old Helen, who had some rudiments of communication but who was prone to severe tantrums. Through persistence and intensive instruction, Sullivan was able to set Helen's mind free to learn language and higher concepts.

Sullivan and Keller are not the only famous teacher–student team to demonstrate the importance of intensive instruction of the deaf-blind. See Personal Perspectives on page 445 for the story of Laura Bridgman and Samuel Gridley Howe.

PROBLEMS NAVIGATING THE ENVIRONMENT

As we discussed in Chapter 11, people who are blind or who have low vision can have significant difficulties with mobility. For people who are deaf-blind, these problems are often even more pronounced. Individuals who are blind and hearing are able to pick up auditory cues that help them in navigation. For example, being able to hear approaching traffic can

FOR INFORMATION on Helen Keller, including many of her letters and papers, visit the website maintained by the American Foundation for the Blind: **www.afb.org/section.asp? sectionid=1**

Personal Perspectives

LAURA BRIDGMAN AND HER TEACHER, SAMUEL GRIDLEY HOWE

ALTHOUGH most people are familiar with the story of Helen Keller, Laura Bridgman (1829–1889) was actually the first documented case of a deaf-blind person to learn language. Laura was struck at the age of two with scarlet fever and left deaf and blind.

Samuel Gridley Howe (1801–1876) was one of the nineteenth century's most daring social activists, reforming schools, prisons, and mental institutions as well as being a member of the "Secret Six" who lent financial support to John Brown's campaign to end slavery in the United States with his ill-fated launching of the raid at Harper's Ferry in 1859. Howe received his medical degree from Harvard University in 1824. After serving a seven-year stint as a surgeon in the Greek civil conflict, he returned to Boston. In 1832, he was named head of the Perkins Institution and Massachusetts School for the Blind (now named the Perkins School for the Blind).

After reading a newspaper account of Laura, Howe visited her parents and convinced them to send the eight-year-old to Perkins in 1837. There, he and his teachers worked painstakingly with Laura for several years. In addition to the goals of teaching her to communicate, Howe viewed Bridgman as a philosophical and religious experiment. By showing that she could learn to communicate, he was debunking the materialists, who held that sensory input was necessary in order to form concepts: "As Laura reached out to the world around her, Howe thrilled to witness the triumph of mind over matter" (Freeberg, 2001, p. 41). With respect to religion, Howe hoped to show that Laura possessed an innate moral consciousness that was intact despite her sensory losses.

Howe held open houses for the public to see the accomplishments of the students at Perkins. Laura soon became the major attraction, drawing hundreds of onlookers. One of the early visitors was Charles Dickens, whose account of his meeting with Laura, which he described in *American Notes*, further publicized the accomplishments of Howe's work with her.

Howe eventually became discouraged because Laura did not progress as far as he had hoped. Although she was able to com-

Laura Bridgman with Samuel Gridley Howe.

municate well, her personality, characterized by immaturity and occasional fits of rage, kept her from becoming the ideal case to prove his philosophical and theological theories.

Although her achievements were not as spectacular as Keller's, Bridgman's accomplishments were extraordinary for the time, a time when many authorities believed that to be deaf-blind was to be mentally retarded. Furthermore, had it not been for Bridgman, Keller might never have received the instruction that unlocked her intellect. Helen's parents were alerted to the potential of teaching their own daughter after reading about Bridgman's accomplishments. Furthermore, Helen's teacher, Annie Sullivan, herself a former student at Perkins, consulted Howe's reports on Laura before embarking on her journey to tutor Helen.

Perhaps most important,

Laura Bridgman's dramatic story drew the public's attention to the wider reform movement that was transforming the lives of many disabled people in nineteenth century America. Howe and other educators invented teaching tools, experimented with curriculum, and built new institutions that helped thousands of people with sensory handicaps to overcome the physical barriers that had always deprived them of an education. . . . Chipping away at centuries of accumulated prejudice and misunderstanding, these students and their teachers began to dismantle one of the greatest barriers faced by the blind and the deaf, the deep-rooted misconception that people with sensory handicaps are unreachable and somehow less than fully human. In the crucial early years of this important reform movement, no person did more to challenge those assumptions and inspire new respect for the disabled than Laura Bridgman. (Freeberg, 2001, pp. 220–221) ∎

Source: Reprinted by permission of the publisher from *The Education of Laura Bridgman: First Deaf and Blind Person to Learn Language* by E. Freeberg, Cambridge, Mass.: Harvard University Press, Copyright © 2001 by the President and Fellows of Harvard College.

UNDERSTANDING THE STANDARDS AND PRINCIPLES What educational approaches are most appropriate for students who are deaf-blind? *(CEC Knowledge and Skills Standards IC4K2, CC4S3, & IC4S1)*

Council for
Exceptional
Children

Braille
A system in which raised dots allow people who are blind to read with their fingertips; each quadrangular cell contains from one to six dots, the arrangement of which denotes different letters and symbols.

Hand-over-hand guidance
A tactile learning strategy for persons who are deaf-blind; the teacher places his or her hands over those of the person who is deaf-blind and guides them to explore objects.

Hand-under-hand guidance
A tactile learning strategy for persons who are deaf-blind; the teacher places his or her hands underneath part of the student's hand or hands while the child is exploring objects.

Adapted signs
Signs adapted for use by people who are deaf-blind; tactually based rather than visually based, such as American Sign Language for those who are deaf but sighted.

Touch cues
Tactual signals used to communicate with persons who are deaf-blind; can be used to signify a variety of messages.

be very helpful when crossing an intersection, and being able to hear such things as buses, trains, and construction noises, can help a person who is blind to identify her or his location. However, people who are both deaf and blind are restricted in their ability to make use of auditory signals for navigating the environment.

Educational Considerations

The major educational needs of infants and preschoolers, as well as of older students, who are deaf-blind fall generally under the categories of communication and orientation and mobility. Both, but especially communication, are required for social interaction. If these skills are taught effectively, then the social interaction of deaf-blind individuals is enhanced considerably (Janssen, Riksen-Walraven, & van Dijk (2004).

In addressing needs for communication and orientation and mobility, practitioners and parents should keep in mind at least two important principles: the importance of direct teaching and the importance of structured routines.

THE IMPORTANCE OF DIRECT TEACHING

Many students with disabilities (e.g., mental retardation, learning disabilities, blindness, deafness) are more reliant than those without disabilities on having teachers teach them directly. Whereas students without disabilities can learn a great deal incidentally (e.g., from seeing or hearing things that happen around them), students with disabilities are often in greater need of having material taught to them directly (see Kauffman, 2002; Kauffman & Hallahan, 2005). As we mentioned in connection with Helen Keller and Laura Bridgman, because of their restricted sensory input, this need for direct teaching of information is even more pronounced for students who are deaf-blind than it is for children with other disabilities.

THE IMPORTANCE OF STRUCTURED ROUTINES

To create a successful environment for learning, it is also critical that teachers and other professionals and parents provide a sense of security for students who are deaf-blind. One of the best ways to create this sense of security is through the use of *structured routines* (Chen, Alsop, & Minor, 2000; Miles, 1998), discussed in detail in Responsive Instruction on page 447.

COMMUNICATION

The hands play a critical role in communication for most students who are deaf-blind. In effect, the hands become the "voice, or the primary means of expression" (Miles, 1999, p. 1). A number of modes of communication that involve touch are used with people who are deaf-blind. **Braille** is the most obvious one. Some other common tactile learning strategies are **hand-over-hand guidance**, **hand-under-hand guidance**, **adapted signs**, and **touch cues** (Chen, Downing, & Rodriguez-Gil, 2000/2001).

Hand–Over–Hand Guidance Hand-over-hand guidance involves the adult placing his or her hand(s) over the child's hand(s) while exploring an object or signing. Although this technique may be necessary, especially for children who have physical disabilities that interfere with movement of their hands, it does have some disadvantages (Chen et al., 2000/2001; Miles, 1999). Some children are resistant to this technique, apparently because they do not like the feeling of loss of control over their hands. Furthermore, some children can become too passive, waiting for someone else's hands to be placed over theirs rather than reaching out on their own.

RESPONSIVE INSTRUCTION

Meeting the Needs of Students with Low-Incidence, Multiple, and Severe Disabilities

The Importance of Establishing Structured Routines

WHAT THE RESEARCH SAYS

Researchers and practitioners from Project PLAI* (Promoting Learning Through Active Interaction) have developed several modules for working with infants who have multiple disabilities and their families (Chen, Alsop, & Minor, 2000; Klein, Chen, & Haney, 2000). One of the modules focuses on establishing predictable routines. Specifically, for infants who are deaf-blind, they have recommended the following objectives:

- Create a predictable routine by identifying at least five daily activities that can be scheduled in the same sequence each day.
- Identify predictable sequences within specific activities (i.e., "subroutines").
- Identify and use specific auditory, visual, tactile, olfactory, and kinesthetic cues to help the infant anticipate familiar activities. (Chen et al., 2000, p. 6)

The following describes how they implemented these objectives with fourteen-month-old Michael, his mother, Cecelia, and older sister, Kate. Michael was born prematurely and only weighed one pound, eight ounces at birth. He was diagnosed with severe ROP (retinopathy of prematurity), cerebral palsy, and a hearing loss of undetermined severity.

An early interventionist helped Cecelia realize that Michael could better understand what was going on around him if his daily events were more predictable. In addition to the early morning and evening routines, Cecelia decided to try to increase the predictability of Michael's routines in several ways. After he finished his morning bottle, he would always get a bath. After the bath, Cecelia would put lotion on him and give him a shoulder and back massage. At bedtime, she would give him his bottle and then Kate would rock him while watching TV. Cecelia also realized that she and Michael had developed "subroutines." For example, after removing Michael's diaper and cleaning him, she would blow on his tummy and say, "Okay, all dry. All dry." Then she would sprinkle powder and put a new diaper on him, say "All done," and give him a kiss while picking him up.

Other predictable routines and subroutines followed. Before going into Michael's room, Cecelia would always announce loudly, "Here comes Mommy." She would touch his shoulders before picking him up. Before putting him in the bath, she would put his foot in the water a couple of times, which helped him to stop screaming when he was placed in the tub. Before Cecelia gave Michael his back massage, she would rub some lotion on her fingers and let him smell it. (Chen, Alsop, & Minor, 2000, pp. 6–7).

APPLYING THE RESEARCH TO TEACHING

Although the above example pertains to infants, structured routines are no less important for school-age children who have multiple disabilities, including deaf-blindness. School routines are particularly important for the student who is deaf-blind because the only way for that child to learn is by doing. The student will be unable to learn through visually observing or hearing stimuli that will assist her or him in making sense of the world. Therefore, the student will be dependent upon the creation of a safe learning environment and trust with the primary instructor (Moss & Hagood, 1995). School routines that would benefit the student who is deaf-blind are as follows:

- *Turn-taking routines.* By keeping interactions balanced ("me, then you"), the student will consistently know when to respond and be more active in his or her learning.
- *Travel or movement routines.* If the student does not feel comfortable moving around the classroom or school, he or she may choose to not move. Lack of mobility decreases opportunities for exploration, social interaction, and independence.
- *Communication routines.* The student who is deaf-blind will rely on tactile communication. The student will be unable to make connections among input without direct interaction with others. Therefore, it is important to establish routines for communication as the student moves from objects to gestures for communication. ■

*Project PLAI was a four-year collaborative project involving California State University-Northridge, SKI-HI Institute at Utah State University, and several early intervention programs, funded by the Office of Special Education Programs, U.S. Department of Education.

This blind child is assisted by a teacher who is using the hand-over-hand technique to help him explore a tray of potato sticks.

Hand-Under-Hand Guidance Hand-under-hand guidance is often recommended as an alternative to hand-over-hand guidance. This technique involves the adult gently slipping his or her hand(s) underneath part of the child's hand(s) while the child is exploring an object. It becomes the tactile equivalent to pointing (Miles, 1999). One of the main advantages of hand-under-hand guidance is that it is noncontrolling, and some authorities believe that when children and adults explore objects and movements together it lays a foundation for language (Miles, 1999).

Adapted Signs Signs used by the Deaf community, such as American Sign Language and Signed English, are visually based, which makes them difficult or impossible to use by people who are deaf-blind, depending on the severity of their visual impairment. For this reason, a variety of tactual versions of signing have been created (Chen et al., 2000/2001). For example, for the reception of signs, the person who is deaf-blind can place his or her hands on the hands of the signer; for the expression of signs, the teacher or parent can hold the hands of the person who is deaf-blind and guide him or her to produce signs.

Touch Cues Touch cues are tactual signals that can convey a number of messages depending on the situation and context. It is important that the touch cues be consistent:

> A child will not be able to decipher the meaning of a touch cue if different people use it for a variety of messages. For example, patting or tapping a child on the shoulder may express any of the following:
>
> ■ positive feedback ("Great job")
> ■ a request or directive ("Sit down")
> ■ information ("Your turn")
> ■ comfort or reassurance ("Don't cry, you're OK")
>
> . . . Touch cues should be used selectively, conservatively, and consistently so that the child can develop an understanding of what they represent. (Chen et al., 2000/2001, p. 3)

ORIENTATION AND MOBILITY

As we learned in Chapter 10, orientation and mobility (O & M) training is critical for those who are blind or who have low vision. The more a person with visual impairment is able to navigate the environment, the more independent she or he is able to become. For people who have both visual impairment and hearing impairment, the need for mobility training is even more important because they are at even greater risk of being unable to navigate their environment.

O & M training for people who have both visual and hearing impairment differs in at least two ways from O & M training for those with only visual impairment. First, adaptations are needed to communicate with people with deaf-blindness (Gense & Gense, 1999). The O & M instructor might need to use such adaptations as an interpreter, adapted signs, and/or touch cues to communicate with the student who is deaf-blind.

Second, it is sometimes necessary to alert the public that a traveler is deaf-blind. Even the best travelers with deaf-blindness occasionally become temporarily disoriented and need assistance. Hearing people with visual impairment can ask for assistance relatively easily. However, people who have both hearing and visual impairment may have a more difficult time communicating their needs to the public, and it will not always be obvious to the public that the person has both a visual and hearing impairment. A long cane can signal vision loss, but it does not indicate hearing impairment. Therefore, some professionals advocate the use of **assistance cards**. Assistance cards are usually relatively small (e.g., 3″ × 6″) and can be held up by the person who is deaf-blind at a busy or unfamiliar intersection. The words on the card indicate that the person is asking for assistance—for example, "Please help me to CROSS STREET. I am both DEAF <u>and</u> VISUALLY IMPAIRED, so TAP ME if you can help. Thank you" (Franklin & Bourquin, 2000, p. 175).

SPECIAL CONSIDERATIONS FOR STUDENTS WITH USHER SYNDROME

Students with Usher syndrome present some special educational challenges because most of them have progressive visual impairment. They might start out having relatively good vision, but their vision inevitably declines to the point at which they are legally, if not totally, blind. The effects of retinitis pigmentosa, which accompanies Usher syndrome, can sometimes be erratic and change rapidly, thus catching the student and his or her family off guard (Miner & Cioffi, 1999). Even when the deterioration occurs slowly over the course of several years, parents and teachers of children with Usher syndrome might neglect the importance of preparing the child for the fact that he or she will one day have substantial visual impairment. Sometimes, they fear that the early introduction of braille and O & M training will stigmatize the child and damage his or her self-concept. However, most authorities now agree that braille and O & M training should not wait until the student can no longer function as a seeing individual.

Considerations for Many Students with Low-Incidence, Multiple, and Severe Disabilities

Some of the devices and methods that we describe here might apply to any of the disabilities we discuss in this chapter. Communication, behavior management, early intervention, transition, employment, family involvement, and normalization are all concerns that are frequently encountered with any of these disabilities.

Augmentative or Alternative Communication

For some individuals with severe and multiple disabilities, oral language is out of the question; they have physical or cognitive disabilities, usually as a result of neurological damage, that preclude their learning to communicate through normal speech. A system of **augmentative or alternative communication (AAC)** must be designed for them.

AAC includes any manual or electronic means by which such a person expresses wants and needs, shares information, engages in social closeness, or manages social etiquette (Beukelman & Mirenda, 1998; Beukelman, Yorkston, & Reichle, 2000; Lloyd, Fuller, & Arvidson, 1997). Students for whom AAC must be designed range in intelligence from highly gifted to profoundly mentally retarded, but they all have one characteristic in common: the inability to communicate effectively through speech because of a physical

Assistance card
A relatively small card containing a message that alerts the public that the user is deaf-blind and needs assistance in crossing the street.

Augmentative or alternative communication (AAC)
Alternative forms of communication that do not use the oral sounds of speech or that augment the use of speech.

UNDERSTANDING THE STANDARDS AND PRINCIPLES   What forms of augmentative or alternative communication might be helpful for individuals with severe and multiple disabilities? *(CEC Knowledge and Skills Standards CC6S1 & IC6S3)*

Council for Exceptional Children

SIMPLIFIED signs are shown at **www. simplifiedsigns.org**
For augmentative and alternative communication, see **www.isaac-online.org**

impairment. Some of these individuals are unable to make any speech sounds at all; others need a system to augment their speech when they cannot make themselves understood because of environmental noise, difficulty in producing certain words or sounds, or unfamiliarity with the person with whom they want to communicate.

Manual signs or gestures are useful for some individuals. But many individuals with severe physical limitations are unable to use their hands to communicate through the usual sign language; they must use another means of communication, usually involving special equipment. However, Nikki Kissane, a University of Virginia undergraduate student who intends to become an orthopedic surgeon, has developed a simplified sign language system. Children and adults with limited speech capabilities can learn and use her simplified signs more easily than traditional signs (see Focus on Concepts on p. 451).

The problems to be solved in helping individuals communicate in ways other than signing include selecting a vocabulary and giving them an effective, efficient means of indicating elements in their vocabularies. Although the basic ideas behind AAC are quite simple, selecting the best vocabulary and devising an efficient means of indication for many individuals with severe disabilities are extraordinarily challenging. As one AAC user put it, "The AAC evaluation should be done with the AAC user involved in the process from step one. It is the augmented speaker who will be using the device every day, both personally and professionally, not the AAC specialist" (Cardona, 2000, p. 237).

A variety of approaches to AAC have been developed, some involving relatively simple or so-called low-technology solutions and some requiring complex or high-technology solutions (Lloyd et al., 1997). Many different direct-selection and scanning methods have been devised for AAC, depending on individual capabilities. The system that is used may involve pointing with the hand or a headstick, eye movements, or operation of a microswitch by foot, tongue, or head movement or breath control. Sometimes, the individual can use a typewriter or computer terminal that is fitted with a key guard so that keys are not likely to be pressed accidentally or use an alternative means for selecting keystrokes. See Success Stories on page 452 about David, a fourth grader who uses an alternative-access keyboard. Often, communication boards are used. A communication board is an array of pictures, words, or other symbols that can be operated with either a direct-selection or scanning strategy. The content and arrangement of the board will vary, depending on the person's capabilities, preferences, and communication needs.

Speed, reliability, portability, cost, and overall effectiveness in helping a person communicate independently are factors to be considered in designing and evaluating AAC (Beukelman & Mirenda, 1998; Lloyd et al., 1997). Some AAC systems are very slow, unreliable (either because of the equipment or a poor match with the abilities of the user), cumbersome, or useful only in very restricted settings. Although people typically think of the equipment and material costs that AAC involves, the real costs must include intensive and extensive instruction. A communication board will not necessarily be useful just because it is available. And the most sophisticated technological solution to communication is not always the one that will be most useful in the long run.

Today, researchers are finding increasingly innovative and creative technological solutions to the problem of nonvocal communication. At the same time, they are recognizing the importance of making decisions that are highly individualized and evidence-based (Schlosser & Raghenvendra (2004). No one is well served by AAC that is not highly reliable from a scientific point of view.

Until rather recently, many practitioners saw AAC primarily as a means of allowing users to demonstrate the language skills they have already acquired. But now researchers and practitioners increasingly emphasize how AAC can be a tool for teaching language—for helping AAC users not only to give voice to what they feel and know about specific tasks, but also to acquire increasingly sophisticated language skills (Nelson, 1998; Oken-Fried & Bersani, 2000; Yoder, 2001).

Researchers are attempting to make it possible for young AAC users to talk about the same kinds of things that other youngsters do (Marvin, Beukelman, Brockhaus, & Kast, 1994). Other efforts are directed at training AAC users to tell those with whom they

FOCUS ON CONCEPTS

Simplified Sign Language

FIGURING out how to communicate effectively with simple gestures has not been an easy task for U.Va. student Nikki Kissane. But thanks to her research efforts, mute children and adults or those with limited speech capabilities have a new simplified communication system that is easier to learn, produce, and understand than existing sign languages. . . .

After witnessing her grandfather suffer a series of strokes and seeing the physiological and emotional difficulties he experienced, Kissane approached psychology professor John Bonvillian to see if she could participate in his ongoing research on sign-language communication for nonspeaking but hearing individuals. . . .

Kissane studied more than 20 sign language dictionaries to identify signs that are "iconic," those clearly resembling the object or action they represent, or "transparent," those that easily convey their meaning. To illustrate, cradling one's arms while gently rocking back and forth would be a transparent sign for "baby," whereas gesturing throwing a ball would be an iconic gesture for "throw."

From her research, Kissane identified about 900 signs for such everyday words as "comb," "book" and "reach" that have the potential of being easily understood and communicated through simple hand and arm gestures. She also created numerous new signs to supplement those she found in her search.

To determine if such signs could be incorporated into a simplified system, she had volunteer U.Va. students view different groups of signs to see which ones they could remember and repeat easily. All signs recalled perfectly by at least 70 percent of the participants were added to a lexicon.

Kissane also observed some classes led by her mother, who teaches elementary school art to children, including several with autism. She gained pointers from her mother on how to draw the gestures.

"I observed a few of the classes to see where autistic children struggle in motor and cognitive skills," Kissane said. ■

Source: Wooten, I. L. (2001, May 18). Student develops new sign language system. *Inside UVA, 31*(18), 12. Reprinted with permission. Photos from *The Daily Progress*, Charlottesville, VA. Reprinted with permission.

Eye

Celebrate

Sleep

communicate how to interact with them more effectively—that is, to train AAC users in pragmatics. Personal Perspectives on page 454 was written by Chris Featherly when he was an eighteen-year-old high school student. His story and others written by AAC users (Oken-Fried & Bersani, 2000) illustrate the value of AAC and issues involved in its use. The fact that Chris Featherly has cerebral palsy, a congenital neurological condition that we will discuss in Chapter 14, is beside the point here. The important thing is that some people have physical limitations that preclude their efficient use of oral language and need an augmented or alternative means of communicating.

SUCCESS STORIES

Special Educators At Work

Mrs Womack, David's mother: "When some teachers hear that ventilator, their tendency is to pamper the child, but I want him treated like a student."

Sixteen-year-old David Womack attends an academic day school for students with severe physical disabilities.

These are the keys to his success:

- *intensive collaboration,*
- *relentless emphasis on technology,*
- *specific goals for independence and academic achievement.*

On the second day of second grade, seven-year-old David Womack was hit by a car as he stepped off the school bus. The accident injured his spinal cord, leaving him with no movement below his neck and with an inability to breathe on his own. After two years of rehabilitation, David was ready to leave the hospital and reenter school. His parents and other members of the IEP team made the decision to enroll nine-year-old David in a special day school for students with intense medical and physical needs. David's achievements are the result of intensive, relentless, and specific special education.

Intensive Collaboration   David's specialized day school is staffed with medical and therapeutic personnel and with teachers who are dually certified as special and general educators. David was the first student dependent on a ventilator to attend the school. He entered his third-grade classroom in a large electronic sip-and-puff wheelchair that he propelled by blowing air through a strawlike mouthpiece. His life-support system, called "the vent," was mounted on the back of his chair and made a loud rhythmic sound. Never more than several feet away was a private-duty nurse who monitored him at all times. "It was so scary," recalls Mrs. Womack. "I could tell everybody was nervous."

The school's task included helping the Womack family adjust to a different life and stimulating David to discover his new potential. Even though the staff was experienced in dealing with difficult physical issues, David presented a challenge, and the presence of the ventilator and the private nurse emphasized his fragility. Says occupational therapist Ginette Howard, "We had to raise everybody's expectations by treating David like a student instead of a patient!"

The school's technology team supported David's classroom learning. Howard and computer teacher Maryann Cicchillo combined their knowledge of instructional software and sophisticated technologies to provide David with the tools to read, write, and compute. Classroom teachers followed their lead, and so did his nurse, Gail Nolan, who was committed to his academic and social growth. David's progress was built slowly but steadily on a foundation of trust.

Relentless Emphasis on Technology   David was frightened to leave the hospital, so the first task was securing his ventilator equipment for classroom use. "We made sure there was a plastic casing over the dials because he was afraid someone might play with the settings," Howard recalls. The second

Users of AAC encounter three particular challenges that are not faced by natural communicators:

1. AAC is much slower than natural communication—perhaps one-twentieth the typical rate of speech. This can result in great frustration for both the AAC users and natural communicators.
2. Users of AAC who are not literate must rely on a vocabulary and symbols that are selected by others. If the vocabulary and symbols, as well as other features of the system, are not well chosen, AAC will be quite limited in the learning and personal relationships it allows.
3. AAC must be constructed to be useful in a variety of social contexts, allow accurate and efficient communication without undue fatigue, and support the individual's learning of language and academic skills.

year, he became more confident and more willing to try new technologies. David progressed from being withdrawn and fearful to trusting and to developing an interest in computer applications. Providing him with computer access became the challenge.

"David has chin supports to keep his head erect, and he can move his mouth," says Howard. She and Cicchillo selected a small alternative-access keyboard that was worked by an electronic wand. With much effort, David would clench a mouthstick in his teeth and gently tap the attached wand on the miniature impulse-sensitive keyboard. Cicchillo ensured that appropriate software was available to David's teachers through the school's network. Gradually, David became accustomed to using the mouthstick and to the expectation that he was independently responsible for his school work.

Specific Goals for Independence and Academic Achievement David's technology sessions have increased his independence as a student. He uses a word prediction and abbreviation/expansion program to reduce the number of keystrokes and to increase his speed in writing assignments. He is eager to try new technologies that challenge his accuracy and increase his speed. "I can't tell you how many times we've explored technology to support homework assignments, to take tests, or complete a paper," says Cicchillo.

"Science is my favorite subject," says David, a quiet young man who speaks in a soft, breathy voice. Dorothy Vann's science lab is fully accessible, with adjustable tables and low sinks. The lab is also equipped with instructional technology that David needs to fully participate. In biology, he views slides through a stereo microscope that utilizes a small attached camera to project video images. "I knew David was capable of doing more than he initially showed us," says Vann.

Working with David has been an evolving process for each of the collaborators. In reflecting on their work with David, Howard and Cicchillo identify a breaking-in period when teachers and the child who is newly ventilator-dependent have to overcome their fears. According to Dorothy Vann, "It takes a while for a child to accept goals for achievement and to believe in his or her own success."

CEC'S STANDARDS: PAVING THE WAY TO SUCCESS

Council for Exceptional Children

ASSESS YOUR STEPS TO SUCCESS in meeting the CEC Knowledge and Skill Base for All Beginning Special Education Teachers of Students in Individualized Independence Curriculums. Use the following questions to reflect on the growth of your own professional knowledge, skills, and dispositions.

REFLECTING ON YOUR OWN PROFESSIONAL DEVELOPMENT

If you were David's teacher...

- WHAT are some areas about educating students with severe disabilities that you would need to know more about?
- WHAT are some specific skills that would help you address David's academic and emotional challenges?
- WHAT personal dispositions do you think are most important for you to develop in teaching students with severe disabilities?

Using the CEC Standards

- WHAT are some ways in which special educators could select, plan, and coordinate the activities of related services personnel to maximize direct instruction for a student with severe disabilities? (IC10S3)
- HOW would you develop a technology plan based on an adaptive technology assessment for a student with a severe disability? (IC8S5)
- WHAT strategies would help you to identify and prioritize areas of the general curriculum and accommodations for a student with a severe disability? (CC7S1) ■

By Jean Crockett

Progress in the field of AAC requires that all of these challenges be addressed simultaneously. AAC is increasingly focused on literacy and the right to use print, including writing, for communication. In many ways the emphasis on basic literacy skills parallels the emphasis on literacy for all students, regardless of disabilities (Yoder, 2001).

The need for AAC is increasing as more people with severe disabilities, including those with TBI and other disabilities, are surviving and taking their places in the community. As more students with severe disabilities are integrated into regular educational programs at all levels, the availability and appropriate use of AAC in such classrooms become more critical issues (Beukelman & Mirenda, 1998; Lloyd et al., 1997). Whatever system of AAC is devised, it must be relatively easy to use, efficient, mechanically reliable, and reliable in communicating the user's thoughts and intentions, not someone else's (Schlosser & Raghenvendra, 2004).

One type of AAC that burst on the scene in the early 1990s is called facilitated communication (FC). FC requires that a "facilitator" physically assist the user in typing out

Personal Perspectives

LIFE WITH CEREBRAL PALSY

Chris Featherly

My name is Christopher Glen Featherly, and I'm going to try to give you a little overview of life with cerebral palsy as I know it.

I'm 18 years old and was born in Fort Worth, Texas. I'm currently attending Bremen High School in Midlothian, Illinois. . . .

When I came from Texas to live with my grandparents at the age of 5, I only had five generic signs for communication. My grandmom wouldn't put up with that, and so she went to the library for a sign language book. Now she learned that there really was something upstairs! The school system wanted me to use a 48-page, three-ring binder of pictures for my communication. Can you see me, using my right hand, to flip between 48 pages to talk to someone? I don't think so! My grandmom took me to Siegel Institute in downtown Chicago for a speech evaluation. They said, "This kid needs a TouchTalker [an AAC device; see www.prentrom.com for descriptions of other devices]. . . ." Well, guess what! The school speech clinician said, "No. He doesn't have language, and if he has it [Touch Talker] he won't

use his own voice to talk." So guess what grandmom did? She took me to Homewood to see another speech therapist. What do you think she said? You got it! She said, "TouchTalker." So back to school, and again the answer was, "No." Grandmom then told them she was going to take me to Shriners. If they said TouchTalker, that would be the mode of communication I would have. Well, what do you think they said? Yup! It was TouchTalker. Now, we knew how school felt about it, which meant it was in our ball park. It was time to save money and purchase it so that I could get stuff out of my head and stuff into it. By now, do you sorta have an idea what kind of grandmom I have?

[Chris's story goes on to describe software and hardware upgrades that he needed as he progressed, and his use of online resources.] ■

Source: Featherly, C. (2000). Life with cerebral palsy. In M. Oken-Fried & H. A. Bersani (Eds.), *Speaking up and spelling it out: Personal essays on augmentative and alternative communication* (pp. 189–193). Baltimore: Paul H. Brookes.

messages on a keyboard. Although FC quickly became very popular and still is used by some, it has been called into serious question because it appears to communicate the facilitator's words, not the words of the person with disabilities. In fact, FC appears to have been discredited by research (Mostert, 2001; National Research Council, 2001). Beukelman and Mirenda, noting that a very small number of people around the world appear to be typing independently after being taught with FC, concluded, "we do not believe that FC works for everyone or even with *most* people" (1998, p. 329). Any AAC device that misrepresents the user's communication demeans the user through pretense. This is not acceptable, as all people with disabilities should be treated with dignity and respect (Yoder, 2001). The goal of AAC should be independent communication in which there is no doubt about the authenticity of the messages, as the National Research Council (2001) points out.

The remarkable increase in the power and availability of microcomputers is radically changing the ability to provide AAC and make sure that the user's words are communicated. New applications of microcomputers may lead to breakthroughs that will allow people with severe disabilities to communicate more effectively, even if they have extremely limited muscle control. Furthermore, existing microcomputer software suggests ways of encouraging children to use their existing language skills. Technological developments will no doubt revolutionize AAC within a few years (Oken-Fried & Bersani, 2000). Loncke (2001) predicts that electronic communication will lead to globalization of AAC, which seems consistent with Chris Featherly's on-line communication (see Personal Perspectives above).

Much information about AAC is now available on various websites. The International Society for Augmentative and Alternative Communication (ISAAC) publishes the profes-

www.ablongman.com/hallahan10e   Behavior Problems **455**

sional journal *Augmentative and Alternative Communication*. ISACC also maintains a website that you might want to explore. Parents need to be aware of the availability of ACC and demand equipment and training that are effective for their child (Snell, 2004).

Behavior Problems

Some individuals who have certain severe or multiple disabilities engage in problematic behaviors. Their behaviors may include self-stimulation, self-injury, tantrums, aggression toward others, or some combination of these. In fact, as the federal (IDEA) definition states, self-stimulation, self-mutilation, tantrums, and failure to respond to social stimuli are prominent features of many severe and multiple disabilities.

We caution that not all people with low incidence, severe, or multiple disabilities exhibit the behavior problems we discuss here. Many people who are deaf-blind and many who have TBI, autism, or other severe or multiple disabilities do not engage in these behaviors. Nevertheless, most of the people who do exhibit these problems to a significant extent have severe and multiple disabilities. Moreover, behaviors of the type that we discuss here add a level of complexity and seriousness to any disability. Thus, finding solutions to these behavior problems is critical to treating the individual with respect and helping the person to participate in typical school and community activities.

SELF-STIMULATION

Self-stimulation can be defined as any repetitive, stereotyped behavior that seems to have no immediately apparent purpose other than providing sensory stimulation. Self-stimulation may take a wide variety of forms, such as swishing saliva, twirling objects, hand-flapping, fixed staring, and the like. Repetitive, stereotyped behavior (sometimes called *stereotypy*) may have multiple causes, including social consequences, in addition to sensory stimulation (Kennedy, Meyer, Knowles, & Shukla, 2000; Rapp, Miltenberger, Galensky, Ellingson, & Long, 1999).

Nearly everyone sometimes engages in some form of self-stimulation, such as lip-biting, hair-stroking, and nail-biting, but not at the high rate that characterizes a disability. Nondisabled infants engage in self-stimulation, and so do nondisabled adults, particularly when they are tired or bored. Only the high rate, lack of subtlety, and social inappropriateness of such self-stimulation differentiate it from the norm.

Self-stimulation becomes problematic when it occurs at such a high rate that it interferes with learning or social acceptability or when it occurs with such intensity that it does injury. Some individuals with autism or other pervasive developmental disability engage in self-stimulation to the exclusion of academic and social learning. In most of these cases, it appears that only intrusive, directive intervention will be successful in helping the individual learn academic and social skills (Kauffman, 2005).

SELF-INJURY

Self-injurious behavior (SIB) is repeated physical self-abuse, such as biting, scratching, or poking oneself, head-banging, and so on. Unchecked, SIB often results in self-mutilation. Self-stimulation can be so frequent and intense that it becomes SIB. For example, Worsdell, Iwata, Conners, Kahng, and Thompson (2000) studied SIB characterized by hand-biting, head- or body-hitting, hand-mouthing, and skin-picking. Hand-mouthing is self-stimulation of the kind that all infants do; even some nondisabled adults can be seen occasionally mouthing their hands. However, hand-mouthing becomes self-injurious for some people with severe developmental disabilities, resulting in serious skin lesions.

FOR MANAGEMENT of behavior problems, see **www.pbis.org**

UNDERSTANDING THE STANDARDS AND PRINCIPLES What can teachers do about behavior problems some individuals with multiple disabilities may exhibit? *(CEC Knowledge and Skills Standards CC5K6, CC5S2, CC5S5, CC5S10, & CC5S11)*

Council for Exceptional Children

Self-stimulation
Any repetitive, stereotyped activity that seems only to provide sensory feedback.

Self-injurious behavior (SIB)
Behavior causing injury or mutilation of oneself, such as self-biting or head-banging; usually seen in individuals with severe and multiple disabilities.

TANTRUMS

Severe tantrums can include a variety of behaviors, including self-injury, screaming, crying, throwing or destroying objects, and aggression toward others. Sometimes, the event that sets off a tantrum is unknown, at least to the casual observer. Often, however, a tantrum is precipitated by a request or demand that the individual do something (perhaps a self-care task or some academic work), and the consequence of the tantrum is that the demand is withdrawn, thus reinforcing the tantrum behavior.

Tantrums impose a handicap on the individual who uses them to avoid learning or doing important things. They stymie socialization, as most people want to avoid interacting with someone who is likely to tantrum. Teachers and others who work most successfully with individuals who have tantrums do not withdraw reasonable demands for performance. What they do is modify their demand or circumstances in some way or alternate their demands for performance in ways that are less likely to set off a tantrum.

AGGRESSION TOWARD OTHERS

Not all aggression toward others is associated with tantrums. Some individuals with severe or multiple disabilities engage in calculated physical attacks that threaten or injure others. Sometimes these attacks come without warning or only after subtle indications of imminent assault that only someone who knows the individual well is likely to perceive. Aggression toward others is disabling because it limits social interactions. For understandable reasons, people tend to avoid those they believe are likely to endanger or hurt them. Research suggests that aggression and other undesirable behavior such as SIB may be followed by attention or other rewarding consequences for individuals with severe and multiple disabilities (Thompson & Iwata, 2001).

LACK OF DAILY LIVING SKILLS

Lack of **daily living skills** refers to the absence or significant impairment of the ability to take care of one's basic needs, such as dressing, feeding, or toileting. Many people with severe and multiple disabilities must be taught the adaptive behavior that is expected of older children and adults. These adaptive behaviors include a wide variety of tasks involving clothing selection and dressing, food preparation and eating, grooming, socializing, using money, using public transportation, playing games or other recreation, and so on (Brown & Snell, 2000).

FUNCTIONAL BEHAVIORAL ASSESSMENT AND POSITIVE BEHAVIORAL SUPPORT

Problem behaviors are often related to a brain disorder or brain injury, even if the disorder is not understood. An example is severe autism, which often includes self-stimulation, self-injury, tantrums, or all of these. However, there is increasing emphasis on analyzing and changing the environments in which problem behavior is exhibited, that is, increasing focus on the immediate and alterable influences on behavior rather than on immutable or historical reasons for behavior (Horner, Albin, Sprague, & Todd, 2000).

In earlier chapters, we introduced the ideas of **functional behavioral assessment (FBA)** and **positive behavioral support (PBS)**, primarily as they apply to students with less severe disabilities (see Chapters 2, 5, 7, and 8). However, these procedures may be particularly important for students with severe and multiple disabilities. FBA entails finding out why or under what circumstances problem behavior is exhibited, and PBS involves creating an environment that supports appropriate behavior.

Daily living skills Skills required for living independently, such as dressing, toileting, bathing, cooking, and other typical daily activities of nondisabled adults.

Functional behavioral assessment (FBA) Evaluation that consists of finding out the consequences (purposes), antecedents (what triggers the behavior), and setting events (contextual factors) that maintain inappropriate behaviors; this information can help teachers to plan educationally for students.

Positive behavioral support (PBS) Systematic use of the science of behavior to find ways of supporting the desirable behavior of an individual rather than punishing undesirable behavior.

FBA often reveals how a student uses self-stimulation, SIB, tantrums, or aggression against others. A student might behave inappropriately to escape or avoid unpleasant or nonpreferred activities or tasks (McCord, Thomson, & Iwata, 2001). In many instances, researchers and practitioners find that the student has no other effective and efficient means of communication. The task, therefore, is to figure out how the student is using unacceptable communication and teach him or her a more effective and efficient and acceptable means of letting others know what he or she wants or is feeling. FBA has led to the discovery that sometimes people with severe and multiple disabilities use inappropriate behavior to communicate a variety of their wants or needs (e.g., "Pay attention to me," "Let me out of here," "There's nothing to do," "There's too much to do," or "I don't want to do that now").

Positive behavioral support (PBS) is the vehicle for teaching a student how to behave more appropriately, making appropriate behavior "work" for their communication. In the case of students with severe and multiple disabilities, making PBS a part of managing behavior across school, home, neighborhood, and community is particularly important (*Families and Disability Newsletter*, 2001; Horner et al., 2000). For a more detailed discussion of PBS for students with multiple or severe disabilities, see the Responsive Instruction on page 458.

Case book Reflection

Refer to the case, *Chase* in your booklet. How did his teachers use functional behavioral assessment and positive behavioral support to manage his outbursts and behavior? Was it effective? Why or why not?

Early Intervention

Most children with multiple and severe disabilities are identified at birth or soon thereafter because their disabilities are very noticeable to parents, physicians, and/or nurses. Some newborns with severe and multiple disabilities require extensive medical treatment and therefore are immediately placed in **neonatal intensive care units (NICUs)**. NICUs are the equivalent of intensive care units (ICUs) for older children and adults, providing around-the-clock monitoring of bodily functions. The NICU staff consists of several specialists, often including specially trained nurses, physicians, respiratory care practitioners, occupational therapists, and social workers. Because NICUs are expensive to staff and administer, not all hospitals have them; therefore, newborns are sometimes transported from one hospital to another that has a NICU. Even though the infant is under constant medical supervision, most authorities agree that parents should be allowed to spend as much time as possible with their newborns so that bonding can take place between the parents and infant. Some NICUs allow parents to "room in" with their babies.

Neonatal intensive care unit (NICU)
A special unit in a hospital designed to provide around-the-clock monitoring and care of newborns who have severe physical problems; staffed by professionals from several disciplines, such as nursing, social work, occupational therapy, respiratory therapy, and medicine; similar to an intensive care unit for older children and adults.

Other children with severe and multiple disabilities might seem typical at birth but are recognized as having pervasive developmental disabilities within the first couple of years of their lives. In the case of very serious TBI, an individual might actually be developing normally until the event that severely damages her or his brain. Therefore, early intervention should be seen as having two meanings: (1) early in the child's life and (2) as soon as possible after the disability is detected.

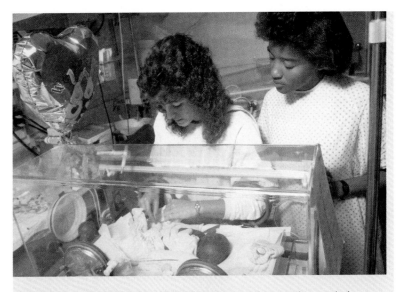

Authorities agree that parents should be encouraged to spend as much time as possible with the infants being cared for in neonatal intensive care units (NICUs).

Meeting the Needs of Students with Low-Incidence, Multiple, and Severe Disabilities

Positive Behavioral Support

WHAT IS POSITIVE BEHAVIORAL SUPPORT?

Recent reauthorizations of the Individuals with Disabilities Education Act require teachers, school systems, and those involved with students who exhibit challenging behaviors to approach problematic behavior through a mechanism called "positive behavioral support." Positive behavioral support (PBS) refers to the process of identifying alternative, acceptable ways to communicate through teaching more appropriate behaviors and/or changing the environment to reduce the likelihood of prompting the undesirable behavior (Kogel, Kogel, & Dunlap, 1996). This approach to behavior management differs fundamentally from traditional behavioral modification plans that focus on the elimination of target behaviors, yet do not take into account possible environmental or personal triggers when doing so. For example, a student's undesirable behavior of banging his head on his desk might be eliminated by placing a baseball cap on his head. Although this might appear to be an acceptable solution, if the student's banging was a sign of boredom or an anxiety-producing peer in the vicinity, the baseball cap solution does not address the function of the behavior, and it is likely that another behavior will manifest in response to the original source of the behavior.

PBS, by contrast is guided by two fundamental assumptions: (1) Each behavior carries a communicative intent, and (2) typically, multiple factors influence the presence of specific behavior. Interventions based upon these assumptions, therefore, include a functional behavioral assessment (FBA) (Horner, Vaughn, Day, & Ard, 1996). FBA seeks to identify the purpose of the behavior and supporting environmental conditions. The results of such assessment lead to the development of multifaceted plans that can include changing situational events, altering events that immediately precede the behavior, teaching alternative responses to the situation, and providing meaningful reinforcers to promote acceptable responses (Horner et al., 1996).

APPLYING THE RESEARCH TO TEACHING

Support strategies such as removing high-frustration activities (e.g., difficult assignments, undesirable directives), selecting functional and meaningful (from the student's perspective) curricula, reducing fear or anxiety about a situation through precorrection (e.g., a teacher might suggest what to do when feeling frustrated), teaching more appropriate ways to make requests or express oneself, using behavior modification to reinforce desired behaviors and communicate nonacceptability, and creating activities that build upon student interest and strength are all a part of implementing PBS.

Based on a synthesis of studies that included PBS, the U.S. Office of Special Education Programs makes the following recommendations to support the behavioral needs of individuals with significant disabilities.

- *Respond to individual needs.* Services and programs should be responsive to the preferences, strengths, and needs of individuals with challenging behavior. In addition, students may benefit from instruction in self-determination skills, social skills, goal-setting, and independent learning skills.
- *Alter environments.* If something in the individual's environment influences the challenging behavior, it is important to organize the environment for success. For example, clearly defined work spaces and quiet work areas may assist a child who is noise-sensitive.
- *Teach new skills to the individual with challenging behavior and members of his or her social network.* Individuals need to be taught alternative, appropriate responses that serve the same purpose as the challenging behavior.
- *Appreciate positive behaviors.* It is important to reinforce and acknowledge all positive behaviors consistently. (U.S. Office of Special Education Programs, 1998, p. 1) ∎

—By Kristin L. Sayeski

The Division for Early Childhood (DEC) of the Council for Exceptional Children (CEC) has established a set of recommended practices for early intervention special education programs (Odom & McLean, 1996; Sandall, McLean, & Smith, 2000). The task force that developed these recommendations relied on six criteria that it considered essential to early intervention programs in special education: (1) research- or value-based practices, (2) family-centered practices, (3) a multicultural perspective, (4) cross-disciplinary collaboration, (5) developmentally and chronologically age-appropriate practices, and (6) adherence to the principle of normalization (McLean & Odom, 1996).

RESEARCH- OR VALUE-BASED PRACTICES

Early intervention programs should be based as much as possible on techniques that research has shown to be effective. Unfortunately, it is not always possible to conduct all the necessary research before an approach or technique is adopted. The task force recommended that when research has not provided definitive evidence of an approach's effectiveness, the approach be based on values held by the early childhood special education community. Some of these value-based practices are providing individualized practices for each child and family, communicating with family members in a nonpaternalistic manner and with mutual respect and caring, making center environments safe and clean, and providing opportunities for families to have access to medical decision making (Strain, Smith, & McWilliam, 1996).

FAMILY-CENTERED PRACTICES

At one time, the prevailing philosophy in early childhood special education programming ignored parents and families at best or viewed them primarily as potential negative influences on the child with disabilities. When early intervention programs did involve parents, the assumption often was that the parents had little to offer and were in need of training to improve their parenting skills. Although it is true that some parents do need to be educated about how to be better parents, to assume that this is always the case is paternalistic and offputting to the majority of parents, who are very capable. For this reason, authorities now recommend that one not assume that parents have little or nothing to offer with respect to how to work with their children. Instead, they emphasize that parents, siblings, and extended family, can be a valuable and integral part of the educational process for young children with disabilities.

As we discussed in Chapters 1 and 2, the federal law, IDEA, also recognizes that parents and families should be central to the educational process for infants and toddlers. The Individualized Family Service Plan (IFSP), in fact, dictates that the family be central in the decision-making process for the child. A family-centered philosophy means taking into account the particular priorities and needs of the family when an educational intervention plan for the child is being developed.

MULTICULTURAL PERSPECTIVE

Given the changing ethnic demographics in the United States, it is critical that all special education programming be culturally sensitive. It is particularly important that early intervention professionals adopt a multicultural perspective because parents are often still coping with the stress of having had their child diagnosed with a disability (McLean & Odom, 1996).

To provide early intervention from a multicultural perspective, the task force recommended practices such as ensuring that:

- someone in the program or immediately available to the program speaks the family's preferred language. . . .
- staff base their communication with family members on principles of mutual respect, caring, and sensitivity. . . .
- and services ensure an unbiased, nondiscriminatory curriculum with regard to disability, gender, race, religion, and ethnic and cultural orientation. (Strain et al., 1996, p. 105)

CROSS-DISCIPLINARY COLLABORATION

Because infants and young children with multiple and severe disabilities by definition have needs in multiple areas, best practice dictates that professionals from several disciplines should be involved. Furthermore, it is critical that these professionals collaborate

UNDERSTANDING THE STANDARDS AND PRINCIPLES What should teachers know with respect to early intervention programs in special education? *(CEC Knowledge and Skills Standards EC4S1, EC7S2, EC7S3, & EC7S4)*

Council for Exceptional Children

Case book Reflection

Refer to the case, *Who Will Help Patrick?* in your booklet. Patrick is living with his foster mother; however, the living conditions are very grave. How does the issue of family play a significant part in the success of a child with multiple and severe disabilities?

in a coordinated way to provide high-quality services. There are different kinds of cross-disciplinary models, but the most critical feature for success is that the professionals in each of the disciplines work collaboratively, not independently. Some authorities also recommend that professionals should be willing to share roles (Strain et al., 1996). For example, the early childhood special education teacher might engage in training activities that are typically conducted by the speech therapist and vice versa.

DEVELOPMENTALLY AND CHRONOLOGICALLY AGE-APPROPRIATE PRACTICES

Developmentally appropriate practice (DAP)
Educational methods for young children that are compatible with their developmental levels and that meet their individual needs; coined by the National Association for the Education of Young Children.

The term **developmentally appropriate practice (DAP)** was first used by the National Association for the Education of Young Children, an organization that focuses on early childhood education for children without disabilities. DAP refers to the practice of using educational methods that are at the developmental levels of the child and that meet the child's individual needs (Bredekamp & Rosegrant, 1992). Many early childhood special educators are in agreement with the notion of DAP, but they believe that it should be balanced with the need for using educational methods that are also chronologically age appropriate. They believe that young children with disabilities should be educated as much as possible alongside their same-age nondisabled peers rather than with much younger nondisabled peers.

PRINCIPLE OF NORMALIZATION

As we discussed in Chapter 2, normalization is the philosophical principle that all people with disabilities should have educational and living environments that are as similar as possible to those of people who do not have disabilities. The DEC of CEC has adopted the philosophy of inclusion wholeheartedly in their statement on inclusion:

> Inclusion, as a value, supports the right of all children, regardless of their diverse abilities, to participate actively in natural settings within their communities. A natural setting is one in which the child would spend time had he or she not had a disability. (Division for Early Childhood, 1993, p. 4, as cited in McLean & Odom, 1996, p. 12)

Sheltered workshop
A facility that provides a structured environment for people with disabilities in which they can learn skills; can be either a transitional placement or a permanent arrangement.

Competitive employment
A workplace that provides employment that pays at least minimum wage and in which most workers are nondisabled.

Transition to Adulthood

Transition to adulthood is a critical time for most people with severe and multiple disabilities. Fortunately, as we noted in Chapter 2, the field of special education has made great strides in developing transition services for people with disabilities. Much of this progress has been made because of a change in philosophy about how people with disabilities are treated, and this change is nowhere more evident than in the treatment of people with severe and multiple disabilities. For example, not too long ago, with respect to employment the best that could be hoped for was to be able to place such individuals in a **sheltered workshop**. Now, however, a much wider range of options is available, including, for some people, **competitive employment** alongside workers who are nondisabled.

CHANGING PHILOSOPHY

We can point to at least two principles of current transition programming that reflect the change in philosophy toward treating people with severe disabilities with more dignity (Westling & Fox, 2000). First, there is an emphasis on **self-determination**. Self-determination

> has been described as "acting as the primary causal agent in one's life and making choices and decisions regarding one's quality of life, free from undue external influence or interference" (Wehmeyer, 1992, p. 305). Self-determination develops over the life span and is associated with reaching adulthood . . . Issues such as accessibility, employment rights, community living, inclusive schooling, mobility, and personal care assistance all stem from the desire of individuals with disabilities to access the activities and lifestyles they desire. (Westling & Fox, 2000, p. 473)

As part of this emphasis on self-determination, professionals have developed a number of what are called **person-centered plans**. Person-centered plans focus on the student's preferences and those of her or his family in planning for the student's future (Brown & Snell, 2000; Giangreco, Cloninger, & Iverson, 1993; Mount & Zwernik, 1988; Vandercook, York, & Forest, 1989).

Second, authorities now recommend that **natural supports** be an integral part of transition planning. Rather than always creating new services for a person's particular needs, the notion of natural supports is to try first to find available resources that already exist in the workplace or the community. With respect to work, this might mean training coworkers to

Case book Reflection

Refer to the case, *Chase* in your booklet. At the end of this case, Chase is about to enter middle school. How might he benefit from early vocational programming? What might you include in his transition plan?

Self-determination
Having control over one's life, not having to rely on others for making choices about one's quality of life; develops over one's life span.

Person-centered plan
A method of planning for people with disabilities that places the person and his or her family at the center of the planning process.

Natural supports
Resources in a person's environment that can be used for support, such as friends, family, and coworkers.

There is a growing range of employment options available to persons with severe and multiple disabilities, including sheltered workshops, but also competitive environments alongside workers who do not have disabilities.

Job coach
A person who assists adult workers with disabilities (especially those with mental retardation), providing vocational assessment, instruction, overall planning, and interaction assistance with employers, family, and related government and service agencies.

Individualized education program (IEP)
IDEA requires an IEP to be drawn up by the educational team for each exceptional child; the IEP must include a statement of present educational performance, instructional goals, educational services to be provided, and criteria and procedures for determining that the instructional objectives are being met.

provide assistance rather than immediately assuming that a **job coach** is required. With respect to community living, this might mean having the person with a disability living in an apartment, with assistance in daily living skills from a neighbor, family member, or paid attendant, rather than living in a residential facility with attendants.

VOCATIONAL PROGRAMMING

As we stated in Chapter 2, each student's **individualized education program (IEP)** must contain a transition plan, beginning no later than age sixteen; and it should begin by age fourteen when appropriate. The transition plan should contain recommendations for how to ready the student for the world of work and/or for postsecondary education or training.

For many students with severe and multiple disabilities, it is advisable that vocational training actually begin in elementary school because it might take several years to acquire all the skills they will need to hold down a job successfully. In elementary school, the training might consist of such things as learning to keep on schedule, building social skills, performing worklike tasks (e.g., helping to take attendance, collecting lunch money), and beginning to learn about different types of jobs.

In secondary school, the focus shifts to involving the student in actual work situations in the community with the help of a job coach. The student should be involved in selecting these placements, and there should be enough variety in the jobs that the student gets a good sample of what kinds of jobs are available and what he or she is good at and likes. In the early stages, this might involve the student volunteering in several different types of placements. Later, it is preferable that the student engage in paid work placements. Being paid adds to the reality of the experience and provides an opportunity for the student to learn how to handle finances.

COMMUNITY AND DOMESTIC LIVING SKILLS

As we noted in Chapter 5, community living skills involve such things as using transportation, shopping, using telephones, managing money, and using the Internet. Domestic living skills include such things as preparing meals, doing laundry, housekeeping, yard maintenance, and so forth.

At one time, community living skills were taught primarily or solely in classroom settings. In other words, teachers arranged their classroom to simulate a community setting, such as an aisle in a grocery store. Authorities now believe that simulations are much inferior to using real community settings (Westling & Fox, 2000). The best place to teach domestic living skills, however, is not necessarily in the student's home. Because students are not that far away from the time when they will move out of their parents' home and because teaching domestic skills is often done in small groups, there are some advantages to using a setting other than their own home. Thus, domestic living skills are often taught in a school setting, such as the home economics classroom and the school cafeteria (Westling & Fox, 2000).

Another reason for using the school as the instructional setting some of the time is to ensure that the student with disabilities has a chance to interact with age-mates who do not have disabilities (Browder & Bambara, 2000; Moon & Inge, 2000). Inclusion in regular school programs provides opportunities for students with disabilities to interact socially with nondisabled peers. And social skills are critical for successful integration into the community and workplace.

The last thirty to forty years have brought enormous strides in preparing people with multiple and severe disabilities to lead productive lives as adults. It was not that long ago that people with multiple and severe disabilities were housed in large residential institutions and had minimal contact with the public. Today, with intensive and extensive instruction and the support of professionals and the community, many of them can aspire to work alongside nondisabled persons and live independently or semi-independently by themselves or in a small **community residential facility (CRF)**.

Community residential facility (CRF)
A place, usually a group home, in an urban or residential neighborhood where about three to ten adults with mental retardation live under supervision.

SUMMARY

WHAT is the definition of low-incidence, multiple, and severe disabilities, and what is their prevalence?

■ Low-incidence, multiple, and severe disabilities are those that occur relatively infrequently and require extensive support in more than one major life activity, such as, mobility, communication, self-care, independent living, employment, and self-sufficiency. Probably 1 percent or fewer of all learners have such low-incidence, multiple, or severe disabilities.

WHAT is traumatic brain injury, and how might it affect education?

■ Traumatic brain injury (TBI) is injury to the brain resulting in total or partial disability or psychosocial maladjustment that affects educational performance.
  ■ It may be the result of closed head injuries or open head injuries.
  ■ It may affect cognition, language, memory, attention, reasoning, abstract thinking, judgment, problem solving, sensory or perceptual and motor disabilities, psychosocial behavior, physical functions, information processing, or speech, all of which are important in school.

HOW is deaf-blindness defined, and what are the special educational problems it entails?

■ Deaf-blindness is defined by significant impairments in both hearing and seeing, although the individual may have some residual hearing or sight.

■ It may be caused by a variety of genetic and chromosomal syndromes, prenatal conditions, and postnatal conditions.
■ The person who is deaf-blind has difficulty accessing information, communicating, and navigating the environment.
■ It requires direct teaching, structured routines, and emphasis on communication and mobility.

WHAT considerations apply to many students with low-incidence, multiple, and severe disabilities?

■ Communication, behavior management, early intervention, and transition to adulthood are concerns that apply to many learners with these disabilities.
  ■ Augmentative or alternative communication (AAC) is important for those who cannot communicate effectively through speech.
  ■ Common behavior problems requiring special management include self-stimulation, self-injury, tantrums, aggression toward others, lack of daily and living skills, all of which may require functional behavioral assessment and positive behavioral support.
  ■ Early intervention should be based on both research and values and be family-centered, multicultural, cross-disciplinary, age-appropriate, and feature normalization.
  ■ Transition to adulthood should honor the concepts of person-centered planning and natural supports, feature vocational programming, and include community and domestic living skills.

APPLYING THE STANDARDS AND PRINCIPLES

■ **WHAT** do you think teachers should be most aware of as they think about **implementing instructional strategies** to meet the academic needs of students with severe and multiple disabilities? *(CEC Content Standards #4 & INTASC Principles #4)*

■ **WHAT** are the benefits of functional behavioral assessment **(FBA)** and positive behavior support **(PBS)**? *(CEC Content Standards #5 & INTASC Principles #5)*

■ **THE parents** of a young child with severe and multiple disabilities express concern about their child's difficulties. They are most concerned about their child's inability to communicate. What would you tell them? *(CEC Content Standard #6 & INTASC Principle #6)*

■ **WHAT** can individuals with severe and multiple disabilities expect as they **transition to adulthood**? *(CEC Content Standards #7 & INTASC Principles #7)*

Council for Exceptional Children

INTASC

Chapter 14

Learners with Physical Disabilities and Other Health Impairments

$\mathcal{J}$im trudged down the steps and across the yard. He felt mad at the world. He was angry at the uncles for bringing him up here, and mad at Mama for letting him come. He thought about going to wait in the truck for the uncles to come back, but his legs wouldn't stop moving down the slope of the yard. Penn had been to the top of the Empire State Building. Penn had been to Independence Hall. Jim had no idea what to say to a boy who had seen the things Penn had seen. And he had no idea what to say to a boy who had polio. When he walked past the rocking chairs, his stomach dropped as if he had jumped off of something high. He took a deep breath and turned around. "Hey, Penn," he said.

"Hey, Jim," said Penn.

The two boys stared at each other and grinned, then shook hands awkwardly, as if a grown-up were making them do it. Jim looked down at Penn's legs before he could stop himself. Penn slapped his right leg twice with an open palm.

"It's this one," he said. "I can't move this one."

"Oh," Jim said. "I'm sorry."

Penn shrugged. "It's okay," he said. "It could've been a lot worse." He kicked his left leg straight out. "This one's fine."

TONY EARLEY
Jim the Boy

QUESTIONS TO GUIDE YOUR READING OF THIS CHAPTER.

- HOW are physical disabilities defined and classified?
- WHAT is the prevalence of physical disabilities, and what is the need for special education?
- WHAT are some major neuromotor impairments?
- WHAT are some major orthopedic and musculoskeletal disorders?
- WHAT other conditions affect health or physical ability?
- HOW can physical disabilities be prevented?
- WHAT are the psychological and behavioral characteristics of individuals with physical disabilities?
- WHAT are prosthetics, orthotics, and adaptive devices?
- WHAT are the major educational considerations for students with physical disabilities?
- WHY is early intervention important, and on what should it focus?
- WHAT are the major issues in transition for students with physical disabilities?

In Western culture, many people are almost obsessed with their bodies. They don't just want to be healthy and strong; they want to be beautiful—well formed and attractive to others. In fact, some people seem to be more concerned about the impression their bodies make than they are about their own well-being. They might even endanger their health in an effort to become more physically alluring. It is not really surprising, then, that people with physical disabilities must fight two battles: the battle to overcome the limitations imposed by their physical conditions and the battle to be accepted by others.

Individuals with physical disabilities or differences are often stared at, feared, teased, socially rejected, or treated cruelly. Sometimes people feel embarrassed about someone else's disability, not seeming to understand the feelings of the person who has the disability. Or people might feel that an acquired physical disability must change someone's personality dramatically. In Tony Earley's (2000) story about Jim and his friend Penn, who had polio, we see Jim's mixed feelings of anger and fear when seeing his pal for the first time after Penn was paralyzed (see p. 465). We probably expect Jim's mixture of anger, fear, and inquisitiveness from a ten-year-old—wondering about death, the permanence of disability, how it feels to have the disability, and so on. But most of us have such feelings and questions, regardless of our age. And most people with physical disabilities share Penn's matter-of-factness and eagerness to be accepted and get on with life.

Although polio has been virtually eradicated by vaccination, many other causes of partial paralysis and other physical disabilities have not been eliminated. Attitudes toward physical disabilities have not changed much in many ways, nor have the problems of having physical disabilities. Children with physical disabilities often face more than the problem of acceptance. For many, accomplishing the simple tasks of everyday living is a minor—or major—miracle.

Definition and Classification

In this chapter, we consider children whose primary distinguishing characteristics are health or physical problems. *Children with physical disabilities or other health impairments* are those whose physical limitations or health problems interfere with school attendance or learning to such an extent that special services, training, equipment, materials, or facilities are required. Children who have physical disabilities might also have other disabilities of any type or special gifts or talents. Thus, the characteristics of children with physical disabilities are extremely varied. The child's physical condition is the proper

Misconceptions About Learners with Physical Disabilities and Other Health Impairments

MYTH Cerebral palsy is a contagious disease.

FACT Cerebral palsy is not a disease. It is a nonprogressive neurological injury. It is a disorder of muscle control and coordination caused by injury to the brain before or during birth or in early childhood.

MYTH Physical disabilities of all kinds are decreasing because of medical advances.

FACT Because of advances in medical technology, the number of children with severe disabilities is increasing. The number of survivors of serious medical conditions who develop normally or have mild impairments, such as hyperactivity and learning disabilities, is also increasing.

MYTH The greatest educational problem involving children with physical disabilities is highly specialized instruction.

FACT The greatest educational problem is teaching people without disabilities about what it is like to have a disability and how disabilities can be accommodated.

MYTH The more severe a person's physical disability, the lower is his or her intelligence.

FACT A person can be severely physically disabled by cerebral palsy or another condition but have a brilliant mind.

MYTH People with epilepsy are mentally ill.

FACT People with epilepsy (seizure disorder) are not any more or less disposed to mental illness than are those who do not have epilepsy.

MYTH Arthritis is found only in adults, particularly those who are elderly.

FACT Arthritic conditions are found in people of any age, including young children.

MYTH People with physical disabilities have no need for sexual expression.

FACT People with physical disabilities have normal sexual urges and need outlets for sexual expression.

MYTH Physical disabilities shape people's personalities.

FACT People with physical disabilities have the full range of personality characteristics found among those who do not have physical disabilities. There are no particular personality characteristics associated with physical disability.

MYTH If a child with a physical disability such as cerebral palsy or spina bifida learns to walk as a young child, then he or she will maintain that ability throughout life.

FACT Continuing intervention through adolescence and adulthood—the entire life span—is required in many cases. Unless they have continued support for ambulation, adolescents or adults might find walking much more difficult or give up walking, even if they learned to walk as children.

Casebook Reflections

Refer to the case *Praying for a Miracle* in your booklet. Peter is very capable academically but suffers from muscular dystrophy. How does his case show the complexities of harmonizing the needs of a child's academic abilities with the needs of a child's disability, which in this case is progressive?

Congenital anomaly
An irregularity (anomaly) that is present at birth; might or might not be due to genetic factors.

Acute
A serious state of illness or injury from which someone often recovers with treatment.

Chronic
A permanent condition; not temporary.

Episodic
Occurring in episodes; a temporary condition that will pass but may recur.

Progressive
A disease or condition that worsens over time and from which one seldom or never recovers with treatment.

concern of the medical profession, but when physical problems have obvious implications for education, teaching specialists are needed. The fact that the primary distinguishing characteristics of children with physical disabilities are medical conditions, health problems, or physical limitations highlights the necessity of interdisciplinary cooperation. There must be communication between physicians and special educators to maintain the child's health and at the same time develop whatever capabilities the child has (Bigge, Best, & Heller, 2001).

Physical disabilities occur with tremendous variety. Children may have **congenital anomalies** (defects they are born with), or they may acquire disabilities through accident or disease after birth. Some physical disabilities are comparatively mild and transitory; others are profound and progressive, ending in total incapacitation and early death. It is difficult to discuss physical disabilities in general, so this chapter is organized around specific conditions that fall into one of three categories: neuromotor impairments, orthopedic and musculoskeletal disorders, and other conditions that affect health or physical ability.

It is important to make distinctions between conditions that are acute or chronic and between those that are episodic or progressive. An **acute** illness or condition may be very serious or severe, but with treatment (which may include hospitalization or medication) it resolves, and the person recovers. Someone with a serious infection or who has a serious accident may, for example, become acutely ill or be in critical condition for a time but recover. However, a **chronic** condition is one that is ongoing. It does not resolve, even with the best treatment; it is an incurable condition. Cerebral palsy is chronic; it cannot be cured. An **episodic** condition is one that recurs, although most of the time the individual can function quite normally. Its occurrence is limited primarily to successive episodes. The episodes do not necessarily become more serious or severe over time. Asthma and seizure disorders (epilepsy), for example, tend to be episodic. However, a **progressive** condition is one that becomes more and more serious or severe over time, usually involving more and more complications or deterioration. Muscular dystrophy is an example of a physical problem that is usually progressive.

Prevalence and Need

Roughly 300,000 students in U.S. public schools are being served under two special education categories related to physical disabilities. About 75,000 of these have orthopedic disabilities, and about 225,000 have other health problems. This does not include students with traumatic brain injury or multiple disabilities or young children who are said to have a developmental delay. The needs of many students with physical disabilities are unmet because the number of children and youths with such disabilities is growing, yet health and social service programs are not.

Part of the increase in the prevalence of physical disabilities might be due to improvements in the identification of, and medical services to, children with certain conditions. Ironically, medical advances have not only improved the chances of preventing or curing certain diseases and disorders, but also assured the survival of more children with severe medical problems. Many children with severe and multiple disabilities and those with severe, chronic illnesses or severe injuries, who in the past would not have survived long, today can have a normal life span. So declining mortality rates do not necessarily mean that there will be fewer individuals with disabilities. Moreover, improvements in medical care might not lower the number of individuals with disabilities unless there is also a lowering of risk factors in the environment—factors such as accidents, toxic substances, poverty, malnutrition, disease, and interpersonal violence (Baumeister, Kupstas, & Klindworth, 1990; Pless, 1994).

Neuromotor Impairments

Neuromotor impairment is caused by injury to the brain or spinal cord (neurological damage) that also affects the ability to move parts of one's body (motor impairment). It may be associated with injury to the brain before, during, or after birth. **Traumatic brain injury (TBI)**, which we discussed in Chapter 13, involves brain damage with an identifiable external cause (trauma) after the birth process. However, brain injury can be acquired from a variety of nontraumatic causes as well: hypoxia (reduced oxygen to the brain, as might occur in near drowning), infection of the brain or its linings, stroke, tumor, metabolic disorder (such as may occur with diabetes, liver disease, or kidney disease), or toxic chemicals or drugs.

In many cases of brain damage, it is impossible to identify the exact cause of the neuromotor impairment. The important point is that when a child's nervous system is damaged, no matter what the cause, muscular weakness or paralysis is almost always one of the symptoms. Because these children cannot move about like most others, their education typically requires special equipment, special procedures, or other accommodations for their disabilities.

CEREBRAL PALSY

Cerebral palsy (CP) is not a disease. It is not contagious, it is not progressive (except that improper treatment can lead to complications), and there are no remissions. Although it is often thought of as a motor problem associated with brain damage at birth, CP is actually more complicated. For practical purposes, CP can be considered part of a syndrome that includes motor dysfunction, psychological dysfunction, seizures, and emotional or behavioral disorders due to brain damage.

Some individuals with CP show only one indication of brain damage, such as motor impairment; others show combinations of symptoms. The usual definition of CP refers to paralysis, weakness, lack of coordination, and/or other motor dysfunction because of damage to the child's brain before it has matured (Batshaw & Perret, 1986; Capute & Accardo, 1996a, 1996b). Symptoms can be so mild that they are detected only with difficulty or so profound that the individual is almost completely incapacitated. Because CP includes such a heterogeneous group of children, the label *cerebral palsy* has been called into question by some. Others have noted that the label "defines groups of children who are desperately in need of a service, and this seems an adequate ground" for continuing to use the label (Bax, 2001, p. 75).

Although there is no cure for CP, advances in medical and rehabilitation technology offer increasing hope of overcoming the disabilities resulting from neurological damage. For example, intensive long-term physical therapy in combination with a surgical procedure in which the surgeon cuts selected nerve roots below the spinal cord that cause spasticity in the leg muscles allows some children with spastic CP to better control certain muscles. Such treatment allows some nonambulatory children to walk and helps others to walk more normally. However, the fact that children are enabled to walk does not mean that they will be able to walk all their lives. Continued services might be required if they are to continue walking as adults (Bottos, Feliciangeli, Sciuto, Gericke, & Vianello, 2001).

Causes and Types   Anything that can damage the brain during its development can cause CP. Before birth, maternal infections, chronic diseases, physical trauma, or maternal exposure to toxic substances or X-rays, for example, can damage the brain of the fetus. During the birth process, the brain can be injured, especially if labor or birth is difficult or

Traumatic brain injury (TBI)
Injury to the brain (not including conditions present at birth, birth trauma, or degenerative diseases or conditions) resulting in total or partial disability or psychosocial maladjustment that affects educational performance; may affect cognition, language, memory, attention, reasoning, abstract thinking, judgment, problem solving, sensory or perceptual and motor disabilities, psychosocial behavior, physical functions, information processing, or speech.

Cerebral palsy (CP)
A condition characterized by paralysis, weakness, lack of coordination, and/or other motor dysfunction; caused by damage to the brain before it has matured.

UNDERSTANDING THE STANDARDS AND PRINCIPLES   What do we know about the causes and types of neuromotor impairments? *(CEC Knowledge and Skills Standard PH2K2)*

Council for Exceptional Children

THE UNITED Cerebral Palsy Association provides information and resources for people with CP and their families: **www.ucp.org**

Advances in medical and rehabilitation technology offer increasing hope of overcoming disabilities associated with cerebral palsy.

complicated. Premature birth, hypoxia, high fever, infections, poisoning, hemorrhaging, and related factors can cause harm after birth. In short, anything that results in oxygen deprivation, poisoning, cerebral bleeding, or direct trauma to the brain can be a possible cause of CP.

Although CP occurs at every social level, it is more often seen in children born to mothers in poor socioeconomic circumstances. Children who live in such circumstances have a greater risk of incurring brain damage because of such factors as malnutrition of the mother, poor prenatal and postnatal care, environmental hazards during infancy, and low birth weight.

The two most widely accepted means of classification specify the limbs that are involved and the type of motor disability. Some individuals have a mixture of various types of CP.

Classification according to the extremities involved applies not just to CP but to all types of motor disability or paralysis. The most common classifications are **quadriplegia** (all four limbs are involved) and **paraplegia** (only the legs are involved).

Likewise, classification by type of movement applies not only to CP, but also to other types of neuromotor disabilities. **Spasticity** refers to stiffness or tenseness of muscles and inaccurate voluntary movement. **Choreoathetoid** is the term applied to abrupt, involuntary movements and difficulty maintaining balance. **Atonic** refers to floppiness or lack of muscle tone.

The important point about CP is that the brain damage affects strength and the ability to move parts of the body normally. The difficulty of movement may involve the limbs as well as the muscles involving facial expressions and speech. As a result, someone with CP might have difficulty moving or speaking or might exhibit facial contortions or drooling. But these results of brain damage do not necessarily mean that the person's intelligence or emotional sensitivity has been affected by the damage affecting muscle control.

Quadriplegia
A condition in which all four limbs are paralyzed

Paraplegia
A condition in which both legs are paralyzed.

Spasticity
Characterized by muscle stiffness and problems in voluntary movement; associated with spastic cerebral palsy.

Choreoathetoid
Characterized by involuntary movements and difficulty with balance; associated with choreoathetoid cerebral palsy.

Atonic
Lack of muscle tone; floppiness.

Associated Disabilities and Educational Implications CP is a developmental disability—a multidisabling condition that is far more complex than a motor disability alone. When the brain is damaged, sensory abilities, cognitive functions, and emotional responsiveness as well as motor performance are usually affected. A high proportion of children with CP are found to have hearing impairments, visual impairments, perceptual disorders, speech problems, emotional or behavioral disorders, mental retardation, or some combination of several of these disabling conditions in addition to motor disability. They might also exhibit such characteristics as drooling or facial contortions.

Some individuals with CP have normal or above-average intellectual capacity, and a few test within the gifted range. Nevertheless, the average tested intelligence of children with CP is lower than the average for the general population. We must be very cautious in interpreting the test results of children with CP, however, as many standardized tests of intelligence and achievement might be inappropriate for individuals with special difficulties in perception, movement, or response speed. Furthermore, the movement problems of a child with CP might become more apparent when the child is in a state of emotional arousal or stress; this can complicate using typical testing procedures, which tend to be demanding and stressful.

The educational problems of children who have CP are as multifaceted as their disabilities. Not only must special equipment and procedures be provided because the children have physical disabilities, but the same special educational procedures and equipment that are required to teach children with vision, hearing, or communication disorders, learning disabilities, emotional or behavioral disorders, or mental retardation are often needed. Careful and continuous educational assessment of the individual child's capabilities is particularly important. Teaching the child who has CP demands competence in many aspects of special education and experience in working with a variety of disabling conditions in a multidisciplinary setting (Bigge et al., 2001; Heller, Alberto, Forney, & Schwartzman, 1996; Tyler & Colson, 1994).

SEIZURE DISORDER (EPILEPSY)

A person has a **seizure** when there is an abnormal discharge of electrical energy in certain brain cells. The discharge spreads to nearby cells, and the effect may be loss of consciousness, involuntary movements, or abnormal sensory phenomena. The effects of the seizure will depend on the location of the cells in which the discharge starts and how far the discharge spreads.

People with **epilepsy** have recurrent seizures (Engel, 1995). About 6 percent of the population will have a seizure at some time during life, but most of them will not be diagnosed as having epilepsy because they do not have repeated seizures (Batshaw & Perret, 1986). Seizures reflect abnormal brain activity, so it is not surprising that they occur more often in children with developmental disabilities (e.g., mental retardation or cerebral palsy) than in children without disabilities (Bigge et al., 2001; Coulter, 1993; Vining & Freeman, 1996).

Causes and Types   Seizures apparently can be caused by almost any kind of damage to the brain. As brain imaging and molecular biology advance, scientists are arriving at a better understanding of risk for epilepsy (Avoli, Rogawski, & Avanzini, 2001). The most common immediate causes include lack of sufficient oxygen (hypoxia), low blood sugar (hypoglycemia), infections, and physical trauma. Certain conditions, such as those just listed, tend to increase the chances that neurochemical reactions will be set off in brain cells (Vining & Freeman, 1996). In many cases, the causes are unknown. Some types of seizures may be progressive; that is, they may damage the brain or disrupt its functioning in such a way that having a seizure increases the probability of having another (Girvin, 1992). Even though the cause of seizures is not well understood, it is important to note that with proper medication, most people's seizures can be controlled.

Seizures can take many forms, and the best way to classify seizures is a matter of debate among neurologists (e.g., Parra, Augustijn, Geerts, & Boas, 2001). However, educators should note that seizures may differ along at least the following dimensions:

- *Duration*: They may last only a few seconds or for several minutes.
- *Frequency*: They may occur as frequently as every few minutes or only about once a year.
- *Onset*: They may be set off by certain identifiable stimuli or be unrelated to the environment, and they may be totally unexpected or be preceded by certain internal sensations.
- *Movements*: They may cause major convulsive movements or only minor motor symptoms (e.g., eye blinks).
- *Causes*: They may be caused by a variety of conditions, including high fever, poisoning, trauma, and other conditions mentioned previously; but in many cases, the causes are unknown.
- *Associated disabilities*: They may be associated with other disabling conditions or be unrelated to any other medical problem or disability.
- *Control*: They may be controlled completely by drugs, so that the individual has no more seizures, or they may be only partially controlled.

Educational Implications   About half of all children with seizure disorders have average or higher intelligence, just as is true for the general population. Among those without

Seizure (convulsion)
A sudden alteration of consciousness, usually accompanied by motor activity and/or sensory phenomena; caused by an abnormal discharge of electrical energy in the brain.

Epilepsy
A pattern of repeated seizures.

MORE INFORMATION about epilepsy is available at **www.efa.org**

mental retardation, however, there seems to be a higher-than-usual incidence of learning disabilities (Besag, 1995). Although many children who have seizure disorders have other disabilities, some do not. Consequently, both general and special education teachers can expect to encounter children who have seizures (see Spiegel, Cutler, & Yetter, 1996). Besides obtaining medical advice about management of the child's particular seizure disorder, teachers should know first aid for epileptic seizures (see Focus on Concepts below). Ignorance about the causes of seizures and about first aid are among the most common misconceptions about epilepsy (Gouvier, Brown, Prestholdt, Hayes, & Apostolas, 1995).

Seizures are primarily a medical problem and require primarily medical attention. Educators are called on to deal with the problem in the following ways:

1. General and special education teachers need to help dispel ignorance, superstition, and prejudice toward people who have seizures and provide calm management for the occasional seizure the child may have at school (Spiegel et al., 1996).

2. Special education teachers who work with students with severe mental retardation or teach children with other severe developmental disabilities need to be prepared to manage more frequent seizures as well as to handle learning problems. The teacher should record the length of a child's seizure and the type of activity the child was engaged in before it occurred. This information will help physicians in diagnosis and treatment. If a student is being treated for a seizure disorder, the teacher should know the type of medication and its possible side effects (Bigge et al., 2001).

Some children who do not have mental retardation but have seizures exhibit learning and behavior problems. These problems might result from damage to the brain that causes other disabilities as well, or they might be the side effects of anticonvulsant medication or

FOCUS ON CONCEPTS

First Aid for Epileptic Seizures

A MAJOR epileptic seizure is often dramatic and frightening. It lasts only a few minutes, however, and does not require expert care. These simple procedures should be followed:

- Remain calm. You cannot stop a seizure once it has started. Let the seizure run its course. Do not try to revive the individual.
- If the person is upright, ease him or her to the floor and loosen his or her clothing.
- Try to prevent the individual from striking his or her head or body against any hard, sharp, or hot objects; but do not otherwise interfere with movement.
- Turn the individual's face to the side so that saliva can flow out of the mouth.
- Do not insert anything between the individual's teeth.

- Do not be alarmed if the individual seems to stop breathing momentarily.
- After the movements stop and the person is relaxed, allow him or her to sleep or rest if he or she wishes.
- It isn't generally necessary to call a doctor unless the attack is followed almost immediately by another seizure or the seizure lasts more than ten minutes.
- Notify the parents, guardians, or next of kin that a seizure has occurred.
- After a seizure, many people can carry on as before. If, after resting, the individual seems groggy, confused, or weak, it may be a good idea to accompany him or her home. ■

Source: Courtesy of Epilepsy Foundation of America.

the result of mismanagement by parents and teachers. Teachers must be aware that seizures of any type can interfere with the child's attention or the continuity of education. Brief seizures might require the teacher to repeat instructions or allow the child extra time to respond. Frequent major convulsions might prevent even a bright child from achieving at the usual rate.

Many students with epilepsy have no learning problems at all. However, some do have learning disabilities, and children with epilepsy more often have emotional or behavioral disorders than do those without epilepsy. In fact, *Epilepsia*, the journal of the International League Against Epilepsy, devoted an entire special issue to learning disabilities (Ayala, Elia, Cornaggia, & Trimble, 2001). If children with epilepsy do have problems in school, their school adjustment can be improved dramatically if they are properly assessed, placed, counseled, taught about seizures, and given appropriate work assignments.

SPINA BIFIDA AND OTHER SPINAL CORD INJURIES

Neurological damage might involve only the spinal cord, leaving the brain unaffected. Spinal cord injury can occur before or after birth, affecting the individual's ability to move or control bodily functions below the site of the injury (Bigge et al., 2001).

During early fetal development, the two halves of the embryo grow together or fuse at the midline. When the closure is incomplete, a congenital midline defect is the result. Cleft lip and cleft palate are examples of such midline defects. **Spina bifida** is a congenital midline defect that results from failure of the bony spinal column to close completely during fetal development. The defect may occur anywhere from the head to the lower end of the spine. Because the spinal column is not closed, the spinal cord (nerve fibers) can protrude, resulting in damage to the nerves and paralysis and/or lack of function or sensation below the site of the defect.

Spina bifida is often accompanied by paralysis of the legs and of the anal and bladder sphincters because nerve impulses are not able to travel past the defect. Surgery to close the spinal opening is performed in early infancy, but this does not repair the nerve damage. Although spina bifida is one of the most common birth defects resulting in physical disability, its causes are not known.

Spinal cord injuries resulting from accidents after birth are also a major cause of paralysis. The basic difference between spina bifida and other spinal cord injuries is that the individual who is injured after birth has gone through a period of normal development and must adjust to an acquired disability.

Educational Implications   The extent of the paralysis resulting from a spinal cord injury depends on how high or low on the spinal column the injury is. Some children with spinal cord injuries are able to walk independently, some need braces, and others have to use wheelchairs. Lack of sensation and ability to control bodily functions, too, will depend on the nature of the injury. Therefore, the implications for education are extremely varied. However, factors other than muscle weakness or paralysis alone affect a child's ability to walk (Bartonek & Saraste, 2001). Careful analysis of motivation and other environmental inducements to walk are critically important.

Some children will have acute medical problems that might lead to repeated hospitalizations for surgery or treatment of infections. Lack of sensation in certain areas of the skin can increase the risk of burns, abrasions, and pressure sores. The child might need to be repositioned periodically during the school day and monitored carefully during some activities in which there is risk of injury.

Because the student with spina bifida has deficiencies in sensation below the defect, she or he may have particular problems in spatial orientation, spatial judgment, sense of direction and distance, organization of motor skills, and body image or body awareness. Lack of bowel and bladder control in some children will require periodic **catheterization**. Many children can be taught to do the procedure known as *clean intermittent catheterization* themselves, but teachers should know what to do or obtain help from the school nurse.

Spina bifida
A congenital midline defect resulting from failure of the bony spinal column to close completely during fetal development.

FOR MORE INFORMATION about spina bifida, see the website of the National Spina Bifida Association of America: **www.sbaa.org**
See also the National Spinal Cord Injury Association: **www.spinalcord.org**

Catheterization
The insertion of a tube into the urethra to drain the bladder.

Orthopedic and Musculoskeletal Disorders

Some children are physically disabled because of defects or diseases of the muscles or bones. Even though they do not have neurological impairments, their ability to move is affected. Most of the time, muscular and skeletal problems involve the legs, arms, joints, or spine, making it difficult or impossible for the child to walk, stand, sit, or use his or her hands. The problems may be congenital or acquired after birth, and the causes can include genetic defects, infectious diseases, accidents, or developmental disorders.

Two of the most common musculoskeletal conditions affecting children and youths are **muscular dystrophy** and **juvenile rheumatoid arthritis**. Muscular dystrophy is a hereditary disease that is characterized by progressive weakness caused by degeneration of muscle fibers (Batshaw & Perret, 1986). The exact biological mechanism that is responsible for muscular dystrophy is not known, nor is there any cure at present. Juvenile rheumatoid arthritis is a potentially debilitating disease in which the muscles and joints are affected; the cause and cure are unknown (Bigge et al., 2001). It can be a very painful condition and is sometimes accompanied by complications such as fever, respiratory problems, heart problems, and eye infections. Among children with other physical disabilities, such as cerebral palsy, arthritis may be a complicating factor that affects the joints and limits movement. These and other conditions can significantly affect a student's social and academic progress at school.

A wide variety of other congenital conditions, acquired defects, and diseases also can affect the musculoskeletal system, such as the spinal curvature known as **scoliosis** or missing or malformed limbs (see Bigge et al., 2001; Heller, Alberto, Forney, & Schwartzman, 1996). In all these conditions, as well as in cases of muscular dystrophy and arthritis, the student's intelligence is unaffected unless there are additional associated disabilities. Regarding the musculoskeletal problem itself, special education is necessary only to improve the student's mobility, to ensure that proper posture and positioning are maintained, to provide for education during periods of confinement to hospital or home, and otherwise to make the educational experience as normal as possible.

Other Conditions Affecting Health or Physical Ability

In addition to those discussed so far, an extremely wide array of diseases, physiological disorders, congenital malformations, and injuries can affect students' health and physical abilities and create a need for special education and related services. The cataloging of these conditions is not important, but special educators should understand the range of physical disabilities and the types of accommodations that might be necessary to provide an appropriate education and related services.

Asthma is an increasingly common lung disease characterized by episodic inflammation or obstruction of the air passages such that the person has difficulty in breathing. Usually, the difficulty in breathing is reversible (i.e., is responsive to treatment). Severe asthma can be life-threatening, and in some cases, it severely restricts a person's activities. The disease can also get better or worse for poorly understood reasons, and the unpredictability of the condition can be difficult to deal with. In Personal Perspectives on page 475, Kathryn Hegarty describes some of her experiences with asthma. Note that she received important support from both her family and her school. Without the special resource class for students with special needs, which she describes as "The Base," she doesn't think she would have been able to go to school.

Congenital malformations and disorders can occur in any organ system, and they may range from minor to fatal flaws in structure or function. In many cases, the cause of the malformation or disorder is not known; in others, it is known to be hereditary or caused by ma-

---

Muscular dystrophy
A hereditary disease characterized by progressive weakness caused by degeneration of muscle fibers.

Juvenile rheumatoid arthritis
A systemic disease with major symptoms involving the muscles and joints.

Scoliosis
An abnormal curvature of the spine.

Asthma
A lung disease characterized by episodic difficulty in breathing, particularly exhaling, due to inflammation or obstruction of the air passages.

CHILDREN with special health needs and their families face common problems. Family Voices (National Coalition for Children with Special Healthcare Needs) provides information at **www.familyvoices.org**

A variety of websites contain information about specific diseases and conditions:

The Asthma and Allergy Foundation of America: **www.aafa.org**

The National Cystic Fibrosis Society: **www.cff.org**

The National Multiple Sclerosis Foundation: **www.nmss.org**

The National Organization for Rare Disorders: **www. rarediseases.org**

Personal Perspectives

THE IMPORTANCE OF FAMILY AND SCHOOL IN COPING WITH ASTHMA

I WAS diagnosed with asthma at the age of two so I don't remember what life was like without it. Fortunately, throughout my younger years the illness never affected me significantly and I was able to do everything other children my age did.

I was lucky to have a supportive family, we had always been very close, but things changed when my asthma got worse. My older brother, Andrew, was very protective, although he had quite a tough time as he was always told to look after me. My Mum and Dad were often shouted at when I was feeling fed up or if I was begging them to discharge me from the hospital. It was when I hit puberty that things started to go wrong. I woke up one morning feeling a bit breathless and I found that my inhaler wasn't helping. My Mum took me to hospital where I was put on a nebuliser. It was the same medication as my inhaler but it was delivered through a breathing mask. I soon felt better and was sent home, although it started to become a regular occurrence. I was put on a very high dose of steroids. The list of possible side effects included weight gain, high blood pressure and brittle bones. . . .

Over the following months my asthma got progressively worse, which involved my having short but frequent stays in the hospital. My school had a facility called "The Base" for pupils who needed to work out of their usual class for a variety of reasons. This meant that on days I was not feeling well I could go there and work would be brought down from my classes so that I could work quietly at my own pace. I could also use this facility if the [elevators] were out of use since it was difficult for me to use the stairs around the school as I would become so breathless.

I certainly wouldn't have been at school half as much without "The Base." I became very friendly with one of the teachers who worked there. She provided not only educational support, but emotional support as well. I would often go in feeling fed up and frustrated. She would sit down and listen while I poured my heart out and told her how awful my life was.

Some days, even walking to the bus stop was too much for me, so the school provided a taxi to take me between home and school. It meant that if I was unwell while I was at school, I could telephone the taxi to pick me up early, or if I hadn't been well during the night I could go in to school later. It gave me a lot of freedom but I didn't abuse it. The school knew that I wanted to be there so I didn't have to feel guilty if I was late or even if I didn't go in at all. . . . [Kathryn also describes her worsening condition, some classmates' misunderstanding, and her lack of social life due to her illness.]

I think the fact that I have such a supportive family has kept me going. I am also extremely grateful to my school. If it hadn't been for "The Base" I would hardly have been there at all. I could have given up a long time ago, but I didn't. I am a fighter because I have had to be. I will always have asthma. It is part of my life but, hopefully, I am over the worst of it. From now on things can only get better. ∎

Source: Hegarty, K., Lyke, T., Doherty, R., & Douglas, S. (2000). "I didn't ask to have this": First-person accounts of young people. In A. Closs (Ed.), *The education of children with medical conditions* (pp. 15–17). London: David Fulton. Reprinted by permission.

---

ternal infection or substance use by the mother during pregnancy. For instance, **fetal alcohol syndrome (FAS)**, which is now one of the most common syndromes involving malformations and mental retardation, is caused by the mother's use of alcohol during pregnancy. Worldwide, FAS is now seen in about 1 in 1000 live births, and the prevalence of other disorders related to alcohol use of women during pregnancy is a serious problem (Archibald, Fennema-Notestine, Gamst, Riley, Mattson, & Jernigan, 2001).

More children die in accidents each year than are killed by all childhood diseases combined. Millions of children and youths in the United States are seriously injured and disabled temporarily or permanently in accidents each year. Many of those who do not acquire traumatic brain injury receive spinal cord injuries that result in partial or total paralysis below the site of the injury. Others undergo amputations or are incapacitated temporarily by broken limbs or internal injuries.

Fetal alcohol syndrome (FAS)
Abnormalities associated with the mother's drinking alcohol during pregnancy; defects range from mild to severe, including growth retardation, brain damage, mental retardation, hyperactivity, anomalies of the face, and heart failure; also called *alcohol embryopathy*.

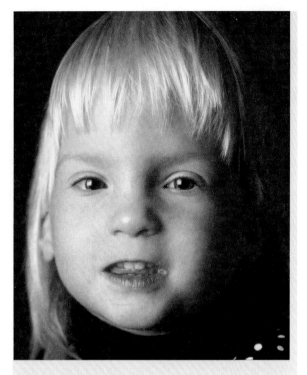

Fetal alcohol syndrome, associated with mothers' alcohol use during pregnancy, results in distinct physical and developmental abnormalities.

Acquired immune deficiency syndrome (AIDS)
A virus-caused illness resulting in a breakdown of the immune system; currently, no known cure exists.

FOR MANY WEBSITES related to FAS, simply enter *fetal alcohol syndrome* as a search term in your web browser. The American Autoimmune and Related Diseases Association provides information about AIDs and related disorders at **www.aarda.org**

Acquired immune deficiency syndrome (AIDS) is often thought to be a disease that merely makes one susceptible to fatal infections. However, children with AIDS often acquire neurological problems as well, including mental retardation, cerebral palsy, seizures, and emotional or behavioral disorders. AIDS is caused by the human immunodeficiency virus (HIV). Although HIV infections can be spread in other ways, the primary means of transmission is through sexual contact. Most of the reported new cases of HIV infections are in minority populations, and almost three-fourths of the new infections in the group aged thirteen to nineteen years are in minority populations. It is clear that "HIV infection in American adolescents has not received the attention it merits over the years" (Rogers, 2001, p. 1).

HIV/AIDS still carries considerable stigma in our society (Murphy, Roberts, & Hoffman, 2002). As children and youths with AIDS and other viral and bacterial infections live longer owing to improved medical treatments, there will be an increasing need for special education and related services. Teachers should be aware that if reasonable procedures are followed for preventing infections, there is no serious concern regarding transmission of HIV in the classroom (Ainsa, 2000; Bigge et al., 2001).

We have already mentioned fetal alcohol syndrome, which results in disabilities acquired by children of mothers who abuse alcohol during pregnancy. The abuse of other substances by mothers also has negative implications for their children. If the mother is a substance abuser, then there is also a high probability of neglect and abuse by the mother after her baby is born. Many women who are intravenous drug users not only risk chemical damage to their babies, but also give them venereal diseases such as syphilis, which can result in disabilities. Children of such mothers are also at risk for being born with AIDS. If the number of substance-abusing mothers increases, then the number of infants and young children with severe and multiple disabilities will increase as well. In spite of the multiple causal factors involved, the prospects of effective early intervention with children who are exposed prenatally to drugs are much better than previously thought. Although the consequences of any drug use during pregnancy may be serious, the near hysteria of the 1980s about the irreversible effects of crack cocaine on infants was not justified. True, many children who are exposed prenatally to drugs will have developmental disabilities. Like the developmental disabilities that have other causes, however, those of children who are exposed before birth to drugs are amenable to modification.

Some students have conditions that require particularly careful treatment because seemingly minor mistakes or oversights can have very serious consequences for them. Programs for students who are medically fragile must be particularly flexible and open to revision. Daily health care plans and emergency plans are essential, as are effective lines of communication among all who are involved with the student's treatment, care, and schooling. Decisions regarding placement of these students must be made by a team that includes health care providers and school personnel as well as the student and his or her parents.

An increasing number of children are returning home from hospitalization able to breathe only with the help of a ventilator (a mechanical device that forces oxygen into the lungs through a tube inserted into the trachea). Many of these children are also returning to public schools, sometimes with the assistance of a full-time nurse. Whether it is appropriate for children who are dependent on ventilators or other medical technology to attend regular classrooms is debatable. Educators and parents together must make decisions in each individual case, weighing medical judgment about danger to the child as well as the interest of the child in being integrated into as many typical school activities as possible with her or his peers.

Prevention of Physical Disabilities

Although some physical disabilities are not preventable by any available means, many or most are. For instance, failure to wear seat belts and other safety devices accounts for many disabling injuries. Likewise, driving under the influence of alcohol or other drugs, careless storage of drugs and other toxic substances, careless storage of firearms, use of alcohol and other drugs during pregnancy, and a host of unsafe and unhealthful practices that could be avoided cause many disabilities (Hanson, 1996).

Teenage mothers are more likely than older women to be physically battered (*Shelter News*, 2001). Teens are also more likely than older women to give birth to premature or low-birth-weight babies, and these babies are at high risk for a variety of psychological and physical problems when they reach school age (Cowden & Funkhouser, 2001). Thus, preventing adolescent pregnancies would keep many babies from being born with disabilities. Inadequate prenatal care, including maternal infections and inadequate maternal nutrition during pregnancy, also contributes to the number of babies born with disabilities. And for young children, immunization against preventable childhood diseases could lower the number of those who acquire disabilities (Hanson, 1996).

Child abuse is a significant contributing factor in creating physical disabilities in the United States, and its prevention is a critical problem. Many thousands of children, ranging from newborns to adolescents, are battered or abused each year. Teachers can play an extremely important role in detecting, reporting, and preventing child abuse and neglect because, next to parents, they are the people who spend the most time with children. If they suspect abuse or neglect, teachers must report it to child protective services under state and local regulations. These vary from one area and state to another, but ordinarily, the teacher is required to report suspected cases of child abuse or neglect to a school administrator, law enforcement officer, or social services official. A professional who fails to report child abuse or neglect may be held legally liable.

Children who are already disabled physically, mentally, or emotionally are more at risk for abuse than are nondisabled children (Vig & Kaminer, 2002). Because children with disabilities are more vulnerable and dependent, abusive adults find them easy targets. Moreover, some of the characteristics of children with disabilities are sources of additional stress for their caretakers and may be contributing factors in physical abuse. These children often require more time, energy, money, and patience than children without disabilities. Parenting any child is stressful; parenting a child with a disability can demand more than some parents are prepared to give. It is not surprising that children with disabilities are disproportionately represented among abused children and that the need for training is particularly great for parents of children with disabilities.

Teenage girls are more likely than older women to give birth to premature or low-birthweight babies, who will be at high risk for learning problems when they reach school age.

Psychological and Behavioral Characteristics

ACADEMIC ACHIEVEMENT

It is impossible to make many valid generalizations about the academic achievement of children with physical disabilities because they vary so widely in the nature and severity of their conditions. The environmental and psychological factors that determine what a child will achieve academically also are extremely varied (Bigge et al., 2001).

Many students with physical disabilities have erratic school attendance because of hospitalization, visits to physicians, the requirement of bed rest at home, and so on. Some learn well with ordinary teaching methods; others require special methods because they have mental retardation or sensory impairments in addition to physical disabilities. Because of the frequent interruptions in their schooling, some fall considerably behind their age peers in academic achievement, even though they have normal intelligence and motivation. The two major effects of a physical disability, especially if it is severe or prolonged, are that a child might be deprived of educationally relevant experiences and that he or she might not be able to learn to manipulate educational materials and respond to educational tasks the way most children do.

Some children with mild or transitory physical problems have no academic deficiencies at all; others have severe difficulties. Some students who have serious and chronic health problems still manage to achieve at a high level. Usually, these high-achieving children have high intellectual capacity, strong motivation, and teachers and parents who make every possible special provision for their education. Children with neurological impairments are, as a group, most likely to have intellectual and perceptual deficits and therefore to be behind their age peers in academic achievement.

PERSONALITY CHARACTERISTICS

Research does not support the notion that there is a certain personality type or self-concept associated with any physical disability. Children and youths with physical disabilities are as varied in their psychological characteristics as nondisabled children, and they are apparently responsive to the same factors that influence the psychological development of other children. How children adapt to their physical limitations and how they respond to social-interpersonal situations greatly depend on how parents, siblings, teachers, peers, and the public react to the children (Bigge et al., 2001; Lerner, Lowenthal, & Egan, 1998; Llewellyn & Chung, 1997).

UNDERSTANDING THE STANDARDS AND PRINCIPLES What determines how children adapt to their physical limitations and how they respond to social-interpersonal situations? *(CEC Knowledge and Skills Standards CC3K3, CC3K4, & PH3K1)*

Council for
Exceptional
Children

Public Reactions   Public attitudes can have a profound influence on how children with physical disabilities see themselves and on their opportunities for psychological adjustment, education, and employment. If the reaction is one of fear, rejection, or discrimination, these children might spend a great deal of energy trying to hide their stigmatizing differences. If the reaction is one of pity and an expectation of helplessness, people with disabilities will tend to behave in a dependent manner. To the extent that other people can see children with physical disabilities as people who have certain limitations but are otherwise just like everyone else, children and youths with disabilities will be encouraged to become independent, productive members of society (see Nabors & Larson, 2002).

Several factors seem to be causing greater public acceptance of people with physical disabilities. Professional and civic groups encourage support and decrease fear of people who are disabled through information and public education. People with physical disabilities are increasingly visible in the media, and they are often portrayed in a more realistic and positive light. Government insistence on the elimination of architectural barriers that prevent citizens with disabilities from using public facilities serves to decrease discrimination. Programs to encourage hiring workers with disabilities help the public to see those with physical disabilities as constructive, capable people. Laws that protect every child's right to public education bring more individuals into contact with people who have severe or profound disabilities. But there is no doubt that many children with physical disabilities are still rejected, feared, pitied, or discriminated against. The more obvious the physical flaw, the more likely it is that the person will be perceived in negative terms by the public.

Public policy regarding children's physical disabilities has not met the needs of most such children and their families. In particular, as successful medical treatment prolongs the lives of more and more children with severe, chronic illnesses and other disabilities, issues of who should pay the costs of treatment and maintenance (which are often enormous) and which children and families should receive the limited available resources are becoming critical.

Children's and Families' Reactions   As we suggested earlier, children's reactions to their own physical disabilities are largely a reflection of how others respond to them (see Olrick, Pianta, & Marvin, 2002; Singh, 2003). Shame and guilt are learned responses; children will have such negative feelings only if others respond to them by shaming or blaming them (and those who are like them) for their physical differences. Children will be independent and self-sufficient (within the limits of their physical disabilities) rather than dependent and demanding only to the extent that they learn how to take care of their own needs. And they will have realistic self-perceptions and set realistic goals for themselves only to the extent that others are honest and clear in appraising their conditions.

However, certain psychological reactions are inevitable for the child with physical disabilities, no matter how she or he is treated. The wish to be nondisabled and to participate in the same activities as most children and the fantasy that the disability will disappear are to be expected. With proper management and help, the child can be expected eventually to accept the disability and live a happy life, even though he or she knows the true nature of the condition. Fear and anxiety, too, can be expected. It is natural for children to be afraid when they are separated from their parents, hospitalized, and subjected to medical examinations and procedures that might be painful. In these situations, too, proper management can minimize emotional stress. Psychological trauma is not a necessary effect of

Children's feelings about their own disabilities are largely a reflection of how they are treated by others, and also of the attitude that their own families take toward them. They are more likely to see themselves as "normal" if they are treated that way, and encouraged to participate in regular activities.

hospitalization. The hospital environment may, in fact, be better than the child's home in the case of abused and neglected children.

Other important considerations regarding the psychological effects of a physical disability include the age of the child and the nature of the limitation (e.g., whether it is congenital or acquired, progressive or not). But even these factors are not uniform in their effects. A child with a relatively minor and short-term physical disability might become more maladjusted, anxious, debilitated, and disruptive than another child with a terminal illness because of the way the child's behavior and feelings are managed. Certainly, understanding the child's and the family's feelings about the disability are important. But it is also true that managing the consequences of the child's behavior is a crucial aspect of education and rehabilitation. Adolescence is a difficult time for most parents, and the fact that a child has a physical disability does not necessarily mean that the family will find a youngster's adolescence more difficult or less difficult (Magill-Evans, Darrah, Pain, Adkins, & Kratochvil, 2001).

Personal Perspectives on page 481 illustrates how family support, school experiences, medical treatment, and attitudes affect the life of a child with a chronic health problem (in this case, diabetes). Besides the school and society at large, the family and its cultural roots are important determinants of how and what children with physical disabilities will learn; therefore, it is important to take cultural values into account in teaching children not only about the academic curriculum but about their disability as well.

Prosthetics, Orthotics, and Adaptive Devices for Daily Living

Many individuals with physical disabilities use prosthetics, orthotics, and other adaptive devices to help them function better on a daily basis. A **prosthesis** is an artificial replacement for a missing body part (e.g., an artificial hand or leg); an **orthosis** is a device that enhances the partial function of a part of a person's body (a brace or a device that allows a person to do something). **Adaptive devices** for daily living include a variety of adaptations of ordinary items found in the home, office, or school—such as a device to aid bathing or hand washing or walking—that make performing the tasks required for self-care and employment easier for the person who has a physical disability.

The most important principles to keep in mind are use of residual function, simplicity, and reliability. For example, the muscles of the arm, shoulder, or back operate an artificial hand. This might be too complicated or demanding for an infant or young child with a missing or deformed upper limb. Depending on the child's age, the length and function of the amputated limb, and the child's other abilities, a passive "mitt" or a variety of other prosthetic devices might be more helpful. Choice of the most useful prosthesis will depend on careful evaluation of each individual's needs. A person without legs may be taught to use his or her arms to move about in a wheelchair or to use his or her torso and arms to get about on artificial legs (perhaps also using crutches or a cane). Again, each individual's abilities and preferences must be evaluated in designing the prosthesis (see Bigge et al., 2001; Heller, Alberto, Forney, & Schwartzman, 1996).

Two points regarding prosthetics, orthotics, and residual function must be kept in mind:

1. Residual function is often important even when a prosthesis, orthosis, or adaptive device is not used. For example, it may be crucial for the child with cerebral palsy or muscular dystrophy to learn to use the affected limbs as well as possible without the aid of any special equipment because using residual function alone will make the child more independent and can help to prevent or retard physical deterioration. Moreover, it is often more efficient for a person to learn not to rely completely on a prosthesis or orthosis, as long as he or she can accomplish a task without it.

Prosthesis
A device designed to replace, partially or completely, a part of the body (e.g., artificial teeth or limbs).

Orthosis
A device designed to restore, partially or completely, a lost function of the body (e.g., a brace or crutch).

Adaptive devices
Special tools that are adaptations of common items to make accomplishing self-care, work, or recreation activities easier for people with physical disabilities.

Personal Perspectives

OVERCOMING A HEALTH CHALLENGE

JESSIE SKINNER I was 3 when I was first diagnosed with diabetes. My Mom gave me my shots until I was 8. The first few times I gave myself shots, it was scary! It got easier as I got older. I went to camp and everyone else was doing their own shots, so I decided to start doing it myself. My diabetes is hard to control. I remember being in the hospital when I was in seventh grade because my blood sugar was high. Close to the end of seventh grade I changed doctors because I didn't feel comfortable adjusting my own insulin. My new doctor was really nice when my Mom was in the room; she'd always compliment me. But when my Mom left the room, she'd tell me, "You'd better start taking your insulin!" I'd tell her, "I am taking my insulin!" I never really felt that she believed me. Once when I was in the hospital, the same thing happened—my blood sugar was really high, but they were doing my shots for me. From that point on, she believed that I was doing my shots on a regular basis.

Once my doctor started believing me, we got closer and I could talk to her better. I wasn't afraid to tell her that I forgot my insulin on a day. Now she wants me to write some things down to help other kids with hard-to-control diabetes. One suggestion is for kids to always tell the truth about skipping their insulin. I learned that the hard way. One day I was mad at my Mom and I skipped my insulin, thinking that I was going to hurt her. The only one I hurt was myself. I got really sick and ended up in the hospital. Then I had to tell the truth. . . .

I think it's important for kids to learn to take care of their medical issues because it makes you more responsible and it helps you to better understand what you have. If you need help, don't be afraid to ask. For me, if my blood sugar is really high, my vision isn't very good. It's good to take a break once in a while and let someone else do the shot, to make sure it's the right dosage. I'll sometimes ask the nurse at school for help.

Another suggestion I have is in dealing with adults who don't understand. My softball coach found out that I had diabetes. This changed my relationship with her a whole lot. The positions that I was good at she no longer let me play. She put me in right field where no balls ever come. I think she was scared and didn't know anything about diabetes. I ended up talking to her and asking her what her problem was. Her response was, "Your diabetes." I asked her why she was holding me back, because it was something that I couldn't help. She told me that she didn't realize that she was treating me any differently than the other kids. Talking with her turned our relationship around. Now we're best friends. We even go skiing together! And now I play all the positions on my softball team.

When kids feel that they're being treated differently, I suggest they talk to the person and ask what's bothering him or her. Don't give up! I didn't, even though I wanted to give up. I now feel good that I didn't. I was so nervous when I approached my coach, because I thought she was going to kick me off the team. I'm afraid to tell other people that I have diabetes because I'm afraid they'll treat me differently. Even though I have a good relationship with my coach now, I still wonder if she looks at me differently. ■

Source: Skinner, J. (1996). Overcoming a health challenge. In L. E. Powers, G. H. S. Singer, & J. Sowers (Eds.), (1996). *On the road to autonomy: Promoting self-competence in children and youth with disabilities* (pp. 255–256). Baltimore: Paul H. Brookes. Reprinted with permission.

2. Spectacular technological developments often have very limited meaning for the immediate needs of the majority of individuals with physical disabilities. It might be years before expensive experimental equipment is tested adequately and marketed at a cost that most people can afford, and a given device might be applicable only to a small group of individuals with an extremely rare condition (Moore, 1985). Even though a device may provide greater ability to participate in ordinary childhood activities, the current cost of some technological devices is clearly a barrier to their widespread use. Common standby prostheses, orthoses, and other equipment adapted to the needs of individuals will continue to be the most practical devices for a long time to come.

We do not mean to downplay the importance of technological advances for people with physical disabilities. Advances in

Casebook Reflections

Refer to the case *Praying for a Miracle* in your booklet. Adaptations are in the planning stages for Peter's house to be made wheelchair accessible. Adjustments have been made for proper equipment to be installed for his bathing and toileting. What other challenges do you foresee?

(a)   (b)

FIGURE 14.1 Rehabilitation engineers are redesigning wheelchairs for use in off-the-street recreational and work environments: (a) chairs suitable for use at the beach or in other soft terrain; (b) a chair specially designed for racing.

THE NORTHWESTERN University Prosthetics Research Laboratory and Rehabilitation Engineering Program is dedicated to the improvement of prostheses and orthoses: **www.repoc.northwestern.edu** Rehabilitation tools and assistive devices may be researched at **www.rehabtool.com**

At Adrian's Adaptive Closet, you will find links to sites that offer clothes adapted for individuals who use wheelchairs: **www.adrianscloset.com**

The site for Wheelchair Net is a community for people who have a common interest in wheelchair technology and its improvement and successful application: **www.wheelchairnet.org/index2.html**

computer technology and applications have provided extraordinary help for many students with disabilities (DeFord, 1998; Lindsey, 2000). Our point here is that the greatest significance of a technological advance often lies in how it changes seemingly ordinary items or problems. For example, technological advances in metallurgy and plastics have led to the design of much more functional braces and wheelchairs. The heavy metal-and-leather leg braces that were formerly used by many children with cerebral palsy or other neurological disorders—cumbersome, difficult to apply, and not very helpful in preventing deformity or improving function—have been largely supplanted by braces constructed of thermoform plastic. Wheelchairs are being built of lightweight metals and plastics and redesigned to allow users to go places that are inaccessible to the typical wheelchair (see Figure 14.1). And an increasing number of computerized devices are improving the movement and communication abilities of people with disabilities.

The greatest problem today is not in devising new or more sophisticated assistive technology but rather in accurately evaluating children and youths to determine what would be most useful and then making that technology available. Most schools do not now make maximum use of available technology. Many children and youths who need prostheses or other assistive devices, such as computers, special vehicles, and self-help aids, are not carefully evaluated and provided with the most appropriate equipment.

Educational Considerations

Too often, we think of people who have physical disabilities as being helpless or unable to learn. It is easy to lower our expectations for them because we know that they are indeed unable to do some things. We forget, though, that many people with physical disabilities can learn to do many or all the things that most nondisabled people do, although sometimes they must perform these tasks in different ways (e.g., a person who does not have the use of the hands might have to use the feet or mouth). Accepting the limitations imposed by physical disabilities without trying to see how much people can learn or how the environment can be changed to allow them to respond more effectively is an insulting and dehumanizing way of responding to physical differences.

Educating students with physical disabilities is not so much a matter of special instruction for children with disabilities as it is of educating the nondisabled population (Closs, 2000). People with physical disabilities solve many of their own problems, but their lives are often needlessly complicated because the nondisabled give no thought to what life is like for someone with specific physical limitations. Design adaptations in buildings, furniture, household appliances, and clothing can make it possible for someone with a physical disability to function as efficiently as a nondisabled person in a home, school, or community.

The objectives of educators and other professionals who work with children and youths with physical disabilities should include autonomy and self-advocacy (Bigge et al., 2001; Bullock & Mahon, 2000). Children with physical disabilities typically want to be self-sufficient, and they should be encouraged and taught the skills they need to take care of themselves to the maximum extent possible. This requires knowledge of the physical limitations created by the disability and sensitivity to the child's social and academic needs and perceptions—understanding of the environmental and psychological factors that affect classroom performance and behavior.

INDIVIDUALIZED PLANNING

Students with complex physical disabilities typically require a wide array of related services as well as special education. The IEPs (individualized education programs) for such students tend to be particularly specific and detailed. The instructional goals and objectives often include seemingly minute steps, especially for young children with severe disabilities (see Bigge et al., 2001; Hanson, 1996; Heller, Alberto, Forney, & Schwartzman, 1996; Lerner et al., 1998). Many of the children under the age of three years who need special education and related services are children with physical disabilities. These children are required by law to have an **individualized family service plan (IFSP)** rather than an IEP. The IFSP must specify how the family will be involved in intervention as well as what other services will be provided. It is clear that parents of children with chronic health conditions might wish that their children did not exist, could be cured, or would improve significantly, although their actual expectations are more realistic (Wolman, Garwick, Kohrman, & Blum, 2001).

Casebook Reflections

Refer to the case *Praying for a Miracle* in your booklet. During elementary and middle school, Peter has been taught in a special school for students with physical disabilities and other health impairments. Looking ahead to the transition years, his principal believes that Peter might benefit from being placed in a mainstream program for the gifted and talented in his local high school. What possibilities might this open? What problems?

Individualized family service plan (IFSP)
A plan mandated by P.L. 99-457 to provide services for young children with disabilities (under three years of age) and their families; drawn up by professionals and parents; similar to an IEP for older children.

UNDERSTANDING THE STANDARDS AND PRINCIPLES What two objectives should professionals who work with children and youth with physical disabilities keep in mind? *(CEC Knowledge and Skills Standards PH4K1, PH4K2, & PH4S1)*

Council for Exceptional Children

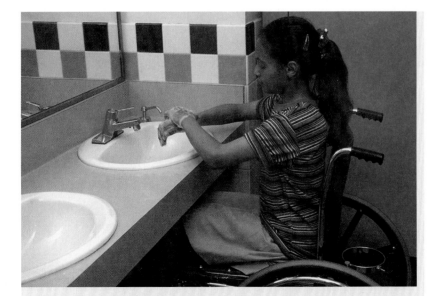

Design adaptations in buildings, furniture, household appliances, and clothing can make it possible for someone with a physical disability to function as efficiently as a nondisabled person in a home, school, or community.

Collaboration and Co-Teaching of Students with Physical Disabilities and Other Health Impairments

"But I'm Not a Nurse!"

Students with physical disabilities and other health impairments often require complex systems of care, including services from health care professionals, related service personnel, and special educators. It is easy for everyone to forget about the students' cognitive and social needs because of the day-to-day physical needs. Even though a student with physical disabilities may have a wide range of services, the least restrictive environment for them may be the general education classroom. It is in this situation that collaboration with a special educator is important for the general education teacher to understand and meet the needs of these students.

WHAT DOES IT MEAN TO BE A TEACHER OF STUDENTS WITH PHYSICAL DISABILITIES AND OTHER HEALTH IMPAIRMENTS?

Special educators who work with students with physical disabilities must have skills related to learning and instruction, as well as skills in determining appropriate assistive technology

devices, positioning, and socialization. According to the Council for Exceptional Children (2001), they should be adept at:

1. Using adaptations and assistive technology to provide individuals with physical and health disabilities full participation and access to the general curriculum
2. Using techniques of physical management to ensure participation in academic and social environments
3. Integrating an individual's health care plan into daily programming
4. Participating in the selection and implementation of augmentative or alternative communication systems

These skills require a broad range of training for special educators, including medical management and extensive collaboration with health care providers and families. With this knowledge, special educators can collaborate with general education teachers to adjust instruction, change the physical en-

EDUCATIONAL PLACEMENT

Children with physical disabilities may be educated in any one of several settings, depending on the type and severity of the condition, the services available in the community, and the medical prognosis for the condition, but most are in regular education settings (Nabors & Lehmkuhl, 2004). If such children ordinarily attend regular public school classes but must be hospitalized for more than a few days, they may be included in a class in the hospital itself. If they must be confined to their homes for a time, a visiting or homebound teacher can provide tutoring until they can return to regular classes. In these cases, which usually involve children who have been in accidents or who have conditions that are not permanently and severely disabling, relatively minor, commonsense adjustments are required to continue the children's education and keep them from falling behind their classmates. At the other extreme, usually involving serious or chronic disabilities, the child might be taught for a time in a hospital school or a special public school class designed specifically for children with physical disabilities.

Today, most children with disabilities are being integrated into the public schools because of advances in medical treatment: new developments in bioengineering, allowing them greater mobility and functional movement; decreases in or removal of architectural barriers and transportation problems; and the movement toward public education for all children. Any placement has positive and negative features, and the best decision for a particular child requires weighing the pros and cons. Working with a special educator to better understand a student's needs and how to meet those needs is imperative. For an example of how teachers can work together, read Making It Work above. Sometimes the benefits of a particular type of placement are either greatly exaggerated or almost completely dismissed.

vironment of the classroom, and communicate successfully with students.

SUCCESSFUL STRATEGIES FOR CO-TEACHING

Jo is a special education teacher of five- and six-year-olds with cerebral palsy and spina bifida. Charlotte is a general education teacher with a group of twenty-eight kindergarten-aged students, some of whom had never had any school experiences. They describe their collaboration experiences.

Jo: We combined the children into two groups. Each group was made up of half of my children and half of Charlotte's children. We'd occasionally put the two groups together. I became an expert in a certain content area. I taught it to two groups, and Charlotte did the same.

Charlotte: Our classes are scheduled for music together because of our collaboration. We had a music teacher come in who taught music to both classes as a large group; however, Jo and I did stay in the classroom to facilitate management needs because it was such a large group for one teacher to handle. In fact, we had to teach the music teacher some management ideas. It was a good experience for the music teacher; she was able to see how you can work with a range and variety of children.

It's important to find someone who has a similar philosophy and treats children the way you do, but it also must be someone you can get along with, who has the same tolerance that you do. Had we not been friendly, liked each other, and respected the way each other did things, Jo and I would not have been successful. We have seen collaborations that were not as successful as ours because they did not develop out of commonalities.

Jo: One of the most demanding things about our collaboration was keeping up with the kids, keeping them on pace, and trying to make it valuable for them educationally. As much as I want this very worthwhile social experience for my special needs kids, am I giving them the multisensory nuts-and-bolts special education that they need? I constantly have to try and strike a balance between the social needs of the children and the intense requirements of their special needs.

Charlotte: The most demanding thing about our collaboration was not working together ourselves, but effectively meeting the needs of the children. That's really the most demanding thing: living up to them. ■

By Margaret P. Weiss

EDUCATIONAL GOALS AND CURRICULA

Educational goals and curricula cannot be prescribed for children with physical disabilities as a group because their individual limitations vary so greatly. Even among children with the same condition, goals and curricula must be determined after assessment of each child's intellectual, physical, sensory, and emotional characteristics. A physical disability, especially a severe and chronic one that limits mobility, may have two implications for education: (1) The child might be deprived of experiences that nondisabled children have, and (2) the child might find it impossible to manipulate educational materials and respond to educational tasks the way most children do. For example, a child with severe cerebral palsy cannot take part in most outdoor play activities and travel experiences and might not be able to hold and turn pages in books, write, explore objects manually, or use a typewriter without special equipment. Among other things, this student might require adapted physical education. Read Responsive Instruction on page 486 for more about adapted physical education.

For children with an impairment that is only physical, curriculum and educational goals should ordinarily be the same as those for nondisabled children: reading, writing, arithmetic, and experiences designed to familiarize them with the world around them. In addition, special instruction might be needed in mobility skills, daily living skills, and occupational skills. That is, because of their physical impairments, these children might need special, individualized instruction in the use of mechanical devices that will help them to perform tasks that are much simpler for people without disabilities. For children with other disabilities in addition to physical limitations, curricula will need to be further adapted (Bigge et al., 2001).

Educational goals for students with severe or profound disabilities must be related to their functioning in everyday community environments. Only recently have educators

THE ATTAINMENT Company creates resources to help people identify the emerging issues in special education and to access the educational materials that will allow them to meet such issues effectively: **www. attainmentcompany.com**

Meeting the Needs of Students with Physical Disabilities and Other Health Impairments

Adapted Physical Education

WHAT IS ADAPTED PHYSICAL EDUCATION?

Adapted physical education (APE) is an instructional service, not a setting or placement. Students receive APE when their disability necessitates a physical education program different from their peers. The difference can be in the form of an alternative activity, an instructional modification or adaptation, or different criteria for success. APE can be part of an integrated program, for students with and without physical disabilities, or can be a stand-alone program for students with disabilities only.

WHO QUALIFIES FOR ADAPTED PHYSICAL EDUCATION?

Any student with an IEP may be eligible for APE. IDEA requires that "physical education services, specially designed if necessary, must be made available to every child with a disability receiving a free appropriate public education." Necessary adaptations are determined by IEP team members. Any student with gross motor skill deficits or limitations in strength, flexibility, or physical fitness should be considered for APE services.

STRATEGIES FOR MAKING ACCOMMODATIONS

Strategies for making accommodations to general physical education classes include (Auxter, Pyfer, & Huettig, 2001):

- Reducing the size of the playing field through reducing the size of the soccer field, goal area, basketball court, or length of a race
- Changing the size of equipment by using larger or more colorful balls, increasing the size of the bat but decreasing weight, using larger rackets, lighter bows, or scoops for catching
- Reducing the playing area by adding more players to the field or court
- Modifying basic rules such as everyone plays seated, less mobile players get two or three bounces to get to the ball in tennis, rest periods or frequent substitutions are allowed, shorten the game, or partner activities
- Using specialized equipment such as a ramp or bumpers for bowling, a batting tee, or a sit-ski for skiing

The overarching aim for APE is for students to have access to activities that will support physical, recreational, and/or leisure goals. APE should take place in the least restrictive environment (LRE). Determining the LRE involves considerations of safety as well as opportunities for meaningful participation. For many students, the LRE will be the general education physical education class. ■

By Kristin L. Sayeski

---

begun to address the problems of analyzing community tasks (e.g., crossing streets, using money, riding public transportation, greeting neighbors) and planning efficient instruction for individuals with severe disabilities. Efficient instruction in such skills requires that teaching occur in the community environment itself.

The range of educational objectives and curricula for children with physical disabilities is often extended beyond the objectives and curricula typically provided for other students in school. For example, very young children and those with severe neuromuscular problems might need objectives and curricula focusing on the most basic self-care skills (e.g., swallowing, chewing, self-feeding). Older students might need not only to explore possible careers in the way all students should, but also to consider the special accommodations their physical limitations demand for successful performance as well (see Bigge et al., 2001).

Although all students can profit from a discussion of death and dying, education about these topics might be particularly important in classrooms in which a student has a terminal illness. Teachers should be direct and open in their discussion of death and dying. Death should not be a taboo subject; nor should teachers deny their own feelings or squelch the feelings of others. Confronted with the task of educating a child or youth with a terminal illness, teachers should seek available resources and turn to professionals in other disciplines for help (Heller, Alberto, Forney, & Schwartzman, 1996; Leaman, 2000).

UNDERSTANDING THE STANDARDS AND PRINCIPLES What should teachers consider when planning educational goals for children with physical disabilities? *(CEC Knowledge and Skills Standards PH5K1, PH5K2, & PH5K3)*

Council for Exceptional Children

Personal Perspectives

WEIGHING THE ISSUE OF PLACEMENT: ONE STUDENT'S PERSPECTIVE

THERE were gains and losses at special school. Some of the positives were small classes and individual tuition to catch up on work I missed when absent, on-site paramedical therapy and medical specialists who visited school, so saving time, energy and having to be off school. There was more specialist equipment available too, some of my own, some for the use of anyone who needed it at any time. The school was fully accessible. I suppose the other thing was that there was less feeling of isolation or difference in relation to being ill or disabled: that was the norm.

On the negative side, special schools then didn't really encourage assertiveness and pride about being disabled, there really was a prevailing medical model of "caring" that could result in childlike dependency. In mainstream schools there is an understanding that kids will experiment with so-called bad habits such as smoking and sex, but staff were horribly shocked and dismayed when I was found smoking. . . . It is ironic that when I was in special school so many of us would have benefited from more liberal and "normal" approaches with opportunities for mainstreaming, but now, when so many of the children who attend special school seem to have far more complex and profound disabilities, they can't take advantage of the progress fully. ■

Source: Hegarty, K., Lyke, T., Doherty, R., & Douglas, S. (2000). "I didn't ask to have this": First-person accounts of young people. In A. Closs (Ed.), *The education of children with medical conditions* (p. 18). London: David Fulton. Reprinted with permission.

LINKS WITH OTHER DISCIPLINES

Many children with physical disabilities will need the services of a physical therapist and/or occupational therapist. (For a description of classroom implications, see Responsive Instruction on page 488.) Both can give valuable suggestions about helping the child use his or her physical abilities to the greatest possible extent, continuing therapeutic management in the classroom, and encouraging independence and good work habits. The teacher should be particularly concerned about how to handle and position the child so that the risk of further physical disability will be minimized and independent movement and manipulation of educational materials can be most efficiently learned.

Specialists in prosthetics and orthotics design and build artificial limbs, braces, and other devices that help individuals who are physically disabled to function more conventionally. By conferring with such specialists, the teacher will better understand the function and operation of a child's prosthesis or orthosis and know what the child can and cannot be expected to do.

Cooperation with psychologists and social workers can be particularly important in the case of a child with a physical disability. Working with the child's family and community agencies is often necessary to prevent lapses in treatment. The child may also be particularly susceptible to psychological stress, so the school psychologist might need to be consulted to obtain an accurate assessment of intellectual potential.

Speech-language therapists are often called on to work with children with physical disabilities, especially those with cerebral palsy. The teacher will want advice from the speech-language therapist on how to maximize the child's learning of speech and language. Individuals of all ages need access to play and recreation, regardless of their physical abilities. Any adequate

Casebook Reflections

Refer to the case *Praying for a Miracle* in your booklet. There is no mention of physical or occupational therapists in this case. What might their role be in assisting Peter? What suggestions might they have to make Peter's transition more successful?

Meeting the Needs of Students with Physical Disabilities and Other Health Impairments

Integrating Physical and Occupational Therapy in General Education Settings

The majority of students with physical disabilities receive related services as a part of their educational program. Related services can include anything from speech-language pathology to counseling to transportation. Two common related services for students with physical disabilities are occupational and physical therapy. Researchers have found that the more integrated these types of services are into education settings, the more effective the outcomes (Karnish, Bruder, & Rainforth, 1995).

PHYSICAL AND OCCUPATIONAL THERAPY

Understanding the differences between physical and occupational therapy can be confusing. Yet a clear understanding of the skills that are supported through these therapies is fundamental for creating the necessary bridge between out-of-class therapy and integrated therapy that supports student learning.

Physical therapy addresses sensory and gross motor functions. Physical therapists can assist students by identifying optimal positions for various tasks; teach students how to move within the classroom and school environment; and develop students' movement, strength, and coordination. Occupational therapists provide support for daily living skills such as dressing, bathing, and toileting as well as fine motor skills (handling small objects, handwriting, oral-motor skills).

CLASSROOM IMPLICATIONS

Despite the different focuses of the two groups, their services can overlap. As a classroom teacher, multidisciplinary collaboration among all services providers is a must. When planning for the integration of physical or occupational services in the classroom, the classroom teacher should consider the following:

- What are educationally relevant services versus medically relevant services? For example, an educationally relevant service would be to work on transfer and handling techniques with the teacher and paraprofessional to position a student for instruction. A medically relevant therapy would be strength building (Szabo, 2000).
- What are the educationally relevant IEP goals, and how can therapy support progress toward those goals? For example, mobility independence, ability to operate assistive technology, improved posture, and improved upper extremity coordination are all therapy goals that directly relate to improved educational outcomes.
- What type of service is necessary: direct, indirect, or both? Direct services involve hands-on treatment provided directly by the therapist. Preferably, these treatments occur within the natural environment (classroom, playground, gym) where the skill is expected. Indirect services, on the other hand, involve consultation or monitoring support. Under a consultation model, the therapist makes recommendations for instructional modifications, activity enhancement, environmental modifications, adaptation of materials, or schedule alterations. It may even include training the classroom teacher in ways to provide direct services. Monitoring involves periodic evaluations of student progress and related training for team members. A combination of direct and indirect services provides both direct services for certain goals or skills and consultation support for others.
- Is peer support appropriate? As students become more skilled, peer support can be solicited. This reduces the dependence a student has on any one individual and encourages interdependence—an important skill as students get older.

By working with therapists to identify ways to support therapy within the classroom, teachers learn ways to reduce the physical challenges students can encounter within general education settings, while fostering the development of necessary physical and occupational skills. ■

By Kristin L. Sayeski

program for children or youths with physical disabilities will provide toys, games, and physical exercise to stimulate, amuse, and teach recreation skills and provide the youngster with options for productive leisure (Bullock & Mahon, 2000). Physical education that is adapted to the abilities and disabilities of students is an important part of every sound school program.

Early Intervention

All people who work with young children with physical disabilities have two concerns: (1) early identification and intervention and (2) development of communication. Identifying signs of developmental delay so that intervention can begin as early as possible is important in preventing further disabilities that can result from lack of teaching and proper care. Early intervention also maximizes the outcome of therapy. Communication skills are difficult for some children with physical disabilities, and they are a critical objective of any preschool program (see Chapter 9). Danielle is a four-year-old who has received intensive language instruction, as well as other modifications to her environment. Read her story in Success Stories on page 490.

Besides communication, the first concern of teachers of young children with physical disabilities should be handling and positioning. Handling refers to how the child is picked up, carried, held, and assisted; positioning refers to providing support for the child's body and arranging instructional or play materials in certain ways. Proper handling makes the child more comfortable and receptive to education. Proper positioning maximizes physical efficiency and ability to manipulate materials; it also inhibits undesirable motor responses while promoting desired growth and motor patterns (Bigge et al., 2001). Proper positioning for one child might not be appropriate for another.

The teacher of young children with physical disabilities must know how to teach gross motor responses—such as head

People with physical disabilities can learn to do many of the things most nondisabled persons do, although sometimes they must perform these tasks in different ways. Educating students with physical disabilities is mostly a matter of educating the nondisabled population of this fact.

control, rolling over, sitting, standing, and walking—and understand how abnormal reflexes that may be a part of developmental disabilities can interfere with learning basic motor skills. If the child has severe neurological and motor impairments, the teacher might need to begin by focusing on teaching the child to eat (e.g., how to chew and swallow) and to make the oral movements that are required for speech (Bigge et al., 2001; Heller, Alberto, Forney, & Schwartzman, 1996). Fine motor skills, such as pointing, reaching, grasping, and releasing, can be critically important. These motor skills are best taught in the context of daily lessons that involve self-help and communication.

Motor skills should be taught not in isolation but as part of daily living and learning activities that will increase the child's communication, independence, creativity, motivation, and future learning. Learning social responsiveness, appropriate social initiation, how to play with others, and problem solving are other important goals for which the teacher must develop instructional strategies.

Transition

Transition involves a turning point, a change from one situation or environment to another. When special educators speak of transition, they typically refer to change from school to work or from adolescence to adulthood. For children with physical disabilities, however, transition is perhaps a more pervasive concern than it is for children with other disabilities. It may involve discharge from intensive care or transition from hospital to home at any age. In fact, transition begins for some newborns immediately after they have been treated with sophisticated medical procedures. Nevertheless, we focus here on the transition concerns of adolescents and young adults with physical disabilities. Clearly, transition planning for many

Special Educators at Work

Jennifer Durrance, Danielle's mother: "Her teacher wrote me notes daily because she knew Danielle couldn't tell me about her day."
After three years of early intervention services, four-year-old Danielle Durrance receives early childhood special education in an inclusive preschool program.

These are the keys to her success:

- **intensive** *early intervention,*
- **relentless** *communication,*
- **specific** *goals addressing physical delays and academic readiness.*

Special educator Leigh Anne Williams teaches typically developing youngsters as well as 3-and 4-year-olds with disabilities or developmental delays. Danielle Durrance is the only child in her class who uses a wheelchair. Her mother, Jennifer Durrance, communicates frequently with Williams to ensure that Danielle receives appropriate instruction and related services in her inclusive preschool program. Since she was 9-months-old, Danielle has prospered from intensive, relentless, and specific special education.

Intensive Early Intervention   Danielle has Cerebral Palsy (CP), a neurological condition that limits her mobility, her speech, and her social interactions. On the day before Halloween, she dabbed white finger-painted ghosts and goblins on black paper. Danielle finished her creation at her standing table, a piece of adaptive equipment that provides her with vertical support for up to 60 minutes each day. While her nine classmates washed their hands, Danielle transferred to her wheelchair with the help of one of the classroom's three instructional assistants. "My assistants take turns lifting Danielle and positioning her to use her walker or the vestibular swing that hangs from the classroom ceiling. They also help with her personal hygiene and we

keep a chart on the bathroom door to be sure we're sharing her physical support," says Williams.

Danielle was born prematurely at 34 weeks gestation and experienced a lack of oxygen during delivery. She weighed only 4 pounds, 4 ounces, at birth and spent 11 days in the hospital. When she was 4-months-old her mother suspected something was wrong. "She couldn't roll over and find a toy that was near her in the crib. You know how babies look at their hands a lot? Well, she would mostly look at one hand; she kept her other hand down." At 6 months, Danielle was not sitting up and it was clear that her eyes were crossed. When she was 9-months-old, developmental tests, including an MRI, confirmed that Danielle had CP and early intervention services began. A special education teacher came to the house to work with Danielle and her parents drove her to physical and occupational therapy several times a week. They also made visits to an ophthalmologist

Relentless Communication   Mrs. Durrance credits effective communication between parents and professionals for Danielle's smooth transition from early intervention services to preschool special education. "At the transition meeting, someone asked if I had a picture of Danielle with me. I really appreciated that. There

students with physical disabilities, including those who are supported by medical technology, is inadequate (Morningstar, Turnbull, Lattin, Umbarger, Reichard, & Moberly, 2001).

Two areas of concern for transition stand out clearly for adolescents and young adults with physical disabilities: careers and sociosexuality. Adolescents begin contemplating and experimenting with jobs, social relations, and sexuality in direct and serious ways. For the adolescent with a physical disability, these questions and trial behaviors are often especially perplexing, not just to themselves but also to their families: Can I get and hold a satisfying job? Can I become independent? Will I have close and lasting friendships? Will anyone find me physically attractive? How can I gratify my sexual needs? Ordinary adolescents have a

was nothing in particular that caused me to feel stressed, but I think teachers should know that many parents feel very nervous at these meetings."

Jennifer Durrance also advises teachers to learn as much as they can about how a child's disability affects her life and her learning:

Know the IEP, especially when a child is served in the regular classroom.

Keep communication a priority. Teachers need to know the parents of the child, too.

Seek information. Know that parents are knowledgeable about their child's disability.

Specific Goals Addressing Physical Delays and Academic Readiness Danielle has attended the Green Valley Preschool Program since August, 1999. According to evaluations using the Carolina Curriculum for Preschoolers with Special Needs, Danielle has progressed in all developmental areas, although her delays in cognition and social adaptation place her approximately 1 year to 1 1/2 years behind her age peers. She remembers objects that have been hidden, understands concepts like empty/full, and add one more. Socially, she follows directions, expresses enthusiasm for work or play, plays games with supervision, and enjoys being with other children. According to her IEP, Danielle's social interactions are limited by her physical delays. Danielle's fine and gross motor skills place her closer to 2 years behind her age peers. She receives occupational and physical therapy to enhance her manipulative and visual motor skills and to improve her mobility and endurance. She also receives speech-language therapy. Receptively, Danielle appears to understand many age-appropriate concepts and vocabulary, but she doesn't often initiate communication, nor does she imitate consistently.

In Spring the IEP team will make decisions for Danielle's programming for the next school year. Together, her parents and her multi-disciplinary team will decide if Danielle should start Kindergarten with her age peers or whether she would benefit more from extended preschool support.

CEC'S STANDARDS: PAVING THE WAY TO SUCCESS.

ASSESS YOUR STEPS TO SUCCESS in meeting the CEC Knowledge and Skill Base for All Beginning Special Education Teachers of Students with Physical and Health Disabilities. Use the following questions to reflect on the growth of your own professional knowledge, skills, and dispositions.

REFLECTING ON YOUR OWN PROFESSIONAL DEVELOPMENT:

If you were Danielle's teacher...

- WHAT are some areas about educating students with physical disabilities that you would need to know more about?
- WHAT are some specific skills that would help you address her academic and physical challenges?
- WHAT personal dispositions do you think are most important for you to develop in teaching students with physical disabilities?

Using the CEC Standards

- WHAT are the roles and responsibilities of medical and related services personnel in educating students with physical disabilities?
- WHAT are some frequent concerns of families of students with physical disabilities and what are some strategies to address these concerns?
- WHAT are some instructional practices, strategies, and adaptations necessary to accommodate the physical and communication characteristics of students with physical disabilities? ■

By Jean Crockett

hard time coming to grips with these questions and the developmental tasks they imply; adolescents with physical disabilities often have an even harder time.

As we pointed out in discussing psychological characteristics, there is no formula for predicting the emotional or behavioral problems a person with a given physical disability will have. Much depends on the management and training the person has received and continues to receive as an adolescent and as an adult. Bottos and colleagues provide the following caution about interventions for cerebral palsy: "Services for individuals with CP should be planned keeping in mind an entire life perspective rather than just the child-focused approach. Reduced contact when children grow up often results in a general deterioration of the quality of life of adults with disabilities and their careers" (2001, p. 526). Andersson and Mattsson (2001) drive the point home. In their study, 35 percent of adults with CP reported decreased walking ability, and 9 percent had stopped walking altogether.

CHOOSING A CAREER

For the adolescent or young adult with physical disabilities, career considerations are extremely important. In working out an occupational goal, the individual's specific abilities, disabilities, and motivation must be assessed carefully. Postsecondary education must be considered in light of the individual's interests, strengths, demands, and accessibility. Some disabilities clearly rule out certain occupational choices. With other disabilities, high motivation and full use of residual function can make it possible to achieve unusual professional status.

One of the greatest problems in dealing with adolescents who have physical disabilities is helping them to attain a realistic employment outlook. Intelligence, emotional characteristics, motivation, and work habits must be assessed at least as carefully as physical limitations. Furthermore, the availability of jobs and the demands of certain occupations must be taken into account. The child who has moderate mental retardation and severe spastic quadriplegia, for instance, is highly unlikely to have a career as a lawyer, a laboratory technician, or a clerk-typist. But what of one who has severe spastic quadriplegia and a bright mind? Such a person might well overcome both the physical limitation and the associated social stigma and be successful in a wide variety of fields in which the work is more mental than physical.

There are no simple conclusions regarding the occupational outlook for students with physical disabilities. Those with mild or transitory disabling conditions might not be affected at all in their occupational choices. Yet some with relatively mild physical disabilities might be unemployed or even unemployable because of inappropriate social and emotional behavior or poor work habits; they might need vocational rehabilitation training to function even in a vocation with limited demands. Some people with severe physical disabilities are able to use their intelligence, social skills, and residual physical abilities to the fullest and become competitive employees (or employers) in demanding occupations.

The outlook for employment of students with physical or multiple and severe disabilities has been improved dramatically by legislation and research and demonstration projects. As we mentioned in Chapter 1, the Americans with Disabilities Act of 1990 requires that reasonable accommodations be made to create equal employment opportunities for people with disabilities. More accessible transportation and buildings, increased skill in using technology to allow people to accomplish tasks at work, and greater commitment to preparing people with disabilities for work are resulting in more personal independence, economic self-sufficiency, and social acceptance, which benefit not only people with disabilities, but the economy and society as well.

We now recognize that preparing for work begins in childhood. Long before adolescence, children, including those with physical disabilities, need to be taught about and to explore various careers. They need to be thinking about what they like to do as well as what they are particularly good at and about the demands and rewards of various kinds of jobs. The objective should be to help students select appropriate training and enter a career that makes maximum use of their abilities in ways that they find personally gratifying.

Supported employment for people with severe disabilities is a relatively new concept that is being adopted widely. In this approach, a person with a severe disability works in a regular work setting. He or she becomes a regular employee, performs a valued function in the same workplace as nondisabled employees, and receives fair remuneration. Training and continued support are necessary—hence the term *supported employment*. For example, a person with disabilities might be hired as a greeter at a store but needs training and continued support in such skills as making eye contact, smiling, welcoming shoppers to the store, and offering a shopping cart or information to customers. Training and continued

A WIDE VARIETY of websites provide ideas and guidance for independent living. These include:

Canine Companions for Independence, a nonprofit organization providing assistance dogs: **www. caninecompanions.org**

A collection of computer-related products and services available to assist people with disabilities: **www. closingthegap.com**

The Independent Living Research Utilization Center: **www.ilru.org**

The Institute on Independent Living: **www. independentliving.org**

Supported employment A method of integrating people with disabilities who cannot work independently into competitive employment; includes use of an employment specialist, or job coach, who helps the person with a disability function on the job.

support might also be required to help the person with disabilities know when to leave people alone and not insist on providing information or assistance that the customer does not want.

New technologies, especially in computing and other electronic devices, offer great promise for enabling students with physical disabilities to achieve personal independence, to acquire education and training that will make them employable, and to find employment. In some cases, the technology is readily available and educators need only to become aware of the software (e.g., software that allows the functions of keys to be altered), find ways in which keystrokes can be saved through subprogramming routines (e.g., macros or find-and-replace features in word processing), or provide substitutions for physical manipulation of materials (e.g., computer graphics programs as substitutes for paper paste-ups or model construction).

Sometimes an individual's ability to use standard equipment is greatly enhanced by a simple modification such as orientation or location. Simply placing a keyboard in a vertical position over a monitor can enhance the ability of someone who uses a headstick to use a computer. A headstick is an adaptive device that allows someone who cannot use his or her hands or feet, but who has control of neck muscles, to use a computer or accomplish other tasks. Teachers must always look for simple, inexpensive or cost-free ways to facilitate the performance of students with disabilities—to prevent an environment designed for people without disabilities from handicapping those who must do things a different way. Overlooking the seemingly obvious is perhaps the way in which we most frequently handicap people with disabilities.

Casebook Reflections

Refer to the case *Praying for a Miracle* in your booklet. Think about Peter once he is out of high school. Do you see him going to college? Why or why not? What job possibilities might he have?

UNDERSTANDING THE STANDARDS AND PRINCIPLES   What do we know about transition to adulthood for students with physical disabilities? *(CEC Knowledge and Skills Standards PH10S1 & PH10S4)*

SOCIOSEXUALITY

Until fairly recently, physical disabilities were assumed to cancel human sexuality. People who were not typical physically, especially if they had limited mobility, were thought of as having no sex appeal for anyone and as having little or no ability or right to function sexually.

Fortunately, attitudes and experiences are changing. It is now recognized that people with disabilities have a right to family life education, including sex education, and to a full range of human relationships, including appropriate sexual expression. Sociosexual education for students with physical disabilities, as with such education for all other children and youths, should begin early, continue through adulthood, and include information about the structures and functions of the body, human relationships and responsibilities, and alternative modes of sexual gratification. Youths with physical disabilities need to experience close friendships and warm physical contact that is not sexually intimate. But it is neither realistic nor fair to expect people with physical disabilities to keep all their relationships platonic or to limit themselves to fantasy. Most physical disabilities, even if severe, do not in themselves kill sexual desire or prevent sexual gratification, nor do they preclude marriage and children. The purpose of special education and rehabilitation is to make exceptional individuals' lives as full and complete as possible. In the case of youths with physical disabilities, this might involve teaching or providing alternative means of sexual stimulation and accepting sexual practices and relationships that are different from the norm. With sensitive education and rehabilitation, satisfying sociosexual expression can be achieved by all but a small minority of people with disabilities.

It is now recognized that people with disabilities have a right to family life education, including sex education, and to a full range of human relationships, including appropriate sexual expression.

Summary

HOW are physical disabilities defined and classified?

- Physical disabilities are physical limitations or health problems that interfere with school attendance or learning to such an extent that special services, training, equipment, materials, or facilities are required.
  - May be congenital or acquired.
  - May be acute or chronic, episodic or progressive.
  - May be accompanied by other disabilities, such as mental retardation and emotional or behavioral disorders, or special gifts or talents.
- Major categories are neuromotor impairments, orthopedic or musculoskeletal disorders, and other conditions that affect health or physical abilities.

WHAT is the prevalence of physical disabilities, and what is the need for special education?

- Less than 0.5 percent of the child population have physical disabilities.
  - About half of these have multiple disabilities.
  - About one-fourth of these have orthopedic problems.
  - About one-fourth of these have chronic health problems.

WHAT are some major neuromotor impairments?

- All involve damage to the brain before, during, or soon after birth.
  - Cerebral palsy, characterized by paralysis, weakness, uncoordination, and/or other motor dysfunction, sometimes by mental retardation or other disabilities
  - Seizure disorder, an abnormal electrical discharge in the brain
  - Spna bifida, the failure of the spinal column to close during fetal development

WHAT are some major orthopedic and musculoskeletal disorders?

- Muscular dystrophy, a degenerative disease causing a progressive weakening and wasting away of muscle
- Juvenile rheumatoid arthritis, acute inflammation around the joints that may cause chronic pain and other complications

WHAT other conditions affect health or physical ability?

- Fetal alcohol syndrome (FAS), now one of the most common causes of malformation and mental retardation, caused by the mother's abuse of alcohol during pregnancy
- AIDS, a life-threatening viral infection that often involves neurological complications such as mental retardation, seizures, cerebral palsy, and emotional or behavioral disorders
- Accidents

HOW can physical disabilities be prevented?

- Safety prcautions, better health care, prevention of pregnancy in early teens, prevention of child abuse

WHAT are the psychological and behavioral characteristics of individuals with physical disabilities?

- No generalizations are possible.
- Much depends on the reactions of family and the public.

WHAT are prosthetics, orthotics, and adaptive devices?

- Prosthetics are artificial body parts.
- Orthotics enhance the function of a body part.
- Adaptive devices aid daily activity.

WHAT are the major educational considerations for students with physical disabilities?

- Education must make the most of the student's assets.
- Education should be as normal as possible and equip the student for daily living as well as employment or further education.

WHY is early intervention important, and on what should it focus?

- Early intervention is important in preventing further disability and maximizing the child's development.
- Early intervention should focus on communication, handling, positioning, and social skills.

WHAT are the major issues in transition for students with physical disabilities?

- Transition may involve movement from one setting to another as well as preparation for adulthood.
  - Choice of and preparation for a career are important issues.
  - Sociosexuality is another critical issue.

APPLYING THE STANDARDS AND PRINCIPLES

- **DESCRIBE** at least two types of **physical disabilities** *(CEC Content Standard #2 & INTASC Principle #2)*

- **DESCRIBE** some **effects a physical disability** might have on a student's education *(CEC Content Standard #3)*

- **HOW** should teachers determine what **instructional methods** to use with students with physical disabilities? *(CEC Content Standard #4 & INTASC Principle #4)*

- **DESCRIBE** a **learning environment** that would be well suited for students with physical disabilities. *(CEC Content Standard #5 & INTASC Principle #5)*

- **HOW** would you **respond to parents** who approached you expressing concern about the future of their high school student with a physical disability? *(CEC Content Standard #10 & INTASC Principle #10)*

Council for Exceptional Children

INTASC

Chapter 15

Learners with Special Gifts and Talents

A genius is not very likely to ever discover himself; neither is he very likely to be discovered by his intimates; they are so close to him that he is out of focus to them and they can't get at his proportions; they cannot perceive that there is any considerable difference between his bulk and their own. They can't get a perspective on him and it is only by a perspective that the difference between him and the rest of their limited circle can be perceived.

MARK TWAIN
The Autobiography of Mark Twain

QUESTIONS TO GUIDE YOUR READING OF THIS CHAPTER . . .

- HOW is giftedness defined?

- WHAT is the prevalence of giftedness?

- WHAT are the origins of giftedness?

- HOW is giftedness identified?

- WHAT are the psychological and behavioral characteristics of students with special gifts?

- HOW do cultural values affect the education of students with special gifts?

- WHAT groups of students with special gifts are neglected?

- WHAT are the major educational considerations for students with special gifts?

- WHAT are the major problems of early intervention for children with special gifts?

- WHAT provisions are made for transition of students with special gifts?

People who have special gifts or the potential for gifted performance can go through life unrecognized. As Mark Twain pointed out (see p. 497), they might seem unremarkable to their closest associates. Sometimes the special talents or gifts of children and youths are not discovered because their families and intimates place no particular value on their special abilities. And sometimes they are not recognized because these young people are not given opportunities or training. Especially in the case of those who are poor or members of minority groups, students with extraordinary gifts or talents may be deprived of chances to demonstrate and develop their potential. How many more outstanding artists and scientists would we have if every talented child had the opportunity and the training necessary to develop his or her talents to the fullest possible extent? We know that we would have more, but we don't know how many.*

Unlike disabling conditions, giftedness is something to be fostered deliberately. Yet giftedness is not without risk of stigma and rejection. Many people have a low level of tolerance for others who eclipse the ordinary individual in some area of achievement. A child who achieves far beyond the level of her or his average peers may be subjected to criticism or social isolation by other children or their parents (Coleman & Cross, 2000; Cross, 1997; Swiatek, 1998).

Some of the problems of giftedness parallel those of disabling conditions. For instance, the definition and identification of children with special gifts or talents involve the same difficulties as those involving mental retardation or emotional or behavioral disorders. But there is an underlying philosophical question regarding giftedness that makes us think differently about this exceptionality: Most of us feel a moral obligation to help people who are at some disadvantage compared to the average person, who have differences that prevent them from achieving ordinary levels of competence unless they are given special help. But with people who have special gifts, we might wonder about our moral obligation to help those who are already accelerated become even better, to distinguish themselves further by fulfilling their highest promise. The desirability or necessity of helping the highest-achieving students become even better is often questioned. Today, the emphasis is on programs to develop the talents of *all* students, with less special attention to those who might be identified as gifted or talented. As some researchers have noted, this trend toward downplaying giftedness might not be very wise (Gallagher, 2000b).

---

*We are indebted to Carolyn M. Callahan, Ph.D., of the University of Virginia for her invaluable assistance in preparing this chapter.

MISCONCEPTIONS ABOUT
Learners with Special Gifts and Talents

MYTH People with special intellectual gifts are physically weak, socially inept, narrow in interests, and prone to emotional instability and early decline.

FACT There are wide individual variations, and most individuals with special intellectual gifts are healthy, well adjusted, socially attractive, and morally responsible.

MYTH Those who have special gifts or talents are in a sense superhuman.

FACT People with special gifts or talents are not superhuman; rather, they are human beings with extraordinary gifts in particular areas. And like everyone else, they may have particular faults.

MYTH Children with special gifts or talents are usually bored with school and antagonistic toward those who are responsible for their education.

FACT Most children with special gifts like school and adjust well to their peers and teachers, although some do not like school and have social or emotional problems.

MYTH People with special gifts or talents tend to be mentally unstable.

FACT Those with special gifts or talents are about as likely to be well adjusted and emotionally healthy as those who do not have such gifts.

MYTH We know that 3 to 5 percent of the population has special gifts or talents.

FACT The percentage of the population that is found to have special gifts or talents depends on the definition of *giftedness* used. Some definitions include only 1 or 2 percent of the population; others, over 20 percent.

MYTH Giftedness is a stable trait, always consistently evident in all periods of a person's life.

FACT Some of the remarkable talents and productivity of people with special gifts develop early and continue throughout life; in other cases, a person's gifts or talents are not noticed until adulthood. Occasionally, a child who shows outstanding ability becomes a nondescript adult.

MYTH People who have special gifts do everything well.

FACT Some people who are characterized as having a special gift have superior abilities of many kinds; others have clearly superior talents in only one area.

MYTH A person has special intellectual gifts if he or she scores above a certain level on intelligence tests.

FACT IQ is only one indication of one kind of giftedness. Creativity and high motivation are as important as indications as general intelligence. Gifts or talents in some areas, such as the visual and performing arts, are not assessed by IQ tests.

MYTH Students who have a true gift or talent for something will excel without special education. They need only the incentives and instruction that are appropriate for all students.

FACT Some children with special gifts or talents will perform at a remarkably high level without special education of any kind, and some will make outstanding contributions even in the face of great obstacles to their achievement. But most will not come close to achieving at a level commensurate with their potential unless their talents are deliberately fostered by instruction that is appropriate for their advanced abilities.

Definition

Students with special gifts excel in some way compared to other students of the same age. Beyond this almost meaningless statement, however, there is little agreement about how giftedness should be defined. Local school systems often have widely differing practices regarding the education of students with special gifts or talents, because the term *gifted* has no clear-cut definition. The disagreements about definition are due primarily to differences of opinion regarding the following questions:

UNDERSTANDING THE STANDARDS AND PRINCIPLES Is there consensus about what *giftedness* means? Why or why not? *(CEC Knowledge and Skills Standard GT1K5)*

Council for Exceptional Children

1. *In what ways do students with a special gift or talent excel?* Do they excel in general intelligence, insight, creativity, special talents, and achievements in academic subjects or in a valued line of work, moral judgment, or some combination of such factors? Perhaps nearly everyone is gifted in some way or other. What kind of giftedness is most important? What kind of giftedness should be encouraged?

2. *How is giftedness measured?* Is it measured by standardized tests of aptitude and achievement, teacher judgments, past performance in school or everyday life, or some other means? If it is measured in any one particular way, some individuals will be overlooked. If past performance is the test, giftedness is being defined after the fact. What measurement techniques are valid and reliable? What measurements will identify those students who have the potential to develop special gifts or talents?

3. *To what degree must a student excel to be considered to have a special gift or talent?* Must the student do better than 50 percent, 80 percent, 90 percent, or 99 percent of the comparison group? The number of individuals with special gifts will vary depending on the criterion (or criteria) for giftedness. What percentage of the population should be considered to have special gifts?

4. *Who should make up the comparison group?* Should it be every student of the same chronological age, the other students in the same school, all students of the same ethnic or racial origin, or some other grouping? Almost everyone is the brightest or most capable in some group. What group should set the standard?

5. *Why should students with special gifts be identified?* What social or cultural good is expected to come from their identification? Is it important to meet individual students' educational needs? Are national economic or security issues at stake? Does identifying these individuals maintain an elite group or social power? By providing special educational opportunities for these students, will others reap personal or social benefits? What criteria will be used to judge whether identifying students with special gifts or talents pays off?

Giftedness or talentedness, like mental retardation, is whatever we choose to make it. Someone can be considered gifted (or retarded) one day and not the next, simply because an arbitrary definition has been changed. There is no inherent rightness or wrongness in the definitions that professionals use (Kauffman & Hallahan, 2005). Some definitions might be more logical, more precise, or more useful than others, but we are still unable to say that they are more correct in some absolute sense. We have to struggle with the concepts of gift and talent and the reasons for identifying individuals with gifts or talents before we can make any decisions about definition. Our definition of giftedness will be shaped to a large extent by what our culture believes is most useful or necessary for its survival. Giftedness is defined, not discovered (see Borland, 1997; Callahan, 1997; Gallagher, 2000a, 2000b, 2002; Heller, Monks, Sternberg, & Subotnik, 2000).

Even the terminology of giftedness can be rather confusing. Besides the word *gifted*, a variety of other terms have been used to describe individuals who are superior in some way: talented, creative, insightful, genius, and precocious, for example.

Precocity
Remarkable early development.

■ **Precocity** refers to remarkable early development. *Precocious* children develop gifts in such areas as language, music, or mathematics at a very young age.

Pedro Sanchez is a soil scientist at the Earth Institute of Columbia University, and a leader in international agroforestry.

Angela Johnson is a children's author and 2003 recipient of the Genius Grant from the John D. and Catherine T. MacArthur Foundation.

Thomas Quastoff, an accomplished bass-baritone classical music singer, was born with multiple physical disabilities caused by the morning sickness drug thalidomyde used by his mother during her pregnancy.

Susan Stroman is the Tony award–winning director and choreographer of such Broadway hits as *Contact* and *The Producers*.

Dr. Nawal Nour is a MacArthur Fellowship recipient and runs the African Women's Health Center, providing healthcare services to women who have been circumcised.

Edward P. Jones is a recipient of a MacArthur Foundation Genius Grant and the author of several books, including the Pulitzer Prize winner, *The Known World* about a black slave owner.

Robert Ballard, an explorer and anthropologist, broadcasts live from his expeditions down the Amazon River via satellite and the Internet to students all over the world.

Jody Williams is coordinator of the International Campaign to Ban Landmines and winner of the Nobel Peace Prize in 1997.

Mattie Stepanek (with his mother Jeni) battled muscular distrophy most of his short life, but he managed to become an accomplished poet along the way.

Bonnie Bessler is an associate professor of molecular biology at Princeton University investigating the chemical signaling mechanisms that bacteria use to communicate with each other.

Insight
The ability to separate and/or combine various pieces of information in new, creative, and useful ways.

Genius
A word sometimes used to indicate a particular aptitude or capacity in any area; rare intellectual powers.

Creativity
The ability to express novel and useful ideas, to sense and elucidate new and important relationships, and to ask previously unthought of, but crucial, questions.

Talent
A special ability, aptitude, or accomplishment.

Giftedness
Refers to cognitive (intellectual) superiority, creativity, and motivation of sufficient magnitude to set the child apart from the vast majority of age peers and make it possible for the child to contribute something of particular value to society.

- **Insight** may be defined as separating relevant from irrelevant information, finding novel and useful ways of combining relevant bits of information, or relating new and old information in a novel and productive way.
- **Genius** has sometimes been used to indicate a particular aptitude or capacity in any area. More often, it has been used to indicate extremely rare intellectual powers (often assumed to be indicated by IQ) or creativity.
- **Creativity** refers to the ability to express novel and useful ideas, to sense and elucidate novel and important relationships, and to ask previously unthought of, but crucial, questions.
- **Talent** ordinarily has been used to indicate a special ability, aptitude, or accomplishment.
- **Giftedness**, as we use the term in this chapter, refers to cognitive (intellectual) superiority (not necessarily of genius caliber), creativity, and motivation in combination and of sufficient magnitude to set the child apart from the vast majority of age peers and make it possible for her or him to contribute something of particular value to society.

The lack of consensus about what *giftedness* means poses problems for government definitions. No federal law requires special education for students with special gifts or talents, although federal legislation encourages states to develop programs and support research. Only if the student has a disability in addition to giftedness does the federal mandate for special education apply (Zirkel, 2003). However most states mandate programs, and the most common elements of state definitions are (1) general intellectual ability, (2) specific academic aptitude, (3) creative thinking ability, (4) advanced ability in the fine arts and performing arts, and (5) leadership ability.

Giftedness (or genius) appears to involve both quantitative and qualitative differences in thinking. "People who are gifted typically work really hard (i.e., they are highly motivated). Of course, quantity alone does not make one a genius. The quality of the quantity matters" (Shermer, 2001, p. 268). Gifted people might think and work more, but they also think and work better than most of us (Goldsmith, 2005; Heller et al., 2000).

The field of special education is beginning to appreciate the many different ways in which giftedness can be expressed in various areas of human endeavor. Likewise, educators are starting to acknowledge the extent to which the meaning of giftedness is rooted in cultural values (Gallagher, 2002; Karnes & Bean, 2001; Sternberg, 1998, 2000). There are many different abilities and many different ways of measuring them. What is considered giftedness, and how it is measured depend to a large extent on what a culture values and believes. Most experts now acknowledge that intelligence is not all there is to giftedness.

Whereas the usual tests of intelligence assess the ability to think deductively and arrive at a single answer that can be scored right or wrong, tests of creativity suggest many different potential answers. Creativity has become an extremely appealing topic of commentary and research in the early twenty-first century (see Lynch & Harris, 2001; Sternberg, 2001; Sternberg & Dess, 2001). A special section of *American Psychologist* featured articles on the creative talents of writers John Irving (Amabile, 2001) and Stephen Donaldson (Ward, 2001), physicist Linus Pauling (Nakamura & Csikszentmihalyi, 2001), scientists Thomas Young (Martindale, 2001) and Charles Darwin (Gruber & Wallace, 2001), and painter Claude Monet (Stokes, 2001).

Recognizing the many facets of human intelligence has led to dissatisfaction with previous conceptualizations of general intelligence that reduced it to a single number (IQ) that was assumed to be unchangeable (Gould, 1996). Sternberg (1997) describes a theory of intelligence that suggests three main kinds of giftedness: analytic, synthetic, and practical.

- *Analytic giftedness* involves being able to take a problem apart—to understand the parts of a problem and how they are interrelated, which is a skill typically measured by conventional intelligence tests.

Children who are gifted may have superior cognitive abilities that allow them to compete with adults of average intellect.

- *Synthetic giftedness* involves insight, intuition, creativity, or adeptness at coping with novel situations, skills that are typically associated with high achievement in the arts and sciences.
- *Practical giftedness* involves applying analytic and synthetic abilities to the solution of everyday problems, the kinds of skills that characterize people who have successful careers.

Old stereotypes of giftedness die hard. For example, many people still hold the myth that those with special gifts or talents are superior in every way, that they make up a distinct category of human beings. This myth may account, in part, for the general public's fascination with particularly creative people and the tendency to fawn over those who distinguish themselves in glamorous lines of work.

A popular idea today is that there are multiple intelligences as described chiefly by Howard Gardner (e.g., Gardner & Hatch, 1989). Others have argued that the concept of multiple intelligences is simply unsupported by research (see www.educationnext.org/20043/18.html). The theory of multiple intelligences is frequently encountered today, but there are few, if any, proven applications of the theory to teaching. This is not to say that intelligence can be reduced to a single score or performance, simply that the popular notion of many multiple intelligences with implications for teaching remains unproven.

Today, most experts in educating those with special gifts and talents suggest that giftedness refers to superior abilities in specific areas of performance, which may be exhibited under some circumstances but not others. So even though giftedness is believed to be a remarkable ability to do something that society values, it is not an inherent, immutable trait that a person necessarily carries for life. Moreover, having a special gift at one thing does not mean that a person is good at everything—or even that someone who is a good thinker about one thing is a good thinker about all things (Kauffman, 2002).

Another significant issue in reconceptualizing giftedness is recognizing that it, like beauty, is something that is defined by cultural consensus. Accordingly, Sternberg and Zhang (1995) propose five criteria for judging whether someone exhibits giftedness:

1. *Excellence*, meaning that the individual must be superior to the peer group in one or more specific dimensions of performance
2. *Rarity*, meaning that very few members of the peer group exhibit the characteristic or characteristics
3. *Demonstrability*, meaning that the person must be able to actually exhibit the excellent and rare ability through some type of valid assessment (i.e., the person cannot just claim to have it)
4. *Productivity*, meaning that the person's performance must lead to or have the potential to lead to producing something
5. *Value*, meaning that the person's performance is highly valued by society

Sternberg and Zhang also suggest that most people intuitively believe that each of these five criteria is necessary and all five together are sufficient to define giftedness. Similar intuitive, consensual definitions appear to have existed in all cultures throughout history (see Hunsaker, 1995; Tannenbaum, 1993, 2000a). Some researchers have suggested that we should speak of *people who exhibit gifted behavior*, rather than of *gifted people*, because people typically demonstrate special gifts only under particular circumstances (Reis & Renzulli, 2001; Renzulli & Reis, 1997, 2000).

Prevalence

It has been assumed in federal reports and legislation that 3 to 5 percent of the U.S. school population could be considered to have special gifts or talents. Obviously, the prevalence of giftedness is a function of the definition that is used. If giftedness is defined as the top x percent on a given criterion, the question of prevalence has been answered. Of course, if x percent refers to a percentage of a national sample, the prevalence of gifted pupils in a given school or cultural group may vary from that of the comparison group, regardless of the criteria that are used to measure performance (Gagne, 2000).

Origins of Giftedness

As defined today, giftedness is not something that sets people apart in every way from people who are average. Instead, it refers to specific, valued, and unusual talents that people may exhibit during some periods of their lives. Therefore, the main factors that contribute to giftedness are really much the same as those that foster any type of behavior, whether typical or exceptional:

1. Genetic and other biological factors, such as neurological functioning and nutrition
2. Social factors, such as family, school, the peer group, and community

We are all combinations of the influences of our genetic inheritances and social and physical environments; to say otherwise is to deny reality (see Gould, 1996; Heller et al., 2000; Shermer, 2001; Sternberg, 1998). Having said this, we must focus on environments that foster gifted performance.

Although giftedness may be determined in part by one's genetic inheritance, whatever genetic combinations are involved are exceedingly complex and not distributed according to race or social class. Genetic differences in abilities apply within various ethnic groups and social classes, not between them (see Gould, 1996; Plomin, 1997; Thompson & Plomin, 2000). However, the fact that children are not born with equal capabilities is obvious:

So, we can conclude there is evidence to support the following statement: There are some youngsters who are born with the capability to learn faster than others those ideas or concepts that modern societies value in children and adults. Such youngsters and their abilities are subject to many social influences and must interact with their environmental context. Therefore, it often becomes difficult to find students with these special talents in a multicultural society. (Gallagher, 2000b, p. 6)

UNDERSTANDING THE STANDARDS AND PRINCIPLES How are individuals with special gifts and talents different from the general population of learners? *(CEC Knowledge and Skills Standard GT2K2)*

Council for
Exceptional
Children

Families, schools, peer groups, and communities obviously have a profound influence on the development of giftedness. Stimulation, opportunities, expectations, demands, and rewards for performance all affect children's learning. For decades, researchers have found a correlation between socioeconomic level and IQ, undoubtedly in part because the performances measured by standard intelligence tests are based on what families, schools, and communities of the upper classes expect and teach.

SEE ERIC Clearing-house on Disabilities & Gifted Education, **www.ericec.org/gifted/ gt_menu.html**

How can families, schools, and the larger culture nurture children's giftedness? Research has shown that parents differ greatly in their attitudes toward and management of the giftedness of their children (Renzulli & Park, 2002; Silverman, 1997). Home and family are critically important, especially in the child's younger years (Subotnik & Arnold, 1994). The following have been found to occur in the families of highly successful persons:

- Someone in the family (usually one or both parents) had a personal interest in the child's talent and provided great support and encouragement for its development.
- Most of the parents were role models (at least at the start of their child's development of talent), especially in terms of lifestyle.
- There was specific parental encouragement of the child to explore, to participate in home activities related to the area of developing talent, and to join the family in related activities. Small signs of interest and capability by the child were rewarded.
- Parents took it for granted that their children would learn in the area of talent, just as they would learn language.

Research has shown that the home and family, especially in a child's younger years, are extremely important.

- Expected behaviors and values related to the talent were present in the family. Clear schedules and standards for performance appropriate for the child's stage of development were held.
- Teaching was informal and occurred in a variety of settings. Early learning was exploratory and much like play.
- The family interacted with a tutor/mentor and received information to guide the child's practice. Interaction included specific tasks to be accomplished, information or specific points to be emphasized or problems to be solved, a set time by which the child could be expected to achieve specific goals and objectives, and the amount of time to be devoted to practice.
- Parents observed practice, insisted that the child put in the required amount of practice time, provided instruction where necessary, and rewarded the child whenever something was done especially well or when a standard was met.
- Parents sought special instruction and special teachers for the child.
- Parents encouraged participation in events (recitals, concerts, contests, etc.) in which the child's capabilities were displayed in public.

How schools can nurture children's giftedness has received too little attention (Borland, Schnur, & Wright, 2000; Heller et al., 2000; Lynch & Harris, 2001). Yet the ways in which schools identify giftedness, group children for instruction, design curricula, and reward performance have profound effects on what the most able students achieve. When schools facilitate the performance of all students who are able to achieve at a superior level in specific areas, giftedness is found among children of all cultural and socioeconomic groups.

Identification of Giftedness

Measurement of giftedness is a complicated matter. Some components cannot be assessed by traditional means; in addition, the particular definition of giftedness will determine how test scores are interpreted. But if it is indeed important to identify giftedness early so that children with special talents will achieve self-fulfillment and be aided in the development of their special potential to make a unique and valuable contribution to society, it is important that appropriate methods be used.

The most common methods of identification include IQ (based on group or individual tests), standardized achievement test scores, teacher nominations, parent nominations, peer nominations, self-nominations, and evaluations of students' work or performances. Typically, some combination of several of these methods is used. Identification practices have been extremely controversial, and best practices have frequently been ignored.

In devising identification procedures that are fair to individuals from all cultural and ethnic groups and all social classes, educators must take into account the varied definitions of giftedness and recognize the effects of cultural variation on children's behavior (Borland et al., 2000; Feldhusen & Jarwan, 2000; Heller et al., 2000). In addressing multicultural differences, it is important to recognize the variations of socioeconomic status, language, and values that occur within various ethnic and cultural groups, not just between them. Hunsaker and Callahan (1995) propose eight general identification principles that will help ensure fairness:

1. Assessments go beyond a narrow conception of talent.
2. Separate and appropriate identification strategies are used to identify different aspects of giftedness.
3. Reliable and valid instruments and strategies are used to assess talent.
4. Appropriate instruments are employed for underserved populations.
5. Each child is viewed as an individual, recognizing the limits of a single score on any measure.

6. A multiple-measure/multiple-criteria approach is followed.
7. Appreciation is shown for the value of the individual case study and the limitations of combinations of scores.
8. Identification and placement are based on individual students' needs and abilities rather than on the numbers who can be served.

The focus of identification methods should be on balancing concern for identifying only those students whose capabilities are markedly above average with concern for including all who show promise for gifted performance.

Psychological and Behavioral Characteristics

Contrary to myth, most students who are gifted are not constantly bored with and antagonistic toward school, if they are given work that is challenging.

Giftedness has been recognized in some form in every society throughout recorded history. In many societies, individuals with special gifts have been stereotyped in one of two ways: (1) as physically weak, socially inept, narrow in interests, and prone to emotional instability and early decline or, in the opposite direction, (2) as superior in intelligence, physique, social attractiveness, achievement, emotional stability, and moral character and immune to ordinary human frailties and defects. Although it might be possible to find a few individuals who seem to fit one stereotype or the other, the vast majority of people with special gifts or talents fit neither.

Nevertheless, stereotypes persist. A still-common misperception is that genius predisposes people to mental illness. For example, in the movie *A Beautiful Mind*, Russell Crowe plays the role of John Nash, a mathematician who had schizophrenia, about whom one movie critic wrote: "John Nash was one of those men both blessed and cursed by genius. It made him smart, it made him fragile" (Hunter, 2001, p. C1). It is important to be aware that some people with special gifts and talents accomplish remarkable things in spite of, not because of, mental illness or physical disability (see Goldsmith, 2005).

Students with special gifts tend to be far ahead of their age peers in specific areas of performance. Many children carrying the label "gifted" learn to read easily, often before entering school—if they have been reared in a literature-rich environment. They may be far advanced in one area, such as reading or math, but not in another, such as penmanship or art (i.e., skills requiring manual dexterity). Contrary to popular opinion, most such students are not constantly bored with and antagonistic toward school if they are given work that is reasonably challenging for them (Gallagher & Gallagher, 1994; Neihart, Reis, Robinson, & Moon, 2002). Some, however, become uninterested in school and perform poorly in the curriculum or drop out (Renzulli & Park, 2002). Not surprisingly, they become upset and maladjusted when they are discriminated against and prevented from realizing their full potential. But such a reaction is not unique to any group of children, whether exceptional or average along any dimension.

Perhaps it should not be surprising that the majority of students who show giftedness enter occupations that demand greater-than-average intellectual ability, creativity, and motivation. Most find their way into the ranks of professionals and managers, and many distinguish themselves among their peers in adulthood. But not all such students enjoy occupational success in demanding jobs; some choose career paths that do not make use of their talents or otherwise fail to distinguish themselves (Manstetten, 2000).

The self-concepts, social relationships, and other psychological characteristics of students with special gifts or talents have been matters of considerable interest. Many of these students are happy, well liked by their peers, emotionally stable, and self-sufficient. They

Casebook Reflection

Refer to the case *Filling Mr. K.'s Shoes—Not!!* in your booklet. Students with exceptional gifts and talents still have emotional and social issues that need to be addressed. How might Susan have changed her approach to address these important issues with her students?

may have wide and varied interests and perceive themselves in positive terms (Coleman & Cross, 2000; Neihart et al., 2002). Gifted students appear to make internal as well as external comparisons of their performance—to see their own *relative* strengths and weaknesses and to see themselves as gifted only in their best or strongest area. "For example, a student with high mathematics achievement will probably have a high math self-concept, but her verbal self-concept may be depressed as a result—regardless of her verbal achievement" (Plucker & Stocking, 2001, p. 542).

Students with intellectual gifts are often acutely sensitive to their own feelings and those of others and highly concerned about interpersonal relationships, intrapersonal states, and moral issues. Using their advanced cognitive abilities appears to help many of these children develop at a young age the social and emotional adjustment strategies that are used by most adults. In short, many (but not all) students with high intellectual gifts are self-aware, self-assured, socially skilled, and morally responsible. Note that the prodigy Gregory Smith (described in our discussion of transition on page 523) is also very concerned about other children and issues of social justice.

However, assuming that gifted students never need education in morality is a terrible mistake. Individuals can and have used their special gifts for nightmarish purposes, as Tannenbaum (2000b) has described. Therefore, it is important to recognize the enormous potential for both good and evil purposes to which special gifts and talents can be put and to help individuals who have such gifts and talents see the value of using them in the service of what is morally right.

Giftedness includes a wide variety of abilities and degrees of difference from average. Moreover, the nature and degree of an individual's giftedness may affect his or her social and emotional adjustment and educational and psychological needs. Consider, for example, that categorizing only people with IQs of 180 or higher as "gifted" is roughly like categorizing as "mentally retarded" only those individuals with IQs of 20 or less. In fact, children who are exceptionally precocious—those whose talents are extremely rare—may constitute a group for which extraordinary adaptations of schooling are required (just as extraordinary adaptations are required for children with very severe mental retardation) (see Gross, 1992, 1993, 2000, 2002).

Child prodigies are children whose development and accomplishments meet or exceed those of adults with extraordinary talent. Child prodigies often astonish others by their talent at an early age, and they often need opportunities that more typical students do not need and would find intimidating. Besides the two prodigies depicted in Personal Perspectives on page 509, Burge (1998) describes Chris Sharma (who won the World Cup in rock climbing at age fifteen), Jennifer Baybrook (who became the first female national yo-yo champion at age seventeen), Alexandra Nechita (who at age twelve showed her paintings in fifty galleries), Sara Chang (who at age eight was a guest violin soloist with Zubin Mehta and the New York Philharmonic), Emily Kumpel (who at age nine used her organizational and public relations savvy to collect thousands of books for school children in South Africa), Jason Crowe (who published a successful newspaper at age eleven), and Justin Miller (a globe-trotting gourmet who by age eight had cooked three times on David Letterman's show).

Cultural Values Regarding Students with Special Gifts and Talents and Their Education

In American culture, it is difficult to elicit sympathy and next to impossible to arrange sustained public support for education that meets their needs for children with special gifts, especially intellectual gifts (Clark, 1997; Gallagher, 2000a, 2002). This is not a peculiarly

Personal Perspectives

TWO PRODIGIES

THE SCIENTIST

Considering her predicament, Carrie Shilyansky's phone voice is surprisingly amiable. "I've got some frozen slugs in my hand, so let me just put them in the freezer quick," she says. As her nonchalance testifies, Carrie knows sea slugs. At 16, she has already studied the creatures for three years, and her research has given scientists insight into the cellular processes behind memory and learning.

Her work with the mollusk—*Aplysia californica* when she talks to her lab buddies—won her second place at the national level in the prestigious Westinghouse Science Talent Search last year. "She is absolutely brilliant," says John Armstrong of Westinghouse. In October, Carrie presented her research, which she hopes eventually to publish, at an annual meeting among thousands of neuroscientists in New Orleans. "It was just amazingly exciting," says Carrie, who lives in San Marino, California.

Her interest in memory began as a child, when she started reading scientific literature to understand how memory works and how information is stored. "People always talk about information and memory," she says. "But they're just sort of these general concepts floating around." She started sitting in on neurobiology seminars at the California Institute of Technology when she was 11. Last fall, when she showed up as a freshman at CalTech, Carrie's advisor remembered her face. "You're the little kid who always used to come sit up front," she said when she met Carrie again.

Carrie began studying sea slugs at a CalTech laboratory where she worked weekends and during breaks at her high school. The creatures, with their simple central nervous systems, make ideal neurobiology subjects. Carrie wanted to study how memory was encoded in the slugs' nervous systems. She tapped them, causing their gills to retract, until they learned the taps weren't harmful. When she changed the frequency of the taps, however, she observed that the slugs had to learn again that the taps were harmless. Scientists had previously thought that only the strength of stimuli such as taps, and not the frequency, affected learning.

Despite her success, Carrie has learned that a young life built around science has its drawbacks. "A big, huge chunk of your social life is just gone because you don't have the time," she says. "There are a lot of times I need to be there for friends and I can't because I need to be in the lab."

THE ORATOR

Adults learned Ayinde Jean-Baptiste had a way with words when he recited part of a sermon by Martin Luther King Jr. to his first-grade class. He was 4 years old. His performance was so powerful that it immediately led to his first gig: delivering the King sermon to a Chicago-area church. In the decade since Ayinde first took the podium, requests for speaking engagements have continued to pour into his Evanston, Illinois, home. He has twice shared a podium with President Clinton—at a celebration of Martin Luther King's birthday and at the inauguration of Kweisi Mfume as president of the National Association for the Advancement of Colored People. At the Million Man March in Washington, D.C., Ayinde addressed hundreds of thousands of men, exhorting them to build their communities and commit themselves to their families.

His speaking, which has helped win him a host of awards—including a $10,000 scholarship and the Chicago NAACP President's Award—takes him around the country to about 25 engagements a year. Said one woman who heard him speak at an awards ceremony: "After two or three sentences, I thought, 'He's really good.' After four or five sentences, he could have sold me swampland."

Ayinde, 15, who has never taken a speech class, practices at home before his family. He memorizes all the speeches he delivers, a strategy (used by the ancient Greeks) that he believes allows the words to flow through him more powerfully. "I enjoy the feeling that I get when people respond to me," he says. "I enjoy being able to spread positivity."

One of the most moving responses came from a young man who approached Ayinde after a 1995 speech in New York City. The man, who remembered Ayinde's talk at the Million Man March, said that in the months after the rally he had conquered his drug addiction and reclaimed his role as a young father.

Ayinde often exhorts young people to value education and to avoid drugs and gangs. "I think the reason that I'm an effective speaker, especially with youth, is that sometimes we listen to each other more readily than we do to adults," he says. "If we're talking with each other about things that we face, it stays with us longer."

Source: K. Burge (1998, April). Prodigies. *U.S. Airways Attaché,* 82–84. Reprinted with permission.

American problem, but there is something self-limiting, if not self-destructive, about a society that refuses to acknowledge and nourish the special talents of its children who have the greatest gifts (see De Hahn, 2000; Tannenbaum, 1993, 2000a). Hunsaker (1995) examined the perception and treatment of giftedness in traditional West African, Egyptian, Greco-Roman, Semitic, Chinese, Mesoamerican, and European Renaissance cultures. He found that few of these cultures used the term *gifted*. Nevertheless, as in contemporary American society, individuals with advanced abilities were viewed with ambivalence:

> They were considered exceptional because of the hopes people had that they would ensure the continued existence of their culture. Their ability was seen as a divine or inherited gift. Great efforts personally and societally were needed to develop their abilities, and special opportunities were generally not available to the socially disadvantaged. Finally, the exceptional were the objects of ambivalent feelings directed toward them as persons and toward their knowledge. Beliefs and feelings about individuals of exceptional ability have not changed a great deal from those we inherited from other cultures. (Hunsaker, 1995, pp. 265–266)

Gallagher (2000a) describes American society's ambivalence toward students with special gifts or talents. Our society loves the good things that people with extraordinary gifts produce, but it hates to acknowledge superior intellectual performance. Opponents of special education for students with special gifts argue that it is inhumane and un-American to segregate such students for instruction and to allocate special resources for educating those who are already advantaged. There is the danger of leaving some children out when only the ablest are selected for special programs. However, it seems impossible to argue against special education for students with special gifts and talents without arguing against special education in general, because all special education involves recognizing and accommodating unusual individual differences (Kauffman & Hallahan, 2005).

Neglected Groups of Students with Special Gifts and Talents

Students who are disadvantaged by economic needs, racial discrimination, disabilities, or gender bias are often overlooked in programs for gifted and talented students. Two facts cannot be ignored:

1. Children from higher socioeconomic levels already have many of the advantages, such as more appropriate education, opportunities to pursue their interests in depth, and intellectual stimulation, that special educators recommend for those with special gifts or talents.
2. There are far too many individuals with special gifts or talents who are disadvantaged by life circumstances or disabilities and who have been overlooked and discriminated against, resulting in a tremendous waste of human potential.

UNDERACHIEVERS WITH SPECIAL GIFTS AND TALENTS

Students can fail to achieve at a level consistent with their abilities for a variety of reasons. Many females achieve far less than they might because of social or cultural barriers to their selection or progress in certain careers. Students who are members of racial or ethnic minorities also are often underachievers because of bias in identification or programming for their abilities. Likewise, students with obvious disabilities are frequently overlooked or denied opportunities to achieve.

Underachievement of children with special gifts or talents can result from any of the factors that lead to underachievement in any group, such as emotional conflicts or a chaotic, neglectful, or abusive home environment. A frequent cause is inappropriate school programs—schoolwork that is unchallenging and boring because these students have already mastered most of the material or because teachers have low expectations or mark students down for their misbehavior. A related problem is that underachievers with special gifts or talents often develop negative self-images and negative attitudes toward school. And when a student shows negative attitudes toward school and self, any special abilities that she or he might have will likely be overlooked (see Montgomery, 2000; Peters, Grager-Loidl, & Supplee, 2000; Reis & McCoach, 2002).

Casebook Reflection

Refer to the case *Never Give Up* in your booklet. Ryan's case underscores the complexities for students who are gifted and talented. How and to what extent do you think Ryan's life experiences might have affected the way he behaved in school? How should life experiences be taken into consideration in devising a behavior management strategy? Do students who are gifted and talented need discipline?

One way of preventing or responding to underachievement is allowing students to skip grades or subjects so that school becomes more nurturing and provides greater interest and challenge. However, acceleration is not always appropriate, nor is it typically sufficient by itself to address the problems of the underachieving student with exceptional abilities. Counseling, individual and family therapy, and a variety of supportive or remedial strategies are possible alternatives or additions to acceleration (see Colangelo & Assouline, 2000; Siegle & McCoach, 2002).

Underachievement must not be confused with nonproductivity. A lapse in productivity does not necessarily indicate that the student is underachieving. Students with extraordinary ability should not be expected to be constantly producing something remarkable. But this points up our difficulty in defining giftedness: How much time must elapse between episodes of creative productivity before we say that someone no longer exhibits giftedness or has become an underachiever? We noted earlier that giftedness is in the performance, not the person. Yet we know that the unrelenting demand for gifted performance is unrealistic and can be inhumane.

STUDENTS LOW IN SOCIOECONOMIC STATUS AND THOSE LIVING IN REMOTE AREAS

Children who are reared in poverty might not have toys, reading materials, opportunities for travel and exploration, good nutrition and medical care, and many other advantages that more affluent families typically provide. Lack of basic necessities and opportunities for learning can mask intelligence and creativity. Many of these children live in inner-city areas, and their families do not have the financial resources to provide the opportunities and early experiences that foster their talents.

Children who live in remote areas might not have access to many of the educational resources that are typically found in more populated regions. Many of those who live in remote areas also experience economic deprivation and lack the advantages that affluent families have.

STUDENTS WITH SPECIAL GIFTS FROM CULTURAL- AND ETHNIC-MINORITY GROUPS

Some ethnic groups, such as many ethnic minorities from Asian countries, are included in programs for gifted students more often than would be suggested by their percentage of the general population. However, some ethnic groups, especially African Americans and Spanish-speaking students, are underrepresented in programs for gifted students.

Among the greatest challenges in the field today are identifying culturally diverse and disadvantaged students with special abilities and including and retaining these students in special programs. Some cultural and ethnic groups have been sorely neglected in programs for students with special gifts or talents. Many African American students with special gifts

UNDERSTANDING THE STANDARDS AND PRINCIPLES Why are some ethnic groups underrepresented in programs for gifted students? *(CEC Knowledge and Skills Standards GT1K5, GT1K10, & GT3K2)*

Council for Exceptional Children

Many gifted individuals have been disadvantaged by life circumstances or other disabilities and thus overlooked and discriminated against, resulting in a tremendous waste of potential.

or talents remain underachievers, even if they recognize the importance of achievement in American society (Borland, 2004; Ford, 1998, 2002).

Appropriate identification and programming for students with special gifts or talents can be assumed to result in approximately equal proportions of all ethnic groups. However, this proportionality will likely be achieved only if renewed efforts are made to do the following:

- Devise and adopt culturally sensitive identification criteria
- Provide counseling to raise the educational and career aspirations of students in underrepresented groups
- Make high-achieving models from all ethnic groups available
- Retain underrepresented ethnic students in programs for gifted students
- Adopt a workable system to ensure the inclusion of underrepresented groups
- Build relationships with the families of minority children

Ultimately, the larger social-environmental issue of making families and communities safe, as well as intellectually stimulating, for children and youths of all cultural and ethnic backgrounds must be addressed (Borland, 2004; Borland & Wright, 2000; Cropper, 1998; Feldhusen, 1998; Gallagher, 1998, 2000a). Equal opportunity for development outside the school environment would help address the underrepresentation of minority students in programs for students with extraordinary abilities.

STUDENTS WITH DISABILITIES AND SPECIAL GIFTS AND TALENTS

FOR ADDITIONAL INFORMATION

about children with disabilities who are also gifted or talented, see **www.uniquelygifted.org**

The education of students with both disabilities and special gifts or talents is emerging as a field. The major goals of the field are the identification of gifted and talented students with specific disabilities, research and development, the preparation of teachers and other professionals to work with such children and youths, the improvement of interdisciplinary cooperation for the benefit of such children and youths, and the preparation of students for adult living. The Responsive Instruction on page 513 provides a summary of the early stages of the research on instructional strategies for twice exceptional students.

Our stereotypic expectations of people with disabilities frequently keep us from recognizing their abilities. For example, if a child lacks the ability to speak or to be physically active or presents a demeanor associated with intellectual dullness (e.g., drooling, slumping, dull eyes staring), we tend to assume that the child has mental retardation. The fact is, students with physical characteristics typically associated with severe mental retardation might be intellectually brilliant; unless this is acknowledged, however, the talents of students with cerebral palsy and other physical disabilities can be easily overlooked. Students with special gifts or talents and impaired hearing also can be overlooked if their communication skills are poorly developed, if their teachers are not looking for signs of talent, or if they are taught by teachers who have limited competence in communicating with people who are deaf.

Some students with learning disabilities or attention deficit-hyperactivity disorder have extraordinarily high intellectual abilities, yet their talents will be missed if those abilities are not properly assessed (Baum, Olenchak, & Owen, 1998; Kaufmann & Castellanos, 2000; Kaufmann, Kalbfleisch, & Castellanos, 2000; Moon, Zentall, Grskovic, Hall, & Stormont, 2001). Shaywitz and colleagues (2001) found that boys with very high IQs and boys with

Meeting the Needs of Students with Special Gifts and Talents

Strategies for the Identification and Instruction of Twice Exceptional Students

WHO ARE "TWICE EXCEPTIONAL" STUDENTS?

The term *twice exceptional* refers to any student who is both gifted and has a disability, such as a learning disability or cerebral palsy. Unfortunately, the identification of gifts or talents can be challenging, as the "disability" characteristics often take center stage (see p. 514). Researchers have identified specific barriers to the identification of giftedness in populations of students with disabilities (Cline & Hegeman, 2001). Challenges can include:

- Focus on assessment of the disability without attention to possible talents
- Stereotypic expectations associated with physical or global intelligence expectations
- Developmental delays particularly evident in certain areas of cognitive ability such as abstract thinking or verbal ability
- Lack of worldly experiences due to disability limitations
- Narrow views of giftedness as global, high intelligence only
- Disability-specific concerns overshadowing possible gifts or talents

To overcome these barriers, these researchers recommend that (1) assessment batteries include information about participation in extracurricular activities, (2) patterns of strengths should be noted in addition to disability-specific reporting, (3) ability should be viewed in terms of experiential opportunities, (4) adaptations and accommodations should be made during testing (e.g., omitting questions about color for a blind student or allowing extended time for a student with learning disabilities), (5) comparisons should be made with other students with similar disabilities, and (6) areas unaffected by the disability should be weighed more heavily (Cline & Hegeman, 2001; Willard-Holt, 1999).

STRATEGIES FOR MEETING THE NEEDS OF TWICE EXCEPTIONAL STUDENTS

To address the issue of underidentification of giftedness in individuals with disabilities, schools need to become advocates for the identification of gifts in all populations of students. Parents, school personnel, and the community should take an active role in supporting the unique needs of students with gifts.

Instructional strategies to foster the development of gifts in twice exceptional students include the following

- Focusing on the development of strengths, interests, and intellectual gifts
- Teaching and encouraging the use of compensatory strategies
- Reducing communication limitations and developing alternative means for communicating
- Helping students shape a healthy, realistic self-concept in which students acknowledge their strengths and weaknesses through open discussions
- Emphasizing high-level abstract thinking, creativity, and problem-solving approaches
- Providing for individual pacing in areas of giftedness and disability
- Establishing high expectations and promoting avenues for self-direction
- Offering instructional options that capitalize on students' strengths (Willard-Holt, 1999) ■

By Kristin L. Sayeski

learning disabilities exhibited similar types of behavior problems, strongly suggesting that gifted students are a very heterogeneous group.

Giftedness occurs in combination with disabilities of nearly every description. Personal Perspectives on page 514 tells the story of a Rhodes Scholar with dyslexia (a reading disability) and attention deficit disorder (ADD). Marie Curie, twice the winner of the Nobel Prize (physics and chemistry), suffered from profound depression (Goldsmith, 2005). Consider also Evelyn Glennie, a deaf percussionist, and Timothy Cordes, a blind medical student. They do not fit the stereotypes we hold. True, they are not typical of people with their disabilities—or of people who do not have their disabilities, for that matter. Fortunately,

Personal Perspectives

RHODES SCHOLAR OVERCOMES DISABILITIES

HEATHER LONG has dyslexia, ADD, and memory recall challenges. Learning to read was difficult for her, but special education during early elementary school, gifted classes in middle and high school, the support of dedicated parents, teachers, and tutors, plus her own hard work and determination helped Long overcome her disabilities and become a Rhodes Scholar.

How are you able to succeed when others with (or without!) similar challenges don't?
I was lucky that my parents got tutors for me as soon as they were alerted to [my challenges] when I was in first or second grade. And my mom stayed home and helped me with my schoolwork. It has not always been easy. Especially in college, there are so many distractions and so much going on that I stay up all night a lot of times, when it is quiet, to do my work. And I don't have a TV in my room.

Also, I have a natural passion for learning. I find that with a lot of gifted people and people with disabilities. It might not be in the traditional learning style, but we are really interested and intrigued in looking at the things around us in a different way.

What have you found most difficult?
Learning to read. I'm still not a speed-reader. This became very apparent when the last Harry Potter book came out. My friends in college were devouring the book in five hours and calling me about it, but it took me another day or two to get through it.

What strategies and accommodations do you use?
Part of it is scheduling—working in my room, not having distractions, working at night. When I was learning Old and Middle English, I went to the library and checked out tapes of people reading the *Canterbury Tales* and *Beowulf*. I also listened to audio books in elementary school, so my eyes couldn't slip around with the words I was reading or the spelling. I'm not really an auditory learner. I'm mostly visual, actually, but it helps me slow down visually when I listen to audio books and read along.

It's also knowing your limits. I want to challenge myself, but I know I can't take a course in which I have to read 1,000 page novels. I just read too slowly. But, I'm good at analyzing poetry.

What did teachers do that helped you?
I give a lot of credit to my second grade teacher. She kept telling the school counselor that "there was something wrong here." She was the first person who really pushed to identify specifically what was going on.

My second to fourth grade tutor, Mrs. Marti, used her creativity to help me learn. The only way to get me interested in spelling was to get out a can of shaving cream and let me use the shaving cream to spell the words. Then it was fun.

I also had a couple of teachers in elementary and middle school who pointed out my strengths—"Even though you are struggling in that area, you are gifted here." For instance, I was good in math but struggling with reading. I realized that, even though I felt I was behind some of my peers, I was not the worst student in the class at everything.

What advice do you offer other students who struggle with similar disabilities?
First, you have to realize it is not necessarily a "disability." There is so much stigma attached to that. You have to see some of your weaknesses as strengths.

Also, don't be afraid to seek help. There are times I wish I had sought help more often and been more open about [my challenges]. Often, you don't realize how many other people have these types of problems as well. I was stunned at the number of my friends who have ADD that I didn't find out about until last year. That was helpful, too—knowing I was not the only one.

What advice do you offer special and gifted education teachers?
It's integral for special education and gifted teachers to alert the regular curriculum teachers to ways they can make classroom settings and evaluations more conducive for varying types of learning. For instance, a college professor used to give really long essay tests — basically a regurgitation of information — until she had a child [of her own] with learning disabilities. Then she realized that might not be the best method of testing everyone. Teachers need to make sure they are not testing all students on the same skills but look at a wide variety.

There are different ways to show talents. Although a student may not be the best in her class at spelling, she may be the best at making a mobile about the book. We are really lucky in America, because we have a system that is evolving more and more to appreciate different ways of learning and incorporate the arts.

The biggest challenge now is to make the case that special and gifted education programs need to exist and to show how beneficial they are for both ends of the spectrum. It is important in a school to have a place where it is okay to do Odyssey of the Mind or Science Olympiad activities or just to do puzzles in the middle of the day.

Anything else you'd like to say?
I've benefited from both gifted and special education. I wish more school districts would recognize and fully fund these programs. These teachers really understand that students learn in different ways. ∎

Source: CEC Today. (July–August–September 2004). "Rhodes Scholar Overcomes Diabilities. CEC, Arlington, VA. Reprinted with permission.

their disabilities were not allowed to preclude their pursuit of their areas of special talent.

We do not want to foster the myth that giftedness is found as often among students with disabilities as among those who do not have disabilities. But clearly, students with special gifts or talents and disabilities have been a neglected population. A key factor in meeting these students' needs is the collaboration of a variety of disciplines and institutions to provide appropriate technology and training.

FEMALES WITH SPECIAL GIFTS AND TALENTS

Clearly, females comprise the largest group of neglected students with special gifts or talents. As Callahan (1991) and Kerr (1997, 2000) point out, some aspects of the way females are treated in U.S. society are changing. Females with extraordinary capabilities today have many opportu-

Students whose disabilities prevent them from speaking or physically expressing themselves may have potential that is not obvious through casual observation.

nities for education and choice of careers that were denied to females a generation ago (see Goldsmith, 2005 for descriptions of outmoded views of females).

Cultural factors work against the development and recognition of females with special gifts or talents. Females simply have not had equal opportunity and motivation to enter many academic disciplines or careers that have by tradition been dominated by males, such as chemistry, physics, medicine, and dentistry. When females have entered these fields, they have often been rewarded inappropriately (according to irrelevant criteria) for their performance. English literature has tended to portray females as wives, mothers, or "weaker" sisters, who are either dependent on males or sacrifice themselves for the sake of males. Such barriers to giftedness in females have only recently been brought forcefully to public attention.

Females lag behind males in many measures of achievement and aptitude (e.g., professional and career achievement, standardized test scores, grades) and tend not to pursue courses of study or careers involving science, engineering, and math (Lubinski, Benbow, & Morelock, 2000). In short, they are underrepresented in many fields of advanced study and in professions and careers that carry high status, power, and pay. We can only presume to know the reasons for their underrepresentation (Kerr, 2000). Factors that have contributed to the situation might include lower parental expectations for females, overemphasis on and glamorization of gender differences, school and societal stereotypes of gender roles, and educational practices that are detrimental to achievement (e.g., less attention to high-achieving girls, expectations of less independence of girls).

Research reviewed by Callahan (1991), Kerr (1997, 2000), and Lubinski and colleagues (2000) suggests that the problems of neglect and underrepresentation of females with exceptional abilities are much more complex than was previously believed. Like underrepresentation of ethnic and cultural minorities, the problems involving females are closely tied to cultural, social, and political issues, and they do not have simple or easy solutions. Nevertheless, the education of females with special gifts or talents might be improved by encouraging females to take risks by enrolling in challenging courses, to make career choices appropriate for their abilities, and to explore avenues that break stereotypical female roles.

Casebook Reflection

Refer to the case *Filling Mr. K.'s Shoes Not!!* in your booklet. How do you think Susan measures up as a teacher of high-achieving or gifted students? In what ways does she reflect what you believe are the ideal characteristics of a teacher of gifted students, and in what way(s) does she fall short?

Special Educators at Work

Noshua: "I felt I could finally be myself!"

Eighteen-year old Noshua Watson is enrolled in a Ph.D. program in economics at Stanford University. She completed high school and college through a residential acceleration program for gifted students.

These are the keys to her success:

- *Intensive and accelerated programming,*
- *relentless, individualized, academic challenges,*
- *specific attention to personal growth and unique abilities.*

At age thirteen, Noshua Watson enrolled in the Program for the Exceptionally Gifted, known as PEG, an acceleration program at Mary Baldwin College in Virginia. Combining high school and college, Noshua was challenged in a supportive environment that encouraged her personal growth. She thrived on campus activities, assisting with research and helping to teach an economics course during her senior year. Noshua credits her success to intensive, relentless, and specific instruction geared to her exceptional learning needs.

Intensive and Accelerated Programming "Acceleration programs like PEG challenge our culture," says Celeste Rhodes, the program's director. "Parents and students must be courageous in their ability to accept uniqueness," she says. Rhodes describes the PEG program as an alternative for the motivated student who might have teenage interests but demonstrates a serious sense of purpose. "You see it in the interviews," she says. "There is an energy, a spark, a drive."

To Rhodes, giftedness is not defined narrowly by IQ but includes multiple measures including consistent achievement over time. "We are accelerating students by four years. That requires a history of discipline, hard work, and high grades." Through a lengthy essay and interview process, an optimal match is sought between student and program. Says Rhodes, "Since we are residential, emotional stability is extremely important." Noshua agrees: "As PEG students, we were ready and eager for the academic rigors, but emotionally and physically, we were not as mature. We were still teenagers with a lot of special needs."

Relentless, Individualized, Academic Challenges Noshua was supported by an individualized curriculum that matched her advanced cognitive skills. Small group instruction was combined with personal mentoring and alternatives such as independent study and accelerated pacing. Noshua was free to choose among the college's liberal arts offerings, but was required to take two PEG level courses—one in literature and one in mathematics. She also took study skills workshops taught by veteran PEG students designed to prepare novices for college-level learning and campus life. Says Noshua, "I was intellectually challenged, but I could socially mature at my own rate, and for me that was really key."

EDUCATIONAL PROGRAMMING ideas for gifted and talented students can be obtained at **www.cloudnet.com/~edrbsass/edexc.htm**

Educational Considerations

The focus of education is now on talent development across the full spectrum of abilities in particular areas of functioning (see Gentry & Owen, 1999; Heller et al., 2000; Tomlinson, Kaplan, Renzulli, Purcell, Leppien, & Burns, 2002). However, this point of view includes the recognition by many that special education for some is necessary to provide equity for students with special gifts or talents. Although there is no federal requirement of special education for gifted students, the National Association for Gifted Children has published program standards that states and localities can use to assess the quality of their services (Landrum, Callahan, & Shaklee, 2001).

All students at all ages have relative talent strengths, and schools should help students to identify and understand their own best abilities. Those whose talents are at exceptionally higher levels than those of their peers should have access to instructional resources and activities that are commensurate with their talents. The one-size-fits-all mentality that is at

Specific Attention to Personal Growth and Unique Abilities For her first two years, Noshua lived in a special dormitory for younger PEG students. Social activities were sponsored and friendships nurtured through residence life. Residential coordinators were sensitive to the needs of adolescents, and they also served as academic advisors. For her last two years, Noshua lived independently in a regular dorm, and her academic advisor was a faculty member in her chosen major of economics.

Selecting educational alternatives to meet her unique abilities is a familiar practice for Noshua and her family. As a youngster, she attended a magnet school and was described as an avid learner who was strong-willed and knew her own mind. She experienced gifted education for the first time in a regional public school program for third through fifth graders. Noshua's family moved in her sixth-grade year; there were no specialized programs for gifted students in her new district. Enrichment classes were held only before and after school, and transportation problems prevented Noshua from attending.

Junior high was not a positive experience. "I was frustrated academically because my guidance counselor said if I wanted to take both French and Spanish, I also had to take an honors math course one level beyond my grade. Socially, I was frustrated because most kids at school just wanted to 'hang out.' My parents wouldn't allow me to do this, and it was hard for me to relate. I guess you could say I was sort of a geek!" she says playfully.

Noshua felt that she could finally be herself after spending three happy summers at a residential camp for gifted students. In eighth grade, she and her parents looked for programs that offered alternatives to conventional high schools. "That's when I heard about PEG, and so did a fellow camper. We graduated from college together last June." As for starting graduate school, she says, "I just love being at Stanford. My life experience has been different, and I'm used to a lot more independence than other people my age."

CEC'S STANDARDS: PAVING THE WAY TO SUCCESS

ASSESS YOUR STEPS TO SUCCESS in meeting the CEC Knowledge and Skill Base for All Beginning Special Education Teachers of Students with Gifts and Talents. Use the following questions to reflect on the growth of your own professional knowledge, skills, and dispositions.

REFLECTING ON YOUR OWN PROFESSIONAL DEVELOPMENT

If you were Noshua's teacher . . .

- WHAT are some areas about educating gifted students that you would need to know more about?
- WHAT are some specific skills that would help you to address her advanced academic needs and social challenges?
- WHAT personal dispositions do you think are most important for you to develop in teaching students with gifts and talents?

Using the CEC Standards

- WHAT are some variations in beliefs, traditions, and values across and within cultures and their effects on relationships among individuals with gifts and talents, families, and schools? (GT3K2)
- WHAT are some services, networks, and organizations for individuals with gifts and talents? (GT10K3)
- WHAT procedures are used in your school system for screening and identifying individuals with gifts and talents? (GT8K4) ■

By Jean Crockett

---

least partly an outgrowth of the inclusion movement reflects a mistaken view of human development. Highly talented young people suffer boredom and negative peer pressure in heterogeneous classrooms. Students at all ages and grade levels are entitled to challenging and appropriate instruction if they are to develop their talents fully. For some, like Noshua Watson, this instruction might be available only in a setting apart from her age mates. Read about Noshua's success in college courses in Success Stories on page 516.

The common belief that students with special gifts or talents do not need education designed for their needs works against talent development. "Contrary to popular belief, talented individuals do not make it on their own. Not only is the process of talent development lengthy and rigorous, but the need for support from others is crucial for ultimate success" (Van Tassel-Baska, 1998, p. 762). As we noted earlier, family support plays a crucial role in the development of talent (Freeman, 2000). However, special school supports also are needed for many students if they are to achieve to their full potential. The consensus of leaders in the field is that special education for students with special gifts or talents should have three characteristics:

UNDERSTANDING THE STANDARDS AND PRINCIPLES What educational approaches are most appropriate for students with special gifts and talents? *(CEC Knowledge and Skills Standards GT4S1, GT4S3, & GT5K4)*

517

1. A curriculum designed to accommodate the students' advanced cognitive skills
2. Instructional strategies consistent with the learning styles of students with extraordinary abilities in the particular content areas of the curriculum
3. Administrative arrangements facilitating appropriate grouping of students for instruction (see Callahan, 2000, 2001; Feldhusen, 1998; Landrum et al., 2001; Lynch & Harris, 2001; Moon & Rosselli, 2000; Tomlinson et al. 2002).

Enrichment

An approach in which additional learning experiences are provided for students with special gifts or talents while the students remain in the grade levels appropriate for their chronological ages.

Acceleration

An approach in which students with special gifts or talents are placed in grade levels ahead of their age peers in one or more academic subjects.

States and localities have devised a wide variety of plans for educating students with special gifts or talents. Generally, the plans can be described as providing **enrichment** (additional experiences provided to students without placing them in a higher grade) or **acceleration** (placing the students ahead of their age peers).

Many variations of enrichment and acceleration have been invented, however, ranging from regular classroom placement, with little or no assistance for the teacher, to special schools offering advanced curricula in special areas such as science and mathematics or the arts. Between these extremes are consulting teacher programs, resource rooms, community mentor programs (in which highly talented students work individually with professionals), independent study programs, special classes, and rapid advancement of students through the usual grades, including early admission to high school or college.

Not every community offers all possible options. In fact, there is great variation in the types of services that are offered within the school systems of given states and from state to state. As one might expect, large metropolitan areas typically offer more program options than small towns or rural areas. New York City, for example, has a long history of special high schools for students with extraordinary gifts and talents.

Some of the educational options for students with high ability, such as acceleration and inclusion, are extremely controversial. Some educators argue that when students with extraordinary abilities are pulled out of regular classes, there is a negative impact on the attitudes and perceptions of the students who are not pulled out (e.g., Sapon-Shevin, 1994). Research findings contradict this assumption (Shields, 1995). No single type of program option meets the needs of all students who have special gifts or talents. Ideally, assessment, identification, and instruction are closely linked, whether students have disabilities or

Accelerated educational programs, particularly in mathematics, have been evaluated favorably and may support early college entrance for some students who are gifted.

special gifts and talents—or both. In including students with disabilities and special gifts and talents, it is important to use strategies that will meet the needs of both types of students. *Making It Work* on page 520 provides a description of one such strategy, called *fractured fairy tales*.

Advances in telecommunications, the presence of computers in the home and classroom, and the call for excellence in U.S. education are three developments with implications for educating the most able students. Telecommunications—including instructional television, telephone conferencing, and on-line sources—are technological means of facilitating the interaction of particularly able students and their teachers over wide geographical areas. These communication systems are important for extending appropriate education to students with special gifts or talents who live in rural and remote areas. The possible uses of computers for enhancing the education of extraordinarily high-performing students are enormous (Dale, 2000). Using software tutorials, accessing data banks, playing or inventing computer games that are intellectually demanding, writing and editing in English and foreign languages, learning computer languages, and solving advanced problems in mathematics are only a few of the possibilities.

ACCELERATION

Acceleration involves moving a student ahead of her or his age peers in one or more areas of the curriculum. It might mean skipping one or more grades or attending classes with students in higher grades for one or a few specific subjects. For high school students, it may mean taking advanced placement (AP) courses (Callahan, 2003). Acceleration has not been used frequently, especially in rural areas. It has been used primarily with students who are extremely intellectually precocious (i.e., those who score 160 or higher on individually administered intelligence tests). Radical acceleration of extremely precocious students, combined with enrichment at each stage of their school careers, appears to offer many of these students the best social experiences as well as academic progress commensurate with their abilities (see Assouline & Lupkowski-Shoplik, 2003; Gross, 2000). For a brief summary of research on acceleration, see Responsive Instruction on page 521.

Opponents of acceleration fear that children who are grouped with older students will suffer negative social and emotional consequences or that they will become contemptuous of their age peers. Proponents of acceleration argue that appropriate curricula and instructional methods are available only in special schools or in regular classes for students who are older than the child with special gifts or talents. Furthermore, proponents argue that by being grouped with other students who are their intellectual peers in classes in which they are not always first or correct, students acquire more realistic self-concepts and learn tolerance for others whose abilities are not as great as their own.

Research on the effects of acceleration does not clearly indicate that it typically has negative effects, but neither does it clearly indicate benefits in all cases (Callahan, 2003; Van Tassel-Baska, 2000). Acceleration appears to be a plan that can work very well but demands careful attention to the individual case and to specific curriculum areas.

ENRICHMENT

Renzulli and his colleagues have developed an enrichment model based on the notion that children exhibit gifted behaviors in relation to particular projects or activities to which they apply their above-average ability, creativity, and task commitment (Reis & Renzulli, 2001; Renzulli & Reis, 2000). Students who are selected into a talent pool through case study identification methods are engaged in enrichment activities that involve individual or small group investigation of real-life problems; they become practicing pollsters, politicians, geologists, editors, and so on. The teacher (1) helps students to translate and focus a general concern into a solvable problem, (2) provides them with the tools and methods necessary to solve the problem, and (3) assists them in communicating their findings to authentic audiences (i.e., consumers of information). Students may stay in the enrichment program as

Collaboration and Co-Teaching of Students with Special Gifts and Talents

"How can I challenge him when half of my students have difficulty reading?"

Working with students with gifts and talents can be especially challenging for classroom teachers, considering the wide range of achievement levels in today's classrooms. Collaboration with a teacher of students with special gifts and talents can help general education teachers challenge all students.

WHAT DOES IT MEAN TO BE A TEACHER OF STUDENTS WITH SPECIAL GIFTS AND TALENTS?

The Council for Exceptional Children (2001) identifies the following skills as important for teachers of the gifted and talented:

1. Teach individuals to use self-assessment, problem solving, and other cognitive strategies
2. Use procedures to increase the individual's self-awareness, self-management, self-control, self-reliance, self-esteem, and self-advocacy
3. Create a safe, equitable, positive, and supportive learning environment in which diversities are valued
4. Create an environment that encourages self-advocacy and increased independence.

SUCCESSFUL STRATEGIES FOR CO-TEACHING OR COLLABORATION

Instruction in a differentiated classroom is based upon student readiness and includes constant assessment of student skill and knowledge, varying of activities or assignments for individuals, and the active exploration of topics at varying levels by individuals or groups of students (Tomlinson, 1995). Assignments vary, instructional support needs vary, and groupings vary. This can be quite difficult to manage as a single classroom teacher with between twenty and thirty students with a wide variety of skills. Teachers of students with gifts and talents can facilitate this process by helping to manage the classroom when groups and individuals are working, by helping to assess student progress, and by helping to collect resources. For example, the following lesson involving "fractured fairy tales" could be very successful with two teachers working together.

Using Fractured Fairy Tales to Explore Fiction Fractured fairy tales are designed to be humorous by changing a familiar story in an unexpected way, such as altering the plot, a character, or setting. One student might decide to make Little Red Riding Hood a tough, strong girl, completely unafraid of the wolf and able to save her grandmother. Another student might select a fictional superhero and create a humorous flaw that causes problems when he or she has to save the day. When the teacher presents a fractured fairy tale, asking a series of questions helps the children to think through the changes and what they mean. Examples include: (1) What characters in this story differ from the original and how? (2) Which events occur in the new one that don't in the original? (3) How do the changes in characters and plot in the new version change the meaning and/or the way you feel about the characters? (4) How does this change the overall effect? When students are asked to change the nature of even a few characters in a fairy tale, they will discover that the smallest change can affect plot. If their changes remove the conflict and suspense from the story, the teacher can take them back to the original story. What moment in the story held the most tension for them? What kept them riveted to the story? This process can apply to the simplest stories as well as to the most advanced novels and plays. The key is to discuss the relationships across story elements and to examine what is gained or lost with each change (Smutny, 2001).

This lesson can be used with students of all achievement and grade levels; however, the instructional support necessary for all students to understand the lesson varies. For example, the collaborating teachers could split students into groups by their understanding of plot, conflict, resolution, and character and the two teachers could work with the groups to either help clarify these concepts and their application to creation of a new fairy tale or to help push students' thinking of perspective and the influence of small changes on these concepts. Together, the teachers can challenge all students to actively explore literature while providing the support that each needs to be successful—an often impossible task for a teacher working alone. ■

By Margaret P. Weiss

long as they have the ability, creativity, and motivation to pursue productive activities that go beyond the usual curriculum for students their age. The model has become known as the *schoolwide enrichment model*. The purpose is to make special programming for students who have such abilities a more integral part of general education.

Tomlinson and colleagues (2002) have developed a parallel curriculum that is designed to challenge all high-ability learners, whether they are in homogeneous or hetero-

RESPONSIVE INSTRUCTION

Meeting the Needs of Students with Special Gifts and Talents

Acceleration

WHAT THE RESEARCH SAYS

Conceptualizations of gifted education focus on the talent identification and development aspects of this educational process (Van Tassel-Baska, 1998). This trend has come about as a result of expanded views of giftedness. Giftedness, once narrowly defined in terms of overall intellectual prowess, now encompasses students with talents in specific academic and nonacademic areas. For example, a student might be gifted in the area of mathematics but not verbal abilities (specific academic giftedness) or a student may be gifted in music or art (nonacademic giftedness). Expanded definitions recognize each of these forms of giftedness and current research has explored ways to promote and foster the development of those specific talents.

One line of research showing promising benefits involves acceleration models of service delivery for highly gifted students. Students in accelerated programs take advanced coursework. Common forms of acceleration are early entrance to school, advanced placement in certain subjects, grade skipping, curriculum compacting (rapid, focused curriculum), college course enrollment while in high school, grade telescoping (reorganizing high school or junior high to reduce the number of years required to finish), and early enrollment into college (Rogers & Kimpston, 1992). Research on acceleration shows that students who took accelerated coursework as preteens selected advanced coursework in high school and college, were accepted to schools with good reputations maintained acceleration into graduate-level programs, and identified productive career paths early (Swiatek & Benbow, 1991).

Skepticism about the efficacy of acceleration can be reduced to two overarching concerns: (1) acceleration leads to academic burnout or academic challenges due to gaps in knowledge and (2) acceleration has negative social and emotional consequences. Large-scale research on these issues involving many studies, however, dispels wholesale acceptance of these concerns (Rogers & Kimpston, 1992; Swiatek & Benbow, 1991). Researchers do recommend that decisions about acceleration be made on an individual basis and that different forms of acceleration be considered. Specific forms of acceleration associated with positive consequences are early entrance to school; grade skipping, particularly in grades 3–6; nongraded or multigraded classrooms; curriculum compacting; grade telescoping; subject acceleration in mathematics; and early admission to college (Rogers & Kimpston, 1992).

APPLYING THE RESEARCH TO TEACHING

Research on acceleration reveals three critical program elements: (1) flexible philosophy in regard to age and student placement, (2) implementation of diagnostic/prescriptive testing, and (3) strong commitment on behalf of administration and teachers (Van Tassel-Baska, 1998).

Schools can foster talent development through the following:

- Embracing national and state content standards that emphasize higher-level concepts, skills, and ideas
- Conducting testing closely linked to instructional practices
- Ensuring that content knowledgeable and skilled teachers provide instruction
- Allowing access to advanced curriculum at whatever age readiness is demonstrated
- Establishing College Board Advanced Placement classes in a range of disciplines
- Offering a variety of acceleration options (Van Tassel-Baska, 1998) ■

By Kristin L. Sayeski

---

geneous classrooms. Their curriculum is a guide to ways of enriching the classroom for all learners based on the idea that intelligence should be more broadly and flexibly defined than it was in the past.

Early Intervention

The giftedness of young children presents special problems of definition, identification, programming, and evaluation (Perleth, Schatz, & Monks, 2000). Although progress has been made in building model programs and providing better services for young children with special gifts, negative attitudes toward such efforts persist. Barriers inhibiting the development of better education for these children include lack of parental advocacy, lack of appropriate teacher training, an emphasis on older students of extraordinary ability, financial constraints, and legal roadblocks such as laws preventing early admission to school. The barriers to early identification and programming for students with special gifts or talents include school policies and ideologies that refuse to advance students in grade beyond their chronological age peers.

Many questions about the education of young children who have special gifts remain unanswered. Relatively little is known about how advantageous it is to identify and program for such children before they are in third or fourth grade or how best to train parents and teachers to work with preschoolers with special abilities.

Although not a panacea, early admission to school and acceleration through grades and subjects offer significant advantages for some young students with special gifts or talents. What many young children with special abilities need most is the freedom to make full and appropriate use of school systems as they now exist. They need the freedom to study with older children in specific areas in which their abilities are challenged. Such children need to be able to get around the usual eligibility rules so that they can go through the ordinary curriculum at an accelerated rate. Unfortunately, relatively few preschoolers with special gifts receive the kind of educational programming appropriate for their abilities.

Preschoolers with special gifts or talents may be intellectually superior and have above-average adaptive behavior and leadership skills as well. Their advanced abilities in many areas, however, do not mean that their development will be above average across the board. Emotionally, they might develop at an average pace for their chronological age. Sometimes, their uneven development creates special problems of social isolation, and adults might have unrealistic expectations for their social and emotional skills because their cognitive and language skills are so advanced. They might require special guidance by sensitive adults who not only provide appropriate educational environments for them, but also discipline them appropriately and teach them the skills required for social competence. They might need help, for example, in acquiring self-understanding, independence, assertiveness, sensitivity to others, friend-making skills, and social problem-solving skills (Perleth et al., 2000).

Transition to Adulthood

For students with special gifts or talents who are achieving near their potential and are given opportunities to take on adult roles, the transitions from childhood to adolescence to adulthood and from high school to higher education or employment are typically not very problematic. Particularly by adolescence, they tend to be aware of their relative strengths and weaknesses. This means that they might not see themselves as gifted in their areas of *relative* weakness even though they perform as well as or better than the majority of their age peers in those areas (Plucker & Stocking, 2001).

In many ways, transitions for these youths tend to mirror the problems in transitions faced by adolescents and young adults with disabilities. Not all adolescents and young adults with special gifts or talents take transitions in stride. Many need personal and career counseling and a networking system that links students to school and community resources (Neihart et al., 2002).

If there is a central issue in the education of adolescents with special gifts or talents, it is that of acceleration versus enrichment. Proponents of enrichment believe that these students need continued social contact with their age peers. They argue that such students should follow the curriculum of their age peers and study topics in greater depth. Proponents of acceleration believe that the only way to provide challenging and appropriate education for students with special gifts and talents is to let them compete with older students. These educators argue that because the cognitive abilities of such students are advanced beyond their years, these students should proceed through the curriculum at an accelerated pace.

Acceleration for adolescents with special gifts or talents can mean enrollment in advanced placement courses, early entrance to college, or enrollment in college courses while they are attending high school (see Callahan, 2003). Some of the most highly gifted students might even be admitted early to graduate study. In the case of the child prodigy who is now a graduate student at the University of Virginia (see Personal Perspectives below), radical acceleration seems to have been an obvious choice. It is difficult to argue against early admission to college and graduate school for an adolescent with Gregory Smith's very unusual intellectual gifts, social maturity, and moral commitments. Other students with

Personal Perspectives

CHILD PRODIGY NOW U.VA. GRAD STUDENT

GREGORY R. SMITH completed one goal May 31 when he received his bachelor's degree from Randolph-Macon College at the age of 13. Now the child prodigy is aiming at another by jumping into the University's graduate studies program.

Smith started the first of two summer classes Tuesday, the day after his 14th birthday. He is pursuing a Ph.D. in mathematics, the first of several doctoral degrees he plans to obtain.

"The University of Virginia has been my first choice all along, Smith said in announcing his decision last week. "It has been my plan since I graduated from high school to apply to U.Va. for my graduate work. I am so excited to have this wonderful opportunity to study at one of our country's best universities."

U.Va. officials have been equally excited about Smith's selection. Gene Block, vice president and provost, said, "Greg will be a wonderful addition to our graduate studies program. His record of intellectual achievement, combined with his dedication to international service, fit well into the U.Va. tradition. We realize that it's important not only to challenge Greg academically but also to provide an environment where he feels at home among peers."

Smith has been recognized as a prodigy since early childhood. Born in West Reading, Pa., he was solving math problems at 14 months and reading by age 2. The family moved to Florida, where he completed his K-12 education in five years, then to Virginia, where at age 10 he enrolled at Randolph-Macon College in Ashland. He graduated cum laude with a degree in mathematics and was a member of Phi Beta Kappa and five other honor fraternities.

Along the way Smith has used the media attention generated by his blazing academic pace to become a vocal advocate for the pursuit of peace and for children's rights around the world. He founded International Youth Advocates and has served as youth ambassador for the Christian Children's Fund

and youth spokesperson for World Centers of Compassion for Children. During the past year, he has traveled throughout the United States and visited six countries on four continents. Humanitarian aid efforts are benefiting orphans in East Timor and youth in Sao Paulo, Brazil, and Smith is helping people in Rwanda build their first public library.

He has met with presidents, including former President Bill Clinton and former Soviet Union President Mikhail Gorbachev, as well as Nobel Peace laureates, such as Ireland's Betty Williams and South Africa's Archbishop Desmond Tutu. His efforts have brought him before the United Nations Security Council and several state legislatures.

One of Smith's goals is to create an international symbol for the child, so that child-occupied buildings in conflict zones can be marked and protected. In addition, he hopes to create recognized safe havens in embattled areas so children will have shelters sanctioned by international law.

"I believe all children are born pure and innocent and only act with violence because we teach them hate and violence," he said. "There must be peaceful parenting to have a peaceful future. It is up to us to create an environment that makes it possible for children to resist the corruptions that take us down violent and immoral paths."

Nominated in 2002 and '03 for the Nobel Peace Prize, Smith has been tapped to co-chair the World of Children Awards with Muhammad Ali. He is among 43 students in the nation to receive scholarships up to $50,000 a year for six years from the Jack Kent Cooke Foundation for his graduate studies.

Smith, who has a website at http://www.gregoryrsmith.com, lives in Albemarle County with his mother, Janet, and father, Robert. ■

Source: Graves, L. (June 13, 2004). Child prodigy now U.Va. grad student. *Inside UVA.* Reprinted with permission.

special gifts or talents who are nonetheless less dramatically different from their age peers may not benefit from radical acceleration.

Acceleration programs, particularly in mathematics, have been evaluated very favorably (Assouline & Lupkowski-Shoplik, 2003). In fact, early entrance to college on a full-time or part-time basis appears to work very well for adolescents, as long as it is done with care and sensitivity to the needs of individual students. It is important to provide counseling and support services for students who enter college early to ensure that they have appropriate, rewarding social experiences that enhance their self-esteem, as well as academic challenges and successes in the courses they take.

Beyond acceleration and enrichment, adolescents with special gifts or talents often need attention to social and personal development if they are to make successful and gratifying transitions to adulthood and careers. Like other groups of students with special characteristics and needs, they may benefit from opportunities to socialize with and learn from other students who have similar characteristics and face similar challenges. They may be able to obtain particular benefit from reflecting on the nature and meaning of life and the directions they choose for themselves. Given proper supports, they can often make use of self-determination and survival skills (see Neihart et al., 2002).

Summary

HOW is giftedness defined?

- Students with special gifts excel in some way compared to others of the same age. However, there is little agreement about how giftedness should be defined. Disagreements about definition include:
  - What is to be measured
  - How it is to be measured
  - The degree to which one must excel
  - The comparison group
  - Reasons for identifying giftedness

  Giftedness is actually whatever we wish to make it.
- There may be different kinds of giftedness, such as analytic, synthetic, and practical intelligence.
- Giftedness may include the qualities of excellence, rarity, demonstrability, productivity, and value.

WHAT is the prevalence of giftedness?

- Prevalence depends on definition; school systems across the nation typically identify about 3 to 5 percent of students as gifted.

WHAT are the origins of giftedness?

- Both biological (primarily genetic) and social factors (e.g., family, school, peer group, community) are involved.
  - No one knows precisely how much each of these two factors contribute to giftedness, especially in the individual case.

- We can alter many social factors but not genetic factors, and more attention needs to be given to how schools foster giftedness.

HOW is giftedness identified?

- Individual intelligence tests have been the traditional means of identifying giftedness.
- More attention is being given now to additional, culturally sensitive identification procedures, including nomination by peers, parents, teachers, and self as well as to interests and accomplishments.

WHAT are the psychological and behavioral characteristics of students with special gifts and talents?

- Gifted students typically learn to read at an early age and achieve other developmental milestones earlier than most children.
- Gifted students are typically good at many things.
- Gifted students typically like school and like learning.
- Gifted students are subject to the same psychological and physical problems of other students.

HOW do cultural values affect the education of students with special gifts and talents?

- Throughout history, all cultures have had the concept of giftedness.
- American culture is ambivalent about giftedness, liking the good things that giftedness brings but disliking in-

tellectual superiority and identifying individuals with intellectual gifts.

WHAT groups of students with special gifts and talents are neglected?

- Underachievers are often overlooked.
- Students who are low in socioeconomic status and those living in remote areas are often unrecognized.
- Students from cultural- and ethnic-minority groups are often neglected.
- Those with disabilities are often not identified.
- Females are underrepresented.

WHAT are the major educational considerations for students with special gifts and talents?

- Acceleration and enrichment are the two most common ways of accommodating gifted students; and both have advantages and disadvantages, proponents and opponents.
  - Acceleration involves moving a student ahead academically to be grouped with older students or those in advanced placement.

- Enrichment involves adding to or altering the curriculum to be more challenging to those with special abilities.

WHAT are the major problems of early intervention for children with special gifts and talents?

- Lack of research to indicate effective ways of identifying giftedness in young children (i.e., before third or fourth grade) is a major problem.
- Early admission to school or radical acceleration is a controversial practice that some adults fear results in psychological problems.

WHAT provisions are made for transition of students with special gifts and talents?

- By adolescence, most gifted students can make an accurate estimate of their relative strengths and weaknesses.
- The problems of gifted adolescents tend to mirror those of students with disabilities of the same age, and many will need personal counseling about further education and career paths.
- Acceleration (including early admission to college) and enrichment (including advanced placement courses) are the two primary accommodations.

APPLYING THE STANDARDS AND PRINCIPLES

- **HOW** would you summarize **what it means to be gifted?** *(CEC Content Standard #1 & #2; INTASC Principle #1 & #2)*

- **HOW** should teachers determine what **instructional methods** to use with students with special gifts and talents? *(CEC Content Standard #4 & INTASC Principle #4)*

- **DESCRIBE** a learning environment in which students with special gifts and talents are likely to thrive. *(CEC Content Standard #5 & INTASC Principle #5)*

Council for Exceptional Children

INTASC

Appendix

CEC CONTENT STANDARDS AND INTASC CORE PRINCIPLES

CEC Special Education Content Standards for All Beginning Special Education Teachers

INTASC Core Principles for General and Special Education Teachers

CEC Special Education Content Standard #1

Foundations   Special educators understand the field as an evolving and changing discipline based on philosophies, evidence-based principles and theories, relevant laws and policies, diverse historical points of view, and human issues that have historically influenced and continue to influence the field of special education and the education and treatment of individuals with exceptional needs both in school and society. Special educators understand how these influence professional practice, including assessment, instructional planning, implementation, and program evaluation. Special educators understand how issues of human diversity can impact families, cultures, and schools, and how these complex human issues can interact with issues in the delivery of special education services. They understand the relationships of organizations of special education to the organization and functions of schools, school systems, and other agencies. Special educators use this knowledge as a ground upon which to construct their own personal understandings and philosophies of special education.

INTASC Principle #1

The teacher understands the central concepts, tools of inquiry, structures of the discipline(s) he or she teaches and can create learning experiences that make these aspects subject matter meaningful for students.

CEC Special Education Content Standard #2

Development and Characteristics of Learners   Special educators know and demonstrate respect for their students first as unique human beings. Special educators understand the similarities and differences in human development and the characteristics between and among individuals with and without exceptional learning needs (ELN). Moreover, special educators understand how exceptional conditions can interact with the domains of human development, and they use this knowledge to respond to the varying abilities and behaviors of individuals with ELN. Special educators understand how the experiences of individuals with ELN can impact families, as well as individuals' ability to learn, interact socially, and live as fulfilled contributing members of the community.

INTASC Principle #2

The teacher understands how children learn and develop and can provide learning opportunities that support the intellectual, social, and personal development of each learner.

CEC Special Education Content Standard #3

Individual Learning Differences   Special educators understand the effects that an exceptional condition can have on an individual's learning in school and throughout life. Special educators understand that the beliefs, traditions, and values across and within cultures can affect relationships among and between students, their families, and the school community. Moreover, special educators are active and resourceful in seeking to understand how primary language, culture, and familial backgrounds interact with the individual's exceptional condition to impact the individual's academic and social abilities, attitudes, values, interests, and career options. The understanding of these learning differences and their possible interactions provide the foundation on which special educators individualize instruction to provide meaningful and challenging learning for individuals with ELN.

INTASC Principle #3

The teacher understands how students differ in their approaches to learning and creates instructional opportunities that are adapted to diverse learners.

CEC Special Education Content Standards for All Beginning Special Education Teachers	INTASC Core Principles for General and Special Education Teachers

CEC Special Education Content Standard #4

Individual Strategies   Special educators possess a repertoire of evidence-based instructional strategies to individualize instruction for individuals with ELN. Special educators select, adapt, and use these instructional strategies to promote challenging learning results in general and special curricula and to appropriately modify learning environments for individuals with ELN. They enhance the learning of critical thinking, problem solving, and performance skills of individuals with ELN and increase their self-awareness, self-management, self-control, self-reliance, and self-esteem. Moreover, special educators emphasize the development, maintenance, and generalization of knowledge and skills across environments, settings, and the life span.

INTASC Principle #4

The teacher understands and uses a variety of instructional strategies to encourage students' development of critical thinking, problem solving, and performance skills.

CEC Special Education Content Standard #5

Learning Environments and Social Interactions   Special educators actively create learning environments for individuals with ELN that foster cultural understanding, safety and emotional well being, positive social interactions, and active engagement of individuals with ELN. In addition, special educators foster environments in which diversity is valued and individuals are taught to live harmoniously and productively in a culturally diverse world. Special educators shape environments to encourage the independence, self-motivation, self-direction, personal empowerment, and self-advocacy of individuals with ELN. Special educators help their general education colleagues integrate individuals with ELN in regular environments and engage them in meaningful learning activities and interactions. Special educators use direct motivational and instructional interventions with individuals with ELN to teach them to respond effectively to current expectations. When necessary, special educators can safely intervene with individuals with ELN in crises. Special educators coordinate all these efforts and provide guidance and direction to paraeducators and others, such as classroom volunteers and tutors.

INTASC Principle #5

The teacher uses an understanding of individual and group motivation and behavior to create a learning environment that encourages positive social interaction, active engagement in learning, and self-motivation.

CEC Special Education Content Standard #6

Communication   Special educators understand typical and atypical language development and the ways in which exceptional conditions can interact with an individual's experience with and use of language. Special educators use individualized strategies to enhance language development and teach communication skills to individuals with ELN. Special educators are familiar with augmentative, alternative, and assistive technologies to support and enhance communication of individuals with exceptional needs. Special educators match their communication methods to an individual's language proficiency and cultural and linguistic differences. Special educators provide effective language models, and they use communication strategies and resources to facilitate understanding of subject matter for individuals with ELN whose primary language is not English.

INTASC Principle #6

The teacher uses knowledge of effective verbal, nonverbal, and media communication technologies to foster active inquiry, collaboration, and supportive interaction in the classroom.

CEC Special Education Content Standards for All Beginning Special Education Teachers

INTASC Core Principles for General and Special Education Teachers

CEC Special Education Content Standard #7

Instructional Planning Individualized decision making and instruction is at the center of special education practice. Special educators develop long-range individualized instructional plans anchored in both general and special curricula. In addition, special educators systematically translate these individualized plans into carefully selected short-range goals and objectives taking into consideration an individual's abilities and needs, the learning environment, and a myriad of cultural and linguistic factors. Individualized instructional plans emphasize explicit modeling and efficient guided practice to assure acquisition and fluency through maintenance and generalization. Understanding of these factors, as well as the implications of an individual's exceptional condition, guides the special educator's selection, adaptation, and creation of materials, and the use of powerful instructional variables. Instructional plans are modified based on ongoing analysis of the individual's learning progress. Moreover, special educators facilitate this instructional planning in a collaborative context including the individuals with exceptionalities, families, professional colleagues, and personnel from other agencies as appropriate. Special educators also develop a variety of individualized transition plans, such as transitions from preschool to elementary school and from secondary settings to a variety of postsecondary work and learning contexts. Special educators are comfortable using appropriate technologies to support instructional planning and individualized instruction.

INTASC Principle #7

The teacher plans instruction based on knowledge of subject matter, students, the community, and curriculum goals.

CEC Special Education Content Standard #8

Assessment Assessment is integral to the decision making and teaching of special educators, and special educators use multiple types of assessment information for a variety of educational decisions. Special educators use the results of assessments to help identify exceptional learning needs and to develop and implement individualized instructional programs, as well as to adjust instruction in response to ongoing learning progress. Special educators understand the legal policies and ethical principles of measurement and assessment related to referral, eligibility, program planning, instruction, and placement for individuals with ELN, including those from culturally and linguistically diverse backgrounds. Special educators understand measurement theory and practices for addressing issues of validity, reliability, norms, bias, and interpretation of assessment results. In addition, special educators understand the appropriate use and limitations of various types of assessments. Special educators collaborate with families and other colleagues to assure nonbiased, meaningful assessments and decision making. Special educators conduct formal and informal assessments of behavior, learning, achievement, and environments to design learning experiences that support the growth and development of individuals with ELN. Special educators use assessment information to identify supports and adaptations required for individuals with ELN to access the general curriculum and to participate in school, system, and statewide assessment programs. Special educators regularly monitor the progress of individuals with ELN in general and special curricula. Special educators use appropriate technologies to support their assessments.

INTASC Principle #8

The teacher understands and uses formal and informal assessment strategies to evaluate and ensure the continuous intellectual, social, and physical development of the learner.

CEC Special Education Content Standards for All Beginning Special Education Teachers	**INTASC Core Principles for General and Special Education Teachers**

CEC Special Education Content Standard #9

Professional and Ethical Practice   Special educators are guided by the profession's ethical and professional practice standards. Special educators practice in multiple roles and complex situations across wide age and developmental ranges. Their practice requires ongoing attention to legal matters along with serious professional and ethical considerations. Special educators engage in professional activities and participate in learning communities that benefit individuals with ELN, their families, colleagues, and their own professional growth. Special educators view themselves as lifelong learners and regularly reflect on and adjust their practice. Special educators are aware of how their own and others' attitudes, behaviors, and ways of communicating can influence their practice. Special educators understand that culture and language can interact with exceptionalities and are sensitive to the many aspects of diversity of individuals with ELN and their families. Special educators actively plan and engage in activities that foster their professional growth and keep them current with evidence-based best practices. Special educators know their own limits of practice and practice within them.

INTASC Principle #9

The teacher is a reflective practitioner who continually evaluates the effects of his or her choices and actions on others (students, parents, and other professionals in the learning community) and who actively seeks out opportunities to grow professionally.

CEC Special Education Content Standard #10

Collaboration   Special educators routinely and effectively collaborate with families, other educators, related service providers, and personnel from community agencies in culturally responsive ways. This collaboration assures that the needs of individuals with ELN are addressed throughout schooling. Moreover, special educators embrace their special role as advocate for individuals with ELN. Special educators promote and advocate the learning and well being of individuals with ELN across a wide range of settings and a range of different learning experiences. Special educators are viewed as specialists by a myriad of people who actively seek their collaboration to effectively include and teach individuals with ELN. Special educators are a resource to their colleagues in understanding the laws and policies relevant to individuals with ELN. Special educators use collaboration to facilitate the successful transitions of individuals with ELN across settings and services.

INTASC Principle #10

The teacher fosters relationships with school colleagues, families, and agencies in the larger community to support students' learning and well being.

Sources: Council for Exceptional Children. (2003). *What every special educator must know: The international standards for the preparation and certification of special education* (5th ed.). Arlington, VA: Author; Council of Chief State School Officers. (1992). *Model standards for beginning teacher licensing, assessment, and development: A resource for state dialogue.* Washington, DC: Author. Available at www.csso.org/content/pdfs/corestrd.pdf.

Glossary

Acceleration   An approach in which students with special gifts or talents are placed in grade levels ahead of their age peers in one or more academic subjects.

Accessible pedestrian signal (APSs)   Devices for people who are blind to let them know when the "walk" signal is on at intersections; can be auditory, tactile, or both.

Accommodations   Changes in the delivery of instruction, type of student performance, or method of assessment which do not significantly change the content or conceptual difficulty of the curriculum.

Acquired apraxia   As in Developmental apraxia, there are problems in motor planning such that the child has difficulty in producing speech sounds and organizing words and word sounds for effective communication. However, the problem is known to be caused by neurological damage.

Acquired immune deficiency syndrome (AIDS)   A virus-caused illness resulting in a breakdown of the immune system; currently, no known cure exists.

Acute   A serious state of illness or injury from which someone often recovers with treatment.

Adaptations   Changes in curricular content or conceptual difficulty or changes in instructional objectives and methods.

Adapted signs   Signs adapted for use by people who are deaf-blind; tactually based rather than visually based, such as American Sign Language for those who are deaf but sighted.

Adaptive behavior   Conceptual, social, and practical skills that people have learned so that they can function in their everyday lives; along with intellectual functioning are considered in making a determination of mental retardation.

Adaptive devices   Special tools that are adaptations of common items to make accomplishing self-care, work, or recreation activities easier for people with physical disabilities.

Adaptive skills   Skills needed to adapt to one's living environment (e.g., communication, self-care, home living, social skills, community use, self-direction, health and safety, functional academics, leisure, and work); usually estimated by an adaptive behavior survey; one of two major components (the other is intellectual functioning) of the AAMR definition.

Adderall   A psychostimulant for ADHD; its effects are longer acting than those of Ritalin.

Adventitiously deaf   Deafness that occurs through illness or accident in an individual who was born with normal hearing.

Advocacy   Action that is taken on behalf of oneself or others; a method parents of students with disabilities can use to obtain needed or improved services.

Affective disorder   A disorder of mood or emotional tone characterized by depression or elation.

Aggression   Behavior that intentionally causes others harm or that elicits escape or avoidance responses from others.

Americans with Disabilities Act (ADA)   Civil rights legislation for persons with disabilities ensuring nondiscrimination in a broad range of activities.

Amniocentesis   A medical procedure that allows examination of the amniotic fluid around the fetus; sometimes recommended to determine the presence of abnormality.

Anoxia   Deprivation of oxygen; can cause brain injury.

Anxiety disorder   A disorder characterized by anxiety, fearfulness, and avoidance of ordinary activities because of anxiety or fear.

Aphonia   Loss of voice.

Apraxia   The inability to plan and coordinate speech.

Aqueous humor   A watery substance between the cornea and lens of the eye.

Asperger syndrome   One of five autistic spectrum disorders; a milder form of autism without significant impairments in language and cognition; characterized by primary problems in social interaction.

Assistance card   A relatively small card containing a message that alerts the public that the user is deaf-blind and needs assistance in crossing the street.

Asthma   A lung disease characterized by episodic difficulty in breathing, particularly exhaling, due to inflammation or obstruction of the air passages.

Astigmatism   Blurred vision caused by an irregular cornea or lens.

Atonic   Lack of muscle tone; floppiness.

Atresia   Absence or closure of a part of the body that is normally open.

Attention deficit hyperactivity disorder (ADHD)   A condition characterized by severe problems of inattention, hyperactivity, and/or impulsivity; often found in people with learning disabilities.

Audiologist   An individual trained in audiology, the science dealing with hearing impairments, their detection, and remediation.

Audiometric zero   The lowest level at which people with normal hearing can hear.

Auditory-verbal approach   Part of the oral approach to teaching students who are hearing impaired; stresses teaching the person to use his or her remaining hearing as much as possible; heavy emphasis on use of amplification; heavy emphasis on teaching speech.

Augmentative or alternative communication (AAC). Alternative forms of communication that do not use the oral sounds of speech or that augment the use of speech.

Auricle   The visible part of the ear, composed of cartilage; collects the sounds and funnels them via the external auditory canal to the eardrum.

Authentic assessment   A method that evaluates a student's critical-thinking and problem-solving ability in real-life situations in which he or she may work with or receive help from peers, teachers, parents, or supervisors.

Autism   One of five autistic spectrum disorders; characterized by extreme social withdrawal and impairment in communication; other common characteristics are stereotyped movements, resistance to environmental change or change in daily routines, and unusual responses to sensory experiences; usually evident before age of 3 years; a pervasive developmental disability characterized by extreme withdrawal, cognitive deficits, language disorders, self-stimulation, and onset before the age of 30 months.

Autism spectrum disorders   Five similar conditions: autism, Asperger syndrome, Rett syndrome, childhood disintegrative disorder, and pervasive developmental disorder not otherwise specified; all involve varying degrees of problems with communication skills, social interactions, and repetitive and stereotyped patterns of behavior.

Autistic savant   A person with severe autism whose social and language skills are markedly delayed but who also has advanced skills in a particular area, such as calculation or drawing.

Baby signs   A system developed to help hearing parents and their infants communicate with each other before spoken language develops; consists of signs from ASL as well as other gestures.

Basal ganglia   A set of structures within the brain that include the caudate, globus pallidus, and putamen, the first two being abnormal in people with ADHD; generally responsible for the coordination and control of movement.

Behavior management   Strategies and techniques used to increase desirable behavior and decrease undesirable behavior. May be applied in the classroom, home, or other environment.

Behavior modification   Systematic control of environmental events, especially of consequences, to produce specific changes in observable responses. May include reinforcement, punishment, modeling, self-instruction, desensitization, guided practice, or any other technique for strengthening or eliminating a particular response.

Behavioral inhibition   The ability to stop an intended response, to stop an ongoing response, to guard an ongoing response from interruption, and to refrain from responding immediately; allows executive functions to occur; delayed or impaired in those with ADHD.

Behavioral phenotype   A collection of behaviors, including cognitive, language, and social behaviors as well as psychopathological symptoms, that tend to occur together in people with a specific genetic syndrome.

Bicultural-bilingual approach   An approach for teaching students with hearing impairment that stresses teaching American Sign Language as a first language and English as a second language and promotes the teaching of Deaf culture.

Braille bills   Legislation passed in several states to make braille more available to students with visual impairment; specific provisions vary from state to state, but major advocates have lobbied for (1) making braille available if parents want it, and (2) ensuring that teachers of students with visual impairment are proficient in braille.

Braille notetakers   Portable devices that can be used to take notes in braille, which are then converted to speech, braille, or text.

Braille   A system in which raised dots allow people who are blind to read with their fingertips; each quadrangular cell contains from one to six dots, the arrangement of which denotes different letters and symbols.

Cataracts   A condition caused by clouding of the lens of the eye; affects color vision and distance vision.

Catheterization   The insertion of a tube into the urethra to drain the bladder.

Caudate   A structure in the basal ganglia of the brain; site of abnormal development in persons with ADHD.

Center-based program   A program implemented primarily in a school or center, not in the student's home.

Central coherence   The inclination to bring meaning to stimuli by conceptualizing it as a whole; thought to be weak in people with ASD.

Cerebellum   An organ at the base of the brain responsible for coordination and movement; site of abnormal development in persons with ADHD.

Cerebral palsy (CP)   A condition characterized by paralysis, weakness, lack of coordination, and/or other motor dysfunction; caused by damage to the brain before it has matured.

CHARGE syndrome   A genetic syndrome resulting in deaf-blindness; characterized by physical anomalies, often including coloboma (abnormalities of the pupil, retina and/or optic nerve), cranial nerves, heart defects, atresia (absence or closure) of the chonae (air passages from nose to throat), retardation in growth and mental development, genital abnormalities, ear malformation and/or hearing loss.

Childhood disintegrative disorder   One of five autistic spectrum disorders; normal development for at least two and up to ten years, followed by significant loss of skills; much more prevalent in males.

Choanae   Air passages from the nose to the throat.

Choreoathetoid   Characterized by involuntary movements and difficulty with balance; associated with choreoathetoid cerebral palsy.

Chorionic villus sampling (CVS)   A method of testing the unborn fetus for a variety of chromosomal abnormalities, such as Down syndrome; a small amount of tissue from the chorion (a membrane that eventually helps form the placenta) is extracted and tested; can be done earlier than amniocentesis but the risk of miscarriage is slightly higher.

Chromosomal disorder   Any of several syndromes resulting from abnormal or damaged chromosome(s); can result in mental retardation.

Chromosome   A rod-shaped entity in the nucleus of the cell; contains genes, which convey hereditary characteristics; each cell in the human body contains 23 pairs of chromosomes.

Chronic   A permanent condition; not temporary.

Chronological age   Refers to how old a person is; used in comparison to mental age to determine IQ. IQ = (mental age ÷ chronological age) × 100.

Classwide peer tutoring (CWPT)   An instructional procedure in which all students in the class are involved in tutoring and being tutored by classmates on specific skills as directed by their teacher.

Cleft palate   A condition in which there is a rift or split in the upper part of the oral cavity; may include the upper lip (cleft lip).

Closed head injury   Damage to the brain that occurs without penetration of the skull; might be caused by a blow to the head or violent shaking by an adult.

Coaching   A technique whereby a friend or therapist offers encouragement and support for a person with ADHD.

Cochlea   A snail-shaped organ that lies below the vestibular mechanism in the inner ear; its parts convert the sounds coming from the middle ear into electrical signals that are transmitted to the brain.

Cochlear implantation   A surgical procedure that allows people who are deaf to hear some environmental sounds; an external coil fitted on the skin by the ear picks up sound from a microphone worn by the person and transmits it to an internal coil implanted in the bone behind the ear, which carries it to an electrode implanted in the cochlea of the inner ear.

Cognition   The ability to solve problems and use strategies; an area of difficulty for many persons with learning disabilities.

Cognitive mapping   A nonsequential way of conceptualizing the spatial environment that allows a person who is visually impaired to know where several points in the environment are simultaneously; allows for better mobility than does a strictly sequential conceptualization of the environment.

Cognitive training   A group of training procedures designed to change thoughts or thought patterns.

Collaborative consultation   An approach in which a special educator and a general educator collaborate to come up with teaching strategies for a student with disabilities. The relationship between the two professionals is based on the premises of shared responsibility and equal authority.

Coloboma   A condition of the eye in which the pupil is abnormally shaped and/or there are abnormalities of the retina or optic nerve; can result in loss of visual acuity and extreme sensitivity to light.

Communication disorders   Impairments in the ability to use speech or language to communicate.

Communication   The process of sharing information.

Communicative function   Acts of communication, such as requesting, rejecting, commenting, arguing, and reasoning.

Communicative Intent   The need to communicate for social reasons; thought to be lacking in most children with autism.

Community residential facility (CRF)   A place, usually a group home, in an urban or residential neighborhood where about three to ten adults with mental retardation live under supervision.

Comorbidity   Co-occurrence of two or more conditions in the same individual.

Competitive employment   A workplace that provides employment that pays at least minimum wage and in which most workers are nondisabled.

Comprehension monitoring   The ability to keep track of one's own comprehension of reading material and to make adjustments to comprehend better while reading; often deficient in students with learning disabilities.

Conduct disorder   A disorder characterized by overt, aggressive, disruptive behavior or covert antisocial acts such as stealing, lying, and fire setting; may include both overt and covert acts.

Conductive hearing impairment   A hearing impairment, usually mild, resulting from malfunctioning along the conductive pathway of the ear (i.e., the outer or middle ear).

Congenital anomaly   An irregularity (anomaly) that is present at birth; might or might not be due to genetic factors.

Congenital cytomegalovirus (CMV)   The most frequently occurring viral infection in newborns; can result in a variety of disabilities, especially hearing impairment.

Congenitally deaf   Deafness that is present at birth; can be caused by genetic factors, by injuries during fetal development, or by injuries occurring at birth.

Connexin-26 gene   A gene, the mutation of which causes deafness; the leading cause of congenital deafness in children.

Constant time delay   An instructional procedure whereby the teacher makes a request while simultaneously prompting the student and then over several occasions makes the same request and waits a constant period of time before prompting; often used with students with mental retardation.

Contingency-based self-management   Educational techniques that involve having students keep track of their own behavior, for which they then receive consequences (e.g., reinforcement).

Continuous performance test (CPT)   A test measuring a person's ability to sustain attention to rapidly presented stimuli; can help in the diagnosis of ADHD.

Continuum of alternative placements (CAP)   The full range of alternative placements, from those assumed to be least restrictive to those considered most restrictive; the continuum ranges from regular classrooms in neighborhood schools to resource rooms, self-contained classes, special day schools, residential schools, hospital schools, and home instruction.

Cooperative learning   A teaching approach in which the teacher places students with heterogeneous abilities (for example, some might have disabilities) together to work on assignments.

Cooperative teaching   An approach in which general educators and special educators teach together in the general classroom; it helps the special educator know the context of the regular classroom better.

Cornea   A transparent cover in front of the iris and pupil in the eye; responsible for most of the refraction of light rays in focusing on an object.

Cortical visual impairment (CVI)   A poorly understood childhood condition that apparently involves dysfunction in the visual cortex; characterized by large day-to-day variations in visual ability.

Co-teaching   A special educator working side-by-side with a general educator in a classroom, both teachers providing instruction to the group.

Cranial nerves   Twelve pairs of nerves that connect the brain with various muscles and glands in the body.

Creativity   The ability to express novel and useful ideas, to sense and elucidate new and important relationships, and to ask previously unthought of, but crucial, questions.

Criterion-referenced testing   Assessment wherein an individual's performance is compared to a goal or standard of mastery, differs from norm-referenced testing wherein an individual's performance is compared to the performance of others.

Cued speech   A method to aid speechreading in people with hearing impairment; the speaker uses hand shapes to represent sounds.

Curriculum-based assessment (CBA)   A formative evaluation method designed to evaluate performance in the particular curriculum to which students are exposed; usually involves giving students a small sample of items from the curriculum in use in their schools; proponents argue that CBA is preferable to comparing students with national norms or using tests that do not reflect the curriculum content learned by students.

Cystic fibrosis   An inherited disease affecting primarily the gastrointestinal (GI) tract and respiratory organs; characterized by thick, sticky mucous that often interferes with breathing or digestion.

Cytomegalovirus (CMV)   A herpes virus; can cause a number of disabilities.

Daily living skills   Skills required for living independently, such as dressing, toileting, bathing, cooking, and other typical daily activities of nondisabled adults.

Deaf clubs   Gathering spots where people who are deaf can socialize; on the decline in the United States.

Decibels   Units of relative loudness of sounds; zero decibels (0 dB) designates the point at which people with normal hearing can just detect sound.

Decoding   The ability to convert print to spoken language; dependent on phonological awareness and phonemic awareness; a significant problem for many people with reading disabilities.

Deinstitutionalization   A social movement starting in the 1960s whereby large numbers of persons with mental retardation and/or mental illness are moved from large mental institutions into smaller community homes or into the homes of their families; recognized as a major catalyst for integrating persons with disabilities into society.

Descriptive Video Service®   A service for use of people with visual impairment that provides audio narrative of key visual elements; available for several public television programs and some videos of movies.

Developmental apraxia   A disorder of speech or language involving problems in motor planning such that the child has difficulty in producing speech sounds and organizing words and word sounds for effective communication. The cause may be unknown.

Developmental delay   A term often used to encompass a variety of disabilities of infants or young children indicating that they are significantly behind the norm for development in one or more areas such as motor development, cognitive development, or language.

Developmentally appropriate practice (DAP)   Educational methods for young children that are compatible with their developmental levels and that meet their individual needs; coined by the National Association for the Education of Young Children.

Diabetic retinopathy   A condition resulting from interference with the blood supply to the retina; the fastest-growing cause of blindness.

Direct Instruction (DI)   A method of teaching academics, especially reading and math; emphasizes drill and practice and immediate feedback; lessons are precisely sequenced, fast-paced, and well-rehearsed by the teacher.

Disability rights movement   Patterned after the civil rights movement of the 1960s, this is a loosely organized effort to advocate for the rights of people with disabilities through lobbying legislators and other activities. Members view people with disabilities as an oppressed minority.

Dopamine   A neurotransmitter, the levels of which may be abnormal in people with ADHD.

Doppler effect   A term used to describe the phenomenon of the pitch of a sound rising as the listener moves toward its source.

Down syndrome   A condition resulting from an abnormality with the twenty-first pair of chromosomes; the most common abnormality is a triplet rather than a pair (the condition sometimes referred to as trisomy 21); characterized by mental retardation and such physical signs as slanted-appearing eyes, hypotonia, a single palmar crease, shortness, and a tendency toward obesity.

Dysarthria   A condition in which brain damage causes impaired control of the muscles used in articulation.

Dysfluencies   Hesitations, repetitions, and other disruptions of normal speech flow.

Early expressive language delay (EELD)   A significant lag in the development of expressive language that is apparent by age 2.

Echolalia   The parroting repetition of words or phrases either immediately after they are heard or later; often observed in individuals with autistic spectrum disorders.

Education for All Handicapped Children Act   Also known as Public Law 94-142, which became law in 1975 and is now known as the Individuals with Disabilities Education Act (IDEA). Retitled in 1990 and reauthorized in 1977 and 2004.

Encephalitis   An inflammation of the brain; can affect the child's mental development adversely.

Encopresis   Bowel incontinence; soiling oneself.

Enrichment   An approach in which additional learning experiences are provided for students with special gifts or talents while the students remain in the grade levels appropriate for their chronological ages.

Enuresis   Urinary incontinence; wetting oneself.

Epilepsy   A pattern of repeated seizures.

Episodic   Occurring in episodes; a temporary condition that will pass but may recur.

Error analysis   An informal method of teacher assessment that involves the teacher noting the particular kinds of errors a student makes when doing academic work.

Evoked-response audiometry   A technique involving electroencephalograph measurement of changes in brain wave activity in response to sounds.

Executive functions   The ability to regulate one's behavior through working memory, inner speech, control of emotions and arousal levels, and analysis of problems and communication of problem solutions to others; delayed or impaired in people with ADHD.

Expressive language   Encoding or sending messages in communication.

External otitis   An infection of the skin of the external auditory canal; also called *swimmer's ear*.

Externalizing   Acting-out behavior; aggressive or disruptive behavior that is observable as behavior directed toward others.

Familiality studies   A method of determining the degree to which a given condition is inherited; looks at the prevalence of the condition in relatives of the person with the condition.

Family activity settings   Activities that families routinely engage in, such as mealtimes and seasonal celebrations; can be focal points for the implementation of PBSs.

Family-centered model   A consumer-driven model that encourages the family to make its own decisions with respect to services while mobilizing resources and supports for the family's goals.

Family characteristics   A component of the Turnbulls' family systems model; includes type and severity of the disability as well as such things as size, cultural background, and socioeconomic background of the family.

Family functions   A component of the Turnbulls' family systems model; includes such things as economic, daily care, social, medical, and educational needs.

Family interaction   A component of the Turnbulls' family systems model; refers to how cohesive and adaptable the family is.

Family life cycle   A component of the Turnbulls' family systems model; consists of birth and early childhood, childhood, adolescence, and adulthood

Family systems theory   Stresses that the individual's behavior is best understood in the context of the family and the family's behavior is best understood in the context of other social systems.

Fetal alcohol effect (FAE)   Abnormalities that are more subtle than those of FAS; caused by the mother drinking alcohol during pregnancy.

Fetal alcohol syndrome (FAS)   Abnormalities associated with the mother's drinking alcohol during pregnancy; defects range from mild to severe, including growth retardation, brain damage, mental retardation, hyperactivity, anomalies of the face, and heart failure; also called *alcohol embryopathy*.

Fingerspelling   Spelling the English alphabet by using various finger positions on one hand.

Formative assessment   Measurement procedures used to monitor an individual student's progress; they are used to compare how an individual performs in light of his or her abilities, in contrast to standardized tests, which are primarily used to compare an individual's performance to that of other students.

Fragile X syndrome   A condition in which the bottom of the X chromosome in the twenty-third pair of chromosomes is pinched off; can result in a number of physical anomalies as well as mental retardation; occurs more often in males than females; thought to be the most common hereditary cause of mental retardation.

Free appropriate public education (FAPE)   The primary intent of federal special education law, that the education of all children with disabilities will in all cases be free of cost to parents (i.e., at public expense) and appropriate for the particular student.

Frontal lobes   Two lobes located in the front of the brain; responsible for executive functions; site of abnormal development in people with ADHD.

Full inclusion   All students with disabilities are placed in their neighborhood schools in general education classrooms for the entire day; general education teachers have the primary responsibility for students with disabilities.

Functional academics Practical skills (e.g., reading a newspaper or telephone book) rather than academic learning skills.

Functional Behavioral Assessment (FBA) Evaluation that consists of finding out the consequences (what purpose the behavior serves), antecedents (what triggers the behavior), and setting events (contextual factors) that maintain inappropriate behaviors; this information can help teachers plan educationally for students.

Functional magnetic resonance imaging (fMRI) An adaptation of the MRI used to detect changes in the brain while it is in an active state; unlike a PET scan, it does not involve using radioactive materials.

Functional magnetic resonance spectroscopy (fMRS) An adaptation of the MRI used to detect changes in the brain while it is in an active state; unlike a PET scan, it does not involve using radioactive materials.

Functional vision assessment An appraisal of an individual's use of vision in everyday situations.

Gastrointenstinal Pertaining to the stomach, intestines, and/or other related organs.

Genius A word sometimes used to indicate a particular aptitude or capacity in any area; rare intellectual powers.

Giftedness Refers to cognitive (intellectual) superiority, creativity, and motivation of sufficient magnitude to set the child apart from the vast majority of age peers and make it possible for the child to contribute something of particular value to society.

Glaucoma A condition often, but not always, due to excessive pressure in the eyeball; the cause is unknown; if untreated, blindness results.

Globus pallidus A structure in the basal ganglia of the brain; site of abnormal development in people with ADHD.

Guardianship A legal term that gives a person the authority to make decisions for another person; can be full, limited, or temporary; applies in cases of parents who have children who have severe cognitive disabilities.

Guide dogs Dogs trained for the purpose of helping people who are blind navigate the environment; generally not recommended for children; they require extensive training for the user.

Handicapism A term used by activists who fault the unequal treatment of individuals with disabilities. This term is parallel to the term *racism*, coined by those who fault unequal treatment based on race.

Hand-over-hand guidance A tactile learning strategy for persons who are deaf-blind; the teacher places his or her hands over those of the person who is deaf-blind and guides them to explore objects.

Hand-under-hand guidance A tactile learning strategy for persons who are deaf-blind; the teacher places his or her hands underneath part of the student's hand or hands while the child is exploring objects.

Heritability studies A method of determining the degree to which a condition is inherited; a comparison of the prevalence of a condition in identical (i.e., monozygotic, from the same egg) twins versus fraternal (i.e., dizygotic, from two eggs) twins.

Herpes simplex A viral disease that can cause cold sores or fever blisters; if it affects the genitals and is contracted by the mother-to-be in the later stages of fetal development, it can cause mental subnormality in the child.

Hertz (Hz) A unit of measurement of the frequency of sound; refers to the highness or lowness of a sound.

Hidden curriculum The dos and don'ts of social interactions that most people learn incidentally or with little instruction but that remain hidden for those with Asperger syndrome.

Home-based program A program delivered primarily in a student's home rather than in a school or center.

Home-note program A system of communication between the teacher and parents; the teacher evaluates the behavior of the student using a simple form, the student takes the form home, gets the parents' signatures, and returns the form the next day.

Homophenes Sounds that are different but that look the same with regard to movements of the face and lips (i.e., visible articulatory patterns).

Hydrocephalus A condition characterized by enlargement of the head because of excessive pressure of the cerebrospinal fluid.

Hyperactive child syndrome A term used to refer to children who exhibit inattention, impulsivity, and/or hyperactivity; popular in the 1960s and 1970s.

Hyperopia Farsightedness; vision for near objects is affected; usually results when the eyeball is too short.

In vitro fertilization The procedure of removing eggs from the mother, fertilizing them with the father's sperm in a laboratory, then returning them to the mother's uterus; used to help infertile couples conceive.

Inborn errors of metabolism Deficiencies in enzymes used to metabolize basic substances in the body, such as amino acids, carbohydrates, vitamins, or trace elements; can sometimes result in mental retardation; PKU is an example.

Incus The anvil-shaped bone in the ossicular chain of the middle ear.

Individualized education program (IEP) IDEA requires an IEP to be drawn up by the educational team for each exceptional child; the IEP must include a statement of present educational performance, instructional goals, educational services to be provided, and criteria and procedures for determining that the instructional objectives are being met.

Individualized family service plan (IFSP) A plan mandated by PL 99-457 to provide services for young children with disabilities (under three years of age) and their families; drawn up by professionals and parents; similar to an IEP for older children.

Individuals with Disabilities Education Improvement Act (IDEA) The Individuals with Disabilities Education Act was enacted in 1990 and reauthorized in 1997 and 2004; it replaced PL 94-142, enacted in 1975. This federal law requires that to receive funds under the act, every school system in the nation must provide a free, appropriate public education for every child between the ages of three and twenty-one, regardless of how or how seriously he or she may be disabled.

Informal reading inventory (IRI)   A method of assessing reading in which the teacher has the student read progressively more difficult series of passages or word lists; the teacher notes the difficulty level of the material read and the types of errors the student makes.

Inner speech   An executive function; internal language used to regulate one's behavior; delayed or impaired in people with ADHD.

Insight   The ability to separate and/or combine various pieces of information in new, creative, and useful ways.

Internalizing   Acting-in behavior; anxiety, fearfulness, with-drawal, and other indications of an individual's mood or internal state.

IQ–achievement discrepancy   Academic performance markedly lower than would be expected on the basis of a student's intellectual ability.

Iris   The colored portion of the eye; contracts or expands, depending on the amount of light striking it.

Itinerant teacher services   Services for students who are visually impaired in which the special education teacher visits several different schools to work with students and their general education teachers; the students attend their local schools and remain in general education classrooms.

Job coach   A person who assists adult workers with disabilities (especially those with mental retardation), providing vocational assessment, instruction, overall planning, and interaction assistance with employers, family, and related government and service agencies.

Juvenile rheumatoid arthritis   A systemic disease with major symptoms involving the muscles and joints.

Kurzweil 1000   A computerized device that converts print into speech for persons with visual impairment; the user places the printed material over a scanner that then reads the material aloud by means of an electronic voice.

Language disorders   Oral communication that involves a lag in the ability to understand and express ideas, putting linguistic skill behind an individual's development in other areas, such as motor, cognitive, or social development.

Language   An arbitrary code or system of symbols to communicate meaning.

Language-based reading impairment   A reading problem that is based on a language problem.

Large-print books   Books having a font-size that is larger than the usual 10-point type; a popular size for large print books is 18-point type.

Larynx   The structure in the throat containing the vocal apparatus (vocal cords); laryngitis is a temporary loss of voice caused by inflammation of the larynx.

Learned helplessness   A motivational term referring to a condition in which a person believes that no matter how hard he or she tries, failure will result.

Least restrictive environment (LRE)   A legal term referring to the fact that exceptional children must be educated in as normal an environment as possible.

Legally blind   A person who has visual acuity of 20/200 or less in the better eye even with correction (e.g., eyeglasses) or has a field of vision so narrow that its widest diameter subtends an angular distance no greater than 20 degrees.

Lens   A structure that refines and changes the focus of the light rays passing through the eye.

Levels of support   The basis of the AAMR classification scheme; characterizes the amount of support needed for someone with mental retardation to function as competently as possible as (1) intermittent, (2) limited, (3) extensive, or (4) pervasive.

Literary braille   Braille symbols used for most writing situations.

Locus of control   A motivational term referring to how people explain their successes or failures; people with an internal locus of control believe that they are the reason for success or failure, whereas people with an external locus of control believe that outside forces influence how they perform.

Long cane   A mobility aid used by individuals with visual impairment, who sweep it in a wide arc in front of them; proper use requires considerable training; the mobility aid of choice for most travelers who are blind.

Low birth weight (LBW)   Babies who are born weighing less than 5.5 pounds; usually premature; at risk for behavioral and medical conditions, such as mental retardation.

Low vision   A term used by educators to refer to individuals whose visual impairment is not so severe that they are unable to read print of any kind; they may read large or regular print, and they may need some kind of magnification.

Magnetic resonance imaging (MRI)   A neuroimaging technique whereby radio waves are used to produce cross-sectional images of the brain; used to pinpoint areas of the brain that are dysfunctional.

Magnifying devices   Often recommended for people with low vision; can be for close vision (e.g., handheld magnifier) or distance vision (e.g., monocular telescope or binocular telescope mounted on eyeglass frames).

Malleus   The hammer-shaped bone in the ossicular chain of the middle ear.

Manifestation determination   Determination that a student's misbehavior is or is not a manifestation of a disability.

Maternal serum screening (MSS)   A method of screening the fetus for developmental disabilities such as Down syndrome or spina bifida; a blood sample is taken from the mother and analyzed; if it is positive, a more accurate test such as amniocentesis or CVS is usually recommended.

Meningitis   A bacterial or viral infection of the linings of the brain or spinal cord; can cause a number of disabilities.

Mental age   Age level at which a person performs on an IQ test; used in comparison to chronological age to determine IQ. IQ = (mental age ÷ chronological age) × 100.

Metacognition   One's understanding of the strategies available for learning a task and the regulatory mechanisms needed to complete the task.

Microcephalus   A condition causing development of a small, conical-shaped head; proper development of the brain is prevented, resulting in mental retardation.

Mild mental retardation   A classification used to specify an individual whose IQ is approximately 55–70.

Milieu teaching   A naturalistic approach to language intervention in which the goal is to teach functional language skills in a natural environment.

Minimal brain injury   A term used to describe a child who shows behavioral but not neurological signs of brain injury; the term is not as popular as it once was, primarily because of its lack of diagnostic utility (i.e., some children who learn normally show signs indicative of minimal brain injury); a term used to refer to children who exhibit inattention, impulsivity, and/or hyperactivity; popular in the 1950s and 1960s.

Mixed hearing impairment   A hearing impairment resulting from a combination of conductive and sensorineural hearing impairments.

Mnemonics   The use of memory-enhancing cues to help one remember something; techniques that aid memory, such as using rhymes, songs, or visual images to remember information.

Moderate mental retardation   A classification used to specify an individual whose IQ is approximately 40–55.

Modifications   Changes made in instruction or assessment to make it possible for a student with a disability to respond more normally.

Molecular genetics   The study of the organization of DNA, RNA, and protein molecules containing genetic information.

Morphology.   The study within psycholinguistics of word formation; how adding or deleting parts of words changes their meaning.

Motor-speech disorder   Loss or impairment of the ability to understand or formulate language because of accident or illness.

Multicultural education   Aims to change educational institutions and curricula so they will provide equal educational opportunities to students regardless of their gender, social class, ethnicity, race, disability, or other cultural identity.

Muscular dystrophy   A hereditary disease characterized by progressive weakness caused by degeneration of muscle fibers.

Mute   Possessing no, or almost no, language; characteristic of many with autism.

Myopia   Nearsightedness; vision for distant objects is affected; usually results when eyeball is too long.

Native-language emphasis   An approach to teaching language-minority pupils in which the student's native language is used for most of the day and English is taught as a separate subject.

Natural supports   Resources in person's environment that can be used for support, such as friends, family, co-workers.

Nemeth Code   Braille symbols used for mathematics and science.

Neonatal intensive care unit (NICU)   A special unit in a hospital designed to provide around-the-clock monitoring and care of newborns who have severe physical problems; staffed by professionals from several disciplines, such as nursing, social work, occupational therapy, respiratory therapy, and medicine; similar to an intensive care unit for older children and adults.

Neurotransmitters   Chemicals involved in sending messages between neurons in the brain.

Newsline®   A service allowing access via touch-tone phone to several national newspapers; available free of charge to those who are visually impaired.

Night blindness   A condition characterized by problems in seeing at low levels of illumination; often caused by retinitis pigmentosa.

Nonverbal learning disabilities   A term used to refer to individuals who have a cluster of disabilities in social interaction, math, visual-spatial tasks, and tactual tasks.

Norepinephrine   A neurotransmitter, the levels of which may be abnormal in people with ADHD.

Normalization   A philosophical belief in special education that every individual, even the most disabled, should have an educational and living environment as close to normal as possible.

Nuchal translucency sonogram   A method of screening for Down syndrome; fluid from behind the fetus's neck and protein from the mother's blood are analyzed.

Nystagmus   A condition in which there are rapid involuntary movements of the eyes; sometimes indicates a brain malfunction and/or inner-ear problems.

Obstacle sense   A skill possessed by some people who are blind, whereby they can detect the presence of obstacles in their environments; research has shown that it is not an indication of an extra sense, as popularly thought; it is the result of learning to detect subtle changes in the pitches of high-frequency echoes.

Open head injury   A brain injury in which there is an open wound in the head, such as a gunshot wound or penetration of the head by an object, resulting in damage to brain tissue.

Optic nerve   The nerve at the back of the eye, which sends visual information back to the brain.

Oralism–manualism debate   The controversy over whether the goal of instruction for students who are deaf should be to teach them to speak or to teach them to use sign language.

Orientation and mobility (O & M) skills The ability to have a sense of where one is in relation to other people, objects, and landmarks and to move through the environment.

Orthosis A device designed to restore, partially or completely, a lost function of the body (e.g., a brace or crutch).

Ossicles Three tiny bones (malleus, incus, and stapes) that together make possible an efficient transfer of sound waves from the eardrum to the oval window, which connects the middle ear to the inner ear.

Otitis media Inflammation of the middle ear.

Otoacoustic emissions Low-intensity sounds produced by the cochlea in response to auditory stimulation; used to screen hearing problems in infants and very young children.

Oval window The link between the middle and inner ears.

Paradoxical effect of Ritalin The now discredited belief that Ritalin, even though a stimulant, acts to subdue a person's behavior and that this effect of Ritalin is evident in people with ADHD but not in those without ADHD.

Paraplegia A condition in which both legs are paralyzed.

Partial participation An approach in which students with disabilities, while in the general education classroom, engage in the same activities as nondisabled students but on a reduced basis; the teacher adapts the activity to allow each student to participate as much as possible.

Peer tutoring A method that can be used to integrate students with disabilities in general education classrooms, based on the notion that students can effectively tutor one another. The role of learner or teacher may be assigned to either the student with a disability or the nondisabled student.

Peer-mediated instruction The deliberate use of a student's classroom peer(s) to assist in teaching an academic or social skill.

Perinatal causes of mental retardation Causes at birth; some examples are anoxia, low birthweight, and infections such as syphilis and herpes simplex.

Perkins Brailler A system that makes it possible to write in braille; has six keys, one for each of the six dots of the cell, which leave an embossed print on the paper.

Perseveration A tendency to repeat behaviors over and over again; often found in people with brain injury, as well as those with ADHD.

Person-centered planning Planning for a person's self-determination; planning activities and services on the basis of a person's dreams, aspirations, interests, preferences, strengths, and capacities; a method of planning for people with disabilities that places the person and his or her family at the center of the planning process; a type of transition model; consumer-driven in that professionals are viewed as working for individuals.

Pervasive Developmental Disorder not Otherwise Specified (PDD-NOS) One of five autistic spectrum disorders; pervasive delay in development that does not fit into any of the other diagnostic categories.

Phenylketonuria (PKU) A metabolic genetic disorder caused by the inability of the body to convert phenylalanine to tyrosine; an accumulation of phenylalanine results in abnormal brain development.

Phonemic awareness One's ability to understand that words are made up of sounds or phonemes.

Phonological awareness The ability to understand that speech flow can be broken into smaller sound units such as words, syllables, and phonemes; lack of such awareness is generally thought to be the reason for the reading problems of many students with learning disabilities.

Phonology The study of how individual sounds make up words.

Play audiometry Use of a gamelike format to test hearing of young and hard-to-test children; the examiner teaches the child to respond to sounds.

Portfolios A collection of samples of a student's work done over time; a type of authentic assessment.

Positive behavioral intervention and supports (PBIS) Positive reinforcement (rewarding) procedures intended to support a student's appropriate or desirable behavior.

Positive Behavioral Support (PBS) Systematic use of the science of behavior to find ways of supporting desirable behavior of an individual rather than punishing the undesirable behavior; positive reinforcement (rewarding) procedures that are intended to support a student's appropriate or desirable behavior

Positron emission tomography (PET) scans A computerized method for measuring bloodflow in the brain; during a cognitive task, a low amount of radioactive dye is injected in the brain; the dye collects in active neurons, indicating which areas of the brain are active.

Postlingual deafness Deafness occurring after the development of speech and language.

Postnatal Occurring in an infant after birth.

Postnatal causes of mental retardation Causes occurring after birth; can be biological (e.g., traumatic brain injury, infections) or psychosocial (an unstimulating environment).

Prader-Willi syndrome Caused by inheriting from one's father a lack of genetic material on the fifteenth pair of chromosomes; leading genetic cause of obesity; degree of mental retardation varies, but the majority fall within the mildly mentally retarded range.

Pragmatics The study within psycholinguistics of how people use language in social situations; emphasizes the functional use of language rather than the mechanics.

Preacademic skills Behaviors that are needed before formal academic instruction can begin (e.g., ability to identify letters, numbers, shapes, and colors).

Precocity Remarkable early development.

Prefrontal lobes Two lobes located in the very front of the frontal lobes; responsible for executive functions; site of abnormal development in people with ADHD.

Prelingual deafness Deafness that occurs before the development of spoken language, usually at birth.

Prelinguistic communication Communication through gestures and noises before the child has learned oral language.

Prenatal causes of mental retardation Causes occurring during fetal development; some examples include chromosomal disorders, inborn errors of metabolism, developmental disorders affecting brain formation, and environmental influences.

Prereferral teams (PRTs) Teams made up of a variety of professionals, especially regular and special educators, who work with regular class teachers to come up with strategies for teaching difficult-to-teach children. Designed to influence regular educators to take ownership of difficult-to-teach students and to minimize inappropriate referrals to special education.

Primary language disorder A language disorder that has no known cause.

Profound mental retardation A classification used to specify an individual whose IQ is below approximately 25.

Progressive A disease or condition that worsens over time and from which one seldom or never recovers with treatment.

Progressive time delay An instructional procedure whereby the teacher makes a request while simultaneously prompting the student and then over several occasions gradually increases the latency between the request and the prompt; often used with students with mental retardation.

Prosthesis A device designed to replace, partially or completely, a part of the body (e.g., artificial teeth or limbs).

Psychoanalytic Related to psychoanalysis, including the assumptions that emotional or behavior disorders result primarily from unconscious conflicts and that the most effective preventive actions and therapeutic intervention involve uncovering and understanding unconscious motivations.

Psychostimulants Medications that activate dopamine levels in the frontal and prefrontal areas of the brain that control behavioral inhibition and executive functions; used to treat persons with ADHD.

Pull-out programs Special education programs in which students with disabilities leave the general education classroom for part or all of the school day (e.g., to go to special classes or resource room).

Pupil The contractile opening in the middle of the iris of the eye.

Pure-tone audiometry A test whereby tones of various intensities and frequencies are presented to determine a person's hearing loss.

Quadriplegia A condition in which all four limbs are paralyzed

Raised dome detectable warnings Bumps in the pavement that are designed to alert people who are blind to unsafe areas.

Reading comprehension The ability to understand what one has read.

Reading fluency The ability to read effortlessly and smoothly; consists of the ability to read at a normal rate and with appropriate expression; influences one's reading comprehension.

Receptive language Decoding or understanding messages in communication.

Reciprocal teaching A cognitive teaching strategy whereby the student gradually assumes the role of co-instructor for brief periods; the teacher models four strategies for the students to use: (1) predicting, (2) questioning, (3) summarizing, and (4) clarifying; a method in which students and teachers are involved in a dialogue to facilitate learning.

Refraction The bending of light rays as they pass through the structures (cornea, aqueous humor, pupil, lens, vitreous humor) of the eye.

Resonance. The quality of the sound imparted by the size, shape, and texture of the organs in the vocal tract.

Response-to-intervention (RTI) or response-to-treatment approach A way of determining whether a student has a learning disability; increasingly intensive levels of instructional intervention are delivered, and if the student does not achieve, at some point, he or she is determined to have a learning disability or is referred for special education evaluation.

Retina The back portion of the eye, containing nerve fibers connected to the optic nerve.

Retinitis pigmentosa A hereditary condition resulting in degeneration of the retina; causes a narrowing of the field of vision and affects night vision.

Retinopathy of prematurity (ROP) A condition resulting in abnormal growth of blood vessels in the eye; caused by factors related to premature birth, including the administration of an excessive concentration of oxygen at birth.

Rett syndrome One of five autistic spectrum disorders; normal development for five months to four years, followed by regression and mental retardation; much more prevalent in females.

Ritalin The most commonly prescribed psychostimulant for ADHD; its generic name is methylphenidate.

Rubella (German measles) A serious viral disease, which, if it occurs during the first trimester of pregnancy, is likely to cause a deformity in the fetus.

Scaffolded instruction A cognitive approach to instruction in which the teacher provides temporary structure or support while students are learning a task; the support is gradually removed as the students are able to perform the task independently.

Schizophrenia A disorder characterized by psychotic behavior manifested by loss of contact with reality, distorted thought processes, and abnormal perceptions.

Scoliosis An abnormal curvature of the spine.

Screen reader Software for computers that magnifies images on the screen, converts text on the screen to speech, or both.

Secondary language disorder A language disorder that is caused by another disorder or disability, such as mental retardation, hearing impairment, or brain injury.

Seizure (convulsion) A sudden alteration of consciousness, usually accompanied by motor activity and/or sensory phenomena; caused by an abnormal discharge of electrical energy in the brain.

Self-determination The ability to make personal choices, regulate one's own life, and be a self-advocate; a prevailing philosophy in education programming for people with mental retardation; having control over one's life, not having to rely on others for making choices about one's quality of life; develops over one's life span.

Self-injurious behavior (SIB) Behavior causing injury or mutilation of oneself, such as self-biting or head-banging; usually seen in individuals with severe and multiple disabilities.

Self-instruction A type of cognitive training technique that requires individuals to talk aloud and then to themselves as they solve problems.

Self-monitoring A type of cognitive training technique that requires individuals to keep track of their own behavior.

Self-regulation Refers generally to a person's ability to regulate his or her own behavior (e.g., to employ strategies to help in a problem-solving situation); an area of difficulty for persons who are mentally retarded.

Self-stimulation Any repetitive, stereotyped activity that seems only to provide sensory feedback.

Semantics. The study of the meanings attached to words and sentences.

Sensorineural hearing impairment A hearing impairment, usually severe, resulting from malfunctioning of the inner ear.

Severe mental retardation A classification used to specify an individual whose IQ is approximately 25–40.

Sheltered workshop A facility that provides a structured environment for people with disabilities in which they can learn skills; can be either a transitional placement or a permanent arrangement.

Sheltered-English approach A method in which language-minority students are taught all their subjects in English at a level that is modified constantly according to individuals' needs.

Short-term memory (STM) The ability to recall information after a short period of time.

Sibshops Workshops for siblings of children with disabilities; designed to help siblings answer questions about the disability and learn to adjust to having a sister or brother with a disability.

Sign language A manual language used by people who are deaf to communicate; a true language with its own grammar.

Signing English systems Used simultaneously with oral methods in the total communication approach to teaching students who are deaf; different from American Sign Language because they maintain the same word order as spoken English.

Slate and stylus A method of writing in braille in which the paper is held in a slate while a stylus is pressed through openings to make indentations in the paper.

Sleep apnea Cessation of breathing while sleeping.

Snellen chart Used in determining visual acuity; consists of rows of letters or Es arranged in different positions; each row corresponds to the distance at which a normally sighted person can discriminate the letters; does not predict how accurately a child will be able to read print.

Social support Emotional, informational, or material aid provided to a person or a family; this informal means of aid can be very valuable in helping families of children with disabilities.

Spasticity Characterized by muscle stiffness and problems in voluntary movement; associated with spastic cerebral palsy.

Specific language impairment (SLI) A language disorder with no identifiable cause; language disorder not attributable to hearing impairment, mental retardation, brain dysfunction, or other plausible cause; also called specific language disability.

Speech The formation and sequencing of oral language sounds during communication.

Speech audiometry A technique that tests a person's detection and understanding of speech, rather than using pure tones to detect hearing loss.

Speech disorders Oral communication that involves abnormal use of the vocal apparatus, is unintelligible, or is so inferior that it draws attention to itself and causes anxiety, feelings of inadequacy, or inappropriate behavior in the speaker.

Speech reception threshold (SRT) The decibel level at which a person can understand speech.

Speechreading A method that involves teaching children to use visual information from a number of sources to understand what is being said to them; more than just lipreading, which uses only visual clues arising from the movement of the mouth in speaking.

Spina bifida A congenital midline defect resulting from failure of the bony spinal column to close completely during fetal development.

Standardized achievement assessment A method of evaluating a person that has been applied to a large group so that an individual's score can be compared to the norm, or average.

Stapes The stirrup-shaped bone in the ossicular chain of the middle ear.

Stereotypic behaviors Any of a variety of repetitive behaviors (e.g., eye rubbing) that are sometimes found in individuals who are autistic, blind, severely mentally retarded, or psychotic; sometimes referred to as stereotypies or blindisms.

Strabismus A condition in which the eyes are directed inward (crossed eyes) or outward.

Strattera A nonstimulant medication for ADHD; affects the neurotransmitter norepinephrine.

Strauss syndrome Behaviors of distractibility, forced responsiveness to stimuli, and hyperactivity; based on the work of

Alfred Strauss and Heinz Werner with children with mental retardation.

Stuttering Speech characterized by abnormal hesitations, prolongations, and repetitions; may be accompanied by grimaces, gestures, or other bodily movements indicative of a struggle to speak, anxiety, blocking of speech, or avoidance of speech.

Subculture A culture that is associated with or part of a larger culture; a culture that is not the entire culture of a nation or other entity. Sometimes called "microculture," but a subculture is not necessarily small or a minority of a larger culture.

Supported competitive employment A workplace where adults who are disabled earn at least minimum wage and receive ongoing assistance from a specialist or job coach; the majority of workers in the workplace are nondisabled.

Supported employment A method of integrating people with disabilities who cannot work independently into competitive employment; includes use of an employment specialist, or job coach, who helps the person with a disability function on the job.

Supported living An approach to living arrangements for those with disabilities and/or mental retardation that stresses living in natural settings rather than institutions, big or small.

Supports Resources and strategies that promote a person's development, education, interests, and personal well-being; critical to the AAMR's conceptualization of mental retardation

Syntax The way words are joined together to structure meaningful sentences; grammar.

Syphilis A venereal disease that can cause mental subnormality in a child, especially if it is contracted by the mother-to-be during the later stages of fetal development.

Systematic instruction Teaching that involves instructional prompts, consequences for performance, and transfer of stimulus control; often used with students with mental retardation.

Tactile map An embossed representation of the environment that people who are blind can use to orient themselves to their surroundings.

Talent A special ability, aptitude, or accomplishment.

Task analysis The procedure of breaking down an academic task into its component parts for the purpose of instruction; a major feature of Direct Instruction.

Teratogens Agents, such as chemicals, that can disrupt the normal development of the fetus; a possible cause of learning disabilities and other learning and behavioral problems.

Text telephone (TT) A device connected to a telephone by a special adapter; allows communication over the telephone between people who are hearing impaired and those with hearing; sometimes referred to as a TTY (teletype) or TTD (telecommunication device for the deaf).

Theory of mind The ability to take another's perspective in a social exchange; the ability to infer another person's feelings, intentions, desires, etc.; impaired in those with ASD.

Thimerosal A preservative, that up until 1999, was used in vaccines as a preservative; contains small traces of mercury, which in higher doses is known to cause neurological defects.

Tiered assignment Assignments varying in difficulty but on a single topic.

Total communication approach An approach for teaching students with hearing impairment that blends oral and manual techniques.

Touch cues Tactual signals used to communicate with persons who are deaf-blind; can be used to signify a variety of messages.

Tourette's syndrome (TS) A neurological disorder beginning in childhood (about three times more prevalent in boys than in girls) in which stereotyped, repetitive motor movements (tics) are accompanied by multiple vocal outbursts that may include grunting noises or socially inappropriate words or statements (e.g., swearing).

Toxins Poisons in the environment that can cause fetal malformations; can result in cognitive impairments.

Transliteration A method used by most sign language interpreters in which the signs maintain the same word order as that of spoken English; American Sign Language (ASL) is also used by some interpreters.

Traumatic brain injury (TBI) Injury to the brain (not including conditions present at birth, birth trauma, or degenerative diseases or conditions) resulting in total or partial disability or psychosocial maladjustment that affects educational performance; may affect cognition, language, memory, attention, reasoning, abstract thinking, judgment, problem solving, sensory or perceptual and motor disabilities, psychosocial behavior, physical functions, information processing, or speech.

Traveling notebook A system of communication in which parents and professionals write messages to each other by way of a notebook or log that accompanies the child to and from school.

Trisomy 21 A type of Down syndrome in which the twenty-first chromosome is a triplet, making forty-seven, rather than the normal forty-six, chromosomes in all.

Tunnel vision A condition characterized by problems in peripheral vision, or a narrowing of the field of vision.

Tympanic membrane (eardrum) The anatomical boundary between the outer and middle ears; the sound gathered in the outer ear vibrates here.

Tympanometry A method of measuring the middle ear's response to pressure and sound.

Unified Braille Code A combination of literary braille and braille codes for technical fields, such as the Nemeth Code for science and mathematics; not yet widely adopted.

Universal design The design of new buildings, tools, and instructional programs to make them usable by the widest possible population of potential users.

Usher syndrome An inherited syndrome resulting in hearing loss and retinitis pigmentosa, a progressive condition characterized by problems in seeing in low light and tunnel vision; there are three different types of Usher syndrome, differing with respect to when it occurs developmentally and the range of the major symptoms of hearing impairment, vision impairment, and balance problems.

Vestibular mechanism   Located in the upper portion of the inner ear; consists of three soft, semicircular canals filled with a fluid; sensitive to head movement, acceleration, and other movements related to balance.

Visual acuity   The ability to see fine details; usually measured with the Snellen chart.

Visual efficiency   A term used to refer to how well one uses his or her vision, including such things as control of eye movements, attention to visual detail, and discrimination of figure from background; believed by some to be more important than visual acuity alone in predicting a person's ability to function visually.

Vitreous humor   A transparent, gelatinous substance that fills the eyeball between the retina and the lens of the eye.

Williams syndrome   A condition resulting from deletion of material in the seventh pair of chromosomes; often results in mild to moderate mental retardation, heart defects, and elfin facial features; people affected often display surprising strengths in spoken language and sociability while having severe deficits in spatial organization, reading, writing, and math.

Working memory (WM)   The ability to remember information while also performing other cognitive operations.

Zero tolerance   A school policy, supported by federal and state laws, that having possession of any weapon or drug on school property will automatically result in a given penalty (usually suspension or expulsion) regardless of the nature of the weapon or drug or any extenuating circumstances.

References

CHAPTER 1

Bateman, B. D., & Linden, M. A. (1998). *Better IEPs: How to develop legally correct and educationally useful programs* (3rd ed.). Longmont, CO: Sopris West.

Bolger, K. E., & Patterson, C. J. (2001). Developmental pathways from child maltreatment to peer rejection. *Child Development, 72,* 549–568.

Bolick, C. (2001, September 5). A bad IDEA is disabling public schools. *Education Week,* pp. 56, 63.

Carr, M. R. (2004, January 4). My son's disability, and my own inability to see it. *Washington Post,* p. B5.

Clark, D. L., & Astuto, T. A. (1988). *Education policy after Reagan: What next?* Occasional paper No. 6, Policy Studies Center of the University Council for Educational Administration, University of Virginia, Charlottesville.

Council for Exceptional Children. (1998). *What every special educator must know* (3rd ed.). Reston, VA: Author.

Crockett, J. B. (1999–2000). Viable alternatives for students with disabilities: Exploring the origins and interpretations of LRE. *Exceptionality, 8,* 43–60.

Crockett, J. B., & Kauffman, J. M. (1999). *The least restrictive environment: Its origins and interpretations in special education.* Mahwah, NJ: Lawrence Erlbaum.

Crockett, J. B., & Kauffman, J. M. (2001). The concept of the least restrictive environment and learning disabilities: Least restrictive of what? Reflections on Cruickshank's 1977 guest editorial for the Journal of Learning Disabilities. In D. P. Hallahan & B. K. Keogh (Eds.), *Research and global perspectives in learning disabilities: Essays in honor of William M. Cruickshank* (pp 147–166). Mahwah, NJ: Lawrence Erlbaum.

Cruickshank, W. M. (1977). Guest editorial. *Journal of Learning Disabilities, 10,* 193–194.

Dupre, A. P. (1997). Disability and the public schools: The case against "inclusion." *Washington Law Review, 72*(3), 775–858.

Finn, C. E., Jr., & Rotherham, A. J. (2001, December 26). Give special ed a road map to success. *Los Angeles Times,* p. B13.

Finn, C. E., Jr., Rotherham, A. J., & Hokanson, C. R., Jr. (Eds.). (2001). *Rethinking special education for a new century.* New York: Thomas B. Fordham Foundation.

Fuchs, D., & Fuchs, L. S. (1994). Inclusive schools movement and the radicalization of special education reform. *Exceptional Children, 60,* 294–309.

Fisher, M. (2001, December 13). Students still taking the fall for D. C. schools. *Washington Post,* p. B1.

Gersten, R., Schiller, E. P., & Vaughn, S. (2000). Preface. In R. Gersten, E. P. Schiller, & S. Vaughn (Eds.), *Contemporary special education research: Syntheses of the knowledge base on critical instructional issues* (pp. ix–xi). Mahwah, NJ: Lawrence Erlbaum.

Gliona, M. F., Gonzales, A. K., & Jacobson, E. S. (2005). Dedicated, not segregated: Suggested changes in thinking about instructional environments and in the language of special education. In J. M. Kauffman & D. P. Hallahan (Eds.), *The illusion of full inclusion: A comprehensive critique of a current special education bandwagon* (2nd ed.) (pp. 135–146). Austin, TX: Pro-Ed.

Goodman, J. F., & Bond, L. (1993). The individualized education program: A retrospective critique. *Journal of Special Education, 26,* 408–422.

Hallahan, D. P., & Kauffman, J. M. (1977). Labels, categories, behaviors: ED, LD, and EMR reconsidered. *Journal of Special Education, 11,* 139–149.

Hallahan, D. P., Lloyd, J. W., Kauffman, J. M., Weiss, M., & Martinez, E. (2005). *Introduction to learning disabilities* (3rd ed.). Boston: Allyn & Bacon.

Hart, B., & Risley, T. R. (1995). *Meaningful differences in the everyday experience of young American children.* Baltimore: Paul H. Brookes.

Heward, W. L. (2003). Ten faulty notions about teaching and learning that hinder the effectiveness of special education. *The Journal of Special Education, 36,* 186–205.

Hendrick, I. G., & MacMillan, D. L. (1989). Selecting children for special education in New York City: William Maxwell, Elizabeth Farrell, and the development of ungraded classes, 1900–1920. *Journal of Special Education, 22,* 395–417.

Hockenbury, J. C., Kauffman, J. M., & Hallahan, D. P. (1999–2000). What's right about special education? *Exceptionality, 8*(1), 3–11.

Howe, K. R., & Miramontes, O. B. (1992). *The ethics of special education.* New York: Teachers College Press.

Huefner, D. S. (1994). The mainstreaming cases: Tensions and trends for school administrators. *Educational Administration Quarterly, 30,* 27–55.

Huefner, D. S. (2000). *Getting comfortable with special education law: A framework for working with children with disabilities.* Norwood, MA: Christopher Gordon.

Hungerford, R. (1950). On locusts. *American Journal of Mental Deficiency, 54,* 415–418.

Itard, J. M. G. (1962). *The wild boy of Aveyron.* (George & Muriel Humphrey, Trans.). Englewood Cliffs, NJ: Prentice-Hall.

Kanner, L. (1964). *A history of the care and study of the mentally retarded.* Springfield, IL: Charles C. Thomas.

Kauffman, J. M. (1995). Why we must celebrate a diversity of restrictive environments. *Learning Disabilities Research and Practice, 10,* 225–232.

Kauffman, J. M. (1999a). Today's special education and its messages for tomorrow. *The Journal of Special Education, 32,* 244–254.

Kauffman, J. M. (1999b). How we prevent the prevention of emotional and behavioral disorders. *Exceptional Children, 65,* 448–468.

Kauffman, J. M. (1999–2000). The special education story: Obituary, accident report, conversion experience, reincarnation, or none of the above? *Exceptionality, 8*(1), 61–71.

Kauffman, J. M. (2002). *Education deform: Bright people sometimes say stupid things about education.* Lanham, MD: Scarecrow Education.

Kauffman, J. M. (2004). The president's commission and the devaluation of special education. *Education and Treatment of Children, 27* 307–324.

Kauffman, J. M. (2005a). *Characteristics of emotional and behavioral disorders of children and youth* (8th ed.). Upper Saddle River, NJ: Merrill Prentice-Hall.

Kauffman, J. M. (2005b). How we prevent the prevention of emotional and behavioural difficulties in education. In P. Clough, P. Garner, & J. T. Pardeck, & F. K. O. Yuen (Eds.), *Handbook of emotional and behavioural difficulties in education* (pp. 366–376). London: Sage.

Kauffman, J. M. (in press). Waving to Ray Charles: Missing the meaning of disability. *Phi Delta Kappan, 86*(6).

Kauffman, J. M., Bantz, J., & McCullough, J. (2002). Separate and better: A special public school class for students with emotional and behavioral disorders. *Exceptionality, 10,* 149–170.

Kauffman, J. M., & Hallahan, D. P. (1997). A diversity of restrictive environments: Placement as a problem of social ecology. In J. W. Lloyd, E. J. Kameenui, & D. Chard (Eds.), *Issues in educating students with disabilities* (pp. 325–342). Hillsdale, NJ: Lawrence Erlbaum.

Kauffman, J. M., & Hallahan, D. P. (2005a). *Special education: What it is and why we need it.* Boston: Allyn & Bacon.

Kauffman, J. M., & Hallahan, D. P. (Eds.). (2005b). *The illusion of full inclusion: A comprehensive critique of a current special educational bandwagon* (2nd ed.). Austin, TX: Pro-Ed.

Kauffman, J. M., & Landrum, T. J. (2006). *Children and youth with emotional and behavioral disorders: A history of their education.* Austin, TX: Pro-Ed.

Kauffman, J. M., McGee, K., & Brigham, M. (2004). Enabling or disabling? Observations on changes in the purposes and outcomes of special education. *Phi Delta Kappan, 85,* 613–620.

Kauffman, J. M., Mostert, M. P., Trent, S. C., & Pullen, P. L. (2006). *Managing classroom behavior: A reflective case-based approach* (4th ed.). Boston: Allyn & Bacon.

Kauffman, J. M., & Wiley, A. L. (2004). How the President's Commission on Excellence in Special Education (PCESE) devalues special education. *Learning Disabilities: A Multidisciplinary Journal, 13* 3–6.

Lloyd, J. W., Forness, S. R., & Kavale, K. A. (1998). Some methods are more effective. *Intervention in School and Clinic, 33*(1), 195–200.

MacMillan, D. L., & Forness, S. R. (1998). The role of IQ in special education placement decisions: Primary and determinative or peripheral and inconsequential? *Remedial and Special Education, 19,* 239–253.

MacMillan, D. L., & Hendrick, I. G. (1993). Evolution and legacies. In J. I. Goodlad & T. C. Lovitt (Eds.), *Integrating general and special education* (pp. 23–48). Columbus, OH: Merrill/Macmillan.

Martin, E. W. (1995). Case studies of inclusion: Worst fears realized. *The Journal of Special Education, 29,* 192–199.

Mock, D. R., & Kauffman, J. M. (2002). Preparing teachers for full inclusion: Is it possible? *The Teacher Educator, 37,* 202–215.

Mock, D. R., & Kauffman, J. M. (2005). The delusion of full inclusion. In J. W. Jacobson, R. M. Foxx, & J. A. Mulick (Eds.), *Controversial therapies for developmental disabilities: Fad, fashion, and science in professional practice* (pp. 113–128). Mahwah, NJ: Lawrence Erlbaum.

Morse, W. C. (1984). Personal perspective. In B. Blatt & R. Morris (Eds.), *Perspectives in special education: Personal orientations* (pp. 101–124). Glenview, IL: Scott, Foresman.

National Center on Educational Restructuring and Inclusion (1995). National study on inclusion: Overview and summary report. *National Center on Educational Restructuring and Inclusion Bulletin, 2*(2), 1–10.

National Research Council. (2001). *Educating children with autism.* Committee on Educational Interventions for Children with Autism. Division of Behavioral and Social Sciences and Education. Washington, DC: National Academy Press.

Richards, P. L., & Singer, G. H. S. (1998). "To draw out the effort of his mind": Educating a child with mental retardation in early-nineteenth-century America. *The Journal of Special Education, 31,* 443–466.

Safford, P. L., & Safford, E. H. (1998). Visions of the special class. *Remedial and Special Education, 19,* 229–238.

Sarason, S. B. (1990). *The predictable failure of educational reform: Can we change course before it's too late?* San Francisco: Jossey-Bass.

Schiller, E. P., & Malouf, D. B. (2000). Research syntheses: Implications for research and practice. In R. Gersten, E. P. Schiller, & S. Vaughn (Eds.), *Contemporary special education research: Syntheses of the knowledge base on critical instructional issues* (pp. ix–xi). Mahwah, NJ: Lawrence Erlbaum.

Smith, J. D. (1998a). Histories of special education: Stories from our past, insights for our future. *Remedial and Special Education, 19,* 196–200.

Smith, J. D. (Ed.). (1998b). The history of special education: Essays honoring the bicentennial of the work of Jean Itard. [Special issue]. *Remedial and Special Education, 19*(4).

Stainback, W., & Stainback, S. (1984). A rationale for the merger of special and regular education. *Exceptional Children, 51,* 102–111.

Stein, M., & Davis, C. A. (2000). Direct instruction as a positive behavioral support. *Beyond Behavior, 10*(1), 7–12.

Stullken, E. H. (1950). Special schools and classes for the socially maladjusted. In N. B. Henry (Ed.), *The education of exceptional children.* Forty-ninth Yearbook of the National Society for the Study of Education (Part 2, pp. 281–301). Chicago: University of Chicago Press.

Trent, J. W. (1998). Defectives at the World's Fair: Constructing disability in 1904. *Remedial and Special Education, 19,* 201–211.

U.S. Department of Education. (1995). *Seventeenth annual report to Congress on implementation of the Individuals with Disabilities Education Act.* Washington, DC: Author.

U.S. Department of Education. (1997). *Nineteenth annual report to Congress on implementation of the Individuals with Disabilities Education Act.* Washington, DC: Author.

U.S. Department of Education. (2002). *Twenty-fourth annual report to Congress on implementation of the Individuals with Disabilities Education Act.* Washington, DC: Author.

Verstegen, D. A., & Clark, D. L. (1988). The diminution of federal expenditures for education during the Reagan administration. *Phi Delta Kappan, 70,* 134–138.

Will, M. C. (1986). Educating children with learning problems: A shared responsibility. *Exceptional Children, 52,* 411–415.

Winzer, M. A. (1986). Early developments in special education: Some aspects of Enlightenment thought. *Remedial and Special Education, 7*(5), 42–49.

Winzer, M. A. (1993). *The history of special education: From isolation to integration.* Washington, DC: Gallaudet University Press.

Winzer, M. A. (1998). A tale often told: The early progression of special education. *Remedial and Special Education, 19,* 212–218.

Yell, M. L. (in press). *The law and special education* (2nd ed.). Upper Saddle River, NJ: Prentice-Hall.

Yell, M. L., & Drasgow, E. (2005). *No Child Left Behind Act: A guide for professionals.* Upper Saddle River, NJ: Merrill/Prentice-Hall.

Yell, M. L., Rogers, D., & Rogers, E. L. (1998). The legal history of special education: What a long, strange trip it's been! *Remedial and Special Education, 19,* 219–228.

Zelder, E. Y. (1953). Public opinion and public education for the exceptional child: Court decisions 1873–1950. *Exceptional Children, 18,* 187–198.

Zigmond, N. (1997). Educating students with disabilities: The future of special education. In J. W. Lloyd, E. J. Kameenui, & D. Chard (Eds.), *Issues in educating students with disabilities* (pp. 377–390). Mahwah, NJ: Lawrence Erlbaum.

Zigmond, N. (2003). Where should students with disabilities receive special education services? Is one place better than another? *The Journal of Special Education, 37,* 193–199.

Zigmond, N., & Baker, J. M. (1995). Concluding comments: Current and future practices in inclusive schooling. *The Journal of Special Education, 29,* 245–250.

CHAPTER 2

Abt Associates. (1976–1977). *Education as experimentation: A planned variation model* (Vols. 3A and 4). Cambridge, MA: Author.

Agran, M., Blanchard, C., & Wehmeyer, M. L. (2000). Promoting transition goals and self-determination through student self-directed learning: The self-determined learning model of instruction. *Education and Training in Mental Retardation and Developmental Disabilities, 35,* 351–364.

Artesani, A. J., & Millar, L. (1998). Positive behavior supports in general education settings: Combining person-centered planning and functional analysis. *Intervention in School and Clinic, 34,* 33–38.

Baker, J. M., & Zigmond, N. (1995). The meaning and practice of inclusion for students with learning disabilities: Themes and implications from the five cases. *Journal of Special Education, 29,* 163–180.

Bank-Mikkelsen, N. E. (1969). A metropolitan area in Denmark: Copenhagen. In R. B. Kugel & W. Wolfensberger (Eds.), *Changing patterns of residential services for the mentally retarded* (pp. 227–254). Washington, DC: President's Committee on Mental Retardation.

Bateman, B. D., & Linden, M. A. (1998). *Better IEPs: How to develop legally correct and educationally useful programs* (3rd ed.). Longmont, CO: Sopris West.

Baxter, J. A., Woodward, J., & Olson, D. (2001). Effects of reformation-based mathematics instruction on low achievers in five third-grade classrooms. *Elementary School Journal, 101,* 529–547.

Bogdan, R. (1986). The sociology of special education. In R. J. Morris & B. Blatt (Eds.), *Special education: Research and trends* (pp. 344–359). New York: Pergamon Press.

Bradley, M. R. (Ed.) (2001). Positive behavior supports: Research to practice. *Beyond Behavior, 11*(1), [special feature].

Browder, D. M., Wood, W. M., Test, D. W., Karvonen, M., & Algozzine, B. (2001). Reviewing resources on self-determination: A map for teachers. *Remedial and Special Education, 22,* 233–244.

Buck, G. H., Polloway, E. A., Kirkpatrick, M. A., Patton, J. R., & Fad, K. M. (2000). Developing behavioral intervention plans: A sequential approach. *Intervention in School and Clinic, 36,* 3–9.

Carpenter, B., & Bovair, K. (1996). Learning with dignity: Educational opportunities for students with emotional and behavioral difficulties. *Canadian Journal of Special Education, 11*(1), 6–16.

Carr, M. R. (2004, January 4). My son's disability, and my own inability to see it. *Washington Post,* B5.

Carta, J. J. (1995). Developmentally appropriate practice: A critical analysis as applied to young children with disabilities. *Focus on Exceptional Children, 27*(8), 1–14.

Carta, J. J., & Greenwood, C. R. (1997). Barriers to the implementation of effective educational practices for young children with disabilities. In J. W. Lloyd, E. J. Kameenui, & D. Chard (Eds.), *Issues in educating students with disabilities* (pp. 261–274). Mahwah, NJ: Lawrence Erlbaum.

Chadsey-Rusch, J., & Heal, L. W. (1995). Building consensus from transition experts on social integration outcomes and interventions. *Exceptional Children, 62,* 165–187.

Condon, K. A., & Tobin, T. J. (2001). Using electronic and other new ways to help students improve their behavior: Functional behavioral assessment at work. *Teaching Exceptional Children, 34*(1), 44–51.

Cook, B. G., Gerber, M. M., & Semmel, M. I. (1997). Are effective school reforms effective for all students? The implications of joint outcome production for school reform. *Exceptionality, 7,* 77–95.

Cook, L., & Friend, M. (1998). Co-teaching: Guidelines for creating effective practices. In E. L. Meyen, G. A. Vergason, & R. J. Whelan (Eds.), *Educating students with mild disabilities: Strategies and methods* (2nd ed., pp. 453–479). Denver, CO: Love.

Crissey, M. S., & Rosen, M. (Eds.). (1986). *Institutions for the mentally retarded: A changing role in changing times.* Austin, TX: Pro-Ed.

Crockett, J. B., & Kauffman, J. M. (1998). Taking inclusion back to its roots. *Educational Leadership, 56*(2), 74–77.

Crockett, J. B., & Kauffman, J. M. (1999). *The least restrictive environment: Its origins and interpretations in special education.* Mahwah, NJ: Lawrence Erlbaum.

Crockett, J. B., & Kauffman, J. M. (2001). The concept of the least restrictive environment and learning disabilities: Least restrictive of what? Reflections on Cruickshank's 1977 guest editorial for the *Journal of Learning Disabilities.* In D. P. Hallahan & B. K. Keogh (Eds.), *Research and global perspectives in learning disabilities: Essays in honor of William M. Cruickshank* (pp. 147–166). Mahwah, NJ: Lawrence Erlbaum.

Cronin, M. E. (2000). Instructional strategies. In P. L. Sitlington, G. M. Clark, & O. P. Kolstoe (Eds.), *Transition education and services for adolescents with disabilities* (3rd ed., pp. 255–283). Boston: Allyn & Bacon.

Cruickshank, W. M. (1977). Guest editorial. *Journal of Learning Disabilities, 10,* 193–194.

Dobbs, M. (2004, April 22). "No child" law leaves schools' old ways behind. *The Washington Post,* A1, A12–A13.

Duhaney, L. M. G., & Salend, S. J. (2000). Parental perceptions of inclusive educational placements. *Remedial and Special Education, 21,* 121–128.

Dupre, A. P. (1997). Disability and the public schools: The case against "inclusion." *Washington Law Review, 72,* 775–858.

Dupre, A. P. (2000). A study in double standards, discipline, and the disabled student. *Washington Law Review, 75*(1).

Dwyer, K. P., Osher, D., & Hoffman, C. C. (2000). Creating responsive schools: Contextualizing early warning, timely response. *Exceptional Children, 66,* 347–365.

Falk, K. B., & Wehby, J. H. (2001). The effects of peer-assisted learning strategies on the beginning reading skills of young children with emotional or behavioral disorders. *Behavioral Disorders, 26,* 344–359.

Fallis, D. S. (2004a, May 23). A dangerous place. Assisted living in Virginia. As care declines, cost can be injury, death. *The Washington Post,* pp. A1, A15–A17.

Fallis, D. S. (2004b, May 24). A dangerous place. A volatile mix of residents. In Vax's assisted living homes, violent preyed on the vulnerable. *The Washington Post,* pp. A1, A6–A7.

Fallis, D. S. (2004c, May 25). A dangerous place. Lost in life and death. Assisted living facility's chaos bred wide neglect. *The Washington Post,* pp. A1, A6.

Fallis, D. S. (2004d, May 26). A dangerous place. Failure to regulate. Weak laws let deficient facilities stay open. *The Washington Post,* pp. A1, A12–A13.

Fennick, E. (2001). Coteaching: An inclusive curriculum for transition. *Teaching Exceptional Children, 33*(6), 60–66.

Fiedler, C. R., & Simpson, R. L. (1987). Modifying the attitudes of nonhandicapped high school students toward handicapped peers. *Exceptional Children, 53,* 342–349.

Finn, C. E., Jr., Rotherham, A. J., & Hokanson, C. R., Jr. (Eds.). (2001). *Rethinking special education for a new century.* New York: Thomas B. Fordham Foundation.

Fox, N., & Ysseldyke, J. E. (1997). Implementing inclusion at the middle school level: Lessons from a negative example. *Exceptional Children, 64,* 81–98.

Fuchs, D., & Fuchs, L. S. (1991). Framing the REI debate: Abolitionists versus conservationists. In J. W. Lloyd, N. N. Singh, & A. C. Repp (Eds.), *The regular education initiative: Alternative perspectives on concepts, issues, and models* (pp. 241–255). Sycamore, IL: Sycamore Publishing.

Fuchs, D., & Fuchs, L. S. (1994). Inclusive schools movement and the radicalization of special education reform. *Exceptional Children, 60,* 294–309.

Fuchs, D., Fuchs, L. S., Thompson, A., Svenson, E., Yanb, L., Otaiba, S. A., Yang, N., McMaster, K. N., Prentice, K., Kazdan, S., & Saenz, L. (2001). Peer-assisted learning strategies in reading: Extensions for kindergarten, first grade, and high school *Remedial and Special Education, 22,* 15–21.

Fuchs, D., Mock, D., Morgan, P. L., & Young, C. L. (2003). Responsiveness-to-intervention: Definitions, evidence, and implications for the learning disabilities construct. *Learning Disabilities Research and Practice, 18,* 157–171.

Fuchs, L. S., Fuchs, D., Eaton, S. B., Hamlett, C. L., & Karns, K. M. (2000). Supplementing teacher judgments of mathematics test accommodations with objective data sources. *School Psychology Review, 29,* 65–85.

Fulk, B. M., & King, K. (2001). Classwide peer tutoring at work. *Teaching Exceptional Children, 34*(2), 49–53.

Furney, K. S., Hasazi, S. B., & DeStefano, L. (1997). Transition policies, practices, and promises: Lessons from three states. *Exceptional Children, 63,* 343–355.

Gallagher, J. J. (1972). The special education contract for mildly handicapped children. *Exceptional Children, 38,* 527–535.

Gallagher, P. A., Rhodes, C. A., & Darling, S. M. (2004). Parents as professionals in early intervention: A parent educator model. *Topics in Early Childhood Special Education, 24,* 5–13.

Gardner, R., Cartledge, G., Seidl, B., Woolsey, M. L., Schley, G. S., & Utley, C. A. (2001). Mt. Olivet after-school program: Peer-mediated interventions for at-risk students. *Remedial and Special Education, 22,* 22–33.

Garrett, J. N., Thorp, E. K., Behrmann, M. M., & Denham, S. A. (1998). The impact of early intervention legislation: Local perceptions. *Topics in Early Childhood Special Education, 18,* 183–189.

Gartner, A., & Joe, T. (1986). Introduction. In A. Gartner & T. Joe (Eds.), *Images of the disabled/disabling images.* New York: Praeger.

Gliona, M. F., Gonzales, A. K., & Jacobson, E. S. (2005). Suggested changes in thinking about instructional environments and in the language of special education. In J. M. Kauffman & D. P. Hallahan (Eds.), *The illusion of full inclusion: A comprehensive critique of a current special education bandwagon* (2nd ed., pp. 135–146). Austin, TX: Pro-Ed.

Greenwood, C. R., Arrega-Mayer, C., Utley, C. A., Gavin, K. M., & Terry, B. (2001). Classwide peer tutoring learning management system: Applications with elementary-level English language learners. *Remedial and Special Education, 22,* 34–47.

Grigal, M., Test, D. W., Beattie, J., & Wood, W. M. (1997). An evaluation of transition components of individualized education programs. *Exceptional Children, 63,* 357–372.

Grim, R. (2004, May 2). No rhyme, for no good reason. *The Washington Post,* p. B8.

Groopman, J. (2003, November 10). Annals of medicine: The Reeve effect. *The New Yorker,* pp. 82–93.

Guterman, B. R. (1995). The validity of categorical learning disabilities services: The consumer's view. *Exceptional Children, 62,* 111–124.

Hall, J. P. (2002). Narrowing the breach: Can disability culture and full educational inclusion be reconciled? *Journal of Disability Policy Studies, 13,* 144–152.

Hallahan, D. P., & Kauffman, J. M. (1994). Toward a culture of disability in the aftermath of Deno and Dunn. *Journal of Special Education, 27,* 496–508.

Hallahan, D. P., Lloyd, J. W., Kauffman, J. M., Weiss, M. P., & Martinez, E. A. (2005). *Learning disabilities: Foundations, characteristics, and effective teaching* (3rd ed.). Boston: Allyn & Bacon.

Halpern, A. S. (1993). Quality of life as a conceptual framework for evaluating transition outcomes. *Exceptional Children, 59,* 486–498.

Helwig, R., & Tindal, G. (2003). An experimental analysis of accommodation decisions on large-scale mathematics tests. *Exceptional Children, 69,* 211–225.

Holbrook, P. J. (2001). When bad things happen to good children: A special educator's views of MCAS. *Phi Delta Kappan, 82,* 781–785.

Hoover, J. J., & Patton J. R. (2004). Differentiating standards-based education for students with diverse needs. *Remedial and Special Education, 25,* 74–78.

Huefner, D. S. (2000). *Getting comfortable with special education law: A framework for working with children with disabilities.* Norwood, MA: Christopher Gordon.

Jakubecy, J. J., Mock, D. R., & Kauffman, J. M. (2003). Special education, current trends. In J. W. Guthrie (Ed.), *Encyclopedia of education* (2nd ed., pp. 2284–2290). New York: Macmillan Reference.

Johns, B. H. (2003). NCLB and IDEA: Never the twain should meet. *Learning Disabilities: A Multidisciplinary Journal, 12*(3), 89–91.

Johnson, E. S., Kimball, K., Brown, S. O., & Anderson, D. (2001). A statewide review of the use of accommodations in large-scale, high-stakes assessments. *Exceptional Children, 67,* 251–264.

Kaiser, A. P. (Ed.) (2000). Special issue: Assessing and addressing problems in children enrolled in Head Start. *Behavioral Disorders, 26*(1).

Kastor, E. (1997, June 19). Ready, willing, and disabled: Women at global forum turn the wheelchairs of progress. *The Washington Post*, p. D1.

Katsiyannis, A., & Magg, J. W. (2001). Manifestation determination as a golden fleece. *Exceptional Children, 68,* 85–96.

Kauffman, J. M. (1989). The regular education initiative as a Reagan-Bush education policy: A trickle-down theory of education of the hard-to-teach. *Journal of Special Education, 2,* 256–278.

Kauffman, J. M. (1999a). Today's special education and its messages for tomorrow. *Journal of Special Education, 32,* 244–254.

Kauffman, J. M. (1999b). How we prevent the prevention of emotional and behavioral disorders. *Exceptional Children, 65,* 448–468.

Kauffman, J. M. (1999–2000). The special education story: Obituary, accident report, conversion experience, reincarnation, or none of the above? *Exceptionality, 8*(1), 61–71.

Kauffman, J. M. (2002). *Education deform: Bright people sometimes say stupid things about education.* Lanham, MD: Scarecrow Education.

Kauffman, J. M. (2003). Appearances, stigma, and prevention. *Remedial and Special Education, 24,* 195–198.

Kauffman, J. M. (2004). The president's commission and the devaluation of special education. *Education and Treatment of Children, 27* 307–324

Kauffman, J. M. (2005a). *Characteristics of emotional and behavioral disorders of children and youth* (8th ed.). Upper Saddle River, NJ: Prentice-Hall.

Kauffman, J. M. (2005b). How we prevent the prevention of emotional and behavioural difficulties in education. In P. Clough, P. Garner, & J. T. Pardeck, & F. K. O. Yuen (Eds.), *Handbook of emotional and behavioral difficulties in education* (pp. 366–376). London: Sage.

Kauffman, J. M., Bantz, J., & McCullough, J. (2002). Separate and better: A special public school class for students with emotional and behavioral disorders. *Exceptionality, 10,* 149–170.

Kauffman, J. M., & Brigham, F. J. (2000). Editorial: Zero tolerance and bad judgment in working with students with emotional or behavioral disorders. *Behavioral Disorders, 26,* 5–6.

Kauffman, J. M., & Hallahan, D. P. (1993). Toward a comprehensive delivery system: The necessity of identity, focus, and authority for special education and other compensatory programs. In J. I. Goodlad & T. C. Lovitt (Eds.), *Integrating general and special education* (pp. 73–102). Columbus, OH: Merrill.

Kauffman, J. M., & Hallahan, D. P. (1997). A diversity of restrictive environments: Placement as a problem of social ecology. In J. W. Lloyd, E. J. Kame'enui, & D. Chard (Eds.), *Issues in ed-*

ucating students with disabilities (pp. 325–342). Hillsdale, NJ: Lawrence Erlbaum.

Kauffman, J. M., & Hallahan, D. P. (2005a). *Special education: What it is and why we need it.* Boston: Allyn & Bacon.

Kauffman, J. M., & Hallahan, D. P. (Eds.). (2005b). *The illusion of full inclusion: A comprehensive critique of a current special education bandwagon* (2nd ed.). Austin, TX: Pro-Ed.

Kauffman, J. M., & Landrum, T. J. (2005). Educational service interventions and reforms. In J. W. Jacobson & J. A. Mulick (Eds.), *Handbook of mental retardation and developmental disabilities.* New York: Kluwer.

Kauffman, J. M., & Landrum, T. J. (2006). *Children and youth with emotional and behavioral disorders: A history of their education.* Austin, TX: Pro-Ed.

Kauffman, J. M., & Lloyd, J. W. (1995). A sense of place: The importance of placement issues in contemporary special education. In J. M. Kauffman, J. W. Lloyd, D. P. Hallahan, & T. A. Astuto (Eds.), *Issues in educational placement: Students with emotional and behavioral disorders* (pp. 3–19). Hillsdale, NJ: Lawrence Erlbaum.

Kauffman, J. M., Lloyd, J. W., Hallahan, D. P., & Astuto, T. A. (1995). Toward a sense of place for special education in the twenty-first century. In J. M. Kauffman, J. W. Lloyd, D. P. Hallahan, & T. A. Astuto (Eds.), *Issues in educational placement: Students with emotional and behavioral disorders* (pp. 379–385). Hillsdale, NJ: Lawrence Erlbaum.

Kauffman, J. M., McGee, K., & Brigham, M. (2004). Enabling or disabling? Observations on changes in the purposes and outcomes of special education. *Phi Delta Kappan, 85,* 613–620.

Kauffman, J. M., Mostert, M. P., Trent, S. C., & Pullen, P. L. (2006).*Managing classroom behavior: A reflective case-based approach* (4th ed.). Boston: Allyn & Bacon.

Kauffman, J. M., & Wiley, A. L. (2004). How the President's Commission on Excellence in Special Education (PCESE) devalues special education. *Learning Disabilities: A Multidisciplinary Journal, 13,* 3–6.

Kavale, K. A., & Forness, S. R. (2000). History, rhetoric, and reality: Analysis of the inclusion debate. *Remedial and Special Education, 21,* 279–296.

Klinger, J. K., Vaughn, S., Schumm, J. S., Cohen, P., & Forgan, J. W. (1998). Inclusion or pull-out: Which do students prefer? *Journal of Learning Disabilities, 31,* 148–158.

Kohler, P. D. (1998). Implementing a transition perspective of education: A comprehensive approach to planning and delivering secondary education and transition services (pp. 179–205). In F. R. Rusch & J. G. Chadsey (Eds.), *Beyond high school: Transition from school to work.* Belmont, CA: Wadsworth.

Kuppers, P. (2001). *Disability and contemporary performance: Bodies on edge.* New York: Routledge.

Lamb, H. R., & Weinberger, L. E. (Eds.). (2001). *Deinstitutionalization: Promise and problems.* San Francisco: Jossey-Bass.

Landesman, S., & Butterfield, E. C. (1987). Normalization and deinstitutionalization of mentally retarded individuals: Controversy and facts. *American Psychologist, 42,* 809–816.

Laski, F. J. (1991). Achieving integration during the second revolution. In L. H. Meyer, C. A. Peck, & L. Brown (Eds.), *Critical issues in the lives of people with severe disabilities* (pp. 409–421). Baltimore, MD: Paul H. Brookes.

Leahy, M. (2004, April 18). A job for Sarah: Can a mildly retarded young woman find success and independence greeting shoppers at Lowe's? *The Washington Post Magazine,* pp. 10–15. 20, 26–30.

Lerner, W., Lowenthal, B., & Egan, R. (1998). *Preschool children with special needs: Children at-risk, children with disabilities.* Boston: Allyn & Bacon.

Lieberman, L. M. (1992). Preserving special education . . . for those who need it. In W. Stainback & S. Stainback (Eds.), *Controversial issues confronting special education: Divergent perspectives* (pp. 13–15). Boston: Allyn & Bacon.

Longmore, P. K., & Umansky, L. (Eds.). (2001). *The new disability history: American perspectives.* New York: New York University Press.

MacMillan, D. L., Widaman, K. F., Balow, I. H., Borthwick-Duffy, S., Hendrick, I. G., & Hemsley, R. E. (1992). Special education students exiting the educational system. *Journal of Special Education, 26*(1), 20–36.

Maheady, L., Harper, G. F., & Mallette, B. (2001). Peer-mediated instruction and interventions with students with mild disabilities. *Remedial and Special Education, 22,* 4–14.

Martella, R. C., Nelson, J. R., & Marchand-Martella, N. E. (2003). *Managing disruptive behaviors in the schools: A schoolwide, classroom, and individualized learning approach.* Boston: Allyn & Bacon.

Martin, E. W. (1994). Case studies on inclusion: Worst fears realized. *Journal of Special Education, 29,* 192–199.

Martin, F. D. (Ed.). (2001). *Significant disability: Issues affecting people with significant disabilities from a historical, policy, leadership, and systems perspective.* Springfield, IL: Charles C. Thomas.

Mathiason, C. S. (1997, February 15). *DPI advocates for a "disability-friendly" International Classification of Impairment, Disability and Handicap (ICIDH).* Retrieved from http://www.escape.ca/~dpi/icicdh.html

McConnell, M. E., Hilvitz, P. B., & Cox, C. J. (1998). Functional assessment: A systematic process for assessment and intervention in general and special education classrooms. *Intervention in School and Clinic, 34,* 10–20.

McCray, A. D., Vaughn, S., & Neal, L. I. (2001). Not all students learn to read by third grade: Middle school students speak out about their reading disabilities. *Remedial and Special Education, 35,* 17–30.

McNeil, L. M. (2000). Creating new inequalities: Contradictions of reform. *Phi Delta Kappan, 81,* 729–734.

Michalko, R. (2002). *The difference that disability makes.* Philadelphia: Temple University Press.

Miller, S. P. (2002). *Validated practices for teaching students with diverse needs and abilities.* Boston: Allyn & Bacon.

Mills, P. E., Cole, K. N., Jenkins, J. R., & Dale, P. S. (1998). Effects of differing levels of inclusion on preschoolers with disabilities. *Exceptional Children, 65,* 79–90.

Mitchell, R. (2004, April 27). Dumbing down our schools. *The Washington Post,* p. A21.

Mock, D. R., Jakubecy, J. J., & Kauffman, J. M. (2003). Special education, history of. In J. W. Guthrie (Ed.), *Encyclopedia of education* (2nd ed., pp. 2278–2284). New York: Macmillan Reference.

Mock, D. R., & Kauffman, J. M. (2002). Preparing teachers for full inclusion: Is it possible? *The Teacher Educator, 37,* 202–215.

Mock, D. R., & Kauffman, J. M. (2005). The delusion of full inclusion. In J. W. Jacobson, J. A. Mulick, & R. M. Foxx (Eds.),

Fads: Dubious and improbable treatments for developmental disabilities (pp. 113–128). Mahwah, NJ: Lawrence Erlbaum.

Moody, S. W., Vaughn, S., Hughes, M. T., & Fischer, M. (2000). Reading instruction in the resource room: Set up for failure. *Exceptional Children, 66,* 305–316.

Moon, M. S., & Inge, K. (2000). Vocational preparation and transition. In M. E. Snell & F. Brown (Eds.), *Instruction of students with severe disabilities* (5th ed., pp. 591–628). Upper Saddle River, NJ: Merrill.

Mostert, M. P., Kauffman, J. M., & Kavale, K. A. (2003). Truth and consequences. *Behavioral Disorders, 28,* 333–347.

Murawski, W. W., & Swanson, H. L. (2001). A meta-analysis of co-teaching research: Where are the data? *Remedial and Special Education, 22,* 258–267.

Nelson, J. R., Roberts, M., Mather, S., & Rutherford, R. J. (1999). Has public policy exceeded our knowledge base? A review of the functional behavioral assessment literature. *Behavioral Disorders, 24,* 169–179

Noell, G. H., Witt, J. C., LaFleur, L. H., Mortenson, B. P., Rainer, D. D., & LeVelle, J. (2000). Increasing intervention implementation in general education following consultation: A comparison of two follow-up strategies. *Journal of Applied Behavior Analysis, 33,* 271–284.

Odom, S. L. (2000). Preschool inclusion: What we know and where we go from here. *Topics in Early Childhood Special Education, 20,* 20–27.

Palmer, D. S., Fuller, K., Arora, T., & Nelson, M. (2001). Taking sides: Parent views on inclusion for their children with severe disabilities. *Exceptional Children, 67,* 467–484.

Palmer, S. B., & Wehmeyer, M. L. (2003). Promoting self-determination in early elementary school: Teaching self-regulated problem-solving and goal-setting skills. *Remedial and Special Education, 24,* 115–126.

Peck, S. (2004). Communication made easier: Facilitating transitions for students with multiple disabilities. *Teaching Exceptional Children, 36*(5), 60–63.

Pisha, B. & Coyne, P. (2001). Smart from the start: The promise of universal design or learning. *Remedial and Special Education, 22,* 197–203.

Pomplun, M. (1997). When students with disabilities participate in cooperative groups. *Exceptional Children, 64,* 49–58.

Pugach, M. C., & Warger, C. L. (2001). Curriculum matters: Raising expectations for students with disabilities. *Remedial and Special Education, 22,* 194–196.

Raspberry, W. (2004, May 3). No child's failure. *The Washington Post,* p. A21.

Ravitch, D. (2003). *The language police: How pressure groups restrict what students learn.* New York: Knopf.

Raynes, M., Snell, M., & Sailor, W. (1991). A fresh look at categorical programs for children with special needs. *Phi Delta Kappan, 73*(4), 326–331.

Rueda, R., Gallego, M. A., & Moll, L. C. (2000). The least restrictive environment: A place or a context? *Remedial and Special Education, 21,* 70–78.

Ruef, M. B., Higgins, C., Glaeser, B. J. C., & Patnode, M. (1998). Positive behavioral support: Strategies for teacher. *Intervention in School and Clinic, 34,* 21–32.

Safran, S. P. (1998). Disability portrayal in film: Reflecting the past, directing the future. *Exceptional Children, 64,* 227–238.

Safran, S. P. (2001). Movie images of disability and war: Framing history and political ideology. *Remedial and Special Education, 22,* 223–232.

Sale, P., & Carey, D. M. (1995). The sociometric status of students with disabilities in a full-inclusion school. *Exceptional Children, 62,* 6–19.

Sasso, G. M. (2001). The retreat from inquiry and knowledge in special education. *Journal of Special Education, 34,* 178–193.

Sasso, G. M., Conroy, M. A., Stichter, J. P., & Fox, J. J. (2001). Slowing down the bandwagon: The misapplication of functional assessment for students with emotional and behavioral disorders. *Behavioral Disorders, 26,* 269–281.

Schwartz, A. A., Jacobson, J. W., & Holburn, S. C. (2000). Defining person centeredness: Results of two consensus methods. *Education and Training in Mental Retardation and Developmental Disabilities, 35,* 235–249.

Scruggs, T. E., & Mastropieri, M. A. (1996). Teacher perceptions of mainstreaming/inclusion, 1958–1995: A research synthesis. *Exceptional Children, 63,* 59–74.

Semmel, M. I., Abernathy, T. V., Butera, G., & Lesar, S. (1991). Teacher perceptions of the regular education initiative. *Exceptional Children, 58*(1), 9–24.

Sitlington, P. L., Clark, G. M., & Kolstoe, O. P. (2000). *Transition education and services for adolescents with disabilities* (3rd ed.). Boston: Allyn & Bacon.

Skiba, R. J., & Peterson, R. L. (2000). School discipline at a crossroads: From zero tolerance to early response. *Exceptional Children, 66,* 335–346.

Smith, B. J. (2000). The federal role in early childhood special education policy in the next century: The responsibility of the individual. *Topics in Early Childhood Special Education, 20,* 7–13.

Smith, J. D. (Ed.). (1998). The history of special education: Essays honoring the bicentennial of the work of Jean Itard [Special issue]. *Remedial and Special Education, 19*(4).

Sprague, J., & Walker, H. (2000). Early identification and intervention for youth with antisocial and violent behavior. *Exceptional Children, 66,* 367–379.

Stainback, S., & Stainback, W. (1992). Schools as inclusive communities. In W. Stainback & S. Stainback (Eds.), *Controversial issues confronting special education: Divergent perspectives* (pp. 29–43). Boston: Allyn & Bacon.

Stancliffe, R. J., Abery, B. H., & Smith, J. (2000). Personal control and the ecology of community living settings: Beyond living-unit size and type. *American Journal on Mental Retardation, 105,* 431–454.

Strain, P. S. (2001). Empirically-based social skills intervention: A case for quality of life improvement. *Behavioral Disorders., 27,* 30–36.

Strain, P. S., & Timm, M. A. (2001). Remediation and prevention of aggression: An evaluation of the Regional Intervention Program over a quarter century. *Behavioral Disorders, 26,* 297–313.

Stroman, D. F. (2003). *The disability rights movement: From deinstitutionalization to self-determination.* Lanham, MD: University Press of America.

Sugai, G., & Horner, R. H. (Eds.), (1999–2000). Functional behavioral assessment. *Exceptionality, 8*(3) [special issue].

Sugai, G., Sprague, J. R., Horner, R. H., & Walker, H. M. (2000). Preventing school violence: The use of office discipline referrals to assess and monitor school-wide discipline interventions. *Journal of Emotional and Behavioral Disorders, 8,* 94–101.

Switzer, J. V. (2003). *Disabled rights: American disability policy and the fight for equality.* Washington, DC: Georgetown University Press.

Thurlow, M. L. (2000). Standards-based reform and students with disabilities: Reflections on a decade of change. *Focus on Exceptional Children, 33*(3), 1–16.

Thurlow, M. L., Nelson, J. R., Teelucksingh, W., & Draper, I. L. (2001). Multiculturalism and disability in a results-based educational system: Hazards and hopes for today's schools. In C. A. Utley & F. E. Obiakor (Eds.), *Special education, multicultural education, and school reform: Components of quality education for learners with mild disabilities* (pp. 155–172). Springfield, IL: Charles C. Thomas.

Tindal, G., Heath, B., Hollenbeck, K., Almond, P., & Harniss, M. (1998). Accommodating students with disabilities on large-scale tests: An experimental study. *Exceptional Children, 64,* 439–450.

Tomlinson, C. A. (2001). *How to differentiate instruction in mixed-ability classrooms* (2nd ed.). Alexandria, VA: ASCD.

Tregaskis, C. (2004). *Constructions of disability: Researching the interface between disabled and non-disabled people.* New York: Routledge.

University of Minnesota. (1999, October). Behavioral outcomes of deinstitutionalization for people with intellectual disabilities: A review of studies conducted between 1980 and 1999. *Policy Research Brief, 10*(1), 1–11.

Utley, C. A., Mortweet, S. L., & Greenwood, C. R. (1997). Peer-mediated instruction and interventions. *Focus on Exceptional Children, 29*(5), 1–23.

Vaughn, S., Bos, C., & Schumm, J. S. (1997). *Teaching mainstreamed, diverse, and at-risk students in the general education classroom.* Boston: Allyn & Bacon.

Vaughn, S., & Fuchs, L. S. (2003). Redefining learning disabilities as inadequate response to instruction: The promise and potential problems. *Learning Disabilities Research and Practice, 18,* 137–146.

Vaughn, S. Moody, S. W., & Schumm, J. S. (1998). Broken promises: Reading instruction in the resource room. *Exceptional Children, 64,* 211–225.

Vaughn, S., Schumm, J. S., & Arguelles, M. E. (1997). The ABCDEs of co-teaching. Teaching *Exceptional Children, 30*(2), 4–10.

Vaughn, S., Elbaum, B., & Boardman, A. G. (2001). The social functioning of students with learning disabilities: Implications for inclusion. *Exceptionality, 9,* 47–65.

Walker, H. M., Ramsey, E., & Gresham, F. M. (2004). *Antisocial behavior in school: Strategies and best practices* (2nd ed.). Pacific Grove, CA: Brooks/Cole.

Walsh, J. M., & Jones, B. (2004). New models of cooperative teaching. *Teaching Exceptional Children, 36*(5), 14–20.

Wehmeyer, M. L., Palmer, S. B., Agran, M., Mithaug, D. E., & Martin, J. E. (2000). Promoting causal agency: The self-determined learning model of instruction. *Exceptional Children, 66,* 439–453.

Weiss, M. P., & Brigham, F. J. (2000). Co-teaching and the model of shared responsibility: What does the research support? In T. E. Scruggs & M. A. Mastropieri (Eds.), *Advances in learning and behavioral disabilities: Educational interventions.* Stamford, CT: JAI Press.

Weiss, M. P., & Lloyd, J. W. (2002). Congruence between roles and actions of secondary special educators in co-taught and special education settings. *Journal of Special Education, 36*(2), 58–68.

Wolfensberger, W. (1972). *The principle of normalization in human services.* Toronto: National Institute on Mental Retardation.

Wyer, K. (2001, Spring). The Great Equalizer: Assistive technology launches a new era in inclusion. *Teaching Tolerance,* Number 19.

Yell, M. L. (1998). *The law and special education.* Upper Saddle River, NJ: Prentice-Hall.

Yell, M. L. (in press). *The law and special education* (2nd ed.). Upper Saddle River, NJ: Prentice-Hall.

Yell, M. L., & Drasgow, E. (2005). *No child left behind: A guide for professionals.* Upper Saddle River, NJ: Merrill Prentice Hall.

Yell, M. L., Rozalski, M. E., & Drasgow, E. (2001). Disciplining students with disabilities. *Focus on Exceptional Children, 33*(9), 1–20.

Yell, M. L., & Shriner, J. G. (1997). The IDEA amendments of 1997: Implications for special and general education teachers, administrators, and teacher trainers. *Focus on Exceptional Children, 30*(1), 1–19.

Zigler, E., Hodapp, R. M., & Edison, M. R. (1990). From theory to practice in the care and education of mentally retarded individuals. *American Journal on Mental Retardation, 95*(1), 1–12.

Zigmond, N. (1995). An exploration of the meaning and practice of special education in the context of full inclusion of students with learning disabilities. *Journal of Special Education, 29,* 109–115.

Zigmond, N. (2003). Where should students with disabilities receive special education services? Is one place better than another? *The Journal of Special Education, 37,* 193–199.

Zigmond, N., & Baker, J. M. (1995). Concluding comments: Current and future practices in inclusive schooling. *Journal of Special Education, 29,* 245–250.

Zigmond, N., Jenkins, J., Fuchs, L. S., Deno, S., Fuchs, D., Baker, J. N., Jenkins, L., & Couthino, M. (1995). Special education in restructured schools: Findings from three multi-year studies. *Phi Delta Kappan, 76,* 531–540.

Zigmond, N., & Miller, S. E. (1992). Improving high school programs for students with learning disabilities: A matter of substance as well as form. In F. R. Rusch, L. DeStefano, J. Chadsey-Rusch, L. A. Phelps, & E. Szymanski (Eds.), *Transition from school to adult life* (pp. 17–31). Sycamore, IL: Sycamore Publishing.

Zurkowski, J. K., Kelly, P. S., & Griswold, D. E. (1998). Discipline and IDEA 1997: Instituting a new balance. *Intervention in School and Clinic, 34,* 3–9.

CHAPTER 3

Artiles, A. J., Trent, S. C., Hoffman-Kipp, P., & Lopez-Torres, L. (2000). From individual acquisition to cultural-historical practices in multicultural teacher education. *Remedial and Special Education, 21,* 79–89, 120.

Artiles, A. J., & Zamora-Duran, G. (Eds.). (1997). *Reducing disproportionate representation of culturally diverse students in special education.* Reston, VA: Council for Exceptional Children.

Ascher, C. (1992). School programs for African-American males . . . and females. *Phi Delta Kappan, 73,* 777–782.

Associated Press. (2004, April 18). Gay teens harassed at school: Persecution leads to law. *Charlottesville Daily Progress,* p. A11.

Banks, J. A. (1997). *Teaching strategies for ethnic studies* (6th ed.). Boston: Allyn & Bacon.

Banks, J. A., & Banks, C. A. M. (Eds.). (1997). *Multicultural education: Issues and perspectives* (3rd ed.). Boston: Allyn & Bacon.

Bateman, B. D. (1994). Who, how, and where: Special education's issues in perpetuity. *Journal of Special Education, 27,* 509–520.

Bell, K. (2004). GLSEN in tough times: Training educators about LGBT issues in a challenging political, economic, and educational climate. *Beyond Behavior, 13*(2), 29–30.

Bennett, L. (2000). Equality by design: Three charter schools try new approaches to integration. *Teaching Tolerance, 17,* 43–49.

Cartledge, G. (2004). Another look at the impact of changing demographics on public education for culturally diverse learners with behavior problems: Implications for teacher preparation. In L. M. Bullock & R. A. Gable (Eds.), *Quality personnel preparation in emotional/behavioral disorders: Current perspectives and future directions* (pp. 64–69). Denton, TX: Institute for Behavioral and Learning Differences at the University of North Texas.

Cartledge, G., & Loe, S. A. (2001). Cultural diversity and social skill instruction. *Exceptionality, 9,* 33–46.

Cho, S., Singer, G. H. S., & Brenner, M. (2000). Adaptation and accommodation to young children with disabilities: A comparison of Korean and Korean American parents. *Topics in Early Childhood Special Education, 20,* 236–249.

Collins, K. (2000). No place for bigotry: An anti-bias club changes the atmosphere at a suburban high school. *Teaching Tolerance, 17.*

Council for Exceptional Children. (1997). Making assessments of diverse students meaningful. *CEC Today, 4*(4), 1, 9.

Council for Exceptional Children. (2000). Improving results for culturally and linguistically diverse students. *Research Connections in Special Education, 7.*

Coutinho, M. J., & Oswald, D. P. (2000). Disproportionate representation in special education: A synthesis and recommendations. *Journal of Child and Family Studies, 9,* 135–156.

Dadurka, D. (2004, April 22). Ruffner's life, work honored. *Charlottesville Daily Progress,* p. A2.

DeGarcia, B. (2004, April 14). Letters to the editor: Montgomery Blair's distinct diversity. *The Washington Post,* p. A24.

Delpit, L. D. (1988). The silenced dialogue: Power and pedagogy in educating other people's children. *Harvard Educational Review, 58,* 280–298.

Delpit, L. (1995). *Other people's children: Cultural conflict in the classroom.* New York: New Press.

Elksnin, L. K., & Elksnin, N. (2000). Teaching parents to teach their children to be prosocial. *Intervention in School and Clinic, 36,* 27–35.

Elliot, B. (2000). Finding my stride: A gay student takes the bold step of being true to himself. *Teaching Tolerance, 17,* 40–41.

Evertson, C. M., & Weinstein, C. S. (Eds.). (in press). *Handbook of classroom management: Research, practice, and contemporary issues.* Mahwah, NJ: Lawrence Erlbaum.

Ford, B. A., Obiakor, F. E., & Patton, J. M. (Eds.). (1995). *Effective education of African American exceptional learners: New perspectives.* Austin, TX: Pro-Ed.

Ford, D. Y. (1998). The under-representation of minority students in gifted education: Problems and promises in recruitment and retention. *Journal of Special Education, 32,* 4–14.

Franklin, M. E. (1992). Culturally sensitive instructional practices for African-American learners with disabilities. *Exceptional Children, 59*, 115–122.

Fuchs, L. S., & Fuchs, D. (1997). Use of curriculum-based measurement in identifying students with disabilities. *Focus on Exceptional Children, 30*(3), 1–16.

Fujiura, G. T., & Yamaki, K. (2000). Trends in demography of childhood poverty and disability. *Exceptional Children, 66*, 187–199.

Fulk, B. M., & King, K. (2001). Classwide peer tutoring at work. *Teaching Exceptional Children, 34*(2), 49–53.

Gallucci, J. P. (2000). Signs of remembrance: A school for the deaf celebrates Dia de los Muertos. *Teaching Tolerance, 18*, 30–31.

Gelman, J. A., Pullen, P. L., & Kauffman, J. M. (2005). The meaning of highly qualified and a clear roadmap to accomplishment. *Exceptionality, 12,* 195–207.

Gersten, R., & Baker, S. (2000). What we know about effective instructional practices for English-language learners. *Exceptional Children, 66*, 454–470.

Gersten, R., Brengelman, S., & Jimenez, R. (1994). Effective instruction for culturally and linguistically diverse students: A reconceptualization. *Focus on Exceptional Children, 27*(1), 1–16.

Gersten, R., & Woodward, J. (1994). The language-minority student and special education: Issues, trends, and paradoxes. *Exceptional Children, 60*, 310–322.

Glazer, N. (1997). *We are all multiculturalists now.* Cambridge, MA: Harvard University Press.

Glazer, N. (1998). In defense of preference. *The New Republic, 218*(14), 18–21, 24–25.

Gollnick, D. M., & Chinn, P. C. (1994). *Multicultural education in a pluralistic society* (4th ed.). New York: Macmillan.

Greenwood, C. R., Arrega-Mayer, C., Utley, C. A., Gavin, K. M, & Terry, B. J. (2001). Classwide peer tutoring learning management system: Applications with elementary-level English language learners. *Remedial and Special Education, 22*, 34–47.

Hadadi, R. (2004, April 14). Letters to the editor: Montgomery Blair's distinct diversity. *The Washington Post*, p. A24.

Hallahan, D. P., & Kauffman, J. M. (1994). Toward a culture of disability in the aftermath of Deno and Dunn. *Journal of Special Education, 27*, 496–508.

Hallahan, D. P., Lloyd, J. W., Kauffman, J. M., Weiss, M., & Martinez, E. (2005). *Introduction to learning disabilities* (3rd ed.). Boston: Allyn & Bacon.

Hammill, D. D. (2004). What we know about correlates of reading. *Exceptional Children, 70*, 453–468.

Harrison, M. M. (2000). Stories waiting to be told: Refugee students find their voices in two Midwestern communities. *Teaching Tolerance, 18*, 39–44.

Hirsch, E. D. (1996). *The schools we need and why we don't have them.* New York: Doubleday.

Hirsch, S. (2004, May 10). Annals of national security: Torture at Abu Ghraib. *The New Yorker*, pp. 42–47.

Horwitz, S. (1998, April 5). Lessons in black and white; crossing color lines in room 406 with Miss Kay and her kids. *The Washington Post*, p. F1.

Hosp, J. L., & Reschly, D. J. (2004). Disproportionate representation of minority students in special education: Academic, demographic, and economic predictors. *Exceptional Children, 70*, 185–199.

Ishii-Jordan, S. (1997). When behavior differences are not disorders. In A. J. Artiles & G. Zamora-Duran (Eds.), *Reducing disproportionate representation of culturally diverse students in special and gifted education* (pp. 27–46). Reston, VA: Council for Exceptional Children.

Jones, C. J. (2001a). CBAs that work: Assessing students' math content-reading levels. *Teaching Exceptional Children, 34*(1), 24–28.

Jones, C. J. (2001b). Teacher-friendly curriculum-based assessment in spelling. *Teaching Exceptional Children, 34*(2), 32–38.

Jones, E. P. (2003). *The known world.* New York: Harper Collins.

Kauffman, J. M. (1999). How we prevent the prevention of emotional and behavioral disorders. *Exceptional Children, 65*, 448–468.

Kauffman, J. M. (2001). *Characteristics of emotional and behavioral disorders of children and youths* (7th ed.). New York: Merrill/Macmillan.

Kauffman, J. M. (2003). Appearances, stigma, and prevention. *Remedial and Special Education, 24,* 195–198.

Kauffman, J. M. & Hallahan, D. P. (2005). *Special education: What it is and why we need it.* Boston: Allyn & Bacon.

Kauffman, J. M., McGee, K., & Brigham, M. (2004). Enabling or disabling? Observations on changes in special education. *Phi Delta Kappa, 85,* 613–620.

Kauffman, J. M., Mostert, M. P., Trent, S. C., & Pullen, P. L. (2006). *Managing classroom behavior: A reflective case-based approach* (4th ed.). Boston: Allyn & Bacon.

Kennicott, P. (2004, May 5). A wretched new picture of America: Photos from Iraq show we are our own worst enemy. *The Washington Post*, pp. C1, C11.

Keogh, B. K. (2003). *Temperament in the classroom: Understanding individual differences.* Baltimore: Brookes.

Keogh, B. K., Gallimore, R., & Weisner, T. (1997). A sociocultural perspective on learning and learning disabilities. *Learning Disabilities Research and Practice, 12*, 107–113.

King, C. I. (2004, February 1). The Kings of Foggy Bottom. *The Washington Post Magazine*, pp. 8–9, 20–25.

Kline, S. A., Simpson, R. L., Blesz, D. P., Myles, B. S., & Carter W. J. (2001). School reform and multicultural learners with emotional and behavioral disorders: Issues, challenges, and solutions. In C. A. Utley & F. E. Obiakor (Eds.), *Special education, multicultural education, and school reform: Components of quality education for learners with mild disabilities* (pp. 118–129). Springfield, IL: Charles C. Thomas.

Leake, D., & Leake, B. (1992). African-American immersion schools in Milwaukee: A view from inside. *Phi Delta Kappan, 73*, 783–785.

Lewis, A. C. (2004). Desegregation and degeneration. *Phi Delta Kappan, 85* 643–644.

MacMillan, D. L., & Reschly, D. J. (1998). Overrepresentation of minority students: The case for greater specificity or reconsideration of the variables examined. *Journal of Special Education, 32*, 15–24.

MacMillan, D. L., Gresham, F. M., Lopez, M. F., & Bocian, K. M. (1996). Comparison of students nominated for prereferral interventions by ethnicity and gender. *Journal of Special Education, 30*, 133–151.

McAfee, M. (2000). Welcome to Park Day School: A bay area teacher shares her independent school's commitment to community. *Teaching Tolerance, 18*, 24–29.

McCourt, F. (1996). *Angela's ashes*. New York: Scribner.

McDonnell, L. M., McLaughlin, M. J., & Morison, P. (Eds.). (1997). *Educating one and all: Students with disabilities and standards-based reform*. Washington, DC: National Academy Press.

Mostert, M. P. (2002). Useless eaters: Disability as handicap in Nazi Germany. *Journal of Special Education, 36*, 155–168.

Mui, Y. Q. (2004, April 4). Beyond black and white: What happens at a high school where everyone is a minority? *The Washington Post Magazine*, pp. 23–31, 45.

Mundy, L. (2002, March 31). A world of their own. *The Washington Post Magazine*, pp. 22–29, 38–43.

Osher, D., Cartledge, G., Oswald, D., Sutherland, K. S., Artiles, A. J., & Coutinho, M. (2004). Cultural and linguistic competency and disproportionate representation. In R. B. Rutherford, M. M. Quinn, & S. R. Mathur (Eds.), *Handbook of research in emotional and behavioral disorders* (pp. 54–77). New York: Guilford.

Oswald, D. P., & Coutinho, M. J. (2001). Trends in disproportionate representation: Implications for multicultural education. In C. A. Utley & F. E. Obiakor (Eds.), *Special education, multicultural education, and school reform: Components of quality education for learners with mild disabilities* (pp. 53–73). Springfield, IL: Charles C. Thomas.

Ovando, C. J. (1997). Language diversity and education. In J. A. Banks & C. A. M. Banks (Eds.), *Multicultural education: Issues and perspectives* (3rd ed., pp. 272–296). Boston: Allyn & Bacon.

Patton, J. M. (1997). Disproportionate representation in gifted programs: Best practices for meeting this challenge. In A. J. Artiles & G. Zamora-Duran (Eds.), *Reducing disproportionate representation of culturally diverse students in special and gifted education* (pp. 59–85). Reston, VA: Council for Exceptional Children.

Pavri, S. (2001). Loneliness in children with disabilities: How teachers can help. *Teaching Exceptional Children, 33*(6), 52–58.

Peck, A., & Scarpati, S. (2004). Literacy instruction and research. *Teaching Exceptional Children, 36*(6), 71.

Pullen, P. L. (2004). *Brighter beginnings for teachers*. Lanham, MD: Scarecrow Education.

Ravitch, D. (2003). *The language police: How pressure groups restrict what students learn*. New York: Knopf.

Reschly, D. J. (2001, July 13). *Overrepresentation, it's not what you think it is: Equal treatment studies*. Presentation at the Office of Special Education Programs Annual Research Project Directors' Conference, Washington, DC.

Rueda, R., & Kim, S. (2001). Cultural and linguistic diversity as a theoretical framework for understanding multicultural learners with mild disabilities. In C. A. Utley & F. E. Obiakor (Eds.), *Special education, multicultural education, and school reform: Components of quality education for learners with mild disabilities* (pp. 74–89). Springfield, IL: Charles C. Thomas.

Schofield, J. W. (1997). Causes and consequences of the colorblind perspective. In J. A. Banks & C. A. M. Banks (Eds.), *Multicultural education: Issues and perspectives* (3rd ed., pp. 251–271). Boston: Allyn & Bacon.

Singh, N. N. (1996). Cultural diversity in the 21st century: Beyond E Pluribus Unum. *Journal of Child and Family Studies, 5*, 121–136.

Singh, N. N., Baker, J., Winton, A. S. W., & Lewis, D. K. (2000). Semantic equivalence of assessment instruments across cultures. *Journal of Child and Family Studies, 9*, 123–134.

Singh, N. N., Ellis, C. R., Oswald, D. P., Wechsler, H. A., & Curtis, W. J. (1997). Value and address diversity. *Journal of Emotional and Behavioral Disorders, 5*, 24–35.

Spencer, J. M. (1997). *The new colored people: The mixed-race movement in America*. New York: New York University Press.

Takaki, R. (1994). Interview: Reflections from a different mirror. *Teaching Tolerance, 3*(1), 11–15.

Taylor, R. L. (1997). *Assessment of exceptional students: Educational and psychological procedures* (4th ed.). Boston: Allyn & Bacon.

Terwilliger, J. (1997). Semantics, psychometrics, and assessment reform: A close look at "authentic" assessments. *Educational Researcher, 26*(8), 24–27.

Thomas, C. (1998, April 22). Do we educate our children or preserve an institution? *Charlottesville Daily Progress*, p. A8.

Thurlow, M. L., Nelson, J. R., Teelucksingh, W., & Draper, I. L. (2001). Multiculturalism and disability in a results-based educational system: Hazards and hopes for today's schools. In C. A. Utley & F. E. Obiakor (Eds.), *Special education, multicultural education, and school reform: Components of quality education for learners with mild disabilities* (pp. 155–172). Springfield, IL: Charles C. Thomas.

Tyler, N. C., Yzquierdo, Z., Lopez-Reyna, N., & Flippin, S. S. (2004). Cultural and linguistic diversity and the special education workforce: A critical overview. *The Journal of Special Education, 38*, 22–38.

Utley, C. A., & Obiakor, F. E. (Eds.). (2001a). *Special education, multicultural education, and school reform: Components of quality education for learners with mild disabilities*. Springfield, IL: Charles C. Thomas.

Utley, C. A., & Obiakor, F. E. (2001b). Learning problems or learning disabilities of multicultural learners: Contemporary perspectives. In C. A. Utley & F. E. Obiakor (Eds.), *Special education, multicultural education, and school reform: Components of quality education for learners with mild disabilities* (pp. 90–117). Springfield, IL: Charles C. Thomas.

Utley, C. A., & Obiakor, F. E. (2001c). Multicultural education and special education: Infusion for better schooling. In C. A. Utley & F. E. Obiakor (Eds.), *Special education, multicultural education, and school reform: Components of quality education for learners with mild disabilities* (pp. 3–29). Springfield, IL: Charles C. Thomas.

U.S. Department of Education. (1997). *Nineteenth annual report to Congress on the implementation of the Individuals with Disabilities Education Act*. Washington, DC: Author.

Van Keulen, J. E., Weddington, G. T., & DeBose, C. E. (1998). *Speech, language, learning, and the African American child*. Boston: Allyn & Bacon.

Walker, T. (2000). Street smart: Sidewalk libraries open a world of learning for urban youth. *Teaching Tolerance, 17*, 22–25.

Welsh, P. (2004, June 20). When the street and the classroom collide. *The Washington Post*, pp. B1, B4.

Wiesel, E. (2004, July 4). The America I love. *Parade*, pp. 4–5.

Wilkins, R. (2001). *Jefferson's pillow: The founding fathers and the dilemma of black patriotism*. Boston: Beacon.

Williams, P. J. (1998a). In living black and white. *Washington Post Magazine*, pp. 19–20, 30.

Williams, P. J. (1998b). *Seeing a color-blind future*. New York: Noonday Press.

Wortham, A. (1992, September). Afrocentrism isn't the answer for black students in American society. *Executive Educator, 14,* 23–25.

CHAPTER 4

Alper, S., Schloss, P. J., & Schloss, C. N. (1996). Families of children with disabilities in elementary and middle school: Advocacy models and strategies. *Exceptional Children, 62,* 261–270.

Anderson, L., Larson, S., Lakin, C., & Kwak, N. (2002, August). Children with disabilities: Social roles and family impacts in the NHIS-D. *DD Data Brief, 4*(1), 1–11.

Bell, R. Q., & Harper, L. V. (1977). *Child effects on adults.* Hillsdale, NJ: Lawrence Erlbaum.

Berry, J. O., & Hardman, M. L. (1998). *Lifespan perspectives on the family and disability.* Boston: Allyn & Bacon.

Blue-Banning, M., Summers, J. A., Frankland, H. C., Nelson, L. L., & Beegle, G. (2004). Dimensions of family and professional partnerships: Constructive guidelines for collaboration. *Exceptional Children, 70,* 167–184.

Bronfenbrenner, U. (1979). *The ecology of human development: Experiments by nature and design.* Cambridge, MA: Harvard University Press.

Bronfenbrenner, U. (1995). Developmental ecology through space and time: A future perspective. In P. Moen, G. H. Elder, & K. Luscher (Eds.), *Examining lives in context: Perspectives on the ecology of human development* (pp. 619–647). Washington, DC: American Psychological Association.

Brooks-Gunn, J., & Lewis, M. (1984). Maternal responsivity in interactions with handicapped infants. *Child Development, 55,* 858–868.

Bryan, T. H., Nelson, C., & Mathur, S. (1995). Homework: A survey of primary students in regular, resource, and self-contained classrooms. *Learning Disabilities Research and Practice, 10,* 85–90.

Bryan, T. H., & Sullivan-Burstein, K. (1997). Homework how-to's. *Teaching Exceptional Children, 29*(6), 32–37.

Burke, P. (2004). *Brothers and sisters of children with disabilities.* London: Jessica Kingsley.

Cottone, E. (1998). *Home-school collaboration: Evaluating the effectiveness of a school-home note program for children with ADHD.* Unpublished doctoral dissertation, University of Virginia, Charlottesville.

Drotar, D., Baskiewicz, A., Irvin, N., Kennell, J., & Klaus, M. (1975). The adaptation of parents to the birth of an infant with a congenital malformation: A hypothetical model. *Pediatrics, 56,* 710–717.

Duis, S. S., Summers, M., & Summers, C. R. (1997). Parent versus child stress in diverse family types: An ecological approach. *Topics in Early Childhood and Special Education, 17,* 53–73.

Dunst, C. J. (2002). Family-centered practices: Birth through high school. *The Journal of Special Education, 36,* 139–147.

Dyson, L. L. (1997). Fathers and mothers of school-age children with developmental disabilities: Parental stress, family functioning, and social support. *American Journal on Mental Retardation, 102,* 267–279.

Epstein, M., Munk, D., Bursuck, W., Polloway, E., & Jayanthi, M. (1999). Strategies for improving home-school communication about homework for students with disabilities. *Journal of Special Education, 33,* 166–176.

Featherstone, H. (1980). *A difference in the family: Life with a disabled child.* New York: Basic Books.

Ferguson, P. M. (2002). A place in the family: An historical interpretation of research on parental reactions to having a child with a disability. *The Journal of Special Education, 36,* 124–130.

Fox, L., Vaughn, B. J., Wyatte, M. L., & Dunlap, G. (2002). "We can't expect other people to understand": Family perspectives on problem behavior. *Exceptional Children, 68,* 437–450.

Gavidia-Payne, S., & Stoneman, Z. (1997). Family predictors of maternal and paternal involvement in programs for young children with disabilities. *Child Development, 68,* 701–717.

Gerlach, E. K. (1999). *Just this side of normal: Glimpses into life with autism.* Eugene, OR: Four Leaf Press.

Hallahan, D. P., & Martinez, E. A. (2002). Working with families. In J. M. Kauffman, M. Mostert, S. C. Trent, & D. P. Hallahan (Eds.), *Managing classroom behavior: A reflective case-based approach* (3rd ed., pp. 124–140). Boston: Allyn & Bacon.

Hanline, M. F., & Knowlton, A. (1988). A collaborative model for providing support to parents during their child's transition from infant intervention to preschool special education public school programs. *Journal of the Division for Early Childhood, 12,* 116–125.

Harry, B. (2002). Trends and issues in serving culturally diverse families of children with disabilities. *The Journal of Special Education, 36,* 131–138.

Jayanthi, M., Bursuck, W., Epstein, M., & Polloway, E. (1997). Strategies for successful homework. *Teaching Exceptional Children, 30*(1), 4–7.

Jayanthi, M., Sawyer, V., Nelson, J., Bursuck, W., & Epstein, M. (1995). Recommendations for homework-communication problems: From parents, classroom teachers, and special education teachers. *Remedial and Special Education, 16,* 212–225.

Kelley, M. L., (1990). *School-home notes: Promoting children's classroom success.* New York: Guilford Press.

Kelley, M. L., & McCain, A. P. (1995). Promoting academic performance in inattentive children. *Behavior Modification, 19,* 357–375.

Keogh, B. K., Garnier, H. E., Bernheimer, L. P., & Gallimore, R. (2000). Models of child-family interactions for children with developmental delays: Child-driven or transactional? *American Journal on Mental Retardation, 105,* 32–46.

Klinger, J., & Vaughn, S. (1999). Students' perceptions of instruction in inclusion classrooms: Implications for students with learning disabilities. *Exceptional Children, 66,* 23–37.

Kraus, S., Maxwell, K., & McWilliam, R. A. (2001). "Practice" makes perfect: Research looks at family-centered practices in early elementary grades. *Exceptional Parent, 31*(3), 62–63.

Lambie, R. (2000). *Family systems within educational contexts: Understanding at-risk and special-needs students.* Denver, CO: Love Publishing Co.

Lehmann, J. P., & Baker, C. (1995). Mothers' expectations for their adolescent children: A comparison between families with disabled adolescents and those with non-labeled adolescents. *Education and Training in Mental Retardation and Developmental Disabilities, 30,* 27–40.

Lessenberry, B. M., & Rehfeldt, R. A. (2004). Evaluating stress levels of parents with disabilities. (2004). *Exceptional Children, 70,* 231–244.

Lucyshyn, J. M., Horner, R. H., Dunlap, G., Albin, R. W., & Ben, K. R. (2002). Positive behavior support with families. In J. M.

Lucyshyn, G. Dunlap, & R. W. Albin (Eds.), *Families and positive behavior support: Addressing problem behavior in family contexts* (pp. 3–43). Baltimore, MD: Paul H. Brookes.

Mahoney, G., & Robenalt, K. (1986). A comparison of conversational patterns between mothers and their Down syndrome and normal infants. *Journal of the Division for Early Childhood, 10,* 172–180.

Mahoney, G., Boyce, G., Fewell, R. R., Spiker, D., & Wheeden, C. A. (1998). The relationship of parent-child interaction to the effectiveness of early intervention services for at-risk children and children with disabilities. *Topics in Early Childhood and Special Education, 18,* 5–17.

McCain, A. P., & Kelley, M. L. (1993). Managing the classroom behavior of an ADHD preschooler: The efficacy of a school-home note intervention. *Child and Family Behavior Therapy, 15*(3), 33–44.

Meadow-Orlans, K. P., Mertens, D. M., & Sass-Lehrer, M. A. (2003). *Parents and their deaf children: The early years.* Washington, DC: Gallaudet University Press.

Meyer, D. J., & Vadasy, P. F. (1994). *Sibshops: Workshops for siblings of children with special needs.* Baltimore: Paul H. Brookes.

Orsmond, G. I., & Seltzer, M. M. (2000). Brothers and sisters of adults with mental retardation: Gendered nature of the sibling relationship. *American Journal on Mental Retardation, 105,* 486–508.

O'Shea, D. J., O'Shea, L. J., Algozzine, R., & Hammitte, D. J. (Eds.). (2001). *Families and teachers of individuals with disabilities: Collaborative orientations and responsive practices.* Boston: Allyn & Bacon.

Parette, H. P., & Petch-Hogan, B. (2000). Approaching families: Facilitating culturally/linguistically diverse family involvement. *Teaching Exceptional Children, 33*(2), 4–10.

Pierro, C. (1995). Talking with your child about disabilities. *Exceptional Parent, 25*(6), 92.

Polloway, E., Bursuck, W., Jayanthi, M., Epstein, M., & Nelson, J. (1996). Treatment acceptability: Determining appropriate interventions within inclusive classrooms. *Intervention in School and Clinic, 31,* 133–144.

Powell, T. H., & Gallagher, P. A. (1993). *Brothers & sisters—A special part of exceptional families* (2nd ed.). Baltimore: Paul H. Brookes.

Roach, M. A., Barratt, M. S., Miller, J. F., & Leavitt, L. A. (1998). The structure of mother-child play: Young children with Down syndrome and typically developing children. *Developmental Psychology, 34,* 77–87.

Scorgie, K., & Sobsey, D. (2000). Transformational outcomes associated with parenting children who have disabilities. *Mental Retardation, 38,* 195–206.

Seaver, A. (2001). Fighting prejudice. *Exceptional Parent, 31*(4), 116.

Seltzer, M. M., Greenberg, J. S., Floyd, F. J., Pettee, Y., & Hong, J. (2001). Life course impacts of parenting a child with a disability. *American Journal on Mental Retardation, 106,* 265–286.

Singer, G. H. S. (2002). Suggestion for a pragmatic program of research on families and disability. *The Journal of Special Education, 36,* 148–154.

Singer, G. H. S., Goldberg-Hamblin, S. E., Peckham-Hardin, K. D., Barry, L., & Santarelli, G. E. (2002). Toward a synthesis of family support practices and positive behavior support. In J. M. Lucyshyn, G. Dunlap, & R. W. Albin (Eds.), *Families and pos-*

itive behavior support: Addressing problem behavior in family contexts (pp. 155–183). Baltimore, MD: Paul H. Brookes.

Skinner, D., Bailey, D. B., Correa, V., & Rodriguez, P. (1999). Narrating self and disability: Latino mothers' construction of identities vis-à-vis their child with special needs. *Exceptional Children, 65,* 481–495.

Turnbull, A. P., & Turnbull, H. R. (2000). Fostering family-professional partnerships. In M. E. Snell & F. Brown (Eds.), *Instruction of students with severe disabilities* (5th ed., pp. 31–66). Columbus, OH: Merrill Prentice-Hall.

Turnbull, A. P., & Turnbull, H. R. (2001). *Families, professionals, and exceptionality: Collaborating for empowerment* (4th ed.). Upper Saddle River, NJ: Prentice-Hall.

CHAPTER 5

AAMR Ad Hoc Committee on Terminology and Classification. (2002). *Mental retardation: Definition, classification, and systems of supports* (10th ed.). Washington, DC: American Association on Mental Retardation.

AAMR. (1999–2004). Fact sheet: Frequently asked questions about mental retardation. Retrieved June 4, 2004 from the World Wide Web: www.aamr.org/Policies/faq_mental_retardation.shtml.

Abbeduto, L., Murphy, M. M., Cawthon, S. W., Richmond, E. K., Weissman, M. D., Karadottir, S., & O'Brien, A. (2003). Receptive language skills of adolescents and young adults with Down or Fragile X syndrome. *American Journal on Mental Retardation, 108,* 149–160.

The Arc. (2001, April 10). Phenylketonuria (PKU). Retrieved July 23, 2004, from www.thearc.org/faqs/pku.html.

Ashbaugh, J. W. (2002). Down the garden path of self-determination. *Mental Retardation, 40,* 416–417.

Bebko, J. M., & Luhaorg, H. (1998). The development of strategy use and metacognitive processing in mental retardation: Some sources of difficulty. In J. A. Burack, R. M. Hodapp, & E. Zigler (Eds.), *Handbook of mental retardation and development* (pp. 382–407). New York: Cambridge University Press.

Beirne-Smith, M., Ittenbach, R. F., & Patton, J. R. (2002). *Mental retardation* (6th ed.). Upper Saddle River, NJ: Merrill/Prentice-Hall.

Belser, R. C., & Sudhalter, V. (2001). Conversational characteristics of children with fragile X syndrome: Repetitive speech. *American Journal on Mental Retardation, 106,* 28–38.

Bray, N. W., Fletcher K. L., & Turner, L. (1997). Cognitive competencies and strategy use in individuals with mental retardation. In W. E. MacLean (Ed.), *Ellis' handbook of mental deficiency, psychological theory, and research* (pp. 197–217). Mahwah, NJ: Lawrence Erlbaum.

Browder, D., Flowers, C., Ahlgrim-Delzell, L., Karvonen, M., Spooner, F., & Algozzine, R. (2004). The alignment of alternate assessment content with academic and functional curricula. *The Journal of Special Education, 37,* 211–223.

Browder, D., & Snell, M. E. (2000). Teaching functional academics. In M. E. Snell & F. Brown (Eds.), *Instruction of students with severe disabilities* (5th ed.). Columbus, OH: Merrill.

Bush, A., & Beail, N. (2004). Risk factors for dementia in people with Down syndrome: Issues in assessment and diagnosis. *American Journal on Mental Retardation, 109,* 83–97.

Butler, F. M., Miller, S. P., Lee, K., & Pierce, T. (2001). Teaching mathematics to students with mild-to-moderate mental retardation: A review of the literature. *Mental Retardation, 39*, 20–31.

Butterworth, J., & Strauch, J. D. (1994). The relationship between social competence and success in the competitive work place for persons with mental retardation. *Education and Training in Mental Retardation and Developmental Disabilities, 29*, 118–133.

Campbell, F. A., Ramey, C. T., Pungello, E., Sparling, J., & Miller-Johnson, S. (2002). Early childhood education: Young adult outcomes from the Abecedarian Project. *Applied Developmental Science, 6*, 42–57.

Carr, J. (1994). Annotation: Long term outcome for people with Down's syndrome. *Journal of Child Psychology and Psychiatry, 35*, 425–439.

Chapman, D. A., Scott, K. G., & Mason, C. A. (2002). Early risk factors for mental retardation: Role of maternal age and maternal education. *American Journal on Mental Retardation, 107*, 46–59.

Council for Exceptional Children (2001). Performance-based Standards. Retrieved June 5, 2001 from www.cec.sped.org/ps/perf_based_stds/index.html.

Cronin, M. E. (2000). Instructional strategies. In P. L. Sitlington, G. M. Clark, & O. P. Kolstoe, *Transition education and services for adolescents with disabilities* (3rd ed., pp. 255–283). Boston: Allyn & Bacon.

Davis, P. K., & Cuvo, A. J. (1997). Environmental approaches to mental retardation. In D. M. Baer & E. M. Pinkerston (Eds.), *Environment and behavior* (pp. 231–242). Boulder, CO: Westview Press.

Davis, S. (1997). *The Human Genome Project: Examining the Arc's concerns regarding the Human Genome Project's ethical, legal, and social implications.* An address presented at the DOE Human Genome Program Contractor-Grantee Workshop VI. Posted on the World Wide Web by the Human Genome Management Information System. Retrieved July 29, 2001, from www.ornl.gov/hgmis/resource/arc.html.

Delquadri, J., Greenwood, C. R., Stretton, K., & Hall, R. V. (1983). The peer tutoring spelling game: A classroom procedure for increasing opportunity to respond and spelling performance. *Education and Treatment of Children, 6*, 225–239.

Dimitropoulos, A., Feurer, I. D., Butler, M. G., & Thompson, T. (2001). Emergence of compulsive behavior and tantrums in children with Prader-Willi syndrome. *American Journal on Mental Retardation, 106*, 39–51.

Drew, C. J., & Hardman, M. L. (2004). *Mental retardation: A lifespan approach to people with intellectual disabilities* (8th ed.). Upper Saddle River, NJ: Merrill/Prentice-Hall.

Dykens, E. (2001). Introduction to special issue. *American Journal on Mental Retardation, 106*, 1–3.

Dykens, E. M., Hodapp, R. M., & Finucane, B. M. (2000). *Genetics and mental retardation syndromes: A new look at behavior and interventions.* Baltimore, MD: Paul H. Brookes.

Evenhuis, H. M. (1990). The natural history of dementia in Down's syndrome. *Archives of Neurology, 47*, 263–267.

Fidler, D. J., Hodapp, R. M., & Dykens, E. M. (2002). Behavioral phenotypes and special education: Parent report of educational issues for children with Down syndrome, Prader-Willi syndrome, and Williams syndrome. *The Journal of Special Education, 36*, 80–88.

Frank, A. R., & Sitlington, P. L. (2000). Young adults with mental disabilities: Does transition planning make a difference? *Education and Training in Mental Retardation and Developmental Disabilities, 35*, 119–134.

Fraser, J., & Mitchell, A. (1876). Kalmuc idiocy: Report of a case with autopsy, with notes on sixty-two cases. *Journal of Mental Science, 22*, 161–179.

Gelb, S. A. (2002). The dignity of humanity is not a scientific construct. *Mental Retardation, 40*, 55–56.

Greenwood, C. R. (1991). Longitudinal analysis of time, engagement, and achievement of at-risk versus non-risk students. *Exceptional Children, 57*, 521–532.

Guralnick, M. J., Connor, R. T., & Hammond, M. (1995). Parent perspectives of peer relationships and friendships in integrated and specialized programs. *American Journal on Mental Retardation, 99*, 457–476.

Hagerman, R. J. (2001). Fragile X syndrome. In S. B. Cassidy & J. E. Allanson (Eds.), *Management of genetic syndromes* (pp. 165–183) New York: Wiley-Liss.

Hatton, D. D., Wheeler, A. C., Skinner, M. L., Bailey, D. B., Sullivan, K. M., Roberts, J. E., Mirrett, P., & Clark, R. D. (2003). *American Journal on Mental Retardation, 108*, 373–390.

Heal, L. W., Gonzalez, P., Rusch, F. R., Copher, J. I., & DeStefano, L. (1990). A comparison of successful and unsuccessful placements of youths with mental handicaps into competitive employment. *Exceptionality, 1*, 181–195.

Hodapp, R. M., & Fidler, D. J. (1999). Special education and genetics: Connections for the 21st century. *Journal of Special Education, 33*, 130–137.

Hof, P. R., Bouras, C., Perl, D. P., Sparks, L., Mehta, N., & Morrison, J. H. (1995). Age-related distribution of neuropathologic changes in the cerebral cortex of patients with Down's syndrome. *Archives of Neurology, 52*, 379–391.

Horner, R. H., Albin, R. W., Sprague, J. R., & Todd, A. W. (2000). Positive behavior support. In M. E. Snell & F. Brown (Eds.), *Instruction of students with severe retardation* (5th ed., pp. 207–243). Upper Saddle River, NJ: Prentice-Hall.

Human Genome Project. (2004a, March 11). Human Genome Project information. Retrieved July 21, 2004 from the World Wide Web: www.ornl.gov/sci/techresources/Human_Genome/home.shtml.

Human Genome Project. (2004b, July 8). Ethical legal and social issues. Retrieved July 21, 2004 from the World Wide Web: www.ornl.gov/sci/techresources/Human_Genome/elsi/elsi.shtml.

Kasari, C., & Bauminger, N. (1998). Social and emotional development in children with mental retardation. In J. A. Burack, R. M. Hodapp, & E. Zigler (Eds.), Handbook of mental retardation and development (pp. 411–433). New York: Cambridge University Press.

Kasari, C., Freeman, S. F. N., & Hughes, M. A. (2001). Emotion recognition by children with Down syndrome. *American Journal on Mental Retardation, 106*, 59–72.

Kaufman, S. Z. (1999). *Retarded isn't stupid, mom!* (Rev. ed.). Baltimore: MD: Paul H. Brookes.

Kuna, J. (2001). The Human Genome Project and eugenics: Identifying the impact on individuals with mental retardation. *Mental Retardation, 39*, 158–160.

Lambert, N., Nihira, K., & Leland, H. (1993). *AAMD Adaptive Behavior Scale-School, 2nd Edition.* Austin, TX: Pro-Ed.

MacMillan, D. L., Gresham, F. M., Bocian, K. M., & Lambros, K. M. (1998). Current plight of borderline students: Where do they belong? *Education and Training in Mental Retardation and Developmental Disabilities, 33,* 83–94.

Mank, D., Cioffi, A., & Yovanoff, P. (2003). Supported employment outcomes across a decade: Is there evidence of improvement in the quality of implementation? *Mental Retardation, 41,* 188–197.

McDonnell, J. J., Hardman, M. L., & McDonnell, A. P. (2003). *An introduction to persons with moderate and severe disabilities* (2nd ed.). Boston: Allyn & Bacon.

Mechling, L. C., Gast, D. L., & Langone, J. (2002). Computer-based video instruction to teach persons with moderate intellectual disabilities to read grocery aisle signs and locate items. *The Journal of Special Education, 35,* 224–240.

Mervis, C. B., Klein-Tasman, B. P., & Mastin, M. E. (2001). Adaptive behavior of 4- through 8-year-old children with Williams syndrome. *American Journal on Mental Retardation, 106,* 82–93.

Moldavsky, M., Lev, D., & Lerman-Sagie, T. (2001). Behavioral phenotypes of genetic syndromes: A reference guide for psychiatrists. *Journal of the American Academy of Child and Adolescent Psychiatry, 40,* 749–761.

Morse, T. E., & Schuster, J. W. (2000). Teaching elementary students with moderate intellectual disabilities how to shop for groceries. *Exceptional Children, 66,* 273–288.

Mortweet, S. L., Utley, C. A., Walker, D., Dawson, H. L., Delquadri, J. C., Reddy, S. S., Greenwood, C. R., Hamilton, S., & Ledford, D. (1999). Classwide peer tutoring: Teaching students with mild mental retardation in inclusive classrooms. *Exceptional Children, 65,* 524–536.

MR/DD Data Brief. (2001, April). Characteristics of service use by persons with MR/DD living in their own homes or with family members: NHIS-D analysis. Research and Training Center on Community Living, Institute on Community Integration, University of Minnesota.

National Institute of Neurological Disorders and Stroke. (2001, July 1). NINDS microcephaly information page. Retrieved July 23, 2004 from www.ninds.nih.gov/healthandmedical/disorders/microcephaly.htm.

National Organization on Disability, & Harris, L. & Associates. (2000). *National Organization on Disability/Harris Survey of Americans with Disabilities.* New York: Author.

Nietupski, J., Hamre-Nietupski, S., VanderHart, N. S., & Fishback, K. (1996). Employer perceptions of the benefits and concerns of supported employment. *Education and Training in Mental Retardation and Developmental Disabilities, 31,* 310–323.

Olney, M. F., & Kennedy, J. (2001). National estimates of vocational service utilization and job placement rates for adults with mental retardation. *Mental Retardation, 39,* 32–39.

Parmar, R. S., Cawley, J. F., & Miller, J. H. (1994). Differences in mathematics performance between students with learning disabilities and students with mental retardation. *Exceptional Children, 60,* 549–563.

Pinel, J. P. J. (2003). *Biopsychology* (5th ed.). Boston: Allyn & Bacon.

Ramey, C. T., & Campbell, F. A. (1984). Preventive education for high-risk children: Cognitive consequences of the Carolina Abecedarian Project. *American Journal of Mental Deficiency, 88,* 515–523.

Ramey, C. T., & Campbell, F. A. (1987). The Carolina Abecedarian Project: An educational experiment concerning human malleability. In J. J. Gallagher & C. T. Ramey (Eds.), *The malleability of children* (pp. 127–139). Baltimore, MD: Paul H. Brookes.

Reynolds, A. J., Temple, J. A., Robertson, D. L., & Mann, E. A. (2001). Long-term effects of an early childhood intervention on educational achievement and juvenile arrest. *Journal of the American Medical Association, 285,* 2339–2346.

Romer, L. T., Richardson, M., Aigbe, E., & Porter, A. (2003). Down the garden path of self-determination: A response to Ashbaugh. *Mental Retardation, 41,* 292–294.

Salzberg, C. L., Lignugaris/Kraft, B., & McCuller, G. L. (1988). Reasons for job loss: A review of employment termination studies of mentally retarded workers. *Research in Developmental Disabilities, 9,* 153–170.

Schweinhart, L. J., & Weikart, D. P. (1993). Success by empowerment: The High/Scope Perry Preschool Study through age 27. *Young Children, 49,* 54–58.

Scott, M. S., Greenfield, D. B., & Partridge, M. F. (1991). Differentiating between two groups that fail in school: Performance of learning disabled and mildly retarded students on an oddity problem. *Learning Disabilities Research and Practice, 6,* 3–11.

Semel, E., & Rosner, S. R. (2003). *Understanding Williams syndrome: Behavioral patterns and interventions.* Mahwah, NJ: Lawrence Erlbaum.

Spinath, F. M., Harlaar, N., Ronald, A., & Plomin, R. (2004). Substantial genetic influence on mild mental impairment in early childhood. *American Journal on Mental Retardation, 109,* 34–43.

Stancliffe, R. J., Abery, B. H., & Smith, J. (2000). Personal control and the ecology of community living settings: Beyond living-unit size and type. *American Journal on Mental Retardation, 105,* 431–454.

Sugai, G., Horner, R., Dunlap, G., Lewis, T., Nelson C. M., Scott, T., Liaupsin, C., Ruef, M., Sailor, W., Turnbull, A. P., Turnbull, H. R., Wickham, D., & Wilcox, B. L. (2000). Applying positive behavior support and functional behavioral assessment in schools. *Journal of Positive Behavior Interventions, 2,* 131–143.

Taylor, H. G., Klein, N., Minich, N. M., & Hack, M. (2000), Middle-school-age outcomes in children with very low birthweight. *Child Development, 71,* 1495–1511.

Taylor, R. L., Richards, S. B., & Brady, M. P. (2005). *Mental retardation: Historical perspectives, current practices, and future directions.* Boston: Allyn & Bacon.

Thomas, C. L. (Ed.). (1985). *Taber's cyclopedic medical dictionary* (15th ed.). Philadelphia: F. A. Davis Co.

Tomporowski, P. D., & Tinsley, V. (1997). Attention in mentally retarded persons. In W. E. MacLean (Ed.), *Ellis' handbook of mental deficiency, psychological theory, and research* (pp. 219–244). Mahwah, NJ: Lawrence Erlbaum.

Turner, G., Webb, T., Wake, S., & Robinson, H. (1996). Prevalence of fragile X syndrome. *American Journal of Medical Genetics, 64,* 196–197.

Warren, S., & Yoder, P. J. (1997). Communication, language, and mental retardation. In W. E. MacLean (Ed.), *Ellis' handbook of mental deficiency, psychological theory, and research* (pp. 379–403). Mahwah, NJ: Lawrence Erlbaum.

Wechsler, D. (2003). *Wechsler Intelligence Scale for Children—IV.* San Antonio, TX: Psychological Corporation.

Wehmeyer, M. L., Palmer, S. B., Agran, M., Mithaug, D. E., & Martin, J. E. (2000). Promoting causal agency: The Self-Determined Learning Model of Instruction. *Exceptional Children, 66,* 439–453.

Westling, D. L., & Fox, L. (2000). *Teaching students with severe disabilities* (2nd ed.). Upper Saddle River, NJ: Merrill.

Wisniewski, H. M., Silverman, W., & Wegiel, J. (1994). Aging, Alzheimer disease, and mental retardation. *Journal of Intellectual Disability Research, 38,* 233–239.

Wolery, M., & Schuster, J. W. (1997). Instructional methods with students who have significant disabilities. *Journal of Special Education, 31,* 61–79.

Wolfensberger, W. (2002a). Needed or at least wanted: Sanity in the Language Wars. *Mental Retardation, 40,* 75–80.

Wolfensberger, W. (2002b). Social role valorization and, or versus, "Empowerment." *Mental Retardation, 40,* 252–258.

CHAPTER 6

Adams, G. L., & Engelmann, S. (1996). *Research on Direct Instruction: 25 years beyond DISTAR.* Seattle: Educational Achievement Systems.

American Psychiatric Association. (2000). *Diagnostic and statistical manual of mental disorders* (4th ed., text rev.). Washington, DC: Author.

Beichtman, J. H., Hood, J., & Inglis, A. (1992). Familial transmission of speech and language impairment: A preliminary investigation. *Canadian Journal of Psychiatry, 37,* 151–156.

Bender, W. N. (2004). *Learning disabilities: Characteristics, identification, and learning strategies* (5th ed.). Boston: Allyn & Bacon.

Bender, W. N., Rosenkrans, C. B., & Crane, M. K. (1999). Stress, depression, and suicide among students with learning disabilities: Assessing the risk. *Learning Disability Quarterly, 22,* 143–156.

Blachman, B. (2001). Phonological awareness. In D. P. Pearson (Ed.), *Handbook of reading research* (pp. 483–502). Mahwah, NJ: Lawrence Erlbaum.

Blackorby, J., & Wagner, M. (1997). The employment outcomes of youth with learning disabilities: A review of findings from NLTS. In P. J. Gerber & D. S. Brown (Eds.), *Learning disabilities and employment* (pp. 57–74). Austin, TX: Pro-Ed.

Brunswick, N., McCrory, E., Price, C. J., Frith, C. D., & Frith, U. (1999). Explicit and implicit processing of words and pseudowords by adult developmental dyslexics: A search for Wernicke's Wortschatz? *Brain, 122*(Part 10), 1901–1917.

Bryan, T., Burstein, K., & Ergul, C. (2004). The social-emotional side of learning disabilities: A science-based presentation of the state of the art. *Learning Disability Quarterly, 27,* 45–51.

Bryan, T. H., Donahue, M., Pearl, R., & Sturm, C. (1981). Learning disabled children's conversational skills—The "TV Talk Show." *Learning Disability Quarterly, 4,* 250–260.

Bryan, T. H., & Sullivan-Burstein, K. (1998). Teacher-selected strategies for improving homework completion. *Remedial and Special Education, 19,* 263–275.

Butler, D. L. (1998). Metacognition and learning disabilities. In B. Y. L. Wong (Ed.), *Learning about learning disabilities* (2nd ed., pp. 277–307). San Diego, CA: Academic Press.

Case, L. P., Harris, K. R., & Graham, S. (1992). Improving the mathematical problem-solving skills of students with learning disabilities. *Journal of Special Education, 26,* 1–19.

Cawley, J. F., Parmar, R. S., Yan, W., & Miller, J. H. (1998). Arithmetic computation performance of students with learning disabilities: Implications for the curriculum. *Learning Disabilities Research and Practice, 13,* 68–74.

Choate, J. S., Enright, B. E., Miller, L. J., Poteet, J. A., & Rakes, T. A. (1995). *Curriculum-based assessment programming* (3rd ed.). Boston: Allyn & Bacon.

Clarizio, H. F., & Phillips, S. E. (1986). Sex bias in the diagnosis of learning disabled students. *Psychology in the Schools, 23,* 44–52.

Cobb, J. (2003). *Learning how to learn: Getting into and surviving college when you have a learning disability* (rev. ed.). Washington, DC: Child & Family Press.

Council for Exceptional Children (2001). Performance-based Standards. Retrieved June 5, 2001 from www.cec.sped.org/ps/perf_based_stds/index.html.

DeFries, J. C., Gillis, J. J., & Wadsworth, S. J. (1993). Genes and genders: A twin study of reading disability. In A. M. Galaburda (Ed.), *Dyslexia and development: Neurobiological aspects of extraordinary brains* (pp. 187–294). Cambridge, MA: Harvard University Press.

Deno, S. L. (1985). Curriculum-based measurement: The emerging alternative. *Exceptional Children, 52,* 219–232.

Deshler, D. D., Schumaker, J. B., Lenz, B. K., Bulgren, J. A., Hock, M. F., Knight, J., & Ehren, B. J. (2001). Ensuring content-area learning by secondary students with learning disabilities. *Learning Disabilities Research and Practice, 16,* 96–108.

Ellis, A. (2001). *Research on educational innovations* (3rd ed.). Larchmont, New York: Eye On Education.

Engelmann, S., Carnine, D., Engelmann, O., & Kelly, B. (1991). *Connecting math concepts.* Chicago: Science Research Associates.

Engelmann, S., Carnine, L., Johnson, G., & Meyers, L. (1988). *Corrective reading: Decoding.* Chicago: Science Research Associates.

Engelmann, S., Carnine, L., Johnson, G., & Meyers, L. (1989). *Corrective reading: Comprehension.* Chicago: Science Research Associates.

Epstein, M. H., Munk, D. D., Bursuck, W. D., Polloway, E. A., & Jayanthi, M. (1998). Strategies for improving home-school communication about homework for students with disabilities. *Journal of Special Education, 33,* 166–176.

Fletcher, J. M., Lyon, G. R., Barnes, M., Stuebing, K. K., Francis, D. J., Olson, R. K., Shaywitz, S. E., & Shaywitz, B. A. (2002). Classification of learning disabilities: An evidence-based evaluation. In R. Bradley, L. Danielson, & D. P. Hallahan (Eds.), *Identification of learning disabilities: Research to practice* (pp. 185–250). Mahwah, NJ: Lawrence Erlbaum.

Flowers, D. L. (1993). Brain basis for dyslexia: A summary of work in progress. *Journal of Learning Disabilities, 26,* 575–582.

Flowers, D. L., Wood, F. B., & Naylor, C. E. (1991). Regional cerebral blood flow correlates of language processes in reading disability. *Archives of Neurology, 48,* 637–643.

Foorman, B. R., Francis, D. J., Shaywitz, S. E., Shaywitz, B. A., & Fletcher, J. M. (1997). The case for early reading intervention. In B. Blachman (Ed.), *Foundations of reading acquisition and dyslexia: Implications for early intervention* (pp. 243–264). Mahwah, NJ: Lawrence Erlbaum.

Forness, S. R., & Kavale, K. A. (2002). Impact of ADHD on school systems. In P. Jensen & J. R. Cooper (Eds.), *NIH consensus conference on ADHD.* Bethesda, MD: National Institutes of Health.

Frostig, M., & Horne, D. (1964). *The Frostig program for the development of visual perception: Teacher's guide*. Chicago: Follett.

Fuchs, D., Fuchs, L., & Burish, P. (2000). Peer-Assisted Learning Strategies: An evidence-based practice to promote reading achievement. *Learning Disabilities Research and Practice, 15*(2), 85–91.

Fuchs, D., Fuchs, L. S., McMaster, K. L., Yen, L., & Svenson, E. (2004). Nonresponders: How to find them? How to help them? What do they mean for special education? *Teaching Exceptional Children, 37,* 72–77.

Fuchs, D., Fuchs, L. S., Thompson, A., Svenson, E., Yen, L. Otaiba, S., Yang, N., McMaster, K. N., Prentice, K., & Kazdan, S. (2001). Peer-assisted learning strategies in reading: Extensions for kindergarten, first grade, and high school. *Remedial and Special Education, 22,* 15–21.

Fuchs, D., Mock, D., Morgan, P. L., & Young, C. L. (2003). Responsiveness-to-intervention: Definitions, evidence, and implications for the learning disabilities construct. *Learning Disabilities Research & Practice, 18,* 157–171.

Fuchs, L. S. (2003). Assessing intervention responsiveness: Conceptual and technical issues. *Learning Disabilities Research & Practice, 18,* 172–186.

Fuchs, L. S., Deno, S. L., & Mirkin, P. K. (1984). The effects of frequent curriculum-based measurement and evaluation of pedagogy, student achievement and student awareness of learning. *American Educational Research Journal, 24,* 449–460.

Fuchs, L. S., & Fuchs, D. (1997). Use of curriculum-based measurement in identifying students with disabilities. *Focus on Exceptional Children, 30*(3), 1–16.

Fuchs, L. S., & Fuchs, D. (1998a). Treatment validity: A unifying concept for reconceptualizing the identification of learning disabilities. *Learning Disabilities Research and Practice, 13,* 204–219.

Fuchs, L. S., & Fuchs, D. (1998b). General educators' instructional adaptation for students with learning disabilities. *Learning Disabilities Quarterly, 21,* 23–33.

Georgiewa, P., Rzanny, R., Hopf, J. M., Knab, R., Glauche, V., Kaiser, W. A., & Blanz, B. (1999). fMRI during word processing in dyslexic and normal reading children. *Neuroreport, 10,* 3459–3465.

Gerber, P. J. (1997). Life after school: Challenges in the workplace. In P. J. Gerber & D. S. Brown (Eds.), *Learning disabilities and employment* (pp. 3–18). Austin, TX: Pro-Ed.

Gerber, P. J., Ginsberg, R., & Reiff, H. B. (1992). Identifying alterable patterns in employment success for highly successful adults with learning disabilities. *Journal of Learning Disabilities, 25,* 475–487.

Gerber, P. J., & Reiff, H. B. (1991). *Speaking for themselves: Ethnographic interviews with adults with learning disabilities*. Ann Arbor, MI: University of Michigan Press.

Goldstein, D. E., Murray, C., & Edgar, E. (1998). Employment earning and hours of high school graduates with learning disabilities through the first decade after graduation. *Learning Disabilities Research and Practice, 13,* 53–64.

Good, R. H., Simmons, D. C., & Kame'enui, E. J. (2001). The importance and decision-making utility of a continuum of fluency-based indicators of foundational reading skills for third-grade high-stakes outcomes. *Scientific Studies of Reading, 5,* 257–288.

Grigorenko, E. L., Wood, F. B., Meyer, M. S., & Pauls, D. L. (2000). Chromosome 6p influences on different dyslexia-related cognitive processes: Further confirmation. *American Journal of Human Genetics, 66,* 715–723.

Hagman, J. O., Wood, F., Buchsbaum, M. S., Tallal, P., Flowers, L., & Katz, W. (1992). Cerebral metabolism in adult dyslexic subjects assessed with positron emission tomography during performance on an auditory task. *Archives of Neurology, 49,* 734–739.

Hallahan, D. P. (1975). Comparative research studies on the psychological characteristics of learning disabled children. In W. M. Cruickshank & D. P. Hallahan (Eds.), *Perceptual and learning disabilities in children. Vol. 1: Psychoeducational practices* (pp. 29–60). Syracuse, NY: Syracuse University Press.

Hallahan, D. P. (1992). Some thoughts on why the prevalence of learning disabilities has increased. *Journal of Learning Disabilities, 25,* 523–528.

Hallahan, D. P., & Bryan, T. H. (1981). Learning disabilities. In J. M. Kauffman & D. P. Hallahan (Eds.), *Handbook of special education* (pp. 141–164). Englewood Cliffs, NJ: Prentice-Hall.

Hallahan, D. P., & Cruickshank, W. M. (1973). *Psychoeducational foundations of learning disabilities*. Englewood Cliffs, NJ: Prentice-Hall.

Hallahan, D. P., Gajar, A. H., Cohen, S. B., & Tarver, S. G. (1978). Selective attention and locus of control in learning disabled and normal children. *Journal of Learning Disabilities, 4,* 47–52.

Hallahan, D. P., Kauffman, J. M., & Ball, D. W. (1973). Selective attention and cognitive tempo of low achieving and high achieving sixth grade males. *Perceptual and Motor Skills, 36,* 579–583.

Hallahan, D. P., Lloyd, J. W., Kauffman, J. M., Weiss, M. P., Martinez, E. A. (2005). *Learning disabilities: Foundations, characteristics, and effective teaching*. Boston: Allyn & Bacon.

Hallahan, D. P., & Mercer, C. D. (2002). Learning disabilities: Historical perspectives. In R. Bradley, L. Danielson, & D. P. Hallahan (Eds.), *Identification of learning disabilities: Research to practice* (pp. 1–67). Mahwah, NJ: Lawrence Erlbaum.

Hallahan, D. P., & Reeve, R. E. (1980). Selective attention and distractibility. In B. K. Keogh (Ed.), *Advances in special education. Vol. 1: Basic constructs and theoretical orientations* (pp. 141–181). Greenwich, CT: JAI Press.

Hallgren, B. (1950). Specific dyslexia (congenital word blindness: A clinical and genetic study). *Acta Psychiatrica et Neurologica, 65,* 1–279.

Hammill, D. D. (1990). On defining learning disabilities: An emerging consensus. *Journal of Learning Disabilities, 23,* 74–84.

Hammill, D. D., & Larsen, S. (1974). The effectiveness of psycholinguistic training. *Exceptional Children, 41,* 5–15.

Hammill, D. D., Leigh, J. E., McNutt, G., & Larsen, S. C. (1981). A new definition of learning disabilities. *Learning Disability Quarterly, 4,* 336–342.

Harris, K. R., Graham, S., Reid, R., McElroy, K., & Hamby, R. S. (1994). Self-monitoring of attention versus self-monitoring of performance: Replication and cross-task comparison studies. *Learning Disability Quarterly, 17,* 121–139.

Henderson, C. (1999). *1999 college freshmen with disabilities: A biennial statistical profile*. Washington, DC: American Council on Education HEALTH Resource Center.

Hitchings, W. E., Luzzo, D. A., Ristow, R., Horvath, M., Retish, P., & Tanners, A. (2001). The career development needs of college students with learning disabilities: In their own words. *Learning Disabilities Research and Practice, 16,* 8–17.

Kaplan, D. E., Gayan, J., Ahn, J., Won, T.-W., Pauls, D. L., Olson, R. K., DeFries, C., Wood, F. B., Pennington, B. F., Page, G. P., Smith, S. D., & Gruen, J. R. (2002). Evidence for linkage and association with reading disability, on 6p21.3–22. *American Journal of Human Genetics, 70,* 1287–1298.

Kavale, K. A. (1988). The long-term consequences of learning disabilities. In M. C. Wang, M. C. Reynolds, & H. J. Walberg (Eds.), *Handbook of special education: Research and practice. Vol. 2: Mildly handicapped conditions.* New York: Pergamon Press.

Keogh, B. K., & Glover, A. T. (1980, November). Research needs in the study of early identification of children with learning disabilities. *Thalamus (Newsletter of the International Academy for Research in Learning Disabilities).*

Kephart, N. C. (1971). *The slow learner in the classroom* (2nd ed.). Columbus, OH: Merrill.

Kibby, M. Y., & Hynd, G. W. (2001). Neurological basis of learning disabilities. In D. P. Hallahan & B. K. Keogh (Eds.), *Research and global perspectives in learning disabilities: Essays in honor of William M. Cruickshank* (pp. 25–42). Mahwah, NJ: Lawrence Erlbaum.

Kirk, S. A., & Kirk, W. D. (1971). *Psycholinguistic learning disabilities: Diagnosis and remediation.* Urbana: University of Illinois Press.

Klingner, J. K., Vaughn, S., Hughes, M. T., Schumm, J. S., & Elbaum, B. (1998). Outcomes for students with and without learning disabilities in inclusive classrooms. *Learning Disabilities Research and Practice, 13,* 153–161.

Klingner, J. K., Vaughn, S., Schumm, J. S., Cohen, P., & Forgan, J. (1998). Inclusion or pull-out: Which do students prefer? *Journal of Learning Disabilities, 31,* 148–158.

Kotkin, R. A., Forness, S. R., & Kavale, K. A. (2001). Comorbid ADHD and learning disabilities: Diagnosis, special education, and intervention. In D. P. Hallahan & B. K. Keogh (Eds.), *Research and global perspectives in learning disabilities: Essays in honor of William M. Cruickshank* (pp. 43–63). Mahwah, NJ: Lawrence Erlbaum.

Kushch, A., Gross-Glenn, K., Jallad, B., Lubs, H., Rabin, M., Feldman, E., & Duara, R. (1993). Temporal lobe surface area measurements on MRI in normal and dyslexic readers. *Neuropsychologia, 31,* 811–821.

Lasley II, T. J., Matczynski, T. J., & Rowley, J. B. (2002). *Instructional models: Strategies for teaching in a diverse society.* Belmont, CA: Wadsworth/Thomas Learning.

Leinhardt, G., Seewald, A., & Zigmond, N. (1982). Sex and race differences in learning disabilities classrooms. *Journal of Educational Psychology, 74,* 835–845.

Levin, J. R. (1993). Mnemonic strategies and classroom learning: A twenty year report card. *Elementary School Journal, 27,* 301–321.

Lewis, B. A. (1992). Pedigree analysis of children with phonology disorders. *Journal of Learning Disabilities, 25,* 586–597.

Lewis, B. A., & Thompson, L. A. (1992). A study of development of speech and language disorders in twins. *Journal of Speech and Hearing Research, 35,* 1086–1094.

Lindstrom, L. E., & Benz, M. R. (2002). Phases of career development: Case studies of young women with learning disabilities. *Exceptional Children, 69,* 67–83.

Lloyd, J. W. (1988). Direct academic interventions in learning disabilities. In M. C. Wang, M. C. Reynolds, & H. J. Walberg (Eds.), *Handbook of special education: Research and practice. Vol. 2: Mildly handicapped conditions.* New York: Pergamon Press.

Lloyd, J. W., Hallahan, D. P., Kauffman, J. M., & Keller, C. E. (1998). Academic problems. In G. Stoner, M. R. Shinn, & H. M. Walker (Eds.), *Intervention for achievement and behavior problems* (pp. 201–239). Silver Spring, MD: National Association of School Psychologists.

Lopez-Reyna, N. A., & Bay, M. (1997). Enriching assessment using varied assessments for diverse learners. *Teaching Exceptional Children, 29*(4), 33–37.

MacMillan, D. L., Gresham, F. M., & Bocian, K. M. (1998). Discrepancy between definitions of learning disabilities and school practices: An empirical investigation. *Journal of Learning Disabilities, 31,* 314–326.

MacMillan, D. L., & Siperstein, G. N. (2002). Learning disabilities as operationally defined by schools. In R. Bradley, L. Danielson, & D. P. Hallahan (Eds.), *Identification of learning disabilities: Research to practice* (pp. 287–333). Mahwah, NJ: Lawrence Erlbaum.

Mastropieri, M. A., & Scruggs, T. E. (1998). Constructing more meaningful relationships in the classroom: Mnemonic research into practice. *Learning Disabilities Research and Practice, 13,* 138–145.

Mastropieri, M. A., Sweda, J., & Scruggs, T. E. (2000). Putting mnemonics to work in an inclusive classroom. *Learning Disabilities Research & Practice, 15,* 69–74.

Mathes, M. Y., & Bender, W. N. (1997). The effects of self-monitoring on children with attention-deficit/hyperactivity disorder. *Remedial and Special Education, 18,* 121–128.

Mathes, P., Torgesen, J. K., Allen, S. H., & Allor, J. H. (2001). *First grade PALS (Peer-Assisted Literacy Strategies).* Longmont, CO: Sopris West.

McCrory, E., Frith, U., Brunswick, N., & Price, C. (2000). Abnormal functional activation during a simple word repetition task: A PET study of adult dyslexics. *Journal of Cognitive Neuroscience, 12,* 753–762.

McGrady, H. J., Lerner, J. W., & Boscardin, M. L. (2001). The educational lives of students with learning disabilities. In P. Rodis, A. Garrod, & M. L. Boscardin (Eds.), *Learning disabilities and life stories* (pp. 177–193). Boston: Allyn & Bacon.

Meese, R. L. (2001). *Teaching learners with mild disabilities: Integrating research and practice.* (2nd ed.). Stamford, CT: Wadsworth.

Montague, M. (1997). Student perception, mathematical problem solving, and learning disabilities. *Remedial and Special Education, 18,* 46–53.

Montague, M., & Graves, A. (1992). Teaching narrative composition to students with learning disabilities. In M. Pressley, K. Harris, & J. T. Guthrie (Eds.), *Promoting academic competence and literacy in schools* (pp. 261–276). New York: Academic Press.

Murawski, W. W., & Swanson, H. L. (2001). A meta-analysis of co-teaching research: Where are the data? *Remedial and Special Education, 22,* 258–267.

National Center for Children in Poverty. (2002). Early childhood poverty: A statistical profile. Retrieved October 4, 2004 from the World Wide Web: www.nccp.org/media/ecp02-text.pdf.

National Joint Committee on Learning Disabilities. (1989, September 18). Letter from NJCLD to member organizations.

Topic: Modifications to the NJCLD definition of learning disabilities. Washington, DC: Author.

Olson, R., Wise, B., Conners, F., Rack, J., & Fulker, D. (1989). Specific deficits in component reading and language skills: Genetic and environmental influences. *Journal of Learning Disabilities, 22,* 339–348.

Paulesu, E., Demonet, J. F., Fazio, F., McCrory, E., Chanonine, V., Brunswick, N., Cappa, S. F., Cossu, G., Habib, M., Frith, C. D., & Frith, U. (2001). Dyslexia: Cultural diversity and biological unity. *Science, 291,* 2165–2167.

Pelkey, L. (2001). In the LD bubble. In P. Rodis, A. Garrod, & M. L. Boscardin (Eds.), *Learning disabilities and life stories* (pp. 17–28). Boston: Allyn & Bacon.

Pennington, B. F. (1990). Annotation: The genetics of dyslexia. *Journal of Child Psychology and Child Psychiatry, 31,* 193–201.

Peterson (2003). *Colleges for students with learning disabilities or ADD (Peterson's colleges with programs for students with learning disabilities or attention deficit disorders)* (7th ed.). Princeton, NJ: Peterson's.

Petryshen, T. L., Kaplan, B. J., Liu, M. F., deFrench, N. S., Tobias, R., Hughes, M. L., & Field, L. L. (2001). Evidence for a susceptibility locus on Chromosome 6q influencing phonological coding dyslexia. *American Journal of Medical Genetics (Neuropsychiatrica Genetics), 105,* 507–517.

Pugh, K. R. Mencl, W. E., Shaywitz, B. A., Shaywitz, S. E., Fulbright, R. K., Constable, R. T., Skudlarski, P., Marchione, K. E., Jenner, A. R., Fletcher, J. M., Liberman, A. M., Shankweiler, D. P., Katz, L., Lacadie, C., & Gore, J. C. (2000). Task-specific differences in functional connections within the posterior cortex. *Psychological Science, 11,* 51–56.

Pullen, P. C. (2002, October 1). Expert connection: Phonological awareness. *TeachingLD.org.* Retrieved from http://TeachingLD.org/expert_connection/phonological.html.

Queen, O. (2001). Blake Academy and the Green Arrow. In P. Rodis, A. Garrod, & M. L. Boscardin (Eds.), *Learning disabilities and life stories* (pp. 3–16). Boston: Allyn & Bacon.

Raskind, M. H., Goldberg, R. J., Higgins, E. L., & Herman, K. L. (1999). Patterns of change and predictors of success in individuals with learning disabilities: Results from a twenty-year longitudinal study. *Learning Disabilities Research and Practice, 14,* 35–49.

Raskind, W. H. (2001). Current understanding of the genetic basis of reading and spelling disability. *Learning Disability Quarterly, 24,* 141–157.

Reiff, H. B., Gerber, P. J., & Ginsberg, R. (1997). *Exceeding expectations: Successful adults with learning disabilities.* Austin, TX: Pro-Ed.

Reynolds, C. A., Hewitt, J. K., Erickson, M. T., Silberg, J. L., Rutter, M., Simonoff, E., Meyer, J., & Eaves, L. J. (1996). The genetics of children's oral reading performance. *Journal of Child Psychology and Psychiatry, 37,* 425–434.

Richards, T. L. (2001). Functional magnetic resonance imaging and spectroscopic imaging of the brain: Application of fMRI and fMRS to reading disabilities and education. *Learning Disability Quarterly, 24,* 189–203.

Rosenshine, B., & Meister, C. (1994). Reciprocal teaching: A review of research. *Review of Educational Research, 64,* 479–530.

Rourke, B. P. (1995). *Syndrome of nonverbal learning disabilities: Neurodevelopmental manifestations.* New York: Guilford Press.

Rueda, R., & Garcia, E. (1997). Do portfolios make a difference for diverse students? The influence of type of data on making instructional decisions. *Learning Disabilities Research and Practice, 12,* 114–122.

Rumsey, J. M., Horwitz, B., Donohue, B. C., Nace, K. L., Maisog, J. M., & Andreason, P. (1999). A functional lesion in developmental dyslexia: Left angular gyral blood flow predicts severity. *Brain and Language, 70*(2), 187–204.

Schulte-Korne, G. (2001). Annotation: Genetics of reading and spelling disorder. *Journal of Child Psychology and Psychiatry, 42,* 985–997.

Schulte-Korne, G., Deimel, W., Muller, K., Gutenbrunner, C., & Remschmidt, H. (1996). Familial aggregation of spelling disability. *Journal of Child Psychology and Psychiatry, 37,* 817–822.

Seligman, M. E. (1992). *Helplessness: On depression, development and death.* San Francisco: W. H. Freeman.

Sexton, M., Harris, K. R., & Graham, S. (1998). Self-regulated strategy development and the writing process: Effects on essay writing and attributions. *Exceptional Children, 64,* 295–311.

Shaywitz, S. E., Shaywitz, B. A., Fletcher, J. M., & Escobar, M. D. (1990). Prevalence of reading disability in boys and girls: Results of the Connecticut Longitudinal Study. *Journal of the American Medical Association, 264,* 998–1002.

Shaywitz, S. E., Shaywitz, B. A., Pugh, K. R., Fulbright, R. K., Constable, R. T., Mencl, W. E., Shankweiler, D. P., Liberman, A. M., Skudlarski, P., Fletcher, J. M., Katz, L., Marchione, K. E., Lacadie, C., Gatenby, C., & Gore, J. C. (1998). Functional disruption in the organization of the brain for reading in dyslexia. *Neurobiology, 95,* 2636–2641.

Short, E. J., & Weissberg-Benchell, J. (1989). The triple alliance for learning: Cognition, metacognition, and motivation. In C. B. McCormick, G. E. Miller, & M. Pressley (Eds.), *Cognitive strategy research: From basic research to educational applications* (pp. 33–63). New York: Springer-Verlag.

Skinner, M. E. (1998). Promoting self-advocacy among college students with learning disabilities. *Intervention in School and Clinic, 33,* 278–283.

Spekman, N. J., Goldberg, R. J., & Herman, K. L. (1992). Learning disabled children grow up: A search for factors related to success in the young adult years. *Learning Disabilities Research and Practice, 7,* 161–170.

Swanson, H. L. (2001). Research on interventions for adolescents with learning disabilities: A meta-analysis of outcomes related to higher-order processing. *Elementary School Journal, 101,* 331–348.

Swanson, H. L., & Hoskyn, M. (1998). Experimental intervention research for students with learning disabilities: A meta-analysis of treatment outcomes. *Review of Educational Research, 68,* 277–321.

Swanson, H. L., & Sachse-Lee, C. (2001). A subgroup analysis of working memory in children with reading disabilities: Domain-general or domain-specific deficiency? *Journal of Learning Disabilities, 34,* 249–263.

Torgesen, J. K. (1977). The role of nonspecific factors in the task performance of learning disabled children: A theoretical assessment. *Journal of Learning Disabilities, 10,* 27–34.

Torgesen, J. K. (1988). Studies of children with learning disabilities who perform poorly on memory span tasks. *Journal of Learning Disabilities, 21,* 605–612.

Torgesen, J. K. (2002). Empirical and theoretical support for direct diagnosis of learning disabilities by assessment of intrinsic processing weaknesses. In R. Bradley, L. Danielson, & D. P. Hallahan (Eds.), *Identification of learning disabilities: Research to practice* (pp. 565–613). Mahwah, NJ: Lawrence Erlbaum.

Torgesen, J. K., & Kail, R. V. (1980). Memory processes in exceptional children. In B. K. Keogh (Ed.), *Advances in special education. Vol. 1: Basic constructs and theoretical orientations.* Greenwich, CT: JAI Press.

Trota, G. A. (2004, Summer). A focus on phonological awareness acquisition and intervention. *Current Practice Alerts*, Sponsored by the Division for Learning Disabilities and Division for Research of the Council for Exceptional Children.

U.S. Department of Education. (2002). *Twenty-fourth annual report to Congress on the implementation of the Individuals with Disabilities Education Act.* Washington, DC: Author.

Vaughn, S., Elbaum, B., & Boardman, A. G. (2001). The social functioning of students with learning disabilities: Implications for inclusion. *Exceptionality, 9*, 47–65.

Vaughn, S., & Fuchs, L. S., (2003). Redefining learning disabilities as inadequate response to instruction: The promise and potential problems. *Learning Disabilities Research & Practice, 18*, 137–146.

Vaughn, S., Gersten, R., & Chard, D. J. (2000). The underlying message in LD intervention research: Findings from research syntheses. *Exceptional Children, 67*, 99–114.

Vaughn, S., Linan-Thompson, S., & Hickman, P. (2003). Response to instruction as a means of identifying students with reading disabilities. *Exceptional Children, 69*, 391–409.

Vaughn, S., Schumm, J. S., & Arguelles, M. E. (1997). The ABCDEs of Co-teaching. *Teaching Exceptional Children, 30*, 4–10.

Wax, I. F., & Kravets, M. (2003). *K & W guide to colleges for students with learning disabilities or attention deficit disorder* (7th ed.). New York: Princeton Review.

Werner, H., & Strauss, A. A. (1941). Pathology of figure-background relation in the child. *Journal of Abnormal and Social Psychology, 36*, 236–248.

Willows, D. M. (1998). Visual processes in learning disabilities. In H. L. Swanson (Ed.), *Handbook of assessment of learning disabilities: Theory, research, and practice* (pp. 147–175). Austin, TX: Pro-Ed.

Witte, R. H., Philips, L., & Kakela, M. (1998). Job satisfaction of college graduates with learning disabilities. *Journal of Learning Disabilities, 31*, 259–265.

Woodward, J., & Baxter, J. (1997). The effects of an innovative approach to mathematics on academically low-achieving students in inclusive settings. *Exceptional Children, 63*, 373–388.

Worling, D. E., Humphries, T., & Tannock, R. (1999). Spatial and emotional aspects of language inferencing in nonverbal learning disabilities. *Brain and Language, 70*, 220–239.

CHAPTER 7

Allsopp, D. H. (1999). Using modeling, manipulatives, and mnemonics with eighth-grade math students. *Teaching Exceptional Children, 32*(2), 74–81.

American Psychiatric Association. (2000). *Diagnostic and statistical manual of mental disorders* (4th ed., text rev.). Washington, DC: Author.

Arnold, L. E., Elliott, M., Sachs, L., Abikoff, H. B., Conners, C. K., Greenhill, L. L., Hinshaw, S. P., Jensen, P. S., Newcorn, J. H., Severe, J. B., Vitiello, B., Bird, H., Wells, K. C., Comarda, A., Elliott, G. R., Hechtman, L., Hoza, B., March, J. S., Pelham, W. E., Swanson, J. M., & Wigal, T. (2003). Effects of ethnicity on treatment attendance, stimulant response/dose, and 14-month outcome in ADHD. *Journal of Consulting and Clinical Psychology, 71*, 713–727.

Barkley, R. A. (1994). Impaired delayed responding: A unified theory of attention-deficit hyperactivity disorder. In D. K. Routh (Ed.), *Disruptive behavior disorders in childhood* (pp. 11–57). New York: Plenum.

Barkley, R. A. (1997). Behavioral inhibition, sustained attention, and executive functions: Constructing a unifying theory of ADHD. *Psychological Bulletin, 121*, 65–94.

Barkley, R. A. (1998). *Attention-deficit hyperactivity disorder: A handbook for diagnosis and treatment.* New York: Guilford Press.

Barkley, R. A., & Murphy, K. R. (1998). *Attention-deficit hyperactivity disorder: A clinical workbook* (2nd ed.). New York: Guilford Press.

Barkley, R. A., Murphy, K. R. & Kwasnik, D. (1996). Psychological adjustment and adaptive impairments in young adults with ADHD. *Journal of Attention Disorders, 1*, 41–54.

Barkley, R. A. (2000a). *A new look at ADHD: Inhibition, time, and self-control* (video manual). Baltimore: Guilford Press.

Barkley, R. A. (2000b). *Taking charge of ADHD: The complete, authoritative guide for parents* (rev. ed.). New York: The Guilford Press.

Bateman, B., Warner, J. O., Hutchinson, E., Dean, T., Rowlandson, P., Gant, C., Grundy, J., Fitzgerald, C., & Stevenson, J. (2004). The effects of a double blind, placebo controlled, artificial food colourings and benzoate preservative challenge on hyperactivity in a general population sample of preschool children. *Archives of Disease in Childhood, 89*, 506–511.

Baumgaertel, A., Wolraich, M. L., & Dietrich, M. (1995). Comparison of diagnostic criteria for attention deficit disorders in a German elementary school sample. *Journal of the Academy of Child and Adolescent Psychiatry, 34*, 629–638.

Biederman, J., Faraone, S. V., Mick, E., Spencer, T., Wilens, T., Kiely, K., Guite, J., Ablon, J. S., Reed, E., & Warburton, R. (1995). High risk for attention deficit hyperactivity disorder among children of parents with childhood onset of the disorder: A pilot study. *American Journal of Psychiatry, 152*, 431–435.

Biederman, J., Wilens, T., Mick, E., Faraone, S. V., & Spencer, T., (1998). Does attention-deficit hyperactivity disorder impact the developmental course of drug and alcohol abuse and dependence? *Biological Psychiatry, 44*, 269–273.

Biederman, J., Wilens, T., Mick, E., Spencer, T., & Faraone, S. V. (1999). Pharmacotherapy of attention-deficit/hyperactivity disorder reduces risk for substance abuse disorder. *Pediatrics, 104*, 20.

Birch, H. G. (1964). *Brain damage in children: The biological and social aspects.* Baltimore: Williams & Wilkins.

Castellanos, F. X. (1997). Toward a pathophysiology of attention-deficit/hyperactivity disorder. *Clinical Pediatrics, 36*, 381–393.

Castellanos, F. X. (2001). Neural substrates of attention-deficit hyperactivity disorder. *Advances in Neurology, 85*, 197–206.

Castellanos, F. X., Lee, P. P., Sharp, W., Jeffries, N. O., Greenstein, D. K., Clasen, L. S., Blumenthal, J. D., James, R. S., Ebens, C. L., Walter, J. M., Zijdenbos, A., Evans, A. C., Giedd, J. N., &

Rapoport, J. L. (2002). Developmental trajectories of brain volume abnormalities in children and adolescents with attention-deficit/hyperactivity disorder. *Journal of the American Medical Association, 288,* 1740–1748.

Cepeda, N. J., Cepeda, M. L., & Kramer, A. F. (2000). Task switching and attention deficit hyperactivity disorder. *Journal of Abnormal Child Psychology, 28,* 213–226.

Chilcoat, H. D., & Breslau, N. (1999). Pathways from ADHD to early drug use. *Journal of the American Academy of Child and Adolescent Psychiatry, 38,* 1347–1354.

Christakis, D. A., Zimmerman, F. J., DiGiuseppe, D. L., & McCarty, C. A. (2004). Early television exposure and subsequent attentional problems in children. *Pediatrics, 113,* 708–713.

Cole, C. L., & Bambara, L. M. (1992). Issues surrounding the use of self-management interventions in the school. *School Psychology Review, 21,* 193–201.

Conners, C. K. (1989a). *Conners Teacher Rating Scale-28.* Tonawanda, NY: Multi-Health Systems.

Conners, C. K. (1989b). *Conners Teacher Rating Scale-39.* Tonawanda, NY: Multi-Health Systems.

Conners, C. K. (1997). *Conners Rating Scales—Revised (CSR-R).* North Tonawanda, NY: Multi-Health Systems.

Conners, C. K. (1999). *Conners Adult ADHD Rating Scales (CAARS).* North Tonawanda, NY: Multi-Health Systems.

Cooper, P. (1999). ADHD and effective learning: Principles and practical approaches. In P. Cooper & K. Bilton (Eds.), *ADHD: Research, practice and opinion* (pp. 138–157). London: Whurr.

Cox, D. J., Merkel, R. L., Kovatchev, B., & Seward, R. (2000). Effect of stimulant medication on driving performance of young adults with attention-deficit hyperactivity disorder. *Journal of Nervous and Mental Disease, 188,* 230–234.

Crenshaw, T. M., Kavale, K. A., Forness, S. R., & Reeve, R. E. (1999). Attention deficit hyperactivity disorder and the efficacy of stimulant medication: A meta-analysis. In T. Scruggs & M. Mastropieri (Eds.), *Advances in learning and behavioral disabilities, Vol. 13* (pp. 135–165). Greenwich, CT: JAI Press.

Cruickshank, W. M., Bentzen, F. A., Ratzeburg, F. H., & Tannhauser, M. T. (1961). *A teaching method of brain-injured and hyperactive children.* Syracuse, NY: Syracuse University Press.

Cruickshank, W. M., Bice, H. V., & Wallen, N. E. (1957). *Perception and cerebral palsy.* Syracuse, NY: Syracuse University Press.

Davies, S., & Witte, R. (2000). Self-management and peer-monitoring within a group contingency to decrease uncontrolled verbalizations of children with attention-deficit/hyperactivity disorder. *Psychology in the Schools, 37,* 135–147.

DuPaul, G. J., Barkley, R. A., & Connor, D. F. (1998). Stimulants. In R. A. Barkley (Ed.), *Attention-deficit hyperactivity disorder: A handbook for diagnosis and treatment* (pp. 510–551). New York: Guilford Press.

DuPaul, G. J., & Eckert, T. L. (1997). The effects of school-based interventions for attention deficit hyperactivity disorder: A meta-analysis, *School Psychology Review, 26,* 5–27.

DuPaul, G. J., Eckert, T. L., & McGoey, K. E. (1997). Interventions for students with attention-deficit/hyperactivity disorder: One size does not fit all. *School Psychology Review, 26,* 369–381.

DuPaul, G. J., & Ervin, R. A. (1996). Functional assessment of behaviors related to attention-deficit hyperactivity disorder: Linking assessment to intervention design. *Behavior Therapy, 27,* 601–622.

DuPaul, G. J., Power, D. T. J., Anastopolos, A. D., & Reid, R. (1998). *ADHD Rating Scale-IV: Checklists, norms, and clinical interpretations.* New York: Guilford Press.

Erhardt, D., & Hinshaw, S. P. (1994). Initial sociometric impressions of attention-deficit hyperactivity disorder and comparison boys: Predictions from social behaviors and from nonbehavioral variables. *Journal of Consulting and Clinical Psychology, 62,* 833–842.

Ervin, R. A., DuPaul, G. J., Kern, L., & Friman, P. C. (1998). Classroom-based functional and adjunctive assessments: Proactive approaches to intervention selection for adolescents with attention deficit hyperactivity disorder. *Journal of Applied Behavior Analysis, 31,* 65–78.

Esser, G., Schmidt, M. H., & Woerner, W. (1990). Epidemiology and course of psychiatric disorders in school-age children—Results of a longitudinal study. *Journal of Child Psychology and Psychiatry, 31,* 243–263.

Evans, S. W., Pelham, W. E., Smith, B. H., Bukstein, O., Gnagy, E. M., Greiner, A. R., Altenderfer, L., & Baron-Myak, C. (2001). Dose-response effects of methylphenidate on ecologically valid measures of academic performance and classroom behavior in adolescents with ADHD. *Experimental and Clinical Pharmacology, 9,* 163–175.

Faraone, S. V., Biederman, J., Spencer, T., Wilens, T., Seidman, L. J., Mick, E., & Doyle, A. E. (2000). Attention-deficit/hyperactivity disorder in adults: An overview. *Biological Psychiatry, 48,* 9–20.

Faraone, S. V., & Doyle, A. E. (2001). The nature and heritability of attention-deficit/hyperactivity disorder. *Child and Adolescent Psychiatric Clinics of North America, 10,* 299–316.

Faraone, S. V., Pliszka, S. R., Olvera, R. L., Skolnik, R., & Biederman, J. (2001). Efficacy of Adderall and methylphenidate in attention deficit hyperactivity disorder: A reanalysis using drug-placebo and drug-drug response curve methodology. *Journal of Child and Adolescent Psychopharmacology, 11,* 171–180.

Feingold, B. (1975). *Why your child is hyperactive.* New York: Random House.

Fergusson, D. M., Horwood, L. J., & Lynskey, M. T. (1993). Prevalence and comorbidity of DSM-III-R diagnoses in a birth cohort of 15 year olds. *Journal of the American Academy of Child and Adolescent Psychiatry, 32,* 1127–1134.

Filipek, P. A., Semrud-Clikeman, M., Steingard, R. J., Renshaw, P. F., Kennedy, D. N., & Biederman, J. (1997). Volumetric MRI analysis comparing subjects having attention-deficit hyperactivity disorder with normal controls. *Neurology, 48,* 589–601.

Forness, S. R., Kavale, K. A. (2002). Impact of ADHD on school systems. In P. Jensen & J. R. Cooper (Eds.), *Attention deficit hyperactivity disorder: State of the science; best practices* (pp. 1–20). Kingston, NJ: Civic Research Institute.

Forness, S. R., Kavale, K. A., & Crenshaw, T. M. (1999). Stimulant medication revisited: Effective treatment of children with ADHD. *Journal of Emotional and Behavioral Problems, 7,* 230–235.

Gillis, J. J., Gilger, J. W., Pennington, B. F., & DeFries, C. (1992). Attention deficit disorder in reading-disabled twins: Evidence for a genetic etiology. *Journal of Abnormal Child Psychology, 20,* 303–315.

Goldstein, K. (1936). The modification of behavior consequent to cerebral lesions. *Psychiatric Quarterly, 10,* 586–610.

Goldstein, K. (1939). *The organism*. New York: American Book Co.

Hale, J. B., Hoeppner, J. B., DeWitt, M. B., Coury, D. L., Ritacco, D. G., & Trommer, B. (1998). Evaluating medication response in ADHD: Cognitive, behavioral, and single-subject methodology. *Journal of Learning Disabilities, 31*, 595–607.

Hallahan, D. P., & Cottone, E. A. (1997). Attention deficit hyperactivity disorder. In T. E. Scruggs & M. A. Mastropieri (Eds.), *Advances in learning and behavioral disabilities, Vol. 11* (pp. 27–67). Greenwich, CT: JAI Press.

Hallowell, E. M., & Ratey, J. J. (1994). *Driven to distraction*. New York: Touchstone.

Hallowell, E. M., & Ratey, J. J. (1996). *Answers to distraction*. New York: Bantam Books.

Hoffmann, H. (1865). Die Geschichte vom Zappel-Philipp [The Story of Fidgety Philip]. *Der Struwwelpeter*. Germany: Pestalozzi-Verlag.

Horner, R. H., & Carr, E. G. (1997). Behavioral support for students with severe disabilities: Functional assessment and comprehensive intervention. *Journal of Special Education, 31*, 1–11.

Hudson, P. (1997). Using teacher-guided practice to help students with learning disabilities acquire and retain social studies content. *Learning Disabilities Quarterly, 20*, 23–32.

Hynd, G. W., Hern, K. L., Novey, E. S., Eliopulos, D., Marshall, R., Gonzalez, J. J., & Voeller, K. K. (1993). Attention deficit hyperactivity disorder and asymmetry of the caudate nucleus. *Journal of Child Neurology, 8*, 339–347.

Kame'enui, E. J., & Carnine, D. W. (1998). *Effective teaching strategies that accommodate diverse learners*. Columbus, OH: Prentice-Hall.

Kanbayashi, Y., Nakata, Y., Fujii, K., Kita, M., & Wada, K. (1994). ADHD-related behavior among non-referred children: Parents' ratings of DSM-III-R symptoms. *Child Psychiatry and Human Development, 25*(1), 13–29.

Kavale, K. A., & Forness, S. R. (1983). Hyperactivity and diet treatment: A meta-analysis of the Feingold hypothesis. *Journal of Learning Disabilities, 16*, 324–330.

Kemp, K., Fister, S., & McLaughlin, P. J. (1995). Academic strategies for children with ADD. *Intervention in School and Clinic, 30*, 203–210.

Kewley, G. D. (1998). Personal paper: Attention deficit hyperactivity disorder is underdiagnosed and undertreated in Britain. *British Medical Journal, 316*, 1594–1596.

Kohn, A. (1993). *Punished by rewards: The trouble with gold stars, incentive plans, A's, praise, and other bribes*. Boston: Houghton Mifflin.

Kucan, L., & Beck, I. L. (1997). Thinking aloud and reading comprehension research: Inquiry, instruction, and social interaction. *Review of Educational Research, 67*, 271–299.

Lambert, N. M., & Hartsough, C. S. (1998). Prospective study of tobacco smoking and substance dependencies among samples of ADHD and non-ADHD participants. *Journal of Learning Disabilities, 31*, 533–544.

Landau, S., Milich, R., & Diener, M. B. (1998). Peer relations of children with attention-deficit hyperactivity disorder. *Reading and Writing Quarterly: Overcoming Learning Difficulties, 14*, 83–105.

Lawrence, V., Houghton, S., Tannock, R., Douglas, G., Durkin, K., & Whiting, K. (2002). ADHD outside the laboratory: Boys' executive function performance on tasks in videogame play and on a visit to the zoo. *Journal of Abnormal Child Psychology, 30*, 447–462.

Leung, P. W. L., Luk, S. L., Ho, T. P., Taylor, E., Mak, F. L., & Bacon-Shone, J. (1996). The diagnosis and prevalence of hyperactivity in Chinese schoolboys. *British Journal of Psychiatry, 168*, 486–496.

Levy, F., Barr, C., & Sunohara, G. (1998). Directions of aetiologic research on attention deficit hyperactivity disorder. *Australian and New Zealand Journal of Psychiatry, 32*, 97–103.

Lloyd, J. W., Hallahan, D. P., Kauffman, J. M., & Keller, C. E. (1998). Academic problems. In R. J. Morris & T. R. Kratochwill (Eds.), *The practice of child therapy* (pp. 167–198). Boston: Allyn & Bacon.

Lou, H. C., Henriksen, L., & Bruhn, P. (1984). Focal cerebral hypoperfusion in children with dysphasia and/or attention deficit disorder. *Archives of Neurology, 41*, 825–829.

Lou, H. C., Henriksen, L., Bruhn, P., Borner, H., & Nielsen, J. B. (1989). Striatal dysfunction in attention deficit and hyperkinetic disorder. *Archives of Neurology, 46*, 48–52.

Manos, M. J., Short, E. J., & Findling, R. L. (1999). Differential effectiveness of methylphenidate and Adderall in school-age youths with attention-deficit/hyperactivity disorder. *Journal of the American Academy of Child and Adolescent Psychiatry, 38*, 813–819.

Marshall, R. M., Hynd, G. W., Handwerk, M. J., & Hall, J. (1997). Academic underachievement in ADHD subtypes. *Journal of Learning Disabilities, 30*, 635–642.

Mathes, M. Y., & Bender, W. N. (1997). The effects of self-monitoring on children with attention-deficit/hyperactivity disorder who are receiving pharmacological interventions. *Remedial and Special Education, 18*, 121–128.

Mercer, C. D., & Mercer, A. R. (1998). *Teaching students with learning problems* (5th ed.). Columbus, OH: Prentice-Hall.

Milberger, S., Biederman, J., Faraone, S. V., Guite, J., & Tsuang, M. T. (1997). Pregnancy, delivery and infancy complications and attention deficit hyperactivity disorder: Issues of gene-environment interaction. *Biological Psychiatry, 41*, 65–75.

MTA Cooperative Group. (1999). A 14-month randomized clinical trial of treatment strategies for attention-deficit/hyperactivity disorder, *Archives of General Psychiatry, 56*, 1073–1086.

Murphy, K. R. (1998). Psychological counseling of adults with ADHD. In R. A. Barkley (Ed.), *Attention-deficit hyperactivity disorder: A handbook for diagnosis and treatment* (pp. 582–591). New York: Guilford Press.

National Institute of Mental Health. (2003). *Attention deficit hyperactivity disorder*. Retrieved September 5, 2004 from the World Wide Web: www.nimh.nih.gov/publicat/adhd.cfm.

Pasamanick, B., Lilienfeld, A. M., & Rogers, M. E. (1956). Pregnancy experience and the development of behavior disorders in children. *American Journal of Psychiatry, 112*, 613–617.

Pelham, W. E. (2000). Implications of the MTA Study for behavioral and combined treatments. *ADHD Report, 8*(4), 9–13, 16.

Pinel, J. P. J. (2003). *Biopsychology* (5th ed.). Boston: Allyn & Bacon.

Pliszka, S. R., Browne, R. G., Olvera, R. L., & Wynne, S. K. (2000). A double-blind, placebo-controlled study of Adderall and methylphenidate in the treatment of attention deficit/hyperactivity disorder. *Journal of the American Academy of Child and Adolescent Psychiatry, 39*, 619–626.

Reid, R., & Harris, K. R. (1992). Self-monitoring of attention versus self-monitoring of performance: Effects on attention and academic performance. *Exceptional Children, 60,* 29–40.

Reid, R., Casat, C. D., Norton, H. J., Anastopoulos, A. D., & Temple, E. P. (2001). Using behavior rating scales for ADHD across ethnic groups: The IOWA Conners. *Journal of Emotional & Behavioral Disorders, 9,* 210–218.

Reid, R., Riccio, C. A., Kessler, R. H., DuPaul, G. J., Power, T. J., Anastopolous, A. D., Rogers-Adkinson, D., & Noll, M. (2000). Gender and ethnic differences in ADHD as assessed by behavior ratings. *Journal of Emotional and Behavioral Disorders, 8,* 38–48.

Richters, J. E., Arnold, L. E., Abikoff, H., Conners, C. K., Greenhill, L. L., Hechtman, L., Hinshaw, S. P., Pelham, W. E., & Swanson, J. M. (1995). NIMH collaborative multisite multimodal treatment study of children with ADHD: Background and rationale. *Journal of the Academy of Child and Adolescent Psychiatry, 34,* 987–1000.

Robison, L. M., Skaer, T. L., Sclar, D. A., & Galin, R. S. (2002). Is attention deficit hyperactivity disorder increasing among girls in the US? *CNS Drugs, 16,* 129–137.

Rohde, L. A., Biederman, J., Busnello, E., Zimmerman, H., Schmitz, M., Martins, S., & Tramontina, S. (1999). ADHD in a sample of Brazilian adolescents: A study of prevalence, comorbid conditions, and impairments. *Journal of the Academy of Child and Adolescent Psychiatry, 38,* 716–722.

Rooney, K. J. (1995). Teaching students with attention disorders. *Intervention in School and Clinic, 30,* 221–225.

Rosenshine, R. (1995). Advances in research on instruction. *Journal of Educational Research, 88,* 262–268.

Rowland, A. S., Umbach, D. M., Catoe, K. E., Stallone, L., Long, S., Rabiner, D., Naftel, A. J., Panke, D., Faulk, R., & Sandler, D. P. (2001). Studying the epidemiology of attention-deficit hyperactivity disorder: Screening method and pilot results. *Canadian Journal of Psychiatry, 46,* 931–940.

Schachar, R., Mota, V. L., Logan, G. D., Tannock, R., & Klim, P. (2000). Confirmation of an inhibitory control deficit in attention-deficit/hyperactivity disorder. *Journal of Abnormal Child Psychology, 28,* 227–235.

Schaughency, E. A., McGee, R., Raja, S. N., Freehan, M., & Silva, P. (1994). Self-reported inattention, impulsivity, and hyperactivity in ages 15 and 18 years in the general population. *Journal of the Academy of Child and Adolescent Psychiatry, 33,* 173–183.

Semrud-Clikeman, M., Steingard, R. J., Filipek, P., Biederman, J., Bekken, K., & Renshaw, P. F. (2000). Using MRI to examine brain-behavior relationships in males with attention deficit disorder with hyperactivity. *Journal of the American Academy of Child and Adolescent Psychiatry, 39,* 477–484.

Shapiro, E. S., DuPaul, G. J., & Bradley-Klug, K. L. (1998). Self-management as a strategy to improve the classroom behavior of adolescents with ADHD. *Journal of Learning Disabilities, 31,* 545–555.

Shelton, T. L., Barkley, R. A., Crosswait, C., Moorehouse, M., Fletcher, K., Barrett, M. S., Jenkins, L., & Metevia, L. (2000). Multimethod psychoeducational intervention for preschool children with disruptive behavior: Two-year post-treatment follow-up. *Journal of Abnormal Child Psychology, 28,* 253–266.

Sherman, D. K., Iacono, W. G., & McGue, M. K. (1997). Attention-deficit hyperactivity disorder dimensions: A twin study of inattention and impulsivity-hyperactivity. *Journal of the American Academy of Child and Adolescent Psychiatry, 36,* 745–753.

Shimabukuro, S. M., Prater, M. A., Jenkins, A., & Edelen-Smith, P. (1999). The effects of self-monitoring of academic performance on students with learning disabilities and ADD/ADHD. *Education and Treatment of Children, 22,* 397–414.

Smith, D. J., & Nelson, J. R., Young, K. R., & West, R. P. (1992). The effect of a self-management procedure on the classroom and academic behavior of students with mild handicaps. *School Psychology Review, 21,* 59–72.

Solanto, M. V. (1998). Neuropsychopharmacological mechanisms of stimulant drug action in attention-deficit hyperactivity disorder: A review and integration. *Behavioural Brain Research, 94,* 127–152.

Solanto, M. V. (2002). Dopamine dysfunction in AD/HD: Integrating clinical and basic neuroscience research. *Behavioural Brain Research, 130,* 65–71.

Spencer, T., Biederman, J., Wilens, T., Harding, M., O'Donnell, D., & Griffin, S. (1996). Pharmacotherapy of attention-deficit hyperactivity disorder across the life cycle. *Journal of the American Academy of Child and Adolescent Psychiatry, 35,* 409–432.

Stevenson, J. (1992). Evidence for a genetic etiology in hyperactive children. *Behavior Genetics, 22,* 337–344.

Still, G. F. (1902). Some abnormal psychical conditions in children. *The Lancet, 1,* 1008–1012, 1077–1082, 1163–1168.

Strauss, A. A., & Werner, H. (1942). Disorders of conceptual thinking in the brain-injured child. *Journal of Nervous and Mental Disease, 96,* 153–172.

Swanson, J., Castellanos, F. X., Murias, M., LaHoste, G., & Kennedy, J. (1998). Cognitive neuroscience of attention deficit hyperactivity disorder and hyperkinetic disorder. *Current Opinion in Neurobiology, 8,* 263–271.

Swanson, J. M., Kraemer, H. C., Hinshaw, S. P., Arnold, L. E., Conners, C. K., Abikoff, H. B., Clevenger, W., Davies, M., Elliott, G. R., Greenhill, L. L., Hechtman, L., Hoza, B., Jensen, P., March, J. S., Newcorn, J. H., Owens, E. B., Pelham, W. E., Schiller, E., Severe, J. B., Simpson, S., Vitiello, B., Wells, K., Wigal, T., & Wu, M. (2001). Clinical relevance of the primary findings of the MTA: Success rates based on severity of ADHD and ODD symptoms at the end of treatment. *Journal of the American Academy of Child and Adolescent Psychiatry, 40,* 168–179.

Swanson, J. M., Sergeant, J. A., Taylor, E., Sonuga-Barke, E. J. S., Jensen, P. S., & Cantwell, D. P. (1998). Attention-deficit hyperactivity disorder and hyperkinetic disorder. *The Lancet, 351,* 429–433.

Szatmari, P. (1992). The epidemiology of attention-deficit/hyperactivity disorder. In G. Weiss (Ed.), *Child and adolescent psychiatry clinics of North America: Attention deficit disorder* (pp. 361–372). Philadelphia: Saunders.

Tankersley, M. (1995). A group-oriented contingency management program: A review of research on the good behavior game and implications for teachers. *Preventing School Failure, 40,* 59–72.

Teicher, M. H., Anderson, C. M., Polcarl, A., Glod, C. A., Maas, L. C., & Renshaw, P. F. (2000). Functional deficits in basal ganglia of children with attention-deficit/hyperactivity disorder shown with functional magnetic resonance imaging relaxometry. *Nature Medicine, 6,* 470–473.

Tripp, G., & Alsop, B. (2001). Sensitivity to reward delay in children with attention deficit hyperactivity disorder (ADHD). *Journal of Child Psychology and Psychiatry, 42,* 691–698.

Vaughn, S., Schumm, J. S., & Arguelles, M. E. (1997). The ABCDEs of Co-teaching. *Teaching Exceptional Children, 30*, 4–10.

Weiss, M., Hechtman, L., & Weiss, G. (2000). ADHD in parents. *Journal of the American Academy of Child and Adolescent Psychiatry, 39*, 1059–1061.

Werner, H., & Strauss, A. A. (1939). Types of visuo-motor activity in their relation to low and high performance ages. *Proceedings of the American Association on Mental Deficiency, 44*, 163–168.

Werner, H., & Strauss, A. A. (1941). Pathology of figure-background relation in the child. *Journal of Abnormal and Social Psychology, 36*, 236–248.

Wilens, T. E. & Biederman, J. (1992). Pediatric psychopharmacology: The stimulants. *Pediatric Clinics of North America, 15*(1), 191–222.

Wilens, T. E., Biederman, J., & Spencer, T. J. (2002). Attention deficit/hyperactivity disorder across the lifespan. *Annual Review of Medicine, 53*, 113–131.

Willcutt, E. G., Chhabildas, N., & Pennington, B. F. (2001). Validity of the DSM-IV subtypes of ADHD. *ADHD Report, 9*(1), 2–5.

Willcutt, E. G., Pennington, B. F., Boada, R., Ogline, J. S., Tunick, R. A., Chhabildas, N. A., & Olson, R. K. (2001). A comparison of the cognitive deficits in reading disability and attention-deficit/hyperactivity disorder. *Journal of Abnormal Psychology, 110*, 157–172.

Wolraich, M. L., Wilson, D. B., & White, J. W. (1995). The effect of sugar on behavior or cognition in children: A meta-analysis. *Journal of the American Medical Association, 274*, 1617–1621.

Woodward, L. J., Fergusson, D. M., & Horwood, L. J. (2000). Driving outcomes for young people with attentional difficulties in adolescence. *Journal of the American Academy of Child and Adolescent Psychiatry, 39*, 627–634.

CHAPTER 8

Achenbach, T. M. (1985). *Assessment and taxonomy of child and adolescent psychopathology*. Newbury Park, CA: Sage.

American Psychiatric Association. (1994). *Diagnostic and statistical manual of mental disorders* (4th ed.). Washington, DC: Author.

Bandura, A. (1973). *Aggression: A social learning analysis*. Englewood Cliffs, NJ: Prentice-Hall.

Bandura, A. (1986). *Social foundations of thought and action: A social cognitive theory*. Englewood Cliffs, NJ: Prentice-Hall.

Bateman, B. D., & Chard, D. J. (1995). Legal demands and constraints on placement decisions. In J. M. Kauffman, J. W. Lloyd, D. P. Hallahan, & T. A. Astuto (Eds.), *Issues in educational placement: Students with emotional and behavioral disorders* (pp. 285–316). Hillsdale, NJ: Lawrence Erlbaum.

Blake, C., Wang, W., Cartledge, G., & Gardner, R. (2000). Middle school students with serious emotional disturbances serve as social skills trainers and reinforcers for peers with SED. *Behavioral Disorders, 25*, 280–298.

Block, A., & Weisz, V. (2004, July 6). Choosing prisoners over pupils. *The Washington Post*, A19.

Bower, E. M. (1981). *Early identification of emotionally handicapped children in school* (3rd ed.). Springfield, IL: Charles C. Thomas.

Bower, E. M. (1982). Defining emotional disturbance: Public policy and research. *Psychology in the Schools, 19*, 55–60.

Brigham, F. J., & Kauffman, J. M. (1998). Creating supportive environments for students with emotional or behavioral disorders. *Effective School Practices, 17*(2), 25–35.

Cheney, D., & Bullis, M. (2004). The school-to-community transition of adolescents with emotional and behavioral disorders. In R. B. Rutherford, M. M. Quinn, & S. R. Mathur (Eds.). *Handbook of research in emotional and behavioral disorders* (pp. 369–384). New York: Guilford.

Cline, D. H. (1990). A legal analysis of policy initiatives to exclude handicapped/disruptive students from special education. *Behavioral Disorders, 15*, 159–173.

Coleman, M., & Vaughn, S. (2000). Reading interventions for students with emotional/behavioral disorders. *Behavioral Disorders, 25*, 93–104.

Colvin, G. (2004). *Managing the cycle of acting-out behavior in the classroom*. Eugene, OR: Behavior Associates.

Cooper, P. (2005). Biology and behaviour: The educational relevance of a "biopsychosocial" perspective. In P. Clough, P. Garner, J. T. Pardeck, & F. K. O. Yuen (Eds.), *Handbook of emotional and behavioural difficulties in education* (pp. 91–105). London: Sage.

Costenbader, V., & Buntaine, R. (1999). Diagnostic discrimination between social maladjustment and emotional disturbance: An empirical study. *Journal of Emotional and Behavioral Disorders, 7*, 1–10.

Council for Exceptional Children (2001). Performance-based Standards. Retrieved June 5, 2001 from www.cec.sped.org/ps/perf_based_stds/index.html.

Coutinho, M. J., Oswald, D. P., Best, A. M., & Forness, S. R. (2002). Gender and socio-demographic factors and the disproportionate identification of minority students as emotionally disturbed. *Behavioral Disorders, 27*, 109–125.

Crockett, J. B., & Kauffman, J. M. (1999). *The least restrictive environment: Its origins and interpretations in special education*. Mahwah, NJ: Lawrence Erlbaum.

Cullinan, D. (2002). *Students with emotional and behavior disorders: An introduction for teachers and other helping professionals*. Upper Saddle River, NJ: Merrill/Prentice-Hall.

Cullinan, D. (2004). Classification and definition of emotional and behavioral disorders. In R. B. Rutherford, M. M. Quinn, & S. R. Mathur (Eds.), *Handbook of research in emotional and behavioral disorders* (pp. 32–53). New York: Guilford.

Duke, D. L., Griesdorn, J., & Kraft, M. (1998, March). *A school of their own: A status check of Virginia's alternative high schools for at-risk students*. Charlottesville, VA: Thomas Jefferson Center for Educational Design.

Duncan, B. B., Forness, S. R., & Hartsough, C. (1995). Students identified as seriously emotionally disturbed in school-based day treatment: Cognitive, psychiatric, and special education characteristics. *Behavioral Disorders, 20*, 238–252.

Edgar, E., & Siegel, S. (1995). Postsecondary scenarios for troubled and troubling youth. In J. M. Kauffman, J. W. Lloyd, D. P. Hallahan, & T. A. Astuto (Eds.), *Issues in educational placement: Students with emotional or behavioral disorders* (pp. 251–283). Hillsdale, NJ: Lawrence Erlbaum.

Epstein, M. H., & Sharma, J. (1997). Behavioral and Emotional Rating Scale (BERS): A strength-based approach to assessment. Austin, TX: Pro-Ed.

Falk, K. B., & Wehby, J. H. (2001). The effects of peer-assisted learning strategies on the beginning reading skills of young children with emotional/behavioral disorders. *Behavioral Disorders, 26,* 344–359.

Farmer, E. M. Z., & Farmer, T. W. (1999). The role of schools in outcomes for youth: Implications for children's mental health services research. *Journal of Child and Family Studies, 8,* 377–396.

Farmer, T. W. (2000). Misconceptions of peer rejection and problem behavior: Understanding aggression in students with mild disabilities. *Remedial and Special Education, 21,* 194–208.

Farmer, T. W., Farmer, E. M. Z., & Gut, D. (1999). Implications of social development research for school based intervention for aggressive youth with emotional and behavioral disorders. *Journal of Emotional and Behavioral Disorders, 7,* 130–136.

Farmer, T. W., Quinn, M. M., Hussey, W., & Holahan, T. (2001). The development of disruptive behavioral disorders and correlated constraints: Implications for intervention. *Behavioral Disorders, 26,* 117–130.

Forness, S. R., & Kavale, K. A. (1997). Defining emotional or behavioral disorders in school and related services. In J. W. Lloyd, E. J. Kame'enui, & D. Chard (Eds.), *Issues in educating students with disabilities* (pp. 45–61). Mahwah, NJ: Lawrence Erlbaum.

Forness, S. R., & Kavale, K. A. (2001). Ignoring the odds: Hazards of not adding the new medical model to special education decisions. *Behavioral Disorders, 26,* 269–281.

Forness, S. R., Kavale, K. A., Sweeney, D. P., & Crenshaw, T. M. (1999). The future of research and practice in behavioral disorders: Psychopharmacology and its school implications. *Behavioral Disorders, 24,* 305–318.

Forness, S. R., & Knitzer, J. (1992). A new proposed definition and terminology to replace "serious emotional disturbance" in Individuals with Disabilities Act. *School Psychology Review, 21,* 12–20.

Freedman, J. (1993). *From cradle to grave: The human face of poverty in America.* New York: Atheneum.

Fuchs, D., Fuchs, L. S., Fernstrom, P., & Hohn, M. (1991). Toward a responsible reintegration of behaviorally disordered students. *Behavioral Disorders, 16,* 133–147.

Furlong, M. J., Morrison, G. M., & Fisher, E. S. (2005). The influences of the school contexts and processes on violence and disruption in American schools. In P. Clough, P. Garner, J. T. Pardeck, & F. K. O. Yuen (Eds.), *Handbook of emotional and behavioural difficulties in education* (pp. 106–120). London: Sage.

Furlong, M. J., Morrison, G. M., & Jimerson, S. (2004). Externalizing behaviors of aggression and violence and the school context. In R. B. Rutherford, M. M. Quinn, & S. R. Mathur (Eds.), *Handbook of research in emotional and behavioral disorders* (pp. 243–261). New York: Guilford.

Garrity, C., Jens, K., Porter, W., Sager, N., & Short-Camilli, C. (1996). Bully-proofing your school: A comprehensive approach. *Reclaiming Youth and Children, 5*(1), 35–39.

Garrity, C., Jens, K., Porter, W., Sager, N., & Short-Camilli, C. (2000). *Bully-proofing your school: A comprehensive approach* (2nd ed.). Longmont, CO: Sopris West.

Godwin, R. (2004, February 2). In my father's footsteps: A thank-you to my big brother. *The Washington Post,* p. C10.

Gresham, F. M., & Kern, L. (2004). Internalizing behavior problems in children and adolescents. In R. B. Rutherford, M. M. Quinn, & S. R. Mathur (Eds.), *Handbook of research in emotional and behavioral disorders* (pp. 262–281). New York: Guilford.

Gresham, F. M., Lane, K. L., McIntyre, L. L., Olson-Tinker, H., Dostra, L., MacMillan, D. M., Lambros, K. M., & Bocian, K. (2001). Risk factors associated with the co-occurrence of hyperactivity-impulsivity-inattention and conduct problems. *Behavioral Disorders, 26,* 189–199.

Hallenbeck, B. A., & Kauffman, J. M. (1995). How does observational learning affect the behavior of students with emotional or behavioral disorders? A review of research. *Journal of Special Education, 29,* 45–71.

Harris, J. R. (1995) Where is the child's environment? A group socialization theory of development. *Psychological Review, 102,* 458–489.

Ialongo, N. S., Vaden-Kiernan, N., & Kellam, S. (1998). Early peer-rejection and aggression: Longitudinal relations with adolescent behavior. *Journal of Developmental and Physical Disabilities, 10,* 199–213.

Ishii-Jordan, S. R. (2000). Behavioral interventions used with diverse students. *Behavioral Disorders, 25,* 299–309.

Jolivette, K., Stichter, J. P., & McCormick, K. M. (2002). Making choices—improving behavior—engaging in learning. *Teaching Exceptional Children, 34*(3), 24–30.

Jones, V., Dohrn, E., & Dunn, C. (2004). *Creating effective programs for students with emotional and behavioral disorders.* Boston: Allyn & Bacon.

Jordan, D., Goldberg, P., & Goldberg, M. (1991). *A guidebook for parents of children with emotional or behavioral disorders.* Minneapolis: Pacer Center.

Kaiser, A. P. (Ed.). (2000). Special issue: Assessing and addressing problems in children enrolled in Head Start. *Behavioral Disorders, 26*(1).

Kamps, D. M., Tankersley, M., & Ellis, C. (2000). Social skills interventions for young at-risk students: A 2-year follow-up study. *Behavioral Disorders, 25,* 310–324.

Kaslow, N. J., Morris, M. K., & Rehm, L. P. (1997). Childhood depression. In R. J. Morris & T. R. Kratochwill (Eds.), *The practice of child therapy* (3rd ed., pp. 48–90). Boston: Allyn & Bacon.

Katsiyannis, A., & Archwamety, T. (1999). Academic remediation/achievement and other factors related to recidivism rates among delinquent youths. *Behavioral Disorders, 24,* 93–101.

Kauffman, J. M. (1999). How we prevent the prevention of emotional and behavioral disorders. *Exceptional Children, 65,* 448–468.

Kauffman, J. M. (2005a). *Characteristics of emotional and behavioral disorders of children and youth* (8th ed.). Upper Saddle River, NJ: Merrill Prentice-Hall.

Kauffman, J. M. (2005b). *Cases in emotional and behavioral disorders of children and youth.* Upper Saddle River, NJ: Merrill Prentice Hall.

Kauffman, J. M. (2005c). How we prevent the prevention of emotional and behavioural difficulties in education. In P. Clough, P. Garner, J. T. Pardeck, & F. K. O. Yuen (Eds.), *Handbook of emotional and behavioural difficulties in education* (pp. 366–376). London: Sage.

Kauffman, J. M., Bantz, J., & McCullough, J. (2002). Separate and better: A special public school class for students with emotional and behavioral disorders. *Exceptionality.*

Kauffman, J. M., Brigham, F. J., & Mock, D. R. (2004). Historical to contemporary perspectives on the field of behavioral disorders. In R. B. Rutherford, M. M. Quinn, & S. R. Mathur (Eds.),

Handbook of research in emotional and behavioral disorders (pp. 15–31). New York: Guilford.

Kauffman, J. M., & Hallenbeck, B. A. (Eds.). (1996). Why we need to preserve specialized placements for students with emotional or behavioral disorders [Special issue]. *Canadian Journal of Special Education, 11*(1).

Kauffman, J. M., & Landrum, T. J. (2006). *Children and youth with emotional and behavioral disorders: A brief history of their education.* Austin, TX: Pro-Ed.

Kauffman, J. M., Lloyd, J. W., Baker, J., & Riedel, T. M. (1995). Inclusion of all students with emotional or behavioral disorders? Let's think again. *Phi Delta Kappan, 76,* 542–546.

Kauffman, J. M., Lloyd, J. W., Hallahan, D. P., & Astuto, T. A. (Eds.). (1995). *Issues in educational placement: Students with emotional and behavioral disorders.* Hillsdale, NJ: Lawrence Erlbaum.

Kauffman, J. M., Mostert, M. P., Trent, S. C., & Pullen, P. L. (2006). *Managing classroom behavior: A reflective case-based approach* (4th ed.) Boston: Allyn & Bacon.

Kauffman, J. M., & Pullen, P. L. (1996). Eight myths about special education. *Focus on Exceptional Children, 28*(5), 1–16.

Kavale, K. A., Forness, S. R., & Mostert, M. P. (2005). Defining emotional or behavioral disorders: The quest for affirmation. In P. Clough, P. Garner, J. T. Pardeck, & F. K. O. Yuen (Eds.), *Handbook of emotional and behavioural difficulties in education* (pp. 38–49). London: Sage.

Kazdin, A. E. (1995). *Conduct disorders in childhood and adolescence* (2nd ed.). Newbury Park, CA: Sage.

Kazdin, A. E. (1997). Conduct disorder. In R. J. Morris & T. R. Kratochwill (Eds.), *The practice of child therapy* (3rd ed., pp. 199–270), Boston: Allyn & Bacon.

Keogh, B. K. (2003). *Temperament in the classroom: Understanding individual differences.* Baltimore: Brookes.

Konopasek, D., & Forness, S. R. (2004). Psychopharmacology in the treatment of emotional and behavioral disorders. In R. B. Rutherford, M. M. Quinn, & S. R. Mathur (Eds.), *Handbook of research in emotional and behavioral disorders* (pp. 352–368). New York: Guilford.

Knowlton, D. (1995). Managing children with oppositional behavior. *Beyond Behavior, 6*(3), 5–10.

Landrum, T. J. (2000). Assessment for eligibility: Issues in identifying students with emotional or behavioral disorders. *Assessment for Effective Intervention, 26*(1), 41–49.

Landrum, T. J., & Kauffman, J. M. (2003). Emotionally disturbed, education of. In J. W. Guthrie (Ed.), *Encyclopedia of education* (2nd ed., pp. 726–728). New York: Macmillan Reference.

Landrum, T. J., Tankersley, M., & Kauffman, J. M. (2003). What's special about special education for students with emotional and behavioral disorders? *The Journal of Special Education, 37,* 148–156.

Lewis, T. (2000). Establishing and promoting disciplinary practices at the classroom and individual student level that ensure safe, effective, and nurturing learning environments. In L. M. Bullock and R. A. Gable (Eds.), *Positive academic and behavioral supports: Creating safe, effective, and nurturing schools for all students.* Reston, VA: Council for Exceptional Children.

Lewis, T. J., & Sugai, G. (1999). Effective behavior support: A systems approach to proactive schoolwide management. *Focus on Exceptional Children, 31*(6), 1–24.

Loeber, R., Green, S. M., Lahey, B. B., Christ, M. A. G., & Frick, P. J. (1992). Developmental sequences in age of onset of disruptive child behaviors. *Journal of Child and Family Studies, 1,* 21–41.

Maag, J. W., & Katsiyannis, A. (1998). Challenges facing successful transition for youths with E/BD. *Behavioral Disorders, 23,* 209–221.

Malmgren, K., Edgar, E., & Neel, R. S. (1998). Postschool status of youths with behavioral disorders. *Behavioral Disorders, 23,* 257–263.

Masia, C. L., Klein, R. G., Storch, E. A., & Corda, B. (2001). School-based behavioral treatment for social anxiety disorder in adolescents: Results of a pilot study. *Journal of the American Academy of Child and Adolescent Psychiatry, 40,* 780–786.

Miller, J. G. (1997). African American males in the criminal justice system. *Phi Delta Kappan, 79,* K1–K12.

Moynihan, D. P. (1995, September 21). "I cannot understand how this could be happening." *Washington Post,* p. A31.

Mueller, M. M., Edwards, R. P., & Trahant, D. (2003). Translating multiple assessment techniques into an intervention selection model for classrooms. *Journal of Applied Behavior Analysis, 36,* 563–573.

Nelson, C. M., & Kauffman, J. M. (1977). Educational programming for secondary school age delinquent and maladjusted pupils. *Behavioral Disorders, 2,* 102–113.

Nelson, C. M., Leone, P. E., & Rutherford, R. B., (2004). Youth delinquency: Prevention and intervention. In R. B. Rutherford, M. M. Quinn, & S. R. Mathur (Eds.), *Handbook of research in emotional and behavioral disorders* (pp. 282–301). New York: Guilford.

O'Mahony, P. (2005). Juvenile delinquency and emotional and behaviorual difficulties in education. In P. Clough, P. Garner, J. T. Pardeck, & F. K. O. Yuen (Eds.), *Handbook of emotional and behavioural difficulties in education* (pp. 142–154). London: Sage.

Osher, D., Cartledge, G., Oswald, D., Sutherland, K. S., Artiles, A. J., & Coutinho, M. (2004). Cultural and linguistic competency and disproportionate representation. In R. B. Rutherford, M. M. Quinn, & S. R. Mathur (Eds.), *Handbook of research in emotional and behavioral disorders* (pp. 54–77). New York: Guilford.

Oswald, D. P., Coutinho, M. J., Best, A. M., & Singh, N. N. (1999). Ethnic representation in special education: The influence of school-related economic and demographic variables. *Journal of Special Education, 32,* 194–206.

Patterson, G. R., Reid, J. B., & Dishion, T. J. (1992). *Antisocial boys.* Eugene, OR: Castalia.

Peacock Hill Working Group. (1991). Problems and promises in special education and related services for children and youth with emotional or behavioral disorders. *Behavioral Disorders, 16,* 299–313.

Presley, J. A., & Hughes, C. (2000). Peers as teachers of anger management to high school students with behavioral disorders. *Behavioral Disorders, 25,* 114–130.

Rhode, G., Jensen, W. R., & Reavis, H. K. (1992). *The tough kid book: Practical classroom management strategies.* Longmont, CO: Sopris West.

Richardson, G. A., McGauhey, P., & Day, N. L. (1995). Epidemiologic considerations. In M. Hersen & R. T. Ammerman (Eds.),

Advanced abnormal child psychology (pp. 37–48). Hillsdale, NJ: Lawrence Erlbaum.

Rogers-Adkinson, D., & Griffith, P. (Eds.). (1999). *Communication disorders and children with psychiatric and behavioral disorders.* San Diego: Singular.

Rutter, M., & Schopler, E. (1987). Autism and pervasive developmental disorders: Concepts and diagnostic issues. *Journal of Autism and Developmental Disabilities, 17,* 159–186.

Sasso, G. M., Conroy, M. A., Stichter, J. P., & Fox, J. J. (2001). Slowing down the bandwagon: The misapplication of functional assessment for students with emotional and behavioral disorders. *Behavioral Disorders, 26,* 282–296.

Serna, L. A., Lambros, K., Nielsen, E., & Forness, S. R. (2000). Head Start children at-risk for emotional or behavioral disorders: Behavioral profiles and clinical implications of a primary prevention program. *Behavioral Disorders, 26,* 70–84.

Shaw, D. S., Owens, E. B., Giovannelli, J., & Winslow, E. B. (2001). Infant and toddler pathways leading to early externalizing disorders. *Journal of the American Academy of Child and Adolescent Psychiatry, 40,* 36–43.

Sheras, P. L. (2001). Depression and suicide in adolescence. In C. E. Walker & M. C. Roberts (Eds.), *Handbook of clinical child psychology* (3rd ed.) (pp. 657–673). New York: Wiley.

Sprague, J., & Walker, H. (2000). Early identification and intervention for youth with antisocial and violent behavior. *Exceptional Children, 66,* 367–379.

Stein, M., & Davis, C. A. (2000). Direct instruction as a positive behavioral support. *Beyond Behavior, 10*(1), 7–12.

Strain, P. S., McConnell, S. R., Carta, J. J., Fowler, S. A., Neisworth, J. T., & Wolery, M. (1992). Behaviorism in early intervention. *Topics in Early Childhood Special Education, 12*(1), 121–141.

Strain, P. S., & Timm, M. A. (2001). Remediation and prevention of aggression: An evaluation of the Regional Intervention Program over a quarter century. *Behavioral Disorders, 26,* 297–313.

Sugai, G., & Horner, R. H. (Ed.). (1999–2000). Special issue: Functional behavioral assessment. *Exceptionality, 8*(3).

Sutherland, K. S., & Wehby, J. H. (2001). Exploring the relationship between increased opportunities to respond to academic requests and the academic and behavioral outcomes of students with EBD. *Remedial and Special Education, 22,* 113–121.

Talbott, E., & Callahan, K. (1997). Antisocial girls and the development of disruptive behavior disorders. In J. W. Lloyd, E. J. Kame'enui, & D. Chard (Eds.), *Issues in educating students with disabilities* (pp. 305–322). Mahwah, NJ: Lawrence Erlbaum.

Tankersley, M., & Landrum, T. J. (1997). Comorbidity of emotional and behavioral disorders. In J. W. Lloyd, E. J. Kame'enui, & D. Chard (Eds.), *Issues in educating students with disabilities* (pp. 153–173). Mahwah, NJ: Lawrence Erlbaum.

Thomas, J. M., & Guskin, K. A. (2001). Disruptive behavior in young children: What does it mean? *Journal of the American Academy of Child and Adolescent Psychiatry, 40,* 44–51.

Timm, M. A. (1993). The Regional Intervention Program: Family treatment by family members. *Behavioral Disorders, 19,* 34–43.

Tolbin, T., & Sprague, J. (1999). Alternative education programs for at-risk youth: Issues, best practice, and recommendations. *Bulletin of the Oregon School Study Council, 42*(4).

U.S. Department of Education. (2000). *Twenty-second annual report to Congress on implementation of the Individuals with Disabilities Education Act.* Washington, DC: Author.

U.S. Department of Health and Human Services. (2001). *Report of the Surgeon General's Conference on Children's Mental Health: A National Action Agenda.* Washington, DC: Author.

Walker, H. M. (1995). *The acting-out child: Coping with classroom disruption.* Longmont, CO: Sopris West.

Walker, H. M., & Bullis, M. (1991). Behavior disorders and the social context of regular class integration: A conceptual dilemma? In J. W. Lloyd, N. N. Singh, & A. C. Repp (Eds.), *The regular education initiative: Alternative perspectives on concepts, issues, and models.* Sycamore, IL: Sycamore Publishing.

Walker, H. M., Forness, S. R., Kauffman, J. M., Epstein, M. H., Gresham, F. M., Nelson, C. M., & Strain, P. S. (1998). Macrosocial validation: Referencing outcomes in behavioral disorders to societal issues and problems. *Behavioral Disorders, 24,* 7–18.

Walker, H. M., Kavanagh, K., Stiller, B., Golly, A., Severson, H., & Feil, E. G. (1998). First Step to Success: An early intervention approach for preventing school antisocial behavior. *Journal of Emotional and Behavioral Disorders, 6,* 66–80.

Walker, H. M., Ramsey, E., & Gresham, F. M. (2003–2004a). Heading off disruption: How early intervention can reduce defiant behavior—and win back teaching time. *American Educator, 27*(4), 6–21.

Walker, H. M., Ramsey, E., & Gresham, F. M. (2003–2004b). How disruptive students escalate hostility and disorder—and how teachers can avoid it. *American Educator, 27*(4), 22–27, 47.

Walker, H. M., Ramsey, E., & Gresham, F. M. (2004). *Antisocial behavior in school: Strategies and best practices* (2nd ed.). Pacific Grove, CA: Brooks/Cole.

Walker, H. M., & Severson, H. H. (1990). *Systematic screening for behavior disorders (SSBD): A multiple gating procedure.* Longmont, CO: Sopris West.

Walker, H. M., Severson, H. H., & Feil, E. G. (1994). *The early screening project: A proven child-find process.* Longmont, CO: Sopris West.

Walker, H. M., & Stieber, S. (1998). Teacher ratings of social skills as longitudinal predictors of long-term arrest status in a sample of at-risk males. *Behavioral Disorders, 23,* 222–230.

Wehby, J. H., Dodge, K. A., & Valente, E. (1993). School behavior of first grade children identified as at-risk for development of conduct problems. *Behavioral Disorders, 19,* 67–78.

White, R. B., & Koorland, M. A. (1996). Curses! What do we do about cursing? *Teaching Exceptional Children, 28,* 48–51.

Wolf, M. M., Braukmann, C. J., & Ramp, K. A. (1987). Serious delinquent behavior as part of a significantly handicapping condition. *Journal of Applied Behavior Analysis, 20,* 347–359.

Wood, F. H. (Ed.). (1990). When we talk with children: The life space interview [Special section]. *Behavioral Disorders, 15,* 110–126.

Yell, M. L., Bradley, R., Katsiyannis, A., & Rozalski, M. E. (2000). Ensuring compliance with the discipline provisions of IDEA '97. *Journal of Special Education Leadership, 13*(1), 3–18.

Yell, M. L., Rozalski, M. E., & Drasgow, E. (2001). Disciplining students with disabilities. *Focus on Exceptional Children, 33*(9), 1–20.

Zanglis, I., Furlong, M. J., & Casas, J. M. (2000). Case study of a community mental health collaborative: Impact on identification of youths with emotional or behavioral disorders. *Behavioral Disorders, 25,* 359–371.

CHAPTER 9

American Speech-Language-Hearing Association. (1991, March). Guidelines for speech-language pathologists serving persons with language, socio-communicative, and/or cognitive-communicative impairments. *ASHA, 33*, 21–25.

American Speech-Language-Hearing Association. (2001). Retrieved September 2001 from http://www.asha.org.

Audet, L. R., & Tankersley, M. (1999). Implications of communication and behavioral disorders for classroom management: Collaborative intervention techniques. In D. Rogers-Adkinson & P. Griffith (Eds.), *Communication disorders and children with psychiatric and behavioral disorders* (pp. 403–440). San Diego: Singular.

Bauman-Waengler, J. (2000). *Articulatory and phonological impairments: A clinical focus.* Boston: Allyn & Bacon.

Bernthal, J. E., & Bankson, N. W. (1998). *Articulation and phonological disorders* (4th ed.). Boston: Allyn & Bacon.

Bernthal, J. E., & Bankson, N. W. (2004). *Articulation and phonological disorders* (5th ed.). Boston: Allyn & Bacon.

Butler, K. G. (Ed.). (1999a). Children's language, behavior, and emotional problems [Special issue]. *Topics in Language Disorders, 19*(2).

Butler, K. G. (Ed.). (1999b). Many voices, many tongues: Accents, dialects, and variations [Special issue]. *Topics in Language Disorders, 19*(4).

Calandrella, A. M., & Wilcox, M. J. (2000). Predicting language outcomes for young prelinguistic children with developmental delay. *Journal of Speech, Language and Hearing Research, 43*, 1061–1071.

Campbell, S. L., Reich, A. R., Klockars, A. J., & McHenry, M. A. (1988). Factors associated with dysphonia in high school cheerleaders. *Journal of Speech and Hearing Disorders, 53*, 175–185.

Cannito, M. P., Yorkston, K. M., & Beukelman, D. R. (Eds.). (1998). *Neuromotor speech disorders: Nature, assessment, and management.* Baltimore: Paul H. Brookes.

Catts, H. W., Fey, M. E., Zhang, X., & Tomblin, J. (2001). Estimating the risk of future reading difficulties in kindergarten children: A research-based model and its clinical implications. *Language, Speech, and Hearing Services in Schools, 32*, 38–50.

Conture, E. G. (2001). *Stuttering: Its nature, diagnosis, and treatment.* Boston: Allyn & Bacon.

Curlee, R. F., & Siegel, G. M. (Eds.). (1997). *Nature and treatment of stuttering: New directions* (2nd ed.). Boston: Allyn & Bacon.

Curlee, R. F., & Yairi, E. (1997). Early intervention with early childhood stuttering: A critical examination of the data. *American Journal of Speech-Language Pathology, 6*, 8–18.

Donahue, M. L., Hartas, D., & Cole, D. (1999). Research on interactions among oral language and emotional/behavioral disorders. In D. Rogers-Adkinson & P. Griffith (Eds.), *Communication disorders and children with psychiatric and behavioral disorders* (pp. 69–97). San Diego: Singular.

Erhen, B. J. (2000). Maintaining a therapeutic focus and sharing responsibility for student success: Keys to in-classroom speech-language services. *Language, Speech, and Hearing in Schools, 31*, 219–229.

Fey, M. E., Catts, H. W., & Larrivee, L. S. (1995). Preparing preschoolers for academic and social challenges of school. In M. E. Fey, J. Windsor, & S. F. Warren (Eds.), *Language intervention: Preschool through the elementary years* (pp. 3–37). Baltimore: Paul H. Brookes.

Foundas, A. L. (2001). The anatomical basis of language. *Topics in Language Disorders, 21*(3), 1–19.

Gillam, R. B., & Hoffman, L. M. (2001). Language assessment during childhood. In D. M. Ruscello (Ed.), *Tests and measurements in speech-language pathology* (pp. 77–117). Boston: Butterworth-Heinemann.

Goldstein, B., & Iglesias, A. (2004). Language and dialectical variations. In J. E. Bernthal & N. W. Bankson (Eds.), *Articulation and phonological disorders* (5th ed., pp. 348–375). Boston: Allyn & Bacon.

Graham, S., Harris, K. R., MacArthur, C., & Schwartz, S. (1998). Writing instruction. In B. Y. L. Wong (Ed.), *Learning about learning disabilities* (2nd ed., pp. 391–424). San Diego: Academic Press.

Guitar, B. (1998). *Stuttering: An integrated approach to its nature and treatment* (2nd ed.). Baltimore: Lippincott Williams & Wilkins.

Hadley, P. A., Simmerman, A., Long, M., & Luna, M. (2000). Facilitating language development for inner-city children: Experimental evaluation of a collaborative, classroom-based intervention. *Language, Speech, and Hearing in Schools, 31*, 280–295.

Hallahan, D. P., Lloyd, J. W., Kauffman, J. M., Weiss, M., & Martinez, E. (2005). *Introduction to learning disabilities* (3rd ed.). Boston: Allyn & Bacon.

Hammer, C. S., & Weiss, A. L. (2000). African American mothers' views of their infants' language development and language-learning environment. *American Journal of Speech-Language Pathology, 9*, 126–140.

Hart, B., & Risley, T. R. (1995). *Meaningful differences in the everyday experience of young American children.* Baltimore: Paul H. Brookes.

Haynes, W. O., & Pindzola, R. H. (1998). *Diagnosis and evaluation in speech pathology* (5th ed.)., Boston: Allyn & Bacon.

Hodson, B. W., & Edwards, M. L. (1997). *Perspectives in applied phonology.* Gaithersburg, MD: Aspen.

Justice, L. M. (2006). *Communication sciences and disorders: An introduction.* Upper Saddle River, NJ: Prentice Hall.

Justice, L. M., & Schuele, C. M. (2004). Phonological awareness: Description, assessment, and intervention. In J. E. Bernthal & N. W. Bankson (Eds.), *Articulation and phonological disorders* (5th ed., pp. 376–411). Boston: Allyn & Bacon.

Kaiser, A. P., Hemmeter, M. L., Ostrosky, M. M., Alpert, C. L., & Hancock, T. B. (1995). The effects of training and individual feedback on parent use of milieu teaching. *Journal of Childhood Communication Disorders, 16*, 39–48.

Kent, R. (2004). Normal aspects of articulation. In J. E. Bernthal & N. W. Bankson (Eds.), *Articulation and phonological disorders* (5th ed., pp. 1–62). Boston: Allyn & Bacon.

Klein, H. B., & Moses, N. (1999). *Intervention planning for adults with communication problems: A guide for clinical practicum and professional practice.* Boston: Allyn & Bacon.

Leonard, L. (2000). *Children with specific language impairment.* Cambridge, MA: MIT Press.

McGregor, K. K. (2000). The development and enhancement of narrative skills in a preschool classroom: Towards a solution to clinician-client mismatch. *American Journal of Speech-Language Pathology, 9*, 55–71.

Nelson, N. W. (1998). *Childhood language disorders in context: Infancy through adolescence* (2nd ed.). Boston: Allyn & Bacon.

Oetting, J. B., & McDonald, J. L. (2001). Nonmainstream dialect use and specific language impairment. *Journal of Speech, Language and Hearing Research, 44,* 207–223.

Owens, R. E., Jr. (2004). *Language disorders: A functional approach to assessment and intervention* (4th ed.). Boston: Allyn & Bacon.

Owens, R. E., Jr., Metz, D. E., & Haas, A. (2000). *Introduction to communication disorders: a life span perspective.* Boston: Allyn & Bacon.

Plante, E., & Beeson, P. M. (1999). *Communication and communication disorders: A clinical introduction.* Boston: Allyn & Bacon.

Prizant, B. M. (1999). Early intervention: Young children with communication and emotional/behavioral problems. In D. Rogers-Adkinson & P. Griffith (Eds.), *Communication disorders and children with psychiatric and behavioral disorders* (pp. 295–342). San Diego: Singular.

Raspberry, W. (2001, August 21). Bi-English education: Low-income children might benefit from early immersion in standards. *Charlottesville Daily Progress,* p. A6.

Robinson, R. L., & Crowe, T. A. (2001). Fluency and voice. In D. M. Ruscello (Ed.), *Tests and measurements in speech-language pathology* (pp. 163–183). Boston: Butterworth-Heinemann.

Rogers-Adkinson, D., & Griffith, P. (Eds.). (1999). *Communication disorders and children with psychiatric and behavioral disorders.* San Diego: Singular.

Ruscello, D. M. (2001). Use of tests and measurements in speech-language pathology: An introduction to diagnosis. In D. M. Ruscello (Ed.), *Tests and measurements in speech-language pathology* (pp. 1–29). Boston: Butterworth-Heinemann.

Snow, C., Burns, M., & Griffin, P. (1998). *Preventing reading difficulties in young children.* Washington, DC: National Academy Press.

Soto, G., Huer, M. B., & Taylor, O. (1997). Multicultural issues. In L. L. Lloyd, D. R. Fuller, & H. H. Arvidson (Eds.), *Augmentative and alternative communication: A handbook of principles and practices* (pp. 406–413). Boston: Allyn & Bacon.

Sowell, T. (1997). *Late-talking children.* New York: Basic Books.

Stothard, S., Snowling, M., Bishop, D., Chipchase, B., & Kaplan, C. (1998). Language impaired preschoolers: A follow-up into adolescence. *Journal of Speech, Language and Hearing Research, 41,* 407–418.

Throneburg, R. N., Calvert, L. K., Sturm, J. J., Paramboukas, A. A., & Paul, P. J. (2000). A comparison of service delivery models: Effects on curricular vocabulary skills in the school setting. *American Journal of Speech-Language Pathology, 9,* 10–20.

Vihman, M. M. (2004). Early phonological development. In J. E. Bernthal & N. W. Bankson (Eds.), *Articulation and phonological disorders* (5th ed., pp. 376–411). Boston: Allyn & Bacon.

Walker, D., Greenwood, C., Hart, B., & Carta, J. (1994). Prediction of school outcomes based on early language production and socioeconomic factors. *Child Development, 65,* 606–621.

Warren, S. F., & Abbaduto, L. (1992). The relation of communication and language development to mental retardation. *American Journal on Mental Retardation, 97,* 125–130.

Williams, A. L. (2001). Phonological assessment of child speech. In D. M. Ruscello (Ed.), *Tests and measurements in speech-language pathology* (pp. 31–76). Boston: Butterworth-Heinemann.

Yairi, E., & Ambrose, N. G. (1999). Early childhood stuttering: Persistency and recovery rates. *Journal of Speech, Language, and Hearing Research, 42,* 1097–1112.

Yoder, P. J., & Warren, S. F. (2001). Relative treatment effects of two prelinguistic communication interventions on language development of toddlers with developmental delays vary by maternal characteristics. *Journal of Speech and Hearing Research, 44,* 224–237.

CHAPTER 10

Acredolo, L., & Goodwyn, S. (2002). *Baby signs: How to talk with your baby before your baby can talk.* Chicago, IL: Contemporary Books.

Aldersley, S. (2002). Least restrictive environment and the courts. *Journal of Deaf Studies and Deaf Education, 7,* 189–199.

Andrews, J. F., Leigh, I. W., & Weiner, M. T. (2004). *Deaf people: Evolving perspectives from psychology, education, and sociology.* Boston: Allyn & Bacon.

Andrews, J. F., & Zmijewski, G. (1997). How parents support home literacy with deaf children. *Early Child Development and Care, 127,* 131–139.

Andrews, J. F., Ferguson, C., Roberts, S., & Hodges, P. (1997). What's up, Billy Jo? Deaf children and bilingual-bicultural instruction in East-Central Texas. *American Annals of the Deaf, 142,* 16–25.

Arnos, K. S. (2002). Genetics and deafness: Impacts on the Deaf community. *Sign Language Studies, 2,* 150–168.

Bell, A. G. (1883). *Memoir upon the formation of a deaf variety of the human race.* New Haven, CT: The National Academy of Sciences.

Blamey, P. J., Sarant, J. Z., Paatsch, L. E., Barry, J. G., Bow, C. P., Wales, R. J., Wright, M., Psarros, C., Rattigan, K., & Tooer, R. (2001). Relationships among speech perception, production, language, hearing loss, and age in children with impaired hearing. *Journal of Speech, Language, and Hearing Research, 44,* 264–285.

Bornstein, M. H., Selmi, A. M., Haynes, O. M., Painter, K. M., & Marx, E. S. (1999). Representational abilities and the hearing status of child/mother dyads. *Child Development, 70,* 833–852.

Brill, R. G., MacNeil, B., & Newman, L. R. (1986). Framework for appropriate programs for deaf children. *American Annals of the Deaf, 131,* 65–77.

Buchino, M. A. (1993). Perceptions of the oldest hearing child of deaf parents. *American Annals of the Deaf, 138,* 40–45.

Cambra, C. (1996). A comparative study of personality descriptors attributed to the deaf, the blind, and individuals with no sensory disability. *American Annals of the Deaf, 141,* 24–28.

Campbell, K. C. M., & Derrick, G. (2001). Otoacoustic emissions. *eMedicine Journal, 2*(7).

Chambers, A. C. (1997). *Has technology been considered? A guide for IEP teams.* Reston, VA: Technology and Media Division/Council of Administrators of Special Education, Council for Exceptional Children.

Charlson, E., Strong, M., & Gold, R. (1992). How successful deaf teenagers experience and cope with isolation. *American Annals of the Deaf, 137,* 261–270.

Council for Exceptional Children (2001). Performance-based standards. Retrieved June 5, 2001 from the World Wide Web: www.cec.sped.org/ps/perf_based_stds/index.html

Easterbrooks, S. (1999). Improving practices for students with hearing impairments. *Exceptional Child, 65,* 537–554.

Elliot, L., Stinson, M., McKee, B., Everhart, V., & Francis, P. (2001). College students' perceptions of the C-Print Speech-to-Text transcription system. *Journal of Deaf Studies and Deaf Education, 6,* 285–298.

Emmorey, K. (2002). *Language, cognition, and the brain: Insights from sign language research.* Mahwah, NJ: Lawrence Erlbaum.

Feldman, H. M., Dollaghan, C. A., Campbell, T. F., Colborn, D. K., Janosky, J., Kurs-Lasky, M., Rockette, H. E., Dale, P. S., & Paradise, J. L. (2003). Parent-reported language skills in relation to otitis media during the first 3 years of life. *Journal of Speech, Language, and Hearing Research, 46,* 273–287.

Gallaudet Research Institute. (2003, January). *Regional and National Summary Report of Data from 2001–2002 Annual Survey of Deaf and Hard of Hearing Children & Youth.* Washington, DC: GRI, Gallaudet University.

Garrick-Duhaney, L. M., & Duhaney, D. C. (2000). Assistive technology: Meeting the needs of learners with disabilities. *Journal of Instructional Media, 27,* 393–401.

Gaustad, M. G., & Kluwin, T. N. (1992). Patterns of communication among deaf and hearing adolescents. In T. N. Kluwin, D. F. Moores, & M. G. Gaustad (Eds.), *Toward effective public school programs for deaf students: Context, process, and outcomes* (pp. 107–128). New York: Teachers College Press.

Goldin-Meadow, S. (2003). *The resilience of language: What gesture creation in deaf children can tell us about how all children learn language.* New York: Psychology Press.

Goodwyn, S. W., Acredolo, L. P., & Brown, C. A. (2000). Impact of symbolic gesturing on early language development. *Journal of Nonverbal Behavior, 24,* 81–103.

Helmuth, L. (2001). From the mouths (and hands) of babes. *Science, 293,* 1758–1759.

Janesick, V. J., & Moores, D. F. (1992). Ethnic and cultural considerations. In T. N. Kluwin, D. F. Moores, & M. G. Gaustad (Eds.), *Toward effective public school programs for deaf students: Context, process, and outcomes* (pp. 49–65). New York: Teachers College Press.

Kaplan, H., Mahshie, J., Mosely, M., Singer, B., & Winston, E. (1993). *Research synthesis on design of effective media, materials, and technology for deaf and hard-of-hearing students* (Tech. Report No. 2). Eugene, OR: National Center to Improve the Tools of Education. (ERIC Document Reproduction Service No. 386 851).

Kluwin, T. N., Stinson, M. S., & Colarossi, G. M. (2002). Social processes and outcomes of in-school contact between deaf and hearing peers. *Journal of Deaf Studies and Deaf Education, 7,* 200–213.

Ladd, P. (2003). *Understanding Deaf culture: In search of Deafhood.* Clevedon, England: Multilingual Matters.

Lane, H. (1984). *When the mind hears: A history of the deaf.* New York: Random House.

Lane, H. (1992). *The mask of benevolence: Disabling the Deaf community.* New York: Knopf.

Lane, H. (2002). Do deaf people have a disability? *Sign Language Studies, 2,* 356–379.

Lane, H., Hoffmeister, R., & Bahan, B. (1996). *A journey into the Deaf world.* San Diego, CA: Dawn Sign Press.

Lederberg, A. R., & Golbach, T. (2002). Parenting stress and social support in hearing mothers of deaf and hearing children:

A longitudinal study. *Journal of Deaf Studies and Deaf Education, 7,* 330–345.

Listening Center at Johns Hopkins. (2004, May 12). Cochlear Implant Candidacy. Retrieved May 20, 2004 from the World Wide Web: www.thelisteningcenter.com/cand1.html.

Lucker, J., Bowen, S., & Carter, K. (2001). Visual teaching strategies for students who are deaf or hard of hearing. *Teaching Exceptional Children, 33*(3), 38–44.

Marschark, M.(2002). *Language development in children who are deaf: A research synthesis.* Alexandria, VA: National Association of State Directors of Special Education (NASDE).

Meadow-Orlans, K. P. (1987). An analysis of the effectiveness of early intervention programs for hearing-impaired children. In M. J. Guralnick & F. C. Bennett (Eds.), *The effectiveness of early intervention for at-risk and handicapped children* (pp. 325–362). New York: Academic Press.

Meadow-Orlans, K. P. (1990). Research on developmental aspects of deafness. In D. F. Moores & K. P. Meadow-Orlans (Eds.), *Educational and developmental aspects of deafness* (pp. 283–298). Washington, DC: Gallaudet University Press.

Meadow-Orlans, K. P., Mertens, D. M., & Sass-Lehrer, M. A. (2003). *Parents and their deaf children: The early years.* Washington, DC: Gallaudet University Press.

Menchel, R. S. (1988). Personal experience with speechreading. *Volta Review, 90*(5), 3–15.

Mitchell, R. E., & Karchmer, M. A. (2004). Chasing the mythical ten percent: Parental hearing status of deaf and hard of hearing students in the United States. *Sign Language Studies, 4,* 138–163.

Moores, D. F. (2002). The law of unexpected consequences. *American Annals of the Deaf, 147,* 84–87.

Mundy, L. (2002, March 31). A world of their own. *Washington Post Magazine,* pp. 22–31.

National Association of the Deaf. (2001, March 26). Newsroom: Captions on TV Not Decreasing. Retrieved May 26, 2004 from the World Wide Web: www.nad.org/infocenter/newsroom/nadnews/NADstatementCaptioning.html.

National Center for Accessible Media. (2004, May 21). Access to Movie Theaters for Patrons who are Deaf, Hard of Hearing, Blind or Visually Impaired. Retrieved May 27, 2004 from the World Wide Web: ncam.wgbh.org/mopix/nowshowing.html.

National Center for Biotechnology Information. (2000, May 1). *Genes and disease: Deafness.* Retrieved May 16, 2004 from the World Wide Web: www.ncbi.nlm.nih.gov/books/bv.fcgi?call= bv.View. ShowSection&rid=gnd.section.123.

Padden, C. A. (1996). Early bilingual lives of Deaf children. In I. Parasnis (Ed.), *Cultural and language diversity and the Deaf experience.* (pp. 99–116). Cambridge, England: Cambridge University Press.

Padden, C., & Humphries, T. (1988). *Deaf in America: Voices from a culture.* Cambridge, MA: Harvard University Press.

Pisha, B., & Coyne, P. (2001). Smart from the start: The promise of Universal Design for Learning. *Remedial and Special Education, 22,* 197–203.

Powers, S. (2003). Influences of student and family factors on academic outcomes of mainstream secondary school deaf students. *Journal of Deaf Studies and Deaf Education, 8,* 57–78.

Prinz, P. M., Strong, M., Kuntze, M., Vincent, M., Friedman, J., Moyers, P., & Helman, E. (1996). A path to literacy through ASL and English for Deaf children. In C. E. Johnson & J. H. V.

Gilbert (Eds.), *Children's language* (Vol. 9, pp. 235–251). Mahwah, NJ: Lawrence Erlbaum.

Quigley, S., Jenne, W., & Phillips, S. (1968). *Deaf students in colleges and universities.* Washington, DC: Alexander Graham Bell Association for the Deaf.

Reagan, T. (1990). Cultural considerations in the education of deaf children. In D. F. Moores & K. P. Meadow-Orlans (Eds.), *Educational and developmental aspects of deafness* (pp. 73–84). Washington, DC: Gallaudet University Press.

Sacks, O. (1989). *Seeing voices: A journey into the world of the deaf.* Berkeley: University of California Press.

Schery, T. K., & Peters, M. L. (2003). Developing auditory learning in children with cochlear implants. *Topics in Language Disorders, 23,* 4–15.

Schirmer, B. R. (2001). *Psychological, social, and educational dimensions of deafness.* Boston: Allyn & Bacon.

Schroedel, J. G., & Geyer, P. D. (2000). Long-term career attainments of deaf and hard of hearing college graduates: Results from a 15-year follow-up survey. *American Annals of the Deaf, 145,* 303–314.

Seal, B. C. (2004). *Best practices in educational interpreting* (2nd ed.). Boston: Allyn & Bacon.

Senghas, A. (2003). Intergenerational influence and ontogenetic development in the emergence of spatial grammar in Nicaraguan Sign Language. *Cognitive Development, 18,* 511–531.

Sheridan, M. (2001). *Inner lives of deaf children: Interviews and analysis.* Washington, DC: Gallaudet University Press.

Siegel, L. (2000). The educational and communication needs of deaf and hard of hearing children: A statement of principle on fundamental educational change. *American Annals of the Deaf, 145,* 64–77.

Siple, L. (1993). Working with the sign language interpreter in your classroom. *College Teaching, 41,* 139–142.

Spencer, P. (2002). Language development of children with cochlear implants. In J. Christiansen & I. Leigh (Eds.), *Cochlear implants in children: Ethics and choices.* Washington, DC: Gallaudet University Press.

Stinson, M. S., & Whitmire, K. (1992). Students' views of their social relationships. In T. N. Kluwin, D. F. Moores, & M. G. Gaustad (Eds.), *Toward effective public school programs for deaf students: Context, process, and outcomes* (pp. 149–174). New York: Teachers College Press.

Stokoe, W. C. (1960). *Sign language structure.* Silver Spring, MD: Linstok Press.

Stokoe, W. C., Casterline, D. C., & Croneberg, C. G. (1976). *A dictionary of American Sign Language on linguistic principles* (2nd ed.). Silver Spring, MD: Linstok Press.

Traxler, C. B. (2000). The Stanford Achievement Test, 9th Edition: National norming and performance standards for deaf and hard-of-hearing students. *Journal of Deaf Studies and Deaf Education, 5,* 337–348.

U.S. Department of Education. (2003). *Twenty-fourth annual report to Congress on the implementation of the Individuals with Disabilities Education Act.* Washington, DC: Author.

Walker, L. A. (1986). *A loss for words: The story of deafness in a family.* New York: Harper & Row.

Wilbur, R. (2000). The use of ASL to support the development of English and literacy. *Journal of Deaf Studies and Deaf Education, 5,* 81–104.

CHAPTER 11

American Foundation for the Blind (2002, November 8). Web developers—Tips & tricks to improve accessibility. Retrieved February 15, 2004 from the World Wide Web: www.afb.org/info_document_view.asp?documentid=1453.

Bailey, J. (2003). Surmounting the Braille reading speed plateau. *Braille Monitor, 46,* 323–325.

Barlow-Brown, F., & Connelly, V. (2002). The role of letter knowledge and phonological awareness in young Braille readers. *Journal of Research in Reading, 25,* 259–270.

Barraga, N. C., & Collins, M. E. (1979). Development of efficiency in visual functioning: Rationale for a comprehensive program. *Journal of Visual Impairment and Blindness, 73,* 121–126.

Barraga, N. C., & Erin, J. N. (2001). *Visual impairments and learning.* (4th ed.). Austin, TX: Pro-Ed.

Berk, L. E. (2005). *Infants and children: Infants through middle childhood* (5th ed.). Boston: Allyn & Bacon.

Blind Babies Foundation. (2002a, September 25). Cortical visual impairment. Retrieved March 6, 2004 from the World Wide Web: www.blindbabies.org/factsheet_cvi.htm.

Blind Babies Foundation. (2002b, September 25). Retinopathy of prematurity. Retrieved March 6, 2004 from the World Wide Web: www.blindbabies.org/factsheet_rop.htm.

Bongers, R. M., Schellingerhout, R., van Grinsven, R., & Smitsman, A. W. (2002). Variables of the touch technique that influence the safety of cane walkers. *Journal of Visual Impairment and Blindness, 96,* 516–531.

Celeste, M. (2002). A survey of motor development for infants and young children with visual impairments. *Journal of Visual Impairment and Blindness, 96,* 169–174.

Chandler, D. L. (2003). People file: To touch the heavens. *Smithsonian, 34*(5), 103–106.

Chen, D. (1996). Parent-infant communication: Early intervention for very young children with visual impairment or hearing loss. *Infants and Young Children, 9*(2), 1–12.

Chen, D. (2001). *Visual impairment in young children: A review of the literature with implications for working with families of diverse cultural and linguistic backgrounds* (CLAS Tech. Rep. No. 7). Champaign, IL: University of Illinois at Urbana-Champaign, Early Childhood Research Institute on Culturally and Linguistically Appropriate Services.

Chen, D., & Dote-Kwan, J. (1999). The preschool years. In K. E. Wolffe (Ed.), *Skills for success: A career education handbook for children and adolescents with visual impairments* (pp. 44–158). New York: AFB Press.

Chong, C. (2000, Fall). Technology, Braille, the Nemeth Code, and jobs. *Future Reflections, 19*(4). Retrieved June 29, 2001 from the World Wide Web: http://www.nfb.org/FR/FR4/FRFA0010.htm

Chong, C. (2004). Appropriate use of the electronic notetaker in school. *Braille Monitor, 47,* 29–31.

Collins, M. E., & Barraga, N. C. (1980). Development of efficiency in visual functioning: An evaluation process. *Journal of Visual Impairment and Blindness, 74,* 93–96.

Corn, A. L., & Koenig, A. J. (1996). Perspectives on low vision. In A. L. Corn & A. J. Koenig (Eds.), *Foundations of low vision: Clinical and functional perspectives* (pp. 3–25). New York: AFB Press.

Corn, A. L., & Koenig, A. J. (2002). Literacy for students with low vision: A framework for delivering instruction. *Journal of Visual Impairment and Blindness, 96,* 305–321.

Corn, A. L., Wall, R. S., Jose, R. T., Bell, J. K., Wilcox, K., & Perez, A. (2002). An initial study of reading and comprehension rates for students who received optical devices. *Journal of Visual Impairment and Blindness, 96,* 322–333.

D'Allura, T. (2002). Enhancing the social interaction skills of preschoolers with visual impairments. *Journal of Visual Impairment and Blindness, 96,* 576–584.

Council for Exceptional Children (2001). Performance-based Standards. Retrieved June 5, 2001 from www.cec.sped.org/ps/perf_based_stds/index.html

Cox, P. R., & Dykes, M. K. (2001). Effective classroom adaptations for students with visual impairments. *Teaching Exceptional Children 33*(6), 68–74.

Dobelle, W. H. (2000). Artificial vision for the blind by connecting a television camera to the visual cortex of the brain. *Journal of the American Society of Artificial Internal Organs, 46,* 3–9.

Ferrell, K. A., & Muir, D. W. (1996). A call to end vision stimulation training. *Journal of Visual Impairment and Blindness, 90,* 364–366.

Fichten, C. S., Judd, D., Tagalakis, V., Amsel, R., & Robillard, K. (1991). Communication cues used by people with and without visual impairments in daily conversations and dating. *Journal of Visual Impairment and Blindness, 85,* 371–378.

Gabias, P. (1992, July). Unique features of guide dogs: Backtracking and homing. *Braille Monitor,* 392–399.

Galati, D., Sini, B., Schmidt, S., & Tinti, C. (2003). Spontaneous facial expressions in congenitally blind and sighted children aged 8–11. *Journal of Visual Impairment and Blindness, 97,* 418–428.

Gillon, G. T., & Young, A. A. (2002). The phonological-awareness skills of children who are blind. *Journal of Visual Impairment and Blindness, 96,* 38–49.

Glaucoma Research Foundation. (2003, July 14). What is glaucoma? Retrieved March 6, 2004 from the World Wide Web: www.glaucoma.org/learn/.

Grice, N. (2002). *Touch the universe: A NASA Braille book of astronomy.* Washington, DC: National Academies Press, Joseph Henry Press.

Groopman, J. (2003, September 29). Annals of Medicine: The bionic eye: Can scientists use electronic implants to help the blind see? *The New Yorker,* pp. 50–54, 67–68.

Harder, A., & Michel, R. (2002). The target-route map: Evaluating its usability for visually impaired persons. *Journal of Visual Impairment and Blindness, 96,* 711–723.

Hill, A. (1997, April). Teaching can travel blind? *Braille Monitor,* 222–225.

Hill, J., & Black, J. (2003). The Miniguide: A new electronic travel device. *Journal of Visual Impairment and Blindness, 97,* 655–656.

Houtenville, A. J. (2003). A comparison of the economic status of working-age persons with visual impairments and those of other groups. *Journal of Visual Impairment and Blindness, 97,* 133–148.

Hull, J. M. (1997). *On sight and insight: A journey into the world of blindness.* Oxford, England: Oneworld Publications.

International Council on English Braille. (2004, February 14). A single Braille code for all English-speaking peoples of the world. Retrieved October 28, 2004 from the World Wide Web: www.iceb.org/ubc.html.

Jernigan, K. (1992, June). Equality, disability, and empowerment. *Braille Monitor,* 292–298.

Jernigan, K. (1994). *If blindness comes.* Baltimore, MD: National Federation of the Blind.

Kleege, G. (1999). *Sight unseen.* New Haven, CT: Yale University Press.

Knott, N. I. (2002). *Teaching orientation and mobility in the schools: An instructor's companion.* New York: American Foundation for the Blind Press.

Koenig, A. J., & Holbrook, M. C. (2000). Ensuring high-quality instruction for students in braille literacy programs. *Journal of Visual Impairment and Blindness, 94,* 677–694.

Kuusisto, S. (1998). *The planet of the blind: A memoir.* New York: Dial Press.

Lansaw, J. (2000, December). Citizenship and the irony at the top of the world. *Braille Monitor,* 963–965.

Leonard, R. (2002). Predictors of job-seeking behavior among persons with visual impairments. *Journal of Visual Impairment and Blindness, 96,* 635–644.

Lewis, S., & Iselin, S. A. (2002). A comparison of the independent living skills of primary students with visual impairments and their sighted peers: A pilot study. *Journal of Visual Impairment and Blindness, 96,* 335–344.

Lewis, V., & Klauber, J. (2002). [Image] [Image] [Image] [Link] [Link] [Link]: Inaccessible Web design from the perspective of a blind librarian. *Library Hi Tech, 20,* 137–140.

Lussenhop, K., & Corn, A. L. (2003). Comparative studies of the reading performance of students with low vision. *RE:view, 34,* 57–69.

Mangold, S. S. (2000, October). Trends in the use of braille contractions in the United States: Implications for UBC decisions. *Braille Monitor,* 813–819.

Maurer, M. (2000, April). Blindness, quotas, and the disadvantages of civil rights. *Braille Monitor,* 287–296.

Maurer, M. (2003). The Federation is attacked for seeking to enhance mobility and safety. *Braille Monitor, 46,* 1–5.

McHugh, E., & Lieberman, L. (2003). The impact of developmental factors on stereotypic rocking of children with visual impairments. *Journal of Visual Impairment and Blindness, 97,* 453–473.

Millar, D. (1996). A consumer's perspective. *Journal of Visual Impairment and Blindness, 90,* 9.

Miller, C. (1999). On the LOOK OUT for functional vision assessment/evaluation. *SEE/HEAR, 4, No. 1.* Retrieved February 20, 2004 from the World Wide Web: www.tsbvi.edu/Outreach/seehear/winter99/fva.htm.

National Federation of the Blind. (2003, July 24,). Blind literacy legislation adopted by states. Retrieved March 14, 2004 from the World Wide Web: www.nfb.org/brailstates.htm.

Ochaita, E., & Huertas, J. A. (1993). Spatial representation by persons who are blind: A study of the effects of learning and development. *Journal of Visual Impairment and Blindness, 87,* 37–41.

Perez-Pereira, M. & Conti-Ramsden, G. (1999). *Language development and social interaction in blind children.* East Sussex, England: Psychology Press, Ltd.

Prevent Blindness America. (1998–2003). Retrieved February 22, 2004 from the World Wide Web: www.preventblindness.org/children/trouble_signs.html.

Rapp, D. W., & Rapp, A. J. (1992). A survey of the current status of visually impaired students in secondary mathematics. *Journal of Visual Impairment and Blindness, 86,* 115–117.

Rumrill, P. D., Roessler, R. T., Battersby-Longden, J. C., & Schuyler, B. R. (1998). Situational assessment of the accommodation needs of employees who are visually impaired. *Journal of Visual Impairment and Blindness, 92,* 42–54.

Rumrill, P. D., Schuyler, B. R., & Longden, J. C. (1997). Profiles of on-the-job accommodations needed by professional employees who are blind. *Journal of Visual Impairment and Blindness, 91,* 66–76.

Ryles, R. (1996). The impact of braille reading skills on employment, income, education, and reading habits. *Journal of Visual Impairment and Blindness, 90,* 219–226.

Schroeder, F. K. (1996). Perceptions of braille usage by legally blind adults. *Journal of Visual Impairment and Blindness, 90,* 210–218.

Schroeder, F. K. (2002). Research and future opportunities for the blind. *Braille Monitor, 45,* 581–586.

Spungin, S. J. (2003). Cannibalism is alive and well in the blindness field. *Journal of Visual Impairment and Blindness, 97,* 69–71.

The Sendero Group. (2000–2003). Sendero Group Shopping Cart: GPS Software v2. Retrieved from March 12, 2004 from the World Wide Web: www.senderogroup.com/shopgps.htm.

The Sendero Group. (2000–2004). Mike's latest perceptions. Retrieved from March 12, 2004 from the World Wide Web: www.senderogroup.com/mikejournal.htm#Q1%202003.

Ulrey, P. (1994). When you meet a guide dog. *RE:view, 26,* 143–144.

Warren, D. H. (1994). *Blindness and children: An individual differences approach.* New York: Cambridge University Press.

Webster, A., & Roe, J. (1998). *Children with visual impairments: Social interaction, language, and learning.* London: Routledge.

Weihenmayer, E. (2001). *Touch the top of the world: A blind man's journey to climb farther than the eye can see.* E. P. Dutton.

Wolffe, K. E., Sacks, S. Z., Corn, A. L., Erin, J. N., Huebner, K. M., & Lewis, S. (2002). Teachers of students with visual impairments: What are they teaching? *Journal of Visual Impairment and Blindness, 96,* 293–303.

Wunder, G. (1993, March). Mobility: Whose responsibility is it? *Braille Monitor,* 567–572.

CHAPTER 12

Adreon, D., & Stella, J. (2001). Transition to middle and high school: Increasing the success of students with Asperger syndrome. *Intervention in School and Clinic, 36,* 266–271.

American Psychiatric Association. (2000). *Diagnostic and statistical manual of mental Disorders* (4th ed., text rev.). Washington, DC: Author.

Asperger, H. (1944). Die autistischen psychopathen im kindersalter. *Archiv für Psychiatrie und Nervenkrankheiten, 117,* 76–136. Translated by U. Frith in U. Frith (Ed.), *Autism and Asperger syndrome* (pp. 37–92). Cambridge, UK: Cambridge University Press, 1991.

Barnhill, G. P. (2001). What is Asperger syndrome? *Intervention in School and Clinic, 36,* 259–265.

Baron-Cohen, S., Leslie, A. M., & Frith, U. (1985). Does the autistic child have a "theory of mind"? *Cognition, 21,* 37–46.

Beale, A. J. (1998). Correspondence. *The Lancet, 351,* 906.

Bedford, H., Booy, R., Dunn, D., DiGuiseppi, C., Gibb, D., Gilbert, R., Logan, S., Peckham, C., Roberts, I., & Tookey, P. (1998). Correspondence. *The Lancet, 351,* 907.

Bell, R. Q., & Harper, L. V. (1977). *Child effects on adults.* Hillsdale, NJ: Lawrence Erlbaum.

Bettelheim, B. (1967). *The empty fortress.* New York: Free Press.

Bleuler, E. (1916). *Lehrbuch der Psychiatrie.* Translated by A. A. Brill (1951). *Textbook of psychiatry.* New York: Dover.

Bock, M. A. (2002, April 30). *The impact of social behavioral learning strategy training on the social interaction skills of eight students with Asperger syndrome* Paper presented at YAI National Institute for People with Disabilities 23rd International Conference on MR/DD, New York.

Bondy, A., & Frost, L. (1994). The Delaware Autistic Program. In S. Harris & J. Handleman (Eds.), *Preschool education for children with autism* (pp. 37–54). Austin, TX: Pro-Ed.

Bondy, A., & Frost, L. (2001). The picture exchange communication system. *Behavior Modification, 25,* 725–744.

Charlop-Christy, M., Carpenter, M., Le, L., LeBlanc, L., & Kellet, K. (2002). Using the Picture Exchange Communication System (PECS) with children with autism: Assessment of PECS acquisition, speech, social-communicative behavior, and problem behavior. *Journal of Applied Behavioral Analysis, 35,* 213–231.

Charlop-Christy, M. H., Schreibman, L., Pierce, K., & Kurtz, P. F. (1998). Childhood autism. In R. J. Morris & T. R. Kratochwill (Eds.), *The practice of child therapy* (3rd ed., pp. 271–389). Boston: Allyn & Bacon.

Chen, R. T., & DeStefano, F. (1998). Vaccine adverse events: Causal or coincidental? *The Lancet, 351,* 611–612.

Courchesne, E., Carper, R., & Akshoomoff, N. (2003). Evidence of brain overgrowth in the first year of life in autism. *Journal of the American Medical Association, 290,* 337–344.

Courchesne, E., Karns, C. M., Davis, H. R., Ziccardi, R., Carper, R. A., Tigue, B. S., Chisum, H. J., Moses, P., Pierce, K., Lord, C., Lincoln, A. J., Pizzo, S., Schreibman, L., Haas, R. H., Akshoomoff, N. A., & Courchesne, R. Y. (2001). Unusual brain growth patterns in early life in patients with autistic disorder. *Neurology, 57,* 245–254.

Eisenberg, L., & Kanner, K. (1956). Early infantile autism, 1943–1955. *American Journal of Orthopsychiatry, 26,* 556–566.

Fombonne, E. (1999). *Epidemiological findings on autism and related disorders.* Paper presented at the First Workshop of the Committee on Educational Interventions for Children with Autism, National Research Council, December 13–14, 1999.

Fombonne, E., Roge, B., Claverie, J., Courty, S., Fremoile, J. (1999). Microcephaly and macrocephaly in autism. *Journal of Autism and Developmental Disorders, 29,* 113–119.

Frith, U. (2003). *Autism: Explaining the enigma* (2nd ed.). Malden, MA: Blackwell Publishing.

Frost, L., & Bondy, A. (2002). *Picture Exchange Communication System training manual* (2nd ed.). Newark, DE: Pyramid Education Products.

Gerhardt, P. F. (2003). Transition support for learners with Asperger syndrome: Toward a successful adulthood. In R. W. Du Charme & T. P. Gullotta (Eds.). *Asperger syndrome: A guide for professionals and families* (pp. 157–171). New York: Kluwer Academic/Plenum Publishing.

Glaeser, B. C., Pierson, M. R., & Fritschmann, N. (2003). Comic Strip Conversations: A positive behavioral support strategy. *Teaching Exceptional Children, 36*(2), 14–19.

Grandin, T. (1995). *Thinking in pictures.* New York: Doubleday.

Hallahan, D. P., Lloyd, J. W., Kauffman, J. M., Weiss, M. P., & Martinez, E. A. (2005). *Learning disabilities: Foundations, char-*

acteristics, and effective teaching (3rd ed.). Boston: Allyn & Bacon.

Hermelin, B. (1976). Coding and the sense modalities. In L. Wing (Ed.), *Early childhood autism.* London: Pergamon.

Herschkowitz, N. (2000). Neurological bases of behavioral development in infancy. *Brain Development, 22,* 411–416.

Hewetson, A. (2002). *The stolen child: Aspects of autism and Asperger syndrome.* Westport, CT: Bergin & Garvey.

Horner, R. H., Albin, R. W., Sprague, J. R., & Todd, A. W. (2000). Positive behavior support. In M. E. Snell & F. Brown (Eds.), *Instruction of students with severe retardation* (5th ed., pp. 207–243). Upper Saddle River, NJ: Prentice-Hall.

Institute of Medicine. (2004). *Immunization Safety Review: Vaccines and Autism.* Washington, DC: National Academies Press.

Kanner, L. (1943). Autistic disturbances of affective contact. *Nervous Child, 2,* 217–250. Reprinted in L. Kanner, *Childhood psychosis: Initial studies and new insights* (pp. 1–43). Washington, DC: V. H. Winston, 1973.

Lainhart, J. E. (2003). Increased rate of head growth during infancy in autism. *Journal of the American Medical Association, 290,* 393–394.

Matson, J. L., Benavidez, D. A., Compton, L. S., Paclwaskyj, T., & Baglio, C. (1996). Behavioral treatment of autistic persons: A review of research from 1980 to the present. *Research in Developmental Disabilities, 7,* 388–451.

McClannahan, L. E., & Krantz, P. J. (1999). *Activity schedules for children with autism: Teaching independent behavior.* Bethesda, MD: Woodbine House.

Mesibov, G. B., Shea, V., & Adams, L. W. (2001). *Understanding Asperger syndrome and high functioning autism.* New York: Kluwer Academic/Plenum Publishing.

Minshew, N. J., Sweeney, J., & Luna, B. Autism as a selective disorder of complex information processing and underdevelopment of neocortical systems. *Molecular Psychiatry, 7*(Suppl. 2), S12–S15.

Mirenda, P. (2003). Toward functional augmentative and alternative communication for students with autism: Manual signs, graphic symbols, and voice output communication aids. *Language, Speech, and Hearing Services in Schools, 34,* 203–216.

Murch, S. H., Anthony, A., Casson, D. H., Malik, M., Berelowitz, M., Dhillon, A. P., Thomson, M. A., Valentine, A., Davies, S. E., & Walker-Smith, J. A. (2004). Retraction of an interpretation. *The Lancet, 363,* 750.

Myles, B. S. (2003). Social skills instruction for children with Asperger syndrome. In R. W. Du Charme & T. P. Gullotta (Eds.). *Asperger syndrome: A guide for professionals and families* (pp. 21–42). New York: Kluwer Academic/Plenum Publishing.

Myles, B. S., & Simpson, R. L. (2001). Understanding the hidden curriculum: An essential social skill for children and youth with Asperger syndrome. *Intervention in School and Clinic, 36,* 279–286.

Myles, B. S., & Simpson, R. L. (2003). *Asperger syndrome: A guide for parents and teachers.* Austin, TX: Pro-Ed.

Nash, J. M. (2002, May 6). The secrets of autism. *Time,* 46–56.

National Research Council. (2001). *Educating children with autism.* Committee on Educational Interventions for Children with Autism. Division of Behavioral and Social Sciences and Education. Washington, DC: National Academy Press.

Ozonoff, S. (1997). Causal mechanisms of autism: Unifying perspectives from an information-processing framework. In D. J.

Cohen & F. R. Volkmar (Eds.), *Handbook of autism and pervasive developmental disorders* (pp. 868–879). New York: John Wiley.

Piven, J. Arndt, S., Bailey, J., & Andreason, N. C. (1996). Regional brain enlargement in autism: a magnetic resonance imaging study. *Journal of the American Academy of Child and Adolescent Psychiatry, 35,* 530–536.

Piven, J., Arndt, S., Bailey, J., Havercamp, S., Andreason, N. C., & Palmer, P. (1995). An MRI study of brain size in autism. *American Journal of Psychiatry, 152,* 1145–1149.

Rogers, M. F., & Myles, B. S. (2001). Using social stories and comic strip conversations to interpret social situations for an adolescent with Asperger syndrome. *Intervention in School and Clinic, 36,* 310–313.

Sacks, O. (1995). *An anthropologist on Mars.* New York: Knopf.

Scheuermann, B., & Webber, J. (2002). *Autism: Teaching does make a difference.* Stamford, CT: Wadsworth Group.

Schuler, A. L. (1995). Thinking in autism: Differences in learning and development. In K. A. Quill (Ed.), *Teaching children with autism: Strategies to enhance communication and socialization* (pp. 11–32). New York: Delmar Publishers.

Schwartz, I., Garfinkle, A., & Bauer, J. (1998). The Picture Exchange Communication System: Communicative outcomes for young children with disabilities. *Topics in Early Childhood Special Education, 18,* 144–159.

Shore, S. (2003). My life with Asperger syndrome. In R. W. Du Charme & T. P. Gullotta (Eds.), *Asperger syndrome: A guide for professionals and families* (pp. 189–209). New York: Kluwer Academic/Plenum Publishing.

Simpson, R. L. (2004). Finding effective intervention and personnel preparation practices for students with autism spectrum disorders. *Exceptional Children, 70,* 135–144.

Simpson, R. L., de Boer-Ott, S. R., & Smith-Myles, B. (2003). Inclusion of learners with autism spectrum disorders in general education settings. *Topics in Language Disorders, 23,* 116–133.

Strock, M. (2004). Autism Spectrum Disorders (Pervasive Developmental Disorders). NIH Publication No. NIH-04-5511, National Institute of Mental Health, National Institutes of Health, U.S. Department of Health and Human Services, Bethesda, MD, 40 pp. Retrieved August 9, 2004 from the World Wide Web: www.nimh.nih.gov/publicat/autism.cfm.

Volkmar, F. R., & Pauls, D. (2003). Autism. *The Lancet, 362,* 1133–1141.

Wing, L. (1981). Asperger syndrome: A clinical account. *Psychological Medicine, 11,* 115–129.

Wakefield, A. J., Murch, S. H., Anthony, A., Linnell, J., Casson, D. M., Malik, M., Berelowitz, M., Dhillon, A. P., Thomson, M. A., Harvey, P., Valentine, A., Davies, S. E., & Walker-Smith, J. A., (1998). Illeal-lymphoid-nodular hyperplasia, non-specific colitis, and pervasive developmental disorder in children. *The Lancet, 351,* 637–641.

Wallin, J. (2004). Visual Supports: PECS. Retrieved August 2004 from the World Wide Web: www.polyxo.com/visualsupport/pecs.html.

Williams, K. (2001). Understanding the student with Asperger syndrome: Guidelines for teachers. *Intervention in School and Clinic, 36,* 287–292.

Wing, L., & Potter, D. (2002). The epidemiology of autistic spectrum disorders: Is prevalence rising? *Mental Retardation & Developmental Disabilities Research Reviews, 8*(3), 151–161.

CHAPTER 13

Adelson, P. D., & Kochanek, P. M. (1998). Head injury in children. *Journal of Child Neurology, 13,* 2–15.

Aitken, S. (2000). Understanding deafblindness. In S. Aitken, M. Buultjens, C. Clark, J. T. Eyre, & L. Pease (Eds.), *Teaching children who are deafblind: Contact, communication, and learning* (pp. 1–34). London: David Fulton Publishers.

Ashley, M. J. (Ed.). (2004). *Traumatic brain injury: Rehabilitative treatment and case management* (2nd ed.). Boca Raton, FL: CRC Press.

Baldwin, V. (1994). *Annual Deaf-Blind Census.* Monmouth: Teaching Research Division. DB-LINK: The National Clearinghouse on Children Who Are Deaf-Blind.

Beukelman, D. R., & Mirenda, P. (1998). *Augmentative and alternative communication: Management of severe communication disorders in children and adults* (2nd ed.). Baltimore: Paul H. Brookes.

Beukelman, D. R., Yorkston, K. M., & Reichle, J. (Eds.). (2000). *Augmentative and alternative communication for adults with acquired neurologic disorders.* Baltimore: Paul H. Brookes.

Bigge, J. L., Best, S. J., & Heller, K. W. (2001). *Teaching individuals with physical, health, or multiple disabilities* (4th ed.). Upper Saddle River, NJ: Prentice Hall.

Boys Town National Research Hospital Genetics Department (2001, February 21). The Collaborative Usher Syndrome Project. Retrieved May 15, 2001 from the World Wide Web: http:/www.boystown.org/btnrh/genetics/usher.htm

Bredekamp, S., & Rosegrant, T. (Eds.). (1992). *Reaching potentials: Appropriate curriculum and assessment for young children.* Washington, DC: National Association for the Education of Young Children.

Browder, D. M., & Bambara, L. M. (2000). Home and community. In M. E. Snell & F. Brown (Eds.), *Instruction of students with severe disabilities* (5th ed., pp. 543–589). Upper Saddle River, NJ: Merrill.

Brown, D. (1996, February). CHARGE. Retrieved May 15, 2001 from the A-Z to Deafblindness on the World Wide Web: http://www.deafblind.com/chargedb.html

Brown, F., & Snell, M. E. (2000). Meaningful assessment. In M. E. Snell & F. Brown (Eds.), *Instruction of students with severe disabilities* (pp. 67–114). Upper Saddle River, NJ: Prentice-Hall.

Cardona, G. W. (2000). Spaghetti talk. In M. Oken-Fried & H. A. Bersani (Eds.), *Speaking up and spelling it out: Personal essays on augmentative and alternative communication* (pp. 237–244). Baltimore: Paul H. Brookes.

CHARGE Syndrome Foundation, Inc. (2001, April 18). Home page. Retrieved May 15, 2001 from the World Wide Web: http://www.chargesyndrome.org/

Chen, D., Alsop, L., Minor, L. (2000). Lessons from Project PLAI in California and Utah: Implications for early intervention services to infants who are deaf-blind and their families. *Deaf-Blind Perspectives, 7*(3), 1–8.

Chen, D., Downing, J., & Rodriguez-Gil, G. (2000/2001). Tactile learning strategies for children who are deaf-blind: Concerns and considerations from Project SALUTE. *Deaf-Blind Perspectives, 8*(2), 1–6.

Christensen, J. R. (1996). Pediatric traumatic brain injury. In A. J. Capute & P. J. Accardo (Eds.), *Developmental disabilities in infancy and childhood: Vol. I. Neurodevelopmental diagnosis and treatment* (2nd ed., pp. 245–260). Baltimore: Paul H. Brookes.

Council for Exceptional Children. (2001). Traumatic brain injury: The silent epidemic. *CEC Today, 7*(7), 1, 5, 15.

Crimmins, C. (2000). *Where is the mango princess?* New York: Knopf.

Dell Orto, A. E., & Power, P. W. (2000). *Brain injury and the family: A life and living perspective* (2nd ed.). Washington, DC: CRC Press.

DePompei, R., & Tyler, J. (2004). Children and adolescents: Practical strategies for school participation. In M. J. Ashley (Ed.), *Traumatic brain injury: Rehabilitative treatment and case management* (2nd ed., pp. 559–580). Boca Raton, FL: CRC Press.

Division for Early Childhood. (1993). DEC position statement on inclusion. *DEC Communicator, 19*(4), 4.

Dykens, E. M., Hodapp, R. M., & Finucane, B. M. (2000). *Genetics and mental retardation syndromes: A new look at behavior and interventions.* Baltimore: Paul H. Brookes.

Families and Disability Newsletter. (2001, June). Positive behavioral support (PBS). Lawrence, KS: University of Kansas Life Span Institute Beach Center on Families and Disability.

Featherly, C. (2000). Life with cerebral palsy. In M. Oken-Fried & H. A. Bersani (Eds.), *Speaking up and spelling it out: Personal essays on augmentative and alternative communication* (pp. 189–193). Baltimore: Paul H. Brookes.

Ford, J., & Fredericks, B. (1995). Perceptions of inclusion by parents of children who are deaf-blind. In N. G. Haring & L. T. Romer (Eds.), *Welcoming students who are deaf-blind into typical classrooms: Facilitating school participation, learning, and friendships* (pp. 37–53). Baltimore: Paul H. Brookes.

Franklin, P., & Bourquin, E. (2000). Picture this: A pilot study for improving street crossings for deaf-blind travelers. *RE:view, 31,* 173–179.

Fraser, R. T., & Clemmons, D. C. (Eds.). (2000). *Traumatic brain injury rehabilitation: Practical, vocational, neuropsychological, and psychotherapy interventions.* Boca Raton, FL: CRC Press.

Freeberg, E. (2001). *The education of Laura Bridgman: First deaf and blind person to learn language.* Cambridge, MA: Harvard University Press.

Gense, D. J., & Gense, M. (1999). The importance of orientation and mobility skills for students who are deaf-blind. Retrieved May 15, 2001 from the DB-LINK Web site on the World Wide Web: www.tr.wou.edu/dblink/o&m2.htm

Giangreco, M. F., Cloninger, C. J., & Iverson, V. S. (1993). *Choosing options and accommodations for children: A guide to planning inclusive education.* Baltimore: Paul H. Brookes.

Hall, B. D. (1979). Choanal atresia and associated multiple anomalies. *Journal of Pediatrics, 95,* 395–398.

Hembree, R. (2000). National deaf-blind child count summary: December 1, 1999 count. Monmouth, OR: National Technical Assistance Consortium for Children and Young Adults who are Deaf-Blind (NTAC), Teaching Research Division, Western Oregon University.

Hodges, L. (2000). Effective teaching and learning. In S. Aitken, M. Buultjens, C. Clark, J. T. Eyre, & L. Pease (Eds.), *Teaching children who are deafblind: Contact, communication, and learning* (pp. 167–199). London: David Fulton Publishers.

Horner, R. H., Albin, R. W., Sprague, J. R., & Todd, A. W. (2000). Positive behavior support. In M. E. Snell & F. Brown (Eds.),

Instruction of students with severe disabilities (pp. 207–243). Upper Saddle River, NJ: Prentice-Hall.

Horner, R. H., Vaughn, B. J., Day, H. M., & Ard, W. R. (1996). The relationship between setting events and problem behavior: Expanding our understanding of behavioral supports. In L. K. Kogel, R. L. Kogel, & G. Dunlap (Eds.). *Positive behavioral support: Including people with difficult behavior in the community* (pp. 381–402). Baltimore: Paul H. Brookes.

Janssen, M. J., Riksen-Walraven, J. M., & van Dijk, J. P. M. (2004). Enhancing the interactive competence of deafblind children: Do intervention effects endure? *Journal of Developmental and Physical Disabilities, 16,* 73–94.

Kauffman, J. M. (2001). *Characteristics of emotional and behavioral disorders of children and youth* (7th ed.). Upper Saddle River, NJ: Prentice-Hall.

Kauffman, J. M. (2002). *Education deform: Bright people sometimes say stupid things about education.* Lanham, MD: Scarecrow Education.

Kauffman, J. M., & Hallahan, D. P. (2005). *Special education: What it is and why we need it.* Boston: Allyn & Bacon.

Kauffman, J. M., Mostert, M. P., Trent, S. C., & Pullen, D. (2001). *Managing classroom behavior: A reflective case-based approach* (4th ed.) Boston: Allyn & Bacon.

Kennedy, C. H., Meyer, K. A., Knowles, T., & Shukla, S. (2000). Analyzing the multiple functions of stereotypical behavior for students with autism: Implications for assessment and treatment. *Journal of Applied Behavior Analysis, 33,* 559–571.

Klein, M. D., Chen, D., & Haney, M. (2000). *Promoting learning through active interaction: A guide to early communication for young children who have multiple disabilities.* Baltimore: Paul H. Brookes.

Kloepfer, H. W., Laguaite, J. K., & McLaurin, J. W. (1996). The hereditary syndrome of congenital deafness and retinitis pigmentosa (Usher's syndrome). *Laryngoscope, 76,* 850–862.

Kogel, L. K., Kogel, R. L., & Dunlap, G. (1996). *Positive behavioral support: Including people with difficult behavior in the community.* Baltimore: Paul H. Brookes.

Light, R., McCleary, C., Asarnow, R., Zaucha, K., & Lewis, R. (1998). Mild closed-head injury in children and adolescents: Behavior problems and academic outcomes. *Journal of Consulting and Clinical Psychology, 66,* 1023–1027.

Lloyd, L. L., Fuller, D. R., & Arvidson, H. H. (Eds.). (1997). *Augmentative and alternative communication: A handbook of principles and practices.* Boston: Allyn & Bacon.

Loncke, F. (2001). Augmentative and alternative communication in the 21st century. *Augmentative and Alternative Communication, 17,* 61.

Marvin, C. A., Beukelman, D. R., Brockhaus, J., & Kast, L. (1994). "What are you talking about?" Semantic analysis of preschool children's conversational topics in home and preschool settings. *Augmentative and Alternative Communication, 10,* 75–86.

McCord, B. E., Thomson, R. J., & Iwata, B. A. (2001). Functional analysis and treatment of self-injury associated with transition. *Journal of Applied Behavior Analysis, 34,* 195–210.

McDonald, S., Togher, L., & Code, C. (Eds.). (1999a). *Communication disorders following traumatic brain injury.* East Sussex, UK: Psychology Press.

McDonald, S., Togher, L., & Code, C. (1999b). The nature of traumatic brain injury: Basic features and neuropsychological consequences. In S. McDonald, L. Togher, & C. Code (Eds.),

Communication disorders following traumatic brain injury (pp. 19–54). East Sussex, UK: Psychology Press.

McLean, M. E., & Odom, S. L. (1996). Establishing recommended practices in early intervention/early childhood special education. In S. L. Odom & M. E. McLean (Eds.), *Early intervention/early childhood special education: Recommended practices* (pp. 1–22). Austin, TX: Pro-Ed.

Melancon, F. (2000). A group of students with Usher syndrome in south Louisiana. *Deaf-Blind Perspectives, 8*(1), 1–3.

Miles, B. (1998). Overview of deaf-blindness. Retrieved May 15, 2001 from the DB-LINK Web site on the World Wide Web: www.tr.wou.edu/dblink/Overview2.htm.

Miles, B. (1999, March 9). Talking the language of the hands. Retrieved June 1, 2001 from the DB-LINK Web site on the World Wide Web: www.tr.wou.edu/dblink/hands2.htm.

Miner, I., & Cioffi, J. (1999, October 25). Usher syndrome in the school setting. Retrieved May 15, 2001 from the DB-LINK Web site on the World Wide Web: www.tr.wou.edu/dblink/usherfulltext.htm.

Moon, M. S., & Inge, K. (2000). Vocational preparation and transition. In M. E. Snell & F. Brown (Eds.), *Instruction of students with severe disabilities* (5th ed., pp. 591–628). Upper Saddle River, NJ: Merrill.

Moss, K., & Hagood, L. (1995, January). Teaching strategies and content modifications for the child with deaf-blindness. *PS News.* Retrieved June 20, 2001 from www.tsbvi.edu/outreach/seehear/archive/strategies.html

Mostert, M. P. (1998). *Interprofessional collaboration in schools.* Boston: Allyn & Bacon.

Mostert, M. P. (2001). Facilitated communication since 1995: A review of published studies. *Journal of Autism and Developmental Disorders, 31,* 287–313.

Mount, B., & Zwernik, K. (1988). *It's never too early; it's never too late.* St. Paul, MN: Metropolitan Council.

National Information Clearinghouse On Children Who Are Deaf-Blind. (2001, May 18). State definitions of deaf-blindness. Retrieved June 9, 2001 from the DB-LINK website on the World Wide Web: www.tr.wosc.osshe.edu/dblink/data/definitions.htm

National Research Council. (2001). *Educating children with autism.* Washington, DC: National Academy Press.

Nelson, N. W. (1998). *Childhood language disorders in context: Infancy through adolescence* (2nd ed.). Boston: Allyn & Bacon.

Odom, S. L., & McLean, M. E. (Eds.), (1996). *Early intervention/early childhood special education: Recommended practices.* Austin, TX: Pro-Ed.

Oken-Fried, M., & Bersani, H. A. (Eds.). (2000). *Speaking up and spelling it out: Personal essays on augmentative and alternative communication.* Baltimore: Paul H. Brookes.

Oley, C. A. (2001). CHARGE association. In S. B. Cassidy & J. E. Allanson (Eds.), *Management of genetic syndromes* (pp. 71–84). New York: Wiley-Liss.

Pease, L. (2000). Creating a communicating environment. In S. Aitken, M. Buultjens, C. Clark, J. T. Eyre, & L. Pease (Eds.), *Teaching children who are deafblind: Contact, communication, and learning* (pp. 35–82). London: David Fulton Publishers.

Persel, C. S., & Persel, C. H. (2004). The use of applied behavior analysis: Traumatic brain injury rehabilitation. In M. J. Ashley (Ed.), *Traumatic brain injury: Rehabilitative treatment and case management* (2nd ed., pp. 403–453). Boca Raton, FL: CRC Press.

Rapp, J. T., Miltenberger, R. G., Galensky, T. L., Ellingson, S. A., & Long, E. S. (1999). A functional analysis of hair-pulling. *Journal of Applied Behavior Analysis, 32,* 329–337.

Sandall, S., McLean, M. E., & Smith, B. J. (Eds.). (2000). *DEC recommended practices in early intervention/early childhood special education.* Longmont, CO: Sopris West.

Savage, R. C. (1988). *Introduction to educational issues for students who have suffered traumatic brain injury. An educator's manual: What educators need to know about students with traumatic brain injury.* Southborough, MA: Author.

Savage, R. C., & Wolcott, G. F. (1994). (Eds.). *Educational dimensions of acquired brain injury.* Austin, TX: Pro-Ed.

Scheetz, N. A. (2001). *Orientation to deafness* (2nd ed.). Boston: Allyn & Bacon.

Schlosser, R. W., & Raghenvendra, P. (2004). Evidence-based practice in augmentative and alternative communication. *Augmentative and Alternative Communication, 20,* 1–21.

Snell, M. E. (2004). What if your child lacks needed communication services and supports? *Exceptional Parent, 34*(2), 41–44.

Strain, P. S., Smith, B. J., & McWilliam, R. A. (1996). The widespread adoption of service delivery recommendations: A systems change perspective. In S. L. Odom & M. E. McLean (Eds.), *Early intervention/early childhood special education: Recommended practices* (pp. 101–123). Austin, TX: Pro-Ed.

Thompson, R. H., & Iwata, B. A. (2001). A descriptive analysis of social consequences following problem behavior. *Journal of Applied Behavior Analysis, 34,* 169–178.

Tyler, J. S., & Mira, M. P. (1999). *Traumatic brain injury in children and adolescents: A sourcebook for teachers and other school personnel* (2nd ed.). Austin, TX: Pro-Ed.

U.S. Department of Education (1999, March 12). Assistance to the States for the Education of Children with Disabilities and the Early Intervention Program for Infants and Toddlers with Disabilities: Final Regulations. *Federal Register, 64*(48), 12422.

U.S. Office of Special Education Programs. (1998). *Positive behavioral support: Helping students with challenging behaviors succeed.* Reston, VA: ERIC/OSEP Special Project, the ERIC Clearinghouse on Disabilities and Gifted Education, the Council for Exceptional Children.

Vandercook, T., York, J., & Forest, M. (1989). The McGill Action Planning System (MAPS): A strategy for building the vision. *Journal of the Association for Persons with Severe Handicaps, 14,* 205–215.

Walther-Thomas, C., Korinek, L., McLaughlin, V. L., & Williams, B. T. (2000). *Collaboration for inclusive education: Developing successful programs.* Boston: Allyn & Bacon.

Wehmeyer, M. (1992). Self-determination and the education of students with mental retardation. *Education and Training in Mental Retardation, 27,* 303–314.

Westling, D. L., & Fox, L. (2000). *Teaching students with severe disabilities* (2nd ed.). Upper Saddle River, NJ: Merrill.

Worsdell, A. S., Iwata, B. A., Conners, J., Kahng, S. W. & R. H. (2000). Relative influences of establishing operations and reinforcement contingencies on selfinjurious behavior during functional analysis. *Journal of Applied Behavior Analysis, 33,* 451–461.

Yoder, D. E. (2001). Having my say. *Augmentative and Alternative Communication, 17,* 2–10.

CHAPTER 14

Ainsa, P. (2000). *Teaching children with AIDS.* Lampeter, Ceredigion, Wales, UK: Edwin Mellen Press.

Andersson, C., & Mattson, E. (2001). Adults with cerebral palsy: A survey describing problems, needs, and resources, with special emphasis on locomotion. *Developmental Medicine and Child Neurology, 43,* 76–82.

Archibald, S. L., Fennema-Notestine, C., Gamst, A., Riley, E. P., Mattson, S. N., & Jernigan, T. L. (2001). Brain dysmorphology in individuals with prenatal alcohol exposure. *Developmental Medicine and Child Neurology, 43,* 148–154.

Auxter, D., Pyfer, J., & Huettig, C. (2001). *Principles and methods of adapted physical education* (9th ed.). Boston, MA: McGraw Hill.

Avoli, M., Rogawski, M. A., & Avanzini, G. (2001). Generalized epileptic disorders: An update. *Epilepsia, 42,* 445–457.

Ayala, G. F., Elia, M., Cornaggia, C. M., & Trimble, M. M. (Eds.). (2001). Epilepsy and learning disabilities. *Epilepsia, 42*(Suppl. 1).

Bartonek, A., & Saraste, H. (2001). Factors influencing ambulation in myelomeningocele: A cross-sectional study. *Developmental Medicine and Child Neurology, 43,* 253–260.

Batshaw, M. L., & Perret, Y. M. (1986). *Children with handicaps: A medical primer.* Baltimore: Paul H. Brookes.

Baumeister, A. A., Kupstas, F., & Klindworth, L. M. (1990). New morbidity: Implications for prevention of children's disabilities. *Exceptionality, 1,* 1–16.

Bax, M. (2001). Editorial: What's in a name? *Developmental Medicine and Child Neurology, 43,* 75.

Besag, F. M. C. (1995). Epilepsy, learning, and behavior in children. *Epilepsia, 36,* 58–63.

Bigge, J. L., Best, S. J., & Heller, K. W. (2001). *Teaching individuals with physical, health, or multiple disabilities* (4th ed.). Upper Saddle River, NJ: Merrill/Prentice-Hall.

Blum, R. W. (1992). Chronic illness and disability in adolescence. *Journal of Adolescent Health, 13,* 364–368.

Bottos, M., Feliciangeli, A., Sciuto, L., Gericke, C., & Vianello, A. (2001). Functional status of adults with cerebral palsy and implications for treatment of children. *Developmental Medicine and Child Neurology, 43,* 516–528.

Brown, R. T. (1993). An introduction to the special series: Pediatric chronic illness. *Journal of Learning Disabilities, 26,* 4–6.

Bullock, C. C., & Mahon, M. J. (2000). *Introduction to recreation services for people with disabilities: A person-centered approach.* Champaign, IL: Sagamore.

Capute, A. J., & Accardo, P. J. (Eds.). (1996a). *Developmental disabilities in infancy and childhood: Vol. 1. Neurodevelopmental diagnosis and treatment* (2nd ed.). Baltimore: Paul H. Brookes.

Capute, A. J., & Accardo, P. J. (Eds.). (1996b). *Developmental disabilities in infancy and childhood: Vol. 2. The spectrum of developmental disabilities* (2nd ed.). Baltimore: Paul H. Brookes.

Closs, A. (Ed.). (2000). *The education of children with medical conditions.* London: David Fulton.

Coulter, D. L. (1993). Epilepsy and mental retardation: An overview. *American Journal on Mental Retardation, 98,* 1–11.

Council for Exceptional Children (2001). Performance-based Standards. Retrieved June 5, 2001 from www.cec.sped.org/ps/perf_based_stds/index.html.

Cowden, A. J., & Funkhouser, E. (2001). Adolescent pregnancy, infant mortality, and source of payment for birth: Alabama residential live births, 1991–1994. *Journal of Adolescent Health, 29,* 37–45.

DeFord, S. (1998, July 26). High tech for the disabled. *Washington Post Education Review, 4,* 30.

Earley, T. (2000). *Jim the Boy* (pp. 203–205). Boston: Little, Brown.

Engel, J. (1995). Concepts of epilepsy. *Epilepsia, 36,* 23–29.

Girvin, J. P. (1992). Is epilepsy a progressive disorder? *Journal of Epilepsy, 5,* 94–104.

Gouvier, W. D., Brown, L. M., Prestholdt, P. H., Hayes, J. S., & Apostolas, G. (1995). A survey of common misconceptions about epilepsy *Rehabilitation Psychology, 40,* 51–59.

Hanson, M. J. (Ed.). (1996). *A typical infant development* (2nd ed.). Austin TX: Pro-Ed.

Heller, K. W., Alberto, P. A., Forney, P. E., & Schwartzman, M. N. (1996). *Understanding physical, sensory, and health impairments: Characteristics and educational implications.* Pacific Grove, CA: Brooks/Cole.

Heller, K. W., Alberto, P. A., & Meagher, T. M. (1996). The impact of physical impairments on academic performance. *Journal of Developmental and Physical Disabilities, 8,* 233–245.

Karnish, K., Bruder, M., & Rainforth, B. (1995). A comparison of physical therapy in two school based treatment contexts. *Physical and Occupational Therapy in Pediatrics, 15*(4), 1–25.

Leaman, O. (2000). Schools and death. In A. Closs (Ed.), *The education of children with medical conditions* (pp. 155–168). London: David Fulton.

Lerner, J. W., Lowenthal, B., & Egan, R. (1998). *Preschool children with special needs: Children at risk, children with disabilities.* Boston: Allyn & Bacon.

Lindsey, J. E. (Ed.). (2000). *Technology and exceptional individuals* (3rd ed.). Austin, TX: Pro-Ed.

Llewellyn, A., & Chung, M. C. (1997). The self-esteem of children with physical disabilities—Problems and dilemmas of research. *Journal of Developmental and Physical Disabilities, 9,* 265–275.

Magill-Evans, J., Darrah, J., Pain, K., Adkins, R., & Kratochvil, M. (2001). Are families with adolescents and young adults with cerebral palsy the same as other families? *Developmental Medicine and Child Neurology, 43,* 466–472.

Michael, R. J. (1995). *The educator's guide to students with epilepsy.* Springfield, IL: Charles C. Thomas.

Moore, J. (1985). Technology is not magic. *Exceptional Parent, 15*(7), 41–42.

Morningstar, M. E., Turnbull, H. R., Lattin, D. L., Umbarger, G. T., Reichard, A., & Moberly, R. (2001). Students supported by medical technology: Making the transition from school to adult life. *Journal of Developmental and Physical Disabilities, 13,* 229–259.

Murphy, D. A., Roberts, K., & Hoffman, D. (2002). Stigma and ostracism associated with HIV/AIDS children carrying the secret of their mothers' HIV + serostatus. *Journal of Child and Family Studies, 11,* 191–202.

Nabors, L. A., & Larson, E. R. (2002). The effects of brief interventions on children's playmate preferences for a child sitting in a wheelchair. *Journal of Developmental and Physical Disabilities, 14,* 403–413.

Nabors, L. A., & Lehmkuhl, H. D. (2004). Children with chronic medical conditions: Recommendations for school mental health

clinicians. *Journal of Developmental and Physical Disabilities, 16,* 1–19.

Olrick, J. T., Pianta, R. C., & Marvin, R. S. (2002). Mother's and father's responses to signals of children with cerebral palsy during feeding. *Journal of Developmental and Physical Disabilities, 14,* 1–17.

Parra, J., Augustijn, P. B., Geerts, Y., & Boas, W. (2001). Classification of epileptic seizures: a comparison of two systems. *Epilepsia, 42,* 476–482.

Pless, I. B. (Ed.). (1994). *The epidemiology of childhood disorders.* New York: Oxford University Press.

Rogers, A. S. (2001). HIV research in American youth. *Journal of Adolescent Health, 29*(Suppl. 3S), 1–4.

Shelter News. (2001, Fall). Battering and teen pregnancy: A connection too real to ignore. Charlottesville, VA: Shelter for Help in Emergency.

Singh, D. K. (2003). Families of children with spina bifida: A review. *Journal of Developmental and Physical Disabilities, 15,* 37–55.

Spiegel, G. L., Cutler, S. K., & Yetter, C. I. (1996). What every teacher should know about epilepsy. *Intervention in School and Clinic, 32,* 34–38.

Szabo, J. L. (2000). Maddie's story: Inclusion through physical and occupational therapy. *Teaching Exceptional Children, 33*(2), 12–18.

Tyler, J. S., & Colson, S. (1994). Common pediatric disabilities: Medical aspects and educational implications. *Focus on Exceptional Children, 27*(4), 1–16.

Vig, S., & Kaminer, R. (2002). Maltreatment and developmental disabilities in children. *Journal of Developmental and Physical Disabilities, 14,* 371–386.

Vining, E. P. G., & Freeman, J. M. (1996). Epilepsy and developmental disabilities. In A. J. Capute & P. J. Accardo (Eds.), *Developmental disabilities in infancy and childhood: Vol. 2. The spectrum of developmental disabilities* (2nd ed., pp. 511–520). Baltimore: Paul H. Brookes.

Wolman, C., Garwick, A., Kohrman, C., & Blum, R. (2001). Parents' wishes and expectations for children with chronic conditions. *Journal of Developmental and Physical Disabilities, 13,* 261–277.

CHAPTER 15

Amabile, T. M. (2001). Beyond talent: John Irving and the passionate craft of creativity. *American Psychologist, 56,* 333–336.

Assouline, S., & Lupkowski-Shoplik, A. (2003). *Developing mathematical talent: A guide for challenging and educating gifted students.* Waco, TX: Prufrock Press.

Baum, S. M., Olenchak, F. R., & Owen, S. V. (1998). Gifted students with attention deficits: Fact and/or fiction? Or, can we see the forest for the trees? *Gifted Child Quarterly, 42,* 96–104.

Borland, J. H. (1997). The construct of giftedness. *Peabody Journal of Education, 72*(3&4), 6–20.

Borland, J. H. (2004). *Issues and practices in the identification and education of gifted students from under-represented groups.* Storrs, CT: National Research Center on the Gifted and Talented.

Borland, J. H., Schnur, R., & Wright, L. (2000). Economically disadvantaged students in a school for the academically gifted: A postpositivist inquiry into individual and family adjustment. *Gifted Child Quarterly, 44,* 13–32.

Borland, J. H., & Wright, L. (2000). Identifying and educating poor and under-represented gifted students. In K. A. Heller, F. J. Monks, R. J. Sternberg, & R. F. Subotnik (Eds.), *International handbook of giftedness and talent* (2nd ed., pp. 587–594). New York: Pergamon.

Burge, K. (1998, April). Prodigies. *U.S. Airways Attache*, 80–87.

Callahan, C. M. (1991). An update on gifted females. *Journal for the Education of the Gifted, 14*, 284–311.

Callahan, C. M. (1997). The construct of talent. *Peabody Journal of Education, 72*(3&4), 21–35.

Callahan, C. M. (2000). Evaluation as a critical component of program development and implementation. In K. A. Heller, F. J. Monks, R. J. Sternberg, & R. F. Subotnik (Eds.), *International handbook of giftedness and talent* (2nd ed., pp. 537–548). New York: Pergamon.

Callahan, C. M. (2001). Evaluating learner and program outcomes in gifted education. In F. A. Karnes & S. M. Bean (Eds.), *Methods and materials for teaching the gifted* (pp. 253–298) Waco, TX: Prufrock Press.

Callahan, C. M. (2003). *Advanced placement and international baccalaureate programs for talented students in American high schools: A focus on science and mathematics*. Storrs, CT: National Research Center on the Gifted and Talented.

Clark, B. (1997). *Growing up gifted: Developing the potential of children at home and at school* (5th ed.). Upper Saddle River, NJ: Prentice-Hall.

Cline, S., & Hegeman, K. (2001). Gifted children with disabilities. *Gifted Child Today, 24*(3), 16–24.

Colangelo, N., & Assouline, S. G. (2000). Counseling gifted students. In K. A. Heller, F. J. Monks, R. J. Sternberg, & R. F. Subotnik (Eds.), *International handbook of giftedness and talent* (2nd ed., pp. 595–608). New York: Pergamon.

Coleman, L. J., & Cross, T. L. (2000). Social-emotional development and the personal experience of giftedness. In K. A. Heller, F. J. Monks, R. J. Sternberg, & R. F. Subotnik (Eds.), *International handbook of giftedness and talent* (2nd ed., pp. 203–212). New York: Pergamon.

Council for Exceptional Children (2001). Performance-based Standards. Retrieved June 5, 2001 from www.cec.sped.org/ps/perf_based_stds/index.html

Cropper, C. (1998). Fostering parental involvement in the education of the gifted minority student. *Gifted Child Today, 21*(1), 20–24, 46.

Cross, T. L. (1997). Psychological and social aspects of educating gifted students. *Peabody Journal of Education, 72*(3&4), 180–200.

Dale, E. J. (2000). Technology for individuals with gifts and talents. In J. E. Lindsey (Ed.), *Technology and exceptional individuals* (3rd ed., pp. 375–407). Austin, TX: Pro-Ed.

De Hahn, E. L. H. (2000). Cross-cultural studies in gifted education. In K. A. Heller, F. J. Monks, R. J. Sternberg, & R. F. Subotnik (Eds.), *International handbook of giftedness and talent* (2nd ed., pp. 549–561). New York: Pergamon.

Feldhusen, J. F. (1998). Programs for the gifted few or talent development for the many? *Phi Delta Kappan, 79*, 735–738.

Feldhusen, J. R., & Jarwan, F. A. (2000). Identification of gifted and talented youth for educational programs. In K. A. Heller, F. J. Monks, R. J. Sternberg, & R. F. Subotnik (Eds.), *International handbook of giftedness and talent* (2nd ed., pp. 271–282). New York: Pergamon.

Ford, D. Y. (1998). The under-representation of minority students in gifted education: Problems and promises in recruitment and retention. *Journal of Special Education, 32*, 4–14.

Ford, D. Y. (2002). Racial identity among gifted African American students. In M. Neihart, S. M. Reis, N. M. Robinson, & S. M. Moon (Eds.), *The social and emotional development of gifted children. What do we know?* (pp. 155–163). Waco, TX: Prufrock Press.

Freeman, J. (2000). Families: The essential context for gifts and talents. In K. A. Heller, F. J. Monks, R. J. Sternberg, & R. F. Subotnik (Eds.), *International handbook of giftedness and talent* (2nd ed., pp. 573–586). New York: Pergamon.

Gagne, F. (2000). Understanding the complex choreography of talent development through DMGT-based analysis. In K. A. Heller, F. J. Monks, R. J. Sternberg, & R. F. Subotnik (Eds.), *International handbook of giftedness and talent* (2nd ed., pp. 67–79). New York: Pergamon.

Gallagher, J. J. (1998). Accountability for gifted students. *Phi Delta Kappan, 79*, 739–742.

Gallagher, J. J. (2000a). Changing paradigms for gifted education in the United States. In K. A. Heller, F. J. Monks, R. J. Sternberg, & R. F. Subotnik (Eds.), *International handbook of giftedness and talent* (2nd ed., pp. 681–693). New York: Pergamon.

Gallagher, J. J. (2000b). Unthinkable thoughts: Education of gifted students. *Gifted Child Quarterly, 44*, 5–12.

Gallagher, J. J. (2002). *Society's role in educating gifted students: The role of public policy*. Storrs, CT: National Research Center on the Gifted and Talented.

Gallagher, J. J., & Gallagher, S. A. (1994). *Teaching the gifted child* (4th ed.). Boston: Allyn & Bacon.

Gardner, H., & Hatch, T. (1989). Multiple intelligences go to school: Educational implications of the theory of multiple intelligences. *Educational Researcher, 18*(8), 4–9.

Gentry, M., & Owen, S. V. (1999). An investigation of the effects of total school flexible cluster grouping on identification, achievement, and classroom practices. *Gifted Child Quarterly, 43*, 224–243.

Goldsmith, B. (2005). *Obsessive genius: The inner world of Marie Curie*. New York: Norton.

Gould, S. J. (1996). *The mismeasure of man* (Rev. ed.). New York: Norton.

Gross, M. U. M. (1992). The use of radical acceleration in cases of extreme intellectual precocity. *Gifted Child Quarterly, 36*, 91–99.

Gross, M. U. M. (1993). *Exceptionally gifted children*. London: Routledge.

Gross, M. U. M. (2000). Issues in the cognitive development of exceptionally and profoundly gifted individuals. In K. A. Heller, F. J. Monks, R. J. Sternberg, & R. F. Subotnik (Eds.), *International handbook of giftedness and talent* (2nd ed., pp. 179–192). New York: Pergamon.

Gross, M. U. M. (2002). Social and emotional issues for exceptionally intellectually gifted students. In M. Neihart, S. M. Reis, N. M. Robinson, & S. M. Moon (Eds.), *The social and emotional development of gifted children. What do we know?* (pp. 19–29). Waco, TX: Prufrock Press.

Gruber, H. E., & Wallace, D. B. (2001). Creative work: The case of Charles Darwin. *American Psychologist, 56*, 346–349.

Heller, K. A., Monks, F. J., Sternberg, R. J., & Subotnik, R. F. (Eds.). (2000). *International handbook of giftedness and talent* (2nd ed.). New York: Pergamon.

Hunsaker, S. L. (1995). The gifted metaphor from the perspective of traditional civilizations. *Journal for the Education of the Gifted, 18*, 255–268.

Hunsaker, S. L., & Callahan, C. M. (1995). Creativity and giftedness: Published instrument uses and abuses. *Gifted Child Quarterly, 39*, 110–114.

Hunter, S. (2001, December 21). Fragile genius of "A Beautiful Mind:" The human enigma within the known patterns of the universe. *Washington Post,* C1, C5.

Karnes, M. B., & Bean, S. M. (Eds.). (2001). *Methods and materials for teaching the gifted.* Waco, TX: Prufrock Press.

Kauffman, J. M. (2002). *Education deform: Bright people sometimes say stupid things about education.* Lanham, MD: Scarecrow Education.

Kauffman, J. M. & Hallahan, D. P. (2005). *Special education: What it is and why we need it.* Boston: Allyn & Bacon.

Kaufman, M. (1998, February 2). The best for the brightest. *Washington Post Magazine,* pp. 18–20, 32–35.

Kaufmann, F. A., & Castellanos, F. X. (2000). Attention deficit/hyperactivity disorder in gifted students. In K. A. Heller, F. J. Monks, R. J. Sternberg, & R. F. Subotnik (Eds.), *International handbook of giftedness and talent* (2nd ed., pp. 621–632). New York: Pergamon.

Kaufmann, F., Kalbfleisch, M. L., & Castellanos, F. X. (2000). *Attention deficit disorders and gifted students: What do we really know?* Storrs, CT: National Research Center on the Gifted and Talented.

Kerr, B. (1997). Developing talents in girls and young women. In N. Colangelo & G. A. Davis (Eds.), *Handbook of gifted education* (2nd ed., pp. 475–482). Boston: Allyn & Bacon.

Kerr, B. (2000). Guiding gifted girls and young women. In K. A. Heller, F. J. Monks, R. J. Sternberg, & R. F. Subotnik (Eds.), *International handbook of giftedness and talent* (2nd ed., pp. 649–658). New York: Pergamon.

Landrum, M. S., Callahan, C. M., & Shaklee, B. D. (Eds.). (2001). *Aiming for excellence: Gifted program standards.* Waco, TX: Prufrock Press.

Lubinski, D., Benbow, C. P., & Morelock, M. J. (2000). Gender differences in engineering and the physical sciences among the gifted: An inorganic-organic distinction. In K. A. Heller, F. J. Monks, R. J. Sternberg, & R. F. Subotnik (Eds.), *International handbook of giftedness and talent* (2nd ed., pp. 633–648). New York: Pergamon.

Lynch, M. D., & Harris, C. R. (Eds.). (2001). *Fostering creativity in children K–8: Theory and practice.* Boston: Allyn & Bacon.

Manstetten, R. (2000). Promotion of the gifted in vocational training. In K. A. Heller, F. J. Monks, R. J. Sternberg, & R. F. Subotnik (Eds.), *International handbook of giftedness and talent* (2nd ed., pp. 439–446). New York: Pergamon.

Martindale, C. (2001). Oscillations and analogies: Thomas Young, MD, FRS, genius. *American Psychologist, 56*, 342–345.

Montgomery, D. (Ed.). (2000). *Able underachievers.* London: Whurr.

Moon, S. M., & Rosselli, H. C. (2000). Developing gifted programs. In K. A. Heller, F. J. Monks, R. J. Sternberg, & R. F. Subotnik (Eds.), *International handbook of giftedness and talent* (2nd ed., pp. 499–521). New York: Pergamon.

Moon, S. M., Zentall, S., Grskovic, J. A., Hall, A., & Stormont, M. (2001). Emotional and social characteristics of boys with AD/HD and giftedness: A comparative case study. *Journal for the Education of the Gifted, 24*, 207–247.

Nakamura, J., & Csikszentmihalyi, M. (2001). Catalytic creativity: The case of Linus Pauling. *American Psychologist, 56*, 337–341.

Neihart, M., Reis, S. M., Robinson, N. M., & Moon, S. M. (Eds.). (2002). *The social and emotional development of gifted children. What do we know?* Waco, TX: Prufrock Press.

Perleth, C., Schatz, T., & Monks, F. J. (2000). Early identification of high ability. In K. A. Heller, F. J. Monks, R. J. Sternberg, & R. F. Subotnik (Eds.), *International handbook of giftedness and talent* (2nd ed., pp. 297–316). New York: Pergamon.

Peters, W. A. M., Grager-Loidl, H., & Supplee, P. (2000). Underachievement in gifted children and adolescents: Theory and practice. In K. A. Heller, F. J. Monks, R. J. Sternberg, & R. F. Subotnik (Eds.), *International handbook of giftedness and talent* (2nd ed., pp. 609–620). New York: Pergamon.

Plomin, R. (1997). Genetics and intelligence. In N. Colangelo & G. A. Davis (Eds.), *Handbook of gifted education* (2nd ed., pp. 67–74). Boston: Allyn & Bacon.

Plucker, J. A., & Stocking, V. B. (2001). Looking outside and inside: Self-concept development of gifted adolescents. *Exceptional Children, 67*, 535–548.

Reis, S. M., & McCoach, D. B. (2002). Underachievement in gifted students. In M. Neihart, S. M. Reis, N. M. Robinson, & S. M. Moon (Eds.), *The social and emotional development of gifted children. What do we know?* (pp. 81–91). Waco, TX: Prufrock Press.

Reis, S. M., & Renzulli, J. S. (2001). The schoolwide enrichment model: Developing students' creativity and talents. In M. D. Lynch & C. R. Harris (Eds.), *Fostering creativity in children, K–8: Theory and practice* (pp. 15–39). Boston: Allyn & Bacon.

Renzulli, J. S., & Park. S. (2002). *Giftedness and high school dropouts: Personal, family, and school-related factors.* Storrs, CT: National Research Center on the Gifted and Talented.

Renzulli, J. S., & Reis, S. M. (1997). The schoolwide enrichment model: New directions for developing high-end learning. In N. Colangelo & G. A. Davis (Eds.), *Handbook of gifted education* (2nd ed., pp. 136–154). Boston: Allyn & Bacon.

Renzulli, J. S., & Reis, S. M. (2000). The schoolwide enrichment model. In K. A. Heller, F. J. Monks, R. J. Sternberg, & R. F. Subotnik (Eds.), *International handbook of giftedness and talent* (2nd ed., pp. 367–382). New York: Pergamon.

Rogers, K. B., & Kimpston, R. D. (1992). Acceleration: What we do vs. what we know. *Educational Leadership, 50*(2), 58–61.

Sapon-Shevin, M. (1994). *Playing favorites: Gifted education and the disruption of community.* Albany: State University of New York Press.

Shaywitz, S. E., Holahan, J. M., Freudenheim, D. A., Fletcher, J. M., Makuch, R. W., & Shaywitz, B. A. (2001). Heterogeneity within the gifted: Higher IQ boys exhibit behaviors resembling boys with learning disabilities. *Gifted Child Quarterly, 45*, 16–23.

Shermer, M. (2001). *The borderlands of science: Where sense meets nonsense.* New York: Oxford University Press.

Siegle, D., & McCoach, D. B. (2002). Promoting positive achievement attitude with gifted and talented students. In M. Neihart, S. M. Reis, N. M. Robinson, & S. M. Moon (Eds.), *The social and emotional development of gifted children. What do we know?* (pp. 237–249). Waco, TX: Prufrock Press.

Shields, C. M. (1995). A comparison study of student attitudes and perceptions in homogeneous and heterogeneous classrooms. *Roeper Review, 17,* 234–238.

Silverman, L. K. (1997). Family counseling with the gifted. In N. Colangelo & G. A. Davis (Eds.), *Handbook of gifted education* (2nd ed., pp. 382–397). Boston: Allyn & Bacon.

Smutny, J. F. (2001). *Creative strategies for teaching language arts to gifted students (K–8).* (ERIC Digest No. E612). Retrieved October 30, 2001 from www.ericec.org.

Sternberg, R. J. (1997). A triarchic view of giftedness: Theory and practice. In N. Colangelo & G. A. Davis (Eds.), *Handbook of gifted education* (2nd ed., pp. 43–53). Boston: Allyn & Bacon.

Sternberg, R. J. (1998). Abilities are forms of developing expertise. *Educational Researcher, 27*(3), 11–20.

Sternberg, R. J. (2000). Giftedness as developing expertise. In K. A. Heller, F. J. Monks, R. J. Sternberg, & R. F. Subotnik (Eds.), *International handbook of giftedness and talent* (2nd ed., pp. 23–54). New York: Pergamon.

Sternberg, R. J. (2001). What is the common thread of creativity? Its dialectical relation to intelligence and wisdom. *American Psychologist, 56,* 360–362.

Sternberg, R. J., & Dess, N. K. (2001). Creativity for the new millennium. *American Psychologist, 56,* 332.

Sternberg, R. J., & Zhang, L. (1995). What do we mean by giftedness? A pentagonal implicit theory. *Gifted Child Quarterly, 39,* 88–94.

Stokes, P. D. (2001). Variability, constraints, and creativity: Shedding light on Claude Monet. *American Psychologist, 56,* 355–359.

Subotnik, R. F., & Arnold, K. D. (Eds.). (1994). *Beyond Terman: Contemporary longitudinal studies of giftedness and talent.* Norwood, NJ: Albex.

Swiatek, M. A. (1998). Helping gifted adolescents cope with social stigma. *Gifted Child Today, 21*(1), 42–46.

Swiatek, M. A., & Benbow, C. P. (1991). Ten-year longitudinal follow-up of ability-matched accelerated and unaccelerated gifted students. *Journal of Educational Research, 83,* 528–538.

Tannenbaum, A. J. (1993). History of giftedness and "gifted education" in world perspective. In K. A. Heller, F. J. Monks, & A. H. Passow (Eds.), *International handbook of research and development of giftedness and talent* (pp. 3–27). New York: Pergamon.

Tannenbaum, A. J. (1997). The meaning and making of giftedness. In N. Colangelo & G. A. Davis (Eds.), *Handbook of gifted education* (2nd ed., pp. 27–42). Boston: Allyn & Bacon.

Tannenbaum, A. J. (2000a). A history of giftedness in school and society. In K. A. Heller, F. J. Monks, R. J. Sternberg, & R. F. Subotnik (Eds.), *International handbook of giftedness and talent* (2nd ed., pp. 23–54). New York: Pergamon.

Tannenbaum, A. J. (2000b). Giftedness: The ultimate instrument for good and evil. In K. A. Heller, F. J. Monks, R. J. Sternberg, & R. F. Subotnik (Eds.), *International handbook of giftedness and talent* (2nd ed., pp. 447–466). New York: Pergamon.

Thompson, L. A., & Plomin, R. (2000). Genetic tools for exploring individual differences in intelligence. In K. A. Heller, F. J. Monks, R. J. Sternberg, & R. F. Subotnik (Eds.), *International handbook of giftedness and talent* (2nd ed., pp. 157–164). New York: Pergamon.

Tomlinson, C. (1995). *Differentiating instruction for advanced learners in the mixed-ability middle school classroom.* (ERIC Digest No. E536). Retrieved October 30, 2001 from www.ericec.org.

Tomlinson, C. A., Kaplan, S. N., Renzulli, J. S., Purcell, J., Leppien, J., & Burns, D. (2002). *The parallel curriculum: A design to develop high potential and challenge high-ability learners.* Thousand Oaks, CA: Corwin.

Van Tassel-Baska, J. (1998). The development of academic talent: A mandate for educational best practice. *Phi Delta Kappan, 79,* 760–763.

Van Tassel-Baska, J. (2000). Theory and research on curriculum development for the gifted. In K. A. Heller, F. J. Monks, R. J. Sternberg, & R. F. Subotnik (Eds.), *International handbook of giftedness and talent* (2nd ed., pp. 345–365). New York: Pergamon.

Ward, T. B. (2001). Creative cognition, conceptual combination, and the creative writing of Sephen R. Donaldson. *American Psychologist, 56,* 350–354.

Willard-Holt, C. (1999). *Dual exceptionalities.* (ERIC Digest No. E574.) Alexandria, VA: ERIC Clearinghouse on Disabilities and Gifted Education.

Zirkel, P. A. (2003). *The law and gifted education.* Storrs, CT: National Research Center on the Gifted and Talented.

Author Index

433–434, 436, 484, 520,
527–530
Courchesne, E., 404
Courchesne, R. Y., 404
Courty, S., 404
Coury, D. L., 237
Couthino, M., 52
Coutinho, M., 90–91, 100,
259
Coutinho, M. J., 91, 270
Cowden, A. J., 477
Cox, C. J., 75
Cox, D. J., 224
Coyne, P., 341
Crane, M. K., 190
Crenshaw, T. M., 235, 237,
256
Crimmins, C., 435
Crissey, M. S., 43
Crockett, J. B., 13, 16, 18–19,
22, 30, 44–45, 52–53, 275
Croneberg, C. G., 330
Cronin, M. E., 44, 152
Cropper, C., 512
Cross, T. L., 498, 508
Crosswait, C., 224, 237
Crowe, T. A., 300–301
Cruickshank, W. M., 16, 45,
171, 183, 211, 226–227
Csikszentmihalyi, M., 502
Cullinan, D., 246, 249,
252–253
Curlee, R. F., 302
Curtis, W. J., 95
Cutler, S. K., 472
Cuvo, A. J., 154

D

Dadurka, D., 101
Dale, E. J., 519
Dale, P. S., 52, 69, 328
D'Allura, T., 387
Darrah, J., 480
Davies, M., 236
Davies, S., 227, 232
Davies, S. E., 402–403
Davis, C. A., 6, 271
Davis, H. R., 404
Davis, P. K., 154
Davis, S., 139
Dawson, H. L., 156
Day, H. M., 458
Day, N. L., 252
Dean, T., 217
de Boer-Ott, S. R., 421–422
DeBose, C. E., 95, 98
DeFord, S., 482
deFrench, N. S., 178
DeFries, C., 178, 219

DeFries, J. C., 178
DeGarcia, B., 88
De Hahn, E. L.H., 510
Deimel, W., 178
Dell Orto, A. E., 433, 435–438
Delpit, L. D., 98
Delquadri, J., 156
Delquadri, J. C., 156
Demonet, J. F., 177
Denham, S. A., 69
Deno, S., 52
Deno, S. L., 179–180
DePompei, R., 435–436
Derrick, G., 326
Deshler, D. D., 202
Dess, N. K., 502
DeStefano, F., 402
DeStefano, L., 71
DeStephano, L., 161
DeWitt, M. B., 237
Dhillon, A. P., 402–403
Diener, M. B., 224
Dietrich, M., 215
DiGiuseppe, D. L., 217
DiGiuseppi, C., 403
Dimitropoulos, A., 149
Dishion, T. J., 263, 273
Division for Early Childhood,
460
Dobbs, M., 59
Dobelle, W. H., 385
Docherty, R., 475, 487
Dodge, K. A., 280
Dohrn, E., 260
Dollaghan, C. A., 328
Donahue, M., 185
Donahue, M. L., 298
Donohue, B. C., 177
Dostra, L., 253
Dote-Kwan, J., 387
Douglas, G., 220
Douglas, S., 475, 487
Downing, J., 446, 448
Doyle, A. E., 219, 237–238
Draper, I. L., 58, 61, 63, 92
Drasgow, E., 29, 58, 74, 277
Drew, C. J., 143, 153
Drotar, D., 110
Duara, R., 177
Duhaney, D. C., 347
Duhaney, L. M. G., 50
Duis, S. S., 112
Duke, D. L., 281
Duncan, B. B., 280
Dunlap, G., 123, 155, 458
Dunn, D., 403
Dunn, E., 260
Dunst, C. J., 116
DuPaul, G. J., 215–216, 225,
227–230, 232, 235

Dupre, A. P., 29, 52, 74–75
Durkin, K., 220
Dwyer, K. P., 74
Dykens, E., 147
Dykens, E. M., 139, 141–142,
145, 147, 149, 443
Dyson, L. L., 112

E

Earley, T., 465–466
Easterbrooks, S., 341
Eaton, S. B., 57
Eaves, L. J., 178
Ebens, C. L., 218
Eckert, T. L., 227, 229–230
Edelen-Smith, P., 232
Edgar, E., 200, 271, 281
Edison, M. R., 43
Edwards, M. L., 300
Edwards, R. P., 277
Egan, R., 69, 478, 483
Ehren, B. J., 202, 290
Eisenberg, L., 402
Elbaum, B., 52–53, 197
Elia, M., 473
Eliopulos, D., 218
Elksnin, L. K., 100
Elksnin, N., 100
Elliot, B., 101
Elliot, L., 348
Elliott, G. R., 215, 236
Elliott, M., 215
Ellis, A., 195
Ellis, C., 277, 280
Ellis, C. R., 95
Emmorey, K., 322, 333
Engel, J., 471
Engelmann, O., 194
Engelmann, S., 194–195
Enright, B. E., 179
Epilepsy Foundation of
America, 472
Epstein, M., 124
Epstein, M. H., 191, 248, 254,
260, 271, 280
Ergul, C., 189
Erhardt, D., 224
Erickson, M. T., 178
Erin, J. N., 363, 386
Ervin, R. A., 227–228
Escobar, M. D., 175
Esser, G., 215
Evans, A. C., 218
Evans, E., 292
Evans, S. W., 235
Evenhuis, H. M., 140
Everhart, V., 348
Everson, J. M., 159
Evertson, C. M., 102

F

Fad, K. M., 75
Falk, K. B., 56, 271
Fallis, D. S., 43
*Families and Disability
Newsletter,* 457
Faraone, S. V., 219, 225, 233,
235, 237–238
Farmer, E. M. Z., 246, 263,
271
Farmer, T. W., 246, 257, 259,
263, 271, 273, 275, 280
Faulk, R., 215
Fazio, F., 177
Featherly, C., 454
Featherstone, H., 110
Federal Register, 347
Feil, E. G., 254, 261, 263,
279–280
Feingold, B., 217
Feldhusen, J. F., 506, 512,
518
Feldman, E., 177
Feldman, H. M., 328
Feliciangeli, A., 469, 491–492
Fennema-Notestine, C., 475
Fennick, E., 55, 73
Ferguson, C., 344
Ferguson, P. M., 112
Fergusson, D. M., 215, 224
Fernstrom, P., 273
Ferrell, K. A., 376
Feurer, I. D., 149
Fewell, R. R., 118
Fey, M. E., 297, 311–312
Fichten, C. S., 372
Fidler, D. J., 147, 149
Fiedler, C. R., 46
Field, L. L., 178
Filipek, P. A., 218, 220
Findling, R. L., 233
Finn, C. E., Jr., 13, 33, 58
Finucane, B. M., 139,
141–142, 145, 147, 149,
443
Fischer, M., 53, 58
Fishback, K., 163
Fisher, E. S., 257
Fisher, M., 13
Fister, S., 230–231
Fitzgerald, C., 217
Fletcher, J. M., 173, 175, 177,
199, 512
Fletcher, K., 224, 237
Fletcher, K. L., 146
Flippin, S. S., 95–96
Flowers, C., 153
Flowers, D. L., 177
Flowers, L., 177

Luk, S. L., 215
Luna, B., 405
Luna, M., 313
Lupkowski-Shoplik, A., 519, 524
Lussenhop, K., 377
Luzzo, D. A., 202–203
Lyke, T., 475, 487
Lynch, M. D., 502, 506, 518
Lynskey, M. T., 215
Lyon, G. R., 173

M

Maag, J. W., 280
Maas, L. C., 218
MacArthur, C., 309
MacMillan, D. L., 26, 29, 69–70, 90, 92, 138, 175
MacMillan, D. M., 253
MacNeil, B., 322
Magg, J. W., 75
Magill-Evans, J., 480
Maheady, L., 56
Mahon, M. J., 483, 488
Mahoney, G., 106, 118
Mahshie, J., 341
Maisog, J. M., 177
Mak, F. L., 215
Makuch, R. W., 512
Malik, M., 402–403
Mallette, B., 56
Malmgren, K., 281
Malouf, D. B., 24
Mangold, S. S., 374
Mank, D., 162–163
Mann, E. A., 158
Manos, M. J., 233
Manstetten, R., 507
March, J. S., 215, 236
Marchand-Martella, N. E., 74
Marchione, K. E., 177
Marschark, M., 329
Marshall, R., 218
Marshall, R. M., 225
Martella, R. C., 74
Martin, E. W., 18
Martin, F. D., 48
Martin, J. E., 44, 151
Martindale, C., 502
Martinez, E., 6, 93, 309, 315
Martinez, E. A., 54, 123, 125, 176, 181, 183, 191, 414
Martins, S., 215
Marvin, C. A., 450
Marvin, R. S., 479
Marx, E. S., 350
Masia, C. L., 268
Mason, C. A., 145
Mastin, M. E., 149

Mastropieri, M. A., 50, 188–189
Matczynski, T. J., 189
Mather, S., 75
Mathes, M. Y., 192, 232
Mathes, P., 197
Mathiason, C. S., 42
Mathur, S., 124
Matson, J. L., 414
Mattson, S. N., 475
Mattsson, E., 492
Mauer, P., 375
Maurer, M., 370–371, 386
Maxwell, K., 116
McAfee, M., 96
McCain, A. P., 125
McCarty, C. A., 217
McClannahan, L. E., 414
McCleary, C., 438–439
McCoach, D. B., 511
McConnell, M. E., 75
McConnell, S. R., 280
McCord, B. E., 457
McCormick, K. M., 271
McCourt, F., 80
McCray, A. D., 53
McCrory, E., 177
McCuller, G. L., 161
McCullough, J., 13, 16, 45, 271
McDonald, J. L., 289
McDonald, S., 438
McDonnell, A. P., 161–162
McDonnell, J. J., 161–162
McDonnell, L. M., 92
McElroy, K., 192
McGauhey, P., 252
McGee, K., 16, 53, 61, 94
McGee, R., 215
McGoey, K. E., 227
McGrady, H. J., 189
McGregor, K. K., 312
McGue, M. K., 219
McHenry, M. A., 300
McHugh, E., 372
McIntyre, L. L., 253
McKee, B., 348
McLaughlin, M. J., 92
McLaughlin, P. J., 230–231
McLaughlin, V. L., 437
McLaurin, J. W., 443
McLean, M. E., 458–460
McMaster, K. L., 174
McMaster, K. N., 56
McNeil, L. M., 61
McNutt, G., 172
McWilliam, R. A., 116, 459–460
Meadow-Orlans, K. P., 116, 322–323, 350

Mechling, L. C., 160
Meese, R. L., 181–182, 193
Mehta, N., 140
Meister, C., 194
Melancon, F., 443
Menchel, R. S., 342
Mencl, W. E., 177
Mercer, A. R., 230
Mercer, C. D., 176, 230
Merchant, N., 429
Merkel, R. L., 224
Mertens, D. M., 116, 323
Mervis, C. B., 149
Mesibov, G. B., 411
Metevia, L., 224, 237
Metz, D. E., 286, 291, 302–303
Meyer, D. J., 116
Meyer, J., 178
Meyer, K. A., 455
Meyer, M. S., 178
Meyers, L., 194
Michalko, R., 47, 64–65
Michel, R., 379
Mick, E., 219, 225, 235, 238
Milberger, S., 219
Miles, B., 440, 444, 446, 448
Milich, R., 224
Millar, D., 379
Millar, L., 75
Miller, C., 363
Miller, J. F., 119
Miller, J. G., 254, 281
Miller, J. H., 157, 185
Miller, L. J., 179
Miller, S. E., 73
Miller, S. P., 57, 157
Miller-Johnson, S., 158
Mills, P. E., 52, 69
Miner, I., 449
Minich, N. M., 143
Minor, L., 446–447
Minshew, N. J., 405
Mira, M. P., 435–436, 438–439
Miramontes, O. B., 22
Mirenda, P., 416, 438, 449–450, 453–454
Mirkin, P. K., 180
Mirrett, P., 147, 149
Mitchell, A., 140
Mitchell, R., 60
Mitchell, R. E., 320, 335
Mithaug, D. E., 44, 151
Moberly, R., 490
Mock, D., 55, 174–175
Mock, D. R., 18–19, 40, 45, 47–48, 50, 52, 249
Moldavsky, M., 147, 149
Moll, L. C., 45

Monks, F. J., 500, 502, 504, 506, 516, 521–522
Montague, M., 183, 191
Montgomery, D., 511
Moody, S. W., 47, 53, 58
Moon, M. S., 71–73, 159, 462
Moon, S. M., 507–508, 512, 518, 522, 524
Moore, J., 481
Moorehouse, M., 224, 237
Moores, D. F., 336, 340
Morelock, M. J., 515
Morgan, P. L., 55, 174–175
Morison, P., 92
Morningstar, M. E., 490
Morris, M. K., 268
Morrison, G. M., 252–253, 257
Morrison, J. H., 140
Morse, T. E., 154
Mortenson, B. P., 55
Mortweet, S. L., 56, 156
Mosely, M., 341
Moses, N., 314
Moses, P., 404
Moss, K., 447
Mostert, M. P., 23, 52, 56, 80, 99, 102, 249, 257, 271, 273, 275–277, 436, 438, 454
Mota, V. L., 220
Mount, B., 461
Moyers, P., 333
MR/DD Data Brief, 161
MTA Cooperative Group, 236
Mueller, M. M., 277
Mui, Y. Q., 88
Muir, D. W., 376
Muller, K., 178
Mundy, L., 89, 340
Munk, D., 124
Munk, D. D., 191
Murawski, W. W., 55, 196
Murch, S. H., 402–403
Murias, M., 231
Murphy, D. A., 476
Murphy, K. R., 221, 239
Murphy, M. M., 147, 149
Murray, C., 200
Myles, B. S., 98, 407, 410–411, 417–420, 423

N

Nabors, L. A., 478, 484
Nace, K. L., 177
Naftel, A. J., 215
Nakamura, J., 502
Nakata, Y., 215

Subject Index

A

AAC. *See* augmentative or alternative communication
AAMR. *See* American Association on Mental Retardation
ABA. *See* applied behavior analysis
Abecedarian Project, 155, 158
Abilities
  discrepancy with achievement, in learning disabilities, 173
  importance of, 7
Academic achievement. *See* achievement
Acadians, Usher syndrome among, 443
Acceleration, 519, 524
  definition of, 518
  research on, 521
Access
  to Internet, 383–384
  to technology, 63–65
Accessible pedestrian signal (APS), definition of, 388
Accommodations
  for assessments, 61, 61*t*
  definition of, 57
  for homework, 124
  in physical education, 486
Achievement
  discrepancy with ability, in learning disabilities, 173
  and emotional/behavioral disorders, 262
  hearing impairment and, 334
  physical disabilities and, 478
  visual impairment and, 369
Acquired apraxia, 303
Acquired immune deficiency syndrome (AIDS), definition of, 476
ACT. *See* American College Test
Acting-out behavior, 263–267
Acute, definition of, 468
ADA. *See* Americans with Disabilities Act
Adaptability, 120
Adaptations, definition of, 57
Adapted physical education (APE), 486
Adapted signs, 448
  definition of, 446
Adaptive behavior
  assessment of, 146
  definition of, 136
  examples of, 136*t*
  and mental retardation, 135–136
Adaptive devices, 480–482
  definition of, 480
Adaptive skills, and ADHD, 224
Adderall, for ADHD, 233
ADHD. *See* attention deficit–hyperactivity disorder
ADHD-Rating Scale-IV, 216

Adult-directed programs, 68
Adulthood. *See* transition to adulthood
Adventitiously deaf, definition of, 322
Advocacy
  definition of, 127
  by parents, 127
  personal perspectives on, 128
  by students, 203
Affective disorder, definition of, 251
African American English, 288–289
African-American students
  and ADHD, 215
  in special education versus total school population, 90*t*
  with special gifts/talents, 511–512
Age, and ability, 8
Aggression, 263–267
  definition of, 263
  with severe/multiple disabilities, 456
AIDS. *See* acquired immune deficiency syndrome
Ali, Muhammad, 523
Alternative teaching, and ADHD, 234
Alzheimer's disease, Down syndrome and, 140
American Association on Mental Retardation (AAMR)
  definition of mental retardation, 135–137
  on self-determination, 152
American College Test (ACT), and learning disabilities, 202
American Foundation for the Blind, 360, 390–391
American School of the Deaf, 25
American Sign Language (ASL), 321, 343–344, 350. *See also* sign language
American Speech-Language-Hearing Association (ASHA), 288, 290, 306
Americans with Disabilities Act (ADA), 27–28
  definition of, 27
Amniocentesis, definition of, 140
Analytic giftedness, 502
Anoxia, definition of, 143
Antecedents, 154
Anxiety disorder, definition of, 251
APE. *See* adapted physical education
Aphonia, definition of, 301
Appalachian English, 290
Applied behavior analysis (ABA), 418–419
Appreciation, teaching, 96
Apraxia, 303
  definition of, 302
APS. *See* accessible pedestrian signal
Aqueous humor, definition of, 362
ARC, 27
Armstrong, John, 509
Articulation disorders, 299–300
ASHA. *See* American Speech-Language-Hearing Association

E

Ear, anatomy and physiology of, 324–326, 325f
Eardrum, definition of, 324
Early expressive language delay (EELD), definition of, 296
Early intervention, 65–69
    for ADHD, 237
    for autism spectrum disorders, 421–422
    for communication disorders, 309–312
    for emotional/behavioral disorders, 277–280
    for giftedness, 521–522
    for hearing impairment, 349–350
    for learning disabilities, 197–199
    for mental retardation, 155–158
    for multiple/severe disabilities, 457–460
    for physical disabilities, 489
    types of programs for, 67–68
    for visual impairment, 385–387
Echolalia, definition of, 398
Education. *See also* general education; special education
    family involvement in, 116–127
Education for All Handicapped Children Act, definition of, 27
EELD. *See* early expressive language delay
Elementary and Secondary Education Act, 58, 277
Eligibility conferences, teachers and, 20
Elitharp, Toni, 418–419
Elyoumni-Pindo, Najia, 330–331
Emotional disorders, 244–283
    with ADHD, 225
    biological factors in, 255–256
    causes of, 254–260
    characteristics of, 262–270
    classification of, 251–253
    cultural factors in, 259–260
    definition of, 249–251
    educational considerations with, 270–277
    family factors in, 256–257
        personal perspectives on, 258
    identification of, 260–262
    misconceptions about, 247
    prevalence of, 253–254
    risk factors for, 254, 255f
    school factors in, 257–258
    terminology on, 248–249, 248f
Emotionally disturbed, definition of, 250
Emotional problems
    with learning disabilities, 189–190
    personal perspectives on, 190
    with traumatic brain injury, 438–439
Employment
    with ADHD, 239
    alternatives, 72t
    with emotional/behavioral disorders, 281
    with mental retardation, 161–163
        future prospects for, 163
    physical disabilities and, 492–493
    with visual impairment, 390–391
Empowerment, psychological, 150

Encephalitis, 144
    definition of, 145
Encoding, 288
Encopresis, definition of, 268
Englemann, Siegfried, 195
Enrichment, 519–521, 524
    definition of, 518
Enuresis, definition of, 268
Environmental influences, and mental retardation, 142–143
Epilepsy, 471–473
    definition of, 471
Episodic, definition of, 468
Error analysis, 180–181
    definition of, 180
    personal perspectives on, 182
Ethical dilemmas, 22
Ethics, of full inclusion, 48–49
Ethnicity, 88
    and ADHD, 215
    versus exceptionality, 90, 90t
    and social support, 121–122
Ethnic-minority groups
    and special education, 89
    and special gifts/talents, 511–512
Evidence, on inclusion, 52–53
Evoked-response audiometry, definition of, 327
Exceptionality
    versus ethnicity, 90, 90t
    orientation to, 4–8
    and special education, 2–37
Exceptional learners
    educational definition of, 8–11
    misconceptions about, 5
    personal perspectives on, 9
    prevalence of, 11–13
    study of, 4
Executive functions
    in ADHD, 221–222
    in autism spectrum disorders, 411–412
    definition of, 221
Expressive language, definition of, 288
Externalizing, 263–267
    definition of, 252
External otitis, definition of, 328
Eye, anatomy and physiology of, 362, 362f

F

Facilitated communication (FC), 453–454
FAE. *See* fetal alcohol effect
Familiality studies, definition of, 178
Families, 104–129
    with ADHD, 239–240
    and asthma, 475
    and early intervention in communication disorders, 311–312
    effect of child with disability on, 108–116
    and emotional/behavioral disorders, 256–257
        personal perspectives on, 258
    with emotional/behavioral disorders, 281

opposition to, 233
research on, 233–236
side effects of, 235
ROP. *See* retinopathy of prematurity
Routine, for deaf-blindness, 446–447
Rowley, Amy, 30
RTI. *See* response to intervention
Rubella, definition of, 143, 442
Ruffner, Adelaide, 100–101
Rural areas, and gifts/talents, 511
Russell, Mia Callahan, 184–185

S

Sacks, Oliver, 443
Sadonis, Cindy, 346
Sarah, 63
SAT. *See* Scholastic Aptitude Test
Scaffolded instruction
definition of, 98
for learning disabilities, 192
Schizophrenia
definition of, 253, 398
identification of, 260
Scholastic Aptitude Test (SAT), and learning disabilities, 202
School
and asthma, 475
and emotional/behavioral disorders, 257–258
language of, 305
School choice, and segregation, 84
Schoolwide enrichment model, 520
Schroeder, Fred, 370–371
Scoliosis, definition of, 142, 474
Screen readers, definition of, 383
Seaver, Abigail, 115
Secondary language disorders, 297–298
definition of, 294
Secondary programming
with emotional/behavioral disorders, 281
with learning disabilities, 201–202
Segregation, versus least restrictive environment, 16
Séguin, Édouard, 25
Seizure
definition of, 471
first aid for, 472
Seizure disorder, 471–473
causes of, 471
educational considerations with, 471–473
types of, 471
Self-advocacy, 203
Self-contained class, 15
Self-determination, 43–44
AAMR on, 152
definition of, 43, 150
and mental retardation, 149–155
and multiple/severe disabilities, 461
personal perspectives on, 153
Self-injurious behavior (SIB), definition of, 455
Self-instruction
definition of, 192

for learning disabilities, 192
Self-monitoring
for ADHD, 232
definition of, 192
for learning disabilities, 192
Self-realization, 151
Self-regulation, 150
definition of, 146
Self-stimulation, definition of, 455
Semantic disorder, 295
Semantics, 288
definition of, 184, 289
Sensorineural hearing impairment, definition of, 328
Sensory acuteness, myth of, 369
Sensory perceptions, abnormal, in autism, 408
Service delivery models
for ADHD, 229–230
for autism spectrum disorders, 421
for emotional/behavioral disorders, 272–275
for hearing impairment, 344–345
for learning disabilities, 196–197
for mental retardation, 155
for visual impairment, 385
Severe disabilities, 428–463
definition of, 430–432
educational considerations with, 449–457
misconceptions about, 431
personal perspectives on, 454
transition for, 72
Severe mental retardation, definition of, 137
Sexuality, physical disabilities and, 493
Shame, cultural, universality of, 80–82
Sharma, Chris, 508
Sheltered-English approach, definition of, 98
Sheltered workshops, 161–162
definition of, 161, 460
Shilyansky, Carrie, 509
Shine, 408
Short-term memory (STM), definition of, 187
SIB. *See* self-injurious behavior
Siblings
adjustment of, 115–116
concerns of, 114t
personal perspectives on, 115
reactions to child with disabilities, 114–116
Sibshops, definition of, 116
Sight, remaining, use of, 376–377
Signing English systems, 342–343
definition of, 342
Sign language, 320, 330–333, 350
definition of, 322
developmental milestones of, 332
grammatical complexity of, 331
interpreters of, working with, 352
neurological foundations of, 333
nonuniversality of, 331–332
simplified, 450–451
Skinner, Jessie, 481
Slate and stylus, 375*f*
definition of, 375*f*